MARKESINIS

THE GERMAN LAW OF OBLIGATIONS

MARKESINIS
The German Law of Obligations

VOLUME II
The Law of Torts:
A Comparative Introduction

B. S. MARKESINIS

THIRD EDITION

WITH CORRECTIONS AND ADDITIONS

CLARENDON PRESS · OXFORD

1997

Oxford University Press, Great Clarendon Street, Oxford OX2 6DP

Oxford New York

Athens Auckland Bangkok Bogota Bombay
Buenos Aires Calcutta Cape Town Dar es Salaam
Delhi Florence Hong Kong Istanbul Karachi
Kuala Lumpur Madras Madrid Melbourne
Mexico City Nairobi Paris Singapore
Taipei Tokyo Toronto Warsaw
and associated companies in
Berlin Ibadan

Oxford is a trade mark of Oxford University Press

Published in the United States
by Oxford University Press Inc., New York

First published 1994
Reprinted with corrections and additions 1997

British Library Cataloguing in Publication Data
Data available

Library of Congress Cataloging in Publication Data
Data available
ISBN 0–19–826768–1
ISBN 0–19–826767–3 (Pbk)

Typeset by Hope Services (Abingdon) Ltd.
Printed in Great Britain
on acid-free paper by
Biddles Ltd., Guildford and King's Lynn

TO MY MOTHER TO WHOM I OWE SO MUCH

CONTENTS

Table of Cases

DECISIONS OF THE FEDERAL CONSTITUTIONAL COURT

DECISIONS OF THE IMPERIAL COURT

DECISIONS OF THE FEDERAL SUPREME COURT

Abbreviations

ABGB	Austrian General Civil Code
AC	Law Reports, Appeal Cases (Decisions of the House of Lords and the Privy Council from 1891)
AcP	*Archiv für die civilistische Praxis*
AfP	*Archiv für Privatrecht*
A. J. Comp. L.	*American Journal of Comparative Law*
ALJR	*Australian Law Journal Reports*
All ER	All England Law Reports
Am. Rep.	American Reports
AOK	*Allgemeine Ortskrankenkasse* (National Health Insurance Scheme)
App. Cas.	Law Reports, Appeal Cases (1875–90)
ATF	Recueil officiel d'arrêts du Tribunal fédéral suisse (can also be referred to as BGE-Entscheidungen des schweizerischen Bundesgerichtes)
AuR	*Arbeit und Recht*
B.	*Beklagter* (defendant)
BayObLG	Bayerisches Oberstes Landesgericht
BB	*Der Betriebsberater*
DB	*Der Betrieb*
BGB	Bürgerliches Gesetzbuch (German Civil Code)
BGBl.	Bundesgesetzblatt (Government Gazette)
BGE	Entscheidungen des schweizerischen Bundesgerichtes (can also be referred to as ATF-Recueil officiel d'arrêts du Tribunal fédéral suisse)
BGH	Bundesgerichtshof (Germany's Federal (Supreme) Court)*
BGHZ	Entscheidungen des Bundesgerichtshofs in Zivilsachen (Decisions of the German Supreme Court in civil matters)
Buffalo L. Rev.	*Buffalo Law Review*
BVerfG	Bundesverfassungsgericht
BVerfGE	Entscheidungen des Bundesverfassungsgerichts (Decisions of the Federal Constitutional Court)
BVerfGG	Bundesverfassungsgerichtsgesetz (Statute of the Constitutional Court of the FRG)

* Before the 're-unification' of 1990, the BGH was the Supreme (Civil and Criminal) Court for Western Germany only.

B.Y.B.I.L.	*British Year Book of International Law*
CA	Decisions of the English Court of Appeal
Cal. L. Rev.	*California Law Review*
Cal. Rptr. 2d	California Reporter, 2nd series (American law reports)
Cal. Rptr. 3d	California Reporter, 3rd series (American law reports)
Campbell L. Rev.	*Campbell Law Review*
Can. Bar Rev.	*The Canadian Bar Review*
Cass.	Cour de cassation
CC	*Code Civil*
CCLT	Canadian Cases on the Law of Torts
Ch.	Law Reports, Chancery Division (from 1891)
Ch. Civ.	Cour de cassation, Chambre Civile
Ch. Civ. 2e	Cour de cassation (French Court of Cassation, 2nd civil chamber)
Ch. Comm.	Cour de cassation, Chambre Commerciale
Ch. Crim.	Cour de cassation, Chambre Criminelle
Ch. D.	Law Reports, Chancery Division (1875–90)
Ch. Mixte	Cour de cassation, Chambre Mixte
Ch. Req.	Cour de cassation, Chambre des Requêtes
Ch. Réun.	Cour de cassation, Chambres Réunies
Cincinnati L. Rev.	*Cincinnati Law Review*
C.L.	*Current Law*
CLJ	*Cambridge Law Journal*
Colum. L. Rev.	*Columbia Law Review*
Connecticut L. Rev.	*Connecticut Law Review*
Cornell L. Rev.	*Cornell Law Review*
Cumb. L. Rev.	*Cumberland Law Review*
D.	Recueil Dalloz (1945–64)
DB	*Der Betrieb*
DC	Dalloz, recueil critique de jurisprudence et de législation (1941–44)
Depaul L. Rev.	*Depaul Law Review*
Dickinson L. Rev.	*Dickinson Law Review*
DLR	Dominion Law Reports
Duke LJ	*Duke Law Journal*
DS	Recueil Dalloz et Sirey (1965–)
D. StR.	Deutsches Steuerrecht
Duq. L. Rev.	*Duquesne Law Review*
EG BGB	Einführungsgesetz zum BGB (introductory law to the BGB)

Encyclopedia	*International Encyclopedia of Comparative Law*, vol. xi (Chief ed. A. Tunc, 1975)
EuGRZ	*Europäische Grundrechtezeitung*
Ex. D.	Law Reports, Exchequer Division (1875–80)
FamRZ	*Zeitschrift für das gesamte Familienrecht*
F. Supp.	Federal Supplement (American law reports)
F. 2d	Federal Reporter, 2nd series (American law reports)
Fordham L. Journ.	*Fordham Urban Law Journal*
Fordham L. Rev.	*Fordham Law Review*
Ga. L. Rev.	*Georgia Law Review*
GG	Grundgesetz (the Constitution of Western Germany)
Harv. L. Rev.	*Harvard Law Review*
Hastings LJ	*Hastings Law Journal*
Haw.	Hawaii Supreme Court Reports
ICLQ	*International and Comparative Law Quarterly*
IDHL	*International Digest of Health Law*
Indiana L. Rev.	*Indiana Law Review*
Indiana LJ	*Indiana Law Journal*
JA	*Juristische Arbeitsblätter*
JCP	*Juris-Classeur Périodique* (also referred to as *SJ* (*La Semaine juridique*))
J. Leg. Stud.	*Journal of Legal Studies*
J. of Law, Econ. and Org.	*Journal of Law, Economics and Organics*
JSPTL	*Journal of the Society of Public Teachers of Law*
JuS	*Juristische Schulung*
JW	*Juristische Wochenschrift* (from 1872 to 1939)
JZ	*Juristenzeitung*
KB	Law Reports, King's Bench (1901–52)
Kentucky LJ	*Kentucky Law Journal*
KG	Kammergericht (Court of Appeal of Berlin)
KUG	Gesetz betreffend das Urheberrecht an Werken der bildenden Künste und der Photographie (translated and abbreviated as the Law on Artistic Creations)
La. L. Rev.	*Louisiana Law Review*
LMCLQ	*Lloyds Maritime and Commercial Law Quarterly*
LQR	*Law Quarterly Review*
LR Ch. App.	Law Reports, Chancery Appeal Cases (1865–75)
LRCP	Law Reports, Common Pleas Cases (1865–75)
LR Ex.	Law Reports, Exchequer Cases (1965–75)
LRHL	Law Reports, English and Irish Appeals (1866–75)

LRQB	Law Reports, Queen's Bench (1865–75)
LT	Law Times Reports (1859–1947)
Maryland L. Rev.	*Maryland Law Review*
Mass.	Massachusetts
Med. R	*Medizin und Recht*
MDR	*Monatsschrift für Deutsches Recht*
Miss. LJ	*Mississippi Law Journal*
Mercer L. Rev.	*Mercer Law Review*
MLR	*Modern Law Review*
N. Carolina L. Rev.	*North Carolina Law Review*
NE	North Eastern Reporter (American law reports)
NJ	*Neue Justiz*
NJSA	New Jersey Statutes Annotated
NJW	*Neue Juristische Wochenschrift*
NW	North Western Reporter (American law reports)
NYU L. R.	*New York University Law Review*
NZLJ	*New Zealand Law Journal*
NZLR	New Zealand Law Reports
ObLG	Oberstes Landesgericht
OGH	Oberster Gerichtshof (Austrian Supreme Court)
OLG	Oberlandesgericht (German Court of Appeal)
OR	Swiss Code of Obligations
Ore. L. Rev.	*Oregon Law Review*
Oxford J. L. Studies	*Oxford Journal of Legal Studies*
P.	Law Reports, Probate Division (1891–)
P. 2d	Pacific Reporter, 2nd series (American law reports)
QB	Law Reports, Queen's Bench (1891–1900; 1952–)
QBD	Law Reports, Queen's Bench Division (1875–90)
RabelsZ	*Rabels Zeitschrift für ausländisches und internationales Recht*
Rev. int. dr. comp.	*Revue international de droit comparé*
Rev. trim. dr. civ.	*Revue trimestrielle de droit civil*
RG	Reichsgericht
RGBl.	Reichsgesetzblatt (Government Gazette)
RGSt	Amtliche Sammlung der Entscheidungen des Reichsgerichts in Strafsachen
RGZ	Entscheidungen des Reichsgerichts in Zivilsachen (Decisions of the German Imperial Court in civil matters)
Rutgers L. Rev.	*Rutgers Law Review*
RVO	Reichsversicherungsordnung (Imperial Insurance Act)

S.	Recueil Sirey
St John's L. Rev.	*St John's Law Review*
San D. L. Rev.	*San Diego Law Review*
S. Ct.	Supreme Court
S.C.R.	Supreme Court Reports
Seton Hall L. Rev.	*Seton Hall Law Review*
SJ	*La Semaine juridique* (also referred to as *JCP* (*Juris-Classeur Périodique*))
So.	Southern Reporter (American law reports)
So. 2d	Southern Reporter, 2nd series (American law reports)
So. Cal. L. Rev.	*Southern California Law Review*
Stan. L. Rev.	*Stanford Law Review*
StGB	Strafgesetzbuch (German Criminal Code)
StVG	Strassenverkehrsgesetz (Road Traffic Act)
Suffolk Univ. L. Rev.	*Suffolk University Law Review*
SW	South Western Reporter (American law reports)
Sydney L. Rev.	*Sydney Law Review*
Temple L. Rev.	*Temple Law Review*
Texas Tech. L. Rev.	*Texas Technical Law Review*
Trib. Civ.	Tribunal Civil
Tulane L. Rev.	*Tulane Law Review*
Tul. L. Rev.	*Tuluna Law Review*
UBC L. Rev.	*University of British Columbia Law Review*
U. Ch. L. Rev.	*University of Chicago Law Review*
UCLA L. Rev.	*University of California Los Angeles Law Review*
U. Fla. L. Rev.	*University of Florida Law Review*
U. Haw. L. Rev.	*University of Hawaii Law Review*
Univ. of Cincinnati L. Rev.	*University of Cincinnati Law Review*
UP L. Rev.	*University of Pennsylvania Law Review*
UTLJ	*University of Toronto Law Journal*
Va. L. Rev.	*Virginia Law Review*
Vand. L. Rev.	*Vanderbilt Law Review*
VersR	*Versicherungsrecht*
Villanova L. Rev.	*Villanova Law Review*
Washburn LJ	*Washburn Law Journal*
Wash. and Lee L. Rev.	*Washington and Lee Law Review*
Wash. L. Rev.	*Washington Law Review*
WHG	Wasserhaushaltsgesetz (German Act on the Use of Water)
Wis.	Wisconsin

Books cited only by the Names of their Authors

IN GERMAN

Deutsch = E. Deutsch, *Haftungsrecht* I (1976).

Esser/Schmidt = J. Esser and E. Schmidt, *Schuldrecht* I (General part, 7th edn., 1992).

Esser/Weyers = J. Esser and H. L. Weyers, *Schuldrecht* II (Special part, 1 and 2, 7th edn., 1992).

Fikentscher = W. Fikentscher, *Schuldrecht* (8th edn., 1992).

Kötz = H. Kötz, *Deliktsrecht* (5th edn., 1991).

Larenz I = K. Larenz, *Lehrbuch des Schuldrechts* I (General part, 14th edn., 1987).

Larenz II = K. Larenz, *Lehrbuch des Schuldrechts* II (Special part, first vol., 13th edn., 1986); II (Special part, 12th edn., 1981).

Medicus = D. Medicus, *Bürgerliches Recht* (15th edn., 1991).

Palandt = O. Palandt, *Bürgerliches Gesetzbuch* (52nd edn., 1992).

IN ENGLISH

Clerk and Lindsell = Clerk and Lindsell, *On Torts* (Gen. ed. R. W. M. Dias, 11th edn., 1986).

Fleming = J. G. Fleming, *The Law of Torts* (7th edn., 1987).

Franklin = M. A. Franklin and R. L. Rabin, *Tort Law and Alternatives* (5th edn., 1992).

Epstein = R. A. Epstein, *Cases and Materials on Torts* (5th edn., 1990).

Harper, James, and Gray = F. V. Harper, Fleming James, Jr., and O. S. Gray, *The Law of Torts* (2nd edn., 1986).

Henderson and Pearson = J. A. Henderson and R. N. Pearson, *The Torts Process* (3rd edn., 1988).

Lawson and Markesinis = F. H. Lawson and B. S. Markesinis, *Tortious Liability for Unintentional Harm in the Common Law and the Civil Law*, 2 vols. (1982).

Posner = R. A. Posner, *Tort Law-Cases and Economic Analysis* (1982).

Prosser, Wade, and Schwartz = W. L. Prosser, J. W. Wade, and V. E. Schwartz, *Cases and Materials on Torts* (8th edn., 1988).

Prosser and Keeton = W. L. Prosser, W. Page Keeton, D. B. Dobbs, R. E. Keeton, and D. G. Owen, *Law of Torts* (5th edn., 1984).

Zweigert, K., and Kötz, H. = *An Introduction to Comparative Law* II (2nd edn., 1987) (Eng. trans. by Tony Weir).

'What is striking and mysterious in comparing two legal systems is the ways they are similar and the ways they are different. Much of what follows will be of immediate use to [Common] lawyers only in so far as the contrasts between German and [Common] law make them more sharply aware of the fundamental character of their own legal system. By seeing how another . . . advanced culture can make entirely different arrangements for things they have always supposed to be matters of course—things that obviously must be this way and not the other—they also may gain a critical outlook and an expanded capacity for adapting their own system's traditional institutions to the practical needs of real life as they evolve. On the other hand, much in this book addresses problems that are virtually identical in both systems. Recognising and solving a problem becomes remarkably easier when it shows up wearing a peculiar foreign costume.'*

* Karl N. Llewellyn, *The Case Law System in America*, English edition by P. Gewirtz and M. Ausaldi (1989), 1. (In Llewellyn's original the word used in the first bracket is 'German' and in the second is 'American'.)

Foreword to the Third Edition

The *German Law of Torts* has, within a remarkably short period, become a classic of European legal literature. Three editions in under eight years: the record speaks for itself. For the monoglot English-speaking reader, Professor Markesinis' book has no peer and no rival.

The reasons for the book's outstanding success are not hard to divine. First is the intrinsic interest and importance of the subject. Only a small part of the German Civil Code is devoted to the law of torts, but it is an important, perhaps increasingly important, part. And the Code itself, described by Maitland as 'the most carefully considered statement of a nation's law that the world has ever seen', is a work well worthy of serious study. That is a truth which our fathers perhaps overlooked, but of which our grandfathers were fully aware.

A distinguished scholarly survey of the tort paragraphs in the German Code would be achievement enough. But it would scarcely earn the widespread acclaim with which successive editions of the book have been greeted. That is the product of the book's second great virtue: its treatment of German tort law not as a series of abstract principles or general theories but as a code of legal rules worked out and refined by practical application in the courts to actual human beings in real situations. So the law comes to life in a way readily understood by the common lawyer, and congenial to him, not as the dream of a legal philosopher but as a source of solutions to practical problems, a system deeply rooted in the untidy earth of ordinary life. This is as much a casebook as a treatise on jurisprudence.

It is, however, the book's third great virtue which assures it a place in the library of the well-armed practitioner (and even judge). That virtue, proclaimed in the full title to the book, lies in the expert and skilful comparisons persistently drawn between the solutions achieved by German judges applying the Code and judges in the United Kingdom and other common law jurisdictions applying rules derived from statute and authority. Problems which have exercised, and often baffled, common law judges—responsibility for economic loss, the scope of duties of care, liability for psychiatric damage, the protection of privacy, environmental liability—are here set in a comparative context which yields fresh insights, suggests new possibilities and stimulates the jaded imagination.

Professor Markesinis has chosen his moment well. As the countries of Western Europe draw closer together, as frontiers disappear and barriers fall, opportunities to learn from the experience of others become more plentiful and the need to take advantage of those opportunities more obvious.

This important book may fairly be seen as contributing to that increase in mutual understanding upon which international harmony and co-operation so closely depend.

Royal Courts of Justice   T. H. BINGHAM
25 March 1994   MR

Foreword to the Second Edition

I AM honoured to be invited to contribute a Foreword to the Second Edition of this remarkable and, certainly to me, most valuable book.

The theoretical case for the study of comparative law has long been made out. The problem now is not *whether* comparative law should be taught in our universities, and studied by our law students. The problem is rather *how* it should be presented, not merely as an aspect of legal culture, but as a subject which is capable of influencing our work, whether as scholars or as practising lawyers in the development, exposition and application of legal principles, in the context of our own domestic legal system.

It must never be forgotten, by those who teach and write about law, that, for those who study it and those who practise it, our own domestic law bristles with difficulties which are hard to master, and problems which are difficult to solve. In working through a heavy university curriculum, and in the helter-skelter of professional life (whether in practice or on the bench), it is not at all easy to accommodate the introduction of material from other legal systems, and especially from civil law systems with which we are unfamiliar. Even in appellate tribunals, it is hard enough to master and to reconcile existing English material—statutes, cases and academic writings. Moreover, in the great majority of cases, the point is a relatively narrow one which is subjected to intensive examination; and it is the practical implications of any particular solution which exercise, perhaps, the greatest influence.

It is only by grasping the practicalities of university study, of professional lawyers' practices, and of work in the courts, that it is possible to conceive an appropriate vehicle for bringing comparative law to bear, as a useful tool, and as an effective influence. For these purposes, books on comparative law which are general in nature, however admirable in themselves, however educational in a cultural sense, are of little direct use. To be influential in a more practical way, comparative law material has to be far more closely focused; and, not only that, it has to be readily comprehensible, practically orientated, and thoroughly reliable, by which I mean both accurate and up to date.

It stands to Professor Markesinis' great credit that he has fully grasped the realities of the situation in which the comparative lawyer finds himself. He understands how necessary it is that work on comparative law should be closely focused, for it to be of practical benefit to English lawyers. He understands how necessary it is that such work should be thoroughly reliable, demonstrating the author's deep and genuine understanding of this subject, set in the practical and theoretical context of its own legal system. He understands how necessary it is that it should be readily comprehensible; for example, despite his own mastery of languages, he recognizes the need to present the primary sources in copious and felicitous translation for the English lawyer. He understands, too, the need for it to be practically useful, by travelling far beyond the provisions of codes to the real cases which trouble the courts and by including reported judgments from those cases, set in their theoretical context as seen by indigenous lawyers.

It is perhaps even more to Professor Markesinis' credit that he is not only capable of mastering fully a substantial topic from a foreign system of law demonstrating his expertise to the satisfaction of leading lawyers from that legal system; he also has the courage to embark upon so exacting a task as the critical exposition of such a topic, and the determination and industry to carry that task through to its fulfilment.

I speak, of course, of the present book, his *Comparative Introduction to the German Law of Torts*. It came as no surprise to me that the first edition of the book was so successful and was so warmly received. I know of no more directly useful book on comparative law than this. It is a book which can not only be usefully consulted by creative lawyers in this country; it is one which is capable of influencing directly the solution of problems with which we have to grapple in our own domestic law. Too often, German law is presented to us as over-theoretical and ridden with concepts. Here, however, we can see German judges at work, tackling the same problems as we have to tackle, coming up with solutions sometimes the same as ours, sometimes different—and, when they are different, sometimes (it may be thought) better than those which we have chosen. It has truly been said that the most beneficent effect of the study of other systems of law is that we learn more about our own. In this book, Professor Markesinis has taught us all how comparative law is best presented to achieve that admirable objective.

I gladly commend this new edition. As with all new editions of successful law books, it has grown in size. But, as the reader will soon discover, this is no mere update; it has involved substantial rewriting, as well as the incorporation of much new and valuable material, from Anglo-American law as well as from German law. In the result, it will be even more useful to us than its predecessor; and I am bold enough to predict that it will be even more successful.

House of Lords   ROBERT GOFF

Foreword to the First Edition

WHEN I was invited to write a few words of introduction to this book I accepted immediately and without any hesitation, even though at that time I had not yet read the manuscript. Lawyers usually are cautious people, but in this case there was no risk involved. Since I knew the author's previous publications dealing with the law of tort on a comparative basis, I had no doubt that his project of a *Comparative Introduction to the German Law of Tort* would be a great success. There were two further reasons why I gladly accepted this invitation. For many years the author co-operated most fruitfully with the late Professor Lawson, who some decades ago was my tutor in Oxford. Both Dr Markesinis and I owe this great comparatist very much, for he had the rare gift of illuminating difficult problems by quick and penetrating observations. The other reason is the author's connection with Cornell Law School, which encouraged and supported this book. This brings back to my memory the wonderful time I spent there working in Rudi Schlesinger's team exploring the common core of legal systems in the area of formation of contracts—a project of comparative law conducted under the auspices of the Cornell Law School which has been favourably received by scholars all over the world.

The present book, I am sure, will not merely serve its immediate purpose of introducing the reader to the German law of tort; no doubt it will also open many new perspectives for the general understanding of this legal system belonging to the civil law. Apart from family law, which has undergone rapid changes in most countries since 1945, the law of liability is an area where many important developments have taken place. Even a superficial look at the index of any of the ninety volumes of the official collection of civil cases decided by the Federal Supreme Court will suffice to confirm this impression: the number of reported cases on problems of civil liability is remarkable. Many of them have given rise to vivid discussion in German legal literature, thus confronting the courts with new ideas. This had led to a fruitful exchange of ideas between bench and scholars unknown in most of the other legal systems. The care with which the Federal Supreme Court considers critical views put forward against its opinions is sufficient evidence of this.

The importance of the law of liability and its special value for academic teaching in the Federal Republic of Germany is further stressed by the somewhat complicated interaction of contract and tort which has reached the point where the boundaries between these two areas of the law have become blurred. The different approaches taken by the German Civil Code in regard to vicarious liability in contractual relations on the one hand, and in the law of tort on the other, have certainly contributed much to the tendency to enlarge the field of contractual liability, thus filling gaps found to exist in the law of tort. However, the much disputed § 831 of the Civil Code dealing with the responsibility of employers for tortious acts committed by their employees in the course of employment which used to be a stumbling-block for plaintiffs in former times has lost much of its significance in actual legal practice, because increasingly the courts have shifted the emphasis on the basic rule contained in § 823 I Civil Code. This means that they will look into the relevant business organization rather than try to establish the employer's fault in the selection or supervision of an individual, thereby depriving the employer of the chance to exculpate himself. The burning problem nowadays is whether purely economic loss must be made good in ordinary negligence cases, where the parties have not been in contractual relations *stricto sensu*. Liability for negligent misstatements is but one group of cases in which this problem has arisen. Here as elsewhere in this book Dr Markesinis has succeeded completely in selecting those cases which are most instructive. Therefore the reader obtains all the information he needs in order to find out how the law stands in such important fields as, for instance, products liability, medical malpractice, and traffic accidents. However, it is the thorough, comparative discussion accompanying each group of cases that makes reading this book a great pleasure even for one already familiar with the material. Although this book was written for students belonging to the Anglo-American legal family I would, therefore, like to recommend it to students of other legal backgrounds as well, because the problems dealt with are of a universal nature in the sense that each developed legal system has to deal with them.

WERNER LORENZ

University of Munich
Faculty of Law

Preface to The German Law of Obligations

Volume II
The Law of Torts

With the appearance of this edition—a corrected third for Volume two and the first of Volume one—the work I started at the Cornell Law School in the early eighties is two thirds on its way to completion. What remains to be written is the third and last of the projected volumes, dealing with the French law of obligations, and the reader will then have a comparative textbook and casebook on the American, English, French, and German law of obligations conceived by one mind though, because of lack of time, increasingly written in collaboration with learned colleagues. In the completion of this Herculean task one must immediately stress the invaluable assistance rendered by those who have tirelessly worked with the translations of close to three hundred leading German decisions. In alphabetical order they are: the late Harry Lawson (who worked closely with me for the production of some twenty-five translations), Kurt Lipstein, Joe Shaw, Irene Snook, and Tony Weir (Lipstein and Weir carrying, in fact, the lion's share of this chore).

A two-volume work which falls just short of two thousand printed pages could, of course, in one sense qualify for the glorified description of a *magnum opus*. In reality, however, it was designed as and remains an introductory work mainly aimed at students. If, occasionally, it provides some assistance to more mature legal practitioners, be they judges or practising lawyers, then this can only be regarded as an extra bonus. In academic terms, however, its greatest ambition was and is its desire to present the information it contains about German law in a way that is intelligible to and usable by Common lawyers. In that sense, the anglicization of German law, which it has attempted in its pages, is also its thesis (to the extent that textbooks are allowed to have a thesis): foreign law is best taught through cases which can be used as springboards into the ever-deeper waters of a foreign culture. How deep these plunges will be, is left to individual teachers; but in these two volumes I have tried to provide secondary (and not always legal) material which will make the experience of understanding foreign law both enjoyable and profitable. Three editions (and a reprint) in the space of less than fifteen years make one feel that one must be on the right track (even though no way near the finishing line).

Oxford 28.X.1996   Basil Markesinis

Preface to the Third Edition and Acknowledgements

WHEN, in the mid 1980s, I first proposed this book to the OUP, doubts about its commercial prospects loomed large. Only Professor Tony Honoré and Mr Richard Hart were willing to back the project to the hilt. Eight years later, academic and commercial reaction to this work have been such as to call for a third and enlarged edition. For a book of this type, size, and price, this must be a 'first' of sorts; and the publishers have decided to mark the success by making this an illustrated edition and giving me the opportunity to make more familiar to Common law readers the faces of some of Germany's great legal minds. For my part, I wish to acknowledge in public my sense of gratitude to these two friends who made sure that the first edition of this book saw the light of day.

The aims of the book are well described in the Prefaces of the two previous editions, so here suffice it to make only three additional points.

The first relates to an observation made by Professor von Bar in his review of the second edition in [1991] CLJ 356. He suggested there that 'this book sets itself and meets the task of developing an up-to-date methodology for the study of comparative law.' This may be too generous a compliment, at any rate to the extent that it ascribes to me, solely, a new methodology for comparative law. For I have always felt that I was, to a considerable degree, attempting to transplant to England the German approach to contemporary comparative law as exemplified in the work of such scholars as Professors Lorenz, Kötz and von Bar (and before them Rabel and Rheinstein). Nevertheless, the book does represent a conscious attempt to put 'into practice' the brand of comparative law I have been trying to promote in the Common law and which contrasts to the 'school' of René David which, it would appear to me, has over-valued broad-ranging descriptions and put a heavy premium on broadening cultural horizons rather than informing the foreign lawyer about the details of another system. To that extent, therefore, the book is best understood if read against the background of my writings published, inter alia, in (1993) 109 *Law Quarterly Review*, (1990) 53 *The Modern Law Review*, 1–21, 1993 *Rabels Zeitschrift*, 438–48, and in the introductory chapter I wrote for a collection of essays (which I also edited) under the title *The Gradual Convergence: Foreign Ideas, Foreign Influences and English Law on the Eve of the 21st Century* and which was also published by the O.U.P. in 1994.

My second observation, self-evident to anyone who knows German law, is that in this book the presentation of the material is not as fairly 'balanced' as it should be if it had been written with a German readership in mind. I have, in other words, given more space to topics which were of personal interest to me or, in my opinion, particularly lent themselves to treatment in classes on foreign law and comparative methodology. This may explain (though not quite justify) why, to give but one example, the space I have devoted to such important paragraphs as 823 II BGB and 826 BGB is smaller than is called for by the volume of case law generated by these important provisions of the Civil Code. Moreover, in order to assist the Common Law reader, especially the relative newcomer to the field, I have significantly enlarged my own contributions to the texts so that now, in its third edition, the book contains, roughly in equal measure, my own material (not always merely legal) and my own personal ideas, alongside the translations of the German texts. This material has consciously attempted to 'anglicize' (but, naturally, not distort) German law in order to make its ideas (though not its concepts) more transplantable into the main body of English law. This 'anglicization' of the German law can be seen as both a source of strength and weakness of this work though I, naturally, think it is the former and not the latter. At this level, however, it is no longer a book about the German law but one also concerned with legal methodology and, in this context, may be fulfilling Professor von Bar's prophecy.

Thirdly, I must stress that although there are, in this book, references to nearly one thousand German and Anglo-American cases (and I do *not* include in this count references and cross-references given in the translated decisions), the treatment of my subject is by no means complete, let alone exhaustive. This is a particularly important *caveat*, especially after Sir Robin Cooke so convincingly castigated the House of Lords (in (1991) 107 *LQR* 46) for making selective use of American material. Rich references to academic literature will, to some extent, make up for my own selectivity.

Books of this size and complexity need a great deal of time to write and also much help from colleagues and students alike. The lack of the first commodity has more than been compensated for by the constant willingness of friends to help whenever assistance was needed. The Prefaces to the first two editions record the names of those who helped with the older versions of the book. Their contribution is neither forgotten nor should it be understated. In particular, the assistance with the translations received from the late Harry Lawson, Kurt Lipstein, Tony Weir and, for the first time in this edition, from Josephine Shaw (a former student and currently Senior Lecturer at Keele University), cannot be adequately acknowledged. My interference with their texts has been occasional only and prompted not by the wish to impose uniformity but by the desire to conform with the advice of Manuel Chrysoloras—the Byzantine scholar who first rendered Greek texts into Latin in Mediaeval Italy. For his views, transmitted to us by his pupil

Cenzio de' Rustici (N. G. Wilson, *From Byzantium to Italy. Greek Studies in the Italian Renaissance* (1992), 11) strikes me as so apposite for anyone involved in technical translations that they deserve to be quoted here in full: '. . . a word for word rendering into Latin is quite inadequate . . . [for this is] not merely absurd, but at times it entirely falsifie[s] the meaning of the Greek. Instead he [Chrysoloras] said that one need[s] to translate according to the sense, on condition that those performing the task should impose upon themselves the requirement not to change in any way the idiom of the Greek. For if anyone did change the Greek idiom in order to speak more clearly or openly to his audience, he would be performing the duty of the commentator, not the translator.' If for 'Latin' one reads 'English' and substitutes 'German' for the word 'Greek', the reader will appreciate not only the wisdom of Chrysoloras' advice but also the difficulties we all had to face in making accessible to English-speaking readers some very difficult German materials.

The writing of this book also benefited greatly from a stream of letters exchanged over the years with Professors Werner Lorenz, Hein Kötz, and Christian von Bar. For not only has it made me envy their enormous and diverse learning, but also admire the tact with which they would write back and correct my misunderstandings and errors while not discouraging me in my task. I hope it will not be considered presumptuous of me to say that in my many dealings with German colleagues—and over the years I have also corresponded fruitfully with (in alphabetical order) Professors Erwin Deutsch, Dieter Giesen, and Bernhard Grossfeld—their assistance has always been given willingly, efficiently, and with incomparable style. I am also grateful to Mr William C. Hoffman of the Cologne Reinsurance Company for kindly contributing a helpful explanatory note on the German liability regime for environmental harm.

My debt to younger colleagues is just as great and it is here sincerely acknowledged since I belong to those who believe that one can learn from one's students at least as much as one teaches them. I am thus grateful to Armin Hauschield (Köln and Austin, Texas), Nancy Morton (Austin, Texas), Mark Tittel (Austin, Texas), Wolfgang Vogt (Osnabrück and London), Graham Wladimiroff (London and Leiden) for much useful 'spade work' incorporated into this edition. By far my greatest debt, however, is to Dr. Bernhard Scheifele (Mannheim and Austin) who joined a learned group of former research assistants which included in the past Dr. Kurt Clausius and Dr. Helmut Nicolaus. Like his predecessors, Dr. Scheifele displayed loyalty, reliability, thoroughness, and great learning; and he also proved a constant source of information and, not infrequently, a better teacher than I, myself, could ever hope to be.

I also gratefully acknowledge the help received from Professor Roy

Mersky, Director of the Tarlton Law Library of the University of Texas (and to Jon Pratter, immensely knowledgeable about their foreign materials), Keith McVeigh, Librarian of the Squire Law Library, and Jules Winterton, Librarian of the Institute of Advanced Legal Studies. Sincere thanks are also due to my two Personal Assistants in London (Mrs Pamela Celentano) and Texas (Mrs Consuelo Akin) who put up with me (and my endless demands related to the writing of this book) with such efficiency and good humour. Last but by no means least I wish to acknowledge a very special debt to Mrs Irene Snook who edited and proof-read the entire book, and who repeatedly demonstrated how admirable Germanic efficiency is at its best, and to Jane Williams for ably and cheerfully seeing this huge and difficult book through all the phases of production.

Grateful thanks are due to the following for permission to reproduce materials over which they hold the copyright: Edward Arnold, for permission to reprint maps nos. 3, 5 and 6 taken from M. Hughes, *Nationalism and Society: Germany 1800–1945* (London 1988); Bismarck Museum, Friedricksruhe, for the painting of Emperor William I and Bismarck; Cambridge University Press for maps nos. 1, 2, 4 taken from Dr Mary Fulbrook's *A Concise History of Germany* (Cambridge 1991); Carl Heymanns Verlag KG and C. H. Beck'sche Verlagsbuchhandlung, publishers of the Entscheidungen des Bundesgerichtshofes in Zivilsachen and the *Neue Juristische Wochenschrift*; the Kölnische Rückversicherungs-Gesellschaft AG for the use of their English version of the Environmental Liability Act; Little, Brown for permission to reprint pages 714, 736–8, 747–8 and 752–4 from von Mehren and Gordley, *The Civil Law System* 2nd edn. (1977); the Niedersächsische Staats- und Universitätsbibliothek in Göttingen for the legal map of Germany during the pre-codification period; Fred B. Rothman and Co. for permission to reprint a number of articles from *The German Civil Code* translated by I. S. Forrester, S. L. Goren and H. M. Ilgen.

October 3rd, 1993
B. S. MARKESINIS

University College London

---

* The references, omitted here to avoid confusion, were to the numbers of the first edition. In this edition the names of those who worked to produce the English versions are given at the beginning of each translated decision.

Preface to the First Edition and Acknowledgements

THIS is the first of three volumes designed to introduce Common lawyers to the Modern French and German law of contract and tort. It focuses on the German law of tort (delict) using the comparative method thus making frequent references to American, English, and French materials. It is hoped that in this way the Common lawyer will not only learn the rudiments of German tort law but will also be able to rethink his own solutions in the light of his experience with the 'foreign' law. Volume two of this series will concentrate on certain aspects of the German law of contracts, while the final volume will be devoted to the French law of obligations, contracts, and torts.

Clearly, both in size and scope, this is a work which goes beyond my own limited capacities and if the first step towards the realization of the project has been accomplished, it is principally due to two factors.

The first is the encouragement and support that I have received over the years from the Dean of the Cornell Law School, Professor Peter Martin. This went beyond asking me to take over the Comparative Law course at Cornell, so ably taught for so many years by Professor Rudi Schlesinger. The support was also manifested in a tangible way by providing funds that made the financing of these translations possible. I hope that by making widely available for the first time such a mass of foreign material, which for four years now I have been collecting and using for my lectures at Cornell, I will encourage a greater interest in modern civil law systems. Interestingly enough, my task was in fact urged upon the American Association of Law Schools some thirty years ago by the great comparatist Max Rheinstein (1 A. J. Comp. L. 95–114 (1952)), but the enormity of the work involved, acknowledged by Rheinstein himself, has obviously deterred many a more able comparatist than myself to undertake it. Dean Martin's insistence that it should, at least, be attempted is the first direct cause of this volume.

The second *sine qua non* was obtaining the help of eminent colleagues in order to translate the complex primary material. No one could have wished for a more distinguished and able team than the one I was fortunate enough to assemble.

Professor F. H. Lawson—no doubt the doyen of Comparative lawyers of his time—and I worked closely during the last seven years of his life in preparing a two-volume book entitled *Tortious Liability for Unintentional Harm in the Common Law and the Civil Law* which was published by the Cambridge University Press in 1982. Cases . . .*, reproduced here, were either first published in that book or were meant to have been included in it but were omitted for reasons of space. Most of the credit for these translations should go to Harry Lawson, and it gives me great pleasure to express once again in public my sincere gratitude for all he taught me during the years I worked with him and for him. Like all other pupils and colleagues I, too, greatly feel the loss caused by his recent death.

I was never taught by Professor Kurt Lipstein and because of his retirement we overlapped in the Cambridge Law faculty only for a couple of years. But like others I have greatly benefited from his willingness to help whenever help was needed. I am very fortunate to have received his most able and willing co-operation in this project and he should be credited for the translations of cases . . .*

Finally, my Trinity colleague Tony Weir also agreed to join us in this effort. His translation of Zweigert and Kötz's *Einführung in die Rechtsvergleichung* is, I think, widely considered to be a landmark in the art of legal translation, so I am delighted that he kindly agreed to contribute the translations of cases . . .*, which bear witness to his unique and enviable style.

The selection of the cases—never an easy task and, in this instance, made even more difficult by the absence of the notion of the 'leading case'—is mine, though I have been guided by willing colleagues and friends. Mine, also, are the introductory sections of each chapter, which are meant to give the reader a general feeling about the background and approach to German law in this field, and the annotations that accompany most decisions.

These vary in size, from the relatively modest note which merely aims at providing the interested student and teacher with further references discussing the point at issue, to the ambitious ones where I have tried, to the best of my ability, to set out the parallel solutions of English and American law. I hope this material, which, alas, has been deliberately compressed for reasons of space, will provide English lawyers with the extra impetus to look more closely at American law and, conversely, renew American interest in English law. To put it differently, there is no reason why one should limit the application of the comparative method to the study of systems that belong to different legal families. This, however, remains a subsidiary aim of the work, my prime purpose remaining the desire to provide an elementary and, I hope, readable account of the German law of torts.

As a result of trying to achieve all these different goals I have discovered rather late in the day that my own additional material now accounts for over a third of the entire book so, I suppose, this work aspires to be both a textbook and case-book for German tort law.

* The references, omitted here to avoid confusion, were to the numbers of the first edition. In this edition the names of those who worked to produce the English versions are given at the beginning of each translated decision.

For all the above, my translation colleagues bear no responsibility. Nor do the following colleagues and former students who have nevertheless helped me in many ways. Thanks are thus due to Professor Dr Hein Kötz for suggestions made in private correspondence and also for his work in this field which has influenced me in a way which is as profound as it will be obvious; to Professor Dr Werner Lorenz, an old friend of Cornell's, to whom I owe a special debt of gratitude for reading through the entire manuscript and giving me the benefit of his acknowledged expertise. And as if all this were not enough, he has most generously contributed a Foreword to my audacious attempt to try and explain his own law to foreign students. Thanks are also due to my colleague and friend Professor Christian von Bar for generous advice and encouragement given whenever requested. Special thanks are due to Messrs Carl Heymanns Verlag KG and C. H. Beck'sche Verlagsbuchhandlung, publishers of the Entscheidungen des Bundesgerichtshofes in Zivilsachen and the *Neue Juristische Wochenschrift* respectively for their generous permission to reproduce here in translated form extracts of some of the judicial decisions published in their learned editions. I also gratefully acknowledge the permission extended by the following authors and publishers to reprint excerpts from the works indicated: Arthur T. von Mehren and James R. Gordley, *The Civil Law System*, 2nd edn., 1977 (Little, Brown and Company) pp. 714, 736–8, 747–8, 752–4; F. H. Lawson and B. S. Markesinis, *Tortious Liability for Unintentional Harm in the Common Law and the Civil Law*, vol. II, 1982 (Cambridge University Press) pp. 54–62, 76–176. Finally, I wish to thank the following pupils of mine who at various times gave me valuable assistance with the collection of the material: Gena Cadieux JD (Cornell), Josephine Shaw BA (Cambridge) and now lecturer in Law at Exeter University, and Mr Helmut Nicolaus of the University of Heidelberg. Last but not least I wish to thank Mrs Laura Cordy for her patience and unremitting work in typing the manuscript, and the publishers for their helpful co-operation at every stage.

B. S. MARKESINIS

Trinity College
Cambridge
10 July 1984

I

Introduction

THE idea of a German supreme court can trace its origins to at least the end
of the fifteenth century and the creation in 1495 of the Reichskammergericht of the Holy Roman Empire which originally sat in Frankfurt.
The prevailing political fragmentation, however, prevented it from exercising any effective influence, especially in the area of the unification of the
law, and even the Emperor himself held his own court in Vienna which
often competed with the Reichskammergericht. A truly central supreme
court had thus to await the unification of Germany which was eventually
realized under Bismarck's strong hand in 1871, when the Second German
Reich came into being, embracing Prussia (which retained a special status
and dominated the new federal state), the kingdoms of Bavaria, Saxony,
and Wurttemberg, eighteen 'lesser' states, the three 'free' cities of Hamburg,
Bremen, and Lübeck and the so-called *Reichsland* (imperial territory) of
Alsace-Lorraine which was ceded to the Empire by the Treaty of Frankfurt
of 10 May 1871 but which for some time thereafter retained a special status
(indeed was until 1879 administered directly from Bismarck's office). This
was a complicated constitutional arrangement, as were many that had preceded it; but before a British lawyer hurriedly condemns it as 'typically'
German, he should pause for a moment and reflect on the difficulties faced
by his Continental counter-parts trying to comprehend the equally complex
constitutional arrangements between England and Wales, Scotland, and
Northern Ireland, not to mention the special status of the Channel Islands.
Here then, again, history provides, if not a convincing justification, at least
an explanation for the existing complications.

We need not reflect here on the extent to which this unification can, some
one hundred and thirty years later, be judged as satisfactory or, even, complete. Certainly, those who know Germany well will be quick to mention
both substantial differences in the language (there are over one hundred
dialects) and lingering mutual suspicions between the various States that

FEDERAL LEVEL

I Supreme Constitutional Court
Bundesverfassungsgericht
(situated in Karlsruhe)

II Supreme Courts (Federal Level)

(1) Administrative Matters
Federal Administrative Court
Bundesverwaltungsgericht
(situated in Berlin)

(2) Financial Matters
Federal Tax Court
Bundesfinanzhof
(situated in Munich)

(3) Labour Matters
Federal Labour Court
Bundesarbeitsgericht
(situated in Kassel)

(4) Social Security Matters
Federal Court of Social Matters
Bundessozialgericht
(situated in Kassel)

(5) Civil and Criminal Matters
Federal Supreme Court
Bundesgerichtshof
(situated in Karlsruhe)
(10 Civil Senates) (5 Criminal Senates)
5 judges, 5 judges,
sitting in sitting in
panels of five
(Grosser Senat)
(Vereinigte Große Senate)

(6) Industrial Property (Patents)
Bundespatentgericht
(Federal Court ranking as a Court of Appeal; appeals from its decisions are heard by the *Bundesgerichtshof*)

LÄNDER LEVEL

III
Administrative Courts of Appeal
Oberverwaltungsgericht

Court of Appeal in Social Matters
Landessozialgericht

Labour Court of Appeal
Landesarbeitsgericht

Court of Appeal
Oberlandesgericht

IV
Administrative Court
Verwaltungsgericht

Tax Court
Finanzgericht

Labour Court
Arbeitsgericht
(§ 566 ZPO)

Court of Social Matters
Sozialgericht
(1 or 3 judges
§ 348 ZPO)

District Court
Landgericht
(General jurisdiction or appeal from *Amtsgericht*)
Civil and Commercial Matters
(1 judge, 2 lay judges)

Criminal Section
(professional and lay judges)

Local or 'County' Court
Amtsgericht

Jurisdiction = up to DM 10,000 special matters (landlord/tenant, matrimonial etc.) divorce etc.:
Familiengericht } 1 judge

Previous German Courts

Reichskammergericht = 1495
Reichsgericht = 1879 (Leipzig) –1945
Bundesgerichtshof = 1953 (Karlsruhe)

form the Federation. Yet again, however, the English lawyer (who has also assumed the role of speaking for the Welshman while ignoring the historically more cosmopolitan Scot or his counter-part from Northern Ireland) can easily overstate the cohesiveness. Happily, the tort lawyer need not explore these fascinating questions in any detail. For present purposes it will suffice merely to say that the political union which was forged in the 1870s made inevitable the legal union that followed.

Even then it was some years before the Reichsgericht came into being on 1 October 1879, this time, however, sitting in Leipzig. This was truly the first supreme court for the whole of Germany, and though other high federal courts subsequently saw the light of day, jurisdiction at the highest level was never divided. The Reichsgericht thus survived until the end of the Second World War (1945). During the next few years, while Germany lay in ruins and under foreign occupation, there was no federal supreme court, and as a result there followed an immediate and disturbing fragmentation of the law administered in the different parts of the country. The first attempts to re-establish some semblance of unity were made in 1947 in the British-occupied zone when a special Court of Justice was entrusted with this task. However, it was not until 1 October 1950, a year after the enactment of the Constitution of Bonn (GG)*, that the Bundesgerichtshof was established, this time in Karlsruhe. The scene was thus set for a 'judicial recovery' from the traumatic years of the Nazi period and the post-war chaos—a recovery which, in some respects, is as admirable as the more publicized 'economic miracle' of the 1950s which so symbolizes the tenacity and determination of the German people.

Though in most respects modelled on the Reichsgericht, the Bundesgerichtshof was no longer accepted as the unique, supreme federal court. The desire for increased specialization, which is an important characteristic of the German judicial structure, meant that along with the Bundesgerichtshof, which became the Supreme Court for civil and criminal matters, four other Supreme Courts also came into being (each at the head of a separate set of courts with its own organization and personnel) dealing respectively with administrative law, financial matters, labour matters, and social legislation (Art. 95 GG). Alongside these, the Federal Constitutional Court (Bundesverfassungsgericht) was entrusted with the task of ensuring the preservation of the new Constitution and the control of the constitutionality of legislation (Arts. 93, 94 GG). These six courts, and the Federal Patent Court (Bundespatentgericht) (which, however, acts and ranks as a

---

* *Grundgesetz* is sometimes literally translated as Basic (Constitutional) Law; and it was so called in German since the belief was that a Constitution (*Verfassung der Bundesrepublik Deutschland*) could only be drafted once Germany was reunited. For the benefit of Anglo-American readers, however, *Grundgesetz* (GG) has in this book been more often rendered as 'the Constitution'.

Court of Appeal) are federal courts; *all* other courts are State courts (i.e.
equipped and maintained by the now sixteen States (Länder)). Two
differences thus spring to mind with the United States where a federal structure has been adopted by the Constitution. First, in Germany unlike the
USA, the Federal Government maintains no federal courts at the first and
second level (the Patent Court, mentioned above, being the only exception).
Secondly, however, in Germany and unlike America, each State has its own
Constitutional Court which is meant to ensure that the *State* constitution
is observed. The patterns of federalism are thus truly almost endless. (See
Fig. 1.)

This proliferation of supreme courts has brought with it the possibility of
jurisdictional conflicts, positive or negative in nature (e.g. two or more
courts asserting or denying jurisdiction over the same dispute, now largely
regulated by the Gerichtsverfassungsgesetz as amended in 1960) as well as
the likelihood of a diverging case-law on matters of substance. To resolve
this latter conflict, and in order to ensure the unity of the federal law, Art.
95 of the Constitution of Bonn provided for the creation of a highest federal
court (Oberstes Bundesgericht) but this, in fact, never came into being, and
a constitutional amendment of 1968 provided, instead, for a 'Common
Senate' (Gemeinsamer Senat) composed of judges from the other five
Supreme Courts. The task of this court is to rule whenever one of the
Supreme Courts proposes to depart from the case-law of another Supreme
Court or a holding of the Common Senate. Since in this work our emphasis
will be on the civil law, the remaining observations will be devoted to the
organization of the civil courts and the civil side of the Bundesgerichtshof.

The lowest court on civil matters is the Amtsgericht of which there are a
large number (approximately 550 in the old West Germany and nearly 200
in the former East Germany). They have (as of March 1993) limited and
specifically ascribed jurisdiction which includes disputes up to the value of
DM 10,000. In addition they deal with such varied matters as disputes
between landlords and tenants; claims for financial support arising from
marital or extramarital relationships; the supervision of guardians, executors, and trustees in bankruptcy; and the handling of various registers
including the all-important land register. Since 1977 all family matters, especially those associated with divorce proceedings, matrimonial property,
alimony, etc., are heard by a special division of the court, the
Familiengericht, and from there an appeal lies directly to the appropriate
Oberlandesgericht. Appeals from all other decisions of an Amtsgericht can
be filed with the appropriate Landgericht provided the amount in dispute
exceeds DM 1200. (See § 511a ZPO.) Though hierarchically an inferior
court (and, in some respects, analogous to the County Court), the
Amtsgericht is thus a court of singular importance to the average citizen

who in his lifetime is usually spared the agony and the cost of the more prolonged or difficult type of litigation.

It is in the Landgericht, however, that one finds the equivalent of the
English High Court, and their large number (just under one hundred in the
former West Germany and an estimated twenty in what used to be East
Germany) brings out clearly the second important characteristic of the
German judicial organization, namely the considerable decentralization in
the administration of justice. The Landgericht is a court of general jurisdiction and sits as either a trial court or a court of review from any
Amtsgericht of its district—a lawyer (*Rechtsanwalt*) representing the parties
before this higher court. The Landgericht is usually divided into sections (or
chambers) each of which includes a presiding judge and two associates (all
three being professional and academically trained judges except those sitting
in the Kammer für Handelssachen (the commercial division) which is composed of one professional judge as president and two laymen experienced in
commercial matters). From these courts an appeal (*Berufung*) lies to one of
the nineteen Courts of Appeal which is called the Oberlandesgericht except
for the one that sits in Berlin, which has always been known as the
Kammergericht. Some Länder (namely Bremen, Hamburg, Hessen,
Saarland, and Schleswig-Holstein) have only one Court of Appeal; others
(e.g. Bavaria) have more. (Bavaria, in fact, also has an *Oberstes
Landesgericht* (ObLG) which handles applications for revision related to
State law.) To these Courts of Appeal five more have been added since re-
unification, one for each new *Land*. Quite exceptionally, a Court of Appeal
can be bypassed and an appeal against a decision of the *Landgericht* can be
lodged directly with the Bundesgerichtshof. This, however, is likely to occur
only where the facts of the case are not in dispute and both parties, desirous
of an early solution to their dispute, are willing to utilize this leap-frogging
procedure (*Sprungrevision*) (§ 566a ZPO).

The Bundesgerichtshof stands, as already stated, at the apex of the judi-
cial hierarchy in civil and criminal matters, now hearing cases from all
courts of the re-united Germany. (Cases from the 'new' Länder can be
found reported from vol. 117 of the BGHZE.) It is divided into ten Civil
Senates (sections) and five Criminal Senates (of which one always sits in
West Berlin). Each Senate specializes in different matters. The Sixth Civil
Senate, for example, deals with problems of delictual liability; the Seventh
Civil Senate with various types of contract and cases of unjust enrichment;
the Eighth Civil Senate handles disputes related to sales of goods, leases, etc.
When deciding a case each Senate is composed of one presiding judge and
four other Supreme Court judges, and the entire Bundesgerichtshof is now
staffed by over one hundred Supreme Court judges who are aided by specialist staff.

obligatoire des précédents en droit privé allemand', 4èmes Journées Franco-
Allemandes, 13–17 juin 1984 in *Rev. intern. dr. comp.* no. spécial, vol. 6, p. 189
(1984). Many of the points made in this section are also discussed in greater detail in
the standard textbooks on the law of civil procedure (*Zivilprozessordnung*). For a
more general discussion of the legal aspects of re-unification see Hailbronner, 'Legal
Aspects of the Unification of the Two German States' 1991 *European Journal of
International Law* no. 2, pp. 18 *et seq.*

2.   THE STYLE AND FORM OF THE JUDGMENTS OF THE BGH[1]

A judgment of the German Supreme Court presents some marked
differences both in style and form from the judgments of, say, the House of
Lords or the French *Cour de cassation*. In terms of length, the contrast is
greater with the French decisions (especially of the Cour de cassation),
which are unparalleled in terseness and peculiarity of grammatical style. For
example, a typical German judgment dealing with a contractual or delictual
matter, will run to about 2000–2500 words—in a minority of cases reaching
the 5000-word range. (Judgments of the Federal Constitutional Court tend
to be much longer.) In length they thus tend to be closer to the average
American decision than to the longer judgments of the House of Lords. One
also acquires the impression—though to my knowledge no empirical study
has been conducted on this matter—that the average decision of the
Reichsgericht was shorter during the nineteenth century and the earlier part
of this century than it has been since the end of the Second World War.

Like the French decisions, but unlike the Anglo-American equivalents,
the decisions of the German Supreme Court are unanimous decisions of the
entire court. Clearly this does not mean that there are never any disagreements between the judges trying a particular case; but it does mean that in
the published decision there are no open dissents. The court decides by simple majority (judges voting in inverted order of seniority, the presiding judge
voting last). Thus, on occasion, the phrasing of the judgment requires very
careful drafting in order to express the compromise formula agreed upon by
the members of the court. By contrast, dissenting judgments are allowed in
the Federal constitutional law and the judges make frequent use of this
right.

Typically the report of a judgment will commence with a couple of paragraphs containing in abstract form the propositions of the law supported by
the decision. This section of the report forms no part of the decision and in
the translations reproduced in this book it has, consequently, been omitted.

---

[1] In this section I have drawn on my article 'Conceptualism, Pragmatism and Courage: A
Common Lawyer Looks at some Judgments of the Federal Court', 34 *A. J. Comp. L.* 349
(1986).

These paragraphs will be followed by references to the articles of the Civil or Criminal Code (or other enactments) that had to be construed and applied in the case. The section of the court that had to decide the case will then be given and this will be followed by the date on which the trial was concluded and the initials of the parties to the action. This is the form adopted in the semi-official reports quoted as BGHZ and followed by the number of the volume and the page on which the decision is reproduced. Other reports—the *NJW*, for example—follow a slightly different order of presentation.

The facts of the case (*Tatbestand*) will then follow—usually an abbreviated form of the judgment of the Court of Appeal. Quite frequently, sections of the legal reasoning of the Court of Appeal will also be reproduced and the court will then indicate whether it agrees or disagrees with the reasoning and/or the result. It will then proceed to consider the grounds for appeal advanced by the appellant and give its own reasons for its conclusions.

The extent to which the facts will be given in detail will vary from case to case; sometimes the court merely states that the facts, as found by the lower court, are inadequate, then gives its opinion on the question of law and finally, refers the case back to the lower courts to discover the relevant facts in the light of the law as stated by the court. But the statement of facts is never as detailed as it is in English (or American) judgments, the court not being obliged to indulge in the kind of detailed consideration of material which is necessary in the Common law in order to decide whether the case before it is covered by an earlier authority or whether, on the contrary, the present facts are materially different and thus justify distinguishing it from earlier precedents.

The legal arguments that follow are presented in an abstract manner which is not always easy for a Common lawyer to follow or even to translate accurately. For first of all, the tone of the argument can be highly conceptual, even metaphysical. Sections of the judgments dealing with the protection of human personality (see below, cases 29–32) are just that, and they will, in turn, generate academic literature which can reach heights of abstraction unthought of in the Common law. The discussion of the notion of 'unlawfulness' in the decision of the Great Senate (below, case 87) provides yet another example of this phenomenon (though this controversial judgment is now regarded as obsolete). Clearly, the decision is incomprehensible (even to a young German lawyer) and some explanation of the problem and the disputes it has generated must precede any study of this case.

Another difference—especially from English decisions—is the detailed consideration of the views of contemporary (and past) academic writers dealing with the subject before the court. In particular, what is usually referred to as the 'dominant opinion' (*herrschende Meinung*), which is the opinion on a certain matter as reflected in the majority of writings and decisions, will enjoy strong persuasive authority. Sometimes judgments contain more than a mere reference to academic literature; they can produce an admirably lucid summary of the views of the academic world, only to add immediately—one suspects with some measure of despair—that the solution to the problem should, in the end, depend on common sense and not theoretical constructions, however admirable they may be. One of the leading judgments on legal cause (case 60)—a subject that has greatly attracted the German legal mind—offers an excellent illustration, and should act as a caution for those who overstress the Germanic tendency towards conceptualism and abstraction. The chicken-pest case (below, case 43) furnishes yet another example of the court's willingness to take into account the views of academic writers, if only to reject them and then offer its own solution. This judgment is, in fact, a teacher's dream in so far as it offers an excellent springboard from which to consider the various theories behind modern products liability law. Moreover, the interesting thing about this dialogue between court and academics is that it helps perpetuate this interaction from which, apparently, both branches of the profession stand to gain. For writers will respond to such judicial criticism and often come up with new theories or modifications of existing theories that may well be later accepted by the court. The overall impression that one gets is one of mutual respect and reciprocal influence and it is not uncommon to find the court expressly adopting the views of a certain writer on a particular problem. Thus, to give but one example, the whole doctrine of contract with protective effects *vis-à-vis* a third party (as a variant of the classical contract in favour of third parties regulated by the BGB in §§ 328 ff.) was largely taken over by the courts from the teachings of Professor Larenz. Another example of this close co-operation between academic writers and the courts can be found in the judicial development of § 242 BGB (good faith) which will be discussed in detail in the second volume of this work.

The previous case-law—especially of the Supreme Court itself—is also considered and quoted in the judgments but again in a manner quite different from that adopted by the Anglo-American courts. Rarely will a quote be given in order to distinguish one case before the court from the previous one. More often, it will be given to show what the established practice of the court is on a particular matter and to reinforce the present argument. Many of the differences with Anglo-American law are obviously due to the doctrine of *stare decisis* which, subject to the rather few special occasions already alluded to in the previous section, is not known to German law. This is not to say, of course, that an inferior court will easily depart from the line taken by the BGH—especially if there is a series of decisions (*ständige Rechtsprechung*) substantially to the same effect. Statute and custom are, therefore, technically the only true sources of law (though *published* preparatory works can be used in order to discover the intention of the legislator as part of the technique of interpretation of any law). On the other hand, it is not unknown for the various State Courts of Appeal to 'rebel' against a particular decision of the Supreme Court. Sometimes—as in the case of the recognition of the general right to one's personality—the rebellion will be short-lived and within a relatively short period of time the Supreme Court will manage to assert its will; in other instances, however, the reaction of the Courts of Appeal may be stronger and more persistent, which can then force the BGH to reconsider its own decision on this matter. As we shall see (below, case 9), this is what happened in the context of the 'cable' cases and the reparation of purely economic loss through § 823 II BGB.

German judges (and lawyers generally) could be accused of leaving nothing to the imagination. Certainly the elegance, humour, and high literary style achieved by some English and American judges are often sacrificed at the altar of accuracy and thoroughness. For example, the Lord Denning type of presentation of facts, with the judge in the middle of the human drama rather than in the role of an impersonal adjudicator, is quite unknown in Germany. Equally, the desire to express in accurate and impersonal terminology a particular problem can deprive the judgment of elegance, even of life. An excellent illustration of this can be found by comparing two rescue cases—one German and one American (below, case 45, compared with *Wagner* v. *International Rly Co.*, 232 NY 176, 133 NE 437 (1921)). The problem and the solution proposed are identical. No wonder, since the policy reasons behind the similar results are the same. But Cardozo J.'s memorable words: 'Danger invites rescue. The cry of distress is the summons of relief . . .' are replaced by dry, causative language of the type which helps create the popularly conceived image of German law and its lawyers.

Like all generalizations, however, the above must be treated with some caution. For the contact with 'reality' and the true forces that shape the law can often be found in the short but clear references to various policy factors that the judges are increasingly making. The fear of 'innumerable claims', if negligently inflicted economic loss were to become compensatable, is clearly voiced in some of the 'cable' cases (9 and 10); and if this is read in conjunction with the writings of modern commentators on this subject one realizes that this policy factor (and others, such as insurance) lie behind the refusal to compensate cases of negligently inflicted economic loss. All of a sudden, the impressive conceptual armoury used by the courts to deny the plaintiff's claim becomes a façade; the concepts are nothing but devices that formulate the conclusions of the judges but do not really explain them.

The 'contact' with the real world and its sufferings is also seen in many contract cases. The revalorization cases of the early and middle twenties, which will be discussed in volume two in connection with § 242 BGB, reveal the German judges at their boldest and most human. Incidentally, this is not only one of the most remarkable areas of judge-made law in a country of codes; it also offers the interested student excellent material for an excursus into sociology, politics, and economics and an opportunity to see how law is shaped by the changing demands of social life. In one of these leading cases the Reichsgericht thus stressed that: 'The first and noblest task of the judge is . . . to satisfy in his decisions the imperative demands of life and to allow himself in this respect to be guided by the experience of life' (see RGZ 100, 129).

3.   THE DELICT PROVISIONS OF THE BGB

§ 823. A person who wilfully or negligently injures the life, body, health, freedom, property, or other right of another contrary to law is bound to compensate him for any damage arising therefrom.

The same obligation attaches to a person who infringes a statutory provision intended for the protection of others. If according to the purview of the statute infringement is possible even without fault, the duty to make compensation arises only if some fault can be imputed to the wrongdoer.

§ 824. A person who maintains or publishes, contrary to the truth, a statement calculated to endanger the credit of another, or to injure his earnings or prospects in any other manner, must compensate the other for any damage arising therefrom, even if he does not know of its untruth, provided he ought to know.

A communication the untruth of which is unknown to the person making it does not thereby render him liable to make compensation, if he or the recipient of the communication has a justifiable interest in it.

§ 825. A person who by fraud or threats, or by an abuse of the relation of dependence, induces a woman to permit illicit cohabitation is bound to compensate her for damage arising therefrom.

§ 826. A person who wilfully causes damage to another in a manner *contra bonos mores* is bound to compensate the other for the damage.

§ 827. A person who does damage to another in a condition of unconsciousness, or in a condition of morbid disturbance of the mental activity, incompatible with a free determination of the will, is not responsible for the damage. If he had brought himself into a temporary condition of this kind by spirituous liquors or similar means, he is responsible for any damage which he unlawfully causes in this condition in the same manner as if negligence were imputable to him; the responsibility does not arise if he has been brought into this condition without fault.

§ 828. A person who has not completed his seventh year of age is not responsible for any damage which he does to another.

A person who has completed his seventh year but not his eighteenth year of age is not responsible for any damage which he does to another, if at the time of committing the damaging act he did not have the understanding necessary to realize his responsibility. The same rule applies to a deaf mute.

§ 829. A person who in any one of the cases specified in §§ 823–6 is by virtue of §§ 827, 828 not responsible for any damage caused by him, must, nevertheless, to the extent that compensation cannot be obtained from a third party charged with the duty of supervision, make compensation for the damage in so far as according to the circumstances—in particular according to the relative positions of the parties—equity requires indemnification, and he is not deprived of the means which he needs for his own maintenance according to his station in life and for the fulfilment of his statutory duties to furnish maintenance to others.

§ 830. If several persons have caused damage by an unlawful act committed in common, each is responsible for the damage. The same rule applies if it cannot be discovered which of several participants has actually caused the damage.

Instigators and accomplices are in the same position as joint-doers.

§ 831. A person who employs another to do any work is bound to compensate for damage which the other unlawfully causes to a third party in the performance of his work. The duty to compensate does not arise if the employer has exercised ordinary care in the choice of the employee, and, where he has to supply appliances or implements or to superintend the work, has also exercised ordinary care as regards such supply or superintendence, or if the damage would have arisen, notwithstanding the exercise of such care.

The same responsibility attaches to a person who takes over the charge of any of the affairs specified in para. 1, sentence 2, by contract with the employer.

§ 832. A person who is bound by law to exercise supervision over a person on account of minority, or of his mental or physical condition, is bound to make compensation for any damage which the latter unlawfully does to a third party. The duty to compensate does not arise if he fulfils his duty of supervision, or if the damage would have occurred notwithstanding the proper exercise of supervision.

The same responsibility attaches to a person who takes over by contract the exercise of supervision.

§ 833. If a person is killed or injured, or the health of a person is affected, or a thing is damaged by an animal, the person who keeps the animal is bound to compensate the injured party for any damage arising therefrom. The duty to make compensation does not arise if the damage is caused by a domestic animal which is intended to serve the profession, the business activities, or the support of the keeper of the animal and if the keeper of the animal has either exercised the requisite care in supervising the animal or if the damage would have occurred notwithstanding the exercise of such care.

§ 834. A person who undertakes to supervise an animal under a contract with the keeper of the animal is responsible for any damage which the animal causes to a third party in the manner specified in § 833. The responsibility does not arise if he has exercised the requisite care in the supervision of the animal, or if the damage would have occurred notwithstanding the exercise of such care.

§ 835. [Repealed.]

§ 836. (1) If, by the collapse of a building or other structure attached to a piece of land, or by the detachment of parts of the building or structure, a person is killed or injured, or the health of a person is affected, or a thing is damaged, and if the collapse or the detachment was caused by defective construction or inadequate maintenance, the possessor of the land is bound to compensate the injured party for any damage arising therefrom. The duty to make compensation does not arise if the possessor has exercised the requisite care for the purpose of averting danger.

(2) A former possessor of the land is responsible for the damage if the collapse or the detachment occurs within one year after the termination of his possession, unless during his possession he exercised the requisite care, or unless a subsequent possessor could have averted the danger by the exercise of such care.

(3) The possessor within the meaning of these provisions is the proprietary possessor.

§ 837. If a person in the exercise of a right possesses a building or other structure on the land of another, the responsibility specified in § 836 attaches to him instead of the possessor of the land.

§ 838. A person who undertakes for the possessor the maintenance of a building or a structure attached to land, or who has to maintain the building or the structure by virtue of a right of use belonging to him, is responsible in the same manner as the possessor for any damage caused by the collapse or the detachment of parts.

§ 839. (1) If an official wilfully or negligently commits a breach of official duty incumbent upon him towards a third party, he shall compensate the third party for any damage arising therefrom. If only negligence is imputable to the official, he may be held liable only if the injured party is unable to obtain compensation otherwise.

(2) If an official commits a breach of his official duty in giving judgment in an action, he is not responsible for any damage arising therefrom, unless the breach of duty is subject to a public penalty to be enforced by criminal proceedings. This provision does not apply to a breach of duty consisting of refusal or delay in the exercise of the office.

(3) The duty to make compensation does not arise if the injured party has wilfully or negligently omitted to avert the injury by making use of a legal remedy.

§ 840. If several persons are together responsible for damage arising from an unlawful act, they are liable, subject to the provisions of § 835, section 3, as joint debtors.

If, in addition to the person liable under §§ 831, 832 to make compensation for the damage caused by another, that other person is also liable, as between themselves only the latter is liable, or in the case provided for by § 829, only the person who has the duty of supervision.

If, in addition to the person liable under §§ 833–8 to make compensation for any damage, a third party is also liable for the damage, as between themselves only such third party is liable.

§ 841. If an official whose public duty requires him to appoint another person for the purpose of acting for a third party or to supervise such an activity or to co-operate in this activity by giving his consent to legal transactions is responsible with the other person for the damage caused by him through neglect of his duties to that other party, between the two of them, is solely liable.

§ 842. The obligation to make compensation for damage on account of an unlawful act directed against the person of another extends to the detriment which the act occasions to his earnings or prospects.

§ 843. If, in consequence of an injury to body or health, the earning capacity of the injured party is destroyed or diminished or an increase of his necessities arises, compensation must be made to the injured party by the payment of a money annuity.

The provisions of § 760 apply to the annuity. Whether, in what manner, and to what amount, the person bound to make compensation has to give security is determined according to the circumstances. Instead of an annuity the victim may demand a lump sum settlement, if a serious reason exists for it.

The claim is not excluded by the fact that another person has to furnish maintenance to the injured party.

§ 844. In the case of causing death the person bound to make compensation must make good the funeral expenses to the person on whom the obligation of bearing such expenses lies.

If the deceased at the time of the injury stood in a relation to a third party by virtue of which he was or might become bound by law to furnish maintenance to him, and if in consequence of the death such third party is deprived of the right to claim maintenance, the person bound to make compensation must compensate the third party by the payment of a money annuity, in so far as the deceased would have been bound to furnish maintenance during the presumable duration of his life; the provisions of § 843, sections 2–3, apply *mutatis mutandis*. The obligation to make compensation arises even if at the time of the injury the third party was only *en ventre sa mère*.

§ 845. In the case of causing death, or of causing injury to body or health, or in the case of deprivation of liberty, if the injured party was bound by law to perform services in favour of a third party in his household or industry, the person bound to make compensation must compensate the third party for the loss of services by the payment of a money annuity. The provisions of § 843, sections 2–4, apply *mutatis mutandis*.

§ 846. If, in the cases provided for by §§ 844, 845, some fault of the injured party has contributed to cause the damage which the third party has sustained, the provisions of § 254 apply to the claim of the third party.

§ 847. In the case of injury to body or health, or in the case of deprivation of liberty, the injured party may also demand an equitable compensation in money for the damage which is not a pecuniary loss.

A like claim belongs to a woman against whom a crime or offence against morality is committed, or who is induced by fraud, or by threats, or by an abuse of a relation of dependence to permit illicit cohabitation.

§ 848. A person liable to restore an object of which he deprived another unlawfully is also liable if it perished accidentally, if its return has become impossible accidentally for any other reason, or if it deteriorated accidentally, unless the destruction, the impossibility to return it for other reasons, or its deterioration, would also have occurred if it had not been taken.

§ 849. If a party can claim damages because he was deprived of an object or because it had been damaged and has suffered in value, he can claim interest on the sum representing damages from the time which serves to determine its taking.

§ 850. Where the person liable to restore an object unlawfully withheld has incurred outlays in respect of that object, he is entitled, as against the injured party, to claim the same rights as the possessor of an object has against the owner for outlays incurred.

§ 851. If a person bound to make compensation for any damage on account of taking or damaging of a moveable compensates the person in whose possession the thing was at the time of the taking or damage, he is discharged by so doing even if a third party was owner of the thing, or had some other right in the thing, unless the right of the third party is known to him or remains unknown in consequence of gross negligence.

§ 852. (1) The claims for compensation for any damage arising from a delict is barred by prescription in three years from the time at which the injured party obtained knowledge of the injury and of the identity of the person liable to make compensation, and without regard to such knowledge in thirty years from doing the act.

(2) If negotiations are pending between the party liable and the party entitled to compensation with regard to the compensation, the running of the period of prescription is interrupted until one of the parties continues the negotiations.

(3) If the person liable has acquired anything by the delict at the expense of the injured party, he is, even after the running of the period of prescription, bound to return it under the provisions relating to the return of unjust enrichment.

§ 853. If by an illegal act a person acquires a contractual claim, the injured party may refuse to perform even if the time has passed for hearing the contractual claim.*

4. OTHER RELEVANT PROVISIONS OF THE BGB

†§ 226. The exercise of a right is inadmissible if it can only have the purpose of causing damage to another.

§ 227. An act required by self-defence is not unlawful.

Self-defence is that defence which is necessary in order to ward off from oneself or another an actual unlawful attack.

§ 228. Anyone who damages or destroys a thing belonging to another in order to ward off from himself or another a danger threatened by it, does not act unlawfully, if the damage or destruction is necessary to ward off the danger and the damage is not out of proportion to the danger. If the person acting is to blame for the danger, he is bound to make good the damage.

§ 229. Anyone who for purposes of self-help takes away, destroys, or damages a thing or for purposes of self-help apprehends an obligor suspected of intending flight or overcomes the resistance of the obligor to an act which the latter is bound to suffer, does not act unlawfully if the help of the authorities cannot be obtained in good time and there is danger that unless he acts at once the realization of the claim will be frustrated or appreciably impeded.

---

* Translation by Forrester, Goren and Ilgen, *The German Civil Code* (1975), reproduced by kind permission of Fred B. Rothman & Co. (1975).

† Taken from F. H. Lawson and B. S. Markesinis, *Tortious Liability for Unintentional Harm in the Common Law and the Civil Law* (1982) II, 54–7.

§ 230. Self-help must not go further than is necessary to ward off the danger.

In case of the seizure of things, in so far as compulsory execution is not effected, leave to distrain must be applied for.

In case of the apprehension of the obligor, in so far as he is not set free again, leave for the precautionary detention of his person must be applied for to the District Court in whose district the apprehension has taken place; the obligor must be brought before the Court without delay.

If the application is delayed or rejected, the restitution of the things seized and the liberation of the person apprehended must follow without delay.

§ 231. Anyone who does one of the acts specified in § 229 under the mistaken assumption that the necessary presuppositions for the exclusion of illegality are in existence, is bound to compensate the other party, even if the mistake is not due to negligence.

§ 249. The person who is bound to make compensation must restore the situation which would exist if the circumstance making him liable to compensate had not occurred. If compensation is to be made for injury to a person or damage to a thing the creditor may demand, instead of restitution in kind, the sum of money necessary to effect such restitution.

§ 250. The creditor may by notice to the person liable to compensate, fix a reasonable period for the restitution in kind with a declaration that he will not accept restitution after the expiration of the period. After the expiration of the period, the creditor may demand the compensation in money if the restitution is not effected in due time; the claim for restitution is barred.

§ 251. If performance in kind is impossible or insufficient to compensate the creditor, the party obliged to provide reparation must do so in money.

The party obliged to provide reparation may do so by paying money only if performance in kind requires disproportionate expenditure. Expenditure incurred in healing an injured animal is not disproportionate for the reason alone that it exceeds its value considerably.

§ 252. The damage to be made good includes also lost profits. Profit is deemed to have been lost which would have been expected with probability according to the ordinary course of things, or according to the particular circumstances, in particular, according to the preparation and provisions made.

§ 253. For an injury which is not an injury to property compensation in money may be demanded only in the cases specified by law.

§ 254. If any fault of the injured party has contributed to the occurrence of the damage, the duty to compensate and the extent of the compensation to be made depend upon the circumstances, especially upon how far the injury has been caused predominantly by the one or the other party.

This applies also if the fault of the injured party was limited to omission to call the attention of the debtor to the danger of unusual serious damage, of which the debtor neither knew nor ought to have known, or to an omission to avert or mitigate the damage. The provision of § 278 applies *mutatis mutandis*.

§ 255. The person who is to make compensation for the loss of a thing or of a right is bound to make compensation only upon an assignment to him of the claims which belong to the person entitled to compensation by virtue of his ownership of the thing or by virtue of his right against third parties.

§ 276. The debtor is responsible, unless otherwise provided, for recklessness and negligence. A person who does not exercise the care required in ordinary intercourse acts negligently. The provisions of §§ 827 and 828 apply.

The debtor may not be released beforehand from responsibility for recklessness.

§ 277. The person who is answerable only for such care as he is accustomed to exercise in his own affairs is not relieved from liability for gross negligence.

§ 278. A debtor is responsible for the fault of his statutory agent, and of persons whom he employs in fulfilling his obligation, to the same extent as for his own fault. The provision of § 276 II does not apply.

Promise of performance for the benefit of a third party

§ 328. (1) A contract may stipulate for performance to a third party, so that the third party acquires a right to demand performance.

(2) In the absence of express stipulation it is to be deduced from the circumstances, especially from the object of the contract, whether the right of the third party shall arise forthwith or only under certain conditions, and whether any right shall be reserved to the contracting parties to take away or modify the right of the third party without his consent.

§ 329. If in a contract one party binds himself to satisfy a creditor of the other party without assuming the debt, it is not to be presumed, in case of doubt, that the creditor shall acquire a direct right to demand satisfaction from him.

§ 330. If, in a contract for life insurance or an annuity, payment of the insurance or annuity to a third party is stipulated for, it is to be presumed, in case of doubt, that the third party shall directly acquire the right to demand the performance. The same rule applies, if in a gratuitous transfer of property the duty to perform the act to a third party is imposed upon the recipient, or if a person, on taking over the whole of another person's property or goods, promises an act of performance to a third party for the purpose of settling the latter's debts.

§ 331. (1) If the performance to the third party is to be made after the death of the person to whom it was promised, in case of doubt the third party acquires the right to the performance upon the death of the promisee.

(2) If the promisee dies before the birth of the third party, the promise to perform to the third party can be revoked or altered only if the right to do so has been reserved.

§ 676. A person who gives advice or a recommendation to another is not bound to compensate for any damage arising from following the advice or the recommendation, without prejudice to his responsibility resulting from a contract or delict.

§ 803. The owner of a thing may deal with it in his discretion and exclude others from any interference, subject to the laws or to the rights of third parties.

**§ 904. [Emergency] The owner of a thing is not entitled to prohibit the interference of another with the thing, if the interference is necessary for the avoidance of a present danger and the damage threatened is disproportionally great compared to the damage caused to the owner by the interference. The owner may demand compensation for the loss suffered by him.

§ 906. [Interference from adjacent land]

(1) The owner of a piece of land is not entitled to prohibit the intrusion of gases, vapours, smells, smoke, soot, heat, noises, shocks and similar interferences emanating from another piece of land to the extent that the interference does not or only immaterially prejudices the use of his piece of land.

(2) The same applies in so far as a substantial prejudice is caused by the use of another piece of land in conformity with local custom and it cannot be prevented by measures, the financing of which can be reasonably expected of users of this kind. If by virtue of this, the owner must tolerate an interference, he may demand from the user of the other piece of land an appropriate settlement in money, if by the interference in conformity with local custom the use of, or income from, his piece of land is prejudiced over and above the expected degree.

(3) The causing of intrusion through a special conduit is not permissible.

§ 907. [Works threatening prejudice]

(1) The owner of a piece of land may demand that on adjacent land no works be installed or maintained as to which it is to be foreseen with certainty, that their existence or use will result in an inadmissible interference with his piece of land. If a plant satisfies the provisions of the State law, which prescribe a certain distance from the boundary or other protective measures, the removal of the plant may not be demanded until the inadmissible interference actually results.

** Taken from I. S. Forrester, S. L. Goren, and H. M. Ilgen, *The German Civil Code*, and reproduced by kind permission of Fred B. Rothman & Co. (1975).

(2) Trees and bushes do not belong to works within the meaning of these provisions.

§ 1004. [Claims for removal and for injunction]

(1) If the ownership is interfered with otherwise than by dispossession or withholding of possession, the owner may demand from the disturber the removal of the interference. If further interference is to be apprehended, the owner may sue for an injunction.

(2) The claim is excluded, if the owner is obliged to tolerate the interference.

5. SOME PRELIMINARY OBSERVATIONS ON THE BGB IN GENERAL AND THE DELICT PROVISIONS IN PARTICULAR

A. The German Civil Code (BGB) was voted by the German Parliament on 1 July 1896, and was promulgated by the Emperor on 18 August of the same year. Its coming into force on 1 January 1900 not only marked the end of the long codification process which had commenced with the appointment of the first Commission on 2 July 1874, but more importantly it also completed the unification of the modern German State. This 'unification process' was even more tortuous and convoluted, but the three landmark dates must surely be 1843, when the German Customs Union abolished the 'internal' customs regulations between the various German States while, at the same time, erecting a common tariff wall to protect the 'internal' economy from foreign competition; 1871 when the German Empire was founded under the strong hand of Bismarck; and 1900 which was the year when the BGB came into force thus putting an end to the existing fragmentation of the legal system.

The extent to which German law was fragmented prior to the codification is rarely fully appreciated. A glance at contemporary maps of Germany would give one an approximate idea of the different systems applicable in Germany on the eve of codification. In reality, however, even this picture would be misleading for two reasons. First because it would convey the impression that there were five legal 'systems' vying for superiority whereas, in fact, alongside these there were—according to a memorandum submitted to the Reichstag—a multitude of other 'systems', mostly hybrids of sorts. Secondly, maps showing the component parts of the German Empire might convey the impression that each 'system' was limited to a particular 'State' or locality which was not the case. For example, the Prussian Code (*Allgemeines Landrecht für die Preussischen Staaten*)—enacted in 1794— applied to only seven of the eleven provinces of Prussia, but it also was in force in some parts of Bavaria and other localities of Germany linked with the Kingdom of Prussia. In fact in 1896, out of an estimated population of forty-two million, eighteen million lived under the Prussian Code; fourteen million were subject to the Common (mainly Roman) German law; seven and a half million inhabitants were subjected to the Napoleonic Code, which was adopted in the Prussian Rhine Province, the Rhenish part of the Grand Duchy of Hesse, and the Bavarian Palatinate; two and a half million lived under a Code enacted by the State of Saxony in 1863, and half a million more were subject to Scandinavian law. Voltaire's quip, that in his time in France one changed one's law as often as, when travelling, a man changed his horses, thus applied to Germany as well.

The picture of diversity was partly mitigated by the enactment of a number of statutes which applied to all the States. The Bill of Exchange Act was the first such Act enacted by various States between 1848 and 1850 and others, dealing with such matters as criminal law, bankruptcy law, and commercial law followed and were later re-enacted as Imperial laws of the Reich.

Further reading

An account of German legal history and of the emergence of the West German State lies clearly outside the scope of this work. German legal history is usually taught either as part of constitutional history—usually called *Deutsche Rechtsgeschichte*—or focuses more on the institutions of private law and is called *Deutsches Privatrecht*. Fehr and Schwerin–Thieme have written treatises using the first title and their popularity and rich references have ensured successive editions. (Fehr's work is now in its 6th edn. (1962).) Mitteis–Lieberich have written on *Deutsches Privatrecht*, a work which is currently in its 9th edn. (1981). Hübner's *Grundzüge des deutschen Privatrechts* (1982 reprint of 1930 edn.) was also translated into English in 1918 and appeared in the Continental Legal History Series under the title *A History of Germanic Private Law*. Other works on the subject have been written by: Coing, *Epochen der Rechtsgeschichte in Deutschland* (4th edn., 1981); Koebler, *Rechtsgeschichte* (3rd edn., 1982); Kroeschell, *Deutsche Rechtsgeschichte* (I, 8th edn., 1987; II, 7th edn., 1989; III, 1st edn., 1989); Laufs, *Rechtsentwicklungen in Deutschland* (4th edn., 1991); Schlosser, *Grundzüge der neueren Privatrechtsgeschichte* (6th edn., 1988); Wesenberg-Wesener, *Neuere deutsche Rechtsgeschichte im Rahmen der europäischen Rechtsentwicklung* (4th edn., 1985) and last but by no means least the excellent work by Wieacker, *Privatrechtsgeschichte der Neuzeit unter besonderer Berücksichtigung der deutschen Entwicklung* (2nd edn., 1967). A more than adequate and very readable account in English of the development of modern European law can be found in von Mehren and Gordley, *The Civil Law System* (2nd edn., 1977) 3–96. For a more detailed account see: J. P. Dawson's classic *The Oracles of the Law* (1967). English accounts of the history of the codification can also be found in Schuster, 'The German Civil Code' 12 *LQR* 17 (1896), Freund, 'The New German Code', 13 *Harv. L. Rev.* 627 (1899–1900), Michael John's excellent *Politics and the Law in Late Nineteenth-Century Germany* (1989). This last work, however, may prove heavy going for those students who know little about 19th century German history. Mary Fulbrook's *A Concise History of*

Germany (1990) offers to all 'beginners' a most readable and informed introduction. For further references see also Zweigert and Kötz, *An Introduction to Comparative Law* (Eng. trans. by T. Weir) I, 138 and 149.

B. The BGB consists of 2385 articles—or, as they are more usually referred to, paragraphs—and is accompanied by the Introductory Law (*Einführungsgesetz zum Bürgerlichen Gesetzbuch*) which, though still in force today, is of less significance than when it came into force in 1900—its main aim being to deal with the transition from the old regime to the new and with matters related to conflict of laws.

The BGB devotes thirty paragraphs (not including § 835 BGB which was repealed) to the law of torts—and they form the twenty-fifth title of the second book dealing with obligations. Contractual obligations, on the other hand, are covered by some 570 paragraphs (§§ 241–811 BGB) of which the first 191 (§§ 241–432 BGB) refer to problems common to all obligations, while the remainder deal with specific contracts such as sale and exchange (§§ 433–515 BGB); gift (§§ 516–34 BGB which, in the civil law systems, is regarded as a contract); lease (§§ 535–97 BGB); basic rules of labour law (§§ 611–630 BGB) and contract of labour and services (§§ 631 *et seq.*, BGB) and others.

The thirty paragraphs devoted to the law of tort represent a marked difference from the five articles devoted to this matter by the French Civil Code (articles 1382–6 CC). This more systematic treatment of a subject is symptomatic of the more exhaustive approach taken by German lawyers in general and also reflects the fact that between 1804—the year of the enactment of the French Code—and 1900—the year when the BGB came into force—legal science had made great forward strides and had also had the chance to consider in greater detail problems which were non-existent or relatively unimportant during the early part of the nineteenth century. The treatment offered by the two Codes on other matters, besides torts, supports the accuracy of this observation. Unjustified enrichment, for example, receives no particular treatment in the French Code, but has eleven articles dedicated to it by the BGB (§§ 812–22 BGB). Similarly, the problems of offer and acceptance have been worked out in France by the courts without any legislative guidance. The BGB by contrast devotes (cross-references not included) thirteen articles to this subject (§§ 145–57 BGB) though, naturally, the case-law has added considerable flesh to these bones.

The fairly detailed regulation of tort law, however, also represents a compromise to a dispute which divided the members of the codifying Commission. For the authors of the first draft had reached the conclusion that widely drafted provisions were necessary in order to achieve full protection against tortious conduct. Indeed, both the Prussian and Austrian Codes contained such general clauses. On the other hand, the more casuistic approach to tort law—well known to Common lawyers—was also the method adopted by Roman law which formed part of the legal heritage of Germany. In addition, many felt that a general clause type of regulation of the matter would only transfer the burden from the shoulders of the legislator to those of the judges and, perhaps, force them to develop the kind of case-law that could be found in France and which was treated with great scepticism by the Germans. In the end, the Code finally opted for a compromise, adopting three general provisions—§§ 823 I, 823 II, and 826 BGB— and some specific provisions dealing with a number of rather narrowly defined tortious situations. Thus § 824 BGB deals with cases where untrue statements damage one's credit; § 825 BGB imposes an obligation to pay compensation on anyone who has indecently induced a female person to have sexual intercourse with him; § 834 BGB deals with the liability of animal supervision; and § 836 BGB deals with liability to ruinous buildings, etc.

A different and, perhaps, more meaningful way of dividing these tort provisions of the Code is as follows. One should first mention the provisions which impose liability for fault. §§ 823 I and II, 824–6, 830, and 839 BGB come under this category and it should be stated immediately that (subject to the minor reservations given below) the Code system of liability is a system of fault-based liability. Then one should mention the provisions of the Code which make liability depend on a rebuttable presumption of fault. §§ 831, 832, 833 (second sentence), 834, 836–8 BGB belong here. Thirdly, one should mention liability for created risks, independent of fault. A number of independent statutes deal with these situations, the most important being certain sections of the Strict Liability Act and the Road Traffic Act extracted below (ch. 3, section B. 3). Finally, in some cases one person is liable strictly but for some other person's fault. In the Common law of vicarious liability we find the best example. As we shall see, German law does not take this view; but various proposals for reform, if enacted, would place vicarious liability in this group. Certain provisions of strict liability statutes (e.g. § 3 of the Strict Liability Act) also fall into this category.

Three further preliminary points must also be made at this stage.

First, it must be stressed that the BGB is a typical product of the Pandectist scholarship, abstract, conceptual, and meticulous in the extreme. It is a Code which addresses itself to lawyers—if not university professors— and thus lacks the vivacity and style of the French or Swiss Codes. Its influence has thus been felt in countries as far apart as Greece and Japan (to mention just two) because of its intellectual power (which once led Maitland to describe it as 'the best code the world has yet seen') rather than to its immediate appeal to the people whose lives it is meant to regulate. Its abstract conceptualism is immediately obvious in the first delict provision—§ 823 I BGB—where the cardinal notion of unlawfulness (*Rechtswidrigkeit*) has provoked rivers of ink to flow in an attempt to give it a precise meaning (see below, ch. 2, section A. 3). In fairness, however, one must equally state that the Common law notion of 'duty' and the French notion of *faute* have given rise to similar difficulties and we shall later stress that for the purpose of comparison these concepts should be avoided where possible and the lawyer should, instead, look for the function they all wish to fulfil.

Second, §§ 823 ff. BGB are not independent and self-sufficient provisions of the Code but must often be read in conjunction with other parts of it, particularly the general part of the law of obligations. Numerous such cross-references will be encountered in the pages that follow, but four important illustrations may be given at this stage.

The question of contributory negligence of the victim, which has recently been the subject of considerable controversy in French law (in particular the *faute de la victime* in the context of article 1384 CC), is essentially regulated by § 254 I BGB which makes the obligation to compensate the negligent plaintiff depend on how far the injury has been *caused* predominantly by the one or the other party (plaintiff/defendant).

Another illustration can be found in the interpretation of the troublesome concept of unlawfulness. This, according to one school of thought (see below, ch. 2, section A. 3), is satisfied whenever one of the interests enumerated by § 823 I BGB has been infringed *in the absence of a legally recognized defence* (*Rechtfertigungsgrund*). But to determine this one must, *inter alia*, look at §§ 227–31, 904 BGB and their interpretation by the case-law.

A third illustration can be found in § 847 BGB which allows monetary compensation for injuries to body or health or for the deprivation of liberty. The full significance of this paragraph can only be appreciated when it is realized that it forms an exception to the general rule enunciated in § 253 BGB which prohibits monetary compensation for harm which is not damage to property *unless* otherwise provided by the Code. As will be explained later on one of the difficulties to which these provisions give rise is whether § 847 BGB can be extended analogically to cover instances other than the ones which it expressly provides for in the light of the categorical phrasing of § 253. This, incidentally, can raise the acutely controversial problem as to whether judges can also make law and not merely interpret the Code and it will be discussed briefly in section 6 of this chapter and also in the section dealing with the judicially created right of privacy (see below, cases 29–32). Finally, to complete this brief list of illustrations, mention should be made of § 278 BGB which has been closely linked with many attempts to circumvent the unfortunate provision of § 831 (discussed in detail in Chapter 3, below).

The final preliminary point is really a warning to the Common lawyer not to expect to find in the law of tort all the material included in his own tort courses. Defamation, for example, is primarily a crime, though it may also have tort consequences if used in conjunction with § 823 II BGB (see also the rather limited provision in § 824 BGB). More importantly, perhaps, trespass to land and nuisance are not normally included in the German law of tort, but in the German law of property—though they may also attract the operation of the law of tort.

History can explain this difference. Roman law—from which most of the Western European systems derive—was, as is well known, a system based on a set of actions and conveyances. But with the progress of time—certainly by the middle of the third century AD—the emphasis shifted steadily from the form of action to the cause of action and from there to the right which the plaintiff was wishing to enforce. As actions became subservient to the rights they were designed to enforce, they inevitably started to move away from the law of actions into the law of property or obligations. The law relating to the formation and extinction of contracts and the law of delict easily slid into the law of obligations. The actions that helped assert proprietary rights caused more difficulties. Yet there was no doubt that in the end these actions, having shed their substantive content and, as a law of mere procedure, being thrust outside the Civil Code, would go with property rather than obligations. Thus, when the civilians, and above all the natural lawyers, began to tackle the work of classifying the law, many parts of it went into quite different pigeon-holes from those which are familiar to Common lawyers with their forms of action abolished only the day before yesterday. Common lawyers must thus be prepared to find much of their law of torts in the civil law of property; the same is also true of the extensions (by analogy) of the proprietary actions dealing with matters which a Common lawyer would expect to find in his law of tort. The tort of nuisance is one such example.

Rei vindicatio was the Roman form of action that helped to establish property rights. That its progenies in modern German (and French) law would be regarded as incidental to ownership and thus be dealt with in the property sections of the codes (the third book of the BGB) is easy to comprehend. The same is true of the *actio confessoria* which helped protect rights less than ownership such as easements and life interests, and the *actio negatoria* which was given to an owner who wished to assert the freedom of his land from an easement. But then came the extension in the medieval and modern law. For suppose your neighbour does not walk across your land under a claim to an easement, but merely sends fumes across your land or makes life unbearable by noise, can he not be said to be really claiming something in the nature of an easement to these things even though no such easement would be recognized by the law? On that fictitious reasoning you can claim the freedom of your land from his encroachment as if it had been an easement, and your action will be an *actio quasi-negatoria*, which will sound in property and not in delict. From the substantive point of view, what will be in issue will be the ambit of ownership, not the personal duty of your neighbour not to commit a delict of encroachment. Incidentally, this attitude of mind led German law and some of its derivatives to restrict the remedy, if no fault were proved in the neighbour, to a declaration or injunction. French and Swiss law, on the other hand, which do not take their classifications so seriously, have found it possible to award damages as well. But to Common lawyers this is the tort of nuisance and hence a tort, for we think instinctively, even now that we have got rid of the forms of actions, of the wrong rather than the right. To the Common lawyer, therefore, the civilian classification is not always easy to understand and one of his first tasks will be to learn how to jump over the barriers of classification which his own system has adopted.

Further reading

For further details see Lawson and Markesinis, *Tortious Liability for Unintentional Harm in the Common Law and the Civil Law* (1982) I, 36–41 and above all, Lawson, *A Common Lawyer Looks at the Civil Law* (1955).

6. THE CONSTITUTIONALIZATION OF PRIVATE LAW

Traditional comparatists have, on the whole, underplayed the importance of public law compared to private law. For at least half of this century this may have been understandable as far as the English comparatists are concerned since, like the rest of the English lawyers they were under the pervading influence of Dicey, who, through his misunderstanding of the French scene, had stunted all interest in administrative law. Yet paradoxically even the French comparatists were (and still are) primarily *privatistes* and one explanation for this must surely be found in the dominant belief of the day that the study of the *civil codes* lay at the core of the legal formation.

In recent times, however, interest in comparative public law has grown; and the impact that the constitutional law background has had on the development of private law is also attracting increased attention. The phenomenon is not limited to Germany. For example, students of American law are aware of the fact that in *New York Times* v. *Sullivan* (376 US 254, 84 S. Ct. 710) the American common law of defamation yielded much ground to the constitutional requirement that free speech be safeguarded. (Attempts to extend these ideas to the area of products liability, e.g. defectively written manuals, have so far failed. On this see: Note, 'Products Liability and the

First Amendment' 59 *Indiana LJ* 503 (1984).) Similarly, the famous (or notorious) decision of *Roe* v. *Wade* (410 US 113, 93 S. Ct. 705 (1973)), by accepting that women had a constitutional right to choose to terminate their pregnancy, had an impact in other areas of tort law—for instance in actions for wrongful birth (see, for instance, *Berman* v. *Allan* 404 A. 2d 8; *Procanik* v. *Cillo* 97 NJ 339, 478 A. 2d 755, 9). For a doctor's negligent failure to warn a pregnant woman of the fact that, say, she was infected by rubella during the critical months of pregnancy, deprived her of her right to abort and thus justified the award of damages (initially for emotional suffering only) in an action for wrongful birth. The constitutionalization of the civil law has, if anything, been even more dramatic and influential in Germany, so it is necessary to describe it, albeit briefly, even in a book devoted to the law of torts.

A principal aim of the Constitution of Bonn of 1949 (Basic Law—*Grundgesetz*) was to establish unequivocally the liberal, social, democratic order of the new state based on the principle of legality (*Rechtsstaat*). The memory of the national-socialist background, with its many attempts to discover and revive traditional Germanic values, had affected the law in almost all its aspects and was still alive, so the framers of the Constitution deliberately placed at the head of the constitutional text nineteen articles dealing with fundamental human rights (*Grundrechte*). (For the Nazi period see: Laufs, *Rechtsentwicklungen in Deutschland*; Weinkauf and Wagner, *Die deutsche Justiz und der National-Sozialismus* (1968). Articles 1–19 are reproduced below at the end of Ch. 2. B. 10.) These rights primarily protect the citizen in his various dealings with the state. To what extent do they also regulate the relations between individuals? This is the so-called problem of *Drittwirkung der Grundrechte* and some authors (including some courts, e.g. the *Bundesarbeitsgericht*) have favoured the *direct* application of these constitutionally proclaimed rights in the area of private law. Thus, for example: BAGE 4, 240 (employees have constitutionally protected rights of free speech against employers); BAGE 1, 258 (labour agreements providing for lower wages for women may be invalidated); BAGE 4, 274 (agreement which gives the employer the right to terminate contract on marriage of his employee may be invalidated). For a more recent example see: BAGE 46, 98. The Federal Labour Court has in many cases maintained this stance despite the *Lüth* decision of the Constitutional Court which, as is explained in the text, refused to follow the 'direct applicability' theory primarily expounded by the author and judge Hans Carl Nipperdey. The prevailing view, however, espoused by the *Bundesverfassungsgericht* (its important *Lüth* decision is reproduced below as case 27) has opted for a theory of *indirect* influence first strongly advocated by the distinguished constitutional lawyer Günter Dürig in 'Grundrechte und Zivilrechtsprechung', *Festschrift zum 75. Geburtstag von Hans Nawiasky* (1956) 158 ff. According to this the basic rights form an 'objective system of values' (*objektive Wertordnung*) which, via the medium of the general clauses of the BGB (e.g. §§ 134, 138, 242, 826, etc.), used and abused by the Nazis (Hedemann, *Die Flucht in die Generalklauseln* (1933); Adami, 'Das Programm der NSDAP und die Rechtsprechung', *Deutsches Recht*, 1939, 486), influence the private law of the land. Thus, an injured party may, irrespective of nationality, by means of a constitutional appeal (*Verfassungsbeschwerde wegen Grundrechts-verletzungen*; art. 93 I, no. 4a, GG), complain of any direct and actual (*unmittelbar und gegenwärtig*) violation of his rights. Such a complaint will be received by the Constitutional Court only after all other remedies have been exhausted; and, if successful, it will lead to the annulment of the offending law, decree, or judgment. (During the first thirty years of the court's life over 50,000 appeals have been considered, the vast majority complaining about violations of fundamental rights.) Where, then, did this constitutionalization of private law most manifest itself? The answer must surely be first and foremost in the area of family law and then in a narrow but no less spectacular way in the creation of a general right of privacy. The latter creation will be considered in more detail in later sections of this book, so at this stage a few general observations will suffice.

What brought about the court revolution of the 1950s in the area of family law was the neglect of article 117 of the Constitution of Bonn of 1949 which proclaimed that all legal norms (including those in the Civil Code) that were incompatible with the newly proclaimed equality of sexes (article 3, II, GG) would have to be abolished by 31 March 1953. This, however, did not happen since—in Professor Rheinstein's words—'the politically domi-nant group [in the ruling Christian-Democratic party included] both Catholic and Protestant [believers] who tend[ed] to identify the Christian pattern of family and society with the ancient pattern of the patriarchal family and general male dominance. [And] they were not overly zealous to implement a command that happened to find expression in the Constitution'. ('The Law of Family and Succession' in A. Yiannopoulos (ed.), *Civil Law in the Modern World* (1965) 25–57, reprinted in his *Gesammelte Schriften* (ed. H. G. Leser) (1972) 212, 219–20.) The combined action of the Constitutional Court (BVerfG NJW 1954, 65; BVerfGE 3, 225) and the Federal Court (in its advisory opinion of 6 September 1953 [BGHZ 11, 34]) declared §§ 1354 BGB (the final word on all matters con-cerning marriage, including residence and domicile, belongs to the husband except where he is abusing this right) and 1387 BGB (husband bears certain litigation costs during marriage) incompatible with the constitutionally pro-claimed complete equality of sexes. More remarkably still and in a manner which, to my knowledge, is unique in the modern civil law systems, the entire law of marriage was pushed into a state of legislative vacuum in which the courts alone fashioned the rules that they deemed compatible with the constitution—a state of affairs that did not come to an end until the *Gleichberechtigungsgesetz* of 18 June 1957, BGBl. 1, 609 (Act Concerning Legal Equality of Men and Women in Matters of Private Law) came into force.

Yet old attitudes die slowly and even though the new Act improved, among other things, the property rights of women after divorce by introducing the system of 'community of acquired benefits' (*Zugewinngemeinschaft*), it left untouched other aspects of male predominance such as the father's pre-eminent powers in the context of parental authority (old § 1627 BGB). But the Constitutional Court had, as it were, tasted blood in its earliest battles with the Bundestag, so it again forced a change in the law, this time through its decision of 29 July 1959 (BVerfGE 10, 59). This process of rejuvenation of German family law was, in a sense, completed by the decision of 29 January 1969 (BVerfGE 25, 157; FamRZ 1969, 196) where the complete equality of legitimate and illegitimate children was established—a result even more remarkable than the previous ones since in this case there was no time limit imposed by the Constitution, as there had been by Art. 117 in the case of equality of the sexes. The intervention was, however, constitutionally inspired, based on Art. 6 V which required that legislation be passed to that effect.

A sketch of great judicial developments even as brief and as inadequate as the above suffices, nevertheless, to support the following statements. First, it shows that accounts (both by English and continental European lawyers) concerning case-law in continental Europe and its significance in the development of the law hardly do justice to the subject. At best, they convey to a Common law reader a diminished picture of the role of the courts in the civil law system and confirm—tacitly at least—his misconception of civil law judges as law bureaucrats mechanically applying the Codes. Bureaucrats (in the sense of civil servants) they may be; automata deprived of will and vision they are not.

Secondly, the study of the case-law itself gives the lie to the statement that the courts are not a creative source of law. Of course, this does not mean that the judge can create law by giving effect to his own personal views or considerations of expediency. Things, however, are different where the constitutional legislator has established a general and enforceable guiding principle (i.e. that of equality) as it did in Art. 3 II of the Constitution. (Contrast with this article 109 of the Weimar Constitution.) In this case the legislator has, in effect, 'transferred part of the law to be regulated by judicial decision' (BGHZ 11, 34). This is perfectly possible according to the Constitution which, though it gives the legislature a *dominant* position in the making of laws, it does not treat it as an *exclusive* one. According to the same decision 'the doctrine of separation of powers which is constitutionally guaranteed is not violated whenever the judge is left to find the law within the parameters of a general norm' (such as that contained in Art. 3 II). Indeed, the decision goes on, Art. 117 I assumes that 'as of 1 April 1953 the judge, through the gradual development of judge-formulated and accepted customary law, will progressively transform the general norms about equality into a more precise and generally binding set of rules'. And the court concludes this part of the judgment by openly admitting that the combined effect of the aforementioned articles of the Constitution is to 'entrust it with the task of bringing about the [constitutionally desired] equality of sexes by means of a judge-made law in the Anglo-Saxon fashion'.

These are bold words and the court, itself, has on different occasions tried to disguise somewhat its creative role. But the disguise is thin at best, as the following statement of the Constitutional Court (taken from the development of the right of privacy) itself shows:

occasionally, the law can be found outside the positive legal rules erected by the state; this is law which emanates from the entire constitutional order and which has as its purpose the 'correction' of written law. It is for the judge to 'discover' this law and through his opinions give it concrete effect. The Constitution does not restrict judges to apply statutes in their literary sense when deciding cases put before them. Such an approach assumes a basic completeness of statutory rules which is not attainable in practice . . . The insight of the judge may bring to light certain values of society . . . which are implicitly accepted by the constitutional order but which have received an insufficient expression in statutory texts. The judge's decision can help realize such ideas and give effect to such values (BVerfGE 34, 269).

Thirdly, the product of these judicial interventions was original and, one must add again, transplantable in the sense that it has been considered and, in some cases, expressly followed by legislative attempts to reform other systems which, like the English, have shown themselves to have been more conservative (backward some might say) in matters of family law. In English, good accounts of the constitutional background can be found in Koch's *A Constitutional History of Germany* (1984) and Kommers' *The Constitutional Jurisprudence of the Federal Republic of Germany* (1989).

7. BIBLIOGRAPHICAL SURVEY

The literature of the German law of torts is vast and growing faster than ever. For present purposes we can ignore references to classic works such as Enneccerus and Lehmann, *Recht der Schuldverhältnisse* (1958). However, for the sake of relative completeness three standard treatises must be mentioned: Staudinger's multi-volume *Kommentar zum Bürgerlichen Gesetzbuch 2. Recht der Schuldverhältnisse* II, 5,

§§ 823–53 (12th edn., 1986), Palandt's *Bürgerliches Gesetzbuch* (47th edn., 1988), and the newer but highly regarded *Münchener Kommentar zum Bürgerlichen Gesetzbuch 3. Schuldrecht* (Special part) 2, §§ 657–853 now in its 2nd edn. (1986). All these are, essentially, reference works which, because of their frequent citations of the case-law, present a particular appeal to practitioners.

More academically oriented, but by no means less authoritative, are five excellent works: Larenz, *Lehrbuch des Schuldrechts* I (General part, 14th edn., 1987), II (Special part, first vol., 13th edn., 1986; the remaining section of the Special part is in its 12th edn., 1981); Esser/Schmidt, *Schuldrecht* I (General part, 7th edn. 1992); Esser/Weyers, *Schuldrecht* (Special part, 7th edn., 1992); Deutsch, *Haftungsrecht* I (1976); Fikentscher, *Schuldrecht* (8th edn., 1992).

Larenz's book is the classic post-war work on the subject, and its author, whose *Methodenlehre der Rechtswissenschaft* (6th edn., 1991) can also be usefully consulted, has justly enjoyed a great reputation in Germany. Esser's work is no less erudite than Larenz's and often gives a different approach to problems of tortious liability; but, to foreign readers at any rate, it may appear more difficult to follow. Deutsch's book is a comparative newcomer in this class of books, but has had considerable impact on both the academic and judicial world. It contains in particular excellent accounts of such topics as 'unlawfulness' and 'culpability' on which the author had earlier written a notable *Habilitation* (*Fahrlässigkeit und erforderliche Sorgfalt*, 1963). Recently, the same author has entered the short textbook market with his informative *Unerlaubte Handlungen und Schadensersatz: Ein Grundriss* (1987).

Because of their smaller size Medicus's *Bürgerliches Recht* (15th edn., 1991) and Kötz's *Deliktsrecht* (5th edn., 1991) would probably be described by an American readership as 'small-horn' books. Their size, however, should in no way detract from their great value; nor does it hide the indisputable scholarship of their authors. Medicus's work is a master-work of conciseness which, despite its size, does not eschew difficult or controversial points and often gives the author's own trenchant criticisms of the law. *Multum in parvo* aptly describes this work. Kötz's book is equally informative, and for a foreign reader even more readable than that of Medicus. Moreover, its author often uses his considerable comparative expertise to criticize in a stimulating and policy-orientated manner the positive law. The present work has been greatly influenced both in content and arrangement of material by these two excellent short books. Finally, from the growing literature that adopts the economic analysis of law, see Adams, *Ökonomische Analyse der Gefährdungs- und Verschuldenshaftung* (1985).

The periodic literature on the subject is enormous and references to it as well as to leading monographs will appear at the head of various sections of this book as well as in its footnotes. However, one work in particular must be singled out: it is von Caemmerer's 'Wandlungen des Deliktsrechts' in *Hundert Jahre deutsches Rechtsleben, Festschrift zum hundertjährigen Bestehen des Deutschen Juristentages, 1860–1960* (1960), reprinted in his *Gesammelte Schriften* (Collected Works) (1968) 452 ff. A long article rather than a book, this masterly account of the changes in the law of delict brought about by the courts, mainly during this century, gives a general view of the whole law of civil responsibility. Von Caemmerer's influence on German delict law is probably unparalleled in our times and, in a sense, it is all the more remarkable since it has been exercised through learned articles rather than a fully fledged treatise—a form of writing so appreciated by the German legal mind.

The English literature on the subject is, on the whole, very poor. The most updated translation of the text of the Code (BGB) is by Forrester, Goren, and Ilgen entitled *The German Civil Code* (1975) (with an up-to-date supplement published in 1981), while certain portions of the BGB have also been included in translated form in Lawson and Markesinis, *Tortious Liability for Unintentional Harm in the Common Law and the Civil Law*, 2 vols. (1982) and von Mehren and Gordley, *The Civil Law System* (2nd edn., 1977).

Until recently English-speaking readers had to content themselves with two books: Rayan's *An Introduction to the Civil Law* (1962) (dealing with French and German law) and Cohn's *Manual of German Law*, 2 vols. (1968, 1971). Though the latter was in many respects the more satisfactory of the two, they were both elementary, their aim being to give the general reader some knowledge of the German legal system as a whole rather than to provide him with a detailed knowledge of a single branch of German law or supply him with further aids for research. They also make little or no use of the rich case-law. More recently, another introductory book has appeared written by Professors Horn, Kötz, and Leyser. It is entitled *German Private and Commercial Law: An Introduction* (1982) and despite some shortcomings (see this author's review in [1982] *Cambridge Law Journal* 360) it is in many respects a very useful book which will, no doubt, be greatly appreciated by the complete beginner. But its delict section (Chapter 9) is largely based on §§ 17–20 of Zweigert and Kötz's *An Introduction to Comparative Law* and if the reader has a choice of reading either of these books, he is advised to use the latter rather than the former work. Nigel Foster's recent *German Law and Legal System* (1993) is the latest book about German law written in English which, in a mere 336 pages provides a brief but good introduction to the entire legal system.

At a more sophisticated level mention should be made of four works. First and foremost is vol. XI of the *International Encyclopedia of Comparative Law* edited by Professor A. Tunc. Some of the leading authorities on the subject have collaborated to produce a book which, though its parts are uneven in some respects, represents a work of great erudition and a veritable mine of information, though it is rapidly becoming out of date.

The second work that must be singled out here is Zweigert and Kötz, *An Introduction to Comparative Law* (2nd edn., 1987). Superbly translated into English by Tony Weir, vol. II achieves a closely knit exposition of the American, English, French, and German law of contract and tort and is indisputably one of the masterpieces of comparative law literature.

Von Mehren and Gordley, *The Civil Law System* (2nd edn., 1977) is the third significant work in this field. A selection of translated cases, accompanied by other supporting material and the authors' own pertinent commentary, has for many years made this work the ideal book for the comparative study of the law—especially for American law schools which are accustomed to operate through case-books.

Lawson and Markesinis, *Tortious Liability for Unintentional Harm in the Common Law and Civil Law*, 2 vols. (1982) should, perhaps, also be added to this section of the bibliography. Though by no means a textbook in the usual format taken by this species of legal works, it is a work essentially for law students. Its main aim is to attempt a 'thematic' exposition of certain problems of the law of torts in America, England, France, and Germany and to single out the similarities rather than the differences that exist between these four legal systems. Each chapter of vol. I contains extensive bibliographical references and vol. II provides a selection of materials (mainly French and German cases). It can be used either on its own or as a 'companion volume' to vol. I.

The literature in English on German law is referred to in various sections of this book. A full list can be found in the impressive work that Professor Szladits has for many years now been conducting for the Parker School in New York. It is published periodically under the title *A Bibliography of Foreign and Comparative Law*. Finally, references to Anglo-American law can be found in the introductory sections of each chapter but especially in the notes that accompany the translated German judgments.

2

Liability under § 823 I BGB

SECTION A. COMMENTARY

I. INTRODUCTORY REMARKS

AMONG the three general provisions of the BGB—§§ 823 I and II, and 826—
§ 823 I has, traditionally, been accorded a special pre-eminence even though
we shall see that § 823 II BGB is nowadays considered as a close rival, and
for some writers, has an even wider potential ambit. Compared with § 826
BGB, § 823 I BGB is both wider and narrower. It is 'objectively' narrower,
in so far as it can be invoked only if one of the enumerated interests (discussed below) has been violated, whereas there is no such limitation with
§ 826 BGB. In practical terms, the 'kind of harm' which is *not* protected by
§ 823 I BGB is economic loss (unless it is consequential upon physical damage), whereas claims for economic loss are the most usual claims brought
under § 826 BGB. § 823 I BGB is, however, 'subjectively' wider than § 826 in
so far as it covers intention as well as negligence, whereas § 826 is limited to
intentional activities which, in addition, must be *contra bonos mores*. On the
other hand, the ambit of § 823 II BGB is made to depend on the notion of
'protective law' (*Schutzgesetz*). Its effect is to give rise to civil liability in the
event of a violation of some statute or other enactment—usually of a criminal nature—if this enactment is a 'protective law' in the sense that will be
explained below. The only additional requirement introduced by this section is that if the protective law in question imposes liability irrespective of
fault, additional civil liability will not be engendered unless the defendant
was also guilty of fault. (See Chapter 4, below.)

For an action to be based on § 823 I BGB the following requirements
must be satisfied: (i) there must be a violation of one of the enumerated
rights or interests, namely, life, body, health, freedom, property, or any
'other right' (*sonstiges Recht*) which was (ii) unlawful, and (iii) culpable
(intentional or negligent), and there must be (iv) a causal link between the
defendant's conduct (which can be an act or an omission) and the plaintiff's
harm as defined by this paragraph. We shall examine these four elements in
turn.

2. THE RIGHTS AND INTERESTS PROTECTED BY § 823 I BGB

Select bibliography

Von Bar, *Gutachten und Vorschläge zur Überarbeitung des Schuldrechts—Deliktsrecht*, herausgegeben vom Bundesminister der Justiz (1980); idem, 'Probleme der Haftpflicht für deliktsrechtliche Eigentumsverletzungen' no. 55 *Mannheimer Vorträge zur Versicherungswissenschaft* (1992); von Caemmerer, 'Wandlungen des Deliktsrechts', op. cit. (select bibliography, above, p. 22); idem, 'Die absoluten Rechte in § 823 I BGB', reprinted in *Gesammelte Schriften* I, 554; idem, 'Das Verschuldensprinzip in rechtsvergleichender Sicht' *RabelsZ* (1978), 1; Canaris, 'Schutzgesetze— Verkehrspflichten—Schutzpflichten' *Festschrift für Larenz* (1983) 27; Deutsch, 'Entwicklung und Entwicklungsfunktion der Deliktstatbestände' *JZ* 1963, 385; idem, 'Freiheit und Freheitsverletzung im Haftungsrecht' *Festschrift Hauss* (1978) 43; idem, 'Entwicklungstendenzen des Schadensrechts in Rechtsprechung und Wissenschaft' *JuS* 1967, 152; idem, 'System und Aufbau der Schadenshaftung im Deliktsrecht' in *Festschrift F. Weber* (1975) 125; idem, 'Die neuere Entwicklung der Rechtsprechung zum Haftungsrecht' *JZ* 1984, 308; *JZ* 1990, 733; Fabricius, 'Zur Dogmatik des "sonstigen Rechts" gemäss § 823 I BGB' *AcP* 160 (1961) 273; Fraenkel, *Tatbestand und Zurechnung bei § 823 I BGB* (1979); Honig, 'Die neuere Entwicklung der Rechtsprechung zum Haftungsrecht' *JZ* 1984, 308; Hübner, 'Zur Reform von Deliktsrecht und Gefährdungshaftung' *NJW* 1982, 2041; Kupisch-Krüger, 'Grundfälle zum Recht der unerlaubten Handlungen' *JuS* 1980, 270, 422, 574, 727, *JuS* 1981, 30, 347, 584, 737; idem, *Deliktsrecht* (1983); Lang, *Normzweck und Duty of Care* (1983); Leser, 'Zu den Instrumenten des Rechtsgüterschutzes im Delikts- und Gefährdungshaftungsrecht' *AcP* 183 (1983) 568; Lorenz, 'Verkehrspflichten zum Schutze fremden Vermögens' 25 *Jahre Kalrsruher Forum* 48 (1983); Löwisch, *Der Deliktsschutz relativer Rechte* (1970); Mertens/Reeb, 'Grundfälle zum Recht der unerlaubten Handlungen' *JuS* 1971, 409, 469, 525, 586; *JuS* 1972, 35; Mertens, 'Deliktsrecht und Sonderprivatrecht. Zur Rechtsfortbildung des deliktischen Schutzes von Vermögensinteressen' *AcP* 178 (1978) 227; Reinhardt, 'Das Subjektive Recht in § 823 I BGB' *JZ* 1961, 713; Schulz, 'Überlegungen zur ökonomischen Analyse des Haftungsrechts' *VersR* 1984, 608; Stoll, *Richterliche Fortbildung und gesetzliche Überarbeitung des Deliktsrechts* (1984); Wussow, *Unfallhaftpflichtrecht* (13th edn., 1985); Zeuner, 'Historische Linien in der Entwicklung des Rechts am Gewerbebetrieb, des allgemeinen Persönlichkeitsrechts und der Verkehrssicherungspflichten' *VersR* 1983, 196. *In English*: Opoku, 'Delictual Liability in German Law' 21 *Int. Comp. L. Quart.* (1972) 230; Zweigert and Kötz, II, 264 ff.

(a) Life

Interference with 'life' here means killing a person, in which case the claim for compensation rests with third parties, their claim being based on §§ 844–6 BGB (see below). This is, of course, the action which an English Common lawyer would describe as the fatal accident action, i.e. the new action given to the 'dependants' of the deceased victim. The question of the deceased's own action—to be brought by his estate—is, of course, another matter and one which, in the civil law systems in general, is related to the part of the law which deals with succession or the administration of the estates.

§§ 844–6 BGB deal, as stated, with the *new* action given to the victim's 'dependants'. They are discussed in greater detail in Chapter 4, below; and the reader is advised to read (if not study) this material at an early stage. Here suffice it to note that § 844 II BGB specifies the 'dependants' by reference to those persons whom the deceased would have been 'obliged to support by law' (*kraft Gesetzes unterhaltspflichtig*). Who these people are can be found in the family law section of the BGB, and obviously include spouses and minor children (§§ 1360, 1602 BGB), all ascendants in the direct line (§ 1601 BGB) and (in certain circumstances) even separated (§ 1361 BGB) and divorced spouses (§§ 1569 ff. BGB), subject always to the detailed provisions contained in the family law book of the BGB. In his meticulousness, the German legislator has also provided at the end of § 844 II BGB that a child conceived but unborn at the time of the injury is not excluded as a potential claimant.

(b) Body and health

These headings cover any adverse interference with the person. Terminological precision has, again, dictated the use of two words—the first signifying any interference with the body of the plaintiff, such as severing his finger, breaking his leg, or external abrasions of the kind typically found in car accident cases, while interference with the plaintiff's health refers to externally provoked malfunctions of his inner body. Internal infections, gastroenteritis, bacterial infection, inhalation of poisonous fumes, etc. would come in this category. Thus the BGH recently held that the transmission of the virus constitutes an injury to health even when it has not yet developed into AIDS (BGH NJW 1991, 1948). In both these instances, the interference must emanate from a source *external* to the plaintiff. Nevertheless, even when this requirement is satisfied, the full extent of the plaintiff's hurt may be partly attributable to the external factors and partly linked with his own constitution as, for example, some kind of dormant cancer. Whether this result, as well, can be attributed to the defendant's conduct is a question of legal cause and will be discussed in § 5, below.

In German law (as in other systems) physical injury is widely compensated. In *The Hua Lien* ([1991] 1 *Lloyd's Rep.* 309, 328–9) Lord Brandon maintained that 'in most claims in respect of physical damage to property [and, one might add, personal injury] the question of the existence of a duty of care does not give rise to any problem, because it is self-evident that such a duty exists and the contrary view is unarguable.' This 'duty' language may not be entirely appropriate to German law, but the general idea expressed by the statement is as true of German law as it is of English and American law. (For exceptions to this rule, dictated by policy, see *Hill* v. *Chief Constable of W. Yorks.* [1988] QB 60; [1989] AC 53 and cf., *Ross* v. *City of N. Y.* 240 NE 2d. 860). There do exist, however, three 'types' of physical injury which have given rise to difficulties which are also known to the Common law. These situations involve nervous shock, pre-natal injuries and claims for 'wrongful life.'

Nervous shock is one kind of interference with a person's health which has given rise to many difficulties in German law, as well as English and American law. Shock may be the result of fear generated for one's own safety and personal integrity or it may be the result of witnessing some gruesome accident. Should recovery here be limited only to nervous shock suffered by close relatives of the victim or to persons who only saw or heard the accident with their own unaided senses (but not to those who some time after the accident became aware of its consequences, perhaps through hearsay)? And should well-intended rescuers, who come to the accident scene to offer their services and are subject to horrifying sights, be all allowed to claim damages for their shock? Three cases dealing with these matters are reproduced below (cases 1 to 3) but here suffice it to say that nervous shock is, clearly, injury to health in the sense of § 823 I BGB, so long as it entails medically recognizable physical or psychological consequences which would not have been suffered by the ordinary, not oversensitive, citizen.

The decision of the BGH of 11 May 1971 (BGHZ 56, 163 = Case 1, below), though not without its critics, is still good law; and it illustrates, especially when read in conjunction with other similar decisions, the strong emphasis that German courts put on the seriousness and extraordinary nature of the shock before they treat it as compensatable (for a more recent confirmation see: BGH NJW 1989, 2317 = Case 2, below). The expression often used is that the shock must be an 'appropriate' and 'understandable' (*verständliche*) consequence of witnessing *or being told* of the accident. The italicised words suggest an area of difference with Anglo-American law; otherwise, however, the terms used imply flexible standards which, more often than not, do not seem to work in favour of plaintiffs. Thus, shock suffered as a result of being told that one's car was damaged has not been allowed. (LG Hildesheim, VersR 1970, 720). Likewise, no compensation was given for shock suffered by the plaintiff when he was told that the police were investigating a close relative. (LG Hamburg NJW 1969, 615.) Further, though a close family relationship with the primary victim will, typically, make it easier for the plaintiff to obtain damages for his nervous shock, it is by no means obvious that this is seen as a rigid, additional condition for recovery. Thus, non-relatives of the prime victim have often been denied recovery (LG Tübingen NJW 1968, 1187; LG Stuttgart VersR 1973, 648). But an accompanying *fiancée* has succeeded; and, in similar circumstances, so might a partner in a 'serious love relationship'. (LG Frankfurt NJW 1969, 2286). If the shock leads to a premature birth, the *nasciturus* may also be entitled to sue for any damages that he may have suffered (BGH NJW 1985, 1391). (For further details see: *Münchener Kommentar* (Grunsky) para. 249 nos. 54 and 54a.)

Can one draw any preliminary conclusions from such a brief sketch? Three, perhaps, can be put forward here, though somewhat tentatively since cases such as those cited above technically have no precedential value and can only serve as indications of how a court might decide a case.

First, German law is more generous than the Common law in cases of distant shock; this *may* be due in part to the absence of juries and a smaller and more closely monitored medical profession which reduces the chances of 'faked' medical evidence. It is also potentially more open-minded towards claims brought by non-relatives. Secondly, in other contexts the greater 'generosity' of German law may be more apparent than real. This seems reasonable enough to infer from the fact that (*a*) many claims which would be unacceptable to the Common law are also rejected by the German courts and (*b*) that damages awarded under this heading to successful claimants seem to be modest. Finally, and from a purely conceptual point of view, it may be worth noting that German courts tend to approach problems of nervous shock in terms of causation (rather than duty). Increasingly, however, German writers are recognising that the demarcation line really depends on policy considerations and that causative language merely provides the technical device to draw these lines rather than explaining why some plaintiffs fall on their wrong side. To this writer, at least, the main attraction of the German approach may, therefore, lie in the fact that it makes the seriousness of the harm the determinative factor rather than basing recovery on such fortuitous elements as the plaintiff's proximity to the scene of the accident or his familial relationship with the primary victim.

Pre-natal injuries is the second kind of 'physical' injury that has given rise to considerable difficulties both in German law and the Common law systems. There are a number of reasons why this is so. First, the *nasciturus*—as the child still in the womb is often called in the civil law systems—though a 'living entity' is not a person. If it is to be accorded legal rights, these may be in conflict with those of the mother (e.g. right to live and to abort). Secondly, it may be thought proper to vest some of these rights immediately (e.g. after a certain period, usually the 24th week of pregnancy, you may not kill the embryo) while others will mature upon live birth. The right to inherit belongs to this category (§ 1923 II BGB). As we shall observe in the notes to cases 3 and 4 (reproduced below), German and English law adopt the same position with regard to the right to sue for injuries sustained while *in utero*. On the other hand, some American courts do not require 'live birth' and are willing to grant tort actions to persons who were merely 'viable' at the time of the injury (even if there was subsequently no live birth). This solution can accentuate the third difficulty that these cases create namely, difficulties with causation and proof.

The protection afforded by German law goes beyond this point as the decision in BGHZ 8, 243 (reproduced below as case 4) clearly shows. In chronological terms this is a pioneering decision, allowing an action to a child born with impairments as a result of a tortious act which took place prior to conception. In the main, the Common law solutions in this context are similar to the German.

The third and last category of 'physical' injury cases which have given trouble to the courts (both in Common law and Civil law jurisdictions) are the so-called 'wrongful life' and 'wrongful birth' cases. These are more modern in origin and raise profound philosophical questions as well as difficult questions of evaluation of damages. This time, developments in this field started in the USA and later spread to European systems. BGHZ 86, 240 (reproduced as case 5) and the decision of the Supreme Court of New Jersey in *Procanik* v. *Cillo* (reproduced as an appendix to the German decision) bring out very clearly the relevant points, so discussion of this topic will be deferred until that point.

Further reading

For nervous shock in German law see, *inter alia*, Berg note to LG Frankfurt of 23 March 1969 published in *NJW* 1970, 515; Von Hippel, 'Haftung für Schockschäden Dritter' *NJW* 1965, 1890; Krüger, 'Der praktische Fall; Bürgerliches Recht— Schadensersatzprobleme bei sogenannten Schockschäden' *JuS* 1986, 214; Münchener Kommentar zum Bürgerlichen Gesetzbuch, Rdnr. 54 vor § 249 and § 823 Rdnr. 57. English: Fleming, 'Distant Shock in Germany and Elsewhere' 20 *A. J. Comp. L.* 485 (1972).

(c) Freedom

Any interference with the person's liberty and freedom of movement will (if the other elements of § 823 I BGB are satisfied) give rise to a civil claim and, often, a criminal action as well. Torts like that of false imprisonment are covered by this heading and include instances of false information given to the police in order to have the plaintiff arrested. However, freedom of religion or speech are not covered by this term. (Fikentscher, *Schuldrecht* (8th edn., 1991) § 103, I, 3 (p. 731); Staudinger, op. cit. (Select Bibliography), §

823, No. 44 ff. etc. *contra* Leinemann, *Der Begriff Freiheit nach § 823 I BGB* (1969).)

(d) Property

(i) Ownership

Ownership, the cardinal property right regulated by §§ 903 ff. BGB is, of course, completely protected by § 823 I BGB against culpable interferences. The interference with the substance of a thing (whether moveable or immoveable), of the type that one would encounter in, say, a traffic accident case, would thus form the typical kind of interference under this heading. But even the *use* of a thing without the permission of its owner, would be actionable, although it did not entail its destruction or damage. Dropping the plaintiff's engagement ring in the river, or grazing one's animals on the plaintiff's land without his permission, would thus be covered by this provision. Incidentally, this right for compensation could arise only if the other elements of § 823 I BGB (and particularly the requirement of fault) were satisfied. In the absence of fault, the owner would have to rely on the remedies given him in the third book of the Code dealing with the law of property. Thus, § 985 BGB gives him a real action for dispossession; or § 1004 BGB which provides a remedy for interferences which do not amount to dispossession (right to demand a cessation of the interference and/or an injunction for the future); or the remedy given by § 906 BGB which is analogous to the Common law injunctions in nuisance cases.

(ii) Possession

Difficulties have arisen with regard to the concept of possession which the Code treats more as a physical relation to a thing than a right. Paragraph 854 BGB thus states that 'possession of a thing is acquired by obtaining *actual* power of control over the thing'.

Possession is thus, clearly, not 'ownership'; but could it be regarded as sufficiently akin to this latter notion to receive protection under the words 'or *other* rights' (*sonstiges Recht*) of § 823 I BGB?

The paragraphs that follow § 854 BGB make clear that possession is given special protection by the law regardless of the possessor's title and this, partly because the law wishes to discourage—within certain limits (see § 859 BGB)—self-redress, but also because possession is often in practice the outward manifestation of ownership. But does a possessor, whose physical relationship with a thing has been disturbed, also have the right to claim monetary compensation under § 823 I BGB?

Professor Medicus gives the following illustration using, incidentally, the statutory notion of 'indirect possession'. This is defined by § 868 BGB and deals with a person exercising factual control over a thing but in pursuance to a contract with another person (the mediate or indirect possessor). The typical example is a lease. Now suppose that a lessee fails to vacate an apartment that has been leased from the lessor who has given him legal notice to terminate the contract. If the lessor forcibly ejects the lessee, the latter's remedies—set out in §§ 859, I, III and 861 BGB—include a limited right of self-help as well as the right to demand the return of possession. But can he also demand damages—for example to cover his expenses for staying in a hotel—under § 823 I BGB? As stated, the position of possessors is, in this respect, not entirely clear, but according to Professor Medicus (*Bürgerliches Recht* (1991) no. 607; see also Esser/Weyers, *Schuldrecht* II, 2 (1992) §§ 551 2*b*) the answer should depend upon whether the possessor is in a position similar to that of an owner, i.e. he has the 'negative' advantage usually associated with ownership (e.g. right to stop others from interfering), but also the 'positive' advantages, namely the right to use and exploit the thing (§ 903 BGB). This would include all lawful possessors but also a *bona fide* possessor during pending litigation. The solution to the hypothetical example, therefore, should be that the lessee could obtain damages for his loss sustained for the period during which—in accordance with the rules of civil procedure (§§ 721, 765*a*. ZPO)—he might have obtained a reprieve from the eviction. (For rich references to recent case-law on this and related matters see Deutsch in *JZ* 1984, 308 ff.; *JZ* 1990, 733 *et seq.*)

Similarly, other limited property rights like servitudes (§§ 1018 ff. BGB) and usufruct (§§ 1030 ff. BGB) should also receive protection by being included under the heading 'other [absolute] rights' of § 823 I BGB.

(*iii*) *Economic loss*

It will have been noticed that the protection of wealth as such is not included in the list of enumerated interests of § 823 I BGB. This does not mean that economic losses will never be compensated. A person who is injured and incurs medical expenses will receive monetary compensation both for his pain and suffering (in accordance with § 847 BGB) and for his economic loss (e.g. medical expenses, lost earnings, etc.). Equally, a person whose car has been damaged in a traffic accident will be able to claim compensation for it, which may also include the cost of hiring a substitute. Finally, to give one last illustration, if the defendant's negligent activities lead to the severing of an electricity cable, thereby causing a power cut which affects the plaintiff's electrically operated egg-hatching machines, the plaintiff will be able to claim both the value of the eggs and the profit he would have made on those eggs which would have statistically hatched into chickens and then been sold (BGHZ 41, 123 = BGH NJW 1964, 720 but see Hager's criticisms in *JZ* 1979, 53 ff.). In all these cases we are talking of economic loss immediately consequential to injury to the person or property and the only problem that the court will have to face will be one of remoteness: how much of the plaintiff's loss to allocate to the defendant's conduct. By contrast, when we move to pure economic loss (*reiner Vermögensschaden*) the difficulties experienced by German law are multiplied; in addition, they are experienced in areas which are well known to Common lawyers. Indeed, it could be argued that in no other area of its law of torts does German law demonstrate such an ideological affinity with the Common law as in its refusal to compensate pure economic loss through the medium of tort rules. Yet, as we shall note below, in both systems this basic premise has, in recent times, come under constant and ingenious attacks with practitioners (and judges) showing in many instances a willingness to probe for weak points in the citadel that would allow the establishment of bridge-heads for the opposing school of thought. Such an attitude, inevitably, gives rise to the question why should this be so; and the question becomes more pressing (and, to some extent has defied a conclusive answer) whenever the problem has been examined against the background of French law (and its derivatives) which have adopted the exact opposite solution, equated for all intents and purposes economic loss with physical injury, and have not incurred the dire consequences that Common lawyers and German lawyers so fear.

Stripped to its essentials, the first argument is that economic loss (like nervous shock), tends to give rise to difficulties of an administrative nature such as, for example, a potentially *indeterminate* number of claims (and, it should be stressed, it is the indeterminacy that matters rather than the number of claims itself), unreliable evidence, and collusive actions. These fears were succinctly voiced as early as 1861 by the great German jurist Rudolf von Jhering who wrote:

What would it lead to if one could be sued in non-contractual relations generally for gross negligence as well as intent! A careless utterance, carrying a tale, giving false information and bad advice, uttering a thoughtless judgment, recommending an undeserving housemaid one used to employ, answering a traveller's question about the way or the time, and so on, in a word, everything and anything, if grossly negligent, would make one liable for the harm it caused in spite of all *bona fides*; and in the course of such an extension the *actio de dolo* would become the veritable scourge of commercial and social intercourse, free conversation would be greatly inhibited, the most innocent word would become a snare! (R. Jhering, 'Culpa in Contrahendo', *Jahrbücher für die Dogmatik des heutigen römischen und deutschen Privatrechts* 4 (1861) 1, 12.)

This clearly echoes what was to become one of the best-known aphorisms of Cardozo J. in his famous judgment in *Ultramares Corp.* v. *Touche, Niven and Co.* 255 NY 170, 174; NE 441, 444 (1931).

Another argument is that 'insurance considerations' favour the non-liability rule. It is useful to put this argument in such a stark manner since lawyers in Europe, especially Continental Europe, are less accustomed to analysing tort cases in an overtly economic manner. The German decisions bear witness to the validity of this assertion, though it is no longer entirely true of academic literature. Yet the assumption that the 'insurance factor' always favours the non-liability rule is simply not correct; and the decision of the Canadian Supreme Court in *Norsk Pacific Steamship Co. Ltd.* v. *Canadian National Railway Co.* [1992] I S.C.R. 1021 (reproduced below, pp. 223–64) contains one of the interesting (if long) judicial discussions of the subject.

In the early 1980s there were signs that English law was slowly relaxing the attitude towards economic loss even though no one was predicting that it would reach the very liberal position of French, Belgian, or Dutch law where tort compensation for pure economic loss is, quite simply, a non-problem. (See Fokkema and Markesinis, 'All or Nothing? The Compensation of Pure Economic Loss in English and Dutch Law' in *Ex Iure* (a collection of essays published in 1987 by Gouda Quint) 63; Herbots, 'Le "Duty of Care" et le dommage purement financier en droit comparé' (1985) *Revue de droit internationale et de droit comparé* 52.) In England the move expressing a dissatisfaction with the status quo received its first major boost in some wide propositions about the tort of negligence in *Anns* v. *Merton London Borough Council* [1978] AC 728, and it peaked with the decision in *Junior Books Ltd.* v. *Veitchi Co. Ltd.* [1983] AC 520. The result reached in this case is arguably fair and right *on its facts*; but some unnecessarily wide and inadequately thought out dicta precipitated a spectacular demise, first by means of clumsy attempts to show that *Junior Books* was not really a case of economic loss at all (*Tate and Lyle Inc. Ltd.* v. *GLC* [1983] 2 AC 509) and then by more sustained attacks (e.g. in *Peabody Donation Fund* v. *Sir Lindsay Parkinson and Co. Ltd.* [1985] AC 210; *Leigh and Sillavan* v. *Aliakmon Shipping Co. Ltd.* [1986] AC 785; *Yuen Kun-yeu* v. *A. G. of Hong Kong* [1988] AC 175) leading to the ignominious statement by a Court of Appeal judge in *Sinaan Contracting Co.* v. *Pilkington Ltd.* (*No. 2*) [1988] 2 WLR 761 at p. 778, that even citing the case served no 'useful purpose'. This process of dismantling *Anns* was completed by the House of Lords in *Murphy* v. *Brentwood D.C.* [1991] I AC 398, a decision, however, which may have created its own considerable difficulties and which has not, on the whole, met with a warm reception from British academics. (See: Markesinis and Deakin, 'The Random Element of Their Lordships' Infallible Judgment: An Economic and Comparative Analysis of the Tort of Negligence from *Anns* to *Murphy*', (1992) 55 *MLR* 619 and further references to academic literature on page 621, n. 15.) The discrediting of *Anns* may, thus, be short lived though the potential 'abandonment' of *Murphy* is unlikely to be followed by a move towards the 'French position' but, rather, signal a move towards a more flexible attitude which will make recovery easier but dependant on factual circumstances grouped under characteristic headings. This approach has already been advocated by a number of academics (e.g. Professor Feldthusen in Canada: *Economic Negligence: The Recovery of Pure Economic Loss*, 2nd edn. (1989); idem, 'Economic Loss in the Supreme Court of Canada: Yesterday and Tomorrow' 17 *Can. Bus. L.J.* 356 (1990–91)); and it can also find some (influential) judicial support in the Common law world. (E.g. in the majority in *Norsk*, op. cit., above, and in Lord Goff's judgment in *The Aliakmon*, [1985] 1 QB 350, 393). It is also largely adopted in this book since it makes the comparative presentation of the rich and varied material more digestible.

In the USA one finds a similar attempt by decisions like *State of Louisiana ex rel. Guste* v. *M/V Testbank* (752 F. 2d 1019 (1985), reproduced in part in the 2nd edn. of this book, pp. 184–203), to halt the more liberalizing rules found in such important decisions as *Petition of Kinsman Transit Co.* (388 F. 2d 821) and *Union Oil Co.* v. *Oppen* (501 F. 2d 558). This attempt to adopt 'bright line' rules (e.g. economic loss is compensatable *only* if connected to physical injury or property damage) seems to have succeeded, though one also finds important decisions in the opposite direction. Thus see: *People Express Airlines* v. *Consolidated Rail* 100 NJ 246, 495 A. 2d 107 (1985); *J'Aire Corp.* v. *Gregory* 598 P. 2d 60 (1979). Selecting cases for inclusion in works such as this is not easy; and, to some extent, it must reflect personal ideas and preconceptions. Nevertheless, the selection has been made on the basis of methodological criteria as well as for the intrinsic merit of the judgments reproduced. In the case of economic loss two leading cases have been selected for special treatment. The first—*Norsk*—comes from Canada and adopts a 'liberal' approach; the second, delivered by the US Supreme Court—*East River*—is more traditional but no less impressive for that. The two decisions may not be as irreconcilable as they appear at first sight if one adopts the more *nuancé* view that recovery for economic loss may be desirable in some factual situations but not in others.

In Germany, too, the rigid anti-compensation rule has been doubted by some academics and severely eroded *in some situations* by the courts themselves, despite strong academic criticism. But, overall, the challenge has, again, been unsuccessful since the non-liability rule was clearly incorporated in the code in accordance with the demands of both the socio-economic environment of the nineteenth century and Roman legal tradition. For the socio-economic environment clearly ranked tactile forms of property above pure economic interests, and what is more, expressed a clear preference for land over moveables. And legal tradition was also hostile towards pure economic loss, since the *lex Aquilia* and classical Roman law formed part of the German Common law and this system of compensation was devised for damage to physical objects.

Many consequences follow from this basic attitude of German law. Here we can only outline a few fundamental points; and further details will be given in the annotations to the translated decisions.

First one must note that as a result of the rigidity of tort law, German contract law has been expanded (many academics would argue excessively), to meet new situations calling for a pro-plaintiff solution. More about this in the notes on the cases dealing with liability for negligent statements and the liability of attorneys towards non-clients.

Secondly, the expansion has often been the result of bold judicial creativity. This creativity has not, as already alluded, been met with 'enthusiasm' by the academic side of the profession. In this context, therefore, the harmonious collaboration between the two sides of the legal profession, so much the hallmark of German law (and so different from English law), has been ruptured.

Thirdly, despite the above, there exist large areas of tort law where no recovery is allowed for pure economic loss and, in this sense, German law is very close to English law in result if not in methodology. The 'cable cases' provide an obvious example; but many others exist. Thus, for example, if the defendant injures the plaintiff's employee, or debtor, the plaintiff has no action in tort for his economic loss. According to the prevailing view, interferences with contractual or quasi-contractual relations are not actionable under § 823 I BGB. (See, however, Koziol, *Die Beeinträchtigung fremder Forderungsrechte* (1967); Löwisch, *Der Deliktsschutz relativer Rechte* (1970); Mincke, 'Forderungsrechte als "sonstige Rechte" im Sinne des § 823 Abs. I BGB' *JZ* 1984, 862). Thus, the famous French decision (Colmar, 20 avril 1955, *D.* 1956, 723), which allowed a football club to claim the economic loss it suffered as a result of the injury of one of its leading players, would be decided differently in Germany. And so would be a number of other such cases which have received more generous treatment at the hands of French courts (though see Professor Durry's remarks in 1976 *Rev. trim. dr. civ.*, 134).

Fourthly, demarcation lines cannot always be drawn easily, especially in cases involving pure economic loss. The distinction between damage to 'property' and economic loss has thus caused many difficulties. For example, A damages B's cable and C's factory comes to a halt. Molten material in his electrically-operated machines solidifies and has to be discarded. This, clearly, is physical damage, actionable under § 823 I BGB. But what if the solidified material can be remelted—no doubt at an extra cost—and reused? In trying to answer this question, German courts have come up with some rather abstract analyses. (See, for example, OLG Hamm NJW 1973, 760 and notes by Isenbeck in *NJW* 1973, 1755; Moschel, *JuS* 1977, I, 5.)

Fifthly, the different methodology—dictated by the Code, German legal history, or legal education should not deter the reader from using 'constructively' the German ideas which may yet be transplantable into the Common law. At the very least, these ideas should provide the Common lawyer with food for thought. This point will be amplified in the sections that follow, and in the notes to the legal malpractice case.

Finally, for the reasons already given, the economic loss cases will be grouped under different headings and discussed separately, the assumption being that different factual situations call for different legal (and economic) analyses and, therefore, different solutions.

Cable cases. The first three cases (BGHZ 29, 65; BGH NJW 1976, 1740; BGH NJW 1977, 2208, cases 8–10) deal with a problem that has also exercised the English courts. Their annotations will bring out particular points and provide the reader with further bibliographical references. Three points, however, should also be made at this stage. The first is the fact that English and German law essentially reach the same result in this factual situation. It is by no means clear what is the right answer to this problem. If—and we need not give a conclusive answer at this point—the law ought to be changed, the question then arises as to *how* this should be done, given the rigid phrasing of § 823 I BGB. Of course, it should be noted that German attorneys have not been short of ideas in their attempt to circumvent the leading tort provision; but the Supreme Court, apart from a brief period of hesitation, has been as quick to reject them as the practising lawyers have been to invent them.

Secondly, the cases are also noteworthy in their relatively open allusion to policy and, in this respect, they can easily be compared with some of the more recent English decisions. The awareness that policy will decide the outcome is also increasingly shared by the academics who have commented on these decisions. Once again, the *Norsk* decision contains a good discussion of the issues.

Finally, both the English and German cases reveal how various legal devices have been used interchangeably in order to produce the desired result. This equivocation between the various elements of liability must be clearly stressed, for it will accustom the Common lawyer to the fact that he must often seek to find in the German theory of legal cause the answers which he tends to produce through the notion of duty. For comparative studies on this subject see: Hilgenfeldt, *Der Ersatz von Vermögensschäden bei der Unterbrechung von Versorgungsleitungen* (1981); Taupitz, *Haftung für Energieleiterstörungen durch Dritte* (1981).

Loss of use. Two cases (BGHZ 55, 153 and BGH NJW 1977, 2264) dealing with this issue are reproduced below (cases 11 and 12). The annotations to them will make it clear that the results achieved by the courts have been seriously questioned by many academics. These cases also show how difficult it is to draw a line between what constitutes an interference with property, actionable under § 823 I BGB, and what should be called pure economic loss.

Damage caused to the product. This is an economic loss which, arguably, should be left to contract rather than tort. Nevertheless, in Germany, tort law is increasingly expanding to cover this type of economic loss. A number of cases reproduced in section B, 14 of this chapter deal with this problem and their annotations will make it obvious to the Anglo-American reader that the problem is not unknown to the Common law world. Perhaps they will also make clear that—to quote Professor Kötz's words (*Deliktsrecht* 5th edn., nos. 65–6)—letting the [tort] bull into the [contract] china shop can create serious demarcation problems and entail unbearable economic consequences. This judicial trend seems well-entrenched; but the literature is divided. Broadly supportive is Hager, 'Zum Schutzbereich der Produzentenhaftung', *ACP* 1984, 413. The judges who have created this case law have also defended it extra-judicially. See: Steffen in *VersR* 1988, 977 and Kullmann in *NJW* 1991, 675. For criticism and further references, see: Kötz, 5th edn., pp. 28 *et seq*. Cf. also the views of the US Supreme Court in *East River Steamship Corp.* v. *Transamerica Delaval, Inc.* Note also that German law seems to have applied different rules to defective chattels (which damage themselves: case 43) and to immovables (case 44).

Economic loss as a result of negligent misstatements. Here, too, we are dealing with economic loss which in the Common law systems will, if at all, be actionable in tort. The development of the *tort* action in England and the United States was largely brought about by the doctrine of consideration which (especially in England) made the expansion of the notion of contract impossible. (See Lord Devlin's judgment in *Hedley Byrne and Co. Ltd.* v. *Heller and Partners Ltd.* [1964] AC 465, 529.) In Germany the pressure was the reverse. A tort action under § 823 I BGB was and is impossible; and an action under § 826 BGB tends to be limited to the most opprobrious forms of misconduct. Though § 826 BGB has, in recent times, received an expansive interpretation, it is still unable to deal with the most common situations. The expansion of contractual or quasi-contractual remedies was the only answer German law could produce. (Note, however, that in both systems great use is made of the notion of reliance which can transcend the classical distinction between contract and tort and in cases like negligent misstatements make it almost meaningless.) A number of translated German decisions deal with this problem which, in recent years, has also occupied the House of Lords in such cases as *Smith* v. *Eric Bush; Harris* v. *Wyre Forest DC* [1990] 1 AC 831 and *Caparo Industries plc* v. *Dickman and Another* [1990] 2 AC 605. Though the results reached by the German courts are often identical to those accepted by the English courts—*Caparo*, for example, would not have been decided differently under German law—the reasoning is different and the sources of the law multiple and highly complex. More about the contractually 'flavoured' methodology will be said in the next sub-section; and the complexity of the sources that must be used by German judges to solve these cases will be discussed in the notes to the translated decisions.

The case that follows (19) deals with a related topic. A notary, solicitor, or attorney is negligent in the drafting of the will of the testator and, as a result, a potential legatee is deprived of the benefit he would have otherwise derived from the will. The lawyer's contractual and/or delictual liability towards his client is not, of course, in doubt. But can he be made liable to the 'third' party/potential legatee? German law (as indeed English and American law) has given a positive answer, but has again justified it in contractual, not delictual terms. Common lawyers have opted for a different justification of the same result, but the comparison of the various cases shows that the problem—the limit of the potential liability—is the same. Incidentally, in these cases liability can often be said to result from what the lawyer *says* (i.e. negligent statement); but it can also result from what the lawyer *does*. In the annotation in this case we shall examine the English and American approaches to the problem. The advantages of contract over tort are set out in section B, the notes to case 19, below.

Economic loss at the borderline of contract and tort. The divide between contract and tort, not always easy to draw, becomes very vague when the tortious conduct produces pure economic loss instead of the more typical physical injury or property damage. This division, explicable by reference to history, is more rigidly maintained by the Common law where some of its jurists have even produced eloquently pithy but, it is submitted, not always persuasive reasons for its maintenance (for example Weir, *International Encyclopaedia of Comparative Law* (1975), XI, ch. 12, 'Complex Liabilities', 5; for a more sceptical approach see Markesinis, 'An Expanding Tort Law—the Price of a Rigid Contract Law' *LQR* 103 (1987) 354, 384 ff.). This is not so in the modern civil law in general and the German law of torts in particular, where contract and tort are seen as species of the wider notion of obligation and where codal provisions or other reasons have forced lawyers, while not abandoning the search for doctrinal clarity, to cross the boundaries more often than English lawyers have in an attempt to find a solution (not necessarily the best one) to a problem. We shall note later on (in the section on products liability and liability for harm caused by third parties) how this has worked out in specific instances of potential liability; here suffice it to sketch two of the main contractual solutions devised to overcome shortcomings of the German law of tort: they are contracts with protective effects *vis-à-vis* third parties (*Verträge mit Schutzwirkung zugunsten Dritter*) and the (untranslatable) concept of *Drittschadensliquidation*; and their treatment in Germany is usually found in books dealing with the law of contract or the 'general part' of the law of obligations.

(i) Contracts in favour of third parties

Contracts in favour of third parties (*Verträge zugunsten Dritter*) giving, under certain circumstances, a third party the right to demand that a promisor in a contract perform his primary obligation to him (and not to the co-contractor/promisee) are regulated by §§ 328–35 BGB. They are similarly recognized by section 302 *Restatement (Second) Contracts*, article 4 of the 1982 Contracts (Privity) Act of New Zealand and, indeed, by other legal systems (e.g. Israel). Not so, however, by the English Common law which has remained rigidly faithful to its doctrine of consideration. (For a recent thoughtful and critical discussion of the English Common law, see: Law Commission 'Privity of Contract: Contracts for the Benefit of Third Parties', Consultation Paper No. 121. See, also, Beatson, 'Reforming the Law of Contracts for the Benefit of Third Parties. A Second Bite at the Cherry' (1992) *Current Law* 1, where one also finds some interesting insights about the Law Commission's research into foreign (including German) law.) But this is not the contractual device that concerns us here. What is of interest here is the judicially created variant of contract with protective effects *vis-à-vis* third parties which brings strangers to a contract under its protective umbrella and allows them to entertain an action for damages for breach of one of the contract's *secondary* obligations. The situations in which this concept has provided a solution originally involved physical injury; and this contractual device enabled the German courts to overcome the restrictive provision of liability for harm caused by third parties found in § 831 BGB (discussed below in Chapter 3). The German equivalent of cases like *Cavalier* v. *Pope* ([1906] AC 428 cf. RGZ 102, 231; see, also, RGZ 127, 218, reprinted below as case 94) show the difference with the more traditional concept of contract in favour of third parties (§§ 328 ff. BGB). For the problem in *Cavalier* v. *Pope* (and the German equivalents) is not whether the plaintiff (wife of the lessee of premises) can sue the lessor for delivery of the leased premises (the *primary* obligation of the contract); but whether she is entitled to claim damages if she is injured as a result of a breach of one of the *secondary* obligations imposed on the lessor by law or the contract (e.g. the duty to keep the premises in good repair). In this and other similar cases the defendant often benefited from the immunity given to him by the narrow rule of 'vicarious liability' found in the tort section of the BGB (§ 831) so the German courts (as is explained below in Ch. 3. 2) had to resort to various contractual devices (including that of contracts with protective effects *vis-à-vis* third parties) in order to provide greater protection for plaintiffs. Clearly, such a convoluted technique was never necessary for the Common law (and, indeed, for those systems (e.g. French) that opt for the true vicarious liability rule). The German 'refinement' of the traditional contract in favour of third parties has thus, understandably, escaped the attention of most Common lawyers. Yet, German law may, in this context as well, hold out some interesting ideas for discerning Common lawyers dealing with the *Ross* v. *Caunters* [1980] Ch. 297 type of situation. (Attorney's liability towards a non-client/third party which has suffered pure economic loss as a result of the attorney's negligence.) The same may be true in cases where a sub-contractor causes, through his negligence economic loss not just to his co-contractor (the general contractor) but also the owner of the building. (E.g., *Junior Books* v. *Veitchi* [1984] AC 520 (England); *J'Aire Corp.* v. *Gregory* 24 Cal. 3rd 799, 598 P. 2d 60 (1979) (USA).) For, it will be argued (in the notes to the relevant German cases), that in all these situations the defendant (attorney or sub-contractor, as the case may be), must not be made more extensively liable towards the third party than he would be if sued by his co-contractor. For this to be achieved, however, the cause of action against such defendants will have to be either contractual or, if tort terminology is chosen, it will have to be made clear that the scope and extent of any tortious duty will have to be determined by the underlying contract between attorney/client or owner/contractor. (See: Lorenz and Markesinis, 'Solicitors' Liability Towards Third Parties; Back into the Troubled Waters of the Contract/Tort Divide' (1993) 56 *MLR* 558 *et seq.*, replying to Beatson, op. cit. (1992) *Current Law*, 1. See, also, Kötz, 'The Doctrine of Privity of Contract' (1990) 10 *Tel Aviv Univer. Studies in Law*, 195.)

Yet the option of framing the action in contract has also crossed the minds of some lawyers. In *Cavalier* v. *Pope*, mentioned earlier on, the possibility was considered but rejected on the grounds that the plaintiff's wife was not a party to the contract of lease. In *J'Aire* the case was initially also pleaded in contract on the ground that the plaintiff could be regarded as an intended beneficiary of the contract between the owner of the premises and the defendants. This point, however, was later abandoned by the plaintiff's attorney, probably in the belief that it would not have succeeded in court. Nevertheless, a Californian commentator has come out in favour of the

contractual approach arguing that it would have been less drastic to dis-
cover a contract in favour of the plaintiff than to grant the plaintiff's claim
by extending tort to cover negligently inflicted economic loss. (Schwartz,
'Economic Loss in American Tort Law: The Examples of *J'Aire* and of
Products Liability' 23 *San D. L. Rev.*, 40 ff. Contrast Rubin's view in 'Tort
Recovery for Negligently Inflicted Economic Loss: A Reassessment' 37
Stan. L. Rev. 1513 (1985). Finally, *Junior Books* v. *Veitchi* has also been seen
by an English tort expert as supportable 'in a legal system which admits that
[a third party] beneficiary of a contract can sue' (Weir, *A Casebook on Tort*,
5th edn. (1983) 34).)

It would appear that German law has found a better practical way round
this problem—at least in the context of building contracts of the type envisaged in both *Junior Books* and *J'Aire*; and it may well be one that the
Royal Institute of British Architects might wish to study carefully. For it is,
I understand, common practice in Germany for contractors, using the general conditions of trade, to assign in advance all claims they may have
against their sub-contractors arising from breach of warranties, rather than
structure the relationship of the parties in such a way as to make it difficult
if not impossible to make the sub-contractor liable to the employer for the
bad quality of the work. But a building owner accepting such an assignment (of the contractor's claims against the sub-contractor) does not
thereby lose his possible claims against the main contractor. (For details
see: BGHZ 62, 351; 67, 101; 74, 258. See, also, § 11 no. 10(a) of the AGB-
Gesetz of 1976 which is the German equivalent of our Unfair Contract
Terms Act 1977.) Indeed, so common this practice appears to be, the *Junior
Books* type of case apparently has not been litigated in the courts. Well-
known academic writers, however, have speculated that, if no assignment
had taken place and/or the main contractor was not worth suing, a result
similar to that reached by the House of Lords would be achieved by
German courts through the medium of contract with protective effects *vis-
à-vis* third parties. (Schlechtriem, 'Deliktshaftung des Subunternehmers
gegenüber dem Bauherrn wegen Minderwerts seines Werks—Eine neue
Entscheidung des House of Lords', *Versicherungsrecht, 25 Jahre Karlsruher
Forum* (1983), 64, 65, especially in view of BGH NJW 1965, 1955 and BGH
NJW 1982, 2431. Neither case, however, deals with building contracts.
Lorenz, 'Some Thoughts about Contract and Tort' in *Essays in Memory of
Professor F. H. Lawson* (1986) 86, 97, seems to agree. On the other hand,
BGH NJW 1981, 1779, case 14 below, in what appears to be an *obiter dic-
tum*, denies a direct action against the sub-contractor.) As stated, the
advantages of this contractually flavoured action will be considered more
carefully below. Here suffice it to state that the contract with protective
effects *vis-à-vis* third parties makes contractual protection possible while

avoiding all the consequences of a fully fledged contract in favour of third parties.

Clearly, then, the above technique goes some way towards solving the kind of problem faced by Anglo-American courts in cases like *J'Aire* and *Junior Books* v. *Veitchi*. However, it also challenges the doctrine of contractual privity which is accepted by German law as it is by the Common law systems. Some kind of workable compromise is thus needed if a right balance is to be preserved between the traditional doctrine and the judicially fashioned deviation. It follows that if the ambit of contract is to be enlarged—as it is by constructions such as the contract with protective effects *vis-à-vis* third parties—special care must be taken so that the expansion is kept under control and the dividing line between contractual and tortious liability is not blurred or, even, abolished. The way German lawyers have grappled with these, at times, incompatible aims is instructive for a number of reasons.

Noteworthy is first of all the fact that we are here faced with a judge-made doctrine. True, courts and academics have tried—as is customary in German law—to pin their views on some article of the Code. Thus, sometimes the expansion of the contract has been based on § 157 BGB. (Broad interpretation of the contract; implied intentions of the parties; end-aim of the transaction. RGZ 87, 292; 98, 213; 106, 126; 127, 218 (an interesting decision); 152, 177. For a time this practice was continued by the BGH. Thus see: BGHZ 1, 383, 386; 5, 378, 384; BGH NJW 1956, 1193.) In others the even more amorphous § 242 BGB (good faith) has been invoked to render respectability to what is a clear example of judicial activism. (Larenz, *Schuldrecht* I (1st edn. 1953), 16. III; idem, NJW 1956, 1193; NJW 1960, 79. Larenz's work changed not only the theoretical foundation of the new concept, but also helped distinguish it from the traditional contract in favour of third parties regulated by §§ 328 ff. BGB.) This problem has greatly exercised academics but the courts, in what I have elsewhere called fits of 'pragmatism' ('Conceptualism, pragmatism and courage: a common lawyer looks at some judgments of the German Federal Court', 34 *A. J. Comp. L.* 349 (1986)) have refused to resolve this 'theoretical' issue, preferring to focus on the narrow aspects of each action before them. (Thus in BGHZ 56, 269, 273 the theoretical basis of the concept was deliberately left undecided; and in BGH NJW 1977, 2073, 2074 it was regarded as irrelevant!)

A second interesting feature is, as we shall see, the emphasis on the relationship between contractual creditor and plaintiff/third party (which is *known* to the defendant/debtor) rather than on the foreseeability of the plaintiff/third party by the contractual debtor/defendant. The weakness of the latter (tort) approach is the potential open-endedness of the liability; an open-endedness which could, given the vagueness of the foreseeability test, lead to the blurring of contractual and tortious liability.

Turning then to the conditions required for the opening of the contractual umbrella we note that they are three. (Rich references to the case-law illustrating these requirements are given by Sonnenschein, 'Der Vertrag mit Schutzwirkung für Dritte—und immer neue Fragen', *JA* 1979, 225.) First, the third party must come into contact with the performance of the contractual debtor and be endangered (or otherwise affected) by any misperformance in (roughly) the same way as the contractual creditor. This is commonly known as the requirement of proximity of performance (*Leistungsnähe*). Secondly, according to what is probably the better view, the contractual creditor must have some interest in protecting the third party, and thirdly, the above two elements must be known to the debtor/defendant at the time of conclusion of the contract (or the commencement of the contractual negotiations).

This, as stated, is a subject rich in case-law where most generalizations are dangerous; not all decisions are clearly reconcilable with one another (as German lawyers readily admit); and where the only discernible trend is for the courts—despite academic doubts—to move towards an expansion of the contractual umbrella. This last point is particularly obvious from recent decisions (taken from what one might describe broadly as the banking/financial area) in which the second (and, in one sense, most important element) of the above requirements has been given a rather too generous interpretation. Cases 16, 17 and 18 illustrate this trend which many (even in Germany) regard as dangerously expansive. The widening of the protective ambit of the contract is obvious not only in the fact that the courts no longer insist that the protected third party may be specifically identified in advance, but also and mainly in the fact that the third party no longer stands in a close, personal, relationship with the creditor. No longer, it seems, is it necessary (in these financial/banking cases) for the creditor to be responsible for the third party 'for better or for worse'—(*Wohl und Wehe*). Instead the paramount question is 'in what circumstances the *objective interests involved* [sic] permit the inference that the parties [debtor/creditor] have [even] implicitly stipulated a duty of care towards third parties' (BGH NJW 1984, 355, 356).

(ii) Drittschadensliquidation

The advantages, if any, that the contractual approach offers over the tort reasoning will be considered in the note to case 19, below. Here, let us look briefly at the other contractually flavoured concept devised by German lawyers to solve cases of pure economic loss in cases like (arguably) *Ross* v. *Caunters* ([1980] Ch. 297) and *The Aliakmon* (*Leigh and Sillavan* v.

Aliakmon Shipping Co. Ltd.: The Aliakmon [1986] AC 785). The judgment of the House of Lords must be read in conjunction with the decision of the Court of Appeal, especially Lord Justice Goff's judgment ([1985] QB 350). This has involved the use of the notion of *Drittschadensliquidation* or, to give it the English name devised by Lord Justice Goff in *The Aliakmon*, transferred loss.

Drittschadensliquidation is a quasi-contractual judge-made doctrine which allows a creditor to a contract to claim (in contract) for loss resulting from the non-execution or bad execution of the contract, which falls not upon him (the creditor) but upon a third party.

The *fons et origo* of this development seems to be a decision of the Court of Appeal in Lübeck (*Seufferts Archiv.* II (1857), 36 at p. 47), where an agent was allowed to claim damages suffered by his 'undisclosed' principal. In practice a more important example of the application of the theory can be found in cases where the risk (but not the property) in goods has passed from the seller to the buyer (e.g. §§ 446 and 447 BGB). In this type of situation German law has for a long time now (see RGZ 62, 331) accepted that the seller can recover damages from the wrongdoer in order to hand them over to the buyer or, which is even more important in practice, assign this claim to the buyer. (Indeed, because of § 281 BGB he is obliged, if requested, to do so.)

The doctrine of transferred loss is based on the all-pervading concept of good faith and is meant to prevent circuity of actions and above all, to ensure that the defaulting party in the contract does not benefit from the fact that in these cases the loss has been shifted (*Gefahrverlagerung, zufällige Schadensverlagerung*) from the creditor to the third party. If this exception to the notion of relativity of contracts had not been accepted, the defaulting party would not be liable to his creditor (since the latter has suffered no loss); nor would he be liable (in contract) to the third party in the absence of any contractual link between them. Like all judge-made rights, however, this right is kept under close scrutiny lest it get out of control and expose the contractual debtor to an unlimited number of claims. Thus, the third party will be allowed to rely on the doctrine only where special relations between him and the creditor to the contract cause the interest (and the loss) to be shifted on to him.

The appropriateness of this theory to solve the kind of problem that faced the English courts in *The Aliakmon* is obvious to a comparative lawyer; and this belief is reinforced by Lord Justice Goff's judgment in the Court of Appeal where the learned judge, in effect, invented his parallel theory of transferred loss without, apparently, being aware of the German counterpart.

Simplifying the facts of *The Aliakmon*, one notes that there the buyer, who had the risk but not the property in the purchased goods, failed in his action against the shipowner whose negligent storage had damaged the goods resulting in the plaintiff's economic loss. BGH VersR 72, 1138 was a decision involving land transport and the Federal Court, following established case-law (starting with RGZ 62, 331; see, also, BGH VersR 1979, 906), had no difficulty in resorting to the theory of *Drittschadensliquidation* and giving the plaintiff a contractually flavoured action. The separation of risk and property, in the context of carriage of goods, is also envisaged by § 447 BGB and, again, the theory of 'transferred loss' provides the plaintiff/buyer with a successful remedy. (In German law the plaintiff in *The Aliakmon* would also succeed by relying on § 281 I BGB. In practical terms this produces the same result as the *Drittschadensliquidation* but a very different result from that reached by the House of Lords.)

What unites the large miscellany of cases which the Germans have systematically brought under the theory of 'transferred loss' are two common elements. (Tagert, *Die Geltendmachung des Drittschadens* (1938) was the first to classify the various instances of transformed loss under various headings. Illustrations are also provided by Ries, 'Grundprobleme der Drittschadensliquidation und des Vertrags mit Schutzwirkung für Dritte' *JA* 1982, 453; Lange, *Schadensrecht, Handbuch des Schuldrechts* i (1979) 278–97.) First is the fact that in these cases the invocation of the floodgates argument—the 'shop soiled' argument of the timorous as Professor Fleming calls it in his *Introduction to the Law of Torts* (2nd edn. 1985, p. 3)—is inappropriate since one person only suffers loss. Secondly, the co-contractor of the defaulting party—in our two examples the testator or the seller of the goods—will have no incentive to sue (or may simply no longer be around to sue!). As German lawyers argue, in these cases the person who has suffered the loss has no remedy while the person who has the remedy has suffered no loss. If such a situation is left unchallenged, the defaulting party may never face the consequences of his negligent conduct; his insurer may receive an unexpected (and undeserved) windfall; and the person on whom the loss has fallen may be left without any redress. The question to my mind is not whether the plaintiffs should be allowed to recover—I believe the answer must be in the affirmative—but whether the defaulting defendants should run the risk of incurring greater liability towards these plaintiffs than they would have incurred had they been sued by their co-contractor. The German reply is negative; and their contractually flavoured solutions offer a neater explanation of this result than the tentative English attempts to harness tort for an answer.

(iii) Some preliminary reactions to the German concepts and techniques

The comparatist must first describe a foreign system to his readership and then see what conclusions can be drawn from it to benefit his national law.

The picture of German law given thus far is, inevitably, a simplified one. The reality is infinitely more complex, if not inscrutable to the foreign observer who treads on perilous ground when expressing a critical view of this system. But even the potentially distorted appreciation of foreign law by the comparatist may be of use to the national lawyer. Four points should, thus, be made at this stage.

First, the test that will determine who is to be included within the protective umbrella of the contract is crucial if the concept of contract with protective effects *vis-à-vis* third parties is to be employed. Most German lawyers agree that the list of such persons must be limited; but they differ greatly as to the criteria that must be employed to achieve this aim and, as a result, as to who precisely enjoys such protection. The traditional emphasis on the creditor's interest to protect the third party/plaintiff seems to me to be the most precise test without being excessively restrictive. In any event in my opinion it is probably more workable to place the emphasis on the relationship between creditor and third party/plaintiff (which is *known* to the debtor/defendant) than to operate, as the Common law does, on the basis of the amorphous foreseeability test applied to the plaintiff/defendant relationship.

Secondly, one might venture the thought that the more recent attempts to enlarge the circle of contractually protected persons threatens to undermine the security and (relative) predictability provided by the older tests. If the current trend remains limited, however, to the banking/financial services, it is understandable if not necessarily justifiable. For in these cases the German courts are essentially faced with variations of the *Hedley Byrne* v. *Heller and Partners* ([1964] AC 465) problem which they cannot solve through tort law because of the restrictive provision of § 823 I BGB. The way they expand contract is thus, essentially, as arbitrary as our own attempts to limit tort duties in similar factual situations. Though the pressures are exerted in different directions in the two systems, the problem is the same: discovering the proper bounds of liability which modern insurance practices tend to expand outwards.

Thirdly, the concept of contract with protective effects *vis-à-vis* third parties and the theory of transferred loss originally had a different area of application: the first was used in cases of physical injury and property damage (mainly in order to avoid the problems created by § 831 BGB); the latter applied to cases of pure economic loss which had not always received full and adequate regulation by the positive law. In this original context the two notions presented one further difference. In the former, the risk of the contractual debtor was *widened* by the inclusion of a third party within the contractual umbrella. For example, in the *Cavalier* v. *Pope* type of situation, the landlord's liability was *extended* to cover injury suffered by the tenant's induces another person to break his contractual obligations towards a third party, he will not be liable under § 823 I BGB towards this third party for his economic loss, though he may be liable to him under § 826 BGB if the other conditions of liability in this paragraph are satisfied.

Three types of situation have given rise to considerable literature and case-law and they must now be examined. The first is related to the possible use of § 823 I BGB within the context of family relations; the second deals with the right of an established and operating business; and the third with the general right to one's personality and privacy. The last two 'rights' are very important judicial creations and seven decisions dealing with them are reproduced below (cases 24–32).

(ii) Delictual protection of family relationships

It is by no means clear to what extent a person's family status and his legal rights thereunder are protected by § 823 I BGB. In some cases, the answer seems clearer than in others. 'Parental power' is, generally, regarded as an 'other' right. Thus, if in the course of his divorce proceedings, a father has lost the right to exercise those powers and refuses to hand the child over to the mother, he may be held liable under § 823 I BGB (see RGZ 141, 319). But do spouses have an *absolute* right *erga omnes* to demand the respect of their marital bond? Though in some cases the BGH has given a positive answer to the above question (see, for example, BGHZ 6, 630 where a wife was given redress (maintenance) against an unfaithful husband), the attitude of the Supreme Court is, on the whole, quite negative. Thus the 'marital intruder' (*Ehestörer*) will not be liable to the husband in tort for enticing his wife away and then causing the husband the cost of instituting adultery and divorce proceedings (BGHZ 23, 279). Neither will the wife be liable to the husband on this ground (BGHZ 23, 215 and, more recently, BGH NJW 1990, 706).

Though this solution has not passed without criticism, it does appear to be correct. As the Supreme Court itself remarked in the above decisions, *vis-à-vis* the parties in the marriage there is no reason for the law of delict to operate, their relationship being the exclusive concern of the provisions of the family law section of the Code; equally, the third party should not be held liable for causing the breach of the marriage, since marital fidelity is something that concerns the spouses and them alone. This approach, that marriage as an institution is subject to its own rules and lies outside the protective ambit of the rules of the law of tort, has also been adopted by even more recent decisions of the Supreme Court (e.g. BGH JZ 1973, 668). However, not all lawyers are convinced by this kind of reasoning and the debate cannot be regarded as having been closed. Nevertheless, it should be made clear that those academics who argue against the established view are only arguing for a limited extension of § 823 I BGB so as to allow certain claims such as, for example, the costs of divorce, delivery of a child born of an adulterous relationship (§ 1615 k in association with § 1615 i III BGB), litigation for illegitimization proceedings (BGHZ 57, 229) and maintenance of the child according to § 1615 b II BGB.

Further reading

Beitzke, *Familienrecht* (26th edn. 1992), § 12 III; Boehmer, 'Zur Ehestörungsklage' *AcP* 155 (1956) 181; Engel, *Der Rückgriff des Scheinvaters wegen Unterhaltsleistungen* (1974); Gernhuber, *Lehrbuch des Familienrechts* (3rd edn., 1980) § 17 II; von Hippel, 'Schadensersatz bei Ehestörung' *NJW* 1965, 664; Jayme, *Die Familie im Recht der unerlaubten Handlungen* (1971); Schwab, *Familienrecht* (6th edn., 1991) § 22; Smid, *Zur Dogmatik der Klage auf Schutz des 'räumlich-gegenständlichen Bereiches' der Ehe* (1983).

(iii) The right of an established and operating business

This is a judge-made right which has developed into a kind of general clause intended to protect commercial enterprises against the infliction of certain types of rather vaguely defined interferences with their economic interests. Its emergence may be due to certain gaps in the delictual provisions of the Code but is, nevertheless, remarkable since in a free-enterprise economy, where free competition is both the justification and the result of the system, the protection afforded to business entities cannot be as extensive as that given to property. It is, perhaps, this type of doubt that lies behind more recent attempts to limit or at least define more carefully the scope of the protection afforded.

The development of this right began only four years after the BGB had come into force when it became recognized that the protection given by the Code in cases of purely economic loss was very limited. § 826 BGB, for example, only caught intentional activities which were contrary to 'public policy'; and § 824 BGB caught only *untrue* statements damaging the *credit* of another person. Nor was § 823 I BGB of any help.

The first cases were mainly concerned with one type of conduct which hindered the business activities of a competing enterprise. The noxious activity typically took the form of the defendant claiming unjustifiably that the plaintiff had no right to use a particular industrial property right (patent, registered design) held by him (the defendant). If the plaintiff ceased his activities, thereby suffering economic loss, but subsequently discovered that the defendant's claim was groundless and also was made in a careless manner, then he should be and was allowed to claim his loss. From the very beginning, therefore, it was made clear, and was subsequently repeatedly confirmed, that this kind of protection could only avail business or commercial enterprises and not, for example, a legal partnership or a trade union or a club. This distinction, which has not passed uncriticized, was perhaps explained by the desire of the courts to keep within reasonable bounds the newly created right which, however, was destined to develop even further.

Three decisions are reproduced below to illustrate the development of this new right and the accompanying annotations show that the literature to which it has given rise is enormous. (To these three cases one should add two of the cable cases (cases 8 and 9) which also contain clear evidence of the court's desire not to extend unduly the ambit of the new right. This is obvious also from the most recent case: BGH JZ 1983, 857.)

The doubts expressed about this right are understandable, not only in view of the fact that court-made rights are typically followed by an expression of concern by the judges that the new right (or tort) be kept within reasonable bounds; they are also explicable by the fact that the new right was soon expanded to cover cases where issues (like freedom of expression) were involved alongside the right of a business enterprise to safeguard its financial interests. This was the case with the extension of the right in order to protect entrepreneurs against criticisms which adversely affected their business but which were not caught by either §§ 824 or 826 BGB. For example, organizing boycotts of the plaintiff's business or making factually true statements about it which the defendant culpably knew would severely affect the plaintiff but which he had no pressing interest to make. As stated, the danger of inhibiting free speech in these cases is considerable; and the need to 'balance' the competing interests before giving judgment is also very great.

The courts' desire to keep matters within manageable bounds was thus also expressed in the form of an imperative that the interference with the established and operating business be 'direct' before it can become actionable under this heading. The notion of directness, however, as Common lawyers know only too well from their experience with the 'remoteness' cases, is an invitation to the judge to hide his own value-judgment behind an apparently unimpeachable concept. Not surprisingly, perhaps, it also gave rise to numerous other attempts to discover the right test. Perhaps, the most often quoted test is in fact one given by the BGH itself. Thus, for the Supreme Court the conduct of the defendant will constitute an invasion of the plaintiff's right if it is 'business-connected' which means, according to this court, that it must be 'in some way directed against the business as such . . . and must not simply affect rights and interests which are separable from the business as a functioning unit'. This formula, as many academics have admitted quite bluntly, is nothing but an empty shell of words, and perhaps the courts should attempt more openly to weigh the reciprocal interests rather than to indulge in the creation of opaque formulae. The right of an established and operating business is further restricted by the subsidiary nature of the right (*Subsidiarität*) which means that the right can only be invoked in the absence of any other relevant provision (on which, for example, see BGHZ 55, 153, below case 11). Finally, since the element of 'unlawfulness' (on which see below 3(*a*)) has to be positively established in each single case, the result is that the new general clause has to receive its precise content by continuous judicial activity. This, in fact, has been happening, as Deutsch points out most clearly in *JZ* 1984, 308.

Further reading

The literature on the subject is enormous; what follows is only a selection. Buchner, *Die Bedeutung des Rechts am eingerichteten und ausgeübten Gewerbebetrieb für den deliktsrechtlichen Unternehmensschutz* (1971); idem, 'Konsolidierung des deliktsrechtlichen Unternehmensschutzes' *DB* 1979, 1069 f.; Canaris, 'Grundrechte und Privatrecht', *AcP* 184 (1984) 201; Fikentscher, 'Das Recht am Gewerbebetrieb (Unternehmen) als "sonstiges Recht" im Sinne des § 823 Abs. 1' *Festgabe für Kronstein* (1967) 261 ff.; Larenz, *Schuldrecht*, II, 632 f.; Neumann-Duesberg, 'Zum Recht am eingerichteten und ausgeübten Gewerbebetrieb' *NJW* 1972, 133 ff.; Raiser, *Das Unternehmen als Organisation* (1969); Schippel, *Das Recht am eingerichteten und ausgeübten Gewerbebetrieb* (1956); Schnug, 'Das Recht am Gewerbebetrieb—ein Fremdkörper im deliktischen Haftungssystem?', *JA* 1985, 440; Schwabe/Canaris, 'Grundrechte und Privatrecht', *AcP* 185 (1985) 1, 9; Schwitanski, *Deliktsrecht, Unternehmensschutz und Arbeitskampfrecht* (1986) 21 ff., 59 ff.; Suppes, *Die Rechtsprechung des BGH zum Recht am eingerichteten und ausgeübten Gewerbebetrieb* (1965); Wiethölter, 'Zur politischen Funktion des Rechts am eingerichteten und ausgeübten Gewerbebetrieb' *Kritische Justiz* 1970, 121; Wolf, 'Das Recht am eingerichteten und ausgeübten Gewerbebetrieb' *Festschrift von Hippel* (1967) 665 ff.

(iv) The general right to one's personality

In Germany, as indeed in the United States, the first attempts to recognise a general right of privacy (and, more generally, a wider protection of the human personality) were made by distinguished academics like Kohler ('Das Recht an Briefen', *Archiv für bürgerliches Recht* VII, 94 ff.) and the famous 'Germanist' Gierke (*Deutsches Privatrecht* I, 707; III, 887) towards the end of the 19th century. On a more regional basis, one must, however, note the Civil Code of Saxony of 1863—greatly admired at the time—which gave judges the *discretion* to award damages in cases involving the 'dissemination of *untrue* statements about a person's life, personal abilities, conduct of office, established business, or other relations.' Of course, the emphasis on *untrue* statements, brings this provision closer to defamation than privacy; but that does not really affect its pioneering nature given the feeling, widely accepted at that time, that interferences with honour, reputation, and other such personal interests should not be vindicated through an action for damages. (See, for example, various *obiter* in RGZ 7, 295, which reflects the view taken by most German courts.) This attitude was also adopted by the Committee which was entrusted with the task of drafting the BGB and which expressed it in uncompromising terms when it stated that 'it [would be] repugnant to the dominant opinion among the population to place non-material values on the same level as property interests and to make good with money interferences with non-material interests. The Code [which was being drafted at the time] should not ignore this view, *especially prevalent among the better circles of society* [*sic*]. Only the worst elements [of society] would try to take advantage [of such a provision]. Pursuit of profit, selfishness, and covetousness would be promoted and wrongful proceedings, started from ulterior motives, would be encouraged.' (Protokolle der Kommission für die Zweite Lesung des Entwurfs des Bügerlichen Gesetzbuchs, vol. I (1897), pp. 622–3).

Clearly, the times were not yet ripe for the recognition of any wide-ranging rights of personality; and the 'toughness' of living conditions at that time made the average citizen quite indifferent towards such 'lesser' interferences with his daily life. Inevitably, therefore, German law opted for a more gradual extension of the protection of the various aspects of the human personality. It was not until the Nazi holocaust demonstrated its utter disregard for human beings, their life, and their dignity, that the need was really felt for greater legal protection; and even then it was strongly resisted by sections of the Press. The next move was thus facilitated by the post-War climate and the newly sanctioned Bill of Rights (contained in the first twenty articles of the Constitution of Bonn of 1949). What happened next is explained in the translated cases and their annotations—more than usually detailed since many comparatists would take the view that the German law of privacy holds some interesting lessons for the English Common law. Here, therefore, only three general observations will be made.

First, one must stress that the absence (until the *Schacht* decision of 1954) of a general right of personality did not mean that the protection afforded by German law (at any rate while the democratic order was respected) was inadequate, let alone non-existent even though the way the courts managed to afford protection was, at times, achieved in a somewhat crude legal manner. When, for example, in 1899 the defendants broke into Bismarck's death chamber and photographed his corpse, public resentment was such that the court that had to hear the case against the photographers *had* to discover a way to deny the offenders the financial advantages of their conduct. In the event, the defendants were forced to hand over to the plaintiffs the negatives of the photographs. The actual decision, however, is more complicated than this summary suggests, since it had to be decided according to the old *Gemeines Recht*—i.e. the *usus modernus Pandectarum*—and was related to a bankruptcy question (since the defendants were insolvent): were the negatives part of their estate? (RGZ 45, 170). By 1907 this rather primitive protection was further extended by the Act on Artistic Creations (*Kunsturhebergesetz*) which, in §§ 22 *et seq.*, prohibited the publication of a person's picture without his consent unless his was a 'public figure' (though see KG JW 1928, 363). The unauthorised publication of private letters was also increasingly restricted, though in the beginning the protection afforded to the 'author' (or, more typically his heirs wishing to prevent publication of letters that were in the possession of their recipients) depended upon whether the letters in question could be considered as 'literary works'. This move started with RGZ 69, 401 where the Imperial Court demonstrated great ingenuity when Nietzsche's sole heiress sought to prevent the publication of letters written by the philosopher which the heirs of the addressee wished to publish. In the absence of a general right of personality, the court reasoned that the ownership in the letters had passed to the addressee (and to his heirs). But if the letters could be regarded as 'artistic creations', they could then be given copyright protection. Thus, to start with, the publication of private facts, lying outside the range of fiduciary relations, received little or no publicity. Fifty years later, however, the Federal Court in the *second* Wagner case (BGHZ 15, 249), which involved the private diaries of Cosima Wagner written during her marriage to the great composer, held that the publication of private notes or records could be enjoined on privacy grounds even if they fell short of the standards of 'literary merit' that would ensure them protection under copyright laws.

Other aspects of the human personality received more clearly defined protection by the Civil Code or other enactments. Thus, § 12 of the BGB protects the human name and § 826 BGB can also, on occasion, be of use. § 824 BGB can give an action against a person who publishes wrong facts which endanger the credit of the plaintiff and which he knows or ought to know are false. Finally, the crime of insult or slander (§ 185 of the Criminal Code) can be used in conjunction with § 823 II BGB to give rise to a civil action.

Secondly, one should note that the new *right* created in 1954 and added to the list of other rights ought to have been modelled on the *interests* of life, body, health, and freedom. If the Code were ever to be redrafted, the protection of personality should be added to the list of those *interests* with which it is more related, rather than be treated as another *right* analogous, perhaps, to that of ownership. One must add, however, that such redrafting of the Code seems unlikely; at any rate, it has failed up to now to materialize since the protection of one person's personality and privacy can mean that another person's freedom of speech can be curtailed. The issues raised by this new right are complicated and one must remember that the right to be protected against an often irresponsible Press must be counterbalanced by the equally important need to preserve the freedom of the Press guaranteed by article 5 of the Constitution (see also § 193 of the Criminal Code). Where the line will be drawn will thus depend on the circumstances of each case and the rich case-law will, at best, provide useful guide-lines but not binding rules. The famous 'Lebach decision' (BVerfGE 35, 202), reproduced in section B. 10 illustrates how difficult it can be to balance on the one hand the right to publish information and, on the other, 'the right to anonymity'. (The anonymity of criminals and, more, generally persons prosecuted for offences has been discussed in a number of cases. Interesting dicta can be found, inter alia, in: OLG Düsseldorf NJW 1980, 599; OLG Hamburg NJW 1980, 842; OLG Hamm NJW 1982, 458; OLG Köln NJW 1987, 2682—the last one linking German domestic law with the European Convention on Human Rights.) It would appear, however, that the more active a person becomes in the 'public domain' the less he will be able to argue successfully that criticisms of his conduct amount to actionable invasions of his privacy. (Thus, see BGHZ 36, 77, 80; BGH NJW 1964, 1471 and many others.)

Finally, as has been already noted, the development of the new right was prompted by the Constitution's protection of the human personality (articles 1 and 2). That this constitutional provision should be given material effect on the civil law plane was desirable and necessary. Less straightforward, however, was the method of widening the remedies available to the aggrieved plaintiff in order to make this protection more complete. Thus, in the first decision that recognized the new right—the *Schacht* case (case 29)—the court decreed, and the plaintiff was content to demand, reparation *in specie* (correction of statement published in a newspaper). In the second important judgment—the *Herrenreiter* case (case 30)—the court argued in favour of the analogical extension of § 847 BGB while in case 31 the court finally decided to base the award of monetary compensation on § 253 BGB in conjunction with article 1 of the Constitution. If natural restitution is insufficient under § 253 BGB—reasoned the court—then that paragraph should be interpreted to allow even monetary compensation. The constitutional text, in its express desire to protect human dignity and personality, makes *this* extension of *this* civil remedy (damages) both desirable and necessary. This last part of the reasoning may be doubtful (see Medicus, 15th edn., no. 615). But given the legislative inactivity in the field, it has repeatedly been upheld by the Federal Supreme Court; indeed, the Constitutional Court itself held in a long and interesting judgment (BVerfGE 34, 269) that this 'extension' in no way violated the constitutional order.

Further reading

On the right of judges to make law see BGHZ 11, 34; BVerfGE 34, 269; BAG NJW 1988, 2816 and the following works: Canaris, *Die Feststellung von Lücken im*

Gesetz—Eine methodologische Studie über Voraussetzungen und Grenzen der richterlichen Rechtsfortbildung praeter legem (2nd edn., 1983); Doehring (ed.), *Richterliche Rechtsfortbildung, Festschrift der Juristischen Fakultät zur 600-Jahr-Feier der Ruprechts-Karls-Universität Heidelberg* (1986); Esser, 'Richterrecht, Gerichtsgebrauch und Gewohnheitsrecht' *Festschrift von Hippel* (1967) 95; idem, 'In welchem Ausmass bilden Rechtsprechung und Lehre Rechtsquellen' 75 *Zeitschrift für vergleichende Rechtswissenschaft* (1975) 67; Flume, Richter und Recht, *Verhandlungen des sechsundvierzigsten deutschen Juristentages* (1966) K5 (1967); Heussner, 'Die Rechtsprechung des Bundesverfassungsgerichts zum Richterrecht', *Festschrift für Hilger/Stumpf* (1983) 317; Larenz, *Methodenlehre der Rechtswissenschaft* (6th edn., 1991) (the relevant pages (341–412) of the 2nd edn. of 1969 can be found translated in *The Role of Judicial Decisions and Doctrine in Civil Law and in Mixed Jurisdictions* (ed. J. Dainow, 1975)). On the right of privacy and personality see Brandner, 'Das allgemeine Persönlichkeitsrecht in der Entwicklung durch die Rechtsprechung' *JZ* 1983, 689; von Caemmerer, 'Der privatrechtliche Persönlichkeitsschutz nach deutschem Recht' *Festschrift von Hippel* (1967) 27; Canaris, 'Grundrechte und Privatrecht' *AcP* 184 (1984) 201; Freund, 'Der persönlichkeitsrechtliche Schutz des Werbeadressaten' *BB* 1986, 409; von Gamm, 'Persönlichkeitsschutz und Massenmedien' *NJW* 1979, 513; Hubmann, *Das Persönlichkeitsrecht* (1967); Larenz, 'Das "allgemeine Persönlichkeitsrecht" im Recht der unerlaubten Handlungen' *NJW* 1955, 521; Max-Planck-Institut für ausländisches und internationales Privatrecht (ed.), *Der zivilrechtliche Persönlichkeits- und Ehrenschutz in Frankreich, der Schweiz, England und den USA* (1970); Mertens, 'Persönlichkeitsrecht und Schadenersatz', *JuS* 1962, 261; Schwerdtner, *Das Persönlichkeitsrecht in der deutschen Zivilrechtsordnung* (1977); idem, 'Der zivilrechtliche Persönlichkeitsschutz', *JuS* 1978, 289; Solyom, *Die Persönlichkeitsrechte. Eine vergleichend-historische Studie über ihre Grundlagen* (1984); Stein, 'Der Schutz von Ansehen und Geheimsphäre Verstorbener' *FamRZ* 1986, 7; Tettinger, 'Der Schutz der persönlichen Ehre im freien Meinungskampf' *JZ* 1983, 317. For a comparative discussion in German see Dworkin, Fleming, Hubrecht, Strömholm, Finzgar and Kübler, *Die Haftung der Massenmedien, insbesondere der Presse, bei Eingriffen in persönliche oder gewerbliche Rechtspositionen* (Arbeiten zur Rechtsvergleichung, 1972); in English: Zweigert and Kötz, op. cit. (select bibliography), II, § 20; Handford, 'Moral Damage in Germany' 27 *ICLQ* 849 (1978); Humphries, *Media and Media Policy in West Germany. The Press and Broadcasting since 1945* (1990); Krause, 'The Right of Privacy—Pointers for American Legislation?' [1965] *Duke L. J.* 481; Lorenz, 'Privacy and the Press—A German Experience', *Butterworths Lectures 1989–90*, 79–119 (1990); Markesinis, 'The Right to be Let Alone Versus Freedom of Speech', 1986 *Public Law* 67; UNESCO Report: 'The Legal Protection of Privacy: A Comparative Survey of Ten Countries', *UNESCO International Social Science J.* 1972, 417. A topic not discussed in this book is employee protection against violations of their privacy by their employers which has increased in recent times as computers enable employers to gather and store much personal information about their workers. German law is ahead of the law in both England and the United States; and it is discussed by Schwarz, 'Privacy in German Employment Law' 15 *Hastings International and*

Comparative Law Rev. 135 (1992)—an article with rich references to the relevant German literature.

3. UNLAWFULNESS AND FAULT

(a) Unlawfulness

Unlike French law, German law has kept the element of fault (*Verschulden*) separate from that of objective unlawfulness (*Rechtswidrigkeit*), the first being understood as an attitude (the attitude of a person who intentionally or negligently causes damage to another) while the second as simply indicating the violation of a legal norm in the absence of a legally recognized excuse. How far these two concepts can actually be kept apart is a matter of considerable controversy and what follows is a bird's-eye view of one of the most hotly debated—but essentially—theoretical areas of the German law of torts.

The traditional school of thought on the matter, which still enjoys much support with the courts, takes the view that the element of unlawfulness is automatically satisfied whenever one of the interests or rights enumerated in § 823 I BGB has been violated. For example, running over the plaintiff or damaging his property is an act which brings about a consequence which deserves the disapproval of the legal order. Unlawfulness, in other words, depends on the harmful result (*Erfolgsunrecht*). The only thing that can remove the 'unlawfulness' is the presence of a legally recognized defence (*Rechtfertigungsgrund*). Action taken in order to repel an actual unlawful act upon oneself or another person is, according to § 227 BGB, such a defence. Equally, the destruction of a thing belonging to another person will, according to § 228 BGB, also be a lawful defence, so long as it does not represent a disproportionate reaction to the threatened danger. Various forms of self-help can, within limits, remove the element of unlawfulness in the defendant's conduct (§ 228 BGB, for example, allows one to destroy the object from which the danger emanates; § 904 allows one—in certain circumstances—to destroy an object *other* than the one which is the source of the danger). §§ 561, 859 and 1029 BGB contain specific applications of the same general rule in the context of possession and ownership. Another legally recognized defence is found in § 34 StGB (necessity).

Consent can also have a bearing on the issue under consideration if it is lawfully given with full knowledge of all the facts and prior to the accomplishment of the activity complained of. How this works in the field of medical operations is a matter of some dispute. For some academics, a properly performed medical operation forms part of the process of healing the plaintiff, it is an act done in his interest and, therefore, the element of unlawfulness is not satisfied. Case-law takes the opposite view, and proper consent must be affirmatively proved (if contested) in order to remove unlawfulness from the activity. It goes without saying that in practice many difficulties can arise, especially in cases of minors, and also in cases concerning the degree of information that the doctor has to supply to the patient (concerning the gravity of his illness) in order to obtain his consent (case 36, in section B deals with this problem), and clearly, the solution must depend to some extent on the likelihood of causing a neurotic plaintiff even greater injuries by revealing to him the full extent of his illness. All that can be said here is that these difficulties are in no way restricted to German law.

If no justification is produced by the defendant, and a protective interest or right has been shown to have been violated, the element of unlawfulness is satisfied and the plaintiff must then go on to prove the defendant's fault. The question whether the defendant acted intentionally or negligently becomes the second phase of the inquiry and more about this will be said in sub-section (b) of this section.

This approach has in fairly recent times been challenged by a host of distinguished academics like Nipperdey, von Caemmerer, Esser, and others. According to these authors, unlawfulness should be determined by looking not at the result of the conduct but at the conduct itself (*Handlungsunrecht*). The mere violation of one of the enumerated interests of § 823 I BGB, if done unintentionally, does not necessarily satisfy the element of unlawfulness. Something more is required to do this and the missing element can be supplied by proof that the defendant's conduct has either failed to measure up to the standard of conduct imposed by a particular imperative rule applicable to the occasion in question (*Verhaltensnorm*), or that it has violated the general duty imposed upon all human beings to take care not to inflict injury on others. The need for such a duty is obvious in every civilized society, and the scope and content of this general duty of care (*allgemeine Sorgfaltspflicht*) should be deduced from § 276 BGB, which imposes upon human beings the obligation to exercise in their ordinary daily affairs (*im Verkehr*) the care that the occasion demands. So the objective approach will determine what the defendant's behaviour should have been. Moreover, in determining this standard, the social utility of the activity in question will have to be taken into account (*Sozialadäquanz*). Indeed, influential authors who favour this type of approach have openly stated that policy considerations should ultimately determine the existence as well as the limits of such duties. When we discuss the 'duties of care' in the next section, ample illustrations will be provided of how all this has worked in practice.

It was inevitable that a system like the German, which flourishes on legal theories, would respond to this approach with a stream of legal literature accepting, condemning, or varying the new theory. For present purposes these variations on the new theme are irrelevant. In any event, all authors

'Die Begriffe Kausalität, Rechtswidrigkeit und Verschulden in ihrer Beziehung zueinander', *Festschrift für Larenz* (1983), 583; Stoll, 'Zum Rechtfertigungsgrund des verkehrsrichtigen Verhaltens' *JZ* 1958, 137; Wiethölter, *Der Rechtfertigungsgrund des verkehrsrichtigen Verhaltens* (1960).

(b) Fault

A number of decisions are given below as illustrations. Generally speaking, however, and subject to one point only, the treatment which this topic receives in German law greatly resembles that found in common law text books.

The difference which sets German law apart can be found in its tendency to analyse the problems of fault in a highly abstract manner and to categorise the various types of fault under five, arguably six, different headings. Thus, a distinction is drawn between: (*a*) *Dolus directus* (*direkter Vorsatz*); (*b*) *dolus eventualis* (*bedingter Vorsatz*); (*c*) gross negligence (*grobe Fahrlässigkeit*); (*d*) ordinary negligence (*mittlere Fahrlässigkeit*) and (*e*) light negligence (*leichte Fahrlässigkeit*). These categories can best be illustrated by means of specific examples. (Ordinary negligence is defined in § 276 BGB and we shall return to it further down. In addition to the above headings, recklessness may form a separate heading of fault).

(*a*) *Dolus directus*. It can come in two forms, e.g. I aim at a child standing behind a house window and I kill it. *Alternatively*, I set fire to a house in order to burn it *knowing* that a young child is inside and knowing (and accepting) that the inevitable result of my burning the house will be the death of the child.

(*b*) *Dolus eventualis*. For instance, I hit a man on the head with the intention of injuring him; but I also realise that he *may* die as a result of the blow. Despite this knowledge, I persist with my action.

(*c*) Negligence. The differences between the three types mentioned above is one of degree. In most *tort* cases the distinction between the various types of negligence (particularly light and average or normal negligence) is of little significance (though see BAGE 42, 130, overturned by BAG NJW 1991, 3275, discussed below in Chapter 3); but it is of some importance for contract law.

A further distinction is made and it seems of particular importance to criminal law. This is between advertent negligence (*luxuria*) and inadvertent negligence (*negligentia*). Sometimes these terms are rendered into English as conscious and unconscious negligence. Adverted negligence comes close to intention (*dolus eventualis*) in the sense that the actor (personally) foresaw the criminal consequences as likely to materialise. The difference, however, is that in the case of *dolus* the actor accepts the result whereas in the case of *luxuria* he does not. (Indeed, he goes ahead with his action in the belief that the criminal event will not materialise). Inadvertent negligence, on the other hand, approximates the notion of *casus*. The difference is that *negligentia* (unlike *casus*) is a form of culpability since the actor could, had he applied himself, foreseen and avoided the consequences of his act.

At the beginning of this section, the state of recklessness (*Leichtfertigkeit*) is suggested as an independent heading of fault. This is because many lawyers would find it difficult to say how it differs in *practice* from gross negligence. The theoretical answer often given is that recklessness is a slightly worse form of conduct than gross negligence, involving a higher degree of deviation from the accepted norm. In practice, however, non-German observers are likely to take the view that their German colleagues are, in this instance, splitting hairs. Additionally, one has the impression that recklessness is a term reserved more for the criminal law while gross negligence is used in the context of civil law—contract and tort (e.g. § 826 BGB).

§ 276 BGB contains the definition of negligence. The person who fails to observe the ordinary care which is required in everyday life is guilty of negligence. This means doing what the reasonable man (or woman) would not have done or not doing what they would have done. As in English and American law, the standard of care is objective and the test—the *bonus pater familias*, as the man on the Clapham omnibus is sometimes called—is wide enough to allow plenty of room for judicial creativity. If the defendant belongs to a particular group or profession he will be judged against the standard expected to be attained by members of that profession. So a general medical practitioner will have to demonstrate the standard of care expected of general medical practitioners and not the standard of the specialized consultant. In our example, however, he will be negligent if he realizes (or ought to realize) that a specialized second opinion on the state of the health of his patient ought to have been obtained but was in fact never obtained.

Personal shortcomings of the defendant will not normally be taken into account and German writers often quote as an illustration of this the learner-driver who commits the kind of error of judgment which his experienced colleagues would have avoided. The reasoning is similar to that given by Lord Denning MR in *Nettleship* v. *Weston* ([1971] 2 QB 691) and it is clear that negligence in these cases does not necessarily involve any moral blameworthiness. One is also tempted to speculate that, as in *Nettleship* v. *Weston*, compulsory motor car insurance may account for this very high (if not unattainable) standard of care. Certainly, one case reproduced below (case 36), which has French and English equivalents, suggests that negligent liability often is strict liability in everything but name. Having stressed the objective standard of the test, one must add that there is also room for certain subjective elements to enter into the equation. Thus, the defendant's conduct will be measured against the conduct of the hypothetical reasonable man who was in the same *external* circumstances as was the defendant.

As stated, the reasonable man is nothing more than the anthropomorphic conception of justice. German judges, like their English, French, and American counterparts, will thus formulate their value-judgment in the light of such factors as the probability of harm, the cost of avoidance, and the magnitude of danger if it is realized. German case-law is very rich on this point and it really serves no purpose to provide further details since the examples and reasoning are very similar to those found in other systems. It is noteworthy, however, that mathematical formulae, which attempt to work out negligence on the basis of a yield–cost analysis, and which are so favoured by many American judges and academics, are increasingly appearing in German legal writings—a fact which suggests that there is here plenty of room for cross-fertilization of ideas. The limitations of these theories, however, are also stressed in Germany and in England.

One should, perhaps, conclude this section by stating that the '*objectiviza-tion*' of negligence represents one of the inroads into the fault principle. The theoretical distinction between fault and risk-based liability is often very blurred in practice, especially where it is aided by a statutory (e.g. §§ 836 and 833(2) BGB) or case-law-created (e.g. § 823 II BGB) reversal of the onus of proof, or the notion of prima-facie proof, which is analogous to our doctrine of *res ipsa loquitur*. This change has involved a transformation or even perversion of traditional doctrines and notions and may be largely due to the impact that the insurance factor has had on the modern law of torts.

Further reading

On this issue see Deutsch, 'Der Begriff der Fahrlässigkeit im Zivilrecht' *Jura* 1987, 505; Esser, 'Die Zweispurigkeit unseres Haftpflichtrechts' *JZ* 1953, 129; for France see Viney, *Le déclin de la responsabilité civile* (1965) and for some comparative observations see Markesinis, 'La perversion des notions de responsabilité civile délictuelle par la pratique de l'assurance' [1983] *Rev. int. dr. comp.* 301 ff.

4. THE DUTIES OF CARE

(a) Generally

It has already been noted how the duty concept has been introduced into the notion of unlawfulness. *Acts*, according to this view, which indirectly infringe one of the protected interests, are not automatically unlawful unless it can be shown that the defendant has failed to satisfy the standard of care demanded by society. This duty-oriented approach becomes even more obviously necessary in the case of liability for omissions. From Roman times to today, it has been well known that liability for an omission could be imposed if a previous duty to act could be discovered. In early times, statute and contract were the main progenitors for duties of affirmative action. Later, the area of liability for omissions was widened, even though technical administrative difficulties, as well as ideological objections (especially in the Common law), strongly militated against such an extension. In German law, one of the most fertile sources of the development of liability for omissions and, indeed, of the whole law of tort, was the development of the idea that a preceding dangerous (or potentially dangerous) activity or state of affairs should give rise to a duty of care. From this idea, the courts slowly but steadily developed the famous *Verkehrssicherungspflichten*. The term *Verkehrssicherungspflicht* is not easy to translate. But its meaning could be summarized by saying that whoever by his activity or through his property establishes in everyday life a source of potential danger which is likely to affect the interests and rights of others, is obliged to ensure their protection against the risks thus created by him.

It has been a matter of some dispute *where* these duties of care should be considered. Should they be examined under the heading of conduct or unlawfulness or even remoteness? For present purposes it is not necessary to enter into these disputes, not least because once again the final *practical* result is not so very different. However, the purpose of these duties of care must be made clear. They are there to delineate the range of relationships which will be protected by careless interference; they are also there to limit (more effectively than the theory of adequate cause can do) the range of persons who could be held liable for a particular harmful result. To put it differently, does the relationship between the parties put one of them under a duty to take care *vis-à-vis* the other? Whether this is so, as well as the precise content of the duty, is a matter of judicial policy which will be largely determined *inter alia* by the kind of factors we have already considered in the previous section, namely gravity of harm, probability of occurrence, cost of prevention and so on. As one would expect, the case-law is extremely rich. And once one excludes theoretical disputes, the factual situations considered and the solutions given to the problems they raise are very similar in American, English, and German law.

The way the rich case-law can be classified may vary. Situations giving rise to risks (and hence, duties) can be and are often classed alphabetically. Alternatively, the duties may be said to derive from family or business relationships, or where no relationship (in the usual sense of the word) exists, this last heading, for example, including a discussion of the problem of products liability. In this section one important group of cases dealing with safety on highways and premises will be examined, and the next section will discuss certain problems related to the law of product liability.

*(b) Traffic safety on highways and places open to the public including danger-
ous premises*

Historically, this is the area where the duties of care made their first appearance and they cover a large number of different factual situations which
have exact equivalents in both English and American law. Thus, plaintiffs
injured on public highways (or, indeed, smaller roads of all types), business
premises, factories, shops, or homes may have a right of action against
those who opened these facilities to the public or are in some way responsible for their upkeep. The following are illustrations from the recent case
law; and they are noticeable for the fact that they have also figured in
Common law litigation. Thus, the President of a sports club who instructed
a 14-year-old boy to mow the playing field with a self-propelled mower
which, according to safety regulations should not be operated by anyone
under 16 years of age, owes a duty of care to children injured nearby. (BGH
NJW RR 1991, 668); the proprietor of a restaurant should foresee that some
of his customers may have difficulty with walking and should thus take
appropriate measures to protect them against the dangers of a very slippery
floor (BGH NJW 1991, 921); organizers of a mass spectacle are under a
duty to ensure that the public is given safe ways to enter and exit the area
where the event is being organized (BGH NJW 1990, 905). Examples such
as these abound in the books; and, of course, it need not be repeated in
detail here that all these are cases of fault-based liabilities.

Such duties are owed towards all people and, therefore, are classified
under the law of delict. But additional contractual liability is not excluded.
As English Common lawyers say when discussing their Occupiers Liability
Act 1957, occupation of premises is a ground of liability not a reason for
excluding other rules of liability. This can be the case, for example, where a
customer is injured in a shop after he has concluded his purchases.
Contractual and tortious duties may, in this case, coexist; but they do not
overlap in the sense that each is subject to its own rules about limitation,
measure of damages, proof, and responsibility for the unlawful conduct of
other persons. Indeed, the tort remedies may be distinctly inferior in these
respects compared with the contractual remedies and that is why, as we
shall see below (Ch. 3, section A.2), the German courts have expanded the
contractual remedies to the time *before* the contract is concluded (in our
case before the customer has agreed to buy the goods); and even to third
parties accompanying the potential purchaser (see below, case 90).

The duty to take reasonable care to protect the entrants of premises (and
their property) is primarily imposed on the owner of the premises but it may
also be imposed upon a hirer or lessee, depending on their degree of control.
The problems here and the solutions they receive by German courts are,

essentially, no different from the ones encountered in Anglo-American law. Thus, for example, a contractual agreement between a landlord and his tenant, that only the latter will be responsible for the maintenance and safety of the premises and be liable to third parties, will have no effect *vis-à-vis* the injured third party, but it may well be valid with regard to the *internal relationship* between owner–lessee (see RGZ 95, 61). Similarly, where the owner has delegated the performance of his duties to a third party, the better view seems to be that he remains answerable for their bad performance and not only responsible for his own fault in selecting and supervising the third party. In English terminology, the duty is a non-delegable duty, and clearly, the desire to afford increased protection to the victim lies behind these rules. Where express statutory law permits such delegation and grants immunity to the delegating person for the bad performance, only then will such an exception be granted. This is often the case with local communities who, for example, are allowed to subcontract to private companies their duty to clear snow from roads and spread salt in order to make them safer. In such cases their responsibility will, normally, be limited to careful selection and supervision.

So far the discussion has been limited to the owner's general liability towards persons injured while on his premises. In principle, German law has not made the sharp distinction that the Common law made between lawful visitors and trespassers, and even less has it opted for the irrational distinctions adopted by the old Common law between different types of lawful visitors. These duties are owed towards all persons, the underlying idea being that the 'occupier' of the land is, usually, in a better position to know the risk and prevent it from materializing, and also to insure against its occurrence. Thus, the 'occupier's' liability towards a trespassing child will, invariably, be upheld, a result which is increasingly accepted as fair in the Common law jurisdictions as well. But liability towards the more obnoxious type of intruders (such as burglars) can and will be limited in various ways. Thus the court may not protect such persons either on the ground that their presence was not foreseeable (causative grounds); or because they may be found guilty of contributory fault (contributory negligence or *volenti* in the Common law); or, finally, because the requisite standard of care has been satisfied by the defendant/occupier (cf. the humanitarian duty in *British Railways Board* v. *Herrington* ([1972] AC 877). Equally, 'no trespass' signs, if clearly phrased, may afford some (or full) protection to the occupier, though other factors (including statutes prohibiting such clauses) may also have to be taken into account. (Note, also, the parents' obligation to look after their children.) The extensive case-law is reviewed by Marburger in *Jura* 1971, 481 and Stoll, *Das Handeln auf eigene Gefahr, eine rechtsvergleichende Untersuchung* (1961) and, on the whole, its comparison with the Common law is both easy and fruitful.

The liability of an occupier of premises may be engaged otherwise than by means of one of the duties of care. §§ 836–8 BGB are, in this respect, particularly noteworthy for two reasons. First, because they can be regarded as particular statutory expressions of the general principle discussed in this section, namely that anyone who exercises a sufficient degree of control over a particular thing (moveable or immoveable) which is likely to cause danger is under a duty to take reasonable care to ensure that this danger does not materialize. Secondly, and more importantly, because they contain rules of presumed fault. In such circumstances it is, therefore, for the defendant to exculpate himself and not—as is normal—for the plaintiff to prove the former's fault.

The overlap between these two sets of rules (§§ 836–8 BGB and the duties of care) is not complete. § 836 BGB—more or less like the analogous rules contained in Art. 1386 of the French Civil Code—deals with collapsing buildings or other structures attached to land. Collapsing walls or scaffolding, falling tiles, window-panes that become detached from their frames, are all included under this heading. But snow falling off roof-tops, tree branches being broken off, or even a falling gravestone which injures a passer-by would be covered not by the aforementioned paragraph of the Code, but by the duties of care. As stated, the precise content of those duties would vary from case to case. The measures necessary to prevent a 'roof avalanche' would depend on a variety of local factors, such as frequency and volume of the snowfalls, the slope of the roof, the frequency of such accidents, and so on (cf. BGH NJW 1955, 300; OLG München, MDR 1965, 905). Damage from collapsing trees or branches might entail liability if proper checks on the state of the health of the trees were not carried out at the correct intervals (BGH NJW 1965, 815); and irregularly maintained gravestones could render liable not only the owners of the burial plots so long as they have control over them (BGH NJW 1971, 2308), but also the cemetery authorities who open this area to the general public (BGHZ 34, 206). Other instances from the very rich case-law, which can in every way be matched by Anglo-American cases, include the following: a self-service store liable to a customer (or potential customer) who slips on a vegetable leaf or other slippery substance (BGH NJW 1976, 712; cf. *Ward* v. *Tesco* [1976] 1 WLR 810); organizers of a motor-car race who fail to take the necessary precautions in order to prevent spectators being injured (BGH NJW 1975, 533; cf. *White* v. *Blackmore* [1972] 2 QB 651); a house-owner held liable to his visitor who is injured by defective banisters (BGHZ 5, 378; cf. *Wheat* v. *Lacon* [1966] 1 QB 355); landowners liable to a plaintiff whose car was damaged by a train passing through an unfenced crossing on the defendant's land (BGHZ 11, 175; cf. *Commissioner for Rly.* v. *McDermott* [1967] 1 AC 169).

With regard to accidents happening on highways or Federal roads, the actions will be directed against the authorities entrusted with their upkeep and maintenance. In the case of Federal roads, this body is one of the States (article 90 of the Constitution). Local towns or districts are responsible for the smaller roads.

Less clear are the legal grounds of liability. Theoretically, this can be justified either by reference to § 823 I or § 839 BGB. The latter, in conjunction with article 34 of the Constitution, makes the State (or other public authority) liable for breaches of official duties. From the State's point of view, this second method is preferable since § 839 I 2 BGB provides that in cases of negligence the official (and the State) will only be liable if the injured party is unable to obtain compensation from elsewhere. But liability under § 839 is not avoided if the victim is entitled to any insurance funds, and this irrespective of whether their source is a private or a public insurance. (See *Münchener Kommentar*, § 839 BGB, § 264; BGHZ 79, 26; BGH NJW 1983, 2181.) In this respect, matters are simplified whenever statute expressly designates such duties imposed on the state as *public law* duties, for in such cases the State is liable under Art. 34 of the Constitution in conjunction with § 839 BGB. By contrast, the situation can become more obscure whenever the nature of the duties has not been expressly designated. (For further details see *Münchener Kommentar* § 839 BGB, para. 156. See, also, BGHZ 68, 217.)

Further reading

For further literature on the 'duties of care' see von Bar, *Verkehrspflichten* (1980) (the leading modern monograph); Canaris, 'Schutzgesetze–Verkehrspflichten–Schutzpflichten' in *Festschrift Larenz zum 80 Geburtstag* (1983) 27; Deutsch, 'Die neuere Entwicklung der Rechtsprechung zum Haftungsrecht', *JZ* 1984, 308, 309–11; Esser, *Grundlagen und Entwicklung der Gefährdungshaftung* (1969); Marburger, 'Die Verkehrssicherungspflicht gegenüber Unbefugten' *Jura* 1971, 481; Mertens, 'Verkehrspflichten und Deliktsrecht' *VersR* 1980, 397; Steffen, 'Verkehrspflichten im Spannungsfeld von Bestandsschutz und Handlungsfreiheit' *VersR* 1980, 409; Stoll, *Das Handeln auf eigene Gefahr, eine rechtsvergleichende Untersuchung* (1961); Westen, 'Zur Frage einer Garantie- und Risikohaftung für sog. "Verkehrspflichtverletzungen"' in *Festschrift von Hippel* (1967) 591.

(*c*) *Problems related to the liability of manufacturers of defective goods*

Select bibliography

Despite its youthful age, this subject has generated an enormous legal literature. The following is a selection.

different from the previous one, will be dominated by the adjustments made by the Product Liability Act of 1989 giving effect to the European Community's Directive of 25 July 1985. (Both documents are reproduced in section B. 15 below, along with the English equivalent enactment.)

The leading judgment of 1968 clearly reflects the preoccupations of academics to find a legal basis for products liability in so far as it devotes much space to the detailed consideration of the various contractual or quasi-contractual theories developed in the 1960s to meet the new situation. If a Common lawyer were to express surprise that this search for a juristic basis would be conducted in the area of contract law rather than tort law he should then consider the following two points.

First, one must repeat what was said earlier on, namely that the law of contracts has proved more pliable and able to expand on the civil law systems than it has in the Common law. The doctrine of consideration is the main reason why the Common law was forced to develop its law of torts. But wherever consideration has been taken somewhat less seriously—e.g. in the United States—the concurrent growth of contractual and delictual remedies has been a notable feature. The UCC doctrine of 'warranty without privity' is one of these developments and, incidentally, brings American law quite close to French law which has developed its strict law of products liability through the law of sales but has also accepted strict or semi-strict tortious liability.

Further reading

For details on this see J. Ghestin, *Conformité et garanties dans la vente* (*produits mobiliers*) (1983); *La responsabilité des fabricants et distributeurs* (1975) (collection of essays, ed. by Professor Gavalda); *La responsabilité civile du fabricant dans les états membres du Marché Commun* (1974) with interesting essays by Professors Bigot (213), Ghestin (17), and Malinvaud (131).

Secondly, one should note the considerable advantages that a plaintiff could obtain if his action was dubbed by German law contractual or quasi-contractual. Two of them should be mentioned here. The first is related to the burden of proof. Though in the civil law systems (unlike the Common law) fault is an element of an action for breach of contract as well as tort, the burden of proof may be different in these two actions. Thus, § 282 BGB provides that, 'If it is disputed whether the impossibility of performance is the result of a circumstance for which the debtor is responsible, the burden of proof falls on the debtor', i.e. if contested, the defendant has to disprove his fault. On the other hand, according to the general rules of tort law, in a product liability case the plaintiff had to show that the product left the defendant's enterprise in a faulty condition and that the defendant, or his legally appointed representative, had not organized his business in such a way as to enable the defect to be detected. The second, and not entirely unrelated, reason that made contractual actions preferable to those founded in tort could be found in § 831 BGB. This deals with the problems of vicarious liability and will be discussed in greater detail below (Ch. 3, section A. 1 and 2). Here suffice it to say that it does not establish a true rule of vicarious liability but makes employers liable for the unlawful acts of their employees only where they are themselves guilty of negligent selection or supervision of the employees. In contrast debtors are, according to § 278 BGB, fully liable for the faults of the persons whom they employ in the execution of their *contractual* obligations. Finally, one should also bear in mind the relatively short period of prescription applicable to tort claims (§ 852 I BGB) (though, admittedly, in some instances the period of limitation may be shorter in contract than it is in tort and this has caused a flight into tort. Thus, see the cases discussed in section 16, below).

Having stated the reasons which prompted German lawyers to turn to the law of contract rather than the law of tort, one should look briefly at the various contractual or quasi-contractual methods advanced by academic writers. The brief comments that follow should be read in conjunction with the relevant passages of the leading case (No. 43) which is reproduced below (Ch. 2, section B. 14).

One way of making the manufacturer liable to the ultimate consumer is by discovering an express or implied guarantee which is directed to the ultimate consumer and on which he relies to his detriment. The difficulties with this approach are the same that eventually forced American lawyers to abandon a similar kind of reasoning—widely prevalent in the United States during the 1950s—but which proved to be inadequate in practice.

A second contractual method can be found in the various attempts to discover a contract in favour of a third party or a contract with protective effects *vis-à-vis* third parties. The first type of contract (*Vertrag zugunsten Dritter*) is regulated by §§ 328 ff. BGB and is not unknown to American lawyers who, since *Lawrence* v. *Fox*, 20 NY 268 (1859), have broken away from the English tradition on this matter. As already explained, this type of contract allows a third party (the ultimate consumer) to require performance of the contract concluded between the creditor and the debtor (for example, the manufacturer and the wholesaler). On reflection, however, this is a rather awkward notion because what the third party (the consumer) needs is not the right to enforce the *prime* contractual obligation (delivery of the thing in exchange for payment of the price) but to demand that he be included under the protective umbrella of the *subsidiary* contractual obligations (in our case to deliver the thing in good order and with clear instruction, etc.). This way of reasoning led German courts to develop, under the influence of Professor Larenz, a variant to the contract in favour of third parties which can be called a contract with protective effects *vis-à-vis* third parties (*Vertrag mit Schutzwirkung für Dritte*). In this way, third parties can be given the protection afforded to the main creditor which emanates from a cluster of subsidiary obligations which would be included in every such contract in accordance with § 242 BGB (contracts to be performed according to good faith).

However, we have already noted the need to keep this expansion of the contractual umbrella under control lest it undermine completely the relativity of the contractual bond. To put it differently, *who* will be treated as a third party and receive such protection? Though as already stated the requirement of 'proximity to the performance' (*Leistungsnähe*), a close relationship (*personenrechtliches Fürsorgeverhältnis*) between the contractual creditor and the third party has been relaxed by some recent decisions, this has not occurred in the context of products liability. Indeed, it is noteworthy that even those authors who have argued in favour of expanding the circle of 'protected' third parties have refused to apply their theories to this area of the law. (See, for example, Canaris, 'Die Produzentenhaftpflicht in dogmatischer und rechtspolitischer Sicht' *JZ* 1968, 494, 499 ff.)

The theory of 'transferred loss' (or, to give its German name, *Drittschadensliquidation*) has also been considered but rejected. In the chicken pest case the Supreme Court, disagreeing with the Court of Appeal, would not allow the veterinarian to demand from the pharmaceutical company (which had sold him the defective vaccine) the loss *suffered by the owner* of the chickens which died as a result of the inoculation. (If such a claim had been recognized it could have been transferred by the veterinarian to the plaintiff and pursued by the latter.)

Further reading

For further details concerning this concept see von Caemmerer in *Gesammelte Schriften* I, 597 ff.; Lorenz, 'Die Einbeziehung Dritter in vertragliche Schuldverhältnisse', *JZ* 1960, 108 ff.; Selb, 'Kritik formaler Drittschadensthese' *NJW* 1964, 1765. More precisely, on the *Vertrag mit Schutzwirkung zugunsten Dritter* see: Esser/Schmidt, op. cit., § 34. IV. 2; Münchener Kommentar—Gottwald, § 328 nos. 60 ff.; Larenz I, op. cit., § 17. II; Schwerdtner, 'Verträge mit Schutzwirkung für Dritte', *Jura* 1980, 493; Strauch, 'Verträge mit Drittschutzwirkung' *JuS* 1982, 823; on the concept of *Drittschadensliquidation* see: Esser/Schmidt, op. cit., § 34. IV. 1; Hagen, *Drittschadensliquidation im Wandel der Rechtsdogmatik* (1971); Peters, 'Zum Problem der Drittschadensliquidation' *AcP* 180 (1980) 329. A short account in English can be found in Markesinis, 'An Expanding Tort Law the Price of a Rigid Contract Law' 103 (1987) *LQR* 354.

In addition to the above contractual theories, the court also dealt with a number of others which share some common elements including the desire to justify a strict or semi-strict type of liability. Two of them deserve a brief look since they are expressly referred to (and rejected) by the court.

The first, advanced by a leading expert in the field (Diederichsen, *Die Haftung des Warenherstellers* (1967) 297 ff., 327 ff., 345 ff.) can, in a rather crass manner but for simplicity's sake, be reduced to two basic propositions: first, that the basic relationship that has to be considered in these cases is that between manufacturer and ultimate consumer, which is one of 'reliance' irrespective of any awareness of any advertisements by the manufacturer so long as the defective goods were purchased from a sales network set up by the manufacturer and were already defective at the time they left his factory; second, that this relation is *sui generis*, not regulated by the written law and has to be shaped in its details by the judge. A corollary to this is that the liability is strict.

The court's dislike of any theory which cannot be pegged on a clear provision of the Code is obvious from the way this theory is dismissed. Equally obvious—and in tune with the court's long-established practice—is its refusal to discover new headings of strict liability in the absence of legislative intervention (see below, ch. 3, section A. 5). A third objection, not mentioned by the court but stressed by academics, is the following. If the manufacturer of goods is to be strictly liable, why should this liability be limited to cases where his goods were sold bearing his name (or through a sales network set up by him) and excluded whenever the same goods were sold unidentified in a department store or, even, bearing the latter's commercial brand?

Lorenz's theory ('Warenabsatz und Vertrauensschutz' *Karlsruher Forum* (1963) 8, especially 14 ff.) shares a number of common points with some other theories also considered and rejected by the court (see the work of Canaris in the Select Bibliography, above p. 80). He, too, for example, puts the emphasis on the relationship between producer and ultimate consumer and he, also, is prepared to attach considerable significance to the reliance that one person (the consumer) places on the conduct of another (the manufacturer). Like other writers, Lorenz also accepts that we are here faced with a *lacuna* in the written law which must be filled in a way that will ensure that the plaintiff is given a protection equal to (if not greater than) that enjoyed by contracting parties (moving towards strict liability). Unlike other authors, however, Lorenz makes a clear attempt to base his solution on a specific provision of the Code and this, in his opinion, is § 122 BGB. This provides that if a declaration of an intention is void, either because it was made in error or because it was not seriously intended, the person who made the declaration must compensate the other party for the damages he has sustained as a result of relying upon the validity of the declaration; (incidentally, the damages in this case cover only the reliance interest and not the progress. To make them strictly liable for such development risks would also run counter to the rationale of imposing such a strict liability in the first place, for it will be remembered, one of the justifications of imposing strict liability on the manufacturer is his ability to detect and avoid the defect. In the present instance, however, by definition this is not possible and the manufacturer's duties are limited to an obligation to warn consumers or even withdraw their products once they become aware (or ought to become aware) of the defect or of their potential harmful consequences. The rules of the leading case have thus not been extended to this category. Article 15(8) of the European Directive gives Member States the option of deleting the defence of state of art contained in Art. 7(e) but the Federal Republic has not exercised this right so the defence has been retained. (Note, however, that the defence is not available under the Pharmaceutical Act; and the relationship between this enactment and the 1988 Bill has not been clarified.) The retention of the state of art defence will not, however, absolve the manufacturer from continuously observing his products and warning users of (and if necessary recalling) products that are subsequently revealed as defective. (BGH NJW 1987, 1009 = WM 1987, 126, is an interesting case since it extends the manufacturer's post-marketing duties concerning his own product to the performance of component parts.)

The Act on Pharmaceutical Products of 1976, in force since 1 January 1978, is the leading exception in this respect. This enactment imposes strict liability on pharmaceutical concerns which introduce into the market drugs for human use or consumption which produce harmful results that go beyond those which current medical opinion regards as acceptable. The risk-based liability is incurred irrespective of whether the damage is the result of bad development, production, or labelling. But like all German laws of strict liability, the Pharmaceutical Products Act lays down certain maxima for monetary compensation (lump sums of up to DM 500,000 or annuities of up to DM 30,000 where one person is killed or injured or, in cases of defects in mass production killing or injuring more than one person, 200 million or 12 million DM respectively per incident), payment of these sums being ensured by obliging the pharmaceutical concerns to create special 'cover funds' (*Deckungsvorsorge*) which, in practice, means taking out liability insurance. Victims who wish to attempt to recover further compensation are, of course, free to make use of the normal fault-based provisions of the Code.

Further reading

For further discussion of the new Act see Deutsch, 'Das Arzneimittelrecht im Haftungssystem' *VersR* 1979, 685; idem, 'Arzneimittelschaden: Gefährdungshaftung, Verschuldenshaftung, Staatshaftung' in *Festschrift Larenz* (1983) 111 (with further references); idem, *Arztrecht und Arzneimittelrecht. Eine zusammenfassende Darstellung mit Fallbeispielen und Texten* (2nd edn. 1991); Kullmann, 'Die Haftungsregelung des § 84 AMG' *PharmaR* 81, 112; Wolter, 'Die Haftungsregelung des neuen AMG' *DB* 1976, 2001. For a comparative discussion in English see: Fleming, 'Drug Injury Compensation Plans', 30 *A. J. Comp. Law* 297 (1982).

(*vi*) *The Product Liability Act 1989.* (For the text of the Act and a brief discussion of its provisions see pages 542–5 below).

5. CAUSATION

French lawyers, paraphrasing Voltaire's dictum about the existence of God, have often teased the Germans by saying that if causation did not exist as a subject it would have to be invented so that German lawyers would have something to exercise their minds. There is a great deal of truth in this state-ment though it could also convey a misleading picture in at least two respects. For, if one is thinking in terms of the volume of the legal literature, the Germans are not alone in having devoted a great deal of effort to this topic. The Americans, for instance, have rivalled this literature in size and, probably, in ingenuity. Secondly, the theoretical preoccupation of German scholars with this subject has not prevented their courts from stating more than once that the solution should, in the end, be one dictated by common sense and equity (see, for example, BGHZ 3, 261, 267; BGHZ 30, 154, 157, etc.).

(*a*) *Conditions and causes*

The Germans (like the Americans and the English but more clearly so than the French) adopt a bifurcated approach to problems of causation by insist-ing that the defendant's conduct (or the event for which he is to be held responsible) cannot claim to be a legal 'cause' of the plaintiff's hurt, unless it is previously established that it is at least a 'condition' (*Bedingung*) of that harm. This leads to a two-phased inquiry, the first being preoccupied with the question whether the defendant's conduct played some role in bringing about the plaintiff's hurt, while the second seeks to discover which of the many conditions of the harm will also be treated as its legal cause. This first phase of the inquiry is strongly causative rather than normative in nature and hence American scholars often refer to it with some justification as the cause-in-fact stage of the inquiry. This labelling of this phase as factual or causative is correct, especially if it is compared with the second phase of the inquiry which is more normative and policy-orientated. This does not mean, however, that it cannot involve issues of valuation and therefore acquire strong normative overtones as well. This becomes clear in those cases where the 'standard' test (to be discussed in the next paragraph) cannot be operated without serious injustice.

The test used to determine whether a particular piece of conduct is a condition of the plaintiff's hurt is that of the *conditio sine qua non*, better known to Common lawyers as the 'but-for' test (also referred to as the *Äquivalenztheorie*). Would the plaintiff's harm have occurred but for the defendant's conduct? If it would, then the defendant's conduct is not a cause of the harm. A doctor who negligently examines (or treats) a patient who dies from another ailment will not be causally linked with (and hence will not be responsible for) that death. Equally, a chemist who negligently renews a prescription without previously consulting the patient's doctor will not be liable once it is shown that the doctor, had he been asked, would certainly have continued the treatment with the same drug (RGSt 15 (1886) 151; RGSt 63 (1929) 211). The point need not be laboured, since it raises no issues which are not already known to a Common law audience. Where the German thoroughness emerges quite clearly is in the effort to determine how the defendant's conduct (or the event complained of) will be deemed to be or not to be a *conditio sine qua non* of the plaintiff's harm. One of the first to attempt an answer to this problem was the Austrian criminal lawyer Glaser who in 1858 (*Abhandlungen aus dem österreichischen Strafrechte* I, 298; translated by Hart and Honoré *Causation in the Law* 2nd edn. (1985), 443) wrote:

If one attempts wholly to eliminate in thought the alleged author (of the act) from the sum of events in question and it then appears that nevertheless the sequence of intermediate causes remains the same, it is clear that the act and its consequences cannot be referred to him . . . but if it appears that, once the person in question is eliminated in thought from the scene, the consequences cannot come about, or that they can come about only in a completely different way, then one is fully justified in attributing the consequences to him and explaining it as the effect of his activity.

This has been termed the method of elimination (*Hinwegdenken*) since it assumes the notional elimination of the propositus from the scene, the other conditions remaining exactly the same. It should be contrasted with a different method—that of substitution—which, far from eliminating the propositus from the scene, assumes, on the contrary, that he was there and acted lawfully, the other conditions remaining the same except in so far as they would have been altered by the lawful conduct of the person in question.

The elimination theory seems more acceptable when the alleged cause is a positive act. What we have to do is to reconstruct the sequence of events, omitting the tortfeasor's conduct. If, despite this, the sequence of events remains unaltered, then the conduct has no causal relation to subsequent events. If, on the other hand, the final result is changed as a consequence of the theoretical suppression of the tortfeasor's act, then that act must have played an active and necessary part in producing the plaintiff's harm. Thus, if A shoots B and A's shot is eliminated, then B's death goes also. In the case of omissions, however, the situation is more complex, for if the 'procedure of elimination without substitution is adopted no omission can ever be treated as a *conditio sine qua non* of an event' (Hart and Honoré, *Causation in the Law* (1959) 403). What is necessary here is the substitution of the act that the defendant omitted. Would the harmful result nevertheless have occurred? If it would, then the defendant's omission is not the cause of the result. Let us look at an example often given by German textbooks to illustrate how the above works in practice.

Suppose that a passenger ship is not properly equipped with lifebuoys and one of its passengers falls into the sea. If the shipowner's wrongful omission is eliminated and the correct conduct is substituted, we must assume that adequate lifebuoys would have been provided. That, in itself, however, provides no solution to the question whether the drowning was connected with the absence of lifebuoys. A partial substitution of the wrongful conduct by lawful conduct is not enough. What we must further do, in addition to eliminating the wrongful omission, is to assume that the ship's crew could and would have used the lifebuoys promptly and that the passenger would have seized one in time. The answer to our question, there-fore, can be provided only if we substitute the right for the wrong conduct and then enquire what further changes would have taken place in that event. In the case of omissions, therefore, *total substitution* (as the above process is sometimes referred to) is, in principle, necessary in order to produce a rea-sonable result (BGHZ 12, 94). Only if all the conditions mentioned above are satisfied, can the drowning be attributed to the absence of lifebuoys.

The above represents little more than a crass abridgement of the difficulties and diverging views that one can find on this subject and, perhaps, one could say that the choice between the elimination and the substitution theories is, in the end, one of policy: the former can lead to more extensive liability (espe-cially in cases of hypothetical causes) and was, apparently, preferred by the Reichsgericht (RGZ 141, 365); the latter can reduce liability within narrow limits and has received the support of the Bundesgerichtshof (BGHZ 10, 6). (For a more detailed analysis consult Honoré, *International Encyclopedia of Comparative Law* XI, ch. 7, 74–6, 79 ff.)

In the examples given up to this point the *conditio sine qua non* rule has been able to produce acceptable results. But there are many instances where the test breaks down completely. This, for example, is the case whenever it can be shown that the event complained of could have been brought about in more than one way. Suppose, for example, that two motor-cyclists simul-

taneously pass the plaintiff's horse in a way that makes it bolt and it is subsequently proved that either of them alone could have caused the fright of the
horse. Or imagine two chemical factories releasing independently of each
other toxic liquids into a nearby river and thus affecting the riparian owner's
fishing-rights. Or, finally, suppose that a garage sells a car which has defective brakes to the plaintiff who, at the critical moment, makes no attempt to
apply them. Would the horse have bolted in our first example but for the conduct of the first motor-cyclist? The answer is yes, because of the way the other
motor-cyclist rode quickly past it. The same reasoning can be applied to our
other examples and it is clear that a strict application of the *conditio sine qua
non* test would hold that neither of the motor-cyclists in the first example, nor
the polluting factories in the second, nor the garage in the third, would be
held liable since each of these acts was a sufficient cause of the plaintiff's hurt.
But, however impeccable the logic of this approach may be, the solution is
patently unjust, and unless we hold liable each of the persons who has done
enough to bring about the harmful result, the victim will remain uncompensated. The word 'enough' supplies the clue for one possible solution, and that
is the adoption of the 'substantial factor' formula which was first applied by
the Minnesota court (*Anderson* v. *Minneapolis St. P and SSMR Co.* 146
Minn. 430, 179 NW 45, 1920) some seventy years ago and has more recently
been sanctioned by the American *Restatement Second, Torts* § 432.2.
According to this theory, the defendant's conduct is a cause of the plaintiff's
harm if it was a material element and a substantial factor in bringing it about.
There is nothing to stop a German judge from following a similar reasoning
and eliminating the insubstantial factors at this stage of the enquiry. On the
whole, however, one is left with the impression that this 'evaluation process'
will be attempted later and at this cause-in-fact stage of the process all activities will be retained as 'conditions' of the plaintiff's harm.

In the last three examples we have been faced with what have been termed
'multiple sufficient causes' in the sense that each is normally 'sufficient' to
produce the harmful result. In the first two examples they have both operated simultaneously and have been positive in nature; in the third example,
the second cause was negative in nature (i.e. failure to apply the brakes). But
the most fiercely debated of 'multiple sufficient causes' are the so-called
'overtaking causes' (see von Caemmerer, 'Das Problem der überholenden
Kausalität' in *Gesammelte Schriften* I, 411). Examples include the case of
the medical practitioner who blinds the patient who would, in any event,
have subsequently become blind; another is the case of a house which is
damaged by a negligently caused explosion of gas but which would, in any
event, have been destroyed by a subsequent bombing attack. In these cases
the second cause, i.e. blindness, bomb attack (commonly referred to as
the 'overtaking' cause but, in actual fact, the cause 'overtaken' by the

'operative' cause for which the tortfeasor is responsible) is sufficient by itself to produce the harmful result in question; in fact, however, it does not do so since the causal process initiated by the tortfeasor prevents, or has already prevented, this from happening. In such cases, can the propositus rely on the second sufficient cause and argue that he did not occasion the whole or part of the harm, or that if he did so, he ought for some other reason (causal or equitable) to be relieved from at least part of the liability? One can envisage a host of possible answers ranging between two extremes, namely, that of completely disregarding the overtaking cause (RGZ 169, 117, 120), and that according to which damages must always be assessed by taking into account events subsequent to the appearance of the cause of action but before trial (BGHZ 10, 6). All these are issues which are hotly debated in Germany and cannot be discussed in an introductory book of this kind. But we shall glance briefly, at the end of this section, at one of these overtaking causes, namely the victim's predispositions.

(b) Legal cause

The simplicity (or apparent simplicity) of the *conditio sine qua non* theory led some authors to consider extending its application to the domain of legal cause. Indeed, this is still the case in the area of criminal law since in that branch of the law the element of fault (invariably intention though there do exist criminal offences where negligence will suffice, e.g. §§ 222, 230 StGB) provides a good corrective device against the risk of extensive liability. But in the context of private law, where liability often does not depend on fault, this theory met with little success—German authors opting instead for one of the variants of the adequate causation theory. (German authors make a distinction between causation giving rise to liability (*haftungsbegründende Kausalität*) and what we would call remoteness of damage (*haftungsausfüllende Kausalität*); the discussions about 'adequacy' only arise under the second heading. See Deutsch, 141; Larenz I, § 27, III, 435; Esser/Schmidt I, § 33, II; Traeger, *Kausalbegriff*, 219. But the point need not be laboured further for the purposes of this book.)

This theory was first expounded by the German physiologist von Kries (*Die Prinzipien der Wahrscheinlichkeitsrechnung; Ueber den Begriff der objektiven Möglichkeit*) and its central idea was simple enough. The defendant's conduct (or specified event for which he is responsible), which must be a condition of the plaintiff's hurt, will further qualify as an adequate cause of that harm if it is such that it significantly increases the risk of the type of harm which actually occurs. Theoretically, this approach tends to achieve a compromise between the extension of liability which the theory of direct consequences (known to Common lawyers from the *Re Polemis* litigation) is *capable* of producing, and the greater restriction of liability which *could* result from the use of the foreseeability theory. For, it could be argued, the adequacy theory can set realistic limits of liability by relying on commonsense notions of causal connection. Put differently, a 'significantly increased probability' is a test less vague than the notion of foreseeability. So, at least, runs the traditional argument for it was eventually realized that the real problem behind these notions is, essentially, one of responsibility and not of causality. A value-judgment, foreign to the notion of causation, could and should in the end determine the difficult cases that reached the courts. This became obvious the moment one had to determine *how* the increased probability of the harm would have to be assessed. Academic writers were quick to offer their views. For von Kries—the originator of the theory—the valuation should be undertaken on the basis of all the circumstances which were known, or ought to have been known, to the originator of the condition at the time of its entry (*ex ante*) and also taking into account *general practical knowledge* (*ex post*) based on experience. Rümelin, on the other hand, advanced the theory of 'objective hindsight'. For him consideration should be given to the whole empirical knowledge of mankind and all the circumstances anywhere to hand at the time the condition occurred, whether they were recognizable by the most *superior* discernment *or* had first become recognizable *ex post* from events following the condition in question.

Von Kries's 'individual foresight' approach proved too narrow for private law cases of objective (no fault) liability and contractual liability; Rümelin's 'objective hindsight' theory was, on the other hand, too wide to exclude with certainty the inequitable results of the condition theory. *The Wagon Mound* I ([1961] AC 388) litigation, for example, would have been decided differently if the objective hindsight test was applied, since it will be remembered, that by the time of the second *Wagon Mound* ([1967] AC 617) trial, scientific opinion had changed with regard to the crucial factor which had led to the fire damage in that case (i.e. possibility of oil igniting in water). So a compromise solution was proposed by yet another author—Traeger (*Kausalbegriff im Zivil- und Strafrecht* (1904), para. 159)—and this came to be adopted by the courts. According to this view, an event is an adequate condition of a consequence if it has in a general and appreciable way enhanced the objective possibility of a consequence of the kind coming about. In deciding this, account is to be taken of (i) all the circumstances recognizable by an 'optimal' observer *at the time the event occurred* and, (ii) the additional circumstances known to the originator of the condition. The factual situation so established must be examined in the light of the whole human experience available at the time the decision is made, to see whether it appreciably favoured the occurrence of the damage-producing event.

A number of cases are reproduced below (see case 60) which show that the case-law is not clear and the problems of applying these tests in practice are not solved. In particular, how much knowledge should be credited to the 'optimal' observer? Professor Larenz takes the example of a plaintiff who is slightly injured by the defendant but who dies as a result of a heart condition from which he is already suffering and continues:

Is the observer to be credited with knowledge of the heart condition if it was then unknown but could have been discovered by a competent physician? Or need the observer know only that the possibility of such a condition was not completely remote? In that event, the fatal outcome was not wholly unlikely and should have been taken into consideration as well. Or should the observer be taken to know that a pillar struck by a truck had been so weakened that ordinary strains would cause it and the entry of the building to collapse, when this knowledge would have been possessed by an expert in building construction but not by an ordinary worker? The more one credits the observer with knowledge of circumstances which produced the event in question but which could be known only with difficulty, the more one expands the area in which consequences are to be adjudged 'adequate'. For the 'optimal' observer described by the Bundesgerichtshof, almost nothing is secret; he is practically omniscient. For the omniscient, the actual course of events is always foreseeable, however abnormal it may have been. If one takes the Bundesgerichtshof's standard of the optimal observer seriously, then the criterion of adequacy loses most of its ability to limit the area of responsibility of the person liable (*Lehrbuch des Schuldrechts* (11th edn., 1976) 354 ff. trans. by von Mehren, in von Mehren and Gordley, *The Civil Law System* (2nd edn., 1977) 586; in the 14th edn. the text can be found on pp. 436–7).

In view of the above, it is not surprising that more recent court decisions have shown a marked inclination to state that the problem they have to solve is not 'exactly one of causality but rather the discovery of a corrective device which can limit the purely logical consequences in the interests of equity' (see BGHZ 30, 154, 157 and also BGHZ 3, 261, 267). Seen in this light, the adequacy theory has proved an inefficient controlling device, von Caemmerer arguing that an exhaustive examination of the case-law of the Reichsgericht shows that only in a handful of cases the court was able (or willing) to deny the existence of a causal link on the basis of this theory (*Das Problem des Kausalzusammenhangs*, in *Gesammelte Schriften* I, 395, 403 ff.). An effort to combine the adequate cause theory with a more normative theory of causation was thus inevitable; the development of the 'scope of the rule' theory was its result.

This theory, first elaborated by Rabel (*Das Recht des Warenkaufs* (1936) 495 ff.) in relation to breaches of *contractual* duties, and more recently, also adopted by tort lawyers, postulates that there should be no recovery if the harm in suit is not within the scope of the rule violated. This may be because the harm is not within the protective purpose of the rule in question (*Schutzzweck der Norm*) (i.e. it is not the mischief the statute was designed to prevent) or, according to a variant, because it has not come about in an unlawful manner (*Rechtswidrigkeitszusammenhang*). Two leading German cases applying this theory are reproduced below (cases 64 and 65); and for a more recent illustration see BGH NJW 1985, 791; BGH NJW 1991, 3275. Here one could add two English examples which can illustrate the above propositions. In *Gorris* v. *Scott* ((1874) LR 9 Ex. 125) a statute provided that sheep carried as deck cargo should be enclosed in proper pens. They were not, and during rough weather they were washed overboard. The plaintiff's claim for damages was dismissed on the ground that the purpose of the requirement of the fencing was to prevent the spreading of contagious disease among the animals and not to safeguard them against the perils of the sea. In other words, the mischief that occurred was not the one the statute wanted to prevent. Two more cases (reproduced below, cases 54 and 55), dealing with the duties of local authorities to inspect the foundations of buildings, also provide an illustration of how this normative theory of causation can be used to exclude compensation.

In other instances the plaintiff may not belong to the class of people the statute intended to protect or, alternatively, the statute may have meant to protect only the general interest and not individual interests. This point is illustrated in the cable case reproduced below (case 9). Finally, the harm may have been inflicted in a manner not envisaged by the statute. In *Close* v. *Steel Co. of Wales Ltd.* ([1962] AC 367), for example, the House of Lords was concerned with the proper construction of a section of the English Factories Act which provided for the 'fencing in' of dangerous machinery. The plaintiff was injured by material which 'flew out' of the machinery and the House of Lords took the view that he could not avail himself of this provision since it was designed to protect workmen from coming into contact with moving parts of the machinery and not to protect them from injury inflicted through fragments flying out of the machine itself. Examples such as these abound in German textbooks. (For more details see Larenz, *Schuldrecht* I, 508 ff.)

It would be futile to add that the new theory has not solved all problems or that it has led to the formulation of a number of variations. But one of its limitations must be stressed. Though the new theory can work well whenever it is easy to assign a particular purpose to a particular rule, it breaks down almost completely when it is difficult or impossible to define with precision the scope of the rule in question. Thus, it works rather well in cases of tortious liability resulting from breach of statutes or subsidiary regulations, and also in the case of some 'nominate torts'. But it becomes almost unworkable in the cases of widely conceived tortious conduct (e.g. liability *contra bonos mores* under § 826 BGB or even § 823 I BGB, on which see Professor Kötz's comments in his *Deliktsrecht*, 74–83). Of course, it can be and has been argued that even in these cases the purpose of the rule that is violated can be discovered since 'all rules of conduct, irrespective of whether they are the product of a legislative act or are a part of the fabric of the court-made law of negligence, exist for a purpose. They are designed to protect *some* persons under *some* circumstances against *some* risks' (Malone, 9 *Stan. L. Rev.* 50, 73 (1956–7)). Yet, as stated, where wrongful conduct is only vaguely defined or definable, it is well-nigh impossible to ascribe a specific purpose to the rule in question, and to invite a judge to do so is to invite him to fix the limits of recovery for himself. This may be desirable whenever reasons of expediency or of policy militate for or against the imposition of liability. In these cases, the 'scope of the rule' theory has the clear advantage of making the judge aware of his quasi-legislative functions in deciding the kind of damage which shall be compensated. But this solution is more doubtful when the harm in suit is one which is clearly recognized but the manner of its infliction is dubious or unusual. Here recourse to the probability or explanatory theories may supply better guidance.

(c) Some special problem areas

It has been noted that causation theories do not really solve all problems. In particular, there are some factual situations which have given rise to considerable difficulties and, incidentally, shown that these theories offer only a conceptual framework within which the judges express their value-judgments. Three of these factual situations will be briefly examined in the remaining part of this chapter. The first deals with the fault of the injured party, the second with rescue cases, and the last with the predispositions of the victim/plaintiff.

(i) Fault of the injured party

It will be noticed that we are using here the continental term 'fault of the injured party' rather than the approximately equivalent Common law term 'contributory negligence'. This is because in the modern civil law fault of the injured party is wider than contributory negligence in so far as it includes intentional activities on behalf of the victim. More importantly, fault of the injured party is often taken to include not only his fault in the production of his hurt but also his failure to minimize its consequences *after* the harmful result has occurred. The German Civil Code makes this distinction most clearly and regulates the fault of the injured party to mitigate his damage in § 254 II BGB. The distinction, however, is more the result of the wish to establish conceptual clarity rather than the desire to dictate a different treatment. Thus in both cases the tortfeasor's responsibility will be taken into account to reduce his damages. It will be noticed that the legislator leaves considerable freedom to the judge to determine how to work out the doctrine—that of the unforeseeable plaintiff. To put it differently, there is often a tendency to rephrase certain problems of legal or 'proximate' cause in terms of legal duty. Given that the same test (foreseeability) determines both the 'remote plaintiff' (illustrated by the leading cases of *Palsgraf* v. *Long Island Rly Co.* (248 NY 339, 162 NE 99, 1928) and *Hay* (*Bourhill*) v. *Young* ([1943] AC 92)) and the 'remote damage', one wonders whether anything is gained by this 'dichotomy' of what is essentially one subject: the subject of remoteness. This, however, is essentially a problem of classification or, as Dean Prosser once observed (*Law of Torts* (4th edn., 1971) 244), to opt for 'duty' rather than 'proximate cause' only restates the problem but does not solve it. The only conceivable advantage of opting for the 'duty' approach is that it can help—in Prosser's words again—'direct attention to the policy issues which determine the extent of the original obligation and of its continuance, rather than to the mechanical sequence of events which goes to make up causation in fact'.

Noting this difference is more important than trying to defend the Common or civil law approach. For, as has been stated in the preceding pages, many problems such as nervous shock and rescue cases will in one system be treated in the causation section of some books and in the duty section of others. The comparatist will have to learn to jump over these artificial hurdles of classification and, in so doing, reflect once again on how policy and not concepts or theories determine the ultimate result.

Further reading

On causation see Brehm, 'Zur Haftung bei alternativer Kausalität' *JZ* 1980, 586; Bydlinski, *Probleme der Schadensverursachung nach deutschem und österreichischem Recht* (1964); von Caemmerer, 'Das Problem des Kausalzusammenhanges im Privatrecht' (1956) reproduced in his *Gesammelte Schriften* I (1968) 395; idem, 'Das Problem der überholenden Kausalität im Schadensersatzrecht' (1962) reproduced in *Gesammelte Schriften* I (1968) 411; Deutsch, 'Die dem Geschädigten nachteilige Adäquanz' *NJW* 1981, 2731; Deutsch and von Bar, 'Schutzbereich und wesentliche Bedingung im Versicherungs- und Haftungsrecht' *MDR* 1979, 536; Frank-Löffler, 'Grundfragen der überholenden Kausalität' *JuS* 1985, 689; Huber, 'Normzwecktheorie und Adäquanztheorie' *JZ* 1969, 677; idem, 'Verschulden, Gefährdung und Adäquanz', *Festschrift Wahl* (1973) 301; von Kries, *Die Prinzipien der Wahrscheinlichkeitsrechnung* (1886); Lang, *Normzweck und Duty of Care* (1983); Larenz, 'Zum heutigen Stand der Lehre von der objektiven Zurechnung' *Festschrift Honig* (1970) 79; *Münchener Kommentar* (Grunsky) op. cit., 3. §249 no. 42; Stoll, *Kausalzusammenhang und Normzweck im Deliktsrecht* (1968); Sourlas, *Adäquanztheorie und Normzwecktheorie bei der Begründung der Haftung nach § 823 I BGB* (1974); Träger, *Der Kausalbegriff im Straf- und Zivilrecht* (1904); Weitnauer, 'Zur Lehre vom adäquaten Kausalzusammenhang' *Festschrift Oftinger* (1969) 321. For further references see Larenz, *Schuldrecht* I, 390. Finally, special reference must be made to the classic work of Hart and Honoré, *Causation in the Law* (2nd edn., 1985).

SECTION B. CASES

I. NERVOUS SHOCK

Case 1
BUNDESGERICHTSHOF (SIXTH CIVIL DIVISION) 11 MAY 1971*
BGHZ 56, 163 = NJW 1971, 1883 = VersR 1971, 905, 1140

On 6 March 1965, when he was sixty-four years old, the plaintiff's husband was fatally injured in a collision with the defendant's motor vehicle. The plaintiff was fifty years old at the time. In this suit she claims damages for the injury to her health which she suffered through the death of her husband.

The Landgericht allowed the claim in full, the Oberlandesgericht in part. The defendant appealed with permission, and his appeal was allowed. The judgments below were vacated, and the case remanded to the Court of Appeal.

Reasons

A . . .
2 (*a*) . . .

(*b*) The Court of Appeal was wrong to find that the plaintiff suffered any real injury to her health as a result of hearing of the accident (see BGH VersR 1966, 283, 285 ff.; OLG Freiburg, JZ 1953, 705, 709).

Apart from a few special instances not here in point, our law consciously rejects any claim for harm due to psychical pain unless it results from injury to the plaintiff's own body or health. This is a policy decision of the legislator. It does not, however, prevent our granting an independent claim to the exceptional person who is 'traumatized' by being involved in an accident, or hearing of one, and who in consequence suffers real damage to body or mind. Nor, if we leave aside the cases of 'purposive neuroses' and supervening causes, for which special rules have been developed, is it an objection to granting such a claim that the only reason the victim's reaction was so severe was that he had a pre-existing organic or psychical weakness which was triggered by the accident. The opposite view is taken by Stoll in his paper for the 45th German Juristentag 1964, 20, but we cannot agree with it, if only because such an unusual reaction normally lies outside the victim's control as well as the defendant's.

On the other hand it is a matter of common knowledge that the pain, grief, and fright arising from a very negative experience can have a very marked effect on one's physiological system and one's ability to cope. Yet to

---

* English version by Tony Weir.

treat such disturbances as invasions of health in the sense of § 823 I BGB would be inconsistent with the binding decision of the legislator (Stoll, idem, 19 ff.). Except in cases where the injury was intended by the actor, liability for harm psychically occasioned, even though it may be adequately caused according to the traditional formula, must be limited to cases where the man in the street, and not only a medical practitioner, would describe it as injury to body and health [reference omitted]. Under certain circumstances, therefore, injuries which are medically ascertainable but do not amount to a 'shock' to the system will go uncompensated. Accordingly, no claim can be made in the normal case of deeply felt grief which, as everybody knows, may have quite serious effects on a person's general well-being.

(c) In the light of these principles, the opinion of the Court of Appeal cannot stand.

The Court of Appeal laid weight on the expert's finding that 'the plaintiff naturally suffered severe psychic shock on first hearing of the death of her husband'. But the court read too much into this. The court had formally asked the expert to report on whether the plaintiff had suffered 'a severe psychic shock which altered her personality and made her depressed, unduly excitable, sleepless, tearful, and apt to shiver on the slightest occasion', taking these terms from the written evidence of Dr C, the plaintiff's general practitioner, evidence of which the expert was somewhat critical. In his reply the expert simply confirmed in general terms that there had been a 'severe psychical shock', though it is doubtful, in view of what he said immediately thereafter, whether he intended this to constitute a medical finding. As to the other symptoms about which he was asked, he made no positive finding, but rather indicated that he himself had not observed them. It would require stronger evidence than this before the Court of Appeal could properly hold that the plaintiff had suffered an injury to health sufficient to ground a claim.

In everyday speech the phrase 'severe psychical shock' denotes a violent temperamental reaction which may have nothing in common with an illness of any kind. Medical men do not use the notion of shock to describe a psychopathological condition. Used to describe a pathological condition (apart from the special case of shock therapy) 'shock' denotes simply an acute disturbance of the circulation [reference omitted] which can result from experiencing an accident or, more rarely, hearing of one. This is naturally of a transitory nature, though it can lead to lasting organic damage. It is by no means clear that the expert believed this to have occurred. A person who experiences an accident, and less often a person who hears of one, may also suffer psychopathological effects. Doctors call this 'neurosis' (not necessarily a purposive neurosis of the kind for which no compensation may be given) or in serious cases even 'psychosis' [reference omitted]. The expert's affidavit does not suggest that he was testifying to any illness of this kind. It is not enough that he did not say there was none: a positive finding is necessary or the plaintiff will fail to meet her burden of proof.

IV. To the extent, therefore, that it grants the plaintiff a claim for damages on her own account, the judgment under appeal cannot be sustained.

When the Court of Appeal re-examines the matter it will need to be convinced, before it can allow the plaintiff's claim even in part, that on hearing of the accident she not only experienced the normal reactions of pain, grief, and depression, but directly suffered a 'traumatic' injury to her physical and psychical health. Further expert evidence may be required, and if the expert testifies to such a condition, it will be necessary to ask to what extent he is relying on the evidence of the general practitioner, which is inadmissible in its present form.

B. I. If, after further investigation, the Court of Appeal holds that the claim should be admitted, the question of the deceased husband's contributory fault will arise. This must be dealt with in a different manner.

1. The Court of Appeal held that in cases like the present one cannot apply § 846 BGB by analogy, and in so holding it was consciously deviating from a view laid down by the Reichsgericht (RGZ 157, 11; RG DR 1940, 163) and supported by some scholars [reference omitted]. We agree with the Court of Appeal on this point: the opinion of the Reichsgericht is unacceptable in the form in which it was expressed. It was certainly right to emphasize that the basic rule of law is that only the direct victim of a tort may sue, a rule to which exceptions are made by §§ 844 and 845 BGB in favour of surviving dependants and persons entitled to services. But it was in error to treat the claim by a third party who suffers injury to his own health when someone else is injured or killed as if this were another case of 'indirect injury to a third party' and to apply § 846 BGB to it by analogy. The difference between this case and those in §§ 844, 845 BGB is essentially that here the third party is affected in one of the legal interests specified in § 823 I BGB and that he is therefore a direct victim with an independent claim of his own under that section. Claims by the indirect victim under §§ 844, 845 BGB presuppose that the primary victim's harm resulted from a tort done to him (BGH VersR 1961, 846, 847) and that is why § 846 BGB provides that any fault on the part of the primary victim which contributed to the harm suffered by the third party must be taken into account in any claim the third party may bring under §§ 844, 845 BGB. This provision is perfectly sensible in relation to claims brought under §§ 844, 845 BGB, but it cannot

apply that view strictly would lead to unjust and inequitable results; the claims of a dead man's survivors result from his death, and if his careless conduct conduced to or accelerated his death, it is only right, in view of their relations with him, that the survivors should have to bear the consequences.

The claim for shock damage which arises in this distinctive manner is a judge-made claim, and though the Court of Appeal would like to extend it beyond the limits set by the Reichsgericht, we are not persuaded by any of the objections which its position on this question has elicited. It only remains to say that, contrary to what is stated in a number of the books, the Reichsgericht was always perfectly clear (see RGZ 162, 321) that cases of shock damage are cases of direct injury to a legal interest protected by § 823 I BGB and not simply instances of indirect harm of the kind covered by §§ 844, 845 BGB.

(c) The present case does not raise the issue of how the decision would be if the occurrence of the harm was wholly or partly independent of any personal relationship, or indeed how far a tortfeasor might be liable at all if the persons suffering the damaging reaction were third parties in no way related to the primary victim.

Case 2

BUNDESGERICHTSHOF (SIXTH CIVIL DIVISION), 4 APRIL 1989*
NJW 1989, 2317

Facts

The plaintiff and her husband had booked a cruise in the eastern Mediterranean scheduled to start on April 26, 1984 and paid the organisers the full price of DM 10,130. On April 21, 1984 the plaintiff's son C, then aged 22, was killed in a road accident. It is not contested by the parties that the defendant is liable in full for the damage resulting from the accident. On account of the pressures placed upon them, the plaintiff and her husband were unable to take the cruise which began one day after the funeral. They were not able to claim reimbursement of the DM 10,130 from the organisers. The plaintiff claimed for the loss of potential support under § 845 BGB arising from her rights as the mother of the victim of the accident and from her husband's corresponding rights which were assigned to her. In addition she claimed compensation for the expenditure on the lost holiday.

Although the LG rejected the claim based on § 845 BGB, it awarded her DM 10,130 as compensation for the holiday expenses. The OLG dismissed the appeals of both parties, but the defendant's appeal to the BGH was suc-

---

* English version by Ms. J. Shaw.

cessful in respect of the lost holiday expenditure. The plaintiff's cross-appeal for the loss of support was denied.

For the following reasons:

I. The OLG accepted the claim brought by the plaintiff for the recovery of money spent on the holiday booked but not taken and made the following findings of law:

As a result of their son's death, the plaintiff and her husband were harmed in respect of their 'right of health' protected by § 823 I BGB. The general view is that damages for pain and suffering are only available in respect of loss in the form of nervous shock which has the degree of severity of an illness. This does not necessarily mean that psychological impairment can only represent an infringement of a right protected by § 823 I BGB when it has the degree of severity of an illness. On the contrary, any form of invasion of the plaintiff's general bodily condition such as the infliction of worry and discomfort is sufficient for there to be damage to the plaintiff's health. Furthermore, the court believed the plaintiff's assertion that she and her husband were psychologically incapable of going on holiday as a result of the death of their son. The principles developed by the case law on the 'Vorhaltekosten' [costs of maintaining a replacement vehicle whenever the plaintiff's own vehicle is out of circulation as a result of an accident] must be applied in this case and, as a result, the expenditure on the holiday must be treated as a recoverable form of damage.

II. The appeal judgment cannot be upheld in law.

1. On the basis of the facts as established, the OLG sees the plaintiff and her husband as having suffered an injury to their right of health protected under § 823 I BGB as a direct consequence of the accident suffered by their son. As a result, it held that the defendant was under a duty to make good the lost expenditure on the holiday as a consequence of the injury.

(a) This approach is not correct as a matter of law. True, the case law has long recognised [references omitted] that the concept of injury to the health within the meaning of § 823 I BGB not only covers physical impairment of the body, but also impairment of a psychological form. However, the law at present denies recovery for mental pain in so far as this is not a consequence of the effects of the injury to the (plaintiff's own) body or the (plaintiff's own) health. Feelings such as sorrow and pain, which are generated by the negative experience itself, are always linked in serious cases with disturbances in the plaintiff's physiological make-up and can, therefore, be directly relevant in a medical sense to the plaintiff's bodily state. To recognise these matters in law as injuries to the plaintiff's health within the meaning of § 823 I BGB . . . would contradict the intention of the legislator to limit tortious liability in § 823 I BGB to clearly defined sets of circumstances by restricting the range of protected interests and the prohibited forms of conduct. In particular, the BGB [never intended] to give a remedy, except where §§ 844 and 845 BGB apply, in cases where the interference with the protected interests of a person has an effect on third parties, unless the latter have suffered an injury in their own right. Thus, precisely in cases such as the present one, the close relatives will normally experience an effect upon their psychological and mental condition on hearing of the victim's death in an accident and as a consequence will suffer not only non-pecuniary, but also pecuniary loss. Nevertheless, the law has restricted recovery for pecuniary loss in the case of the person 'indirectly' injured by a death to the more precisely defined types of loss set out in §§ 844 and 845 BGB. This legislative determination in favour of a basic limitation of tortious liability to recovery by the person 'directly' injured, would be undermined if those types of psychological and mental effects resulting from the experience of the death of a close relative amounted to recoverable injury to health under § 823 I BGB simply because they are recognised by medical science. Consequently, this court has, since its decision in BGHZ 56, 163 [references omitted], only recognised a right to compensation in these types of cases for those types of psychologically inflicted impairments which have psycho-pathological effects lasting for some time, which exceed by some degree the already not inconsiderable detriment caused by a painful trauma for a person's general state of health, and which can therefore 'be regarded in accordance with the general view as injuries to the body or to the health of the victim' [references omitted]. For this reason it is wrong for the OLG to take the view, in cases such as the present one where the loss is in the nature of psychological pressure upon the relatives as a result of the death, that even in the context of psychological injuries any invasion of the plaintiff's general bodily condition, or any infliction of worry and discomfort would suffice even if it did not display the severity of an illness. This point of view is not even supported by the references cited by the OLG itself such as Thomas in Palandt in *BGB Kommentar*, 48th Edition, § 823 note 3b. In that commentary upon the law relating to injuries to mental and bodily health through psychological effects [reference omitted] it is stated that 'in accordance with the protective purpose of § 823 I BGB a claim for compensation should exist only where the injury to health exceeds, in the type and degree, that which close relatives must expect to suffer by way of impairment in these kinds of cases.' In making this statement, Thomas also cited the judgment of this court of May 11 1971 (NJW 1971, 1883 [other references omitted]). The court confirms the approach taken there according to which the only psychological impairments which will amount to injuries to health under § 823 I BGB are those which display the characteristics of an obvious pathology and which will, therefore, be seen by the general public as injuries to the body or the health of the victim [references omitted]. Findings of fact to this effect were not discussed by the OLG and were not advanced by the plaintiff.

(*b*) If an injury to the health of the plaintiff or her husband within the meaning of § 823 I BGB as a consequence of the fatal accident involving their son cannot be established, then it may be left open whether, if such psychological impairments did in the particular circumstances of this case lead to a genuine injury to the plaintiff's health in the sense defined above, lost expenditure on a holiday which was booked but not taken could be brought within the scope and purpose of the legal norm which has been violated [references omitted]. There is also no need to decide whether, for example, recovery for such a form of detriment is excluded as a form of recoverable compensation for injury to health because experience would indicate that regardless of whether the psychological and physical impairments which they might have suffered as a result of the traumatic event had the degree of severity of an illness as required by § 823 I BGB, parents would not, normally, go on holiday one day after the funeral of their child.

2. The appeal judgment is further unsustainable on other legal grounds. Consideration should be given in this context to § 844 I BGB. Even if with respect to this claim for damages (which here accrues to a third party due to his duty to bear the funeral costs) one could give the term 'funeral' expenses a wide meaning to include all expenditures associated with an appropriate and dignified burial, the presence of proximate cause (*Zurechnungszusammenhang*) would be questionable. This is because the plaintiff, according to her own pleadings, failed to take the holiday because of the psychological pressures she was experiencing as a result of the accident and not because of the timing of the funeral.

However, even if the focus were solely upon the funeral, it must be held that expenditure upon a holiday which is booked but not taken falls outside the protective scope of § 844 I BGB. For as exceptions to the general principle of the law of tort, that only persons who are directly injured by an accident will normally have a claim for compensation, §§ 844 and 845 BGB are to be narrowly interpreted. This means that in the context of § 844 I BGB it is the duty of the victim's heirs to bear the costs of the funeral which must form the focus of attention; but the concept of funeral expenses cannot be extended to cover expenditure which has been wasted because the third party (plaintiff) had to attend the funeral. Even if, exceptionally, § 844 I BGB can be construed as encompassing also the recovery of the travelling expenses of close relatives to attend the victim's funeral [references omitted], compensation for the above types of expenditure would go beyond the scope of liability set by the legislator. This court finds itself precluded from giving a wider interpretation of § 844 I BGB both by the terms of the law, itself, and the place of § 844 I BGB within the [wider] systematic framework of the law of tort.

Notes to Cases 1–2

This case raises four important points.

   1. The first is connected with the problem of distant shock. Endorsing the view of earlier courts—of which RGZ 133, 270 is reproduced below as case 3—the court took the view that recovery should not be confined to eye-witnessing relatives but should also be allowed where the injurious effect was distant (*Fernwirkung*). This point, though not seriously contested, has been reaffirmed by the Federal Court in its judgment of 5 February 1985 (BGHZ 93, 351 = NJW 1985, 1390 with note by Deubner at p. 1392). In that case the plaintiff was *en ventre sa mère* when the latter was told of her husband's serious injuries in a traffic accident. As a result, the mother suffered severe physiological and psychological reactions which affected the birth process and led to the plaintiff being born seriously impaired. The child's claim for a declaratory judgment that she was entitled to damages was accepted, the court rejecting the defendant's argument that there was no causal nexus between the mother's shock and the plaintiff's injury. This is one of the crucial issues in nervous shock cases and is discussed more fully in the notes to the next case. For a summary of German law see Ch. 2, A. 2, (*c*), above.

   2. The second point decided by the Federal Court was that recovery should be limited to cases of nervous shock, i.e. cases where there was a recognizable medical illness. To put it differently, mere fright, anguish, distress, or grief will not suffice. In Germany, a recent attempt to enlarge the definition of compensatable harm to include pain, grief, and other expenses connected with the 'inconvenience' suffered as a result of the death of a close relative was firmly rebuffed by BGH NJW 1989, 2317 and is, for this reason, reproduced above as case (2). The dividing line, however, between nervous shock with *recognised* medical symptoms, and 'ordinary' pain and grief is more easy to state than to apply; and it can be manipulated in favour of the plaintiff by an able lawyer and a sympathetic court. (Cf. *Toms* v. *McConnell*, 45 Mich. App. 647, 207 NW 2d 140 (1973). Contrast Lord Justice Bingham's criticism of the term and note his preference for 'psychiatric damage intending to comprehend within it all the relevant forms of mental illness, neurosis, and personality change', [1988] QB 304, 317. Mere pain, grief, and sorrow, however, are again regarded as non-compensatable, ibid. p. 320. See, also, *De Franceschi* v. *Storrier* (1989) 85 ALR 1). Case (2) shows how, with the help of a wider, teleological interpretation of all the relevant provisions of the Code, this temptation has been avoided by German law. In this context, therefore, German law greatly resembles the English

approach, though the juxtaposition of the German and English decisions (e.g. *Hinz* v. *Berry* [1970] 2 QB 40, 42) reveals some interesting differences in writing style. (Cf. in this respect, the comments of Professor Kötz in *La Sentenza in Europa: Metodo Tecnica e Stile* (1988), Einführungsvortrag, 129.) The diversity of American solutions makes comparisons with the law in the USA more difficult, especially since nowadays one detects two diametrically different trends.

3. The first trend manifested itself in the early 1980s and was mostly to be found in the Western States of the USA. Those courts which followed it, inclined towards a wide (but erratic) interpretation of *Dillon*; and they seemed willing to consider sympathetically claims for 'emotional distress' *un*accompanied by obvious physical manifestations. See *Molien* v. *Kaiser Foundation Hospitals*, 27 Cal. 3d 916, 616 P. 2d 813 (1980); *Whitmore* v. *Euroways Express Coaches Ltd*, *The Times*, 4 May 1984. In the *Molien* case the main controlling device introduced by the court was the requirement that the emotional harm suffered by the plaintiff be 'serious'. This was defined in *Rodrigues* v. *State*, 52 Haw. 156, 472 P. 2d 509 (1970) (and approved by *Molien*) as '*serious mental* distress . . . found where a reasonable man, *normally constituted*, would be unable to *adequately cope with the mental stress engendered by the circumstances of the case*'. If the italicized words are properly utilized this may be sufficient: but the Hawaiian courts have certainly not taken it seriously: see the amazing case of *Campbell* v. *Animal Quarantine Station* 63 Haw. 587, 632 P. 2d 1066 (1981) where five plaintiffs recovered a total of $1000 for their anguish suffered when they were told over the phone that their ageing dog had died the previous day after it had been forgotten in an unventilated van for over an hour exposed to the Hawaiian sun! These decisions may well furnish one reason for the appearance of the second and more restrictive trend of cases (which was also, surprisingly perhaps, initiated by the California Supreme Court) towards the end of the 1980s. This newer trend, which not only returns to a more traditional understanding of the meaning of nervous shock but also radically restricts the range of claimants under the *Dillon* v. *Legg* rule, will be discussed briefly in the notes that accompany the translation of the second German decision on nervous shock.

4. *Molien*, allowing recovery for mental anguish even in the absence of physical injury, now seems to be accepted by some ten states with the Texas Supreme Court joining this move in its majority decision in *Moore* v. *Lillebo* 722 SW 2d 683 (1986). It remains to be seen whether this emerging 'independent' cause of action for pure emotional distress will displace the *Dillon* v. *Legg* rule. On this see the notes to the next German case and, *inter alia*, Nola and Ursin, 'Negligent Infliction of Emotional Distress: Coherence Emerging from Chaos' 33 *Hastings LJ* 583 (1982); Hughes, 'Recovering

Damages for Mental Anguish in Wrongful Death Suits: The Elimination of the Physical Injury/Physical Manifestation Requirement' 18 *Texas Tech. L. Rev.* 893 (1987). An interesting compromise is proposed by Miller, 'The Scope of Liability for Negligent Infliction of Emotional Distress: Making "the Punishment Fit the Crime"' *U. Haw. L. Rev.* 1 (1979). Cases such as these prompt many questions. Here are some:

(*i*) How does one define mental anguish that merits compensation? Texas courts understand the term to imply 'a relatively high degree of mental pain and distress. It is more than mere disappointment, anger, resentment, or embarrassment, although it may include all of these . . .', *Trevino* v. *Southwestern Bell Tel. Co.*, 582 SW 2d 584 (Tex. Civ. App. 1979). But *Rodrigues* (cited above) shows that it is easier to formulate a test than to apply it.

(*ii*) What is the legal position of absent members of a community hit by a natural disaster? See Labin, 'Dealing with Disasters: Some Thoughts on the Adequacy of the Legal System' 30 *Stan. L. Rev.* 281 (1978).

(*iii*) What if the victim suffers mental anguish because physical harm *may* follow the negligently caused event, e.g. in the case of a man who had a homosexual relationship with another man who, unbeknown to him, was infected by AIDS? Courts have allowed damages for fear of future cancer—cancerphobia—as a result of exposure to toxic substances, e.g. *Jackson* v. *Johns-Manville Sales Corp.*, 781 F. 2d 394 (1986); *Herber* v. *Johns-Manville Corp.*, 785 F. 2d 79 (1986); *Eagle-Pitcher Indus. Inc.* v. *Cox*, 481 So. 2d 517, rev. denied, 492 So. 2d 1331 (1985). On this see: Gale and Goyer, 'Recovery for Cancerphobia and Increased Risk of Cancer' 15 *Cumb. L. Rev.* 723 (1985); Dworkin, 'Fear of Disease and Delayed Manifestation Injuries: A Solution or a Pandora's Box?' 53 *Fordham L. Rev.* 527 (1984); Note, 'Tort Liability for the Transmission of AIDS Virus: Damages for Fear of AIDS and Prospective AIDS' 45 *Wash. and Lee L. Rev.* 185 (1988).

5. The final issue raised by this case is a difficult one. It concerns the plaintiff's deceased husband's own fault which the court said had to be taken into account when calculating the plaintiff's damages. Now the plaintiff's claim in this case was an *independent* claim based on § 823 I BGB and not a *derivative* (wrongful death) claim based on § 846 BGB. It is, therefore, difficult to see how the victim's own contributory fault could be imputed to his wife. (See the discussion in Chapter 4.) The court bypassed this difficulty by basing its decision on the pervading notion of good faith (embodied in § 242 BGB), but its reasoning is hardly convincing. (See the cogent criticisms of Fleming in 20 *A. J. Comp. Law* 485, 488–9 (1972).)

Common law courts do not appear to have faced this problem squarely *in the context of nervous shock*, though *Dillon* v. *Legg* contains some confused views on the subject. (The majority, at p. 916, asks the question whether the contributory negligence of the victim *and* the plaintiffs should affect their claims whereas the minority, at p. 928, asks the very different question whether the deceased child's negligence can affect the living plaintiffs' claims. The better answer would appear to be that any *dependents'* claims (under Wrongful Death Statutes) should be affected by the contributory negligence of the deceased; but *personal* claims for nervous shock should, probably, be unaffected.) However, the point may arise in 'rescue' cases and in those States which still recognize actions for 'loss of consortium' or loss of 'parental or children's companionship'. In the first instance, and perhaps also in the second, the tendency is to treat the claims as *independent* and, therefore, *not* to impute contributory negligence. See *Mallett* v. *Dunn* [1949] 2 KB 180 (England); *Feltch* v. *General Rental Co.*, 383 Mass. 603, 421 NE 2d 67 (1981), reviewing the contradictory American case-law. See also *Handeland* v. *Brown*, 216 NW 574 (1974) (Iowa, 1974) and compare the views of the majority and the dissent. Imputed contributory negligence is discussed in detail in Gregory, Kalven, and Epstein, 716 ff., especially 730 ff.

Case 3

REICHSGERICHT (SIXTH CIVIL DIVISION) 21 SEPTEMBER 1931[*]
RGZ 133, 270 = JZ 1929, 914 (with a note by Bezold and Plum)

On 5 October 1929 the second defendant, driving the car belonging to his father, the first defendant, mounted the pavement and killed the plaintiffs' seven-year-old son. In criminal proceedings he was sentenced to nine months' imprisonment. The plaintiffs now sued both defendants as joint and several debtors for liquidated damages in respect of the cost of medical attempts to save the child's life, burial, and loss of business profits, and asked for a declaration of liability in respect of loss of future maintenance and services by the plaintiffs' son as well as for damages arising from the nervous breakdown of the plaintiff wife. The defendants paid RM 850 and alleged to have discharged their liability thereby.

The District Court of Cologne held the defendants jointly and severally liable to make periodic payments to the plaintiffs to the extent that the deceased would have been obliged during his estimated life-span to provide them with maintenance and services; in other respects it dismissed the claim. On appeal the Court of Appeal of Cologne allowed the claim for RM 1200 in respect of loss of business profits due to the reduced earning capacity of the plaintiff wife and held that the costs of attempted medical care and of the burial had been discharged; in addition it held the defendants liable as joint and several debtors to compensate the plaintiffs in respect of the loss

[*] English version by Kurt Lipstein.

suffered by them as a result of the past or future injury to the health of the plaintiff mother arising from the accident, including the present or future loss of services, until she reached the age of sixty-five. The appeal by the defendants was successful in part for the following

Reasons

... in this appeal the question is only whether the defendants are also liable for the effects of the plaintiff wife's nervous breakdown which she suffered upon receiving the news of the accident, but which she did not witness herself ... the Court of Appeal found that the emotional excitement on hearing of her child's death caused the plaintiff wife's nervous breakdown, which had affected her earning capacity and was likely to continue to do so in the future.

The Court of Appeal has held correctly that the damage in question is not indirect in the sense that it is only covered by the duty to compensate under § 823 BGB in the exceptional circumstances of §§ 844, 845 BGB. Indirect damage is that damage suffered by a person who is not himself a victim of a tort but is only affected by its reflex effect upon his assets. In the present case, however, the plaintiff wife herself has been injured in her health by the tort, and the plaintiffs sue in respect of this injury to health. It has never been stated in the practice of the Reichsgericht that the legal interests or rights enumerated in § 823 I BGB must be violated directly and that an indirect violation does not suffice [reference]; the view to the contrary, put forward by the appellants, is unfounded. However, two questions must be examined in such cases; firstly, whether the causal nexus can still be regarded as adequate and, if this question should be answered in the affirmative; secondly, whether the indirect violation could be foreseen. The Court of Appeal has examined both questions and has answered them in the affirmative.

It is normally to be expected that a fatal accident of her child will greatly excite the mother emotionally, and it is not unusual if a grave emotional excitement of this kind results in a nervous breakdown which affects the capacity to work. Thus adequate causality exists [reference]. One can go even further and add ... that this result could be foreseen. The contention of the appellants that the second defendant could not even have known whether the seven-year-old boy had any parents cannot be accepted. The question is not whether the defendant could know but whether he ought to have considered the shock of the parents and the possible effects of the shock. In answering these questions in the affirmative the Court of Appeal has not broadened the concept of negligence excessively.

These statements only apply to liability according to the general rules of tort. In the case of the second defendant, his liability under § 823 BGB has been sufficiently justified by the judgment of the Court of Appeal. For, having regard to findings of fact of the accident, it cannot be doubted that the second defendant caused it negligently . . . On the other hand, the Court of Appeal has not given sufficient grounds for holding the first defendant liable, as it does on the basis of § 831 BGB. The appellants point out rightly that it has not been established at all whether and now the first defendant had appointed the second defendant to carry out this 'task'. . . . The fact that the first defendant denied the claim to a limited extent only does not permit the conclusion that he appointed his son to carry out the task. In so far as the claim is based on the injury to her health suffered by the plaintiff wife, the defendants have denied its substance throughout. The Court of Appeal will therefore have to examine again whether the first defendant has incurred liability, which it had held to be the case without restricting it to the provisions of the Act on Motor Vehicles.

If the defendant should only be liable under § 7 of the Act on Motor Vehicles, in addition to the conditions set out above in which liability to compensate the plaintiff wife in respect of injury to her health would exist, the problem would arise whether this injury to her health had occurred 'in the course of operating' the motor vehicle. The courts below have held that it did. From their point of view this finding was superfluous, since judgment against the defendants was based on §§ 823, 831 BGB. However, the affirmative answer to this problem cannot be approved. The Court of Appeal itself refers to the decision of the Reichsgericht [reference] where that court refused to regard as an injury to health 'in the course of operating' a railway, a mental illness suffered by a father as a result of the shock occasioned by a railway accident involving his daughter. This decision is in keeping with the constant practice of the Reichsgericht in applying the Act on the Tortious Liability of the Reich.* The onset of the mental illness was not directly connected with the operational process or with a specific installation of the operation; nor could it be traced to a danger peculiar to the operation of railways [reference], but it could have happened as a result of any accident or fright. The Court of Appeal believes however . . . that the words in § 7 of the Law on Motor Vehicles bear a different meaning from the corresponding words in § 1 of the Law on the Tortious Liability of the Reich. The . . . [reference] legislative history of § 7 shows clearly, however, that in this respect the Law on the Tortious Liability of the Reich was copied deliberately by the Law on Motor Vehicles in order to make use of the extensive practice and literature on the law on liability. . . . Nevertheless it is conceivable that in individual cases the determination may differ as to

* Ed. note. This is Professor Lipstein's rendering of the term 'Reichshaftpflichtgesetz'. Elsewhere in the text the words Imperial Act on Liability have been used in the knowledge and belief that in this context the word Reich indicates that the enactment applies to the whole of the Empire.

whether an accident is to be regarded as having occurred 'in the course of operating', given the technical differences between operating railways and motor vehicles. It is difficult to perceive, however, how a difference can be established in the present case. In both situations the question is whether the effect of a shock suffered by a relative on the occasion of an operational accident is still to be regarded itself as an injury to health in the 'course of operating'. The difference in the types of operations is irrelevant for this purpose . . . Accordingly the first defendant can be held liable under § 831 BGB for the nervous breakdown of the plaintiff wife if the conditions for its application should have been fulfilled but not under the Law on Motor Vehicles. It is a different question, not in issue here, whether the determination must be different, if the plaintiff wife had been present where the accident occurred and whether in such a case the opinion expressed in [reference] can be maintained [reference].

It follows that the judgment against the first defendant must be quashed and the case referred back. On the other hand the appeal of the second defendant must be rejected.

Notes to Case 3

For a number of reasons this is a very important case.

1. First of all it shows the tendency of German law (and modern civil law in general) to use normative concepts of causation in cases where Common lawyers would more evidently have recourse to the notion of duty of care. Note, however, that this was not always so: *Victorian Rly* v. *Coultas* (1883) 13 App. Cas. 222, 226 (the earliest English case on nervous shock, decided before the concept of duty had started its meteoric rise). This equivocation between 'duty' and 'remoteness' will figure in other cases as well (e.g. economic loss, rescue etc.) and is discussed, *inter alia*, by Fleming, 'Remoteness and Duty: the Control Devices in Liability for Negligence' 31 *Can. Bar. Rev.* 471 (1953) (a seminal article) and Lawson and Markesinis I, ch. 2. See also Prosser's remarks at 244–5.

2. Secondly, the case addresses itself to the key issue of distant nervous shock and opts for the more liberal view according to which compensation is not limited to persons suffering shock as a result of witnessing the accident. This approach, which has been followed many times since (e.g. RGZ 157, 11; BGH NJW 1971, 1883, BGHZ 93, 351 = NJW 1985, 1390, and further references and commentary by von Hippel, in 'Haftung für Schockschäden Dritter', *NJW* 1965, 1890) places German law in a more pioneering position when compared with the English and American law. For the former demanded until recently that the plaintiff heard or saw the accident with his own unaided senses. In the early 1980s, however, the House of Lords awarded damages to a mother and wife who rushed to

the hospital to see her injured family a few hours *after* the accident had occurred and then suffered shock (*McLoughlin* v. *O'Brian* (1983) AC 410). The decision though criticized (by among others Weir, *A Casebook on Tort* (6th edn., 1983) 76–7. For reactions on the more recent case law see 7th edn. (1992), pp. 88–90) is remarkable for its open allusion to policy arguments. Equally noticeable is the judicial turnabout *vis-à-vis* the value of the 'floodgates' argument which up to that point had received an almost exaggerated respect. (Cf. on this point the pioneering remarks of Tobriner, J. in *Dillon* v. *Legg* 68 Cal. 2d 728, 441 P. 2d 912 (1968).) The liberating effect of *McLoughlin* was neither immediate nor radical in its effects, though in the early 1990s two interesting decisions at first instance extended the leading case. Thus, in *Hevican* v. *Ruane* [1991] 3 All ER 65 compensation was granted to a father who suffered nervous shock as a result of being told of his son's death and subsequently seeing his body in the mortuary. And in *Ravenscroft* v. *Rederia Aktiebolaget Transatlantic* [1991] 3 All ER 73 the same result was reached in the case of a mother who, however, never saw the body of the killed son. These decisions, however, have now been discredited by the even more recent pronouncements in *Alcock* v. *Chief Constable of the South Yorkshire Police* [1992] 1 AC 310 with the House of Lords sounding a cautious retreat from all earlier pronouncements. The facts of the case that gave rise to this retrenchment were, admittedly, difficult involving claims by relatives and friends of the victims of the Hillsborough Stadium disaster, some of whom saw on live television the spectators crushed to death against the stadium railings that were meant to prevent the crowds from getting onto the football pitch. The reason for this horrifying accident was the decision taken by the police locally to allow extra people to enter a restricted area without foreseeing the sudden surge of the crowd which caused the disaster. A carefully argued decision of the Court of First Instance in favour of *some* of the claimants (in the first, test action) was overturned both by the Court of Appeal and the House of Lords relying largely on the usual grounds advanced against nervous shock. However, unlike some recent American pronouncements, the House of Lords did not limit (potential) recovery to close relatives. The key sections of Lord Keith's leading speech deserves to be quoted in full since it provides a sensible test for solving this aspect of the problem and one which, incidentally, is likely to produce results approximating those of German law. He said (at p. 397):

As regards the class of persons to whom a duty may be owed . . . I think it sufficient that reasonable foreseeability should be the guide. I would not seek to limit the class by reference to particular relationships such as husband and wife or parent and child. The kinds of relationship which may involve close ties of love and affection are numerous . . . They may be present in family relationships or those of close friendship, and may be stronger in the case of engaged couples than in that of persons who have been married to each other for many years. It is common knowledge that such ties exist, and reasonably foreseeable that those bound by them may in certain circumstances be at real risk of psychiatric illness if the loved one is injured or put in peril. The closeness of the tie would, however, require to be proved by a plaintiff, though no doubt being capable of being presumed in appropriate cases. Psychiatric damage to [a bystander] would not ordinarily be within the range of reasonable foreseeability, but could not perhaps be entirely excluded from it if the circumstances of a catastrophe occurring very close to him were particularly horrific.

Alcock is an interesting decision which will repay careful reading. Here, for lack of space, two further points will be mentioned. *First*, neither the decision (nor the commentators) seem to have considered the consequences of a pro-plaintiff judgment against *possible* media defendants for showing such scenes on live television. Would, for example, liability depend on whether 'identifiable' victims were shown on the screen (not the case here)? What effect would 'warning notices' have? More importantly, would such (potential) liability have a 'chilling effect' on news reporting and thus amount to a restriction on free speech? In the USA such an argument would, probably, have a crucial effect on the issue of liability, but in England it might prove less decisive. *Secondly*, the overruling of some of the earlier, more liberal decisions (e.g. *Hevican, Ravenscroft*) will, inevitably, cast doubts over some interesting dicta which they contained. In *Ravenscroft*, for example, Mr Justice Ward stressed that the need to prove 'psychiatric illness' and 'causation' were hurdles that 'not many [litigants] will jump' and this would, inevitably, allay 'fears of the floodgates opening too wide' ([1991] 3 All ER 73, 76). It is submitted that there is much to be said for the view that psychiatric injury can, nowadays, be treated as a form of injury in its own right, that the plaintiff need not be seen as a 'secondary victim' of the accident, and that the seriousness of the injury, coupled with rigid causal proof can be workable controlling devices, sufficiently countering the fear of numerous suits. (See Markesinis and Deakin, *Tort Law* 3rd edn. ch. 2).

Comparative lawyers accustomed to the fact that ideas these days tend to move from West to East (and no longer the other way round) will be surprised to see that American law is in this area rather more timid than English or even German law. True, the original impact rule, which insisted on contemporaneous personal injury before nervous shock was compensated, was increasingly found to be too rigid and nowadays it has gone out of fashion. (*Woodman* v. *Dever*, 367 So. 2d 1061 (Fla. App. 1979) shows its unfairness; and *Payton* v. *Abbott Labs.*, 386 Mass. 540, 437 NE 2d 171, 176 (1982), discusses judicial dissatisfaction with the rule. Florida, however, still retains this rule: *Champion* v. *Gray*, 478 So. 2d 17 (1985).) Most jurisdictions, in conformity with s. 313 of the *Restatement* (*Second*) *of Torts*, still require the plaintiff to be in the danger zone before he can recover (Henderson and Pearson, 567; Prosser, Schwartz, and Wade, 407; see also *Rickey* v. *Chicago Transit Authority*, 98 Ill. 2d 546, 457 NE 2d 1 (1983); *Stadler* v. *Cross*, 295 NW 2d 552 (Minn., 1980) and the courts of some twenty jurisdictions). The pioneering decision of *Dillon* v. *Legg* (above) is thus still the subject of mixed feelings: see, for example, Pearson, in 34 *U. Fla. L. Rev.* 477 (1982).

Dillon, which nevertheless contains one of the best discussions on the subject, extended recovery to bystanders (outside the immediate danger zone) provided (1) the 'plaintiff was located near the scene of the accident . . . (2) the shock resulted from a direct emotional impact upon plaintiff from the sensory and contemporaneous observance of the accident, as contrasted with learning of the accident from others after its occurrence, [and] (3) . . . plaintiff and the victim were closely related . . .' (441 P. 2d 912 at 920). The requirements of 'physical proximity', 'temporal proximity' and 'relational proximity' have been the subject of much discussion, both inside and outside the courtroom. Nowadays, there is a tendency to give this last requirement a very narrow interpretation—certainly narrower than that adopted, in theory at least, by German law—wherever (in the USA) the decisions of the California Supreme Court in *Eldon* v. *Sheldon* 758 P. 2d 582 (1988) and *Thing* v. *La Chusa* P. 2d 814 (1989) are used as models. For the first denied the plaintiff recovery for his shock upon seeing his injured girl friend on the grounds that he was not married to her while the second reached the same result in the case of a mother who suffered shock in circumstances not dissimilar to those in *McLoughlin*).

A similar, narrowing tendency *may* be developing for the other two kinds of 'proximity' (spatial and temporal) stressed by *Dillon*. (See Prosser *On the Law of Torts*, 5th edn. (1984), 366 and supplements.) These requirements of 'nearness, hearness, and dearness' have certainly proved difficult to define as, indeed, the dissent in *Dillon* had predicted (p. 926). Californian courts have thus much vacillated and the confusing case-law—reviewed in *Justus* v. *Atchison*, 19 Cal. 3d 564, 565 P. 2d 122 (1977), and by Quai-Smith, 'The Negligent Infliction of Emotional Distress' 19 *Indiana L. Rev.* 809, 818 ff. (1986)—has not been unravelled (as it could have been) by the decision of the Supreme Court of California in *Ochoa* v. *Superior Court* 39 Cal. 3d 159, 703 P. 2d 1 (1985). Thus cases like *Justus* suggest that only plaintiffs who have observed the accident will be allowed to recover. See also *Parsons* v. *Superior Court*, 81 Cal. App. 3d 506, 146 Cal. Rptr. 495 (1978) and contrast this with the *McLoughlin* judgment. On the other hand, in *General Motors Corp.* v. *Grizzle* 642 SW 2d 837 (Tex. App. 1982) a mother, who arrived at the scene shortly after the accident and saw her injured daughter, succeeded in her action for damages. All one can say, therefore, is that spatial and temporal proximity will remain crucial factors even though they are likely to be understood differently by different courts. See, for example, *Cohen* v. *McDonnell Douglas Corp.*, 389 Mass. 327, 450 NE 581 (1983). However, these problems, too, must now be approached bearing in mind the restrictive philosophy of decisions like *Thing* v. *La Chusa* P. 2d 814 (1989) though beyond that it is dangerous to attempt any specific predictions.

3. Cases such as *Sanchez* v. *Schindler*, 651 SW 2d 249 (1983) suggest yet a different approach which relies on a wider interpretation of the Wrongful Death Statute (in that case, the Texas version) and allows parents the right to recover damages for mental distress resulting from the death of their child. This solution—praised by some Texan commentators (e.g. Mendel in 26 *South Texas Law Journal*, 305 (1985))—is, however, dubious. For not only is it contrary to the intentions of Lord Campbell's Act (on which the Texas Wrongful Death Statute is, apparently, based); but, more importantly, it produces the strange result of making the parents' right of recovery depend on their child's death.

4. Finally, note how articulate the Anglo-American decisions are about the policy issues which have justified first the strict and then more relaxed treatment of claims for nervous shock. The best discussions in America can be found in *Amaya* v. *Home Ice, Fuel and Supply Co.* 59 Cal. 2d 295, 29 Cal. Reptr. 33 (1963); *Dillon* v. *Legg* (above), and in England, *McLoughlin* v. *O'Brian* (above) including the judgments in the Court of Appeal: (1981) QB 599. By contrast the German decisions give little away about policy. There is no doubt, however, that the same policy reasons are at work in this system as well, and contemporary writers are prepared to admit that the problem is not one of causation but one of policy. (See von Hippel in *NJW* 1965, 1890 at 1891. Huber in *Festschrift E. Wahl*, 301 ff. agrees.) Thus, increasing reliance can be found on more normative theories of causation (like the *Normzweck* approach); and even the contractual concept of *Vertrag mit Schutzwirkung für Dritte* has been mentioned as a possible source of inspiration. See Berg in *NJW* 1970, 515.

5. Though articulated in different ways the policy reasons are mainly three. First is the fear of fraudulent or vexatious claims. Tobriner J.'s answer (in *Dillon* v. *Legg*, above) that '. . . the possibility that fraudulent assertions may prompt recovery in isolated cases does not justify a wholesale rejection of the entire class of claims in which that potentiality arises' seems to be winning the day. Secondly is the 'floodgates' argument which has prompted the development of numerous rules of thumb (impact theory, danger zone theory; relatives only can recover etc.). Though not without some merit, this objection, too, is falling into disfavour as an increasing number of dicta in English decisions (dealing with economic loss as well as

nervous shock) clearly suggest, though the California cases of *Eldon* and *La Chusa* show that it still finds favour with cautiously-inclined judges. Finally, one might argue with Professor Atiyah (*Accidents, Compensation and the Law* (3rd edn., 1980) 80) that '. . . the claims of such a person [i.e. one who suffers distress and/or shock as a result of witnessing an accident] must have a low priority when it is remembered that thousands of victims with physical injury go uncompensated every year because they are injured in accidents not caused by negligence'.

6. In this note the approach of three systems was compared briefly. Is there any other factor (not mentioned above) that has to be borne in mind when explaining the differences between them? Could the absence of civil juries in England and the European continent explain why these systems can afford to disregard the floodgates argument more easily than, perhaps, American courts can? To what extent can this ebb and flow of the law be linked to changing attitudes in society? Could the decisions of the Supreme Court of California in *Eldon* v. *Sheldon* 758 P. 2d 582, denying damages for nervous shock to the plaintiff who actually *witnessed* the death of his girl friend (with whom he had a 'stable and significant relationship') be linked to policy factors such as the State's need (real or perceived) to discourage extra-matrimonial cohabitation? Would not this argument appeal more to the wave of 'conservative' judges who were appointed (or elected) from about the mid-eighties onwards? Incidentally, this 'conservative' approach found favour with some French judges in the 1940s, 50s, and 60s (in the slightly different context of wrongful death actions), but was abandoned in the early 70s as being legally unconvincing and morally sanctimonious. For further details on this see: Lawson and Markesinis, *Tortious Liability for Un-Intentional Harm in the Common Law and the Civil Law* I, (1982), ch. 2. The importance of such background factors in the development of American tort law is fully explored in Professor Fleming's *The American Tort Process* (1988), his observations being particularly useful to European lawyers trying to understand tort law in America.

7. References to the extensive periodic literature can be found in Prosser, Wade, and Schwartz, 408–9, to which add: Chesley, 'The Increasingly Disparate Standards of Recovery for Negligently Inflicted Emotional Injuries' 52 *Cincinnati L. Rev.* 1017 (1983); Dupuy, 'Negligent Infliction of Emotional Distress', 53 *Louisiana L. Rev.* 555 (1992); Hughes, 'Recovering Damages for Mental Anguish in Wrongful Death Suits: The Elimination of the Physical Injury/Physical Manifestation Requirement' 18 *Texas Tech. L. Rev.* 893 (1987); Rose, 'Negligent Infliction of Emotional Distress: Formulating the Psycho-Legal Inquiry' 18 *Suffolk Univ. L. Rev.* 401 (1984); Quai-Smith, 'The Negligent Infliction of Emotional Distress: A Critical Analysis of Various Approaches to the Tort in Light of *Ochoa* v. *Superior*

Court' 19 *Indiana L. Rev.* 809 (1986); Comment, 'Negligent Infliction of Mental Distress: A Jurisdictional Survey of Existing Limitation Devices and Proposals Based on an Analysis of Objective Versus Subjective Indices of Distress' 33 *Villanova Law Rev.* 781 (1988); Sitzman, '*Marlene F.* v. *Affiliated Psychiatric Medical Clinic Inc.*: Negligent Infliction of Emotional Distress Bounces Out of Bounds', 22 *Pacific Law Journal* 189 (1990). For a discussion of English and Commonwealth cases see: Trindade, 'The Principles Governing the Recovery of Damages for Negligently Caused Nervous Shock' [1986] *CLJ* 476.

2. PRE-NATAL INJURIES

Case 4

BUNDESGERICHTSHOF (SECOND CIVIL DIVISION) 20 DECEMBER 1952*
BGHZ 8, 243 = NJW 1953, 417 = JZ 1953, 307
(with an approving note by R. Schmidt)

On the occasion of the birth of a previous child, the plaintiff's mother was a patient in the defendant hospital from 29 August until 9 September 1946. On that day she received a blood transfusion which was administered by Dr A who was an employee of the hospital where the donor had first offered himself for this purpose. Dr A had called for a blood test which did not disclose any syphilitic infection, but had not conducted any further examination of the donor. When the donor was again examined in January 1948, the Wassermann test was positive. The defendant hospital, on learning this, recalled all those patients who had been recipients of the donor's blood. It appeared after a further examination that as a result of the transfusion the plaintiff's mother had been infected with syphilis and that, in consequence the plaintiff, who was born on 13 October 1947, was suffering from congenital syphilis.

The plaintiff applied for a declaration that the defendant hospital was liable to pay damages in respect of all damage caused to her now or which might arise in the future as a result of the infection of her mother with syphilis on the occasion of the blood transfusion on 9 September 1946, and for the payment of damages for pain and suffering. The judgments by the courts below allowing the claim were upheld for the following

Reasons

The Court of Appeal has found that the mother of the plaintiff was infected with syphilis because the medical officer at the defendant hospital, when carrying out the blood transfusion on 9 September 1946, did not follow the

* English version by Kurt Lipstein.

measures prescribed by the order and the guide-lines of the Reichsminister of the Interior dated 5 March 1940 concerning the examination of donors of blood. According to the Court of Appeal the omission to take these measures was due to the fact that the medical staff of the hospital had not been informed of the guide-lines published by the Minister of the Interior. It is undisputed that the Chief Medical Officer, Dr X, who was a member of the defendant's board in 1940, failed to give notice to the departments of surgery and gynaecology of the hospital of the order and the guide-lines of the Reichsminister of the Interior. This Division has had occasion to state before in the judgment of 27 February 1952 [reference], which had rejected a second appeal by the defendant in an action by the mother of the plaintiff, that this situation involves not only contractual negligence towards the plaintiff's mother who had been received by the hospital as a patient under the medical insurance scheme but also a tort by the defendant hospital committed by Dr X, a member of the board, for whom the defendant is responsible according to § 31 BGB. In the present case liability for the damage suffered by the plaintiff can only arise in tort. Such a claim is well founded in the present case.

1. The act of the defendant hospital is to be found in the failure to take the necessary precautions on the occasion of the blood transfusion administered to the mother of the child at a time before the child was conceived. Thereby the defendant has violated a legal duty incumbent upon it. Even if at first this act affected directly the health of the mother alone, the same act had nevertheless caused subsequently an injury to the health of the plaintiff as well, who was born on 13 October 1947. The appellant defendant is wrong in arguing that the injury is indirect with the result that it cannot render the defendant liable. For a claim for damages to arise it suffices if the act causing the damage violates directly or indirectly one of the protected interests or absolute rights set out in § 823 I BGB, provided only that a causal nexus exists in the meaning of the theory of adequate causation between the act creating the damage and the resulting violation of a protected interest [reference]. This can be assumed to exist in the present case, for it is common experience that an infection of a married woman with syphilis is likely to transmit this illness later on to a child conceived by her.

2. The appellant objects above all that in the present case the application of § 823 I BGB is logically excluded because at the time when the act causing damage occurred the plaintiff was not in an intact state which could have been violated by an act causing damage. The appellant argues that § 823 I presupposes logically that damage can only be claimed by those who were intact at one time. If such a state never existed, however, because the egg or the foetus was already sick from the moment of conception as a result of the

mother's illness, no interference had ever occurred with the state of health of a child born subsequently. The same view had been expressed in a decision of the Third Civil Division of this court [reference]. Upon enquiry, however, the Third Division has replied that it no longer maintains this view, and therefore this Division is not bound by the above-mentioned decision. The arguments of the appellant cannot be accepted. They are based on a purely concrete manner of thinking which proceeds on the whole from the individual rights, ownership, and the other absolute rights enumerated in § 823 I BGB but does not pay sufficient attention to the special character of the values of life to which § 823 I BGB refers above all. The difference between these values of life and individual rights on the other hand was stressed by the Reichsgericht as early as 1902, following the observations of Planck [reference]. These values of life themselves are clearly not individual rights, instead it is only possible to state that every individual is entitled to have them granted to him, just as the Constitution of Bonn speaks of the right of every person to life and physical integrity [reference].

Absolute rights are clearly determined by law. Accordingly it is logically impossible, e.g. to damage property before any property has come into being. However, it is fundamentally wrong in law to apply to interference with the values of life protected by § 823 I BGB the principles concerning the distinction between injurious acts affecting absolute rights and injurious acts causing damage to other resources. Therefore one must also reject the observations of Rudolf Smend [reference], according to whom, in the case of injury to health the circumstances in which that tort can be committed must be interpreted in the same distinctive manner as in the case of a violation of individual absolute right, as distinct from that of damage to other resources.

The view rejected here is met by the decisive argument that it pays insufficient attention to the special character of the values of life protected by § 823 I BGB. These values precede the legal system. They express the individuality of human beings as part of nature and of creation. They represent life itself, the essence of all that is alive and derive their substance from it. Every human being has a right to these values of life and is therefore entitled to expect that organic growth will not be disturbed or curtailed by human hand. Every deprivation or disturbance by human beings which hinders or curtails natural growth and natural development constitutes a violation of these protected interests. Thus injury to health has been described accurately as 'causing a disturbance of the internal processes of life' [reference]. Common parlance too adopts this attitude in describing a child, such as the plaintiff, whose health was severely impaired at birth, as being a sick child, that is to say as a child whose internal processes of life are disturbed and who has not been endowed with that degree of health with which creation and nature has predisposed the living organism of a human being. In this respect the legal order must follow the phenomenon of nature; it cannot and must not disregard the facts of nature. What is an injury or a curtailment of health cannot therefore be determined by the logical concepts of legal techniques, but is, like the gift of health itself, predetermined by creation and nature which must be recognized as natural reality by the legal system, if it is to derive therefrom any legal conclusions in law.

Following these considerations it is not possible to apply to the health of human beings, which is protected by § 823 I BGB the legal principles based on formal legal technique which governs the violation of individual rights.

It is not possible, either, to agree with the appellant who argues that § 823 I presupposes the existence of a physical person and that it cannot therefore be applied to injuries affecting those who were not yet conceived when the tort was committed, since in such a case 'another person' in the meaning of § 823 I BGB does not exist . . . the plaintiff was conceived in the body of the mother who suffered from syphilis and developed in it as a human being affected by syphilis by absorbing the illness. This would not have happened without the tortious act or omission of the defendant; in short without it she would not have become a person suffering from syphilis.

The object of the argument is thus not damage to a foetus or to an unborn child, but the damage which the plaintiff has suffered by the fact that she was born a sick person affected by syphilis. As stated before, her damage is connected by a link of adequate causation with the infection with syphilis of her mother by the defendant. This damage was suffered by the plaintiff when she was born and constituted an injury to her health. Thus the conditions of § 823 I BGB exist for allowing the claim.

Case 5

BUNDESGERICHTSHOF (SIXTH CIVIL DIVISION) 11 JANUARY 1972*
BGHZ 58, 48 = NJW 1972, 1126 = JZ 1972, 363
(with an approving note by H. Stoll = VersR 1972, 372)

On 7 June 1964, the plaintiffs, husband and wife, were severely injured in a collision between their motor car and that of the defendant, who was solely to blame. At the time of the accident, the plaintiff wife was six months pregnant. On 16 September 1964 she gave birth to a child, the third plaintiff, who was a spastic because he suffered from brain damage. The parties disputed as to whether this was caused by the injury to the mother. Both instances below allowed the claim. A second appeal by the defendant was unsuccessful for the following

---

* English version by Kurt Lipstein.

Reasons

A. . . .

B. *The action by the third plaintiff for a declaration*

I. The Court of Appeal has assumed without discussion that the plaintiff could demand damages under § 823 I BGB for injury to his health, although he was not yet born at the time when the defendants committed the tort. Clearly the Court of Appeal relied on the decision of the Bundesgericht of 20 December 1952 [reference] which had no hesitation in applying § 823 I BGB, even if a child which was born with a defect was not even conceived when the tort was committed against the mother.

This approach, which was adopted by the judgment appealed against, must be applied. In the present case, too, the plaintiff must be treated as 'another person' in the meaning of § 823 BGB, whose health was injured by the defendant; for the purpose of this provision establishing liability the plaintiff is a 'human being' even if he was injured before birth *en ventre sa mère* [references]. Similarly § 25 of the Nuclear Energy Act of 23 December 1959 refers to injury to a human being, but includes in this term also those who have suffered injuries to their health before birth and even before their conception [references]. The fact that the plaintiff suffered the injury to her health before birth cannot be determining if these preceding processes provided by nature and by creation are considered in their own setting.

The objections against applying § 823 BGB, which are mainly conceptual, must and can be overcome; true, in cases of this kind it does not assist that the liability of a tortfeasor does not presuppose the existence at the time of his action of the object, the violation of which leads to liability (distance tort). In the cases now under consideration the (illegal) act injures the foetus directly; the only 'distance' consists in that between this injury and the moment in which the injuries to health become apparent when the child is born, that is to say the moment in which the object of the liability first reaches its existence. In particular, difficulties arise in applying § 823 BGB if it is considered that at the time of the injury the foetus was not yet a human being and cannot therefore be regarded as 'another person' [references].

Nevertheless, no objections exist against applying § 823 BGB, a view shared in the literature, albeit for a number of different reasons [references].

1. The provision of § 823 BGB protects the right of a human being, once born, to the integrity of his body and his health; nobody is allowed to injure the health of a human being. It is unnecessary in the present case to consider

the question as to whether in the case of an injury to the foetus the protected interest is the health and corporeal integrity of a person alive (later on) or whether a right of a foetus to integrity and health is to be recognized [references]. In the present case the issue is not one of compensation for damage which the foetus has suffered—if it were to be granted limited legal personality (see § 844 II BGB, second sentence)—but the injury to health which the child has suffered, being born alive but sick [reference]. In these circumstances it is only necessary to take into account in favour of the tortfeasor that this claim for damages does not arise, if no live birth occurs [references], or if the injury to the foetus has disappeared by the time of the child's birth and has therefore not affected the health of the newly born. It is also clear that the claim for damages only comes into being with the birth, irrespective of the conceptual ground on which it is based (see reference). Apart from this, the fact that the injury was suffered by the foetus before a human being came into being and before legal personality was acquired does not preclude the application of § 823 BGB. This cannot be doubted, not only if, for instance, the tortfeasor injures a pregnant woman intentionally or if the injury is caused by a professional mistake of a gynaecologist who examines her or of the midwife or the doctor etc., in the course of the birth, but also before its conception. The foetus is destined to enter life as a human being; it is identical with the child born subsequently, a fact of nature which the law concerning liability must take into account. Therefore an injury to the foetus becomes an injury to the health of a human being, at least upon birth, for which the tortfeasor must pay damages under § 823 BGB.

2. Nor do any doubts against the applications of § 823 BGB arise in the light of the legal system as a whole. In this connection it need not be considered that by the prohibition of abortion, i.e. of its destruction, criminal law provides a certain protection for the foetus. The fact that a mere injury to the foetus, which is in issue here, is not punishable does not exclude the view that a human being is protected in private law at least as far as a claim for damages is concerned, if an injury to his health is derived from preceding damage inflicted during his embryonic state. Even at that stage of his development he is exposed to dangers and to biological damage which result later on in injuries to his health in the meaning of § 823 BGB; he therefore requires protection. Private law protects developing human beings by numerous special provisions. It accords therefore with its spirit if for the purposes of the law relating to liability in tort developing life is also capable of being injured, with the result that the human being who is born subsequently has the same rights to damages as the person who is injured only at the moment after he has seen the light of day.

II. . . .

1 . . .

2 (*a*) . . .

   (*aa*) . . . If the Court of Appeal should have assumed that the damage alleged by the child was only a 'reflected damage' resulting from the injuries which the defendant has inflicted upon the mother, it would have been wrong in law. The claim for damages in issue in this case is a claim of the child and not part of the mother's claim for damages [references]. As regards legal liability, two injured parties stand side by side, with the result that each claim must be examined separately [references]. . . .

   (*b*) . . .

III. On the basis that the paralysis of the plaintiff child was caused by the accident, the consequences must also be attributed to the defendant.

   It cannot be doubted that these consequences are connected by a link of adequate causation with the accident for which the defendant is to blame. It is impossible equally to fault the view of the Court of Appeal that the defendant's negligence extended not only to the injuries suffered by the mother but also to those of the embryo and therefore of the child. This does not follow simply because the defendant is to blame for having injured the mother and is therefore liable for all consequential damage suffered by her. However, the child need not prove that the defendant could foresee the possibility of injuring a pregnant woman or an embryo as such. It need not be considered here whether this means that mother and child constitute a 'unit of life' [references]. It suffices to render the person liable who inflicted the injury if he should have realized the possibility of a damaging result in general; it need not be foreseeable what form the damage would take in detail and what damage might occur [references].

Notes to Cases 4 and 5

   1. For evidentiary and conceptual reasons Common law courts originally displayed a marked reluctance to sanction damages for pre-natal injuries. The evidentiary obstacles were primarily connected with the difficulties of establishing a causal link between accident and foetal injury. (Note the grotesque results in *Montreal Tramways* v. *Léveillé* [1933] 4 DLR 339 (Quebec) where club-feet, a congenital defect, were treated as the result of a traffic accident! For a more troublesome (and recent) example see: *Mulcahy* v. *Eli Lilly and Co.* 386 NW 2d 67 (1986).) The conceptual difficulties were connected with the foreseeability of the victim (in this case the foetus) and, more importantly, with its legal status which over the years has raised many conceptual, religious, medical, and philosophical issues recently highlighted further in the US by *Roe* v. *Wade* 410 US 113, 93 S. Ct. 705 (1973). Thus,

for the purposes of property, and particularly inheritance, the foetus has traditionally been treated as a person: *Estate of Trattner* 394 Pa. 133, 145 A. 2d 678 (1958). On the other hand, in criminal law the killing of a foetus has not been treated as homicide: *People* v. *Green*, 79 Ill. 2d 103, 402 NE 2d 203 (1980). (Can you think of any policy reasons justifying this different treatment? Which, if any, apply to tort law?)

2. The traditional hostile view of the courts can be found clearly expressed in *Dietrich* v. *Inhabitants of Northampton* 138 Mass. 14 (1884). One of the earliest decisions to make a break with this approach was *Bonbrest* v. *Kotz* 65 F. Supp. 138 (DDC 1946) which, interestingly enough, also referred to Justinian's *Digest* and Blackstone's *Commentaries* (ibid. 140). The change in other Common law jurisdictions came later. For Australia see *Watt* v. *Rama* [1972] VR 353; for Canada see *Duval* v. *Seguin* [1973] 40 DLR 3d 666; and for England see *Congenital Disabilities (Civil Liability) Act* 1976. Once again, therefore, German law blazed the trail.

3. *Todd* v. *Sandidge Construction Co.*, 341 F. 2d 75 (1964) can, in some respects, be treated as an equivalent to case 5; *Renslow* v. *Mennonite Hospital*, 67 Ill. 2d 348, 367 NE 2d 1250 (1977) an analogue to case 4. But see comments in paragraph 4, below. (Contrast, however, *Albala* v. *City of New York*, 54 NY 2d 269, 429 NE 2d 786 (1981).) Note also that whereas *Todd* permits recovery even where the foetus is born dead (so long as it was viable at the time of the accident), the German decision and the English Act (reproduced below) require that the child be born alive. Which of these variants do you prefer and why? (See Bryan J.'s views in *Todd* and compare them with Fleming's, 154–5.) On the 'born alive' requirement the American courts seem divided. Most have taken the view that live birth is not necessary for a wrongful death action. Thus *Volk* v. *Baldazo*, 103 Idaho 570, 651 P. 2d 11 (1983); *Dunn* v. *Rose Way, Inc.*, 333 NW 2d 830 (Iowa 1983). Others, however, probably under the influence of *Roe* v. *Wade* 410 US 113, 93 S. Ct. 705 (1973), have held that live birth is a prerequisite of recovery; *Hardin* v. *Sanders*, 538 SW 2d 336 (Mo. 1976); *Justus* v. *Atchison*, 19 Cal. 3d 564, 565 P. 2d 122 (1977). A number of recent decisions have adopted this position, often reaching this result on the ground that a stillborn foetus is not a 'person' under applicable wrongful death legislation. Thus: *Witty* v. *American Gen. Capital Dist., Inc.*, 727 SW 2d 503 (Texas 1987); *Milton* v. *Carey Medical Center*, 538 A. 2d 252 (Me. 1988); *Giardina* v. *Bennett* 545 A. 2d 139 (N. Jersey 1988)—criticized in 21 *Rutgers L. Journ.*, 227 (1989).

4. When comparing the American and German cases the reader should note that the issues of 'viability' and 'live birth' are often discussed in the context of who can sue. Putting the emphasis on 'live birth' means that the *child* that was injured while a foetus or because of an injurious act to its mother prior to conception can sue for its injuries; and this is the point

made in case no. 5. But if one accepts that viability at the time of the injury will suffice to give rise to a cause of action then two questions may arise: (i) the *estate* of the unborn child might have a right to claim pecuniary compensation survival action and (ii) its survivors might wish to sue invoking the appropriate Wrongful Death Statutes. To a non-American lawyer the first possibility appears little short of monstrous (cf. *Scott* v. *Kopp*, 494 Pa. 487, 491, 431 A. 2d 959, 961 (1981)), whereas the second, where it is allowed, represents a marked departure from English law which, through the medium of Lord Campbell's Act of 1846, originally inspired the USA. (Some American jurisdictions in fact go even further and allow punitive damages to be claimed under Wrongful Death Statutes. See: Moeller, 'Punitive Damages in Wrongful Death Actions', 39 *The Univ. of Kansas L. Rev.*, 199 (1990).) A further problem of such awards to the survivors of the still-born foetus is that they may be cumulated with personal claims that the survivors may have (for example for shock or loss of companionship) and thus, *in effect*, lead to double compensation. Most American courts (and law students) however, do not seem to accept this as a legitimate concern. (For further references to these points see Harper, Fleming James Jr., and Gray, *The Law of Torts* 2nd edn. (1986) iii. 677–80. See also: Kodilinye, 'Tortious Liability for "In Utero" Injuries', 3 *Caribbean L. Rev.* 122 (1993); McCavitt, 'The "Born Alive" Rule: A Proposed Change to the New York Law Based on Modern Medical Technology', 4 *New York Law School Law Rev.* 609 (1991); Note, 'Negligent Infliction of Prenatal Death: New York's Unrecompensed Injury after *Tebbut* v. *Vizostak*' 19 *Connecticut L. Rev.* 365 (1987); Robertson, 'Toward Rational Boundaries of Tort Liability for Injury to the Unborn: Prenatal Injuries, Preconception Injuries and Wrongful Life' *Duke LJ* 1401 (1978); Note, 'Wrongful Death of a Fetus: Does a Cause of Action Arise When There is No Live Birth?' 31 *Villanova L. Rev.* 669 (1986); Batchelor, 'The Expansion of the Viable Fetus Wrongful Death Action' 11 *Campbell L. Rev.* 91 (1988); Wilhelm, 'Protection of Prenatal Life through Wrongful Death Statutes', 15 *Univ. of Dayton L. Rev.*, 157 (1989).)

5. In the USA, the law concerning survival of actions and Wrongful Death Statutes is complicated. To an outside observer, the topic also appears to be inadequately covered in the law curriculum. The following summary may thus be of some use to lawyers who wish to compare the German cases here reproduced with their American analogues but find themselves confused by the somewhat sloppy use of terms by many State courts.

(i) When someone dies, his estate can claim the damages he could have claimed for the period he remained alive after the accident. In the USA this is commonly referred to as the 'survival action' and in England as the Law Reform Action. If the victim dies instantly, only funeral costs can be claimed. In the USA the claim for such expenses may depend on whether the estate was legally obliged to incur them.

(ii) If the injured person is compensated while alive and later dies, his dependants will not be able to bring a claim under the Wrongful Death Statutes. The same is true if the injured person allows his claim to become statute-barred or, otherwise, settles his claim with the defendant. In a very narrow area of American maritime law the position may be different. See: *Miles* v. *Apex Marine Corp.*, 777 S. Ct. 317 (1990); *Sea-Land Services* v. *Gaudet*, 417 US 573, 94 S. Ct. 806 (1974). *Gaudet* (allowing dependants of deceased longshoreman to recover damages for loss of companionship) nowadays applies only to *widows* of *longshoremen* who died in *territorial waters* i.e. within a marine league from the shore. The distinction between such cases and all other maritime death cases is so bizarre that it must indicate a good chance that the Supreme Court will overrule *Gaudet* when it next has the chance to do so.

(iii) If the deceased dies without having been compensated through his personal action, certain dependant relatives may have a cause of action under the Wrongful Death Statutes. This will depend primarily on the wording of the relevant (State) statute, whether it lists the claimants as proper dependants, whether it has mutually exclusive classes of beneficiaries, and so forth.

(iv) In England, compensation for wrongful death is governed by the Fatal Accidents Act of 1846 as repeatedly amended. Many American statutes, passed from about the 1860s onwards, are modelled on the English Act. With significant exceptions (see, for example, *Moragne* v. *State Marine Lines* 398 US 375, 90 S. Ct. 1772; *Gaudette* v. *Webb* 362 Mass. 60, 254 NE 2d 222 (1992)), American courts take the view that there is no Common law (i.e. non-statutory) right to recover for a fatal accident.

(v) In wrongful death cases, English courts have always allowed only claims for monetary losses. No compensation has been given for *dommage morale*, loss of companionship, solatium etc., though, since 1982 there is the possibility to claim a small, fixed amount for bereavement.

(vi) In some USA jurisdictions, the wording of the statute has been interpreted to allow bereavement claims. But since this is a question of statutory interpretation, this extension, though 'novel' to English eyes, cannot be regarded as wrong.

(vii) Some US statutes also allow punitive damages. The award of punitive damages to the dependants, even when authorized by statute, is, *de lege ferenda* very dubious.

Addendum: The Congenital Disabilities (Civil Liability) Act 1976

1 (1) If a child is born disabled as the result of such an occurrence before its birth as is mentioned in subsection (2) below, and a person (other than the child's own mother) is under this section answerable to the child in respect of the occurrence, the child's disabilities are to be regarded as damage resulting from the wrongful act of that person and actionable accordingly at the suit of the child.

(2) An occurrence to which this section applies is one which:

(a) Affected either parent of the child in his or her ability to have a normal, healthy child, or

(b) affected the mother during her pregnancy, or affected her or the child in the course of its birth, so that the child is born with disabilities which would not otherwise have been present.

(3) Subject to the following subsections, a person (here referred to as 'the defendant') is answerable to the child if he was liable in tort to the parent or would, if sued in due time, have been so; and it is no answer that there could not have been such liability because the parent suffered no actionable injury, if there was a breach of duty which, accompanied by injury, would have given rise to the liability.

(4) In the case of an occurrence preceding the time of conception, the defendant is not answerable to the child if at that time either or both of the parents knew the risk of their child being born disabled (that is to say, the particular risk created by the occurrence); but should it be the child's father who is the defendant, this subsection does not apply if he knew of the risk and the mother did not.

(5) The defendant is not answerable to the child, for anything he did or omitted to do when responsible in a professional capacity for treating or advising the parent, if he took reasonable care having due regard to then received professional opinion applicable to the particular class of case; but this does not mean that he is answerable only because he departed from received opinion.

(6) Liability to the child under this section may be treated as having been excluded or limited by contract made with the parent affected, to the same extent and subject to the same restrictions as liability in the parent's own case; and a contract term which could have been set up by the defendant in an action by the parent, so as to exclude or limit his liability to him or her, operates in the defendant's favour to the same, but no greater, extent in an action under this section by the child.

(7) If in the child's action under this section it is shown that the parent affected shared the responsibility for the child being born disabled, the dam-

ages are to be reduced to such extent as the court thinks just and equitable having regard to the extent of the parent's responsibility.

2. A woman driving a motor vehicle when she knows (or ought reasonably to know) herself to be pregnant is to be regarded as being under the same duty to take care for the safety of her unborn child as the law imposes on her with respect to the safety of other people; and if in consequence of her breach of that duty her child is born with disabilities which would not otherwise have been present, those disabilities are to be regarded as damage resulting from her wrongful act and actionable accordingly at the suit of the child.

3 (1) Section 1 of this Act does not affect the operation of the Nuclear Installations Act 1965 as to liability for, and compensation in respect of, injury or damage caused by occurrences involving nuclear matter or the omission of ionizing radiations.

(2) For the avoidance of doubt anything which:

(a) affects a man in his ability to have a normal, healthy child; or

(b) affects a woman in that ability, or so affects her when she is pregnant that her child is born with disabilities which would not otherwise have been present

is an injury for the purposes of that Act.

(3) If a child is born disabled as the result of an injury to either of its parents caused in breach of a duty imposed by any of ss. 7 to 11 of the Act (nuclear site licensees and others to secure that nuclear incidents do not cause injury to persons, etc.), the child's disabilities are to be regarded under the subsequent provisions of that Act (compensation and other matters) as injuries caused on the same occasion, and by the same breach of duty, as was the injury to the parent.

(4) As respects compensation to the child, s. 13(6) of the Act (contributory fault of person injured by radiation) is to be applied as if the reference there to fault were to the fault of the parent.

(5) Compensation is not payable in the child's case if the injury to the parent preceded the time of the child's conception and at that time either or both of the parents knew the risk of their child being born disabled (that is to say, the particular risk created by the injury).

4 (1) References in this Act to a child being born disabled or with disabilities are to its being born with any deformity, disease or abnormality, including predisposition (whether or not susceptible of immediate prognosis) to physical or mental defects in the future.

(2) In this Act:

(a) 'born' means born alive (the moment of a child's birth being when it first has a life separate from its mother), and 'birth' has a corresponding meaning; and

(*b*) 'motor vehicle' means a mechanically propelled vehicle intended or adapted for use on roads.

(3) Liability to a child under s. 1 or 2 of this Act is to be regarded:

(*a*) as respects all its accidents and any matters arising or to arise out of it; and

(*b*) subject to any contrary context or intention, for the purpose of construing references in enactments and documents to personal or bodily injuries and cognate matters.

as liability for personal injuries sustained by the child immediately after its birth.

(4) No damages shall be recoverable under either of those sections in respect of any loss of expectation of life, nor shall any such loss be taken into account in the compensations payable in respect of a child under the Nuclear Installations Act 1965 as extended by s. 3, unless (in either case) the child lives for at least forty-eight hours.

(5) This Act applies in respect of births after (but not before) its passing, and in respect of any such birth it replaces any law in force before its passing, whereby a person could be liable to a child in respect of disabilities with which it might be born; but in s. 1(3) of this Act the expression 'liable in tort' does not include any reference to liability by virtue of this Act or to liability by virtue of any such law.

(6) . . .

5 . . .

6(1) . . .

7 [This Act applies to England, Wales, Northern Ireland, but *not* Scotland.]

3. 'WRONGFUL LIFE'

Case 6

BUNDESGERICHTSHOF (SIXTH CIVIL DIVISION) 18 JANUARY 1983*
BGHZ 86, 240, JZ 1983, 447 with note by Deutsch
at 651; JuS 1984, 434, note by Fischer

The first plaintiff, born on 24 February 1977, is the legitimate daughter of the second and third plaintiffs (henceforth called the plaintiffs). The first plaintiff suffered severe damage to her health because the second plaintiff, her mother, had caught German measles (rubella) during the first weeks of

* English version by Kurt Lipstein.

her pregnancy. The plaintiffs charge the defendant gynaecologist with having failed to diagnose the mother's illness with the result that the pregnancy—which had been desired in principle—had not been terminated.

The child and her parents ask for a declaration that—subject to a statutory assignment—the defendant is liable 'to pay compensation in respect of all the damage which they have suffered or will suffer in the future as a result of the second plaintiff's infection with German measles during her pregnancy'.

The District Court dismissed the first plaintiff's claim but granted the parents the declaration which they had sought. The Court of Appeal of Munich rejected the first plaintiff's appeal and, upon the defendant's appeal, rejected the parents' claim as well [reference].

Upon a second appeal by the three plaintiffs the decision of the Court of Appeal was quashed in so far as the claims of the parents were concerned for the following

Reasons

A

The Court of Appeal has held that the claims of all the plaintiffs are unsubstantiated. In particular it has held:

I. Even if an error had occurred in the treatment of the patient, the defendant had not injured a protected interest or a right of the first plaintiff. It was true that according to a constant practice an act could result in damages if the party whose health had been adversely affected had not been born or not been conceived at the relevant time. In the present case, however, the defendant had not caused the injury to the first plaintiff; instead he was responsible for the fact that the first plaintiff was alive and enjoyed legal capacity. The foetus had no right to its abortion if only for the reason that, in so far as the abortion was legally admissible, the decision was that of the mother alone. Furthermore, the alternative between existence and no existence could not be expressed in legal terms of damage. Finally, by impeding an abortion the defendant had not violated a law for the protection of the plaintiff.

Admittedly the contract for treatment concluded between the defendant and the second plaintiff also exercised a protective effect in favour of the first plaintiff. However, the defendant's duty to explain to the second plaintiff the risks in the pregnancy itself and the possible injury to the foetus was only incumbent upon him in the interest of the second plaintiff.

II. In the opinion of the Court of Appeal the claims of the parents amount to a claim for a declaration by the second plaintiff in respect of non-pecuniary damages (owing to the difficult birth requiring a Caesarian 'wrongful *life*' actions have failed in all three systems—the decisions of the California Court of Appeal in *Curlender*, above, being the boldest. The issue finally came before the California Supreme Court in *Turpin* v. *Sortini*, 31 Cal. Rptr. 3d 220, 643 P. 2d 954 (1982) which disagreed with *Curlender* that damages for pain and suffering should be awarded to the child. The Supreme Court, however, was prepared to grant the child damages for special costs connected with its handicap. This could be seen as a step both forwards and backwards: forwards in so far as it represented a move closer towards accepting in principle claims for wrongful life; backwards in that it stopped short of considering the full consequences of such a move. This, plus a certain tendency to inflate where possible the parents' claims, may suggest that the move towards recognizing wrongful action claims is slowly but steadily gaining pace. Until that happens it is worth considering the arguments put forward against the recognition of such claims. (*Turpin* v. *Sortini* has now been followed by the Supreme Court of Washington in *Harbeson* v. *Parke-Davis Inc.*, 98 Wash. 2d 460, 656 P. 2d 483 (1983), the Supreme Court of New Jersey in *Procanik* v. *Cillo*, 97 NJ 339, 478 A. 2d 755 (1984) and cf. *Viccaro* v. *Milunsky* 406 Mass. 777, 551 NE 2d 8. The issues are discussed in a note in 71 *Calif. L. Rev.* 1278 (1983) and in the literature given above.)

(i) In *Gleitman* v. *Cosgrove*, 49 NJ 22, 227 A. 2d 689 (1967) the court refused to recognize claims for wrongful life on the ground that damages would be impossible to assess. This point was also taken in the *McKay* case, above. Do you think that it is decisive? Have not English courts for many years awarded damages for 'loss of expectation of life' (now abolished by the Administration of Justice Act 1982)? Do you agree with Kaus J. in *Turpin* v. *Sortini* above '. . . that there is a profound qualitative difference between the difficulties faced by a jury in assessing general damages in a normal personal injury . . . and the task before a jury in assessing general damages in a wrongful life case'?

(ii) A second reason which is often given is that the child/plaintiff has not suffered a 'legally cognizable injury'. This is often presented in philosophical terms, namely that 'impaired life' is preferable to 'non life'. A host of constitutional arguments, especially after *Roe* v. *Wade*, above, can be used to strengthen this point (see *Berman* v. *Allan*, 80 NJ 421, 404 A. 2d 8 (1979) though as *Procanik* v. *Cillo* admits *Roe* v. *Wade* also improved the mother's right to claim for wrongful birth; see also Stephenson LJ in *McKay*, 902), but do you really find them convincing? In any event, why should the court decide this question and not someone else, e.g. the parents, or the plaintiff himself wherever this is possible?

(iii) *McKay* also tried to justify its result in terms of 'duty'. True, in one sense it may be grotesque to say that a doctor owes the foetus a duty to kill it; but if such a duty can, under circumstances, be owed to the mother, why can it not be owed to the foetus? In any event, is not the duty language here demonstrating an unwillingness on the part of the judge to decide the real policy issues?

(iv) Alternatively, in cases with facts like those of *McKay* (foetus *already* infected by rubella; doctor negligently fails to discover it and to tell the mother who, had she known, would have had an abortion) one could argue that there is 'no damage'. (In this sense Weir in a critical note of the *McKay* decision in 41 CLJ 225, 227 (1982).) For damage is to make something worse, not to make *simpliciter*; and the fact is that in this case if the doctor had done his duty the child would not have been better, but she would not have been at all. (Weir's comparison of *McKay* with the defective premises case of *Dutton* v. *Bognor Regis* [1970] 1 QB 373 is, in conceptual terms, interesting if not convincing; but the analogy totally underestimates the human and philosophical aspects of the *McKay* type of case.)

It is difficult to deny that these arguments have some strength; equally it is impossible to accept them as conclusive. If that is so, could it be that at present the courts (and public opinion) are not yet ready to cope with this problem and are merely grasping at any argument or concept that is available? Would you be prepared to bet that, say, in ten years' time the law will still be the same?

3. In part 2 of its judgment the court states that in this case [it] 'is confronted for the *first time* [italics supplied] with the problem of . . . "wrongful life"'. This is not so, however, with claims brought by the parents—the so-called 'wrongful birth' actions which had occupied the courts before 1983 and several times since. (See, for example, BGH NJW 1984, 2625; NJW 1984, 688; NJW 1985, 2749; NJW 1985, 671 with note by Deutsch. For a comparative study of American and German law see Deutchler, *Die Haftung des Arztes für die unerwünschte Geburt eines Kindes* ('*wrongful birth*') (1984). See, also, Franzki, 'Neue Dimensionen in der Arzthaftung: Schäden bei der Gebursthilfe und *Wrongful Life* als Exponenten einer Entwicklung?' *VersR* 1990, 1181.) In fact the first such claim (brought by a distraught father against a *pharmacist* who negligently sold him enzymes instead of the requested contraceptives) was upheld by the Court of First Instance of Itzehoe (LG Itzehoe, FamRZ 1969, 90; VersR 69, 265. In actual fact there exists a strange case which can, probably, claim to be the first to raise the question of the cost of maintaining an unwanted child. Thus, in 1924 the Reichsgericht imposed on a mental institution the cost of maintaining an unwanted child conceived by one of its nurses who had sexual intercourse with a mentally retarded patient (RGZ 108, 87.). This decision was fiercely criticized but it was not until 1980 that the Supreme Court was given the chance to look at these problems in detail (BGHZ 76, 249). The

is either pending or about to be completed. As one would have expected, many of these statutes have been challenged on constitutional grounds (mainly for allegedly violating the due process and equal protection clauses of the Constitution) but, in the main, they have been unsuccessful. See, for example, *Hickman* v. *Group Health Plan, Inc.* 396 NW 2d 10 (1986). Very few States (e.g. Maine) have expressly refused to follow this trend and have enacted legislation allowing wrongful life and wrongful birth actions along the lines of *Procanic*.

Thirdly, in the USA these tort actions were, as is made clear in *Procanic*, greatly facilitated by *Roe* v. *Wade*. In the late 1980s *Roe* was progressively eroded by the prevailing 'conservative' climate of the day; and this, undoubtedly, assisted the passing of the statutes mentioned in the previous paragraphs. Matters, however, may again be about to change, though few can tell how such changes will affect this part of tort law. This, incidentally, is a (wider) aspect of American law which European lawyers (teachers and practitioners) tend to underestimate, often to their detriment. For changing views on, for example, such (*apparently* non-political) topics as *forum non conveniens*, can have important consequences for transnational litigation.

Addendum 1

The terminology used by the courts is not always clear; indeed some courts have condemned the use of the word 'wrongful' and have attempted to avoid labels altogether. See: *Burke* v. *Rivo* 406 Mass. 764, 551 NE 2d 1 (1990); *Viccaro* v. *Milunsky* 406 Mass. 777, 551 NE 2d 8 (1990). The (inexperienced) reader may also not realize that often many *different* claims are involved. The following may thus be of use:

1. *Wrongful life claim*. Action brought by the handicapped child; it includes among other things, a claim for pain and suffering and for extraordinary medical expenses.

2. *Wrongful birth claim*. Brought by the parents in the above-mentioned situation and includes claims for emotional harm and medical expenses. The cost of bringing up the child tends to be the major item of such claims.

3. *Wrongful conception* (*or pregnancy*) *claim*. Brought by parents for the birth of a healthy but unplanned child.

4. *Wrongful death claims* (known in English law as the Fatal Accident Acts claims). Brought, in England, by the dependants of a deceased person—in most cases the breadwinner. In the USA claims for *speculative* dependency are allowed, though sometimes the award is made to compensate the loss of 'future companionship'.

5. *Parents' personal claims*. Often the parents of an injured person (typically a child) have their own claims, for example for shock for witnessing (or more controversially) of being told of the accident. So-called 'loss of consortium' claims may be included in this category.

6. *Foetal injuries claims*. Typically to be made by a foetus once born alive.

Jurisdictions which do not require 'live birth', but content themselves with 'viability' at the time of the injury, may allow these claims to be brought by the estate.

7. *Pre-conception claims*. Claims made by a child for an injurious act (e.g. defective blood transfusion) to the mother prior to conception.

Though awards made under these headings may often be low (by US standards at any rate), the *total* amount for all or most of these headings may soon mount up. Litigants (and some courts) are not always aware of the danger of double compensation. Thus, despite frequent references to appealing ideas and attractive ideals, gold-digging actions are possible if not, indeed, frequent.

Addendum 2

Procanik by Procanik v. Cillo 97 NJ 339, 478 A. 2d 755 (1984)

I. . . . the complaint contains three counts. In the first count, Peter, through his guardian *ad litem*, seeks damages for birth defects and impaired childhood; in the second count, his parents seek damages for emotional distress and extraordinary medical expenses attributable to Peter's defects; and in the third count, his parents assert a claim for malpractice against their former attorneys.

The defendant doctors, Joseph Cillo, Herbert Langer, and Ernest P. Greenberg, are board-certified obstetricians and gynaecologists who apparently conduct a group practice. On June 9, 1977, during the first trimester of her pregnancy with Peter, Mrs Procanik consulted the defendant doctors and informed Dr Cillo 'that she had recently been diagnosed as having measles but did not know if it was German measles'. Dr Cillo examined Mrs Procanik and ordered 'tests for German Measles, known as Rubella Titer Test'. The results 'were "indicative of past infection of Rubella"'. Instead of ordering further tests, Dr Cillo negligently interpreted the results and told Mrs Procanik that she 'had nothing to worry about because she had become immune to German Measles as a child'. In fact, the 'past infection' disclosed by the tests was the German measles that had prompted Mrs Procanik to consult the defendant doctors.

Ignorant of what an accurate diagnosis would have disclosed, Mrs Procanik allowed her pregnancy to continue, and Peter was born on December 26, 1977. Shortly thereafter, on January 16, 1978, he was diagnosed as suffering from congenital rubella syndrome. As a result of the doctors' negligence, Mr and Mrs Procanik were deprived of the choice of terminating the pregnancy, and Peter was 'born with multiple birth defects', including eye lesions, heart disease, and auditory defects. The infant plaintiff states further that 'he has suffered because of his parents' impaired capacity to cope with his problems', and seeks damages for his pain and suffering and for his 'impaired childhood'.

In April 1983, while this matter was pending in the Appellate Division, Peter moved to amend the first count to assert a claim to recover, as special damages, the expenses he will incur as an adult for medical, nursing, and related health care services. In its opinion, the Appellate Division denied without prejudice leave to amend. Although this claim was not raised before the trial court and not considered by the Appellate Division, fairness, justice, and judicial efficiency persuade us to consider the claim for special damages.

The complaint, which was filed on April 8, 1981, contains two other counts. In the second count, Peter's parents seek damages for their emotional distress and for the extraordinary medical expenses attributable to Peter's birth defects. Before the trial court they stipulated, however, that they knew they had a potential cause of action by January 1978, nearly three years before instituting suit. The trial court ruled, therefore, that the parents' claim was barred by the two-year statute of limitations . . . Before us, however, the parents contend that their claim is derived from Peter's claim and that [the statute], which tolls the statute of limitations during infancy, protects their claim. Hence, the parents ask us to recognize their claim.

In the third count, the parents assert a claim for malpractice against their former attorneys, alleging that they consulted defendant attorney Harold A. Sherman, who undertook to advise them of their legal rights. Mr Sherman consulted with defendant attorneys Greenstone, Greenstone & Naishuler, a professional corporation specializing in medical malpractice claims. After conferring with Mr Goldsmith of that firm, Mr Sherman advised the parents on May 2, 1979 that they did not have a cause of action, and he never informed them that this Court had granted certification in *Berman* v. *Allan* on September 5, 1978.

In *Berman*, 80 NJ 421, 404 A. 2d 8, which was decided on June 26, 1979, we recognized that parents may recover for emotional distress for the 'wrongful birth' of a child born with birth defects. The defendant attorneys, however, never advised Mr and Mrs Procanik that they had a cause of action, and the two-year statute of limitations ran on their claim on January 16, 1980. The trial court did not rule on the attorney malpractice claim, and that issue is not before us.

II. In this case we survey again the changing landscape of family torts. See *Schroeder* v. *Perkel*, 87 NJ 53, 71, 432 A. 2d 834 (1981). Originally that landscape presented a bleak prospect both to children born with birth defects and to their parents. If a doctor negligently diagnosed or treated a pregnant woman who was suffering from a condition that might cause her to give birth to a defective child, neither the parents nor the child could maintain a cause of action against the negligent doctor. *Gleitman* v. *Cosgrove*, 49 NJ 22, 227 A. 2d 689 (1967).

Like the present case, *Gleitman* involved a doctor who negligently treated a pregnant woman who had contracted German measles in the first trimester of her pregnancy. Reasoning from the premise that the doctor did not cause the infant plaintiff's birth defects, the *Gleitman* Court found it impossible to compare the infant's condition if the defendant doctor had not been negligent with the infant's impaired condition as a result of the negligence. Measurement of 'the value of life with impairments against the nonexistence of life itself' was, the Court declared, a logical impossibility. Id. at 28, 227, A. 2d 689. Consequently, the Court rejected the infant's claim.

The Court denied the parents' claim for emotional distress and the costs of caring for the infant, because of the impossibility of weighing the intangible benefits of parenthood against the emotional and monetary injuries sustained by them. Prevailing policy considerations, which included a reluctance to acknowledge the availability of abortions and the mother's right to choose to terminate her pregnancy, prevented the Court from awarding damages to a woman for not having an abortion. Another consideration was the Court's belief that '[i]t is basic to the human condition to seek life and hold on to it however heavily burdened'. 49 NJ at 30, 227 A. 2d 689.

In *Berman*, the parents sought to recover for their emotional distress and for the expenses of raising a child born with Down's Syndrome. Relying on *Roe* v. *Wade*, above, 410 US 113, 93 S. Ct. 705, 35 L. Ed. 2d 147, the Court found that public policy now supports the right of a woman to choose to terminate a pregnancy. *Berman* v. *Allan*, above, 80 NJ at 431–2, 404 A. 2d 8. That finding eliminated one of the supports for the *Gleitman* decision—i.e. that public policy prohibited an award for depriving a woman of the right to choose whether to have an abortion. Finding that a trier of fact could place a dollar value on the parents' emotional suffering, the *Berman* Court concluded 'that the monetary equivalent of this distress is an appropriate measure of the harm suffered by the parents'. 80 NJ at 433, 404 A. 2d 8.

Nonetheless, the Court rejected the parents' claim for 'medical and other expenses that will be incurred in order to properly raise, educate, and supervise the child'. Id. at 432, 404 A. 2d 8. The Court reasoned that the parents wanted to retain 'all the benefits inhering in the birth of the child—i.e. the love and joy they will experience as parents—while saddling defendants with enormous expenses attendant upon her rearing'. Id. Such an award would be disproportionate to the negligence of the defendants and constitute a windfall to the parents. Id.

The *Berman* Court also declined to recognize a cause of action in an infant born with birth defects. Writing for the Court, Justice Pashman reasoned that even a life with serious defects is more valuable than non-existence, the alternative for the infant plaintiff if his mother chose to have an abortion. Id. at 429, 404 A. 2d 8.

More recently we advanced the parents' right to compensation by permitting recovery of the extraordinary expenses of raising a child born with cystic fibrosis, including medical, hospital, and pharmaceutical expenses. *Schroeder* v. *Perkel*, above, 87 NJ at 68–9, 432 A. 2d 834. No claim on behalf of the infant was raised in that case, id. at 61, 432 A. 2d 834, and we elected to defer consideration of such a claim until another day. Id. at 66, 432 A. 2d 834. That day is now upon us, and we must reconsider the right of an infant in a 'wrongful life' claim to recover general damages for diminished childhood and pain and suffering, as well as special damages for medical care and the like.

III. [1, 2] The terms 'wrongful birth' and 'wrongful life' are but shorthand phrases that describe the causes of action of parents and children when negligent medical treatment deprives parents of the option to terminate a pregnancy to avoid the birth of a defective child. See *Schroeder* v. *Perkel*, above, 87 NJ at 75–6, 432 A. 2d 834 (Handler J. concurring and dissenting). In the present context, 'wrongful life' refers to a cause of action brought by or on behalf of a defective child who claims that but for the defendant doctor's negligent advice to or treatment of its parents, the child would not have been born. 'Wrongful birth' applies to the cause of action of parents who claim that the negligent advice or treatment deprived them of the choice of avoiding conception or, as here, of terminating the pregnancy. See Comment, '"Wrongful Life": The Right Not To Be Born' 54 *Tul. L. Rev.* 480, 484–5 (1980); A. Capron, 'Tort Liability in Genetic Counseling' 79 *Colum. L. Rev.* 618, 630–57 (1979).

[3] Both causes of action are distinguishable from the situation where negligent injury to a foetus causes an otherwise normal child to be born in an impaired condition. See e.g. *Smith* v. *Brennan*, 31 NJ 353, 157 A. 2d 497 (1960); W. Prosser, *Law of Torts* § 55 at 335–8 (4th edn., 1971). In the present case, the plaintiffs do not allege that the negligence of the defendant doctors caused the congenital rubella syndrome from which the infant plaintiff suffers. Neither do plaintiffs claim that the infant ever had a chance to be a normal child. The essence of the infant's claim is that the defendant doctors wrongfully deprived his mother of information that would have prevented his birth.

Analysis of the infant's cause of action begins with the determination whether the defendant doctors owed a duty to him. The defendant doctors do not deny they owed a duty to the infant plaintiff, and we find such a duty exists. See *Berman* v. *Allan*, above, 80 NJ at 444, 404 A. 2d 8 (Handler J. concurring and dissenting); *Gleitman* v. *Cosgrove*, above, 49 NJ at 50, 227 A. 2d 689 (Jacobs J. dissenting). In evaluating the infant's cause of action, we assume, furthermore, that the defendant doctors were negligent in treating the mother. Moreover, we assume that their negligence deprived the parents of the choice of terminating the pregnancy and of preventing the birth of the infant plaintiff.

Notwithstanding recognition of the existence of a duty and its breach, policy considerations have led this Court in the past to decline to recognize any cause of action in an infant for his wrongful life. The threshold problem has been the assertion by infant plaintiffs not that they should not have been born without defects, but that they should not have been born at all. *Gleitman* v. *Cosgrove*, above, 49 NJ at 28, 227 A. 2d 689. The essence of the infant's cause of action is that its very life is wrongful. *Berman* v. *Allen*, above, 80 NJ at 427, 404 A. 2d 8. Resting on the belief that life, no matter how burdened, is preferable to non-existence, the *Berman* Court stated that the infant 'has not suffered any damage cognizable at law by being brought into existence'. Id. at 429, 404 A. 2d 8. Although the premise for this part of the *Berman* decision was the absence of cognizable damages, the Court continued to be troubled, as it was in *Gleitman*, by the problem of ascertaining the measure of damages. Id. at 428, 404 A. 2d 8.

The courts of other jurisdictions have also struggled with the issues of injury and damages when faced with suits for wrongful life. . . .

Even when this Court declined to recognize a cause of action for wrongful life in *Gleitman* and *Berman*, dissenting members urged recognition of that claim. . . . Extending through these opinions is an awareness that damages would be appropriate if they were measurable by acceptable standards.

Recently we recognized that extraordinary medical expenses incurred by parents on behalf of a birth-defective child were predictable, certain, and recoverable. *Schroeder* v. *Perkel*, above, 87 NJ at 68–9, 432 A. 2d 834. In reaching that conclusion, we discussed the interdependence of the interests of parents and children in a family tort:

> The foreseeability of injury to members of a family other than one immediately injured by the wrongdoing of another must be viewed in light of the legal relationships among family members. A family is woven of the fibres of life; if one strand is damaged, the whole structure may suffer. The filaments of family life, although

individually spun, create a web of interconnected legal interests. This Court has recognized that a wrongdoer who causes a direct injury to one member of the family may indirectly damage another. [Id. at 63–4, 432 A. 2d 834.]

When a child requires extraordinary medical care, the financial impact is felt not just by the parents, but also by the injured child. As a practical matter, the impact may extend beyond the injured child to his brothers or sisters. Money that is spent for the health care of one child is not available for the clothes, food, or college education of another child.

Recovery of the cost of extraordinary medical expenses by either the parents or the infant, but not both, is consistent with the principle that the doctor's negligence vitally affects the entire family. . . .

[4] Law is more than an exercise in logic, and logical analysis, although essential to a system of ordered justice, should not become an instrument of injustice. Whatever logic inheres in permitting parents to recover for the cost of extraordinary medical care incurred by a birth-defective child, but in denying the child's own right to recover those expenses, must yield to the injustice of that result. The right to recover the often crushing burden of extraordinary expenses visited by an act of medical malpractice should not depend on the 'wholly fortuitous circumstance of whether the parents are available to sue'. *Turpin* v. *Sortini*, above, 31 Cal. 3d at 328, 643 P. 2d at 965, 182 Cal. Rptr. at 348.

[5] The present case proves the point. Here, the parents' claim is barred by the statute of limitations. Does this mean that Peter must forgo medical treatment for his blindness, deafness, and retardation? We think not. His claim for the medical expenses attributable to his birth defects is reasonably certain, readily calculable, and of a kind daily determined by judges and juries. We hold that a child or his parents may recover special damages for extraordinary medical expenses incurred during infancy, and that the infant may recover those expenses during his majority.

Our decision is consistent with recent decisions of the Supreme Courts of California and Washington. The Supreme Court of California has held that special damages related to the infant's birth defects may be recovered in a wrongful life suit. *Turpin* v. *Sortini*, above, 31 Cal. 3d at 238, 643 P. 2d at 965, 182 Cal. Rptr. at 348. Following *Turpin*, the Supreme Court of Washington has held that either the parents or the child may recover special damages for medical and other extraordinary expenses incurred during the infant's minority, and that the child may recover for those costs to be incurred during majority. *Harbeson* v. *Parke-Davis*, 98 Wash. 2d 460, 656 P. 2d 483 (1983).

In restricting the infant's claim to one for special damages, we recognize that our colleagues, Justice Schreiber and Justice Handler, disagree with us and with each other. From the premise that 'man does not know whether non-life would have been preferable to an impaired life', at 369, Justice Schreiber concludes that a child does not have a cause of action for wrongful life and, therefore, that it is 'unfair and unjust to charge the doctors with the infant's medical expenses'. At 370 Justice Handler reaches a diametrically opposite conclusion. He would allow the infant to recover not only his medical expenses, but also general damages for his pain and suffering and for his impaired childhood.

We find, however, that the infant's claim for pain and suffering and for a diminished childhood presents insurmountable problems. The philosophical problem of finding that such a defective life is worth less than no life at all has perplexed not only Justice Schreiber, but such other distinguished members of this Court as Chief Justice Weintraub, *Gleitman*, above, 49 NJ at 63, 227 A. 2d 689 (Weintraub CJ dissenting in part), Justice Proctor, *Gleitman*, above, 49 NJ at 30, 227 A. 2d 689, and Justice Pashman, *Berman* v. *Allan*, above, 80 NJ at 429, 404 A. 2d 8. We need not become preoccupied, however, with these metaphysical considerations. Our decision to allow the recovery of extraordinary medical expenses is not premised on the concept that non-life is preferable to an impaired life, but is predicated on the needs of the living. We seek only to respond to the call of the living for help in bearing the burden of their affliction.

[6] Sound reasons exist not to recognize a claim for general damages. Our analysis begins with the unfortunate fact that the infant plaintiff never had a chance of being born as a normal, healthy child. Tragically, his only choice was a life burdened with his handicaps or no life at all. The congenital rubella syndrome that plagues him was not caused by the negligence of the defendant doctors; the only proximate result of their negligence was the child's birth.

The crux of the problem is that there is no rational way to measure non-existence or to compare non-existence with the pain and suffering of his impaired existence. Whatever theoretical appeal one might find in recognizing a claim for pain and suffering is outweighed by the essentially irrational and unpredictable nature of that claim. Although damages in a personal injury action need not be calculated with mathematical precision, they require at their base some modicum of rationality.

Underlying our conclusion is an evaluation of the capability of the judicial system, often proceeding in these cases through trial by jury, to appraise such a claim. Also at work is an appraisal of the role of tort law in compensating injured parties, involving as that role does, not only reason, but also fairness, predictability, and even deterrence of future wrongful acts. In brief, the ultimate decision is a policy choice summoning the most sensitive and careful judgment.

From that perspective it is simply too speculative to permit an infant plaintiff to recover for emotional distress attendant on birth defects when that plaintiff claims he would be better off if he had not been born. Such a claim would stir the passions of jurors about the nature and value of life, the fear of non-existence, and about abortion. That mix is more than the judicial system can digest. We believe that the interests of fairness and justice are better served through more predictably measured damages—the cost of the extraordinary medical expenses necessitated by the infant plaintiff's handicaps. Damages so measured are not subject to the same wild swings as a claim for pain and suffering and will carry a sufficient sting to deter future acts of medical malpractice.

As speculative and uncertain as is a comparison of the value of an impaired life with non-existence, even more problematic is the evaluation of a claim for diminished childhood. The essential proof in such a claim is that the doctor's negligence deprives the parents of the knowledge of the condition of the foetus. The deprivation of that information precludes the choice of terminating the pregnancy by abortion and leaves the parents unprepared for the birth of a defective child, a birth that causes them emotional harm. The argument proceeds that the parents are less able to love and care for the child, who thereby suffers an impaired childhood. *Schroeder* v. *Perkel*, above, 87 NJ at 72, 432 A. 2d 834 (Handler J. concurring and dissenting) *Berman* v. *Allan*, above, 80 NJ at 434, 404 A. 2d 8 (Handler J. concurring and dissenting).

[7, 8] Several considerations lead us to decline to recognize a cause of action for impaired childhood. At the outset, we note the flaw in such a claim in those instances in which the parents assert not that the information would have prepared them for the birth of the defective child, but that they would have used the information to prevent that birth. Furthermore, even its advocates recognize that a claim for 'the kind of injury suffered by the child in this context may not be readily divisible from that suffered by her wronged parents'. *Berman* v. *Allan*, above, 80 NJ at 445, 404 A. 2d 8 (Handler J. concurring and dissenting). We believe the award of the cost of the extraordinary medical care to the child or the parents, when combined with the right of the parents to assert a claim for their own emotional distress, comes closer to filling the dual objectives of a tort system: the compensation of injured parties and the deterrence of future wrongful conduct.

The final issue is whether the time-barred claim of Mr and Mrs Procanik may be revived as a claim that derives from the infant's timely action. At one time Mr and Mrs Procanik had independent claims for their emotional distress, *Berman* v. *Allan*, above, 80 NJ 421, 404 A. 2d 8, and for the extraordinary medical expenses arising from Peter's multiple birth defects. *Schroeder* v. *Perkel*, above, 87 NJ 53, 432 A. 2d 834.

[9, 10] The trial court ruled that the parents' claims were barred by the two-year period of limitations contained in NJSA 2A: 14–2. Although the parents recognize that their claim, if viewed as independent, is time-barred, they contend that the claim should be viewed as derivative from the infant's claim and, therefore, that it should not have been dismissed. In making that contention, they rely on NJSA 2A: 14–2.1, which pertains to a parent who 'has a claim for damages suffered by him because of an injury to a minor child caused by the wrongful act, neglect or default of any person . . .'. A parent in such a case may commence an action 'within the same period of time as provided' for the commencement of the minor's action. Just three years ago, however, in *Schroeder* v. *Perkel*, above, 87 NJ 53, 432 A. 2d 834, we declared that the parents' claim was independent from that of the child's. The defect in the parents' argument in the present case is that their right to recover is not 'because of injury' to their child, but because of direct injury to their own independent rights. Consequently, the parents' right to recover is not derivative from the claim of the child and is, therefore, barred by NJSA 2A: 14–2.

Our decision today recognizes Peter's right to recover the extraordinary expenses necessitated by his birth defects and also recognizes that the parents, even if they had instituted a timely action, could not recover a second time for those expenses. Finally, Peter's right to recover the costs of his health care is separate from his parents' claim for their own pain and suffering, and recognition of Peter's right to recover does not resuscitate the expired independent claim of the parents.

HANDLER J. concurring in part and dissenting in part.

[An interesting dissent which is not reproduced here because of lack of space but one which merits careful reading.]

Case 7

BUNDESGERICHTSHOF (SIXTH CIVIL DIVISION) 27 NOVEMBER 1984*
NJW 1985, 671

1. If an abortion undertaken on grounds of distress, including economic factors, fails by reason of the doctor's fault, he is in general liable to the mother for the maintenance costs of the child, as in the case of an unsuccessful attempt at sterilization.

2. The mother's claim will fail if she refuses to resubmit immediately to another abortion attempt which is medically safe and legally permissible, but not if she later refuses to have an abortion on other grounds, such as the medical grounds in this case.

3. The doctor is not liable if the mother changes her mind and makes a positive decision, despite the possibility of abortion provided by § 218a StGB, to bear the child to term.

4. A claim for damages for pain and suffering may lie in cases of failed abortion.

Facts

From 17 November 1978 the plaintiff, an unmarried professional woman of 35, was under the care of the defendant gynaecologist in B. On 19 December he diagnosed her as pregnant. After proper medical examination and advice Dr K, a specialist in internal ailments, obtained an abortion licence form and ticked the box marked 'Social Reasons' for a pregnancy in its second month. On 9 January 1979 the defendant undertook an abortion by means of curettage, there being a tumour in the womb, but apparently could not ascertain whether the operation was effective since the sample was insufficient for a pathological examination. On 16 January he made a manual examination of the plaintiff without discovering that the pregnancy was still continuing. On 8 February he again examined the plaintiff who was complaining of pains in the nether regions, and after palpitation attributed her increase in weight to growth of the tumour. He then gave the plaintiff a sealed envelope containing an admission order to the A hospital recommending an operation for 'uterus myomatosus'. Whether the plaintiff ever went to the hospital is disputed, but it is clear that she was not examined or treated. On 12 February she telephoned the defendant to say that she was again wondering whether to have an operation, and he told her to report to the hospital forthwith. The plaintiff, however, waited until the father of the

* English version by Tony Weir.

child returned from abroad, and only went to the G hospital on 2 March, when she was examined by the head of the gynaecological section. He found the pregnancy continuing—indeed, he said he heard the child's heartbeats—and confirmed the existence of the tumour. The plaintiff reported this to the defendant and after a further examination he again advised an operation, though whether for the tumour or also for an abortion is disputed. At any rate on 12 March the plaintiff signed a consent form for an operation. The next day, however, she went to a third hospital and sought out Prof. M who gave her a complete examination and advice on the whole situation, including abortion. She then went to the defendant's clinic but left the next day after refusing to have the operation. From 16 to 31 March she was treated as an in-patient by Prof. M. On 13 July the child was born by Caesarian section, and a hysterectomy performed. At first the plaintiff paid her sister to look after the child, but since then she has been looking after it herself with the help of DM 300 per month from the father. The plaintiff sued the defendant for the failed abortion and claimed the cost of maintaining the child and damages for pain and suffering; she also sought a declaration that the defendant was liable for any further harm.

The Landgericht granted the claim: the Kammergericht dismissed it. Then plaintiff's appeal was now allowed, and the case remanded.

Reasons

I. The court below did not determine whether the defendant could or should have known that the pregnancy had not been interrupted, because it was of the view that even if there had been medical negligence it did not cause the damage in issue. Essentially its views were as follows:

The principles applied by the Bundesgerichtshof in cases of failed sterilization were inapplicable to claims for unsuccessful abortions, which could only succeed if the mother's decision to terminate could no longer be carried out. Here the plaintiff could still have had an abortion on medical grounds. In any case the child was no longer 'unwanted' at the time it was born, which was a precondition of any claim. It emerged from a note by Prof. M on the treatment and advice given to the plaintiff that the plaintiff had told him that she had decided to have the child, seeing that in view of the state of her womb no subsequent pregnancy would be possible and she wanted to take her only chance of having a baby. So of her own free will she had changed her mind and decided to bear the child. The plaintiff could not claim damages for pain and suffering for at most the defendant had failed to terminate an existing pregnancy, and its continuation, though painful, did not make the plaintiff's bodily condition any the worse.

II. This is not altogether correct in law. Furthermore procedural errors vitiate the crucial finding that it was by reason of a change of heart rather than under the pressure of circumstance that the plaintiff decided to bear the child.

1. For the purposes of the appeal we must assume that the defendant was at fault in failing to discover that the attempt to terminate the pregnancy on 9 January 1979 had been unsuccessful, and in failing to proceed to a further abortion attempt in accordance with the plaintiff's continuing wishes and as permitted within the first twelve weeks by § 218a III and § 2 III StGB. Contrary to the views of the respondent and of the court below, such fault leading to the birth of a child whose birth should have been forestalled can give rise to liability towards the mother for the cost of maintaining the child and for damages for the pain and suffering attributable to the corporeal burden of pregnancy.

(a) The defendant had bound himself by contract with the plaintiff to terminate her pregnancy. As this Senate has already decided, a medical contract to perform an abortion not punishable under § 218a StGB is valid in law [references] . . .

It is a question of respecting the grave dilemma of the mother who, if the pregnancy continues, is faced with all manner of burdens affecting her socially, economically, and spiritually [references]. Thus abortion for social reasons is to be treated exactly like abortion on other grounds . . .

(b) If the permitted abortion fails because of the doctor's negligence and the child is born contrary to the mother's wish, the very risk is realized which the abortion was designed to avoid, for she wanted to shed the burden of bearing and caring for the child. When an abortion is undertaken for social reasons the cost of the child's maintenance is one of the burdens sought to be avoided. In such cases the protection afforded by the medical contract normally extends to the economic aspect. If the abortion fails by reason of the doctor's negligence the costs of maintenance are an attributable consequence (on maintenance costs resulting from the birth of an unwanted child, see BGHZ 76, 249 ff. = NJW 1980, 1450; NJW 1984, 2625). A failed abortion differs from a failed sterilization, in that it does not frustrate plans of a couple or single woman to avoid conception in the first place, but the result should be no different in law. A woman's decision to have a legitimate abortion is also a decision with critical implications for her whole future, and the law recognizes the state of conflict in which she finds herself. The doctor who agrees to perform the abortion engages himself to implement her decision within the limits of the medically possible, and if by negligence he breaches this contractual duty he will be liable in damages. The marital status of the woman is wholly irrelevant; what matters is the situation of conflict brought about by the prospect of a legitimate abortion and the medical contract to put an end to it.

2. The plaintiff's claim for damages is good notwithstanding that the father has met his statutory obligations by making maintenance payments. Such payments do not cover all that is needed by way of upbringing. The mother still has to provide care and attend to the child's well-being, services whose economic components are money's-worth. The situation is the same as where an attempt at sterilization has failed, and the principles laid down by this Senate as to compensation for maintenance costs are equally applicable here. It follows that the plaintiff has a claim for what she paid her sister over and above the payments made by the father while she was looking after the child. On other points relating to the mother's maintenance costs and the effect of the father's contributions, reference may be made to the principles laid down in BGHZ 76, 259 (269 ff.) = NJW 1980, 1452, from which one can deduce rules for apportioning the responsibilities between father and unmarried mother. There is no risk of double compensation, as the mother's claim for damages covers only her residual expenditures on maintenance. Whether the father has any claim for damages against the doctor, and whether § 218a StGB is designed to protect only the mother's interests, are questions which need not now be resolved, as no such claim has been made.

3. Nor is the plaintiff's claim affected by the fact that she did not immediately take the defendant's advice to have an operation for the tumour in February 1979. Admittedly if the failure of an abortion is discovered within twelve weeks of the conception the mother can be expected to submit to a second abortion attempt, if legitimate in the circumstances. There is such a disproportion between the unpleasantness of a second simple operation and the economic, social, and psychological problems whose prospect justifies an abortion on social grounds that it would be inconsistent and dishonest for the mother to claim damages for maintenance from the doctor whose error she should have helped to correct. But that was not the case here . . .

4. Finally the defendant cannot invoke the plaintiff's failure to undergo another attempt in March 1979 when she knew that the abortion had failed. Such an operation could no longer be on social grounds, since much more than twelve weeks had elapsed since the conception (§ 218a III StGB), but could only be on medical or possible eugenic grounds (§ 218a I and II no. 1 StGB) depending on the risk to the health of mother and child posed by the uterine tumour. Even if this method of avoiding the difficulties, fear of which underlay her original decision to have an abortion, were open to the plaintiff, nevertheless her failure to use it does not relieve the defendant, because his (assumed) negligence had now put her in a quite different decisional situation. The plaintiff was now in the fifth month of pregnancy, and had a quite different sense of the child as a new and independent life. Abortion was now not a fairly simple procedure performed *per vaginam* but

involved actual incision in the belly. These factors transformed the situation in which the plaintiff had to decide whether to have the child or not. She could reasonably feel that it was no longer responsible to do what she had been prepared to do in her distress at the outset of the pregnancy. Such an attitude commands respect and sympathy, quite apart from any possible differences which a scientist or moralist might find or suppose in the vital quality of a foetus after the first three months. The lawyer must concentrate on the pregnant mother and the factors germane to a decision whether or not to bear the child, as seen by her. If the plaintiff's decision to keep the child, although an abortion on medical grounds was still possible, was made, as she alleges, because an abortion now would be 'murder', it does not break the chain of causation between the defendant's negligence and the harm resulting from the child's birth, namely the cost of maintaining it.

5. It would be different if, after Prof. M had told her that she would never have a child unless she carried this one to term, the plaintiff had determined to keep it because she wanted one child at any rate. This was the finding of the court below. The legal basis of the defendant's liability would then collapse, for it is only for failure to prevent the birth in the interest of freeing the mother from distress that he could be liable. If she was ready to incur such distress because she wanted the child whatever the cost, the last thing she would want would be the protection due to her under the contract with the defendant. The link of attributability (*Zurechnungszusammenhang*) between the fault of the defendant and the burdensome consequences for the plaintiff, namely the birth of the child and the cost of maintaining it, would then be lacking. (On this and the question when a child is in the legal sense 'wanted' or 'unwanted', see BGH NJW 1984, 2625.) Unfortunately the finding of the court below to this effect is vitiated, as the appellants claim, by procedural error.

. . .

One must ascertain whether the plaintiff changed her mind and decided to keep the child for the reasons alleged by the defendant, whatever the ensuing economic situation. In principle it is for the defendant to establish the exceptional circumstances which might displace the normal link of attributability between the medical negligence and the harm in question. In the instant case, indeed, it may be that the uncontested note of Prof. M speaks so strongly for the defendant's contention that it is for the plaintiff, if she can, to weaken its inferences. It is for the court below to raise this matter with the parties and to elicit proper evidence. But the defendant's allegations cannot be regarded as uncontested.

6. The lower court's reasons for rejecting the plaintiff's claim for pain and suffering are also flawed.

(*a*) If any fault of the defendant in not discovering the failure of the abortion and in not proceeding to a timely second attempt led to bodily injury to the plaintiff a concurrent claim for damages in tort would lie under § 823 I BGB. The plaintiff's claim for damages for pain and suffering would then be admissible (§ 847 BGB).

(*b*) This court has held that a pregnancy and birth induced against the will of the woman can constitute bodily injury giving rise to damages for pain and suffering even if the case is physiologically straightforward and free from complications (BGH NJW 1980, 1452). It has also allowed such a claim where, as here, the pregnancy itself was due not to the fault of the doctor but to the decision or deliberate risk-taking of the mother, though only for pain and suffering in excess of that entailed in a natural and uncomplicated confinement (BGHZ 86, 240 (248) = NJW 1983, 1371). Furthermore the physical, and perhaps more importantly mental, anguish of a pregnant woman due to the continuation of the pregnancy, if attributable to the doctor's failure to terminate it in time, may in a particular case constitute an invasion of her corporeal integrity serious enough to justify an award for pain and suffering. Here the plaintiff has been through much physical and mental suffering, as is cogently witnessed by the series of medical examinations and treatments consequent on the failure of the abortion, the difficult personal decisions it rendered necessary, and the manifest and ever-present danger to her health. Even if the plaintiff would in any case have had to submit to an operation on the tumour, a fair award in money may be payable, contrary to the view of the court below, which fails to appreciate how much more the plaintiff here had to suffer than in a 'normal' pregnancy free from complications.

Notes to Case 7

1. In the (former) West Germany abortion was regulated since 1976 by §§ 218–219d of the German Criminal Code and was legal—broadly speaking—if: (*a*) the continuation of the pregnancy poses serious danger to the life or physical or mental health of the woman which cannot be averted in any other reasonable way; (*b*) the child is likely to be born with severe defects which would make it unreasonable for the woman to continue with the pregnancy; (*c*) the pregnancy was the result of an illegal act on the woman and (*d*) the pregnancy results in serious hardship that cannot be otherwise avoided. For a translation of the relevant texts see 27 IDHL 562 (1976); and for an excellent discussion of some of the issues see Mary Ann Glendon's *Abortion and Divorce in Western Law* (1987). On the other hand, in what used to be East Germany, a much more liberal regime prevailed until recently with the consequence that in practice the State met all such

expenses. When in 1990 Germany was re-united, the regime in the East was expressly retained in force by the re-unification treaties until such time as a new law were passed by the German Parliament. Such an Act was, indeed, passed in 1992, but the (mainly) Catholic Government of the State of Bavaria and 249 deputies of the ruling Christian Democratic Party immediately challenged its constitutionality. On 28 May, 1993 the Constitutional Court ruled that abortion was in principle illegal, though it allowed it to remain unpunishable if carried out during the first three months of the pregnancy and provided certain carefully laid down guidelines had been observed. Among these is the obligation to seek 'counselling' before the operation can be carried out, the purposes of such counselling being to try and dissuade the woman from proceeding with her plan to abort. The decision has sparked off a debate similar to that found in the USA (though, probably, not of the same intensity) and has fuelled the fear that its main effect will be to deny State funds to clinics carrying out abortions for the poor thus making them available only to those who can afford the $250–$700 that are usually required for the operation. The decision, thirty pages long and fairly legalistic in tone, has been reported in NJW 1993, 1751 and EuGRZ 1993, 229; and it has already spawned the first article by Hermes and Walther, entitled 'Schwangerschaftsabbruch—zwischen Recht und Unrecht' NJW 1993, 2337–2347.

2. The principal case shows that the cost of maintenance of the child can be claimed if the (failed) abortion was decided on for social/economic reasons. (The BGH has repeatedly held that in principle it is not immoral to sue for maintenance of one's own child: BGH NJW 1984, 2625.) Damages for pain and suffering may also be claimed. The case also considers the difficult point of whether—time permitting—the mother may be under an obligation to submit herself to a second abortion. The academic literature on all these points is divided. See, for example, Deutsch, *NJW* 1985, 674; Stürner, *FamRZ*, 753; Waibl, *NJW* 1987, 1513.

3. BGH NJW 1985, 2749 (also reported in FamRZ 1985, 1008 and JZ 1986, 137) raised a different issue. There the mother/plaintiff, who had had four previous complicated pregnancies, decided to interrupt her fifth pregnancy when she discovered it in the eighth week. The abortion was unsuccessful but by the time this was discovered it was too late to have a second abortion. The pregnancy was uneventful and resulted in a healthy child being born. The mother's claim for pain and suffering was successful but her attempt to obtain maintenance failed on the ground that the purpose of the contract (to carry out an abortion) was to prevent injury to the mother and the child and no such injury had, in fact, resulted. The same solution would have been reached if the purpose of the abortion was a eugenic one but the child that had been born was healthy.

4. English law, as well, has experienced difficulties with this topic. In *Scuriaga* v. *Powell* (1979) 123 SJ 406, a negligently performed abortion failed to terminate the plaintiff's pregnancy and, as a result, she gave birth to a healthy child. The court took the view that she was entitled to damages for loss of earnings, for pain and suffering, *and* for diminution of her marriage prospects. In *Udale* v. *Bloomsbury Area Health Authority* [1983] 1 WLR 1098, which had analogous facts, the mother was allowed damages for pain and suffering and discomfort but was denied damages for the cost of rearing the child until it was 16. The main reason for this was the metaphysical argument that it was impossible to value the life of the child in order to set it off against the considerable financial disadvantages that its unwanted birth brought to its family. On the other hand, a more recent English case—*Thake* v. *Maurice* [1985] 2 All ER 513—granted to the parents of a healthy child, born after an unsuccessful vasectomy operation, the cost of its upkeep. Adopting a reasoning which is very similar to that of the majority in *Sherlock* v. *Stillwater Clinic* 260 NW 2d 169, 174–5 (1977), Peter Pain J. held that the birth of a healthy child was not always 'a blessing' (p. 526). For an interesting (and more recent) decision from the USA see *Marciniak* v. *Lundborg* 153 Wis. 2d 59, 450 NW 2d 243. Realism thus seems to have prevailed over metaphysical arguments though, in the absence of a ruling from a superior court, the point cannot yet be regarded as conclusively settled. On this and related matters see: Grubb, 'Conceiving: A New Cause of Action?', *Current Legal Problems*, Special Issue, (1988) 121 ff.; Reichman, 'Damages in Tort for Wrongful Conception: Who Bears the Cost of Raising the Child?' 3 *Sydney L. Rev.* 568 (1985).

4. ECONOMIC LOSS ('CABLE CASES')

Case 8

BUNDESGERICHTSHOF (SIXTH CIVIL DIVISION) 9 DECEMBER 1958*
BGHZ 29, 65 = NJW 1959, 479
(with an approving note by H. Lehman in NJW 1959, 670)

The plaintiff was the owner of a factory. In September 1955 an employee of the defendant, a civil engineer, operating an excavator on the premises of M, an enterprise engaged in graphic work, damaged a subterranean power cable belonging to the electricity works in E, which led from M's works to the plaintiff's factory. At approximately 9.40 a.m. on 18 June 1956, another employee of the defendant excavating a pit intended for an oil-tank cut the cable once again at a distance of about 60 metres behind the previous break.

---

* English version by F. H. Lawson and B. S. Markesinis.

As a result production in the plaintiff's factory was interrupted until 6.30 a.m. on 19 June.

The plaintiff contended that the power cable, which from the place of the break onwards served only the graphic enterprise and his factory, was part of his enterprise from an economic point of view. The defendant, in cutting the cable had interfered illegally and culpably with his enterprise and was liable for the damages caused by the interruption of production. Alternatively, he contended that the defendant had failed to observe the necessary care for the safety of others. The defendant argued that the plaintiff's enterprise had only been indirectly affected by the cutting of the cable and that only direct interference would have rendered him liable. He also contended that he had exercised the necessary care in selecting and supervising his employees.

The Landgericht in Bielefeld and the Court of Appeal of Hanover allowed the claim. Upon a further appeal the claim was dismissed for the following

Reasons

1. The courts below both held the defendant liable in damages on the ground that by cutting the power cable leading to the plaintiff's factory with the result that the supply of power was interrupted, the defendant had illegally and culpably interfered with the plaintiff's established and active commercial or industrial enterprise. The Court of Appeal held the defendant liable on the basis of § 823 I BGB in conjunction with § 831 BGB in as much as the defendant had failed to produce sufficient evidence to exculpate himself. It also held him liable on the basis of § 823 I BGB alone for having failed to observe the required care for the safety of others (*Verkehrssicherungspflicht*).

The appellant objects against the treatment of the cutting of the power cable as an interference with an established and active commercial or industrial enterprise.

The appeal must be successful in the result

(*a*) The Reichsgericht has acknowledged in the constant practice that the right in an existing commercial or industrial enterprise is 'another right' in the meaning of § 823 I BGB.

As early as its decision RGZ 58, 29 it has regarded the right in an established and active commercial or industrial enterprise as an individual right which can be violated directly; any direct disturbance or interference with the commercial or industrial enterprise is, therefore, a violation of a right protected by § 823 I BGB. During the ensuing period the Reichsgericht at first accorded the protection of § 823 I BGB to an established and active commercial or industrial enterprise only if interference involved the *exist-*

ence of the commercial or industrial enterprise; that is to say if an enterprise was in fact obstructed, if it was alleged to be illegal, or if its restriction or closure was demanded; sometimes the Reichsgericht has expressed it in the terms that the bases of the commercial or industrial enterprise must be directly affected [references]. According to this practice, which was developed in dealing with problems of competition and boycott, acts which damaged the commercial or industrial enterprise indirectly only were not regarded as illegal acts in the meaning of § 823 I BGB. Examples are: if the person carrying on a commercial or industrial enterprise is only deprived of economic profit [references], or if the relationship with suppliers is affected detrimentally [reference] or that with the range of customers [reference], or, finally, if only the prospect of gain is diminished or endangered [references]. The protection of § 823 I BGB was granted in those cases especially where the termination of the commercial or industrial activity of another was demanded on the ground that the activity violated an industrial or commercial right protected by law of the person seeking the termination (design, patents), and it appeared later on that no such right existed, the allegation to this effect having been made falsely due to the objector's negligence at least [references]; further, e.g. if in the course of a boycott, clients had been prevented from entering an eating-house by picketing and by force [references].

The strict requirements for protecting the right in an established and active commercial or industrial enterprise were relaxed by the subsequent practice of the Second Civil Division of the Reichsgericht, the final indication appeared already in the decision of 7 June 1929 [reference] where an order of the local Sickness Insurance Office that no payments would be made for certain branded medicines was treated as an act endangering deliberately the commercial or industrial enterprise engaged in the production of the branded medicines, seeing that the full effect of the order of the local Sickness Insurance Office was to force the producer to curtail production. In its decision of 9 October 1934 [reference] the Second Division abandoned clearly the principle that *only* the existence of the enterprise was being protected and expressed the view that it sufficed to render § 823 I BGB applicable in making the law concerning trademarks and competition if a claim for damages was based on a culpable interference with the commercial or industrial activity of another. This was confirmed by the same division in its decision of 19 December 1938 [references]; the court stated there that in so holding it took into consideration that every owner of an enterprise could demand to be protected against illegal disturbances which prevented his enterprise from devoting its full potential based on the totality of its components and means employed, even if the disturbance did not threaten the existence of the enterprise as such [references]. The Second Division considered further [references] whether the same principle did not apply also outside the sphere of the law of competition and designs. In its decision of 3 October 1936 [reference] the First Division of the Reichsgericht expressly approved the view of the Second Division that for the purpose of applying § 823 I BGB a direct attack on the existence of the enterprise was not required where the commercial or industrial activity of another had been interfered with culpably (but see to the contrary the Fifth Division of the Reichsgericht [reference]).

According to the practice of the Bundesgerichtshof, the protection of § 823 I BGB is granted in respect of any interference with the right of an established and active commercial or industrial enterprise, if it constitutes a direct interference with the commercial or industrial activity, even if it does not involve competition and industrial property rights [references]. In the decision cited here [reference] it is stated that the right in an existing commercial or industrial enterprise—like ownership—must be protected by § 823 I BGB against direct interference not only in its substantive existence but also in its various manifestations, which include the entire sphere of commercial and industrial activity. This practice must be followed.

(b) In consequence of the practice of the court to range the right in an existing or commercial industrial enterprise among the number of 'other rights' mentioned in § 823 I BGB this right is placed on an equal footing for the purpose of protection with the other protected legal interest and rights enumerated there, i.e. life, health, liberty, and property. Therefore it must also be examined in the case of a violation of a right in an existing commercial or industrial enterprise whether its consequences, for which damages are claimed, are covered by the protection of the law (the decision of this division [references]). Admittedly in so far as the protection of an established and active commercial or industrial enterprise is concerned, the question is not unlike the above-mentioned fundamental judgment of this division regarding the limits of liability, as to whether damage complained of resulted from the violation of a protected interest, the safeguarding of which is the purpose of the law. The reason is that when § 823 I BGB was formulated, the legislature had not yet envisaged the protection of established and active commercial or industrial enterprises. In the present case, the question as to the limits of liability is therefore to be considered and decided mainly from the angle as to what is the object of protection accorded by the practice of this court to established and active commercial or industrial enterprises.

The notion of a commercial or industrial enterprise includes everything which in its totality enables the enterprise to develop and to operate in the economy. Thus it includes not only the premises and the land used by it, machinery and tools, furniture and stock but also business connections, the circle of clients, and debtors. The protection accorded and gradually extended by the practice of the courts to established and active commercial or industrial enterprises is intended to safeguard the enterprise against legal interference with its economic activity and functioning. Even if the Bundesgerichtshof in a previous decision [reference] regarded the individual situation in which the commercial or industrial activity is carried out as determining the extent of the area of commercial or industrial activity, nevertheless all the cases in which the Bundesgerichtshof had held that a right in an established and active commercial or industrial enterprise had been violated involved the protection of those characteristics of a commercial or industrial enterprise which are specifically its own. The objects of protection are the substance and the emanations of the commercial or industrial enterprise to the extent that they constitute its natural and characteristic features of economic and technical activities.

(c) Then as now, as the Court of Appeal has observed correctly, the interference with the sphere of the commercial or industrial enterprise must be direct if § 823 I BGB is to apply [references]. The plaintiff is wrong when he refers to the decision of the Reichsgericht [references] in support of a view to the contrary; it was held there only that to restrict the right in an established and active commercial or industrial enterprise to the protection of its substance was too narrow and that every culpable interference with the commercial or industrial activity of another was sufficient to render § 823 I BGB applicable; the requirement that the interference must be direct was not affected thereby. It is true, of course, as the Court of Appeal has stated, that the notion of 'direct interference' has not been defined by the practice of the courts. Baumbach and Hefermehl [references] point out correctly that the difficulties in drawing the line between direct and indirect interference are particularly great in the case of such a complex legal term as enterprise. Contrary to the view of the appellant the purely linguistic distinction between 'indirect' and 'direct' cannot yield the criteria for the necessary delimitation of these notions. The question as to when interference with the right in an established and active commercial or industrial enterprise is direct cannot be answered either by reference to the doctrine of causality alone, and the absence of so-called intermediate causes is also not decisive, as the Court of Appeal has pointed out in agreement with the practice of the Bundesgerichtshof [references; *contra* RGZ 163, 21, 32 where the court relied on directness of the causal nexus; similarly the Court of Appeal of Munich, 21 March 1956, NJW 1956, 1769]. The suggestion of Larenz [reference] in his note to the aforementioned decision of the Court of Appeal of Munich—upon which both parties rely in support of their legal position—does not lead to a sufficiently clear limitation of direct and indirect interference. Larenz argues that whether an interference is direct must be determined teleologically, i.e. in the sense that the act of interference must have the purpose of restricting the commercial or industrial activity, and that, consequently, the purpose must disclose the direction towards inflicting damage upon the commercial or industrial enterprise. Inasmuch as Larenz wishes to treat as 'direct' every interference with a commercial or industrial enterprise the purpose of which is, or at least could have been, to reduce or to affect detrimentally the difficulties become obvious immediately when the interference was due to negligence. Nevertheless it is not possible to agree with Baumbach and Hefermehl [references] that in view of the existing difficulties of delimitation the requirement that the interference must be direct should be abandoned and that instead the effect of the interference upon the sphere of activity should be decisive in favour of the retention of the requirement of directness [references].

The Court of Appeal, relying on the decision of this Division dated 14 April 1954 [reference] is of the opinion that the notion of directness was characterized by its objective. From this it concluded that a workable delimitation could be established in the case of intentional acts; if they were committed negligently it was sufficient if in the circumstances the act might have been intended to affect the commercial or industrial enterprise adversely and the person so acting had been aware of this consequence of his act, but had hoped that the consequence would not materialize. The Court of Appeal held that in the present case a negligent interference causing liability to pay damages had in fact taken place. This Division in the decision cited above has held that an act to constitute a violation of the right in a commercial or industrial enterprise must somehow be directed against the enterprise as such. For this reason this Division did not regard as illegal interference in a commercial or industrial enterprise the fact alone that one unfounded claim for the restitution of a parcel of land attached to the enterprise had been raised by a claimant seeking restitution under the Military Government no. 52, resulting in the administration of the land by trustees. The reason was that the attack was directed against the owner of the enterprise, but not against the enterprise itself, even if thereby it may have caused damages to the commercial or industrial enterprise indirectly. Similarly it is not an interference with commercial or industrial activities if as a result of injuries to persons an enterprise is deprived of the personnel which is indispensable for its operation [reference]. These decisions which require that in order to be covered by § 823 I BGB an attack must be directed against the industrial or commercial enterprise itself indicate the general approach of the predominant practice. It is to avoid an excessive extension of the right in an established and active commercial or industrial enterprise which would run counter to the casuistic enumeration in the German legal system of situations constituting torts. Voices have been raised by courts and in legal literature which advocate a return to the older practice of the Reichsgericht according to which only an interference with an industrial or commercial enterprise which affects its substance is to be regarded as an attack against an absolute right [references]. These opinions are clearly inspired by the view that, in the words of Lehman [reference], the recognition of an excessively broad general protection of commercial or industrial enterprise might easily lead to a surreptitious creation of rules.

Certainly the protection which was originally accorded only to the existence of a commercial or industrial enterprise was extended when subsequently the Reichsgericht and then the Bundesgerichtshof in a constant practice have held that every illegal direct interference with commercial or industrial activity constitutes a violation of an established and active commercial or industrial enterprise which is protected by § 823 I BGB even if the attack is directed not against its existence but against any one of its emanations. This does not mean that by the circuitous route of protecting commercial or industrial enterprises protection is being granted to contractual rights which, in contrast to absolute rights, only bind certain persons and are therefore not 'other rights' in the meaning of § 823 I BGB [references] or that economic aspects as a whole are being protected, although these are only given protection by the law of tort in special circumstances, e.g. by § 826 BGB; to protect either of these would be alien to the present legal system. In addition the need to enquire carefully in connection with the question of illegality whether, having regard to the principle of balancing the respective interests and duties, the defendant can perhaps rely on special grounds of justification [reference] has a restrictive effect. In fact the extent and the limits within which the right in an established and active commercial or industrial enterprise is to be protected must be determined precisely by an appropriate amplification of the notion that the interference must be 'direct'.

Direct interference with the right in an existing commercial or industrial enterprise against which § 823 I BGB provides a remedy is only that which is somehow directed against the enterprise as such, i.e. which is aimed at the enterprise and does not affect rights or legal interests which can be detached from the enterprise without difficulty. All the cases in which the Bundesgerichtshof acknowledged that a right in an established and active commercial or industrial enterprise had been violated involved interferences of this kind which were aimed at the enterprise. Just as an injury to an employer or the destruction of or damage to a lorry belonging to an enterprise is not specifically connected with the enterprise, the cutting of the cable by the defendant or his employee operating the tractor is not so connected either; the defendant's enterprise operating the excavator had damaged a power cable which apart from supplying power to the graphic working of M, almost by chance serves in addition the plaintiff's enterprise only, although it could equally well have been intended to supply electric current to other customers. Furthermore the supply of electric current by a cable and the right to receive it does not constitute a natural characteristic of an established and active commercial or industrial enterprise, but represents a relationship based on the duty to supply current incumbent upon the public supply undertaking, identical with that which connects, e.g. household and members of the professions with the electricity works. Consequently the fact that a cable has been damaged on land not belonging to the enterprise concerned resulting in a cut in the electricity supply cannot, in the absence of special circumstances which do not exist here, be regarded as an interference aimed at the area of operation of the enterprise concerned. It is true that when the defendant's excavator cut the power cable leading to the plaintiff's factory, the material and technical bases were already affected whereby the plaintiff could and did receive electric power from the electricity works in accordance with the contract existing between them. However this does not constitute interference with an established and active commercial or individual enterprise; to do so would exceed the range of protection accorded to commercial or industrial enterprises by the practice of the courts; instead the issue involves a violation of property in the cable belonging to the electricity works and of the right of the plaintiff against the electricity works for the supply of electric power, limited by the latter's general conditions of trade.

If, therefore, the plaintiff's claim cannot be based on a violation of his right to an established and active commercial or individual enterprise, it cannot be supported either, contrary to the view of the Court of Appeal, on the ground that the defendant had violated the required care of the safety of others [*Verkehrssicherungspflicht*].

Case 9

BUNDESGERICHTSHOF (SIXTH CIVIL DIVISION) 8 JUNE 1976*
BGHZ 66, 388 = NJW 1976, 1740 = VersR 1976, 1043

The defendant company, which ran a building enterprise, was on 23 November 1973 carrying out excavations on private property in the Württemberg town W. An electric cable was negligently damaged. This led to a 27-minute interruption of the current used in the plaintiff's manufacturing business. The plaintiff estimated that the interruption led, through a

---

* English version by F. H. Lawson and B. S. Markesinis.

failure of production, to a loss of DM 1157. The plaintiff claims that amount as damages from the defendant.

Both lower instances rejected the claim. The plaintiff is granted leave to apply for review, but is unsuccessful for the following reasons:

I. 1. The appellate court is of opinion that:

(*a*) The claim can find no support in § 823 I BGB; for not property of the plaintiff's was damaged or destroyed by the electricity failure. Moreover, no legal injury was done to the plaintiff's right of an established and active business, since there was no direct interference with it.

(*b*) Moreover, the appellate court rejects a claim for compensation under § 823 II BGB; for the defendant's contravention of § 18 III of the Baden-Württemberg Building Regulations (LBauO) did not constitute a breach of an enactment designed for the plaintiff's protection. The provision says: 'Public spaces, supply, run-off and warning apparatuses and also hydrants, survey marks, and boundary marks must be protected during the process of building and, where necessary, be kept accessible subject to the necessary precautions.'

In essentials the appellate court says: The language of this provision contemplates damage only to things, not persons. Moreover, the Regulations as a whole belong to the law of *public* security and order. § 18 III cannot be assumed to afford to electricity users a claim to compensation not otherwise provided for, all the more since it would lead to a great and intolerable extension of liability. It would also be consistent with the fact that § 1 II no. 1 of the Regulations affords no private law right to compensation where a similar accident occurs in the course of building in places open to public traffic. This reasoning is in open conflict with the BGH decision of 12 March 1968 about the corresponding regulations of Land Nordrhein-Westfalen.

It is against this reasoning (i.e., of BGH NJW 1968, 1279) that this appeal is lodged. In support of the appeal a question is raised whether, contrary to the principles laid down by BGHZ 29, 65 (74) = NJW 1959, 479, an interruption of electricity supply is not to be regarded as an invasion of the right of an established and active business, in the sense of § 823 I BGB.

II. The appeal is unsuccessful.

1. The Senate deciding the case agrees with the appellate court in holding that the plaintiff cannot invoke § 18 III 1 of the Regulations as a protective enactment for the purposes of § 823 II BGB. In so far as this runs counter to the principles of the aforementioned decision of the BGH of 12 March 1968, the Court rejects them. The decision of 12 March 1968 is not followed.

(*a*) [Earlier decisions elsewhere are in agreement.]

(*b*) There are convincing reasons for approving the appellate decision. That certain provisions of the Regulations, especially those for the protection of neighbours, can be treated as protective enactments for the purposes of § 823 II BGB does not stand in the way. For no such purpose can be detected in favour of electricity users.

(*aa*) The provision of the Regulations here in question is not an enactment for the protection of the plaintiff. Although admittedly most rules of a public law character operate in a general way to protect and further the interest of individual citizens, it does not follow that that *general* operation also specifies the cases where a protective enactment in question affords *him* an *individual protection*. That is not difficult to establish if the protective function of a rule can be detected in the statement of its purpose; but if, as often happens with recent enactments, the *travaux préparatoires* give only an imperfect indication or none at all, it is of no use to consider legislative purpose in the abstract: nor has this been done so far by the Federal High Court, despite some ambiguous formulations. In the last resort the question must be attacked directly, whether the creation of an individual claim for compensation appears meaningful, sensible, and tolerable in the light of the whole system of liability. Only by doing so can a development, rightly feared by the appellate court, be avoided, namely that the increasing tendency to base claims on § 823 II BGB might undermine Parliament's ruling *against* a general liability for purely economic loss. In this connection it may be useful to ask whether in such cases an individual claim for an injunction would be sensible and tolerable.

(*c*) There is no need to go further into these aspects of the decision; for it appears from what has been said that the appellate court properly decided that the Regulations afforded no individual protection to users of electricity against possible economic damage.

(*aa*) According to the basic principle of liability laid down by federal law there is, as a rule, no liability for indirect damage (economic damage that a third party suffers by mere reflex operation through injury to another's property); and this includes damage to an electricity user resulting from damage to a cable owned by an electricity supplier. That the failure to afford compensation is not felt to be intolerable is shown *inter alia* by the fact that the responsibility of electricity suppliers even for vital failures is excluded by regular nation-wide conditions of supply. Although the possibility cannot be absolutely excluded that this principle may be set aside by protective *Land* legislation, nevertheless, such legislation should be interpreted to extend protection only if the need for it arises from a

state of affairs in the law of the *Land* which could not have been anticipated on a federal level. Since that is obviously not the case here, the constitutional distribution of powers makes it unlikely that the *Land*
legislator wantonly intended to extent protection by action repugnant to
the federal rule.

(*bb*) But even apart from this constitutional aspect, based on the concept of constitutional demarcation of authority, the appellate decision
must be approved. There is nothing to be said for the view that the
Regulations, when regulating building, intended to afford to electricity
users an abnormal individual protection when a cable is damaged. The
appellate court rightly points to the lack of any corresponding provision
in § 1 II of the LBauO (*Landesbauordnung*), where danger to cables is
especially to be anticipated, that is to say, where works are conducted in
places open to public traffic. In other fields also electricity users have no
individual protection, for instance where cables are endangered in traffic,
mining, or agricultural accidents. The possibility that a building regulation intends to afford a protection so much out of line in this particular
field is very remote. The official statement of motives leading to the
Regulations here in question lends no assistance. Moreover, it is noticeable that the basic duty of care already existed in the general law and was
not originally created by the Regulations as part of *Land* law. Its inclusion in § 18 III only serves to sum up precautions required to be taken in
works regulated by statute, and to form a basis for prosecution. There is
nothing to show that an arbitrary individual protection was aimed at,
alien to federal law and as part of a generally inappropriate set of regulations.

2. The appellate court also appropriately rejects any liability to compensate
for an interference with the plaintiff's business. It finds itself in agreement
with the Senate decision of 1959 which dealt with a case on all fours with
this one. The Senate, on reconsideration, holds fast in principle to its decision in spite of some loudly expressed academic criticism. The need to
relate to a trade, as established by the 1959 judgment, which is denied in
cases such as the present one, is essential if the protection provided by case-
law in the event of a violation of the right of an established and active business is not to be enlarged into a general delictual rule for the protection of
traders. The highest court has always taken this point into account
although the boundaries of this 'residual right' affording special protection
to traders have never been fully defined and much could be said in favour
of a restrictive application of this delictual rule. In any event, matters cannot be otherwise in the case of a power cut of this nature which affects
everyone and which is liable to cause widespread financial loss to persons

who do not exercise any trade and to whom the general law of delict affords no claim for damages.

The above cannot be countered with the argument that where damage is caused by an electricity failure a distinction between physical and economic damage makes little sense. In fact the Senate has so far awarded damages for physical damage in business according to § 823 I BGB. This, it must be admitted, somewhat surprising limitation—von Caemmerer calls it 'crude'—rests on a binding general decision of the delictual law in force. It is impossible to recognize any reason for departing from it in favour of businesses. In any event, might not the danger of less foreseeable and perhaps much greater physical damage involved in such accidents justify a partial exemption of the tortfeasor from a risk that the electricity supplier frees himself from with state approval? But the present case affords no occasion for such an examination, since physical damage is neither manifest nor even doubtful.

Case 10

BUNDESGERICHTSHOF (SIXTH CIVIL DIVISION) 12 JULY 1977*
NJW 1977, 2208 = JZ 1977, 721 = VersR 1977, 1006

The defendant was carrying out earth removal operations required in the construction of an aqueduct and reservoir for the city B and the local water authority. In the course of the works a mechanical digger operated by one of the defendant's men damaged an electric cable which supplied several concerns. As a result current to the plaintiff's business was interrupted for 32 minutes, and the work of its 1385 employees brought to a halt.

The Landgericht and the Oberlandesgericht dismissed the claim for damages. The plaintiff's appeal was also dismissed.

Reasons

I. 1. The Court of Appeal held that the plaintiff had no tort claim under § 823 I BGB, since no legal interest protected by this rule had been invaded: in having to pay wages when no work could be done owing to the lack of current the plaintiff suffered a purely economic loss. The court also held that there had been no invasion of an established and operative business. Furthermore, no claim arose under § 823 II BGB, for although there was a provincial regulation regarding the safeguarding of electric cables during building operations (§ 18 III Provincial Building Ordinance of Baden-Württemberg—BadWürttBauO), it did not have the character of a protective law (*Schutzgesetz*) in favour of customers supplied from the national electricity grid.

* English version by Tony Weir.

2. This is perfectly in line with the decision of this court.

(*a*) This court has frequently stated the preconditions which must be met before damages are payable for affecting a business (BGHZ 29, 65; 41, 123; 66, 388, 393). Those principles involve the conclusion that the damage done by the defendant's mechanical digger to the electric cable was not an invasion of the plaintiff's business as such, since there is lacking the requirement of intimate connection with the business (*Betriebsbezogenheit*). In a similar case (BGHZ 29, 65, 74) the court said that the breaking of an electric cable supplying a factory is no more intimately connected with the business than injury to its employees or damage to its vehicles: it is not an essential characteristic feature of an established and operative business that it have an uninterrupted supply of electricity, especially as all the other customers connected to the same cable have the same legal relationship with the utility that supplies the current. We need not dwell on this point since even the appellant does not contest it.

(*b*) Although it had previously held otherwise (see, for example, NJW 1968, 1279), this court in its decision of 8 June 1976 (BGHZ 66, 388) stated that § 18 III BadWürttBauO (and the similar provisions of the building ordinances of other Länder) are not protective laws in favour of subscribers who suffer economic loss through a lack of current due to damage to a cable. Accordingly there are no legal objections to the view of the Court of Appeal, which evidently was unaware of that decision. Nor, indeed, does the appellant himself contest this part of the judgment.

II. The plaintiff also puts forward a contractual claim both in his own right and by assignment. The Court of Appeal rejected this. The underlying facts are that representatives of the parties had a meeting on site with representatives of the water authority and the city, that the plaintiff's business manager and the city representative drew attention to the presence of the main electric cable where the earthworks were about to begin and stressed how vital it was for the plaintiff's business, and that the defendant's clerk of works was then told that any digging in the neighbourhood of the cable must be done by hand rather than by machine. The Court of Appeal analysed these facts correctly, and its holding that the plaintiff was not drawn into the protective ambit of the contract of services between the water authority and the defendant cannot be faulted.

1. Case-law recognizes that persons not immediately involved in a contract may yet be drawn within its protective ambit, with the result that although they cannot bring a claim for performance, as would be the case if it were a true contract for the benefit of third parties under § 328 I BGB, they may nevertheless have a contractual claim for damages if they suffer harm owing

to faulty conduct by the debtor in breach of contract (on this see BGHZ 49, 350; NJW 1975, 344; NJW 1954, 874; BGH VersR 1955, 750; NJW 1956, 1193; NJW 1959, 1676; BGHZ 51, 91, 96).

The cases agree that whether third parties are to be included in the protective area of a contract when they were not involved in its formation and have not been expressly covered by the parties, depends on the meaning and purpose of the contract and its construction in accordance with the principle of good faith (§ 157 BGB) (see BGHZ 56, 269, 273); in the long run what is critical is not so much the relationship between the contractors themselves as the special relationship between the creditor and the third party whose inclusion is in question (see especially BGHZ 51, 91, 96). In order to avoid an intolerable extension of contractual duties of care beyond what the principle of good faith can demand of the debtor of the contractual performance, the court has frequently observed that the duties of care and protection can only be extended beyond the actual parties to the contract if the principal creditor (here the water authority) has some responsibility for the well-being of the third party, as owing him protection and care (see especially BGHZ 51, 91, 96; NJW 1974, 1189). This requirement, which is needed so as to avoid blurring the line between contractual and tortious liability in an insupportable manner and contrary to the will of the legislature, is normally present only when there is a legal relationship of a personal nature between the contractual creditor and the third party, such as commonly arises in family relationships, in employment, and in landlord and tenant cases (see BGHZ 51, 91, 96).

2. Contrary to the appellant's contention, the Court of Appeal acted consistently with these principles in holding that the requirements for including the plaintiff in the protective area of the contract for work between the defendant and the water authority were not satisfied in this case.

(*a*) In particular the water authority here was in no way responsible for the well-being of the plaintiff. For the contractual creditor, the plaintiff was only one of a large number of subscribers that might be affected by damage to the cable. As this court said in its judgment of 3 November 1961 (VersR 1962, 86, 88), contractual duties must not be extended in cases where faulty work or failure to take security measures could cause harm to people of all kinds—houseowners, tenants, entrepreneurs, and so on—for then the class of people protected by the contract would be unlimited and unenforceable. The mere fact that the plaintiff's business was apt to suffer a considerable economic loss through interruption of the electricity supply does not justify holding that the water authority which could itself suffer if the plaintiff was damaged, must look out for its well-being. Even if it be true that the contractual creditor had a certain interest in the safety of the cable, this interest was only a general one, and not one solely or predominantly related to the needs of the plaintiff for which the plaintiff could claim protection from the creditor.

(*b*) Nor can it be said that the meeting on site modified the contract of works between the defendant and the water authority. The water authority was bound to give such instructions before the work started in order to enable the defendant to take the necessary steps to protect the utility cables (including telephone cables—§ 317 StGB), and the special reference to the harm the plaintiff might suffer if the current were interrupted was insufficient to bring it within the protective area of the contract contrary to the principles already stated. It is important that at the time he concludes the contract, the contractual debtor should be able to see what risk he is undertaking, and this would be impossible if the creditor could later determine what third parties were to be included in its protective area by making a unilateral declaration to the debtor or to some unauthorized employee.

3. The Court of Appeal was also right to hold that the plaintiff had no assigned claim for damages from the water authority. The requirements of *Drittschadensliquidation* are not met (BGHZ 51, 91, 93 ff.). There is no special legal relationship between the plaintiff and the water authority, the defendant's contractual creditor, such as would justify holding that in law it was not the creditor but the plaintiff who suffered the harm. Only if, at the time of the wrong, the creditor's interest is vested in, or has passed to, the third party, does the party liable have to make good to the creditor what is lost by reason of the creditor's legal and economic relations with the third party. Apart from a few exceptional cases (e.g. BGHZ 40, 91, 100) this only applies when the creditor has contracted on the third party's account (e.g. BGHZ 25, 250, 258) or when the object which the debtor was to safeguard belonged not to the creditor but to the third party (as in BGHZ 15, 224). No such fact situation is present here (see also NJW 1959, 479). We need not now enquire what the case would be if the defendant contractor had undertaken by contract a specific duty of care towards the third party since, as has been stated, no such agreement is shown to have been made.

Notes to Cases 8–10

1. These cases represent one facet of the wider problem of compensability of purely economic loss which remains, both in German and Anglo-American law, a central topic of the law of torts: (i) because it impinges (as cases 15 and 19 also show) on the uneasy relationship between contract and tort and (ii) because the decisions on this topic show how judicial fashions change *vis-à-vis* the concepts used to limit liability for negligence. We shall

return to these more general points later; here suffice it to make a few general remarks about these 'cable cases'.

2. The factual situation is, typically, the following: A damages B's property and as a result C, (and, perhaps, others) suffer economic loss. Cases 8, 9, and 10 fall into this pattern and find an excellent English equivalent in *Spartan Steel* v. *Martin and Co.* [1973] 1 QB 27 and an American parallel in *Beck* v. *FMC Corporation and Niagara Mohawk Power Corporation*, 385 NYS 2d 956; aff'd, 369 NE 2d 10 (1977). A factual variant, raising analogous problems, is the following: A, a water company usually under a contractual obligation with a local authority B to provide water and maintain proper water pressures, fails to do so. As a result of this, firemen are unable to extinguish a fire that breaks out and consumes C's house. In all but four American jurisdictions C's claims against A are turned down, *H. R. Moch Co.* v. *Rensselaer Water Co.*, 247 NY 160, 159 NE 896 (1928) being, perhaps, the *locus classicus*. These negative results of Anglo-American and German law call for a comment, not least because they are in stark contrast with the attitude taken by other systems (e.g. the French).

3. It is interesting to compare case 9 with *Spartan Steel*, above, and discover the true reasons that lie behind these judgments. Which of these judgments do you find most convincing? How many of the reasons given by Lord Denning MR, whose judgment is extracted below, can also be found in the German decision? Zweigert and Kötz I, § 5, maintain that 'style' is one of the most important distinguishing features between Common law and modern civil law (though they do not specifically discuss judicial styles). How different do you find the style of: (i) the American and German judgments; (ii) the American and English judgments?

4. A policy factor which gets short shrift in these judgments is the insurance factor. The American water cases display an amazing ingenuity in utilizing every legal concept under the sun to turn down these claims while at the same time avoiding talking openly about insurance considerations. In these cases two types of insurance can be envisaged: loss insurance (which would justify the status quo) and liability insurance (which would argue in favour of a change in the law). Which of the two is cheaper and more efficient and why? A good discussion of the insurance factor can be found in 51 *Cornell Law Rev.* 142 (1965) and, most recently, in the decision of the Canadian Supreme Court in *Norsk Pacific Steamship Co. Ltd.* v. *Canadian National Railway Co.* [1992] 1 S.C.R. 1021 (extracts of which are reproduced below, pp. 223–64). The insurance aspect of the case are also increasingly considered by the German legal literature which seems divided as to whether a change in the law is desirable. For further details see Hagar, 'Haftung bei Störung der Energiezufuhr' *JZ* 1979, 53 and Bürge, 'Die Kabelbruchfälle . . .' *Juristische Blätter* 1981, 57. The two most thorough

monographs on the subject are by Hermann, *Zum Nachteil des Vermögens* (1979) and Taupitz, *Haftung für Energieleiterstörungen durch Dritte* (1981).

5. In England the attitude of the courts towards economic loss has vacillated in the late 1970s and early 1980s and, on the whole, the same can be said of other Common law jurisdictions like Canada, Australia, and New Zealand. The cable cases, however, in England have remained unaffected so one is forced to cope with some fine distinctions they have provoked and which can also be found in America.

One situation where recovery is allowed is where the plaintiff can prove that his economic loss is immediately consequential upon damage to property. Cf. *Newlin* v. *New England Tel and Tel*, 316 Mass. 234, 54 NE 2d 929 (1944) (USA); *SCM (UK) Ltd.* v. *W. J. Whittal and Son Ltd* [1971] 1 QB 337 (England); and BGHZ 41, 123 and, more recently, BGH VersR 85, 1147 (Germany). This distinction helps to keep litigation under control, but it is crude and it has not passed uncriticized. (See the powerful dissenting judgment of Edmund Davies LJ in the *Spartan Steel* case.) The comparison of two American cases, *Beck* (above) and *Dunlop Tire and Rubber Corp.* v. *FM Corp.* 53 App. Div. 2d 150, 385 NYS 2d 971 (1976), offers a good illustration of the problem.

In *Beck* an explosion in factory A (FMC) damaged an electric power plant B (Niagara Mohawk) which supplied electricity to C (a Chevrolet plant). During the power cut, C laid off its hourly-paid work-force, and refused to pay it. D, one of the workers, sued B for breach of warranty and negligence, and A for negligence. The contract-based action was dismissed on the convincing ground that D was only an *incidental* beneficiary of the contract between B and C. The tortious actions against A and B were dismissed on the ground that no duty was owed by either of them to D. The reasoning begs the question, but the court let the cat out of the bag when it said that any '. . . contrary determination would unduly extend the liability of this defendant to an indefinite number of potential beneficiaries'.

Dunlop's facts were slightly different, though the action arose out of the same incident at FMC's factory. In *Dunlop* the explosion in A, besides damaging the power company B, also caused stones and debris to fall on C's (Dunlop's) plant. (Dunlop was about a mile closer to the centre of the explosion that Chevrolet was in the *Beck* case.) C (Dunlop) sustained lost profits of $170,000 due to the power cut and a further $16,445 due to the power cut as well as the prejudicial effect that the explosion had on its machinery. With regard to the latter, the court felt that *Beck*'s case did not apply since C's claim was not 'vicarious or derivative' (by which the court must have meant ricochet). But is C's tortious action in *Dunlop* really different from that of D in *Beck*? Was *Beck* adequately distinguished, or was the real reason for granting the claim in *Dunlop* connected with the fact that it was closely linked with material damage? This crucial point is only raised as a secondary point by the court.

Dunlop's first and main claim for their purely economic loss was rejected. This time, however, causative language was used.

> Logically [said the court] if damage from the loss of power was foreseeable, then the interruption of production was also foreseeable and the lost profits resulting from the interruption should be compensatable, if proved and if, indeed, lost profits are recoverable at all in a tort action. However, while there is some limited authority that lost profits may be recovered [citations] such damages are subject to the general rule of certainty which requires that the plaintiff prove the extent of the damage and the causal relationship between the defendant's negligence and the damage.

And the court concluded: 'A stoppage in production . . . does not necessarily result in lost profits and the damage which a manufacturer may sustain for a 24-hour shut-down of electrical power may well be too remote and speculative to be compensated.' Can this reasoning be squared with that in *Beck*? The reasoning of the *Dunlop* court suggests that the floodgates of litigation can be controlled through the medium of foreseeability and remoteness. If that is so why use (as *Beck* did) the duty concept and frustrate recovery in *all* cases?

6. If distinctions are to be made what about the following situations?

(*a*) A damages B's cable which has been installed to service *only* C's factory. Can C recover? The point does not appear to have been decided in either England or Germany but an Australian case has given an affirmative answer. *Caltex Oil (Australia) pty* v. *The Dredge 'Willemstad'* (1976) 11 ALR 227. Here the floodgates argument cannot be invoked. Could this case be solved by applying Lord Goff's theory of 'transferred loss' or the Germanic equivalent of *Drittschadensliquidation*? (See discussion above, p. 187.)

(*b*) If A damages B's cable and C's molten material solidifies during the power cut *and* has *to be thrown away*, C has suffered material damage and can therefore recover damages for it (and for consequential loss of profits). But what if the solidified material can be remelted and used after the restoration of the power? A German court (OLG Hamm NJW 1973, 760) held that this was not interference with *property* since there was no permanent interference with its *substance*. The reasoning appears too abstract and conceptual, and perhaps it would be more convincing to accept that there is material damage. That the damage was only temporary should thus only influence the quantum of damages rather than the characterization of the loss as material or economic. On these points see Möschel, 'Der Schutzbereich des Eigentums nach § 823 I BGB' *JuS* 1977, 1, 5; Isenbeck, note on OLG Hamm in NJW 1973, 1755.

7. Case 9 also considers whether a claim can be based on § 823 II BGB (see discussion in text, Chapter 4). In the late 1960s the Supreme Court held that it could: BGH NJW 1968, 1279. The State Court of Appeals refused, however, to follow suit (see, for example, BayObLG NJW 1972, 1085; OLG Hamm NJW 1973, 760; OLG Saarbrücken VersR 1976, 176) and in the end forced the Supreme Court to recant. The answer, however, once again depends on unexpressed policy views about the issues. How else can one explain the fact that identically phrased statutory provisions have received different characterizations in Germany, Austria, and Switzerland? On this see the exhaustive treatment of Bürge in *Juristische Blätter* 1981, 57.

Addendum: Extracts from Lord Denning MR's judgment in *Spartan Steel* v. *Martin and Co.* [1973] 1 QB 27, 36.

At bottom I think the question of recovering economic loss is one of policy. Whenever the courts draw a line to mark out the bounds of duty, they do it as matter of policy so as to limit the responsibility of the defendant. Whenever the courts set bounds to the damages recoverable—saying that they are, or are not, too remote—they do it as matter of policy so as to limit the liability of the defendant.

In many of the cases where economic loss has been held not to be recoverable, it has been put on the ground that the defendant was under no duty to the plaintiff. Thus where a person is injured in a road accident by the negligence of another, the negligent driver owes a duty to the injured man himself, but he owes no duty to the servant of the injured man—see *Best* v. *Samuel Fox and Co. Ltd* [1952] AC 716, 731; nor to the master of the injured man—*Inland Revenue Commissioners* v. *Hambrook* [1956] QB 641, 660; nor to anyone else who suffers loss because he had a contract with the injured man—see *Simpson and Co.* v. *Thomson* (1877) 3 App. Cas. 279, 289; nor indeed to anyone who only suffers economic loss on account of the accident—see *Kirkham* v. *Boughey* [1958] 2 QB 338, 341. Likewise, when property is damaged by the negligence of another, the negligent tortfeasor owes a duty to the owner or possessor of the chattel, but not to one who suffers loss only because he had a contract entitling him to use the chattel or giving him a right to receive it at some later date—see *Elliott Steam Tug Co. Ltd.* v. *Shipping Controller* [1922] 1 KB 127, 139 and *Margarine Union GMBH* v. *Cambay Prince Steamship Co. Ltd* [1969] 1 QB 219, 251-2.

In other cases, however, the defendant seems clearly to have been under a duty to the plaintiff, but the economic loss has not been recovered because it is *too* remote. Take the illustration given by Blackburn J. in *Cattle* v. *Stockton Waterworks Co.* (1875) LR 10 QB 453, 457, when water escapes from a reservoir and floods a coalmine where many men are working. Those who had their tools or clothes destroyed could recover, but those who only lost their wages could not. Similarly, when the defendants' ship negligently sank a ship which was being towed by a tug, the owner of the tug lost his remuneration, but he could not recover it from the negligent ship, though the same duty (of navigation with reasonable care) was owed to both tug and tow—see *Société Anonyme de Remorquage à Hélice* v. *Bennetts* [1911] 1 KB 243, 248.

In such cases if the plaintiff or his property had been physically injured, he would have recovered: but, as he only suffered economic loss, he is held not entitled to recover. This is, I should think, because the loss is regarded by the law as too remote—see *King* v. *Phillips* [1953] 1 QB 429, 439–40.

On the other hand, in the cases where economic loss by itself has been held to be recoverable, it is plain that there was a duty to the plaintiff and the loss was not too remote. Such as when one ship negligently runs down another ship, and damages it, with the result that the cargo has to be discharged and reloaded. The negligent ship was already under a duty to the owners of the cargo, and they can recover the cost of discharging and reloading it, as it is not too remote—see *Morrison Steamship Co. Ltd* v. *Greystoke Castle* (*Cargo Owners*) [1947] AC 265. Likewise, when a banker negligently gives a reference to one who acts on it, the duty is plain and the damage is not too remote—see *Hedley Byrne and Co. Ltd* v. *Heller and Partners Ltd* [1964] AC 465.

The more I think about these cases, the more difficult I find it to put each into its proper pigeon-hole. Sometimes I say: 'There was no duty.' In others I say: 'The damage was too remote.' So much so that I think that the time has come to discard those tests which have proved so elusive. It seems to me better to consider the particular relationship in hand, and see whether or not, as a matter of policy, economic loss should be recoverable, or not. Thus in *Weller and Co.* v. *Foot and Mouth Disease Research Institute* [1966] 1 QB 569 it was plain that the loss suffered by the auctioneers was not recoverable, no matter whether it is put on the ground that there was no duty or that the damage was too remote. Again in *Electrochrome Ltd* v. *Welsh Plastics Ltd* [1968] 2 All ER 205, it is plain that the economic loss suffered by the plaintiffs' factory (due to the damage to the fire hydrant) was not recoverable, whether because there was no duty or that it was too remote.

So I turn to the relationship in the present case. It is of common occurrence. The parties concerned are: the electricity board who are under a statutory duty to maintain supplies of electricity in their district; the inhabitants of the district, including this factory, who are entitled by statute to a continuous supply of electricity for their use; and the contractors who dig up the road. Similar relationships occur with other statutory bodies, such as gas and water undertakings. The cable may be damaged by the negligence of the statutory undertaker, or by the negligence of the contractor, or by accident without any negligence by anyone, and the power may have to be cut off whilst the cable is repaired. Or the power may be cut off owing to a short circuit in the power house and so forth. If the cutting-off of the supply causes economic loss to the consumers, should it as matter of policy be recoverable? And against whom?

The first consideration is the position of the statutory undertakers. If the board do not keep up the voltage or pressure of electricity, gas, or water—or, likewise, if they shut it off for repairs—and thereby cause economic loss to their consumers, they are not liable in damages, not even if the cause of it is due to their own negligence. The only remedy (which is hardly ever pursued) is to prosecute the board before the magistrates. Such is the result of many cases, starting with a water board—*Atkinson* v. *Newcastle and Gateshead Waterworks Co.* (1877) 2 Ex. D. 441; going on to a gas board—*Clegg, Parkinson and Co.* v. *Earby Gas Co.* [1896] 1 QB 592; and then on to an electricity company—*Stevens* v. *Aldershot Gas, Water and District Lighting Co. Ltd* best reported in (1932) 31 LGR 68; also in 102 LJKB 12. In those cases the courts, looking at the legislative enactments, held that Parliament did not intend to expose the board to liability for damages to the inhabitants *en masse*: see what Lord Cairns LC said in *Atkinson* v. *Newcastle and Gateshead Waterworks Co.* 2 Ex. D. 441, 445 and Wills J. in *Clegg, Parkinson and Co.* v. *Earby Gas Co.* [1896] 1 QB 592, 595. In those cases there was indirect damage to the plaintiffs but it was not recoverable. There is another group of cases which go to show that, if the board, by their negligence in the conduct of their supply cause direct physical damage or injury to person or property, they are liable: see *Milnes* v. *Huddersfield Corporation* (1886) 11 App. Cas. 511, 530 by Lord Blackburn; *Midwood and Co. Ltd* v. *Manchester Corporation* [1905] 2 KB 597; *Heard* v. *Brymbo Steel Co. Ltd* [1947] KB 692 and *Hartley* v. *Mayoh and Co.* [1954] 1 QB 383. But one thing is clear: the statutory undertakers have never been held liable for economic loss only. If such be the policy of the legislature in regard to electricity boards, it would seem right for the Common law to adopt a similar policy in regard to contractors. If the electricity boards are not liable for economic loss due to negligence which results in cutting off the supply, nor should a contractor be liable.

The second consideration is the nature of the hazard, namely cutting off the supply of electricity. This is a hazard which we all run. It may be due to a short circuit, to a flash of lightning, to a tree falling in the wires, to an accidental cutting of the cable, or even to the negligence of someone or other. And when it does happen, it affects a multitude of persons: not as a rule by way of physical damage to them or their property, but by putting them to inconvenience, and sometimes to economic loss. The supply is usually restored in a few hours, so the economic loss is not very large. Such a hazard is regarded by most people as a thing they must put up with—without seeking compensation from anyone. Some the e are who install a stand-by system. Others seek refuge by taking out an insurance policy against breakdown in the supply. But most people are content to take the risk on themselves. When the supply is cut off, they do not go running round to their solicitor. They do not try to find out whether it was anyone's fault. They just put up with it. They try to make up the economic loss by doing more work next day. This is a healthy attitude which the law should encourage.

The third consideration is this: if claims for economic loss were permitted for this particular hazard, there would be no end of claims. Some might be genuine, but many might be inflated, or even false. A machine might not have been in use anyway, but it would be easy to put it down to the cut in supply. It would be wellnigh impossible to check the claims. If there was economic loss on one day, did the claimant do his best to mitigate it by working harder next day? And so forth. Rather than expose claimants to such temptation and defendants to such hard labour—on comparatively small claims—it is better to disallow economic loss altogether, at any rate when it stands alone, independent of any physical damage.

The fourth consideration is that, in such a hazard as this, the risk of economic loss should be suffered by the whole community who suffer the losses—usually many but comparatively small losses—rather than on the one pair of shoulders, that is, on the contractor on whom the total of them, all added together, might be very heavy.

The fifth consideration is that the law provides for deserving cases. If the defendant is guilty of negligence which cuts off the electricity supply and causes actual physical damage to person or property, that physical damage can be recovered: see *Baker* v. *Crow Carrying Co. Ltd.* (unreported) 1 February 1960; Bar Library

Transcript No. 45, referred to by Buckley LJ in *SCM (UK) Ltd.* v. *W. J. Whittall and Son Ltd.* [1971] 1 QB 337, 356; and also any economic loss truly consequential on the material damage; see *British Celanese Ltd.* v. *A. H. Hunt (Capacitors) Ltd.* [1969] 1 WLR 959 and *SCM (UK) Ltd.* v. *W. J. Whittall and Son Ltd.* [1971] 1 QB 337. Such cases will be comparatively few. They will be readily capable of proof and will be easily checked. They should be and are admitted.

These considerations lead me to the conclusion that the plaintiffs should recover for the physical damage to the one melt (£368), and the loss of profit on that melt consequent thereon (£400): but not for the loss of profit on the four melts (£1,767), because that was economic loss independent of the physical damage.

5. ECONOMIC LOSS (LOSS OF USE; OTHER POSSIBLE HEADINGS)

Case 11

BUNDESGERICHTSHOF (SECOND CIVIL DIVISION) 21 DECEMBER 1970*
BGHZ 55, 153 = NJW 1971, 886 = VersR 1971, 418

The defendant Federal Republic of Germany was the owner of a navigable channel which connected a mill with the port of B. During the night of 21 October 1965 part of the wall forming the bank collapsed bringing down part of the external wall of a dwelling-house based on it. In order to prevent a further collapse of the house, its owner, acting in accordance with an order of the competent authority, the City of B inserted beams as support. Two of these were inserted between the two banks of the channel immediately upon its surface. Thus the channel was effectively closed until the bank of the channel was provisionally restored during the middle of 1966. As a result the plaintiff's motor vessel *Christel* was immobilized at the mill; nor could the plaintiff approach the mill with his other vessels, as he was contractually bound to do, in order to carry goods to and from the mill. He claimed damages amounting to DM 31,061 for loss of earnings.

The Landgericht Stade and the Court of Appeal of Celle allowed the claim. Upon a second appeal, the claim was rejected in part for the following

Reasons

I. . . .

II. . . .

1. The Court of Appeal is correct in holding that the case of a culpable violation of the duty incumbent upon the defendant by its constitutionally appointed organs to maintain the channel, § 823 I, §§ 89, 31 BGB must be

---

* English version by F. H. Lawson and B. S. Markesinis.

considered as forming the basis of the claim, and not, as the appellant contends § 839 BGB in conjunction with Art. 34 of the Federal Constitution (GG) . . .

Prior to and at the time of the collapse of the wall forming the bank the duty to maintain it was vested (by State) in a particular authority. The culpable violation of this duty gives rise to claims under § 823 I BGB [references] . . .

2. . . . it follows from the existing duties of the defendant [references] to keep the channel open to navigation that it is also obliged to prevent the threatening collapse of the wall of the channel by suitable safety measures which the owner must tolerate . . .

In the special circumstances the duty of the defendant to secure the navigability of the channel included not only the duty to restore it when obstructed or rendered impassable, but also the duty to remedy by suitable measures any immediate danger which endangered the navigability of the channel owing to the state of the walls or the banks.

3. As the Court of Appeal has held with justification, the authority constitutionally appointed by the defendant has culpably violated this duty . . .

The appellant is wrong in contending that the culpable violation of this duty was the adequate causation for the closure of the channel and therefore for the losses of the plaintiff resulting therefrom. It is true that the immediate cause for closure of the channel was the order of the city of B of 22 October 1965 and the propping-up of the house, street no. 10 in the execution of this order. Both were only the adequate consequence of the preceding violation of the duty incumbent upon the authority constitutionally appointed by the defendant. For it is not outside common experience that the failure to secure a defective wall of a bank which supports an external wall of a building, can lead to consequences of this kind.

4. The Court of Appeal denies that the provisions concerning the duty to maintain a waterway constitute a protective law in the meaning of § 823 II BGB. This is correct in law [references]. Nevertheless it holds the defendant liable in damages for the loss incurred by the plaintiff through the closure of the channel because the conduct of its constitutionally appointed organ in violation of its duty is to be regarded as an inadmissible interference with an established and active commercial or industrial enterprise. This reasoning, and partly also the result, are open to legal doubts.

(a) Liability based on interference with the right to an established and active commercial or industrial enterprise is subsidiary in character and is incurred only if no other remedy exists, and if the rules in force governing a certain topic viewed as a whole disclose the existence of a gap, which must be closed with the help of § 823 I BGB [reference]. An examination of the case from this angle leads to the following conclusions.

As regards the plaintiff's motor vessel *Christel*, any claim for damages on the ground of interference with a right to an established and active commercial or industrial enterprise is ruled out to the extent that damage to property has occurred which leads to loss. For property is damaged not only if the substance of an object is adversely affected but also by any other actual interference with the right of an owner [references]. In the present case property of the plaintiff in the motor vessel *Christel* has been damaged inasmuch as the vessel was forced to remain at the loading stage of the mill because the channel was closed. It was consequently unable to move beyond that area of the channel between the loading-stage and the beams which formed a bar. It was therefore practically eliminated as a means of transport and was incapable of normal use. The 'imprisonment' of the vessel therefore constituted a factual interference with this vessel which affected the rights of the plaintiff as an owner. In denying an interference with property in a similar case the Reichsgericht [reference], contrary to the present Division, clearly proceeded from the assumption that an interference with property in the meaning of § 823 I BGB can exist only in an interference with the substance of an object, but not in any other kind of interference [reference]. Such a narrow interpretation of § 823 I BGB does not, however, accord with the purpose of this provision. This is to protect the rights enumerated therein against any culpable illegal violation. The defendant, who is responsible for the conduct of its constitutionally appointed representative (§§ 89, 31 BGB), who, in violating its duty caused damage, is therefore liable to pay compensation to the plaintiff for the damage arising from the 'imprisonment' of the motor vessel *Christel*: § 823 I BGB. To this extent any liability of the defendant is excluded on the ground of illegal culpable interference with the rights of the plaintiff in an established and active commercial or industrial enterprise. Moreover it must remain undecided as to whether any such interference has taken place at all.

As regards the claim for damages in respect of the river boats which could not use the channel the answer must be different. To this extent the defendant has not interfered with the property of the plaintiff for the reason that the river-boats were not affected in their capacity of means of transport by the closure of the channel and were thus not diverted from their natural use. This conclusion is not altered by the fact that the plaintiff was unable to dispatch the river-boats to the loading-stage of the mill while the channel was closed. This cannot be regarded as an interference with property, but is a restriction of the plaintiff in the enjoyment of the common use of the channel together with all others who engage in shipping.

Such common use is not, however, 'another right' in the meaning of § 823 I BGB [reference].

(*b*) Therefore the question as to whether the violation of their duty by the constitutionally appointed authority is to be regarded as an inadmissible interference with an established and active commercial or industrial enterprise is only relevant in respect of the plaintiff's claim for damages arising out of the closure of the channel. This court disagrees with the Court of Appeal which answered the question in the affirmative. The appellant is, however, wrong in arguing that in the present no right of the plaintiff in an established and active commercial or industrial enterprise has been violated if only for the reason that such a violation cannot be committed by an omission. The rights and legal interest which are protected by § 823 I BGB can also be violated through an omission [reference]. The appellant is right, however, in contending that the observations of the Court of Appeal as to whether in the present case the defendant has directly interfered with the plaintiff's established and active commercial or industrial enterprise is not open to legal objections, at least in so far as they concern the amount of damages in issue.

It is recognized by the practice of the courts that not every illegal and culpable interference with the business activity of another gives rise to claims for damages in accordance with § 823 I BGB. Instead, this is only the case if the interference touches directly the sphere of the commercial or industrial enterprise, therefore centred on the enterprise and does not affect rights or protected interests which can be separated without difficulty from the commercial or industrial enterprise [references]. In the present case no such interference aimed at the plaintiff's enterprise has taken place. The navigability of a waterway does not fall within the ambit of the commercial enterprise of a person engaged in shipping. A temporary closure of a waterway which also concerns others engaged in shipping does not therefore interfere with the plaintiff's commercial enterprise. The Court of Appeal wishes to come to a different conclusion in the present case on the ground that the plaintiff's vessels had used the channel, before its closure, more than others engaged in shipping—at times almost exclusively—and that the closure has temporarily prevented the plaintiff from complying with his contractual obligations towards the mill; but this reasoning cannot be accepted. The existence of such obligations does not mean that the navigability of a waterway, which a person engaged in shipping has to use within the framework of his contractual obligations, is to be regarded as falling within the sphere of that person's commercial enterprises. The contrary opinion of the Court of Appeal cannot be supported either by the consideration that at the time when the river-wall collapsed the journeys of the plaintiff's vessel on behalf of the mill represented an important part of the plaintiff's commercial activities. The question as to what falls within the commercial enterprise of a person engaged in shipping cannot be determined by the fact that one or several of his vessels are principally employed on certain river routes, seeing that this depends on the offers to load them made by third parties. The Court of Appeal is therefore wrong in holding that in the present case the defendant is liable to pay damages for having interfered with the plaintiff's established and active commercial enterprise also in so far as he could not for a time use the channel for his vessels. If this opinion were accepted it would mean that common users would be protected under the heading of 'any other rights' of § 823 I BGB, if only by the circuitous route of a right in an established and active commercial or industrial enterprise.

It follows that the judgment appealed against is only to be upheld to the extent that it declares the plaintiff's claim arising out of the 'imprisonment' of the motor vessel *Christel* to be justified (DM 24,086). The additional claim (DM 6965) must be dismissed.

Case 12

BUNDESGERICHTSHOF (SIXTH CIVIL DIVISION) 21 JUNE 1977*
NJW 1977, 2264 = VersR 1977, 965

The defendant was the liquidator in the bankruptcy of a limited partnership and of its deceased partner D who was personally liable. The partnership had conducted the business of a major petrol depot. In May 1972, a motorized petrol tanker belonging to a third party attended the depot in order to take on petrol. Owing to the negligence of the tanker's driver, a fire broke out, but the partnership as owners of the premises and the deceased partner were also to be blamed for having failed to prevent the negligent handling of the loading process by the driver of the tanker. Fearing that the fire might spread to the depot as a whole, the police ordered the temporary closure of the plaintiff's business premises for two hours and blocked for another three hours the access roads in order to keep them clear for the fire brigade. The plaintiff, on whose premises work had stopped for five hours, claimed damages representing wages paid and general expenses incurred in respect of the period of closure. He sued the defendant, the owner of the tanker and his employee.

The Court of First Instance and the Court of Appeal of Bamberg gave judgment for the plaintiff. Upon a second appeal by the defendant the judgment of the Court was quashed and the case was referred back to the Court of First Instance for the following

---

* English version by Kurt Lipstein.

Reasons

I. The Court of Appeal is of the opinion that the bankrupt is liable to pay damages because he has negligently damaged the established and active commercial enterprise of the plaintiff ('another right' in the meaning of § 823 I BGB). It held that in view of the existing danger to life the police could not allow the persons necessary to run the plaintiff's business to remain; thus the head office of the enterprise had ceased to function between 8.30 a.m. and 10.30 a.m. Thus the fire had directly affected the running of the plaintiff's enterprise. Therefore the non-productive expenditure of wages and other running costs covering the five hours during which business was interrupted, as alleged by the plaintiff, constituted a direct damage to be compensated in accordance with § 823 I BGB. In this respect it held that the claim for damages was well founded. The Court of Appeal refrained therefore from determining whether the claim could also be maintained on the ground that the plaintiff's property in the business premises had been violated or on the basis of § 823 II BGB in conjunction with the Decree concerning Inflammable Liquids of 5 June 1970 (henceforth called the Decree) [reference].

II. The arguments cannot be supported in law for several reasons. It must be objected in the first place that the Court of Appeal has wrongly simplified the account of the facts referred to in the plaintiff's pleadings seeking to establish liability. A distinction must be drawn between the first period of two hours during which the business premises of the plaintiff were in immediate danger and were evacuated upon the order of the police and the ensuing period when, because of the fire in the tank depot, vehicles of the police and the fire brigade only blocked the (public) access road to the plaintiff's business premises, as a result of which, as the plaintiff alleges, no vehicles could leave the premises, thus making it impossible to supply the building lots for which he was responsible.

These two situations must be considered separately from the legal point of view. During the first period the plaintiff's premises and his power to dispose of them were directly curtailed. Subsequently however, the plaintiff was only prevented from enjoying the common use of a public highway, although he may have been particularly affected, since his premises border on to it, particularly as it provided the only access. The facts as found by the Court of First Instance do not disclose whether this interruption of traffic was damage resulting from the dangerous situation which threatened the plaintiff's premises or was the result of the measures to remove the danger.

1. Damage resulting from the closure of the business premises during the final two hours

(*a*) In this respect it is altogether questionable why the Court of Appeal was able to affirm that an interference with an established and active commercial enterprise had occurred. It is noted in the judgment and admitted that the Bundesgerichtshof regards it as imperative that the interference must be aimed at the enterprise [references] and that the Bundesgerichtshof is concerned above all to counter any excess, contrary to the legal system, of this special remedy in tort [reference]. The requirement that the interference must be aimed at the enterprise, to be meaningful, can only be understood in the sense that he who interfered must have violated those duties of conduct incumbent upon him in view of the particular needs of protection of a commercial or industrial enterprise. Nothing else can be deduced either from the dogmatic considerations contained in the aforementioned decision of this Division [reference], contrary to the Court of Appeal. It is necessary, however, to enlarge on this aspect. Precisely for the reason that the special remedy in tort created by the practice of this court is only intended to fulfil a need peculiar to commercial or industrial enterprise, it only concerns a situation not covered otherwise [references] which must give way to other legal grounds [references]. For this reason alone it was therefore wrong for the Court of Appeal, without considering other grounds for the claim, to proceed immediately to an examination as to whether a right in an established and active commercial or industrial enterprise had been violated.

(*b*) In fact, to the extent that it is based on the temporary evacuation on the order of the police and the acute danger of a fire and an explosion which was the reason for it, the plaintiff's claim for damages is justified under § 823 I BGB because his ownership and possession were infringed.

It is true that the substance of the premises and of the installations of the enterprise were not touched; this, however, is not essential [references]. As this Division has already stated in its decision of 14 February 1967 [references], the deprivation of an object, even if unaccompanied by damage or destruction, may constitute a violation of ownership in the meaning of § 823 I BGB [references]; the same applies to interference with an object which renders its use impossible [references]. On the other hand the mere fact that an object was endangered physically was not always treated as a violation of property [references]. This Division cannot share that view in a case such as the present where the existence of an acute danger obviously precluded any use, at least for a while. Moreover the right of ownership of the plaintiff (§ 903 BGB) was seriously restricted by the order of the police to evacuate the premises, even if only temporarily. For both these reasons those responsible for the fire in the petrol depot are liable for the violation of another's protected legal interest.

Thus the claim, to the extent considered at this stage, is justified as a violation of property (§ 823 I BGB). It need not be decided here whether the same result could be reached by applying § 823 II BGB in conjunction with the Decree or with § 309 of the Criminal Code.

2. Damage resulting from the blocking of the public access road

According to the plaintiff's pleadings . . . after the evacuation of his premises at the orders of the police had come to an end, he was prevented from dispatching his vehicles loaded with materials because the feeder road providing access to the business premises of the plaintiff continued to be blocked by vehicles of the police and of the fire brigade. Their presence, it would appear, no longer served the direct purpose of protecting the plaintiff's premises but in order to secure and to guard the place of the fire itself (see above, Introduction to **II**). It would seem that in the opinion of the Court of Appeal, the plaintiff's claim in respect of the ensuing loss was justified. This Division cannot accept this conclusion even in principle— unlike in the situation dealt with in (1), above.

(*a*) As stated previously, there are no indications that the damage is connected with the temporary danger to and evacuation of the premises of the plaintiff's enterprise. Consequently the damage cannot, to this extent, be the result of the violation of property examined in (1), above. It would also be wrong to regard the short-time interruption of public traffic on the access roads to the plaintiff's premises as an interference with the ownership of business premises. The difference from the case decided by the Bundesgerichtshof in [reference] (an inland waterways vessel being detained for months in a channel of a river) is obvious. The plaintiff has not put forward this view either; further, it is unnecessary to take into account that the Court of First Instance—the Court of Appeal left the question open— rightly requested the negligent conduct of the bankrupt owners of the petrol depot as involving several violations of provisions of the Decree. The reason is that there are no indications that these provisions of § 309 of the Criminal Code are intended to provide protection individually for traffic users [reference] whose freedom of movement is restricted temporarily as a result of the closure of a road for the purpose of extinguishing a fire and for safety measures. It is insufficient that the plaintiff, as the owner of neighbouring premises, was particularly affected by the closure.

The special remedy intended to cover a situation not provided for otherwise, namely for interference with a facility and an active or commercial or industrial enterprise cannot assist either. It is not the purpose of this special remedy to provide businessmen with a claim for damages in respect of losses which others would have to bear in similar circumstances without being able to make any claim. This applies at all events where the common user of a public highway is obstructed temporarily. For it is recognized that a common user is not 'another right' protected by § 823 I BGB [reference]. This principle must not be evaded by granting protection to an established and active commercial or industrial enterprise. For the same reason any such interference must not be regarded as aimed at an enterprise [reference]. In the absence of evidence to the contrary it cannot be so aimed if every other interested person is exposed to the same impediment and must bear his own losses having regard to the substantive principles which attribute liability in damages. Such is the case where the common user of a public highway is interrupted temporarily. As regards the provisions of the Decree and of § 309 of the Criminal Code this conclusion was reached before. The same applies to infringements of the law which typically leads to a temporary standstill of traffic, in particular if provisions of the Road Traffic Regulations are contravened. In such cases the practice of the courts has attributed to the guilty party accidents suffered by others which resulted from a continuing situation creating a danger [reference]. On the other hand, it would seem that claims for damages by such users of a public highway have never been allowed under § 823 II BGB in conjunction with the traffic regulations which had been violated, if the claimants suffered pecuniary losses as a result of a hold-up of traffic following an accident. Here the argument applies once again that the purpose of traffic regulations cannot be to provide protection to that extent, seeing that such adverse consequences must be accepted without compensation by every person using public highways as a matter of chance.

(b) If this is so, no special right can exist either viewed from the perspective of a right in an established and active commercial or industrial enterprise. Instead those carrying on a commercial or an industrial enterprise can be expected to bear without compensation such losses as does everyone else living under the same law who suffers severe pecuniary damage through loss of time. This applies certainly to such restrictions in the common user of a public highway which, while they may be particularly serious for a commercial or industrial enterprise, remain on the whole within those limits which other road users must also tolerate without compensation. This applies in the present case. In view of the facts the question must not be decided here possibly in the light of the law relating to expropriation or of sacrifice for the public good as to whether a tort by a private person may so affect a common user adversely as to require that person to pay damages, at least when the interference is of long or even indeterminate duration [reference].

In such a case the commercial or industrial enterprise would be seriously prejudiced while any interference which may even last for several weeks would have to be tolerated without compensation [reference], and it would then have to be considered whether a tort had been committed by interference with an established and active commercial or industrial enterprise.

III. 1. . . .

The Court of First Instance, to which the issue will be referred back to determine the amount of damages will have to take into account in particular that the plaintiff cannot, as he has done hitherto, specify his damages in the abstract in accordance with the extent of his expenses which have turned out to be useless. No legal rule requires that all expenses which have become useless as a result of the damaging event must be compensated, [reference] . . . Instead the Court of First Instance will have to examine on its own to what extent the plaintiff has been lastingly deprived of profits as a result of those incidents of interference with his business which give rise to a claim for damages.

Case 13

BUNDESGERICHTSHOF (SECOND CIVIL DIVISION) 9 APRIL 1984*
NJW 1984, 2569

Facts

In the summer of 1980 the plaintiff started to construct an inner harbour wall about 230 metres long out of steel shuttering. The employer and owner of the harbour was the city. On 16 March 1981 while building operations were still in train, the barge TS on entering the harbour collided with and damaged the part of the wall which had been constructed. The plaintiff repaired the wall and sued the defendant as owner of the barge for its expense in so doing, claiming both in its own right and as assignee of the city.

The Rhine Navigation Court held the claim admissible, but the Rhine Navigation Court of Appeal dismissed it. The Bundesgerichtshof reversed and remanded.

Reasons

1. The owner of a ship is answerable for damage done to a third party by the fault of any of the crew in the execution of his functions (§ 3 (1) BinnSchG). Not only must causative fault on the part of a crew-member be shown but that person must actually be liable to the third party [references]. The relevant basis of liability here is § 823 I BGB.

* English version by Tony Weir.

2. The Court of Appeal did not decide whether any of the crew were at fault in the collision with the coffer-dam, nor whether the navigational signs at the harbour entrance had been correctly positioned by the city, as the plaintiff alleged. For the purposes of this appeal both assumptions must be made in favour of the plaintiff.

3. According to the Court of Appeal the plaintiff cannot complain of damage to property because the plaintiff did not own the part of the wall which was damaged: it belonged to the city.

The piles driven into the harbour bed were firmly attached to it and formed an essential component of the harbour itself, which was vested in the city. The piles were not there as a merely temporary measure: they were to remain there for the duration of the works. It is irrelevant that at the time of the accident the city had not yet accepted the half-built wall. Important as acceptance is for the contractual relations between the plaintiff and the city (see §§ 640 ff. BGB) it is irrelevant to the question of the ownership of the constructed part of the wall. That falls to be determined by §§ 94, 946 BGB, as the court below correctly stated. This turns on objective factors (permanent fixture to the soil) and not on the attitudes of the contractor and owner of the land. To the extent that these have a role to play under § 95 BGB, the appellant is bound by the finding that the piles were driven into the ground for the duration and not for subsequent removal, so that there can be no question of this being 'a purely temporary measure' [references].

4. The Court of Appeal further held that the plaintiff could not base a claim on interference with possession. It held:

At the time of the accident the plaintiff was certainly still in possession of the standing portion of the wall; for the purpose of executing its building operations, it had direct physical control of the building site, the piles already installed, and the wall, on which they were still working. But possession is protected by § 823 I BGB only in so far as it confers a right to possession, use, or enjoyment. The claim under § 823 I BGB is geared in principle to the replacement of the injury to possession, not to injury to the thing itself; but the plaintiff's claim is addressed to injury to the thing itself so that it does not lie under the heading of interference with possession.

Contrary to the view of the Court of Appeal the plaintiff's possession of the coffer-dam is a sufficient basis for its claim, on the factual assumptions made for the purposes of this appeal (2. above). The plaintiff was still bound to complete the work after it had been damaged (see §§ 631, 644 BGB). Until the city accepted it, the plaintiff bore the risk of having to repair at its own expense any damage to the wall caused by third parties, and until that was done the city was bound neither to accept the work nor pay the agreed fee. Thus the plaintiff's possession of the wall was associated with responsibility for its condition. This is enough to support a claim for the cost of the repairs. The case is akin to those where a tenant or lessee is contractually liable to the landlord or lessor for damage done to the thing by a third party. The tenant and lessee have been granted a claim for damages against the third party based on their possession [references]. Those are admittedly cases of 'liability-harm' [reference], whereas here it is by reason of his duty of performance *vis-à-vis* the site owner that the possessor suffers. Nevertheless, this is equally a consequential loss attributable to invasion of a legally protected interest, and it is irrelevant that it is purely economic in nature [reference]. The Court of Appeal was in error to suppose that in NJW 1970, 38 ff. the Sixth Civil Senate had held that a building contractor had no claim based on possession against another contractor for damaging work done by the first contractor and not yet accepted. On the contrary, the judgment expressly left this question open, the first contractor in that case being no longer in possession of the work. . . .

Case 14

BUNDESGERICHTSHOF (SEVENTH CIVIL DIVISION) 23 APRIL 1981*
NJW 1981, 1779

In 1973 as the general building contractor for the District of M the plaintiff built a centre for the disabled. The plaintiff delegated to the defendant the tiling operation of the proposed structure. For this purpose they agreed that the standard contract VOB\B (1952) should apply, but they made special provision concerning delivery and conditions and warranties in respect of legal or physical defects. According to the list of work to be done, the surrounds of the swimming pool of the Special School were to be covered with tiles made of artificial stone which were to be 'non-slip as a cover of the bottom'. The architect K, who was appointed by the District of M, selected the tiles from samples submitted by the defendant.

When the swimming pool was opened, it appeared that the tiles submitted by the defendant did not prevent slipping. At first the District asked the plaintiff to remedy the defect free of cost. The plaintiff refused and referred the District to its remedy against the architect.

Thereupon the District instructed the plaintiff by an additional contract and against further payment to replace the unsuitable tiles by others which prevented slipping. The plaintiff once again employed the defendant for the fixed price of DM 7992 and received in return DM 9000 from the District. To the latter extent the District claimed damages from the architect on the ground that he made a mistake in selecting the tiles. The latter's Insurance Company paid this sum in full and in subsequent proceedings sued the plaintiff for the payment of two-thirds of this amount. The District Court of

* English version by Kurt Lipstein.

Essen, by a decision of 5 November 1976 condemned the plaintiff to pay one half of the amount (i.e. DM 4500). The plaintiff accepted this and, in turn, claimed compensation from the defendant.

The District Court rejected the claim. The Court of Appeal of Düsseldorf gave judgment in favour of the plaintiff for DM 1500. Upon leave to lodge a second appeal the judgment of the District Court was restored.

Reasons

The Court of Appeal allowed the plaintiff's claim to the extent of one half of the sum paid to the Insurance Company of the architect on the ground that the defendant's performance was fundamentally defective in the meaning of § 13 nos. 1 and 7 of the standard contract. It held that in selecting the tiles both the defendant as well as the clerk of the works had failed, in violation of their duty according to § 4 no. 3 of the standard contract, to make an examination and to give advice; as a result the work had been defective.

The liability of the defendant in respect of defects was not ruled out by the fact that the plaintiff had not asked the defendant to remedy the defect. It was true that, had the owner of the building sued the plaintiff as the principal contractor for damages in respect of defects, the plaintiff would have been obliged to give the defendant in his capacity of sub-contractor the opportunity to make good the defect. However, instead of asking for the defects to be remedied the District M had instructed the plaintiff to replace the defective tiles by non-slip tiles and had demanded with justification that the architect should pay for the expenses in remedying the defects. In the opinion of the Court of Appeal the plaintiff had been under an obligation to compensate in part the architect's insurance company and had been unable to rely in relation to the latter, upon its right to ask for the defect to be removed—even if the claims of limitations or if liability had been restricted by agreement. As between the principal building contractor and the sub-contractor it would be inequitable if the latter, who was the real cause of the damage, could effectively plead that he had not been asked to remedy the defect, while the principal contractor was precluded from relying on this defence. If the latter was liable to pay, he should also be entitled to hold the sub-contractor liable for the consequence of the defect.

The conclusions of the Court of Appeal cannot be accepted. They are contrary to the particular legal nature of sub-contracting.

1. Since no question arises as to claims sounding in tort, the plaintiff's claims against the defendant can only result from the instructions given on 4 April 1973. The contract of the general or principal building contractor with the sub-contractor is an independent contract to perform building operations; it creates mutual rights and duties which are independent of those

which may exist between the owner of the building or others connected with the building operation and the principal building contractor and of the extent to which they rely on them [references].

The liability of the principal building contractor does not as such have any repercussions upon his contractual relationship with the sub-contractor. Neither the letter appointing the sub-contractor nor the documents accompanying the contract provide, in addition to liability for defects, for liability of the sub-contractor by way of recourse in the sense that he must assume liability for pecuniary obligations of the principal contractor, if the sub-contractor is liable in the last resort for the basis of this obligation. Such a right of recourse cannot be derived either from a general liability for a breach of contract by a positive act. If the breach of contractual duties to examine and to advise does not result in more than a defective performance, any liability of the sub-contractor—as the Court of Appeal does not fail to recognize—can only be based on the responsibility for defective performance (see §§ 4 no. 3 and 13 no. 3 of the standard contract); it cannot be based in addition on the failure to observe the general duty to protect the other party to the contract against loss [references].

2. Since the defendant fitted tiles on the surround of the swimming pool which were not anti-slip and thus were contrary to the contract and unsuitable, without having drawn the attention of the plaintiff that the tiles selected by the architect in the presence of the clerk of the works were unsuitable, the plaintiff has a claim to have the tiles replaced or—if the defendant should refuse to do so—for damages in remedying the defect. However, the plaintiff has forfeited this claim not only because he failed to invite the defendant to remedy the defect, as required by § 13 no. 7 of the standard contract [reference], but also because he gave additional instructions, accompanied by the promise of payment, to exchange the tiles for others [reference]. Thereby any claim for damages according to § 13 no. 7 of the standard contract was lost [reference].

3. It is true that the principal contractor is liable for the culpable acts of the sub-contractor as his aid in performing the contract; however they are not co-debtors of the owner of the building and of others connected therewith as regards their liability for defects. The sub-contractor owes his duty to the main contractor, not to the owner of the building, and thus § 421 BGB does not apply. A claim by the architect of the building owner against the main contractor for partial compensation cannot therefore be brought against the sub-contractor at the same time. The plaintiff, too, did not acquire a claim for partial compensation against the defendant by repaying to the architect and his insurance company half of the expenses in remedying the defects.

4. The plaintiff cannot either base his claim on considerations of equity.

(*a*) It is true that according to § 242 BGB reasons of equity may result in the reduction or even in the rejection of claims. On the other hand, reasons of equity cannot create claims which do not exist in law or in contract [reference].

(*b*) The rejection of the claim by the District Court is also not inequitable.

When the plaintiff received, on 20 June 1974, the additional order, he was not prevented from requesting the defendant to replace the tiles on the ground of liability for defects, seeing that they were clearly defective [references]. If the plaintiff should have regarded this as inequitable, having regard to the additional order received from the owner of the building, he could at least have reserved his right of recourse, in case the architect who was involved in the wrong selection should be sued by the owner of the building in respect of the defects in the building which were partly caused by the architect, but by the architect, who would ask for partial compensation, if sued by the owner of the building. A main or general contractor can provide adequately for such a risk in his contracts with the sub-contractors. If he fails to do so, he cannot shift the legal consequences to the sub-contractor on the ground that they are inequitable.

The plaintiff as the main contractor has received a higher remuneration than the sub-contractor in respect of the same performance. The fact that as the main contractor he received a higher remuneration is justified, in particular, by the higher risk run by the main contractor as a co-debtor side by side with the architect and other specialists.

Notes to Cases 11–14

1. Purely economic loss can result from an infinite variety of factual situations—the cable cases, discussed above, offering but one example. Many other instances can be given. Unfair competition is one example, indeed the only instance of economic loss which has troubled some systems (e.g. the French). Financial loss can also result from the death of a key employee. French law is, in theory, more generous than English and German law which deny such claims (see also Ch. 4, section A). Economic loss can also be occasioned to the ultimate purchaser of a defective product who, though not actually injured by it, is forced to spend money to put the defect right. The point is discussed in cases 48–54. The same can happen where a local authority fails to exercise a statutory right to inspect the foundations of buildings under construction with the result that cracks appear on the ceilings causing loss of heat (and, hence, higher electricity bills) or requiring redecoration. This type of economic loss is discussed in cases 54, 55 where one will find a spectacular U-turn by the English courts which has brought them closer to German solutions. Cases 11 and 12 deal with the situation

where no property is damaged, but its owner is deprived of its use. Technically the loss is again purely financial but the decisions reproduced above rightly adopted a more subtle approach.

2. The canal case, like the cable cases, explores various ways of allowing the claim. One is the judge-made right of an established and operating business (discussed above), but its subsidiary nature prevents it from being invoked if there is another applicable rule. The plaintiff's argument that he was entitled to expect the proper maintenance of the canal did not fare better, the court refusing to hold that the statutory obligation to maintain the canal was a protective norm and therefore actionable under § 823 II BGB (see below, Chapter 4). Do you share this interpretation? (In Germany it has not pleased everyone: see Medicus, op. cit., but cf. Möschel *JuS* 1977, 1, 3.) The crux of the decision lies clearly in its teleological interpretation of § 823 I BGB. Interference with property, reasoned the court, must be taken to include not only interference with its substance but also with the rights and the authority of the owner. This is sensible enough, but demarcation lines must also be drawn. For the court the dividing line was between the vessel trapped for an indefinite time and the vessel which, though unable to perform its contract, has retained its freedom of movement. The distinction is repeated and refined in the next case, 10, the crucial factor here being the duration of the interference. Both judgments raise as many problems as they solve and that, perhaps, explains why they have remained, if one can borrow the French expression, *arrêts d'espèce*. Must the interference be complete or prolonged, or both, before it is actionable? What if the vessel could return to its starting-point but by means of a circuitous and very expensive route? Why is an obstruction of someone else's waterway that hinders the use of my vessel actionable, while the interference with someone else's cable that stops me from using my machinery is not? Casuistry appears to have kept alive for so long the rule prohibiting the compensation of purely economic loss. It also explains why there are so many exceptions to the rule and why the law has become so difficult to present in a simple way. (See also BGH JZ 1983, 857; BGH NJW 1983, 812, and Deutsch, *JZ* 1984, 308–9.)

3. It has been impossible to find an *exact* factual equivalent in English and American law. English law has, in some instances, used the tort of public nuisance. In *Rose v. Miles* (1815) 4 M and S 101, 103; 105 ER 773, a barge-owner navigating a creek obstructed by the defendant's barges was allowed to claim his extra costs for unloading the cargo from his barges and transporting it by land to its ultimate destination, since in Lord Ellenborough's view he had suffered greater damage than other members of the public who might have been contemplating using the creek. The decision, incidentally, has impeccable origins that can be traced back to *Iveson v. Moore* (1699) 1 Ld. Raym. 486 (another case allowing recovery for purely

economic loss resulting from highway obstructions). Analogous cases in the USA have taken a similar stand, see *In re China Union Lines Ltd*, 285 F. Supp. 426 (1967) and *In Re Lyra Shipping Co. Ltd*, 360 F. Supp. 1188 (1973). Both these decisions, however, were recently overruled by the Court of Appeals for the 5th Circuit in its decision *State of Louisiana* v. *M/V Testbank* of 11 Feb. 1985: 752 F. 2d 1019, extracts of which are reproduced below. One can hazard a guess, however, that the German solution would appeal to those jurisdictions which are moving towards recognizing claims for economic loss. The following casuistry may support this statement.

(i) Negligent interference with existing contracts with resulting economic loss has not been traditionally actionable in the USA. *Robins Dry Dock and Repair Co.* v. *Flint* 275 US 303, 48 S. Ct. 134 (1927) is the *locus classicus* for the proposition. *Re Kinsman Transit Co.*, 388 F. 2d 821 (1968) marked a strong move towards the other direction, even though in that case the plaintiff's claim was rejected on causative grounds. (See, generally, Note, 'Negligent Interference with Contract: Knowledge on a Standard for Recovery' 63 *Va. L. Rev.* 813 (1977).) See also the interesting Canadian case of *Seaway Hotel Ltd.* v. *Craggs (Canada) Ltd.* (1959) 21 DLR 2d 264.

(ii) Even in the absence of contract the parties may negligently be deprived of a prospective economic benefit. Their plight has not been dealt with consistently by the courts. Frustrated beneficiaries who lose their legacies due to the negligence of a lawyer advising the testator can usually recover (see case 19 and its notes); but in other cases the courts have not been so generous. In *Weller* v. *Foot Mouth Disease* [1966] 1 QB 569, a live virus escaped from the defendant's laboratory due to their admitted negligence and caused a cattle disease. As a result, cattle auctions were prohibited for a period of time and the plaintiffs, cattle auctioneers, tried to claim their lost profits from the defendants. Their action failed. In *Rickards* v. *Sun Oil Co.* 23 NJ Misc. 89, 41 A. 2d 267 (Sup. Ct. 1945) a ship crashed into and destroyed a bridge which provided the only access to a small island town. The island businessmen claimed their lost profits for the period when outsiders could not visit their town but the action was turned down on the grounds that the damage was not foreseeable. (Do you agree with this or would it have been better to deny the claims on the grounds that the type of loss incurred (purely economic loss) was not recognized by the law?)

(iii) Loss of a chattel is not treated as economic loss. A bailee, for example, who has negligently lost the bailed chattel will be responsible to the bailor for its value. Bailment, however, is very 'close' to contract so the theoretical difficulties concerning compensation are in this case minimized.

(iv) Where the tort of negligence fails the plaintiff, the older tort of nuisance may come to his aid. Obstructions on the highway—including access to the highway—may thus be actionable in nuisance, and here recovery of purely economic loss has traditionally been allowed. This could provide a remedy in the kind of factual situation envisaged in case 12; though the duration of the obstruction would again be crucial. *Rose* v. *Miles* (1815) 4 M and S 101 is also interesting. There the plaintiff's barges were prevented from navigating on a public navigable creek. The court allowed him to claim the extra cost he incurred by having to convey his goods overland. Cf. *In Re Lyra Shipping Co. Ltd.*, 360 F. Supp. 1188 (1973).

4. Older cases dealing with particular problems of economic loss must nowadays be constantly reviewed against the background of recent, wide pronouncements on the subject, e.g., *Union Oil Co.* v. *Oppen* 501 F. 2d 558 (1974); *J'Aire Corp.* v. *Gregory* 24 Cal. 3d 799, 598 P. 2d 60; *Junior Books* v. *Veitchi Co.* [1982] 3 WLR 477. Other relevant 'economic loss' cases are reviewed by Markesinis, 'An Expanding Tort Law: The Price of a Rigid Contract Law' 103 [1987] *LQR* 354; Robertson, 'Recovery in Louisiana Tort Law for Intangible Economic Loss: Negligence Actions and the Tort of Intentional Interference with Contractual Relations' 46 *Louisiana L. Rev.* 737 (1986); Goldberg, 'Recovery for Pure Economic Loss in Tort: Another Look at *Robins Dry Dock* v. *Flint*' 20 *The Journal of Legal Studies* 249 (1991); Gonynor, 'The *Robins Dry Dock* Rule: Is the "Bright Line" Fading?' 4 *University of San Francisco Maritime Law Journal* 85 (1992); Jutras, 'Civil Law and Pure Economic Loss: What are we Missing?' 12 *The Canadian Business Law Journal* 295 (1986–7); Tetley, 'Damages and Economic Loss in Marine Collision: Controlling the Floodgates' 22 *Journal of Maritime Law and Commerce* 539 (1991).

5. For a discussion of the issues raised by cases 13 and 14 see the text in Chapter 2, 2(e), and cf. the decisions of *Junior Books* v. *Veitchi* [1983] AC 520 and the *J'Aire* decision reproduced in the second addendum.

Addendum 1

State of Louisiana ex rel. Guste v. *M/V Testbank* 752 F. 2d 1019 (1985)

Facts

In July 1980 two vessels collided in the Mississippi River Gulf Outlet. A large quantity of toxic chemicals was lost overboard one of the ships and, fearing greater contamination, the authorities closed the outlet to navigation for about twenty days. Fishing, shrimping, and other 'related' activities were also suspended for a short while in a surrounding area of about four hundred square miles. Forty-one lawsuits were filed and were eventually consolidated. The plaintiffs came under various (fairly) distinct categories namely: commercial fishermen; recreational fishermen; operators of marinas; bait and tackle shops; cargo terminal operators; restaurants etc. The Court of First Instance dismissed all the claims save those brought by the commercial fishermen. A panel of the Court of Appeal affirmed, but since a minority felt that the problem of the compensability of pure economic loss was ripe for re-examination, the case was heard by the full Court of Appeals sitting *en banc*. The majority judgment, affirming the decisions below, was delivered by Judge Higginbotham. Six judges dissented and the dissent was delivered by Judge Wisdom. The entire decision takes up 34 printed pages and will repay careful reading. For reasons of space, only key extracts have been reproduced in this book.

Patrick Higginbotham, Circuit Judge:

[The judge began with the *Robins* decision and argued that the rule enunciated in that case should be restated more widely to cover the (admittedly different) facts of this case. He then relied heavily on earlier decisions of the Fifth and (to a lesser extent Fourth and Second) Circuits in order to show that the law is well settled and any change would be inappropriate. The extracts that follow (pp. 1028–1032) contain the crux of the majority position and are reproduced without their footnote references.]

IV. Plaintiffs urge that the requirement of physical injury to a proprietary interest is arbitrary, unfair, and illogical, as it denies recovery for foreseeable injury caused by negligent acts. At its bottom the argument is that questions of remoteness ought to be left to the trier of fact. Ultimately the question becomes who ought to decide—judge or jury—and whether there will be a rule beyond the jacket of a given case. The plaintiffs contend that the 'problem' need not be separately addressed, but instead should be handled by 'traditional' principles of tort law. Putting the problem of which doctrine is the traditional one aside, their rhetorical questions are flawed in several respects.

Those who would delete the requirement of physical damage have no rule or principle to substitute. Their approach fails to recognize limits upon the adjudicating ability of courts. We do not mean just the ability to supply a judgment; prerequisite to this adjudicatory function are pre-existing rules, whether the creature of courts or legislatures. Courts can decide cases without pre-existing normative guidance but the result becomes less judicial and more the product of a managerial, legislative or negotiated function.

Review of the foreseeable consequences of the collision of the SEA DANIEL and TESTBANK demonstrates the wave upon wave of successive economic consequences and the managerial role plaintiffs would have us assume. The vessel delayed in St. Louis may be unable to fulfil its obligation to haul from Memphis, to the injury of the shipper, to the injury of the buyers, to the injury of their customers. Plaintiffs concede, as do all who attack the requirement of physical damage, that a line would need to be drawn—

somewhere on the other side, each plaintiff would say in turn, of its recovery. Plaintiffs advocate not only that the lines be drawn elsewhere but also that they be drawn on an *ad hoc* and discrete basis. The result would be that no determinable measure of the limit of foreseeability would precede the decision on liability. We are told that when the claim is too remote, or too tenuous, recovery will be denied. Presumably then, as among all plaintiffs suffering foreseeable economic loss, recovery will turn on a judge or jury's decision. There will be no rationale for the differing results save the 'judgment' of the trier of fact. Concededly, it can 'decide' all the claims presented, and with comparative if not absolute ease. The point is not that such a process cannot be administered but rather that its judgments would be much less the products of a determinable rule of law. In this important sense, the resulting decisions would be judicial products only in their draw upon judicial resources.

The bright line rule of damage to a proprietary interest, at most, has the virtue of predictability with the vice of creating results in cases at its edge that are said to be 'unjust' or 'unfair.' Plaintiffs point to seemingly perverse results, where claims the rule allows and those it disallows are juxtaposed—such as vessels striking a dock, causing minor but recoverable damage, then lurching athwart a channel causing great but unrecoverable economic loss. The answer is that when lines are drawn sufficiently sharp in their definitional edges to be reasonable and predictable, such differing results are the inevitable result—indeed, decisions are the desired product. But there is more. The line drawing sought by plaintiffs is no less arbitrary because the line drawing appears only in the outcome—as one claimant is found too remote and another is allowed to recover. The true difference is that plaintiffs' approach would mask the results. The present rule would be more candid, and in addition, by making results more predictable, serves a normative function. It operates as a rule of law and allows a court to adjudicate rather than manage.

V. That the rule is identifiable and will predict outcomes in advance of the ultimate decision about recovery enables it to play additional roles. Here we agree with plaintiffs that economic analysis, even at the rudimentary levels of jurists, is helpful both in the identification of such roles and the essaying of how the roles play. Thus it is suggested that placing all the consequence of its error on the maritime industry will enhance its incentive for safety. While correct, as far as such analysis goes, such *in terrorem* benefits have an optimal level. Presumably, when the cost of an unsafe condition exceeds its utility there is an incentive to change. As the costs of an accident become increasing multiples of its utility, however, there is a point at which greater accident costs lose meaning, and the incentive curve flattens. When the accident costs are added in large but unknowable amounts the value of the exercise is diminished. With a disaster inflicting large and reverberating injuries through the economy, as here, we believe the more important economic inquiry is that of relative cost of administration, and in maritime matters administration quickly involves insurance. Those economic losses not recoverable under the present rule for lack of physical damage to a proprietary interest are the subject of first party or loss insurance. The rule change would work a shift to the more costly liability system of third party insurance. For the same reasons that courts have imposed limits on the concept of foreseeability, liability insurance might not be readily obtainable for the types of losses asserted here. As Professor James has noted, '[s]erious practical problems face insurers in handling insurance against potentially wide, open-ended liability. From an insurer's point of view it is not practical to cover, without limit, a liability that may reach catastrophic proportions, or to fix a reasonable premium on a risk that does not lend itself to actuarial measurement.' James, above, at 53. By contrast, first party insurance is feasible for many of the economic losses claimed here. Each businessman who might be affected by a disruption of river traffic or by a halt in fishing activities can protect against that eventuality at a relatively low cost since his own potential losses are finite and readily discernible. Thus, to the extent that economic analysis informs our decision here, we think that it favours retention of the present rule.

VI. Plaintiffs argue alternatively that their claims of economic losses are cognizable in maritime tort because the pollution from the collision constituted a public nuisance, and violated the Rivers and Harbors Appropriation Act of 1899 and Louisiana law. We look to each in turn.

1. [1] Plaintiffs seek to avoid the *Robins* rule by characterizing their claims as damages caused by a public nuisance. They suggest that when a defendant unreasonably interferes with public rights by obstructing navigation or negligently polluting a waterway he creates a public nuisance for which recovery is available to all who have sustained 'particular damages.' As defined at common law such damages are those which are substantially greater than the presumed-at-law damages suffered by the general public as a result of the nuisance. *See generally Restatement* (*Second*) *of Torts* §§ 821B, 821C (1977); Prosser, 'Private Action for Public Nuisance' 52 *Cal. L. Rev.* 997 (1966). Characterizing the problem as one of public nuisance, however, does not immediately solve the problems with plaintiffs' damage claims for pure economic losses. As Dean Prosser has explained, 'courts have not always found it at all easy to determine what is sufficient "particular damage" to support [a] private action [for a public nuisance], and some rather fine lines have been drawn in the decisions.' W. Prosser, *Law of Torts* § 88 (4th edn.

1971). In drawing such lines today we are unconvinced that we should abandon the physical damage limitation as a prerequisite to recovery for economic loss.

The problem in public nuisance theory of determining when private damages are sufficiently distinct from those suffered by the general public so as to justify recovery is as difficult, if not more so, as determining which foreseeable damages are too remote to justify recovery in negligence. In each case it is a matter of degree, and in each case lines must be drawn. With economic losses such as the ones claimed here the problem is to determine who among an entire community that has been commercially affected by an accident has sustained a pecuniary loss so great as to justify distinguishing his losses from similar losses suffered by others. Given the difficulty of this task, we see no jurisprudential advantage in permitting the use of nuisance theory to skirt the *Robins* rule.

[2] Were we to allow plaintiffs recovery for their losses under a public nuisance theory we would permit recovery for injury to the type of interest that, as we have already explained, we have consistently declined to protect. Nuisance, as Dean Prosser has explained, is not a separate tort subject to rules of its own but instead is a type of damage. W. Prosser, *Law of Torts* § 87 (4th edn. 1971). Our decisions under *Robins* have emphasized the nature of the interest harmed rather than the theory of recovery. As we noted in *Dick Meyers Towing*, '[r]ephrasing the claim as a public nuisance claim does not change its essential character'. *Dick Meyers*, 577 F. 2d at 1025 n. 4. Thus we conclude that plaintiffs may not recover for pure economic losses under a public nuisance theory in maritime tort.

2. [3] Plaintiffs' arguments that the Rivers and Harbors Appropriation Act affords them an avenue of relief are foreclosed by Supreme Court decision. Plaintiffs suggest that both Section 10 of the Act, which prohibits the obstruction of navigable waters, and Section 13 of the Act, which prohibits the deposit of refuse into navigable waters, have been violated, and that such violations provide a basis for civil liability. In *California* v. *Sierra Club*, 451 US 287, 101 S. Ct. 1775, 68 L. Ed. 2d 101 (1981), the Court held that the Rivers and Harbors Appropriation Act did not authorize private actions to be brought for violation of its provisions. Accordingly, plaintiffs' claims under the Rivers and Harbors Act may not be maintained.

3. Plaintiffs also urge that their economic losses are recoverable as state law claims in negligence, nuisance or under the Louisiana Environmental Affairs Act of 1980. Because established principles of general maritime law govern the issue of recovery in this case, we reject these state law theories.

[4] The claims all involve a collision on a navigable waterway of the United States and the resulting damages, and hence are within the admiralty

and maritime jurisdiction of the federal courts. *See e.g. Foremost Insurance Co.* v. *Richardson*, 457 US 668, 102 S. Ct. 2654, 73 L. Ed. 2d 300 (1982). Under the Admiralty Extension Act our jurisdiction extends to the claims for shoreside damages as well as to those directly involving the waterway.

[5, 6] It is well-settled that the invocation of federal admiralty jurisdiction results in the application of federal admiralty law rather than state law. *See e.g. Kossick* v. *United Fruit Co.*, 365 US 731, 81 S. Ct. 886, 6 L. Ed. 2d 56 (1961); *Freeport Sulphur Co.* v. *S/S Hermosa*, 526 F. 2d 300, 302 n. 2 (5th Cir. 1976). While our maritime decisions are informed by common law developments in the state courts, there is no requirement, as in diversity cases, that state law be adopted. Indeed the federal interest in protecting maritime commerce is often best served by the establishment of uniform rules of conduct. We believe that such is the case here. The *Robins* rule has proved to be a workable and useful tool in our maritime jurisprudence. To permit recovery here on state law grounds would undermine the principles we seek to preserve today. Accordingly, we decline to adopt plaintiffs' state law claims as theories of recovery.

VII.

[7] In conclusion, having re-examined the history and central purpose of the doctrine of *Robins Dry Dock* as developed in this circuit, we remain committed to its teaching. Denying recovery for pure economic losses is a pragmatic limitation on the doctrine of foreseeability, a limitation we find to be both workable and useful. Nor do we find persuasive plaintiffs' arguments that their economic losses are recoverable under a public nuisance theory, as damages for violation of federal statutes, or under state law.

Accordingly, the decision of the district court granting summary judgment to defendants on all claims for economic losses unaccompanied by physical damage to property is AFFIRMED.

WISDOM, Circuit Judge, with whom ALVIN B. RUBIN, POLITZ, TATE, and JOHNSON, delivered a powerful dissent which was reproduced on pages 189–203 of the second edition of this book. In this edition, the judgment has been omitted to make room for extracts from the *Norsk* decision.

Notes to Testbank

Even a cursory look at this decision will show that it raises at least as many questions as it purports to answer. Here are some.

1. Why did the court not refer to any recent decisions of the ninth circuit—notably *J'Aire Corp.* v. *Gregory*—which reached a different result? Is it because the ninth circuit is regarded as being too *avant garde*? Or is it because someone (judge, attorney, legal assistant?) did not do his 'homework' properly?

2. In the *Robins* case Holmes J. referred to a famous English decision—*Cattle* v. *Stockton Waterworks Co.*—in order to buttress his position. At the time when *Testbank* was decided, English law was paying considerably less attention to the 'floodgates' argument which was espoused by the majority. Why were not these cases cited? Is it again a question of an excusable (because of the volume of work) or inexcusable omission? Or is it a symptom of the fact that American judges nowadays seem to be less and less interested in what happens in England, Canada, Australia, or New Zealand? If the latter is the reason for this 'splendid isolation' do you find it convincing? In the event, English law has now moved back to a more conservative position; though the Supreme Court of New Jersey has sided with the minority in *Testbank*. See: *People Express Airlines* v. *Consolidated Rail*, 100 NJ 246, 495 A. 2d 107 (1985).

3. The majority states (at p. 1024) that 'This circuit has consistently refused to allow recovery for economic loss absent physical damage to a proprietary interest.' Is this entirely correct? (Cf. Judge Wisdom's judgment on pp. 1040 ff. and references given in the text and the footnotes.)

4. Do you agree with the majority that the case of the commercial fishermen is both different and stronger than that of the other claimants? Note that the fishermen who have not yet caught the fish cannot complain if someone else catches them; and if they cannot complain if someone else catches them, why should they be able to claim damages if someone else kills them? (See Epstein, 8 *J. Leg. Stud.* 49, 52 (1979).)

5. Which interpretation of *Kinsman* judgment do you find: (*a*) more accurate and (*b*) preferable: that adopted by the majority or the minority?

6. What do you think of the majority's quasi-jurisprudential argument (pp. 1028–929) that its position allows the courts to 'adjudicate' whereas the minority's view 'accepts a rule of *management* which can strain the limits of adjudication'? (Italics added.)

7. The emphasis placed by the majority on the impact of insurance practice on modern tort law is most welcome (see p. 1029). But is its apparently unqualified preference for first party insurance always preferable? (See Professor Atiyah's comment in (1985) 3 *Oxford J. L. Studies* 485, 489: '. . . it is really high time (in both England and America) that lawyers informed themselves about such fundamental matters of insurability in new tort cases and saw to it that the courts were also informed.' See also Rizzo in 11 *J. Leg. Stud.* (1982) where the author's economic analysis suggests that the majority's preference for first party insurance is wrong in situations like *Testbank*.)

8. The majority states (p. 1028): 'Those who would delete the requirement of physical damage have no rule of principle to substitute.' Is this strong point countered effectively by the minority? Cf. the interesting compromise proposed by MacGrath in (1985) 3 *Oxford J. L. Studies* 350.

9. Both majority and minority consider the applicability of the tort of Public Nuisance. Do you find these parts of the judgments clear? More precisely, is it accurate to suggest that pure economic loss is not recoverable in Public Nuisance?

10. The minority seems to have merged the requirements of the tort of Negligence and the tort of Public Nuisance by apparently being prepared to allow recovery where the plaintiff has suffered loss which is both foreseeable and 'particular'. Does the addition of 'particular' (in the sense of different in kind and/or degree from that suffered by the general public) help matters? Can one call the loss suffered by a restaurant owner within the 'restricted' area 'particular' damage but deny this term to a restaurant owner situated in New Orleans (which was not within the restricted zone)?

11. Finally, should one try to solve the *Testbank* type of disaster by means of statute or international treaties imposing strict liability on the carriers of the polluting substances subject to certain monetary limits? On this see: Gaskell, '*The Amoco Cadiz*' 3 *Journal of Energy and Natural Resources Law*, 169 (1985).

Addendum 2

J'Aire Corp. v. *Gregory* 24 Cal. 3d 799, 598 P. 2d 60, 157 Cal. Reptr. 407 (1979)

Bird CJ: Appellant, a lessee, sued respondent, a general contractor, for damages resulting from the delay in completion of a construction project at the premises where appellant operated a restaurant. Respondent demurred successfully and the complaint was dismissed. This court must decide whether a contractor who undertakes construction work pursuant to a contract with the owner of premises may be held liable in tort for business losses suffered by a lessee when the contractor negligently fails to complete the project with due diligence.

The facts as pleaded are as follows. Appellant, J'Aire Corporation, operates a restaurant at the Sonoma County Airport in premises leased from the county of Sonoma. Under the terms of the lease the county was to provide heat and air conditioning. In 1975 the county entered into a contract with respondent for improvements to the restaurant premises, including renovation of the heating and air-conditioning systems and installation of insulation.

As the contract did not specify any date for completion of the work, appellant alleged the work was to have been completed within a reasonable time as defined by custom and usage (Civ. Code, § 1657). Despite requests that respondent complete the construction promptly, the work was not completed within a reasonable time. Because the restaurant could not operate during part of the construction and was without heat and air-conditioning for a longer period, appellant suffered loss of business and resulting loss of profits.

Appellant alleged two causes of action in its third amended complaint. The first cause of action was based upon the theory that it was a third-party beneficiary of the contract between the county and respondent. The second cause of action sounded in tort and was based upon negligence in completing the work within a reasonable time. Damages of £50,000 were claimed.

Respondent demurred on the ground that the complaint did not state facts sufficient to constitute a cause of action. The trial court sustained the demurrer without leave to amend and the complaint was dismissed. On appeal only the sustaining of the demurrer to the second cause of action is challenged.

. . . The only question before this court is whether a cause of action for negligent loss of expected economic advantage may be maintained under these facts.

Liability for negligent conduct may only be imposed where there is a duty of care owed by the defendant to the plaintiff or to a class of which the plaintiff is a member (*Richards* v. *Stanley* (1954) 43 Cal. 2d 60, 63, 271 P. 2d 23). A duty of care may arise through statute or by contract. Alternatively, a duty may be premised upon the general character of the activity in which the defendant engaged, the relationship between the parties, or even the interdependent nature of human society. Whether a duty is owed is simply a shorthand way of phrasing what is 'the essential question— whether the plaintiff's interests are entitled to legal protection against the defendant's conduct' (*Dillon* v. *Legg* (1968) 69 Cal. Rptr. 72, P. 2d 912).

This court has held that a plaintiff's interest in prospective economic advantage may be protected against injury occasioned by negligent as well as intentional conduct. [Reference omitted.] For example, economic losses such as lost earnings or profits are recoverable as part of general damages in a suit for personal injury based on negligence. Where negligent conduct causes injury to real or personal property, the plaintiff may recover damages for profits lost during the time necessary to repair or replace the property. [Reference omitted.]

Even when only injury to prospective economic advantage is claimed, recovery is not foreclosed. Where a special relationship exists between the parties, a plaintiff may recover for loss of expected economic advantage through the negligent performance of a contract although the parties were not in contractual privity. [*Biakanja*, *Lucas*, and *Heyer*] held that intended beneficiaries of wills could sue to recover legacies lost through the negligent preparation of the will. [Reference omitted.]

In each of the above cases, the court determined that defendants owed plaintiffs a duty of care by applying criteria set forth in *Biakanja* v. *Irving*. [Reference omitted.] Those criteria are (1) the extent to which the transaction was intended to affect the plaintiff, (2) the foreseeability of harm to the plaintiff, (3) the degree of certainty that the plaintiff suffered injury, (4) the closeness of the connection between the defendant's conduct and the injury suffered, (5) the moral blame attached to the defendant's conduct, and (6) the policy of preventing future harm. [Reference omitted.]

Applying these criteria to the facts as pleaded, it is evident that a duty was owed by respondent to appellant in the present case. (1) The contract entered into between respondent and the county was for the renovation of the premises in which appellant maintained its business. The contract could not have been performed without impinging on that business. Thus respondent's performance was intended to, and did, directly affect appellant. (2) Accordingly, it was clearly foreseeable that any significant delay in completing the construction would adversely affect appellant's business beyond the normal disruption associated with such construction. Appellant alleges this fact was repeatedly drawn to respondent's attention. (3) Further, appellant's complaint leaves no doubt that appellant suffered harm since it was unable to operate its business for one month and suffered additional loss of business while the premises were without heat and air-conditioning. (4) Appellant has also alleged that delays occasioned by the respondent's conduct were closely connected to, indeed directly caused its injury. (5) In addition, respondent's lack of diligence in the present case was particularly blameworthy since it continued after the probability of damage was drawn directly to respondent's attention. (6) Finally, public policy supports finding a duty of care in the present case. The wilful failure or refusal of a contractor to prosecute a construction project with diligence, where another is injured as a result, has been made grounds for disciplining a licensed contractor (Bus. 6 Prof. Code, § 7119). Although this section does not provide a basis for imposing liability where the delay in completing construction is due merely to negligence, it does indicate the seriousness with which the Legislature views unnecessary delays in the completion of construction.

In the light of these factors, this court finds that respondent had a duty to complete construction in a manner that would have avoided unnecessary injury to appellant's business, even though the construction contract was with the owner of a building rather than with appellant, the tenant. It is settled that a contractor owes a duty to avoid injury to the person or property of third parties. As appellant points out, injury to a tenant's business can often result in greater hardship than damage to a tenant's person or property. Where the risk of harm is foreseeable, as it was in the present case, an injury to the plaintiff's economic interests should not go uncompensated merely because it was unaccompanied by any injury to his person or property.

To hold under these facts that a cause of action has been stated for negligent interference with prospective economic advantage is consistent with the recent trend in tort cases. This court has repeatedly eschewed overly rigid Common law formulations of duty in favour of allowing compensation for foreseeable injuries caused by a defendant's want of ordinary care. See, e.g., *Dillon* v. *Legg* [reference omitted]; *Rowland* v. *Christian* [reference omitted]; cf. *Brown* v. *Merlo* [reference omitted] (liability of automobile driver for injury to non-paying passenger); *Rodriguez* v. *Bethlehem Steel Corp.* [reference omitted] (liability for loss of consortium). Rather than traditional notions of duty, this court has focused on foreseeability as the key component necessary to establish liability: 'While the question whether one owes a duty to another must be decided on a case-by-case basis, every case is governed by the rule of general application that all persons are required to use ordinary care to prevent others from being injured as the result of their conduct . . . Foreseeability of the risk is a primary consideration in establishing the element of duty' (*Weirum* v. *RKO General, Inc.* [reference omitted]). Similarly, respondent is liable if his lack of ordinary care caused foreseeable injury to the economic interests of appellant.

In addition, this holding is consistent with the legislature's declaration of the basic principle of tort liability, embodied in Civil Code, § 1714, that every person is responsible for injuries caused by his or her lack of ordinary care. (See *Rowland* v. *Christian* [reference omitted].) That section does not distinguish among injuries to one's person, one's property, or one's financial interests. Damages for loss of profits or earnings are recoverable where they result from an injury to one's person or property caused by another's negligence. Recovery for injury to one's economic interests, where it is the foreseeable result of another's want of ordinary care, should not be foreclosed simply because it is the only injury that occurs.

Respondent cites *Fifield Manor* v. *Finston* [reference omitted] for the proposition that recovery may not be had to negligent loss of prospective economic advantage. *Fifield* concerned the parallel tort of interference with contractual relations. There a non-profit retirement home that had contracted with Ross to provide him with life-time medical care sued a driver who negligently struck and killed Ross. The plaintiff argued it had become liable under the contract for Ross's medical bills and sought recovery from the driver, on both a theory of direct liability and one of subrogation. Recovery was denied.

The critical factor of foreseeability distinguishes *Fifield* from the present case. Although it was reasonably foreseeable that defendant's negligence might cause injury to Ross, it was less foreseeable that it would injure the retirement home's eco-nomic interest. Defendant had not entered into any relationship or undertaken any activity where negligence on his part was reasonably likely to affect plaintiff adversely. Thus, the nexus between the defendant's conduct and the risk of the injury that occurred to the plaintiff was too tenuous to support the imposition of a duty owing to the retirement home. In contrast, the nexus in the present case between the injury that occurred and respondent's conduct is extremely close. *Fifield* does not entirely foreclose recovery for negligent interference with prospective eco-nomic advantage.

Respondent also relies on *Adams* v. *Southern Pac. Transportation Co.* [reference omitted]. In *Adams* plaintiff employees were held unable to sue the railroad whose cargo of bombs exploded, destroying the factory where they worked. It should be noted that the Court of Appeal in *Adams* clearly believed that plaintiffs should be permitted to maintain an action for negligent interference with prospective economic interests. It reluctantly held they could not only under the belief that *Fifield* pre-cluded such recovery. Adhering to the *Fifield* rule, the Court of Appeal in *Adams* did not determine whether the railroad owed plaintiffs a duty of care. In the present case, plaintiff's injury stemmed directly from conduct intended to affect plaintiff and was more readily foreseeable than the damage to the employer's property in *Adams*. To the extent that *Adams* holds that there can be no recovery for negligent interfer-ence with prospective economic advantage, it is disapproved.

The chief dangers which have been cited in allowing recovery for negligent inter-ference with prospective economic advantage are the possibility of excessive liability, the creation of an undue burden on freedom of action, the possibility of fraudulent or collusive claims, and the often speculative nature of damages . . . Central to these fears is the possibility that liability will be imposed for remote consequences, out of proportion to the magnitude of the defendant's wrongful conduct.

However, the factors enumerated in *Biakanja* and applied in subsequent cases place a limit on recovery by focusing judicial attention on the foreseeability of the injury and the nexus between the defendant's conduct and the plaintiff's injury. These factors and ordinary principles of tort law such as proximate cause are fully adequate to limit recovery without the drastic consequence of an absolute rule which bars recovery in all such cases. Following these principles, recovery for negligent interference with prospective economic advantage will be limited to instances where the risk of harm is foreseeable and is closely connected with the defendant's conduct, where damages are not wholly speculative and the injury is not part of the plaintiff's ordinary business risk.

Accordingly, this court holds that a contractor owes a duty of care to the tenant of a building undergoing construction work to prosecute that work in a manner which does not cause undue injury to the tenant's business, where such injury is reasonably foreseeable. The demurrer to appellant's second cause of action should not have been sustained. The judgment of dismissal is reversed.

Notes to J'Aire

1. For some time now, California has supplanted New Jersey in its role as trend-setter in the USA. The decisions of its Supreme Court attract particular attention. *J'Aire* is no exception and it is, therefore, regrettable that it has not been thought out fully; indeed, it is a shame that so many of its legal protagonists gave evidence of sloppiness which in the classroom would have earned them low marks.

2. Take, first, counsel for the plaintiffs. The case was originally argued in contract (first cause of action) and tort (second cause of action). Under laboratory conditions, one would have been inclined to argue that, given the nature of the plaintiff's loss (pure economic loss), the first cause of action was more likely to produce a pro-plaintiff decision. Yet in the judgment we are laconically told that 'on appeal only the sustaining of the demurrer [by the trial court] to the second cause of action [was] challenged.' Many a teacher may have spent much time speculating what strategic reasons may have led to this decision. Yet the answer is much more mundane; and we owe it to Professor Schwartz who had the brilliant idea of asking the attorney in question why he did this, only to be told that 'contracts were never my strong point at [law] school.' (Schwartz, 'Economic Loss in American Tort Law: the Examples of J'Aire and of Products Liability', 23 *San Diego L. Rev.* 37, 43 (1986)). If one is willing to treat this as an answer containing an element of the truth, it can give rise to much comparative discussion about the 'compartmentalised' way law is taught in American law schools.

3. So let us turn to the judgment of the Chief Justice. Early in her judgment, she tells us that 'This court has held that a plaintiff's economic advantage may be protected against injury occasioned by negligent . . . conduct.' Two illustrations are given to support this proposition, one of economic loss flowing from personal injury, the other from property damage. Neither is appropriate, for in both these cases economic loss causes no difficulties, the limits of recovery being set by the rules of factual and legal cause. The problem we are discussing here, and which confronted the court in *J'Aire*, is the (different) problem of *pure* economic loss. (How right those Germans are with their desire to be precise with the terms = _reine_ Vermögensschäden.) If

this were a tutorial essay, one would be inclined to scribble in the margin 'not relevant'.

4. The Chief Justice continues in similar vein, placing great reliance on the decisions in *Biakanja, Lucas,* and *Heyer*. These, however, are cases of legal malpractice; they involve different types of relationships, different kinds of insurance arguments, and do not raise the spectre of unlimited liability which (indirectly) plays such a determinative role in pure economic loss cases. The decision thus compares unfavourably with the more subtle and carefully researched judgment of La Forest in *Norsk*, extracts of which are reproduced below.

5. The actual result in *J'Aire* may be supportable; indeed it may be reasonable, provided it is produced through contract (or, at least, a tort action, shaped in its scope and consequences by the underlying contract). This point is discussed in greater detail in the notes to the legal malpractice cases; and is made even more obvious when considered against the background of German law (also discussed briefly in these notes).

6. One final (minor) point—interesting from the point of view of comparative methodology. German lawyers studying the Common law always have some difficulty with the notion of duty of care. Conversely, Common lawyers cannot find this key concept in the codal provision which, instead, talks of 'protected interests'. The following sentence from Chief Justice Bird's judgments is, therefore, particularly interesting: 'Liability for negligent conduct may only be imposed where there is a duty of care . . . whether a duty is owed is simply a short hand way of phrasing what is the essential question—whether the plaintiff's *interests* are entitled to legal protection . . .'. Comparatists should rejoice at such sentences and treat them as the literary equivalents of musical cadenzas. For they offer a chance to escape the strictures imposed by textbooks, and an excellent opportunity to attempt one's own excursus into legal history, drafting techniques, and the merits and demerits of comparing systems via their concepts or through the functions which their concepts are meant to perform.

Addendum 3

Norsk Pacific Steamship Co. Ltd. v. *Canadian National Railway Co.* [1992] 1 S.C.R. 1021

Summary of the facts

The New Westminster Railways Bridge, which spans the Fraser River near Vancouver and carries a *single* track, is owned by the Department of Public Works of Canada (PWC). A barge, towed by a tug owned by the defendants (Norsk), and negligently navigated by its captain, damaged the bridge, necessitating its closure for several weeks while it was being repaired. As a result of this closure, the Canadian National Railway (CNR), who were the plaintiffs in this action, had to re-route traffic over another bridge, incurring considerable additional expense. CNR, who accounted for 86 per cent of the use of the bridge, had a licence contract with PWC which, *inter alia*, obliged them to provide PWC with inspection, consulting, maintenance, and repair services for the bridge as and when requested by PWC and at PWC's expense. Since the marine traffic using the Fraser river was, at the site of the bridge, heavy and had, in the past, occasioned structural damage to the bridge leading to its closure, the licence agreement between CNR and PWC provided that the former could not claim damages from the latter in the event of closure of the bridge in an emergency. Finally, one should, perhaps, note that CNR owned the land (and tracks) on *either side* of the bridge (but not the rails on the damaged bridge). CNR's tort action for its economic losses was accepted at First Instance, by the Court of Appeal, and by four judges out of seven in the Supreme Court.

[Three long judgments were delivered in this case by McLachlin, Stevenson, and La Forest JJs. For reasons of space, only extracts from one of them is reproduced here. They are taken from the 'dissent' since it, arguably, provides one of the most thorough judicial discussions of the problem of pure economic loss; but the case will be best understood if read in its entirety.]

La Forest J. (dissenting)—This case concerns recovery in tort for economic loss. Though some of the arguments are framed as if the case turned on the broad question whether such damages are generally recoverable, the specific issue is much narrower. It is whether a person (A) who contracts for the use of property belonging to another (B) can sue a person who damages that property for losses resulting from A's inability to use the property during the period of repair. (I call this 'contractual relational economic loss', a convenient if somewhat barbarous phrase.)

The issue arises in a context where a barge collided with a bridge while being pulled by the defendants' tug, thereby preventing the plaintiff (CN) from making use of it. Ordinarily, a person whose operations are disrupted by damage to a bridge belonging to another cannot at common law pursue the person who caused the damage. But the plaintiff claims that it may do so by reason of its particular relationship with the owner of the bridge and with the tortfeasor. As in the case of three other railways, it has a contractual right to use the bridge for railway purposes, but the plaintiff relies on additional facts to establish its special relationship. It is by far the major user of the bridge, which is a central link in its operations, so much so that many of those who operated on the river, including the master of the defendants' tug, thought it belonged to the plaintiff. As well, CN's contract requires it to repair and maintain the bridge when necessary at the request of the owner; CN also owns land close to the bridge.

The courts below and my colleagues, Justices McLachlin and Stevenson, are all of the view that CN's claim should be upheld. But this unanimity is more apparent than real, for they do so for different reasons and, indeed, there is significant disagreement on the determining issues. I take the opposite view. For sound policy reasons, the courts have established a clear rule (the 'bright line' rule) that persons cannot sue a tortfeasor for suffering losses to their contractual rights with the owner of property by reason of damages caused to that property by the tortfeasor. That rule, I have no doubt, may be subject to exceptions for clear and overriding policy reasons, but as I will indicate, I have been unable to determine any reason for excluding CN from the general rule in the present case.

[A detailed statement of the facts follows at this stage taking up 7 full columns of the S.C. Reports.]

The Issues

It is crucial at the outset to set forth precisely what is, and what is not in issue in this appeal. The issue is not whether economic losses are recoverable in tort, as my colleague McLachlin J. seems to frame it in her analysis. For reasons I shall explore later, I would have thought it clear that they are indeed recoverable in certain cases. And, though the parties disagree with respect to the points in issue, they did not frame them in that way in their factums in this Court.

The appellants (defendants) argue that the question in this appeal is whether a duty of care can arise between A (the defendants here) and C (the plaintiff CN here) where A negligently damages the property of B (PWC here) that results in a contractual disruption and conseque it economic loss to C. The appellants contend that the nature of CN's relationship with PWC is merely contractual and that this fact is dispositive of the case.

CN concedes that a contractual interest *simpliciter* does not justify recovery, but it disagrees with the appellants' description of the damage suffered as being merely contractual disruption. Its argument proceeds essentially on two broad fronts which overlap to some degree.

The first front can be termed the alternative interests argument. CN first argues that its <u>interest</u> is more than a mere contractual one. To this end, it put forward essentially two arguments: first that it suffered from a transferred loss of use; and, secondly, that it is involved in a common adventure with PWC. These arguments are centred on the relationship between the plaintiff and the property owner, i.e., between CN and PWC. They represent an attempt to <u>avoid</u> the application of the rule barring recovery for mere contractual interests.

The second broad front on which CN proceeds may be termed the 'special relationship' front. Here it argues that, even if the Court rejects its alternative interests argument and finds that its <u>interest</u> is merely contractual, the existence of other factors is sufficient to constitute a special relationship with the tortfeasor and to ground recovery for its contractual claims. In particular, it points to the high degree of subjective and objective foreseeability in this case as sufficient to constitute a special relationship between Norsk and CN, but other factors are invoked as well. These arguments are largely centred on the plaintiff-tortfeasor relationship, i.e., the relationship between CN and Norsk. They represent an attempt to qualify the application of the contractual relational economic loss rule.

CN's two strands of argument overlap, so that the factors that underlie its alternative interests arguments are also at times invoked in support of the existence of a special relationship or, more broadly, of proximity. It thus builds its argument on the allegedly particular characteristics of its relationship with the property owner on the one hand and the tortfeasor on the other. The appellants, on the other hand, consider that the contractual nature of the plaintiff's relationship with the property owner is dispositive of the case.

Part I of the analysis in this judgment examines the appellants' contention and focuses on the narrow problem of contractual relational economic loss. In my view, this question has been unhelpfully bound up with the larger question of pure economic loss. The first part of these reasons retraces these developments and sets forth the rationale for considering this narrow issue as a separate problem.

Part II examines CN's arguments to the effect that it has more than a mere contractual interest. My conclusion is that it does not.

Part III returns to the issue of contractual relational economic loss. It examines the various proposals that have been made to relax the bright line rule excluding recovery for contractual relational economic loss, including those set forth by my colleagues McLachlin and Stevenson JJ.

Part IV examines the rationale for the exclusionary rule. My conclusion is that the bright line rule excluding recovery for economic loss owing to interference with contractual relations that results from damage to a third party's property should not be modified, at least on the facts of this case. I should underline from the outset that this conclusion is not a rejection of recovery for pure economic loss in general terms. It is limited, for reasons that will be set forth, to cases where property damage to a third party has occurred and where the plaintiff's interest is contractual.

Analysis

Part I: The Need to Recentre the Analysis on Contractual Relational Economic Loss

To phrase the key issue in this case as a simple one of 'is pure economic loss recoverable in tort?' is misleading. I do not doubt that pure economic loss is recoverable in some cases. It does not follow, however, that all economic loss cases are susceptible to the same analysis, or that cases of one type are necessarily relevant to cases of another. Nor does it follow that the constellation of policy concerns that have grown up around the issue of economic loss can be ignored. The fact is that different types of factual situations may invite different approaches to economic loss, and it seems to me to be at best unwise to lump them all together for purposes of analysis. Professor Feldthusen distinguishes five different categories of economic loss cases which involve different policy considerations: see Feldthusen, 'Economic Loss in the Supreme Court of Canada: Yesterday and Tomorrow' (1990–91), 17 *Can. Bus. L.J.* 356, at pp. 357–8. They are as follows:

1. The Independent Liability of Statutory Public Authorities;
2. Negligent Misrepresentation;
3. Negligent Performance of a Service;
4. Negligent Supply of Shoddy Goods or Structures;
5. Relational Economic Loss.

The present case fits into his fifth category. In my view, both policy and precedent justify narrowing the focus in the present case to loss cases of the kind described in that category.

Professor Feldthusen considers that the cases and strong policy reasons support a general rule precluding recovery of all relational loss, which he frames in the following terms: 'The recovery of pure economic loss will be precluded in negligence when it is consequent upon an injury to the person or property of a third party': see Feldthusen, *Economic Negligence* (2nd edn. 1989), at p. 200. He recognizes, however, that such a rule would be subject to a number of specific exceptions.

In general terms, we are here concerned with relational loss resulting from property damage, and I need not consider relational loss arising out of personal injury. Turning then to an examination of the category of cases in which the initial damage is to property, it is apparent that contract is not the only relation that can lead to losses. If the property is publicly owned, users may not be required to contract for its use. Thus persons who regularly use an ordinary bridge or other publicly maintained facility have no contractual right to do so but may nevertheless suffer damages by having to find alternative routes for themselves or their goods, and their suppliers or customers may also suffer damage. Those suffering such damage will ordinarily not recover: see *Bethlehem Steel Corp. v. St. Lawrence Seaway Authority*, [1978] 1 F.C. 464, (claims for loss of profits owing to ships being held up after a bridge destroyed and a canal obstructed were refused, as was a claim for extra shipping costs arising out of the same accident); *Star Village Tavern v. Nield* (1976), 71 D.L.R. (3d) 439 (Man. Q.B.), (recovery by tavern owner suffering losses owing to bridge closure refused). To impose such indeterminate liability on tortfeasors is almost unthinkable as the cases make clear. The courts have similarly refused recovery in other cases of relational economic loss; see, for example, *Weller & Co. v. Foot & Mouth Disease Research Institute*, [1966] 1 Q.B. 569, as explained by *S.C.M. (United Kingdom) Ltd. v. W. J. Whittall and Son Ltd.*, [1971] 1 Q.B. 337, at p. 342, and *Spartan Steel & Alloys Ltd. v. Martin & Co. (Contractors) Ltd.*, [1973] Q.B. 27.

Where the government is able to sue as owner (as in this case and as in most bridge cases), I can see no reason for any difference in treatment depending on whether use is based on contract or not. In my view, contractual relational economic loss cases are perhaps best conceived as a variant of relational loss. At least in terms of result, the different types of relational economic loss cases generally appear to be dealt with in the same way by the courts. As will become evident, many of the underlying policies are, in my view, the same. Nevertheless, most of the reported cases involve claims for contractual relational economic loss, probably because most of the others appear obvious. To avoid possible doctrinal confusion, I propose as much as possible to narrow the focus to contractual relational economic loss only.

Policy

Cases of contractual relational loss have a number of specific characteristics that differentiate them from other economic loss cases, and certainly from other non-relational loss cases. The first is that in such cases, the right of action of the property owner already puts pressure on the defendants to act with care. The deterrent effect of tort law, to the extent that it survives the advent of widespread insurance, is already present. In this case PWC collected substantial damages. Consequently, Norsk was already under a substantial incentive to take care with respect to the bridge since its liability to the bridge owner would and did require the payment of substantial damages. In most cases of this type, imposing further liability cannot reasonably be justified on the grounds of deterrence (unless a policy of full internalization of all losses resulting from accidents to the party who could have avoided the accident is to be pursued at all costs).

This is a critical difference with respect to the other types of economic loss cases. Professor Feldthusen underlines the importance of this first key aspect of contractual relational economic loss cases, in the following passage dealing with relational loss generally ((1990–91), 17 *Can. Bus. L.J.* 356, at p. 377):

. . . in each of [the first four] categories [identified above], the issue is whether the law of negligence applies at all to sanction the defendant's careless conduct. Relational loss cases are different because the defendant will be held liable to the victim of physical damage. The issue is whether *additional* liability to third parties is warranted. The better analogy is not to how the claim in *Hedley Byrne* or *Rivtow Marine* was resolved, but to how an additional claim brought by the best customer of the plaintiffs in each of those cases would have fared. [Emphasis added.]

I come now to a second distinction. A firm exclusionary rule in this area does not have the effect of necessarily excluding compensation to the plaintiff for his or her loss. Rather, it simply channels to the property owner both potential liability to the plaintiff and the right of recovery against the tortfeasor. The property owner is both entitled to recover from the tortfeasor and potentially liable under contract to the plaintiff. Here, the licence agreement explicitly rejected any liability, so the plaintiff cannot recover under it against PWC. In contracts between sophisticated parties such as those in the case at bar, who are well advised by counsel, such exclusions of liability often result from determinations regarding who is in the best position to insure the risk at the lowest cost.

A third distinction is that perfect compensation of all contractual relational economic loss is almost always impossible because of the ripple effects which are of the very essence of contractual relational economic loss. This aspect has been recognized as critical from the very beginning. It is in this sense that the solution to cases of this type is necessarily pragmatic and involves drawing a line that will exclude at least some people who have been undeniably injured owing to the tortfeasor's admitted failure to meet the requisite standard of care.

In other types of economic loss cases, ripple effects may not be of concern. Thus cases like the present are significantly different from the situation in *Rivtow Marine Ltd.* v. *Washington Iron Works*, [1974] S.C.R. 1189, in which Rivtow was the sole victim of the type of damage for which it claimed. Full compensation of all those to whom a private law duty is owed is also realistically possible in the situation dealt with in *Kamloops* (*City of*) v. *Nielsen*, [1984] 2 S.C.R. 2. In cases like the present, claims that the denial of recovery in the type of case here would be 'unjust' must take into account that other 'just' claims are inevitably denied in this type of case.

Finally, contractual relational economic loss cases typically involve accidents. This distinguishes them from both products liability economic loss cases like *Rivtow*, in which by definition there is no accident, and negligent misrepresentation cases like *Hedley Byrne & Co.* v. *Heller & Partners Ltd.*, [1964] A.C. 465. This aspect is of fundamental importance with respect to tests of liability founded on the foreseeability of an individual plaintiff or an ascertained class of plaintiffs, which I shall discuss in Part III.

In light of these substantial differences between contractual relational economic loss cases and other pure economic loss cases, I agree with Professor Feldthusen, that 'it assists little, if at all, to generalize on the basis of proximity from other types of economic loss cases to the relational loss cases' ((1990–91), 17 *Can. Bus. L.J.* 356, at p. 376). For the purposes of the present case, it is not necessary to proceed to an exhaustive categorization of economic loss cases. There is, in my view, at the very least a clear difference between economic loss in three types of cases.

In the first type, which involves what has been termed consequential economic loss, the plaintiff claims for economic loss in addition to his claims for property damage or personal injury. Focusing on the issue of remoteness of damage, the courts have established guidelines regarding the availability of damages for economic loss in these cases.

In the second type, which can be termed non-relational economic loss, the plaintiff claims for pure economic loss unrelated to any personal injury or property damage suffered by either the plaintiff or any third party. The law in this area is developing. In view of my analysis of the issues in this case, it is not necessary for me to say much about these cases. I doubt, however, that this group can be analyzed in terms of a single rule. The extract from Professor Feldthusen above contends that this group can be further broken down into four distinct categories. It is sufficient to say that I fully support this Court's rejection of the broad bar on recovery of pure economic loss in *Rivtow* and *Kamloops*. I would stress again the need to take into account the specific characteristics of each case. I agree with McLachlin J. that *Murphy* v. *Brentwood District Council*, [1991] 1 A.C. 398, does not represent the law in Canada.

The present case, however, is of a third type. It involves a claim for contractual relational economic loss by the plaintiff as a result of damage caused to someone else's property.

Precedent

The English Background

It is helpful to retrace the development of the so-called rule against recovery of pure economic loss in order to place the argument in this case in context. The debate has often been obscured because of the existence of at least two different versions of the rule, one narrow and one broad. American cases have occasionally addressed specifically the issues in this case in terms of the breadth or narrowness of the economic loss rule. Particularly instructive in this regard is the recent case of *State of Louisiana* v. *M/V Testbank*, 752 F. 2d 1019 (1985).

The original formulation of the rule of the categorical exclusion of economic loss in cases such as *Cattle* v. *Stockton Waterworks Co.* (1875), L.R. 10 Q.B. 453, was narrow. In its narrow formulation, the rule excludes claims for negligent interference with contractual relations <u>where a third party's property has been damaged</u> and where the damage to the plaintiff's <u>contractual relations</u> is caused as a result of that property damage. The rule thus applies to exclude recovery for a plaintiff's pure economic loss flowing from the property owner's property damage, damage which I have termed contractual relational economic loss.

The development of the original narrow rule is well set out in *Candlewood Navigation Corp.* v. *Mitsui O.S.K. Lines Ltd.* (*The Mineral Transporter*), [1986] A.C. 1, at pp. 15–17, a case that dealt with a time charterer's claim for economic loss. Because of the importance of clearly understanding this development, I reproduce Lord Fraser of Tullybelton's account in that case *in extenso*:

This issue is one of fundamental importance in maritime law and in the law of negligence generally. <u>There is a long line of authority in the United Kingdom for the proposition that a time charterer is not entitled to recover for pecuniary loss caused by damage by a third party to the chartered vessel. The reason is that a time charterer has no proprietary or possessory right in the chartered vessel; his only right in relation to the vessel is contractual</u>: see *Scrutton on Charterparties and Bills of Lading*, 19th edn. (1984), p. 47. The proposition in relation to a time charterer is thus only one example of the more general principle stated by Scrutton LJ in *Elliott Steam Tug Co. Ltd.* v. *Shipping Controller* [1922] I K.B. 127, 139–40:

'At Common law there is no doubt about the position. <u>In case of a wrong done to a chattel the Common law does not recognize a person whose only rights are a contractual right to have the use or services of the chattel for purposes of making profits or gains without possession of or property in the chattel.</u> Such a person cannot claim for injury done to his contractual right: see on this point the judgment of Blackburn J. in *Cattle* v. *Stockton Waterworks Co.* (1875) L.R. 10 Q.B. 453, where a contractor making a tunnel on K's land claimed against a wrongdoer to K's land, whose wrong made his contract less profitable, and was held not entitled to recover. It is for this reason that underwriters cannot sue directly a wrongdoer against property they have insured, but must proceed in the name of the assured, as explained by Lord Penzance in *Simpson* v. *Thomson* (1877) 3 App. Cas. 279, 289. It is for this reason also that charterers under a charter not amounting to a demise do not and cannot sue in the Admiralty Court a wrongdoer who has sunk by collision their chartered ship. The same principle was applied by Hamilton J. in *Remorquage à Hélice* (*Société Anonyme*) v. *Bennetts* [1911] I K.B. 243, to prevent the owner of a tug suing the wrongdoer who had sunk his tow, whereby he had lost the benefit of his contract of towage.'

The general principle was stated in *Cattle* v. *Stockton Waterworks Co.*, L.R. 10 Q.B. 453, a case which had nothing to do with ships or maritime law. The facts have been summarised sufficiently for the present purpose in the passage just cited from

Scrutton LJ's judgment in *Elliott*'s case. The reason for the decision appears from the following passage from the judgment of the Court of Queen's Bench which was delivered by Blackburn J., at pp. 457–8, where, after stating that the court would have been glad to avoid giving effect to the rule against permitting the contractor to sue, he went on to say:

'But if we did so, we should establish an authority for saying that, in such a case as that of *Fletcher* v. *Rylands* (1866) L.R. 1 Ex. 265, the defendant would be liable, not only to an action by the owner of the drowned mine, and by such of his work-men as had their tools or clothes destroyed, but also to an action by every work-man and person employed in the mine, who in consequence of its stoppage made less wages than he would otherwise have done. And many similar cases to which this would apply might be suggested. It may be said that it is just that all such per-sons should have compensation for such a loss, and that, if the law does not give them redress, it is imperfect. Perhaps it may be so. But, as was pointed out by Coleridge J., in *Lumley* v. *Gye* (1853) 2 E. & B. 216, 252, courts of justice should not "allow themselves, in the pursuit of perfectly complete remedies for all wrong-ful acts, to transgress the bounds, which our law, in a wise consciousness as I con-ceive of its limited powers, has imposed on itself, of redressing only the proximate and direct consequences of wrongful acts." In this we quite agree. No authority in favour of the plaintiff's right to sue was cited, and, as far as our knowledge goes, there was none that could have been cited.'

It is apparent from that citation that the court in *Cattle*'s case regarded the rule as a pragmatic one dictated by necessity.

The same appears even more clearly from the other foundation case in this branch of the law, *Simpson & Co.* v. *Thomson* (1877) 3 App. Cas. 279 which was a Scottish appeal arising out of a collision between two ships belonging to the same owner. The House of Lords held that the underwriters, who had paid the insurance due on one of the ships which was lost and which was not to any extent to blame for the acci-dent, had no right of action against the owner of the other ship which was solely to blame, because they (the underwriters) had no independent right of action but only such right as they might have derived from the owner of the lost ship in whose place they stood. He had no right of action, as owner of the innocent ship, against himself as owner of the negligent ship. Lord Penzance gave a rather fuller statement of the reasons behind the rule against allowing the underwriters to sue, at pp. 289–90:

'But in the argument at your Lordships' Bar the learned counsel for the respon-dents took their stand upon a much broader ground. They contended that the underwriters, by virtue of the policy which they entered into in respect of this ship, had an interest of their own in her welfare and protection, inasmuch as any injury or loss sustained by her would indirectly fall upon them as a consequence of their contract; and that this interest was such as would support an action by them in their own names and behalf against a wrongdoer. This proposition virtually affirms a principle which I think your Lordships will do well to consider with some care, as it will be found to have a much wider application and signification than any which may be involved in the incidents of a contract of insurance.

The principle involved seems to me to be this—that where damage is done by a wrongdoer to a chattel not only the owner of that chattel, but all those who by contract with the owner have bound themselves to obligations which are rendered more onerous, or have secured to themselves advantages which are rendered less beneficial by the damage done to the chattel, have a right of action against the wrongdoer although they have no immediate or reversionary property in the chattel, and no possessory right by reason of any contract attaching to the chattel itself, such as by lien or hypothecation.

This, I say, is the principle involved in the respondents' contention. If it be a sound one, it would seem to follow that if, by the negligence of a wrongdoer, goods are destroyed which the owner of them had bound himself by contract to supply to a third person, this person as well as the owner has a right of action for any loss inflicted on him by their destruction.

But if this be true as to injuries done to chattels, it would seem to be equally so as to injuries to the person. An individual injured by a negligently driven carriage has an action against the owner of it. Would a doctor, it may be asked, who had contracted to attend him and provide medicines for a fixed sum by the year, also have a right of action in respect of the additional cost of attendance and medicine cast upon him by that accident? And yet it cannot be denied that the doctor had an interest in his patient's safety. In like manner an actor or singer bound for a term to a manager of a theatre is disabled by the wrongful act of a third person to the serious loss of the manager. Can the manager recover damages for that loss from the wrongdoer? Such instances might be indefinitely multiplied, giving rise to rights of action which in modern communities, where every complexity of mutual relation is daily created by contract, might be both numerous and novel.'

These two cases of *Cattle*, L.R. 10 Q.B. 453, and *Simpson*, 3 App. Cas. 279, have stood for over a hundred years and have frequently been cited with approval in later cases, both in the United Kingdom and elsewhere. They show, in their Lordships' opinion, that the justification for denying a right of action to a person who has suffered economic damage through injury to the property of another is that for reasons of practical policy it is considered to be inexpedient to admit his claim. [Emphasis added.]

Lord Fraser felt it was unnecessary to refer to all the many cases in which either or both of the cases of *Cattle* and *Simpson & Co.* v. *Thomson* (1877), 3 App. Cas. 279, have been cited but he did go on to note the favourable treatment given to the narrow rule in Scotland, Canada and the United States.

Subsequently, in the second stage of the development of the rule, it was greatly broadened. The remarks of Mason J. in *Caltex Oil (Aust.) Pty. Ltd.* v. *The Dredge 'Willemstad'* (1976), 11 A.L.R. 227 (H.C.), are illuminating, in that they illustrate the passage from the narrow rule discussed in the above passage to a broader rule (at p. 269):

None the less before *Hedley Byrne* the influence of the early cases was strong and it seems to have been generally considered that financial loss not consequential upon property damage could not be recovered. For the most part the cases concerned a claim by a plaintiff that he suffered a loss or lost a profit under a contract because the defendant's negligent conduct damaged or destroyed property of the other contracting party thereby putting an end to the contract or rendering it unprofitable. Yet the cases were thought to establish a general principle relating to the recovery of pure economic damage. [Emphasis added.]

As Mason J. notes, in its broad formulation, the rule was said to exclude all claims in negligence for pure economic loss, i.e., economic loss in the absence of property loss or personal injury loss, to the plaintiff in question. The crucial factor of property damage to a third party that existed in the early cases fell completely out of the picture. Interestingly, the same evolution appears to have occurred with respect to the holding in *Robins Dry Dock & Repair Co.* v. *Flint*, 275 U.S. 303 (1927), in the United States, which I shall more fully discuss later. The result was that until 1963, it was generally felt that no recovery would lie for pure economic loss.

A new stage in the development of the law on economic loss opened with the great case of *Hedley Byrne* v. *Heller, supra.* The speeches of the Law Lords were principally concerned with the problem of liability for negligent words, rather than with the issue of economic loss itself. As Atiyah notes, the problems of liability for negligent misstatements and the problem of economic loss had become entangled before *Hedley Byrne* and with both problems arising again in that case, it is perhaps not surprising that in subsequent cases, the two issues have not always been completely distinguished: see Atiyah, 'Negligence and Economic Loss' (1967), 83 *L.Q. Rev.* 248; see also the discussion of *Hedley Byrne* in Stapleton, 'Duty of Care and Economic Loss: A Wider Agenda' (1991), 107 *L.Q. Rev.* 249, at pp. 259–61.

Only two of the Lords in *Hedley Byrne*, Lord Hodson and Lord Devlin, dealt specifically with the issue of economic loss. Both rejected the broad exclusionary rule. It was clear that henceforth economic loss was recoverable at least in some circumstances. With *Hedley Byrne* to guide the way, the broad rule came increasingly under attack in a variety of situations during this third phase.

Many recent cases on economic loss have approached the problem at a very high level of generality. They have addressed the question of whether we should abandon the broad rule altogether. Many examples of the broad interpretation of *Cattle* and the other early cases can be pointed to: see, for example, *Abramovic* v. *Canadian Pacific Ltd.* (1989), 69 O.R. (2d) 487, at p. 492; *Kamloops (City of)* v. *Nielsen, supra*, at p. 28. My colleague, McLachlin J., I may say, interprets *Cattle* broadly in this manner, although she recognizes that the case dealt with relational losses.

The result of this broad approach is that cases on relational economic loss are bound up with other types of economic loss cases which raise different policy concerns. This leads to all types of economic loss cases being canvassed in order to resolve the case at hand. The judgment of the Court of Appeal in this case has been criticized for its undifferentiated approach to the issue of pure economic loss. Professor Feldthusen (1990–91), 17 *Can. Bus. L.J.* 356, writes, at p. 375:

> The main effect of this scatter-gun approach is to obscure the state of the authorities on relational loss, and to present instead the accurate, but largely irrelevant, impression that recovery of economic loss is often allowed in negligence.

In the second phase, cases decided on the narrow facts of contractual relational economic loss had been interpreted very broadly to exclude liability for all pure economic loss. Now, it was argued, the rejection of the broad rule in cases like *Hedley Byrne* and *Rivtow* should eliminate the specificities of economic loss in all cases. Today CN urges us to extend this approach to include contractual relational economic loss cases.

In my view, the precedents support a distinct approach to the issue of contractual relational economic loss. The original exclusionary rule developed in such cases and was expressed in narrow terms. In addition, the recognition that *Cattle* stands for a narrow rule has never completely disappeared. Recent cases have referred to *Cattle* and the early cases as establishing the narrow rule: see the extracts from *Candlewood, supra*; *Leigh and Sillavan Ltd.* v. *Aliakmon Shipping Co.*, [1986] A.C. 785, at p. 809; *Murphy* v. *Brentwood District Council, supra*, at p. 485. Cases that frame and treat the question in terms of the narrow rule have generally upheld it. The major exception is *Caltex*, which I will discuss at length later.

[There follows a brief review of Canadian and U.S. law before La Forest turns his attention to the civil law systems.]

Civil Law Systems

Since my colleagues have also supported their conclusions by forays into comparative law, and notably their understanding of the civil law experience, I find it necessary to enter into some discussion of that experience. I say at the outset that it does not seem to me to provide as much comfort for my colleagues' views as they seem to derive from it.

It is undeniable that not all legal systems have isolated cases like the present as presenting specific problems. Some civil law systems do not apply any particular rules either to pure economic loss cases or to contractual relational economic loss cases. The opinions of my colleagues in this case particularly rely on the law of France and Quebec. The argument from French and Quebec law is really about the floodgates argument. Since those systems allow recovery for pure economic loss without breaking down, the argument goes, we should not be deterred by floodgates arguments: see Jutras, 'Civil Law and Pure Economic Loss: What Are We Missing?' (1986–87), 12 *Can. Bus. L.J.* 295, at p. 310. In my opinion the relevant comparative reference is to contractual relational economic loss, not to the broad question of pure economic loss. To consider comparative law at the level of generality of 'economic loss' is not, in my view, helpful. I have already explained why I think the cases grouped under the rubric of economic loss deserve a more refined analysis. The same narrowing of the question should be employed in the recourse to comparative law. The legal system of every society faces essentially the same problems and solves these problems by quite different means, though often with similar results: see Zweigert and Kötz, *Introduction to Comparative Law, Volume I—The Framework* (2nd edn. 1987), at p. 31. While some of these systems have not retained the concept of 'economic loss' as a limiting factor, they have generally not recognized claims of the type put forward here.

Second, the French and Quebec approach involves applying the same criteria to a case of this type as to any other tort claim. Although some scholars argue that the Common law should change its focus entirely to a concern with causation as the limiting factor (see Tetley, 'Damages and Economic Loss in Marine Collision: Controlling the Floodgates' (1991), 22 *J. Mar. Law & Com.* 539, at p. 584), this does not appear to me to be an advisable option. Our current causality test of foreseeability is clearly insufficient to control liability. The directness criterion was rejected in *Overseas Tankship (U.K.) Ltd.* v. *Morts Dock & Engineering Co.* (*The Wagon Mound*), [1961] A.C. 388, for determinations as to remoteness and does not seem to me to provide much predictive value: see *S.C.M. (United Kingdom) Ltd.* v. *W. J. Whittall and Son Ltd.*, *supra*, at p. 343.

A close examination of French law in this area reveals that the floodgates problem is resolved by the use of a number of control devices such that liability is very rare. French delict doctrine treats the question of *dommage par ricochet* in relation first to the requirement that the injury suffered must have a 'personal character'; see Viney, 'Les obligations: La responsabilité: conditions' (1982), in Ghestin, *Traité de droit civil*, nos. 288 *et seq*. Undoubtedly, in general terms, French law allows generous recovery for *dommage par ricochet*: see Viney, at no. 309. However, with respect to persons who were contractually linked to the initial victim, Viney writes as follows, at no. 312:

> [Translation] The courts have from time to time had before them claims made by some customer, supplier or creditor, or by a partner, employee or employer, of the initial victim when the latter's death endangers their interests. <u>In general, the courts have so far been very hesitant to allow such claims, especially those made by a creditor, employer or partner; but at the same time a more liberal solution may well be envisaged in the case of employees who are thrown out of work by the employer's death.</u>
>
> The position in French law is no more harsh in this respect than that of foreign systems of law, which generally refuse to take into consideration this type of repercussive damage. . . . [Emphasis added.]

The distinction of the case of the employee is not specifically justified, but the most obvious rationale for distinguishing that particular case is surely that the employee is least able to protect himself or herself from the consequences of the accident. As for mere *créanciers* of the primary victim like CN, recovery is generally denied. The 1975 Cour de cassation case which left open the issue of recovery for a creditor whose debtor died as result of the defendant's fault, Cass. civ. 2e, June 25, 1975, Bull. II no. 195, eventually returned to that court in 1979: see Cass. civ. 2e, February 21, 1979, Bougues-Montès, J.C.P. 1979, IV, 145. The finding that the damages were indirect and hence unrecoverable was, as noted by Durry, partly justified by the fact that the lender should have protected himself by contract by requiring his debtor to contract life insurance; see 'Obligations et contrats spéciaux' (1979), 77 *Rev. trim. dr. civ.* 610. Larroumet speaks of recovery in such cases (other than in cases of contracts concluded *intuitus personae*) as an [translation] 'academic hypothesis' and notes that [translation] 'it is rarely found in the cases': see Bordeaux, May 17, 1977, D.1978, I.R. 34, note Larroumet.

Cases in which contractual relational economic loss have been awarded as a result of property damage to a third party are even more rare. These cases are admittedly also subject to the same basic framework of analysis. However, the Cour de

Cassation exercises its control over the lower courts' determinations of causality; see Starck, *Droit civil: Obligations: I. Responsabilité délictuelle* (3rd edn. 1988), by Roland and Boyer, at no. 851. Recovery is rarely allowed. Durry describes the state of the law in this area as follows, 'Obligations et contrats spéciaux' (1976), 74 *Rev. trim. dr. civ.* 132, at p. 134:

> [Translation] Physical repercussive damage to one who is neither parent, relative, fiancé or mistress of the immediate victim responds to a well-known dialectic: though in principle compensation may be obtained it in fact rarely is.

Markesinis' comparative examination of English and French law in this area (Markesinis, 'La politique jurisprudentielle et la réparation du préjudice économique en Angleterre: une approche comparative', [1983] *Rev. int. dr. comp.* 31, at pp. 44–5), also points out the remarkable similarity of result despite the different analytical approaches:

> [Translation] The first point to note is that French judges are fully aware of these dangers. Some fifty years ago the Tribunal civil of Bordeaux indicated it had no doubts on the matter when it said 'that extending entitlement to damages to everyone who might in some way suffer tangible or intangible injury from a quasi-delict *would amount to creating a kind of social disorder which can never be the purpose of the law*' . . . Accordingly, what is special about this judgment is that it *openly* expresses the philosophy of many judgments which have followed and which, though *in theory* they admit the possibility of compensation, have in many if not all cases proceeded to a denial of the right of action in practice. Consequently, what is interesting in these cases is to examine the method used to arrive at the result which English law obtains in a generally and rigidly applicable manner.
>
> A variety of 'causal' dispositions, which sometimes seemed to involve duplication, have been skilfully (and at times arbitrarily) used to attain this result. In some cases, it is said that the victim assumed the risk; in other cases, that the injury suffered is only indirect; and in still others, that it is only hypothetical and not certain; but in all cases, the possibility of compensation is recognized in theory. [Emphasis added.]

Recovery has been allowed in a few contractual relational economic loss cases. The first is where the contract that is disturbed is *intuitus personae*, i.e., a personal service contract where the particular individual cannot be replaced. In one case, a soccer club recovered for damages incurred as a result of the death of a star player: see Cour d'appel de Colmar (Ch. détachée à Metz), April 20, 1955, D.1956.723 (*Football Club de Metz c. Wiroth*). Even here, however, the law is not certain: recovery was denied to an opera director for the loss caused by an injury to the leading tenor: see Cass. civ. 2ᵉ, November 14, 1958, G.P. 1959.1.31 (*Demeyer c. Camerlo*). In a preliminary procedure at first instance, recovery was allowed to employees whose unemployment was caused by the tortfeasor who damaged their hair salon: see Trib. gr. inst. Nanterre, October 22, 1975, G.P. 1976.1.392 (*Brunet c. Rico et Caisse mutuelle d'assurance et de prévoyance*).

Marcailloux v. *R.A.T.V.M.*, Cass. civ. 2ᵉ, April 28, 1965, D.S. 1965.777, cited by McLachlin J., involved a traffic accident that led to a traffic jam. The person who caused the accident was held liable for damages of 39 francs to the local transport authority for the loss of receipts caused by the resulting delay to the circulation of its vehicles. It is unclear what distinguishes this claim from other potential traffic jam claims. The note by Professor Esmein in the *Marcailloux* case observes that the characterization of a particular damage as direct or indirect, far from being a factual inquiry, is simply the statement of a conclusion as to recovery; in this regard, it plays a similar function to the concept of proximity in our law. See Note under Cass. civ. 2e, April 28, 1965, D.S. 1965.777.

In Quebec, the expansive interpretation of 'another' in art. 1053 of the Civil Code of Lower Canada referred to by McLachlin J. has served to shift the analysis to the terrain of causality: see Baudouin, *La responsabilité civile délictuelle* (3rd edn., 1990), at no. 177. Baudouin recognizes the difficulty of generalizing with respect to determinations of directness but he considers that a trend toward an exclusion of liability is discernible, *supra*, at no. 354:

> [Translation] The problem of determining what is 'direct' damage is complex and here again any attempt at generalization would be presumptuous. However, one trend seems to be clear. The courts will not recognize loss the immediate source of which is not the fault itself but some other injury already caused by the fault. In other words, damage resulting from damage, repercussive damage, 'second degree' damage, is indirect.

However, as the author recognizes, this is at most a trend. He further notes that Quebec courts have tended to consider causality as a question of fact: *supra*, at no. 349. This would constitute a significant difference with the French regime. However, the author notes that the decision of this Court in *Morin* v. *Blais*, [1977] 1 S.C.R. 570, considered the question of causality to constitute a question of law. Recovery of contractual relational economic loss has been allowed in a few cases in Quebec. Employers have been allowed to recover for the loss of the services of their employees.

In my view, the French and Quebec experience remains inconclusive. Although the cases are theoretically not subject to any special requirements for recovery, cases of recovery of contractual relational economic loss are few. The rarity of the cases has resulted in little doctrinal discussion of the issues raised and the brevity of the reasons makes the grounds for determination difficult to analyse. While French law does not establish an absolute bar, it is very close to establishing a *de facto* bar through the use of the dual requirements of directness and proof of causality. The number of cases in which recovery has been allowed is very few when one considers that relational losses occur as a result of practically every accident causing property damage in the commercial area.

Furthermore, one is at pains to establish the grounds for distinguishing successful claims from other relational claims. What little doctrinal discussion there is appears to be both keenly aware of the potential for open-ended liability and conscious that recovery is generally denied. Such analysis also points to factors entering into the directness and causality analysis that would exclude CN's claim, factors such as the *intuitus personae* nature of the contractual relationship and the inability of the plaintiff to protect itself through contract or otherwise. I shall have occasion to consider such factors later.

In addition, civil law scholars have remarked on the lack of emphasis in French and Quebec law on the problems raised by the nature of particular protected interests; see Jutras, *supra*, at pp. 295–6 and 310–11. In civil law systems such as the German system which, unlike the French system, have focused significant attention on the problems posed by the nature of different protected interests (see Limpens, Kruithof and Meinertzhagen-Limpens, 'Liability for One's Own Act', in *International Encyclopedia of Comparative Law*, vol. XI, *Torts*, ch. 2, IV.), recovery is denied for contractual relational claims based on the type of damage; see Markesinis, *A Comparative Introduction to the German Law of Torts* (2nd edn. 1990), at pp. 39 *et seq.* Other civil law systems have strict exclusionary rules. Switzerland apparently excludes *le dommage par ricochet*, allowing only recovery for wrongful death; see Herbots, 'Le "duty of care" et le dommage purement financier en droit comparé' [1985], *Rev. dr. int. et dr. comp.* 7, at p. 32.

What conclusions can be drawn from the civil law? First, I think there is general agreement that economic loss cases cannot simply be subjected to the same analysis as cases involving other types of damage: see Atiyah, *supra*, at p. 270. No one is suggesting, after all, that we modify the rules adopted in *Hedley Byrne* for an undifferentiated *Donoghue* test in economic loss cases.

There remains the argument that French and Quebec experience puts the lie to the floodgates problem in this area. In my view, this is simply not borne out. First of all, as Markesinis points out, French judges are acutely aware of the potential for unlimited liability. They use different analytical tools to reach much the same result.

One can of course attempt to meet the floodgates argument by contending that recovery for contractual relational economic loss will remain exceptional even if the exclusionary rule is relaxed. This is perhaps the most that can be drawn from the civil law experience: the replacement of an exclusionary rule with what amounts to very close to a *de facto* bar will not lead to many cases being brought forward. Unlike the civil law rules in these areas, however, the traditional control devices in our tort law have been elaborated to deal with damages that are generally by their nature limited.

I am principally concerned about the relative advisability of attempting to draw a line within the group of contractual claimants as opposed to distinguishing based on the nature of the interest at stake. Specifically, I am concerned about the nature and the workability of the criteria used to distinguish valid claims. In my view, any incursions into the exclusionary rule should be carefully justified on policy grounds. With respect to this question, I do not find any theory put forward in either France or Quebec that would aid in making distinctions amongst contractual claimants on valid policy grounds; see the discussion by Mayrand JA of the difficulties in making the directness determination with respect to 'victims by ricochet' in *J.E. Construction Inc.* v. *General Motors du Canada Ltée*, [1985] C.A. 275, at pp. 278–9.

To the extent that recovery has been allowed, the inability of doctrine to elucidate the characteristics leading to recovery or to a finding of directness gives the lie to the idea that allowing recovery in a few cases of this nature will provide material for an *ex post* rationalisation that the court is incapable of formulating beforehand. I do not share McLachlin J's confidence that turning this issue over to the Common law to decide cases on the basis of proximity will lead to the gradual formation of categories of recovery that make sense in policy terms, and nothing in the civil law experience with findings of directness leads me to greater confidence in this regard: see Herbots, *supra*, at p. 21.

The narrow exclusionary rule distinguishes between property claims and contract claims and excludes the latter in cases of property damage. This bright line test has been in the past extended to the wider field of pure economic loss; in this wider field, it is in retreat in a number of areas. In my view, this case presents the court with the following problem: should the court eliminate the bright line test in the narrow area of contractual relational economic loss in favour of a test that will discriminate differently, this time amongst the class of contractual claimants, those who merit recovery and those who do not? If yes, what criteria should govern recovery?

Before dealing further with the question of contractual relational economic loss, however, it is necessary to consider a different set of arguments advanced by the respondent.

Part II: Alternative Interest Theories

Introductory Remarks

CN argues that its case does not rest on a mere contractual interest. It seeks to avoid the application of the narrow exclusionary rule by arguing that it has alternative interests at stake that differentiate it from the ordinary contractual claimant. It does not seek to place itself under a long-standing exception to the exclusionary rule enunciated in *Simpson & Co.* v. *Thomson, supra*, at p. 290, which involves cases allowing recovery to a plaint. Twith a proprietary or possessory interest. If CN could argue that its interest in the bridge was analogous to the interest of a demise charterer in the chartered ship, it would be able to recover since it would be, *vis-à-vis* third parties, the temporary owner of the bridge; see *Scrutton on Charterparties and Bills of Lading* (19th edn. 1984), at pp. 47–52; *Baumwoll Manufactur von Carl Scheibler* v. *Furness*, [1893] A.C. 8 (H.L.); *The 'Father Thames'*, [1979] 2 Lloyd's Rep. 364. A demise charterer's interest typically entirely supplants the interest of the owner of the ship, even in the repair of physical damage: see *Candlewood, supra*, at p. 18. For example, in *Rivtow*, the plaintiff was a demise charterer. No argument was directed to contesting Rivtow's interest.

CN's licence agreement gives it no proprietary or possessory interest. This state of affairs was surely not entirely fortuitous in light of the fact that the existence of such an interest was a central consideration in the *Gypsum Carrier* case. CN's contract with PWC establishes no proprietary or possessory interest in the bridge, and it did not attempt to argue that its contract resembled that of a demise charterer.

Unable to contend for the existence of a possessory right to the bridge, CN, we saw, put forward essentially two arguments to the effect that its interest is more than that of a mere contractor. First, it says, it suffered from a transferred loss of use. Secondly, it maintains, it is involved in a common adventure with PWC. These arguments are centred on the relationship between the plaintiff and the property owner, i.e., between CN and PWC.

the plaintiff because of their contract. A true transferred loss case requires that the risk of <u>property damage</u> have passed, as in the case of goods damaged in transit after the risk (but not the property) has passed to the buyer. In such a case, unless the buyer is given a right of action, the carrier will be liable to neither party: not to the seller because he has suffered no loss, nor to the buyer who has no protected interest; see Fleming, *The Law of Torts* (7th edn. 1987), at pp. 164–5.

Even in that type of case, recovery was denied in the recent House of Lords decision in *Leigh and Sillavan Ltd.* v. *Aliakmon Shipping Co.*, *supra*, essentially on the ground that contract law provided a sufficient protection in the circumstances of that case. It was only the particular variation of the contract to which the buyers agreed that deprived them of their usual right of action.

The present is not a true transferred loss case. PWC has collected for the property damage it has sustained. The transferred loss claimed in this case is thus not with respect to the property damage claim. Rather, it is a claim for the transferred <u>loss of use, or transferred economic loss</u>.

In these circumstances, I fail to see how the respondent suffered a transferred loss such as to create an alternative protected interest to its contractual interest.

Common Adventure or Joint Venture

MacGuigan JA refers, at p. 167, to the finding of the trial judge that recovery is supported by 'the CNR's role in supplying materials and inspection and consulting services for the bridge, and CNR's preponderant usage of the bridge, recognized even in the periodic negotiations for routine maintenance closings'. CN argues that these findings bring into play the 'common adventure' cases: see *Morrison Steamship Co.* v. *Greystoke Castle (Cargo Owners)* (*The Greystoke Castle*), [1947] A.C. 265; *Aktieselskabet Cuzco* v. *The Sucarseco*, 294 U.S. 394 (1935).

I disagree. In my view, the appellants are correct in arguing that there was no common adventure in this case. The parties agreed that the bridge was owned, operated and maintained by the PWC. PWC was, by contract with the railways, obligated to operate and maintain the bridge.

CN's preponderant usage of the bridge and participation in negotiations over bridge closure do not justify a finding of common adventure. I can see no reason to allow recovery based simply on the plaintiff's status as a principal client. Undoubtedly, many suppliers of services consult with their principal clients with respect to planning necessary interruptions of supply so as to minimize disruption. While this is certainly good business practice, it does not establish a finding of common adventure.

CN also argues that paragraph 10 of its licence agreement (cited *supra*), together with its provision of materials for repairs, is sufficient to constitute a 'common adventure' between itself and PWC. In my view, that provision is far from sufficient to create an alternative interest. While it does provide that CN will make emergency repairs, it provides both for prior approval and reasonable reimbursement by Canada. The consulting services, inspections, maintenance and repairs are subject to a similar regime. These provisions merely provide for the establishment of further contractual relations between CN and PWC. CN is both a supplier to PWC and a contractor for services from PWC. None of the clauses provides for any joint responsibility for property losses. It would be curious if a bridge user could found a contractual loss claim on the fortuitous circumstance that it also was the company hired to fix the bridge on occasion.

There is no case for a common adventure that equates to the relationship between ship and cargo in a general average case. In cases of common adventure, A, the ship, has suffered damage which is recoverable against the wrongdoer C. B is <u>bound to contribute</u> to A's loss and seeks to recover the amount of its contribution from the wrongdoer: see *The Greystoke Castle, supra*, at p. 304, *per* Lord Simonds (dissenting). In *The Sucarseco, supra*, the United States Supreme Court considered a claim by owners of undamaged cargo against the non-carrying ship arising out of a collision. The cargo owners claimed for damages in the amount of their contributions to the general average. In allowing the claim, Hughes CJ carefully distinguished the case before him from a general contractual claim (at pp. 404–5):

> This is not a case of an attempt, by reason of 'a tort to the person or property of one man,' to make the tortfeasor liable to another 'merely because the injured person was under a contract with that other, unknown to the doer of the wrong.' See *Robins Dry Dock & Repair Co.* v. *Flint*, 275 U.S. 303, 309; *Elliott Steam Tug Co.* v. *Shipping Controller* [1922] I KB 127, 139, 142; *The Federal No. 2*, 21 F. (2d) 313. Here, cargo as well as ship was placed <u>in jeopardy</u>. That jeopardy was due in part to the negligence of the vessel against which the claim is made. The fact that the vessel and the cargo under the 'Jason clause' bear their proportionate shares of the expenses gives *Sucarseco* no ground for a contention that the expenses themselves, or the share that cargo bears, were not occasioned directly by the tort. <u>In the light of the nature of the general average contributions</u>, and of the event which made them necessary, the fact that they were made under the stipulation in the 'Jason clause' is no more a defense to *Sucarseco* than is the fact that the cargo was placed on board under a contract to carry it. [Emphasis added.]

Earlier in his reasons, the Chief Justice had underlined that the Jason clause 'in no way changes the essential features of general average contributions' (at p. 402). In addition to the other distinctions with respect to the case at bar, the contractual clause in these cases largely serves to reaffirm the application of a special legal regime.

The Greystoke Castle, supra, is very similar to *The Sucarseco* and the House of Lords in fact relied on the American case. It involves the law of general average and is easily distinguishable from this case. I would confine Lord Roche's dictum, at p. 280, to cases of general average and common adventure narrowly defined: see *Murphy* v. *Brentwood District Council, supra*, at p. 460, *per* Lord Keith. At the very least, a requirement exists that the expenses be incurred in avoiding or mitigating personal or property damage threatened by the defendant's negligence: see Fleming, *supra*, at p. 164.

These cases involve discretionary decisions made in the common interest that impose cost disproportionately amongst those who benefit from the decision. In the words of Hughes CJ in *The Sucarseco, supra*, at pp. 402–3: 'It must still appear that voluntary and successful sacrifices have been made or extraordinary expenses incurred on behalf of those interested in the adventure in order to avert a common imminent peril, with resulting benefit to the adventure upon which the burden of such sacrifices and expenses appropriately rests.' In my view, these general average cases are not applicable to the facts of this case. There was no common imminent peril. CN was not required to contribute to PWC's loss. The loss fell exactly where the contract between CN and PWC attributed it. It cannot suffice that losses were incurred by both parties, for that is always the case in this type of situation.

With respect to CN's voluntary contributions to bridge maintenance, which constitute the principal extra-contractual aspect of the relationship between the plaintiff and the property owner in this case, it should be remembered that CN and the other railways were paying a low price under the contract, merely sufficient to cover PWC's costs. In return, PWC's repair obligations under the contract were not particularly strict. In the event of the complete or partial destruction of the bridge or any damage thereto, the decision to replace or repair was entirely at Canada's discretion. Canada was under no obligation to rebuild, replace or repair such destruction or damage and the railway was not entitled to claim any compensation or damages. No time limits for repairs were provided for. It thus made perfect commercial sense for CN to voluntarily inspect and repair the bridge on occasion in its own interest, especially since it must, in any event, maintain the necessary manpower and equipment to repair its own bridges in the area. CN may have provided some maintenance services when it suited its purposes, but it cannot be said that CN operates and maintains the bridge. The railway had no obligation to provide any service without being paid. It also had no obligation to contribute financially in any manner to compensate any losses incurred by PWC. CN's voluntary contributions are not such as to constitute a joint venture.

It remains unclear to me how the Court is to proceed to establish the existence of a joint venture other than by looking at the contractual relationship between the plaintiff and the property owner. McLachlin J. considers that the evidence in this case is sufficient to establish the existence of a joint venture. With respect, I am unable to agree. None of the traditional indicia of a joint venture is present either through contract or extra-contractually. There was no legal entity in the nature of the partnership. There was no joint undertaking of any commercial enterprise. There was no duty to share both profits and losses. In my view, where the contractual or extra-contractual relationship between the parties excludes any form of possible joint liability or contribution in cases of loss of this type, a finding of the existence of a joint venture in this context is excluded.

In conclusion, I do not find the respondent's arguments to the effect that it had more than a mere contractual interest convincing. CN's entitlement to use the bridge finds its sole source in the contract. The contract sets out the full extent of CN's rights: without the contract, CN would be trespassing. It has wisely not argued the existence of any possessory interest. Its transferred loss is merely the transfer of a loss of use and is a less compelling case for recovery than the loss incurred by a time charterer. This case does not involve a common adventure such as exists in the cases dealing with general average contributions. As a result, I cannot accept the rationale for recovery set forth by McLachlin J., at pp. 1162–3, to the effect that the purpose of allowing recovery in this case is to permit 'a plaintiff whose position for practical purposes, *vis-à-vis* the tortfeasor, is indistinguishable from that of the owner of the damaged property, to recover what the actual owner could have recovered'.

CN's recovery in the courts below, however, was not founded on a different interest than the typical contractual claimant; rather, it was founded on greater proximity with respect to the same interest. As a result, I propose to return to the issue of contractual relational economic loss. I will first examine the various proposals to relax the bright line rule. Then I will consider the rationale behind that rule in light of the proposals.

Part III: The Proposed Tests

CN argues that even if we reject its 'alternative interests' argument and find its <u>interest</u> merely contractual, the existence of other factors is sufficient to constitute a special relationship with the tortfeasor and to ground recovery for its contractual claims in this case. In particular, it points to the high degree of subjective and objective foreseeability in this case as sufficient to constitute a special relationship between Norsk and CN, but other factors are invoked as well. The respondent does not deny the existence of the rule in *Cattle*. It contends, however, that the rationale for *Cattle* is simply that the <u>mere</u> disruption of contractual rights without more is insufficient to ground recovery. These arguments represent an attempt to <u>qualify</u> the application of the contractual relational economic loss exclusionary rule.

My colleague McLachlin J. has set forth guideposts for the search for the answer to the issue in the case at bar. In brief, she underlines the need for limits to liability, the need for the limits to be reasonably clear and the need for the rule to respond to considerations of policy and fairness. She also recognizes that a single rule for all economic loss cases is probably unattainable. I am in substantial agreement with her on these points but I consider that a number of additional aspects are relevant to the choice of a rule in this area.

First, with respect to the need for limits to liability, it is important to underline that perfect justice is not possible in this area; it is impossible to compensate everybody who suffers loss owing to their contractual relationships with the property owner. Some losses, which were undoubtedly incurred as a result of a defendant's negligence, are going to remain uncompensated. The challenge, then, is to come up with a rule that divides the winners and the losers in the best possible manner.

A good test should distinguish on a rational basis between potential plaintiffs, all of whom were injured by the defendants' negligence. The plaintiff's proposed rule should offer a convincing and practical rationale for distinguishing its claim from those other claims, contractual or otherwise, which are to be rejected. Victims whose claims are to be denied must perceive a minimum of justice in the result. In my view, none of the theories that involve the acceptance of CN's claim but which would lead to the rejection of the claims of the other railways can be accepted as just from this perspective.

A test for recovery in cases of economic loss to contractual entitlements caused by property damage to another party should reflect the characteristics of this type of litigation, described in Feldthusen, *Economic Negligence, supra*, at pp. 207–8:

> The defendants in this type of case are not typically heinous wrongdoers, but rather individuals and enterprises engaged in common and useful social activity.

> The same is true of the plaintiffs who are inadvertently harmed by some unfortu-
> nate and often inevitable consequence of modern life. Few important moral, social
> or symbolic issues are involved. Here, if anywhere, the economists' suggestion that
> the law should devise rules which permit the occasionally incompatible activities
> of plaintiffs and defendants to continue at the lowest possible total social cost
> should be taken seriously. This includes rules which encourage *both parties* to take
> cost-efficient accident prevention measures. And in respect of the unavoidable
> accidents which remain, it suggests that the loss should be borne by the party who
> can insure against it at the lowest cost. [Emphasis in original.]

This description is pertinent in the present case. A good rule should thus place some
incentive on both parties to act in an economically rational manner to reduce total
accident costs.

The rule must, of course, also confront the problem of indeterminacy. It is often
suggested that this is the only problem the rule must confront. This was perhaps natural in light of the importance of potential indeterminate liability in negligent misrepresentation cases and the fact that the breakthrough in allowing recovery for
economic loss came in *Hedley Byrne*. However, this confusion between the two
issues tended to obscure the variety of issues raised in different kinds of economic
loss cases. If the principal reason lying behind the broad exclusionary rule for pure
economic loss is the concern over indeterminate liability, then the exclusionary rule
can be easily discarded in favour of a more direct test of whether liability would be
indeterminate. The plaintiff's case here is essentially built on this proposition and
they offer this Court a wide variety of factual distinctions which they contend
respond to the concern about indeterminate liability. As the above discussion indicates, I do not agree with that approach; a rule in this area should serve to do more
than simply exclude indeterminate liability. However, in contractual economic loss
cases, the proposed rule must certainly confront this issue.

What then does it mean for a particular liability to be determinate? The first critical question is whether the liability needs to be determinate before or after the accident. It is important to underline that since most claims of this nature occur in the
commercial area, the requisite certainty should exist before the accident occurs. A
company like CN should be able to consult legal counsel and receive reasonably
clear advice with respect to potential recovery in the case of an accident that it as
common as a ship hitting a bridge. So should a company like Burlington Northern
Railway. Even more importantly, when the shoe is on the other foot, CN should also
be able to get some reasonably clear guidance from counsel with respect to its potential liabilities in a case where a train derails and damages a factory. Estimating such
liability is, of course, a key aspect to the pricing of insurance for potential tortfeasors. Under the exclusionary rule, liability is determinate before the accident; unless
the contract is such as to create a joint venture or a possessory interest, all parties are
aware that no recovery will lie for damage to those contractual interests.

The second important point is that the objection is not simply to a large number
of claims since an accident may injure a large number of people or cause extensive
property damage. But in physical damage cases, the number of potential first-victim
claims is usually foreseeable even when large. Even more importantly, it is rare for

multiple physical damage claims to ripple down a chain; physical injury to one person rarely gives rise to physical injury to others down a chain: see Stapleton, *supra*, at p. 255. Such ripple effects are on the contrary the very essence of contractual relational economic loss. The concern is that the volume of claims is indeterminate and therefore difficult and expensive to insure against.

A third important consideration is the indeterminacy of each claim. Recovery for contractual expectancies requires analysis of who bore the loss. What would happen if CN effectively passed on any increased costs incurred owing to the unavailability of the bridge to its customers? Refusing to address this question could result in a very expensive tort case leading to compensation for a party who suffered no loss. In a multi-stage chain of contracts, it becomes very difficult to analyse the economic effects of an accident on a particular link in the chain. A related concern is with false or inflated claims: see *Spartan Steel, supra*.

The problem with this case from the perspective of indeterminacy is that it involves a type of accident that will very likely lead to a great number of claims. It so happens that on the facts of this case, the number of injured parties is small. The fact that Norsk was fortunate enough to hit a bridge with few users does not make its potential liability for contractual relational economic loss any less indeterminate. Its liability after the accident is, of course, determinate; but beforehand, when potential tortfeasors are looking for insurance, they and their insurance company do not know which bridge will be hit. It seems odd to establish one set of rules for negligent tortfeasors who hit busy bridges—liability for economic loss is excused because of indeterminacy—and a different set for those who hit bridges used by few users.

I turn to an examination of the proposed tests. The principal authority in the Commonwealth allowing recovery for contractual relational economic loss is *Caltex, supra. Caltex* involved an oil refinery and pipeline owned by the Australian Oil Refinery ('AOR') that carried oil to a terminal owned by the plaintiff Caltex. While oil was moving through the pipeline between the refinery and the Caltex terminal a dredge negligently damaged the pipeline. AOR was compensated for its loss as property owner.

Under the terms of the Caltex-AOR contract, the oil in the pipeline was owned by Caltex but was at the risk of AOR. Caltex claimed against the dredge and its owners for its economic loss resulting from the damage, specifically the expense to which it was put in arranging for continued supply of its terminal either by ship or road. One of the questions before the court was whether the plaintiff could recover damages for economic loss sustained as a result of damage negligently caused to the property of a third party. Although all five judges held that the right to economic loss must rest on something more than mere foreseeability they all agreed that the plaintiff must succeed. Each, however, suggested different approaches for the appropriate test to be applied. I shall examine the various proposed rules under the headings set out below.

Foreseeability of the Individual Plaintiff or of an Ascertained Class of Plaintiffs

CN heavily stressed the defendants' undoubtedly high level of subjective and objective knowledge that CN as a particular company would suffer loss. My colleague

Stevenson J. relies on this factor as his principal ground for finding liability in this case. There is no question that Norsk knew and ought to have known that CN would suffer loss. Indeed, the facts reveal that the tug captain thought CN would suffer even more than it did, since he erroneously thought the bridge belonged to it. I am unable to see the importance of this 'excess of foresight' in policy terms, however.

First, the subjective view of the defendants with respect to the ownership of the bridge is obviously not sufficient to ground a claim. Such an error does not, of course, negate the defendants' duty with respect to the actual owner of the property. Why should it have the effect of creating new duties in the absence of a protected interest? It remains true, however, that Norsk could reasonably foresee that a specific plaintiff, CN, would suffer loss as a <u>contractual</u> claimant. Should this factor distinguish CN from other contractual claimants?

Two judges in *Caltex* suggested versions of an individual plaintiff test, at least one that would allow recovery in this case. At the level of a general test for all cases of pure economic loss, Mason J. adopted what can be termed the specific individual test. 'A defendant', he held at p. 274, 'will then be liable for economic damage due to his negligent conduct when he can reasonably foresee that a specific individual, as distinct from a general class of persons, will suffer financial loss as a consequence of his conduct'. Gibbs J. also incorporated the known plaintiff test into his analysis as a necessary but not sufficient condition for liability (at p. 245). As he saw it, the existence of a common adventure or physical propinquity may have supporting roles, but are neither necessary nor sufficient. The ascertained class test would allow recovery where the defendant knows or has the means of knowing that the persons likely to be affected by his or her negligence consist of a definite number of persons.

In *Candlewood, supra*, at p. 24, the House of Lords rejected the individual plaintiff test and the ascertained class of plaintiffs test in the following terms:

Their Lordships have carefully considered these reasons for the decision in the *Caltex* case, 136 C.L.R. 529. With regard to the reasons given by Gibbs and Mason JJ, their Lordships have difficulty in seeing how to distinguish between a plaintiff as an individual and a plaintiff as a member of an unascertained class. The test can hardly be whether the plaintiff is known by name to the wrongdoer. Nor does it seem logical for the test to depend upon the plaintiff being a single individual. Further, why should there be a distinction for this purpose between a case where the wrongdoer knows (or has the means of knowing) that the persons likely to be affected by his negligence consist of a definite number of persons whom he can identify either by name or in some other way (for example as being the owners of particular factories or hotels) and who may therefore be regarded as an ascertained class, and a case where the wrongdoer knows only that there are several persons, the exact number being to him unknown, and some or all of whom he could not identify by name or otherwise, and who may therefore be regarded as an unascertained class? Moreover much of the argument in favour of an ascertained class seems to depend upon the view that the class would normally consist of only a few individuals. But would it be different if the class, though ascertained, was large? Suppose for instance that the class consisted of all the pupils in a particular school. If it was a kindergarten school with only six pupils they might be regarded as constituting an ascertained class, even if their names were unknown to the wrongdoer. If the school was a large one with over a thousand pupils it might be suggested that they were not an ascertained class. But it is not easy to see a distinction in principle merely because the number of possible claimants is larger in one case than in the other. Apart from cases of negligent misstatement, with which their Lordships are not here concerned, they do not consider that it is practicable by reference to an ascertained class to find a satisfactory control mechanism which could be applied in such a way as to give reasonable certainty in its results.

In *Kamloops, supra*, Wilson J. also questioned the advisability of the individual plaintiff test. At pages 30–1, she stated:

> It is quite apparent that Gibbs and Jacobs JJ, and possibly Stephen J. also, were seeking some means of permitting recovery for pure economic loss while avoiding the undesirable consequences of applying the reasonable foreseeability rule, namely indeterminate liability to an indeterminate class. They saw the solution in limiting foreseeability to specific individuals rather than members of a class. I am not sure, however, that their exception solves the problem. It may make the class determinate but it gives no guarantee that it will be small.

Both Lord Fraser of Tullybelton's unanimous opinion and Wilson J.'s majority opinion stressed the practical difficulties in applying such a test. I agree that the practical difficulties of applying such a test are considerable to say the least.

In my view, problems also exist at the level of principle. In the absence of any malicious intent on the part of the defendant, of what significance is the fact that the defendant knew that the individual plaintiff would suffer? In my view, its only role is to limit liability. The individual plaintiff or class of plaintiff or special relationship test serves a very different and more focused policy function in the context of the negligent misrepresentation cases where it has been employed: see *Hedley Byrne, supra; Candler* v. *Crane, Christmas & Co.*, [1951] 2 KB 164. Professor Feldthusen remarks as follows on its function in those cases ((1990–91), 17 *Can. Bus. L.J.* 356, at pp. 376–7):

> . . . the duty of care is derived from a business relationship between the parties which antedates, and is independent from, the negligent act. The assumption of responsibility or special relationship duty tests and the known limited class remoteness test were developed to deal with transaction-specific negligence. The defendant makes <u>a reflective transactional undertaking</u> to a third party which affects (and is probably intended to affect) the plaintiff. The defendant is actually contemplating advice or service and its consequences in the transaction. It makes some sense to speak of parties known to be at risk from the contemplated transaction. The entire thrust of misrepresentation and services law is to limit liability to contemplated transaction-specific situations. One may describe this in proximity language, but it is a different use of the proximity principle than in a relational case. [Emphasis added.]

Those cases involve the defendant's making a representation <u>voluntarily</u>. It makes sense to impose upon the defendant a requirement that he or she put his or her mind to the question of who might be affected, since the defendant has the opportunity to reflect on this issue before making the representation: see *Haig* v. *Bamford, supra*.

Here we are dealing with an <u>accident</u>. There is no intention to affect the plaintiff; rather the effect on the plaintiff is merely a result of the accident. Norsk cannot be said to contemplate a particular act of negligence, a particular plaintiff or a particular loss in the same sense as a bank manager who provides financial information. Knowledge of the individual plaintiff serves solely to eliminate 'indeterminate liability': it operates arbitrarily both in terms of singling out defendants and in terms of singling out plaintiffs.

In the context of an accident, this criteria has thus no link with fault or with a lack of care; surely no one is suggesting tort law should strive to protect bridges with high profile users more than bridges used by anonymous users, or that defendants who damage bridges with high profile users are more guilty than others. Its sole function is to distinguish one plaintiff from another and thus 'solve' the indeterminacy problem, a function that could be as effectively performed by a rule based on the colour of CN's trains.

Allowing CN's claim to be distinct from the other contractual victims by virtue of its particular foreseeability as an individual victim would in my view give rise to an unjust rule owing to its sheer arbitrariness. It serves neither to distinguish particularly meritorious victims, nor to single out particularly careless tortfeasors. Its sole function is to reduce the class of claimants to a small group, a function that could be equally well performed by any other factual distinction. Further, the test would have the effect of singling out the wrong parties for relief. It would offer a premium to notoriety, a premium for which I can find no legal or social justification, particularly since such persons are most likely to advert to the matter and to contract out or insure against the harm.

The Defendant's Foresight with Respect to the Specific Nature of the Loss Incurred by the Plaintiff

The second factor put forward as founding proximity is that Norsk foresaw the specific nature of the loss incurred by CN. The argument based on the foreseeability of the specific nature of the loss would presumably found recovery for all three railroads, so it sits rather awkwardly with CN's unique relationship claim. It is also clearly insufficient to function on its own as a limit on indeterminate damages, since even if there were thousands of users of the bridge, the specific nature of the losses incurred would be foreseeable for all users. In practically all cases of this type, the defendant will be aware that the 'specific nature of the loss' will be the loss of use of the property he or she has damaged.

Additionally, the tortfeasor does not actually know the specific nature of the loss, since the allocation of the loss will depend primarily on the terms of the contract between the plaintiff and the property owner as well as on other contracts between the plaintiff and the other parties. It is certain that Norsk knew that CN's <u>use of the bridge</u> would be interrupted. What is less clear and in fact quite doubtful is whether

Norsk knew about the <u>allocation of risk of bridge failure</u> in the contract between CN and PWC.

It is thus incorrect to say that, because Norsk knew that CN's use of the bridge would be interrupted, it knew the 'precise nature of the loss' CN would incur. The precise nature of the loss, and in fact whether any loss is incurred at all, would be a result of the contractual allocation of risk, of which Norsk would normally be unaware. In many cases of contractual relational loss, the variety of contractual entitlements will be much greater and more complex.

Physical Propinquity

The third factor that is said to found proximity is the physical proximity of CN's property to the accident. CN's property is closely joined to the bridge on both sides of the river and the bridge forms an integral part of its railway network. CN relies here primarily on the judgment of Jacobs J. in *Caltex*. Jacobs J. there recognized that where the plaintiff's loss arises solely from a contractual relationship with a third party, recovery will be denied (at p. 279). However, he held, at p. 279, that if the damage arose owing to 'physical effect on the person or property of the plaintiff, it will not be irrecoverable simply because it is economic loss'. The judge, at p. 278, defined physical effect short of physical injury as an act or omission that prevents physical movement of a person or physical movement or operation of property. In that case, the physical effect was the immobilization of the flow of crude oil through the pipeline.

CN does not, in my view, meet this physical effect test, even if such a test were adopted. Its trains have certainly not been immobilized. Its land has not been damaged and it makes no sense to speak of its being immobilized. In the absence of such a 'physical effect', physical propinquity of property cannot constitute an alternative potential interest. As the appellants rightly point out, the other railways suffered identical damages despite not owning any property in physical propinquity to the accident.

The application of this test would also lead to minimal damages even if it were met. Jacobs J. describes the damages that flow from his test as being limited to those resulting from the physical effect. In the *Caltex* case, the quantification of the damage was conceded. No inquiry was required as to whether all the crude oil for which alternative arrangement had to be made was 'at the time of the incident already in physical propinquity to the place of the incident'. In the case at bar, however, damages under this test would presumably be recoverable only as regards those trains that were in 'physical propinquity' to the bridge when the barge hit the bridge. How close they would have to be is a matter for speculation.

My colleague McLachlin J. has adopted a geographic proximity factor as one element of her proximity analysis. With respect, I am unable to discern any policy significance in the fact that a particular plaintiff owns property in proximity to an accident.

Proximity

The fourth approach taken by the respondent is more general and involves deciding economic loss cases on the basis of proximity. To this end it puts forward not only the three above-mentioned factors regarding its relationship with Norsk but also the aspects of its relationship with PWC which I examined, i.e., the alleged common adventure and the transferred loss. In fact, it provides the Court with a lengthy list of factors which, it alleges, create the necessary proximity in this case.

Stephen J. in *Caltex* adopted this approach. My colleague McLachlin J. also relies on this approach. I agree with Stevenson J. that the concept of proximity is incapable of providing a principled basis for drawing the line on the issue of liability for the reasons expressed by him (at p. 1178). As he notes, it expresses a result, rather than a principle.

The Argument from Morality

Stephen J.'s opinion in *Caltex*, at p. 255, rejects the exclusionary rule since it possesses the 'unattractive quality of being quite unresponsive to the grossness of the wrongdoer's want of care in its exclusion of non-consequential economic loss'. In a similar vein, McLachlin J. at p. 1159 criticizes the contractual allocation of risk argument on the ground that it 'overlooks the historical centrality of personal fault to our concept of negligence or 'delict' and the role this may have in curbing negligent conduct and thus limiting the harm done to innocent parties, not all of whom are large enterprises capable of maximizing their economic situation'. With respect, liability in this particular area should not be established based on the court's perception of the extent of the defendant's moral fault.

Liability is very often vicarious in cases like the present one. Vicarious liability is not based on the breach of any personal duty owed by the employer, but on his or her employee's tort being imputed to him or her: see Fleming, *supra*, at p. 341. As Fleming notes, '[t]he hallmark of vicarious liability . . . is that it is based neither on any conduct by the defendant himself nor even on breach of his own duty'. This makes it unrealistic in this context to calibrate liability on the degree of fault of the tortfeasor.

Second, to the extent that the concern about fault is linked to deterrence, the deterrent effect of tort law is already present owing to the tort action of the property owner. In my view, cases like the present do not fall to be decided on the grounds of personal fault. Rather they concern the effort to deter accidents and to allocate losses in a reasonable and efficient manner.

CN's Argument

CN, of course, concedes that a line must be drawn and that not all losses can be compensated. It suggests, however, that the line be situated somewhere on the other side of its recovery. It suggests that although its own and at least some other contractually based claims should be allowed, the Court should re-erect a bright line barrier excluding all plaintiffs who are not contractually linked with the property owner victim. In particular, co-contractors of CN, whatever the circumstances with respect to foreseeability and other traditional tort doctrines, 'clearly cannot recover' owing to the lack of a direct contractual relationship with PWC. It is unclear to me why drawing a new bright line around potential claimants in this manner is a significantly better solution.

Part IV: A Refined Proximity Analysis in Contractual Relational Economic Loss Cases

The crucial problem with the various formulations of the proximity test examined so far is that they look at the problem strictly from the perspective of the defendant. The defendant's negligence places it in a position of liability *vis-à-vis* the entire world. However, if it can show that its liability would be indeterminate, it can be excused. In my opinion, given the eminently pragmatic and policy basis of decisions about liability in this area, the situation of both the defendant <u>and the plaintiff</u> needs to be examined in cases of this kind. In particular, the plaintiff's ability to foresee and provide for the particular damage in question is a key factor in the proximity analysis.

The Legitimacy of this Type of Consideration

In my view, it is legitimate to consider which party is the better loss bearer in this type of case. This term requires definition. Determining which party is best able to <u>bear</u> the loss essentially involves asking which party is in a better position to predict the frequency and severity of CN's economic loss when bridges are damaged, and to plan accordingly. Analysis of loss bearing ability emphasizes how the parties deal with accidents that tort law has not succeeded in preventing, rather than with preventing accidents.

The question of which party is best able to bear the loss should be distinguished from the question of which party is best able to avoid the accident's occurring. Analysis of the issues pertaining to deterrence, or accident avoidance, involves the question of the relative ability of parties to act in a way that will reduce the risk of occurrence of the type of accident in question and is widely recognized as relevant in tort law. In my view, analysis of loss <u>bearing</u> ability is particularly relevant in determining whether proximity exists in the context of contractual relational economic loss cases.

Tort law has not generally given much consideration to analysis of loss bearing ability. This type of approach is obviously ill-suited to personal injury cases. In property damage cases involving the primary liability of the tortfeasor, the courts have often rightly been more concerned to ensure deterrence by placing liability on the party best able to avoid the accident's occurring. Under modern conditions, deterrence may, of course, be difficult to effect through tort law; nonetheless, placing liability on the injurer serves to internalize the costs of accidents legitimately to the accident-causing activity. In many cases, loss shifting to the better loss bearer runs squarely into the powerful objection that it is not also the better risk avoider. When the case involves the question whether that party will be held liable <u>at all</u>, the concern for deterrence overrides the concern about loss-bearing ability. Thus, in cases involving primary liability for accidents, tort law has given priority to preventing accidents by requiring those who cause accidents to pay for their damage or more likely to pay for insurance.

Consideration of loss bearing ability is by no means entirely absent from the cases, however, and it has been increasingly recognized in recent cases. In *Leigh and*

Sillavan Ltd. v. *Aliakmon Shipping Co.*, *supra*, at p. 819, Lord Brandon relied on the fact that the plaintiff had open to it an adequate avenue of protection in contract in refusing liability. A recent article by Stapleton, *supra*, at pp. 270–1, has suggested a formulation that seems to me to encapsulate this aspect of that case and may well be of more general application, as the author suggests, in cases of economic loss. She writes:

> The power of this neglected argument [that the plaintiff had available to it an adequate avenue of protection] is that it does not depend on a circular proposition about where 'principle' or precedent has in the past drawn the tort boundary. It is an argument explaining where that boundary should, on clear and stated principle, be placed. In our agenda of considerations, then, about where a tort duty in respect of economic loss should be recognised, we could place alongside the necessary (but not sufficient) condition of the absence or controllability of floodgates problems, a second requirement: the necessary but not sufficient condition that the plaintiff did not have, nor could reasonably be expected to have acquired, protection against the risk of economic loss.

In *Smith* v. *Bush*, [1990] 1 AC 831 (H.L.), the House of Lords, in allowing recovery in a case where a purchaser acquired defective property in reliance on the competence of a professional adviser, considered whether the plaintiff could have protected herself by contract. Prompted by the *Unfair Contract Terms Act 1977*, 1977 (UK), c. 50, the House expressly acknowledged the difficulty purchasers of small houses have in affording a second survey. The issue of indeterminacy became by the same token of lesser concern, since the ambit of liability was confined to a relevant vulnerable subset of property acquirers—those buying modest dwellings: see Stapleton, *supra*, at pp. 278–79. Moreover, as I noted in reference to comparative law, in those systems that in theory allow recovery for relational economic loss, recovery has apparently been denied in some cases where the plaintiff had adequate means of protecting itself.

Increasingly, our courts have openly addressed the issue of insurance as one of these policy concerns. In *Lamb* v. *Camden London Borough Council*, [1981] QB 625 (C.A.), at pp. 637–38, Lord Denning MR wrote as follows:

> On broader grounds of policy, I would add this: the criminal acts here—malicious damage and theft—are usually covered by insurance. By this means the risk of loss is spread throughout the community. It does not fall too heavily on one pair of shoulders alone. The insurers take the premium to cover just this sort of risk and should not be allowed, by subrogation, to pass it on to others. . . . It is commonplace nowadays for the courts, when considering policy, to take insurance into account. It played a prominent part in *Photo Production Ltd.* v. *Securicor Transport Ltd.* [1980] AC 827. The House of Lords clearly thought that the risk of fire should be borne by the fire insurers who had received the full premium for fire risk—and not by Securicor's insurers, who had only received a tiny premium. That, too, was a policy decision. . . .
>
> So here, it seems to me that if Mrs Lamb was insured against damage to the house and theft, the insurers should pay the loss. If she was not insured, that is her misfortune.

See also Fleming, *supra*, at p. 202 and p. 224.

The judges in *Caltex* implicitly or explicitly deny the importance of insurance considerations in resolving the pragmatic question of where to draw the line in this type of case. Four of the five judgments did not consider insurance issues at all. Stephen J. explicitly denies the court any role in this regard. In his view, the task of the courts remains that of fixing loss rather than spreading loss, and if this is to be altered it is a matter for direct legislative action rather than for the courts (at p. 265).

With respect, I do not agree with Stephen J. that the consideration of insurance changes the task of the courts from loss fixing to loss spreading. Insurance considerations are merely one element in an analysis of where it is appropriate to fix the loss, in a case where a solution is necessarily pragmatic. Many of the extensions of tort liability that have occurred over the last 50 years would have been inconceivable in the absence of insurance. Many cases have referred to insurance considerations to justify extending liability: see, for example, Laskin J. in *Rivtow*, *supra*, at p. 1221. To reject, as does Stephen J., the open consideration of insurance as 'covert judicial action' is paradoxical, since what is proposed is to bring insurance considerations into the open rather than merely expressing conclusions in terms of proximity. Fleming notes that Stephen J.'s concern that the new policy dimension may appear more germane to the legislative than to the judicial function, but responds, in my view accurately, that 'the change in perspective is dictated by inescapable external developments, to ignore which would be deliberately short-sighted and self-defeating': see Fleming, *supra*, at p. 11. I agree with my colleagues McLachlin J. and Stevenson J. that insurance deserves to be considered in cases of this kind; however, I disagree with them as to its relevance.

In the context of contractual relational economic loss, policy concerns with respect to which party can best bear the loss are particularly important for three reasons. First, policy concerns with respect to deterrence and cost internalisation are generally at least substantially met by the tortfeasor's primary liability to the property owner. In cases where the property damage is inconsequential, it might make sense to impose additional liability on deterrence grounds; that is not the case here, however, and I expressly reserve that question.

Second, they can be raised since current law denies recovery; rather than pose the risk of a revolutionary result, the approach merely articulates another policy lying behind a well-established rule. In some areas of the law, an examination of relative loss bearing ability might lead to arguments for fundamental changes in the law, changes best left to Parliament. Here, however, such considerations simply serve to establish a new rationale, or perhaps more accurately, to articulate explicitly an underlying rationale for a long-standing rule in an area of the law where the importance of policy considerations is now clearly recognized. As the law of torts has evolved, the courts have not been averse to modifying their mode of analysis of cases and have not waited for the legislature to do so. One imagines with difficulty a statute henceforth requiring the courts to take such considerations into account.

Finally, in this field the crucial problem remains that of limiting liability. All recognize that recovery of this type of claim must remain exceptional, if only because the potential number of claims of this type is practically unlimited. In these circumstances, a significantly higher threshold for recovery is, in my view, entirely justified.

In other areas of tort law, where the trend has been towards extending liability, placing an onus on the plaintiff is inconceivable. In this area, however, there is an overriding need for strict controls on potential liability.

In my view, it is legitimate for these reasons to consider explicitly the ability of the
plaintiff to bear the risk of loss in this type of case.

Turning then to an application of these criteria to this case, a determination of
which party is the better loss bearer is relatively straightforward. CN is undoubtedly
in a better position to bear the loss than Norsk. First, in light of the significant information available regarding bridge failure and CN's long use of the bridge, CN was
probably at least equally competent in terms of estimating the potential risks of
bridge failure. This aspect seems to me to be clear in light of the facts.

Second, CN would clearly be in a better position than PWC to estimate the potential costs of bridge failure to CN's operations. CN knows exactly how much use it
gets out of the various bridges crossed by its trains. It also knows what the alternatives are in cases of bridge failure. Norsk, of course, is very poorly placed to estimate
the value of the use that various people and companies get out of the bridges that
cross the rivers its tugs sail on. It is also poorly placed to estimate the potential costs
to those users of an interruption in bridge service. Unlike the first factor, which
depends to a large degree on the facts of each case, this factor tends to weigh heavily
in favour of the defendant in almost every case of this type.

Third, CN was better placed to protect itself from the consequences of those
losses. This point requires further discussion. It is hard to imagine a more sophisticated group of plaintiffs than the users of railway bridges. These parties have access
to the full range of protective options: first party commercial insurance or self-insur-
ance, contracts both with the bridge owner and with the railway's customers.

Insurance

My colleague McLachlin J. rejects the idea that insurance considerations justify a
denial of liability and relies on an article by Bishop: see Bishop, 'Economic Loss in
Tort' (1982), 2 *Oxf. J. Legal Studies* 1. Bishop argues that the insurance argument
must overcome two difficulties in the context of economic loss. First, he states that
to eliminate recovery for economic loss would reduce the incentive to take care.
With respect, I do not find this argument persuasive in the context of relational economic loss cases, since the primary liability of the tortfeasor to the owner of the
bridge is largely sufficient to create incentives to take care. This, as I noted earlier, is
one of the key distinguishing features that justifies separate treatment of relational
economic loss cases.

Bishop's second argument is that insurance is unavailable at reasonable cost. He
argues in particular that insurance for loss of profits is not available. Insurance companies understandably refuse to insure profitability. However, that is not the issue
here. CN is not claiming for loss of profit, but rather for the costs occasioned by the
interruption of its access to the bridge. That risk is analogous to a business interruption. Many businesses have interruption insurance covering interruption caused by
factors other than breach of contract: see Waddams, *The Law of Damages* (2nd edn.
1991), at § 14.330. Even if insurance is not available in the commercial market, CN is
ideally situated to self-insure.

Undoubtedly in certain cases, an affected business will not have purchased insurance. However, as James has noted, if the business community accepts a rule of non-liability for indirect economic losses without securing insurance protection against them by a relatively inexpensive method, then this fact at least suggests that these losses do not present a social problem serious enough to justify the cost to society in providing for their compensation by the most expensive method in its arsenal—liability based on fault: see James, *supra*, at p. 114. In other words, if the business community is insured, then there is no point in shifting the loss from one insurance company to another at high cost. If the business community is not insured, then that reveals that other ways of defraying such losses are perceived as superior to insurance and the problem is not that serious.

Conclusions about the insurance market are of course somewhat tentative and it would behoove lawyers, as Atiyah notes, to inform themselves about fundamental matters of insurability in new tort cases and to see to it that courts are also informed: see Atiyah, 'Note: Economic Loss in the United States' (1985), 5 *Oxf. J. Legal Studies* 485. However, the weight of opinion is certainly to the effect that first-party insurance is a cheaper and more effective method of protecting against loss than liability insurance, particularly where the liability is of uncertain amount; see *Photo Production Ltd.* v. *Securicor Transport Ltd.*, [1980] AC 827, at p. 851; Smillie, 'Negligence and Economic Loss' (1982), 32 *U.T.L.J.* 231, at pp. 240–2; James, *supra*, at pp. 113–16. In my opinion, the burden of showing otherwise must rest on those who would have the court overturn a long-standing rule excluding recovery.

Contract

I agree with McLachlin J. that in many cases the contractual allocation of risk does not supply a rationale for refusing recovery. Inequality of bargaining power is in fact only one of a number of reasons why contract may not be a real alternative in a given case. In many cases, protecting oneself from economic losses through contract is not possible. In the cases involving interruptions in services provided by utilities, the service is often supplied by a monopoly supplier on standard form contracts. Any shifting of the risk from consumer to utility company may even be statutorily excluded. Such cases involve contracts in name only. Or again, the risk which materializes may be so unusual that the parties never contemplated it. Though there may be other reasons for denying liability, in all of these cases the argument from the contractual allocation of risk is not convincing.

In this case, however, it is. The facts in this case establish that all parties were well aware of the risk of bridge failure. CN knew what it was doing. The very bridge at issue here had been damaged on a number of previous occasions, and various studies of the problem had been carried out. CN participated actively in at least one of these studies. CN was even aware of the traditional legal rule; as I noted, it brought a very similar claim for bridge failure in similar circumstances in 1973 for which recovery was denied.

The risk of bridge failure could have been borne by PWC, which also has a right of action in tort. The economic losses of contractual users of the bridge would then likely have been made good under the contract. The property owner is able to collect these losses from the tortfeasor subject to the limiting principles of tort damages. If

PWC contracted to provide bridge services and is unable to do so because of the negligence of the tug and has to pay damages as a result, it can collect for those damages from the tug owner: see Fleming, *supra*, at p. 226. Liability in the contractual relational economic loss case is <u>channelled</u> rather than <u>denied</u>.

In many cases, contracting parties are not willing to insure performance; the contractual allocation of risk in this case is probably typical in that risk is allocated to the potential victim of interrupted service, who benefits from a lower price and who is best placed to take other measures to deal with accidental interruption of contractual benefits. That such an arrangement is so frequent despite the fact that under current law it precludes recovery by the contracting party is significant. That such an arrangement existed in this case despite the fact that CN's identical claim had been refused in 1973 is doubly significant.

CN's ability to protect itself through contract is not limited to its contract with the property owner. CN can also protect itself to some degree through its contractual arrangements with its clients, suppliers and others. It can plan ahead for the case of unavailability of the property in question. Denying recovery will provide incentives to all parties to act in ways that will combine to minimize the impact of losses once they occur, while still providing the critical incentive to the tug to avoid causing accidents in the first place.

In my view, a denial of recovery in this case is justified in light of CN's overwhelmingly superior risk bearing capacity on the facts of this case.

Before leaving the issue of CN's ability to protect itself, it should be noted that the rule proposed by my colleagues will <u>still</u> require parties such as CN to protect themselves since they will never know before the particular accident whether they will be part of the determinate class. It is to say the least difficult to predict whether a particular railway bridge will be knocked out by someone who knows you by name. Alternatively, it is difficult to know whether of the many possible bridges that will be damaged, the one that will be damaged is the one next to which you own property. As a result, the only solution for the prudent railway will be to purchase insurance. Presumably, the cost of this insurance will reflect the value the insurance company places on the possibility of its recovering from the tortfeasor.

The critical effect of allowing recovery is that it would <u>also</u> require defendants in Norsk's position to insure for potential contractual relational economic loss as well, since they will obviously never know beforehand whether the bridges damaged by its tugs will be used by plaintiffs whose name it knows or who have property nearby. The principal beneficiaries of the rule proposed by my colleagues would be insurance companies, who would benefit from the existence of a new and highly uncertain risk against which companies likely to inflict property damage would need to insure.

The rules suggested by my colleagues thus will require that <u>both</u> parties insure at considerable additional social cost. The only gain will be a slight reduction in the plaintiff's first party insurance costs to take into account the possibility that the insurance company will recover from a tortfeasor under the new doctrine.

A further practical difficulty should be noted. In cases where the tortfeasor is either not insured or insufficiently insured with respect to the initial property damage or personal injury claim or the relational claim or both, serious problems will arise with respect to the primacy of one type of claim over another. For example, if the tortfeasor is liable for both a $500,000 personal injury claim and $500,000 in relational claims but his total assets and insurance only cover half of that amount, the actual compensation of the personal injury claim will presumably be halved in order to allow recovery for a relational claim which as noted will often involve recovery for a subrogated insurance company: see Feldthusen, *Economic Negligence*, *supra*, at p. 207.

Conclusion

It is unclear to me why the current state of the law on contractual relational economic loss, which channels claims to the property owner, is unsatisfactory at least in the commercial area involving sophisticated parties. It is also unclear whether significant amounts of court time should be expended in distinguishing between contractual relational economic loss sufferers—those who are proximate to the tortfeasor and those who are not.

There is no question that the outcome of cases of this nature under the exclusionary rule depends upon the terms of the contract. This operates in two ways: the contract may create a possessory interest or a joint venture or it may provide for an indemnity from the property owner. The question to be resolved is whether allowing the contract to determine whether the plaintiff has the requisite interest and where the loss falls is more arbitrary, unfair or unworkable than the various tests referred to above.

The arguments against recovery in this case can be summed up as follows. First, the arguments for recovery are weak. It is not necessary to impose liability to ensure that tortfeasors like Norsk are dissuaded from damaging bridges. The increase in deterrence that would result from imposing the additional liability called for in this case would not likely have much impact on the behaviour of potential tortfeasors. The only purpose served by recovery in this case to which the judgment of McLachlin J. refers, at pp. 1162–63, is 'the purpose of permitting a plaintiff whose position for practical purposes, *vis-à-vis* the tortfeasor, is indistinguishable from that of the owner of the damaged property, to recover what the actual owner could have recovered'. In my view, the argument that CN is indistinguishable from the owner founders on the fact that CN does not qualify under the well-established cases in which the law provides for recovery by the contracting party where it in fact has a proprietary or possessory interest. CN's interest is merely contractual.

CN argues that restricting recovery to the owner or person in possession is based on pragmatism not logic, and therefore to require logical support for an exception to a pragmatic rule which in a particular case results in an injustice, is in itself illogical. In my view, cases such as *Rivtow* and *Kamloops* which have allowed recovery for pure economic loss have established criteria that do provide logical support for an exception to a pragmatic rule.

The argument that Norsk was at fault and CN was innocent and that fault should justify recovery is also unconvincing here. Fault alone cannot justify recovery in this area since some admittedly injured claimants will have their claims denied. Since the whole exercise in this kind of situation involves drawing a line amongst those who are undeniably injured by the tortfeasor who was undeniably at fault, appeals to fault beg the question. The defendants were equally at fault with respect to other claims that will be denied. CN is unable to show any special damage different in kind from that suffered by the other potential contractual claimants. None of the factual distinctions the company puts forward has any relevance with respect to the defendants' fault.

The second group of reasons focus on the weaknesses of the proposed rules that would allow recovery. The tests that would allow recovery do not meet the criteria that a rule should have in this area. The concept of a 'special relationship' is not applicable to cases involving accidents. None of the facts put forward by CN as indicative of its special relationship has any other policy significance than to attempt to meet, after the fact, the problem of indeterminate liability. The individual plaintiff test would presumably preclude recovery by the other railways that suffered losses identical in nature to those suffered by CN. If the test were extended to cover a foreseeable class of plaintiffs such as users of the railway bridge, it would simply restate the general requirement that the plaintiff be foreseeable and recovery would be allowed whether the users of the bridge were four or four thousand. The proximity test has practically no predictive value; it remains impossible to say whether that test would lead to recovery for the other railways in this case, let alone its application in other cases.

Finally, there are the reasons supporting the exclusionary rule. These are, of course, essentially pragmatic, as has been recognized in cases of this type from the very beginning. First, denial of recovery places incentives on all parties to act in ways that will minimize overall losses, a legitimate and desirable goal for tort law in this area. Second, denial of recovery allows for only one party carrying insurance rather than both parties. Third, it will result in a great saving of judicial resources for cases in which more pressing concerns are put forward. The difficult job of drawing the line is at least done quickly without a great deal of factual investigation into the various factors that found proximity. The right to recover can be most often determined from the face of the contract. Fourth, it also eliminates difficult problems of sharing an impecunious defendant's limited resources between relational claims and direct claims. Fifth, the traditional rule is certain, and although like any pragmatic solution, borderline cases may cause problems, the exceptions to the rule in cases of joint ventures, general average contributions, and possessory and proprietorial interests are reasonably well defined and circumscribed. This case, in my view, does not even constitute a borderline case in this respect, since CN has no property interest of any kind. The consequence of that certainty is that contracting parties can be certain of where the loss with respect to the unavailability of property will lie in the absence of any contractual arrangement.

I add one final consideration. This case is one of maritime law, which in large measure encompasses a global system. The bright line exclusionary rule against recovery has for nearly a century been in effect in that system, and continues to be followed by the major trading nations, in particular Great Britain and the United States. In making arrangements for allocating risks in essentially maritime matters, those engaged in navigating and shipping should, as much as possible, be governed by a uniform rule, so that they can plan their affairs ahead of time, whether by contract or insurance against possible contingencies.

In my view, to justify recovery in cases of this nature, the plaintiff would, at the very least, have to respond effectively not only to the concern about indeterminacy but also show that no adequate alternative means of protection was available. Other concerns may also need to be met. At the very least, the requirement that the plaintiff not have had any commercially reasonable method of protecting itself is an important addition to what remains a conceptually difficult *ex post facto* inquiry into the 'determinate nature' of the particular victim and damage from the perspective of the defendant.

The question of whether recovery should be allowed in the residual cases in which these two barriers are overcome does not require an answer in the context of this case. Individuals and small businesses may be incapable of effectively protecting themselves in any meaningful fashion. In some cases, of course, contractual relational economic loss may occur in a different form such as loss of salary and the failure to protect against it by first-party insurance cannot be said to lead to an inference of social unimportance. In such cases, however, the indeterminacy problem is often very acute. If the number of potential individual plaintiffs is great, recovery will be denied on the grounds of 'indeterminacy', even though the plaintiffs may not have had any real ability to protect themselves. Where the plaintiff passes the indeterminacy tests, it will often be sophisticated. The argument that recovery should be denied to those who could have protected themselves does not support a bright line in and of itself. Rather, it complements the indeterminacy analysis. It suggests that those who are most likely to emerge from the indeterminacy analysis are those with the ability to protect themselves and questions the advisability of a rule with the effect of allowing recovery to only that group of contractual claimants, rather than denying recovery to all.

The exclusionary rule is not in itself attractive. It excludes recovery by people who have undeniably suffered losses as a result of an accident. It also leads to some arbitrary but generally predictable results in cases at the margin. The results with respect to time charters may be 'capricious', but time charterers know their rights and obligations from the start and can act accordingly. The rule only becomes defensible when it is realized that full recovery is impossible, that recovery is in fact going to be refused in the vast majority of such claims regardless of the rule we adopt, and when the exclusionary rule is compared to the alternatives. In my view, it should not be disturbed on the facts of this case.

I should add a few words about McLachlin J.'s suggestion that the essential difference between her approach and mine lies in the flexibility allowed by her approach. She characterizes my approach as providing for recovery depending exclusively on the terms of the formal contract between the plaintiff and the property owner. She considers an approach based on the terms of the contract involves a 'rigid categorization which denies the possibility of recovery in new cases which may not meet the categorical test' (at p. 1164), a problem that is avoided under the proximity test she sets forth.

I do not see the essential difference between our two approaches as that between certainty and flexibility. In my view, the key difference is between a principled flexibility, which adheres to a general rule in the absence of policy reasons for excluding its application, and arbitrariness. Among the policy factors considered in the course of this opinion that might justify relaxing the rule are the ability of the plaintiff to protect itself and the quantum of property damage caused by the tortfea-sor with its attendant impact on the issue of deterrence. I have not found it necessary to consider the precise role of these factors in this case since CN was clearly able to protect itself and the property damage sustained was sufficient to afford deterrence. Whether such factors would in fact provide workable criteria sufficient to provide for recovery despite the strong arguments in favour of the long standing exclusion-ary rule, based on certainty and other factors, is an open question. What I have decided is that in the absence of all of these factors, there is no reason to disturb the rule.

Thus I do not say that the right to recovery in all cases of contractual relational economic loss depends exclusively on the terms of the contract. Rather, I note that such is the tenor of the exclusionary rule and that departures from that rule should be justified on defensible policy grounds. The Court should do more than simply establish a rule that allows judges to resolve cases as they see fit. That, as I see it, is the effect of the approach proposed by my colleague.

Disposition

I would allow the appeal and dismiss the claim for damages.

Notes to Norsk

1. One must again warn the reader that the extracts reproduced above only convey part of the picture and that the strengths and weaknesses of this decision will only become fully apparent when all *three* of its judgments are carefully read.

2. Omitted from the extracts are the sections on the current state of Canadian law; but they, too, should be read by anyone who wishes to see how Canadian law has departed from the English 'model' and adopted a less hostile view towards pure economic loss. The divergences between major Common law jurisdictions (Australia, Canada, New Zealand and, of course, the United States) must also be noted. Also noteworthy is the fact that English, Canadian, Australian and New Zealand courts refer to each others decisions *and* to American decisions. Nowadays, however, it is rare to find American courts referring to English or Commonwealth decisions. Is this due to over-work? too much 'local' material? growing 'local' confidence (or arrogance) which encourages the belief that they have 'nothing to learn' from other (closely related) systems? All three? Is this 'divergence' a healthy phenomenon? or are there areas of the law where it should be avoided?

4. The 'swing' judgment in this case was delivered by Stevenson J. yet, strangely, it is the least effective of them all. For, first, his decision is, essen-tially, a variation of the views of Gibbs and Mason JJ in *Caltex Oil (Aust.) Pty* v. *The Dredge Willemstad* (1976) 136 C.L.R. 529. (The plaintiff should recover because the defendant knew or ought to have known that a 'specific individual . . . as opposed to a general or unascertained class of the public'

was likely in this instance to suffer the foreseeable kind of loss.) This approach has never met with much approval; and it seems to place too great a premium on 'notoriety'. (For more criticisms see: pp. 1107–1112.) The second draw-back of Stevenson J.'s judgment is that it weakened the overall result of the case by expressly disapproving of Mclachlin J.'s proximity test (p. 1178). Thus, the most disturbing aspect of the case as a whole is that it has not left us with a clear *ratio decidendi*. For the proximity test advocated by the majority is espoused only by three justices out of seven; and if one looks at the case *purely from a Common law point of view* (and thus removed from the majority camp the Quebec judge), one is left with only two justices out of six advocating proximity as the appropriate controlling device. Those who like 'bright line rules' will, no doubt, stress this point as *Norsk*'s major defect.

5. Notwithstanding the force of the above-mentioned objection one must also stress the many areas where majority and minority found common ground. Thus both agreed that the 'more flexible approach set out in *Anns*' was preferable to the *Murphy* reasoning, which was expressly stated as not representing the law in Canada (pp. 1054, 1163). In the words of La Forest J., who delivered the minority judgment; 'I fully support this court's rejection of the broad bar on recovery of pure economic loss . . .' (p. 1054). The dispute thus centred around what was termed 'relational economic loss', i.e. economic loss suffered by the plaintiff as a result of property damage caused to a third party. Secondly, all agreed that 'the law of tort does not permit recovery for *all* economic loss' (p. 1163). Thirdly, there was full agreement that cases like *Norsk* required a discussion of the underlying economic and wider policy considerations. Fourthly, all three judgments accepted Stevenson J.'s view that 'the case at bar is a good example of how useful comparative law can be' (p. 1174). Finally, both majority and minority came within a whisker of bringing the case within the ambit of the rule in *Morrison Steamship Co.* v. *Greystoke Castle* [1947] AC 265, long recognized as one of the allowable 'exceptions' to the non-liability rule. Where they disagreed was in 'the test for determining joint venture.'

6. The case is a shining example of comparative law 'in practice' since the judgments quote 32 academic writers (covering seven countries) and 62 decisions (from five different, international, jurisdictions). La Forest J.'s use of the rich material led him to conclude that (*a*) even the most liberal foreign systems (i.e. the Romanistic group) are 'acutely aware of the potential for unlimited liability'; (*b*) they avoid it by establishing 'a *de facto* [if not *de iure*] bar' to recovery; (*c*) they do this through a rich variety of 'causal' devices, and (*d*) that the civilian experience could be taken to support the view (promoted by the majority) that 'recovery for contractual relational economic loss [could] remain exceptional even if the exclusionary rule [were] relaxed'

(p. 1985). *This is an important concession since it shows that the 'floodgates' argument, currently in vogue with the House of Lords, is not empirically substantiated.*

7. For a number of commentators *Norsk* scores heavily (both in methodology and content) over its British contemporary 'leading' judgment— *Murphy*. On this see, Fleming, 'Economic Loss in Canada' (1993) *Tort L. Rev.* 68–74; Markesinis, 'Compensation for Negligently Inflicted Pure Economic Loss: Some Canadian Views' (1993) 109 *LQR* 5–12, and decide which of the two judgments—the English or the Canadian: (*a*) provides you with a better introduction to the problem of economic loss; (*b*) comes up with the most satisfactory answer. Consider also the potential impact that research assistants (Clerks) may have in the style and thoroughness of a judgment.

6. ECONOMIC LOSS (NEGLIGENT STATEMENTS)

Case 15

BUNDESGERICHTSHOF (SIXTH CIVIL DIVISION) 12 FEBRUARY 1979[*]
WM 1979, 548 = NJW 1979, 1595

The plaintiff claims damages from the defendants, an international bank, for loss suffered as a result of inaccurate information supplied to her by their German branch (and concerning the creditworthiness of a third party).

Towards the end of 1970 the plaintiff was looking for a profitable way to invest some DM 130,000 and a finance broker, L, recommended the hotel P, built by U and opened to the public a few months earlier. U had financed his hotel by a number of loans including one for 2.5 million DM raised from the defendants and secured by a land charge. U, requiring a further 3.5 million DM, decided to raise this from private individuals with the help of advertisements and brokers offering 12 per cent interest on all loans as well as a land charge for security. More precisely, he registered a land charge for 3.5 million DM in favour of the defendants which was divided into smaller parts each securing sums of DM 10,000 and DM 25,000. The defendants, in consideration for the usual fee, were willing to assign these 'part land charges' to lenders and place the funds in a blocked account for U until the completion of all formalities. On 3 February L, the broker, gave the plaintiff the following information which was written on the defendants' paper but gave neither date nor address: 'Hotel P, George U. This is a newly built luxury hotel, with some 440 beds and conforming with international standards, was officially opened in June 1970 in the presence of many dignitaries. So

---

[*] English version by F. H. Lawson and B. S. Markesinis.

far as we know it has already entered into long-term arrangements with a number of international travel agencies. It is owned by U, whom we know as a client and as a competent business man. U also owns a hotel in Tenerife and two sanatoria run by reputable persons. Owing to a great increase in building costs, U needs a further 3.5 million DM which is to be found on the open market. Any money advanced for this purpose will be credited to a blocked account with our bank, and after the notary has confirmed that the terms of the contract have been complied with, it will be credited to the hotel's current account. We ourselves have in the past made substantial payments to U against security but, due to an increase in building costs, U's liquidity is, at present, tight.'

On 17 February, 1971 the plaintiff paid DM 130,000 which the defendants immediately credited to U's account. Three days earlier the defendants had asked U to repay their loans by 23 February and on 16 March they extended the repayment date to the end of May 1971. Meanwhile U was getting deeper and deeper into financial difficulties and on 23 December he applied for a composition with his creditors. Four months later bankruptcy proceedings followed. Both plaintiff and defendant withdrew from the auction of the hotel and the plaintiff will receive nothing from the bankrupt's estate.

The plaintiff brought an action claiming DM 65,000 since legal aid was granted to her only for this amount due to her contributory negligence. She argues that her loss is due to the defendant's letter which gave information which they knew to be false. The defendants deny that the information was wrong and also deny liability on the grounds that they had not entered into any contract to supply her with information.

The Court of First Instance awarded the plaintiff DM 32,500, and ruled that she should bear the rest of the loss herself because of her contributory negligence. The defendants' appeal was rejected and their further appeal on points of law is also dismissed.

Reasons

I. The Court of Appeal accepted that the defendant is liable according to the law of contract. Their appeal on points of law fails.

1. The Court of Appeal found that the defendants knowingly and deliberately composed the notice (quoted above) and put it into circulation with the view to its being shown to potential private lenders to U.

(*a*) The Court of Appeal (also) found that the information it contained was both in form and content intended to reach a circle of private potential investors. Stripped to its essential the notice gives information which is intended to appeal to private individuals. This is true both of the description of U and of his other businesses. For instance, the reference to the official opening of the hotel in the presence of local dignitaries could only have aimed at making his business appear reliable in the eyes of private persons. Much of this material would clearly have been written in a different way if the document had been intended to be used solely for internal banking purposes. Its contents make sense only if they are seen as aiming from the outset to attract private prospective investors. And this is corroborated by the statement in the notice that the money lent would be transferred from the blocked account with the defendants to the hotel's account only after a notary had confirmed that the terms of the contract had been complied with. This method of concluding a contract is less important to a bank than the encumbrances which are not mentioned in the notice. But it is calculated to dispel doubts that may arise in the mind of an individual, inexperienced in money matters, reading the preceding passages which explain why the extra sums are required. The outward appearance of the notice also speaks in favour of this interpretation. Thus, it bears the business name and the description of the defendant but gives no indication of the person addressed, or the date or any other details that usually accompany letter-writing.

This interpretation is not only possible, but, indeed, necessary, the more so when one realizes that the defendants, who were asked to handle the loan, were aware that only private individuals would be considered as lenders. The appeal is thus not able to reveal any error of law committed by the Court of Appeal when characterizing the sense and purpose of the notice.

The argument that the Court of Appeal failed to take into account the fact that the defendants gave this kind of information in response to enquiries made by banks is also unsuccessful for if this is taken to imply that the defendants supplied information to banks only, it runs clearly counter to the defendants' submissions before the lower court. There the defendants maintained that information concerning U was given only to individuals making specific enquiries . . . On the appellate level, therefore, one must assume that the defendants gave information not *only* but *also* to banks. This does not necessarily run counter to the Court of Appeal's interpretation. Since only private individuals would be considered as lenders, the banks must have enquired on their behalf and thus the information so acquired must have been destined only for their clients and not for themselves.

(*b*) Once it is accepted, as it must be, that the information supplied by the defendants was meant for potential investors, one must then also accept the further finding of the Court of Appeal, namely that the defendants circulated this information so that it would be presented to a group of prospective investors. The assumption that the defendants intended to give the information to individual enquirers only, and had not agreed to its being passed on to other interested parties, is inconsistent with the purpose of preparing the information, namely to appeal to a group of individuals who might be interested in becoming lenders. Given that the defendants were themselves substantial creditors of U, and were anxious to relieve him of his financial difficulties, their intention was to bring the information to the notice of as many prospective lenders as possible. The assertion that the defendant supplied information concerning U only to individual enquirers does not rule out the possibility that the bank, in conformity with its purpose, approved of the information being passed on to other lenders. In any event, the defendants have failed to adduce any evidence to show that their notice had been brought to the attention of only a small group of individuals. The Court of Appeal was thus free to look at the objective contents of the notice.

2. The Court of Appeal was also not in error in finding that the defendants were fully aware that their information would be of great importance to the recipients and would be used as a basis of important investments. Since its prime purpose was to help attract finance for the hotel P, it is obvious that it was intended to help prospective investors to decide whether to lend money to U to the extent of at least DM 10,000 and was designed with that purpose in mind . . .

3. The Court of Appeal considered the information given to have been false in so far as it concealed facts which ought to have been disclosed. Thus, the reference to U's other properties created the impression that they also were available as additional security even though in actual fact they were already encumbered up to the hilt. The reference to the defendants' own substantial secured loans to U was also false since they had already called for their repayment at the time when the information (in the notice) reached the plaintiff . . . The inaccuracy of the notice is evident from a number of other undisputed facts such as, for example, the concealment of the various charges on the sanatoria properties. To a lender such information is particularly important when making up his mind as to whether to make a loan or not . . . Contrary to the view advanced in this appeal, it must be said that it is customary to mention all substantial charges when information is given about land by a bank. According to the findings of the Court of Appeal, when the information was issued by the defendants, the entire hotel facilities as well as the sanatoria had not been paid for and U was no longer in a position to honour any bills drawn for them. These circumstances, which would normally point towards an extremely delicate economic situation, should have been made clear by the defendants at the time of issuing of their notice

since they would have had great bearing on the decision of the lenders. The defendants did not argue that they were unaware of the above, indeed this would have been unlikely for a bank like theirs, whose function it is to grant credit to borrowers. Nor did the defendants fulfil their duties by stating in their notice that U was faced with liquidity problems since this would not normally indicate to a private individual that bills had already been protested. All these findings are sufficient to characterize the information as false.

II. All the factual elements necessary to impose contractual liability for negligent advice are thus satisfied. According to the cases where information is supplied by a bank a contractual or quasi-contractual relationship already exists between the bank and the enquiring party whenever the information supplied by the bank is of manifest significance to the inquiring party and it is clear that the latter will be relying on it in making substantial capital allocations (cf. decision of the Senate of 6 July 1970, WM 1970, 1021 . . .). The situation in this present case is just that. In this case the bank addresses itself to a quite clearly defined group of prospective lenders who are interested in advancing money for a specific project. The information is aimed at this group, which the defendants wish to attract, and which they know will use this information to make vital economic decisions. This being clearly the purpose of the information it can make little difference in law whether the seeker (of the information) directs himself to the bank or the bank to him. Given the purposes to be achieved by the information, the bank must realize that the persons likely to rely on it must understand it in the sense of a legally binding declaration (the distributor of the notice is a mere messenger). That is why in this case good faith causes a contractual relation to arise when a potential addressee has relied on it in making his decision. The appellant's argument, unsubstantiated by the facts of this case, that the information was only intended for banks, is immaterial since this does not preclude the fact that banks were then allowed to pass it on. The Court of Appeal is indeed wrong in treating this as a case of 'information to whom it may concern'. The Supreme Court has repeatedly insisted that it is, in principle, not possible to assume that a bank when giving information is willing to put itself under an obligation to an indeterminate and incalculable number of persons . . . However, this is not the case here for, though the information is directed to persons still unknown to the bank, those persons can be determined by virtue of their interest and form part of a calculable group of persons.

III.

1. Given that a contract to supply information was thus concluded by the parties, it became incumbent upon the defendants to supply objectively cor-

rect information. This the defendants negligently failed to do (§§ 276, and 278 BGB) since as bankers they knew, or ought to have known, that the facts they failed to mention in their notice were important for the lenders in order to reach their decision.

2. The appeal before this court also claims unsuccessfully that the Court of Appeal erred on the aspect of causation . . . Practical experience however shows that the plaintiff would not have made U a loan if the defendants had given her adverse information by disclosing to her U's actual financial status.

IV. The argument raised in this appeal, that the defendant's negligence is overshadowed by the plaintiff's contributory fault in so far as she accepted the advice of the finance broker L against the advice of her bank and her tax accountant, cannot affect the judgment currently under appeal. For the Court of Appeal, in its exercise of its judicial functions, concluded all legal and factual aspects of the case, and the appellants can point to no legal error prejudicial to them. Their argument that these facts should, from a point of view of law, be now differently appraised cannot thus be accepted.

Case 16

BUNDESGERICHTSHOF (SECOND CIVIL DIVISION) 28 FEBRUARY 1977*
BGHZ 69, 82

The plaintiff, in the course of current business transactions delivered limestone to the building firm GmbH, until the latter was declared bankrupt on 7 August 1973. GmbH had agreed in 1972 that the claims of the plaintiff arising from its sales should be settled by directly debiting its account, and had on 13 September 1972 given a revocable instruction to the defendant *Volksbank*, where it kept an account, to pay the creditor upon the receipt of its invoices and to debit its account with the defendant. It is disputed whether GmbH authorized the plaintiff in addition to collect its claims. During the period in issue here the plaintiff, who had no business relations with the defendant, lodged with the *Bank für Gemeinwirtschaft*, where it had a giro account, the following invoices to be collected by directly debiting the account of GmbH with the defendant: on 30 May 1973 for deliveries on 29 May amounting to DM 13,100.25; on 6 June for deliveries on 31 May amounting to DM 15,672.83; on 14 June for deliveries on 13 June amounting to DM 15,672.83; on 14 June for deliveries on 13 June amounting to DM 6016.88; on 20 June for deliveries on 19 June amounting to DM 12,835.18; and on 27 June for deliveries on 26 June amounting to DM 17,468.75. All these invoices carried the imprint: 'The recipient of the

* English version by Kurt Lipstein.

payments holds an authorization from the debtor to collect the amounts outstanding.' When the invoices were received by the defendant the account of GmbH was overdrawn. Therefore the defendant did not credit the plaintiff. For reasons which form the object of a dispute between the parties, the invoices remained for the time being with the defendant and were only returned on 29 June 1973 to the *Bank für Gemeinwirtschaft* which had submitted them. According to the plaintiff he only got to know on 4 July 1973 that the invoices had not been paid, because on this day his account with the *Bank für Gemeinwirtschaft* had been debited again to the amount of the invoices previously credited to his account.

In the present proceedings the plaintiff claims damages in respect of losses suffered by him in that he continued to supply goods to GmbH on 13, 19, and 26 June 1973, to the value of DM 36,321.81 which remained unpaid. The plaintiff contends that if the defendant had returned the invoices immediately on 30 May 1973, the plaintiff would have known of the failure to pay by 8 June 1973 at the latest. He would then only have made the subsequent deliveries against pre-payment.

The Court of First Instance at Osnabrück and the Court of Appeal at Oldenburg rejected the claim. Upon a second appeal by the plaintiff the judgment below was quashed and the case referred back for the following

Reasons

The plaintiff in setting out the facts has shown conclusively that he has suffered damage because the defendant bank kept the invoices submitted to it for direct debit until the end of the month without taking action. If, instead, it had returned the invoices immediately, the plaintiff would have known on 8 June 1973 at the latest that no further payments could be expected. The plaintiff would then not have made the deliveries which remained unpaid for. . . . The plaintiff in asking the defendant to compensate him for this loss is also established conclusively, contrary to the views expressed by the courts below; its basis is contractual.

1. The Court of Appeal has held correctly that the plaintiff was not entitled to claim any performance by the defendant which may lead to claims for damages. No direct contractual relations are created between the creditor and the debtor's bank as a result of direct debiting. Thus the situation is similar to that of giro proceedings. In the latter situation the fact that the transferor and the recipient of the transfer maintain giro accounts with different banks did not create a direct contractual relationship between the recipient and the bank of the transferor nor do the legal relationships between the transferor and his bank or between the individual banks constitute contracts in favour of the recipient of the transfer as a third party. The

situation is no different in direct debit proceedings; they are a kind of 'transfer in reverse'. The recipient (creditor) is only contracting with his own bank. The debtor bank, which receives the invoices for payment, only acts upon instructions which the creditor bank (or another bank interposed by it) gives in its own name within the framework of giro activities between the banks concerned (again not in favour of the creditor). The debtor, on his part, either instructs his bank in writing to credit directly invoices submitted by a particular creditor (procedure of direct crediting); as in the case of instructions to transfer money it constitutes an instruction (general in these circumstances) in the meaning of §§ 665, 675 BGB within the contract of giro between himself and his bank, with which the creditor is not concerned. Alternatively the debtor authorizes the creditor in writing to collect the payments which are due by way of debiting his account with the debtor bank ('Procedure authorizing Collection'). Thereby, too, the creditor does not obtain a claim against the debtor bank. The procedure of direct debiting serves mainly the interest of the creditor in settling his affairs and involves additional risks for the debtor; in the light of the interests involved no reason exists for assuming that the debtor wishes to grant to the creditor more rights than he would enjoy if the payments were made by bank transfer. Finally, the Agreement between the Principal Organizations of Credit Institutions concerning the Principle of Direct Debiting [references] only creates rights and duties between the credit institutions involved. Contractual claims by clients of banks for performance by the banks concerned are not to be derived from this Agreement according to Part IV no. 1 of the Agreement itself. Contrary to some other legal problems arising from the procedure of direct debiting this represents essentially the general opinion [references].

2. The plaintiff's claim for damages is, however, presented conclusively from the point of view that a protective duty has been violated. It is to be derived in favour of the creditor of the direct debit from the legal relationship arising between the banks involved in carrying out the procedure of direct debit.

Claims for damages arising from a violation of a protective duty can arise in general if a legal relationship between two parties is not sufficient to fulfil the requirements of § 328 BGB, but where the inclusion of certain third parties in its protective sphere is indicated according to good faith by the purpose of the contract and in view of the apparent effect upon them of the contractual performance. In order to avoid a flood of claims of this kind to an incalculable extent and to establish limits beyond which the protection of third parties is restricted to the law of tort, the practice of the courts has stated repeatedly that such an inclusion of third parties can normally be considered only if the internal relationship between the creditor and the debtor discloses aspects of a personal law character and shows that the creditor acts on behalf of a third party for whom he shares responsibility and to whom he owes a duty of care. In so far as characteristics of a personal law nature are thus required, the principles developed in the light of individual agreements as to what should apply according to good faith, are unnecessarily narrow where—as in the present case—bulk transactions of a certain type are in issue which follow a uniformly practised procedure provided on a general scale for legal transactions based upon the confidence that they will be settled properly and with due regard for the interests involved. In these circumstances the inclusion of third parties in the protective sphere of the contractual relations in issue may be possible and indicated according to good faith, if the mechanism entails for the third party who employs it certain risks inherent in it and if the participants charged with handling the mechanism can be called upon without further discussion to keep these risks down. Such is the case in so far as in direct debit proceedings the debtor bank must return invoices because the payments cannot be made in the absence of funds. According to the Agreement of the Banks concerning direct debits, invoices exceeding DM 1000 not met by payment must be returned together with a notice of dishonour either on the same day to the first payor (the creditor's bank) or latest on the second working day by the reverse process of claiming payment from the first payor, accompanied by a notification by telegram, telephone, or telex (Part II no. 1 para. 2). This solution may have been adopted primarily in the interest of the creditor bank concerned. When the invoices are submitted to it, it credits the creditor's account with the amount to be debited (subject to a proviso) and normally allows the creditor to dispose of it. Therefore it runs the risk of losing that sum when the invoices are not honoured if the customer has disposed of the amount in the meantime and is no longer able to repay it. Consequently the creditor bank has an interest that the 'critical' interval between crediting the amount and a possible failure to honour the invoices is kept short; the debtor bank should therefore immediately provide the necessary information by returning the dishonoured invoices or in some other way, on the strength of which the creditor can be debited again. The interest of the creditor is, however, involved to an even greater extent since he issued the instruction to collect the debt. Firstly, he will be interested quite generally, having regard to his business arrangements, not to be surprised by a re-debiting; instead he wishes to be informed in good time that the amount credited to him provisionally on the strength of the invoices is not at his disposal in reality. Secondly, if he employs the procedure of direct debiting for the purpose of collecting outstanding monies, he will normally be engaged in current business relations with the debtor. If these relations extend over a longer period he has a considerable interest which goes beyond collecting whatever amount may have fallen due, to receive early notice of any difficulties in the operation of these relations. The fact that invoices are not honoured is often an alarm signal that the debtor is in payment difficulties. If the creditor is not notified in time but remains ignorant because the invoices are not dealt with, he will continue the business relationship in good faith and will be prevented, to his detriment, from discontinuing them or from continuing them subject to the usual measures of security. While not sharing an identical interest, the creditor bank and the creditor nevertheless share what is at least an equal interest, based on a similarity of risks, in the immediate return of unpaid invoices after having received and examined them, or in immediate notification. Every bank if interposed as the creditor's bank, must protect this interest of the creditor as if it were its own in relation to all other participating banks, having regard to the contractual fiduciary relationship with its own customer, since every bank acts from case to case either as the creditor or the debtor bank in the many proceedings of direct debiting; all other banks are aware of this and treat it as a matter of course. For these special reasons and because legal relationships rely upon the observance of the practice of the banks confirmed by the Agreement on Direct Debits, the duty to return dishonoured invoices constitutes not only a contractual obligation of the debtor bank towards the creditor bank which was created between the banks themselves in virtue of the Agreement, but also a protective obligation of the debtor bank, based on good faith, in favour of the particular creditor claiming a direct debit. In individual cases where the creditor bank sends invoices to the debtor bank direct this protective duty is based on the legal relationship between the two banks which is created in respect of the individual direct debit on the basis of the giro contract. If, however, additional banks are interposed in carrying out direct debiting procedures between the creditor bank and the debtor bank, this protective duty is based upon the legal relationship between the bank which is the last to be interposed and the debtor bank. The reason is that interposed banks, too, are bound, having regard to the chain of contractual relations which leads back to the creditor bank, to follow through to the debtor bank the obligation of the creditor bank to protect the interests of the creditor. From this follows naturally that the duty of protection incumbent upon the debtor bank for the benefit of the creditor of the direct debit is not excluded by Part IV no. 1 of the Agreement on Direct Debits, contrary to the contention of the defendant, although the Agreement is intended to create 'only rights and duties between the participating credit institutions'. The protective duty is not based upon the Agreement but on the legal relationships described above, their contractual purpose and the principle of good faith, and moreover this duty would also have to be recognized if the agreement between the banks did not exist. For the same reason the claims for damages of the creditor of the direct debit against the debtor bank are not affected by the internal special arrangement of Part IV no. 2 of the Agreement, if the protective duty has been violated.

In the present case the defendant bank, by failing to handle the invoices for a long time, has therefore violated the protective duty incumbent upon it and must compensate the plaintiff for the loss resulting therefrom, unless the defendant . . . had retained the invoices with the express consent of the plaintiff's manager . . .

Case 17

BUNDESGERICHTSHOF (FOURTH CIVIL DIVISION) 28 AUGUST 1982*
NJW 1982, 2431

The plaintiff, a Danish private bank, claims damages against the defendant because it was induced by an expert valuation made by the defendant and by information supplied by him to the Danish Consul in Munich to grant a credit which could not be recovered later on. The firm of P was the owner of a considerable area of building land. It intended to develop it by building an extensive holiday village. The project had been approved in principle in planning proceedings. No detailed building plans had, however, been drawn up. Only a draft existed which had been prepared by a private architect appointed by the firm of P in agreement with the local commune. At the request of the firm of P the defendant submitted on 10 August 1974 an expert opinion in which he concluded that the area of building land as a whole had a commercial value of DM 200,000,000. On 19 December 1974 the Danish Consul telephoned the defendant and informed him that the Consulate had received an enquiry as to whether the defendant was in fact an officially appointed and sworn expert. Upon receiving an affirmative reply, the Consul asked whether the expert valuation of the area of the holiday village, which the defendant had supplied, was still valid; in so doing he referred to the growing fall of prices in the market of immovables. The defendant replied that he had not heard anything since in this matter. However, in the meantime the proceedings for the approval of the plans should have been advanced. If so, the increased readiness of building operations was a positive factor which balanced the negative development on the market for immovable property. In particular the fact had to be taken into account that according to the practice of planning consent prevailing now, other projects of this kind would no longer receive approval. At the Consul's request the defendant wrote a letter to the Danish Consulate in which he stated: 'In supplementation of my detailed expert opinion of 10

* English version by Kurt Lipstein.

August 1974 I confirm that the value of the object mentioned above has remained unchanged to the present time. The negative effects of the general development on the market of immovable properties are balanced by the fact that the land is ready to be built upon. Moreover, no consent for further comparable projects in the German region of the Alps can be expected either at present or in the future.' On 6 June 1975 the plaintiff entered into a contract for a loan of DM 15,000,000 with the firm of P. The two managers of the firm and the Danish firm of N became independently liable sureties; the Danish Export Council on its part became a surety for the last mentioned firm. In addition the loan was secured by a charge amounting to DM 18,000,000 on the immovable property of the firm of P. On 14 March (August ?) 1975 the net loan amounting to DM 14,305,000 was paid over. Subsequently the project of the holiday village was not pursued and the interest which had fallen due was not paid. Consequently the loan agreement was rescinded. Based on its charge over the land the plaintiff levied execution against it by way of a sale by auction and bought it on offering DM 1,900,000. The plaintiff contends that the firm of P had sought contacts with sources of money in order to obtain a loan of at least DM 15,000,000 for its planned holiday village. In this connection the firm had entered into negotiations with the Danish firm of N. It had held out the possibility of an order for the delivery of 600 prefabricated houses, if N would assist P in obtaining a credit of DM 15,000,000. In a letter of 28 September 1974 P had not set out its financial situation and the state of the project; in this connection P had referred to the annexed expert valuation by the defendant. N had approached the Danish Ministry of Commerce in order to obtain a guarantee by the State; for this purpose it had submitted the expert valuation by the defendant. The Ministry of Commerce had interposed the plaintiff as a bank, which was to be secured by way of reinsurance by a guarantee of the Danish State. In order to ascertain whether the conditions existed for granting the loan the Danish Export Credit Council had instructed the Danish Consul in Munich to obtain details from the defendant; it had been agreed between the Export Council and the plaintiff that the Consul had told the defendant expressly that a Danish enterprise intended to participate in the project by way of a guarantee or by granting a credit.

The plaintiff's claim was rejected by the courts, below. Upon a second appeal the judgment was quashed and the case referred back for the following

Reasons

1. The Court of Appeal holds that the plaintiff is not entitled to damages in its own right. In making his enquiry the Consul had not made it clear that he acted as the plaintiff's agent. The information was not information 'for

those whom it may concern' which might have the consequence that the defendant was liable in contract 'to any third party'.

From the point of view taken by the Court of Appeal, it should also have been examined whether the plaintiff was included in the protection sphere of the contract. The practice of the courts—and to a great extent also the literature—acknowledges the admissibility of contracts with protective effects for the benefit of third parties [references]. The articles by Ziegler [reference] and Sonnenschein [reference] to which the defendant refers do not cause this Senate to deviate from this well established legal rule. Since the Consul obviously lacked any personal interest in examining the creditworthiness of the firm of P, it could be assumed, at least if it was denied that the Consul acted in the name of another, that future suppliers of credit were to be included in the protection sphere of the contract. The Court of Appeal should have examined the claim from this point of view as well.

In this connection the Court of Appeal adds: the expert valuation had clearly anticipated and assumed an expected development—namely the award of the necessary consent, division, and sale—although in law the possibility of developing the land had not yet been assured. The estimate of a value which was only expected to materialize could not as such have been of interest to third parties, especially credit institutions. However, on p. 2 of the expert valuation, the defendant stated expressly that he had been instructed to ascertain the 'commercial value at the relevant time'. It is true that in carrying out the instruction to supply an expert valuation the defendant had to take the future development into consideration. According to the customs of trade the (present) commercial value of an immovable is determined not only by the factual circumstances at the time when the valuation is made, but also by the expectation of future events (e.g. that it will be capable of development as building land). It is obvious that a credit institution which intends to secure a future loan by a mortgage of charge will be interested in the commercial value of the land to be encumbered. As the Court of Appeal has found, the Consul made it clear to the defendant that the information given by him was required for the purpose of deciding whether the loan was to be granted. The Consul was not content with the information given over the telephone, but asked for a written confirmation; thereby he demonstrated to the defendant that his expert opinion was to serve as the basis of a far-reaching decision. The question as to whether the defendant made it sufficiently clear in his expert opinion that the planning permits necessary for the development of the area in issue may be important in assessing the blameworthiness of the defendant and any possible contributory negligence on the part of the plaintiff, but it is irrelevant for determining whether the plaintiff can make any claims at all because the contract for the supply of information has been violated.

2. The Court of Appeal regards it as possible that in concluding the contract for the supply of information the Consul asked as a representative of the Danish State. If this point of view is adopted the question arises as to whether the Danish State can claim damages from the defendant because the contract to supply information has been violated. According to the plaintiff's pleadings, the Danish Export Council—apparently as representing the Danish State—became a surety for the credit to be granted. The plaintiff contends that the Export Credit Council had assigned to the plaintiff any possible claims for damages by the Danish State against the defendant; by way of a subsidiary argument the plaintiff relies also on this claim for damages. By the reference back the plaintiff is enabled to amplify its pleadings in this respect and especially to set out to what extent the Danish State has suffered damage. It will be useful if in this connection the plaintiff provides some information concerning the legal position of the Export Credit Council, and in particular whether it is an organ of the State which became a surety in the name of the Danish State and also whether on the latter's behalf it has assigned the claim to the plaintiff.

Case 18

BUNDESGERICHTSHOF (FOURTH CIVIL DIVISION) 2 NOVEMBER 1983*
NJW 1984, 355

The defendant is an officially appointed sworn expert for building construction and for valuing land and buildings. On 5 September 1977 he was asked by S, a merchant, to supply an expert opinion concerning the market value of and the estimated income from premises in N. The meeting, in the course of which the defendant received the order, was attended by S, who was accompanied by the plaintiff and by L, a banker. In his written opinion dated 19 September 1977 the defendant intimated that the apartment house erected in 1953 would bring in a gross annual income of DM 91,990 and a net annual income of DM 68,918. He assessed the market value of the premises at DM 1,447,715. The opinion failed to take into account that the premises are subject to restrictions connected with social housing. On 15 November 1977, the plaintiff bought the house on his own account for DM 540,000; S did not participate in the purchase. The premises were conveyed, but the transfer of title was not entered in the land register. The plaintiff financed the purchase by arranging for a loan of DM 500,000 from the City Savings Bank in N, which was secured by a charge on the newly acquired premises. By a contract dated 27 June 1978 the sale agreement of 15 November 1977 was rescinded *in toto* with effect from 1 July 1978. On 28 May 1978, the defendant wrote a letter to B, who was then interested in

* English version by Kurt Lipstein.

acquiring the premises, which contained, *inter alia*, the following passage: 'Mr S instructed me on 5 September 1977 to value the premises. He indicated clearly in the presence of witnesses that he or the connections behind him intended to acquire the premises with a view to converting them into ownership flats. I do not know whether the premises were put up by private finance or whether they represent social housing. It is not the task of a sworn expert to consider this question. I took great care in ascertaining the rental values in the neighbourhood and, having consulted the City administration in N, I came to conclusion that the value of DM 7.50 per square metre is entirely appropriate . . .' The plaintiff alleges that the defendant knew that he and the witness S intended to acquire the premises together. He had bought the premises relying on the accuracy of the defendant's opinion. When the first rents had come in he had found out that the gross value of the income amounted only to DM 25,729.08, which meant that the income was substantially less than the annual payments of interest. For this reason, he had been compelled to rescind the contract of sale. If the defendant had assessed the annual income from the premises incorrectly, the plaintiff would not have bought the premises. As a result he would not have been liable to pay the agent's fee of DM 17,982; local charges of DM 3,973.09; interest on the loan amounting to DM 25,479.76 and notary's fees of DM 6,170.93 totalling DM 53,605.78. He claims this sum.

The District Court rejected the claim. An appeal to the Court of Appeal of Nuremberg was unsuccessful. Upon a second appeal the judgment below was quashed and the case referred back for the following

Reasons

The Court of Appeal denies that the instruction given to the defendant by the witness S to supply an expert opinion constitutes a contract in favour of third parties. No serious objections can be raised against this view. The circumstances indicate that the defendant only intended to assume a duty to perform an act—namely the duty to supply an expert opinion—in favour of the witness S; at least no legal reasons exist for criticizing the court below which found the facts in having interpreted the agreement to this effect.

These considerations alone do not exclude the *locus standi* of the plaintiff to prosecute his claim for damages. It is necessary, in addition, to examine whether the plaintiff is included in the area protected by the contract. It is recognized today, both in the literature and by the practice of the courts, that a contractual obligation may create duties of care towards third parties who themselves are not entitled to seek performance of the principal obligation. As this Senate has stated [reference] this consideration applies also to contracts with officially appointed and sworn experts. The circumstances of the present case indicate the need to examine the facts from this point of view.

It is undisputed that the witness S, accompanied by the plaintiff, called upon the defendant. According to the plaintiff the defendant knew that the premises were to be purchased jointly by S and the plaintiff. The Court of Appeal, it is true, was not convinced that this allegation was correct; consequently it cannot be taken into account by this court. However, the defendant does not deny to have known that a consortium behind the witness S was contemplating the purchase of the premises. He said so clearly in his letter of 28 May 1978. He has also adhered to this account of the facts in the present dispute; he merely claims that he was not aware who belonged to this group. However, this fact is not decisive. Duties of care can also be created in favour of those persons who are not mentioned by name to the other contracting party. Nor is it necessary that the contracting party should know the correct number of persons to whom a duty of care is owed. The practice of the Federal Supreme Court has recognized in several cases that a contract includes a duty of care towards third parties even if the party owing the duty of care was ignorant of the number and the names of the persons to whom the duty was owed [references]. It is essential, however, that the group to whom the duty of care is owed should be capable of being determined objectively . . .

The District Court was of the opinion that the present contract did not include a duty of care towards third persons for the reason that the witness S did not himself owe a duty of care and protection towards the plaintiff. This consideration, too, does not exclude the *locus standi* of the plaintiff. In principle the parties are free to fashion a contract; they are only restricted in their freedom of choice by the binding rules of law and by the moral requirements to be observed in accordance with § 138 BGB. The parties are therefore at liberty to determine which persons are to be included in the duty of care owed by the contract; they can even extend this duty of care to persons who are not in the charge of either 'for better or for worse' [reference]. This cannot be doubted in so far as the parties have inserted express provisions. Where the extent of the duty of care is to be implied from the unequivocal conduct of the parties, the conclusion must be the same; for in the absence of rules requiring the observance of particular formalities an implied declaration of intention is equivalent to one which is express. It is true that in several instances the Federal Supreme Court, in deciding whether a certain person is owed a duty of care by virtue of a contract, has examined whether the other contracting party, to whom the duty of care was owed, was in charge of that person for better or for worse [references]. These decisions must not, however, be interpreted in the sense that the Federal Supreme Court affirmed the legality of this type of contract only in these circumstances. Instead they only concern the question in what circumstances the objective interests involved permit the conclusion that the parties have implicitly stipulated a duty of care towards third parties—i.e. where neither any express statements by the parties nor their conduct otherwise offer any concrete evidence. Even within this approach which relies on typical situations the practice of the Federal Supreme Court [references] requires only that normally, but not always, a contracting party should have been in charge for better or for worse of the person to whom the duty of care is owed. It is another question, however, whether an extension of the duty of care arising from a contract beyond the contracting parties must be presumed having regard to the special circumstances of the particular case. It often happens when an expert is being engaged that the opinion to be supplied is to serve as a basis for a decision by persons who are not linked to the expert by contract [references]. In such a case the court ascertaining the facts must examine in accordance with the general principles of interpretation in the light of the circumstances whether the contracting parties intended to create a duty of care in favour of that person. In this connection, too, it may be relevant whether the instructing party was charged with the care of the third party in question; it is not, however, a necessary prerequisite for holding that such a duty of care exists. In the present case it will have to be considered that an interested party who asks for an expert opinion to form the basis of a decision by a certain group, will normally seek to protect not only his personal interests but also those of the other members of the group; consequently it will not normally be his intention, in entering into the contract, to limit the duty to pay compensation to damage which he suffers personally. In this connection the interests of the expert must also be taken into account; he must not be burdened unreasonably with the duty to pay compensation to third parties; it cannot be expected according to good faith (para. 157 BGB) that the other contracting party will assume such an obligation. In this respect it will have to be considered that the damage which may be suffered by a group of buyers in acquiring a house, if the expert opinion was wrong in estimating its value, are not normally higher than those which would be suffered in similar circumstances by an individual buyer.

Whether in an individual case the duty of care arising under the contract extends to third parties is a matter of interpreting the contract.

2. The Court of Appeal has examined the question whether in his expert opinion the defendant indicated expressly or by implication that he intended to be liable 'to whom it concerns' for the accuracy of his report; it found that he did not. No legal reasons exist for contesting this view; in fact no indications exist that the defendant intended to assume liability towards persons who did not belong to the group of buyers behind the witness S.

3. No legal objections can be raised either against the rejection by the Court of Appeal of near-contractual liability of the expert. Those who commission

an opinion frequently use the expert opinion of an officially appointed and sworn expert by referring to this opinion in their negotiations with third parties, e.g. in order to justify as vendors the amount of the purchase price demanded or in order to demonstrate that a certain object is credit-worthy. If an expert must assume that his expert opinion will be used for such purposes and is intended to serve as a basis for important financial transactions by third parties, he may be liable to these third parties for the accuracy of the expert opinion (see for this aspect the decision of the Federal Supreme Court [reference] concerning a bank reference and a certificate by a chartered accountant). No such use was, however, envisaged in the present case nor has it occurred in fact. The expert opinion was merely intended to inform the witness S and the group of buyers behind him; it was not meant to support statements in negotiations with third parties.

II. By way of a subsidiary argument the Court of Appeal states that the claim would have to be rejected, even if the plaintiff had a *locus standi*. In calculating the annual income he was not obliged to examine whether the house contained apartments which had been financed privately or by social housing aid. Since his instructions did not provide any relevant information, he was entitled to assume that the apartments had been financed privately; consequently he was only bound to rely on 'the rental obtainable on the free housing market for the apartments of the premises'. These statements cannot be supported in law. An expert opinion must be based on facts and not on guesses or assumptions. Therefore the defendant could only proceed on the assumption that the apartments had been financed privately, if he had reached the conclusion that this assumption was correct. If the expert is ignorant of the relevant circumstances for coming to a conclusion, he must enquire of those instructing him and must, if necessary, also make other investigations (as, for instance, by making enquiries with the authorities). If these attempts remain fruitless he may base his expert opinion on assumptions, but he must indicate this clearly in his opinion. Every expert valuer of premises must know that in assessing the rental of an apartment and, as a result of the income of an apartment house, the legal status of the apartments according to the Rent Control legislation is determining. The fact that the defendant has failed to take this into account may support the charge of negligence. The defendant argues in defence that even if the apartments had been financed privately the rents stated by him would not have been recoverable without further action; it would have been necessary to initiate proceedings for an increase in rents in accordance with § 2 of the Act regulating the Amount of Rent; in many cases this would have involved litigation. This pertinent argument only serves to increase the charge of negligence against the defendant. Precisely for the reason that the owner of the underscores '. . . the German willingness, indeed eagerness, to extend tort protection . . . [despite] the Civil Code's categorical exclusion of tort damages for pure economic loss and the great weight reputedly given by German law to theoretical orthodoxy over pragmatism.' (Fleming (1989) 105 *LQR*, 508.) In this trend (rather than in the details of German law) may also lie the greatest lesson for the Common lawyer who, additionally, would not have to go to the same pains to justify similar results if (or when) he decided to adopt a more flexible attitude towards pure economic loss. Finally, many of the ideas, notions, and trends discussed in this section are also evident in two other areas of economic loss. The first is concerned with the consequences of mistakes made by lawyers (and is discussed in the next section); the other deals with damage caused *to* products (and is considered by the cases reproduced in section 15 and the notes that accompany them).

In the light of these introductory remarks, it is self-evident that summaries such as the one that follows are bound to be somewhat crass. Their main aim must be to serve as signposts for further study of the law; if they also succeed in making the reader 'think', that can only be regarded as a welcome bonus.

2. At first sight, German law is cautious and conservative. § 676 BGB provides that 'A person who gives advice or a recommendation to another is not bound to compensate for any damage arising from following the advice or recommendation, without prejudice to his responsibility arising from contract or delict.' Since the main tort provision (§ 823 I BGB) excludes, as we have seen, pure economic loss from its list of protected interests, liability in *tort* can only be based on § 824 BGB or § 826 BGB. The first has minimal importance, while the second also has a limited application. This is despite the fact that in recent times the courts have widened the meaning of intention (in § 826 BGB) to include not only *dolus directus* but also *dolus eventualis* (a notion somewhat akin to our concept of reckless behaviour). Thus, in one decision (BGH NJW 1987, 1758–9) the court eased the fault requirement stating that (for the purposes of liability under § 826 BGB) it would suffice to show that the auditor expected his report to be used in connection with credit negotiations and that (if it were incorrect) it would cause harm to the relying creditor. Professor von Bar has, in fact, gone further by arguing that 'a person who gives information off the cuff must . . . recognise that it could be false; and the very fact that he still goes ahead and gives that information demonstrates that he has reckoned with the possibility of damage to others and has accepted it.' ('Liability for Information and Opinions Causing Pure Economic Loss to Third Parties' in *The Growing Convergence* (ed. B. S. Markesinis) O.U.P. (1993). See, also, Palandt-Thomas, § 826 no. 8 c.bb.)

Because of the above strictures of the tort provisions of the Code the courts have had recourse to the notion of contract with protective effects *vis-à-vis* third parties with the result that the liability of auditors has been taken significantly further than the wording of § 826 could even possibly justify. Liability, essentially, depends upon reliance on the report; and whether this was reasonable or not depends on the contract (commissioning the audit report) as well as all other relevant circumstances. Thus, third parties may be able to sue for damages under contracts to which they are not signatories (BGH JZ 1986, 1111); or where their protection under the contract commissioning the report arises not from its wording but from necessary implication (BGH NJW 1987, 1758, 9). The Federal Court has also made it clear that for the protective effects to arise, it is no longer necessary for the requirement of '*Wohl und Wehe*' (for better or for worse) to be fulfilled. (See BGHZ 69, 82, 86; BGH NJW 1984, 355, 356.) The BGH has also moved away from the view that third party protection must be denied because of the (potential) conflict of interests between the principal of the commissioning report and the third parties (BGH NJW 1987, 1758-9). In this context, of particular interest is a decision of the BGH in 1985 where one reason given for the enlargement of the auditor's liability was the existence of mandatory liability insurance according to § 54 of the Accountants' Regulations (*Wirtschaftsprüferordnung, WPO*). (See, BGH WM 1985, 450, nos. 6 and 8). Also relevant may be the fact that under the WPO the auditors are allowed to make use of the General Commissioning Terms for Chartered Accountants (*Allgemeine Auftragsbedingungen für Wirtschaftsprüfer*) which restrict or (in certain circumstances) eliminate their liability. Statutes such as the General Conditions of Business of 1977 (the German equivalent to the (British) Unfair Contract Terms Act of the same year) may also help define the ambit of liability and thus, *de facto*, limit litigation by reference to the amount of insurance coverage. (See: BGH NJW 1987, 1758, 1760.) One should finally add that if third parties are entitled to sue auditors, they can be opposed by all the defences that may be available to auditors as a result of their contracts with the commissioning company. The contractual nature of this action makes this point obvious, whereas it would be more problematic if the action were tortious in nature. (These observations will be best understood if read in conjunction with the text in Chapter 2, 2 (*d*) (iii), above, and the notes to case 12. For further details about the topics discussed above see: Assmann, 'Grundfälle zum Vertrag mit Schutzwirkung für Dritte' *JuS* 1986, 885; Bamm, 'Entwicklungstendenzen der Expertenhaftung' *JZ* 1991, 373; Ebke, 'Die Haftung des Wirtschaftsprüfers für fahrlässig verursachte Vermögensschäden Dritter', *WM* 1991, 398; Lang, 'Die Rechtsprechung des Bundesgerichtshofes zur Dritthaftung der Wirtschaftsprüfer und anderer Sachverständiger', *WM* 1988, 1001; Müller, 'Wirtschaftsprüfer und vereidigte Buchprüfer als Sachverständige und Gutachter', *WPK-Mitt* 1991, 3.)

3. The 'Common law' regime just described is, as indicated at the beginning of this section, modified wherever the statutory regime takes precedence. This is the situation in the *Caparo* type of case where the result reached by the House of Lords would also be acceptable to German law. (*Caparo*, it will be recalled, dealt with a 'statutory' audit, prepared for the company but relied upon (to their detriment) by (*a*) existing and (*b*) potential shareholders of the said company. The Court of Appeal allowed the first (but not the second) to recover their losses, but the House of Lords overturned the decision denying both categories of plaintiff all redress against the negligent accountants.) The German result would be dictated by § 323 of the Commercial Code (HGB) which specifically regulates the legal position of auditors in the case of 'mandatory audits' (*Pflichtprüfungen*), i.e. the formation audit, the annual audits and 'special' reports, and which restricts the auditor's liability for negligent breach of his duties to the company only. (For an English version of the text see: *Business Transactions in Germany*, Gen. Ed. Ruester, N.Y., Matthew Bender (1990). For a more detailed account in German see: Ebke, *Wirtschaftsprüfer und Dritthaftung* (1983), esp. pp. 38–43; 56–60.) Shareholders and potential shareholders are, thus, excluded for the purview of this paragraph; and they are also denied an action under § 823 II BGB because § 323 HGB is not regarded as a protective norm (*Schutzgesetz*). (This has been well-established for some time. See: *Aktiengesetz Kommentar*, 13th edn. by Baumbach, Hueck and Schulze (1968) § 168, no. 7; *Aktiengesetz Kommentar* by Gessler, Hefermehl, Eckhardt and Kropff, vol. III (1973) § 168, no. 31; *Kölner Kommentar zum Aktiengesetz* by Zoellner, vol. II (1971), § 168, no. 16. These are commentaries on § 168 of the *Aktiengesetz* which is now to be found as § 323 of the Commercial Code, quoted in the text above.) This restrictive interpretation is reinforced by § 340b (5) of the *Aktiengesetz* which deals with the potential liability of auditors in the event of mergers. For in this second instance, liability is expressly extended towards 'the companies participating in the merger *and* their shareholders'. (Emphasis added.)

4. Negligent statement situations can take an infinite variety of factual forms. These have been systematically analysed by Lorenz, 'Das Problem der Haftung für primäre Vermögensschäden bei der Erteilung einer unrichtigen Auskunft', *Festschrift K. Larenz* (1973) 575. Here suffice it to divide them into two groups.

In the first, the defendant makes a statement (usually a report) to the person who asked for it (and, invariably, paid for it) but knows that it will be relied upon by a specified third person. OLG München BB 1956, 866 is such a case and it is discussed along with other similar cases in Lawson and Markesinis, I, 83 ff. It finds an excellent parallel in *Glanzer* v. *Shepard* 233 NY 236, 135 NE 275 (1922). That German law based its solution on contract whereas the American law opted for tort is mostly a matter of 'emphasis', as Cardozo J. put it, adding that if necessary he, too, could have based his decision on contract. (For further German decisions see, *inter alia*, BGH WM 1965, 287; BGH WM 1963, 913.)

Real difficulties appear in the second type of situation where A commissions the (negligently prepared) report from B and then shows it to others who rely on it to their detriment. Case 15 is such a case and it is here that the problem of 'indeterminate liability', so well identified by Cardozo J. in *Ultramares Marine* v. *Touche Niven and Co.* 255 NY 170, 174 NE 441 (1931), rears its ugly head. The courts, if they abandon strict adherence to the privity requirement (as they are nowadays inclined to do), are, in such cases, forced to seek a balance between liability resting on pure foresight (or some equivalent concept) and liability based only on a form of direct nexus between the representor and the representee of the kind found in the aforementioned decision of the Court of Appeal of Munich or in the *Glanzer* decision. (Another possibility is to rely on statutory enactments such as ss. 11 and 12 of the (American) Securities Act of 1932 or s. 18 of the Securities Exchange Act of 1934; but such actions have been of limited use to ordinary investors or creditors besides suffering from the drawback of a short—one year—limitation period.) For the protection currently afforded by federal securities law see Kraakman, 'Gatekeepers: The Anatomy of a Third-Party Enforcement Strategy?' 2 *J. of Law, Econ. and Org.* 53 (1986).

The USA provides, as one would expect, the greatest variety of court-devised techniques to avoid the strictures of the *Ultramares* rule. Thus some courts, while not overruling *Ultramares*, appear to be extending the rationale of the *Glanzer* decision (third party can recover if he is the end and aim of the transaction). See, for example, *White* v. *Guarente* 43 NY 2d 356, 372 NE 2d 315 (NY 1977); *Credit Alliance Corp.* v. *Arthur Anderson and Co.*, 476 NYS 2d 539 (1984); reversed in 483 NE 2d 110, 493 NYS 2d 435 (1985) (duty of care owed to limited class of foreseen users). Yet other courts proclaim a rigid adherence to the principle of the great case. See: *Toro Co.* v. *Krouse, Kern and Co. Inc.*, 827 F. 2d 155 (1987). A more flexible approach is that advocated by the *Restatement (Second) of Torts*, para. 552 (1972) which rejects the private requirement and renders accountants liable not only to those persons whom they intended to influence but also towards the persons whom the accountants know that their *clients* intended to influence. *Rusch Factors Inc.* v. *Levin*, 284 F. Supp. 85 (1968) offers an early illustration, the court in that case being influenced by a tentative draft of the Restatement. Note that the *Rusch* decision (at p. 93) talks of an '*actually* foreseen and *limited* class of persons' [italics supplied]. Whereas the German decision, while agreeing with the idea that the identity of the relying person need not be known to the representor, insists that he must be 'part of a calculable group of persons'. Ohio (*Hadden View Investment Co.* v. *Coopers and Lybrand* (436 NE 2d 212, 70 Ohio St. 2d 154 (1982)) and New Hampshire (*Spherex Inc.* v. *Alexander Grant and Co.*, 122 N.H. 898, 451 A. 2d 1308 (1982)) are among the states that have adopted this rule. Yet a third group of courts has adopted and adapted the multi-criteria test advocated in the legal malpractice case of *Biakanja* v. *Irving* (320 P. 2d 16 (1958) discussed below). *Raritan River Steel Co.* v. *Cherry, Beckaert & Holland*, 79 NC App. 81, 339 SE 2d 62 (1986), a decision of the Court of Appeal of North Carolina, offers one of the best illustrations. Finally, a number of recent decisions seem to be moving towards the adoption of the most liberal test namely that of pure foreseeability. Thus see: *H. Rosenblum Inc.* v. *Adler* 93 NJ 324, 461 A. 2d 138 (1983); *Citizens State Bank* v. *Timm, Schmidt and Co.* 335 NW 2d 361 (1983); *International Mortgage Co.* v. *John P. Butler Accountancy Corp.* 223 Cal. Rptr. 218 (1986). There is, of course, something to be said for and against each of these approaches with the Restatement rule offering, perhaps, the best combination of predictability and flexibility and with the last two tests enjoying the wider support from the pro-plaintiff lawyers including, invariably, the authors of notes and articles in law journals. *Ultramares*, however, as reiterated by *Credit Alliance*, is apparently still favoured by most courts.

5. English law, too, has vacillated on this topic in a manner which has been as confusing as it is difficult to summarize with any pretence to accuracy. The modern law starts with *Candler* v. *Crane Christmas and Co.* [1951] 2 KB 164 which, though denying recovery to the plaintiff, opened the door for future developments through the prophetic dissent of Denning LJ (as he then was). Some fifteen years later heresy was transformed into orthodoxy by the seminal judgment of the House of Lords in *Hedley Byrne and Co. Ltd.* v. *Heller and Partners Ltd.* [1964] AC 465 where the rule was settled that there would be liability for careless statements causing pure economic loss provided there was a 'special relationship' between the plaintiff and the defendant *and* there was no disclosure of liability. 'Special relationship' has obviously been a key phrase; and it has been subsequently interpreted to include a friend giving advice seriously though *not* in a professional context (*Chaudhry* v. *Prabhaker* [1989] 1 WLR 29). Earlier attempts to narrow the *Hedley Byrne* rule only to cases where the party making the statement professed to give that kind of advice or held himself out as possessing special skills also proved unsuccessful. See: *Mutual Life and Citizens' Assurance Co. Ltd.* v. *Evalt* [1971] 3 AC 793; *Esso Petroleum Co. Ltd.* v. *Mardon* [1976] QB 501.

The 1960s and 1970s found the English courts in an imaginative and expansionist mode. This can be seen in English administrative law, but it is also obvious in the decisions dealing with liability for negligent misstatement. Thus, in *Ministry of Housing and Local Government* v. *Sharp* [1970]

QB 223 two further extensions were made to the *Hedley Byrne* principle. (In *Hedley Byrne* A made a false statement to B who relied on it to his detriment; in *Sharp* A made the statement to B (who never repeated it to C) but it was C who suffered the loss and was allowed to recover. Secondly, in *Hedley Byrne* the plaintiff's loss was actual expenditure whereas in *Sharp* the harm suffered was failure to recover a sum that had become due). And a potentially more far-reaching extension came in *JEB Fasteners Ltd.* v. *Marks, Bloom and Co.* [1981] 3 All ER 289 where liability was not based on the *Hedley Byrne* rule (which requires the establishment of a 'special relationship') but on the more amorphous neighbourhood rule of *Donoghue* v. *Stevenson* [1932] AC 562 (which also provided the justification for the legal malpractice rule of *Ross* v. *Caunters* [1980] Ch. 297, though in the latter case the economic loss was not caused by a false statement but by a negligent attestation of a will.

More recently, however, this expansionist mood has been checked; and in some cases it has been accompanied by severely restricting dicta found in a long series of decisions expressing disapproval of the liberal tendencies which peaked with the decision of the House of Lords in *Junior Books* v. *Veitchi* [1938] AC 520 (a case also involving pure economic loss, though caused by negligent deeds, not words). In the context of negligent misstatements, the leading judgment can be found in *Caparo* v. *Dickman* [1970] 2 AC 605 where the House of Lords overruled an interesting and well thought-out judgment of the Court of Appeal by refusing to hold that the auditors of a company owed a duty of care towards the shareholders of the company who suffered losses by purchasing shares in that company by relying on that report. The judgments of at least two Lords (Bridge and Jauncey) suggest that liability can only arise if the statement was both intended to be relied upon for a particular purpose and was, in fact, relied upon, something which, in the opinion of their Lordships, was not satisfied in this case. See, also, *Al Saudi Banque* v. *Clarke Paxley* [1990] Ch. 313 (company auditors not liable to a bank who lent to the company on the strength of their report); *The Morning Watch* [1990] 1 Lloyd's Rep. 547 (Lloyds Register, reporting on the condition of a vessel at the request of the owner, not liable to potential purchaser who relies on their report). As always, the plethora of dicta, often with relatively minor verbal variations, may one day enable a shift to more liberal positions, analogous to those one finds in some leading German judgments. For the time being, however, the following statements may provide a general indication of the current state of English law. Thus, in *Smith* v. *Eric Bush; Harris* v. *Wyre Forest District Council* [1990] AC 831, 865, Lord Griffiths stressed 'that in cases where the advice has not been given for the specific purpose of the recipient acting upon it, it should only be in cases when the adviser knows that there is a high degree of probability that some other identifiable person will act upon the advice that a duty of care should be imposed.' Likewise, in *Caparo Industries Plc* v. *Dickman* [1990] 2 AC 605, 621 Lord Bridge argued that in these cases it is essential to prove 'that the defendant knew that his statement would be communicated to the plaintiff, either as an individual or as a member of an identifiable class, specifically in connection with a particular transaction or transactions of a particular kind (e.g. in a prospectus inviting investment) and that the plaintiff would be very likely to rely on it for the purpose of deciding whether or not to enter upon that transaction or upon a transaction of that kind.' See, also, Lord Oliver's remarks at p. 652.

As a postscript one might add that inadequate consideration has been given to a point raised by Lord Justice Bingham in the *Caparo* case ([1989] 1 QB 653, 689 *et seq.*) namely that the finding of a duty situation in such cases will by no means always lead to liability. For most claims would very likely fail (or would be settled at a very early state in the proceedings) on the grounds that no negligence can be proved or that the causation link between negligent misstatement and the loss has not been established. *Banque Financière de la Cité* v. *Westgate Insurance Ltd.* [1991] 2 AC 249 supports this assertion though, given the paucity of case law on this point, this view in the text is only advanced as a tentative one.

Further reading

For further readings on the Common law see Franklin, (3rd edn.) 248 ff. (4th edn.) 347 ff.; Henderson and Pearson, 1129–37; Prosser, Wade, and Schwartz, 1035 ff.; Prosser in 19 *Vand. L. Rev.* 231 (1966); Craig in 92 *LQR* 213 (1976). For German law see Larenz, above; Lammel, 'Zur Auskunftshaftung' *AcP* 1979, 337; Musielak, *Haftung für Rat, Auskunft und Gutachten* (1974); Scheerer, 'Probleme der Haftung der Kreditinstitute für die Erteilung von Auskünften in Deutschland und Frankreich unter besonderer Berücksichtigung der Haftungsfreizeichnungsklauseln' *Festschrift Bärmann* (1975). Rich references to recent American decisions and the policies that lie behind them can be found in Bilek, 'Accountants' Liability to the Third Party and Public Policy: A Calabresi Approach', 39 *Southwestern Law Journal* 689 (1985). See also: Achampong, 'Common Law Liability of Accountants for Negligence to Non-Contractual Parties: Recent Developments' 91 *Dickinson L. Rev.* 677 (1987); Blaney, 'The Citadel Falls? Liability for Accountants in Negligence to Third Parties Absent Privity: *Credit Alliance Corp.* v. *Arthur Andersen and Co.*' 59 *St John's L. Rev.* 348 (1985); Casazza, '*Rosenblum Inc.* v. *Adler*: CPA's Liability at Common Law to Certain Reasonably Foreseeable Third Parties Who Detrimentally Rely on Negligently Audited Financial Statements' 70 *Cornell L. Rev.* 335 (1985); Davies, 'The Liability of Auditors to Third Parties in Negligence' 14 *University of N.S. Wales Law Journal* 171 (1991); Chapman, 'Limited Auditors' Liability: Economic Analysis and the Theory of Tort Law' 20 *Canadian Business Law Journal* 180 (1992); Nicholson, 'Third Party Reliance on Negligent Advice' (1991) 40 *ICLQ*, 551; Gormley, 'The Foreseen, the Foreseeable, and Beyond: Accountants' Liability to

Nonclients' 14 *Seton Hall L. Rev.* 528 (1984); Pace, 'Negligent Misrepresentation and the Certified Public Accountant: An Overview of Common Law Liability to Third Parties' 18 *Suffolk Univ. L. Rev.* 431 (1984); Causey, 'Accountants' Liability in an Indeterminate Amount for an Indeterminate Time to an Indeterminate Class' 57 *Miss. LJ* 379 (1987).

7. ECONOMIC LOSS (LEGAL MALPRACTICE)

Case 19

BUNDESGERICHTSHOF (SIXTH CIVIL DIVISION) 19 JANUARY 1977*
NJW 1977, 2073 = VersR 1977, 638

The defendant is an attorney who represented the plaintiff's father in divorce proceedings. In January 1972 the plaintiff's father and mother met in the defendant's office, where they signed a divorce agreement drawn up by the defendant. It contained the following clause:

§ 6. As to the house, the parties agree that the half belonging to Mrs M is to be trans-ferred to the three children in equal parts. Mr M hereby agrees not to sell his half but to transfer it to his present legitimate children. An appropriate notarial contract to this effect is to be concluded immediately after the divorce is final. Mr M further promises that once the divorce is final he will indemnify Mrs M against any liabilities arising from the house or its construction. . . .

A divorce decree was granted in February 1972, and the defendant, in the name of the plaintiff's father, thereupon waived any rights of appeal, as did the mother's attorney. The plaintiff's mother now refuses to transfer her interest in the property to the plaintiff and his siblings.

The plaintiff claims damages for breach of the defendant's duty as attorney. The Landgericht rejected the claim but the Oberlandesgericht allowed it. The defendant was permitted to appeal, but his appeal was dismissed.

I. [the reasoning of the Court of Appeal.]

II. Despite the appellant's contentions, this reasoning is sound in law.

1. [The defendant was in breach of his duty as attorney.]

2. Nor is there anything wrong in law with the Court of Appeal's holding that although there was no contract between the plaintiff and the defendant, the plaintiff could sue the defendant for damages for his faulty breach of contract.

(*a*) The Court of Appeal found that there was here a contract with pro-tective effect for third parties and that the plaintiff's claim arose therefrom. We do not have to decide whether this is so.

* English version by Tony Weir.

(*aa*) Certainly an important factor pointing in that direction is that the plaintiff was the son of the attorney's client and was entitled to care and protection from him (compare BGHZ 61, 227, 233). The usual problem in cases of contracts with protective effects for third parties is whether the victim was someone the debtor could expect to be harmed by a breach of the contract. That is not the problem here. The very words of § 6 of the divorce agreement drawn up by the defendant show that the children were its sole beneficiaries, the only people apt to suffer if the agreement proved invalid.

The only question here is how far the protective effect of this contract works in favour of the children, in particular whether they have any claim for damages for breach of contract in their own right. Now the contract between client and attorney is such, given its nature and structure, that it can only be very seldom, whether one interprets the contract extensively or invokes § 242 BGB (see BGHZ 56, 269, 273; NJW 1975, 977), that the duties it generates can be sued on by third parties, for the fiduciary relationship between client and attorney makes it strongly bilateral and self-contained [references omitted]. Thus the fact that third parties have an interest in what an attorney does will not normally lead to any extension of his liability, even if those persons are named or known to him. However, an exception must be made where a contract drafted by the attorney is designed to vest rights in third parties specified therein, especially third parties who, as in the present case, are represented by the client. It is true that most of the cases where the courts have granted third parties a claim for damages arising out of a contract to which they were not parties have involved personal injury or property damage and its consequences (BGHZ 49, 350, 355; NJW 1955, 257; [other references omitted]), but it is not impossible for a third party to have a personal claim for economic loss caused by breach of subsidiary contractual duties (NJW 1968, 1929; BGH NJW 1975, 344). In drawing the line here one must certainly apply an especially stringent test: the circle of persons to whom the protective effect of a contract extends is to be narrowly drawn, so as to avoid blurring the line between contractual and tortious liability in an unacceptable manner (BGHZ 66, 51, 57; NJW 1974, 1189). It must always be borne in mind, in claims for purely economic loss, that the debtor is not to be made liable for the mere ricochet effect of his conduct on third parties.

(*bb*) Despite this, we cannot, on the special facts of the present case, fault the Court of Appeal's holding that the plaintiff was drawn into the protective ambit of the attorney's contract. The respondent invokes a decision of this court of 6 July 1965 (NJW 1965, 1955), but this is not quite in point. The court there did allow the daughter of a client to sue the attorney although she was not herself a party to the contract, but the court was reluctant to categorize the contract as one with protective effect for third parties [references omitted]. Contracts with protective effect for third parties are concerned with breach of subsidiary duties by the contractor (see BGH NJW 1975, 344), whereas in that case the question was really whether the attorney could be made liable towards the client's daughter, the third party, for a breach of specific duties of performance [reference omitted]. Our case is clearly distinguishable.

(b) The plaintiff might also base his claim here on the concept of *Drittschadensliquidation*, a doctrine which borders on, if it does not actually overlap, the area of application of the doctrine of contracts with protective effect for third parties (see BGHZ 49, 350, 355). It would have been quite proper for the defendant's client to indemnify his son, the plaintiff, for the harm he had suffered, and one could then infer from the fact that he brought suit as his son's statutory representative that he was making an assignment of his own claim which the plaintiff, on the threshold of majority, could implicitly accept. But we need not pursue the matter here.

(c) In whatever legal or doctrinal category one puts the present litigated facts, the result must be that the plaintiff has a direct claim against the defendant attorney for compensation for the harm which he suffered as a result of the defendant's failure to tell his father of the need to implement the agreement in § 6 of the divorce document. Any other conclusion would be inconsistent with the meaning and purpose of the attorney's contract here and of the father–son relationship between the client and the plaintiff of which the defendant was well aware.

Addendum: White v. Jones

(Extracts from the transcript of the judgment of the Court of Appeal. A summary of the decision appeared in *The Times* of 3 March, 1993; the case has now been reported in [1993] 3 WLR 730).

Facts

The testator had two daughters: Carol White and Pauline Heath. When his wife died in January 1986 a family quarrel ensued as a result of which the testator proceeded to cut both his daughters out of his estate. In his will, executed in March 1986, he distributed his rather modest estate in various ways among three of his grandchildren and Mrs White's first husband. Soon afterwards a reconciliation took place and the testator, regretting his rash action, informed his two daughters of the will and of his intention to change it. Both he and Mr Heath (a different son-in-law) contacted Mr Jones of the firm of defendant solicitors and gave both oral and written instructions for a new will under which the two daughters would inherit approximately two-thirds of the estate, the remainder being equally divided among all (five) grandchildren. Despite repeated communications, Mr Jones remained inactive though, in mid-August, and before leaving for his annual holiday, he did write an internal memo to a member of the firm's probate division informing him of the need to prepare a new will. A proposed meeting with the testator on 17 September never took place since the latter died a few days earlier. The two daughters, having failed to reach an amicable settlement between them as to the way the estate should be divided, sued the solicitors. At First Instance, Turner J dismissed their action, holding that though the solicitors had committed a serious wrong, they owed no duty of care to the plaintiffs. A unanimous Court of Appeal (consisting of the Vice Chancellor, and Lord Justices Farquarson and Steyn) reversed the decision.

The VICE CHANCELLOR . . .

The liability question

I start with some preliminary observations. First, the present case concerns the consequences in law of a solicitor's failure to prepare a will. In my view there is no distinction in principle between this case and a case, such as *Ross* v. *Caunters*, where the solicitor's failure lies in not warning the client about formal witnessing requirements. On this I cannot agree with the Judge. There is a difference of degree in that with the latter case the proposal to benefit the beneficiary has proceeded further. In the latter case the will has been drawn up by the solicitor and signed by the testator with the beneficiary named therein. In the former case the matter has not proceeded beyond the stage of the solicitor accepting instructions. It is possible the client might have changed his mind before executing the will. I do not think this can be a crucial difference when considering whether a liability in negligence exists, although it may be very material when considering whether a beneficiary has proved he has suffered loss through the solicitor's negligence. In both cases the solicitor is in breach of his professional duty in carrying out his client's instructions for the preparation and execution of a will, in the one case by doing nothing, in the other case by doing his work badly or incompletely. Hereafter I shall draw no distinction between these two cases, and for convenience I shall refer to the question whether in such cases a solicitor can be liable to an intended beneficiary as 'the liability question'.

Knowledge of the testator's intentions

Second, in the present case the prospective beneficiaries played some part in the steps taken by the testator towards the preparation of a new will. They were aware of his wishes, they were aware of his instructions to the solicitors, and they even acted as a channel of communication between him and Mr Jones. Those features are strictly irrelevant when considering the liability question. Let me explain why. There may be cases when a prospective beneficiary can show reliance on a solicitor's advice in circumstances where a liability in negligence will clearly follow, on classic *Hedley Byrne*

([1964] AC 465) principles. For example, if a prospective beneficiary is present when the will is being signed and in response to a question the solicitor assures him it is in order for the prospective beneficiary's wife to be a witness.

That is not this case. Here there is no question of any reliance of that nature. So I put 'reliance' cases on one side. Where reliance is present the law is not in doubt. Short of reliance, in my view awareness by an intended beneficiary of what the testator is doing cannot itself make the solicitor liable to the beneficiary if otherwise he would not be liable. Similarly in respect of assistance given by a prospective beneficiary to the testator in instructing the solicitor. It cannot be that if there are two intended beneficiaries, one of whom knows of the testator's plans and his instructions to the solicitor and the other of whom does not, the negligent solicitor is liable to the former beneficiary but not the latter. That cannot be the touchstone of liability. The two cases must stand or fall together. Absent reliance as already mentioned, the solicitor must be liable in both cases or neither. In other words, the answer to the liability question must be applicable alike to the case where a prospective beneficiary is not even aware of his would-be benefactor's intentions as to a case where he is.

Robertson v. Fleming

Third, Mr Matheson submitted that we are bound, by the House of Lords decision in *Robertson* v. *Fleming* (1861) 4 Macq. 167, to answer the liability question in favour of the solicitors. I do not agree. In that case all their lordships stated, or implicitly accepted, that in the absence of a contract between them a solicitor was not liable to an intended beneficiary. In rejecting the contrary view Lord Campbell LC (at p. 177) expressed himself forthrightly:

> If this were law a disappointed legatee might sue the solicitor employed by a testator to make a will in favour of a stranger, whom the solicitor never saw or before heard of, if the will were void for not being properly signed and attested. I am clearly of opinion that this is not the law of Scotland, nor of England, and it can hardly be the law of any country where jurisprudence has been cultivated as a science. . . .

Lord Cranworth (at pp. 184–185) made an observation to the same effect.

I need hardly note that the law has moved on since 1861. This case was decided before *Donoghue* v. *Stevenson* [1932] AC 562, before *Hedley Byrne*, and before *Murphy* v. *Brentwood*. These twentieth century decisions of the House of Lords establish that there can be a liability in negligence in circumstances where the contrary view was regarded as axiomatic in the nineteenth century. In this regard *Robertson* v. *Fleming* does no more than apply the then established law on negligence to the particular case of a claim by a third party against a solicitor. What it does not do and cannot do is throw any light upon the answer to be given to the liability question by an application of the principles which, in the case of *Donoghue* v. *Stevenson*, have subsequently become part of the bedrock of the English law of negligence.

An open question

Fourth, neither in *Caparo Industries Plc* v. *Dickman* [1990] 2 AC 605 nor in *Murphy* v. *Brentwood* did the House of Lords expressly or implicitly doubt the correctness of *Ross* v. *Caunters*. In the *Caparo* case (at p. 636) Lord Oliver of Aylmerton noted that it gave rise to certain difficulties of analysis. However, in the *Murphy* case (at p. 486) he expressly left open the possibility that outside the reliance cases there may be cases, such as *Ross* v. *Caunters*, where there is a duty to take reasonable care to avoid pecuniary loss. In my view the position is simply that the House of Lords has left open the correctness of *Ross* v. *Caunters*; their lordships have expressed neither approval nor disapproval.

The effect of the solicitors' argument

Fifth, in considering the liability question it is of the utmost importance to keep in mind that if there is no liability the result, as pointed out by Sir Robert Megarry V-C in *Ross* v. *Caunters* (at p. 303), is striking: the only person who has a valid claim against the solicitor has suffered no loss, and the only person who has suffered a loss has no valid claim. The executors can sue the solicitor for damages for professional negligence, but they can recover only nominal damages because the estate has suffered no loss. All that has happened is that, by reason of the negligence, on the testator's death the estate passes to a different beneficiary. The intended beneficiary suffers a loss, but he has no right of recourse against the solicitor for the professional negligence which caused his loss. It would be a sorry reflection on English law if, indeed, that is the position today.

Foreseeability

The House of Lords' decision in *Caparo* v. *Dickman* established that, for there to be a duty to take reasonable care to avoid causing damage of a particular type to a particular person or class of persons, three factors must coalesce: foreseeability of damage, a close and direct relationship characterized by the law as 'proximity' or 'neighbourhood', and the situation must be one where it is fair, just and reasonable that the law should impose the duty of the given scope upon the one party for the benefit of the other. In the present case there is no difficulty over the first of the three headings. A solicitor must foresee that if he fails to prepare a will as instructed by his client, and arrange for it to be duly executed, the disappointed beneficiaries will suffer financial loss. After the client's death nothing can be done to remedy the solicitor's negligence. The estate will pass to those entitled under any valid unrevoked will and, subject thereto, to those entitled on an intestacy. In the nature of things it will then be too late for the solicitor to prepare a will. Furthermore the solicitor must foresee that the payment of damages to his deceased client's estate would achieve nothing. This would not provide a means of recompensing the client for the solicitor's professional negligence. Any money paid to the estate would simply pass under the very testamentary dispositions which fail to carry out the testator's instructions. Money paid to the estate would not go to the disappointed beneficiaries.

A special relationship

I turn next to consider whether there is between a solicitor and intended beneficiary a relationship of proximity and whether it is fair, just and reasonable that there should be a liability imposed on the solicitor to compensate the intended beneficiary. I shall consider these two headings together, because there is no real demarcation line between them. They shade into each other. Both involve value judgments.

Under the third heading the court makes its assessment of the requirements of fairness, justice and reasonableness. Likewise, although less obviously, built into the concept of proximity or neighbourhood is an assessment by the court that in a given relationship there 'ought' to be liability for negligence. These two headings are no more than two labels under which the court examines the pros and cons of imposing liability in negligence in a particular type of case. This is well illustrated in the instant case where some of the points which fall for consideration could happily be considered under either heading.

Mr Matheson submitted the authorities establish that, in cases of pure economic loss, there is no liability for damages in negligence unless there is actual and foreseeable reliance by the plaintiff on the defendants. Reliance is a prerequisite to the existence of the necessary close and direct relationship. I do not agree. As I read the speeches in the recent House of Lords decisions, their lordships have emphasised the importance of reliance in pure economic loss cases. But I do not find in those speeches any indication, still less express statement, that in all cases reliance is a prerequisite to the existence of liability. Indeed, the thrust of the speeches in *Caparo* v. *Dickman* and *Murphy* v. *Brentwood* is against any attempt to lay down hard-and-fast boundary lines.

I can take, as one example of a case where there was no reliance, the decision of the Court of Appeal in *Ministry of Housing and Local Government* v. *Sharp* [1970] 2 QB 223. There the local authority's officer negligently issued a clear official search certificate to a would-be buyer of land. The buyer completed his purchase on the strength of the certificate. In consequence the Ministry lost the benefit of a charge for repayment of compensation previously registered by it in the local land charges register. There was no question of the Ministry relying on anything done by the local authority or the officer. Nevertheless the court held the local authority liable in damages to the Ministry for the negligence of its official. I see no difficulty with this decision. A buyer is entitled to rely on the accuracy of a search certificate. A duty of care is owed to him. He has a remedy against those concerned if he suffers loss by an error in a carelessly prepared certificate. It would be remarkable if, when the local authority's duties are carried out negligently, a buyer has a remedy but an incumbrancer does not.

Nor is there an analogy between the shareholders and future investors in *Caparo* v. *Dickman* and intended beneficiaries in the instant case. In the *Caparo* case the House of Lords decided there was no reason in policy or in principle why the necessary close relationship should be held to exist either between the auditors and future investors or between the auditors and existing shareholders in respect of future purchases of shares. The statutory duties of auditors were not imposed by Parliament for the protection of investors in the market, and as a buyer of further shares an existing shareholder stands in no different position from any other investing member of the public: see Lord Bridge of Harwich at pages 623D–F and 627E–F, Lord Oliver at pages 642F–H, 649H–650C and 653E–G and Lord Jauncey of Tullichettle at pages 662A–D. The present case is quite different. The very purpose of the employment of the solicitor is to carry out the client's wish to confer a particular testamentary benefit on the intended beneficiary. There is no other purpose. If the solicitor negligently fails to achieve that purpose, justice requires there should be some remedy available.

A further point taken by Mr Matheson was that since the testator is under no duty to confer a gratuitous benefit on his intended beneficiaries, there is no reason to impose on the testator's professional adviser a duty which goes further than that on the testator. A testator does not owe a duty of care to his beneficiaries. If he fails to make a will, or if he makes a will but carelessly fails to have it properly witnessed, the disappointed beneficiaries cannot sue the testator for damages for breach of a duty of care. So, runs the argument, why should the disappointed beneficiaries be able to sue the testator's solicitor when they cannot sue the testator himself, however careless he may have been?

In my view there is here a feature of fundamental importance in this case. In general, and always leaving reliance cases on one side, a solicitor owes a professional duty of care to his client and no one else. He is subject to professional rules and standards, and he owes duties to the court as one of its officers. But within that framework it is to his client alone that he owes a duty to exercise the standard of skill and care appropriate to his status as a solicitor. Thus, in general, when acting for a seller of land a solicitor does not himself owe a duty of care to the buyer: see *Gran Gelato Limited* v. *Richcliff (Group) Ltd* [1992] Ch. 560. In the ordinary course of adversarial litigation a solicitor does not owe a duty of care to his client's opponent: see *Al-Kandari* v. *J. R. Brown & Co* [1988] QB 665, per Lord Donaldson of Lymington MR at p. 672 and per Bingham LJ at p. 675. Further, and a little closer to the present case, when advising a client about a proposed dealing with his property in his lifetime a solicitor does not owe a duty of care to a prospective beneficiary under the client's will who may be prejudiced by the dealing: see *Clarke* v. *Bruce Lance & Co* [1988] 1 WLR 881. I observe, in passing, that the lifetime dealing there did not have as its object the benefit of the plaintiff to whom the property had been specifically given under an existing will.

So one asks oneself: is the position different regarding instructions for the preparation and execution of a will? if so, why? After all, such instructions are no more than one particular type of instructions given by clients to a solicitor. Why should a solicitor be liable to a third party in such a case but not in others? These are pertinent questions. Before attempting to answer them I must mention another point also urged by Mr Matheson. He submitted it would not be fair or reasonable to impose liability on the solicitor in favour of the intended beneficiary, because that would be to give the beneficiary the benefit of a claim for professional negligence for services under a contract not made by him and in respect of which he has made no payment.

I think it must be frankly recognised that if the court holds a solicitor liable to an intended beneficiary, what the court is doing is fashioning an effective remedy for the solicitor's breach of his professional duty to his client. I do not shrink from this. If this sounds heretical to some, I pray in aid the observation of Deane J. in the High Court of Australia in *Hawkins* v. *Clayton* (1988) 62 ALJ 240, 259, in a case concerned with a solicitor's liability to make reasonable efforts to locate the executor named in a will held by him in safe custody when he learns of the testator's death:

'The law of contract and the law of tort are, in a modern context, properly to be seen as but two of a number of imprecise divisions, for the purpose of classification, of a general body of rules constituting one coherent system of law.'

Here, a coherent system of law demands there should be an effective remedy against the solicitor. The law of contract is unable to provide the remedy. In some cases, where the purpose of a contract is to confer a benefit on a third party, the purpose can be achieved in the event of breach, by the court making an order compelling the party in breach specifically to perform his obligation to make a payment or confer some other benefit on a third party: see *Beswick* v. *Beswick* [1968] AC 58. That route is not available here. The solicitor did not agree to confer a benefit on the intended beneficiary. He agreed to take steps to enable his client to do so. Specific performance of that agreement is no longer possible once the client has died. I have, indeed, considered whether a remedy for breach of contract could be shaped whereby, the client having lost the opportunity to make a gift to the intended beneficiary, (1) his estate should be regarded as having lost a sum equal to the amount of the intended gift, and (2) the executors should hold that sum, when recovered from the solicitor, upon trust for the intended beneficiary.

In the end I can see no need for the law to grapple with the difficulties raised by this and other possibilities when there is to hand a simple remedy in negligence. Instructions to prepare a will are different from other instructions to a solicitor. The failure to carry them out properly results in the client's purpose being thwarted but leaves the client's estate with no effective remedy. There is good reason why the solicitor should be liable for a third party in this very special situation. If the mistake, such as faulty witnessing, is discovered in the client's lifetime and corrected, the third party will suffer no loss. The cost of preparing and signing a new will would be recoverable by the client from the solicitor. But it is different if the client dies at a time when, because of a breach of the solicitor's professional duty, the will for whose preparation the solicitor was responsible has not been duly prepared and signed. Then it is eminently fair, just and reasonable that the solicitor should be liable in damages to the intended beneficiary. Otherwise there is no sanction in respect of the solicitor's breach in his professional duty. Thus there is a special relationship between the solicitor and intended beneficiary which should attract a liability if the solicitor is negligent.

It is true that the effect of holding the solicitor liable to the intended beneficiary will be to enable him to take advantage of the professional duty owed by the solicitor to the client. But if the solicitor was not so liable, he would go Scot free. He could commit a breach of his professional duty with impunity. That cannot be right. That cannot accord with the objectives the law seeks to attain when imposing upon solicitors and other professional advisers a duty to exercise due professional skill and care. The resources of the law must be sufficient to fill what otherwise would be a serious lacuna. As Bingham LJ observed in *Simaan General Contracting Co* v. *Pilkington Glass Ltd (no. 2)* [1988] 1 QB 758, 782:

'Just as equity remedied the inadequacies of the Common law, so has the law of torts filled gaps left by other causes of action where the interests of justice so required'.

Other objections

Mr Matheson raised several further points which, he submitted, showed that the liability question cannot be answered in favour of the intended beneficiaries without giving rise to unacceptable distortions in the law. He contended the anomalies would be such that the remedy would be capricious in operation. He submitted, first, that to impose liability on the solicitor would be effectively to double the size of the client's estate. This is incorrect. The damages are payable to the disappointed intended beneficiary, not to the deceased's estate. Those entitled to the deceased's estate receive a windfall in the sense that the deceased did not intend the estate should go to them. But that does not assist the solicitor's case. That is the direct and foreseeable consequence of the solicitor's breach of his duty of his client. Because of his negligence the client's money did not reach the right pockets. The law is requiring him to put that right in the only way it can be done.

A further objection concerned the effect of an agreement between the solicitor and client releasing the solicitor from liability for negligence or limiting the extent of his liability. It was said that if a duty of care to an intended beneficiary exists, this duty is independent of the solicitor's duty to his client. Accordingly an agreement of this nature between solicitor and client would not affect the solicitor's duty to the intended beneficiary. This would be an unfair result. I agree that unless the duty to the beneficiary is correspondingly limited, the result would be unfair. However, I can see no overriding reason why the duty should not be limited in this way. Nor did Robert Goff LJ in *Leigh and Sillavan* v. *Aliakmon Shipping Co. Ltd.* [1985] 1 QB 350, at 397, where he outlined a principle of transferred loss. This approach did not altogether find favour with Lord Brandon of Oakbrook when the case reached the House of Lords ([1986] AC 785, 819–20). So this is an important subject which would call for careful examination if, which seems unlikely, it were ever to arise in practice in this field. It can be safely left until then.

Another objection concerned conflicting interests of potential beneficiaries. There is no difficulty here. The preparation by a solicitor of a second will in favour of different beneficiaries is not a breach of any duty owed by the same solicitor to the prospective beneficiaries under an earlier will also prepared by him. The duty on the solicitor to prospective beneficiaries is to exercise professional skill and care in carrying out the testator's instructions, giving him all necessary and appropriate advice. The duty goes no further than that. When the first will has been duly prepared and executed, the solicitor has fully discharged his duties and obligations to the beneficiaries under that will. He owes no obligation to them which would inhibit him from subsequently accepting and carrying out instructions from his client to draw up a new will with different legacies.

Once it is appreciated that the solicitor's duty goes as far as I have shortly stated but not further, I do not see any scope for difficulties over conflicts of interest. The making of a new will and its terms may well affect the existing potential beneficiaries differently: the proposed changes may be advantageous to one, prejudicial to another and neutral so far as a third is concerned. The solicitor's duty throughout remains as I have stated. The fact that this duty is also owed to an intended beneficiary does not alter its nature.

Mr Matheson raised the spectre of the solicitor being liable to an indeterminate class. The intended beneficiaries might include persons unborn at the date of the testator's death; and their interests might not vest finally for many years. I do not agree. Liability is not to an indeterminate class. Liability is to the particular beneficiary or beneficiaries whom the client intended to benefit through the particular will. If a case of negligence should ever occur where an intended beneficiary was not born when the client died, for example, the intended beneficiaries might embrace all the testator's grandchildren whenever born, any difficulties this may cause can then be faced and resolved. This factor, of possible difficulties in imagined and unusual cases, cannot weigh heavily in the scales when set against the ordinary case in which the intended beneficiaries are a small number of identified people. The development of the law should be principled and coherent, but there must be room for special cases in which some loose ends, or even jagged edges, may be inevitable.

In this regard it is sensible to remember that *Ross* v. *Caunters* was decided in 1979. In practice the decision does not seem to have given rise to problems. Furthermore, the decision has generally been welcomed, or at least not made the subject of criticism, by the leading commentators: see, for example, Atiyah, *An Introduction to the Law of Contract*, 4th edn., p. 395; Fleming, *The Law of Torts*, 7th edn., p. 167; Salmond & Heuston on the *Law of Torts*, 20th edn., pp. 215, 217; Treitel, *The Law of Contract*, 8th edn., p. 539; and Winfield and Jolowicz on *Tort*, 13th edn., pp. 88, 96, 106.

Finally, it was said there are insurmountable difficulties over periods of limitation. If an intended beneficiary has a cause of action against a negligent solicitor, time would run either from the date when the will was made or ought to have been made or from the date of death. The first of these possibilities would be unsatisfactory; a beneficiary intended to take under a will can hardly be said to suffer loss during the testator's lifetime. The second would be unsatisfactory, because it would mean that time might not begin to run indefinitely, subject only to the 15 year longstop under section 14B of the Limitation Act 1980. Again these are points best left to be resolved in a case in which they call for decision. If there are problems here, this would not be the first instance of difficulties over limitation in the field of negligence. Even if there are difficulties, as to which I express no view, this does not militate significantly against the existence of a liability in negligence in this type of case.

In my view *Ross* v. *Caunters* is still good law. I venture to echo Sir Robert Megarry's prophecy (at p. 321) that wherever the bounds of negligence become finally drawn, they will be wide enough to give an affirmative answer to the liability question.

The solicitor's liability to his client

For completeness I mention that some argument was addressed to us in support of the proposition that a solicitor's liability to his client lies only in contract; he is not also liable in tort. It was submitted that the decision of Oliver J. to the contrary in *Midland Bank Trust Co. Ltd* v. *Hett, Stubbs & Kemp* [1979] Ch. 384 was wrong. The decision of the Court of Appeal in *Groom* v. *Crocker* [1939] 1 KB 194 has never been overruled (see *Lee* v. *Thompson* (1989) 40 EG 89), and it derives more recent support from the approach of Lord Scarman in *Tai Hing Cotton Mill Ltd* v. *Liu Chong Hing Bank Ltd* [1986] AC 80, 107. It is not necessary to pursue this point. The conclusion on the liability question must be the same whether the solicitor is liable to his client in contract alone or in both contract and tort.

Inter vivos gifts

I have confined my observations to intended testamentary benefits. In *Ross* v. *Caunters* Sir Robert Megarry (at pp. 322–3) summarised his conclusions in terms equally applicable to a case where the solicitor is instructed to carry through a transaction of gift to a third party during the client's lifetime. I see no reason to doubt that a similar principle applies to such case, because the same difficulty arises after the client's death. However, that is not a matter I need pursue on this appeal.

Breach of duty

During the hearing of the appeal the solicitors applied for leave to adduce further evidence with a view to seeking a retrial. We refused that application, for the reason set out in the judgment of Farquharson LJ.

As already mentioned, the Judge concluded that Mr Jones and his firm were in breach of their professional duty in not exercising due diligence in the preparation of Mr Barratt's will. A month elapsed from 17 July, when Mr Jones received the written instructions he had asked for, until he left the office for his holiday. Thereafter a fifth week passed before Mr Barratt went away on holiday. There was no evidence before the Judge on the firm's usual practice when carrying out instructions to prepare a will. Mr Jones's explanation for the delay in preparation of what was, after all, a very simple will was that when he received the letter of instructions he was suspicious and did not believe the letter truly set out Mr Barratt's wishes. When he received the letter he telephoned Mr Barratt who, in effect, confirmed this and said that he still wanted to leave something to his former son-in-law Peter Gould. According to Mr Jones, he told his client he was shortly to go on holiday; he was heavily committed and would be unable to see Mr Barratt until after his return.

The Judge rejected this explanation. This is hardly surprising, having regard to the terms of Mr Jones's internal memorandum of the 16 August. There is nothing in the memorandum to suggest that Mr Jones had any thought that Mr Barratt might have been subject to undue influence. The Judge concluded that if the reason for inaction was not idleness, it was concern on Mr Jones's part that his (Mr Jones's) friend Peter Gould would end up with nothing if the will were changed. He acquitted Mr Jones of deliberate dishonesty in his evidence, although his conduct at the time invited censure.

Given these findings I can see no ground which would justify this court interfering with the Judge's overall conclusion that there was a breach of professional duty by the defendant firm in carrying out Mr Barratt's instructions. The letter of instructions was incomplete to the extent that it did not set out who were to be the executors, nor did it contain residuary gifts. But I think the Judge was entitled to conclude that Mr Jones effectually convicted himself out of his own mouth. By feeling obliged to put forward specious justifications for his delay, Mr Jones recognised implicitly that Mr Barratt had not received the professional service to which he was reasonably entitled.

Damages

I can see no reason to doubt that if Mr Jones and the probate department had got on with the matter as they should have done a new will, under which each plaintiff would have benefited at least to the extent of the £9,000, would have been signed by Mr Barratt before he went on holiday. The firm already had in its files the details of Mr Barratt's estate obtained for the March 1986 will. The respects in which the new instructions were incomplete were largely formal, and a brief meeting at most would have sufficed to deal with them. Mr Barratt was anxious to put right without delay what he perceived as a wrong done by him to his daughters.

In expressing the contrary view the Judge relied heavily on the evidence of Mrs Ducros, who used to live at 86 Whitecroft Road, as demonstrating there was an element of uncertainty about Mr Barratt's precise intentions. I am unable to agree there was any relevant uncertainty. Mrs Ducros' evidence was that at Maxine's wedding on 16 August Mr Barratt wanted to unburden himself. He told her that 'the girls', meaning his two daughters, would be alright, that the house would be sold and divided between them, and that the grandchildren would have about £200 each from the building society. This, of course, does not tally neatly with the letter of instructions. But the factor common to both is that the girls were to be far and away the major beneficiaries. The discrepancies do not suggest either that Mr Barratt was in such a state of indecision he might not have made a new will at all or that under his new will the daughters might not have received at least the sum of £9,000, whether by way of pecuniary legacies or as residuary legatees or as specific legatees of the house. On this point the Judge was drawing an inference from primary facts found by him. I have to part company from him on the proper inference.

Accordingly I would allow this appeal, set aside the Judge's order, and enter judgment for each plaintiff in the sum of £9,000.

Notes to Case 19

1. Lawyers can through their negligence harm the interests of: (i) their clients and (ii) third parties. Increased litigation under the first heading, spurned no doubt by liability insurance becoming compulsory (as it is in Germany or France) or widespread (as it is in England and the USA), has led in some countries (e.g. the USA) to the flourishing of courses on Professional Responsibility. England, on the other hand, still refuses to follow suit, steadfastly clinging to archaic immunities accorded to barristers (but not solicitors who, in fact, *have* to be insured) for work done in court (see *Rondel* v. *Worsley* [1969] 1 AC 191). In those cases, where liability is possible in theory (but by no means easily engaged in practice), two problems have attracted the attention of the courts. The first is connected with the difficulties of assessing what would the chances have been of the disgruntled client/plaintiff but for the negligence of his legal adviser. The second is connected with the curious, if not unjustified, willingness of some American courts to set the standard of expected care at a very low level (note, for example, *Lucas* v. *Hamm* 56 Cal. 2d 583, 364 P. 2d 685 (1961) where the court was prepared to characterize as non-negligent an attorney who failed to take proper notice of the rule against perpetuities on the ground that it is widely misunderstood by the profession!). (For a compara-

tive study of the problems of professional malpractice (including medical malpractice which is treated with less indulgence by the courts) see chapter 6 of vol. XI of the *International Encyclopedia of Comparative Law.*)

Case 15 deals with the second type of situation and it invites comparison with such cases as *Biakanja* v. *Irving* 49 Cal. 2d 647, 320 P. 2d 16 (1958) (pleaded in tort), *Lucas* v. *Hamm,* above, (pleaded in contract *and* tort) and *Heyer* v. *Flaig* (74 Cal. Rptr. 225; 443 P. 2d 161 (1969)) decided in tort in the USA, and *Ross* v. *Caunters* [1980] Ch. 297 (pleaded in tort only) in England. Similarities and differences must again be stressed.

2. The first point to note is, again, the tendency of German law to base its solution on contract. That contract cannot easily explain all such cases is obvious not only by the court's own review of the precedents but also by a certain unease it experiences in utilizing the notion of contract with protective effects *vis-à-vis* third parties or the theory of 'transferred loss' (*Drittschadensliquidation*), both briefly explained above (Ch. 2, section A, A. 2. (*d*) (*iii*) (*e*)). The first German decision on the subject—BGH NJW 1965, 1955; JZ 1966, 141 note Lorenz—relied on the notion of contract with protective effects *vis-à-vis* third parties and found for the plaintiff, though one is inclined to believe that the theory of transferred loss might have been an even more appropriate device. (This case is discussed in English by Lorenz in 'Some Thoughts about Contract and Tort' *Essays in Memory of Professor F. H. Lawson* (1986) 86 ff.) Incidentally, the granting of an action against the attorney (for a sum equal to the void legacy) can in practice result in a 'double-legacy'—a point that has troubled some commentators. (See Kegel, 'Die "lachenden Doppelerben": Erbfolge beim Versagen von Urkundspersonen', *Festschrift für Flume* (1978) I, 545. This argument, however, has been rejected both in England (*White* v. *Jones, supra*) and in Germany (see: BGH 12 June 1979, *Zeitschrift für das Gesamte Familienrecht* 1980, 133 and Lorenz and Markesinis (1993) 56 MLR 558 *et seq.*)

3. The contract versus tort approach must not only be noted but also examined, especially since some American decisions (e.g. *Heyer* v. *Flaig* 74 Cal. Rptr. 225; 443 P. 2d 161 (1969)) have gone as far as suggesting that the distinction may be meaningless. It is submitted that it is not, and American law may be the poorer for ignoring some of the practical consequences of a proper doctrinal characterization. Here are some:

(*a*) *Jurisdiction.* The choice-orientated approach adopted by conflicts rules in cases of contract seems more appropriate in these types of cases than the *locus* of the accident tort approach. In any event, it would be odd if the dispute between plaintiff and defendant/debtor were subject to one rule and the relationship between defendant/debtor and creditor were governed by a different law. (See Fig. 2.) We can, of course, again allow the contractual relationship to influence the tort action (as Tobriner J. suggested in

Heyer v. *Flaig* 70 Cal. 2d 223, 449 P. 2d 161 (1969)); but why not opt more openly for the more straightforward contractual reasoning? (The potential impact that the choice of contract or tort can have on jurisdiction can be seen in factual variations of cases such as *Bryant Electric* v. *City of Fredericksburg* 762 F. 2d 1192 (1985) and *Blake Construction Co.* v. *Alley* 353 SE 2d 726 (1987) both of which represent variations on the *J'Aire* and *Junior Books* theme.)

(*b*) *Liability for omissions.* Traditional tort theory would deny liability where the debtor/defendant has remained inactive rather than acted badly. A contractual solution could make the defendant/debtor liable both for non-feasance and misfeasance. Should this be regarded as excessively onerous for the defendant/debtor it may still be avoided through the use of *Drittschadensliquidation* or the German notion of contract with protective effects *vis-à-vis* third parties, since this, it will be remembered, makes the debtor liable only for the bad or delayed performance of the *secondary* obligations of the contract. (The first German case was one of omission: BGH NJW 1965, 1955; JZ 1966, 141 (with note by Lorenz). Cf. the factually almost identical cases of *Gartside* v. *Sheffield Young and Ellis* [1983] NZLR 37 and Hof Amsterdam, NJ 1985, 40—the last two resorting to tort doctrine.)

(*c*) *Measure of damages.* The tort and contract measure of damages probably remains different despite Lord Denning's attempt to propose a compromise in *H. Parsons (Livestock) Ltd.* v. *Ottley Ingham and Co. Ltd.* ([1978] QB 791). A contractual solution would favour the award of full expectation damages to the plaintiff/third party and this, again, is supported by German law. In the USA a tort solution would further justify a claim for punitive damages. Such a ridiculous claim was, in fact, made in *Heyer* v. *Flaig*.

(*d*) *The limitation period.* Both the length and starting point of the limitation period differ in contract and tort. It is submitted it would be impracticable if one relationship (plaintiff–defendant/debtor) were subject to one rule and the other relationship (debtor–creditor) governed by a different rule. This appears to be in principle the correct starting point but it must be admitted that in some cases it may cause problems. Thus, in the frustrated beneficiary type of case the right of the beneficiary to sue the testator lawyer is not identical to that of the testator since the harm suffered by each is different. Also, if the contractual period of limitation were to apply in exclusion of all tort remedy, it could harm the beneficiaries' interests in those systems where the contractual period of limitation is not substantially longer than the tort period of limitation.

(*e*) *The standard of care.* Few lawyers in England or in the USA seem to have considered points (*a*)–(*d*). More concern, however, has been shown about the standard of care that would be appropriate to the tort action and whether it would be different from that found in the debtor–creditor (contractual) relationship. German law, proceeding on contract theory, has not experienced this difficulty; and German writers, considering a hypothetical (for them) tort action have had no difficulty in saying that the tort standard of care should be determined by the contract. (Schlechtriem, Lorenz, op. cit.) American courts have taken a similar view; and both Lord Roskill (in *Junior Books*) and Robert Goff LJ (in *The Aliakmon*) saw little difficulty in adopting this reasoning in English law. Of course, the contractual solution avoids at a stroke these real or imaginary difficulties.

(*f*) *Exemption clauses/defences.* It has never been doubted in German law that the contractual debtor can oppose against the third party/plaintiff all defences, etc., he may have against the contractual creditor. The contractual solution makes this answer indisputable. In an *obiter dictum* in *The Aliakmon* Robert Goff LJ suggested that something similar should happen where the action was founded in tort ([1985] QB 350 at pp. 397–8) but details have not been worked out. Strangely enough, at least one first instance judgment in England has considered a variant to this problem.

In *Southern Water Authority* v. *Carey* ([1985] 2 All ER 1077) the court was not asked to decide whether the defendant sub-contractor (debtor) could oppose against the owner/plaintiff (third party) the exemption clauses that he (the sub-contractor) had in his contract with the main contractor (creditor); instead the court was faced with a claim by the sub-contractor to oppose against the owner a clause which the main contractor had in his contract with the owner. The court thought he could do so and, I believe, the solution displays a misunderstanding of how this triangular relationship should work. It is submitted that had a contractual explanation been used this misunderstanding would not have occurred.

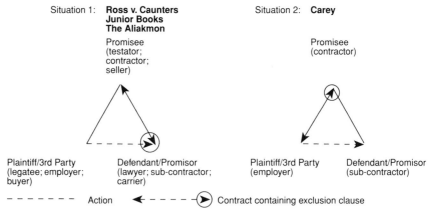

Fig. 2

In *Carey* the plaintiffs (or, rather, their predecessors in title) engaged the first defendants as consulting engineers and the second defendants as main contractors in the building of certain sewage works. The second defendants in turn engaged the third and fourth defendants as sub-contractors. Clause 30 of the work contract between the plaintiffs and the second defendants (main contractors) contained an exemption clause. Subsection (VI) of this clause stated that 'for the purposes of this sub-clause the Contractor contracts on his own behalf and on the behalf of and as trustee for his sub-contractors, servants and agents'. The main contractors having ceased trading, the action for defective workmanship and materials proceeded against the two sub-contractors. At this stage it is worth noting that while the fourth defendant/sub-contractor had in his contract with the main contractor a term almost identical to Clause 30 of the main contract, the third defendants/sub-contractors, when negotiating with the main contractor, had insisted on their own, different, limitation clause. (Though we are nowhere told in what respect the two sets of terms differed, one must assume that the contractor's terms were more advantageous to the defendants/sub-contractors than their own terms, for otherwise why did they try to invoke their protection?) The Court, applying the tort reasoning of *Junior Books*, accepted that the plaintiff had a cause of action. Unlike *Junior Books*, however, the plaintiff was faced with a defence put forward by the defendant. This was based on an exclusion clause contained not in his (the sub-contractor's) contract with the main contractor (in which case the position could have been similar to *The Aliakmon*), but on the exclusion clause contained in the contract between the plaintiff and the main contractor (and which the third defendant/sub-contractor had, as stated, rejected). Diagrammatically the difference from *The Aliakmon* case can be shown as in Fig. 2.

As stated, the court was prepared to allow a tort action by the employer against the sub-contractor but was also willing to give the latter the protection of the clause contained in the contract between employer and main contractor. One reason was that the nature of this limitation clause was relevant in defining the scope of the duty of the sub-contractor in tort. Another explanation was the use of the notion of *volenti*. The judge expressly excluded the latter concept (ibid. at p. 1085a); but later in his judgment he appears to have come very close to accepting it (or something very similar to this concept) since he said: 'As the plaintiffs . . . did . . . choose to limit the scope of the sub-contractor's liability, I see no reason why such limitation should not be honoured.' (Ibid. at pp. 1086 f.) Is the reasoning of this decision and its result acceptable? I confess I have doubts as to both.

It is first of all interesting to note that in *Carey* the court did not follow *The Eurymedon* (*New Zealand Shipping Co. Ltd.*) v. *A. M. Satterthwaite and*

Co., *The Eurymedon* [1975] AC 154) reasoning in order to achieve its result. The artificiality of the contractual reasoning in that case has been noted by many lawyers; but it was reaffirmed by the Privy Council in *Port Jackson Stevedoring Pty. Ltd.*, *The New York Star* v. *Salmond and Spraggon (Australia) Pty. Ltd.* ([1981] 1 WLR 138) so the judge in *Carey* was obviously anxious not to challenge it openly. On the other hand, it was not used either, so those opposed to *The Eurymedon* result and reasoning might be able to argue that in future it may be limited to the special shipping context of such cases. This still, however, leaves open the question of how to explain *Carey*.

One could, *de lege ferenda*, construe *Carey* as a case of contract in favour of third party (and, for brevity's sake I include in this term the contract with protective effects *vis-à-vis* third parties). After all, *Carey* is, in one respect, very similar to *Junior Books*; the owner could be seen as the third party beneficiary of the contract between sub-contractor (promisor) and main contractor (promisee). This construction, of course, is unacceptable *de lege lata* given the English notion of privity. But even if it were accepted it would still not explain the second part of *Carey* namely the allowing to the promisor the defences that the promisee had against the third party. For in contracts in favour of third parties it is the reverse that is allowed: namely the promisor can oppose against the third party the defences *he* has in *his* contract with the promisee.

Can one then justify the outcome through tort reasoning? The judge in *Carey* did so by allowing the tort action to be shaped by the contract to which the plaintiff was a party but the defendant was not. In this he was clearly influenced by certain dicta contained in Lord Roskill's judgment in *Junior Books* v. *Veitchi*. (Lord Roskill refers there to 'a relevant exclusion clause in the *main* contract'.) With respect I do not find Lord Roskill's dicta as obvious as that, my inclination being to interpret them as referring to the *second* contract (sub-contractor–main contractor) and *not* to the *first* contract (between contractor and owner). I incline in favour of this view largely because Lord Roskill seemed to rely heavily in his relevant passage on *Hedley Byrne*; and there, apart from the fact that there were no contractual relations *stricto sensu*, the exemption clause was inserted by the second bank/defendant when replying to the plaintiff's bank and not by the plaintiff's bank (which was merely transmitting the information) to the plaintiff. The clause, in other words, was in the second not the first relationship. My own understanding of the Roskill dictum is also shared by the Court of Appeal in *Muirhead* v. *Industrial Tank Specialities Ltd.* ([1986] QB 507; Reynolds in (1986) 10 *LMCLQ* 97, 106 probably agrees). On the other hand, it must be admitted that this is not how the judge understood it in *Carey*; and his interpretation also has the important support of Professor

Treitel (in (1986) 10 *LMCLQ* 294, 302). Clearly, therefore, the dictum has led to some confusion and should be clarified at the earliest possible opportunity. Nevertheless, even if it were eventually to be classified in the way it was understood in *Carey* it still does not, in my opinion, justify the actual outcome *in that case*. For in that case we were in fact faced with an interesting variant to the problem we have been discussing. Because in *Carey* the judge was faced with *two* sets of exemption clauses, one in the contract between owner and main contractor and one in the contract between main contractor and sub-contractor; and he allowed the sub-contractor the benefit of the first clause even though at the time of conclusion of the relevant contracts the sub-contractor had rejected it in favour of his own clause. I see no commercial reason justifying this result; nor do I think we can say that the plaintiff assented to a limited liability when the defendant, at the time of the making of the contracts, rejected the relevant limitation clause.

4. Contract or tort, the new action must be kept under control, especially where third parties/non-clients are concerned. American decisions are legion—see, for example: *Victor* v. *Goldman* 74 Misc. 2d 685, 344 NYS 2d 672 (1973); *Pelham* v. *Griesheimer* 93 Ill. App. 3d 751, 417 NE 2d 882 (1981), aff'd. 92 Ill. 440 NE 2d 96 (1982); *Guy* v. *Liederbach* 459 A. 2d 744, 501 Pa. 47 (1983); *Needham* v. *Hamilton* 459 A. 2d 1060 (App. DC 1983); *Flaherty* v. *Weinberg* 303 Md. 116, 492 A. 2d 618 (1985); *Walker* v. *Lawson* 514 NE 2d 629 (Ind. App. 1987); *Stinson* v. *Brand* 738 SW 2d 186 (Tenn., 1987); *Mentzer and Rhey Inc.* v. *Ferrari* 367 Pa. Super. 123, 532 A. 2d 484 (1987); *Hale* v. *Groce* 304 Or. 281, 744 P. 2d 1289 (1987); *Simon* v. *Zipperstein* 32 Ohio St. 3d 74, 512 NE 636 (1987). *Schreiner* v. *Scoville* 410 N.W. 2d, 679 (Iowa: 1987); *Licatae* v. *Spector*, 225 A. 2d, 28 (1966: Connecticut) 61 ALR 4th 63–501 suggests that a majority of jurisdictions now favour plaintiffs—at least in the *Ross* v. *Caunters* type of situation. The end result, however, is not all that different from the more restrictive European (German and English) approach. Nevertheless the question remains whether the multi-criteria test enunciated in *Biakanja* v. *Irving* is more workable and (on balance) fairer than the contractual third party beneficiary doctrine. In this context consider: (i) why the six factors mentioned in *Biakanja* (320 P. 2d 16, 19) were subsequently reduced to five (the requirement that 'moral blame [be] attached to the defendant's conduct' has been dropped); (ii) whether the various criteria are cumulative or whether one of them is particularly important; (iii) that equal uncertainty seems to prevail on the requirements needed to be satisfied for the invocation of the third party beneficiary doctrine. In particular, who must intend to confer a benefit on the third party: the promisee (better view) or the promisee *and* the promisor? From the vast literature see: Bauman, 'Damages for Legal Malpractice', 61 *Temple L. Rev.* 1127 (1988); idem, 'Lawyer Liability to Non-Clients', 97 *Dickinson L. Rev.* 267 (1993);

Boston, 'Liability of Attorneys to Non-Clients in Michigan: a re-examina-
tion of *Fridman* v. *Dozore* and a rule of limited liability', 68 *Univ. of Detroit
L. Rev.* 307 (1991); Dugdale, 'Solicitors' Liability to Third Parties' [1984]
NZLJ 316 ff.; Eisenberg, 'Attorneys' Negligence and Third Parties' 57
NYUL Rev. 126 (1982); Gross, 'Contractual Limitations on Attorney
Malpractice Liability: An Economic Approach' 75 *Kentucky LJ* 793
(1986–7); Hazard, 'Lawyer Liability in Third Party Situations: The Meaning
of the *Kaye Scholer* Case', 26 *Akron L. Rev.* 395 (1993); Hilliker, 'Attorney
Liability to Third Parties: A Look to the Future' 36 *Depaul L. Rev.* 41
(1986); Keeton, 'Professional Malpractice' 17 *Washburn LJ* 445 (1978);
Markesinis, 'Fixing Acceptable Boundaries to the Liability of Solicitors' 103
(1987) *LQR* 346; idem, 'Doctrinal Clarity in Tort Litigation: A Comparative
Lawyer's Viewpoint', 25 *The International Lawyer* 953 (1991); Morley,
'Privity as a Bar to Recovery in Negligent Will-Preparation Cases' 57 *Univ.
of Cincinnati L. Rev.* 1123 (1989); Peterson, 'Extending Legal Malpractice
Liability to Non-clients' 61 *Wash. L. Rev.* 761 (1986); Probert and
Hendricks, 'Lawyer Malpractice: Duty Relationships Beyond Contract' 55
The Notre Dame Lawyer 708 (1980); Rolph, 'Solicitors' Liability to Non-
clients in Negligence', 15 *The Advocates' Quarterly*, 129 (1993); Rubenstein,
'Attorney Malpractice in California: The Liability of Who Drafts an
Imprecise Contract or Will' 24 *UCLA Law Review* 422 (1976); Walker,
'Attorney Liability to Third Parties for Malpractice: The Growing
Acceptance of Liability in the Absence of Privity' 21 *Washburn LJ* 48
(1981–2). Gates, 'Lawyers' Malpractice' 37 *Mercer L. Rev.* (1986) gives inter-
esting statistical information.

8. 'OTHER RIGHTS' (FAMILY RELATIONSHIPS)

Case 20

BUNDESGERICHTSHOF (FOURTH CIVIL DIVISION) 30 JANUARY 1957*
BGHZ 23, 215 = NJW 1957, 670 = JZ 1957, 342

The parties married in 1941. On 24 March 1949 a child was born.
Thereupon the plaintiff husband petitioned for a divorce, the wife cross-
petitioned, and the marriage was dissolved on the ground that both were to
be blamed, in the case of the wife because she had committed adultery.
After the divorce, the plaintiff sought and obtained a decree to the effect
that the child was illegitimate.

The plaintiff now claimed DM 1130.05 from the defendant representing
the legal costs of the bastardy proceedings.

---

* English version by Kurt Lipstein.

The Court of First Instance rejected the claim. An appeal to the Court of Appeal of Schleswig and a second appeal to the Bundesgerichtshof were without success for the following

Reasons

The Court of First Instance and the Court of Appeal have rejected the plaintiff's claim for damages representing his costs arising out of the bastardy proceedings on the ground that civil law does not allow a claim for damages in respect of such costs against a spouse who is guilty of a breach of fidelity.

I. The question was already debated at the time when the Civil Code was being drafted as to whether a spouse who was not the guilty party to a divorce should be allowed compensation in respect of those losses suffered by him as a result of the other spouse's dereliction of marital obligations. The Report of the Committee drafting the Civil Code (Motive) [reference] shows that the answer at the time was negative, principally because it was thought that such claims were incompatible with the nature of marriage and that to allow them would be tantamount to a penalty for a divorce; the latter had been deliberately omitted from the Civil Code contrary to its treatment in previous laws. The Reichsgericht adopted this view in its decision reported in [reference] and it was mainly followed by the literature and by the practice of the courts [references].

After the collapse in 1945 an opinion to the contrary made itself felt [references].

II. This Division considered as early as 21 March 1956 [reference] the question as to whether in addition to the claims which the civil law makes available in its provision on family law for the violation by a spouse of the duty of fidelity, further claims can be based on such a violation. This Division gave a negative answer in so far as the application of § 823 BGB was concerned. Although this decision has been criticized, this Division, having examined the question afresh, sees no reason for abandoning this practice. The following are the principal considerations that apply.

1. Civil law contains numerous provisions dealing with the duties arising from marriage and with their contravention [references]. Their specific regulation indicates a general principle that thereby the question was to be solved exclusively and finally as to what are the consequences of a violation of marital obligations.

2. The conclusion is in accordance with the ideas aired at the time when the Civil Code was drafted and as they are set out in the Report of the Committee drafting the BGB [reference].

3. That the provisions in the title on family law are exhaustive is borne out by the consideration that the regulation of the patrimonial relations between spouses would lose much of its meaning, if §§ 823 ff. BGB were to apply. For the duty to pay damages in accordance with the rules on obligations would much exceed the duties laid down by the provisions regulating family law. As a result the provisions regulating family law would become largely superfluous.

4. It is true that the conclusion of a marriage has consequences bearing on family law as well as on the law of property. In principle, however—in accordance with the principle which also found expression in § 888 II of the Code of Civil Procedure—a distinction must be drawn between the duties of the spouses which concern family law and those which involve proprietary rights resulting from the marriage. Those which are purely in the nature of family law, such as the duty to live together and the duty of fidelity, are confined to conduct in accordance with these duties, and if any consequences are to accompany their violation, they cannot be found in the law of obligations; instead, having regard to the nature of the marriage, they must be contained in the provisions of family law proper dealing with such violations. It is incompatible with the nature of marriage as well as with present-day moral sentiment which has not changed in this respect since the time when the Civil Code was drafted, to equate marriage with a transaction in the nature of property law.

5. It is true that in principle an interpretation of the law must be approved which serves to maintain a marital community in keeping with the solemn vows of marriage. This Division has constantly emphasized that aspect, particularly in its practice dealing with § 48 of the Marriage Act. However, to apply the rule on damages of the law of obligations to conjugal misconduct leads to undesirable results.

(*a*) First of all, an award for damages for a violation of matrimonial duties would equal a penalty in practice. For example, as a result of the unjustified refusal of the wife to cohabit, the blameless husband is forced to rely on a paid help to run the household, and the court gives judgment against the wife on the ground of a violation of § 1353 BGB to make monthly payments to the husband which correspond approximately to the cost of the help until cohabitation is resumed. This would mean in effect that by means of fines the wife is being compelled to resume cohabitation, with the difference that the money does not accrue to the State, as it does in the cases enumerated in § 888 I of the Code of Civil Procedure, but to the husband, and that in addition § 888 I of the Code of Civil Procedure would cease to have effect.

(*b*) It must be admitted that there are no reasons in equity why a guilty spouse should not bear the costs of proceedings to contest the legitimacy of the child conceived in adultery. The extent of the liability to damages of the guilty spouse is not, however, limited to this aspect, for this liability can only be either recognized or denied in principle. Consequently, if recognized, the blameless spouse could demand in accordance with the principle laid down in § 249 BGB to be placed in every respect in the same position as would have existed if the occurrence which gave rise to the claim for damages, and therefore also the ensuing divorce, had never taken place. The blameless party would be entitled not only to adequate or equitable maintenance by the guilty spouse but to a sum which enables him, contrary to the provisions on maintenance in §§ 58 and 59 of the Marriage Act, to maintain the same living standard as if the marriage still subsisted. In addition the blameless spouse would be entitled on the death of the guilty spouse to be treated as regards the estate of the latter as if the marriage had still existed at that time, leaving open the question as to whether in relation to the estate the blameless spouse is to be regarded as an heir or only as entitled to a compulsory portion (*Pflichtteilsberechtigter*).

(*c*) Among those who hold that claims for damages lie, some deny that they lie against a guilty spouse, among them in particular Schwab, while Boehmer, modifying his previous opinion [reference], now wishes to restrict it to the situation where the marriage subsists [references]. Leaving aside the consideration that the law of obligations hardly supports the distinction introduced by Boehmer, the refusal to allow a claim for damages against the guilty spouse is ineffective as soon as the co-respondent is sued for damages; the latter, who would be jointly liable in tort together with the guilty spouse, could claim a contribution from the guilty spouse under § 426 BGB. In this connection the question would arise further as to whether § 254 BGB may be applicable with the result that possibly the guilty spouse must shoulder the greater part of the damages or even the total amount.

(*d*) To allow a claim for damages may lead to the abuse of the grounds for divorce for base motives in order to make personal gains, a not unusual phenomenon, as the Report of the Committee drafting the Civil Code pointed out.

(*e*) Another consequence will be in all probability that the number of lawsuits between spouses will increase greatly. In many instances the proceedings for divorce and those for maintenance, if any, will be followed by an action for damages.

(*f*) In the proceedings for damages the need will arise frequently to make, first of all, exact findings concerning the history of the marriage and the conduct of the spouses. For contrary to the opinion of Boehmer it is common experience that in many cases a divorce is granted not on the ground of adulterous relations with a third party, but despite the existence of such relations for other reasons connected with the person of the guilty spouse alone, such as persistent refusal to comply with matrimonial duties.

(g) Apart from the fact that such suits for damages are prosecuted in a manner which is far from pleasant and constitute an excessive burden for the parties and the courts, the accusatorial character of the proceedings does not offer the same degree of reliability as do divorce proceedings.

(h) Finally, as the Report of the Committee drafting the Civil Code has equally pointed out, the assessment of damages in respect of the loss caused by the adulterous conduct and by the divorce must always remain more or less arbitrary. This, however, makes the law extraordinarily uncertain.

6. Boehmer's reference to § 893 of the Code of Civil Procedure does not convince. This provision does not create an independent right to damages but only makes it clear that the right to damages existing according to the rules of civil law is not affected by the rules on levy of execution laid down by the Code of Civil Procedure [reference].

III. The foregoing considerations, which lead to the rejection of a claim for damages based on § 823 BGB, apply also if it is alleged, as indeed it is in the present case, that the adulterous conduct constitutes an intentional infliction of damage contrary to decent morals. It is true that as early as in its decision in [reference] the Reichsgericht had admitted that a married woman may be liable under § 826 BGB, and in its decision in [reference] it has accepted the application of § 826 BGB in a case where a married woman had committed adultery resulting in the birth of a child, a consequence which the wife and the co-respondent had considered possible. The practice of the courts and the literature have also followed this opinion of the Reichsgericht to a considerable extent [reference].

The present Division cannot accept this view. It is contradicted by the fact that the provisions dealing with family law regulate exhaustively the consequences of the violation of matrimonial duties and of a divorce. Instead this Division agrees with the opinions of Giesecke [reference] and of Boehmer [reference] that, if claims for damages for violation of marital duties brought on the basis of § 823 BGB are to be rejected having regard to the provision dealing with family law, the same must apply to claims brought on the strength of § 826 BGB. This Division has already held in its decision [reference] that provisions dealing with family law may also exclude the application of § 826 BGB.

Case 21

BUNDESGERICHTSHOF (FOURTH CIVIL DIVISION) 8 JANUARY 1958*
BGHZ 26, 217 = NJW 1958, 544 = JZ 1958, 247

The defendant entertained an adulterous association with the plaintiff's wife over a lengthy period, and a child was born on 21 September 1953. By a judgment of 17 May 1955 it was declared that the child was not the legitimate issue of the plaintiff and on 11 November 1955 the defendant, by a public document, recognized the child as his own and undertook to pay a monthly sum of DM 50 as maintenance. The marriage of the plaintiff with the mother was dissolved on 5 January 1956 by a decree which declared both to be guilty; but the wife's degree of blame was held to be predominant.

The plaintiff claimed DM 1457 from the defendant consisting of his expenses in connection with the birth of the child, its maintenance, the costs of the action to have it declared illegitimate, and reimbursement of his repayments to the city of Nürnberg of a child's allowance.

The Court of Appeal of Nürnberg allowed the claim. Upon appeal the decision below was reversed in part only for the following

Reasons

I. . . .

II. According to § 1715 BGB the natural father is under an obligation to reimburse the mother for the expenses of her delivery. The expenses of the delivery were paid by the plaintiff in ignorance of the fact that the defendant was the real father of the child. By these payments the obligations of the defendant towards the child's mother were also discharged. It is true that in principle a natural father is not relieved of his obligation under § 1715 BGB by the fact that a third party has paid the expenses of the delivery. However, considering the purpose of this provision, which only envisages the normal case of the delivery of an unmarried woman, different considerations must apply if and to the extent that the expenses of the delivery have been paid by the husband of the woman. Thus as a result of the plaintiff's payment the defendant has been saved the payment of the expenses of delivery, without good legal reason, and at the plaintiff's cost. In accordance with § 812 BGB the defendant must therefore reimburse the plaintiff for this sum . . .

III. On the other hand the appeal is justified in respect of the expenses, claimed by the plaintiff, for the perambulator, the baby's bed, its clothes, the contributions to the sickness insurance totalling DM 210 since these

---

* English version by Kurt Lipstein.

expenses must be regarded as part of the expenses of maintaining the child (§ 1708 I, second sentence) and since under § 1710 I BGB maintenance is to be provided by means of money payments; for the period in question these expenses are already covered by the maintenance payments awarded above (**I**). The plaintiff cannot either claim these expenses on the ground that they represent damages in tort; in this respect the observations set out below apply here as well . . .

IV. Further, the appeal is well founded in so far as the defendant has been condemned to reimburse the plaintiff for the costs arising from the proceedings to contest the legitimacy of the child.

This Division has already dealt several times with the question as to whether a third party can be held liable for the pecuniary losses caused to one spouse as a result of the relations of a third party with the other spouse which are adulterous or in violation of matrimonial fidelity. This Division has denied that such a claim for damages exists [references]. These decisions have been criticized by writers [references]. However, these attacks do not provide any reason for this Division to change its previous practice. Instead the following comments may be made.

1. The decision of 6 February 1957 is being misinterpreted if it is understood to lead to the inevitable conclusion that no damages can be claimed for injuries to a spouse, such as infection with a venereal disease of a wife who had been the victim of rape, even if the requirements of §§ 823 ff. BGB have been complied with. As the reasons set out in para. 3 of this decision [reference] show clearly, this Division has only rejected claims for damages in so far as they are derived from 'the destruction of the marriage'. If, however, no liability in damages arises from the 'destruction of the marriage', it is irrelevant whether the damage caused by the destruction of the marriage is adequate or not.

2. The marital duties which arise mutually between spouses, in particular the duty of fidelity, are personal obligations of the spouses, having regard to the nature of marriage. Therefore they can only be violated by a spouse and not by a third party [reference].

3. § 172 of the Criminal Code, which only provides the possibility for punishing adultery, does not offer any guidance as to the existence of a duty to pay damages. Other violations of marital duties are not punishable according to German criminal law.

4. It is true that in principle a duty to contribute presupposes a duty to pay damages on the part of the person found to contribute [references]. Boehmer affirms in principle that a spouse is liable in damages, but wishes to prevent any enforcement while the marriage persists, with the result that

the principles established by the Bundesgerichtshof [reference] would apply without difficulty. However, as Beitzke remarks appositely, the principle of § 242 BGB requires that if a claim lies against the third party involved in the break-up of the marriage in respect of the loss suffered by the other spouse in consequence of the break-up, the third party must not bear the payment of these damages alone; instead his associate, namely the other spouse, who as a rule is principally to blame, must bear his share (see the case decided by the Bundesgerichtshof in [reference] where an exemption clause agreed between the spouses could not deprive the third party of his right to contribution). It is generally agreed that in assessing the amount of contribution the principle of § 254 BGB applies [reference].

5. The provision of § 1359 BGB does not provide any guidance, since in principle it does not bear upon the duty of marital fidelity; it is also impossible to assume that as regards the latter, a spouse is only liable to apply the same degree of diligence as he applies to his own affairs. If this were so, the guilty spouse to a divorce would also have to be held responsible for every other pecuniary damage which the other spouse suffers as a result of the divorce. This conclusion is ruled out in all likelihood, despite the aim stressed generally by Beitzke 'to tie a person to the marriage, once it has been concluded, by the threat of liability in damages'.

6. The liability to pay damages laid down by § 1298 BGB in respect of breach of promise referred to by Beitzke does not assist either. On the contrary, the fact that the legislature deemed it necessary to insert this provision appears to indicate that in principle claims for damages arising out of duties imposed by family law are to lie only when the law so provides expressly.

7. The enactment of this provision also militates against the assumption that a general duty to pay damages exists in family law, as Boehmer suggests now, while denying that liability in damages arises under §§ 823 ff. BGB in the case of a guilty spouse. However, until now such claims for damages, as well as those for the violation of other protected interests, have been based exclusively on these provisions, unless allowed expressly by other rules, and claims for damages have been denied in principle where § 1353 BGB has been violated [reference]. Provisions such as those contained in s. 151 of the Swiss Civil Code are unknown in German law.

8. Article 6 of the German Constitution (Fundamental Law) does not support a claim to damages either. Leaving aside that the marriage as such is not directly affected by the fact whether damages are paid after its breakdown or not, article 6 of the Constitution does not concern the personal relationship between the spouses. Boehmer, too, believes that by allowing claims for damages 'no tendency towards the enforcement of the duty to comply' is being shown.

9. Equally nothing can be deduced from the rules on maintenance after divorce; in so far as they concern the position of the wife, Beitzke describes them as being in total contradiction to Art. 3 of the Constitution. The question is, however, irrelevant in the present case, since the claims here are not brought by the wife.

10. Finally it remains uncertain, despite the arguments of Boehmer, how the amount of damages is to be assessed when a marriage has been broken up culpably. If the duty to reimburse the costs of the proceedings to contest the legitimacy of the child is to be based on the protective function of § 1353 BGB, as Boehmer seems to hold, no persuasive reason exists for denying the existence of a duty to pay damages for any other pecuniary losses arising from the break-up of the marriage, a result which Boehmer himself regards as 'impossible'. Any general requirement such as that 'the damages claimed must be limited to the protective purpose of the protective rule in question does not permit a clear assessment of the damages. The likely consequences of such a view would be many disputes, the outcome of which must be quite uncertain; such a result does not seem to be desirable for the law's sake as well.'

V. The Court of Appeal holds that a claim for damages against the defendant in respect of the costs of the proceedings to contest the legitimacy of the child cannot be supported in law as distinct from the costs of divorce proceedings; in the latter case the mutual relations between the spouses provide the basis, the husband is faced in the first instance with his unfaithful partner, with whom prima-facie matrimonial matters should be thrashed out alone while the co-respondent figures behind the wife and can only be reached through the latter. On the other hand, the co-respondent was directly involved in the claim for damages in respect of the procreation of the child, and in the triangle formed by the relationship between the husband, the child, and the third party, the wife figured either not at all or only as a fictional centre. Therefore the issue was not the protection of the marriage as a community of life but the legal relationship between father and child. Moreover, the attack on the legitimacy of the child and the ensuing consequences were independent of the continuation of the marriage.

These considerations, too, cannot support a claim for damages against the defendant based on the costs of the proceedings to contest the legitimacy of the child. First of all, in considering the relations between the husband, the child, and the third party, the wife cannot be excluded; for these relations cannot exist without the wife and her unfaithful conduct, just as the third party and his adulterous relationship with the wife were decisive in the case of the divorce. Claims arising out of the procreation of the child fall therefore into the sphere of family law, just as much as those based on adultery and on a divorce ensuing therefrom. The fact that a marriage may continue independently of an act of adultery and of the bastardization of a child does not alter the nature of the claims arising therefrom which fall within the sphere of family law. Finally, if the third party were to be held liable in damages, the wife would be under a duty to contribute, as explained in IV(4), above.

Case 22

BUNDESGERICHTSHOF (SIXTH CIVIL DIVISION) 22 FEBRUARY 1973*
JZ 1973, 668 (with approving note by Manfred Löwisch) = NJW 1973, 991 = VersR 1973, 442

The plaintiff married in 1965 and was still married at the time of the action, living together with his wife. From 1 October 1968 until 10 October 1968 the wife remained absent from the marital home at the invitation of the defendant with whom she stayed in his flat. It was not disputed that acts incompatible with marital fidelity occurred during the time; according to the plaintiff's allegation adulterous intercourse occurred as well.

The plaintiff contended that by the adulterous conduct of the defendant his general right of personality and his right to the undisturbed existence of the marital community had been violated. He claimed DM 10,000 with interest as 'compensation and satisfaction' to be paid either to himself or alternatively to a charity. The claim was rejected in all three instances for the following

Reasons

I. The Court of Appeal assumes, in accordance with the plaintiff's pleadings, that the plaintiff's wife and the defendant committed adultery. Nevertheless, it rejected the claim and held as follows:

The plaintiff was wrong in referring to the practice of the Bundesgerichtshof according to which a person whose right of personality had been injured can in certain circumstances demand pecuniary damages as compensation for his non-pecuniary damage. This claim too—like that for pain and suffering—was a claim for *damages*, while its function of providing satisfaction was only ancillary. No room existed in addition for a separate claim for satisfaction as understood by the plaintiff. A claim for damages—on whatever grounds—was excluded since special family relations were involved. To this extent the Court of Appeal follows the practice initiated by the decision of the Bundesgerichtshof [reference] and holds that the same principles must apply to non-pecuniary and pecuniary damage (and injury to health). Above all, the damage alleged to be suffered by the plaintiff was caused by the unfaithful conduct of his own wife.

* English version by Kurt Lipstein.

The Court of Appeal believes that any payment to the plaintiff is ruled out in particular for the reason that his marriage continues. The fact that the payment would inevitably also benefit indirectly the wife, who was equally or principally to blame, was clearly unacceptable.

Similarly payment to a third party was excluded. According to the Court of Appeal it would amount to the imposition of a penalty upon the defendant which was not supported in law.

The Court of Appeal admitted that an intrusion into marital life of the kind alleged in the present case constitutes a violation of the general right of personality of the deceived spouse. However, here again the considerations applied which also excluded other claims based on tort.

II. These considerations cannot be faulted, at least in the result.

1. The plaintiff bases his claims on the fact that the defendant was an accomplice to the breach of fidelity for which the plaintiff's wife was to be blamed. According to a constant practice of the Bundesgerichtshof, maintained until now in the face of attacks by some writers [references], no claims in tort are allowed by the law in force in cases of 'intrusion of a marriage' either against the guilty spouse or against the intruding third party. The Fourth Division of the Bundesgerichtshof last reaffirmed this practice in its decision of 3 November 1971 [reference] supported by detailed reasons and accompanied by an account of the present views of writers. In that decision the Fourth Division has given a comprehensive account of its reasons for denying unconditionally and generally that matters of intrusion into marriage involve legal interests protected by the law of tort under § 823 I BGB. The Fourth Division points out that without the co-operation of one of the spouses no interference with the marriage can occur and that, therefore, it constitutes essentially an internal marital matter, which is not sought to be protected by inclusion among the situations attracting liability in tort. In view of its strong link with the conduct of the unfaithful spouse the participation of the third party must be coloured by it as well. It is inadmissible to divide their activities into misbehaviour of the spouse governed by matrimonial law and a tort committed by the third party rendering him liable to pay damages. The Fourth Division has pointed out further that it is difficult, having regard to the multiplicity of possible acts of interference with marital relations, to establish suitable limits for any such liability and that the necessary enquiries, as required in the individual case, would have undesirable effects in various respects. For this reason disputes arising out of marital misconduct are treated exclusively as matrimonial matters, even where third parties are involved. The Division sees no reasons for deviating from these principles. They militate also against the present claim for payment as satisfaction for the non-pecuniary loss of the offended spouse. Even

among those writers who are opposed to the practice of the Bundesgerichtshof only very few believe that such a payment is allowed by the law as it stands [references].

2. Contrary to the appellant's main contention, the claim cannot succeed either if in applying § 823 I BGB emphasis is placed on the violation of the plaintiff's general right of personality rather than on that of the integrity of the marital community. It is true that according to the practice of the Bundesgerichtshof, particularly of this Division, a claimant whose general right of personality has been severely infringed may be awarded pecuniary damages for his non-pecuniary loss, provided that additional conditions have been met [references]. However, in so far as the right of personality of a spouse has been infringed because a third party acting together with the other spouse has interfered with the right to the integrity of the marital community, as in the present case, any claims for damages in tort must be denied for the reasons stated above which rule out liability in tort when the right to the integrity of the marital community has been violated. In many cases where a marriage has been subject to interference, and probably in all cases of adultery, the conditions enumerated above will exist for holding that the right of personality has been severely infringed. Therefore, the Court of Appeal, too, assumes that such a violation of the right of personality has occurred. To take such a view of the law would, however, run contrary to the requirements based on the evaluation of the narrower sphere of family law [reference]. This applies at any event in those cases where, as in the present, the violation of the right of personality is restricted to an interference with the matrimonial community of life and fidelity by a third party with the necessary participation of the other spouse.

3. Contrary to the plaintiff's contention no reason exists for taking a different view of the law either because of a fundamental change of public opinion, or because of a conflict with the values expressed by superior norms of the Constitution.

(a) The refusal to enforce matrimonial conduct by public measures, already apparent in the Preparatory Materials for the BGB [reference], has been reinforced still further. An enforceable claim for damages would be equal to such a measure; for this reason it has been recommended expressly as a means of 'deterrence' [reference]. The increased aversion of the legislature to such measures is shown by the fact that the provision of a penalty according to the former § 172 of the Criminal Code—which had been hedged around already by narrow conditions (not applicable here)—was abrogated; it is irrelevant in the present connection that this change in the law only took place after the alleged act of adultery.

(*b*) The rejection of the claim for damages in a case such as the present does not contravene either the values of superior norms of the Constitution on which the Bundesgerichtshof relied in its practice relating to the right of personality. The limits of the general right of personality recognized and protected by § 823 I BGB are flexible. They can always be drawn only with reference to other areas which are protected by law. In the present case these emerge from the observations made above.

The legislature has refrained from enforcing proper marital conduct directly or indirectly by public measures (see also § 888 II of the Code of Civil Procedure), including any penalties and equivalent measures for adultery, and has contented itself with the protection provided by family law. Having regard to the special character of this subject-matter, it cannot be included that the importance of the protection of the personality has been misunderstood and has not been taken into account sufficiently. Instead it expresses the conviction that highly personal relations should not be regulated by law, which is at least compatible with constitutional law and corresponds to modern ethics.

(*c*) Finally, a conclusion to the contrary cannot be based either on the protection of marriage provided by Art. 6 I of the Constitution, which the appellant rightly does not cite. Admittedly marriage is a human institution which is regulated by law and protected by the Constitution and which, in turn, creates genuine legal duties. Its essence, however, consists in the readiness, founded in morals, of the parties to the marriage to create and to maintain it. The provision of Art. 6 I of the Constitution is only intended to protect and to promote this unit, which has its origins in a sphere which precedes law; article 6 does not refer to the personal relations between spouses [references]. Consequently it does not support any demand for the punishment of marital infidelity, nor of third parties who are indispensable participants. It need not be examined here whether different considerations might apply in respect of totally different attacks against the sexual integrity of a spouse (by threats, fraud, or force) if the general law should not provide adequate remedies for compensation.

Case 23

BUNDESGERICHTSHOF (FOURTH CIVIL DIVISION) 19 DECEMBER 1989*
NJW 1990, 706

1. A man may not sue his divorced wife in tort for the economic loss due to his making maintenance payments to an apparently legitimate daughter actually the product of the wife's adultery.

* English version by Tony Weir.

2. § 826 BGB may be applicable if, in addition to the adultery, there is some other very improper and harmful conduct.

Facts: The parties, married in 1953, were divorced by judgment of 24 April 1959 on the ground of the fault of the present plaintiff (then defendant). During the marriage two daughters were born, first B and then, on 22 March 1957, S. After the divorce custody of the daughters was awarded to the defendant, and acting as their statutory representative, she sued the present plaintiff for maintenance payments in 1960, 1964 and 1965. In 1960 she garnished the plaintiff's earnings as well as the disability pension which the plaintiff received while occasionally unemployed through TBC. From the summer of 1966, the plaintiff paid maintenance money for the children by agreement and without court order. In 1986 the plaintiff sued for a declaration that S was illegitimate, and the Amtsgericht in W held that S was not the child of the plaintiff.

The plaintiff now sues the defendant for damages in respect of the maintenance payments he has made since the divorce in respect of the child who was not his and whom he was not bound to support. He alleged that in making the claim for maintenance as the daughter's legal representative, the defendant had represented that he was the father of the child. The defendant replied that she had never doubted the legitimacy of S, and had never noticed the lack of resemblance between her and the plaintiff, which was not at all obvious. The Landgericht dismissed the claim, and the Oberlandesgericht dismissed the plaintiff's appeal, as did the Bundesgerichtshof.

Reasons

I. The court below held it doubtful that the plaintiff had any tort claim for economic loss against his ex-wife on the ground of the illegitimacy of the child S. Founding on the constant decisions of the Bundesgerichtshof the court inclined to the view that the sanctions for anti-matrimonial conduct were to be found in family law exclusively, and that the law of delict afforded the plaintiff no further claim.

Even had claims for damages not been excluded by the provisions of family law, the court below would have dismissed the claim, for the defendant had not deceived the plaintiff in such a way as to render her liable in damages, either by making the claims for maintenance which, until the finding of illegitimacy, were vested in her daughter S, or through any culpable failure to disclose: the defendant was under no duty to confess her adultery or admit the possibility that S might have another father. Finally, claims in tort failed for lack of the requisite *mens rea*: it had not been shown that the defendant had appreciated that the plaintiff was not the father of S, and the mere fact of promiscuity, as to which no findings were made as regards the time of conception, did not establish that she had.

II. We agree with the result reached by the court below.

1. There is no doubt that the plaintiff has suffered economically as a result of the defendant's conduct: for years he has been paying maintenance which he did not owe. As the apparent father of S he was burdened with paying for her upkeep, until the judgment of 25 March 1987 finally declared that S was illegitimate and that it was her true father who had always been liable to make the payments [references].

2. Nevertheless, the law of tort does not permit the plaintiff to sue his ex-wife for this economic loss (BGHZ 80, 235 [238] = NJW 1981, 1445).

(*a*) When the BGB was in draft the question was already being ventilated whether an innocent spouse (as the law then was) could claim compensation for harm due to breach by the other spouse of the duties assumed on entering the marriage, and since that time it has often been the subject of judicial decision and academic discussion.

Such a claim was originally rejected as incompatible with the nature of marriage, on the view that to grant it would amount to penalising divorce in a way which the BGB, in conscious deviation from prior law, had elected not to follow (see BGHZ 23, 215 [216] = NJW 1957, 670 = LM § 823 (Af) BGB no. 5, with references to the Motive to the BGB, vol. 4, p. 615).

In its first decision on the matter (31 March 1956), the Bundesgerichtshof declared that claims for damages for spousal infidelity under § 823 BGB were ousted by the provisions of family law regarding such conduct. This was criticised, but in BGHZ 23, 215 ff. = NJW 1957, 670 the court adhered to its view, and relied *inter alia* on the following considerations: The BGB contains many provisions on the duties assumed on marriage and the consequences of their breach (especially the Marriage Act, and §§ 1353, 1361, 1933, 2077, 2335 BGB); the very existence of this special set of rules indicates that in principle the consequences of a breach of spousal duties are to be determined exclusively in terms of those rules. It is true that the personal and economic consequences of getting married must be kept distinct. Those which appertain purely to family law, such as the duty to live together and the duty of fidelity, are fulfilled by appropriate conduct. Should such duties be breached, the consequences are to be drawn not from the law of obligations but, consistently with the nature of marriage, from the provisions of family law relating to such breaches.

In its judgment of 6 February 1957 (BGHZ 23, 279 ff. = NJW 1957, 671) the court applied to the third party adulterer the principle that the antimatrimonial conduct of a spouse did not give rise to any claim for damages in the law of obligations independently of the provisions of family law, especially the Marriage Law (and compare BGHZ 26, 217 ff. = NJW 1958, 544). Again it stated: 'Although antimatrimonial conduct can undeniably cause harm to the "innocent" spouse, especially if it leads to divorce, the law does not afford any compensation outside the provisions of family law, so anti-matrimonial conduct cannot be treated as an unlawful act grounding a claim for damages under §§ 823 ff. BGB.'

In 1971 the BGH returned to the question (BGHZ 57, 229). Again it rejected the view expressed by academics [Boehmer in many articles, Beitzke, Dölle, Gernhuber and Jayme] that breaches of marriage vows should trigger liability under § 823 I BGB, and asserted that marriage is not one of the relationships whose breach can give rise to general claims for compensation for economic harm. In more detail it confirmed that it would adhere to the view that marriage vows were not among the rights protected by the law of tort in § 823 I BGB. Since the consortium of the spouses could only be disrupted by the participation of one of them, such breaches constitute essentially a matter internal to the marriage, not under the intended protection of the law of torts (BGHZ 57, 229 [232] = NJW 1972, 199).

In a judgment of 22 February 1973 (NJW 1973, 991), the Sixth Civil Senate of the Bundesgerichtshof adopted the view of the Fourth Senate (as it then was). Then the question was whether damages could be claimed on the basis of an invasion of the right of human personality rather than an invasion of the integrity of the community of marriage. The court refused to allow this, on the ground that the rather fluid limits to the general right of human personality had to be drawn in the light of other legal provisions, in this case the considerations stated by the Fourth Civil Senate (as in BGHZ 57, 229 = NJW 1977, 199), and though in many cases of antimatrimonial behaviour there would be a serious invasion of the right of personality—perhaps always in the case of adultery—yet to impose liability in tort would conflict with the more specific prescriptions of family law.

(b) In BGHZ 80, 235, the mother of a child conceived out of wedlock made false representations to the father and thereby induced him to marry her. This senate made the general observation, in line with the decisions of the Bundesgerichtshof, that obligational claims, especially tort claims for damages, are ousted by the exclusive special rules of family law, the Supreme Court having uniformly held that a husband whose wife had committed adultery and borne a child could not bring an action in tort against the wife or the third party for compensation for the economic harm he suffered as a result of the apparent legitimacy of the child (BGHZ 80, 235 [238] = NJW 1981, 1445). Because of the peculiar facts in that case, however, the point did not fall for decision, but in the present case it does. A pointer in the same direction is the decision of this court on 4 November 1987 (NJW 1988, 2032) that the personal duties arising from the community of marriage can only be fulfilled by the free moral choice of the parties, and that even indirect compulsion by the state, such as a penalty clause or damages, must be excluded.

In this case, where after a divorce the apparent father is suing his ex-wife (not the real father) for damages in respect of the maintenance he has for years been paying for a child not his, this senate has again considered the matter afresh. We adhere to the holdings which the Supreme Court has increasingly confirmed since the introduction of the BGB (on the significance of continuity of holdings and legal certainty, see Grosser Senat, BGHZ 85, 64 [66] = NJW 1983, 228). We endorse the view that matrimonial difficulties which affect the inner social and sexual life of the partners, adultery being the chief of these, represent a matter internal to the marriage which is not within the protective ambit of the rules of tort [references].

This view was formed by the Bundesgerichtshof under the previous law of marriage; ideas have changed, but the view is even more strongly justified after the first reform law of marriage. Whereas under prior law (§ 58 I and II Marriage Act) the party whose adultery led to divorce and who was solely or principally at fault faced sanctions in regard to maintenance—either the loss of a claim for maintenance or liability to provide it—under the present law 'fault' which leads to the breakdown of the marriage does not in principle bar the 'guilty' spouse from claiming maintenance if in need, save under § 1579 nos. 6 and 7 BGB in cases of hardship. If there was no liability in tort for adultery under prior law which provided for financial sanctions for such conduct, there is no reason now that the fault principle has given way to the principle of the breakdown of marriage to deviate from the previous decisions and allow claims for damages in tort for conduct which impairs the marriage. This senate therefore adheres all the more strongly to its previous position that it is incompatible with the essence of marriage to apply the law of damages to internal matrimonial matters; marriage and family law oust the law of tort.

Thus not only claims based on § 823 II BGB but all suchlike claims in tort between divorced spouses are excluded if the right alleged to be invaded is the 'very core of marriage' and the 'interest it seeks to protect' or 'marriage as an ideal legal interest' (Gernhuber) or the 'personal moral bond of marriage' (Soergel-Lange), the 'right to fidelity in marriage' (Gernhuber, Enneccerus-Lehmann) or 'the maintenance of sexual fidelity' (Wacke), the 'right to the protection and continuance of the matrimonial community of living' (Berg, Lüke), the 'absolute right of the spouses to complete and exclusive consortium' (Dölle) or—based on § 1353 BGB—a 'claim to enjoin conduct which disturbs the marriage in the area of personal duties of marriage' (Jayme).

The sanctions of tort law may, by contrast, apply to marriage in its external objective and spatial aspects (BGHZ 6, 360 ff. = NJW 1952, 975; BGHZ

34, 80 ff. = NJW 1961, 504), normally vulnerable only by third parties, or, as the Fourth Senate (as it then was) stated in BGHZ 26, 217 [221] = NJW 1958, 544, to the invasion of other legal rights, as for example damage to the health of a spouse through infection resulting from adultery (see Tiedemann, NJW 1988, 729).

But as to the internal mutual relations of the spouses inherent in their matrimonial and sexual community, claims for damages in tort are excluded for the reasons given. Thus adultery by itself cannot be treated as conduct generating liability in damages. If, as in the present case, the wife breaches her duty of fidelity, commits adultery and conceives a child which, until a declaration of illegitimacy, rates as the child of the husband who then pays for her maintenance, he cannot after successfully establishing the illegitimacy of the child use the law of tort to claim compensation for the expense he has been put to because the child was apparently his (BGHZ 80, 235 [238] = NJW 1981, 1445).

3. (a) But the fact that claims for damages under the general law of tort in respect of the consequences of adultery are ousted by the provisions of marriage and family law does not mean that if there are further aggravating factors the special tort rule of § 826 BGB may not be applicable. § 826 BGB is a 'rule of law at a higher level', providing a general standard applicable throughout the whole of private and public law, and comparable in this respect with the all-pervasive principle of § 242 BGB. It is true that the former Fourth Civil Senate deviated from the jurisprudence of the Reichsgericht (RGZ 152, 397 ff.) and held that claims arising from antimatrimonial conduct were barred under § 826 BGB as well (BGHZ 23, 217 [221] = NJW 1958, 544), but that was a case in which there were no special circumstances over and above the adultery which, combined with it, constituted causing harm *contra bonos mores*. Such factors were, by contrast, present in the case decided by the Reichsgericht (Warn. 1935 no. 184) where the adulterous wife and her lover conspired by false statements to procure the dismissal of the husband's claim for a declaration of the illegitimacy of the adulterine child. The Reichsgericht was right to allow a claim for damages under § 826 BGB in that case (and see RGZ 152, 397 [400]). In exceptional cases, therefore, § 826 BGB can apply to disruption of the internal and sexual relationship of husband and wife, especially through adultery, if in addition to the adultery the errant spouse is guilty of further immoral damaging conduct, characterised by an intention, albeit a qualified intention, to cause harm. Whether conduct is immoral under § 826 BGB depends on the standards inherent in that text, not on those appropriate to the spousal community. This is not the case when the wife merely fails to make spontaneous avowal of her act of adultery and leaves the husband in the

belief that the child is his. The mere fact that the wife concealed her infidelity does not amount to an immoral wrong in the sense of § 826 BGB, for there is no duty, sanctioned by the law of damages, to tell one's spouse of one's adultery (RGZ 152, 397 [401]). To require a spouse to make such disclosure would normally be excessive, especially as she would quite often find herself in an insoluble dilemma, for disclosure would not only affect her own interests but also imperil the child's interest in maintenance.

There might, by contrast, be a claim under § 826 BGB if a wife who had conceived a child in adultery made false statements or outright denials in order to dispel her husband's doubts about its paternity, or if she prevented her husband by deceit or otherwise, say by duress, from pursuing a claim for a declaration of illegitimacy.

(b) No such conduct by the defendant has been established in this case or appears from the facts in evidence.

(aa) The plaintiff himself has not alleged that during the period when he was in contact with the child S he ever expressed any doubts about her paternity which the defendant allayed by false statements or otherwise. He rather claims to have been deceived by the fact that the defendant 'never made an issue of paternity' and did not volunteer an admission of her adultery. This is not enough to meet the requirements of § 826 BGB.

(bb) Nor does the conduct of the defendant in 'energetically asserting the apparent rights' of her daughter in several court cases constitute an immoral wrong under § 826 BGB, as the plaintiff alleges.

As the statutory representative of S the defendant sued in April 1960 for monthly maintenance payments of DM 75, which the plaintiff had earlier agreed in writing to make. In 1964 the defendant sought an increase to DM 100 per month and in May 1965 a further increase to DM 130, as well as demanding a like sum for her daughter B, who was four years older. The total sums claimed were in line with the figures in the Düsseldorf Tables for the maintenance by persons in the second and third income groups of children between six and ten years old (S) and between ten and fourteen (B), and the amounts were manifestly reasonable.

Nor is § 826 BGB satisfied by the defendant's conduct in garnishing the plaintiff's wages and then his pension when he did not punctually pay the sums he had agreed or been ordered to pay. The daughter S needed the payments to meet her living needs. Until declared illegitimate, she ranked as the legitimate child of the plaintiff (§ 1593 BGB) and he was liable for her maintenance under §§ 1601, 1602, 1603 BGB. As the child's statutory representative, the defendant was bound to see to making these claims in the interests of the child, and in making and enforcing the maintenance claims she was acting in justified pursuance of the interests of the child. If, instead of parental control being vested in the defendant, a curator had been appointed (§§ 1629 II, 1795 I no. 3, 1903 BGB) to claim the maintenance payments and resist the claim for a declaration of illegitimacy, such curator would likewise have been bound, until the illegitimacy was established, to sue the defendant for the maintenance payments if necessary, and to enforce them by execution if not voluntarily met (§§ 1915, 1793, 1833 BGB). Such conduct by the curator would not have been essentially different from what the defendant did. This shows that in pursuing maintenance claims for S the defendant remained within the limits of the means and methods provided by the legal system and that she cannot on that ground be found guilty of an immoral wrong under § 826 BGB.

(cc) Alternatively the appellant seeks to found his claim for damages on the principles developed by this court in BGHZ 80, 235 ff. = NJW 1981, 1445. He alleges that the defendant's failure to make requisite disclosure and her implicit assertion of his paternity by suing for maintenance prevented the plaintiff from seeking an earlier declaration of illegitimacy, and that this was in law tantamount to the fraudulent inducement to marry in that case.

This is not acceptable. In BGHZ 80, 235 = NJW 1981, 1445 the defendant had conceived the child before marriage and not as a result of adultery in breach of marriage vows, so the facts there were essentially different from this case, where the central question is whether breach of the marriage vows can generate a claim in tort. Furthermore, in that case the mother of the child had expressly and indeed in writing misrepresented the facts by assuring the plaintiff that during the statutory period of conception she had had congress 'with him and him alone' and so deliberately allayed his doubts about the paternity of the child about to be born. She thus induced the plaintiff to enter the marriage and procured that the child was born legitimate and would be maintained by the plaintiff until a declaration of illegitimacy. Such deceitful conduct on the part of the mother constituted conduct apt to generate liability in damages for intentionally causing harm in an immoral manner under § 826 BGB as explained. No comparably harmful conduct apart from the adultery itself can be laid at the door of the defendant here.

Notes to Cases 20–23

1. The fourth book of the BGB deals with family law, but problems of family life have also tried to penetrate the law of torts under the heading of 'other rights' of § 823 I BGB. (The first decision on the matter was decided by the BGH on 26 June 1952 (BGHZ 6, 360 = NJW 1952, 975) and it was rendered as a result of an action brought by a betrayed wife who sought an

injunction to stop her husband's mistress from residing in the marital home. Though the court recognized that delictual protection should be afforded to the spatial and material sphere of matrimony—*räumlich-gegenständlicher Bereich der Ehe*—it did not decide whether this should be achieved by means of § 823 I BGB or through the direct application of Art. 6 of the Constitution by virtue of Art. 1 III of that enactment. As a result of this, wives have been given the right to enter the premises of a company run by the husband (BGHZ 34, 80, 87) or to insist that they be allowed to work at the family bakery (BGHZ 35, 302, 304).) Such attempts have, on the whole, met with varied, perhaps modest success but this has not discouraged litigation. The proper role of tort law in the context of disrupted family relations has also given rise to a lively literature which can be found (along with a neat summary of the various views) in Medicus, nos. 616 *et seq.*, pp. 369–70. Cases 20–23 come from this area of the law and also show how German judges bring together different parts of their Code and thus try to retain an 'internal balance' in the Code. (Earlier cases are reviewed by Markovitz, 'Marriage and the State: A Comparative Look at East and West German Family Law' 24 *Stanford L. Rev.* 116 (1971).) Overall, however, the BGH—rejecting academic suggestions—has shown a preference for the view that 'marriage is not one of the relationships whose breach can give rise to general claims for compensation for economic harm'. (See BGHZ 27, 229; BGH NJW 1973, 991; BGHZ 80, 235; BGH NJW 1990, 706 = Case no. 23, above.)

2. The 'innocent spouse's' losses can be pecuniary or non-pecuniary. The former include such items as the cost of delivery of the child (discussed in case 21), its maintenance, the cost of illegitimization (not allowed by cases 20 and 22), and of divorce proceedings; the latter can refer to the breakdown of the marriage or nervous or other illness resulting from such upheavals. Those who argue against the trend shown in the cases reproduced above are really arguing in favour of a wider recognition of the first type of loss, not the second.

3. These and other analogous cases raise many points. Here are some: If the 'innocent husband'/plaintiff pays for the cost of delivery of the child, the natural father is enriched by a corresponding amount and must, therefore, pay the former that amount. The reasoning given for this in case 21 (but not the final result) has been doubted (see Medicus, 304). Likewise, maintenance paid by the 'innocent husband'/plaintiff for an illegitimate child may be claimed from the natural father *after* the child has been declared as illegitimate. The old case-law (BGHZ 24, 9 ff.) is now embodied in § 1615b BGB. But a husband's tort action against a divorced wife for the economic loss due to his making maintenance payments to an apparently legitimate daughter (who was actually the product of the wife's adultery) will fail. So

held the BGH in NJW 1990, 706, Case 23 above, restating its motto: 'Marriage and family law oust the law of tort.' A claim under § 826 BGB might, however, succeed if the requirement of immorality *of this provision* were satisfied. Mere marital infidelity will, thus, not do. It would be otherwise, however, if, for example, it could be proved that the woman and her lover had conspired to procure the dismissal of the husband's claim for a declaration of illegitimacy: RGZ 152, 397 which, apparently, is still good law. (For further details, the reader must consult books on family law.) BGH NJW 1990, 706 contains some interesting dicta which explain this preeminence of § 826 BGB. The costs of divorce are usually shared by the spouses—§ 93a I ZPO—but the 'innocent spouse' can subsequently claim his share of the divorce costs from the 'marital intruder'. But no damages can be claimed for the act of infidelity (case 22).

4. Some of these points may not arise at all in Common law jurisdictions; others do, and often receive similar solutions. In the US, for example, attorneys' fees are borne by the parties unless otherwise provided for by statute. To that extent, therefore, case 20 has no equivalent. In England there seems to be no case which has awarded costs or compensation for the expense of proving a child to be illegitimate, though *Halsbury*, vol. 13, 4th edn., § 970, does not in terms exclude the possibility. Disavowing a child born in legal wedlock can also receive a different treatment. In England it is possible but not easy, there being a presumption of legitimacy. In the United States the answers are more varied, some States adopting irrebuttable presumptions of legitimacy, others imposing a short period of time following birth within which the illegitimization proceedings must be brought (*Pounds* v. *Schori* 377 So. 2d 1195 (La. 1979) (six months); cf. *Singley* v. *Singley* 140, So. 2d 546 (La. App. 1962) where a child was born more than three hundred days after separation of husband and wife and the husband was permitted to disavow). (See Clark, *Law of Domestic Relations*, 172 (1968).) But if the father refuses to disavow a child, no one else will normally be allowed to do so. (See *Petitioner F.* v. *Respondent R.* 430 A. 2d 1075 (Del. 1981), where a natural father, who sued for custody of the child which was conceived while its mother was married to another man, had his action dismissed for lack of standing to sue.)

5. The problem discussed in case 22 is still known in some American jurisdictions under the name of criminal conversation. *Kremer* v. *Black* 201 Neb. 467, 268 NW 2d 582 (1978) is an example. But most States have abolished such actions and much criticism is still made against those who recognize it. The action is no longer known in English law. (It was abolished by the Law Reform (Miscellaneous Provisions) Act 1970, s. 5.) In the Commonwealth, the action for enticement was abolished somewhat later. Thus in Australia this was done by the Family Law Act 1975, s. 120. In New Zealand on the

other hand the action for enticement was enshrined in legislative form as late as 1975 (see Domestic Actions Act 1975, s. 3); but it was abolished five years later by the Family Proceedings Act 1980, s. 190. For further discussions one must consult family law textbooks as well as older editions of Tort treatises.

9. 'ESTABLISHED AND OPERATING BUSINESS'

Case 24

REICHSGERICHT (FOURTH CIVIL DIVISION) 27 FEBRUARY 1904*
RGZ 58, 24

Three designs were entered in the Register of Designs on behalf of the defendant firm . . . In the summer of 1901 the defendant, under threats of an action for damages and a criminal prosecution, forbade the plaintiff to copy the designs. He did so, at all events by a letter of 2 September concerning carpets, mats, and rugs made of jute pile and, under the same date, by letters to two of the plaintiff's weaving managers. The plaintiff alleged that the defendant had also forbidden the manufacture at an earlier date. In consequence the plaintiff had already, on 10 June 1901, discontinued the manufacture of jute pile in his business. On 15 September 1901 the defendant prosecuted the plaintiff for an offence against section 10 of the Act of 1 June 1891, whereupon a preliminary enquiry was instituted against the plaintiff.

Before that enquiry was concluded the plaintiff sued the defendant claiming that he should (i) agree to a cancellation of the design and (ii) pay compensation for the damage arising from the prohibition against manufacture and the prosecution. The claim under (i) was based on the fact that the design was already, at the time of the notice, a matter of common knowledge. The defendant admitted that claim.

The Landgericht granted the claim. On appeal by the defendant the Oberlandesgericht made the order to pay compensation depend on the failure of the proprietor of the defendant firm to deny on oath his knowledge of the design when the notice was sent. On application for review that judgment was set aside for the following

Reasons

The Court of Appeal starts with the statement that the plaintiff ceased manufacturing the articles corresponding to these designs in consequence of the defendant's demand referring to their registration and that, as a result, the defendant was not entitled to contend that the plaintiff was not forced to

---

* English version by F. H. Lawson and B. S. Markesinis.

accede to his demand. No precise moment is indicated when the demand and the cessation occurred and it is left undecided whether they had not, as the plaintiff alleged, already taken place before the defendant's letter of 2 September 1901 to the plaintiff and his weaving managers. The Court of Appeal finds that the defendant's designs had been wrongly registered since they were not entitled to protection and that, therefore, the defendant had no right to prohibit the plaintiff's business activity. For the damage, however, occurring to the plaintiff from the stopping of production and the prosecution, the court is prepared to make the defendant liable only if there was knowledge of the lack of justification and not merely negligent ignorance. It considers that the evidence so far obtained does not point to knowledge at the critical time and so decides to tender an oath to the defendant proprietors of the firm. According to the original form of the oath, each of the two partners was to swear that on 2 September 1901 he did not know that the registered article was a matter of previous knowledge. The form of the oath was later modified to read that each of them should swear that 'It is not true that at the time when the plaintiff was required by our company to stop manufacturing the objects protected by our designs nos. 156083, 156084 and 156465, I knew . . .'. Even if one assumes that the appellate judge's view of the law is to be approved, this form of oath must still give rise to doubt. For no precise moment is indicated to the swearer as to which he must affirm on oath the truth of the fact of his ignorance; it is left to his conscience to consider which moment to specify among several possible incidents to which his sworn ignorance would refer. Thus the formulation of the oath contains a serious degree of subjective uncertainty. Whether that alone would suffice to justify setting aside the appellate decision may be left undecided. But there are further grounds. The compensation to which the plaintiff is entitled as a result of the prosecution also depends on the oath. According to the accompanying criminal records the prosecution bears the date 4 September 1901. Hence that moment is decisive for liability under the prosecution. The present uncertain form of oath has its basis in the fact that so far there has been no finding about the factual correctness of the disputed allegation of the plaintiff that the stopping of production consequent on the defendants' demand had already taken place on 10 June 1901. If now the oath is refuted, so that the bad faith of the defendant partners is established, there is clearly no interest in specifying more closely the moment when their knowledge began. Assuming, however, that the oath is sworn and also that the request mentioned in the oath occurred *before* 4 September, in particular on 10 June 1901, it is obvious that the earlier moment of ignorance would be quite irrelevant to the claim for compensation arising out of the prosecution. These considerations would be enough to lead to a setting-aside of the contested judgment.

The setting-aside, however, must also result for a second and more comprehensive reason. The Court of Appeal makes an error of law when it denies the applicability of § 823 I BGB and, therefore, is prepared to make the defendants' liability depend only on their knowledge that their design lacks protection. At the time when the defendants, invoking their right to have their design protected and threatening civil and criminal proceedings, forbade the production of the jute pile in question, the plaintiff had already taken up the manufacture of those objects in its business, although there is up to now no certainty of the extent to which that had happened. The defendants, therefore, are chargeable with having encroached on the established business of the plaintiff by virtue of a right that did not belong to them and hence in a manner contrary to law. The plaintiff, who claimed that he already at that time had ten looms devoted to the manufacture and would, but for the prohibition, have extended the application to 50 looms, believes that the defendant's conduct constitutes also an invasion of his property rights, in that it had unlawfully hindered the full use of manufacturing installations owned by him. That view can indeed not be approved. Against the property itself of the plaintiff, which was never in question, no invasion was intended or directed. It was and remained in its content and legal signification the same as if the plaintiff had done his manufacturing not on his own but on some one else's looms. On the other hand, it is both accurate and to the point when the appellant, associating itself with the plaintiff's explanation of first instance, adopts the point of view that the business was disturbed.

§ 823 I BGB obliges anyone who recklessly or negligently injures the life, body, health, freedom, property, or other right of another contrary to law to make good all damage that ensues.

It is acknowledged that it is not the liability for doing economic damage as such that is here in question, but only that economic damage which is a consequence of the violation of the particular legal interests and rights specified by the Code. Hence the question is whether the defendants have violated such a particular legal interest or right of the plaintiff.

One can first of all consider the injury as an interference with the plaintiff's freedom inasmuch as the plaintiff was reduced by outside interference with his will to discontinue the manufacture of jute pile. But this point of view would not lead to the desired result. Admittedly, in the dispute about the meaning attached to freedom by the Code, notable authors have expressed the view that it must be understood quite generally as the free exercise of the will. But even if one were willing to follow that broadest interpretation, finding a basis for compensation would always presuppose an unlawful injury to the free exercise of the will, and it is out of the question that the Code intends to declare the encroachment on another's will unlawful for the reason only that there is no particular right so to encroach. The encroachment on the free exercise of the will would acquire the character of unlawfulness only through the form in which it occurs, such as deceit, threats, force, and these facts would also have to include, as in § 826 BGB (which was applied by the Court of Appeal), at least the defendant's consciousness of the legal invalidity of the registration of the designs. (Cf. Decisions of the Reichsgericht in Civil Cases, vol. 48, 123.)

Then there is the view that the law raised the interests mentioned by it (life, body, health, and freedom) to the status of objects of an especial right to them and through the words 'or a similar right' intended to extend its protection beyond those expressly mentioned to other vital interests. This did not find favour in the case-law of the Reichsgericht. It has been held already that the theory which wished to construct from the not yet limited range of particular interests, special rights to personality and individuality to an extent which has not yet been determined finally does not appear particularly suitable as a basis for interpreting the law. Thus, for instance, it has been denied that either the freedom to do business or the faculty to exploit one's labour without hindrance is protected by § 823 I BGB. There is no need to go further into this matter. For as distinct from the legal possibility of pursuing the occupation of one's choice, as it is accorded generally by § 1 of the Gewerbeordnung, it has already been accepted in several decisions of different Senates that a subjective right is to be recognized to an actually established and active business which is capable of being directly infringed. And, it has already been held that attacks on the exercise of a business can lead to an injunction [references follow]; but they can also found a claim for compensation arising from injury to the exercise of a business. This view formed the basis, in part, of the judgment delivered by the Senate on 25 June 1891 (RGZ 28, 248, especially 247, 249) before the enactment of the Wettbewerbsgesetz (Act on Unfair Competition). That the exercise of a business can be the object of legal advice under § 823 I BGB was decided by the IV Civil Senate in a judgment of 6 March 1902 and the VI Civil Senate in a judgment of 29 May 1902 (RGZ 51, 369, in particular 373), and also in a judgment of 14 December 1903 (RGZ 56, 271) though with some reservations. This Senate believes that it ought in principle to take the same position. That the established independent exercise of a business not only involves the free manifestation of the will of the person exercising it, but that will has also found in it its embodiment as an object, is the firm foundation for the acceptance of a subjective right to that exercise. Disturbances and encroachments aimed directly against the exercise of a business may therefore be looked upon as injuries falling under § 823 I BGB. Such an attack, directed against the exercise of a business, clearly exists when the legal admissibility of that exercise is denied to a certain extent and its restriction demanded on the ground of an industrial property right to the contrary. That attack is, however, contrary to law when the alleged protected industrial property right does not in truth exist, because it is no longer a question of permitted competition. The law under certain conditions puts at the disposal of persons exercising a business valuable exclusive rights in the form of the protection of patents and designs, by virtue of which they can secure the products of their inventive activity against attacks by way of parallel competition and reserve them for their own advantage. It is only a counterpart of their privileged position that they also answer for the existence of the right they enjoy to the self-seeking restriction of the free exercise of their business by their opponents, and must not only enjoy the advantages but also bear the risks that are involved in the assertion of such exclusive rights to patents and designs. In taking that view this Senate believes that it does not dissent from the opinion expressed by the VI Senate especially in the second of its decisions, mentioned above. Admittedly the protection of the exercise of a business against unfair competition is said in that decision to be found according to positive law in the provisions of the Wettbewerbsgesetz, of § 823 II BGB in combination with the penal rules concerning defamation and undermining credit, as well as in §§ 824 and 826 BGB, whereas the notion is rejected that any disturbance or encroachment on another person in the exercise of his business constitutes a violation of a law falling, as contrary to law, under § 823 I BGB. That, however, is not to deny that in some circumstances such an attack may be seen to be an injury contrary to law. The VI Civil Senate did not, as now, have to decide the particular case where the encroachment of another's exercise of his business was based on an alleged exclusive industrial property right that did not in reality exist.

Accordingly, the contested judgment cannot be upheld, since by not applying § 823 I BGB it contravenes the law. But on the merits itself no decision is possible. The Court of Appeal has so far only found that, apart from the results of the submission to the oath, the knowledge of the invalidity of their design on the part of the defendants has not been proved. On the other hand the question whether that ignorance is to be treated as negligence or whether there is a sufficient excuse has not yet been examined. Even so the Court of Appeal has indeed affirmed the causal connection between the demand of the defendants which, as stated before, remained somewhat uncertain, and the suspension of the plaintiff's business. It will, however, have to be investigated in addition whether on this occasion the plaintiff's conduct also constitutes contributory negligence that would justify the application of § 254 BGB. Wherein the legal defect in the defendants' design consisted has not yet been sufficiently elucidated. According to certain indications it does not appear to be excluded that already from the start the plaintiff at least suspected the invalidity of the registration and in course of time soon obtained a more exact knowledge of it . . .

Case 25

REICHSGERICHT (SIXTH CIVIL DIVISION) 19 DECEMBER 1918*
RGZ 94, 248 = JW 1919, 247 and approving note by Kirchenbauer

On 10 June 1908 a design was entered in the designs register of the Patent Office under no. 342454 on behalf of defendant 2a for socks, the upper portions of which were in whole or in part made of wool, but the lower portions of non-woollen material. The defendant transferred his right to that design to defendant 1, the partnership H. B., which he operated in common with defendant 2b. On 21 March 1911, defendant 1 sent to the firm L. & S. in D, which had obtained from the plaintiff the right to retail his socks, a letter in which, referring to the registered design, it warned them against retailing the socks received from the plaintiff, ordered them to withdraw the offers made by them, and threatened them with a claim for compensation. According to the plaintiff's allegation defendant 1 had sent letters to the same effect to two other firms whom the plaintiff had appointed retailers of his socks. The plaintiff also asserted that defendant 1 had completely succeeded in the aim pursued in his letter, since his customers had, in consequence of defendant 1's letters, cancelled their substantial orders.

The plaintiff also alleges that in consequence he has suffered substantial damage. He demands RM 16,000 in part payment for the damage averring that the proprietors of defendant 1, namely the defendants 2, had known when sending the letters that their design was not entitled to protection, since, *inter alia*, it lacked novelty.

The defendants, who allege that they were convinced of the validity of the design when they sent the letters and are even now convinced of it, demand the dismissal of the action and offer to show that the plaintiff has no claim whatever against the defendants.

The Landgericht declared the claim justified in principle, but the Court of Appeal invited both defendants 2 to swear upon oath that they were unaware, when they warned the firm L. & S. and two other firms against infringement of the design no. 342454, that already before giving notice of the design socks were being manufactured and put into circulation of which the upper portion was of whole or part made of wool and the lower portion of non-woollen material. If the two defendants swear the oath, the action should be dismissed; if they do not, the claim should be declared justified in principle.

* English version by F. H. Lawson and B. S. Markesinis.

On the plaintiff's application for review, the appeal of the defendants against the judgment at first instance was rejected for these

Reasons

1. The Court of Appeal, in agreement with the judge at first instance, starts correctly from the position that the defendants' conduct constituted an attack on an established business and that this must be regarded as a legal interest protected by § 823 I BGB. That view conforms to the standing case-law of the Reichsgericht (cf. RGZ 58, 24; 64, 52).

The Oberlandesgericht then sets out the content of the defendants' design and finds that in preliminary proceedings brought by the defendants 1 and 2a against the present plaintiff before the Landgericht of Chemnitz, defendant 2a was ordered to approve the cancellation of the registered design no. 342454.

The Court of Appeal attaches no importance to that condemnation for the purposes of the present dispute. In particular it holds that the judgment in that preliminary proceeding, both at first instance and on appeal, ordered the cancellation of defendant 2a's design only because the inventive idea constituted by the socks had not been disclosed in the notice. It followed that the defendants could not have known this legal reason for the invalidity of the design; and, accordingly even apart from the presence of especial circumstances the existence of which was not alleged, they were not bound to make enquiries in that direction.

These considerations should obviously serve to deny negligence in what the Court of Appeal regarded as the objectively unlawful conduct of the defendants. Even so far the explanations of the Court of Appeal do not seem free from objection. It looks as though the Oberlandesgericht attaches to the registration of a design an importance that it does not possess.

In contrast to principles of patent law, whereby the grant of a patent (and the consequent entry in the patent register according to § 19 of the Patents Act) confers on the patent-holder without more ado the exclusive right to manufacture industrially the object of the invention, to put it into circulation, and sell it (§ 4 Patents Act), the person on whose behalf a design is entered in the register of designs acquires an exclusive right to copy the design industrially and put it in circulation only if it serves the purpose of work or use by a new structure, arrangement, or preparation. In other words, the entry in the register of designs confers on the person entering it no right of exclusive use that could empower him to invade another's established business unless the presuppositions exist that are set out in § 1 GebrMustG.

There can therefore be a negligent attack on another's business if anyone on whose behalf a design is registered forbids a tradesman only on the basis of that fact to retail such objects to which the design refers. Whoever makes himself guilty of an attack on another's business on the basis of a design registered for him can therefore in certain circumstances even act negligently within the meaning of § 823 I BGB if he does not convince himself of the efficacy of his design before he seeks registration. For, in contrast to the provisions of §§ 20 ff. of the Patents Act governing the grant of a patent, this is not ordered on the basis of an official examination into whether the material presuppositions exist on which § 1 GebrMustG affords to a design a claim to legal protection. The Patent Office must under § 3 GebrMustG order the entry of the design in the register of designs as soon as only the formal presuppositions of § 2 of the Act are fulfilled (cf. also the Reichsgericht decision of 27 February 1900, Via. 347/99).

2. It now appears from the foregoing reasons that the Court of Appeal's opinion that the defendant cannot be charged with negligence on the ground that he had not known of the legal inefficacy of this design is not free from objection. Moreover, its further considerations give occasion for appreciable legal doubt.

In particular, the Court of Appeal went on to say that in both the sets of preliminary proceedings concerning the design no. 342454 brought by the defendants against B1 (Landgericht Köln) and the present plaintiff (Landgericht Chemnitz) it was alleged that the object of the design was not new at the time of the notice. But in both cases that question did not give rise to a judicial decision. The proceedings against B1 ended with a settlement and in that against the present plaintiff, the newness of the design was assumed. In the proceedings against B1, the witnesses K and Sch. had indeed said at their examination of April 1911 that as long ago as twenty-five years their range had included socks of which the lower portion was made of cotton and the upper of woollen yarn. From that the Court of Appeal drew the further conclusion that the evidence of the two witnesses proved the lack of newness of the object of the design here in question. Since, however, their examination took place only after defendant 1's warning letter was sent out, since the latter was under no obligation to enquire what those witnesses would say, and since the defendants could not be held to blame for not waiting for the examination of the witnesses before sending out their warning letter, they could not be charged with negligent behaviour. Nor were they bound, once they knew what the witnesses had said, to withdraw their warning by a corresponding recall, since it appears to be excluded that the statements of the witnesses K and Sch. would have shaken their conviction of the newness of their design. Thus, the defendants were not shown to be negligent in failing to withdraw their warning once they knew of the witnesses' statements.

In these statements it appears even more clearly than in the considerations of the Court of Appeal discussed under (1) that it misunderstood the meaning of the registration of a design. Since that registration conferred on the person registering only a purely formal, but not a material right, he exercised it, as the Senate has already declared in its judgment of 3 July 1916, at his peril and responsibility, in so far as concerns the newness and previous use of the design. Hence 'anyone who in reliance on a design encroaches on another's business by a trenchant prohibition against producing and selling the wares and thereby causes damage must constantly examine with the utmost care whether and for how long he is entitled to do it.'

If one starts from this fundamental standpoint the conduct of the defendant 1 is already shown to have been negligent by the fact that, although in the preliminary proceedings against B1 the witnesses K and Sch. had alleged that the object of the design had been openly used in Germany, they had nevertheless sent out the warning letters here in question. For the defendants were bound to take into account that witnesses K and Sch. would confirm the correctness of the then defendant B1's statements.

However, the defendants were guilty of a quite exceptionally gross negligence when, after the examination in April 1911 of the witnesses K and Sch. . . . the absence of newness in the object of the design was established, all the same they did not withdraw their warning.

The Court of Appeal, which considers the defendants not obliged to make such a recall, thereby contradicts its own explanations. In particular it lays especial and decisive emphasis on the fact that the warning had already been sent out before the examination of the witnesses K and Sch. From that it follows that even from the Court of Appeal's standpoint the warning letters should not have been sent after the examination of the witnesses. But if that is correct, a recall of the warning letters was under all circumstances essential once the examination of the witnesses had taken place.

The appellate decision, which thereby wrongly denied the negligence of the defendants, is therefore set aside for infringement of § 823 BGB.

Case 26

BUNDESGERICHTSHOF (FIRST CIVIL DIVISION) 26 OCTOBER 1951*
BGHZ 3, 270 = NJW 1952, 660 = JZ 1952, 227 and partially approving and partially critical note by H. Kleine

The ladies' journal 'C' is published by the plaintiff. The defendant is the publisher of the weekly *Church and Life,* the church bulletin for the bishopric of M. Each issue of this journal includes for each deanery a 'supplement' composed and printed locally, in which notices, mainly of religious ser-

---

* English version by F. H. Lawson and B. S. Markesinis.

vices and other deanery news, are published. In the deanery supplement for O, an article was published entitled 'The Select Readings of the P. Circle for Every Family', in which the moral conduct of the illustrated journals appearing in the post-war period was criticized. The article contains, *inter alia*, expressions to the effect that the publishers exploited the apparent collapse of the concepts of decency and dignity, had replaced honest commercial competition and market calculation by unscrupulous reliance on the primitive instincts of a wearied people; the plaintiff's ladies' journal 'C' was described very critically; Christian readers of the ladies' journal 'C' in receiving the journal, neglected their duty towards the honour of their wives and daughters, and the upbringing of their adolescent children. In addition it states that a Christian could obtain from other journals a picture of the world and a new point of view towards such matters. For the last few months there appeared regularly each week at the wish of the bishop the 'Select Readings of the Circle' which, in richness, up-to-dateness, and make-up is not inferior to the products of other enterprises and are more value for money. It then names a number of journals which form a 'medley' which offered every responsible thinking Christian joy and relaxation by providing moments of reflection in the evenings and on holidays. Information about these Select Readings was available at each parish office or the headquarters of the P. Circle.

The 'Select Readings of the P. Circle' mentioned in that article is distributed by the 'Catholic L. e.V.' in M, which receives the net profit if any. The 'P. Circle' and the 'Catholic L. e.V.' are economically independent of the defendant.

The above-mentioned article in the deanery's supplement appeared anonymously. The plaintiff company holds the defendant company answerable for the statements made against itself and its journal contained in that article, charging the defendant with breaches of certain statutory regulations [references]. The defendant first knew of the article objected to after its appearance, but has declared that it entirely agrees with the article and declines to withdraw the criticism of the plaintiff's journal printed in it.

The plaintiff claimed that the defendant be ordered to refrain from making and to recall the above-mentioned statements. The plaintiff also asked for a declaration that the defendant is liable to pay compensation and the right to publish the judgment.

Both instances below dismissed the action. The application for review led to the decisions being set aside and the case referred back to the lower court for these

Reasons

The applicant for review cannot successfully object that the Court of Appeal looked upon the statements in dispute as comments and not allegations of fact in the sense of § 14 UWG (*Unlauterer Wettbewerbs-gesetz*), § 824 BGB, §§ 186, 187 StGB. The Court of Appeal did not fail to perceive that an allegation of a fact can be hidden under the form of a comment. Even if the protection of a reputation intended by the legislator requires the fluctuating boundary between allegations of fact and value-judgments or mere statements of opinion to be drawn as broadly as possible in favour of allegations of fact, since every comment rests ultimately on external or internal facts, yet it remains a prerequisite that the disapproving judgment takes as its starting-point tangible occurrences susceptible of proof, since otherwise a proof of truth or falsehood, as it is envisaged by § 186 StGB, § 824 BGB, and § 14 UWG, is logically excluded. The applicant starts from the position that no evidence whatever can be adduced for the truth of the contested statements. Comments, however, which do not admit of proof of truth, which are not related to definite probable acts, are not allegations of fact in the sense of the above-mentioned statutory provisions. It must, indeed, be conceded to the applicant that the complaint of exploitation can contain an allegation of fact. However, in the present case that complaint does not rest on specifically detailed acts but alleges that the apparent collapse of 'decency and dignity' is being exploited. If one connects this statement with the further complaints, according to which the personalities standing behind the plaintiff are accused of 'unscrupulous exploitation of the instincts of a wearied people', the view taken by the Court of Appeal must be approved that the expressions in question do not so much conceal a complaint of provable business dishonesty, but rather amount to a moral judgment on the general behaviour and business activity of the persons in question, and, therefore are value-judgments unaccompanied by examinable facts.

The same applies to the further critical statements of the plaintiff's journal and of the statement that 'Christian readers of the journal in receiving the journal neglected their duty towards the honour of their wives and daughters and the upbringing of their adolescent children'. In agreement with the principles established by the Reichsgericht's decisions in civil and criminal cases on distinguishing between value-judgments and allegations of fact, the Court of Appeal has quite accurately regarded those utterances as general expressions of disapproval, which have not for their object examinable acts of those involved [references follow].

III. In examining, however, the question of who may be sued, the Court of Appeal allows itself to be influenced by erroneous considerations of law which affect its further legal assessment of the facts. Neither the defendant's responsibility under press legislation nor its declaration of willingness to hold itself responsible for the article published without its knowledge justifies the Court of Appeal in assuming that the defendant must be treated as though it composed or authorized the article. The Court of Appeal failed to realize that the provisions of the Press law bear only on criminal law, not on civil law. The civil liability of the publishing house for infringements committed by its publications is defined by the general principles (RGZ 50, 109, 110; RG JW 1917, 713). In this purpose it is to be assumed that the publisher of periodicals is normally not in a position, and is also not in general bound, to scan the publication before it appears. As a rule responsibility for the contents is borne by the editor, whose name must appear on each number under the strict provisions of § 7 of the Press Act. The publisher, however, is liable for a fault of the editor, if the latter is subject to his instructions, and it is therefore a question of employer's liability. He may then try to prove that he is not to be blamed under § 831 BGB (RGZ 148, 154, 161). The publisher who did not know before publication of an injurious utterance made public by a periodical published by him is, as a rule, liable in damages only in so far as general provisions make him responsible for the faults of third persons. The publisher is, however, independently of any question of fault, the right defendant in a claim for an injunction under § 1004 BGB, against a disturber if a leaflet which is inserted in his publication unlawfully affects a third person and that injurious result is at least indirectly traceable to his will, since he has the possibility of exercising influence on the content of the sale of the inserted leaflet [references follow].

. . . The defendant's declaration that makes the contested utterances her own, combined indeed with an approval of all the circumstances under which the article complained of appeared, is not without importance for the decision of the claim for an injunction. The defendant has refused to tone down the criticism of the plaintiff's journal in the article in the deanery supplement and has expressed the view that the criticism was, even in its present rigour, required by its opposition to the plaintiff's journal, and was covered by the protection of justified interests. It has also announced that it considered itself justified in publishing similar or equivalent statements in the future. That, however, makes it a 'disturber' in the sense of § 1004 BGB, since it has made these declarations in knowledge of the attacks, which have already occurred and must here be assumed to have been unlawful—and does not deny its ability to prevent the insertion of deanery supplements with a content not approved by it. From that admission of the defendant there follows a risk of further impairment and thereby its liability to be made defendant in proceedings for an injunction, without any need so far to examine its responsibility for the existing publications.

IV. The Court of Appeal denied any infringement of provisions protecting competition on the ground that those provisions presuppose acting with a competitive purpose, whereas the defendant in its conduct complained of acted not with a competitive intention but exclusively on religious ground without a gainful purpose.

The contention of the applicant for review, that the Court of Appeal misunderstood the concept of acting with a competitive purpose, is unfounded. Relying on a decision of the Reichsgericht [reference], the applicant puts forward the view that where business men were engaged in a competitive struggle any act which is objectively apt to further one's own or another's competition suffices to fulfil the factual characteristics of acting for competitive purposes, without any need to examine the subjective disposition of the actor. The applicant fails here to recognize that the Reichsgericht, in the decision referred to, treated the knowledge that another's competition was being furthered only as an indication that the then defendant was pursuing, along with other aims, also competitive purposes. That additional presupposition, however, was required because according to a constant practice concept 'with competitive purposes' requires a subjective intention directed towards competition [references].

The Senate cannot accept the dissenting view put forward by Reimer [reference] in view of the wording of the Act. Although an intention directed to furthering competition by oneself or another does not need to be the only or an essential aim of the act, yet that competitive purpose must not be neglected as completely irrelevant compared with the principal motives [references].

It may, indeed, generally be correct that experience points to a competitive intention when competitors make statements in commercial intercourse which are objectively apt to further one's own or another's competition. It is not, however, a mistake of law when the Court of Appeal does not consider this evidentiary rule, which is not imperative and is merely found empirically to correspond as a rule to the truth, to be decisive in the particular case which concerns information in a church bulletin.

Whether the factual characteristics of acting 'for a competitive purpose' are fulfilled is a matter for the unfettered appreciation of the judge of fact. The Court of Appeal was not wrong in inferring from the circumstance that no reference to the church bulletin published by the defendant was contained in the article and that no financial connection exists between the defendant and the 'P. Circle' or the 'Catholic L. e.V.' selling its select readings that there was no intrinsic probability of a competitive intention to be proved by the defendant. When accordingly, the Court of Appeal—starting from the pastoral duties of the bishop, on whose instructions the defendant acted as the publisher—came to the conclusion that the controversial article would, according to the honest conviction of the defendant, serve only its fight against what it considered the extraordinarily corrupting and dangerous world of journals and magazines, those considerations did not offend against the legal principles laid down by the Reichsgericht for the subjective requirement of acting for competitive purposes [reference].

On the other hand the applicants' complaint for review is well founded that the Court of Appeal ought not to have neglected to take up the offer to provide evidence of the testimony of named witnesses that the controversial article was prepared on the defendant's instructions by the publicity manager of the 'P. Circle' for competitive purposes and was provided for the deanery supplement [details follow].

V. The considerations also by which the Court of Appeal rejects §§ 823 I and II, 826, in combination with § 1004 BGB, as grounds of claim do not stand up to legal review.

. . . First it must be objected that the Court of Appeal regards as decisive whether the defendant acted with a defamatory intent—a question which can be relevant only when the protection of reputation is in issue—without examining whether there was a direct attack on the plaintiff's business through an unlawful impairment of its business activity, which falls within § 823 I BGB. Even utterances which do not fulfil the requirements of defamation but describe the position of a business undertaking, its products, or other performance and thereby disturb the free development of the undertaking, can constitute a direct attack on the right protected by § 823 I BGB to carry on an established business. Since § 14 UWG and § 824 BGB only allow claims arising from allegations of fact, legal protection against injurious comments which do not bear the taint of immorality and therefore do not fall within the general clause of § 1 UWG, § 826 BGB would be incomplete if they could not be treated as injurious acts violating the right to conduct a business.

The Reichsgericht, it must be admitted, affirmed the existence of that right in its earlier decisions only when the attack was aimed directly against the existence of the business. A diminution of the economic profit or of the prospects of gain was not regarded as sufficient [references]. Yet, in later decisions the Reichsgericht went further in the field of the law of trade marks and competition and considered, for the purpose of an injunction, that any unlawful impairment of business activity was sufficient, if it constituted a direct interference with the sphere of the business [references].

But there remains no substantial reason to restrict the concept of the protection of business activity to the field of competition and industrial property. Just as property is protected by § 823 I BGB against direct attack, in all its individual emanations—for instance the impairment of the unrestricted power of disposal—so also, according to this protective provision, the right to an established and active business must be protected against direct disturbances not only in its substance but also in its individual aspects, including the whole field of business activity.

The contested article which, supported by the highest ecclesiastical authority, strongly warns everyone, but especially the Christian reader, against the plaintiff's journal, and couples that warning with a derogatory reference to the persons behind the plaintiff. It displays a direct attack on the plaintiff's protected right to an undisturbed development of its business activity. This interference with the protected legal sphere of the plaintiff, which infringes the protection of business activity afforded by the law, would only not be illegal if the defendant had a special justification for the interference [references].

For this purpose, contrary to the view of the Court of Appeal, it is not of vital importance whether the facts point to punishable defamation, for it is not the protection of a reputation but the plaintiff's right to unimpeded business activity that is in question. If aspects of unfair competition are absent, such as attach as a rule to a critical comparison of industrial products for competitive purposes, an objective criticism of the plaintiff's journal would not be contrary to law even if it had adverse consequences for the plaintiff since Art. 5 of the Constitution allows anyone to express such criticism in the exercise of his right to the free expression of his opinion. But comments disturbing business, which depart from the field of objective criticism, are only not illegal if in accordance with their content, form, or accompanying circumstances they are objectively necessary to protect legally approved interests.

§ 193 StGB, it is true, provides a justification only where defamation is concerned. Yet that rule governs the special case of conflicts of interests which can arise in the protection of reputation, in accordance with an overriding legal doctrine which assumes importance wherever in a conflict between different interests the injury to one legal interest must be accepted. All comments affecting a business which factually fall within § 823 I BGB can be justified as protecting justified interests if the protection keeps within the limits fixed by law. These limits must be drawn according to the principle of balancing interests and duties that govern all conflicts of interests [references].

The conflict between the interest pursued and the legally protected interest that is to be sacrificed to it must be balanced by observing the principles that the Reichsgericht has developed for overriding necessity. The conflict of values can only be resolved in this way, whereby he who can effectively protect a justified interest only by interfering with another's legally protected interest must choose the least violation of law, the most considerate means. Thus injurious utterances are covered by the protection of justified interests only if according to their content, form, and accompanying circumstances they constitute the indicated and necessary means of attaining the legally approved purpose [references].

A mistake as to the need for the severity and extent of the attack on a protected legal good, if innocent, only excludes fault and thereby liability for damages, but not the substantial unlawfulness of the attack [references follow].

It is to be noted that whoever proposes to encroach on another's legal sphere for the sake of his own interests, or of those especially dear to him, must carefully examine whether the injury which he proposes to inflict is necessary as to severity and extent in order to further those interests appropriately. If he neglects that examination, which must take into account the scale of protection of the legal interest under attack, an excessive amount of injury, which is always illegal, cannot be excused even if there is a mistake as to its necessity.

These legal principles were misunderstood by the Court of Appeal. It assumed, indeed quite rightly, that the defendant, as publisher of a bulletin issued by a high ecclesiastical dignitary, held no exceptional legal position, but that its conduct was to be judged according to all applicable legal provisions. The Court of Appeal is also correct in holding that the interests involved in the struggle of the Church against a degenerate Press of which it disapproved affected so closely the defendant as publisher of the Church bulletin that it must be accorded an especial right to protect those interests (RGSt 63, 229 [231]; RGZ 115, 77 [80]). But the Court of Appeal misunderstands the limits to the pursuit of justifiable interests when it considers that the assumed excess in degree of injury is justified on the ground that the defendant acted exclusively for an ethically objectionable purpose and not with a defamatory intent. Even moral motives afford no right to sacrifice the protected interests of another beyond the necessary limits. The view of the law taken by the Court of Appeal, which makes the unlawfulness of the utterances in issue depend on the personal convictions and intentions of the injuring party, would render the right to reputation and the right to an established business defenceless against the grossest attack, if the perpetrator acted not for objectionable reasons but only with the aim of enforcing more effectually the interest pursued by him by excessive attacks which are objectively unnecessary. The Court of Appeal overlooks the fact that the decisions of the Reichsgericht which it cites in support of its opinion to the contrary (RG JW 1914, 368, 371; RGSt 40, 317), deal only with criminal liability—which always presupposes fault—but not with the objective unlawfulness of unduly injurious utterances.

It is also a matter for criticism that the Court of Appeal, contrary to its opinion that the defendant must be treated as though it had prepared or occasioned the article, chooses to justify the conduct of the defendant within the scope of § 193 StGB by the particular state of conflict in which it found it after the publication of the article. If the defendant had no right to express its condemnation in its existing form at the time the article appeared, that right, which the defendant claims also for future publications, cannot be deduced from its position after the publication. The defendant could, when the plaintiff approached it with a request for the withdrawal of the article, reflect at leisure whether the utterances objected to exceeded the measure permitted for the furtherance of its interests; as a champion of ecclesiastical interests its special concern should have been to examine carefully whether the general character of the plaintiff's journal justified such a severe denigration combined with a general attack on the reputations of its publisher and distributors. If the attack was objectively excessive, the defendant, which approved that excess, is in no way excused, as the Court of Appeal wrongly assumes, by the fact that, even if the form of expression were toned down, an objectively necessary contravention of law remains; for only an objectively necessary attack on the interests of others not the unnecessary, so-called excess is justified by the protection of justified interests.

Whether an injurious attack goes beyond the degree objectively permitted for the protection of interests is a question of fact. The Court of Appeal made no finding on it. Starting from its mistaken opinion that for the utterances complained of also to be objectively unlawful only the subjective conviction of the defendant was decisive that they were necessary, the Court of Appeal considered that the question was irrelevant whether an objectively unnecessary excessive attack existed. In this connection the Court of Appeal is of the opinion that it could not be its task 'to take up a position in the fight between two contesting philosophies of life represented here in the publications in question (the plaintiff's journal and the article for which the defendants were responsible) to examine the correctness of the value-judgments contained in them'. That is correct only in so far as the Court of Appeal is not bound to press judgment on the worth or worthlessness of the philosophical aims pursued by the parties, in so far as they are in opposition. If, however, it must be conceded to the plaintiff's journal, as is to be inferred from the reasoning in the judgment under appeal, that it may discuss questions relating to the philosophy of life, the Court of Appeal cannot refuse to decide whether the attack directed by the defendant against this journal, objectively considered, in respect of its content, form, and accompanying circumstances, falls within the limits of legally permitted promotion of interests. In this connection it is to be noted that the permitted degree of attack is to be determined differently when it is directed against a journal with a generally licentious content from when it concerns a journal whose pursuit of serious endeavours is—in whole or in part—not to be denied. For that determination the decisive factor is not single contributions to the journal but its general character. When dealing afresh with the dispute, the Court of Appeal must . . . examine . . . whether the plaintiff's journal (if assimilated to magazines generally regarded as of a scandalous type) has exploited in an unscrupulous and ethically reprehensible way the moral decline of the population for selfish and mercenary ends. In this connection the Court of Appeal will also have to consider that the wide-ranging moral condemnation of the persons behind the plaintiff and its publishing enterprise has been published in the defendant's periodical. Press attacks, however, have such incalculable and profound effects that the limits within which other legal interest may be violated by the promotion of interests of one's own must be drawn especially narrowly (RGSt 63, 92 [94]).

On this view of the law it can be left undecided whether the plaintiff as a company can be regarded as capable of being defamed. It is true that the doubts expressed by the Landgericht in that regard cannot be regarded as removed by the formal assignment, since the claim to forbear from uttering defamatory statements, being of a highly personal nature, cannot be assigned [reference]. Yet, if the unlawfulness of the statements in dispute is established, a basis is provided for an action under § 823 I BGB, so that no discussion is needed as to whether the defendant also infringed a statute serving to protect the plaintiff in the meaning of § 823 II BGB, since no wider claims would arise from that protective provision.

Notes to Cases 24–26

1. These three cases deal with the 'right of an established and operating business' which the German courts have added to the list of protected interests mentioned in § 823 I BGB. A brief account of the emergence of this new right can be found above in Ch. 2, section A. 2 (*e*) (iii). As in all judge-made rights one finds here, on the one hand the desire to expand the law and, on the other, the need to set workable and reasonable limits. The element of 'directness' is here relied upon and is extensively discussed in case 8, above. In the end, however, there is little doubt that policy dictates the results. Case 11, above, is also interesting in so far as it shows that the courts treat this as a residual right to be invoked only where there is no other remedy available to a deserving plaintiff. (A point clearly established in the important decision of 21 June 1966, BGHZ 45, 296 = NJW 1966, 1617 = JZ 1967, 174.) If, however, a particular factual situation is covered by a specific statutory rule (say, § 824 or § 826 BGB), then that rule must be applied; and if one of its conditions is not satisfied, one cannot fall back on this new right. As already stated, only 'business-connected' interests will be protected by this right. What exactly this means is difficult to say and, ultimately, it is for the courts to decide. Thus, see the most recent cases cited by Deutsch in *JZ* 1984, 308, 309.

2. The cases reproduced above have no exact equivalents in the Common law, the points they raise falling to be discussed under different headings of the law. Thus *Kaplan* v. *Helenhart Novelty Corp.* 182 F. 2d 311 (2nd Cir.

1950) is, to a point, factually analogous to cases 24 and 25, though the decision in that case went in favour of the defendant who had acted in good faith when he gave notice of an alleged infringement of the patent. For further discussion see Choate and Francis, *Patent Law* (2nd edn., 1981) and Rosenberg, *Patent Law Fundamentals* (2nd edn., 1980). Case 26, on the other hand, would raise issues which the Common law would, in part at least, discuss under the heading of defamation and freedom of expression. Many cases discussed in the next section (Constitutionalization of Private Law) deal with this issue. See, for example, BVerfGE 25, 256; BGH NJW 1984, 1956; BGH NJW 1985, 1620.

10. THE 'CONSTITUTIONALIZATION' OF PRIVATE LAW

Case 27

FEDERAL CONSTITUTIONAL COURT (FIRST SENATE) 15 JANUARY 1958*
BVerfGE 7, 198

1. Basic rights are primarily to protect the citizen against the state, but as enacted in the Constitution (GG) they also incorporate an objective scale of values which applies, as a matter of constitutional law, throughout the entire legal system.

2. The substance of the basic rights is expressed indirectly in the rules of private law, most evidently in its mandatory provisions, and is best effectuated by the judges' use of the general clauses.

3. Basic rights may be infringed by a judicial decision which ignores the effect of basic rights on private law (§ 90 Act on Constitutional Court Procedure (BVerfGG)). Judicial decisions on private law are subject to review by the Constitutional Court, only in respect of such infringements of basic rights, not for errors of law in general.

4. Rules of private law may count as 'general laws' which may restrict the basic right of freedom of expression under Art. 5 II GG.

5. Such 'general laws' must be interpreted in the light of the especial significance in a free democratic state of the basic right to freedom of expression.

6. The basic right in Art. 5 GG protects not only the utterance of an opinion as such, but also the effect it has on others.

7. The expression of an opinion favouring a boycott does not necessarily infringe proper conduct (*boni mores*) under § 826 BGB; depending on all the

* English version by Tony Weir.

circumstances such an expression may be justified as a matter of constitutional law.

Disposition

The decision of the Landgericht Hamburg of 22 November 1951 infringes the complainants' basic right under Art. 5 I, 1 GG and is therefore vacated. The matter is remitted to the Landgericht Hamburg.

Reasons

At the opening of 'German Film Week' on 20 September 1950 the complainant, then a Senator of the Free and Hanseatic City of Hamburg and Head of the State Press Office, gave an address, in his capacity as President of the Hamburg Press Club, to an audience of film distributors and directors. He said, *inter alia*:

The person least likely to restore the claim to morality which the German film forfeited during the Third Reich is the man who directed 'Jud Süss' and wrote the script for it. If this very man is chosen to represent the German film industry, who can tell what harm we may suffer throughout the world? True he was acquitted in a formal sense in Hamburg, but substantially the judgment was a condemnation. We must call on the distributors and cinema owners to show character—not cheap, but worth the price. And I want the German film to show character as well. If it shows character in its imagination, visual daring and sterling craftsmanship, it will merit every assistance and achieve what it needs in order to survive: success with the public here in Germany and abroad.

Domnick-Film-Produktion GmbH immediately challenged the complainant to justify these charges against Veit Harlan, under whose direction and with whose screen-play they were making 'Unsterbliche Geliebte'.

On 27 October 1950 the complainant released an 'open letter' to the Press by way of reply which contained the following:

The court did not gainsay the fact that for much of the Hitler régime Veit Harlan was the 'Nazi film-director no. 1' or that his film 'Jud Süss' showed him to be a committed exponent of the Nazis' murderous purge of the Jews. Some businessmen here and abroad may not be opposed to Veit Harlan's re-emergence, but the moral integrity of Germany must not be destroyed by hard-faced money-makers. Harlan's return can only reopen wounds barely healed, and resuscitate diminishing distrust fatal to German reconstruction. For all these reasons it is not only the right but the duty of all decent Germans to protest against, and even to boycott, this ignominious representative of the German film industry.

Domnick-Film-Produktion GmbH and Herzog-Film GmbH (the distributor of 'Unsterbliche Geliebte' in the Federal Republic), obtained an interlocutory injunction from the Landgericht Hamburg . . . and the

Oberlandesgericht dismissed the complainant's appeal. At the complainant's request the two film companies were required to bring suit within a certain time. They did so, and on 22 November 1951 the Landgericht Hamburg issued the following judgment:

The defendant is ordered, on pain of fine or imprisonment as determined by the court, to refrain (1) from calling on theatre managers and film distributors not to programme the film 'Unsterbliche Geliebte' and (2) from calling on the German public not to go to see the film . . .

B. I.

The complaint is admissible since the preconditions for the application of § 90 II, 2 BVerfGG are satisfied (decision before exhaustion of legal remedies).

II.

The complainant alleges that the Landgericht's judgment infringes his basic right to free expression of opinion as laid down in Art. 5 I, 1 GG.

The judgment of the Landgericht, an act of the public power of *judicature*, could infringe the complainant's basic right by its *content* only if the court was bound to take account of the complainant's basic right.

By enjoining the complainant from making statements apt to lead others to endorse his views about Harlan's re-emergence and to follow him in discriminating against Harlan's films, the judgment clearly restricts the complainant's freedom of expression of opinion. The Landgericht granted the injunction as a matter of private law order on the basis that the complainant's statements were tortious under § 826 BGB. Thus the public power has restricted the complainant's freedom of expression on the basis of the plaintiff's private law claim. This can constitute an infringement of the complainant's basic right under Art. 5 I, 1 GG only if the applicable rules of private law are so substantially affected that they can no longer support the judgment.

The question whether basic rights affect private law, and if so in what manner, is much debated [references]. The extreme positions are, on the one hand, that basic rights constrain only the state, and, on the other, that basic rights (or at any rate the most important of them) prevail against everyone in private legal relations. Previous decisions of this Court support neither of these extreme positions, the conclusions drawn by the Federal Labour court in its decision of 10 May 1957 (NJW 1957, 1688) from our decisions of 17 and 23 January 1957 (BVerfGE 6, 55 and 6, 84) being unwarranted. Nor is it necessary today to deal with all aspects of the debated question of the 'effect on third parties' (*Drittwirkung*) of basic rights. The matter can be properly resolved by the following considerations:

1. There is no doubt that the main purpose of basic rights is to protect the individual's sphere of freedom against encroachment by public power: they are the citizen's bulwark against the state. This emerges from both their development as a matter of intellectual history and their adoption into the constitutions of the various states as a matter of political history: it is true also of the basic rights in the Basic Law, which emphasizes the priority of human dignity against the power of the state by placing the section on basic rights at its head and by providing that the constitutional complaint (*Verfassungsbeschwerde*), the special legal device for vindicating these rights, lies only in respect of acts of the public power.

But far from being a value-free system [references] the Constitution erects an objective system of values in its section on basic rights, and thus expresses and reinforces the validity of the basic rights [references]. This system of values, centring on the freedom of the human being to develop in society, must apply as a constitutional axiom throughout the whole legal system: it must direct and inform legislation, administration, and judicial decision. It naturally influences private law as well; no rule of private law may conflict with it, and all such rules must be construed in accordance with its spirit.

The legal content of basic rights as objective norms informs private law by means of the rules which directly control this area of law. Just as new rules must conform to the value-system of the basic rights, so existing and older rules receive from it a definite constitutional content which thereafter determines their construction. From the point of view of substantive and procedural law a dispute between private citizens on the rights and duties that arise from rules of conduct thus influenced by the basic rights remains a dispute of private law. It is private law which is interpreted and applied even if its interpreters must follow the public law of the constitution.

The influence of the value-system of the basic rights is clearest in those rules of private law which are mandatory (*zwingendes Recht*) and form part of *ordre public* in the wide sense, i.e. those rules which in the public interest apply to private legal relations whether the parties so choose or not. Such provisions, being functionally related and complementary to public law, are especially exposed to the influence of constitutional law. 'General clauses', such as § 826 BGB, by which human conduct is measured against extralegal standards such as 'proper conduct' (*gute Sitten*), allow the courts to respond to this influence since in deciding what is required in a particular case by such social commands, they must start from the value-system adopted by the society in its constitution at that stage of its cultural and spiritual development. The general clauses have thus been rightly described as 'points of entry' for basic rights into private law [references].

The judge is constitutionally bound to ascertain whether the applicable rules of substantive private law have been influenced by basic rights in the manner described; if so, he must construe and apply the rules as so modified. This is what is meant by saying that the civil judge is bound by the basic rights (Art. 1 III GG). If he issues a judgment which ignores this constitutional influence on the rules of private law, he contravenes not only objective constitutional law by misconceiving the content of the objective norm underlying the basic law, but also, by his judgment, in his capacity as a public official, contravenes the Constitution itself, which the citizen is constitutionally entitled to have respected by the judiciary. Quite apart from any remedies he may have to correct this error in the courts of private law, the citizen can invoke the Federal Constitutional Court by means of a *Verfassungsbeschwerde.*

The Constitutional Court must determine whether the reach and effect of the basic rights in private law has been correctly ascertained by the regular courts. But this is also the limit of its investigation: it is not for the Constitutional Court to check judgments of civil courts for errors of law in general; the Constitutional Court simply judges of the 'radiant effect' of the basic rights on private law and implements the values inherent in the precept of constitutional law. The function of the *Verfassungsbeschwerde* is to test *all* acts, whether of the legislature, the executive or the judiciary, for 'compatibility with the Constitution' (§ 90 BVerfGG). The Federal Constitutional Court is certainly not to act as a court of review, much less overreview, for the civil courts, but neither may it abjure consideration of such judgments entirely or leave uncorrected any instance which comes to its notice of the misapplication of the rules of basic rights.

2. The basic right to freedom of expression of opinion (Art. 5 GG) seems to pose special problems with regard to the relationship between basic rights and private law. As in the Weimar Constitution (Art. 118), this right is constitutionally guaranteed only within the limits of 'general laws' (Art. 5 II GG). Before inquiring what laws are 'general laws' in this sense, one might suppose that the constitution's reference to such laws must be to such laws as judicially construed, with the result that no judicial construction of such a law which limited the basic right could be regarded as a 'breach' of the basic right.

This is not, however, the sense of the reference to 'general laws'. The basic right to freedom of expression, the most immediate aspect of the human personality in society, is one of the most precious rights of man (Declaration of the Rights of Man and Citizen (1789) Art. 11). It is absolutely essential to a free and democratic state, for it alone permits that constant spiritual interaction, the conflict of opinion, which is its vital element (BVerfGE 5, 85 (205)). In a certain sense it is the basis of freedom itself, 'the matrix, the indispensable condition of nearly every other form of freedom' (Cardozo).

Given this fundamental importance for the free democratic state of freedom of expression of opinion, it would be illogical for a constitution to make its actual scope contingent on mere statute (and thus necessarily on the holdings of courts construing it). What was said earlier about the relationship between basic rights and private law applies here also: general laws which have the effect of limiting a basic right must be read in the light of its significance and always be construed so as to preserve the special value of this right, with, in a free democracy, a presumption in favour of freedom of speech in all areas, and especially in public life. We must not see the relationship between basic right and 'general laws' as one in which 'general laws' by their terms set limits to the basic right, but rather that relationship must be construed in the light of the special significance of this basic right in a free democratic state, so that the limiting effect of 'general laws' on the basic right is itself limited.

In its function as ultimate guardian of the basic rights through the medium of the *Verfassungsbeschwerde*, the Federal Constitutional Court must therefore have the power to supervise the decisions of courts whose application of a general law in this area may unduly restrict the scope of the basic right in the individual case. This Court must be competent to uphold as against *all* organs of public power, including the civil courts, the special value it represents for a free democracy, and thus to reconcile, as required by constitutional law, the conflicting restrictive tendencies of the basic right and the 'general laws'.

3. The concept of 'general' law has always been controversial. Leaving on one side the question whether the concept may not be due to an error in the drafting of Art. 118 of the 1919 Constitution [reference], we may note that it was then construed to include all which 'do not forbid an opinion as such and do not envisage the expression of opinion as such', but rather 'serve to protect a legal interest which deserves protection without regard to any particular opinion', and protect 'a community value superior to the activity of freedom of opinion' [reference]. Exponents of the Grundgesetz agree with this [reference: 'laws which do not inhibit the purely intellectual effect of a mere expression of opinion'].

If the term 'general laws' is so understood, we may state the protection of the basic right as follows:

It is unacceptable to hold that the Constitution protects only the expression of opinion, and not its inherent or intended effect on others, for the whole point of an expression of *opinion* is to have 'an effect on the environment of ideas' [reference]. Thus value-judgments, which always have an intellectual aim, namely to persuade others, are protected by Art. 5 I, 1 GG; indeed it is the stance of the speaker as expressed in the value-judgment by which he hopes to affect others which is principally protected by this basic right. To protect the expression and not to protect its effect would be a nonsense.

In this sense the expression of opinion is free in so far as its effect on the mind is concerned; but that does not mean that one is entitled, just because one is expressing an opinion, to prejudice interests of another which deserve protection against freedom of opinion. There has to be a 'balance of interests'; the right to express an opinion must yield if its exercise infringes interests of another which have a superior claim to protection. Whether such an interest exists in a particular case depends on all the circumstances.

4. From this point of view the rules of private law may perfectly well be ranked as 'general laws' in the sense of Art. 5 II GG. If this has not been done by commentators hitherto [reference], that is simply because basic rights have been considered good only as against the state, so it was natural to consider as 'general laws' having limiting effect only those laws which regulated state activity *vis-à-vis* the individual, that is, laws of a public law nature. But if the basic right to free expression of opinion affects relations of private law as well and favours free expression of opinion against the fellow-citizen also, then rules of private law which operate to protect superior legal interests must also be taken into account as possibly limiting the basic right. After all, if provisions of criminal law designed to protect honour or other essential aspects of human personality can set limits to the exercise of the fundamental right to freedom of expression, it is not obvious why similar provisions of private law should not equally do so.

Case 28

FEDERAL CONSTITUTIONAL COURT (FIRST SENATE) 24 FEBRUARY
1971*
BVerfGE 30, 173

Reasons

The complainant seeks constitutional review of the injunction obtained by the adopted son and sole heir of Gustaf Gründgens, actor and theatre director, against the printing, distribution, or publication of a book by Klaus Mann entitled *Mephisto, a Novel, or How to Get on in the World.*

The author left Germany in 1933 and published the novel in Amsterdam in 1936 (Querido Verlag). Seven years after his death in 1949 it was published in East Germany.

The novel portrays the rise of Hendrik Höfgen, a talented actor who in order to make a career for himself as an artist in collusion with Nazi pow-

* English version by Tony Weir.

ers, is false to his true political leanings and rides roughshod over all human and ethical considerations. The psychological, intellectual, and sociological factors which made such a career possible are all laid out.

The model for Hendrik Höfgen was the actor Gustaf Gründgens, one of the Hamburger Kammerspieler in the 1920s, when he was a friend of Klaus Mann and briefly married to his sister Erika. Gründgens and his career are reflected in numerous characteristics of Hendrik Höfgen, including his physical appearance, the plays he acted in, and his appointments as State Councillor and Director-General of the State Theatre of Prussia.

Of the relationship between the fictional Höfgen and the real Gründgens Klaus Mann wrote in *The Turning Point* (New York, 1942):

I visualize my ex-brother-in-law as the traitor *par excellence*, the macabre embodiment of corruption and cynicism. So intense was the fascination of his shameful glory that I decided to portray Mephisto-Gründgens in a satirical novel. I thought it pertinent, indeed, necessary to expose and analyse the abject type of the treacherous intellectual who prostitutes his talent for the sake of some tawdry fame and transitory wealth.

Gustaf was just one among others—in reality as well as in the composition of my narrative. He served me as a focus around which I could make gyrate the pathetic and nauseous crowd of petty climbers and crooks.

In the revised version which appeared in Germany in 1948 (*Der Wendepunkt*), we find at p. 334:

The third book published during my exile, in 1936, *Mephisto*, deals with an unsympathetic character. Why did I write it? The actor I portray has talent, but not much else going for him. He has none of those moral qualities which form what is commonly spoken of as 'character'. Instead of 'character' Hendrik Höfgen has only ambition, vanity, passion for publicity and desire for effect. He is not a man but a posturer.

Was such a figure worth writing a novel about? Yes, indeed. For the posturer represents and symbolises the regime, posturing, false and unrealistic. In a state run by liars and dissemblers the actor has a triumphant role. *Mephisto* is the story of a career in the Third Reich.

In a perceptive review in *Das Neue Tagebuch* in 1937 Herman Kesten rightly suggested that perhaps the author wanted to show a real actor among the bloody amateurs in the horror play. He went on: 'The author goes further: he gives us a paradigm of the "fellow-traveller", one of the millions of petty crooks who themselves commit no grand crime but sup with murderers, not principals but accessories after the event; they do not kill but conceal the corpse, and in order to get more than they deserve lick the blood of the innocent from the boots of the mighty. This host of petty toadies and bootlickers are the prop of the powerful.'

This is exactly the type I wanted to draw: I couldn't have stated my intentions better myself. *Mephisto* is not, as some people have maintained, a *roman-à-clef*. The infamously brilliant and cynically ruthless go-getter, who is the central figure of my satire may have certain traits in common with a certain real actor still allegedly with us. Is my character Councillor and Director-General Höfgen a portrait of the friend of my youth, Councillor and Director-General Gründgens? Not entirely. There are many differences between Höfgen and my erstwhile brother-in-law. But even if the character were closer to the original than it is, Gründgens is not the 'hero' of my tract for the times, since it is not about an individual at all but about the type. Others could have served as a model just as well. My choice fell upon Gründgens not because he was outstandingly awful (indeed he was rather better than many another idol of the Third Reich) but simply because I happened to know him well. It was precisely our earlier acquaintance which led me to make a novel out of the incredible, fascinating and fantastic story of his rise and fall.

II.

1. In August 1963 the complainant announced the publication of *Mephisto*, and suit was brought by the adoptive son and sole heir of Gustaf Gründgens, who died in October 1963. The claim alleged that anyone at all familiar with German theatre in the 1920s and 1930s would link Höfgen with Gründgens; that in addition to many recognizable facts the novel contained many hurtful fictions which helped to give a false and highly derogatory picture of Gründgens's character. The novel was not a work of art but a *roman-à-clef* written to avenge Gründgens's marriage to Mann's sister Erika, which he believed dishonourable.

The plaintiff sought an injunction forbidding the reproduction, distribution, and publication of *Mephisto* on pain of punishment.

The claim was rejected by the Landgericht Hamburg. Thereupon, in September 1965, the complainant published the novel with a foreword stating 'All characters in this novel are types, not portraits. K.M.' On 23 November 1965 the plaintiff obtained an interlocutory injunction from the Hanseatic Oberlandesgericht in Hamburg and the following foreword was included:

TO THE READER

Klaus Mann wrote this novel in Amsterdam in 1936, having left Germany voluntarily on grounds of conscience. In it he gives a critical view, animated by his hatred of Hitler's dictatorship, of contemporary conditions in the German theatre. While there are undeniable resemblances to actual figures of the day, the characters are primarily creatures of the author's imagination. This is especially true of the principal character, whose conduct and beliefs are at any rate largely imaginary. That is why the author prefaced the book with the explanation: 'All characters in this work are types, not portraits.'

. . .

This Court must determine whether in applying the rules of private law the judicial decisions under attack misconceived the meaning of the basic rights of whose infringement the complainant complains or infringed the basic rights themselves [references]. Such constitutional 'fall-out effects' depend principally on the scope of the right to artistic freedom (Art. 5 III, 1 GG) and the right to freedom of expression (Art. 5 I GG), and especially on the relationship between these rights and the protection afforded by these decisions to the human personality of the late Gustaf Gründgens under Art. 1 I and 1 II, 1 GG.

III.

Art. 5 III, 1 GG declares that along with science, research, and teaching, art is free. By its terms and intention the guarantee in Art. 5 III, 1 is an objective value-laden basic norm regulating the relationship between art and the state. It also guarantees the individual freedom of the artist.

1. The field of 'art' must be determined by the distinctive structural features of the artistic enterprise. The essence of artistic endeavour lies in the free creative process whereby the artist, in his chosen communicative medium, gives immediate perceptible form to what he has felt, learnt, or experienced. Artistic activity involves both the conscious and the unconscious, in a manner not rationally separable. Intuition, imagination, and knowledge of the art all play a part in artistic creation; it is not so much communication as expression, indeed the most immediate expression of the artist's individuality.

The freedom guaranteed covers the artistic creation as regards both the work produced and the effect produced by it. The two form an indissociable unity. The exhibition and dissemination of the work are as important as its creation for art as the specifically artistic enterprise; indeed, the 'area of effect', public access to the work of art, is the ground in which Art. 5 III GG is rooted. A glance back at the artistic policy of the Nazi regime shows that to guarantee merely the individual rights of artists cannot ensure the freedom of art: the basic right would prove hollow unless it extends from the personal zone of the artist to the area of impact.

2. It is not here possible to give an exhaustive definition of the scope of the constitutional guarantee of freedom of art in all its various forms. Nor is it necessary for the case in hand, since it is common ground in the courts below, between the parties and probably all experts, that the novel in question ranks as a work of art. We may therefore concentrate on factors relevant to the appraisal of an example of the narrative art which by dealing with actual events courts the risk of conflicting with the rights and interests of the persons portrayed.

In putting real events in a work of art the artist 'recreates' them for he sunders them from their actual context and places them in a novel setting dominated by his concern for striking presentation rather than by their own actuality. Artistic unity may, and sometimes must, prime the truth of the occurrence.

The role and purpose of Art. 5 III, 1 GG is above all to give protection against encroachment by the public power on any specifically artistic undertakings, actions, and decisions. One cannot without inhibiting the free development of the creative artistic endeavour prescribe how the artist should react to reality or reproduce his reactions to it. The artist is the sole judge of the 'rightness' of his response. To this extent the guarantee of artistic freedom means that one must not seek to affect the manner in which the artist goes about his business, the material he selects, or the way in which he treats it, and certainly not seek to narrow the area in which he may operate or lay down general rules for the creative process. As to narrative works of art the constitutional guarantee means that the artist must be free to choose and treat his topic free from attempts by the state to limit the area of specifically artistic judgment by rules or binding value-judgments. This applies also, indeed especially, when the artist is dealing with actual events: 'committed art' is not excluded from the constitutional guarantee.

3. Art. 5 III, 1 GG is a comprehensive guarantee of the freedom of artistic activity. Thus where intermediaries are needed in order to establish relations between the artist and the public they too are protected by the constitutional guarantee. As a product of the narrative art needs to be reproduced, distributed, and published in order to have any effect on the public, the publisher's function as intermediary is indispensable, so the constitutional guarantee extends to his activity as well. Thus, as publisher of the novel, the complainant may invoke the basic right contained in Art. 5 III, 1 GG (see also BVerfGE 10, 118, (121); 12, 205 (260) on the freedom of the Press).

4. Art having its special nature and rules, its guarantee by Art. 5 III, 1 GG is absolute. The clear terms of that provision foredoom any attempt to limit it, whether by narrowing the idea of art in the light of one's value-judgments or by extending or invoking the limitations applicable to other constitutional provisions.

The Bundesgerichtshof was quite right to state that Art. 5 II GG which limits basic rights under Art. 5 I is inapplicable here. The different guarantees in Art. 5 GG are systematically separated, and this shows that the limitations in Art. 5 II are inapplicable to matters covered by Art. 5 III, since Art. 5 III is a *lex specialis* in relation to Art. 5 I. Nor is it acceptable to sever parts of a narrative work of art, call them expressions of opinion under Art. 5 I and then apply to them the limitations laid down in Art. 5 II. Nor do the *travaux préparatoires* of Art. 5 III support the view that the authors of the

Constitution regarded freedom of art as a subspecies of freedom of expression or opinion.

. . .

Nor can one accept that the freedom of art is limited under Art. 2 I, 2 GG by the rights of others, by the constitutional order or by the moral law. Such a view would be incompatible with the constant holding of this Court that Art. 2 I GG is subsidiary and the individual freedoms special [references] in a manner which bars the extension of the community priority of Art. 2 I, 2 GG in the light of the use of Art. 2 I GG. Nor are these limitations applicable to the area of effect of works of art.

5. Yet there are limits to this freedom. The freedom incorporated in Art. 5 III, 1 GG, like all basic rights, is rooted in the Constitution's conception of man as a responsible person free to develop within society [references]. The absolute nature of the guarantee of artistic freedom means that its limits are to be found only within the Constitution itself. The freedom of art is not subject to mere statute, it cannot be qualified by the general legal system or be at the mercy of any vague clause about essential interests of state and society which lacks constitutional basis and is uncontained by the rule of law. If the guarantee of artistic freedom gives rise to any conflict, it must be resolved by construction in terms of the order of values enshrined in the Basic Law and in line with the unitary system of values which underlies it. As part of this system of basic rights the freedom of art is co-ordinate with the dignity of man as guaranteed by Art. 1 GG, the supreme and controlling value of the whole system of basic rights (BVerfGE 6, 32 [41]; 27, 1 [6]). Given the effect which a work of art may have on the social plane, the guarantee of artistic freedom may come into conflict with the area of human personality, equally protected by the Constitution.

A person's claim to respect and value may be affected by an artist's use of details of character and career of actual people as in addition to being an aesthetic reality, such a work also has existence in the realm of social facts and the social effects are not dissipated by being artistically transmuted. Such social effects while taking place beside the artistic effects must nevertheless be appraised with regard to the scope of the guarantee of Art. 5 III, 1 GG, since in the work of art the 'real' and 'aesthetic' worlds are unified.

6. The courts below were right in this connection to invoke Art. 1 I GG in their appraisal of its protective effect on the area of personality of the late actor Gustaf Gründgens. It would be inconsistent with the constitutional mandate of the inviolability of human dignity, which underlies all basic rights, if a person could be belittled and denigrated after his death.

Accordingly an individual's death does not put an end to the state's duty under Art. 1 I GG to protect him from assaults on his human dignity.

In addition the Bundesgerichtshof and Oberlandesgericht held that Art. 2 I GG also had radiant protective effects in private law for Gründgens, though to a degree diminished by his death. However, only a living person is so entitled: the right of personality cannot survive death. An essential pre-condition of the basic right under Art. 2 I GG is the existence of at least a potential or a future person. It is irrelevant that a person may be affected during his lifetime by what the legal situation will be after his death, though this weighed with the Bundesgerichtshof. It is no derogation from the freedom of action and self-determination guaranteed by Art. 2 I GG to hold that the protection of the personality expires on death.

7. The resolution of the tension between the protection of the personality and the right to the artistic freedom cannot turn solely on the 'social' effects of a work of art but must also take account of specifically aesthetic considerations. The conception of man which underlies Art. 1 I GG is as much infused with the guarantee of freedom in Art. 5 III, 1 GG as the latter is influenced by the value implicit in Art. 1 I GG. The individual's claim to social respect and value is not superior to artistic freedom, but neither can art simply ignore the individual's claim to proper respect.

Only by weighing all the circumstances of the given case can one decide whether the publication of a work which artistically deploys true details about an actual person poses a serious threat of encroachment on the protected area of his personality. One consideration must be whether and how far the artistic treatment of the material and its incorporation into the work as an organic whole have made the 'copy' independent of the 'original' by rendering objective, symbolical, and figurative what was individualized, personal, and intimate. If such an aesthetic appraisal reveals that the artist has indeed produced, or even intended to produce, a 'portrait' of the 'original', the outcome will depend on the extent of the artistic alienation and how seriously the 'falsification' damages the reputation or memory of the subject.

IV.

This Court must therefore decide whether in balancing the protection afforded by Art. 1 I GG to the personality of the late Gustaf Gründgens and his adopted son against the guarantee of artistic freedom under Art. 5 III, 1 GG the courts below have upheld the principles just stated. However, in this Court the opinions on that matter are equally divided, so it cannot hold that the decisions under attack infringed the Constitution (§ 15 II, 4 BVerfGG).

. . .

3. This Court has always held that a *Verfassungsbeschwerde* empowers it to review judicial decisions only within narrow limits, and that in particular it cannot review the facts as found and evaluated, the construction of mere law or its application in the individual case, which are matters for the regular courts [references]. These principles apply equally when review is sought of the balancing of the protection afforded to the parties to a civil suit by Art. 1 I of Art. 5 III, 1 GG.

. . .

This Court is not, like a court of appeal, empowered to substitute its own opinion of the case for that of the proper judge. In cases like these it can only hold that the basic right of the losing party has been infringed if the judge has either failed to recognize that it is a case of balancing conflicting basic rights or has based his judgment on a fundamentally false view of the importance, and especially the scope, of either of those rights.

When the judgements under attack are so tested, it emerges that the Oberlandesgericht and the Bundesgerichtshof recognized that a balancing act was required in order to resolve the tension between the rights emanating from Art. 1 I GG and Art. 5 III, 1 GG, and that the judgments as a whole do not seem to be based on a fundamentally erroneous view of the importance or scope of the two basic rights.

Notes to Cases 27–28

1. The constitutionalization of private law is an important and modern development of the law which, on the whole, though studied by national lawyers (especially in Germany and the USA) has received little attention from comparatists. One reason for this may be the fact that comparatists have, traditionally, been private lawyers; and even their groupings of legal systems into families has often been attempted with private law primarily in mind. Clearly, in a case-book on tort, one cannot give this topic the attention it deserves. The reader should, therefore, read these two decisions in conjunction with the brief comments contained in paragraph six of Chapter 1 and treat them as providing the constitutional background to the privacy cases discussed in the next section.

2. The significance of cases 27 and 28 goes beyond the status of freedom of expression in Germany. Arguably, the most important part of *Lüth* is its 'doctrine of interaction' (*Wechselwirkungslehre*) which shows that the basic human rights contained in Arts. 1–19 of the Constitution of Bonn of 1949 do not have a *direct* effect in relations between private citizens. Rather, the impact they have is via the mandatory rules (*ius cogens*) of private law and, especially, the various general clauses of private law (e.g. §§ 138, 242, 823 I and 826 BGB) which must be interpreted in conformity with the fundamental values of the Constitution. The practical result is that the judge balances

the various competing interests before reaching his decision, freedom of expression (Art. 5 of the Constitution) being a cardinal but *not absolute* value (as this is made clear by para. II of that same article as well as by Art. 20). The *Lüth* doctrine was finally and conclusively incorporated into the civil law by the *Höllenfeuer* decision of 21 June 1966 (BGHZ 45, 296 = NJW 1966, 1617 = JZ 1967, 174) which was also a case dealing with the balancing of the right of an established and operating business against freedom of expression. The result is that

in a public law action between an individual and the state, a constitutional right can directly override an otherwise applicable rule of public law. In private law disputes between individuals, in contrast, constitutional rights [are] said to 'influence' rules of civil law rather than actually to override them. A certain intellectual content 'flows' or 'radiates' from the constitutional law into the civil law and affects the interpretation of existing civil law rules. In such cases the rules of private law are to be interpreted and applied in [the] light of the applicable constitutional norm, but it is nonetheless the civil law rules that are ultimately to be applied. (Quint, 'Free Speech and Private Law in German Constitutional Theory' 48 *Maryland L. Rev.* 247, 263 (1989).)

3. *Lüth* accepts that even in such cases the dispute 'remains substantially and procedurally a dispute of civil law' (BVerfGE 7, 198, 205–6). What, then, is the precise role of the Constitutional Court? The answer is not, apparently, entirely clear. According to the *Mephisto* case (BVerfGE 30, 173, 197) the 'evaluative' process of the competing interests was to be left to the civil law judges, with the Constitutional Court retaining the right to intervene only if the civil law decision was based on a fundamental misconception of the basic rights. In some subsequent decisions, however, the Constitutional Court has permitted itself a greater latitude for review, especially whenever there was a 'serious' invasion of a basic right. See the *Deutschland-Magazin* case (BVerfGE 42, 143) where the civil court's decision was not disturbed and the *Echternach* decision (BVerfGE 42, 163) where the State Court decision was reversed. As the court put it (ibid. 168), 'The more a civil court's decision infringes the predicates of free existence and action that are protected by a basic right, the more searching must be the Constitutional Court's investigation to determine whether the infringement is constitutionally justified.' (Translation by P. Quint, op. cit., 322.) These and subsequent important decisions (notably in the *Böll* case (BVerfGE 54, 208) and the *Wallraff* case (BVerfGE 66, 131)) are discussed by Quint, 302 ff.

4. *Lüth*, still regarded as the leading case, can be compared with *NAACP v. Claiborne Hardware Co.* 458 US 886 (1982). Note, however, that the careful evaluative process advocated by *Lüth* (and also found in the *Lebach* case) is absent from *Claiborne*. This preference for *ad hoc* balancing tech-

niques has not, on the whole, found much favour with American courts in first amendment disputes. What are the merits and demerits of these differing approaches? What other differences with US law do these German decisions reveal? Consider, for example, the following remarks made by Professor Quint in his thoughtful comparative study, op. cit. 247, 273–5 (notes omitted):

[A comparative] examination . . . indicates that the force of the American Constitution in disputes between individuals is in some instances weaker and in some instances stronger than the effect of the German Basic Law under the doctrine of the *Lüth* case. In those actions between individuals in which state action is found to exist, the United States Constitution supersedes the 'private law'. In contrast, in German cases involving disputes between individuals, the Basic Law only 'influences' the rules of private law. The values of private law remain present in the balance and must be accommodated. Moreover . . . the fact that the action remains a private law action may have a significant limiting effect on the scope of the Constitutional Court's review. In these respects, therefore, the impact of the Basic Law on disputes between individuals appears weaker than the impact of the American Constitution in those disputes in which state action would be found under American doctrine.

In contrast, in those private disputes in which state action does not exist under American doctrine, the impact of the German Basic Law becomes stronger than that of the United States Constitution. Where there is no state action in American law, the United States Constitution ordinarily has no effect at all. Under American doctrine, therefore, if there is state action, constitutional rights theoretically apply with full vigour; if there is no state action, there are no constitutional rights. Under the German Basic Law, however, the fact that a certain dispute of private law lies beyond where the state action would be drawn under the United States Constitution has no particular meaning. The rules of private law are still 'influenced' by the basic rights of the Constitution. Thus the German Constitution continues to have an impact in cases in which no state action would be found under American law.

This difference between German and American doctrine is perhaps most notable in the area of contractual relations—particularly private employment contracts—in which the United States Constitution generally has no impact. In these cases the German Basic Law can have some force. [See BAGE 47, 363—the application of unconstitutional rights in private legal relations under German law] . . . doctrine is not exhausted, however, by its 'influence' on those contractual relationships in which the United States Constitution does not ordinarily apply. Indeed, the 'influence' of the German Constitution on the norms of private law may even lead, in some circumstances, to something that looks very much like the judicial creation of a constitutional tort action by one private person against *another private person* to redress a constitutional violation—another use of constitutional rights that is generally unknown in American doctrine. With respect to the right of free speech, this result was first suggested by the *Blinkfüer* case, a decision that resembles *Lüth* in certain important respects [BVerfGE 25, 256].

5. The *Lüth* and *Mephisto* cases give some indication of how this balancing act is carried out. The first case deals with speech which may affect—indeed aims at affecting—another person's economic interests; the second involves reputation. There is a third category of cases which deals with internal security, treason, and sedition in relation to free speech. This is exemplified by the *Spiegel* seizure case of 5 August 1966 (BVerfGE 20, 162). Cases like this, as well as decisions banning extreme political parties, e.g. the neo-Nazi party (BVerfGE 2, 1) or the Communist party (BVerfGE 5, 85) invite comparison with Anglo-American law and many suggest that the suppression of extreme political activity, even in the absence of 'imminent lawless action' (cf. *Brandenburg* v. *Ohio* 395 US 444, 447 (1969)), may be the result of the German experience in the 1930s. Clearly, at first sight German law appears to be less tolerant than American law; but, it must be stressed again, the decisions of the Federal Constitutional Court must always be seen against the background of the German experience between the two Wars *and* Art. 21 II of the Constitution of 1949 which enables the banning of political parties which aim at abolishing the existing liberal-democratic order. Lack of space makes the further examination of this topic impossible.

6. *Lüth*, as stated, was a case dealing with an invitation to boycott films made by a former Nazi sympathizer. Lüth won, and in the balancing process the 'purity' of his motives (the wish to protect the cultural interests of the community rather than to make money for himself) seemed to have weighed heavily in his favour. In other instances, however, where excessive economic pressure was applied and monetary gain was at stake, the courts, though following the *Lüth* dictate that the relevant interests should be balanced, in the end showed less favour for free speech. The *Blinkfüer* case of 26 February 1969 (BVerfGE 25, 256) is a case in point where the Axel Springer Publishing House tried to stop news dealers from handling a left-wing periodical by threatening to stop supplying them their papers if they continued to handle the periodical in question. The action for damages by the owners of the periodical—desisted on grounds that it impinged on Springer's freedom of expression—failed in the civil courts but succeeded in the Constitutional Court for the reasons indicated above. Other cases, dealing with boycotts and illustrating the courts' balancing process, include BGH NJW 1985, 1620 = JZ 1985, 587; BGH NJW 1984, 1956.

7. The *Mephisto* case is different, dealing with protection of reputation and the clash this can provoke with free speech. Like other cases, e.g. the *Schmid-Spiegel* decision of 25 January 1961 (BVerfGE 12, 113), it contrasts sharply with cases like *New York Times* v. *Sullivan* (376 US 255 [1964]), though before the reader draws any adverse comparative conclusions he should bear in mind the more detailed, complicated, and inter-related provisions of the German Constitution.

Freedom of expression is limited by Art. 5 II of the Constitution by the 'provisions of the general laws'—in practice §§ 186–7 of the Criminal Code which deal with the crimes of insult and defamation. But it may also be limited by other constitutional provisions e.g. Art. 1 (protecting the inviolable dignity of human beings) and Art. 2 (protecting the free development of personality). *Lüth* required the courts to balance freedom of expression and personal reputation given the facts of each case. In *Mephisto* the Constitutional Court is balancing two different *constitutional freedoms* and by a narrow majority came down in favour of human dignity enshrined in Art. 1 of the Constitution—a protection that endures even after death. (In another important case involving the well-known writer Heinrich Böll (BVerfGE 54, 208) the action was based on both Arts. 1 and 2 of the Constitution; see, also, JZ 1990, 37—a case concerning the painter *Emil Nolde*.)

8. These cases and the Privacy decisions reproduced in the next section, require frequent references to the human rights provisions of the Constitution, so Arts. 1–19 are reproduced in the addendum that follows. The translations are by the Press and Information Office of the Federal Government in Bonn and were kindly supplied by the Cultural Office of the German Embassy in London. Teachers should also set them in their proper historical context in which the ghosts of the Nazi period, combined with the cold-war climate of the 1950s and 1960s, provided an environment which Anglo-American scholars may often find difficult to appreciate. Thus the *Lüth* controversy was provoked by Veit Harlan's record as a film director during the Nazi era. One of his films in particular, apparently produced under the general overview of Josef Goebbels (the propaganda minister of the Third Reich), was so violently anti-Jewish that its circulation was, in the post-war era, treated as a criminal offence. Such a record led another post-war criminal court to find Harlan guilty of crimes against humanity, though in the end he was acquitted on the ground that he was acting under 'duress'. He was also classified as 'exonerated' in the de-Nazification proceedings and, after a brief interlude, attempted to re-enter the cinema world with the (politically innocuous) film that provoked the present litigation. The facts of the *Mephisto* novel, written by Klaus Mann, son of the well-known author Thomas Mann, are given in the judgment. But the character in the novel was largely modelled on Gustaf Gründgens (an actor and, ultimately, director of the Prussian State Theatre) who was a protégé of Hermann Göring's. Gründgens, along with many others (including some eminent academics) who collaborated, benefited, or willingly tolerated the Nazi regime survived, often completely unaffected, into the post-war era. Gründgens, in fact, died naturally in 1963 whereas Klaus Mann committed suicide in 1949. Interesting historical background can be found in: K. Mann, *Der Wendepunkt: Ein Lebensbericht* (1981).

9. A compressed but interesting comparative account of American, English, and German law can be found in Barendt's *Freedom of Speech* (1985) (paperback with an updating postscript 1987); Humphries, *Media and Media Policy in West Germany. The Press and Broadcasting since 1945* (1990); Kommers, *The Constitutional Jurisprudence of the Federal Republic of Germany* (1989).

Addendum

The Constitution of the Federal Republic of Germany, 8 May 1949 (as subsequently amended)

1. Basic Rights

Article 1 (Protection of human dignity)
(1) The dignity of man shall be inviolable. To respect and protect it shall be the duty of all state authority.
(2) The German people therefore acknowledge inviolable and inalienable human rights as the basis of every community, of peace and of justice in the world.
(3)* The following basic rights shall bind the legislature, the executive, and the judiciary as directly enforceable law.

Article 2 (Rights of liberty)
(1) Everyone shall have the right to the free development of his personality in so far as he does not violate the rights of others or offend against the constitutional order or the moral code.
(2) Everyone shall have the right to life and to inviolability of his person. The liberty of the individual shall be inviolable. These rights may only be encroached upon pursuant to a law.

Article 3 (Equality before the law)
(1) All persons shall be equal before the law.
(2) Men and women shall have equal rights.
(3) No one may be prejudiced or favoured because of his sex, his parentage, his race, his language, his homeland and origin, his faith, or his religious or political opinions.

Article 4 (Freedom of faith and creed)
(1) Freedom of faith, of conscience, and freedom of creed, religious or ideological (*weltanschaulich*), shall be inviolable.
(2) The undisturbed practice of religion is guaranteed.
(3) No one may be compelled against his conscience to render war service involving the use of arms. Details shall be regulated by a federal law.

* As amended by federal Act of 19 March 1956 (*Federal Law Gazette* I, p. 111).

Article 5 (Freedom of expression)
(1) Everyone shall have the right freely to express and disseminate his opinion by speech, writing, and pictures and freely to inform himself from generally accessible sources. Freedom of the press and freedom of reporting by means of broadcasts and films are guaranteed. There shall be no censorship.
(2) These rights are limited by the provisions of the general laws, the provisions of law for the protection of youth, and by the right to inviolability of personal honour.
(3) Art and science, research and teaching, shall be free. Freedom of teaching shall not absolve from loyalty to the Constitution.

Article 6 (Marriage, Family, Illegitimate children)
(1) Marriage and family shall enjoy the special protection of the state.
(2) The care and upbringing of children are a natural right of, and a duty primarily incumbent on, the parents. The national community shall watch over their endeavours in this respect.
(3) Children may not be separated from their families against the will of the persons entitled to bring them up, except pursuant to a law, if those so entitled fail or the children are otherwise threatened with neglect.
(4) Every mother shall be entitled to the protection and care of the community.
(5) Illegitimate children shall be provided by legislation with the same opportunities for their spiritual development and their place in society as are enjoyed by legitimate children.

Article 7 (Education)
(1) The entire educational system shall be under the supervision of the state.
(2) The persons entitled to bring up a child shall have the right to decide whether it shall receive religious instruction.
(3) Religious instruction shall form part of the ordinary curriculum in state and municipal schools, except in secular (*bekenntnisfrei*) schools. Without prejudice to the state's right of supervision, religious instruction shall be given in accordance with the tenets of the religious communities. No teacher may be obliged against his will to give religious instruction.
(4) The right to establish private schools is guaranteed. Private schools, as a substitute for state or municipal schools, shall require the approval of the state and shall be subject to the laws of the *Land*. Such approval must be given if private schools are not inferior to the state or municipal schools in their educational aims, their facilities, and the professional training of their teaching staff, and if segregation of pupils according to the means of the parents is not promoted thereby. Approval must be withheld if the economic and legal position of the teaching staff is not sufficiently assured.

(5) A private elementary school shall be permitted only if the education authority finds that it serves a special pedagogic interest, or if, on the application of persons entitled to bring up children, it is to be established as an inter-denominational or denominational or ideological school and a state or municipal elementary school of this type does not exist in the commun[ity] (*Gemeinde*).

(6) Preparatory schools (*Vorschulen*) shall remain abolished.

Article 8 (Freedom of assembly)

(1) All Germans shall have the right to assemble peaceably and unarmed without prior notification or permission.

(2) With regard to open-air meetings the right may be restricted by or pursuant to a law.

Article 9 (Freedom of association)

(1) All Germans shall have the right to form associations and societies.

(2) Associations, the purposes or activities of which conflict with criminal laws or which are directed against the constitutional order or the concept of international understanding, are prohibited.

(3) The right to form associations to safeguard and improve working and economic conditions is guaranteed to everyone and to all trades, occupations, and professions. Agreements which restrict or seek to impair this right shall be null and void; measures directed to this end shall be illegal. Measures taken pursuant to Article 12a, to paragraphs (2) and (3) of Article 35, to paragraph (4) of Article 87a, or to Article 91, may not be directed against any industrial conflicts engaged in by associations within the meaning of the first sentence of this paragraph in order to safeguard and improve working and economic conditions.[1]

Article 10[2] (Privacy of posts and telecommunications)

(1) Privacy of posts and telecommunications shall be inviolable.

(2) This right may be restricted only pursuant to a law. Such law may lay down that the person affected shall not be informed of any such restriction if it serves to protect the free democratic basic order or the existence or security of the Federation or a *Land*, and that recourse to the courts shall be replaced by a review of the case by bodies and auxiliary bodies appointed by Parliament.

Article 11 (Freedom of movement)

(1) All Germans shall enjoy freedom of movement throughout the federal territory.

(2)[3] This right may be restricted only by or pursuant to a law and only in

---

[1] Last sentence inserted by federal Act of 24 June 1968, *Federal Law Gazette* I, p. 709.
[2] As amended by federal Act of 24 June 1968, ibid.
[3] Inserted by federal Act of 24 June 1968, ibid. I. 710.

cases in which an adequate basis of existence is lacking and special burdens would arise to the community as a result thereof, or in which such restriction is necessary to avert an imminent danger to the existence or the free democratic basic order of the Federation or a *Land*, to combat the danger of epidemics, to deal with natural disasters or particularly grave accidents, to protect young people from neglect or to prevent crime.

Article 12[4] (*Right to choose trade, occupation, or profession*)
(1) All Germans shall have the right freely to choose their trade, occupation, or profession, their place of work and their place of training. The practice of trades, occupations, and professions may be regulated by or pursuant to a law.
(2) No specific occupation may be imposed on any person except within the framework of a traditional compulsory public service that applies generally and equally to all.
(3) Forced labour may be imposed only on persons deprived of their liberty by court sentence.

Article 12a[5] (*Liability to military and other service*)
(1) Men who have attained the age of eighteen years may be required to serve in the Armed Forces, in the Federal Border Guard, or in a Civil Defence organization.
(2) A person who refuses, on grounds of conscience, to render war service involving the use of arms may be required to render a substitute service. The duration of such substitute service shall not exceed the duration of military service. Details shall be regulated by a law which shall not interfere with the freedom of conscience and must also provide for the possibility of a substitute service not connected with units of the Armed Forces or of the Federal Border Guard.
(3) Persons liable to military service who are not required to render service pursuant to paragraph (1) or (2) of this Article may, when a state of defence (*Verteidigungsfall*) exists, be assigned by or pursuant to a law to specific occupations involving civilian services for defence purposes, including the protection of the civilian population; however, it shall not be permissible to assign persons to an occupation subject to public law except for the purpose of discharging police functions or such other functions of public administration as can only be discharged by persons employed under public law. Persons may be assigned to occupations—as referred to in the first sentence of this paragraph—with the Armed Forces, including the supplying and servicing of the latter, or with public administrative authorities; assignments to occupations connected with supplying and servicing the civilian population

---

[4] As amended by federal Acts of 19 March 1956, ibid. I. 111, and 24 June 1968, ibid. I. 709.
[5] Inserted by federal Act of 24 June 1968, ibid. I. 710.

shall not be permissible except in order to meet their vital requirements or to guarantee their safety.

(4) If, while a state of defence exists, civilian service requirements in the civilian public health and medical system or in the stationary military hospital organization cannot be met on a voluntary basis, women between 18 and 55 years of age may be assigned to such services by or pursuant to a law. They may on no account render service involving the use of arms.

(5) During the time prior to the existence of any such state of defence, assignments under paragraph (3) of this Article may be effected only if the requirements of paragraph (1) of Article 80a are satisfied. It shall be admissible to require persons by or pursuant to a law to attend training courses in order to prepare them for the performance of such services in accordance with paragraph (3) of this Article as presuppose special knowledge or skills. To this extent, the first sentence of this paragraph shall not apply.

(6) If, while a state of defence exists, the labour requirements for the purposes referred to in the second sentence of paragraph (3) of this Article cannot be met on a voluntary basis, the right of a German to give up the practice of his trade or occupation or profession, or his place of work, may be restricted by or pursuant to a law in order to meet these requirements. The first sentence of paragraph (5) of this Article shall apply *mutatis mutandis* prior to the existence of a state of defence.

Article 13 (*Inviolability of the home*)

(1) The home shall be inviolable.

(2) Searches may be ordered only by a judge or, in the event of danger in delay, by other organs as provided by law and may be carried out only in the form prescribed by law.

(3) In all other respects, this inviolability may not be encroached upon or restricted except to avert a common danger or a mortal danger to individuals, or, pursuant to a law, to prevent imminent danger to public safety and order, especially to alleviate the housing shortage, to combat the danger of epidemics, or to protect endangered juveniles.

Article 14 (*Property, Right of inheritance, Expropriation*)

(1) Property and the right of inheritance are guaranteed. Their content and limits shall be determined by the laws.

(2) Property imposes duties. Its use should also serve the public weal.

(3) Expropriation shall be permitted only in the public weal. It may be effected only by or pursuant to a law which shall provide for the nature and extent of the compensation. Such compensation shall be determined by establishing an equitable balance between the public interest and the interests of those affected. In case of dispute regarding the amount of compensation, recourse may be had to the ordinary courts.

Article 15 (Socialization)

Land, natural resources, and means of production may for the purpose of socialization be transferred to public ownership or other forms of publicly controlled economy by a law which shall provide for the nature and extent of compensation; the third and fourth sentences of paragraph (3) of Article 14 shall apply *mutatis mutandis*.

Article 16 (Deprivation of citizenship, Extradition, Right of asylum)

(1) No one may be deprived of his German citizenship. Loss of citizenship may arise only pursuant to a law, and against the will of the person affected only if such person does not thereby become stateless.

(2) No German may be extradited to a foreign country. Persons persecuted on political grounds shall enjoy the right of asylum.

Article 17 (Right of petition)

Everyone shall have the right individually or jointly with others to address written requests or complaints to the appropriate agencies and to parliamentary bodies.

Article 17a[6] (Restriction of basic rights for members of the Armed Forces etc.)

(1) Laws concerning military service and substitute service may, by provisions applying to members of the Armed Forces and of substitute services during their period of military or substitute service, restrict the basic right freely to express and to disseminate opinions by speech, writing, and pictures (first half-sentence of paragraph (1) of Article 5), the basic right of assembly (Article 8), and the right of petition (Article 17) in so far as this right permits the submission of requests or complaints jointly with others.

(2) Laws for defence purposes including the protection of the civilian population may provide for the restriction of the basic rights of freedom of movement (Article 11) and inviolability of the home (Article 13).

Article 18 (Forfeiture of basic rights)

Whoever abuses freedom of expression of opinion, in particular freedom of the press [paragraph (1) of Article 5], freedom of teaching [paragraph (3) of Article 5], freedom of assembly [Article 8], freedom of association [Article 9], privacy of posts and telecommunications [Article 10], property [Article 14], or the right of asylum [paragraph (2) of Article 16] in order to attack the free democratic basic order, shall forfeit these basic rights. Such forfeiture and the extent thereof shall be pronounced by the Federal Constitutional Court.

---

[6] Inserted by federal Act of 19 March 1956, ibid. I. 111.

Article 19 (Restriction of basic rights)

(1) In so far as a basic right may, under this Basic Law, be restricted by or pursuant to a law, such law must apply generally and not solely to an individual case. Furthermore, such law must name the basic right, indicating the Article concerned.

(2) In no case may the essential content of a basic right be encroached upon.

(3) The basic rights shall apply also to domestic juristic persons to the extent that the nature of such rights permits.

(4) Should any person's right be violated by public authority, recourse to the court shall be open to him. If jurisdiction is not specified, recourse shall be to the ordinary courts. The second sentence of paragraph (2) of Article 10 shall not be affected by the provisions of this paragraph.[1]

II. 'PRIVACY'

Case 29

BUNDESGERICHTSHOF (FIRST CIVIL DIVISION) 25 MAY 1954*

BGHZ 13, 334 = NJW 1954, 1404 = JZ 1954, 698

(with an approving note by Helmut Coing)

The D Company published on 29 June 1952 in its weekly journal . . . an article by K. B. with the title 'Dr H.S. & Co.' and the sub-title 'Political considerations concerning the foundation of a new bank'. The article contained a comment concerning the new Bank for Foreign Trade founded by Dr S in H, and expressed itself in that connection in opposition to Dr S's political activity during the national-socialist regime and the years after the war.

On the instructions of Dr S the plaintiff, an attorney, sent to the defendant company a letter of 4 July 1952, saying, *inter alia*:

I represent the interests of Dr S. In terms of § 11 of the Press Act I hereby require the following correction of the above-mentioned article in your issue of Sunday the 6th instant:

   1. It is incorrect that . . .

   2. . . .

This claim for correction is made under the Press Act, in combination with the BGB, and also the law of copyright.

I ask you to inform me by telephone or in writing on or before midday Saturday 5 July 1952, of your confirmation of the unrestricted execution of the required correction, failing which legal proceedings will be taken.

---

[1] Last sentence inserted by federal Act of 24 June 1968, ibid. I. 710.

* English version by F. H. Lawson and B. S. Markesinis.

The defendant company gave the plaintiff no answer. But in the issue of 6 July it published, along with sundry expressions of opinion by readers on K. B.'s article, the following under the heading 'Letters from Readers'.

Dr H.S. & Co.

To the . . . [name of journal]

I represent the interests of Dr H.S.

 1. It is incorrect . . .

 2. . . . .

   Dr M, Attorney

In the contents of 1 there was no reproduction of or extracts from the appropriate Nuremburg judgment concerning Dr S which the plaintiff had introduced in his letter of 4 July 1952. Otherwise they were unaltered.

The plaintiff sees in this kind of publication an injury to his right of personality. The publication of his letter, written in his capacity of attorney for Dr S, under the heading 'Letters from Readers' and with its contents falsified by the omissions and the choice of title, constitutes a deliberate misleading of the public. The incorrect impression was thus created that this was a mere expression of opinion by a reader on the previous article on Dr S, as was the case with other readers' letters printed under the same rubric. The plaintiff, however, had kept clear of taking any political attitude and had acted only as an attorney within the scope of his instructions. From a professional standpoint alone the conduct of the defendant company was intolerable. An attorney must be able to ensure that demands for correction made in his client's name must not be circulated in a misleading manner.

The plaintiff demanded that the defendant company be ordered to recall in its next issue under 'Letters from Readers' its statement that the plaintiff had sent a reader's letter to the defendant company in the matter of 'Dr H.S. & Co.'.

The defendant company takes the view that it was not bound to agree to the plaintiff's demand for a correction, because his letter did not conform to the requirements set out in § 11 of the Press Act. It lay therefore within its discretion whether and at what place in its journal to print the communication.

The Landgericht granted the claim under § 823 II BGB, in combination with §§ 186, 187 StGB. The Oberlandesgericht rejected the claim. According to the Court of Appeal's opinion there was, in the abbreviated publication of the plaintiff's letter under the rubric 'Letters from Readers', no lawful disparagement of the plaintiff. The method of this publication certainly contained an incorrect statement of fact. The incorrect statement that the plaintiff had sent a reader's letter to the defendant company was, however, not apt to injure his credit, nor to bring him into contempt or lower his dignity in public opinion.

The appeal led to a restoration of the Landgericht's judgment for these

Reasons

The Court of Appeal was in error in failing to examine whether the plaintiff's claim was justified on the basis of a disparagement of his personality rights. It dismissed the action only because it did not consider as proved the objective presuppositions (elements) of a delict in the sense of §§ 823 II, 824 BGB in combination with §§ 186, 187 StGB. This objection is rightly made in the appeal.

It can be left undecided whether the plaintiff's letter of 4 July 1952 was a written work in the sense of § 1 of the Copyright Act and hence fell within the protection of copyright. The Reichsgericht has, indeed, constantly made the protection of correspondence to depend on whether it showed the individual form required for the protection of copyright (RGZ 41, 43 [48]; 69, 401 [403]). On the other hand it has been rightly pointed out in the academic literature that a need for the recognition of a personality right in respect of the use of one's own notes exists equally even when that protection cannot be derived from the personality right of the author, on the ground that they do not possess the form given by an individual intellectual activity . . . The Reichsgericht believed that it must deny such a protection of personality independent of copyright to publications of correspondence because the German law then in force contained no positive statutory provisions on a general personality right (RGZ 79, 397 [398]; 82, 333 [334]; 94, 1; 102, 134; 107, 277 [281]; 113, 414; 123, 312 [320]). It has indeed, in many decisions on § 823 BGB, approved of the protection of personality rights (RGZ 72, 175; 85, 343; 115, 416; 162, 7), but in principle it has recognized personality rights with an absolute power of exclusion only for certain specified personality interests. In the literature, Gierke and Kohler had already pleaded for the recognition of a comprehensive personality right . . .

Moreover, now that the Basic Law [Constitution of 1949] has recognized the right of a human being to have his dignity respected (Art. 1), and also the right to free development of his personality as a private right, to be universally respected in so far as it does not infringe another person's right or is not in conflict with the constitutional order or morality (Art. 2), the general personality right must be regarded as a constitutionally guaranteed fundamental right.

No further discussion is needed here of whether and how far the protection of this general personality right, the limitation of which requires a balancing of interests, is restricted in particular cases by justified private or public needs, which outweigh the interest in the inviolability of the exclusive sphere of personality; for in this present case it is not evident that the defendant company has any interests worth protecting, which it could use to justify the conduct objected to by the plaintiff. On the contrary, by the defendant company's choice of a way of publishing the request for correction, omitting essential parts of the letter, interests of the plaintiff in the nature of personality rights have been infringed.

Every verbal expression of a definite thought is an emanation from the author's personality, even when the protection of copyright cannot be attributed to its form. It follows that in principle only the author is entitled to decide whether and in what form his notes are communicated to the public; for every publication of the notes of a living person under his name is rightly regarded by the public as proceeding from a corresponding direction of his will. The nature of the notes and the method of their communication is subject to the criticism and valuation of public opinion, which draws conclusions from those circumstances about the author's personality. While an unauthorized publication of private notes constitutes—as a rule—an inadmissible attack on every human being's protected sphere of secrecy, a modified reproduction infringes the personality rights of the author because such unauthorized alterations can spread a false picture of his personality. In general, not only unauthorized omissions of essential parts of the author's notes are inadmissible, but also additions through which his notes presented for publication only for certain purposes acquire a different colour or tendency from what he expressed in the form chosen by him and the kind of publication he had allowed.

In so far as they concern works protected by copyright, those legal principles have long been inferred by the courts from the creator's enjoyment of the personality right of an author, which is only a particular phenomenon of the general personality right (RGZ 69, 242 [244]; 79, 397 [399]; 151, 50). As regards the protection of personality the interest of the author in notes which are protected by copyright is essentially the same.

In the present case the plaintiff had unambiguously sent to the defendant company only a demand for correction and, indeed, in his character as attorney for Dr S. Thereby the defendant company was only empowered by the plaintiff either to publish the text in an unshortened form or, restricting itself to the required correction, to make clear that there had been a demand for correction. Since the plaintiff does not ask for his original desire for correction to be carried out, it is unnecessary for the purpose of this decision to consider whether his letter of 4 July 1952 conformed to the conditions of the Press Act. If, in agreement with the Court of Appeal, this had to be denied, the only consequence would be that the defendant company had a right to refuse altogether to publish the letter. But it was not entitled to publish it under the rubric 'Letters from Readers' and, moreover with the omission of the passages that would clearly show that the plaintiff was not putting forward his personal opinion in favour of Dr S but wished to obtain a correction under the Press law.

The Landgericht's decision is to be approved, that this mode of publication—and also the placing of the correction side by side with five other letters on the article on Dr S published by the defendant company—was bound to produce the impression on an impartial reader that the plaintiff's letter gave his personal attitude to the controversy about Dr S. That misleading impression was also not dispelled by the literal reproduction of the plaintiff's introductory sentence; for that sentence, in its generally accepted character, told the reader only that the sender was Dr S's attorney. It did not make sufficiently clear that the content also of the letter in question referred to his instructions as attorney and that it had been composed by him not as a private person but in the exercise of his profession.

Accordingly the Court of Appeal was not in error in holding that the publication of the letter of corrections in shortened form under the rubric 'Letters from Readers' contained an untrue statement of facts. This also means that through the mode of publishing it, the letter acquired a meaning not in conformity with its original composition and that this form of publication did not correspond to what the plaintiff had alone given permission for, namely broadcasting to the public the letter of correction in the form he had chosen.

The Landgericht was right in regarding the publication complained of, which according to its findings had become known to an extraordinarily wide circle of persons, as a continuing disparagement and therefore that the demand for revocation was justified.

Case 30

BUNDESGERICHTSHOF (FIRST CIVIL DIVISION) 14 FEBRUARY 1958*
BGHZ 26, 349 = NJW 58, 827 (with a partially approving and partially critical note by
Larenz = JZ 1958, 571 and an approving article by H. Coing in JZ 1958, 558)

The plaintiff is co-owner of a brewery in X. He is active as a gentleman†
show-jumper ('*Herrenreiter*'). The defendant Limited Partnership is the manufacturer of a pharmaceutical preparation which is widely reputed as being able to increase sexual potency. To advertise this preparation in the Federal Republic, and in particular in K, it disseminated a poster with the picture of a show-jumper. Its basis was an original photograph of the plaintiff, which had been taken by a press agency at a show-jumping competition. The plaintiff had not given permission for the use of his portrait.

The plaintiff claimed damages from the defendant for the damage which

* English version by F. H. Lawson and B. S. Markesinis.
† Ed. note. This is a literal translation of the German text but it should be understood as referring to an 'amateur' and not a 'professional' rider.

he suffered as a result of the dissemination of the poster. He alleged that in the given circumstances he could only claim as damages what he would have obtained if he had allowed the defendant to use his portrait. As his professional and social position did not allow him, and his financial means did not compel him, to dispose of his portrait for advertising purposes, and in particular for the defendant's preparation, he would have done this, if at all, only for a fair price, at a rough estimate DM 15,000 at the very least.

The plaintiff applied for an order that the defendant pay by way of damages a fair sum to be fixed by the court.

The defendant denied any fault and pleaded that, after touching up, the plaintiff's features were not recognizable in the poster; and that it had not itself designed or produced the poster nor obtained the portrait from S, but had ordered it from the H advertising agency, which it had trusted as a respectable, competent, and reliable firm, not to injure the rights of third persons. The defendant could not have known that the poster had been designed on the basis of a photograph, or that the photograph showed a 'gentleman' rider. Only as the case developed did it discover that it really concerned a portrait of the plaintiff. Thereupon it prohibited without delay any further use of the advertisement.

The Landgericht ordered the defendant to pay DM 1000 to the plaintiff by way of damages. The Oberlandesgericht ordered the defendant to pay DM 10,000 to the plaintiff. The defendant's further appeal was unsuccessful for these

Reasons

I. The Court of Appeal, in agreement with the Landgericht, found that the depiction of the rider in the poster allowed the plaintiff's person to be recognized despite the retouching. It rightly concluded that the dissemination of the poster without the plaintiff's permission injured his personality rights, namely his right to deal with his portrait, and that the defendant must compensate him under § 823 II BGB in combination with § 2 of the Act on Artistic Creations, if it was found to blame (cf. RG JW 1929, 2257, BGHZ 20, 345, 347 ff.). The Court of Appeal came to that conclusion seeing that the defendant had not observed the care required in the circumstances, since it had obtained in the course of its business the poster prepared by the H advertising agency without making certain that the person depicted had agreed to the intended use of his portrait.

The appellant's attacks on these findings must fail [further discussion not reproduced].

II. In awarding compensation to the plaintiff the Court of Appeal had in mind the licence fee which he could have demanded if a suitable contract

had been arrived at between the parties. It held that it was justified in applying a method of assessing damages developed for breaches of copyright,
because it was hard for the plaintiff to show whether and to what degree
there had been any pecuniary loss. In contrast to the Landgericht, which
had thought DM 1000 to be sufficient, the Court of Appeal decided that
DM 10,000 was the more appropriate figure.

Although the appeal is unsuccessful in the result, it must be conceded that
the Court of Appeal's reasoning is not entirely appropriate to the peculiar
facts of the case.

1. The appellant does not dispute that, even where there is an injury to the
personality right to one's portrait, the damage can be estimated according
to the payment that would presumably have been arranged if there had been
a contract. Nevertheless the appellant argued that this method of assessing
damages, which the Senate in its judgment of 8 May 1956 (BGHZ 20, 345
ff.—Dahlke) declared admissible for the unauthorized publication of a portrait, could not be used if it was established that the person portrayed
would, for special reasons, never have allowed his portrait to be used for
advertising purposes.

If in the case under appeal pecuniary damage had actually been in question, this attack would not have been well founded. For according to settled
case-law and academic opinion, where a claim to an appropriate compensation, is recognized, it is not a question of applying the *general* provisions of
the law of damages but of its customary supplementation to make good
injury to valuable exclusive rights, based on the equitable consideration that
the defendant should not be better off that he would have been if his application for permission had been granted. The claim to appropriate compensation is therefore granted in all cases of unpermitted invasion of exclusive
rights where permission is usually made dependent on payment and where,
having regard to the kind of the right which has been violated, the invasion
is habitually allowed according to the customs of daily life only—if at all—
against compensation (BGHZ 20, 345, 353 ff.). It is not at all necessary for a
contract actually to have come into existence if the invader's conduct was
otherwise unobjectionable.

2. It must, however, be agreed that the Court of Appeal, by the method of
assessment it chose, did not really try to work out the economic loss to the
plaintiff, but rather to adjust the satisfaction due to him to his non-material
disparagement. In particular the reasoning by which it arrived at the
amount of the damage to the plaintiff shows that according to its opinion
also he did not suffer any tangible pecuniary loss. In truth he claims not
compensation for a non-existent pecuniary loss but an appreciable satisfac-

tion for an unlawful attack on his personality protected by § 22 of the Act on Artistic Creations and Arts. 1 and 2 of the Constitution. He demands satisfaction for the fact that a widely disseminated poster, by making him, one might almost say, 'ride' for the purpose of advertising the defendant's tonic—and a sexual one at that—humiliated him and made him an object of ridicule. In such a situation it is absurd to award damages on the basis of a fictitious licence agreement. This way of estimating damage is appropriate only if one can start with the doing of some kind of pecuniary damage and all that is left is to alleviate the often difficult task of proving its amount. It fails if no pecuniary prejudice at all is in question. It fails also in the present case because it would assume that the plaintiff had done something that not only he, but all others of the same professional and social standing, must consider harmful and as a continuing degradation of his personality. It must convey an imputation that the plaintiff would, after all, voluntarily and for a large sum of money place himself in the unworthy position against which he is defending himself.

The plaintiff's claim therefore cannot be supported by the Court of Appeal's chosen method of assessment, helped out by the fiction of a loss of licence fee.

3. Moreover, basing the claim on unjustified enrichment is precluded because the plaintiff did not experience any pecuniary disadvantage and there is thus no pecuniary shift of the kind envisaged by §§ 812 ff. BGB.

4. If, therefore, the kind of assessment adopted by the Court of Appeal fails, and it is shown that the plaintiff in truth suffered no pecuniary damage, the decisive question comes to be whether he can demand compensation for the immaterial damage which he has suffered as a result of the invasion of his personality following the appearance of his picture in the advertisement. On the facts before it the Senate answers that question in the affirmative.

This Senate has already said in its decision in BGHZ 13, 334, 338 that the sacredness of human dignity and the right to free development of the personality protected by Art. 1 of the Constitution are also to be recognized as a civil right to be respected by everyone in daily life, in so far as that right does not impinge upon the rights of others and is not repugnant to constitutional order or the moral law. This so-called general right to one's personality also possesses legal validity within the framework of the civil law and enjoys the protection of § 823 I BGB under the designation of 'other right' (cf. also BGHZ 24, 12 ff.).

Articles 1 and 2 of the Constitution protect—and indeed must be applied by the courts in the administration of justice—what is called the concept of human personality; they recognize in it one of the supra-legal basic values of the law. Thereby they are directly concerned with the protection of the inner realm of the personality which, in principle, only affords a basis for the free and responsible self-determination of the individual and an infringement of which produces primarily so-called immaterial damage, damage expressed in a degradation of the personality. To respect this inner realm and to refrain from invading it without authorization is a legal command issuing from the Basic Law itself. And it follows from the Constitution that in cases of invasion of this sphere, protection must be given against damage characteristic of such an invasion.

On the limited field of portrait protection this was established in 1907 by the special rules contained in §§ 22 ff. of the Act on Artistic Creations, long before the Constitution came into force and at a time when the civil law did not as yet protect a general personality right. For the protection afforded by § 22, according to which portraits may be distributed or shown publicly only with the subject's consent, rests in essence on the fundamental principle of a person's freedom in his highly personal private life, in which the outward appearance of human being plays an essential part. The unauthorized publication of a portrait constitutes, as has long been recognized in legal literature, an attack on the freedom of self-determination and the free expression of the personality. The reason why a third person's arbitrary publication of a portrait is not allowed is that the person portrayed is thereby deprived of his freedom to dispose by his own decision of this interest in his individual sphere.

Once the violation of the right to one's picture is seen as affecting one's personality it is possible to seek an answer to the question how to compensate immaterial damage in § 847 BGB. This allows an equitable compensation in money for non-pecuniary loss in cases of 'deprivation of liberty'. It is true that deprivation of liberty is here understood to mean deprivation of freedom of bodily movement, as well as compulsion to act, by means of force or threats, whereas § 22 of the Act on Artistic Creations deals with deprivation of the free and responsible exercise of will. Already, however, before the Basic Law came into force, the opinion was often expressed that any attack on the undisturbed exercise of the will was to be regarded as an injury to freedom in the sense of § 847 BGB. Now that the Constitution guarantees a comprehensive protection to the personality and recognizes human dignity and the right to free development of the personality as a fundamental value, it has done away with the dogma held by the original draftsmen of the BGB that there can be no civil law protection of general personality right; and since a protection of 'inner freedom' without a right to compensation for immaterial damage would be in great part illusory, it would be intolerable to refuse compensation for that immaterial damage. Moreover, there is no obvious reason why § 847 BGB should not be extended by analogy to such attacks as injure the right to free exercise of the will, especially where that deprivation of intellectual liberty, just like deprivation of bodily freedom, renders natural restitution impossible. Where such blameworthy depreciations of the personality right are in question, the effective legal protection offered by the Constitution can, in the absence of any special legal provision, be attained only through its inclusion in the injuries mentioned in § 847 BGB, since their injurious consequences are of necessity primarily immaterial.

This view is not at variance with the sense of § 35 of the Act on Artistic Creations. Of course the injured party can claim under it a penalty for the injury to his right to his portrait, and with it to have his immaterial loss made good, only in criminal proceedings and on condition that the injury was intended; but that special provision shows only that as early as 1907 the legislator regarded an infringement of § 22 as so far-reaching and threatening that it was considered necessary to grant expressly to the injured party a claim to compensation for the disparagement. The restriction of the criminal law claim for a penalty to intentional injuries accords with the legislator's limitation of the threat of punishment for an infringement of § 22 to intentional interference. However, that does not mean that the same must apply to the civil law claims to compensation that are not regulated in the Act on Artistic Creations. On the contrary, since the Constitution now recognizes the general personality right as significant for civil law and has afforded a general civil law protection appreciably exceeding the narrow regulation of § 35 of the Act on Artistic Creations, the special provision of § 35 can no longer be cited in opposition to a more extensive civil law protection of the right to one's portrait. The general provisions of the BGB concerning delicts come into operation instead. That means that, at any rate since the Constitution came into force, by an analogous application of § 847 BGB, any blameworthy injury to the right to one's own portrait involves a duty to make good immaterial damage also.

In so far as the Senate, following the case-law of the Reichsgericht, decided in the *Dahlke* case (BGHZ 20, 345, 352 ff.) that immaterial damage cannot give rise to a money claim in the absence of express legal provision, its opinion cannot be upheld in the light of the foregoing discussions. The statement was *obiter*, since the facts disclosed pecuniary damage, which could be estimated on the basis of the usual licence fee.

III. The compensation to be paid to the plaintiff was fixed by the Court of Appeal at DM 10,000. Although starting from a possible assessment according to the satisfaction that might have been paid in a case of contract on the usual terms, the court's arguments fully apply also to fixing the amount of an equitable compensation under § 847 BGB. They also show that the court really awarded the plaintiff compensation for the immaterial damage that had resulted.

As the Grosse Zivilsenat explained in its decision of 6 July 1955 (BGHZ 18, 149), the claim for damages for pain and suffering offers the injured party an appropriate compensation for the depreciation of life (or personality) which is not of a pecuniary kind. But it also takes account of the notion that the doer of damage owes the injured party satisfaction for what he has done to him. It was emphasized in the decision that 'satisfaction', which forms an integral part of the award for compensation for immaterial damage, must take into account all the relevant circumstances. This Senate adheres to this view in this present case. If one therefore moves on from that position, it follows that the Court of Appeal was not in error in taking all the relevant circumstances into account in fixing the amount of damages. In particular, that court explained that the fact that the plaintiff had never been ready to take part in any advertising must be a factor in deciding the amount to be paid. It considered it especially serious that the advertisement was for an aphrodisiac, and so was not to be compared with advertisements for other products. The court was right in taking the view that persons would be unlikely to allow their likeness to be used on a poster for this purpose and so run a risk of being recognized by a wider or narrower public, exposing themselves to the innuendos to which the defendant's preparation would give rise. The Court of Appeal also took the plaintiff's social and business position into account, pointing to the fact that he moved in a social circle the members of which were for the most part known to each other and where the risk of making oneself an object to ridicule was especially great. When, after considering and giving weight to all these special circumstances relevant to amount of damages for pain and suffering, the Court of Appeal regarded the sum of DM 10,000 as appropriate compensation (§ 287 ZPO), it cannot be found to have acted contrary to law.

Case 31

BUNDESGERICHTSHOF (SIXTH CIVIL DIVISION) 19 SEPTEMBER 1961*
BGHZ 35, 363 = NJW 1961, 2059 (with approving notes by W. Rötelmann = *NJW* 1962, 736 and H. Hubmann = *VersR* 1962, 350, 562)

The plaintiff is a professor in the law faculty of the University of G at which he holds a chair of international and ecclesiastical law. From a stay in Korea he had brought with him a ginseng root, which he placed at the disposal of his friend Professor H, a pharmacologist, for research. The latter mentioned in a scientific article on ginseng roots that he had come into possession of genuine Korean ginseng roots 'through the kind assistance' of the

* English version by F. H. Lawson and B. S. Markesinis.

plaintiff. This led to the plaintiff being described in a popular scientific article, which appeared in the year 1957 in the *H and W* journal, along with Professor H and other scientists, as one of the best-known ginseng researchers of Europe.

The defendant company dealt in a tonic containing ginseng. In its advertisement for this tonic the plaintiff was referred to as an important scientist expressing an opinion on its value, and in an editorial note, printed in immediate connection with an advertisement in another journal, allusion was made to its use as an aphrodisiac. Both the advertisement and the journal were very widely distributed.

The plaintiff claimed that he had suffered an unauthorized attack on his personality right; and that the advertisement gave rise to the impression that he had, for payment, issued an opinion on a controversial topic in a department of knowledge not his own, and unprofessionally lent his name to advertising a doubtful product. He had suffered damage to his reputation as a learned man and been made an object of ridicule to the public and above all to his students. In reliance on BGHZ 26, 349 (*Herrenreiter*) he claimed DM 10,000 as satisfaction for the harm done to him.

The Landgericht awarded him DM 8000 as damages for pain and suffering. The appeals to both the Court of Appeal and the Bundesgerichtshof were unsuccessful for these

Reasons

1. By invoking the plaintiff's scientific authority in its advertising to encourage belief in the effectiveness of its preparation for the mentioned purposes, the defendant company unlawfully disparaged his personality right (§ 823 I BGB). The reference to researches by the plaintiff, which lacked any objective foundation, was in the circumstances calculated to make him an object of ridicule in society and lessen his scholarly reputation. Moreover, he was bound to feel outraged by the way his name was used in advertising a preparation recommended as a sexual stimulant. The defendant company's conduct was also blameworthy. Before using the plaintiff's name for its advertisement it ought to have sought his agreement or at least to have ascertained whether and where he had stated what was asserted in its advertisement. The information in a popular article in the *H and W* journal ought in no way to have been adopted unseen; it was moreover substantially altered. The Court of Appeal rightly characterized the defendant's conduct as irresponsible. Likewise approval must also be given to the Court of Appeal's finding that the defendant company was also responsible for the note in the *M* journal which adopted in somewhat modified form the contents of the advertisement. Even if it was the advertising agency employed by the defendant company that caused the note to appear, the information

contained in it depended on material supplied by the defendant company. At the very least, the defendant company had not supervised the advertising agency as was necessary.

2. The senate also agrees with the Court of Appeal's view that the plaintiff has a claim to compensation for immaterial damage. The case is, in its main lines, very similar to those decided by the Bundesgerichtshof and reported in BGHZ 26, 349 (*Herrenreiter*) and 30, 7. In both cases the way a product was advertised attacked the protected sphere of the personality right of persons who claimed compensation for the unlawful injury. In both the conditions for compensation for material damage were absent or at any rate not proved. If, in the circumstances, no permission to use a name or portrait for advertising purposes is in question, it is not possible to estimate pecuniary compensation on the lines of a licence fee according to the principles governing so-called unilateral acquisition without permission. The First Civil Senate awarded damages for pain and suffering to the plaintiff in the case decided by it and reported in BGHZ 26, 349 and also regarded an award of so-called 'immaterial damages', with its function of satisfaction, as the adequate compensation that the law must afford to a plaintiff for the violation of his personality right. From the decision reported in BGHZ 30, 7 it must be taken that the standpoint of the Fourth Civil Senate is at least not at variance with that of the First Civil Senate.

This Senate agrees with the First Civil Senate that satisfaction may be awarded to a person affected by the blameworthy infringement of his personality right. It is indeed stated in § 253 BGB that money compensation can be claimed for non-pecuniary damage only in cases expressly designated by the law. When the BGB established that enumeration principle, the high value of the protection of human personality and its special sphere had not received the recognition that it enjoys according to Arts. 1 and 2 I of the Constitution. From the standpoint of the BGB, the protection of property interests always stood in the foreground, whereas the personal worth of a human being received only insufficient and fragmentary protection. In recognizing a general personality right of mankind and granting it the protection of § 823 I BGB, the courts drew for civil law purposes the consequences resulting from the rank the Constitution assigned to the worth of human personality and the protection of its free development. That protection, however, would be incomplete and full of loopholes if an infringement of the personality right did not give rise to a sanction adequate to the violation. Just as the restriction of protection by the law of delict to specific legal interests of a human being has proved too narrow to afford the protection of personality required by the Constitution, so a narrowing of immaterial damages, for immaterial loss to cover only injury to specifically mentioned legal interests, no longer conforms to the value-system of the Constitution. For Art. 1 declares it to be an urgent obligation on the public power to protect the sacred dignity of the human being. Article 2 I puts the right of a human being to free development of his personality at the head of the fundamental rights. If the law of delict, in protecting the personality right in the non-material realm, retreated completely to a position where it merely protected the particular personality interests mentioned in Art. 2 II, which are emanations from the personality right, the civil law would not be paying attention to the value-decision of the Constitution. The elimination of damages for immaterial loss from the protection of personality would mean that injury to the dignity and honour of a human being would remain without any sanction of the civil law, which deals with the disturbance of essential values and makes the doer of injury owe satisfaction to the victim for the wrong done to him. The law would then renounce the strongest and often only instrument calculated to ensure respect for the personal worth of the individual.

3. That does not mean that the legal consequences of injuries to body, health, and freedom on the one hand and the violation of the personality sphere on the other hand must be exactly the same or at least largely correspond to each other. A need for differentiation is already indicated by the fact that the factual aspect of an injury to a general personality right is much less specific than where body, health, or freedom is injured. That means that there are many marginal cases where the question is whether the case is one included in the generalized description of violation of the personality and whether, if it does, the unlawfulness is not excluded by the competing rights of the 'offender', among which the right to free expression of opinion deserves particular attention. It is precisely where a so-called balancing of interest must take place that the limits of what is allowed are not always easy to fix. If for every overstepping of the limits, however petty, compensation for immaterial loss were to be awarded to the person affected, there would be a danger that unimportant injuries would be used inappropriately to make a gain. The purpose of awarding satisfaction would then be stultified. It must further be observed that it is more difficult to apply the general criterion of monetary value to measure immaterial injuries to the personality right than the consequences of bodily injuries. In injuries to the general personality right the satisfaction function of damages for pain and suffering advances into the foreground as that of compensation recedes. Hence it will always be necessary to look at the kind of injury to the personality right to see if the person affected, whose injury cannot otherwise be redressed, should be granted satisfaction for the wrong he has suffered. That will in general only be the case when the doer of damage is blamed for a serious fault or when an injury to a personality right is objectively significant.

Only when such disturbances are serious may the civil law, taking seriously the protection of personality and its value as such, react against the injury by granting satisfaction to the person affected. Insignificant injuries do not call for satisfaction. Having regard to the special character of an injury to a personality right Swiss law, which has devoted greater attention than the BGB to legal protection of the personality (cf. Art. 49 I of the Swiss Code of Obligations) also restricts damages for immaterial loss to serious cases.

4. The conditions for an award of immaterial damages especially occur when—as in a present case—there is a wanton attack on the personality right of another person out of a desire to increase the force of one's commercial publicity. Such an unfair attempt to succeed can be effectively countered only if it is burdened with the risk of an appreciable loss, and on the other hand, anyone who seeks to make money out of an unfair invasion of the sphere of another's personality must not feel hurt if he is forced to pay a money compensation. For the plaintiff the outrage inflicted—in particular since the object was recommended for specific purposes—was not at all insignificant, the more so because he ran the risk of readers assuming that he had lent his name for a money consideration. The award of a money compensation by way of satisfaction was justified by the seriousness of the attack as well as by the seriousness of the fault.

The amount of satisfaction to be given was for the judge of fact to assess. It could be attacked on appeal only if it rested on an incorrect finding of the applicable law or if the judge of fact overlooked essential points of view. No such defects, however, are here apparent. The Court of Appeal did right in attaching importance to the spread of publicity, which extended to Austria and Switzerland. It was also an essential factor in fixing the amount of the satisfaction that the defendant company continued the advertising complained of even *after* being warned by the plaintiff, thus displaying an especially reckless attitude. On the other hand, the Court of Appeal observed in the defendant company's favour that the mention of the name in the advertisement was not especially prominent, so that it might not have been noticed by the cursory reader.

Case 32

BUNDESVERFASSUNGSGERICHT (FIRST DIVISION) 5 JUNE 1973*
BVerfGE 35, 202

The petitioner had participated in an armed robbery of an arsenal of the German armed forces in the course of which several soldiers on guard duty were killed or severely wounded. The culprits were arrested after a prolonged

* English version by F. H. Lawson and B. S. Markesinis.

search and were convicted. The petitioner was convicted as an accessory and sentenced to six years' imprisonment. A German television station commissioned a documentary play based on the crime, its planning, and detection and the background of the culprits, including the petitioner whose homosexual tendencies were stressed. The play showed a likeness of the petitioner and mentioned him frequently by name. The petitioner who had served two-thirds of his sentence and was soon to be released sought an injunction prohibiting the television company from broadcasting the play pending a decision on the merits of his claim that the play violated his right of personality.

The District Court of Mainz dismissed the action for an injunction on the grounds that the petitioner was 'relatively a personality of contemporary history' and could therefore not rely on the right to the protection of his personality. The Court of Appeal of Koblenz [reference] affirmed this decision by weighing the respective interests of an individual to be protected against the unauthorized publication of his likeness in accordance with §§ 22 and 23 of the Act on the Protection of the Copyright in Works of Art and Photographs (henceforth cited as KUG) as a projection of the right to his personality covered by Arts. 1 and 2 I, of the Constitution on the one hand and the need for objective pictorial information concerning persons in public life, which is recognized in § 23 KUG and must be interpreted in the freedom to express opinions and the liberty of broadcasting stations to provide information, protected by Art. 5 I of the Constitution on the other hand. The Court of Appeal held that in this conflict the right to provide information must prevail, especially since the trial had been concluded. The petitioner was 'relatively a personality of contemporary history'; his interest in social reintegration had to give way to the interest of the public in general to receive a truthful account of the facts and the persons involved . . .

The German Federal Constitutional Court quashed the decisions of the two courts below on the ground that Art. 2 I in conjunction with Art. 1 I of the Constitution had been violated and issued a temporary injunction prohibiting the broadcasting of the play in question to the extent that it mentioned the petitioner by name and reproduced a likeness of him.

Reasons

A. . . .

B. . . .

II. For the present case the Court of Appeal has held correctly that several fundamental rights affect the application of private law and that they lead in opposite directions. The right to one's personality guaranteed by Art. 2 I in conjunction with Art. 1 I of the Constitution conflicts with the freedom of broadcasting stations to provide information, in accordance with Art. 5 I, sentence 2 of the Constitution.

1. On the one hand, a televised broadcast of the kind in issue here concerning the origins, execution, and detection of a crime which mentions the name of the criminal and contains a representation of his likeness necessarily touches the area of his fundamental rights guaranteed by Art. 2 I in conjunction with Art. 1 I of the Constitution. The right to the free development of one's personality and human dignity safeguard for everyone the sphere of autonomy in which to shape his private life by developing and protecting his individuality. This includes the right 'to remain alone', 'to be oneself' within this sphere [reference], to exclude the intrusion of or the inspection by others [reference]. This includes the right to one's likeness and to one's utterances [reference] and even more to the right to dispose of pictures of oneself. Everyone has the right in principle to determine himself alone whether and to what extent others may represent in public an account of his life or of certain incidents thereof.

However, according to the constant practice of the Federal Constitutional Court, not the entire sphere of private life enjoys the *absolute* protection of the above-mentioned fundamental rights [references]. If an individual in his capacity as a citizen living within a community enters into relations with others, influences others by his existence or activity, and thereby impinges upon the personal sphere of other people or upon the interests of communal life, his exclusive right to be master of his own private sphere may become subject to restrictions, unless his sacrosanct innermost sphere of life is concerned. Any such social involvement, if sufficiently strong may, in particular, justify measures of public authorities in the interest of the public as a whole—such as the publication of pictures of a suspect person in order to facilitate a criminal investigation (§ 24 KUG). However, neither the interest of the State to clear up crimes nor any public interest always justifies an infringement of the personal sphere [reference]. Instead, the pre-eminent importance of the right to the free development and respect of personality, which follows from its close connection with the supreme value enshrined in the Constitution, i.e. human dignity, demands that any intrusion of the right of personality which may appear necessary to protect such interest, must always be balanced against the protective rule laid down in Art. 2 I in conjunction with Art. 1 I of the Constitution. Accordingly, it must be determined in the individual case by weighing the particular interests whether the pursuit of the public interest merits precedence generally and having regard to the features of the individual case, whether the proposed intrusion of the private sphere is required by this interest in this form and extent, and whether it is commensurate with the importance of the case [references].

These principles, which were developed by the courts in respect of measures taken by public authorities, must be observed equally when the courts have to determine conflicting interests on the basis of private law. In the course of such a determination the courts are not precluded from taking into account the special position accorded to the media represented by broadcasting and television by virtue of their organization regulated by public law and their public functions.

2. In this respect the consideration is decisive, as the Court of Appeal has pointed out correctly, that the broadcast in dispute serves a function, the free exercise of which on its part is directly protected by a provision in the Constitution. Freedom of information by broadcasts in accordance with Art. 5 I, second sentence of the Constitution (freedom to broadcast), like the freedom of the press, of expression and information is a basic constituent element of a liberal-democratic order [references] . . .

Only when the exercise of the freedom to broadcast conflicts with other protected legal interests, the purpose of the individual broadcast, the manner of its presentation, and its actual foreseeable effect may become relevant. The Constitution has regulated possible conflicts between the freedom to broadcast and the interests of individual citizens, of groups and of the community as a whole, by referring to the legal system as a whole; according to Art. 5 II of the Constitution the emission of broadcasts is subject to the restrictions imposed by the general law. According to the constant practice of the Federal Constitutional Court the need expressed by this provision to take other protected legal interests into account must not render the freedom to broadcast a relative one; instead the laws which restrict the freedom to broadcast must in turn be interpreted in the light of the constitutional guarantee and must, if necessary, be equally restricted in order to ensure that the freedom of broadcasting is safeguarded adequately [reference]. Consequently the opposing protected legal interests must be balanced against each other in each individual case in the light of general and specific considerations.

III. 1. The general laws referred to by Art. 5 II of the Constitution include also the provisions of §§ 22, 23 of the Act on the Copyright in Works of Plastic Art and Photography of 9 January 1907 (RGBl. 1907) maintained by § 141 no. 5 of the Copyright Act of 9 September 1956 (BGBl. I 1273), which formed the basis of the judgment in issue before this court. These provisions, the wording and the original purpose of which related originally to the right to one's own likeness, have for a long time been interpreted by the courts and by writers to apply also to reproductions of one's likeness, whether accompanied by the person's name or not, as well as to the representation of a person by an actor on a stage [references]. The general approach to these provisions has changed since the Constitution came into force to the effect that the right to one's likeness is regarded as an aspect, as a special feature of the general right of personality which was derived from Arts. 1 and 2 of the Constitution [references].

These provisions are in accordance with constitutional law; their somewhat flexible character gives sufficient scope for applying them in keeping with the Constitution and it has been shown in practice that it is possible, in balancing the interest, as required by § 23 KUG, to take sufficient account of the reflex effect of the relevant fundamental rights. In this context, it is irrelevant from the point of view of constitutional law which factual element of § 23 KUG serves as the balancing factor [references].

2. In cases of conflict, such as the present, the general principle applies, on the one hand, that in applying §§ 22 and 23 KUG to televised broadcasts the freedom to broadcast must not be restricted excessively. On the other hand, as distinct from other general laws in the meaning of Art. 5 II of the Constitution, it is a special feature of the present case that the restriction of the freedom to broadcast serves in turn to protect an important concern of the Constitution; the interest of the person affected to prohibit the publication of his likeness or any representation of his person, which must be protected with the framework of § 23 KUG, is directly enhanced by the constitutional guarantee of the protection of personality. In solving this conflict it must be remembered that according to the intention of the Constitution both constitutional concerns are essential aspects of the liberal-democratic order of the Constitution with the result that neither can claim precedence in principle. The view of humanity taken by the Constitution and the corresponding structure of the community within the State require both the respect for the independence of individual personality and the guarantee of a liberal social atmosphere; the latter cannot be realized at the present time unless communications are unimpeded. In case of conflict both concerns of the Constitution must be adjusted, if possible; if this cannot be achieved it must be determined which interest must be postponed having regard to the nature of the case and to any special circumstances. For this purpose, both concerns of the Constitution, centred as they are on human dignity, must be regarded as the nucleus of the system of constitutional concerns. Accordingly, the freedom to broadcast may have the effect of restricting any claims based on the right of personality; however, the damage to 'personality' resulting from a public representation must not be out of proportion to the importance of the publication upholding the freedom of communication [reference]. Furthermore it follows from these guiding principles that the required weighting of interests must take into account the intensity of the infringement of the personal sphere by the broadcast on the one hand; on the other hand, the specific interest which is being sensed by the broadcast and is capable of being thus served, must be

assessed and examined as to whether and to what extent it can be satisfied even without any interference—or a less far-reaching interference—with the protection of personality.

IV. 1. In the light of these general principles the following criteria are relevant from the point of view of constitutional law in assessing televised broadcasts of the kind in issue here.

(a) A public report of a crime in which the name, a likeness, or a representation of the culprit is provided will always constitute a severe intrusion of his personal sphere, seeing that it publicizes his misdeeds and gives from the outset a negative slant to his person in the eyes of those to whom the report is addressed. It may be different if the report is designed to create sympathy for the culprit, as for instance in order to achieve a new trial, a pardon, or some other assistance . . .

(b) Disregarding the possibility of an additional infringement by the manner of the representation (polemics, falsification), even a report which seeks to be objective and factual, if televised constitutes normally a much greater invasion of the private sphere than an oral or written report published in the press or over the radio. This is so, in the first place, because the visual impression and the combination of a picture and word is much stronger, but mainly because television commands a much greater audience than the cinema and the theatre, resulting in a special position. Consequently there is a special reason 'for watching over the observation of the limits established by the law and to prevent an abuse [sic] of the right of personality which had become more vulnerable. In this respect the law must not give way to technical developments' [reference].

(c) If for the above-mentioned reasons alone a special need exists for protection against violations of the right of personality by televised broadcasts reaching such a wide audience, it must be remembered that the broadcast performance of a documentary play entails specific dangers . . .

In conclusion it can be stated that television broadcasts reporting on a crime naming, depicting, or representing the culprit, especially in the form of a documentary play, will normally constitute a serious invasion of his sphere of personality.

2. On the other hand weighty considerations suggest that the public should be fully informed of the commission of crimes including the person of the culprit, and of the facts which led to them. Crimes, too, are part of contemporary history, the presentation of which is altogether the task of the media. Moreover the violation of the general legal order, the infringement of protective legal interests of the citizens involved or of the community, sympathy with the victims and their relatives, fear of the repetition of such crimes, and the desire to prevent them create a fully justified interest in receiving

detailed information concerning the deed and the criminal. This interest will be all the greater the more the criminal act is unusual having regard to the special features of the object of the attack, the manner in which it was carried out, or the severity of the consequences. Where serious crimes of violence are involved, such as that represented in the play in issue, the interest to receive information is based not only on general curiosity and sensationalism but on serious reasons for asking who were the perpetrators, what were their motives, what was done to detect and to punish them, and for preventing similar crimes. For this purpose the desire to know only the facts will be predominant, but as time passes the interest increases to receive a more searching interpretation of the deed, its background, and its social setting. Not least is the legitimate democratic desire in determining to control the organs of the State and public authorities responsible for security and order, the prosecution and the criminal courts . . .

3. In balancing generally the interest in receiving information as circumscribed above by televised reporting within these limits against the invasion of the sphere of personality of the culprit which must follow inevitably, the interest in receiving information must generally prevail in so far as current reporting of crimes is concerned. He who breaks the peace established by law, attacks or violates by his act and its consequences his fellow citizens or legally protected interests of the community, must not only suffer the criminal punishment provided by the law. He must also accept, as a matter of principle, that the public interest in information caused by himself by his own deed is being satisfied in the usual manner in a community which observes the principle of freedom of communication. Moreover, the control of the prosecution and of the criminal proceedings which is assured thereby also benefits the culprit. However, the interest to receive information does not prevail absolutely. The importance of the right to personality, which is a corner-stone of the Constitution, requires not only that account must be taken of the sacrosanct innermost personal sphere [reference] but also a strict regard for the principle of proportionality. The invasion of the personal sphere is limited to the need to satisfy adequately the interest to receive information, and the disadvantages suffered by the culprit must be proportional to the seriousness of the offence or to its importance otherwise for the public. Consequently, it is not always admissible to provide the name, a picture, or any other means of identifying the perpetrator.

It is obvious that the right of personality is only postponed if the reporting is objective and if the interpretation is serious; it is different if the account seeks to be sensational, is intentionally one-sided or misleading. On the other hand, objective reporting of a serious crime justifies not only the publication of the name or of a likeness of the perpetrator; it also includes his personal life in so far as it is directly connected with the act, provides clues about his motive or the setting, and seems relevant for assessing the guilt of the perpetrator in the light of modern criminal law. The actual question as to where the limits are to be drawn in fact seeing that in principle the interest to receive information by reports of contemporary events must prevail, can only be answered having regard to the circumstances of the individual case.

4. The reflex effect of the constitutional guarantee of personality does not, however, allow the media of communication, apart from contemporary reporting, to deal indefinitely with the person of the criminal and his private sphere. Instead, when the interest in receiving information has been satisfied, his right 'to be left alone' gains increasing importance in principle and limits the desire of the mass media and the wish of the public to make the individual sphere of his life the object of discussion or even of entertainment. Even a culprit, who attracted public attention by his serious crime and has gained general disapproval, remains a member of this community and retains his constitutional right to the protection of his individuality. If with the prosecution and conviction by a criminal court the act attracting the public interest has met with the just reaction of the community demanded by the public interest, any additional continued or repeated invasions of the personal sphere of the culprit cannot normally be justified.

5. (a) The time-limit when the reporting of current events which is admissible in principle becomes subsequently an inadmissible account or discussion cannot be stated generally; certainly it cannot be stated in months and years so as to cover all cases. The decisive criterion is whether the report concerned is likely to cause the culprit considerable new or additional harm, compared with the information which is already available.

(b) In order to determine the time-limit more clearly, the interest in reintegrating the criminal into society and to restore his social position may be treated as the decisive point of reference.

(c) Altogether a repeated televised report concerning a serious crime which is no longer justified by the interest to receive information about current events is undoubtedly inadmissible if it endangers the social rehabilitation of the culprit. The vital chance necessary for the existence of the culprit and the interest of the community to restore his social position must prevail in principle over the interest in a discussion of the crime. Whether and to what extent any exceptions are conceivable such as in the case of an overriding historical interest, of scholarly or other broadcasts which are addressed to a limited range of viewers need not be examined here.

V. 1. Examined in the light of the criteria of constitutional law, the decisions appealed against cannot be maintained. The district court has sought to balance the interests of the petitioner and the broadcasting station exclusively by reference to §§ 22, 23 KUG without taking notice of the reflex effect of the fundamental rights contained in Art. 2 I in conjunction with Arts. 1 and 5 I of the Constitution.

The Court of Appeal did realize that a conflict exists between the freedom to broadcast by virtue of Art. 5 I of the Constitution and the guarantee of personality by virtue of Art. 2 I and Art. 1 of the Constitution; in balancing, having regard to § 23 KUG, between the right to one's likeness and the interest of the public to receive information it did take the reflex effect of these fundamental rights into consideration. In solving this conflict it did not, however, apply correctly the criteria which are to be derived from the existing constitutional provisions for the determination of cases such as the present, but have not been formulated hitherto by the Constitutional Court; above all, it did not attribute to the interest in rehabilitation the importance which it deserves from the point of view of constitutional law.

2. If sufficient account is taken of the effect of the provisions of the Constitution which are relevant in the present case upon the general law the conclusion must be reached that the petition of the complainant must succeed . . .

Case 33

OBERLANDESGERICHT OF COLOGNE, 2 JUNE 1987
NJW 1987, 2682

Facts

The plaintiff had been a city official and director of the city's Office for Foreigners. In this capacity, he granted residence permits to a number of Syrians who, it emerged, were planning terrorist activities in the Federal Republic. The State Prosecution Authorities decided to investigate the plaintiff's conduct on the suspicion that he had taken a bribe. The investigations were carried out on behalf of the city authorities . . . by the Federal Office of Criminal Investigations (BKA). This body produced its final report in April 1983. After further investigations, the State Prosecution Authorities began proceedings against the plaintiff in January 1985. The Landgericht and the Oberlandesgericht, as the appellate court, rejected the charge at a preliminary stage, refusing to allow it to be taken to trial. A key sentence in the decision of the LG which was approved by the OLG ran as follows: 'Above all there is absolutely no evidence which could form the basis at trial of proof of payments of money to the accused in exchange for certain actions which were in breach of his conditions of service.'

The defendant is the publisher of a major news magazine. In its issue of

21 February 1983 an article appeared concerning the plaintiff under the title 'In the Foreigners' Office there is lively trade in illegal residence permits. Amongst those who have benefited from this are Syrian terrorists.' The article contained a picture of the plaintiff with the sideline: 'Suspended Office Director—did he know about the terrorist activities?'. The text of the article began with a paragraph about a 'three-man Syrian commando group' and its tasks. Then it continued: 'Commando chief F knew his way around the border city in North Rhine-Westfalia. For Marks 3000, he bought himself a thirteen-month residence permit . . .'. Later-on in the article appeared the following statement: 'An internal enquiry conducted by the Federal Office of Criminal Investigations (BKA) is investigating how the applications came to be made and the permits granted'. A Director of Criminal Investigations had informed the Federal Office for the Protection of the Constitution, the Federal Information Service, the Interior Ministry, and the criminal authorities of the *Land*, that 'the Syrian terrorist R had been able, using intermediaries, to obtain a residence permit from the Foreigners' Office in Aachen for a payment of DM 300 before his arrival in Germany.' The article went on a few lines later: 'In fact, when a raid was conducted at the offices, documents about the expelled Syrians R and A were discovered. The Director had once more granted the permits personally. Whether he knew of the terrorist activities of both Syrians is not yet known.' The plaintiff brought an action claiming that he was innocent of the accusations and that the article represented a serious invasion of his general right of privacy. He claimed damages for pain and suffering of at least DM 10,000, plus interest.

The LG rejected the claim. The plaintiff's appeal was successful for the following

Reasons:

1. The defendant publishing company published a picture of the plaintiff, identified him by name, position, place of work, and age, and also alleged that he provided residence permits in return for money in his capacity as Director of the city's Foreigners' Office. This insulting allegation is to be considered under § 823 II BGB, read in conjunction with § 186 of the Criminal Code. It is not covered by the defence of legitimate interest (§ 193 of the Criminal Code). The allegation is also to be seen as untrue, since the plaintiff asserts this point and the defendant, who carries the burden of proving that the allegation is true, has not been able to discharge it, nor will he be able to do so following the result of the criminal proceedings. The defendant has further infringed the plaintiff's right to his own image (§ 22 KUG) and thus committed a tortious act within the meaning of § 823 I BGB. The question whether a picture of a city official who is suspected of bribery but for which

there is no proof, is a picture in the 'public domain' (§ 23 I Nr. 1 KUG) [and thus a defence under this Act] need not be decided. For in any case the defendant has infringed a legitimate interest of the plaintiff within the meaning of § 23 II KUG in so far as it published the picture together with the improper text. The picture and text together represented a publication which claimed that the plaintiff was guilty before he had been judged by the competent criminal court and, consequently, infringed the general right of privacy in the form of the presumption of innocence guaranteed by Art. 6 II of the European Convention on Human Rights.

2. The words accompanying the text requires closer scrutiny.

(a) This contains the allegation that the plaintiff has taken bribes and gives details of this allegation. It is to be found in the headline itself, which talks of a lively trade in residence permits within the Office for Foreigners. Although the headline does not use the plaintiff's name, the reader is nonetheless alerted to his identity by the picture and the sideline that accompanies it. This contains his name and then asks the question whether he has been aware of the terrorist activities. It is presumed that all along he was responsible for the 'trade in residence permits', and the only doubt that is allowed is related to whether he knowingly took bribes from terrorists. According to the standard established by the OLG (AfP 1976, 132), the headline contains a separate statement. It represents a brief report which is intended to make the reader curious about the text that follows but which is capable of independent evaluation, particularly if taken in conjunction with the picture and the picture sideline. Consequently, it can be expected that readers will have relied on this brief report. Of course it is possible to assume that the average reader of the magazine will be a careful and critical reader. However, it is unrealistic to assume that, given the quantity of information offered by each issue of the magazine, readers will only ever read the headlines *in conjunction* [emphasis added] with the full text which accompanies them. The allegation in the headline is, moreover, formulated in such a way that the meaning it conveys can no longer be altered by the rather weaker comments made in the text. Such a text would, at most, be a contradiction of the headline.

However, there is in fact no contradiction between the headline and the text. The text contains what is promised by the headline, provided one does not only read those comments which could be put forward to support the defendant's case, but rather reads it in context.

Immediately after the alarming warning that a Syrian terrorist commando armed with explosives has penetrated the Federal Republic, comes the news that the commando chief R is very familiar with the border city in North Rhine-Westfalia, and has bought himself a thirteen-month residence permit for DM 3000. The fact that the 'seller' was the plaintiff is suggested not only by the headline, but also by the picture and the sideline that accompanies it since the linking element is the 'Syrian terrorists' and the 'terrorist activities'. In this way the idea of a 'lively trade' is fleshed out with these details.

Later in the article the same events are related in a different form. A Director of Criminal Investigations at the BKA had 'informed' the Office for the Protection of the Constitution, the Federal Information Office, and the criminal authorities of the *Land* that the Syrian terrorist R had obtained a residence permit with the help of intermediaries at the Office for Foreigners having paid them DM 300 before he entered the Federal Republic. This is apparently one and the same set of events which are referred to in the two quite separate parts of the text. The attentive reader will recognize this fact, even though in the second discussion the Syrian is referred to by only one of the three parts of his name and the DM 3000 is reduced to DM 300, perhaps as a consequence of an oversight. The text employs in this instance a different method of relating the story, compared to the account of the same facts in the earlier part of the article. Whereas in the headline and the earlier part of the article the perspective is that of an author who is precisely informed about the events and who is establishing what has occurred, here it is the Director of Criminal Investigations who is the mouthpiece. It would be quite wrong to conclude from this that the author and the defendant have done no more than communicate, in an impartial manner, a few details from amongst the many uncovered by the investigations. That would contradict not only the clear meaning which is given to the article by the headline and the first paragraphs, but is also something which is denied by the defendant itself. For the telex sent by the BKA Director is announced as an internal communication on the part of the BKA which 'reveals' the ways in which the applications came to be made and the permits granted. And revealing means exposing what actually occurred. The style of presentation chosen thus gives the impression that the defendant is only alleging later in the article what the Director has 'stated'. The figure of the 'Director of Criminal Investigations' thus lends an appearance of authenticity to the allegation.

The fact that it was the plaintiff, himself, who was involved in the trade in residence permits and not, for example, another employee of the Office for Foreigners is made clear once more. For, not only is he presented as the Director of the Office for Foreigners who [personally] made the decision on 70 to 80 per cent of the applications made by Arabs; but also that the documents pertaining to the Syrians R and A were discovered when his offices were raided by the police; the Director, once more, granted the permits personally.

The fact that the Syrians R and A, who are both terrorists, are mentioned in the same context gives the reader the impression that both R and A bribed the plaintiff.

The allegation that the plaintiff had taken bribes from Syrian terrorists is in no way diminished or weakened by another statement contained in the article that the State Prosecution Authorities are conducting, with the support of the BKA, a wider criminal investigation against a further eleven defendants for bribery, corruption and breach of the Act on Foreigners, and that these defendants included the previous Director of the Foreigners' Office. This part of the text may be unobjectionable since, while it identifies the defendants, it does not prejudice their cases. However, it does not have the effect of reversing the content of the whole of the rest of the article by stating that the investigations are yet to reveal whether the plaintiff has in fact committed the criminal offences of which he is accused.

In fact, the shadow is further cast on the plaintiff as a result of a further statement that 'the investigators thought' that, beyond the permits granted to the Syrian terrorists A and R, the plaintiff may have received further payments of between DM 500 and 3000 per permit 'generously' granted to other Turks, Iranians, and Syrians. Of course, this in no way revokes or qualifies the allegation regarding bribery by the two Syrians. What must be assessed is whether the author and the defendant are not themselves adopting what the investigators 'believe' in the same way that they allowed the 'Director of Criminal Investigations' to speak for them. This point should not, however, be regarded as being at the heart of the decision, for it is not relevant to the decision.

The LG based its rejection of the claim principally on the fact, also referred to by the defendant in its defence, that it was apparent from the article that the plaintiff was still being investigated but that his guilt was not yet definitively established. It is true that the article does not refer to a completed process of investigation, and so does not state that it can with certainty be expected that the plaintiff will be found guilty. This, however, is not the issue. What is decisive is that the defendants in some parts of the article makes allegations about the guilt of the plaintiff with the—understandable—encouragement to the readers that they should believe them. Furthermore, these allegations are made without any reference to the fact that (first) the plaintiff contested his guilt or (secondly) to the points which he was putting forward in his own defence.

(b) The defendants did not act in the defence of legitimate interests.

(aa) They did not examine with necessary care the truth of its allegation. On the contrary they made this allegation despite having insufficient information at their disposal. In their written statements the defendants relied upon the following matters:

- a criminal investigation was being conducted into the plaintiff's activities in 1982 on the grounds of suspicion of bribery;
- the investigations were conducted not only by the state prosecuting authorities but also by the Federal Office of Criminal Investigations (BKA);
- the plaintiff was removed from his position as Director of the Foreigners' Office and moved to another office;
- he was later (although after the appearance of the article) temporarily suspended from office.

The defendants could have reported all these matters without infringing the duty to check the truth. These matters did not represent, however, the basis for alleging that the plaintiff had been bribed by Syrian terrorists and for fleshing out this allegation with further details.

During the litigation, the defendants did not say what other information they had at their disposal. The article indicates that the defendants had succeeded in discovering certain details from the investigation documents. It must be doubted whether 'the investigating authorities', that is the state prosecuting authorities or the officials of the BKA, had told the defendants what they 'believed'. The final report of the BKA was not yet available. As the decision of the Chamber in Case No. 15 U 177/85 indicated, it was only completed in April 1983. After the report was issued, the state prosecuting authorities continued their investigations for a further two years before they decided to initiate criminal proceedings, which eventually were not allowed to develop into a full trial. As it appears from the decisions of the LG and the OLG which did not allow the case to go to full trial, there was no proof in the form of witnesses or documentary evidence of the allegation that the plaintiff had taken money. The defendant should have concluded, from what it read in the investigation documents, that the grounds for suspicion were not sufficient in order to allege publicly that the plaintiff had been bribed by Syrian terrorists. Once the criminal proceedings were brought, the defendant could have reported these (i.e. the nature of the charges).

In circumstances where the investigatory authorities are considering in depth the suspicion that a criminal act has been committed, and that point is not contested by the defendant but rather confirmed, the duty incumbent upon the media to check the truth of what they report does not allow them to elaborate the grounds for suspicion which they have not gleaned from their own research, but merely derived in a partial and fragmentary manner from the documents relating to an investigation into specific allegations about the guilt of the person in question. This is no longer a case where the media is trying to rouse the awareness of the public in order to bring the truth to light. Consequently, it can only be said that there is a legitimate public interest in the information in so far as the public should be informed of the investigatory activities of the authorities, which was one of the issues covered by the defendant in a short paragraph in its article. To run ahead of the investigating authorities and to communicate its own conclusions from the investigations, even before the authorities have themselves formed a final conclusion, includes a significant risk of misinformation without a corresponding recognisable utility in the provision of such information even though it might be more attractive for readers to be given definite results rather than questions and problems.

Even where an investigation is still in the process of being conducted, there may be situations in which the media may go beyond the information provided to them in this context. This would be the case, for example, where the media are criticising the authorities for dragging their feet in an investigation, or where they are objecting to the presence of irrelevant influences upon the investigation, or the withholding of certain evidence. None of these factors apply here. The defendant only sought to publish the information which it had discovered from the investigation documents and which it had prepared in its own way for publication.

The defendant may not derive a defence from the fact that after extensive further investigations the state prosecuting authorities did decide to bring proceedings against the plaintiff and in fact did seek to claim that the plaintiff was guilty of the acts which the defendant had earlier 'established'. At the time of the publication of the article these allegations were not allowed to be made. Nor is it permissible from today's perspective to repeat them. The intervening time is irrelevant.

Should these arguments be considered incorrect, it is likewise possible to argue that the defendant did not act, from a wider legal perspective, in the defence of a legitimate interest.

(*bb*) The standard which governs press, radio, and television reports of criminal activities which certain (identified) persons are said to have committed, where these persons are the subject of criminal investigations, is increasingly the standard of the 'presumption of innocence' [references omitted]. The presumption of innocence is a principle recognised in all states which adhere to the rule of law, and it has been defined more precisely in Art. 6 II European Convention on Human Rights (ECHR). This provision is applicable law in the Federal Republic. The addressees of this provision are, *inter alia*, criminal judges and the investigation authorities, which, for example, must exercise a corresponding degree of caution when making statements to the press; the media are not covered by this provision. However, the effects of the presumption of innocence extend into the realm of privacy and demand that this right is formulated in such a way as to protect the presumption of innocence and that consequently the presumption of innocence is seen as a protected interest for all persons. If the right of personality is understood in these terms, it places limits upon reports of criminal activities, as a counterbalance to the freedom of the press. It was in this sense that this court applied the presumption of innocence in its earlier decision (AfP 1985, 293) which considered proceedings brought by the same plaintiff against another newspaper.

Under Art. 6 II ECHR the presumption of innocence operates in favour of the 'accused person'. This phrase should not, however, be understood in a strictly technical sense as it is under the rules of criminal procedure. Undoubtedly a suspect is also covered by this provision. Furthermore, the practice of the European Court of Human Rights would appear to cover also an accused person ('*Beschuldigter*') as defined by the rules of criminal procedure (see Peukert, EuGRZ 1980, p. 260 who argues that the presumption of innocence should also apply in the preliminary proceedings). In any case, there is no cause for regarding the presumption of innocence, as one aspect of the general right of personality, as arising only once the proceedings themselves begin, since the particular need for protection of a person subject to criminal investigation, who will be required to defend himself in criminal proceedings, arises already at an earlier stage of the procedure, in particular because prejudgments made by the press can have an effect beyond the official inquiries. The plaintiff, who was a person under suspicion at the time when the article was published, was therefore under the protection of the presumption of innocence. This has the effect that when the press alleges the guilt of such a person, and base that allegation on substantial grounds of suspicion, it will not itself be acting on the basis of a legitimate interest. It even follows from the presumption of innocence that such allegations are unlawful right up to the time when the criminal court makes its decision, regardless of whether they are true or untrue. The civil law cause of action which forms the basis for resisting prejudicial statements is consequently to be derived from §§ 823 I and 1004 BGB. A reason for such a strict application of the presumption of innocence can be found *inter alia* where the criminal proceedings are not yet concluded and where the proceedings are for an injunction or for some other form of interim order. The fact that the question of truth is irrelevant means that the person who has undermined the presumption of innocence cannot bring evidence that the person who is subject to investigation is in fact guilty. This prevents a situation in which parallel and competing investigations into the guilt of that person are undertaken in the context of the civil and criminal proceedings; it also prevents the judge in the civil proceedings coming to a different conclusion to the criminal court.

Where, however, the criminal proceedings conclude, as here, in favour of the accused, whether he is found not guilty or whether the proceedings never come to trial, then there are no grounds for not including the question of truth. An untrue presumption of guilt constitutes a particularly serious breach of the presumption of innocence. Only on this basis can the severity of the invasion of the right of privacy be evaluated. The appropriate provision for such a case, which is a *lex specialis vis-à-vis* § 823 I, is therefore § 823 II BGB read in conjunction with § 186 of the Criminal Code; from this conclusion follows a reversal of the burden of proof. The presumption of innocence must be assessed as a matter of law in the context of the defence of legitimate interests and must therefore be evaluated against the fundamental principle of the freedom of the press; this evaluation will generally result in the conclusion that the press is not acting in the defence of legitimate interests where it is alleging the guilt of the person under investigation.

There may be exceptions to this principle where there are circumstances of particular urgency which influence the conduct of the press. For example, those cases which were mentioned above as regards the question of qualifications of the duty to check the truth of statements could be repeated here. However, it must be stated that in this case there are no grounds for recognising an exception. The defendant did not act in the defence of legitimate interests when it alleged that the plaintiff had been bribed by Syrian terrorists.

3. The tort committed by the defendants represents a serious breach of the right of privacy, which justifies the award of damages for pain and suffering under § 847 BGB. The effects of the breach were serious for the plaintiff. This is all the more so since, apart from the words and text, he was exposed to public scrutiny and a negative judgment by the public as a result of the publication of his picture. This makes the interference with the right of privacy more serious than it would have been had it involved the mere citation of a person's name. Also, the fault of the defendant, or more precisely the negligence of those who acted on their behalf, is also to be seen as gross. This is the case because its actions went beyond those laid down in No. 12 of the Press Code established by the German Press Council, which is to be seen as the correct measure of journalistic care. The interference suffered by the plaintiff cannot be made good by any means other than the award of damages for pain and suffering. The short report printed in the '*Rückspiegel*' in Issue No. 20/86, which stated that the OLG had finally rejected the admissibility of the proceedings had only a very small compensatory effect.

4. The defendants are responsible for the unlawful and negligent acts of the persons who acted on their behalf. In the case of this article, the story was of a highly sensitive nature, and a constitutionally appointed representative under § 31 BGB should have been required to check it, for which the defendant is unconditionally liable. § 31 BGB is applicable to *Kommanditgesellschaften*. It is not clear whether this control actually took place. If it did not, then the fault of the defendants lies in an organisational failure for which the defendants are responsible by virtue of § 823 BGB. In addition, the defendant is responsible for the departmental editor under § 831 BGB.

5. Damages for pain and suffering in the amount of DM 10,000 appear to be appropriate in all the circumstances.

Case 34

OBERLANDESGERICHT HAMBURG 21 MAY 1987
NJW 1988, 737

Facts

The plaintiff claims damages for immaterial harm resulting from a headline in the defendant's national daily newspaper. The Landgericht allowed the claim in part. The plaintiff's appeal was allowed in part, and the defendant's appeal was dismissed.

Reasons

I. The defendant is guilty of a culpable invasion of the plaintiff's right of personality (§ 823 I BGB).

1. The principal invasion of the plaintiff's right consists in the fact that the main headline in the 19 May 1986 issue of the defendant's newspaper B was so drafted as to suggest that the plaintiff would accept or had accepted DM 80,000 in return for being portrayed in the nude. This would be the impression received by any reader of this number of the newspaper who did not go on to read the full text of the article on the front page. The Landgericht was right to state that such readers would be very numerous. Headlines in this newspaper are set up in order to stimulate interest and curiosity about the article in question and induce readers to buy the paper. That is clear from the layout in this issue. The main headline can be read from quite a distance and can therefore be taken in by a person seeing the paper on a news-stand or being read by someone else.

The front page is so laid out that the reader learns the truth very gradually. The words 'K Nude—DM 80,000' were readable from a great distance. Persons closer-to could see the text 'K Nude. She wants DM 80,000.' Adjoining the headline is a coloured picture of the plaintiff unclad down to the bosom; only closer inspection reveals this to be a drawing. Below the picture one sees, in somewhat larger letters, the words 'No smile, the cool look—K in the P-Calendar'. Even this does not tell the reader that there was no question of the plaintiff seeking a fee for publicity. The reader is throughout led to believe what the headline suggests. Only when the small print begins does the reader learn the truth, and then only if close enough to read it. The great majority of those unable to read this small print, especially those who do not buy the paper, will conclude to the discredit of the plaintiff that she was ready for a fee to display her body in the nude, partly because of what they have read, but partly also because they expect sensations from the B newspaper. Most readers will never learn the unsensational fact of the matter, namely that the plaintiff was actually claiming damages for having been so portrayed.

Even those who read the text below the drawing would have the same impression, for in the main they would conclude that the plaintiff allowed herself to be portrayed in the nude in the P-Calendar and was now demanding a fee for it. It is quite unlikely that anyone who did not have the paper in his hands would read the full text on page one and appreciate the truth of the matter, which was revealed only in its final sentence.

2. As drafted—and the defendant is responsible for its drafting—the headline invaded the rights of the plaintiff. It is true that any newspaper report is capable of being misunderstood by a cursory reader or of giving rise to false inferences. That is why this court has decided that one must put up with such negative reactions if a press report is accurate and not misleading; on a balancing of the interests involved, such invasions of the personality are not unlawful, for it would constitute a grave constraint on the basic right of freedom of the press if publishers were held responsible for misinterpretations which are, after all, hardly foreseeable. This applies particularly to readers who simply go by the titles of articles in the middle of a paper or journal and pay no heed to the text; the press need not concern itself with such cursory readers.

But it is different when headlines on the front page are calculated to excite the interest of people with no mind to read anything else in the paper, such as those who are wondering whether to buy the paper or glancing at a copy read by someone else in a train or a bus. Such a headline must be considered on its own, independently of the body of the article it heralds, for it can be foreseen that it will often be read cursorily in this way, and the press must certainly strive to avoid recognisable risks of likely misunderstandings, as indeed this court had already said. That is the case here.

3. The defendant was at fault. There was an obvious risk that the mention of the well-known plaintiff's name in conjunction with the idea of nudity and a

sum of money would conjure up derogatory assumptions affecting her right of personality. Yet gravely at fault though the responsible editors were, it is not established with sufficient certainty that they deliberately intended to cause the harm.

II. An award of damages for pain and suffering (*Schmerzensgeld*) is justified in this case.

1. The Bundesgerichtshof has always held that even where there has been an unlawful and culpable invasion of the right of personality, the victim can claim money damages for immaterial harm only when the gravity of the invasion makes such a *solatium* absolutely necessary. Whether such an invasion is sufficiently grave depends on all the facts of the case, including the seriousness and intrusiveness of the invasion, the dissemination of the publication, the duration of the harm to the victim's interests and reputation, the nature of and reasons for the defendant's conduct and the degree to which he was to blame.

2. Given the very wide circulation of the B newspaper, the headline must have been taken in by a very large number of people who read no further. Thus the misapprehension we have indicated must have been very widely disseminated. The harm to the plaintiff's reputation as a political figure well-known at home and abroad was grave and longlasting, and her name in the leading headline of the B paper, which would immediately command attention, placed her in a context highly prejudicial to her honour as a woman, diminished her seriousness as a politician and reduced her standing as a public figure. Apart from this, what was published in the B newspaper was not independently defamatory: it was the way the front page was laid out which induced the false impression of what the article went on to state.

The wrong was not, however, as great as might be expected from publication in the B newspaper, for anyone who read the whole of the front page would learn the truth of the matter.

The informational value of the fact that the plaintiff was claiming damages from P cannot be invoked here, for it was trivial. This fact could have been communicated quite licitly without infringing the plaintiff's rights at all, but the fact that the infringement might have been avoided does not mitigate the infringement which occurred. It is, on the other hand, relevant that the B newspaper did publish a correction on the front page of its edition of 24 July 1986. This certainly amounts to an attempt to allay the consequences so far as those who were misinformed by the headline are concerned, but it cannot be said that it significantly diminished, much less neutralised, the effect of the publication in invading the plaintiff's rights: the correction was published in an unobtrusive manner which had none of the dramatic effect of the original publication, and in any case it can have reached only B's regular readers, and not the many other people who were affected by the original invasion of the plaintiff's right of personality.

III. The appropriate sum to award by way of solatium is DM 10,000. The proven defamation is a weighty one, which set the plaintiff as a woman and well-known public person in a most degrading light. Those who read the headline and not the full article were left with the impression that the plaintiff was ready to let herself be portrayed in the nude for a fee—an impression quite at variance with the public esteem in which the plaintiff was held. This was calculated to do lasting harm to the plaintiff's reputation and standing. This needs no elucidation. It is equally obvious that because the plaintiff is a prominent politician, the adverse effect on her is much greater than it would be on a simple citizen known only to a few intimates. Finally, one must remember that those who drafted the headline must have been aware, had they been taking the proper care, of the grave risk of invading the plaintiff's right of personality. On the other hand, this invasion was not the result of a report which was actually false, as we have said above, and this also must be taken into account in determining the amount of solatium. Given that in this case the true facts were given to those who read the newspaper, the invasion was not as serious as it would have been had it resulted from false statements in *both* the headline *and* the text. Further, the defendant's published correction went some way towards reducing the damage. Taking all these points into consideration, we must say that the sum awarded by the Landgericht does not seem adequate compensation for the way the plaintiff's right of personality has been infringed. On the other hand, the plaintiff's demand for at least DM 30,000 does not seem appropriate on the facts of this case.

Notes to Cases 29–34

1. The first of these cases marks a real turning-point in German tort law by creating the new all-embracing right of personality and privacy. It is derived from a somewhat strained—but in the event successful—interpretation of the Constitution of Bonn of 1949 the relevant provisions of which are reproduced in the addendum to cases 27 and 28. The linking of the development of the civil law with the Constitution has already been noted. Here suffice it to mention two further points of interest. First, it reveals that both in Germany and in the United States the constitutional background has had a marked but different influence on the law of defamation and privacy. Thus, whereas in Germany this has often led to a greater protection of privacy, in America the emphasis on freedom of speech has often had the reverse effect. We shall return to this important point later on. Secondly, the interaction of public and private law has been maintained through these

years, the Constitutional Court often being called to decide disputes which involved privacy questions. Thus, in BVerfGE 34, 269 it was called upon to consider the constitutionality of the award of monetary compensation in cases of infringement of this new right (see above, Ch. 2, section A.2(*e*)(iv)); BVerfGE 35, 202, is reproduced above as case 32. For other instances see BVerfGE 54, 129; BVerfGE 54, 148; BVerfGE 54, 208 etc.

2. At the risk of becoming repetitive one must stress that these judgments, and indeed the constitutional provisions mentioned above, can only be fully understood if one bears in mind the utter contempt shown towards human dignity by the Nazi regime. It was ironical therefore that the breakthrough decision of 1954 was indirectly connected with one of its former sympathizers. (BVerfGE 7, 198 and BVerfGE 30, 173 also involved former Nazis.) For the mysterious Dr S of that judgment was Dr H. H. G. Schacht, an undoubtedly distinguished economist and financier who played an important role in the restoration of a stable currency after the devastating German inflation of 1923. From 1923 to 1930 he served as president of the Reichsbank and became a supporter of the Nazi party. When Hitler came to power, Schacht played a leading role in the rearmament programme, but from 1938/9 onwards he was urging Hitler to reduce expenditure for armaments as the only way to balance the budget and reduce inflation which had begun to rise again. In July 1944 he was confined to a concentration camp until the end of the war and then he was one of the principal accused at the first Nuremberg trial. He was acquitted at the trial only to be brought subsequently before the German People's court at Stuttgart under the 'denazification' laws. Sentenced to eight years' detention in a labour camp, Schacht appealed against his conviction and resumed a highly successful and respected career as a financier.

3. Soon after the first decision, the BGH reaffirmed its stand in an interesting case brought as a result of the publication of Cosima Wagner's private letters and diaries (BGHZ 15, 249); and, again, two years later in the 'Dahlke' case (BGHZ 20, 345). A year later, the BGH declared its willingness to take the same stand when the interference with the plaintiff's privacy was merely negligent. There followed the landmark case of the 'Gentleman rider' (case 30) which, along with the case of the professor of canon law (case 31), settled the problem of the theoretical basis of monetary compensation for violations of the new right which had not been decreed until that moment. During these years litigation increased at a considerable rate and in the process a number of issues were clarified. The following are but illustrations. BGHZ 24, 72 (communication of medical reports without the patient's consent may amount to a violation of the right); BGHZ 27, 284 (recording a conversation with the speaker without his knowledge and consent may also infringe the new right); BGH NJW 1965, 685 (fictitious

interview with a well-known figure of international society); BGHZ 39, 124 (statements made about a television broadcaster can be actionable under this heading even though they could also have founded an action on defamation (§ 185 StGB in conjunction with § 823 II BGB)). *Vis-à-vis* this last point, however, the better view is that an action for violation of the right of privacy has a residual character and will, normally, be available only if there is no other specific rule that covers the point (e.g. protection of name (§ 12 BGB); artistic creations, etc. § 97 of the Copyright Act). (BGHZ 30, 7, 11). § 823 I BGB will also be chosen instead of § 823 II BGB in conjunction with the Criminal Code as the only way of awarding *Schmerzensgeld* (§ 847 BGB) to the victim (cf. OLG Düsseldorf NJW 1980, 599). For further amusing instances see OLG Frankfurt NJW 1982, 648: defendant produced a sticker depicting *two* cranes, copulating, accompanied by, *inter alia*, the word 'Lusthansa'; Lufthansa, which has a crane as an emblem, sued but failed. In OLG Frankfurt NJW 1985, 1649 a different company produced a sticker with the letters BMW accompanied by the words 'Bums Mal Wieder'. In one sense this could be taken to mean 'Bump [or bang] once again', but *bummsen* can, in colloquial German, mean 'to fuck' so the famous motor-car company *successfully* sued for an injunction. Though the decision was reversed on appeal (see BGHZ 91, 117; 98, 94), the extension of these rules to cover legal (as well as physical) persons is not in doubt: BVerfGE 21, 362; BGH NJW 1974, 1762; BGH NJW 1975, 1882; BGHZ 78, 24.

4. If, in accordance with the above, it is established that the plaintiff's claim can proceed on the grounds that his right of privacy has been interfered with, then the court is obliged to consider the merits of the claim in the light of all the surrounding circumstances. The difficulties involved in balancing competing values are fully exposed and considered in case 32 which shows *inter alia* that not only celebrities but also ex-convicts have, in certain circumstances, rights of privacy. Finding the *via media* in such circumstances is by no means an easy task, but it is one that is performed with admirable clarity and courage of opinion by the Constitutional Court. The approach in such matters being casuistic it is difficult to state hard and fast rules, but perhaps two threads of thought are discernible in the judgments. First, freedom of expression will, on the whole, prevail over the right of privacy where the publication, broadcast, etc. aim at educating and informing the public rather than pursuing mere sensationalism or trying to satisfy the public's taste for gossip. Secondly, the chances of success of a privacy claim tend to decrease as the public profile of the plaintiff increases. But even public figures can seek protection of their privacy in appropriate circumstances. (See case 32 and BGHZ 36, 77, 80.)

5. German law on disclosure of true private facts is particularly interest-

ing not least because its position is so diametrically different from that found in the USA. It thus offers excellent material for reflective comparisons about the basic values and attitudes of these two societies. Two points deserve particular attention. First is the Germanic tendency to distinguish the disclosed facts according to whether they belong to (a) the 'intimate' (b) the 'private' or (c) the 'social' sphere of the plaintiff—the first receiving almost total protection, the last little or none. Though the need to make such distinctions is accepted both by academics and courts (see Schwerdtner, *Münchener Kommentar*, 2nd edn., I (1984) para. 12 BGB no. 231; Thomas in Palandt *Bürgerliches Gesetzbuch*, 51st edn. (1992) para. 823 no. 178; Ricker in *NJW* 1990, 2098) it will also strike Common lawyers as Germanic in its approach and unworkable in practice. On the other hand the German material should also prompt reflection on the merits of according even to public figures some degree of privacy and seclusion. Two decisions of the Federal Court, dealing with the unauthorised tapping of a telephone conversation between two prominent leaders of the Christian Democratic party, clearly illustrate these points. For in the first (BGH JZ 1979, 349) the Court held that even politicians are entitled to rights of privacy, whereas in the second (BGH JZ 1979, 351) the point was made that these rights would be overridden only where there was a real and serious interest to inform the public. First Amendment admirers may cringe at such decisions; but in the light of many successes of investigative journalism directed against German public figures, any outright condemnation of German law would be unfounded.

6. Monetary compensation is often the plaintiff's main demand. The difficulties created here by § 253 BGB—overcome by cases 30 and 31 and not to be found in any other system—have been discussed above (ch. 2, section A.2(e)(iv)). But the intrusion into the plaintiff's privacy must also be grave and objectively serious, otherwise the courts would be inundated with frivolous claims; the point is raised in ch. 4, section A.3(e), and is illustrated by case 113, below. Moreover, the size of the monetary compensation (whenever it is sought which is by no means always) is modest as is shown by an analysis of all published cases for the period 1980 to 1993 (see below subsection 8).

7. Injunctive relief, though not specifically provided for by the tort provisions of the Code, has for a long time now (see RGZ 60, 6) also been available on the analogy of § 1004 BGB (taken from land law). Indeed, the Code of Civil Procedure (ZPO) in a number of provisions (e.g. 920 II, 935, 937 II, 940, 944 etc.) contains rules which are meant to facilitate the granting of this remedy which, however, does not resolve the merits of the dispute but only provides interim relief. Thus the procedure can be quick, entirely oral, and in very urgent cases even oral argument may be waived (§ 937 II ZPO).

Again, in cases of urgency, the remedy can be granted by the Presiding judge sitting alone (§ 944 ZPO) and even the plaintiff's burden of proof may be eased in various ways. Though this remedy suffers from one main drawback—it can only be claimed in those cases where the plaintiff has advance warning of an imminent publication of offending material—the way it has been shaped by German law seems sufficiently interesting to warrant more attention by English specialists than it has hitherto received. (For details on this subject see: Schwerdtner, *Münchener Kommentar* 2nd edn. I, (1984) para. 12 no. 322; Baumbach/Lauterbach/Albers/Hartmann, *Zivilprozessordnung* 50th edn. (1992), commentary on the paragraphs mentioned above.) On the other hand, the idea is unlikely to appeal to American lawyers who, in their desire to leave the Press totally unfettered can (in the eyes of a foreign observer at least) appear to be excessively worried by *all* notions of 'prior restraint'.

8. At the time when this manuscript was being sent to the Press the Lord Chancellor's department issued a Consultation paper entitled *Infringement of Privacy*. It provides a full and readable account of this topic and, in its recommendations, it goes beyond the Calcutt suggestions by advocating the introduction (subject to some important constraints) of a general right of privacy. Just as importantly, it contains a number of subsidiary points and assumptions that can (to some extent) be tested by applying the comparative method. Thus, first it gives a 'guesstimate' of the number of cases that are likely to come before the English courts if the new right is recognised. This is estimated to be 'in the hundreds rather than the thousands' (p. 52). Secondly, while not suggesting a mandatory figure of damages, the paper implies (at p. 45) that a sum in the region of £3000 might be an appropriate guideline for judges. Finally (at p. 42) the paper boldly recommends the availability of injunctions, though it is conscious of the 'chilling effect' this remedy may have on investigative journalism. The following data, discussed by my research pupil Mr Wolfgang Vugt in a paper currently prepared for publication, is derived from *all* published German decisions handed down between 1980 and 1993. Since it may be of special interest to researchers, full details of the cases are provided. Thus:

First, the total number of cases for this period is 122. Given that the German right of privacy is not 'hedged' in by the kind of limitations proposed by the Lord Chancellor's paper, the estimates of litigation contained in the latter document may, in the light of the German experience, be on the pessimistic side. Overall, however, it is unlikely that the new right of privacy will create an excessive load for the courts or an unbearable burden on the Press.

Secondly, in 25 cases 'moral damages' were granted by the German courts showing, as the Lord Chancellor's paper implicitly suggests, that damages may not, necessarily, be the remedy most sought after by affected plaintiffs. These are the following (amount—in DM—awarded is given in parenthesis after the reference): LG Stuttgart, 1983 AfP 292 (5,000); OLG Stuttgart, 1983 AfP 291 (10,500); OLG Düsseldorf, 1984 AfP 229; BGH, 1985 AfP 111 (10,500); OLG Frankfurt, 1986 AfP 140 (2,000); OLG Köln, 1987 AfP (10,000); OLG Frankfurt, 1987 AfP 526 (10,000); OLG Köln, 1986 AfP 347 (10,000); LG Hamburg, 1987, AfP 633 (5,000); LG München, 1987 AfP 634 (20,000 to two plaintiffs); OLG Köln, 1987 AfP 602 (5,000); LG Lübeck, 1987 AfP 721 (1,600); OLG Hamburg, 1987 AfP 703 (3,000); OLG Hamburg, 1988 AfP 247 (10,000); OLG Köln, 1987 NJW 2682 (10,000); BGH, 1988 AfP 30 = 1988 VersR 497 (amount to be fixed); BGH, 1988 AfP 34 (amount to be fixed); AG Kaufbeuren, 1988 AfP 277 (500); OLG Oldenburg, 1989 AfP 556 = 1989 NJW 400 (4,000); OLG Karlsruhe, 1989 VersR 1097 (3,000); LG Köln, 1991 AfP 757 (8,000); OLG Frankfurt, 1992 NJW 441 (2,000); LG Köln, 1992 AfP 83 (6,000); OLG Hamburg, 1992 AfP 376 (10,000); LG Bonn, 1992 AfP 386 (10,000). At (approximately) DM 7–7,500 the average German figure is almost identical to the amounts envisaged by the Lord Chancellor's paper.

Thirdly, these sums refer to damages for 'moral damages'. Where plaintiffs can prove additional, pecuniary losses they, too, may be recoverable. Thus in OLG München 1988 NJW 915, the plaintiff complained of being photographed while sunbathing in the nude in the famous *Englischer Garten*. It was alleged that the subsequent publication of the photograph in a local paper resulted in the plaintiff failing to obtain a wage increase which was in the pipeline. The lost 'benefit' was awarded in the form of damages. No doubt, the same solution should be adopted by English law as well.

Fourthly, in some cases where the complaining plaintiff has not suffered any loss but the defendant has made a gain (at the expense of the former), the measure of damages may be restitutionary rather than compensatory, recovery being allowed on the basis of § 812 BGB. Thus see: OLG Hamburg, 1983 AfP 282 (DM 4,000); BGH 1987 GRUR 128 (5,500); LG München, 1987 AfP 634 (1360); OLG Karlsruhe, 1989 AfP 558 = 1989 VersR 259 = 1989 NJW 401 (500); BGH, 1993 VersR 66 (amount to be fixed). Sometimes, such actions for account succeed under different provisions (e.g. the Copyright Act). See: BGH, 1987 AfP 508. An equal number of courts, however, have failed to make an award under this heading. See: OLG Frankfurt, 1984 AfP 115; OLG Hamburg, 1985 AfP 120; AG Bonn, 1990 AfP 64; AG Hamburg, 1991 AfP 659; OLG Hamburg, 1992 AfP 159.

Fifthly, in 30 cases injunctions were sought and granted, sometimes initially following the expedited procedure described above. There are some lessons here for English law; and some key structural differences with American law must also be noted. The cases granting injunctions were:

OLG Hamburg, 1981 AfP 356; OLG München, 1981 AfP 360; OLG
München, 1982 AfP 230; LG Köln, 1983 AfP 414; OLG München, 1985
AfP 209; OLG München, 1986 NJW 1260; OLG Hamburg, 1987 AfP 518;
OLG Frankfurt, 1987 AfP 528; LG Oldenburg, 1987 NJW 1419; BGH,
1987 AfP 508; OLG Hamburg, 1987 AfP 703; LG Oldenburg, 1987 AfP
537; OLG Hamburg, 1988 AfP 143; LG Berlin, 1988 AfP 168; OLG Hamm
1988 AfP 258; BVerfG, 1990 NJW 1980; OLG Hamburg, 1989 GRUR 666;
OLG Hamburg, 1991 AfP 437 (partial granting of injunction); OLG
München, 1991 AfP 435; OLG Frankfurt, 1991 GRUR 49; BGH, 1990 AfP
209; OLG Hamburg, 1991 AfP 626; OLG Hamburg, 1991 AfP 537; LG
Köln, 1991 AfP 757; OLG München, 1992 AfP 78; OLG Hamburg, 1991
AfP 537; OLG Hamburg, 1993 AfP 576; BGH, 1993 VersR 614; BVerfG,
1993 NJW 1463; LG Hamburg, 1993 AfP 679.

Finally, an almost equal number of decisions have refused plaintiffs the
injunctions they had sought, demonstrating that German courts take the
balancing act they are expected to perform between the competing interests
very seriously. These are: BGH, 1980 AfP 154; OLG Hamburg, 1982 AfP
177; OLG Hamburg, 1983 AfP 466; OLG Köln, 1985 AfP 293; OLG
Oldenburg, 1988 AfP 82; LG Oldenburg, 1987 AfP 720; LG Oldenburg,
1987 AfP 720; LG Oldenburg, 1988 AfP 167; OLG Frankfurt, 1989 AfP
402; OLG Karlsruhe, 1989 AfP 542; OLG Celle, 1989 AfP 575; LG Berlin,
1989 AfP 59; OLG München, 1989 AfP 570; LG Köln, 1989 766; OLG
Köln, 1989 AfP 764; OLG München, 1990 AfP 214; BGH, 1990 AfP 209;
BVerfG, 1990 AfP 192; OLG Frankfurt, 1990 AfP 229; OLG Hamburg,
1991 AfP 533; OLG Düsseldorf, 1991 AfP 424; OLG München, 1991 AfP
534; BGH, 1991 AfP 410; BGH, 1991 AfP 410; BGH, 1991 AfP 416 = 1991
VersR 433; OLG Hamburg, 1992 AfP 279; BGH, 1992 AfP 140; OLG Celle,
1992 AfP 295; KG Berlin, 1992 AfP 302; BGH, 1993 VersR 66; OLG
Hamburg, 1992 AfP 267.

9. English law, on the whole, compares unfavourably with German law.
True, many aspects of the human personality and privacy are protected by a
multitude of existing torts, but this means fitting the facts of each case in the
pigeon-hole of an existing tort and this process may not only involve
strained constructions; often it may also leave a deserving plaintiff without a
remedy. Thus, trespass or nuisance can, at times, help (see *Bernstein* v.
Skyviews and General Ltd. [1978] QB 479) but these old torts have their own
limitations (e.g. actions in nuisance are only available to persons having an
interest in land). An ingenious attempt to extend the tort of passing-off met
with only a cautious response (*Sim* v. *H. J. Heinz Co. Ltd.* [1959] 1 WLR
313). Defamation will, more often, be invoked, though this again will not
always work (especially when the defence of truth is available). In the celebrated case of *Tolley* v. *Fry* [1931] AC 333, an amateur golfer was depicted

without his permission on a poster advertising chocolate bars while playing golf. He was not described as a bad golfer; nor was he made to advertise a cheap product. But his action succeeded because the court was able to discover an innuendo: the advertisement conveyed the impression that he had 'prostituted' his amateur status for gain, something which carried (carries?) a stigma in the English way of thinking. That this was really a 'privacy' case, however, can be demonstrated by asking what the position would have been if the golfer depicted on the poster had been a celebrated professional. *De lege ferenda* he, too, should have received some legal protection against the unauthorized use of his picture; but the way the *Tolley* decision was phrased suggests that this action would have failed—and if this is so the tort of defamation is clearly inadequate for this purpose. The limitations of the tort of defamation also become obvious where the defence of truth is available. If, for example, a case like *Melvin* v. *Read* 112 Cal. App. 285, 297 P. 91 (1931) were to arise in England the plaintiff would almost certainly be left without protection. Likewise with facts similar to those in *Briscoe* v. *Reader's Digest Association Inc.* 483 P. 2d 34 (1971). English law thus does not encourage citizens to forgive even once, let alone seventy times seven! *Re X* ([1984] 1 WLR 1422) is, perhaps, the case that best brings out the unforgiving and casuistic mentality of English law.

10. In 1968, Mary Bell, a juvenile, was convicted of manslaughter and sentenced to detention for life. In 1984, she was released on licence and, some time later, gave birth to a daughter who was made a ward of court at the initiative of the local authority. Somehow this became known to the Press and an application was made by her mother and the local authority to the High Court for an injunction prohibiting the disclosure of the identity and present whereabouts of *both* child and parents. The application, made on the ground that any such disclosure would be detrimental to the family's newly found peace and stability, was accepted by Balcombe J. and an order prohibiting publication of the said information (but not of the fact of the birth) was duly granted.

In an earlier wardship case (*Re X* [1975] Fam. 47), it was attempted, for the first time, to use the wardship jurisdiction in this type of situation in order to prohibit the publication of a book concerning the ward's deceased father and containing material which, as the defendants conceded, was likely to cause her serious psychological damage if it ever came to her notice. A unanimous Court of Appeal took the view that freedom of speech should prevail. In the event, therefore, the carefully balanced judgment of the trial judge was reversed, Lord Denning MR declaring that 'it would be extending the wardship jurisdiction too far and infringing too much upon the freedom of the Press for us to grant an injunction in this case' (ibid. 59). Roskill LJ echoed similar views, though he felt that in appropriate circumstances a balancing of the competing interests might have to be attempted. Sir John Pennycuick was also anxious to preserve, at least 'in exceptional circumstances' (ibid. 61), the right to make such an order in favour of the ward. In his view, it was the courts' clear duty to attempt to balance the competing interests, even though in this instance freedom of speech prevailed.

One could of course try to reconcile these decisions by reference to their particular facts, even though to the reader of the law reports a clear distinction is not all that obvious. (The preference for free speech in the earlier *Re X* case is even more remarkable considering that the offending parts of the book—a mere eight pages—could have been removed at a very small cost which the parents of the ward were more than willing to meet.) Could one then look at the second *Re X* decision, delivered almost ten years after the earlier one, as reflecting a greater sensitivity to human privacy, especially in the light of adverse reactions—national and international—to the telephone tapping case of *Malone* v. *Metropolitan Police Commissioner* ([1979] Ch. 344)? Linking these two cases may strike some people as odd; but, it is submitted, one can legitimately treat *Re X* as a privacy case or, more precisely, as a case dealing with that type of privacy which Judge Cooley described as 'the right to be let alone' (*Tort* (2nd edn., 1889), 29).

Seen in this light, *Re X* is a remarkable decision since it protects the anonymity of the (innocent) child and, at the same time, the anonymity of the mother/ex-criminal. Remarkable and yet typical of the way that protection is afforded by pushing into existing tort pigeon-holes certain fact situations; and where tort law cannot afford a remedy, by extending an inherent jurisdiction which was meant for many things but was hardly devised as a substitute for a non-existent tort of violation of privacy.

Re X, however, also makes the patchy nature of the protection most obvious. Thus, the mother's anonymity is only incidentally protected. And once the wardship ends (through the death of the child or its reaching the age of 18), the protection will disappear. The Rehabilitation of Offenders Act 1974 will in this case afford no protection (s. 5); and mother and child will run the risk of having their lives destroyed because some popular tabloid feels that the revelation of their new identity may interest its gossip-thirsty readership. The limited nature of the protection is also obvious when one considers that the nature of the infringement of the judge's order would render liable for contempt proceedings only those who were aware of it in the first place. To put it differently, a publication of the identity of Mary Bell by another newspaper which independently made the same discovery and published it before the delivery of the judgment would go unpunished. Are these really acceptable results? Should a young girl of 17 be entitled to protection against her mother's distant past but lose it once she has become 18? Should an ex-criminal—*par excellence* of the Mary Bell type—who committed the crime just barely after attaining the age of criminal capacity (10), be haunted by it for the rest of her life?

11. Sections of the Press have shown equal insensitivity in another area where, it is submitted, the plaintiff's right to be left alone should prevail over the public's interest to know. This involves the identification of victims of sexual offences.

The development of the law in this area is typical of the incremental growth of the Common law. First, no anonymity whatsoever was granted to these unfortunate victims. Then s. 4 of the Sexual Offences (Amendment) Act 1976 granted anonymity to victims of rape offences (as defined narrowly by s. 7(2) of the Act). Victims of 'lesser' sexual offences (such as unlawful sexual intercourse, incest, or buggery), anxious to be left alone to forget their traumatic experiences, were, in fact, left unprotected as far as their privacy was concerned. The Criminal Justice Act 1987 extended anonymity to cases involving conspiracy to rape and burglary with intent to rape; but in the House of Lords the Minister from the Home Office thought that any further extension of the anonymity laws would be 'the thin end of the wedge'. The Calcutt Report disagreed, but the Home Office was, mysteriously it would seem, adamant. And then, quite unexpectedly and with very little publicity, the official attitude changed. The Sexual Offences (Amendment) Act 1991 made it possible to extend by statutory instrument anonymity to all cases of sexual offences; and Statutory Instrument 1336/1992 brought this protection into existence in October 1992. In this branch of the law, the incremental growth of English law has, surely, not been one of its strengths; and the adverse consequences that both the media and anonymous government circles feared would follow any extension of the anonymity laws have failed to materialise. (For further details on the absurdities of the old law see the second edition of this book, pages 320–1; for comparisons with US law see below. See, also, Villa-McDowell, 'Privacy and the Rape Victim: The Inconsistent Treatment of Privacy Interests in The Recent Supreme Court Cases' 2 *Southern California Review of Law and Women's Studies*, 293 (1992).)

12. Telephone tapping, sophisticated eavesdropping, and data banks can also make great intrusions into human privacy. *Malone* v. *Metropolitan Police Commissioner* [1979] Ch. 344 considers the first type of intrusion and after a long, erudite, but timid judgment reaches a negative result. The main argument against recognition of a new right was that such a step could only be taken by the legislator. American readers of *Roberson* v. *Rochester Folding Box Co.* 171 NY 538, 64 NE 442 (1902) will find nothing novel in this. Moreover, constitutional orthodoxy may be on the side of such caution. But tort students should ask themselves whether it is acceptable in the

light of Parliament's inability or unwillingness to face up to the problem. JUSTICE—a non-political pressure group for law reform—had this to say in 1970 about English law: 'English law does . . . provide a remedy for some kinds of intrusion into privacy, but it is certainly not adequate to meet activities of a society which is perfecting more and more sophisticated techniques for intrusion. The present law in the field of privacy is uncoordinated and unsatisfactory, and a strong case . . . exists for the creation by means of statutory provision of comprehensive protection for the right of privacy.' In 1993, despite increasing concern and an ever-growing literature, the position remains the same. (For a comparison with American law see Brittan, 'The Right of Privacy in England and the USA' 37 *Tul. L. Rev.* 235 (1963). For a fuller account of English law see Seipp, 'English Judicial Recognition of a Right of Privacy' *Oxford J. L. Studies* (1983) 324 ff.)

13. The comparison of German and American Law is, in more ways than one, an intellectually rewarding exercise for both systems present considerable similarities (e.g. both have a written Constitution and both can claim a prodigious literature on the subject) and even greater differences in outcome (which can, again, be traced to their Constitutions and the fact that each was attempting to address problems relevant to their particular political backgrounds). The following summary of the law in the United States is taken from an Excursus that Professor David Anderson of the University of Texas at Austin contributed to chapter seven of Markesinis and Deakin, *Tort Law* 3rd edn. (1994).

'Invasion of Privacy'

Although it has no counterpart in English law, the American tort law of invasion of privacy is related closely enough to defamation to deserve a brief mention here. Many libel suits in the United States are combined with claims for invasion of privacy. To some extent privacy law is an outgrowth of changes in the law of defamation. At one time a truthful statement made without adequate justification might have been actionable as defamation in either the US or England, but as truth became an absolute defence, at least in the United States, the need for some other remedy became apparent.

'Invasion of privacy' is an umbrella term encompassing four distinct American torts. In addition, American law recognises other 'rights of privacy' that are not torts and are beyond the scope of this discussion. For example, a constitutional 'right of privacy' protects against governmental interference in such personal matters as abortion and contraception (*Roe* v. *Wade*, 410 US 113 (1973); *Griswold* v. *Connecticut*, 381 US 479 (1965)), and 'privacy' statutes that restrict governmental acquisition and use of certain types of personal information (e.g. Privacy Act of 1974, 5 U.S.C. s. 552a (1992)).

Of the four privacy torts, the one closest to the core of the privacy concept is the cause of action for public disclosure of embarrassing private facts. A person may recover damages for a disclosure that would be highly offensive to a reasonable person and is not of legitimate public concern (Restatement (Second) of Torts s. 652D (1977)). Sexual activities and medical abnormalities are among the kinds of disclosures that are most often litigated. The matter need not have been completely secret before the defendant's disclosure. Even the most intimate secrets usually are known to one's closest friends and family, so it is enough that the defendant has disclosed publicly a matter that previously was known only to such a limited circle (*Sipple* v. *Chronicle Publishing Co.*, 154 Cal. App. 3d 1040, 201 Cal. Rptr. 665 (1984); *Dias* v. *Oakland Tribune, Inc.* 139 Cal. App. 3d 118, 188 Cal. Rptr. 762 (1983); *Melvin* v. *Reid*, 112 Cal. App. 285, 297 P. 91 (1931)). On the other hand, matters of official record may be disclosed with impunity, even if they were previously unknown by the public (*Howard* v. *Des Moines Register & Tribune Co.*, 283 N.W. 2d 289 (1979), cert. denied 445 UKS. 904 (1980)).

The central issue is what facts are 'private', and the law has defined that term so narrowly—and the concept of legitimate public concern so broadly—that very few disclosures are actionable. Courts look to contemporary mores to determine what reasonable people would find highly offensive. From that point of reference, disclosures of such matters as one's income or net worth (*Wolf* v. *Regardie*, 553 A. 2d 1213 (D.C. App. 1989); *Schoneweis* v. *Dando*, 231 Neb. 180, 435 N.W. 2d 666 (1989)), personal idiosyncrasies (*Virgil* v. *Time, Inc.*, 527 F. 2d 1122 (9th Cir. 1975), cert. denied 425 UK.S. 998 (1976); *Sidis* v. *F-R Publishing Corp.*, 113 F. 2d 806 (2nd Cir.), cert. denied 311 U.S. 711 (1940)), illegitimacy (*Heath* v. *Playboy Enterprises Inc.*, 732 F. Supp. 1145 (1990)), or medical diagnosis (*Davis* v. *Monsanto Co.*, 627 F. Supp. 418 (1986); *Child Protection Group* v. *Cline*, 350 S.E. 2d 541 (1986); *Meetze* v. *Associated Press*, 230 S.C. 330, 95 S.E. 2d 606 (1956)) usually are held not to be sufficiently offensive.

The concept of legitimate public concern is inspired by First Amendment values, and therefore is interpreted expansively. The public usually is held to have a legitimate interest in the identity of victims of crimes (including rape and other sex offences) (*The Florida Star* v. *B.J.F.*, 491 U.S. 524 (1989); *Cox Broadcasting Corp.* v. *Cohn*, 420 U.S. 469 (1975)), the sexual activities and medical problems of public officials (*Hubert* v. *Harte-Hanks Texas Newspapers Inc.*, 652 S.W. 2d 546 (1983); *Kapellas* v. *Kofman*, 1 Cal. 3d 20, 81 Cal. Rptr. 360, 459 P. 2d 912 (1969)), and the marital difficulties of celebrities (*Carlisle* v. *Fawcett Publications Inc.*, 201 Cal. App. 2d 733, 20 Cal. Rptr. 405 (1962)). Courts are reluctant to second-guess an editor's judgement that a matter is of legitimate public concern; some judges have

These are impressive credentials for a right of privacy, but we should recognize that we do not have at issue here an action for the invasion of privacy involving the appropriation of one's name or photograph, a physical or other tangible intrusion into a private area, or a publication of otherwise private information that is also false although perhaps not defamatory. The version of the privacy tort now before us—termed in Georgia 'the tort of public disclosure', 231 Ga. 62, 200 SE 2d 130—is that in which the plaintiff claims the right to be free from unwanted publicity about his private affairs, which, although wholly true, would be offensive to a person of ordinary sensibilities. Because the gravamen of the claimed injury is the publication of information, whether true or not, the dissemination of which is embarrassing or otherwise painful to an individual, it is here that claims of privacy most directly confront the constitutional freedoms of speech and press. The face-off is apparent, and the appellants urge upon us the broad holding that the press may not be made criminally or civilly liable for publishing information that is neither false nor misleading but absolutely accurate, however damaging it may be to reputation or individual sensibilities.

It is true that in defamation actions, where the protected interest is personal reputation, the prevailing view is that truth is a defence; and the message of *New York Times* v. *Sullivan* 376 US 254 (1964); *Garrison* v. *Louisiana* 379 US 64 (1964); *Curtis Publishing Co.* v. *Butts* 388 US 130 (1967), and like cases is that the defence of truth is constitutionally required where the subject of the publication is a public official or public figure. What is more, the defamed public official or public figure must prove not only that the publication is false but that it was knowingly so or was circulated with reckless disregard for its truth or falsity. Similarly, where the interest at issue is privacy rather than reputation and the right claimed is to be free from the publication of false or misleading information about one's affairs, the target of the publication must prove knowing or reckless falsehood where the materials published, although assertedly private, are 'matters of public interest' (*Time Inc.* v. *Hill*, above, 385 US 387–8).

The court has nevertheless carefully left open the question whether the First and Fourteenth Amendment require that truth be recognized as a defense in a defamation action brought by a private person as distinguished from a public official or public figure. Garrison held that where criticism is of a public official and his conduct of public business, 'the interest in private reputation is overborne by the larger public interest, secured by the Constitution, in the dissemination of truth', 379 US 72–3 [footnote omitted], but recognized that 'different interest may be involved where purely private libels, totally unrelated to public affairs, are concerned: therefore, nothing we say today is to be taken as intimating any views as to the impact of the constitutional guarantees in the discrete area of purely private libels', id., at 72 n. 8. In similar fashion, *Time* v. *Hill*, above, expressly saved the question whether truthful publication of very private matters unrelated to public affairs could be constitutionally proscribed (385 US 383 n. 7).

Those precedents, as well as other considerations, counsel similar caution here. In this sphere of collision between claims of privacy and those of the free press, the interests on both sides are plainly rooted in the traditions and significant concerns of our society. Rather than address the broader question whether truthful publication may ever be subjected to civil or criminal liability consistently with the First and Fourteenth Amendments, or to put it another way, free from unwanted publicity in the press, it is appropriate to focus on the narrower interface between press and privacy that this case presents, namely whether the State may impose sanctions on the accurate publication of the name of a rape victim obtained from public records—more specifically, from judicial records which are maintained in connection with a public prosecution and which themselves are open to public inspection. We are convinced that the State may not do so.

In the first place, in a society in which each individual has but limited time and resources with which to observe at first hand the operations of his government, he relies necessarily upon the press to bring him in convenient form the facts of those operations. Great responsibility is accordingly placed upon the news media to report fully and accurately the proceedings of government, and official records and documents open to the public are the basic data of governmental operations. Without the information provided by the press most of us and many of our representatives would be unable to vote intelligently or to register opinions on the administration of government generally. With respect to judicial proceedings in particular, the function of the press serves to guarantee the fairness of trials and to bring to bear the beneficial effects of public scrutiny upon the administration of justice. [Reference.]

Appellee has claimed in his litigation that the efforts of the press have infringed his right to privacy by broadcasting to the world the fact that his daughter was a rape victim. The commission of crime, prosecutions resulting from it, and judicial proceedings arising from the prosecutions, however, are without question events of legitimate concern to the public and consequently fall within the responsibility of the press to report the operations of government. . . .

The developing law surrounding the tort of invasion of privacy recognizes a privilege in the press to report the events of judicial proceedings. The Warren and Brandeis article, *supra*, noted that the proposed new right would be limited in the same manner as actions for libel and slander where such a publication was a privileged communication: 'the right to privacy is not invaded by any publication made in a court of justice . . . and (at least in many jurisdictions) reports of any such proceedings would in some measure be accorded a like privilege.'

Addendum 2

The Florida Star v. *B.J.F.* Supreme Court of the United States, 1989. 491 US 524, 109 S.Ct. 2603, 105 L.Ed. 2d 443, 16 Med. L. Reptr. 1801.
JUSTICE MARSHALL delivered the opinion of the Court.

Florida Stat. s. 794.03 (1987) makes it unlawful to 'print, publish, or broadcast . . . in any instrument of mass communication' the name of the victim of a sexual offense. Pursuant to this statute, appellant *The Florida Star* was found civilly liable for publishing the name of a rape victim which it had obtained from a publicly released police report. The issue presented here is whether this result comports with the First Amendment. We hold that it does not.

I. *The Florida Star* is a weekly newspaper which serves the community of Jacksonville, Florida, and which has an average circulation of approximately 18,000 copies. A regular feature of the newspaper is its 'Police Reports' section. The section, typically two to three pages in length, contains brief articles describing local criminal incidents under police investigation. On October 20, 1983, appellee B.J.F. reported to the Duval County, Florida, Sheriff's Department (the Department) that she had been robbed and sexually assaulted by an unknown assailant. The Department prepared a report on the incident which identified B.J.F. by her full name. The Department then placed the report in its press room. The Department does not restrict access either to the press room or to the reports made available therein.

A *Florida Star* reporter-trainee sent to the press room copied the police report verbatim, including B.J.F.'s full name, on a blank duplicate of the Department's forms. A *Florida Star* reporter then prepared a one-paragraph article about the crime, derived entirely from the trainee's copy of the police report. The article included B.J.F.'s full name. It appeared in the 'Robberies' subsection of the 'Police Reports' section on October 29, 1983, one of fifty-four police blotter stories in that day's edition. The article read: '[B.J.F.] reported on Thursday, October 20, she was crossing Brentwood Park, which is in the 500 block of Golfair Boulevard, enroute to her bus stop, when an unknown black man ran up behind the lady and placed a knife to her neck and told her not to yell. The suspect then undressed the lady and had sexual intercourse with her before fleeing the scene with her 60 cents, Timex watch and gold necklace. Patrol efforts have been suspended concerning this incident because of lack of evidence.'

In printing B.J.F.'s full name, *The Florida Star* violated its internal policy of not publishing the names of sexual offense victims.

[B.J.F. sued both the newspaper and the Sheriff's Department. The latter settled for $2,500. The *Star*'s motion to dismiss was denied.]

At the ensuing day-long trial, B.J.F. testified that she had suffered emotional distress from the publication of her name. She stated that she had heard about the article from fellow workers and acquaintances; that her mother had received several threatening phone calls from a man who stated that he would rape B.J.F. again; and that these events had forced B.J.F. to change her phone number and residence, to seek police protection, and to obtain mental health counseling. In defense, *The Florida Star* put forth evidence indicating that the newspaper had learned B.J.F.'s name from the incident report released by the Department, and that the newspaper's violation of its internal rule against publishing the names of sexual offense victims was inadvertent.

At the close of B.J.F.'s case, and again at the close of its defense, *The Florida Star* moved for a directed verdict. On both occasions, the trial judge denied these motions. He ruled from the bench that s. 794.03 was constitutional because it reflected a proper balance between the First Amendment and privacy rights, as it applied only to a narrow set of 'rather sensitive . . . criminal offenses.' At the close of the newspaper's defense, the judge granted B.J.F.'s motion for a directed verdict on the issue of negligence, finding the newspaper per se negligent based upon its violation of s. 794.03. This ruling left the jury to consider only the questions of causation and damages. The judge instructed the jury that it could award B.J.F. punitive damages if it found that the newspaper had 'acted with reckless indifference to the rights of others.' The jury awarded B.J.F. $75,000 in compensatory damages and $25,000 in punitive damages. Against the actual damage award, the judge set off B.J.F.'s settlement with the Department.

The First District Court of Appeal affirmed in a three-paragraph *per curiam* opinion. . . . The Supreme Court of Florida denied discretionary review.

The Florida Star appealed to this Court. We noted probable jurisdiction, and now reverse.

II. The tension between the right which the First Amendment accords to a free press, on the one hand, and the protections which various statutes and common-law doctrines accord to personal privacy against the publication of truthful information, on the other, is a subject we have addressed several times in recent years. Our decisions in cases involving government attempts to sanction the accurate dissemination of information as invasive of privacy, have not, however, exhaustively considered this conflict. On the contrary, although our decisions have without exception upheld the press's right to publish, we have emphasized each time that we were resolving this conflict only as it arose in a discrete factual context.

The parties to this case frame their contentions in light of a trilogy of cases which have presented, in different contexts, the conflict between truthful reporting and state-protected privacy interests. [The Court briefly reviewed *Cox Broadcasting, Oklahoma Publishing*, and *Daily Mail*.]

Appellant takes the position that this case is indistinguishable from *Cox Broadcasting*. Alternatively, it urges that our decisions in the above trilogy, and in other cases in which we have held that the right of the press to publish truth overcame asserted interests other than personal privacy, can be distilled to yield a broader First Amendment principle that the press may never be punished, civilly or criminally, for publishing the truth. Appellee counters that the privacy trilogy is inapposite, because in each case the private information already appeared on a 'public record,' and because the privacy interests at stake were far less profound than in the present case. In the alternative, appellee urges that *Cox Broadcasting* be overruled and replaced with a categorical rule that publication of the name of a rape victim never enjoys constitutional protection.

We conclude that imposing damages on appellant for publishing B.J.F.'s name violates the First Amendment, although not for either of the reasons appellant urges. Despite the strong resemblance this case bears to *Cox Broadcasting*, that case cannot fairly be read as controlling here. The name of the rape victim in that case was obtained from courthouse records that were open to public inspection, a fact which Justice White's opinion for the Court repeatedly noted (noting 'special protected nature of accurate reports of *judicial* proceedings') (emphasis added). Significantly, one of the reasons we gave in *Cox Broadcasting* for invalidating the challenged damages award was the important role the press plays in subjecting trials to public scrutiny and thereby helping guarantee their fairness. That role is not directly compromised where, as here, the information in question comes from a police report prepared and disseminated at a time at which not only had no adversarial criminal proceedings begun, but no suspect had been identified.

Nor need we accept appellant's invitation to hold broadly that truthful publication may never be punished consistent with the First Amendment. Our cases have carefully eschewed reaching this ultimate question, mindful that the future may bring scenarios which prudence counsels our not resolving anticipatorily. See, e.g., *Near* v. *Minnesota* (hypothesizing 'publication of the sailing dates of transports or the number and location of troops'); see also *Garrison* v. *Louisiana* (endorsing absolute defense of truth 'where discussion of public affairs is concerned,' but leaving unsettled the constitutional implications of truthfulness 'in the discrete area of purely private libels'); *Landmark Communications Inc.* v. *Virginia*, 435 US 829, 838 (1978); *Time, Inc.* v. *Hill*, 385 US 374, 383, n. 7 (1967). Indeed, in *Cox Broadcasting*, we pointedly refused to answer even the less sweeping question 'whether truthful publications may ever be subjected to civil or criminal liability' for invading 'an area of privacy' defined by the State. Respecting the fact that press freedom and privacy rights are both 'plainly rooted in the traditions and significant concerns of our society,' we instead focused on the less sweeping issue of 'whether the State may impose sanctions on the accurate publication of the name of a rape victim obtained from public records—more specifically, from judicial records which are maintained in connection with a public prosecution and which themselves are open to public inspection.' We continue to believe that the sensitivity and significance of the interests presented in clashes between First Amendment and privacy rights counsel relying on limited principles that sweep no more broadly than the appropriate context of the instant case.

In our view, this case is appropriately analyzed with reference to such a limited First Amendment principle. It is the one, in fact, which we articulated in *Daily Mail* in our synthesis of prior cases involving attempts to punish truthful publication: '[I]f a newspaper lawfully obtains truthful information about a matter of public significance then state officials may not constitutionally punish publication of the information, absent a need to further a state interest of the highest order.' According the press the ample protection provided by that principle is supported by at least three separate considerations, in addition to, of course, the overarching 'public interest, secured by the Constitution, in the dissemination of truth.' The cases on which the *Daily Mail* synthesis relied demonstrate these considerations.

First, because the *Daily Mail* formulation only protects the publication of information which a newspaper has 'lawfully obtain[ed],' the government retains ample means of safeguarding significant interests upon which publication may impinge, including protecting a rape victim's anonymity. To the extent sensitive information rests in private hands, the government may under some circumstances forbid its nonconsensual acquisition, thereby bringing outside of the *Daily Mail* principle the publication of any information so acquired. To the extent sensitive information is in the government's custody, it has even greater power to forestall or mitigate the injury caused by its release. The government may classify certain information, establish and enforce procedures ensuring its redacted release, and extend a damages remedy against the government or its officials where the government's mishandling of sensitive information leads to its dissemination. Where information is entrusted to the government, a less drastic means than punishing truthful publication almost always exists for guarding against the dissemination of private facts. See, e.g., [*Landmark Communications*] ('much of the risk [from disclosure of sensitive information regarding judicial disciplinary proceedings] can be eliminated through careful

internal procedures to protect the confidentiality of Commission proceedings');
[*Oklahoma Publishing*] (noting trial judge's failure to avail himself of the opportunity, provided by a state statute, to close juvenile hearing to the public, including members of the press, who later broadcast juvenile defendant's name); [*Cox Broadcasting*] ('If there are privacy interests to be protected in judicial proceedings, the States must respond by means which avoid public documentation or other exposure of private information').

A second consideration undergirding the *Daily Mail* principle is the fact that punishing the press for its dissemination of information which is already publicly available is relatively unlikely to advance the interests in the service of which the State seeks to act. It is not, of course, always the case that information lawfully acquired by the press is known, or accessible, to others. But where the government has made certain information publicly available, it is highly anomalous to sanction persons other than the source of its release. We noted this anomaly in *Cox Broadcasting*: 'By placing the information in the public domain on official court records, the State must be presumed to have concluded that the public interest was thereby being served.' The *Daily Mail* formulation reflects the fact that it is a limited set of cases indeed where, despite the accessibility of the public to certain information, a meaningful public interest is served by restricting its further release by other entities, like the press. As *Daily Mail* observed in its summary of *Oklahoma Publishing*, 'once the truthful information was "publicly revealed" or "in the public domain" the court could not constitutionally restrain its dissemination.'

A third and final consideration is the 'timidity and self-censorship which may result from allowing the media to be punished for publishing certain truthful information'. *Cox Broadcasting* noted this concern with overdeterrence in the context of information made public through official court records, but the fear of excessive media self-suppression is applicable as well to other information released without qualification, by the government. A contrary rule, [denying] protection to those who rely on the government's implied representations of the lawfulness of dissemination, would force upon the media the onerous obligation of sifting through government press releases, reports, and pronouncements to prune out material arguably unlawful for publication. This situation could inhere even where the newspaper's sole object was to reproduce, with no substantial change, the government's rendition of the event in question.

Applied to the instant case, the *Daily Mail* principle clearly commands reversal. The first inquiry is whether the newspaper 'lawfully obtain[ed] truthful information about a matter of public significance.' It is undisputed that the news article describing the assault on B.J.F. was accurate. In addition, appellant lawfully obtained B.J.F.'s name. Appellee's argument to the contrary is based on the fact that under Florida law, police reports which reveal the identity of the victim of a sexual offense are not among the matters of 'public record' which the public, by law, is entitled to inspect. But the fact that the state officials are not required to disclose such reports does not make it unlawful for a newspaper to receive them when furnished by the government. Nor does the fact that the Department apparently failed to fulfil its obligation under s. 794.03 not to 'cause or allow to be . . . published' the name of a sexual offense victim make the newspaper's ensuing receipt of this information unlawful. Even assuming the Constitution permitted a State to proscribe *receipt* of information, Florida has not taken this step. It is clear, furthermore, that the news article concerned 'a matter of public significance,' in the sense in which the *Daily Mail* synthesis of prior cases used that term. That is, the article generally, as opposed to the specific identity contained within it, involved a matter of paramount public import: the commission, and investigation, of a violent crime which had been reported to authorities. See *Cox Broadcasting* (article identifying victim of rape-murder); [*Oklahoma Publishing*] (article identifying juvenile alleged to have committed murder); [*Daily Mail*] (same); cf. [*Landmark Communications*] (article identifying judges whose conduct was being investigated).

The second inquiry is whether imposing liability on appellant pursuant to s. 794.03 serves 'a need to further a state interest of the highest order.' [*Daily Mail*] Appellee argues that a rule punishing publication furthers three closely related interests: the privacy of victims of sexual offenses; the physical safety of such victims, who may be targeted for retaliation if their names become known to their assailants; and the goal of encouraging victims of such crimes to report these offenses without fear of exposure.

At a time in which we are daily reminded of the tragic reality of rape, it is undeniable that these are highly significant interests, a fact underscored by the Florida Legislature's explicit attempt to protect these interests by enacting a criminal statute prohibiting much dissemination of victim identities. We accordingly do not rule out the possibility that, in a proper case, imposing civil sanctions for publication of the name of a rape victim might be so overwhelmingly necessary to advance these interests as to satisfy the *Daily Mail* standard. For three independent reasons, however, imposing liability for publication under the circumstances of this case is too precipitous a means of advancing these interests to convince us that there is a 'need' within the meaning of the *Daily Mail* formulation for Florida to take this extreme step. Cf. *Landmark Communications* (invalidating penalty on publication despite State's expressed interest in nondissemination, reflected in statute prohibiting unauthorized divulging of names of judges under investigation).

First is the manner in which appellant obtained the identifying information in question. As we have noted, where the government itself provides information to the media, it is most appropriate to assume that the government had, but failed to utilize, far more limited means of guarding against dissemination than the extreme step of punishing truthful speech. That assumption is richly borne out in this case. B.J.F.'s identity would never have come to light were it not for the erroneous, if inadvertent, inclusion by the Department of her full name in an accident report made available in a press room open to the public. Florida's policy against disclosure of rape victims' identities, reflected in s. 794.03, was undercut by the Department's failure to abide by this policy. Where, as here, the government has failed to police itself in disseminating information, it is clear under *Cox Broadcasting*, *Oklahoma Publishing*, and *Landmark Communications* that the imposition of damages against the press for its subsequent publication can hardly be said to be a narrowly tailored means of safeguarding anonymity. Once the government has placed such information in the public domain, 'reliance must rest upon the judgment of those who decide what to publish or broadcast,' [*Cox Broadcasting*] and hopes for restitution must rest upon the willingness of the government to compensate victims for their loss of privacy, and to protect them from the other consequences of its mishandling of the information which these victims provided in confidence.

That appellant gained access to the information in question through a government news release makes it especially likely that, if liability were to be imposed, self-censorship would result. Reliance on a news release is a paradigmatically 'routine newspaper reporting techniqu[e].' [*Daily Mail*] The government's issuance of such a release, without qualification, can only convey to recipients that the government considered dissemination lawful, and indeed expected the recipients to disseminate the information further. Had appellant merely reproduced the news release prepared and released by the Department, imposing civil damages would surely violate the First Amendment. The fact that appellant converted the police report into a news story by adding the linguistic connecting tissue necessary to transform the report's facts into full sentences cannot change this result.

A second problem with Florida's imposition of liability for publication is the broad sweep of the negligence per se standard applied under the civil cause of action implied from s. 794.03. Unlike claims based on the common law tort of invasion of privacy, civil actions based on s. 794.03 require no case-by-case findings that the disclosure of a fact about a person's private life was one that a reasonable person would find highly offensive. On the contrary, under the per se theory of negligence adopted by the courts below, liability follows automatically from publication. This is so regardless of whether the identity of the victim is already known throughout the community; whether the victim has voluntarily cal.ed public attention to the offense; or whether the identity of the victim has otherwise become a reasonable subject of public concern—because, perhaps, questions have arisen whether the victim fabricated an assault by a particular person. Nor is there a scienter requirement of any kind under s. 794.03, engendering the perverse result that truthful publications challenged pursuant to this cause of action are less protected by the First Amendment than even the least protected defamatory falsehoods: those involving purely private figures, where liability is evaluated under a standard, usually applied by a jury, of ordinary negligence. See *Gertz* v. *Robert Welch, Inc.* We have previously noted the impermissibility of categorical prohibitions upon media access where important First Amendment interests are at stake. See *Globe Newspaper Co.* v. *Superior Court*, 457 US 596, 608 (1982) (invalidating state statute providing for the categorical exclusion of the public from trials of sexual offenses involving juvenile victims.) More individualized adjudication is no less indispensable where the State, seeking to safeguard the anonymity of crime victims, sets its face against publication of their names.

Third, and finally, the facial under-inclusiveness of s. 794.03 raises serious doubts about whether Florida is, in fact, serving, with this statute, the significant interests which appellee invokes in support of affirmance. Section 794.03 prohibits the publication of identifying information only if this information appears in an 'instrument of mass communication', a term the statute does not define. Section 794.03 does not prohibit the spread by other means of the identities of victims of sexual offenses. An individual who maliciously spreads word of the identity of a rape victim is thus not covered, despite the fact that the communication of such information to persons who live near, or work with, the victim may have consequences equally devastating as the exposure of her name to large numbers of strangers.

When a State attempts the extraordinary measure of punishing truthful publication in the name of privacy, it must demonstrate its commitment to advancing this interest by applying its prohibition evenhandedly, to the small time disseminator as well as the media giant. Where important First Amendment interests are at stake, the mass scope of disclosure is not an acceptable surrogate for injury. A ban on disclosures effected by 'instrument[s] of mass communication' simply cannot be defended on the ground that partial prohibitions may effect partial relief. See [*Daily Mail*] (statute is insufficiently tailored to interest in protecting anonymity where it restricted only newspapers, not the electronic media or other forms of publication, from identifying juvenile defendants); *id.*, at 110 (Rehnquist, J., concurring in judgment) (same); cf. *Arkansas Writers' Project, Inc.* v. *Ragland*, 481 US 221, 229 (1987); *Minneapolis Star & Tribune Co.* v. *Minnesota Comm'r of Revenue*, 460 US 575, 585 (1983). Without more careful and inclusive precautions against alternative forms of dissemination, we cannot conclude that Florida's selective ban on publication by the mass media satisfactorily accomplishes its stated purpose.

III. Our holding today is limited. We do not hold that truthful publication is automatically constitutionally protected, or that there is no zone of personal privacy within which the State may protect the individual from intrusion by the press, or even that a State may never punish publication of the name of a victim of a sexual offense. We hold only that where a newspaper publishes truthful information which it has lawfully obtained, punishment may lawfully be imposed, if at all, only when narrowly tailored to a state interest of the highest order, and that no such interest is satisfactorily served by imposing liability . . . under the facts of this case. The decision below is therefore reversed.

Addendum 3

S. D. Warren and L. D. Brandeis, 'The Right to Privacy' 4 *Harv. L. Rev.* 193 (1890).

Of the desirability—indeed of the necessity—of some such protection, there can, it is believed, be no doubt. The press is overstepping in every direction the obvious bounds of propriety and of decency. Gossip is no longer the resource of the idle and the vicious, but has become a trade, which is pursued with industry as well as effrontery. To satisfy a prurient taste the details of sexual relations are spread broadcast in the columns of the daily papers. To occupy the indolent, column upon column is filled with idle gossip, which can only be procured by intrusion upon the domestic circle. The intensity and complexity of life, attending upon advancing civilization, have rendered necessary some retreat from the world, and man, under the refining influence of culture, has become more sensitive to publicity, so that solitude and privacy have become more essential to the individual; but modern enterprise and invention have, through invasions upon his privacy, subjected him to mental pain and distress, far greater than could be inflicted by mere bodily injury.

Nor is the harm wrought by such invasions confined to the suffering of those who may be made the subjects of journalistic or other enterprise. In this, as in other branches of commerce, the supply creates the demand. Each crop of unseemly gossip, thus harvested, becomes the seed of more, and in direct proportion to its circulation, results in a lowering of social standards and of morality. Even gossip apparently harmless, when widely and persistently circulated is potent for evil. It both belittles and perverts. It belittles by inverting the relative importance of things, thus dwarfing the thoughts and aspirations of a people. When personal gossip attains the dignity of print, and crowds the space available for matters of real interest to the community, what wonder that the ignorant and thoughtless mistake its relative importance. Easy of comprehension, appealing to that weak side of human nature which is never wholly cast down by the misfortunes and frailties of our neighbours, no one can be surprised that it usurps the place of interest in brains capable of other things. Triviality destroys at once robustness of thought and delicacy of feeling. No enthusiasm can flourish, no generous impulse can survive under the blighting influence.

Addendum 4

Gordon Kaye (by Peter Froggatt his next friend) v. *Andrew Robertson and Sport Newspapers Ltd.* Court of Appeal 23 February 1990

JUDGMENT*

Glidewell LJ

The Plaintiff, Mr Gordon Kaye, is a well-known actor, the star of a popular television comedy series. This formed the basis of a stage show in which the Plaintiff was appearing in January 1990. The show finished its run in London on 27 January 1990. Thereafter it was due to appear in Australia with the Plaintiff in the lead.

Mr Peter Froggatt is a theatrical agent and a personal friend of Mr Kaye. Since Mr Kaye is at present incapable of managing his own affairs, in this action Mr Froggatt is his next friend.

On 25 January 1990 Mr Kaye was driving his car on a road in London during a gale, when a piece of wood became detached from an advertisement hoarding, smashed through the windscreen of the Plaintiff's car and struck him on the head. The Plaintiff suffered severe injuries to his head and brain. He was taken to Charing Cross Hospital where he was on a life support machine for three days. He was then in intensive care, until on 2 February he was moved into a private room, forming part of Ward G at the hospital.

It was apparent that there was intense interest amongst Mr Kaye's fans and consequently in many newspapers and in television in Mr Kaye's progress and condition. For fear that his recovery might be hindered if he had too many visitors, and to lessen the risk of infection, the hospital authorities placed notices at the entrance to the ward asking visitors to see a member of the staff before visiting. Mr Froggatt agreed with the hospital authorities a list of people who might be permitted to visit

---

* Reproduced from the *Report of the Committee on Privacy and Related Matters* Cmn. 1102, 1990, Appendix I.

Mr Kaye, and this was pinned up outside his room. A similar notice to that outside the ward was pinned on the door of the room itself.

The first Defendant is the editor and the second Defendant company is the publisher of *Sunday Sport*, a weekly publication which Mr Justice Potter, from whose decision this is an appeal, described as having 'a lurid and sensational style'. A copy of a recent edition of *Sunday Sport* which was put in evidence before us shows that many of the advertisements contained in it are for various forms of pornographic material. This indicates the readership it seeks to attract.

Until 13 February 1990, Mr Kaye had not been interviewed since his accident by any representative of a newspaper or television programme. On that day, acting on Mr Robertson's instructions, a journalist and a photographer from *Sunday Sport* went to Charing Cross Hospital and gained access to the corridor outside Ward G. They were not seen nor intercepted by any of the hospital staff. Ignoring the notices on the door to the ward and on the Plaintiff's door, they entered the Plaintiff's room. Mr Kaye apparently agreed to talk to them and according to a transcript that we have heard of a taped record they made of what transpired, did not object to them photographing various cards and flowers in his room. In fact a number of photographs, both in colour and monochrome, were taken of the Plaintiff himself showing the substantial scars to his head amongst other matters. The taking of the photographs involved the use of a flashlight.

After some time members of the nursing staff of the hospital learned what was happening. They attempted to persuade the journalist and the photographer to leave, but without success. Security staff were called, and the representatives of *Sunday Sport* were ejected.

Medical evidence exhibited by Mr Froggatt to his affidavit in this action says that Mr Kaye was in no fit condition to be interviewed or to give any informed consent to be interviewed. The accuracy of this opinion is confirmed by the fact that approximately a quarter-of-an-hour after the representatives of *Sunday Sport* had left his room, Mr Kaye had no recollection of the incident.

According to Mr Robertson's affidavit, he regards what he and his staff had achieved as, 'A great old-fashioned scoop'. He makes it clear in his affidavit that he realised that a number of newspapers were interested in interviewing and taking photographs of Mr Kaye, and some of them would 'pay large sums of money for the privilege'. He says, disingenuously, 'I do not think it unreasonable to attempt a direct approach in order to get a free interview. The Plaintiff only had to refuse'.

The Defendants made it clear that they intended to publish an article in *Sunday Sport* about the interview with the Plaintiff, using one or more of the photographs that had been taken. A draft of the article as originally prepared is exhibited to Mr Robertson's affidavit. It was intended to be in two parts, a front page lead with a banner headline and a full story inside the newspaper. The wording of both parts of the article made it clear that the Defendants were saying that Mr Kaye had agreed to be interviewed and to be photographed and described the interview and pictures as exclusive to *Sunday Sport*.

On Friday, 16 February, 1990, upon Mr Froggatt undertaking by Counsel to issue by noon on Monday, 19 February, 1990 and serve on the Defendants the writ in this action together with an undertaking in the usual form as to damages, Mr Justice

Potter on an application made on behalf of the Plaintiff by Mr Froggatt granted an injunction against the Defendants in the following terms:

'1. The Defendants and each of them whether by themselves, their servants or agents or otherwise be restrained from publishing, distributing, or causing to be published or distributed by any means howsoever or by otherwise exploiting:

   (a) any photographs or part of any photographs taken of the Plaintiff at the Charing Cross Hospital on 13 February 1990;

   (b) any statement made by the Plaintiff in the presence of any servant or agent of the Second Defendants at Charing Cross Hospital on 13 February 1990 or any summary or record thereof until trial or further order;

2. The Defendants and each of them be restrained whether by themselves, their servants or agents or otherwise from passing off any photograph or part of a photograph taken of the Plaintiff at Charing Cross Hospital on 13 February 1990 as a photograph consented to by the Plaintiff and from passing off any statement made by the Plaintiff in the presence of any servant or agent of the Second Defendants in Charing Cross Hospital on 13 February 1990 as a statement voluntarily given by the Plaintiff to *The Sunday Sport* until trial or further order;

3. The Defendants and each of them be restrained whether by themselves, their servants or agents or otherwise from publishing or causing to be published any statement to the effect that the Plaintiff had posed for a photograph for publication in *The Sunday Sport* and/or had given an interview to *The Sunday Sport* while in Charing Cross Hospital for treatment until trial or further order;'

The Judge also ordered the Defendants to deliver up 'any tape-recording, notes of interview or photographs obtained or taken by any servant or agent of the second Defendants in Charing Cross Hospital on 13 February 1990 and any copies of negatives thereof'.

The Defendants appealed against the Judge's order. We heard the appeal on Friday, 23 February, 1990. At the conclusion of the hearing we announced our decision which was to the effect that the appeal was allowed to the extent that we discharged the order made under heads 1 and 2 set out above, and that we substituted for the order under head 3 an order in the following terms:

'The Defendants and each of them be restrained until trial or further order whether by themselves their servants or agents from publishing, causing to be published or permitting to be published anything which could be reasonably understood or convey to any person reading or looking at the Defendants' *Sunday Sport* newspaper that the Plaintiff had voluntarily permitted any photographs to be taken for publication in that newspaper or had voluntarily permitted representatives of the Defendants to interview him while a patient in the Charing Cross hospital undergoing treatment'.

In place of the order for delivery up, we accepted an undertaking from the Defendants' solicitors

'that the material referred to in paragraph 4 of the aforesaid order will be kept in safe custody by the Defendants' Solicitors with the proviso that they shall be entitled to release it to the 1st Defendant to be used in any way which complies with the terms of the injunction aforestated'.

I now give my reasons for arriving at this decision.

It is well-known that in English law there is no right to privacy, and accordingly there is no right of action for breach of a person's privacy. The facts of the present case are a graphic illustration of the desirability of Parliament considering whether and in what circumstances statutory provision can be made to protect the privacy of individuals. In the absence of such a right, the Plaintiff's advisers have sought to base their claim to injunctions upon other well-established rights of action. These are:

1. Libel
2. Malicious falsehood
3. Trespass to the person
4. Passing off.

The appeal canvassed all four rights of action, and it is necessary to deal with each in turn.

1. *Libel* The basis of the Plaintiff's case under this head is that the article as originally written clearly implied that Mr Kaye consented to give the first 'exclusive' interview to *Sunday Sport*, and to be photographed by their photographer. This was untrue: Mr Kaye was in no fit condition to give any informed consent, and such consent as he may appear to have given was, and should have been known by *Sunday Sport*'s representative to be, of no effect. The implication in the article would have the effect of lowering Mr Kaye in the esteem of right-thinking people, and was thus defamatory.

The Plaintiff's case is based on the well-known decision in *Tolley* v. *J. S. Fry & Sons Ltd* [1931] AC 333. Mr Tolley was a well-known amateur golfer. Without his consent, Fry published an advertisement which consisted of a caricature of the Plaintiff with a caddie, each with a packet of Fry's chocolate protruding from his pocket. The caricature was accompanied by doggerel verse which used Mr Tolley's name and extolled the virtues of the chocolate. The Plaintiff alleged that the advertisement implied that he had received payment for the advertisement, which would damage his reputation as an amateur player. The Judge at the trial ruled that the advertisement was capable of being defamatory, and on appeal the House of Lords upheld this ruling.

It seems that an analogy with *Tolley* v. *Fry* was the main plank of Mr Justice Potter's decision to grant injunctions in this case. Mr Milmo for the Defendants submits that, assuming that the article was capable of having the meaning alleged, this would not be a sufficient basis for interlocutory relief. In *William Coulson & Sons* v. *James Coulson & Co* [1887] 3 TLR 46 this court held that, though the High Court has jurisdiction to grant an interim injunction before the trial of a libel action, it is a jurisdiction to be exercised only sparingly. In his judgment the Master of the Rolls said:

'Therefore to justify the court granting an interim injunction it must come to a decision upon the question of libel or no libel, before the jury decided whether it was a libel or not. Therefore the jurisdiction was of a delicate nature. It ought only to be exercised in the clearest cases, where any jury would say that the matter complained of was libellous and where if the jury did not so find the court would set aside the verdict as unreasonable'.

This is still the rule in actions for defamation, despite the decision of the House of Lords in *American Cyanamid* v. *Ethicon* [1975] AC 396 in relation to interim injunctions generally. This court so decided in *Herbage* v. *Times Newspapers Limited and others*, unreported but decided on 30 April 1981.

Mr Milmo submits that on the evidence we cannot be confident that any jury would inevitably decide that the implication that Mr Kaye had consented to give his first interview to *Sunday Sport* was libellous. Accordingly, we ought not to grant interlocutory relief on this ground.

It is in my view certainly arguable that the intended article would be libellous, on the authority of *Tolley* v. *Fry*. I think that a jury would probably find that Mr Kaye had been libelled, but I cannot say that such a conclusion is inevitable. It follows that I agree with Mr Milmo's submission and in this respect I disagree with the learned Judge. I therefore would not base an injunction on a right of action for libel.

2. *Malicious Falsehood* The essentials of this tort are that the Defendant has published about the Plaintiff words which are false, that they were published maliciously, and that special damage has followed as the direct and natural result of their publication. As to special damage, the effect of s. 3 (1) of the Defamation Act 1952 is that it is sufficient if the words published in writing are calculated to cause pecuniary damage to the Plaintiff. Malice will be inferred if it be proved that the words were calculated to produce damage and that the Defendant knew when he published the words that they were false or was reckless as to whether they were false or not.

The test in *Coulson* v. *Coulson* applies to interlocutory injunctions in actions for malicious falsehood as it does in actions for defamation. However, in relation to this action, the test applies only to the requirement that the Plaintiff must show that the words were false. In the present case I have no doubt that any jury which did not find that the clear implication from the words contained in the Defendant's draft article were false would be making a totally unreasonable finding. Thus the test is satisfied in relation to this cause of action.

As to malice I equally have no doubt from the evidence, including the transcript of the tape-recording of the 'interview' with Mr Kaye in his hospital room which we have read, that it was quite apparent to the reporter and photographer from *Sunday Sport* that Mr Kaye was in no condition to give any informed consent to them interviewing or photographing him. Moreover, even if the journalists had been in any doubt about Mr Kaye's fitness to give his consent, Mr Robertson could not have entertained any such doubt after he read the affidavit sworn on behalf of Mr Kaye in these proceedings. Any subsequent publication of the falsehood would therefore inevitably be malicious.

As to damage, I have already recorded that Mr Robertson appreciated that Mr Kaye's story was one for which other newspapers would be willing to pay 'large sums of money'. It needs little imagination to appreciate that whichever journal secured the first interview with Mr Kaye would be willing to pay the most. Mr Kaye thus has a potentially valuable right to sell the story of his accident and his recovery when he is fit enough to tell it. If the Defendants are able to publish the article they proposed, or one anything like it, the value of this right would in my view be seriously lessened, and Mr Kaye's story thereafter be worth much less to him.

I have considered whether damages would be an adequate remedy in these circumstances. They would inevitably be difficult to calculate, would also follow some time after the event, and in my view would in no way be adequate. It thus follows that in my opinion all the preconditions to the grant of an interlocutory injunction in respect of this cause of action are made out. I will return later to what I consider to be the appropriate form of injunction.

3. *Trespass to the Person* It is strictly unnecessary to consider this cause of action in the light of the view I have expressed about malicious falsehood. However I will set out my view shortly. The Plaintiff's case in relation to this cause of action is that the taking of the flashlight photographs may well have caused distress to Mr Kaye and set back his recovery, and thus caused him injury. In this sense it can be said to be a battery. Mr Caldecott, for Mr Kaye, could not refer us to any authority in which the taking of a photograph or indeed the flashing of a light had been held to be a battery. Nevertheless I am prepared to accept that it may well be the case that if a bright light is deliberately shone into another person's eyes and injures his sight, or damages him in some other way, this may be in law a battery. But in my view the necessary effects are not established by the evidence in this case. Though there must have been an obvious risk that any disturbance to Mr Kaye would set back his recovery, there is no evidence that the taking of the photographs did in fact cause him any damage.

Moreover, the injunction sought in relation to this head of action would not be intended to prevent another anticipated battery, since none was anticipated. The intention here is to prevent the Defendants from profiting from the taking of the photographs, i.e. from their own trespass. Attractive though this argument may appear to be, I cannot find as a matter of law that an injunction should be granted in these circumstances. Accordingly, I would not base an injunction on this cause of action.

4. *Passing off* Mr Caldecott submits (though in this case not with any great vigour) that the essentials of the tort of passing off, as laid down by the speeches in the House of Lords in *Warnink* v. *J. Townsend & Sons* [1979] AC 731 are satisfied here. I only need say shortly that in my view they are not. I think that the Plaintiff is not in the position of a trader in relation to his interest in his story about his accident and his recovery, and thus fails from the start to have a right of action under this head.

Forms of Injunction

Before I turn to consider the form of an interim injunction which should be granted, I must comment that apart from the initial draft of the article intended to be printed in *Sunday Sport* which was before the Judge, two other versions have subsequently appeared. A second was put before Mr Justice Potter, and a third before us. Both the second and third versions use words which do not imply so clearly as did the original version of the article that the Plaintiff consented to be interviewed and photographed by *Sunday Sport*. Nevertheless, in my view the later articles are irrelevant for present purposes. The fact that at one time the Defendants envisaged printing the original article is sufficient to entitle the Plaintiff to an injunction which prohibits the

Defendants from publishing an article which contains the implication which was to be read into that original article.

In relation to the injunctions granted by Mr Justice Potter, the wording of the first injunction was in my view wider than was necessary to prevent the Defendants doing that which was objectionable, i.e. publishing material from which the objectionable implication could be drawn.

The second injunction granted by Potter J. was based upon the tort of passing off. I have already said that in my view the evidence does not prove the commission of this tort. It was for these reasons, that in common with my brethren, I took the view that the first and second injunctions should be discharged. We considered that the third injunction was in general satisfactory but needed some amendment, and basing ourselves on the Plaintiff's right of action in malicious falsehood, we granted the injunction in the terms set out above.

I therefore concluded that, to the extent I have indicated, the Defendants' appeal should be allowed, but that they should be subject to an injunction in the terms which we have already announced.

Bingham LJ

I have had the benefit of reading in draft the judgment prepared by Glidewell LJ. I agree with it, and with the order made.

Any reasonable and fair-minded person hearing the facts which Glidewell LJ has recited would in my judgment conclude that these Defendants had wronged the Plaintiff. I am therefore pleased to be persuaded that the Plaintiff is able to establish, with sufficient strength to justify an interlocutory order, a cause of action against the Defendants in malicious falsehood. Had he failed to establish any cause of action, we should of course have been powerless to act, however great our sympathy for the Plaintiff and however strong our distaste for the Defendants' conduct.

This case nonetheless highlights, yet again, the failure of both the Common law of England and statute to protect in an effective way the personal privacy of individual citizens. This has been the subject of much comment over the years, perhaps most recently by Professor Markesinis (*The German Law of Torts*, 2nd edn. 1990 page 316) where he writes:

'English law, on the whole, compares unfavourably with German law. True, many aspects of the human personality and privacy are protected by a multitude of existing torts but this means fitting the facts of each case in the pigeon-hole of an existing tort and this process may not only involve strained constructions; often it may also leave a deserving Plaintiff without a remedy.'

The Defendants' conduct towards the Plaintiff here was 'a monstrous invasion of his privacy' (to adopt the language of Griffiths J. in *Bernstein* v. *Skyviews Ltd* [1978] QB 479 at 489G). If ever a person has a right to be let alone by strangers with no public interest to pursue, it must surely be when he lies in hospital recovering from brain surgery and in no more than partial command of his faculties. It is this invasion of his privacy which underlies the Plaintiff's complaint. Yet it alone, however gross, does not entitle him to relief in English law.

The Plaintiff's suggested cause of action in libel is in my view arguable, for reasons which Glidewell LJ has given. We could not give interlocutory relief on that ground. Battery and assault are causes of action never developed to cover acts such as these: they could apply only if the law were substantially extended and the available facts strained to unacceptable lengths. A claim in passing off is hopeless. Fortunately, a cause of action in malicious falsehood exists, but even that obliges us to limit the relief we can grant in a way which would not bind us if the Plaintiff's cause of action arose from the invasion of privacy of which, fundamentally, he complains. We cannot give the Plaintiff the breadth of protection which I would, for my part, wish. The problems of defining and limiting a tort of privacy are formidable, but the present case strengthens my hope that the review now in progress may prove fruitful.

Leggatt LJ

I agree with both judgments that have been delivered. In view of the importance of the topic I add a note about the way in which the Common law has developed in the United States to meet the need which in the present case we are unable to fulfil satisfactorily.

The recognition of a right to privacy seemed to be in prospect when Lord Byron obtained an injunction to restrain the false attribution to him of a bad poem: *Byron* v. *Johnston* [1816] 2 Mer. 29. But it was not until 1890 that in their article *The Right to Privacy* 4 *Harv. L. Rev.* 193 Warren and Brandeis reviewed a number of English cases on defamation and breaches of rights of property, confidence and contract, and concluded that all were based on a broader common principle. They argued that recognition of the principle would enable the courts to protect the individual against the infliction by the press of mental pain and distress through invasion of his privacy. Since then the right to privacy, or 'the right to be let alone', has gained acceptance in most jurisdictions in the United States.

It is manifested in several forms: see Dean Prosser, *Torts*, 4th edn., 1971. One example is such intrusion upon physical solitude as would be objectionable to a reasonable man. So when in *Barber* v. *Time Inc.* [1942] 159 S.W. 2d 291 the Plaintiff was confined to a hospital bed, the publication of her photograph taken without consent was held to be an invasion of a private right of which she was entitled to complain. Similarly, a so-called 'right of publicity' has developed to protect the commercial interest of celebrities in their identities. 'The theory of the right is that a celebrity's identity can be valuable in the promotion of products, and the celebrity has an interest that may be protected from the unauthorised commercial exploitation of that identity. "The famous have an exclusive legal right during life to control and profit from the commercial use of their name and personality"': *Carson* v. *Here's Johnny Portable Toilets Inc.* [1983] 698 F. 2d 831 at page 835.

We do not need a First Amendment to preserve the freedom of the Press, but the abuse of that freedom can be ensured only by the enforcement of a right to privacy. This right has so long been disregarded here that it can be recognised now only by the Legislature. Especially since there is available in the United States a wealth of experience of the enforcement of this right both at common law and also under statute, it is to be hoped that the making good of this signal shortcoming in our law will not be long delayed.

Addendum 5

The impact of the Kaye *decision on the English law of privacy*

1. Used skilfully the *Kaye* decision offers an excellent starting point for a comparative discussion of the protection of privacy and its clash with the interest of free speech. Consider the following points. *First*, the argument advanced by the media that a law protecting privacy would bar them from investigating suspect conduct by politicians (*The Times*, 28 November 1989, leading article) is clearly inapplicable in cases such as *Kaye* which involved an ordinary citizen's moral right 'to be let alone by strangers with no public interest to pursue [while recovering in hospital] from brain surgery and in no more than partial command of his faculties.' (*per* Bingham LJ, p. 103 of the Calcutt Report). If the two situations require a different treatment (and in most respects they do though remember that German law allows even public figures a degree of privacy), it is for lawyers and the Press to try and devise rules that can distinguish between them rather than for the latter to foil all efforts by the former to regulate the problem. *Secondly*, the valiant attempts of the Court of Appeal to come up with some protection are notable for revealing the contortions that have to be undertaken in order to provide a remedy. This must, *thirdly*, lead us to consider the limitations of the traditional torts. Trespass, for example, has been advocated by one leading practitioner (see: Prescott, (1991) 54 *MLR* 802). But how effective would it be, especially in light of the restricted availability of punitive damages in English law? *Fourthly*, one must consider whether other systems (such as the German and French) are worse off for having provided a remedy in precisely this kind of situation (for illustration see Markesinis, (1990) 53 *MLR* 802; (1992) *MLR* 118). *Fifthly*, consider the refusal of the English courts to create a right of privacy. Does this conform with the view widely held on the Continent of Europe (and, indeed, among many Common lawyers) that our courts can create new law or adapt outdated solutions when circumstances require it? Thus, is our law any worse off for the fact that this timid approach was ignored on many occasions when there was a need for modernisation (cf., for example, the transformation of English administrative law in the sixties and seventies)? *Sixthly*, consider the proven ability of the Press to frustrate the six attempts (made in England between 1961 and 1989) to legislate on this matter. Is this a healthy state of affairs? The answer must surely be negative, especially when one takes note of the intemperate language used by some newspaper editors to express their distrust of our judiciary. And is not the Press adopting double standards when it asks for judicial intervention whenever it wishes to avoid high jury awards in defamation cases? Moreover, it must be the height of hypocrisy to express distrust towards *both* judges and jury and then to claim that the Press, itself, is the best judge of its own misconduct.

2. The timing of the *Kaye* litigation, arguably, had a decisive impact on the drafting of the Calcutt Report ('Report of the Committee on Privacy and Related Matters', Cm. 1102) which was published in June of 1990. The recommendations of this (first) Report, referring to the creation of new criminal and civil offences, are reproduced in paragraph 4, below (for reasons of space, its other recommendations, referring to the regulation of Press conduct and Press complaints, have been omitted). But this document, coupled

with the follow-up Report prepared by Sir David Calcutt (entitled 'Review of Press Self-Regulation' Cm. 2135, January of 1993, and essentially reconfirming its earlier recommendations and concluding that self-regulation is not working) and a 'Consultation Paper' published by the Lord Chancellor's Department in July 1993 (entitled 'Infringement of Privacy' and going a step further by recommending the establishment of a general tort of privacy) provide some of the most recent and thorough discussions of this topic and can be read with profit by lawyers from most systems that have to face these issues. The specific recommendations they make may provide the last chance (for the foreseeable future) to regulate this topic in a more balanced way. If the Press succeeds in frustrating this attempt, the ball will be back in the judges' court. If they then decide to act, history will justify their intervention; Continental European law could inspire it; and the average citizen would probably welcome it.

3. For further readings see: Bedingfield, 'Privacy or Publicity? The enduring confusion surrounding the American tort of invasion of privacy' (1992) 55 *MLR* 111; Louciades, 'Personality and privacy under the European Convention on Human Rights' (1990) *B.Y.B.I.L.* 175; Markesinis, 'Subtle ways of legal borrowing: some reflections on the Report of the Calcutt Committee "On Privacy and Related Matters"'; *Festschrift für Werner Lorenz zum siebzigsten Geburtstag* (1990) 717; idem, 'Our patchy law of privacy—time to do something about it' (1990) 53 *MLR* 802; idem, 'The Calcutt Report must not be forgotten' (1992) 55 *MLR* 118.

4. *Calcutt Committee Report: Summary of Recommendations*

Physical intrusion

1. The following acts should be criminal offences in England and Wales:
   (a) entering private property, without the consent of the lawful occupant, with intent to obtain personal information with a view to its publication.
   (b) placing a surveillance device on private property, without the consent of the lawful occupant, with intent to obtain personal information with a view to its publication; and
   (c) taking a photograph, or recording the voice, of an individual who is on private property, without his consent, with a view to its publication and with intent that the individual shall be identifiable.[1]

2. It should be a defence to any of these proposed offences that the act was done:
   (a) for the purpose of preventing, detecting or exposing the commission of any crime, or other seriously anti-social conduct; or
   (b) for the protection of public health or safety; or
   (c) under any lawful authority.

[1] For the purpose of these offences we would define private property as any private residence, together with its immediate curtilage (garden and outbuildings), but excluding any adjacent fields or parkland. In addition, it should cover hotel bedrooms (but not other areas in a hotel) and those parts of a hospital or nursing home where patients are treated or accommodated. (In such cases the lawful occupant should be regarded as the relevant Health Authority or proprietor.) For the offence [described in 1(c), above] to be committed it would not be necessary for the offender himself to enter on to private property. To these offences the ordinary principles of criminal responsibility would apply, and it would therefore be necessary to show that the defendant knew or was reckless as to the fact that private property was involved before he could be guilty of an offence (paragraph 6.34).

3. An individual having a sufficient interest should be able to apply for an injunction against the publication of any material obtained by means of any of these criminal offences or, if the material has already been published, for damages or an account of profits.

4. Further consideration should be given to the extent to which the law in Scotland needs to be extended to cover the proposed offences and civil remedy and how this might best be done.

Legal restrictions on press reporting

5. Consideration should be given to amending the legislation on the non-identification of minors in England and Wales to eliminate any inconsistencies or uncertainties.

6. The statutory prohibition on identifying rape victims in England and Wales should be extended to cover the victims of the sexual assaults listed at Appendix H.[2]

7. In any criminal proceedings in England and Wales, the court should have the power to make an order prohibiting the publication of the name and address of any person against whom the offence is alleged to have been committed, or of any other matters likely to lead to his or her identification. This should only be exercised if the court believes that it is necessary to protect the mental or physical health, personal security or security of the home of the victim.

8. After consulting the press and broadcasting authorities, the Press Complaints Commission (see 11 below) should issue early guidance on jigsaw identification.

Right of reply

9. A statutory right of reply should not be introduced.

Tort of infringement of privacy

10. A tort of infringement of privacy should not presently be introduced.

Press Complaints Commission

11. The press should be given one final chance to prove that voluntary self-regulation can be made to work.

[2] The list includes:
(a) procurement of intercourse with a woman by threats (Sexual Offences Act 1956 s. 2)
(b) procurement of intercourse with a woman by false pretences (Sexual Offences Act 1956 s. 3)
(c) administering drugs to obtain intercourse with a woman (Sexual Offences Act 1956 s. 4)
(d) intercourse with girls under 13 (Sexual Offences Act 1956 s. 5)
(e) intercourse with girls under 16 (Sexual Offences Act 1956 s. 6)
(f) intercourse with mental defectives etc. (Sexual Offences Act 1956 ss. 7 and 8; Mental Health Act 1959 s. 128)
(g) incest (Sexual Offences Act 1956 ss. 10 and 11; Criminal Law Act 1977, s. 54)
(h) buggery with a woman (Sexual Offences Act 1956 s. 12)
(i) buggery with a male person (Sexual Offences Act 1956 s. 12 as qualified by Sexual Offences Act 1967)
(j) indecent assault on a female (Sexual Offences Act 1956 s. 14)
(k) indecent assault on a male (Sexual Offences Act 1956 s. 15)
(l) assault with intent to commit buggery (Sexual Offences Act 1956 s. 16)
(m) burglary with intent to rape (Theft Act 1968 s. 10)

12. The Press Council should be disbanded and replaced by a Press Complaints Commission.
13. The Press Complaints Commission should concentrate on providing an effective means of redress for complaints against the press.
14. The Press Complaints Commission should be given specific duties to consider complaints both of unjust or unfair treatment by newspapers or periodicals and of unwarranted infringements of privacy through published material or in connection with the obtaining of such material.
15. The Press Complaints Commission should publish, monitor and implement a comprehensive code of practice for the guidance of both press and the public.
16. The Press Complaints Commission should operate a hot line for complainants on a 24-hour basis.
17. Press Complaints Commission adjudications should, in certain cases, include a recommendation that an apology be given to the complainant. The precise form of the apology, including whether it should be given publicly or privately, could also be prescribed. Where a complaint concerns a newspaper's refusal to give an opportunity to reply to an attack made on a complainant or to correct an inaccuracy, the Press Complaints Commission should be able to recommend the nature and the form of reply or correction including, in appropriate cases, where in the paper it should be published.
18. The Press Complaints Commission should have an independent chairman and no more than 12 members, with smaller sub-committees adjudicating on complaints under delegated powers.
19. Appointments to the Press Complaints Commission should be made by an Appointments Commission with explicit freedom to appoint whoever it considers best qualified. The Appointments Commission itself should be independently appointed, possibly by the Lord Chancellor.
20. The Press Complaints Commission should have clear conciliation and adjudication procedures designed to ensure that complaints are handled with the minimum of delay. Whenever practical it should first seek conciliation. There should also be a fast track procedure for the correction of significant factual errors. The Commission should also have a specific responsibility and procedure for initiating inquiries whenever it thinks it necessary.
21. Complaints committees should have delegated power to release adjudications, subject to a right of appeal for either party to the full Press Complaints Commission before publication.
22. The Press Complaints Commission should not operate a waiver of legal rights.
23. If the industry wishes to maintain a system of non-statutory self-regulation, it must demonstrate its commitment, in particular by providing the necessary money for setting up and maintaining the Press Complaints commission.

Statutory complaints procedures

24. If the press fails to demonstrate that non-statutory self-regulation can be made to work effectively, a statutory system for handling complaints should be introduced.
25. If maverick publications persistently decline to respect the authority of the Press

Complaints Commission, the Commission should be placed on a statutory footing. It should be given sufficient statutory powers to enable it to require any newspaper, periodical or magazine to respond to its enquiries about complaints and to publish its adjudications as directed. It should be able to recommend the payment of compensation.

26. The Government should set the budget for any statutory Press Complaints Commission and provide the money which it should then reclaim from the industry. The industry should set up a funding body which would apportion the cost between, and collect the money from, various industry bodies or individual publications.

Press Complaints Tribunal

27. Should the press fail to set up and support the Press Complaints Commission, or should it at any time become clear that the reformed non-statutory mechanism is failing to perform adequately, this should be replaced by a statutory tribunal with statutory powers and implementing a statutory code of practice.

28. There should be two separate triggers for the replacement of the Press Complaints Commission by a Press Complaints Tribunal.

29. A Press Complaints Tribunal should perform two distinct functions. First, it should attempt conciliation and investigate complaints. Secondly, where necessary, it should resolve disputes by ruling whether there had been a breach of the code of practice. This should be reflected in its structure and procedures.

30. The Press Complaints Tribunal should be able to award compensation. Unless the complainant can show financial loss, the amount of compensation should be limited by statute. This limit should be periodically reviewed.

31. In privacy cases, the Press Complaints Tribunal should be able to restrain publication of material in breach of the code of practice by means of injunctions. No injunction should be granted if the publisher could show that he had a good arguable defence.

32. The Tribunal chairman should be a judge or senior lawyer appointed by the Lord Chancellor. He should sit with two assessors drawn from a panel appointed by the Home Secretary.

12. UNLAWFULNESS AND FAULT

Case 35

REICHSGERICHT (FIRST CIVIL DIVISION) 14 JANUARY 1928*
RGZ 119, 397 = JW 1928, 1049 with approving note by M. Pappenheim

On 23 October 1921 at noon, the German three-masted schooner *Lisbeth*, on a journey through the English Channel to Göteborg, ran aground on the northern tip of the Dutch island of Texel on a sandbank. On 26 October it became a total loss. The plaintiff owner of the vessel sued the defendant

* English version by Kurt Lipstein.

captain of the ship claiming damages on the ground that he negligently caused the loss of the vessel. The District Court of Altona and the Court of Appeal of Kiel rejected the claim. Upon a second appeal the judgment of the Court of Appeal was confirmed for the following

Reasons

The Court of Appeal has found as a fact that during the voyage when the accident occurred, the defendant had not handled the vessel in accordance with the practice of an experienced and able captain of a sailing-ship applying normal care. If the defendant had applied that care required in the circumstances of a normal, proper, and conscientious captain of a sailing-ship, the stranding could have been avoided. However, the defendant lacked the necessary experience and could not possess it in view of his education and previous activity. The plaintiff, himself an old and experienced captain of sailing-vessels, had been well aware of the limits of the defendant's capacity when he appointed him. In particular the plaintiff had known that the defendant was not sufficiently qualified for discharging the specialized task of commanding the sailing-vessel *Lisbeth* and was completely inexperienced, especially for navigating in the North Sea. It was true that the plaintiff had not believed that he would suffer damage by appointing the unsuitable defendant; he had, however, been grossly negligent in failing to perceive the danger to the ship as a result of the defendant's lack of qualification. In so far as the defendant in his written application for the post had stated that he had been in possession of a schooner and was experienced in handling vessels of this kind, the plaintiff had by no means been misled thereby. Considering that the plaintiff was fully cognizant of the extent of the nautical qualification of the defendant, the defendant's own statement was of little importance. It offended against good faith if the plaintiff, who was well aware when he appointed the defendant that the latter, a young captain without any experience in navigating sailing vessels in the North Sea, would be unable to deal with difficult situations, having regard to his training and experience, now claimed damages against him because the defendant had proved unequal to the task. This held good too if the standard of care required of the defendant was put as that of a normal, proper, and conscientious captain of a sailing-vessel, without regard to the degree of experience possessed by men such as the defendant.

These statements of the Court of Appeal are mainly factual . . . On the strength of these facts the Court of Appeal could conclude, without violating the law, that the defendant was not liable to the plaintiff. The facts as found by the Court of Appeal show that in concluding the contract appointing the defendant the plaintiff knew of the particular personal circumstances of the defendant and took them into account. This indicates a tacit agreement to the effect that in assessing the duty of care incumbent upon the defendant in relation to the plaintiff, the latter's special circumstances are of essential importance [reference]. As between the parties, the plaintiff could only demand such nautical activities of the defendant which did not exceed the degree of nautical capacity and experience which was known to the plaintiff. The defendant is not liable for any circumstances resulting in damage which arise outside these limits, having regard to the special nature of the contract between the parties. It makes no difference that the defendant . . . should have known that he was not equal to the appointment assumed by him. The findings of the fact by the Court of Appeal show clearly that the accident could not have been avoided even if the defendant, conscious of his nautical deficiencies, had acted with special precaution and care, seeing that objectively he lacked the capacity for doing so. On the other hand, the plaintiff in deciding to appoint the defendant, was fully aware of the extent of the defendant's nautical qualifications and was not influenced by the fact that he applied for the post and accepted it without reservations.

These observations suffice to support the judgment appealed against. It may be observed, however, that the additional considerations of the Court of Appeal are not free from error. The Court of Appeal states that, leaving aside the special character of the relationship of the parties in issue, according to the general principles of law the defendant had not acted culpably because he had applied all that care expected of a person with his nautical experience.

The Court of Appeal bases its opinion on the view that within the circle of the captains of sailing-ships several groups exist, graded according to their nautical experience. A person belonging to the group of nautical experience similar to that of the defendant could not have avoided the mistakes which caused the accident, even if he had applied the proper standard of care. These considerations conflict with the dominant view in practice and in the literature. This holds that the term 'the care required in human relations' must be determined according to an objective standard, which is the requirement in regular and proper human relations, having regard to the individual circumstances. Thus the justified demands of human relations determine what measure of circumspection and care must be applied in order to avoid damage. It is normally to be gauged by reference to the view of a certain limited circle of persons and by the typical qualities of the group of persons who represent a specific range of human relations [references]. Accordingly § 511 of the Commercial Code requires the care of a proper 'sailor'. If, as in the present case, the command of a sailing-vessel is in issue, the special features of navigating a sailing-vessel and the care of a proper captain of a sailing-vessel is required. Since the just and reasonable requirements of trade form the basis, it is evident that neither the care of a particularly experienced nor that of an inexperienced captain of a sailing-vessel can serve as a standard. Instead that standard of care is decisive which a proper and conscientious captain of a sailing-ship, endowed with normal knowledge, capacity, and experience, is accustomed to apply. If the circle of captains of sailing-ships as defined above were to be divided into groups according to the degree of nautical experience of individual members, the objective standard would become distorted by the introduction of personal circumstances. A group of experienced captains of sailing-vessels, who are incapable of measuring up to serious tasks and who fail in case of need would be useless in trade . . . Although the reasoning of the Court of Appeal contains an error of law, no ground exists for questioning its decision which, as shown above, is supported by other legally valid reasons.

Case 36

BUNDESGERICHTSHOF (SIXTH CIVIL DIVISION) 9 JUNE 1967*
JZ 1968, 103 = VersR 1967, 808

On 6 January 1961 early in the morning, while it was still dark and raining slightly, R, a miner aged 27 years, was cycling to his place of work on an illuminated road. Shortly before he had reached a turning, the defendant motorist ran into R from behind, catapulting him onto the side of the road where he was hit and killed by a motor car travelling in the opposite direction.

The plaintiffs, assignees by subrogation of the claims of R's widow born in 1936 and of his two children born in 1954 and 1958, sued the defendant on the ground that he was alone responsible for the accident, having driven without due care and with a dirty windscreen. The defendant denies any responsibility. He had been blinded by an oncoming car owing to defective vision, of which he had been unaware hitherto and therefore failed to see R. Moreover, R was himself to be blamed because he was cycling without an illuminated rear light and was too far left on his side of the road.

The District Court, relying on the Road Traffic Act, gave judgment for the plaintiffs, limited to the amount payable under that Act, and granted a declaration asked for within the limits of liability set by the Road Traffic Act. On appeal by the plaintiffs the Court of Appeal of Hamm held the defendant liable to pay full damages on the ground of liability for negligence and rejected the plea of contributory negligence. A second appeal by the defendant was unsuccessful for the following

Reasons

I. 1. The Court of Appeal starts from the premiss that prima facie the defendant appears to have been negligent. The defendant, driving with dimmed

---

* English version by Kurt Lipstein.

lights, ran into the cyclist because he did not see him. In these circumstances common experience leads to the conclusion that the defendant acted negligently inasmuch as he drove either without sufficient care or at a speed incompatible with his field of vision.

2. The defendant does not contest this prima-facie evidence. He only questions the view taken by the Court of Appeal that the defendant had not discharged the burden of proof incumbent upon him thereafter to show as a serious possibility that the events may have taken place without any negligence on his part.

(*a*) The Court of Appeal assumes in favour of the defendant that owing to the special light conditions at the time of the accident he was blinded due to a defect of vision of which he was ignorant. Nevertheless it held that he had not discharged his burden of proof. The Court of Appeal held correctly that the test is whether the defendant could at least realize the limits of his vision, and it is convinced that he could.

This conclusion is based on the consideration that like every motorist the defendant must at least be aware of his individual powers of vision [references]. In determining negligence it is therefore irrelevant in law what the circumstances are which affect an abnormal individual vision. Thus a motorist so affected is treated no differently from one whose vision is perfect. The latter, too, is expected to know the limits of his vision, a knowledge obtained not by means of exact figures, but through his own experience. In determining whether the defendant was negligent the question is therefore not whether he knew or ought to have known of his defect of vision . . . but whether he ought to have known the effect of this defect and therefore the limits of his individual capacity to see. The Court of Appeal has answered this in the affirmative without committing an error of law. This determination is all the more valid since according to the experts the defendant was born with this defect of vision and as he had driven a motor car since 1956.

If, however, the defendant could recognize that his personal vision was limited he could and should have so adjusted his driving, especially his speed so as to satisfy the requirements of traffic and to be able to stop, if necessary. The Court of Appeal has held correctly that the defendant has not shown that he has complied with this requirement.

II. The Court of Appeal rules out any contributory negligence on the part of the cyclist R.

1. The Court of Appeal was unable to find that the rear light of the bicycle did not show. It has also not blamed R for having ridden too far left on his side of the road. The judge of fact adopted the allegation of the plaintiffs

that R wanted to turn left into the side street and had therefore moved to the middle of the road. The District Court had pointed out that R took this route daily on his way to work . . .

2. The further allegation of the defendant that R had not indicated his intention to turn left by raising his left arm was rejected as irrelevant by the Court of Appeal because on the defendant's own admission he had not seen R at all.

The defendant objects that the presumed conduct of R had been dismissed as the cause of the accident. He argues that it was not decisive that he had failed to see the cyclist but that it was decisive whether he would have seen R if he had indicated his intended change of direction by raising his left arm. Common experience supported this conclusion; moreover a presumption operated against the cyclist since the latter had violated § 11 I of the Traffic Regulations (StVO), i.e. had failed to indicate his direction.

In the result the Court of Appeal was right. The purpose of § 11 I of the Road Traffic Regulations is to eliminate the dangers which threaten—apart from the person making the turn—the traffic behind and in the opposite direction. It is intended to draw the attention of these road-users to the imminence of the traffic manœuvre, to make them use care, and thereby to avoid the danger of accidents. This was not the case here. The collision did not occur because the defendant in his motor car overtook the cyclist on his left side without noticing the latter's intention to turn; it occurred because in proceeding straight ahead he did not see the cyclist . . . It is not, however, the purpose of the protective rule which imposes the duty to indicate a change of direction, to ensure that the person subject to this duty is noticed in the traffic irrespective of his intention to make a turn.

Case 37

BUNDESGERICHTSHOF (SIXTH CIVIL SENATE) 7 FEBRUARY 1984
BGHZ 90, 96

On 3 July 1979 the plaintiff was admitted to the S hospital of the defendant Regional District for unexplained pain in his right femur. The first examination was carried out by Dr K, the Duty Doctor. He also discussed with the plaintiff that in order to exclude the possibility of a tumour, a colonoscopy was indicated. Subsequently it was carried out by Dr B, the Senior Medical Officer. In the course of it, the sigmoid colon was perforated and the defendant abandoned the investigation. After an X-ray picture had confirmed the injury, the plaintiff was operated on immediately—complications subsequently occurred.

The plaintiff sued the defendants for adequate damages for pain and suffering as well as for a declaration that they were liable to compensate him for all present and future material and mental damage. He stated that he had not effectively agreed to the colonoscopy and alleged that he had not been informed sufficiently of the character of the investigation or of any possible risks nor that it might be accompanied by considerable pain. He had suffered much pain when the instrument had been inserted in the intestine and had said so at the time. The perforation of the intestine had been caused by a culpable mistake of the second defendant in carrying out the colonoscopy.

The defendant contended that before the colonoscopy the investigation had been sufficiently explained to the plaintiff. They were of the opinion that in view of the fact that complications occurred extremely rarely, it had not been necessary to inform the plaintiff of the risk of a perforation of the intestine. They denied that by this treatment they committed a medical error.

The District court held that 'the claim raised in the action is justified in principle'. The Court of Appeal dismissed the appeal of the defendants, declared that the plaintiff's claim for damages for pain and suffering was justified in principle and allowed the action for a declaration in respect of material damage; as regards mental injuries in the future, it referred the case back to the District court. Upon a second appeal by the defendants the case was referred back to the Court of Appeal.

Reasons

I. The Court of Appeal has interpreted the judgment of the District Court to the effect that it decided not only the claim for damages for pain and suffering by an interim judgment in principle, but also the plaintiff's action for a declaration. Contrary to the District Court, which held the second defendant to have committed an error in his treatment, it regards the claim as well founded on the ground that the medical investigation which resulted in the injury to the plaintiff was illegal because the plaintiff had not been given sufficient information and because therefore his consent was invalid. In so holding, the Court of Appeal argued essentially as follows: It is possible to agree with the District Court that the information had to be given concerning the risk of a perforation of the intestine as a result of a colonoscopy since complications occurred seldom. However, the plaintiff should have been informed that in certain circumstances the investigation could cause the plaintiff considerable pain. This should have been done, in particular because the diagnostic measure was not of vital importance. No such information had been given. Without having to consider the question as to whether the plaintiff had risked his consent during the colonoscopy or whether the second defendant had, in treating the plaintiff, committed an error, he was liable according to §§ 823 I, 847 BGB to pay damages for pain and suffering. The defendant Regional District was liable according to § 831 BGB for the second defendant as its agent in performing his duties. It was not sufficient for the Regional District to plead as a defence that the second defendant was a specially competent doctor of long experience; nor was the fact that the medical heads of department had regularly called together the doctors working in their department, including the second defendant, for instruction and further education. A proper organization of a hospital required also that the doctors should be given advice concerning the general principles governing the duty to provide information and to control their observation by random inspection. This had been omitted. In addition, the liability of both defendants for the material damage resulted from a violation of the contract for medical treatment. As regards future mental damage, a further investigation of a factual kind was necessary.

II. The reasoning of the decision under appeal cannot stand up to legal scrutiny.

1. The Court of Appeal has held rightly that the information given to the plaintiff about the proposed colonoscopy was incomplete because she did not also tell the plaintiff that this diagnostic investigation might have disagreeable effects, psychological as well as physical. The plaintiff was aware of this having learnt about the technique of colonoscopy. However, he should also have been told that in certain circumstances this might cause him considerable pain.

A patient who has not experienced colonoscopy previously and has not heard about it from others could not expect this or even regard this as normal. For a patient to decide whether to consent to a physical investigation, it is relevant, among other considerations, what he must accept in the course of it and what pain he will have to suffer which exceeds that to be expected in connection with a diagnostic medical examination. This knowledge must not be withheld from him merely because he might be frightened and might object to what is normally a harmless investigation or because he may stiffen and thereby make the investigation more difficult for himself and the doctor. It is for the doctor to calm a frightened patient and so to explain to him the need for a painful investigation that he can be certain of the patient's consent and co-operation. In the case of a colonoscopy this may include the information that the doctor would immediately abandon the investigation should he find the pain intolerable. Since neither the duty doctor at first examination nor the second defendant before the start of his investigation told the plaintiff what might ensue, the plaintiff's consent was invalid and the colonoscopic investigation was illegal because he was not aware of all the circumstances affecting his decision.

2. It does not necessarily follow therefrom, as the Court of Appeal assumes incorrectly, that the second defendant is vicariously liable for the injuries to the person of the plaintiff as a result of the perforation of the intestine. The facts as found by the Court of Appeal so far are insufficient for holding the second defendant liable for having provided defective information concerning the unpleasantness of a colonoscopy.

(a) In as far as the required information of the patient was held to have been incomplete because he was not told before the proposed diagnostic investigation of the possibility of considerable pain (without resulting in a serious and permanent injury to his health), it is not immediately obvious that the patient, if correctly informed, would have declined the investigation. It is even less obvious in the case of a patient who is not normally given to complain of pain. In the present case the plaintiff has described himself in the course of proceedings as a man who is not really hypersensitive; moreover, he has not argued that he had been insufficiently informed because he had not been told of the possibility of pain in the course of the investigation. In these circumstances the mere allegation by the plaintiff that he would have declined to undergo the investigation for fear of pain would be insufficient to accept this account (see the decision of this Senate of 7 February 1984, reported below, BGHZ 90, 103 and the order of this Senate of 27 October 1981—VI Z R 63/81, VersR 1982, 74, 75 = NJW 1982, 700). Since the plaintiff made no such allegation, the fact that the defendants have not pleaded expressly that the plaintiff would have consented to the investigation in any case, cannot be held against them. Instead, the plaintiff's pleadings until now are insufficient to support the conclusion that his right to decide himself whether to agree to the investigation had been violated on the legal ground relied upon by the Court of Appeal.

(b) In addition, this Court must accept that in the view of the Court of Appeal the risk of which the plaintiff should have been informed, namely that the investigation might be accompanied by considerable pain, did not materialise in his case. It is true that the plaintiff has made allegation to this effect, but to the detriment of the defendants, who denied from the outset that the investigation had been accompanied by considerable pain; the Court of Appeal did not make any findings to this effect. Evidence taken on this question was not taken into account by it. If, however, the colonoscopy did not cause the plaintiff considerable pain, the investigation also did not cause him any injury. Even if his right to determine himself whether to agree to the investigation has been violated in some respects, he did not suffer any personal injury for which compensation would have to be paid. This conclusion is not vitiated by the fact that in carrying out the colonoscopy leading to the perforation of the sigmoid colon an entirely different and remote risk materialised provided that the latter did not have to be disclosed (for details see *infra* III). The reason is that the damage arising therefrom falls outside the sphere of protection of the rule establishing liability which imposes a duty upon the doctor to pay damages for a physical investigation which is illegal in the absence of a valid consent by the patient.

(*aa*) It is unnecessary in the present case to determine the question of law as to whether no connection exists between the illegality of the physical investigation of the patient in the absence of effective information and the resulting physical injury whenever culpably the basic risks inherent in the investigation have not been set out, but another link has materialised which did not have to be explained to the plaintiff (affirmatively the Court of Appeal Karlsruhe, Med. R. 1983, 180, 192 with a concurring note by Kern; Kern-Laufs, *Die ärztliche Aufkläurungspflicht*, 1983, p. 151 ff.; *contra*: Mutons in *Münchener Kommentar* p. 823 no. 423). Certain objections could be raised against this view because in the case of medical investigations involving risks which are not quite inconsiderable, the right of the patient to determine himself whether to agree to the investigation and who also agrees without any knowledge and without any information, always includes his freedom of decision for or against an investigation covering his body as a whole.

(*bb*) The objections set out here do not apply in the present case.

Admittedly, the action of the second defendant does not cease to be illegal for the reason only that the plaintiff's consent certainly covered an investigation free of pain. The consent of a patient to a medical investigation is not a declaration of intent which can be divided into one concerning the violation of personal integrity on the one hand and another, on the other hand, which involves exposing oneself voluntarily to danger by accepting certain possible risks (see however Kern-Laufs loc. cit. and Med. R. loc. cit.). It is true that in substance it covers both (see Deutsch, NJW 1982, 2585 and in *Arztrecht und Arzneimittelrecht* p. 42 no. 42), but this only defines the legal significance of the declaration of intent. However, it has no bearing on the question as to what is the substance of the declaration made to the doctor in consenting to the medical investigation. The substance is clear: if the consent is valid, it applies without restriction. If it is refused (or what is the same, if it is invalid for failure to receive sufficient information), the declaration of intention means, and cannot be interpreted otherwise, that the patient will not agree to the medical measures, as advised, that is to say in their entirety (similarly Mertons in *Münchener Kommentar* loc. cit.). The motives for his refusal are legally irrelevant as is the question whether hypothetically he would consent to all investigations without complications. If he did not give his consent, he did not consent either to an investigation which was illegal and to which he did not agree, but which was successful. At best the disregard of his right to determine himself whether to undergo the investigation did not result in any damage.

It is possible, however, that in such cases the claim for damages may not succeed for a different legal reason. The duty to supply information concerning the remote damages of considerable pain is designed to protect the patient's right to decide freely whether he will consent to the medical investigation, having regard to the advantages of a diagnostic assessment of his state of health and to the physical unpleasantness which he will experience if he undergoes the investigation.

The medical duty of contract which is to provide information concerning the potential danger of considerable pain is therefore not designed to facilitate the independent decision of the patient whether he is willing to accept possible dangers to his health. Instead it is to enable the patient to decide whether he is willing to face a potential temporary impairment of his well-being as a result of sudden pain. In such cases, a connection between the illegality consisting of the doctor's neglect of his duty and that consisting of the violation of the patient's right to determine himself whether to undergo a medical investigation exists only if the risk of a painful treatment has materialised. If apart from this no risk of any damage to health exists, having regard to the fact that the investigation does not present any danger of which the patient should have to be informed, the failure to inform him of the possibility of pain cannot form the basis of liability in respect of a complication which occurred nevertheless in the course of the diagnostic investigation (see Steffen in *Verhandlungen des 52. Deutschen Juristentags* vol. II Part I p. 15; similarly in another connection Giesen, *JZ* 1992, 448, 454 with reference to the decision of this Senate of 16 June 1981, VI | R 38/40 = VersR 1981, 954 = NJW 1981, 2513; for criticism of the denial of a link of illegality in general see Mertens loc. cit.).

In the present case the plaintiff cannot, therefore, base his claims for damages on the ground that he was not informed of possible pain in the course of the colonoscopy.

Case 38

BUNDESGERICHTSHOF (SIXTH CIVIL DIVISION) 9 DECEMBER 1958*
BGHZ 29, 46

The plaintiff was a patient in the hospital for nervous diseases in L. He claims damages against the local authority in respect of the consequences of electric-shock treatment.

The plaintiff was a chronic alcoholic. When his mental powers continued

* English version by Kurt Lipstein.

to deteriorate, he received unsuccessful treatment for alcoholism in the summer of 1954. He was then received by the hospital for nervous diseases. There medicinal treatment had no lasting effect. For this reason the assembled medical staff suggested that the plaintiff should receive a series of electric-shock treatments. Dr N, the head of the neurological psychiatric department, discussed this method of treatment in October 1954 with the plaintiff's brother and sister and with his wife. They consented to the electric-shock treatment. The parties disagree as to what was said during the remaining part of this discussion.

After receiving shock treatment on five occasions without incident, the plaintiff suffered a complicated comminuted fracture of the head of the left femur when he received his sixth and last treatment on 2 November 1954. As a result his left leg, which was already deformed since birth (club-foot and atrophy), was shortened. In addition a so-called false joint appeared in the area of the head of the femur.

The plaintiff contends as follows: he had been given shock treatment without his consent and had not been informed of the dangers of this treatment. Moreover he had not consented validly since he had lacked the capacity at the time. A guardian, who would have acted in his place, had not yet been appointed. His brother and sister and his wife had not consented validly either to the shock treatment since they, too, had not been informed of the nature and the attendant danger. The plaintiff continued, further, that the treatment had been carried out inexpertly; in particular no drugs relaxing the muscles had been administered, although this was necessary in order to prevent injuries resulting from cramp.

The plaintiff has asked that the defendant should pay DM 2931 as compensation and an adequate sum for pain and suffering. He has asked, further, for a declaration that the defendant is obliged to compensate him for all damage which may arise in the future.

The defendant contends as follows: The plaintiff and his relatives had agreed to the shock treatment. They had been warned that this treatment carried a certain risk. No duty to provide this information existed, for the methods of shock treatment had been greatly improved since the early days when this treatment was first applied, and the danger of injurious consequences was extremely low. The treatment had been carried out correctly and with the help of the most modern appliance, . . . which caused a mild effect of the cramps. Any use of muscle relaxing drugs had been ruled out because the plaintiff's heart, his circulation, his liver, and his lungs had not functioned properly.

The District Court of Landau dismissed the claim. In the course of his appeal the plaintiff abandoned his claim for pain and suffering but maintained his claim for damages amounting to DM 2931 and for a declaration.

The Court of Appeal of Neustadt allowed the claim to the extent that it had not passed to the Social Insurance by way of subrogation and granted the declaration. On the second appeal by the defendant, the judgment of the Court of Appeal was quashed and the case referred back for the following

Reasons

I. The Court of Appeal starts from the proposition that by accepting the plaintiff in their hospital in L a contract had been concluded between the parties. By virtue of this contract the plaintiff was entitled, as against the defendant authority responsible for the hospital, to be treated expertly by the doctors employed by it. This proposition cannot be faulted, nor has the appellant done so. According to the Court of Appeal the evidence does not disclose any violation of the standards of medical care . . .

The Court of Appeal regards the doctor who administered the treatment as liable on the ground that he acted in the absence of a legally valid consent. The Court of Appeal left it undecided whether the plaintiff was legally capable of acting or physically capable of expressing his wishes and therefore able to give a valid consent. The Court of Appeal believes that the question as to whether the plaintiff consented is irrelevant, because he had not been informed of the possible danger accompanying the treatment. In considering the duty of a medical practitioner to inform the patient, the Court of Appeal relied on the principles enunciated by this Division [reference] following the practice of the Reichsgericht and held that the plaintiff or his legal representative should have been informed of the risks connected with shock treatment. It is not clear whether the plaintiff's wife and his brother and sister were given sufficient details of the danger. It seems that the Court of Appeal regarded this question as irrelevant, because none of those persons had been appointed the plaintiff's guardian at that time. As a result the Court of Appeal held that Dr N had acted negligently and in breach of contract for having administered electro-shock to the defendant without any real consent; the defendant was responsible for his according to § 278 BGB.

II. . . . Doctors and lawyers agree that the consent of the patient is required before medical treatment can take place, especially if it interferes with the body. Apart from special, exceptional cases, none of which is in issue here (e.g. where there is danger in delay), any interference with the body of a patient is only lawful if the patient consents. This follows from Art. 2 II of the Constitution which guarantees integrity of the person to everybody. A right to compel treatment, as it was being discussed under National Socialism, but as always rejected by the Reichsgericht [reference], is not being called for by anybody today.

Opinions are divided as to the nature of this consent, whether and to what extent it presupposes, in particular, that the patient is aware of his condition and whether, therefore, he must be informed of the nature of his illness as well as of the character, importance, and possible deleterious consequences of the treatment. This question of the duty of a medical adviser to give information . . . can no longer be answered by relying on the advice of Hippocrates to conceal most from the patient and not to tell him anything of what awaits or threatens him. This advice cannot be reconciled with modern ideas about the calling of a medical practitioner and the right of patients to self-determination [reference]; also it no longer serves as a guide-line for medical conduct . . .

It is unnecessary in the present case to decide to what extent the patient must be informed, for if it is correct . . . that the plaintiff was capable of act-ing, he was informed of the nature of his illness and also of the nature of the treatment, at least at the start of the sixth application of the electro-shock treatment which led to the injury and is therefore essential for the present purpose. The discussion can therefore be limited to the question which has given rise to most doubts, as to whether and to what extent the information to be given to the patient must also include the potentially dangerous conse-quences of the treatment.

1. In response to the demand for such information it is pointed out in med-ical circles, first of all, that a patient is often incapable of understanding the nature and the consequences of the treatment; that since any serious illness affects the person as a whole and causes a disturbance, not only physically but also emotionally, he is unable to assess rationally the advantages and the disadvantages of the proposed medical treatment or to force himself into reaching a decision free from uncontrollable moods, fears, and prejudices [references]. This aspect is important in assessing the legal position inas-much as naturally the information is only indicated if the patient is capable of appreciating the kind, purpose, and consequences of the treatment and to come to a decision, for only a patient who is able to do this can validly con-sent to the proposed treatment. These problems did not arise in the case decided previously by this Division, for it was found in that case that the patient was able to consent validly to the electro-shock treatment because his state of depression did not affect his judgment or his ability to act freely . . . [reference].

The question whether a sick person can act freely in the sense set out above is primarily one to be answered by the medical profession. In most cases a court cannot decide it without medical witnesses or experts. However, even if a patient lacks the ability to act freely, the need for consent remains. This must be given by the person who, after having been given the necessary information, must decide instead of the patient himself whether the operation should take place. According to the opinion of some medical practitioners the nearest relatives of the sick and incapable person are not necessarily qualified to do so. It is true that they are the persons with the strongest and humanly closest interest in the well-being of the patient. However, as long as the law has not conferred upon them the right to decide upon the treatment of a patient who is incapable of acting himself, the practice current in many hospitals to obtain the consent of the nearest relative to the treatment of the patient cannot suffice, even if a consultation with the relatives, where danger exists in delay, may be a relevant means of ascertaining the presumed intention of the patient. In the *absence* of a dangerous situation which requires immediate or speedy action, it is necessary to appoint a guardian for the patient, who must decide in the place of the sick person whether the planned medical action is to take place. Such an appointment of a guardian is possible under § 1910 BGB if the sick person is unable as a result of his infirmity to handle his affairs in the particular circumstances . . .

2. . . . . as regards information to be given to a patient, the position of the doctor has been compared with that of the lawyer. It is said that it is unsatisfactory to treat the relationship between medical adviser and patient as a contract of service, seeing that the relationship is distinguished by a special human characteristic and often touches the deepest and most confidential areas of human feeling. It is alleged that a legal relationship *sui generis* is created in which the personality of the patient plays an important role which must not be overlooked and that the personal relationship between doctor and patient is the basis of a successful treatment . . . lawyers are said to be too formalistic and do not consider sufficiently the real situation.

. . . observations to this effect cannot be accepted. It is unimportant for the purpose of the problem of a medical practitioner's duty of information whether in law the relationship between doctor and patient is regarded as a contract of service or as a relationship *sui generis*. For, irrespective of the legal characterization of this relationship a court cannot and must not, in examining this question, regard the doctor and the patient merely as parties to a private law contract. If a court wishes to ascertain the nature and extent of the duty to provide information required by a doctor, all the circumstances of the individual case must be assembled and considered. The court must not overlook either that the relationship between doctor and patient presupposes profound confidence, that it is strongly based on a human relationship, in which the doctor comes to the aid of the patient, and that, therefore, it constitutes much more than a contractual relationship. . . .

The health of the patient is the doctor's principal concern. It is his duty to restore it and to preserve it. It is reasonable that a conscientious doctor often regards himself as entitled, or even as obliged, to assist by interfering physically if the life and the health of his patient is at stake. Nevertheless, these efforts must find their limit if they conflict with the right of the patient to determine the fate of his body. This situation can arise if the doctor begins a treatment without having informed the patient of its nature and consequences [reference].

It is true that a sick person, who consults a medical practitioner or visits a hospital in order to seek relief for his illness also often consents in advance to a limited extent to the administration of physical treatment which is necessary as a means of recovery. It cannot be concluded therefrom, however, that the patient is not interested in being told in broad terms about the proposed treatment, the usual development, the likely result, and possible danger to his health arising from this treatment. Not being an expert in medical matters, the patient also regards the doctor as an adviser and expects normally to be instructed by him in these matters and to be advised. Only if the patient is aware of his situation, and knows broadly what his consent to the administration of physical medical treatment implies can his consent satisfy the meaning and purpose which is to absolve the administration of physical treatment from the charge of illegality and to shift part of the doctor's responsibility to the patient.

It is true that cases will arise in which the patient wishes to be relieved of his sufferings in all circumstances and indicates clearly that he places his full confidence in the doctor. In such a case the doctor may be justified, in view of the clear wish of the patient, in omitting to provide further information. In such a case . . . the patient looks to the doctor as the authority which relieves him from considering the matter on his own and assuming responsibility himself. The patient does not really wish to know but wants to comply. This does not, however, apply normally, for in many, if not most cases the patient wants to know his situation and thus the prognosis and the risks of the intended operation or of another medical administration of physical treatment and wants to decide himself whether this treatment is to take place. If the doctor respects the patient's right to decide himself, the confidence of the latter in the doctor will be enhanced rather than diminished. A sick person may have very good reasons . . . for refusing to undergo an operation and thus possibly for accepting responsibility for a considerable shortening of his life [reference]. The freedom and dignity of human personality require that this wish of the patient is to be respected.

All this shows that in protecting the freedom of a patient to decide for himself, the courts are far from paying homage to what is a formal principle only. On the contrary, they protect a right enshrined in the Constitution, which is to be respected and applied as much as the right to health. In the present context of the decision concerning the duty of a medical adviser to provide information too, much more is at stake than purely formal matters, for in this connection, too, substantive considerations are in issue as to how the responsibility for treatment is to be decided reasonably and justly between doctor and patient [reference].

3. . . . attention has been drawn . . . to the dangers to the health and to the recovery affecting in particular those suffering from psychosis, if they are informed of their illness. It is said, *inter alia*, that only the medical expert and not the court can decide, having regard to the special situation in the individual case, to what extent a patient can be informed of the risks involved in the administration of physical treatment. It was the duty of the medical practitioner to calm the patient and to dispel the fear of an operation and not to produce the opposite effect by providing detailed information. Unrestricted information concerning possible complications would so deter and frighten a sufferer from a psychosis who was willing in principle to undergo the treatment that in most cases he would refuse his consent to shock treatment and would thus deprive himself of the chance of recovery [reference].

In determining the duty to provide information the above-mentioned consideration cannot be attributed the degree of importance which the medical profession ascribes to it. If the provision of information to a patient who is capable of acting is unlikely to endanger his health or his recovery, and if only the serious possibility exists of the patient refusing his consent to the treatment, contrary to his true interest, it follows that the medical adviser is not relieved of his duty to draw the patient's attention to the typical dangers connected with the treatment . . . the information serves to invite the patient to decide himself. In making up his mind he is to be given the opportunity of considering not only the chances of recovery but also the deleterious effects of the treatment which are not too remote. Only if the patient knows this too, can his consent relieve the doctor of part of his responsibility. Admittedly the doctor must seek to calm the patient and to set his mind at ease, following the information. The doctor may also seek to influence him to undergo urgently needed treatment by patient persuasion and by a discussion of his fears and objections, as well as by pointing out forcibly the disadvantages if the treatment does not take place. On the other hand, the medical adviser must not seek to influence the decision of the patient by concealing relevant facts from him [reference].

The real difficulty is presented by the problem . . . whether and to what extent the duty to provide information must give way to other duties and interests, if serious objections exist against informing the patient having regard to his personality and his mental state, especially if by providing the information his health or even his life may be endangered. The previous decision of this Division has been understood wrongly to state that the Federal Supreme Court regards this circumstance as irrelevant. Admittedly it is stated in the reasons given by the judgment, following the practice of the Reichsgericht [reference]: if, as a result of the information the mood or the general well-being of the patient should be affected adversely, this fact must be accepted as an inevitable disadvantage. The passage in question does not state, however, as has been thought erroneously, that exhaustive information is to be given even if, as a result, the life or the health of the patient is seriously endangered. The principle has been stated meanwhile by this Division in its decision of 10 February 1956 [reference] where it is stated that a doctor is not obliged to prejudice recovery by excessive information. The question as to how such a case is to be judged in law [reference] and how the doctor must act in this situation was irrelevant in the previous case. It need not be decided here either, for, then as now, neither the defendant nor the doctor in charge has pleaded that in this respect doubts existed as to whether the patient should be informed. If a medical adviser has failed to point out the typical dangers connected with the administration of physical treatment, the burden of proof is on him to show good reasons for having omitted to provide information [reference].

This court cannot agree with the claim of the medical profession to decide on their own whether and to what extent in the individual case a patient is to receive information if it is implied thereby that the courts are precluded altogether from reviewing the medical decision. The question as to whether in a particular case the patient received sufficient information touches upon the sphere of law; upon it depends the determination of the legal question, to be decided by the court, as to whether he has validly consented to the treatment. Naturally, the court in determining questions of this kind, will rely extensively on expert medical assistance. This is true . . . in particular in assessing the capacity of the patient to give his consent, but also when the question is whether complete information would have resulted in injury to the plaintiff's health or would have seriously endangered recovery. The court cannot be deprived of the power to review the question whether the doctor has complied with his duty to provide information and whether the patient has validly consented to the treatment.

4. According to the judgment of the Federal Supreme Court, information must only be provided where typical dangers exist inherent in the treatment, that is to say dangers which are normally connected with it and the occurrence of which can be expected according to medical experience and research. . . . The assumption is incorrect that the Federal Supreme Court requires a sick person to be made aware of every possible side-effect of the treatment. No such requirement has ever been laid down. Instead it is

acknowledged that a doctor is not obliged to draw the patient's attention to those dangers which can be avoided without difficulty, having regard to modern standards of operating techniques [reference]. Nor is he required to advise the patient that in unfavourable conditions even the smallest operation may result in some complications, despite all precautionary measures. Generally every patient knows this, and no special warning is necessary [reference].

5. In conclusion, it appears that the problem of the duty to provide a patient with information incumbent upon medical advisers as a condition for the validity of the patient's consent to the treatment continues to be governed basically by the principles which predominate in practice and in the literature.

III. In applying these principles to the facts of the present case the Court of Appeal rightly assumed that according to medical experience complications may arise in the course of electro-shock treatment. . . . Even incurable mental disease can be alleviated thereby at a stroke and sometimes cured; an electric current causes a cramp, accompanied by a sudden cramp-like contraction of all the muscles of the body and by a temporary loss of consciousness. This cramp-like tension can result in damage to joints and bones

. . .

In its previous decision the Federal Supreme Court assumed on the basis of the expert evidence and of the factual findings of the Court of Appeal that at the time of the treatment then in issue, i.e. in the year 1951, complications arose in seven per cent of the cases of electro-shock treatment and that, consequently, it was normally required to inform the patient of this possibility . . . in the present case the question is only what the rate of complications appeared to be in 1954, when the plaintiff received electro-shock treatment. As regards this question the plaintiff, in agreement with statements made by some doctors, has argued as follows: like every therapeutic measure shock treatment had become less dangerous with increasing experience and with improvements in technical handling. For some time, and certainly in 1954, complications had become extremely rare and only occurred in one out of a thousand cases of shock therapy. This objection is relevant, for it is correct that the dangerous nature of the physical treatment cannot be assessed by reference to the frequency of complications during the early stages of a new therapy, when the necessary experience was still lacking. Instead the state of medical science and experience is determining which exists at the time of the particular medical treatment in issue [reference]. The Court of Appeal, too, adopted this view. It stated:

The court realizes that the dangers arising from shock treatment may have been less in 1954 than in 1951. . . . In examining the question of the need to provide information it is impossible to rely on the positive experience of one medical expert which, moreover, extends to the present time. It must be considered that at the relevant time, in 1954, the Siemens-Convulsator III which was used in treating the plaintiff was . . . a new instrument, the effects of which had not yet been tested by an extensive practice. In determining a duty to provide information and the extent of the information to be provided, the state of experience at the particular time must supply the standard. Even if in 1954 fractures, injuries to the spine, and other damage had become so rare as no longer to count as typical, they still occurred to an extent which made it appear necessary to draw attention to them.

These observations of the Court of Appeal give rise to legal criticism. Even if in 1954 the application of shock methods as practised in the hospital for nervous diseases led only very seldom to complications, these complications nevertheless remain typical of shock treatment, for injuries of this kind . . . occur precisely on the occasion of this treatment, and at no other. This does not, however, assist in determining the duty of the medical adviser to inform the patient, for it is also unnecessary to draw attention to typical injuries, if they occur in extremely rare cases only and if it can be assumed that a reasonable patient would not consider such injuries seriously in deciding to give his consent. This would be the case if, as the defendant contends, in 1954 complications occurred in less than one in a thousand cases of shock treatment where the Siemens-Convulsator III was used. In such cases information must only be given if the patient enquires specifically about possible dangers. Since the Court of Appeal has found that this did not happen, it should have ascertained the rate of complications in 1954 accompanying this method of treatment. . . . The fact that the Court of Appeal came to the conclusion, without exhausting [these] sources of further evidence, that injuries still occurred at that time to an extent which made it necessary to inform the patient to this effect discloses . . . an error of law. Consequently the judgment under appeal cannot be upheld on the basis of the reasons set out therein . . .

Case 39

BUNDESGERICHTSHOF (SIXTH CIVIL DIVISION) 15 APRIL 1975*
NJW 1975, 1161 = JZ 1975, 535 = VersR 1975, 831

The defendants accuse the plaintiff of having offered indecent periodicals and picture magazines on their railway bookstalls. After the third defendant, a student of theology, had lodged a complaint with the police he went on the morning of 4 July 1971 together with the other defendants, a lawyer and two acquaintances, to the railway bookstall of the plaintiff in B and invited the sales assistant to remove from the shelves within one hour those

* English version by Kurt Lipstein.

publications which he described as indecent. When he found upon his return that they had not been removed, the third defendant took twenty-four newspapers and periodicals from the shelves and from a stand and took them in front of the railway station, where the fourth defendant defaced them with paint. In addition he wrote in paint on the display window of the kiosk 'Away with filthy pornography'. Meanwhile the first defendant, in the presence of the second defendant, engaged in discussion with passers-by.

On the same evening the first and third defendant went to the plaintiff's kiosk at the railway station in H and made the same demand that all the publications described by them as pornographic were to be removed within an hour. Finding upon their return that their demand had not been complied with, the third defendant began to go through the papers on the newsstand, as a result of which some periodicals fell onto the ground. Using a megaphone he invited passers-by to lodge a complaint against the plaintiff. The first defendant protested against the sale of pornographic publications by holding up a poster.

The plaintiff demands that the defendants should be prohibited from removing from their outlets publications or other objects without any intention of purchasing them, from soiling or damaging them or from affecting them physically.

The district court allowed the claim. The defendants appealed unsuccessfully to the Court of Appeal of Karlsruhe. Their further appeal was rejected for the following

Reasons

The Court of Appeal regards the claim for an order of prohibition as justified under §§ 823 I, 1004 I BGB. It holds correctly that the defendants, acting together, violated the plaintiff's property and interfered with his established and operating business. The appellants do not contest that they acted as trespassers in the meaning of § 1004 I BGB, even if they did not themselves act against the plaintiff. It is only disputed whether the defendants acted illegally and whether a danger exists of a repetition. The Court of Appeal answered both questions in the affirmative. It held that the acts of the defendants were not justified as self-defence nor as permissible defence of others, even if . . . the publications concerned were indecent in the meaning of the wording then in force of § 184 of the Criminal Code and were therefore a danger to young persons according to § 6 of the Act against the Distribution of Publications Endangering Young Persons. In the opinion of the Court of Appeal the infringements of the law committed so far and the conduct of the defendant indicated the likelihood of a repetition. In the result the appeal must fail.

I. 1. The Court of Appeal holds correctly that the defendants cannot seek to justify their acts by relying on the right of self-defence or the defence of others (§ 227 BGB) even if the plaintiff . . . should have contravened § 84 of the Criminal Code or the Act against the Distribution of Publications Endangering Young Persons by displaying and selling the publications to which the defendants took exception. This right of self-help does not enable citizens to maintain morals and order, even if the order is protected by criminal law. Their maintenance is the task of the competent organs of the State; the ordinary citizen must not assume their function. In a State governed by law it is indispensable that the maintenance and protection of orderly community life is to be entrusted primarily to the organs of the State bound to observe the Constitution and not to private initiative [references].

As a matter of principle, an individual can only confront actively a disturbance of public order, even if it involves a criminal act, by relying on his right of self-defence or of defending others . . . if the perpetrator of the disturbance attacks at the same time individual interests which are protected as such [references].

(*a*) Contrary to the contention of the appellants this is not necessarily the case if § 184 of the Criminal Code or §§ 3, 4, 6 of the Act against Distribution of Publications Endangering Young Persons are infringed. Certainly § 184 of the Criminal Code in the wording of 20 July 1971, which applies in the present case, punishes advertising and selling indecent publications in order to protect modesty, morals, and decency in sexual matters in the interest of the community as a whole [references]. The penal sanction sought to protect the sexual feelings current in the community, not the particular notion of morals and decency held by an individual, which may even clash with the sanction. The individual was included in the sphere of protection of the sanction indirectly only inasmuch as normally he benefits from it too. For this reason he was not accorded the right, in the case of contraventions of § 184 of the Criminal Code, to avail himself of the right under § 172 of the Code of Criminal Procedure to apply for the initiation of proceedings to force a prosecution.

Similarly, the Act against the Distribution of Publications Endangering Young Persons in providing for the protection of children and adolescents only serves the State as a guardian. It is the function of the State, not of the individual citizen, to safeguard the order which these provisions seek to protect.

(*b*) Naturally this does not rule out the possibilities that an infringement against these provisions may coincide with an attack against individual interests 'susceptible of self-defence' with the result that the citizen concerned himself or another may intervene in order to fend off *this* attacker.

However, this presupposes a situation in which precisely the protected individual interests are affected by the dangers connected with the 'attack' and that thus the protected sphere of the individual is touched by the coincidence of 'attack' and individual interest; the fact alone that the order protected by the criminal law has been disturbed is insufficient. Those relying on the right of self-defence or to defend others must prove that a conflict of the kind described above exists.

The Court of Appeal holds correctly that the pleadings of the defendants are deficient in this respect. In particular they cannot rely on the argument that merely by offering for sale in their kiosks at railway stations publications—assumed to be a criminal act—they have directly violated the right of personality of the defendants by attacking their honour or otherwise, even if the defendants may have regarded the display of such publications as a sufficient slight of their person, as a threat to their intimate feelings or to their family life.

It is unnecessary in the present case to examine the restrictions imposed by our law upon the trade in pornography by the protection of the personality of the individual and of its dignity [references]. In the present case . . . periodicals and picture magazines, the publication of which was prohibited and punishable, are said to have been offered for sale on the shelves of the premises together with the usual range of publications available at a railway bookstall. However, no customer was compelled against his will to take more than fleeting notice of these publications; his personal attention was not drawn to them, nor were they advertised obtrusively. The personality of the individual which is protected by the Constitution was only affected by this confrontation quantitatively and qualitatively as part of an anonymous public, no more than an individual member of the community is troubled by disturbances of public order. The personality of the customer is neither disregarded nor injured in an insulting manner, nor are his protected intimate feelings injured, even if it is remembered that the protection of personal integrity, both physical and mental, must be rated highly.

It is true that human personality and its free expression through self-determination and self-reliance, guaranteed by the Constitution and the legal order, also requires citizens among themselves to respect the innermost sphere of the individual [references]. This precept does not imply, however, that every citizen who is worried or disturbed by a public disregard of general morals and of criminal law by another is entitled for *this reason only* to proceed against the attacker by way of self-help, unless the attack is directed against himself; in the present case an individual citizen has first sought a confrontation in order to make public interests his own private affair. Such an assumption of an 'office of censor' would indeed run counter to the constitutional guarantee. Instead it must remain for the State itself, which is primarily charged with adjusting such tensions, to select the place, the time, and the extent of any action against the violation of morals and of law within the community.

(*bb*) The same applies to the claim of the fourth defendant, the father of the child, who relies on the right of self-defence or of the defence of others, on the ground that the attack is directed against the right to educate a child (see Art. 6 of the Constitution). In this respect, too, no evidence has been adduced to show that the conduct of the plaintiff constitutes a direct danger to the task of the fourth defendant to educate his child . . .

(*cc*) This Division does not agree with the arguments of the appellants that the courts, by decreeing the prohibition asked for by the plaintiff, would protect a criminal activity by the plaintiff. The question whether the competent public authorities can proceed against the plaintiff, having regard to his trade in the publications objected to, is not affected by a judgment in the terms applied for. This judgment is confined to preventing conduct by the defendants which is to be disapproved by law for the sake of orderly community life and against whom the plaintiff may defend himself by a claim to desist placed at his disposal by private law. Nor is it an abuse of law if the plaintiff resorts to the courts by bringing an action against the defendants.

Notes to Cases 35–39

1. These cases illustrate certain problems that German law discusses under the headings of 'unlawfulness' and *culpa*. Their theoretical treatment has been sketched above (Ch. 2, section A.3) but it is, again, at the level of concrete cases and specific issues that the similarities become obvious and any comparison with the Common law becomes meaningful. A number of points call for special comment.

2. The standard of care expected of the defendant is discussed in cases 35 and 36. In case 35 the plaintiff's claim failed because he himself knew that the defendant was not fully competent. A second reason why the claim failed can be traced in the facts as found by the lower courts: the accident would have occurred even if the defendant had been properly qualified. In other words, the defendant's negligence is not even a condition (let alone a legal cause) of the harm. (See Ch. 2, section A.5 (*a*), and English cases cited there.) But the importance of the judgment is in its second half where (as in case 36) it is stated that the standard of care will be determined objectively by reference to the behaviour of the reasonable man. Here, the basic idea is the same in American, English, and French law, though many formulations have been proposed and the terminology is slightly different. (The Common law searches for the behaviour of the 'reasonable man' who, in the context

of the tort of defamation, becomes the 'ordinary man' in order to accommodate a certain amount of loose thinking (note that in these days of proclaimed sex equality lawyers have still to introduce the notion of the 'reasonable woman'), while the civil law systems refer to the *'bonus pater familias'*.) In practice, however, these are merely expressions of the anthropomorphic conception of justice as perceived by judges and/or juries.

Numerous statements can be quoted from all systems showing that the legal system neither expects the behaviour of the model citizen who is the paragon of all true virtue nor is prepared to countenance the attitudes of the most callous, timorous, or indecisive members of its society. As Harper, James Jun., and Gray put it (*The Law of Torts* 2nd edn. (1986) 389–90): 'As everyone knows, this reasonable *person* [*sic*] is a creature of the law's imagination. He is an abstraction. He has long been the subject of homely phrase and witty epigram.' (Equally, however, courts have applied the ordinary standards of care even to persons of exceptional skill and perception, *Fredericks* v. *Castora* 360 A. 2d 696, 241 Pa. Super. 211 (1976).) In *Hall* v. *Brooklands Club* [1933] 1 KB 205, 224, Greer LJ stressed the need to remain in touch with the average community standards when he described the reasonable man as ' "the man in the street" or "the man in the Clapham omnibus", or, as I recently read in an American author, "the man who takes the magazines at home, and in the evening pushes the lawn-mower in his shirt sleeves" '. However, the reader must also take note of the clear trend discernible in all systems to raise standards in an effort to keep abreast with the quicker tempo and increased hazards of modern life. Thus, in certain areas of tort law—notably traffic accidents which account for a major part of litigation in all advanced legal systems—the presence of obligatory insurance may be the reason of an almost complete equation of negligence with near-strict liability. Case 36 is a good illustration of this tendency and one can find even clearer examples in French (Grenoble, 4 décembre 1978, *JCP* 1980, II, 19340) and English law (*Roberts* v. *Ramsbottom* [1980] 1 WLR 823). In the latter case the English court held 'negligent' a 75-year-old man who had a stroke a few minutes before setting off on a drive that was to lead to a series of accidents culminating in his being taken to hospital where his brain haemorrhage (of which he had had no previous forewarning) was finally discovered. In the court's view nothing less than a complete loss of consciousness would have sufficed to exculpate him from liability. (Cf. *Breunig* v. *American Family Insurance Co.* 173 NW 2d 619 (1970): defendant lost control of her car believing that God had taken control of the steering wheel. He had not and the plaintiff was injured. The plea of insanity was rejected and defendant was held liable.) Other cases like *Henderson* v. *Jenkins* [1970] AC 282 (car brakes defective due to an undiscoverable hidden defect which led to an accident) and *Nettleship* v. *Weston* [1971] 2

QB 691 (learner-driver held to be 'negligent' for failing to attain the standard of competence of an experienced driver; likewise with American law: Gregory *et al.*, 152) lend credence to theories which attempt to ascribe such *perversions* of traditional concepts to modern insurance practice. (In this sense B. S. Markesinis, 'La Perversion des notions de responsabilité civile délictuelle par la pratique de l'assurance' (1983) *Rev. int. dr. comp.* 301.) In America standards have also been dramatically raised in cases involving children causing accidents while engaged in 'adult activities'. *Dellwo* v. *Pearson* 259 Minn. 452, 107 NW 2d 859 (1961) is such a case and has proved particularly influential in automobile cases. See *Prichard* v. *Veterans Cab. Co.* 63 Cal. 2d 727, 408 P. 2d 360 (1965); also Henderson and Pearson, 363–4 with further references. Children are judged by adult standards when they are defendants. By what standards should they be judged when they are the plaintiffs and a question of contributory negligence arises? See *Reiszel* v. *Fontana*, 35 AD 2d 74, 312 NYS 2d 988 (1970).

3. For fuller discussions of American law see Franklin, 43 ff.; Henderson and Pearson, 319 ff.; Epstein, 129 ff.; Posner, 197 ff.; Prosser, *et al.*, 149 ff. For England see Clerk and Lindsell, 405 ff. The impact of modern insurance on the modern law of torts has been the subject of an excellent dissertation by Professor Viney of the University of Paris in the mid sixties (*Le déclin de la responsabilité individuelle* (1965)); and the theme is taken up again in her most recent treatise on the subject, *Traité de droit civil* (ed. J. Ghestin IV), *Les obligations, la responsabilité civile* (1982). Finally, for an excellent comparative discussion of the notion of fault and the changed attitudes towards it see Tunc, *La responsabilité civile* (1981).

4. Case 38 (and, indeed, case 77, below) touches upon one of the most troublesome aspects of medical malpractice law—a topic which has generated heated debates and lends itself for inclusion in courses on advanced torts. The huge American literature can be found in such works as Wadlington, Waltz, and Dworkin, *Law and Medicine* (1980), and Curran and Shapiro, *Medicine and Forensic Science* (3rd edn. 1982). *Making Health Care Decisions, President's Commission for the Study of Ethical Problems in Medicine*, US Government Publishing Office (1982) is a three-volume report full of useful information on the subject. *Comment to Medical Care* is the title of the equally interesting study published by the Law Reform Commission of Canada in 1980. English law, on the other hand, has only recently been awoken to these problems and this late interest is reflected in a rather meagre (but growing) literature. Margaret Brazier's *Medicine, Patients and the Law* 2nd edn. (1992) provides a most readable introduction to the whole subject. Mason and McCall-Smith's *Law and Medical Ethics* 2nd edn. (1987) gives a good summary (at 140–59), on the whole, supportive of the current rather conservative approach of the English courts. By con-

trast Ian Kennedy's stimulating Note in 47 *MLR* 454 (1984) is critical of this attitude. (See also Kennedy's excellent essays collected under the title *Treat Me Right* (1988).) Well worth reading also is Robertson's 'Informed Consent to Medical Treatment' 97 *LQR* 102 (1981) and Andrew Grubb's 'A Survey of Medical Malpractice Law in England: Crisis? What Crisis?', 1 *Journ. of Contemporary Health Law and Policy* 75 ff. (esp. 93–111) (1985). For a comparative study of English and American law on this point see: Schwartz and Grubb, 'Why Britain Can't Afford Informed Consent', 15 *Hastings Center Report* (1985); for Anglo-German law see Shaw, 'Informed Consent: A German Lesson', 35 *ICLQ* 864 (1986).

5. Lawful consent is required for otherwise the interference with the patient's body would be 'unlawful' according to the view taken by German case-law (*contra* Laufs in *NJW* 1969, 529 arguing that in this case the doctor's conduct is not objectively aimed at 'injuring' the body but as 'curing' and that, therefore, § 823 I BGB is inapplicable). Unlike the English Common law, which expects the patient to prove non-disclosure, German law casts on to the doctor the burden of proving the patient's consent. (Deutsch, *Arztrecht und Arzneimittelrecht*, 2nd edn. (1991) 39.) The action will, typically, be based on § 823 I BGB. In the Common law systems on the other hand total absence of consent or fraudulently obtained consent will justify an action in battery. In practice, however, negligence actions are much more common than trespass to the person because: (i) the rules on limitation and causation in trespass are thought to be too oppressive to defendant/doctors and (ii) intentional torts are usually not covered by insurance. See *Cobbs* v. *Grant* 8 Cal. 3d 229, 502 P. 2d 1 (1972); likewise in England, though see *Freeman* v. *Home Office* [1983] 3 All ER 589. Consent is thus crucial, but the problems it raises are far from solved. One could, perhaps, categorize the cases into three groups.

The first includes situations where the answers are *reasonably* clear. For example, in the case of an infant or a young child consent must come from those responsible for his care (usually the parents) §§ 1626, 1631 BGB (Germany); *Zoski* v. *Gaines* 271 Mich. 1, 260 NW 99 (1935) (USA); *S.* v. *McC.*; *W.* v. *W.* [1972] AC 29, 37 (per Lord Hodson) (England). Older children, mature enough to understand the implications of their consent, are free to give it themselves: *Lacey* v. *Laird* 166 Ohio St. 12, 139 NE 2d 25 (1956) (USA); BGHZ 29, 37 (Germany); *Family Law Reform Act 1969*, § 8 (16 years) (England). On this see Skegg in 36 *MLR* 370 (1973) and [1969] *Recent Law* 295 (NZ). An operation on an unconscious adult will usually be defended on the grounds of necessity.

A second group of cases are controversial (and have this in common with the next group); but they also deal with problems which are relatively new to medical science and social life in general. For example, whose consent is necessary for the prescription of a contraceptive pill: parent's or child's? In *Gillick* v. *West Norfolk and Wisbech Area Health Authority* the Court of Appeal ruled that no contraceptive, abortion advice, or treatment could be given to a girl under 16 years of age without her parents' consent save in a case of an emergency or after a court order (*The Times* 21 December 1984) but the decision was overruled by the House of Lords by a three to two majority: [1985] 3 All ER 402; [1986] AC 112 discussed by Professor Glanville Williams in 1985 *New Law Journal* pp. 1156 ff.; Kennedy, 'The Doctor, the Pill, and the Fifteen-Year-Old-Girl' in *Treat Me Right* (1988) 52 ff. Transplant surgery can also raise nice problems. See, for example, *Hart* v. *Brown* 29 Conn. Supp. 368, 289 A. 2d 386 (1972). Two related issues have also occupied modern courts and received similar answers. The first is connected with abortion and the father's 'rights' or 'interests'. Can he seek an injunction—acting in his own right or on behalf of the foetus—and prevent the mother from aborting? (If the foetus were viable, the father's action could also be seen as attempting to prevent the commission of a crime.) Two courts—in *Paton* v. *British Pregnancy Advisory Service* [1979] 276, involving an action by a *husband*, and in *C.* v. *S.* [1987] 1 All ER 1230, involving an action by the *boyfriend* of the mother—have shown a marked reluctance to challenge a medical decision, properly reached, about an abortion; and, in general, would prefer to leave it to the criminal law to challenge the legality of such a decision in the criminal courts where a jury would make the decision and not a judge sitting alone. The European Commission on Human Rights agreed, 3 EHRR 410 (1980).

What of a girl under age who wishes to have an abortion? Is her parents' consent necessary? The answer would appear to be negative so long as the girl is mature enough to understand what is being proposed: *Re P. (a Minor)* (1981) 80 LGR 301. But if the law appears to be settled, the ethical controversies are unlikely to end that easily. See Kennedy, 'A Husband, a Wife, and an Abortion', in *Treat Me Right* (1988) 42 ff.

The third group of cases deals with what is, perhaps, the thorniest aspect of the problem of consent—what exactly need be disclosed for consent to be valid? 'Medicine', wrote an international expert on this subject, 'is a discipline which is enriched by . . . joint international contribution. . . . The same is true of the law governing medical practice.' (Giesen and Hayes, 'The Patient's Right to Know—A Comparative View' (1992) 21 *Anglo-American L.R.* 101–22. See also, Giesen, 'Zwischen Patientenwohl und Patientenwille', *JZ* 1987, 282). Judicial decisions from both Canada and, especially, the antipodes, confirm the accuracy of the statement and the value of the method, so the summary that follows is comparative in nature and not focused on one system in particular.

To the question of how much information must be disclosed to the patient before his consent to medical treatment can be legally valid three answers are possible. The first, basically, leaves the decision to 'a responsible body of medical men skilled in that particular art.' This is known as the *Bolam* test from the leading English case of *Bolam* v. *Friern Hospital Management Committee* [1957] 1 WLR 582 and is the most paternalistic in nature. This test was, essentially, re-affirmed by four out of five law lords in *Sidaway* v. *Royal Bethlem Hospital Governors* [1985] 1 AC 871. (Lord Scarman dissented in favour of the doctrine of informed consent.) Though three of the judges (Lords Bridge, Keith and Templeman) made comments which have encouraged those who believe that English law is too indifferent to the patients' interests, the tone of the judgment was set by Lord Diplock who insisted that medical opinion remained 'determinative' in such matters. This can be seen by the next important case—*Gold* v. *Haringey Area Health Authority* [1988] QB 481 where the Court of Appeal overruled a more pro-plaintiff judgment by Schiemann J. ([1987] 1 FLR 125) by insisting that 'the Judge was not free, as he thought, to form his own view of what warning and information ought to have been given, irrespective of any body of responsible medical opinion to the contrary.' (Per Lloyd LJ at p. 490.) One reason why English law takes such a conservative view was given by Lord Denning in *Whitehouse* v. *Jordan* [1980] 1 All ER 650, 658, and is connected with the fear of increased malpractice litigation. However, such statistics as do exist in America and Germany do not seem to support this fear and further empirical studies are needed before a conclusive view can be expressed.

This English position is rejected by most Common law jurisdictions which adopt the so-called doctrine of 'informed consent' taking the view that the doctor must disclose as much information as a reasonable patient would require to make an informed choice and frequently add, for good measure, that the doctor 'should not lightly make the judgment that the patient does not wish to be fully informed.' This last quotation comes from the leading Australian case of *F.* v. *R.* (1983) 33 SASR 189, 193; and the same ideas are, essentially, found in many American jurisdictions (for example *Canterbury* v. *Spence* 464 F 2d 772 (1972); *Crain* v. *Allison* 443 A. d 558 (1982)) and Canada (*Reibl* v. *Hughes* [1980] 2 SCR 880; *White* v. *Turner* 120 DLR 3d 269). Both these positions have been rejected by many decisions of Continental European systems on the grounds that they violate the patient's right of self-determination. (Rich references to French, German, and Swiss law are given by Giesen and Hayes, op. cit., above, in notes 70–72; and the whole matter is exhaustively considered by Giesen in *International Medical Malpractice Law* (1988). For details on French law see: Guillot, *Le Consentement éclaire du patient: autodétermination ou paternalism* (1986).) This position has, as stated, been forcefully stressed by German courts which, in the light of the recent past, have been only too conscious of the dangers of ignoring human dignity and not preventing unwarranted medical interferences with the body and health of human beings. Thus, from the beginning of the post-War period, courts have stressed that 'proper respect for the patient's right of self determination will further rather than damage the patient's trust in his doctor' and 'to respect the patient's own will is to respect his freedom and dignity as a human being.' (BGHZ 29, 46, 53–56. See, also, BGHZ 90, 96; 90, 103.) Thus, the principle of full disclosure is repeatedly stressed (see BGH VersR 1980, 428, 429; NJW 1984, 1397); and in one case, involving *diagnostic* treatment, the court took the view that even a 0.5 per cent chance of a particular risk occurring should be disclosed (OLG Hamm VersR 1981, 686; other decisions have specified that an even lower risk—0.1%—must be disclosed. See BGH NJW 1994, 793, 4). In the case of *therapeutic* operations disclosure will be geared to the patient's individual circumstance such as his level of understanding (BGH NJW 1980, 633) and even the attending doctor's degree of experience (OLG Köln VersR 1982, 453). The urgency of the situation is also a factor that can be taken into account (BGH VersR 1972, 153); and even the defence of 'therapeutic privilege' (no revelation of risks since patient might not be able to 'handle' adverse news) has been treated with caution, as a decision of the BGH of 28 November 1957 clearly shows. (BGHSt 11, 111, 114 and compare similar statements in *Meyer Estate* v. *Rogers* (1991) 6 CCLT 2d 114.) Beyond stating the above general, guiding principles, one must advise the reader to consult particular instances where the courts have applied them to different factual situations. The following are recent illustrations. A patient must, as a general rule, be warned of the possibility of stiffening of the shoulders as a result of an injection containing cortisone, even if this is a very slight risk; but he need not be informed of the remote danger of fatal sepsis: BGH NJW 1989, 1533. A doctor who wishes to undertake a vaginal delivery, even though the danger to mother and child dictates a caesarian operation, has a duty to warn the expecting mother of the accompanying risks. If the doctor maintains that the expecting mother refused a caesarian section, he has the burden of proving that he furnished her with the required warning: BGH NJW 1992, 741. If a doctor fails to provide the patient with the required information concerning the nature and the difficulty of an operation, he is not free from liability merely because the harm which actually occurs is not one against which the doctor was obliged to warn: BGH NJW 1991, 2346. Before performing cosmetic surgery he must inform the patient especially carefully and thoroughly of the odds of the operation failing to produce the desired results (in this case removing wrinkles under the chin): BGH NJW 1991, 2349. Properly informing a patient about an operation entails explaining to him the urgency of such an operation. The doctor has the burden of proving that he provided a thorough and accurate explanation: BGH NJW 1990, 2928. (For further discussion of these topics see:

Deutsch, *NJW* 1980, 1305; idem, *NJW* 1984, 1802; Laufs and Kern, *JZ* 1984, 631. More detailed discussions can also be found in the standard treatises written by Professor Deutsch, *Arztrecht und Arzneimittelrecht* 2nd edn. 1991 and Professor Giesen, *Arzthaftungsrecht* 3rd edn. 1990.)

One further point related with informed consent which has troubled the courts of many systems is linked to the problem of causation that arises in such cases. For, once it has been decided that inadequate information has been given to the patient, the next point that arises is whether had there been proper disclosure this particular patient would have gone ahead with the proposed medical treatment. Once again, the doubt has centred as to how this question should be answered: objectively, by discovering the reaction of the hypothetical, reasonable man? Or by finding how this particular patient would have reacted. It would be impossible to deny that the question does not lend itself to an easy answer. Equally, however, it is noteworthy that despite the dangers of self-serving evidence (which arise if the test is to be subjective) many courts have adopted it as the right criterion. Thus see: New Zealand: *Smith* v. *Auckland Hospital Board* [1964] NZLR 191 CA; Australia: *Ellis* v. *Wallsend District Hospital* (1989) 17 NSWLR 553, 560; *Rogers* v. *Whittacker* (1991) 23 NSWLR 601; Germany: BGHZ 90, 103, 111, 112; BGHZ 90, 96, 101, 102. Indeed, German courts have tried to counter the argument that patients may, with hindsight, attempt to manipulate the evidence so they insist that it is for the patient to substantiate his allegation that he would not have consented to the operation even if properly informed 'in those [cases] where the reasons adduced [by the patient] for refusing treatment are not altogether comprehensible in the light of the specific facts of the case.' In other words, in such cases it is for the patient to come up with plausible reasons for refusing the treatment had he known the risks in advance.

6. German law recognizes in § 227 BGB the privilege of self-defence against persons (*Notwehr*) and against things (*Notstand*). In § 228 BGB it also recognizes (in certain circumstances) the right of a person to interfere with objects which belong to another person and from which the danger emanates (§ 904 BGB) in order to prevent harm to his own interests or those of others. Where this is the case the 'unlawfulness' of the act disappears and the actor cannot be sued under § 823 I BGB. We are here talking of situations which have exact counterparts in the Common law. See, for example, Fleming, 78–80, 90–2; and Prosser and Keaton, 124 ff.

Case 39, however, attempts to put the privilege of self-defence to a novel use and the dislike of the legal order for self-help is clearly shown in the judgment of the German court. Compare in this respect § 140 of the *Restatement Second, Torts*, which also states that there will be no privilege to use force to prevent the commission of a misdemeanour.

Problems not dissimilar to those faced by the court in the above case have arisen in the US in the context of occupations of nuclear plants by nuclear protestors, but the defence of 'competing harms' raised by the intruders has met with the same fate. An interesting case with such facts is *Commonwealth v. Bregman* 13 Mass. App. Ct. 373, 433 NE 2d 457 (1982).

13. DUTIES OF CARE

Case 40

BUNDESGERICHTSHOF (SIXTH CIVIL SENATE) 19 FEBRUARY 1991*
NJW 1991, 2340

1. Costs incurred by close relatives in visiting the victim in hospital (costs of travel and necessary overnight accommodation, increased maintenance costs, loss of earnings) can be included in the cost of the victim's treatment and claimed under § 823 I BGB only if such visits are medically necessary and the expense unavoidable. Loss of earnings and housework is compensable only if the work could not be done before or after the visit. Further economic losses are not compensable (restriction of previous holdings of this Senate, most recently BGHZ 106, 28 = NJW 1989, 766; NJW 1990, 1037 = VersR 1989, 1308 with further references).

2. Quantum of damages for pain and suffering—what the trial judge must find.

Facts

The plaintiff sues the defendant for breach of his duty of safety. On 17 May 1986, when the plaintiff was barely six years old, he was playing on an undeveloped building-plot of land belonging to the defendant and suffered serious injuries in an accident when a concrete ring on the land, about 1.2 metres broad and weighing 750 kg., fell on him. The land was readily accessible at the time. The plaintiff suffered a double fracture of the pelvis and damage to his urinary tract. The injury to his sphincter has caused incontinence, and there may be further sequelae. The plaintiff claimed DM 50,000 as damages for pain and suffering in addition to a further appropriate sum of at least DM 50,000. In addition, he claims DM 12,209.10 in respect of costs incurred by his parents in visiting him in hospital (travel DM 6,463.10, increased maintenance expenses DM 5,246 and overnight accommodation DM 500) as well as DM 40,800 lost earnings by the father and DM 9,768 as the value of the housework foregone by the mother while making the visits. For private medical treatment as an outpatient, not made good by the Krankenkasse, he claims DM 1,759.56, and a lump sum of DM 500 for inci-

---

* English version by Tony Weir.

dental expenses. He also claims a declaration that the defendant is liable for any further harm, material or immaterial.

The Landgericht rejected the claim. The plaintiff's appeal succeeded in part: the Oberlandesgericht granted the declaration, and awarded the plaintiff DM 25,000 as damages for pain and suffering plus a lump sum DM 200 for incidental costs. His further appeal was also successful in part. The case was remanded for reconsideration of the unliquidated claim for damages for pain and suffering as well as the special damages of DM 38,968.66.

Reasons

I. 1. The court below accepted that the defendant was in breach of his duty of safety to the plaintiff (§ 823 I BGB):

The defendant's land was dangerous to children, since wedges holding the concrete ring could easily be removed and the ring set in motion. It was the dangerous insecurity of the concrete ring which injured the plaintiff. The land was readily accessible, either by a garden gate from the property leased by the plaintiff's parents, or by a lane. Furthermore, the fence dividing it from the highway was broken at this point, and cars were actually being parked on the land.

2. On the view that the defendant's fault was not very grave, the court below held that DM 25,000 was an appropriate sum for damages for pain and suffering, notwithstanding that the claim had been certified at first instance as worth DM 100,000.

3. There was no sufficient legal basis for the mother's claim for the value of the housework she had been prevented from doing, and the court below held that the plaintiff must further specify and prove the other unadmitted items of loss.

II. Some of the appellant's criticisms of the judgment of the court below are sound.

1. The grounds on which court below concluded that the defendant was liable under § 823 I BGB were quite correct. If the owner of land knows or ought to know that, notwithstanding his prohibitions, children use his land as a playground and may play with dangerous objects there and get injured by them, he must take effective steps and lasting precautions to save them from the consequences of their inexperience and fecklessness [references]. The facts found by the court below justify the conclusion that the defendant, who admitted to knowing that children often played on the land and climbed over the things on it, was in breach of this duty of safety. He should also have realised that the concrete ring which injured the plaintiff was so placed and so insecurely fixed that despite its great weight children could set it in motion, as occurred, and be exposed to great danger, and it should

have been obvious that notwithstanding the danger, children would play with so inviting an object.

2. As to the material loss claimed, the court below was correct to reject the claim in respect of the father's loss of earnings and the value of the housework the mother was unable to do. However, the total rejection of the claims for travel costs, increased maintenance, and overnight accommodation was not justified.

(a) The law of tort is based on the principle that a claim may be brought only by the person whose interests are protected by the rule infringed, and then only to the extent that he personally suffers harm. Only in the exceptional cases provided by §§ 844, 845 BGB may there be compensation for economic losses resulting 'indirectly' from the invasion of the interests of others. The Bundesgerichtshof has, however, regularly made an exception for the cost of visits by close relatives to the sickbed of the injured party and, because of their intimate connection with the cost of the victim's recovery, treated them as part of the injury to *his* health (most recently BGHZ 106, 28 [30] = NJW 1989, 706; NJW 1990, 1037 = VersR 1989, 1308).

(b) We adhere to the principle of these decisions, especially as it has long become established in practice. It remains the case, however, apart from the exceptional cases where a third party has a statutory right to sue (§§ 844, 845 BGB), that the victim's claim for damages in tort basically covers only compensation for harm suffered by him personally, so claims for expenditure by a visitor depend essentially on who the visitor is. The mere fact that a third party is affected economically is not enough. Clearly no claim lies in respect of visits by persons not in the near family who attend out of a sense of social or similar duty. The rule of tort is not intended to compensate for such expenditures. But even as regards the expenses of those within the class of 'near family' there are limitations. It must always be borne in mind that such expenses, which do not cost the injured victim himself anything, are only exceptionally and on special factual grounds chargeable to the person causing the injury, for otherwise the door would be opened, *contra legem*, for the compensation of mere economic harm suffered by persons only 'indirectly' affected by the tort.

Previous decisions have therefore always restricted compensation to claims by the 'nearest family' in respect of visits to a patient actually hospitalised, for only such visits can properly be regarded as both necessary for the recovery of the victim and also intimately connected with the cost of his cure, and so distinguished from expenses incurred either in law or in fact by those 'indirectly' affected as a result of the injury to the victim, which are not compensable under the law of tort. Indeed, the only visiting costs incurred by close relatives which can be compensated consistently with the

Code are those which are medically necessary for the recovery of the patient in his existing condition, and only those which are unavoidably incurred. Where there is no such medical necessity, hospital visits even by close relatives cannot be compensated, however desirable as regards the psychic or physical condition of the patient, and the same is true of expenses which might have been avoided. Here the general rule laid down in §§ 249 ff. BGB is not the sole consideration; the limits must be more tightly drawn because the law of tort is in principle restricted to the 'direct' victim. Previous decisions of this Senate which go any further than this will no longer be followed.

(c) The detailed result of this in relation to the holdings below which are criticised by the appellant is as follows:

(aa) *Travel costs* form an expense necessarily involved in hospital visits, provided the cheapest means of transport is used and other economies observed. The court below regarded such expenses as harm to the plaintiff only to the extent that they had been met by the Krankenkasse, but as the appellant argues, this is inconsistent with § 287 Code of Civil Procedure, as the court did not ask why the Krankenkasse limited its payments or whether its limits were in line with the criteria of tort law as explained. The vouchers tendered by the plaintiff in support of this claim seem an adequate basis for evaluation under § 287 Code of Civil Procedure, at any rate so far as the number of visits is concerned.

(bb) Exceptionally a claim may be made for *overnight accommodation* in connection with visits, provided it is unavoidable. The documentation of such expenses tendered by the plaintiff is sufficient to permit evaluation under § 287 Code of Civil Procedure.

(cc) The *cost of meals* taken by close relatives while visiting hospital out of town depends essentially on the individual needs of the visitor. These determine whether in fact the cost of meals was 'greater' than those taken at home. In order to respect the non-compensability of the loss incurred by 'indirect' victims, compensation here must be limited to the unavoidable *increase* in the cost of meals. Only such increase is intimately enough connected with expenditures for the cure of the primary victim to be brought within § 823 I BGB. From this point of view the court below must evaluate the harm under § 287 Code of Civil procedure, on further evidence supplied by the parties, if necessary.

(dd) As to the claim for DM 40,000 in respect of the father's *loss of earnings*, the following applies: This Senate has repeatedly held that loss of earnings suffered by the visitor is capable of being regarded as part of the cost of cure of the injured party for which the person causing the injury must pay, subject to the general duty to mitigate damage, which requires, *inter alia*, that a self-employed person change his hours of work within reasonable limits (see NJW 1985, 2757 = VersR 1985, 784 [785]). Recovery for such losses is however limited to those so closely related to the cost of curing the victim that they can be seen as being truly costs of the visit; examples might be the loss by an employee of remuneration or perquisites if he can take time off work only on unpaid leave and cannot make it up later, or loss by a self-employed person directly attributable to the hospital visit and incapable of being made good in any other way. Beyond this, loss of income resulting from the fact that visiting hospital made the work more difficult cannot be treated as part of the victim's costs of cure to be made good under the law of delict, for this would, contrary to the Code, amount to liability for harm suffered by persons only indirectly affected.

In the present case, according to the plaintiff, the father, in employment as a manager, lost income because the hospital visits hindered him in developing a parallel practice as an independent accountant and tax adviser. Such a loss cannot be treated as part of the loss to the plaintiff which has to be made good. Leaving aside the question whether it was medically necessary for the patient to have the father by his side at the very time the latter needed to devote to his practice, losses such as these which are attributable to the fact that the visits to hospital left less time for the rapid development or extension of his business cannot be regarded as costs of the visit in the sense mentioned. The same would be true of delay in advancement or preferment in office. Such economic losses are harm suffered by third parties which is not compensable by the law of delict.

(*ee*) Nor can *interruption of housework* by the mother be taken into account. The appellant refers to the decision of the Senate of 10 October 1989 (VersR 1989, 1247), but in that case the expenditure claimed was in respect of nursing the victim, an increase in his need which was compensable under § 843 BGB. Here the plaintiff claims compensation for the time his mother could not spend on housekeeping because she was visiting him in hospital. In accordance with the principles just laid down for treating lost time at work as one of the costs of the visit, compensation in tort cannot be given when work lost through the visit can be made up before or afterwards. This was obviously possible in this case, since no substitute home help was employed.

(*ff*) In rejecting the plaintiff's claim for damages in respect of the *cost of private medical treatment* the court below insisted on too stringent a proof of the expenditures and thus misapplied § 287 Code of Civil Procedure. Whether a person who has statutory health insurance may claim the cost of private medical treatment depends on the circumstances of the individual case (VersR 1970, 129; VersR 1989, 54), and the decisive point is whether a reasonable man in the position of the victim would regard such private medical treatment as necessary. The nature of the injury and the victim's standard of living are especially relevant, but the court below did not consider these points, nor did it investigate the plaintiff's assertion that doctors had advised him to go to a 'special clinic' for private medical treatment.

(*gg*) The fact that the court below allowed the plaintiff a lump sum in respect of incidental expenses of only DM 200 discloses no errors of law in the plaintiff's disfavour, and his appeal made no further mention of it.

3. The appellant is correct in arguing that as regards the quantum of damages for pain and suffering the court below misapplied § 287 Code of Civil Procedure.

(*a*) It is true that the judge of fact has a good deal of discretion in determining damages for pain and suffering, and his award cannot normally be criticised simply as being too high or, as here, too low. But this judicial discretion has its limits: the judge must show that in trying to reach a figure appropriate to injuries of that kind and duration he took all the relevant circumstances into account, and he must respect rules of law, canons of logic and the teachings of experience. The judge must also state the factual basis of his evaluation so that it may be seen that he has kept within these limits (invariable holdings, most recently NJW 1989, 773 = VersR 1988, 943).

(*b*) The appellant is right to complain of the way the court below dealt with his claim for damages for pain and suffering. This is especially true as regards the declaration of the Landgericht on 21 August 1989 when it gave full reasons for adopting the figure of DM 100,000 as the value of his claim under this head. On the plaintiff's appeal, the court below agreed that this sum was appropriate, thereby adopting the reasons given, which thus ceased to be the mere assertions of the plaintiff, as the court below later held in the judgment under appeal. While it was not finally bound to this sum, the court should certainly have indicated in the judgment under appeal why it had come to so very different a conclusion on unchanged evidence. If in the absence of different evidence a later evaluation of the damages differs widely from an earlier one, the law of procedure as well as candour to the parties requires the court to indicate at least the critical points of difference. Only so can a court on appeal ascertain whether the court below regarded its earlier judgment as lying outside the discretion proper to the judge of fact or whether both sums lay within it (see NJW 1989, 773 = VersR 1988, 943). Since such considerations are lacking in the judgment of the court below, it must therefore be vacated as inconsistent with § 287 Code of Civil Procedure, without prejudice to the power of the court on remand, if it gives sufficient reasons, again rejecting the claim for unliquidated damages for pain and suffering.

Case 41

BUNDESGERICHTSHOF (SIXTH CIVIL DIVISION) 13 FEBRUARY 1990*
NJW 1990, 726

Facts

The plaintiff is a firm trading under the name of Margot H, its owner. Mrs H and her husband were joint owners of a detached house which was built by the defendant in 1977/78. From 1980 onwards, the plaintiff firm was running a kitchen furniture studio from the basement rooms of the house which it rented from the owners. In the time that followed there were repeated leakages of water into these rooms. On July 26, 1982 water again leaked into the basement of the house and damaged the show furniture and associated display items. The plaintiff calculated the loss which it had incurred at DM 53,385. It claimed compensation from the defendants in this amount, arguing that the defendant had defectively constructed the basement floor and basement walls which had caused the leakages. Both the Landgericht and the Oberlandesgericht rejected the claim. The plaintiff appealed to the BGH which quashed the judgment of the Court of Appeal and referred the case back to the lower court.

For the following

Reasons

I. The OLG rejected both the contractual and the tortious claims brought by the plaintiff.

It held that the plaintiff was not a party to the oral building contract concluded with the husband alone. As a commercial tenant, she was also not covered by the protective scope of this contract; for the defendant could not have foreseen that the basement rooms of a detached house which were intended to be used for leisure purposes (e.g. fitness training, hobbies or parties) would be used for the display of furniture. The OLG argued that the plaintiff had no claim in tort because, after the earlier numerous leakages of water, she had acted at her own risk when she once again displayed furniture in the basement and should have foreseen further danger of water damage. Her careless conduct amounted to such a degree of contributory negligence that the defendant was wholly exonerated from responsibility.

II. The appeal decision cannot be upheld on all counts.

* English version by Ms J. Shaw.

1. The OLG is correct to reject the contractual claims for damages brought by the plaintiff.

(*a*) It is not contested that when the husband concluded the building contract with the defendant, he did not say expressly that he was acting as the plaintiff's representative. As the OLG found, it could not be implied from the circumstances (§ 164 I 2 BGB) that the contract was also intended to be concluded in the name of the plaintiff. The plaintiff's appeal did not contest this evaluation of the facts as flawed in law; rather it sought merely to contrast its own evaluation which is basically irrelevant from the perspective of this court's task as an appellate body. Contrary to the view put forward by the appellants, it was not sufficient for there to be a contract concluded in the name of the plaintiff that she was the joint owner of the land on which the house was built [references omitted], especially since it is not contested that at the time of the conclusion of the building contract the defendant did not know this fact.

(*b*) There are, further, no grounds in law for challenging the view of the OLG that there were no protective effects to be derived from the building contract (concluded between the husband of the plaintiff and the defendant) in favour of the plaintiff, giving her autonomous contractual claims against the defendant in respect of the damage caused to the furniture and display items brought into the basement rooms.

(*aa*) It may be left open for the purposes of this decision whether in the case of a building contract concluded in respect of the construction of a dwelling house, the relatives of the [builder's] client as well as any joint owners of the land to be built upon will always fall within the protective scope of the contract [references omitted]. For such protection can only be of significance in respect of the infliction of loss which results from the fact that the persons in question come into contact with the work of the building contractor precisely in their capacity as family members or joint owners. This was not the case here. The plaintiff suffered the damage to the furniture and display items in the basement for which she seeks compensation neither in her capacity as a joint owner of the house, nor in her position as the wife of the client, but as the commercial tenant of the basement.

(*bb*) In its judgment of 28 October 1986 (NJW 1987, 1013) [other references omitted] this Division left open the question of whether the tenant is covered by the protective scope of a contract concluded between the client and an architect for the construction of a building [references omitted]. This question should be answered in the negative in respect of a contract with a building contractor such as the one in question here. First, there is no need for such a person to be covered, because in these circumstances the tenant will normally enjoy sufficient protection through his contractual claims against the landlord [references omitted]. Second, any other conclusion would mean that the contractual obligations of the building contractor would be unreasonably extended to cover risks which were not foreseeable for the contractor, without there being the possibility of the obligations being subject to clear delimitation on the basis of standards capable of being measured objectively [references omitted].

(*cc*) Since in the instant case the contractual claims would fail because there was insufficient proximity between the legal interests of the plaintiff which were impaired by the leakage of water and the contractual obligations of the defendant, it is no longer decisive in this context for the court to determine whether a commercial usage of the basement rooms by the plaintiff constituted a breach of the building regulations.

2. The conclusion of the OLG that the plaintiff has no claim in tort does not withstand legal scrutiny. The BGH must assume that the defendant was negligent in constructing the basement floor and the basement walls defectively, since the OLG left this matter open, and it must also assume that this breach of duty was the cause of the leakage of water on 26 July 1982 which resulted in a flood of water several centimetres deep in the basement.

(*a*) The OLG correctly assumes, on the basis of the judgment of this Chamber of 28 October 1986 (NJW 1987, 1013) [other references omitted], that the defendant is in principle subject to a tortious duty of care in respect of the items of property brought into the basement by the plaintiff.

(*aa*) In that case this Chamber held that an architect of a house was in principle liable in tort to the tenant in circumstances where, as a result of the defective performance of his duties in respect of the house, he did not offer the type of protection which is to be expected against bad weather. As a result of damp caused by rain, damage was caused to the tenant's property. The position in law of the building contractor must be just the same. His duty of care is likewise not restricted to those risks arising directly from the house and endangering those who use the house and their property. For the building should, in normal circumstances at least, provide protection against threatening external dangers and the users of the house bring their property into the building precisely in reliance upon such protection. There may be an exception in cases of special circumstances involving, for example, the use of the cheapest method of construction (see the judgment of 28 October 1986). However, there were no factual circumstances in the present case requiring the application of this exception. On the contrary, in the application made by the plaintiff to this court, the building was described as 'one of the most generously proportioned and most luxurious properties' in the area.

(*bb*) In these circumstances, in matters of liability one must basically apply the same principles related to the performance of the duties owed by both the architect and the building contractor under their respective contracts for work and services as those which apply to the manufacture and dissemination of products which are intended to eliminate certain dangers but which are unsuitable for this purpose [references omitted]. For just as in the case of such products, where the purchaser takes no other precautionary measures in respect of his interests in reliance upon the protective effects of the product he has bought, so the owner or tenant of a building will regard his property as adequately protected from the effects of bad weather if they have been brought indoors, and he would not think of taking additional measures. Of course, it is the case that it is only the law of contract which protects the interest of use or financial interest of the plaintiff ('*Nutzungs- oder Äquivalenzinteresse*'); a mere interference in *this* interest will not give rise to a claim in tort [references omitted]. If, however, the construction of a house is also intended to eliminate dangers threatening those interests of the plaintiff which are given absolute protection, then any impairment of these interests attributable to the defective performance of a duty will amount to an interference in the integrity of the plaintiff's property ('*restitutio in integrum*'), and will be actionable under § 823 I BGB.

(*cc*) There is no need in this case for a final decision to be made on whether the building contractor can only be exonerated from his liability in tort where he makes good the defects in the work by providing a performance which is intended to eliminate the danger in question, even where the client no longer has an effective contractual claim to the removal of the defect because the time limit for bringing such an action has expired, or whether the (additional) responsibility of the contractor also lapses where he has given unambiguous information to persons relying upon the security provided by the performance of his duties that the work in question would provide only inadequate protection [references omitted]. For it is not in dispute in this case that the defendant had not clearly informed either the plaintiff or her husband before the leakage of water on 26 July 1982 that the floor and walls were unsuitable for the purposes of eliminating the dangers resulting from water entry.

(*dd*) The existence of the defendant's duty of care in tort is likewise not undermined by his claim that the plaintiff had used the basement rooms for displays in contravention of the building regulations. This fact does not place the plaintiff, who was using the basement to the house on the basis of a valid tenancy agreement, outside the sphere of persons whom the defendant should have protected against water damage occurring in the vicinity of the basement by building in a workmanlike fashion [reference omitted].

(*b*) The plaintiff's application is right to question the view of the OLG that she had no claims for compensation in tort against the defendant because she had acted at her own risk by bringing kitchen furniture into the basement rooms and that notwithstanding the fault of the defendant, she was overwhelmingly contributorily negligent.

(*aa*) The fact that the OLG denied the plaintiff's claims for compensation stating that she had acted at her own risk and did not balance her fault against the (assumed) negligence of the defendant, indicates that the OLG has followed the later case law of the Reichsgericht [references omitted] which saw 'acting at one's own risk' as a form of consent to the interference with the plaintiff's interests which acts as a justification. This interpretation has already been held by this Division in its judgment of 14 March 1961 (BGHZ 34, 355 at 360) [other references omitted] as appropriate for use only in exceptional cases such as dangerous sports, as a realistic and legally correct evaluation of conscious risk-taking. If there is no such exceptional situation, as in this case, then according to the established case law of the Chamber there is merely a question to be assessed under § 254 I BGB, as to what extent the victim through his conduct has contributed to the dangerous situation in which the defendant's own conduct led to the occurrence of damage [references omitted]. In contrast to the view put forward by the OLG, this makes it necessary for the court to weigh up against each other the causally relevant contributions made by each party in order to assess the degree to which the defendant is liable.

(*bb*) The arguments so far advanced here do not provide a justification, on the basis of the passing comments made by the OLG as regards the matter of the plaintiff's contributory negligence, for an evaluation of the respective contributions to conclude in a complete exoneration of the defendant from liability. Of course it is only the role of this court, when reviewing the decision of the judge of fact, merely to assess whether he has fully and correctly taken into account all relevant circumstances within the framework of § 254 I BGB, and has not breached any rules of logic or empirically derived principles [references omitted]. The OLG has not, however, remained within these limits as so defined.

3. (*a*) The OLG assumes that after the leakages of water on 18 May 1981, as well as on 7 and 10 August 1981, which preceded the occurrence of damage on 26 July 1982, in each case the defendant carried out repair work. However, even taking this as a starting point, there is insufficient basis for the conclusion that in July 1982 the plaintiff no longer relied upon the basement area being waterproofed. For the plaintiff, whom the OLG was prepared to acknowledge in its judgment of 22 July 1988 in the context of proceedings brought in respect of the water leakages of 7 and 10 August

1981 was still relying on the basement being waterproof after the leakage of 18 May 1981, argued in this case that the defendant had stated that the cause of the water leakages in August 1981 was a wall duct for pipes which was not waterproof. Since the OLG both accepted that the fact that the wall being not waterproof was the cause of that loss and also assumed that the defendant had undertaken damp-proofing work on the wall duct in order to remove the defect, there exist no sufficient grounds in fact for the view that in July after the repair work the plaintiff should have expected the basement area no longer to be watertight. The OLG was wrong to state that this point could be derived from the fact that previous renovation works undertaken by the defendant had proved to be inadequate. In the first place the repair works, as the OLG itself accepted, were carried out on other weaknesses in the damp-proofing; second, even multiple unsuccessful attempts to carry out repairs by a contractor do not as such destroy the reliance of the client that the work previously undertaken to eliminate the defect will have finally succeeded.

(b) It was in truth appropriate for the plaintiff to rely as such upon the ultimate elimination of the danger from water, since the defendant, as the plaintiff stated in her claim and as she sought to prove in her application for a hearing of witnesses, 'announced to the plaintiff that the waterproofing was complete' after finishing the improvement work following the water entry of August 1981, and 'guaranteed to the plaintiff that the basement was now waterproof'. It is a breach of the principle of good faith (§ 242 BGB) for the defendant to argue that the plaintiff could not rely upon such statements. The statements by the plaintiff were, despite the views of the OLG, sufficiently substantiated, all the more since it was principally the task of the defendant to demonstrate the circumstances in which the plaintiff could be said to be contributorily negligent. In any case, the OLG should not have reached the conclusion, as the plaintiff's appeal correctly asserts, that the plaintiff should have anticipated future dangers arising from water, before it had evaluated the witness testimony offered by the plaintiff.

Case 42

BUNDESGERICHTSHOF (SEVENTH CIVIL DIVISION) 11 OCTOBER 1990*
NJW 1991, 562

Facts

In 1979/80, the plaintiff and his wife had a new building built on a piece of land belonging to them. The first defendant was responsible for carrying out the structural work on the building. The supervision of the building work on site was entrusted to the second defendant, an architect. Since no proper

* English version by Ms J. Shaw.

damp insulation was fitted, the basement of the building became very damp. The plaintiff had rented this and other parts of the building to a company (F Ltd), which he ran. F Ltd had stored machines in the damp rooms, and these rusted as a result of the damp. The plaintiff claimed compensation from the defendant for the loss which he suffered as a result of the defective building work. He calculated his loss to be DM 139,697.84. In so far as the plaintiff sought to claim in respect of damage which had accrued to F Ltd, his claim rested upon a deed of assignment dated January 18, 1982 the text of which covered only the claims against the first defendant.

The Landgericht held the defendants liable for the defects and held them to be jointly and severally liable in the amount of DM 19,298.93. The plaintiff appealed claiming a further DM 91,793.22 in damages. The Oberlandesgericht accepted the appeal in part, holding the defendants liable for a further DM 31,381.03. The second defendant appealed to the Bundesgerichtshof, and the appeal was accepted to the extent that he had been held liable for damages in the amount of DM 31,022.50 in respect of the damage to the machines. His appeal against the finding of liability failed.

Reasons

I. The OLG is of the view that the defendant is liable to the plaintiff, and that he must pay 50 per cent of the compensation in respect of the damage caused to the machines.

1. The external insulation of the walls of the basement in contact with the ground was said to be defective. As the architect responsible for on-site supervision of the work, the defendant breached his duty to supervise adequately the performance of the damp-proofing work which experience had taught was particularly delicate and significant in terms of the loss which would be caused by defective work. He was, therefore, jointly responsible for the defective damp-proofing. The defendant's appeal concedes this point.

2. The OLG further held on the basis of expert reports and witness statements that the defects in the damp-proofing, taken in conjunction with certain other defects, had caused the damp in the basement and that it was to this that the rust on the machines was attributable. [Procedural point omitted].

II. The OLG also stated that the plaintiff could claim compensation from the defendant in respect of the damage caused to his property, either through the principles of *Drittschadensliquidation*, or on the basis of the claims duly assigned to him by F Ltd on the basis of a contract with protective effects for third parties or on tortious grounds. The plaintiff has, it is said, become the owner of the claim against the defendant as a consequence of the assignment; this was the appropriate interpretation of the deed of assignment. The final point was that assignment did not contravene the prohibition on contracting with oneself.

1. The Court leaves open the question of whether the damage to the machines may be claimed from the defendant according to the principles of *Drittschadensliquidation*. It may also remain open whether F Ltd may derive claims as a third party on the basis of the protective effects of the construction contract concluded between the parties.

2. It is clear in any case that the plaintiff has a tortious claim. The defendant has breached the duty of care which he owed to F Ltd in that he did not ensure, when performing the role of supervising the building work which was entrusted to him, that the first defendant installed the damp insulation in the basement free from defects.

(*a*) According to the case law of the BGH, an architect may be liable in tort on the basis of a breach of his supervisory obligation for the loss thereby caused. Thus, for example, the architect responsible for the building work was held liable in tort for the loss caused by the collapse of a roof or ceiling [references omitted]; the same applies to the damage caused to a person using a staircase which proved to be unsafe [references omitted]. The tortious responsibility of the architect was also accepted for loss caused by damp to the property of third parties resulting from inadequate damp-proofing or a defective roof [references omitted]. This tortious responsibility of the architect is derived from the fact that during the construction process he not only owes duties on the basis of the contract with the builder, but he also owes duties of care in tort to third parties who are expected to come into contact with the building. For, in the normal course of events, such persons may rely on the architect carrying out in the proper way those tasks which will secure their protection against loss in the future [reference omitted]. That, also, applies to the tenant of a building. The fact that such a person may be, in certain circumstances, less worthy of protection than other third parties who only occasionally come into contact with the building, is no obstacle to a finding that the architect is liable. Of course, in normal circumstances the tenant will have a claim for compensation against the landlord where loss is inflicted by events such as those at issue. That factor makes no difference, however, to the architect's duty of care. Even for the builder himself, claims in tort are not in principle excluded by the fact that there are parallel claims in contract [references omitted]. Nor, however, is the tenant prevented from pursuing claims in tort against the architect, even though he may have a contractual claim against the landlord. The contractual liability of the landlord is not intended to exclude tortious claims against other persons who inflict loss on the tenant.

The liability of the architect is not excluded by the fact that it is in the first instance the main building contractor who is responsible for the building works. The Division has rejected this argument also to the extent that the architect owes a duty of care to safeguard the building site [references omitted]. Just as the architect may be responsible for the safety of the building site within the framework of the tasks which he has undertaken to perform, so the supervisory obligations which are intended to protect the residents of the building and their property may generate a duty of care.

This line of case law is likewise not challenged in the literature [references to literature omitted]. While it is possible to find in the literature signs of a move towards restricting the duty of care [references to literature omitted], there is no need in this case to take a definitive position on this matter. It may be doubtful in individual cases how far the duty of care of the architect extends. The Sixth Division has already referred to this point [reference omitted]. In any event, there is such a duty where the supervisory obligations in respect of the building work are specifically intended to avoid the occurrence of particularly dangerous types of errors on the part of the building contractor which are likely to arise.

(b) In this case the defendant was obliged, with respect to the protection of the tenant, to ensure that the damp-proofing was properly carried out. As a type of building work which is particularly risky, the architect was under a duty to take special care [references omitted]. The fact that the damp-proofing was not carried out properly was particularly likely to cause unexpected damage which could be significant to the property of those using the building.

(c) The liability of the architect is likewise not excluded by the fact that the defendant stated in his pleadings that the use of the storage rooms in question for commercial purposes was a breach of the planning regulations. It is not necessary to decide whether and in what conditions the protective scope of the defendant's duty of care is limited by the fact that the storage of the machines was prohibited under the planning regulations and was therefore unlawful. For in these circumstances there is no justification for a restriction upon the defendant's liability because the use of the rooms for storage was provided for under planning regulations and other local bye-laws. On the facts as given, it cannot make a difference whether the damage occurred to machines used for commercial purposes, the storage of which was not permitted, or to machines stored for other purposes, which were permitted. The decisive factor is rather that the rooms in question were not fit for the purpose which they were intended—as storage space.

(d) The liability is further not excluded because F Ltd may have occupied the rooms in question before they had been inspected in accordance with either the contract or the relevant building regulations. It is possible for liability based on the breach of a duty of care to be restricted where the activity in question has occurred without the knowledge or intention of the person subject to the duty. Such is not the case here. It is not alleged that the defendant was not in agreement with the occupation of the rooms or that he warned against it.

(*e*) The OLG was also right to hold that the plaintiff did not have to inform the defendant of the intention to store items intended for use in his business in the basement. The defendant must have anticipated the usage of the basement for these purposes.

3. The claim for compensation brought by F Ltd is restricted to the claim for so-called *restitutio in integrum* [references omitted]. The plaintiff claimed no more with his request for the recovery of the costs of repair and the costs of providing an expert report. The deliberations of the OLG concerning the contributory negligence of F Ltd contain no errors of law and there is no appeal against them.

14. PRODUCT LIABILITY

Case 43

BUNDESGERICHTSHOF (SIXTH CIVIL DIVISION) 26 NOVEMBER 1968*
BGHZ 51, 91 = NJW 1969, 269 (with approving notes by Diederichsen = JZ 1969, 387 and E. Deutsch = VersR 1969, 155)

On 19 November 1963 the plaintiff, who ran a chicken-farm, had her chickens inoculated against fowl pest by the vet, Dr H. A few days later fowl pest broke out. More than 4000 chickens died and over 100 had to be slaughtered.

The plaintiff claimed compensation for the damage from the defendants, vaccine manufacturers, whose vaccine XY had been used by the vet. This he (the vet) acquired from the defendants in 500 cm bottles at the beginning of November 1963. The bottles came from batch ALD 210, which the defendant company had had inspected on 18 October 1963 at the public Paul-Ehrlich Institute in Frankfurt-am-Main; and the batch had been released by them for public use. The defendant had subsequently and in the course of its business poured the contents into receptacles normally used in commerce. As regards receptacles with lower than 500 cm capacity that is done by airtight closure under negative pressure; larger bottles were filled by the defendants 'openly' but in a closed room under ultraviolet radiation.

When a few days later, on 22 November 1963, Dr H inoculated the chickens at R's farm, fowl pest broke out there. At about this time fowl pest also

* English version by F. H. Lawson and B. S. Markesinis.

broke out in three other poultry farms in Württemberg which had had their chickens inoculated with the defendant company's vaccine from batch ALD 210. When the Stuttgart Veterinary Inspection Officer had several bottles of that batch inspected by the Federal Research Institute for virus diseases in animals, there were found in some bottles bacterial impurities and still active ND (Newcastle Disease) viruses, which had not been sufficiently immunized. Moreover, the Paul-Ehrlich Institute established that some of the bottles sent to it for inspection were not sterile and ND virus could be detected in them.

The defendant company disputed the claim that the outbreak of fowl pest was to be traced to the use of its vaccine; and in any case the defective sterility of the bottles was not the cause. For this it invoked the opinion supplied to it by Dr E of the Federal Research Institute for Virus Diseases. It put forward evidence exonerating it from liability for its workers in and the director of its virus section.

The Landgericht and the Oberlandesgericht declared the claim well founded. The defendant company's appeal was unsuccessful for the following

Reasons

The Court of Appeal started by finding that the vaccine supplied to Dr H was contaminated by bacteria, and that the outbreak of fowl pest was to be traced to it. Even the defendant company's expert, Professor Dr E, could not exclude the possibility that the contamination had arisen through carelessness on the part of persons employed by the defendant company in the bottling. For their fault the defendant company must be liable under § 278 BGB to the vet, the buyer of the vaccine. He, however, was entitled to be compensated for the damage done to the plaintiff. Since he had assigned his claim for compensation to the plaintiff, the action was well founded.

I. The principles governing the claims for damage suffered by a third person (*Drittschadensliquidation*) cannot be applied to the present case.

1. In principle, the only person who can claim compensation for damage under a contract is the one to whom the damage occurred in fact and who, in law, has to bear it. If the damage occurs to a third party, the doer of it is liable to him—apart from certain exceptions—only in delict. This distinction between the more favourable liability in contract and the more restricted liability for delict is imbedded in the existing system of liability law and is not a mere theoretical dogma. Only in special cases have the courts admitted exceptions, namely where special legal relations between the creditor under the contract and the beneficiary of the protected interest cause the interest to be 'shifted' on to the third party, so that as a matter of

law the damage is done to him, and not to the creditor. From it the doer can derive no benefit to the third party's detriment: he must make good to the creditor the damage to the third party. That applies—apart from the rare cases of responsibility for risks (BGHZ 40, 91, 100)—where the creditor has contracted for the third party's account (BGHZ 25, 250, 258), or where the thing that the debtor promised to take care of belonged not to the creditor but to the third party (BGHZ 15, 224).

(*a*) This is no such exceptional case. No 'union of interests' between the vet (who made the contract) and the third party (i.e. the plaintiff) is created by indirect agency. Dr H had not bought the vaccine to the order or for the benefit of the plaintiff. When he ordered and obtained it from the defendant company he did not yet know for which farmer he would use it. A vet invariably buys his medicines for himself like a contractor in respect of his materials and not for his patients or employers, even if he requires them to perform an order already given to him.

Moreover, this is not one of the cases where the thing placed in the debtor's care belonged not to the creditor but to a third party. Of course Dr H may have had imposed on him a 'duty of care' (*Obhutspflicht*) concerning the plaintiff's chickens. But it is a condition for claiming for damage suffered by a third party (*Drittschadensliquidation*) that the duty of care exists between creditor and debtor (BGHZ 40, 101). That was not the case here.

(*b*) The Court of Appeal also acts on these principles. It is also aware that in principle the manufacturer and supplier of a thing which has been sold again to a third party does not need, merely on the basis of the contract of sale, to make good damage occurring to a third party (BGHZ 40, 104, 105). All the same it believed that in the present case it could permit the claim in respect of the damage suffered by the third party. Here the faultless condition of the vaccine was of special interest to the plaintiff, on whose chickens it was to be used. The vet could not check the condition of the vaccine, but had to rely on careful manufacture by the defendant company. The latter must therefore have proceeded on the assumption that a duty of faultless delivery rested on it in favour not merely of the vet but also of whomever happened to keep chickens.

(*c*) These considerations do not justify treating this as a case for claiming damage as suffered by a third party (*Drittschadensliquidation*). Already in its judgment (BGHZ 40, 90) the Bundesgerichtshof has emphasized that a contract of sale cannot be interpreted in accordance with the requirement of good faith so as to afford a basis for compensation to a third party injured through defects in the thing bought. In that decision it departed from the judgment of the Reichsgericht in RGZ 170, 246. The Court of Appeal has also be due to causes that are inherent in the company's methods of production, and in particular in the method of bottling. In the present case there is no need to adopt a comprehensive attitude to the problems of products liability. Here, only the following considerations apply.

(*a*) The claim in the action could be granted without further discussion if the view of Diederichsen in his *Die Haftung des Warenherstellers* (1967) could be followed, that the manufacturer must be liable for every kind of defects in the product without reference to fault, as in the liability for risks or results ('strict liability'). He believes that this can be derived from the existing law by 'considerations of legal sociology or legal theory'. It is however doubtful whether his standpoint can be supported on grounds of legal policy and, at any rate, liability without fault is incompatible with the present law of (civil) liability. To extend the liability for risks regulated in particular enactments—mostly subject to different ceilings—to products liability is forbidden to judges. It is rather for the legislator to decide whether or how far a stronger objective liability should be imposed on the manufacturer.

(*b*) Nor is it legally possible—apart from special cases—to afford to the ultimate recipient a direct claim for damages on the assumption that contract of warranty was concluded directly, albeit tacitly, between him and the producer. The fact that the producer allows his goods to be distributed as his invention, that is to say with his label, in original packaging, with his trade name or trademark, and so on, cannot, *as a rule*, be considered as a declaration that he intends to make himself responsible to users for careful manufacture (cf. RGZ 81, 1). Normally, even the advertisement of branded goods which are advertised with particular emphasis on the ultimate user, contains no indication of any willingness to be liable for any defects in the goods (BGHZ 48, 118, 122–3). Moreover, that cannot be assumed even when the appreciably wider question is asked whether the manufacturer is willing to be directly liable to the ultimate user of his product.

(*c*) There is also no question of a claim for damages being accorded for a breach of alleged duties of protection consequent on a 'social contract'. No business relations exist between manufacturer and recipient nor are they intended to be started and, eventually, to be concluded. The relations which certainly exist on the sociological plane have not enough legal weight for claims for liability to be made from a special legal relation. That applies also to Weimer's attempt to derive a producer's liability from the general rule in § 242 BGB.

2. Special consideration is merited by the idea that recognition should be given to a special quasi-contractual relation between manufacturer and

user, resting on statute and developed from the notion of confidence. In fact the relations that have come into existence between the buyer of a dangerous product and its manufacturer, before the occurrence of the damage, would seem to be closer than those that bring the latter into relations with 'everyman' when—and not before—he is actually injured. As regards the claims for compensation of a buyer, on the other hand, it should be considered whether they also arise from contract law if he bought the goods not directly from the manufacturer but through a dealer.

(*a*) Starting from the special legal relationship between manufacturer and acquirer of goods, Lorenz at the *Karlsruher Forum* 1963 was the first to state the opinion that the manufacturer must be liable under § 122 BGB to answer for the confidence in his product, strengthened by advertising, that he has awakened in its users. Those ideas were mentioned by the Eighth Civil Senate of the Bundesgerichtshof at the close of its judgment of 13 July 1963 (BGHZ 40, 91, 108), but without committing itself to any position. In its judgment BGHZ 48, 118, it declined to accept advertisement as a possible source of liability. In the struggles for the all-important customer (*König Kunde*), advertisements have become more and more extensive and more and more significant from a business point of view. This, however, does not yet mean that they have acquired the meaning of a promise of legal liability. Moreover, no reasonable user understands it to be so: and Lorenz has not followed up his idea.

(*b*) Lorenz's basic idea provided the foundation for the attempts to derive the manufacturer's liability from a duty to satisfy the confidence placed by the user and made the basis for a claim corresponding to the legal principles developed for *culpa in contrahendo*.

It is however doubtful whether these considerations can hold water, so as to afford the user a claim for damages which, like the claim in delict, cannot be excluded automatically, but on the other hand would not be threatened by exoneration under § 831 BGB. The Senate has already, in its judgment of 21 March 1967 (VI ZR 164/65) reacted against the attempts to base the liability of a third person, not a party to a supposed contract, on the fact that his confidence was sought; and it emphasized that they would break, with dire consequences, through the boundary drawn between liability based on a contractual obligation and that arising from delict. Whether the doubt there expressed against an extension of liability for 'positive breach of contract' ('*positive Vertragsverletzung*') tells also against a subjection of the producer to a liability on the analogy of contractual liability need not be finally decided in this case. Nor need the question be gone into of how such a quasi-contractual claim should be afforded to a person injured by the product if he did not buy it but damage occurred through its use by himself or another person. In the case now to be decided there is no question of a number of legally successive sale contracts in which the seller, in fact, is often the mere 'distributor' of the manufacturer in which case a breaking of the veil suggests itself. Here between the plaintiff and the defendant company stood a vet, who had alone to decide which vaccine to use. The plaintiff had placed confidence in him and not in any advertisement. She was not, herself, in a position to buy the vaccine directly or in the market: the defendant company could deliver it only to the vet and only he might use it . . . That, of itself, excludes the idea that a quasi-contractual relation existed between the parties. The plaintiff was not a 'consumer' of the vaccine, nor even a 'user' of it, but, from a legal point of view, 'only' a sufferer of damage. As such she is limited to her claim in delict.

III. According to the Court of Appeal's finding of fact the conditions of liability under § 823 BGB are fulfilled. The vaccine supplied by the defendant company was defective and the cause of the disease to the chickens. Even if, as explained above, the rules of contract law are not applicable, nevertheless the starting-point must be that the defendant company has committed a fault. If anyone when using an industrial product for its declared purpose suffers injury in one of the legal interests protected by § 823 I BGB, through the defective manufacture of the product, it is for the manufacturer to explain the antecedents that caused the defect and thereby to show that he was not to blame for it.

1. It is not in question that even in 'product liability' the injured party must prove that the damage was caused by a defect in the product. The plaintiff had therefore to show that the fowl pest broke out among her chickens because the vaccine originated with the defendant company and contained active viruses when delivered.

That proof was considered by the Court of Appeal to have been furnished. [An explanation followed.]

2. The Court of Appeal, having to ascertain why the vaccine contained live viruses, started from the fact that both the Paul-Ehrlich Institute and the Federal Research Institute found bacteria in the bottles examined by them. It based its conclusions in essence on Professor Dr E's opinion. He declared it highly probable that the bacteria had found their way into the bottles at the manual pouring of the vaccine from the large containers into the bottles. It has been observed on various occasions that viruses which—as here— have been killed by the addition of formaldehyde can, under certain conditions, become reactivated. It was therefore possible that the bacteria here had reactivated the virus. On the basis of these explanations of the expert, the Court of Appeal believed it could find that the contamination of the bottles by bacteria was the cause of reactivation. It pointed out also that no

damage arose from the part of the batch that was not contaminated by bacteria, whereas that was the case with the bottles used by Dr H and in the district of Heilbronn, and in which the bacteria were found. Even Dr E held it possible that the contamination of the vaccine was caused by 'human error' on the part of one of the persons employed by the defendant company in bottling the vaccine.

3. The appellant attacked this conclusion of the Court of Appeal, but without success.

It is indeed correct that the Court of Appeal considered no fault of the defendant company itself as proved. It accepted that it was probably only an employee that was to blame for the damage. A liability of the defendant company, cannot, as we have seen, be established by applying the law of contract, as set out in § 278 BGB. That does not, however, necessitate sending the dispute back to the judge of fact. For it would still be for the defendant company to exonerate itself even if the plaintiff can rely on § 823 BGB.

(aa) This results from the fact that the plaintiff's claim for compensation is also based on § 823 II BGB. For the defendant company, by delivering the dangerous bottles of vaccine infringed a protective enactment. This vaccine, a medicine in the sense of the Medicines Act of 16 May 1961 (§ 3 III AMG), was capable of producing in the chickens injurious, even fatal, effects. § 6 AMG prohibits the putting of such vaccines into circulation. That provision—like § 3 LebMG (cf. RGZ 170, 155, 156 on § 4 LebMG) which applies to foods dangerous to health—constitutes an enactment for the protection of endangered human beings or animals. If, however, an infringement of a protective enactment is proved, it is presumed to be the result of fault. The infringer therefore must produce facts sufficient to disprove his fault (Senate judgment of 12 March 1968—VI ZR 178/66). The owner of the business did not produce that proof so long as a possible cause, falling within the scope of his responsibility and which might point to fault remained unelucidated (Senate judgments of 3 January 1961—VI ZR 67/60 and 4 April 1967—VI ZR 98/65).

(bb) This rule governing the burden of proof would, however, also apply if the plaintiff could here base a claim for damages only on § 823 I BGB. In that case also it would be for the defendant to exonerate itself. It is true that the injured party who relies on § 823 I BGB will have to allege and if necessary prove not only the causal connection between his damage and the conduct of the doer, but also his fault (BGHZ 24, 21, 29). However, the possibility of proving the subjective conditions depends appreciably on how far the injured party can elucidate the detailed course of events. That is however especially difficult when it relates to antecedents which played a part in the business of manufacturing the products. The courts for a long time came to the help of the injured party by contenting themselves with proof of a chain of causation, which, according to human experience, indicates an organizational fault in the manufacturer. All the same, one cannot stop at this point in considering claims for damages for 'product liability'. All too often the owner of a business can show that the defect in the product might have been caused in a way that does not point to his fault—evidence which generally relies on activities in his business and which is difficult for the injured party to disprove. In consequence, when damage has arisen within the range of the manufacturer's business risks, he cannot be regarded as exonerated merely because he points out that the defect in the product might have arisen without any organizational fault of his. This is required in the area of 'product liability' in order to protect the interests of the injured party—whether ultimate acquirer, user, or third party; on the other hand, the interests of the producer allow him to demand that he may prove his lack of fault.

This rule of evidence indeed only operates as soon as the injured party has proved that his damage falls within the scope of the manufacturer's organization and risks, and indeed is satisfied by the existence of an objective defect or of unbusinesslike conduct. This proof is required of the injured party even when he sues the doer of damage for breach of protective and subsidiary duties arising from a contract or the negotiations for one (Senate judgments of 16 September 1961—VI ZR 92/61 and 18 January 1966—VI ZR 184/64). It is the same if he claims against the producer for breach of his duty of care. However, once he has provided this evidence, the producer is better able to explain the facts or to bear the consequences of being unable to offer an explanation. He surveys the field of production, determines and organizes the manufacturing process and the control of delivering the finished products. The size of the business, its complicated, departmentalized organization, its involved technical, chemical, or biological processes and the like make it practically impossible for the injured party to ascertain the cause of the defect. He is therefore unable to lay the facts before the judge in such a way that he can decide with certainty whether the management is to be blamed for neglect or whether it is a case of a mistake in manufacture for which a workman is at fault, or a single breakdown that may happen at any time, or defect in development that was unforeseeable in the existing state of technology or science. But if the unknown cause lies within the scope of the producer, it is also within the scope of his risks. In that case it is appropriate and expected of him that the risk of not being able to prove his innocence should lie with him.

Such rules of evidence have always been applied to contractual or quasi-contractual relations of a special legal character between injured party (creditor) and doer of damage (debtor) (BGHZ 48, 310, 313). No obvious reason can be given why they should not also apply to delict, if the reasons for them apply. In certain connections § 831 BGB already imposes on the employer the proof of exoneration—the same applies to liability cases under §§ 832, 833, 834 BGB, and above all to §§ 836 ff. Here, indeed, the law requires a person damaged through the collapse of a building to prove that the damage was 'the consequence of defective erection or defective maintenance', but lays on the possessor etc. the burden of proving that he had done everything to avoid the dangers that could attach to his building. The reversal of the burden of allegation and proof ordered in these provisions does not always proceed from a presumption of fault in the doer of damage. It rests in the main on the thought that the doer is in a better position than the injured party to throw light on the events relevant to the charge of negligence, so that it is just to impose on him the risk of being unable to do so. The Senate has already in its judgment of 1 April 1953 (VI ZR 77/52) indicated that the plaintiff cannot be required to prove—as a rule an almost impossible task—that the thing that caused the damage came into circulation through the fault of the owner of the business or his agents. Above all, the Senate has already in its judgment of 17 October 1967 (VI ZR 70/66) declared that it is for the producer to exonerate himself, if the injured party can give no detailed information about the management's blameable breaches of duty. The modern development of production, which is distributed among persons or machines that are hard to identify at a subsequent stage and rests on finishing processes capable of being inspected and controlled only by specialists, demands a development of the law of evidence in the direction already indicated in § 836 BGB . . .

In any case—as with the recognized shifting of the burden of proof for 'positive breach of contract'—it always depends on the interests at stake in the groups of cases from time to time under consideration. The question whether the assumption of the risk of proof can be imputed in the case of the owner of a small business, where the manufacturing processes can be easily surveyed and examined (family and one-man businesses, agricultural producers, and the like), need not be considered here. In cases of the present kind it is in any case for the manufacturer to exonerate himself.

4. The defendant company has not furnished that proof of exoneration.

(a) According to Professor Dr E's opinion submitted by the defendant company, it is possible that carelessness on the part of someone concerned with the bottling led to the contamination of the bottles. He considered the process of filling containers over 500 ccm by manual pouring and not, as happens with the smaller containers, by means of an apparatus as an 'older method' which was indeed 'tolerable', but needing improvement. For this manual pouring there must at least be constructed a correspondingly superior 'clean work bench' with UV radiation. In addition the 'modest apparatus outfit' of the business must be increased by installing dry sterilizers, so that the larger containers could be better sterilized, above all without long interruption. He also pointed out that in the process of autoclave without a temperature and pressure gauge no control could be exercised over whether the high temperature needed for the sterilization under pressure was really attained. Moreover, he recommended the use of tubes showing changes of colour. He also advised that the filling-room be examined for its germ content from time to time by exposing dishes of agar or blood.

The expert then was of opinion that in spite of these suggestions for improvement, the manufacturing methods of the defendant company were 'not unsatisfactory' and fulfilled the 'normal requirements'. Moreover, the method of bottling guaranteed a sufficient degree of security, even though it needed to be improved. Finally, he was of opinion that the defendant company had not carelessly neglected any of the necessary precautions. The bacterial contamination could indeed have been caused by defective observance of the required precautions, but could have occurred even if they had been observed.

(b) The expert's view of the required degree of care cannot be approved. Even he starts by saying that in the manufacture of vaccines in which the effect of living viruses must be immunized 'the highest possible security' must be required. For that very reason vaccine works are subjected to strict public supervision (§ 10 AMG together with the provisions of Land law still operative under § 5). The defects mentioned by him in the equipment of the defendant company's business, above all as regards manual bottling, are in conflict with a finding that the management were not guilty of careless conduct. The improvements recommended by him were not at all far-fetched and imposed on the company requirements that were neither technically nor financially excessive. The possibility cannot be excluded that those additional precautions would have averted the bottling of dangerous vaccine.

Case 44

BUNDESGERICHTSHOF (SIXTH CIVIL DIVISION) 11 JULY 1972*
BGHZ 59, 172 = NJW 1972, 2217 = VersR 1972, 1075

On 12 October 1961 the plaintiff, a farmer's wife born in 1920, went to a hospital for a minor gynaecological operation to be carried out by its director. Dr M, his assistant, injected the plaintiff with an anaesthetic called Estil to be employed for a short narcosis, which was produced by the defendant.

* English version by Kurt Lipstein.

Dr M injected it in the bend of the plaintiff's left arm. By accident, the anaesthetic, which was to be administered intravenously only, was injected into an artery. This led to a serious disturbance of the plaintiff's circulation and necessitated, finally, the amputation of her upper arm.

Beginning in August 1960 Estil had been subject to clinical tests, first in one and then in several hospitals. As early as 8 December 1960 an accidental injection into a patient's artery had resulted in the amputation of an arm. Estil was registered with the Senator for Health in Berlin on 23 January 1961 and was put on sale on 1 April 1961. Instructions attached to each package contained the sentence in bold type: 'Intra-arterial injection must be avoided with certainty'. After the accident involving the plaintiff, the warning attached to the package was increased twice. On 9 February 1962 the defendant withdrew Estil from sale.

Meanwhile a number of such accidents had occurred, most of them involving the loss of an arm, but also some affecting the kidneys, in one case with lethal effect. The plaintiff claimed damages from the defendant. The Court of First Instance rejected the claim, but the Court of Appeal of Stuttgart allowed it. A second appeal by the defendant was unsuccessful for the following

Reasons

I. The Court of Appeal holds the defendant to be liable in tort (§ 823 I BGB) because he has caused the loss of the plaintiff's arm by having culpably violated in his capacity of producer of medicines his public duty of care. The appeal against this decision fails in the result.

1. (*a*) The Court of Appeal reaches this view primarily because it holds that thorough clinical tests had not been carried out before Estil was put on the market. Such tests were required in order fully to recognize the dangerous nature of Estil, i.e. its arterial intolerance and the fact that an intra-arterial injection could not be avoided with certainty. If these tests had been carried out, so the Court of Appeal believes, the incident suffered by the plaintiff would not have happened.

(*b*) This Division agrees with the appellant that the arguments of the Court of Appeal cannot be accepted in their entirety. It may be true that further clinical tests were indicated. It is also clear that if the tests had not yet come to an end, the medicament would not yet have been in free circulation and would not have been administered to the plaintiff. Nevertheless, it seems doubtful whether, regarded from this point of view, the incident which affected the plaintiff can be attributed in law to the defendant as a breach of duty. The incident suffered by the plaintiff was caused exclusively by the arterial intolerance of the medicament, as the Court of Appeal found without committing a mistake of law. In order to obtain further certainty further clinical tests with human beings would hardly have been the most suitable means, especially since incorrect injections are less likely to occur among medical specialists and since greater care is applied in an experimental situation than in general practice, for which the medicament was meant at least as much. However, at the time when it was put on the market, the defendant was not at all in doubt, as the Court of Appeal itself stated in another connection and, as he states, he decided for this reason to include a warning in the notice attached to the package, an unusual measure from his point of view. The general danger of intra-arterial injections by accident, especially in the arterial area, was not to form the object of experiments with human beings, least of all by a medicament which would cause necessarily most severe damage in such circumstances. Moreover, applying that degree of care which must be expected absolutely of a manufacturer of such a medicament, this danger could be gleaned already at that time from the medical literature, as the expert opinions show upon which the Court of Appeal relied in another connection.

2. It is unnecessary to enlarge on this point, since the decision of the Court of Appeal is well founded in law on the ground of insufficient information concerning the dangerous nature of the medicament.

(a) The Court of Appeal holds it against the defendant, above all, that he was content to include a general warning in a notice included in the package and in the prospectus sent to medical men without having indicated in any way the serious, possibly irreparable, consequences of a misdirection of the injection into the artery, although he was well aware of them.

In the opinion of the Court of Appeal, there was all the more reason to do so since according to the unanimous opinion expressed in specialist medical circles an accidental intra-arterial injection could not be avoided with certainty, especially if administered in the bend of the arm; the danger inherent in particular in the bend of the arm in this respect could not have escaped the attention of the research department, directed by a medically qualified person, of the defendant's enterprise. Instead the defendant had recommended for the first time only in the notices dispatched after 16 October 1961—i.e. after the incident involving the plaintiff—to make injections in the lower arm for preference and, moreover, at first only 0.5 ccm as an experimental dose; even then he had not mentioned the nature of the possible danger. He had done so only in the third version of the notice—when called upon by the authorities—from January 1962 onwards, i.e. shortly before the product was withdrawn.

The Court of Appeal found further: If the defendant had, as was his duty, drawn the attention of every medical person to the existing risk in such a forcible manner from the beginning or at least after the Congress of Anaesthetists held on 8 October 1961 (where the Estil incidents were discussed) Dr M would have avoided the bend of the arm, and if he had approached the artery nevertheless, he would have noticed it at any rate while making an experimental preliminary injection. Thus the incident would have been avoided.

(*b*) These arguments cannot be invalidated by the appellant. The opinion of the Court of Appeal cannot be faulted in law that the defendant had violated his public duty of care (duty to inform) as a manufacturer of medicaments [references] inasmuch as he failed to indicate openly in the notice included in the package and in the medical prospectus the absolute arterial intolerance of Estil known to him.

It has been recognized for a long time by the practice of the courts that it is the duty of a manufacturer, the violation of which may render him liable to third parties for any ensuing damages, to give an effective warning of specific dangers emanating from a product brought on the market [references].

The requirements are especially strict for providing information about possible danger connected with medicaments. The Court of Appeal is correct in holding that in the face of this principle any consideration of the interest of the manufacturer to promote sales is excluded. The Court of Appeal was therefore right in requiring as information sufficient for the practising medical profession that the consequences of intra-arterial injections (almost certain total loss of the extremity) should be set out clearly together with the advice that the well-known practice of injecting Estil in the bend of the arm must be abandoned, because in the opinion of all the expert advice at the disposal of the Court of Appeal the danger of a misdirected injection is much increased, given the special nature of the anatomical situation. The Court of Appeal, in so holding, agrees in the essential point with numerous decisions which in deciding claims for damages against medical practitioners have found as a fact that an injection of Estil in the bend of the arm is altogether inappropriate. Several of these decisions have been upheld on appeal to this Division [references].

According to the findings of the Court of Appeal, especially in so far as they are based on expert testimony called for by the court and on its foundations, the arterial intolerance to Estil—which could have been proved easily by experiments carried out on the ear of a rabbit—exceeded by far the dangers which accompany generally an accidental intra-arterial injection with other medicaments. The fact that the same may have been true for a few other medicaments which had to be injected intravenously, such as Presuren, which was no longer advertised for sale later on, makes no difference; in the present case a special source of danger existed which the doctor using the medicament did not expect unless his attention was specifically drawn to it. This is all the more valid since according to its purpose as indicated by the advertisements of the manufacturer (the defendant), the medicament was to be used above all in general practice, i.e. by doctors without special qualifications in anaesthetics. This danger was further increased because Estil, intended for brief narcosis, is subject to a quick breakdown in the body and must be injected quickly in one move by a wide-bore needle and under heavy pressure.

No legal objections can be raised if the Court of Appeal holds in the light of these considerations that medical practitioners ought to have been informed of the full extent of the risk in selecting this medicament because only thus would they have been warned particularly to use the utmost care and not to use it at all in case of doubt.

(aa) The appellant fails inasmuch as he wishes to show with reference to the statistical material, previously presented to the judge, but not so found in detail by the latter that on the average other anaesthetic methods disclose for other reasons an even higher quota of incidents. The old medical maxim above all not to create more harm (*primum nil nocere*) militates against the acceptance a priori of a certain quota of incidents. Instead every recognizable source of danger—especially, however, one which is already well known—must be eliminated in dealings with patients, be they diagnostic, anaesthetic, or therapeutic, if and in so far as it can be reasonably avoided; this applies even if actual danger is only to be expected to materialize in relatively few instances. The duty to avoid danger is primarily incumbent upon the doctor, for subject to agreement with the patient, he determines the treatment. However, to impose this duty upon him *alone* would not correspond to the peculiarities of modern pharmaceutical specialization. Here the responsibility, and with it the duty of care, of the manufacturer increases to the extent in which the production of the medicament is based on development which cannot be repeated easily by the medical practitioner or even understood; also the manufacturer himself, through intensive advertising among the medical profession, seeks and achieves to influence a choice in favour of his medicament and no other.

This Division need not decide whether—as the Court of Appeal finds in the alternative—already at the time of the incident involving the plaintiff it was improper to put Estil on the market because it was known that the danger connected therewith was disproportionately high (see now § 6 I of the Medicaments Act which in this respect merely gives statutory authority to a previously recognized duty of care towards the public). The decision under appeal is already supported by the conclusion that the defendant has not complied sufficiently with his clear duty of care towards the public to inform freely medical practitioners who wish to use the medicament of the specific danger and to warn them against it. Especially if it were conceded in favour of the defendant that the continuing marketing of Estil could still be justified having regard to its special narcotic advantages, it was necessary to acquaint the medical profession clearly and explicitly. Only thus could a medical practitioner balance correctly the risk which is connected to a greater or lesser degree with the use of every medicament against the benefit for the patient hoped for in the individual case, and could, if necessary, give proper advice to the patient in making up his mind. The conditions required for such weighing to take place were not provided by the defendant when he drew attention in bold type for the need to avoid intra-arterial injections with certainty. This is particularly valid because, as the defendant has stressed constantly, this requirement is a matter of course where narcotic medicaments are being used. This notice did not bring home that a special danger was to be avoided or had to be accepted for special reasons.

(*b*) Contrary to the view of the appellant, the Court of Appeal is also not wrong in not conceding to the appellant that he could rely on the publications in medical journals to provide the medical profession with information about Estil. Leaving aside the Court of Appeal's apposite consideration that those general medical practitioners who are mainly concerned with using the medicament do not all read specialized publications regularly, the court could deduce from the files to which it referred that those publications did not justify the defendant to treat them as being of unlimited objectivity, for in accordance with an alleged custom he had inspired these reports himself and had paid for them . . .

(*c*) As regards the question whether the insufficient information was the cause of the damage, the Court of Appeal concluded that a warning of the kind which it regarded as indicated would have prevented the incident involving the plaintiff.

(*aa*) This, too, cannot be faulted in law as far as the result is concerned. It could be expected that, as a typical and intended consequence of an adequate notice, no conscientious doctor would have made an injection in the bend of the elbow, but would on finding another suitable vein, have applied the highest possible attention commensurate with the highly dangerous nature of the remedy and would, in appropriate cases have abandoned the use of the medicament altogether. The latter was particularly appropriate in the present case as the appellant emphasizes since . . . the chief medical officer had expected in any case that the well-tried anaesthetic Evipan would be applied.

If this had happened, the typical increase in danger resulting from the failure to give a warning would have been excluded. It was for the defendant to prove that exceptionally, despite the application of extreme care, a misdirected injection would have taken place which according to prevailing medical opinion could never be avoided with *absolute* certainty . . .

(*cc*) Finally the appellant argues, though unsuccessfully, that a manufacturer of medicaments can only be held liable for the application of his product in accordance with its prescribed use; to inject a medicament intended for intravenous application in an artery was to apply it contrary to its prescribed use, the consequences of which could not be attributed to the manufacturer.

This is only correct in so far as an intentional misapplication (e.g. oral, instead of external as prescribed) is in issue. In such circumstances the occurrence of unforeseen acts may break the chain of causation. However, even to that extent the manufacturer is not exempt from giving appropriate warning, as the case may be, against likely wrong use, e.g. by a clear notice 'for external use' (see now § 10 VI 3 of the Medicaments Act). Such a duty to give notice is precisely in issue here. It is all the more important where it is necessary to prevent not an intentional but a negligent misapplication ('missing it') if, as found in the present case, this possibility is not totally remote and must have surprisingly severe consequences. The question as to whether the medical practitioner also acted negligently remains irrelevant as long as the manufacturer is to be blamed specifically for not having forestalled such mistakes of the medical attendant which are not beyond all expectation. According to general opinion, which is also supported by the provision of § 840 I BGB, the fact that another person has also caused the illegal act does not exonerate the tortfeasor either altogether or in part. Thus in the result the Court of Appeal has rightly held that the defendant is liable in tort for the incident involving the plaintiff.

II. . . .

Case 45

BUNDESGERICHTSHOF (SIXTH CIVIL DIVISION) 15 DECEMBER 1978*
BGHZ 75, 75 = BB 1979, 1257 = NJW 1979, 2036

In 1969 the plaintiff gave an order to the G firm to carry out the glazing of his house. Thereupon the firm inserted 'I–Glass' units which had been manufactured under licence by the defendant. The delivery took place on 9 October 1969 by way of the F Company, which had ordered the material from the defendant and taken delivery on 7 October 1969. In September

* English version by Tony Weir.

1974 the plaintiff detected condensation on a part of the inserted plates. At the end of October 1974 the defendant was notified of claims by the plaintiff. The defendant, in a letter of November 1974, asserted that the limitation period affecting the warranty had already elapsed. When that letter reached the plaintiff by way of the G firm on 14 November 1974, he learnt for the first time that the defendant included in its publicity a declaration under the heading 'warranty', which read, *inter alia*, as follows:

The manufacturers of 'I–Glass' warrant—for five years from the date of the first delivery—that under normal conditions the transparency of 'I–Glass' will be vitiated neither by the formation of film nor by the deposit of dust in the space between the plates . . . This warranty creates an obligation only to replace the defective 'I–Glass' units . . . The group of European 'I' manufacturers . . . have established a warranty fund to insure quality and warranty. This fund serves to provide extraordinary insurance of the 'I' warranty and makes it ultimately independent of local conditions and circumstances. The warranty fund therefore supports the warranty issued by each 'I–Glass' licensee . . .

The plaintiff in his action begun in January sued the defendant on his producer's warranty. He at first demanded twelve substitute glass units. In May 1977, he had the plates he objected to changed and claimed compensation for the cost of the materials. The lower courts rejected his claim. On his application for review the Bundesgerichtshof set aside the appellate judgment and sent the case back for reconsideration for these

Reasons

1. The Court of Appeal is of opinion that no direct contractual relation came into being between the defendant manufacturer and the plaintiff as ultimate acquirer of the glass plates. Whether that is correct may be left undecided: for the judgment under review cannot be upheld because by virtue of a contract between the defendant and the F Company a warranty came into existence for the benefit of the plaintiff as ultimate acquirer (contract for the benefit of their parties).

(*a*) . . .

(*b*) . . . The defendant's warranty attached on the date of the first delivery, namely that of the glass to the F Company. Thus it is obvious that the contractual intention of the defendant also relates back to that moment. That answers to the interest of the middleman, who acquires advantages for himself as well as from the creation of the warranty in favour of the ultimate acquirer. If, that is to say, one of the defects covered by the warranty occurs, he will be free from his own liability to the other party in so far as the manufacturer is responsible for the defect by virtue of his duty to perform the warranty. Accordingly everything speaks in favour of the F Company's intending to establish the warranty as early as possible, in order to assure itself of the indirect exemption from liability connected therewith and its independence of later contingencies (e.g. the question whether the ultimate acquirer had notice as a third party of the warranty). The fact that the warranty fund set up intended the liability assumed by the defendant to be independent of local conditions and circumstances does not stand in the way. That turn of phrase emphasizes the *material security* of the warranty, but says nothing about the *person to whom* the defendant intended to direct his offer to make good the warranty. The custom sought by the warranty is not put in doubt on the ground that it initially operated on the middlemen in their relations with the manufacturer, for the last middleman will as a rule indicate to the ultimate acquirer the advantages implied in the warranty, in order to obtain a customer.

(*c*) As the interests of all concerned speak in favour of creating the warranty at once by means of a contract for the benefit of third parties (§ 328 BGB), it must follow that the defendant and the F Company intended to enter into a contract of that kind . . .

That the person of that third party was not ascertained when they made the contract does not affect the result. For the contracting parties the identity of the future ultimate acquirer played (to start with) no role. The agreement that whoever should happen to be the ultimate acquirer should be the third party beneficiary was enough. That made him sufficiently ascertainable.

2. The plaintiff claimed in good time under the warranty offered by the contract for his benefit.

It is true that the defendant learnt of the occurrence to which the warranty applied only after the limitation period had run out. Since the F Company had taken delivery of the glass plates from the defendant on 7 October 1969, the five-year limitation period had already run out when the defendant obtained on 28 October 1974 knowledge of the complaint. That, however, is of no significance since according to the clear wording of the warranty, the period referred to is the period within which the material damage envisaged must occur and not the period within which the claim must be made.

The only decisive factor therefore is that the defect appeared in September 1974—and so within the warranty period. That at that moment the plaintiff's claim against the G firm was already time-barred, because it was based on VOB/B standard contract, is irrelevant. The warranty was to be valid 'independent of local conditions and circumstances', and therefore irrespective of the contractual arrangements of the ultimate acquirer with the glazier.

3. If the glass plates manufactured by the defendant turn out to have the defect alleged by the plaintiff (which must be taken for granted for present purposes), it should make no difference to the plaintiff's action that he no longer demands their replacement but compensation.

The defendant's warranty is intended to give greater effect to the claims for defects that the ultimate acquirer has against the person (the glazier) employed by him to do the work. The contract of warranty is, therefore, ancillary to a warranty arising from a contract for work and labour. In the present case the plaintiff's contract with the G firm was one of sale and work concerning non-fungible goods; for the glass plates had been prepared to fit the special dimensions of the window-frames in the plaintiff's house. That the defendant's contract with the F Company is one of sale is irrelevant. The decisive factor is the economic function the warranty has to perform for the ultimate acquirer as third-party beneficiary.

The plaintiff was at liberty to remedy the defects himself—assumed to exist for the purposes of the present appeal—and to demand monetary compensation from the defendant.

4. The plaintiff's claim under the warranty is not statute-barred. As has already been explained, the warranty was intended to give greater effect to the ultimate acquirer's claim for defective delivery based on the contract of work against the builder carrying out his order. In accordance with that purpose, the claim under the warranty becomes statute-barred at the same moment as the corresponding claim of the ultimate acquirer. Here the glazing of all the windows in a house amounts to a building contract. The limitation period for a contract of work is five years. Accordingly, claims under the warranty also are subject to a five-year limitation. That the plaintiff agreed with the G firm that standard conditions of VOB/B should apply makes no difference. The warranty here for the ultimate acquirer was to be 'independent of the circumstances of the particular case'. It was to give greater effect to his claims of the final acquirer under the warranty arising from the contract of work and therefore according to its sense and purpose should in no way be subject to the agreed curtailment of the limitation period applicable to a contract of work.

The defendant by his warranty agreed to be responsible for all defects appearing within the limitation period. Accordingly, that period for claims under the warranty cannot be taken to run from the delivery, fixing or acceptance of the glass. The better view is that the sense and purpose of the warranty require it to begin only with the discovery of the defect (cf. also BGH NJW 1979, 645). Otherwise defects which were first detected towards the end of the warranty limitation period could in many cases not be successfully invoked before the limitation operated. That is precisely shown in the present case.

The plaintiff here detected the defect in September 1974—within five years from the delivery of the plates—the subject of the action started in January 1977. Thereby the limitation was interrupted in good time.

5. In view of these considerations, the appellate judgment must be set aside. The case must be sent back to the Court of Appeal, which must now inquire whether and how far the plates were defective and what the substitute plates cost.

Case 46

BUNDESGERICHTSHOF (SIXTH CIVIL DIVISION), 7 JUNE 1988*
BGHZ 104, 323

Facts

The defendants manufacture carbonated soft drinks which they bottle in reusable bottles manufactured by DB and Co. and which they market *inter alia* under the trade mark 'Fri.' The parents of the plaintiff, who, at the time of the accident was three years old, purchased a crate of lemonade produced by the defendants on September 5, 1981 from the drinks retailer F. Two days later, on September 7, 1981, when the plaintiff took one of the bottles out of the crate in the basement of his parents' house, it exploded. The plaintiff lost his right eye and part of the sight in his left eye as a result of injuries received from glass splinters. The remains of the glass were not preserved after the accident.

The plaintiff claimed damages for part of his pain and suffering from the defendants in the amount of DM 6,000. In support of his case he claimed that as manufacturers, the defendants are responsible for an injury to his health which occurred when one of their products was being used for the purposes for which it was intended. He could not be expected to prove that the defect in the bottle occurred after it had been marketed by the defendants, since this would be impossible for him in practice. The numerous other comparable cases in which bottles containing products manufactured by the defendants or other producers of mineral water products had exploded showed that this accident did not merely involve a 'stray incident'. Rather, they demonstrated that technical precautions which could have been taken in the bottling process were not in fact taken, even though the dangers must have been known.

The defendants contested the plaintiff's description of the accident. In their view the bottle of lemonade did not explode, but rather it either fell out

---

* English version by Ms J. Shaw.

of the plaintiff's hands or was banged against another object when it was lifted out of the crate. The bottle of lemonade was free from defects when it left the defendants' business. This was guaranteed by the technical installations and organisation of the defendants' business. The fact that the cause of the accident could not be clarified since the remains of the bottle were not preserved, was a matter for which the plaintiff must take responsibility.

The LG gave judgment for the plaintiff. The OLG rejected the claim, and allowed the defendants' appeal on the basis that the plaintiff had no claims against the defendants arising from the accident. The plaintiff's application to the BGH was successful and led to the quashing of the judgment and the remittance of the case to the lower court for decision.

For the following

Reasons

I. The OLG considers that it is not proven that the lemonade bottle was already defective when it was marketed by the defendants. In the view of the OLG, the lack of proof falls as a burden upon the plaintiff. The essential findings of that court are as follows: the reversal of the burden of proof developed by the case law for product liability did not extend either to the defective nature of the product or to the proof of a causal link between the defect and the damage which gives rise to liability, but concerns merely the question of fault. There is also no possibility of a lessening of the burden of proof using the rules governing *prima facie* proof. It is true that there is no question of inappropriate handling of the product by the plaintiff. According to the evidence given by the expert witness Dr Sch., what caused the accident was excessive pressure within the bottle as a result of it being insufficiently filled, or an existing crack in the glass which led to the bursting of the bottle as a result of a small increase in pressure caused by the movement of the contents as it was removed from the crate. However, it could not be excluded that the damage to the bottle such as might here be considered to be the causal factor for the explosion of the bottle could have been caused only after the bottle had been marketed by the defendant. Consequently, the plaintiff must incur the typical difficulties regarding proof which are faced by a consumer who is injured by a product which has been passed along a rather lengthy chain of manufacture and distribution. A lessening of the burden of proof can be of no assistance to the victim as regards evidence of the causal connection. That would lead to a form of strict liability for the manufacturer which is not recognised under the present law, since it would be practically impossible for the defendant to provide the necessary proof.

II. The arguments put forward by the OLG are not, as a matter of law, in all respects convincing.

1. The OLG clearly regards the liability of the defendants as being feasible where it could be said that both possible causes which the expert witness said might explain the explosion of the lemonade bottle—namely excessive pressure inside the bottle as a result of it being insufficiently filled or a crack in the glass—were *already* present at the time when the bottle was marketed by the defendant. In reaching that conclusion, the OLG placed limits which were too restrictive upon recovery. At the present time, it cannot be excluded that the defendants as the manufacturers might still be responsible for the explosion of the lemonade bottle, including an explosion of the violence which caused the severe injuries suffered by the plaintiff in this case, even where the direct cause of the accident was a hairline crack which only appeared in the glass after the bottle had been put into the marketing chain leading to the plaintiff by the defendant. In this case there would be no question of considering the issue which the OLG took to be central, namely the burden of proving whether the defect in question was present or absent at the time when the bottle left the defendant's business.

(*a*) As the manufacturers of carbonated lemonade, the defendants are subject to a duty under the principles of the law of tort to ensure, within the limits of what is technically possible and economically reasonable, that consumers do not suffer any impairment of their health as a consequence of their products. This duty covers not just the concern that the drink which they manufactured should be fit for consumption; it also makes the defendants responsible for ensuring that the containers in which their lemonade is marketed do not cause injuries, whether to the consumer or to other persons concerned with the transport of the product [references omitted]. This applies also to the danger of the bursting of the glass bottle chosen by the defendants for their product as a consequence of a defect in the material or of excessive pressure which can lead—as the present case shows—to very serious injuries. Those types of accidents may be rare, even when measured against the high turnover in drinks and the common usage of that type of lemonade bottle—even in reusable containers. Still, as the experience of the court and the evidence of the expert witness demonstrate, they do occur and have long been known to the drinks industry as a specific risk inherent in such products.

It was the task of the defendants to deal with this risk within the limits of what was technically possible and financially reasonable. The responsibility of the defendants is not undermined by the fact that in addition to used bottles which it prepared for refilling, it also used brand new reusable glass bottles manufactured by DB and Co. for its lemonade. Even with regard to these new bottles, they assumed responsibility for the product when they made use of them; consequently it was for the defendants to ensure that when the bottles were delivered they would withstand the demands of being transported and of being used in the normal way by the purchaser. The defendants were also not solely a bottling concern in respect of which the responsibility for the use of the bottles might have been differently evaluated [reference omitted]. The defendants decided how the drink would be put together, specifying in particular the level of carbonation which in turn determined the degree of pressure in the interior of the bottle; they also specified the type, get up, and usage of the chosen packaging material. Consequently, the defendants are not simply responsible for ensuring that this material and the level of internal pressure to which the bottles were subject once filled were appropriate, but also for ensuring that the composition of the bottles was satisfactory bearing in mind the demands which could be expected to be placed upon them in the context of distribution and consumption. The type of defects which in the view of the expert witness were likely to be responsible for the eye injuries suffered by the plaintiff are amongst those which it is for the defendant, if possible, to eliminate using appropriate methods of production and control.

(b) In this context the defendants must take into account that even if the bottles were not damaged when they left the manufacturer's sphere of control, they may [subsequently] be damaged and left in a state in which they might explode on the way to the consumer. For the product must not only be capable of withstanding impacts arising in the context of normal and intended usage such as knocks, pressures, heat, cold, etc.; such bottles must also be capable of standing up to all types of foreseeable and normal usage [see OLG Frankfurt VersR 1985, 890; Borer, 'Produkthaftung: Der Fehlerbegriff nach deutschem, amerikanischem und europäischem Recht (1986) p. 26]. Of course, it cannot be expected that the manufacturer should take precautions against all types of instances in which its bottles of drink are handled carelessly. The limits of the type of care which the manufacturer would be expected to demonstrate are exceeded in circumstances where the inappropriate handling of the bottle deviates from what is normally foreseeable. However, the defendants must take into account not only the distance which the bottle must travel before it reaches the consumer and the length of time between production and consumption, all of which means that there are uncertainties as to how the bottles will be handled, but also the [possibility of a] great variety of different consumers coming into contact with the bottles. The defendants may not rely upon the fact that the bottles will be sensibly and gently handled during transport and storage.

(c) Of course, the defendants cannot be reproached for having used reusable glass bottles in the first place for bottling their lemonade, even though there remains a residual risk of injury from such bottles, in particular where they are not handled carefully by distributors or consumers. In principle, the defendants are entitled to expect the users, themselves, to take care to avoid injury from glass breakages, because these are inherent risks in the material itself. The same cannot be said of the risks of an explosive breakage of the bottle such as occurred in this case. The average consumer does not anticipate such a risk; even an appropriate warning on the bottle would not change the expectations of consumers in this respect in any lasting way. The consumer cannot in general protect himself against the bottle through acting more carefully where it has already been damaged or where it is subject to excessive internal pressure. The serious injuries which are in particular likely to occur if there is an explosive breakage of the glass are completely disproportionate to the obligations in respect of the product which the consumer can be expected to assume when handling it as an aspect of the general risks of life. It is true that there is much to be said, in the light of the information put forward so far in this case, for the fact that, having regard to the great number of reusable bottles with the same features used by manufacturers of carbonated drinks, there are extremely few accidents caused by exploding bottles which have suffered prior damage. Consequently, there are no grounds for raising legal doubts about the admissibility of using such bottles on the grounds of any general level of risk. On the other hand, the specific risks of an explosive breakage cannot for these reasons simply be ignored by the manufacturer; the consequences of such an accident are too serious for this to be the case. On the contrary, the manufacturer of drinks must be regarded as subject to an obligation within the realms of what is economically reasonable and technically possible to eliminate such specific risks leading to serious injuries in so far as is possible. The type of measures which can be expected of the manufacturer include introducing a significant reduction in the level of carbonation, as was suggested by the expert witness in this case, using a type of bottle which is not as dangerous when it breaks, making use of caps which automatically release excessive pressure, and other appropriate measures.

(*d*) In this case, it can be concluded from the above that the OLG must first examine the question of whether and to what extent the defendants could be reasonably expected, at the relevant time when the bottle was put on the market, to take these types of precautions against their bottles exploding where the glass was damaged, even if only when it was being transported to the consumer. In judging what it is economically reasonable to expect of the manufacturer it is necessary to take into account *inter alia* the customs of consumers and sales potential for a product altered to take into account these matters. However, it must [also] be taken into account that it is the basic safety needs of consumers which are being counterpoised to these economic factors. The burden of going forward with the evidence and of proving that a method of production which eliminates the risk of lemonade bottles exploding is possible and reasonable and of demonstrating that there is a breach of duty on the part of the defendants falls upon the plaintiff, who is not protected by any easing of the burden in this respect. Should the OLG come to the conclusion that the defendants could have eliminated those types of risks of exploding bottles even at the time of the accident, and that the defendants had negligently closed their minds to this possibility in spite of the risk which had long been known in this branch of industry, then it is clear that the defendants are responsible for the injuries to the plaintiff even where the bottle exploded not because of excessive pressure because it had not been filled up, but because the glass had been damaged, even during transport to the consumer.

2. It is only where it can be said that the defendants are not subject to a duty to take such precautions with a view to eliminating the risk discussed above at the time when the bottle was put into circulation that it would be relevant, for the purposes of determining whether the defendants are liable, to consider the question which the OLG placed at the centre of its analysis. This [question] was whether, alongside the possibility that it was excessive pressure caused by the bottle having been insufficiently filled (which would certainly be a defect in manufacture on the part of the defendants) the other possible cause of the damage (namely a crack in the glass) should also be regarded as occurring in the defendants' sphere of production. To put it differently, did the bottle, when it was put on the market, already have the defect which actually triggered the explosion? However, even in this context the arguments of the OLG are not sustainable.

(*a*) The OLG cannot, without erring in law, exclude the possibility that the lemonade bottle in question was free from defects when it was marketed by the defendants.

(*aa*) The applicants' submissions to this court seek to rely, without avail, upon the rules of *prima facie* proof in order to demonstrate that the defect which led to the breakage of the bottle was already present when the product was marketed. The plaintiff argues that it is possible to see that the occurrence of the loss is typical—a feature which it must display if there is to be an easing of the burden of proof and which is in principle necessary for the purposes of demonstrating a defect in the product [references omitted]—from the fact that there have been repeated similar accidents in the past involving lemonade bottles marketed by the defendants, as well as lemonade and mineral water bottles manufactured by others, but despite this the defendants had not taken any care to ensure that adequate controls were placed upon the bottles which it put on the market.

Additionally, the plaintiff argues that it has satisfied the conditions of *prima facie* proof because the defendants have neither identified nor proven a serious possibility of the lemonade bottle suffering damage after it left their business premises.

As this court has repeatedly stated [references omitted], the rules on *prima facie* proof are of no assistance where it cannot be excluded that the condition which caused the danger only arose after the product left the manufacturer's business premises. There is nothing to counter the arguments put forward by the OLG that it could not be excluded that the damage was caused to the bottle after it had been finally marketed by the defendants. There remains the possibility that a third party for whom the manufacturer is not responsible—such as a distributor or a retailer—damaged the lemonade bottle by handling it incorrectly.

(*bb*) Even the arguments led by the plaintiff in his appeal whereby the damaging occurrence resulted in the product destroying itself so that the reasons for the difficulties in proving the case were the responsibility of the defendants do not justify allowing the modifications in the burden of proof sought by the plaintiff. It cannot be said that the *defendants* are frustrating the plaintiff's attempts to prove his case because it cannot be excluded that it was not the defendants but a third party who was responsible for the bursting of the bottle and consequent destruction of the means of proof.

(*cc*) The plaintiff likewise derives no assistance from the reversal of the burden of proof developed in case law of the BGH in particular for cases of medical malpractice involving gross negligence in the treatment process. This case law is based on the proposition that the difficulties experienced by the plaintiff in clarifying exactly what happened during the treatment process which result from the error in treatment can be traced back to the fact that the range of possible causes for the plaintiff's misfortune is either widened or displaced because of the particular likelihood that the error in question would cause loss and to the fact that the failure of the treatment is especially likely as a consequence of the serious medical error [references omitted]. The situation here is not comparable to such a serious error in treatment. The re-use of used lemonade bottles without adequate controls against prior damage to the glass does not in itself represent an elementary error which on these grounds alone would justify an easing of evidentiary difficulties including potentially a shifting of the burden of proof. For it was established by the OLG that the defendants screened the bottles by putting them under an initial pressure of 6.0 bar.

(*b*) It is crucial to determine in this case which party is burdened with the consequences of the fact that the exact cause of the defect and the point at which it arose remain unclarified, and in this context it is correct to adopt the starting point of the OLG, namely that it is in principle the task of the plaintiff not only to prove the defect in the product and the causal link between the defect and the injury to the plaintiff, but also to prove that the defect in question arose within the manufacturer's sphere of control for which the defendants are responsible. The courts have so far always refused to extend the principles of the reversal of the burden of proof regarding the issue of fault to the issue of objective attribution of the injury to the action ('*objektiver Zurechnungszusammenhang*') of loss [references omitted]. A generalised form of reversal of proof would turn the manufacturer's tortious liability into a form of strict liability ['*Erfolgseinstandshaftung*'] for all consequences for which it would be necessary to find some specific legitimation in the substantive law.

However, it does not follow from the above—as the OLG assumes—that modifications of the evidentiary burdens (amounting to a reversal of the burden of proof regarding the attribution of a harmful defect in the product to the manufacturer's sphere of control) are always excluded.

The objections to a presumption of a causal link working against the manufacturer will exceptionally become weaker *inter alia* where the defect in the product which has been established is typically one which arises within the manufacturer's sphere of control. In such cases, and precisely for this reason, the manufacturer (who is required wherever possible to eliminate such risks in order to avoid the infliction of serious loss) is under an obligation, for the sake of the consumer, to assure himself before the product is put on the market that it is free of such defects. This is so where the victim has demonstrated that the manufacturer's attempts to ensure the 'safety status' of the product have been inadequate. In such a case there is no significant hardening of the substantive duties imposed upon the manufacturer if he is required to demonstrate—as it were, in order to ensure the performance of the duty to ensure the 'safety status' of the product which he has not so far fulfilled—that the defect occurred only after he had put the product on the market. The manufacturer would be acting in bad faith if, in the context of litigation and in order to exonerate himself, he were able to rely upon the absence of data regarding the state of the products when they were put on the market which should precisely be available by law in order to ensure the substantive protection of the consumer.

(*aa*) By opening up such a possibility of reversing the burden of proof regarding the existence of a causal link in the field of product liability, this court is building on principles which it has already developed regarding the easing of the evidentiary burden within the law of tort. In this context it is not accepted that every breach of duty which leads to the occurrence of damage remaining unexplained will necessarily lead to the imposition of a burden upon the tortfeasor. There is no general rule that the risk of non-clarification will fall upon the party which has caused it as a consequence of a breach of duty [references omitted]. If it were the case that a failure on the part of the defendants to institute adequate controls upon the re-use of bottles in order to ensure that they will not burst merely represented a breach of their general duty of care to manufacture products which can be used without harming the consumer's health, then there would be no reason to relieve the plaintiff, as the victim, of the burden of proving that the non-existent controls were responsible for the accident, simply because of this breach on the part of the defendants of a duty of care to which they were subject [reference omitted].

(*bb*) However, the position is different where the duty on the part of the manufacturer to eliminate the risk is precisely focused on the clarification of an ambiguous state of affairs or an unclarified feature of the product and is a duty which is imposed upon the manufacturer for the protection of the consumer precisely in order to ensure, through a timely and exact investigation and control of the status of the product, that it is free of risks typically found in such products and which can no longer be discovered once the product has been put on the market by the manufacturer. If the manufacturer is in this way required to produce and preserve data on the inquiries made into the safety of the product, because he is not permitted to burden the consumer with the unclarified status of the product and the risks inherent in that status, then this in no way changes the material duties imposed upon the manufacturers, but rather confirms them. This is so where the manufacturer has breached this duty and so carries the burden of proving that the proper provision of data at the time of the inspection of the product would have ensured that it was guaranteed free of defects. To this extent, there is a conflict of interests which is comparable to that arising in those cases in which the doctor is required, for the purposes of protecting his patient, to provide written reports in order to ensure that there is prompt clarification of the patient's state of health. This clarification serves to avoid dangerous developments and cannot be drawn up belatedly. In these cases, too, this court has imposed upon the doctor who wrongfully fails to ensure that there is such a report the burden of proof in respect of what actually occurred where as a consequence of the breach of duty the clarification of what is in any case a probable causal connection between the negligence of the doctor and the injury to the plaintiff is made more difficult or impossible and the provision of a report is required precisely because of the increased risk of the procedure undertaken in that particular case [reference omitted]. The general essence of the principle of law underlying these decisions can also be applied exceptionally in respect of the constellations of fact described above concerning product liability in order to ease the burden of proof upon the consumer in respect of the causal connection and can go so far as to shift the burden of proof upon the manufacturer.

(cc) The preconditions for the application of the principles regarding the reversal of the burden of proof are fulfilled, having regard to the facts as they are to be understood for the purposes of this appeal hearing. By selling the returnable bottles, the defendants put on the market a product which, because of its particular features (glass containers which are used several times and which are subject to considerable internal gas pressure) reveals an enhanced tendency to cause damage. In respect of such bottles, which may have been used many times over a period of many years, and which may therefore have already been damaged and are therefore likely to explode, the defendants, as the manufacturers, are subject to a duty of examination and report preservation in that they must inspect the state of the glass of every bottle before it is put on the market with a view to ensuring that it is not likely to burst and to ensure that only undamaged bottles leave the manufacturers' place of business. For if the manufacturer of soft drinks uses not only new bottles but also, as here, re-used bottles, then if there is no report preservation there will be no basis for judging the state of the glass and whether and to what extent it is capable of withstanding not only the high internal gas pressure to which it will be subjected but also the considerable demands which will be placed upon it during its journey to the consumer; these are risks which the manufacturer must take into account. It is precisely because serious injuries to the health of a victim can occur where there has been a prior impairment of the glass leading to a risk of explosion and because the risk of such impairments is greater where the previously used bottles are re-used, that the manufacturer is subject to a duty to investigate the condition of the bottles which is so far unknown to him, and thereby to provide for himself and for the consumer information regarding the resistance to explosion of the glass.

It has been established by the OLG that there was no comprehensive method of identifying the already damaged bottles within the defendant's firm; in particular, subjecting the bottles for a short period of time to pressure of 6.0 bar was not a sufficient form of control. Consequently, there appears to have been a breach by the defendants of their duty of report preservation with the resulting possibility of a reversal of the burden of proof. It is a precondition for this duty to ensure the 'safety status' of the bottles that some form of reliable means of identifying already damaged bottles is both technically possible and economically reasonable for the defendants; while this can be assumed for the purposes of this appeal, it has so far not been adequately clarified. If there was such a duty of examination and report preservation, then if it was a hairline crack in the glass which caused the explosion of the bottle, it is to be assumed until the defendants have proved the contrary that the damage to the bottle existed already before it was put on the market by the defendants and could have been dis-covered through a proper inspection [reference omitted].

III. The judgment of the OLG must therefore be quashed and the issue returned to the OLG for a further hearing and decision. It is for the OLG to clarify—where necessary after having heard the parties once again and hav-ing taken the advice of an expert witness—whether the defendants could have prevented the explosion of the bottles in the hands of the consumer where the glass had been damaged, by taking reasonable measures in the context of the manufacture of the products (the lemonade) or, if this was neither possible nor reasonable, whether it could have ensured through appropriate and reasonable controls and report preservation that damaged bottles were not once more put on the market. In such a case the defen-dants, as the manufacturers, are required to prove that the absence of such controls and some means of securing the safety status of the products was irrelevant to the loss which occurred. If, however, at that time it could not be demanded of the defendants that they provide such a 'safety status', then the burden resulting from the unexplained cause of the damage will fall upon the plaintiff.

Case 47

BUNDESGERICHTSHOF (SIXTH CIVIL SENATE) 19 NOVEMBER 1991*
NJW 1992, 1039

1. The reversal of the burden of proof of fault in cases of product liability applies to small as well as large businesses, in this case to a restaurant (application of BGHZ 51, 91 = NJW 1969, 269).

2. Evidence and proof of fault in cases under § 823 II BGB.

Facts

After the wedding breakfast held at the second defendant's restaurant on 29 July 1989, the plaintiff and some of the 54 guests suffered from salmonella poisoning. Germs of *salmonella enteritis* were later found not only in the

---

* English version by Tony Weir.

vanilla ice-cream but also in the pudding and custard prepared the previous evening by the first defendant and her daughter, who were found to be carriers of salmonella. The plaintiff claimed back the DM 3,000 she had paid the second defendant for the wedding feast; from both defendants she claimed damages for pain and suffering in the amount of DM 1,500 and a further DM 800 because the start of the honeymoon was delayed for four days by reason of the illness.

The Landgericht held both defendants jointly and severally liable for DM 1,500 as damages for pain and suffering, but rejected the rest of the claim. All parties appealed to the Oberlandesgericht, which ordered the second defendant to repay the DM 3,000 paid for the wedding feast, but rejected the rest of the claim. On the plaintiff's appeal the decision rejecting the claim for damages for pain and suffering against the second defendant was vacated. The second defendant's ancillary appeal was rejected.

Reasons

A. [Procedural.]

B. The court below dismissed the claim for damages for pain and suffering against both defendants.

It held that the first defendant was not liable under §§ 823 I, II BGB in conjunction with § 230 Criminal Code and/or § 8 LMBG for serving meals contaminated with salmonella, because the plaintiff could adduce no proof that the first defendant was at fault. According to the experts' reports, there were three ways the salmonella could have got into the pudding: from the hands of the salmonella-carriers, from the equipment used in making the pudding or from the ingredients used, especially the eggs. It could be neither proved nor disproved that the salmonella got into the pudding from the hands of the first defendant or her daughter. The rules regarding the burden of proof in cases of product liability did not affect the first defendant since she was not the owner of the restaurant. Nor did they affect the second defendant, since they are inapplicable to the owners of small family businesses, where proof of the subjective elements of delict is not particularly difficult: it is relatively simple to make a pudding and to understand how it is made. Furthermore, the plaintiff could sue the second defendant on the basis of the contract between them. The second defendant could not be made liable under § 831 BGB, for he had shown that he was free from fault as regards the conduct of his wife and daughter. As against this, the claim that the second defendant return the money paid for the wedding feast was allowed on the basis of § 635 BGB. The second defendant had failed to prove that neither he nor any of those who helped him perform the contract were responsible for the salmonella, for it was possible that his wife or daughter had been salmonella carriers before they started to prepare the pudding, and should therefore have washed their hands more carefully. Although there was nothing wrong with the rest of the meal and only a few of the guests were rendered ill, the entire sum paid could be reclaimed since the feast was to be regarded as a single event.

The court below rejected the claim for damages in respect of the lost honeymoon as not representing an economic loss.

II. The plaintiff's appeal.

1. The plaintiff's appeal from the dismissal of his claim for damages for pain and suffering against the second defendant is justified (a), but the court below was right to reject the similar claim against the first defendant (b).

(a) *The second defendant's liability.* The reasons given by the court below for denying the second defendant's liability for the immaterial harm suffered by the plaintiff are not good in law.

(*aa*) In providing food infected with salmonella, the second defendant as owner of the restaurant contributed to the injury to the plaintiff's health. Liability under §§ 823 I, 847 BGB must therefore be considered, as it was by the court below. It is a precondition of liability under these provisions that the defendant be chargeable with some fault. The burden of proof of fault normally lies on the victim, but in the area of product liability the Bundesgerichtshof has developed the exceptional principle that if a product is defective when he puts it into circulation the producer must establish and prove by evidence that he was not at fault as regards the defect in the product which harmed the consumer (BGHZ 51, 91 [103 ff.] = NJW 1969, 269; BGHZ 80, 186 [196 ff.] = NJW 1981, 1603). For the purposes of product liability the second defendant was unquestionably the producer of the meals prepared in his restaurant, so the application of this principle falls for consideration. This is not a case, to use Brüggemeier's words (VersR 1983, 116 ff.) of 'transferring the rules of product liability to the providers of services', for the wedding feast involved much more than the mere provision of services: services were indeed involved, but the main thing was the supply of the meals.

When the burden of proof in the area of product liability was first reversed in the so-called '*chicken-pest*' case (BGHZ 51, 91 = NJW 1969, 269), the Bundesgerichtshof took into account the evidentiary difficulty which a plaintiff normally faces in a suit against a manufacturer. The court based its reversal of the burden of proof on the fact that since the producer oversees the sphere of production and organises the production process and quality control, he is in much the better position ('*näher dran*') to explain what actually happened and to bear the consequences of lack of proof. If the cause of the lack of explanation falls within the producer's area of responsibility, it seems appropriate and fair under these decisions that he bear the risk of being unable to prove that he was not at fault (BGHZ 51, 91 [105] = NJW 1969, 269; for comparable conflicts of interests, see BGHZ 67, 383 [387] = NJW 1977, 501, etc.)

(bb) In the 'chicken-pest' case, which certainly involved industrial production, the court deliberately left open the question whether the risk of inability to disprove fault should also be imposed on the owner of a small business—a family operation or one-man concern—where the methods of production are uncomplicated and simple to understand. In its judgment of 30 April 1991 (BGHZ 114, 284 = NJW 1991, 1948—Aids) the court again declined to decide whether the principle as to proof applies only to industrial mass production, but it did hold it applicable in a case where an infusion solution for use in a hospital became unsterile either during or after the preparation (BGH NJW 1982, 699), and the Eighteenth Civil Senate of the Oberlandesgericht Frankfurt has applied it in a case, rather like the present, of a gypsy salad infected with salmonella in a restaurant (19 February 1979, VersR 1982, 151).

Writers are divided on the question, but by far the majority opinion is that in cases like the present, the burden of proof should be reversed [references]. This court is of the view that there is no compelling reason to exempt small businesses such as personally-run restaurants and cafés from the evidential burden.

The underlying idea which gave rise to this reversal of proof in cases of product liability, namely the consumer's ignorance of how the producer manufactures his products or organises his business, is of general application, whether the business is big or small, the method of production industrial or personal. It is quite true that what happens in a family-run café is more easily understood than what goes on in a factory geared to mass production. It is also true, as the court below noted, that making a pudding is quite a simple operation calling for no specialist knowledge, comprehensible even by the injured customer. But that does not alter the fact that production takes place in the owner's area of control, and that the restaurateur can monitor the process more easily than the customer. He is in the better position to discover and investigate sources of error. The consumer is an outsider who is normally in no position to know how individual dishes are prepared, what ingredients the patron uses or where he obtains them, nor can he tell what steps are taken to maintain hygiene in the kitchen. Given these considerations, it seems right and fair to put on the second defendant the burden of disproving fault.

This court is well aware that it may seem harsh to place the burden of proof on small businesses which cannot be expected to have the same facilities for control as a big industrial concern, but this difference is largely offset by the fact that it is much easier for the owner of a small business than for the manager of a large industrial concern to oversee its organisation, to discover any faults in the system of production and to adduce the necessary proof.

Another consideration is that there are no really satisfactory criteria for distinguishing sensibly between large and small and middle-sized businesses. To go by the number of employees would lead to capricious results, especially as there is often little relation between the size of the workforce and the structure of the enterprise. Indeed, in family and one-man businesses it is often immaterial whether any person outside the family is employed or not.

The Product Liability Act of 1 January 1990, based on principles applicable throughout the EC, does not draw any distinction between large and small businesses or make liability turn on whether the production is industrial or personal [references]. To draw such a distinction in claims for immaterial harm which are not covered by the Act and still fall under § 823 BGB would not be right.

(*cc*) The court below gave a further reason for not reversing the burden of proof in this case, namely that the plaintiff had a contractual claim against the 'producer'. This is an error. The Bundesgerichtshof decided in the '*Schwimmerschalter*' case (BGHZ 67, 359 [362 f.] = NJW 1977, 379) that the reversal of the burden of proof is not excluded by the mere fact that consumer and producer were in contractual relations; to hold otherwise would lead to unacceptably capricious results, as it is often a matter of mere chance whether there is any contract between the victim and the producer, whether any contractual claim has prescribed (§§ 477, 638 BGB) or whether a contractual claim would be barred by an exclusion clause. Cases in the Supreme Court have consistently held that claims in contract and tort co-exist, each following its own rules (BGHZ 67, 359 [362] = NJW 1977, 379; BGHZ 86, 256 [258] = NJW 1983, 810). In the present case, the reversal of the burden of proof in tort cannot depend on whether the plaintiff or other wedding guests have contractual claims for damages against the second defendant.

The court below was therefore wrong to hold that the plaintiff had the burden of proving that the second defendant failed to show the care required by the circumstances. It should rather have inquired whether the second defendant had managed to exculpate himself.

(*dd*) The mere fact that the food provided for the wedding guests was infected with salmonella does not of itself demonstrate any fault on the part of the second defendant. As has been said, the court below was unable to determine how the salmonella got into the pudding and custard, in which it was undoubtedly present, whether from the eggs or some other source. In particular, it is not known whether or not the first defendant and her daughter were already carriers of salmonella when they prepared the pudding. Infection from the kitchen equipment, according to the court below, 'could be ruled out', but there is the possibility that the salmonella got into the pudding from ingredients bought in by the second defendant.

In such a case, what matters is what steps the second defendant took to ensure a properly hygienic method of preparation. On this point the court below found, in connection with another matter, that the second defendant had exculpated himself, and the appellant does not question this. But the court below did not advert to the precautions taken by the second defendant to minimise the use of tainted ingredients, or ask what checks the patron of a restaurant should make on the products he buys in. The duties imposed on the producer and retailer of food products are onerous (constant holding, see BGHSt 2, 384 etc.), but only within the limits of what is possible for the defendant. A small business cannot be treated just like a large one (references). This does not relieve the small café proprietor of responsibility towards his guests: if with the means at his disposal he cannot ensure that the food he serves is wholesome, then he may have to stop serving it. In general, however, if he obtains his supplies from a reliable source, he need go in for quality control only when on the particular facts a test is called for. This matter requires further elucidation on remand.

(b) *Liability of the first defendant.* The plaintiff's appeal from the dismissal of his claim for damages for pain and suffering against the first defendant must fail.

(aa) The first defendant cannot be made liable under § 823 I BGB because the plaintiff cannot prove that she was at all at fault in preparing the infected pudding. The mere fact that it was infected does not establish fault. Nor is the burden of proof reversed against the first defendant since she did not own the restaurant and therefore was not the 'producer' of the noxious sweet. Only the owner is affected by such reversal: it does not apply to subordinate employees, nor even to all managers, but only to those whose role and position in the firm is such that they can be seen as its representative [references], especially those with a capital stake in the business, such as partners (see BGH NJW 1975, 1827).

(bb) Nor can the first defendant be made liable under § 823 II BGB in relation to § 21 8 no. 1 of the Food Act. Not only is it doubtful whether she can be said to have 'produced' the pudding, but there was no proof of fault, as the court below was right to find. The appellant blames the defendant for not using a recipe which would have heated the pudding to over 75° and thus have killed all the germs. This does not establish fault. Like the court below, we can leave aside the question whether the risk of salmonella poisoning makes it obligatory for cafés to heat puddings above 75°, for in view of the possibility that the dishes in which the pudding was placed were infected by the hands of the defendant or her daughter, it was not shown that cooking the pudding as recommended by experts would have prevented the spread of the salmonella. Contrary to the view of the appellant, the fact that there was a breach of § 8 Food Act does not imply any negligence on the part of the second defendant. The decisions do hold that where a protective law has been infringed, it is usually for the defendant to assert and prove facts which repel an inference of negligence (BGHZ 51, 91 [103 ff.] = NJW 1969, 269; BGH VersR 1967, 685; BGH NJW 1985, 1774 = VersR 1985, 452, 453), but this only applies when the protective law is so detailed in its prescriptions that one can properly infer that there must have been negligence (BGH VersR 1984, 270 [271]). If the protective law merely prohibits a stated injurious result, the mere fact that such a result occurs is no indication of negligence.

That is the situation here. § 8 Food Act simply forbids the preparation and circulation of noxious food products. It contains no detailed prescriptions of conduct whose neglect might indicate fault, so one cannot infer any fault on the part of the second defendant from the mere fact of the infraction. It follows that the plaintiff must adduce full proof of the intentional or negligent failure by the first defendant to take the precautions required by the circumstances.

2. The appellant must also fail in her appeal against the rejection of her claim for damages for the delay to the honeymoon. The court below was right to deny that this constituted economic harm. As this court held in BGHZ 86, 212 = NJW 1983, 1107, the pleasure of a holiday foregone owing to personal injury is not to be commercialised, though it may be taken into account as an element of damages for pain and suffering . . .

Notes to Cases 43–47

1. Traffic accidents, product liability, medical malpractice: this surely must be the trilogy of tort subjects that attracts most attention these days. (The trilogy would be a tetralogy but for the fact that 'accidents at work' have in some systems (e.g. French, German) effectively been removed from the province of the law of tort.) The practical importance of these topics is indisputable—though the first two are by far the most often litigated. The theoretical importance of these subjects is, *inter alia*, evidenced by the fact

that much of the modern economic analysis of tort law has grown from the working of tort law in the area of the first two topics. The economic point is already obvious in the pioneering judgment of Traynor J. in *Escola* v. *Coca-Cola Bottling Co. of Fresno* 24 Cal. 2d 453, 150 P. 2d 436 (1944); and of course was to become a central theme in such celebrated and controversial books as Calabresi's *The Costs of Accidents* (1970). And as if all this were not enough, product liability sits uneasily on the boundary between contract and tort, in a way which makes the traditional strict dichotomy of these two parts of the law of obligations look more than usually unjustifiable (a favourite theme developed by Professor Atiyah in many of his works).

Not surprisingly the literature on the subject is enormous. In the US, in addition to the two major treatises of Hursh and Bailey, *American Law of Products Liability* (1974) and Furmer and Friedman's *Products Liability* (rev. edn., 1974) (both of which have regularly published supplements) the subject receives particular attention in all the textbooks. Thus Franklin, 482–600 (a particularly good section of this excellent case-book); Epstein, 611–729 ff.; Henderson and Pearson, 707–841 ff.; Posner, 633 ff.; and Prosser, Wade and Schwartz, 696–854 (a most systematic and informative account). Outside the US the literature is poorer but growing. Waddams's *Products Liability* (Toronto, 1974) is a comprehensive but now somewhat dated monograph. Fischer and Powers, *Products Liability: Cases and Materials* contains much up-to-date material and thoughtful comments and questions. Miller and Lovell's *Products Liability* (Toronto, 1977) is the only monograph in English law. Markesinis and Deakin, *Tort Law* (3rd edn. 1994) gives at 522–64 an account of the contract and tort solutions of English law and also cites further literature, while Miller's *Product Liability and Safety Encyclopedia* (1979) addresses itself more to the practitioner (while also quoting many of the European proposals). The German law is discussed in Ch. 2, section A.4(*c*), above, where one can find extensive bibliographical references to German literature. The cases reproduced here must, therefore, be read in close conjunction with the above and these notes are, for reasons of space, kept to a minimum.

2. In this area of the law more than in others, the student of German law will be irresistibly tempted to make comparisons with developments in the US. Many reasons can be adduced to explain this.

First, it is a matter of fact that German academics have used American law quite extensively in their writing in this area of tort law. The interest first manifested itself in the early 1930s when the great Ernest Rabel encouraged two of his most brilliant students—Kessler (subsequently Professor at the Yale Law School) and Wahl—to take note of the emerging American doctrines (*Die Fahrlässigkeit im nordamerikanischen Deliktsrecht* (1932) and

Vertragsansprüche Dritter im französischen Recht (1935) published in vols. 6 and 9 of the *Beiträge zum ausländischen und internationalen Privatrecht*). By the 1960s this approach received further impetus—with the work of Professor Lorenz (in *Festschrift Nottarp* (1961), 59) leading the way—as the belief grew that the richness of American law might be of use to the emerging German law of product liability (Lorenz's many articles on the subject clearly show this influence). The American influence on current European proposals for law reform is also noticeable.

A second reason which invites comparison between German and American (but not English) law is the willingness of both systems to experiment with contractual notions and devices in an attempt to satisfy the ever-growing demands of modern consumers. Thus contractual experiments are discussed in case 43 and the concepts used are explained Ch. 2, section A.4(c), above. This leading case may—to the approval of most commentators—have turned attention away from contract to tort; but contractual solutions—especially in the form of 'implied warranties'—are still alive as case 45 shows. This use of contract, on occasion, offered procedural and substantive advantages to plaintiffs; and it may still provide the better answer in certain cases of damage *to* the product (i.e. cases of purely economic loss). Cf. on this the decision of the US Supreme Court in *East River SS Corp.* v. *Transamerica Delaval* 476 US 858, 106 S. Ct. 2295 and decisions nos. 48–54. But it also has its drawbacks when physical injury or property damage is involved as the Americans discovered after *Henningsen* (*Henningsen* v. *Bloomfield Motors Inc.* 32 NJ 358, 161 A. 2d 69 (1960)). See *Greenman* v. *Yuba Power Products Inc.* 59 Cal. 2d 47, 377 P. 2d 897 (1963).

3. Treating the ultimate purchaser as a third-party beneficiary—as case 45 does—can also involve an obvious fiction (see Traynor's remarks in the *Escola* case, above). But such fictions are impossible in English law where contractual warranties in the absence of any privity and contracts in favour of third parties have been denounced as a result of a rigid adherence to the doctrine of consideration. If such notions were known to English law they would explain in a satisfactory manner cases like *Junior Books Ltd.* v. *Veitchi Co. Ltd.* [1983] AC 520, and avoid some of the problems created by that decision (cf. Weir, *A Casebook on Tort* (5th edn., 1983), 33–4); but to treat the ultimate consumer as a third-party beneficiary of the contract between the manufacturer and the wholesaler or retailer would involve an impossible stretching of that notion (Weir, op. cit., 21).

On the other hand, American law, which has freed itself from the shackles of consideration, accepts the notion of warranty without privity; and section 2–318 of the UCC (reproduced below) expressly authorizes such contractually flavoured actions. As we shall see, its use is considerable where the damage is *to* the product and the usual tort remedies are not (according to the prevailing view) appropriate or available. By means of a short digression, it is also worth noting that the French law of products liability was, for many years, based largely on the extension of the original contractual action between seller and buyer to cover even the ultimate purchaser. (On this see J. Ghestin, *Conformité et garanties dans la vente* (1983) and the earlier contributions of Professors Ghestin and Viney in *La responsabilité des fabricants et distributeurs*, collection of essays published by *Economica* (1975).) The national legislation that has been inspired by the European Directive has now, of course, based liability in tort.

4. The comparison of German and American law also reveals some differences. Some, e.g. the use of civil juries, the contingent fee system of remuneration of attorneys, the absence of a developed welfare system, the role of the pro-plaintiff bar and judiciary (on which, *inter alia*, see Neely, *The Product Liability Mess* (1988))—may account for larger awards and increased litigation. (John Fleming's *The American Tort Process* (1988) admirably explains how the institutional framework in the USA has influenced the development of American tort law and made it so different from English law.) Others, concerning warning notices, for example, are on questions of emphasis in degree. Yet others may be more apparent than real. In this group one could place the discussions about the *nature* of liability. For, as we have seen in German law, it was, until recently, fault-based liability and not, as now provided by the American *Restatement Second, Tort* § 402A (reproduced below), strict liability. In one sense it is churlish to minimize this difference between the two systems since some German writers (e.g. Kötz) have argued that the reluctance of German law to acknowledge openly a risk-based liability can only help increase costs and complicate matters in an area of the law which is in any event not known for its simplicity. On the other hand even Kötz admits that the burden of proof cast by German law is a *probatio diabolica*, in effect making this a strict liability subject. And in the USA there is by no means unanimity that the introduction of strict liability has led to a decrease in the complexity of product liability litigation. See Ver Steeg, 'Strict Liability and Judicial Resources' 3 *J. Legal Studies* 217 (1974). Moreover, in practice, negligence and strict liability are almost always pleaded in the alternative in a way that would make it a mistake to assert that strict liability has completely displaced the older rules of negligence. See Rheingold, 'Proof of Defect in Product Liability Cases' 38 *Tenn. L. Rev.* 325 (1971). (The main advantage for the plaintiff of winning the case on negligence rather than on strict liability is, of course, that he is entitled to claim huge punitive damages.)

5. The classifications made in German law between defect in construction (cases 43 and 48), defect in design, defect in marketing (warnings etc.) (case 44), and development risks have exact equivalents in American law. Reference must thus be made to the cases extracted and noted in the case-books quoted above, § 1, and in the early exposition of German law (above, Ch. 2, A.4(c)).

15. CONSUMER LEGISLATION AND DEFECTIVE PRODUCTS

(i) *EEC Council Directive* of 25 July 1985, on the approximation of the laws, regulations and administrative provisions of the Member States concerning liability for defective products

THE COUNCIL OF THE EUROPEAN COMMUNITIES,

Having regard to the Treaty establishing the European Economic Community, and in particular Article 100 thereof,

Having regard to the proposal from the Commission,

Having regard to the opinion of the European Parliament,

Having regard to the opinion of the Economic and Social Committee,

Whereas approximation of the laws of the Member States concerning the liability of the producer for damage caused by the defectiveness of his products is necessary because the existing divergences may distort competition and affect the movement of goods within the common market and entail a differing degree of protection of the consumer against damage caused by a defective product to his health or property;

Whereas liability without fault on the part of the producer is the sole means of adequately solving the problem, peculiar to our age of increasing technicality, of a fair apportionment of the risks inherent in modern techno-logical production;

Whereas liability without fault should apply only to movables which have been industrially produced; whereas, as a result, it is appropriate to exclude liability for agricultural products and game, except where they have under-gone a processing of an industrial nature which could cause a defect in these products; whereas the liability provided for in this Directive should also apply to movables which are used in the construction of immovables or are installed in immovables;

Whereas protection of the consumer requires that all producers involved in the production process should be made liable, in so far as their finished product, component part or any raw material supplied by them was defec-tive; whereas, for the same reason, liability should extent to importers of products into the Community and to persons who present themselves as producers by affixing their name, trade mark or other distinguishing feature or who supply a product the producer of which cannot be identified;

Whereas, in situations where several persons are liable for the same damage, the protection of the consumer requires that the injured person should be able to claim full compensation for the damage from any one of them;

Whereas, to protect the physical well-being and property of the consumer, the defectiveness of the product should be determined by reference not to its fitness for use but to the lack of the safety which the public at large is entitled to expect; whereas the safety is assessed by excluding any misuse of the product not reasonable under the circumstances;

Whereas a fair apportionment of risk between the injured person and the producer implies that the producer should be able to free himself from liability if he furnishes proof as to the existence of certain exonerating circumstances;

Whereas the protection of the consumer requires that the liability of the producer remains unaffected by acts or omissions of other persons having contributed to cause the damage; whereas, however, the contributory negligence of the injured person may be taken into account to reduce or disallow such liability;

Whereas the protection of the consumer requires compensation for death and personal injury as well as compensation for damage to property; whereas the latter should nevertheless be limited to goods for private use or consumption and be subject to a deduction of a lower threshold of a fixed amount in order to avoid litigation in an excessive number of cases; whereas this Directive should not prejudice compensation for pain and suffering and other non-material damages payable, where appropriate, under the law applicable to the case;

Whereas a uniform period of limitation for the bringing of action for compensation is in the interests both of the injured person and of the producer;

Whereas products age in the course of time, higher safety standards are developed and the state of science and technology progresses; whereas, therefore, it would not be reasonable to make the producer liable for an unlimited period for the defectiveness of his product; whereas, therefore, liability should expire after a reasonable length of time, without prejudice to claims pending at law;

Whereas, to achieve effective protection of consumers, no contractual derogation should be permitted as regards the liability of the producer in relation to the injured person;

Whereas under the legal systems of the Member States an injured party may have a claim for damages based on grounds of contractual liability or on grounds of non-contractual liability other than that provided for in this Directive; in so far as these provisions also serve to attain the objective of effective protection of consumers, they should remain unaffected by this

Directive; whereas, in so far as effective protection of consumers in the sector of pharmaceutical products is already also attained in a Member State under a special liability system, claims based on this system should similarly remain possible;

Whereas, to the extent that liability for nuclear injury or damage is already covered in all Member States by adequate special rules, it has been possible to exclude damage of this type from the scope of this Directive;

Whereas, since the exclusion of primary agricultural products and game from the scope of this Directive may be felt, in certain Member States, in view of what is expected for the protection of consumers, to restrict unduly such protection, it should be possible for a Member State to extend liability to such products;

Whereas, for similar reasons, the possibility offered to a producer to free himself from liability if he proves that the state of scientific and technical knowledge at the time when he put the product into circulation was not such as to enable the existence of a defect to be discovered may be felt in certain Member States to restrict unduly the protection of the consumer; whereas it should therefore be possible for a Member State to maintain in its legislation or to provide by new legislation that this exonerating circumstance is not admitted; whereas, in the case of new legislation, making use of this derogation should, however, be subject to a Community stand-still procedure, in order to raise, if possible, the level of protection in a uniform manner throughout the Community.

Whereas, taking into account the legal traditions in most of the Member States, it is inappropriate to set any financial ceiling on the producer's liability without fault; whereas, in so far as there are, however, differing traditions, it seems possible to admit that a Member State may derogate from the principle of unlimited liability by providing a limit for the total liability of the producer for damage resulting from a death or personal injury and caused by identical items with the same defect, provided that this limit is established at a level sufficiently high to guarantee adequate protection of the consumer and the correct functioning of the common market;

Whereas the harmonization resulting from this cannot be total at the present stage, but opens the way towards greater harmonization; whereas it is therefore necessary that the Council receive at regular intervals, reports from the Commission on the application of this Directive, accompanied, as the case may be, by appropriate proposals;

Whereas it is particularly important in this respect that a re-examination be carried out of those parts of the Directive relating to the derogations open to the Member States, at the expiry of a period of sufficient length to gather practical experience on the effects of these derogations on the protection of consumers and on the functioning of the common market,

HAS ADOPTED THIS DIRECTIVE:

Article 1

The producer shall be liable for damage caused by a defect in his product.

Article 2

For the purpose of this Directive 'product' means all movables, with the exception of primary agricultural products and game, even though incorporated into another movable or into an immovable. 'Primary agricultural products' means the products of the soil, of stock-farming and of fisheries, excluding products which have undergone initial processing. 'Product' includes electricity.

Article 3

1. 'Producer' means the manufacturer of a finished product, the producer of any raw material or the manufacturer of a component part and any person who, by putting his name, trade mark or other distinguishing feature on the product presents himself as its producer.

2. Without prejudice to the liability of the producer, any person who imports into the Community a product for sale, hire, leasing or any form of distribution in the course of his business shall be deemed to be a producer within the meaning of this Directive and shall be responsible as a producer.

3. Where the producer of the product cannot be identified, each supplier of the product shall be treated as its producer unless he informs the injured person, within a reasonable time, of the identity of the producer or of the person who supplied him with the product. The same shall apply, in the case of an imported product, if this product does not indicate the identity of the importer referred to in paragraph 2, even if the name of the producer is indicated.

Article 4

The injured person shall be required to prove the damage, the defect and the causal relationship between defect and damage.

Article 5

Where, as a result of the provisions of this Directive, two or more persons are liable for the same damage, they shall be liable jointly and severally, without prejudice to the provisions of national law concerning the rights of contribution or recourse.

Article 6

1. A product is defective when it does not provide the safety which a person is entitled to expect, taking all circumstances into account, including:

(*a*)   the presentation of the product;

(*b*)   the use to which it could reasonably be expected that the product would be put;

(*c*)   the time when the product was put into circulation.

2. A product shall not be considered defective for the sole reason that a better product is subsequently put into circulation.

Article 7

The producer shall not be liable as a result of this Directive if he proves:

(*a*)   that he did not put the product into circulation; or

(*b*)   that, having regard to the circumstances, it is probable that the defect which caused the damage did not exist at the time when the product was put into circulation by him or that this defect came into being afterwards; or

(*c*)   that the product was neither manufactured by him for sale or any form of distribution for economic purpose nor manufactured or distributed by him in the course of his business; or

(*d*)   that the defect is due to compliance of the product with mandatory regulations issued by the public authorities; or

(*e*)   that the state of scientific and technical knowledge at the time when he put the product into circulation was not such as to enable the existence of the defect to be discovered; or

(*f*)   in the case of a manufacturer of a component, that the defect is attributable to the design of the product in which the component has been fitted or to the instructions given by the manufacturer of the product.

Article 8

1. Without prejudice to the provisions of national law concerning the right of contribution or recourse, the liability of the producer shall not be reduced when the damage is caused both by a defect in product and by the act or omission of a third party.

2. The liability of the producer may be reduced or disallowed when, having regard to all the circumstances, the damage is caused both by a defect in the product and by the fault of the injured person or any person for whom the injured person is responsible.

Article 9

For the purpose of Article 1, 'damage' means:

(*a*) damage caused by death or by personal injuries;

(*b*) damage to, or destruction of, any item of property other than the defective product itself, with a lower threshold of 500 ECU, provided that the item of property;

(i) is of a type ordinarily intended for private use or consumption, and

(ii) was used by the injured person mainly for his own private use or consumption.

This article shall be without prejudice to national provisions relating to non-material damage.

Article 10

1. Member States shall provide in their legislation that a limitation period of three years shall apply to proceedings for the recovery of damages as provided for in this Directive. The limitation period shall begin to run from the day on which the plaintiff became aware, or should reasonably have become aware, of the damage, the defect and the identity of the producer.

2. The laws of Member States regulating suspension or interruption of the limitation period shall not be affected by this Directive.

Article 11

Member States shall provide in their legislation that the rights conferred upon the injured person pursuant to this Directive shall be extinguished upon the expiry of a period of 10 years from the date on which the producer put into circulation the actual product which caused the damage, unless the injured person has in the meantime instituted proceedings against the producer.

Article 12

The liability of the producer arising from this Directive may not, in relation to the injured person, be limited or excluded by a provision limiting his liability or exempting him from liability.

Article 13

This Directive shall not affect any rights which an injured person may have according to the rules of the law of contractual or non-contractual liability or a special liability system existing at the moment when this Directive is notified.

Article 14

This Directive shall not apply to injury or damage arising from nuclear accidents and covered by international conventions ratified by the Member States.

Article 15

1. Each Member State may:
(*a*) by way of derogation from Article 2, provide in its legislation that within the meaning of Article 1 of this Directive 'product' also means primary agricultural products and game;
(*b*) by way of derogation from Article 7(*e*), maintain or, subject to the procedure set out in paragraph 2 of this Article, provide in this legislation that the producer shall be liable even if he proves that the state of scientific and technical knowledge at the time when he put the product into circulation was not such as to enable the existence of a defect to be discovered.

2. A Member State wishing to introduce the measure specified in paragraph 1(*b*) shall communicate the text of the proposed measure to the Commission. The Commission shall inform the other Member States thereof.

The Member State concerned shall hold the proposed measure in abeyance for nine months after the Commission is informed and provided that in the meantime the Commission has not submitted to the Council a proposal amending this Directive on the relevant matter. However, if within three months of receiving the said information, the Commission does not advise the Member State concerned that it intends submitting such a proposal to the Council, the Member State may take the proposed measure immediately.

If the Commission does submit to the Council such a proposal amending this Directive within the aforementioned nine months, the Member State concerned shall hold the proposed measure in abeyance for a further period of 18 months from the date on which the proposal is submitted.

3. Ten years after the date of notification of this Directive, the Commission shall submit to the Council a report on the effect that rulings by the courts as to the application of Article 7(*e*) and of paragraph 1(*b*) of this Article have on consumer protection and the functioning of the common market. In the light of this report the Council, acting on a proposal from the Commission and pursuant to the terms of Article 100 of the Treaty, shall decide whether to repeat Article 7(*e*).

Article 16

1. Any Member State may provide that a producer's total liability for damage resulting from a death or personal injury and caused by identical items with the same defect shall be limited to an amount which may not be less than 70 million ECU.

2. Ten years after the date of notification of this Directive, the Commission shall submit to the Council a report on the effect on consumer protection and the functioning of the common market of the implementation of the financial limit on liability by those Member States which have used the option provided for in paragraph 1. In the light of this report the Council, acting on a proposal from the Commission and pursuant to the terms of Article 100 of the Treaty, shall decide whether to repeal paragraph 1.

Article 17

This Directive shall not apply to products put into circulation before the date on which the provisions referred to in Article 19 enter into force.

Article 18

1. For the purposes of this Directive, the ECU shall be that defined by Regulation (EEC) no. 3180/78, as amended by Regulation (EEC) no. 2626/84. The equivalent in national currency shall initially be calculated at the rate obtaining on the date of adoption of this Directive.

2. Every five years the Council, acting on a proposal from the Commission, shall examine and, if need be, revise the amounts in this Directive, in the light of economic and monetary trends in the Community.

Article 19

1. Member States shall bring into force, not later than three years from the date of notification of this Directive, the laws, regulations and administrative provisions necessary to comply with this Directive. They shall forthwith inform the Commission thereof.

2. The procedure set out in Article 15(2) shall apply from the date of notification of this Directive.

Article 20

Member States shall communicate to the Commission the texts of the main provisions of national law which they subsequently adopt in the field governed by this Directive.

Article 21

Every five years the Commission shall present a report to the Council on the application of this Directive and, if necessary, shall submit appropriate proposals to it.

Article 22

This Directive is addressed to the Member States.

(ii) The German Product Liability Act of 15 December 1989*

§ 1. *Liability*

(1) If, as a result of a defect of a product, a human being is killed, is injured or affected in his health, or a thing is damaged, the producer† is obliged to compensate the person who suffered the damage for the ensuing harm. In the case of damage to property this rule applies only if an object other than the defective product is damaged and if this object is normally intended for private use or consumption and has been used by the injured party primarily for this purpose.

(2) The obligation to pay damages is excluded if:

1. the producer has not put the product into circulation;
2. it is to be assumed, having regard to the circumstances, that the product was not yet defective when it was put into circulation;
3. the producer has neither manufactured the product for sale or for any other form of distribution for a consideration nor has manufactured or distributed it in the course of his occupational activities;
4. the defect is due to the fact that at the time when the producer put the product into circulation it complied with mandatory legal provisions;
5. the defect could not yet be discerned, having regard to the state of art [literally: science and technique] at the time when the producer put the product concerned into circulation.

(3) In addition, the maker of the part of the product is exempt from the obligation to pay compensation if the defect was caused by the construction of the product into which the part was inserted or by the instructions of the maker of the product. Sentence 1 applies *mutatis mutandis* to a producer of a basic substance (*Grundstoff*).

(4) The person who has suffered the harm has the burden of proving the defect and its causal connection with the harm. In a dispute as to whether

---

* Translated by Kurt Lipstein. According to § 19 of this Act the new regime came into force on 1 January 1990.

† Unless otherwise indicated, the word '*Hersteller*' has been rendered, here and elsewhere in the book, interchangeably as producer or manufacturer.

the obligation to pay compensation is excluded according to sub-paragraphs (2) or (3), the producer bears the burden of proof.

§ 2. *Products*

Product in the meaning of this Act includes every moveable object, even if it forms part of another moveable or of an immovable as well as electricity. Produce of the soil, of animal husbandry, bee-farming, fishing, and hunting are exempt, unless they have undergone the first stage of processing.

§ 3. *Defects*

(1) A product is defective if it does not provide that degree of safety which can be justifiably expected, having regard to all the circumstances, in particular

(*a*) its presentation;
(*b*) its use which may be reasonably expected;
(*c*) the time when it was put into circulation.

(2) A product is not defective for the sole reason that later on an improved product was put into circulation.

§ 4. *Producer*

(1) Producer in the meaning of this Act is the person who has manufactured the final product, a basic substance or a component part of the product. Furthermore, whoever represents himself as a producer by attaching his name, trademark or other distinctive mark is regarded as the producer.

(2) Notwithstanding sub-paragraph 1, a person is also treated as a producer who, within the range of his commercial activity, imports into the area covered by the Treaty for the Establishment of the European Economic Community a product with a view to sale, hire, hire-purchase or any other form of distribution.

(3) If the manufacturer of the product cannot be ascertained, every distributor is treated as its producer, unless he indicates to the injured party within one month of receiving the latter's relevant request who is the producer or the person who supplied him with the product. The same applies to an imported product in respect of which the person referred to in sub-paragraph (2) cannot be ascertained, even if the name of the producer is known.

§ 5. *Several tortfeasors*

If several producers are co-liable for the damage, they are jointly and severally liable. Between the debtors themselves, in the absence of provisions to the contrary, the liability to pay compensation and its extent depends upon the circumstances, in particular as to whether the damage has been caused predominantly by one or the other of them; furthermore §§ 421–5, 426 sub-paragraph 1, second sentence and sub-paragraph 2 BGB apply.

§ 6. *Reduction of liability*
(1) If the injured party is partly to be blamed for having caused the damage, § 254 BGB applies; if an object has been damaged, any blame attached to the person exercising physical control over it is treated as that of the injured party.

(2) If the damage has been caused at the same time by a defect of the product and by the act of a third party, the liability of the producer is not reduced. § 5 second sentence applies.

§ 7. *Extent of damages in case of death*
(1) In case of death, the expenses incurred in an attempt to restore health must be compensated together with the pecuniary loss suffered by the deceased in consequence of the loss or reduction of his earning capacity or of his increased needs. Damages also include the funeral expenses payable to the person responsible for them.

(2) If at the time of injury the deceased was connected with a third party by a relationship which rendered him, actually or potentially, liable by law to maintain that person, and if the third party lost his right to maintenance in consequence of the death, he is entitled to damages in so far as the deceased during the period of his life expectancy would have been liable to maintain him. This liability arises also if the third party was conceived at the time of death but not yet born.

§ 8. *Extent of damages in case of injury to the person*
If injury was caused to the body or to health, the expenses incurred in restoring health must be compensated together with the pecuniary loss suffered by the injured party resulting from the temporary or permanent loss or reduction of his earning capacity or from his increased needs.

§ 9. *Damages by way of periodical payments*
(1) Damage arising in the future as a result of the total or partial loss of earning capacity and of increased needs together with the damages payable to a third party in accordance with § 7 sub-paragraph (2) is to be compensated by periodical payments.

(2) § 843 sub-paragraphs 2–4 BGB apply.

§ 10. *Maximum rate of damages*
(1) If death or injury to the person has been caused by a product or by prod-

ucts of the same kind affected by the same defect, the liability to pay damages is limited to a maximum of DM 160 million.

(2) If the damages payable to several injured parties exceed the maximum rate set out in sub-paragraph (1), the individual damages are reduced in proportion of their total to the maximum rate allowable.

§ 11. *Extent of compensation in case of damage to goods*
Where goods are damaged, the person who suffered the damage has to bear the loss up to DM 1125.

§ 12. *Limitation of actions*
(1) An action according to § 1 shall not be brought after the expiration of three years from the time when the claimant knew or could have known of the damage and of the person liable to pay damages.

(2) Time does not run if negotiations are pending between the persons liable to pay and to receive compensation until the continuation of the negotiations has been abandoned.

(3) Furthermore, the provisions of the BGB relating to limitation of actions apply.

§ 13. *Extinction of claims*
(1) A claim according to § 1 is extinguished after the expiration of ten years from the date when the producer against whom the claim is made has put the product into circulation. This does not apply where a law suit or summary proceedings are pending.

(2) Sub-paragraph (1), sentence 1 does not apply to a claim which has become *res judicata* or to a claim covered by another executory title. The same applies to a claim which is the subject-matter of an out-of-court settlement or which has been recognised by a legal act.

§ 14. *Mandatory character*
The liability of a producer in accordance with the Act cannot be excluded or restricted in advance. Any agreement to the contrary is void.

§ 15. *Liability according to other legal provisions*
(1) If, due to the application of a pharmaceutical product destined for human use and sold in the area of application of the Pharmaceutical Products Act, a person is killed or his body or health otherwise affected, the provisions of the Product Liability Act will not be applicable.

(2) Liability in accordance with other provisions remains unaffected.

Notes

The Act establishes a parallel regime of liability which can be similar or more extensive to that found in the 'Common law' (based on § 823 BGB and described above, Ch. 2, 4 (*c*)). Under the Act, liability depends on the product being 'defective', i.e. not meeting the degree of safety normally required from such a product. Whether this will *in practice* lead to different results than the case law built on § 823 I BGB is a matter of some doubt. (See Kötz, *Deliktsrecht*, nos. 460–1). § 2 of the Act provides a list of situations where liability can be excluded. § 4 is worthy of special attention since it defines the persons likely to be liable; and it *may* be rendering non-manufacturers more extensively liable than they are under the 'Common law' regime. Finally, note that (like all German strict liability statutes) the Act sets limits to the amounts of damages that can be claimed under it. Compensation for pain and suffering (immaterial damages) also presupposes that the claim is based on the *tort* provisions of the Code so they are *not* claimable under the Act. For a fuller discussion see references given in Ch. 3, 5(*b*). It is, of course, left to the plaintiff to decide whether he will base his claim on the 'Common law' regime and/or that established by the Act.

(iii) The [UK] Consumer Protection Act 1987

I. *Product Liability*

1 (1) This Part shall have effect for the purpose of making such provision as is necessary in order to comply with the product liability Directive and shall be construed accordingly.

(2) In this part, except in so far as the context otherwise requires

'agricultural produce' means any produce of the soil, of stock-farming or of fisheries;

'dependant' and 'relative' have the same meaning as they have in, respectively, the Fatal Accidents Act 1976 and the Damages (Scotland) Act 1976;

'producer', in relation to a product, means

(a) the person who manufactured it;

(b) in the case of a substance which has not been manufactured but has been won or abstracted, the person who won or abstracted it;

(c) in the case of a product which has not been manufactured, won or abstracted but essential characteristics of which are attributable to an industrial or other process having been carried out (for example, in relation to agricultural produce), the person who carried out that process;

'product' means any goods or electricity and (subject to subsection (3) below) includes a product which is comprised in another product, whether by virtue of being a component part or raw material or otherwise; and 'the product liability Directive' means the Directive of the Council of the European Communities, dated 25 July 1985, (no. 85/374/EEC) on the approximation of the laws, regulations and administrative provisions of the member States concerning liability for defective products.

(3) For the purposes of this Part a person who supplies any product in which products are comprised, whether by virtue of being component parts or raw materials or otherwise, shall not be treated by reason only of his supply of that product as supplying any of the products so comprised.

2 (1) Subject to the following provisions of this Part, where any damage is caused wholly or partly by a defect in a product, every person to whom subsection (2) below applies shall be liable for the damage.

(2) This subsection applies to

(a) the producer of the product;

(b) any person who, by putting his name on the product or using a trade mark or other distinguishing mark in relation to the product, has held himself out to be the producer of the product;

(c) any person who has imported the product into a member State from a place outside the member States in order, in the course of any business of his, to supply it to another.

(3) Subject as aforesaid, where any damage is caused wholly or partly by a defect in a product, any person who supplied the product (whether to the person who suffered the damage, to the producer of any product in which the product in question is comprised or to any other person) shall be liable for the damage if—

(a) the person who suffered the damage requests the supplier to identify one or more of the persons (whether still in existence or not) to whom subsection (2) above applies in relation to the product;

(b) that request is made within a reasonable period after the damage occurs and at a time when it is not reasonably practicable for the person making the request to identify all those persons; and

(c) the supplier fails, within a reasonable period after receiving the request, either to comply with the request or to identify the person who supplied the product to him.

(4) Neither subsection (2) nor subsection (3) above shall apply to a person in respect of any defect in any game or agricultural produce if the only supply of the game or produce by that person to another was at a time when it had not undergone an industrial process.

(5) Where two or more persons are liable by virtue of this Part for the same damage, their liability shall be joint and several.

(6) This section shall be without prejudice to any liability arising otherwise than by virtue of this Part.

3 (1) Subject to the following provisions of this section, there is a defect in a product for the purposes of this Part if the safety of the product is not such as persons generally are entitled to expect; and for those purposes 'safety', in relation to a product, shall include safety with respect to products comprised in that product and safety in the context of risks of damage to property, as well as in the context of risks of death or personal injury.

(2) In determining for the purposes of subsection (1) above what persons generally are entitled to expect in relation to a product all the circumstances shall be taken into account, including

(a) the manner in which, and purposes for which, the product has been marketed, its get-up, the use of any mark in relation to the product and any instructions for, or warnings with respect to, doing or refraining from doing anything with or in relation to the product;

(b) what might reasonably be expected to be done with or in relation to the product; and

(c) the time when the product was supplied by its producer to another;

and nothing in this section shall require a defect to be inferred from the fact alone that the safety of a product which is supplied after that time is greater than the safety of the product in question.

4 (1) In any civil proceedings by virtue of this Part against any person ('the person proceeded against') in respect of a defect in a product it shall be a defence for him to show

(a) that the defect is attributable to compliance with any requirement imposed by or under any enactment or with any Community obligation; or

(b) that the person proceeded against did not at any time supply the product to another; or

(c) that the following conditions are satisfied, that is to say
   (i) that the only supply of the product to another by the person proceeded against was otherwise than in the course of a business of that person's; and
   (ii) that section 2(2) above does not apply to that person or applies to him by virtue only of things done otherwise than with a view to profit; or

(d) that the defect did not exist in the product at the relevant time; or

(e) that the state of scientific and technical knowledge at the relevant time was not such that a producer of products of the same description as the product in question might be expected to have discovered the defect if it had existed in his products while they were under his control; or

(f) that the defect
    (i) constituted a defect in a product ('the subsequent product') in which the product in question had been comprised; and
    (ii) was wholly attributable to the design of the subsequent product or to compliance by the producer of the product in question with instructions given by the producer of the subsequent product.

(2) In this section 'the relevant time', in relation to electricity, means the time at which it was generated, being a time before it was transmitted or distributed, and in relation to any other product, means

(a) if the person proceeded against is a person to whom subsection (2) of section 2 above applies in relation to the product, the time when he supplied the product to another;

(b) if that subsection does not apply to that person in relation to the product, the time when the product was last supplied by a person to whom that subsection does apply in relation to the product.

5 (1) Subject to the following provisions of this section, in this Part 'damage' means death or personal injury or any loss of or damage to any property (including land).

(2) A person shall not be liable under section 2 above in respect of any defect in a product for the loss of or any damage to the product itself or for the loss of or any damage to the whole or any part of any product which has been supplied with the product in question comprised in it.

(3) A person shall not be liable under section 2 above for any loss of or damage to any property which, at the time it is lost or damaged, is not

(a) of a description of property ordinarily intended for private use, occupation or consumption; and

(b) intended by the person suffering the loss or damage mainly for his own private use, occupation or consumption.

(4) No damages shall be awarded to any person by virtue of this Part in respect of any loss of or damage to any property if the amount which would fall to be so awarded to that person, apart from this subsection and any liability for interest, does not exceed £275.

(5) In determining for the purposes of this Part who has suffered any loss of or damage to property and when any such loss or damage occurred, the loss

or damage shall be regarded as having occurred at the earliest time at which a person with an interest in the property had knowledge of the material facts about the loss or damage.

(6) For the purposes of subsection (5) above the material facts about any loss of or damage to any property are such facts about the loss or damage as would lead a reasonable person with an interest in the property to consider the loss or damage sufficiently serious to justify his instituting proceedings for damages against a defendant who did not dispute liability and was able to satisfy a judgment.

(7) For the purposes of subsection (5) above a person's knowledge includes knowledge which he might reasonably have been expected to acquire

(a) from facts observable or ascertainable by him; or
(b) from facts ascertainable by him with the help of appropriate expert advice which it is reasonable for him to seek;

but a person shall not be taken by virtue of this subsection to have knowledge of a fact ascertainable by him only with the help of expert advice unless he has failed to take all reasonable steps to obtain (and, where appropriate, to act on) that advice.

(8) Subsections (5) to (7) above shall not extend to Scotland.

6 (1) Any damage for which a person is liable under section 2 above shall be deemed to have been caused

(a) for the purposes of the Fatal Accidents Act 1976, by that person's wrongful act, neglect or default;
(b) for the purposes of section 3 of the Law Reform (Miscellaneous Provisions) (Scotland) Act 1940 (contribution among joint wrongdoers), by that person's wrongful act or negligent act or omission;
(c) for the purposes of section 1 of the Damages (Scotland) Act 1976 (rights of relatives of a deceased), by that person's act or omission; and
(d) for the purposes of Part II of the Administration of Justice Act 1982 (damages for personal injuries, etc., Scotland), by an act or omission giving rise to liability in that person to pay damages.

(2) Where

(a) a person's death is caused wholly or partly by a defect in a product, or a person dies after suffering damage which has been so caused;
(b) a request such as mentioned in paragraph (a) of subsection (3) of section 2 above is made to a supplier of the product by that person's personal representatives or, in the case of a person whose death is caused wholly or partly by the defect, by any dependant or relative of that person; and

(c) the conditions specified in paragraphs (b) and (c) of that subsection are satisfied in relation to that request,

this Part shall have effect for the purposes of the Law Reform (Miscellaneous Provisions) Act 1934, the Fatal Accidents Act 1976 and the Damages (Scotland) Act 1976 as if liability of the supplier to that person under that subsection did not depend on that person having requested the supplier to identify certain persons or on the said conditions having been satisfied in relation to a request made by that person.

(3) Section 1 of the Congenital Disabilities (Civil Liability) Act 1976 shall have effect for the purposes of this Part as if

(a) a person were answerable to a child in respect of an occurrence caused wholly or partly by a defect in a product if he is or has been liable under section 2 above in respect of any effect of the occurrence on a parent of the child, or would be so liable if the occurrence caused a parent of the child to suffer damage;

(b) the provisions of this Part relating to liability under section 2 above applied in relation to liability by virtue of paragraph (a) above under the said section 1; and

(c) subsection (6) of the said section 1 (exclusion of liability) were omitted.

(4) Where any damage is caused partly by a defect in a product and partly by the fault of the person suffering the damage, the Law Reform (Contributory Negligence) Act 1945 and section 5 of the Fatal Accidents Act 1976 (contributory negligence) shall have effect as if the defect were the fault of every person liable by virtue of this Part for the damage caused by the defect.

(5) In subsection (4) above 'fault' has the same meaning as in the said Act of 1945.

(6) Schedule 1 to this Act shall have effect for the purpose of amending the Limitation Act 1980 and the Prescription and Limitation (Scotland) Act 1973 in their application in relation to the bringing of actions by virtue of this Part.

(7) It is hereby declared that liability by virtue of this Part is to be treated as liability in tort for the purposes of any enactment conferring jurisdiction on any court with respect to any matter.

(8) Nothing in this Part shall prejudice the operation of section 12 of the Nuclear Installations Act 1965 (rights to compensation for certain breaches of duties confined to rights under that Act).

7 The liability of a person by virtue of this Part to a person who has suffered damage caused wholly or partly by a defect in a product, or to a dependant or relative of such a person, shall not be limited or excluded by any contract term, by any notice or by any other provision.

8 (1) Her Majesty may by Order in Council make such modifications of this Part and of any other enactment (including an enactment contained in the following Parts of this Act, or in an Act passed after this Act) as appear to Her Majesty in Council to be necessary or expedient in consequence of any modification of the product liability Directive which is made at any time after the passing of this Act.

(2) An Order in Council under subsection (1) above shall not be submitted to Her Majesty in Council unless a draft of the Order has been laid before, and approved by a resolution of, each House of Parliament.

9 (1) Subject to subsection (2) below, this Part shall bind the Crown.

(2) The Crown shall not, as regards the Crown's liability by virtue of this Part, be bound by this Part further than the Crown is made liable in tort or in reparation under the Crown Proceedings Act 1947, as that Act has effect from time to time.

(iv) Notes on the consumer protection enactments

1. Individually, each of these texts has inspired many articles in legal journals and many more will no doubt follow. The critical comparison of the texts is, if anything, an even more difficult task and one that cannot be undertaken within the confines of this book. Here, however, are some basic points with the main emphasis naturally being placed on German law (described briefly in section A.4(c) above).

2. The Directive is the progenitor of the three texts reproduced above and is, itself, the result of (*a*) the consumer movement that gained momentum in Europe in the late 1960s and 1970s as well as (*b*) the EC Commission's desire to harmonize the law within the EEC. The first provides the political motive, the second the excuse for the European Community's intervention. Both points are important though the EEC would stress the latter. But have the national laws been harmonized? Cf. for example the attitudes of the Member States towards the defence of the state of art. Existing differences are also (to some extent) maintained where existing laws (e.g. the German Pharmaceuticals Act) are more generous to consumers. Otherwise, has the Directive frozen existing national laws? Put differently, has the national legislator been deprived of the right to pass future legislation that is more gener-

ous to the consumer than is the text of the Directive? And what about national case-law? Can it improve the consumer's lot and remain faithful to the spirit of the Directive?

3. The Directive creates no direct rights but obliges the Member States to implement it by national laws. England and Germany are among the countries which have done so. But what if the text of a national law departs from the text (and intentions) of the Directive? For example, s. 4(1)(c) of the UK Act says that the producer is not liable if he proves 'that the state of scientific and technical knowledge at the relevant time was not such that a producer of products of the same description as the product in question might be expected to have discovered the defect if it had existed in his products while they were under his control'. On the other hand, Art. 7(c) of the Directive gives the producer immunity if he proves 'that the state of scientific and technical knowledge at the time when he put the product into circulation was not such as to enable the existence of the defect to be discovered'. The Confederation of British Industry prefers the subjective wording of the Act; the Directive, by contrast, has opted for an objective wording, while the UK government has tried to argue that *its* wording states more clearly the intentions of the Directive (see Lord Lucas of Chilworth, HL Deb. vol. 487 c. 785 (14 May 1987)). What do you think? Other (permissible) derogations include the exemption from strict liability for the producers of primary agricultural products (where the farming lobby is strong, as it is in England, this derogation has not been taken up) and the possibility of limiting damages for a particular effect (10 million ECU, or about £40 million).

4. The Confederation of British Industry strongly and successfully opposed the abandonment of the defence of the state of art. One of its arguments was that inventiveness would be stifled and industry would suffer. Has the German pharmaceutical industry—one of the best in the world—suffered by adopting the opposite view? Did anyone do a comparative study of the two systems, look at the insurance situation, study the market? Or do British businessmen like British lawyers go into a tizzy when the words change and reforms are mentioned?

5. The Product Liability law now has many sources. As stated, the old tort rules to some extent remain in force; and they are expected to co-exist along with the new regime. Indeed, the old law is still relevant for damages *to* products and other forms of economic loss. Additionally, contract law remains alive; and here not only liability is strict; it is also not subject to any state of art defence. The different sources of product liability law have also given rise to much confusion in the USA as a quick glance at any specialized book will reveal.

6. Each European state has, following its own drafting techniques, implemented the Directive in a different way. Assuming that this was quite genuinely inevitable and preferable to giving the text of the Directive direct effect, what should happen when there is a significant difference between the wording of the Directive and a national enactment? The Directive, for example, excludes from the regime of strict liability primary agricultural products so long as they have not undergone 'initial processing'. The UK legislation, on the other hand, has excluded from strict liability agricultural produce before it has undergone an 'industrial process'. Does the use of hormones, pesticides, fertilizers, additives, etc. remove the exemption and subject these products to strict liability? In the case of the above examples the answer is probably a negative one; but the exception for its strict liability regime must surely be lost when, say, vegetables or fruit are frozen in a factory. Compare the wording of the English, French, and German Acts with the Directive and decide which of them is closer to the 'model'.

7. In one of the best Hamlyn Lectures ever given, Professor Honoré thundered that 'England does not have a genuine legal culture'. Anyone who compares academic law in our Universities at the turn of the century with, say, the situation in Germany at that time will immediately appreciate the validity of this condemnation. But Professor Honoré attributes this state of affairs in part to our inability to make laws 'as clear, elegant, and rational as they could be'. (*The Quest for Security: Employees, Tenants, Wives* (1982), 119.) True though this may be about Common law statutes, what do you think of *modern* civil law statutes? The French text (still not accepted by Parliament) is exceptionally long and complicated. It is also inelegant in that it purports to add 29 product liability articles to the French Civil Code when a mere 5 cover the entire law of torts. Are the French (and the Germans for that matter) following our (bad) example? Compare in this respect the equally long-winded French Road Traffic Act of 1987.

8. There is no doubt that the Directive and its national progenies will add to the complexity of the law; but will the new enactment make it substantially different from how it was before this costly exercise was undertaken? For countries like Germany and France the answer is, on the whole, negative. The Italians and the Greeks, however, may find that membership of the EC also carries with it some responsibilities. Nevertheless, the Directive does take a more open stand on some issues. Here are some:

(*a*) Liability is now strict in theory as well as in practice (except for development risks in non-pharmaceutical products). All that the victim will have to show is that the product was defective and the defect caused his injury. This is not to say that all will be plain sailing since (a) causation (despite presumptions) may be difficult to prove and (b) the Directive (and the national laws) retain quite an array of defences. For details see the texts.

(b) When is a product defective? Note again the different national formulations as well as the Directive's emphasis on 'user expectations'. Can American case-law help in this respect?

(c) Finally, note some new, technical (and from the consumer's point of view) improved rules. Thus the German Act (to some extent) clarifies who is subject to the new strict liability regime. Clearly manufacturers of finished products, component parts, and new materials are subject to the new regime (§ 4 I of the 1989 Act reflecting Art. 3(1) of the Directive). But the Directive (Art. 3(1)) and the 1989 Act (§ 4 I) resolves an ambiguity that existed in German law prior to 1989 by subjecting anyone 'who presents himself as the producer by affixing to a product his name, tradename, or other distinguishing feature'. Dealers were also not *normally* liable for not testing products (BGH NJW 1980, 119), though there was a greater inclination to find dealer-importers liable given the difficulty of enforcing judgments against foreign manufacturers. Immunity, however, seemed the rule rather than the exception (BGH NJW 1987, 1009). Again, the new regime is stricter. § 4 III of the 1989 Act thus follows Art. 3 III of the Directive, making the supplier liable under the Act whenever the producer cannot be identified. Finally, the Act (§ 13) following Art. 11 of the Directive provides that an action under the new law will expire ten years after the producer has put the actual product that caused the harm into circulation. This is the absolute outer limit for § 12 I of the Act (again following the Directive: Art. 10 provides for a limitation period of three years from the moment when the claimant knew or ought to have known of the damage.)

In the many happy hours of reading that will be necessary to understand the emerging law, the following articles in English may help (detailed references to the German literature are given in Ch. 2, section A.4(c) above): Borrie, 'Product Liability in the EEC' 9 *Dublin University Law Journal* 82 (1987); Dielmann, 'The European Economic Community's Council Directive on Product Liability' 20 *The International Lawyer* 1391 (1986); Lord Griffiths, De Val, and Dormer, 'Development in English Product Liability Law: A Comparison with the American System' 62 *Tulane L. Rev.* 353 (1988); Newdick, 'The Future of Negligence in Product Liability' 103 (1987) *LQR* 288; Stapleton, 'Product Liability Reform—Real or Illusory?' (1985); Whittaker, 'The EEC Directive on Product Liability' *Yearbook of European Law* 233 (1985); Whittaker, 'European Product Liability and Intellectual Products' 105 (1989) *LQR* 125.

16. DAMAGE CAUSED TO THE PRODUCT

Case 48

BUNDESGERICHTSHOF (EIGHTH CIVIL DIVISION) 24 NOVEMBER 1976*
BGHZ 67, 359 = NJW 1977, 379 = JZ 1977, 343 (with critical notes by M. Lieb and B.
Rengier = VersR 1977, 358)

Facts

The D firm—insured by the plaintiff company—were manufacturers among other things of tin covers for transformers. The defendant produces cleansing and degreasing apparatus for industrial products, in which through heating and evaporation perchlorhylene oil is washed out and separated from the parts to be cleansed. A ballcock connected to a switch, which the defendant alleges to have obtained from a foreign supplier, prevents the filaments, normally covered with fluid, from being exposed to the air.

After the D firm had, on 29 January 1969, ordered such cleansing apparatus for about DM 20,000, the defendant confirmed the order on 4 February 1969 with the addition: 'Warranty: according to our enclosed conditions of sale and delivery.'

No. VIII of those conditions of delivery—in so far as is relevant here—runs as follows:

VIII. liability for defective delivery:

1. All those parts are to be made good or replaced without charge at our choice to be exercised fairly, which within twelve months of the delivery are proved unusable or the usefulness of which is seriously affected in consequence of circumstances existing before the passing of the risk—in particular owing to defective design, inferior materials, or defective construction . . .

9. Further claims of the buyer or the party giving the order, in particular a claim for compensation for damage caused not to the delivered object itself but by the latter indirectly will in no case be accepted by us.

After the apparatus had been set up and put into operation at the beginning of June 1969 the used oil in the apparatus ignited because a switch operated by a ballcock had not switched off the filaments in time and they had become overheated. The plaintiff company, which had paid to the D firm, its insured, a sum of DM 70,971, made a claim for compensation against the defendant on the ground that the switch had failed in consequence of a defect in manufacture or construction; the D firm had had to spend that amount for the repair of the cleansing and electrical apparatus as well as the elimination of corrosion of the metal stocks. The defendant

* English version by F. H. Lawson and B. S. Markesinis.

stated that the fire had happened only through an excessive supply of petroleum, and denied that it was liable for the damage caused by the fire, and in addition points to the formal exclusion of liability for all claims for compensation and in that respect invokes the operation of prescription in that the order for payment was first made on 23 June 1972.

Both courts below rejected the claim. Upon the plaintiff company's application for review, the judgment of the court was quashed and the case referred back to the Court of Appeal for the following

Reasons

I. . . .

II. . . .

1. The decision of the Court of Appeal must be opposed in the result to the effect that the plaintiff company's claims in contract for damages did not exist according to its pleadings, because they were time-barred under § 477 BGB. [Details follow.]

2. On the other hand, the further considerations of the Court of Appeal that also from the delictual point of view the plaintiff's action is without foundation according to its own pleadings, does not stand up to legal examination.

(*a*) An objective breach of duty by the defendant causing damage resulting from a fire by delivering defective cleansing apparatus has been sufficiently established by the plaintiff company and proved by experts. [Details follow.]

(*b*) Since to this extent the plaintiff company claims against the defendant as the producer of the apparatus, it was for the latter, regarded from the point of view of so-called 'product liability', to exculpate itself by proving absence of fault, a circumstance that lay entirely within its sphere of influence and of which the plaintiff who could rely only on conjecture, could not be unaware (BGHZ 51, 91; Senate judgments of 28 September 1970—VIII ZR 166/68 = WM 1970, 1418, 1420—LM BGB § 433 no. 36 and of 24 November 1971—ZR 81/70 = WM 1972, 106 = NJW 1972, 251). In this connection, it can be assumed in favour of the defendant that the ballcock switch, the failure of which, according to the plaintiff's account, started the fire, was obtained from a third party and only incorporated in the apparatus manufactured by it. If that switch was of itself free from defect, but its performance was too weak or otherwise unsuited for the apparatus, it is a matter of a so-called defect of the construction, characteristic 'product liability' (see judgment of 20 September 1970). But even if there was nothing wrong with the construction and only the switch showed a defect, the defendant would be required—without prejudice to the question which additional claims the plaintiff might perhaps have against the producer of the switch—to exculpate himself from any fault in respect of such defect of production; for after the defendant ordered and incorporated this switch which was necessary for the operational safety of the apparatus to be sold, the responsibility for a defect-free working of the switch—as between the parties—fell exclusively within the ambit of the defendant, who alone could control the workmanship and incorporation of the switch, whereas the D firm was deprived of such a possibility of examining it.

(c) The Court of Appeal's view based on that of the Landgericht, that the 'legal institution of product liability' had been developed for a disposition of goods involving several stages and could not therefore be applied if—as here—direct contractual relations existed between producer and ultimate consumer, is at variance with the law. A genuine concurrence existed between a claim for damages for breach of contract and that for a tort, with the consequence that each claim follows its own legal rules and the injured party is, as a matter of principle, free to choose the basis on which to put forward his claim. In particular he is not prevented from falling back on delictual liability, if contractual claims are no longer available either because the period of limitation has run out or because an exemption clause is restricted to contractual liability (cf. the applicability of § 852 BGB alongside of § 477 BGB dealt with in the judgment of the Senate of 24 May 1976 = BGHZ 66, 315 = WM 1976, 839). If the injured party bases his claim on a tort of the producer, the mere circumstance that direct contractual relations exist between them or in any case have existed, does not exclude the application of the principles of concurring the reversal of the burden of proof of fault developed for claims against a producer (cf. also the judgment of the Senate of 28 September 1970—VIII ZR 166/68). In so far as in this connection Count von Westphalen in his criticism (BB 1976, 1097) of the judgment of the Senate of 24 May 1976 openly expresses the opinion that the Senate, on facts like the present, has retreated from the principles of evidence governing product liability, overlooks the fact that the subject of the dispute then decided was a typical case of a claim arising out of a chain of dealings against a firm which had neither manufactured the product nor had distributed it as a detached agency of the manufacturing firm, and that for this reason there was no room to introduce the principles of product liability; that was also to be deduced from the unabridged statement of facts in the judgment reported in WM 1976, 839.

(d) Contrary to the view of the Court of Appeal the plaintiff has also alleged in sufficient detail the existence of the property of the D firm and damage resulting from it. [Details follow.]

(*e*) The Court of Appeal declares as regards the cost of repairing the cleansing apparatus, that in any case there was no interference with property, because, according to the plaintiff's statement, the apparatus was originally delivered in a defective condition and therefore the D firm was never the possessor or owner of an object free from defects. This view is based on a mistake of law. It is indeed correct that both the Reichsgericht (RG JW 1905, 367) and the Bundesgerichtshof (BGHZ 39, 366) denied a claim of the owner of a building for damage to property based on the defective erection of a building (§ 823 I BGB) in respect of that particular building, when the materials used in the building were defective and when, with the completion of each phase, each time a further defectively produced portion passed into the landowner's ownership (cf. also OLG Karlsruhe 1956, 913; Schafer in *Staudinger, BGB*, 10/11 edn. § 823, n. 49). It is essential in these cases that the defect in the object transferred was inherent beforehand to the object as such; it was therefore completely useless to the owner from the start and that the defect was identical with the damage complained of (cf. Duns/Kraus, *Haftung für schädliche Ware* (1969) p. 66). In such a case the damage to an object of another is in fact already excluded conceptually; only economic damage exists for which § 823 I BGB does not provide redress (BGHZ, above).

That is however not so here. Apart altogether from the fact that the above-mentioned considerations of the Court of Appeal concern only the damage to the cleansing apparatus itself, but not the damage caused by the fire to other property of the D firm, the defendant here had transferred to the D firm the ownership of an apparatus which was otherwise free from fault and only contained a regulating device which was defective as regards a limited function—the failure of which caused further damage to the whole apparatus after ownership has passed. In such a case it does not matter that from the formal point of view the purchaser only acquired property which was defective at the outset (cf. Diederichsen, *VersR* 1971, 1078, 1098; Schlechtriem, *VersR* 1973, 581, 589). Instead, it is decisive that the danger arising from the accompanying delivery of the switch resulted in damage exceeding that represented by the defect only after title had passed and thereby the property of the purchaser, otherwise from defect. (Duns and Kraus, op. cit., 66; Schmidt-Salzer, *Entscheidungssammlung Produkthaftung*, 30 ff.). In cases of that kind—especially when the injured party has acquired the ownership on the basis of a contract of sale—there is no reason to restrain him from having recourse to claims in tort. That is true all the more so since, if the injured party wishes to retain the apparatus (perhaps in order to maintain production) and only wants compensation for the cost of repairs, he cannot rely on a contractual claim to compensation because the law of warranties in sale (§§ 459 ff. BGB) does not provide for damages beyond the express warranties of quality (§§ 463, 480 II BGB). Moreover, claims for breach of contract by a positive act (*positive Vertragsverletzung*), arising out of the delivery of defective objects, are restricted to compensation for damage caused to other legally protected interests but do not cover damage to the object of the sale itself [reference]; thus, to that extent the buyer would be largely without a remedy if he could not fall back on claims in tort.

The Senate does not fail to recognize that in some cases the boundary may be difficult to draw between a defect affecting the transferred object as a whole and a limited defect which later on causes new damage to the object transferred which was otherwise free from defect, as for instance when what was to begin with a limited defect expands like a 'creeping disease' and afterwards takes hold of the entire object (cf. Schlechtriem, op. cit. 589; Duns/Kraus, op. cit., 66 fn. 7). In the present case it is not necessary to set down unambiguous criteria for delimiting the two given the small value of the ballcock and the total value of the cleansing apparatus sold for some DM 20,000.

(*f*) Finally, the claim for compensation put forward by the plaintiff, in so far as it is based on tort, is not excluded on legal grounds. The short period of limitation of § 477 BGB is not applicable to such a claim (see judgment of this Senate of 24 May 1976—ZR 10/74). The same applies to the disclaimer of liability regulated in section VIII no. 9 of the defendant's general conditions of delivery, which it may be assumed in the defendant's favour, were incorporated in the contract. Whether such a disclaimer also includes claims in tort, in so far as they are connected with the defective performance, is a question of interpretation in the light of the individual case (cf. BGH judgment of 23 April 1970—VII ZR 150/68 = JZ 1970, 903). Since the Court of Appeal—consistently with its point of view—did not attempt an interpretation of the general delivery conditions, this Senate can itself interpret this clause (see Senate judgment of 25 June 1975—VIII ZR 244/73 = WM 1975, 895 = NJW 1974, 1693). For this purpose it must be taken into account not only that exemption clauses being exceptions from liability provided by dispositive law—must in principle be construed narrowly, but also in the present case that according to the so-called 'obscurity rule' any remaining doubts as to the extent of the provisions contained in the general conditions of trade must be interpreted against the party who drafted them and makes use of them. In the present case the exemption clause is found in a section of the general conditions of trade which is headed 'Liability for defects in delivery' and which regulated in particular the contractual warranty by the seller, and therefore by modifying §§ 450 ff. BGB and §§ 377 ff. HGB regulates the contractual claims for a warranty. It need not be decided whether the buyer's or contracting party's disclaimer which is mentioned only in no. 9 also includes claims for compensation for breach of contract by positive act arising from a defective delivery. In any case there is no sufficiently clear provision that claims for a blameworthy injury to the legal interests protected by § 823 I BGB are to be excluded. If this had been the defendant's intention, it ought to have been indicated to the D firm by an unambiguously formulated clause that the latter's legal position was being further restricted to an appreciable degree, for example as regards any claims arising from a negligent bodily injury or a destructive threatening the existence of an entire business.

In so far as this Senate stated in the decision BGHZ 64, 355 that the exclusion of liability contained in section II no. 5 of the 'General Conditions for the supply of Electrical Power from the Low Tension Network (AVB)', embraces not only contractual but also delictual claims for damage arising from the break in the supply of current, those statements relate to a state of facts and interests which is not comparable with the present case. Quite apart from the fact that the AVB are regarded as a legal enactment (BGHZ 9, 390) and that for this reason the so-called 'obscurity rule' cannot be invoked for its interpretation (cf. judgment of the Senate of 21 October 1958—VIII ZR 145/57 = NJW 1959, 38), the exclusion of liability in no. II 5 AVB takes account of the circumstance that the energy undertakings can only perform the task allotted to them of providing the public with cheap current, if they are as far as possible exempt from liability; this particular task demands the widest possible exemption from liability with the consequence that—as far as admissible—claims for compensation are included in whatever legal form (judgment of this Senate of 9 June 1959—VIII ZR 61/58 = NJW 1959, 1423 = LM BGB § 138 [Cc] no. 2). On the other hand in the present case, which involves a shift from the seller to the buyer by means of general trade conditions, these considerations do not apply.

III. The decision of the dispute depends therefore on whether the plaintiff succeeds in proving that a defective or unsuitable switch caused the fire. To that extent the dispute requires a further clarification of facts.

Case 49

BUNDESGERICHTSHOF (EIGHTH CIVIL SENATE) 11 JANUARY 1978*

NJW 1978, 1051

Facts

The defendant ran a sandpit. On February 1, 1973 she delivered to the plaintiff 6m³ of sand which was intended to be used as the outer cladding to

---

* English version by Ms J. Shaw.

the plaintiff's newly constructed house. The plaintiff had the outer cladding applied in spring 1973, and subsequently damage in the cladding began to appear which were attributable to certain mineral impurities present in the sand delivered by the defendant. Alleging that the defendant had quarried the impure sand, which was unsuitable for use as an outer cladding, out of a new sandpit without first examining it to see whether it was pure, the plaintiff brought a claim for compensation against the defendant on January 8, 1974. Notice of the claim was served upon the defendant on February 21, 1974. The LG rejected the claim on the grounds that it was barred by the statute of limitations. The OLG rejected the plaintiff's appeal. The permitted appeal to the BGH was likewise unsuccessful.

For the following

Reasons

[In Point **I.**, the court agreed with the conclusion of the OLG that the plaintiff had no claim against the defendant in respect of the delivery of the impure and therefore defective sand based on the statutory guarantees applicable to the sale of goods, either because such a claim was not possible, or because it was no longer possible since the time limit for bringing the action had expired (§ 477 BGB).]

II. Finally, the plaintiff also has no claim based on *damage to his property* (§ 823 I BGB) which is not subject to brief limitation periods and which is consequently not out of time (§ 852 BGB [references omitted]). The question which has been debated in the literature and which the plaintiff's application places at the forefront of this case concerns the circumstances in which a client has claims against a building contractor for damage to his property based on defects in the construction of a building. Such a general question, however, is not at issue here because the defendant was not working as a building contractor but had only delivered the defective sand on the basis of a contract of sale, and it was the plaintiff who then used the sand, mixed with other building materials, to apply the cladding to his house which was previously unclad [references omitted]. Even the judgment of this court of November 24, 1976 (BGHZ 67, 359 [other references omitted]) and the question which arose in that case as to whether a purchaser, who had bought a technical installation from the seller which contained no defects, with the exception of a faulty safety switch, could bring a claim against the seller when the failure of the switch resulted in damage to the installation itself, concerns an entirely different set of factual circumstances which do not apply here.

What is decisive here is that according to the findings of the OLG, which are correct in law, the plaintiff's building, which previously did not have an external cladding, did not suffer a reduction in value as compared to what it was previously worth, as regards either its physical substance or use as a dwelling house. Accordingly, the present case is to be distinguished also from factual circumstances which were present in the judgment of the BGH of November 6, 1963 (BB 1964, 65). The plaintiff's application is incorrect on this point. For that case involved a finished house which already had an outer cladding, but which subsequently suffered a reduction in its value as a result of damage from smoke and soot emanating from neighbouring land. The financial burden suffered by the plaintiff, as a consequence of what he argued was the need to remove the cladding, therefore represents pure economic loss and therefore represents an interference with an interest which is not protected by § 823 I BGB. Since, moreover, the mere fact of delivering what was, from the beginning, defective sand does not in itself represent property damage to this building material, then the only remaining question is whether the plaintiff has suffered property damage as regards those building materials (chalk, cement) which originally belonged to him and which were mixed with the defective sand to form the outer cladding, and which consequently became worthless. The OLG correctly denied this claim. The plaintiff overlooks the fact that when the outer cladding was manufactured, his original property interest in the building materials which he provided lapsed as a consequence of the mingling (§ 948 BGB) and the processing (§ 950 BGB) of the materials, and that he acquired a new, albeit impaired, property interest in the cladding material. Therefore there is no loss which can be defined as property damage affecting the plaintiff in respect of which he could claim compensation under § 823 I BGB [reference omitted].

Case 50

BUNDESGERICHTSHOF (EIGHTH CIVIL DIVISION) 5 JULY 1978*
NJW 1978, 2241

On 21 January 1975 the plaintiff bought a used motor car from the defendant. A so-called 'Order Form' in standard form provided that the motor car was being delivered as 'used, as inspected, every warranty being excluded'. A handwritten addition noted '. . . is being delivered in an unexceptionable technical condition'. On the reverse side of the form the defendant's general conditions of trade were set out which are provided in article VII [Warranties].

1. No warranty is given in respect of the objects sold. This does not apply if and to the extent that the seller has provided a warranty in writing by a separate letter of guarantee.
2. No right exists to demand a return of the price in return for the goods [*Wandelung*], a reduction of the price [*Minderung*] or damages.

* English version by F. H. Lawson and B. S. Markesinis.

On 28 March 1975 the plaintiff, while driving the motor car, suffered an accident due to a blow-out of a rear tyre which was not of the type required by law to be fitted to this type of car. He sued the defendant for damages. The latter pleaded *inter alia* that the period of limitation had run.

The Court of First Instance and the Court of Appeal of Bamberg allowed the claim. A second appeal was rejected for the following

Reasons

I. The appeal is rejected. The appellant is correct, it must be admitted, in objecting to the view of the Court of Appeal that the defendant is liable to pay damages to the plaintiff under § 463 I BGB. For that claim is caught by the period of limitation, contrary to the opinion of the Court of Appeal.

1. (*a*) The Court of Appeal is right in regarding the statement that the motor car was being delivered in an unexceptional technical condition as a guarantee of a quality in the meaning of § 459 II BGB, i.e. as a guarantee that at the time of delivery the vehicle is technically in order, ready to be used and safe in operation. The question as to whether such details contained in a contract of sale of the object sold only serve to describe it (§ 459 I BGB) or whether they warrant a certain quality (§ 459 II BGB) is a matter of factual appreciation in the individual case, provided that—as in the present case—the statements are not of the type which are normally made in connection with such transactions. The interpretation reached by the Court of Appeal is possible, conforms to the principles laid down by the practice of the courts concerning the assurance of the existence of certain qualities [references], and therefore binds this court. Moreover it is convincing. A purchaser from an appointed dealer of a certain manufacturer of a used car of this particular make is interested, above all, that the car should at least conform to the official rules for permitting the car to be used on the roads (§§ 18 ff. of the Decree concerning the Admission of Motor Vehicles for Use on Roads) and can be put into operation without any hesitation. If the dealer in used cars, contrary to the practice in the trade with second-hand cars, confirms in addition that the car's condition is technically unexceptionable, it is at least likely that he undertakes thereby to be responsible for any possible damage, if those conditions are not present. The argument of the appellant is inapposite to the effect that it cannot possibly be assumed that the defendant intended to warrant the technically unexceptionable condition of *all* parts of the used car, seeing that thereby the plaintiff would be in a much more advantageous position than if he had bought a new car. Clearly the Court of Appeal did not wish to attribute to the contractual statements of the defendant such an extensive meaning; it interpreted them and could interpret them to warrant *operational readiness and safety* . . .

Since by fitting tyres which did not conform to the permit for operating the car, the permit had become invalid (§§ 18(1), 19(2), 21 of the Decree concerning the Admission of Motor Vehicles for Use on Roads) and since, moreover, the vehicle . . . fitted with tyres which did not comply with the legal requirement, was no longer operationally safe, the defendant is liable to pay to the plaintiff damages for having failed to perform the contract (§ 463 first sentence BGB).

(*b*) The Court of Appeal is also correct in holding that the liability of the defendant for promised qualities has not been excluded either by the standard clause 'used, as inspected, every warranty being excluded' or by the exemption clause of the general conditions of trade reproduced on the reverse side of the standard contract. This Division has stated repeatedly that an exemption clause in a standard contract does not affect the liability of a seller for the absence of stipulated qualities [references]. If the seller is unwilling to remain subject to the risk of liability in accordance with the provisions of the law, he must indicate this unequivocally and in a manner intelligible to the buyer—with particular reference to the promises made— in the text of the contract or otherwise at the conclusion of the contract [reference]. This had not happened in the present case. Therefore, the defendant cannot plead either that his declaration, which amounts to a stipulation as to quality, was not made in the form prescribed by article VII no. 1 of its general conditions of trade ('. . . by a separate letter of guarantee') [reference].

2. However, the claims for damages available to the plaintiff under § 463 I BGB are caught by the period of limitation. The Court of Appeal believes that the period of limitation amounting to six months according to § 477 I BGB had only begun to run when the plaintiff was able to perceive the cause of the accident with the necessary degree of certainty following the receipt on 23 September 1975 of the written information by the manufacturer of the tyre. However, this view of the law is erroneous.

(*a*) It is true that this Division has raised the question several times— although it was not decisive in the final resort—whether in certain circumstances in order to prevent gross injustice or a curtailment of buyers' rights the period of limitation for claims for damages in respect of warranties arising out of a sale, instead of beginning to run from the delivery of the object sold, should not start at a later moment only, e.g. when the damage occurred, when the buyer could become aware of it, or quite generally when it becomes possible in the individual case to raise such claims so as to interrupt the period of limitation [references]. These considerations, however, concerned without exception the question of liability for damage arising out of defects of the goods sold (*Mangelfolgeschäden*). In typical cases this often manifests itself in other legally protected assets of the buyer only a considerable time after the object sold has been delivered, or the damage may only occur at a later time.

In the present case, however, the issue is exclusively one of damages for *failure to perform*. It is unnecessary to dilate on this in respect of costs of repair, reduced value, and loss of use; the same applies to the cost of expert opinions relating to the existence of defects, for these are necessarily the consequences of defects, they are directly connected with remedying the defects, and—like profits lost as a result of the defects [references]—they reduce the value of the consideration received by the buyer in return for the price [reference].

(*b*) It need not be decided here as to whether to this extent, despite the clear wording of § 477 I BGB, a case exists in certain circumstances for postponing to a later date the moment when the period of limitation begins to run [references]. For even if this were to be assumed in favour of the plaintiff, the time for bringing a claim would have passed . . .

II. Since the contractual claims of the plaintiff against the defendant are caught by the period of limitation, the reasons given by the Court of Appeal do not support the decision under appeal. However, the decision is right for different reasons. The claim is well founded in tort (§ 823 I BGB); in this respect the defence that the period of limitation has run is ineffective, since the claim in tort is not subject to the short period of limitation [reference].

1. The Court of Appeal expresses doubts as to whether an action in tort lies—without going into details—because the plaintiff had acquired the motor car in a defective condition. His property was threatened from the outset with the danger of further losses through an accident. The fact that this threat had materialized did not constitute a separate violation of property. This view cannot be accepted.

(*a*) It is true that in the decision referred to by the Court of Appeal [reference] the Bundesgerichtshof rejected the claim of the owner of a building based on the violation of his property because the building has been badly constructed (§ 823 I BGB); it rejected the claim in respect of this building in particular, if the materials used for the building were defective and if, as the building work progressed, each time another defectively constructed section became the property of the owner of land [reference]. These cases are characterized by the fact that the defect of the object delivered was inherent in it as a whole, that the latter was therefore altogether useless to the owner from the beginning and that the defect was identical with the damages claimed [reference].

(*b*) With reference to this case, this Division in its decision of 24 November 1976 [case 48, above] has distinguished the case where the seller transferred to the buyer title in an object which was unexceptionable in general and merely included a defective control instrument (a safety switch)—the function of which was limited—the failure of which after title has passed caused further damage to the installation as a whole. In that case this Division accepted that property had been damaged illegally. It regarded as decisive that the cause of the danger represented by the contemporaneous supply of a defective switch had only materialized in damage exceeding the defect itself after title had passed and that as a result the property of the buyer, which was in every other respect free from defects, had been damaged as a whole. Rengier [reference] and Schubert [reference] criticize this decision on the ground that even small, limited defects render the entire object sold defective from the outset, as well as useless having regard to the danger of its destruction connected therewith. Weitnauer [reference] does not deny that property has been violated—illegally on the facts—but argues that a subsequent destruction of the installation does not constitute damage; in his opinion the latter event had only laid bare damage which had occurred previously. The value of an installation, the self-destruction of which as a result of a defect could be expected, was 'nil' from the beginning.

These objections—which are substantially identical—are not convincing in the opinion of this Division and do not persuade it to abandon its position in [reference]. Above all, it is not correct that in commerce a danger-ridden installation is treated as valueless. This might perhaps be so if the defect in question is absolutely incapable of detection and must lead to the destruction of the entire installation. No such case is in issue here. As Rengier and Schubert have pointed out, it may be difficult in individual cases to distinguish between a defect which affects the object transferred in its entirety from the beginning and a limited defect which only later on caused additional damage to an object which is otherwise free from defect. This Division has already stressed this in its decision of 24 November 1976 [reference], but the unequivocal facts of that case did not make it necessary to establish detailed criteria of delimitation. This Division is also not persuaded by the view of Rengier and Schubert that in allowing a claim in tort, the Bundesgerichtshof undermines the provisions of the law of sale concerning damages for non-performance (§ 463 BGB) as well as the rule concerning the limitation of this action laid down in § 477 BGB. A real concurrence of actions exists between the claim for damages for breach of contract and that in tort; in the latter case—leaving aside the special aspects of products liability—the claimant bears the burden of proof that the tortfeasor is to be blamed, unlike in the case of a claim in contract (§ 282 BGB). It follows that each of these two claims is governed by its own rules [reference]. In cases such as that which this Division had to decide [reference] no reason exists for denying the injured party recourse to claims in tort and thus for placing the party causing the damage in a better position than a third party who had incorporated a defective individual part into an object of a sale after its delivery to the buyer which led to the destruction of the latter.

(c) The case to be decided now—damage to a purchased motor vehicle arising out of an accident due to the fitting of a tyre contrary to the regulations—must in the opinion of this Division be treated similarly. On the one hand, the motor car which the plaintiff bought from the defendant was defective as far as the rear tyres were concerned. On the other hand, the car as a whole remained a valuable asset. Only after ownership had passed, a cause of danger resulting from this defect resulted in different and much higher damage compared with the original defect when an accident occurred in actual circulation. If the course of events had been different, especially if the tyres had been changed in time, this damage, which is different in substance from that of having tyres fitted which were contrary to the regulations, would have been avoided. Therefore it must be held that the defendant has violated the plaintiff's property illegally . . . It would seem that also the Sixth Division of the Bundesgerichtshof in its decision of 30 May 1978 [reference], which is to be published, proceeded from the above-mentioned view of this Division.

2. (a) [The court considered the culpability of the defendant] . . .

(b) [The court considered the contributory negligence of the plaintiff] . . .

3. Finally, faced with a claim for damages based on tort (§ 823 I BGB) the defendant cannot rely either on the exemption clause in the standard contract form (article VII of the defendant's general conditions of trade) and on the fact that the plaintiff bought the vehicle 'as inspected'. It is true that in all trade with second-hand cars a very wide exclusion of liability accords with the customs of this branch of business; this Division has described it as 'more or less a requirement of economic reason' [reference]. On the other hand, in the present case the defendant gave an express assurance by a personal statement that the used car was in an 'unexceptional technical condition'. If the defendant also intended to exclude similar claims for damages based on tort, thus rendering his assurance largely ineffective in this area of liability and therefore of no value for this buyer, he should have stated this unequivocally. The simple reference, made in standard form in connection with the arrangement concerning contractual warranties to the effect that 'no right exists to demand . . . damages' is certainly insufficient to embrace such an extensive exclusion of liability, having regard to the special features

of the present case. The further question can remain undecided as to whether generally, even in the absence of special assurances, exemption clauses of the kind employed here in the trade with second-hand cars also cover claims for damages in tort [reference].

Case 51

BUNDESGERICHTSHOF (SIXTH CIVIL DIVISION) 18 JANUARY 1983
BGHZ 86, 256

A motor car manufactured by the defendant was sold by the L garage to the plaintiff in February 1976. The throttle on this car was defective in that the accelerator-pedal did not always spring back after being depressed. On 12 May 1976 the plaintiff tried to repair it, but in vain. In June 1976 the gas-pedal broke off and he installed another pedal of his own devising.

On 5 July 1976 the plaintiff had an accident in B, allegedly because the car accelerated after he had removed his foot from the pedal. The front of the car was damaged. The plaintiff had the car repaired, and a new gas-pedal from the factory was installed. A few weeks later there was another accident when the car struck a fence while being reversed by the plaintiff's wife, then his fiancée. This accident also, according to the plaintiff, was due to the fact that the vehicle accelerated unexpectedly because the gas-pedal stuck. This time it was the rear end of the car which was damaged. The cost of repairs to the plaintiff's car on these two occasions totalled DM 3742.

[Here follow technical details of the defect, according to the two expert reports procured by the plaintiff.]

The plaintiff argues that the damage was due to a defect in construction and that the defendant is liable therefore: in respect of the repairs to his car and the garden fence, as well as the cost of the two expert reports, he claims a total of DM 4443. The Landgericht rejected his claim for the cost of repairing the car (in the amount of DM 3742). The plaintiff's appeal was dismissed. On his further appeal to this court, the decision below is reversed and the case remanded.

Reasons

The judgment of the Court of Appeal is wrong in law.

1. Certainly the Court of Appeal was right to hold that where a purchased chattel suffers damage because of the faulty construction or manufacture of a component part, its purchaser may have a claim in tort against the manufacturer on the basis of an invasion of his rights as property-owner (§ 823 I BGB).

(*a*) It is true that tortious duties are not imposed, like guarantees in the law of sales, in order to protect a contractor's expectations of utility and value in the acquisition of an undefective thing (see BGHZ 77, 215, 218 with references; BGHZ 80, 186, 188). They rather relate to the interest which people have in the integrity of their belongings or possessions, in not having them adversely affected by the chattel which the manufacturer puts into commerce (*Integritätsinteresse*). Such tortious duties to guard against damage or disturbance may be imposed on the manufacturer not only as regards other property of the acquirer which may be imperilled by faults in construction or production of the manufactured item, but also as regards that item itself. In principle, the purchaser's interest in having the purchased item undamaged and undisturbed is as much worth protection as his interest in the safety of the rest of his property; the manufacturer must therefore respect this interest as well (see Bruggemeier *WM* 1982, 1294, 1303). Accordingly, it is not a precondition of tortious liability that other goods or interests of the consumer or of third parties should necessarily have been affected by the thing which is put into commerce with a defective component (*contra*, Schlechtriem [reference omitted]). The manufacturer may be held liable to the consumer in tort if the impairment or disturbance of the manufactured item constitutes harm which it was the manufacturer's duty under the law of tort to avoid out of respect for the interest of the owner or possessor in the safety of his property.

(*b*) Where the loss due to the defective nature of the thing simply reflects the acquirer's interest in its utility and value, the case is different, for as we have said, duties in tort are not imposed in order to reinforce the purchaser's expectation that he will have the value and use of an object without a defect. This expectation is protected by the law of contract exclusively, save in cases under § 826 BGB where the harm is caused deliberately. It would be wrong to say that whenever a person acquires a defective thing his rights as owner are thereby invaded, and thus invoke the law of tort. Such harm cannot, as is generally acknowledged, ground a claim in tort (see RG JW 1905, 367, 368; compare BGHZ 39, 366; 55, 392; 67, 359, 364; BGH judgments of 11 Jan. 1978, NJW 1978, 1051; 5 July 1978, NJW 1978, 2241, 2242). If the only harm in issue is the undervalue due to the original defect and existing from the time of acquisition, that is simply a case of disappointed contractual expectations, and the law of tort has no role to play (so Duns/Kraus, *Haftung für schädliche Waren* (1969), 66). But the harm may not be *substantially identical* (*stoffgleich*) with the undervalue of the thing in that the defect impairs the owner's interest in its value and usability; it may take the form of an invasion of the consumer's interest in the integrity of his property and possessions which the manufacturer may in the circumstances be under a duty to respect. The manufacturer can then in principle be subjected to delictual products liability, and this is so even when there is a concurrent contractual claim under the law of warranty or replacement [references omitted], for it is accepted law that the rules of tort and contract apply concurrently and independently neither excluding the other (BGHZ 67, 359, 362; constant holding).

Of course liability in tort must not be permitted to unhinge the law of contract. But that will not happen in cases like the present if tort liability is carefully restricted to the integrity interest, appropriately distinguished in each case from the interest in usability and value. There is no conflict with the refusal of courts to impose liability in damages for positive breach of contract in cases of so-called consequential loss due to defects except where the purchaser has suffered damage to property other than the purchased item (BGHZ 77, 215, 217; so, too, for the contract of services, BGH 4 March 1971, NJW 1971, 1131, not reported on this point in BGHZ 55, 392). This judicial extension of warranties in sales (§§ 459 ff. BGB) was undertaken in order to reinforce, not to exclude, in cases where a special relationship existed, the protection of integrity provided by the law of tort. The tort liability of the supplier or manufacturer for damage due to defects in the purchased thing is not thereby blocked off (*contra*, apparently, Diederichsen, *NJW* 1978, 1281, 1286 [other references omitted]).

2. We realize that there will occasionally be practical difficulties in distinguishing the case where the harm in suit is substantially identical with the diminution in value of the thing due to an original defect which, as we have said, should be dealt with by the law of contract, from the case, subject to the law of tort where the damage or disturbance to the thing, defective owing to the manufacturer's negligence, goes beyond the owner or possessor's interest in the usability and value of the thing and affects his interest in the integrity of his property. Sometimes the defect will be so radical that from the very beginning the thing is really worthless and that therefore the 'damage' to the thing when the defect manifests itself is 'substantially identical' (see the cases in RG JW 1905, 367 and BGHZ 39, 366). Such cases will be relatively rare. Much commoner will be the case where the defect originally affects a more or less distinct part of the thing. Even so, one must find criteria of distinction which are of practical utility [reference omitted].

(*a*) In BGHZ 67, 359 the thermostat in a dry-cleaning machine was defective and unable to perform its safety function with the result that the machine overheated and burnt out. The Eighth Civil Senate allowed a claim in tort essentially because the defective thermostat was functionally distinct and, in relation to the machine as a whole, relatively trivial in value. These criteria may or may not be capable of extrapolation beyond the facts of that case [references omitted], but as the court below clearly recognized, they certainly cannot of themselves determine when the supplier or manufacturer of a partially defective product is liable. The manufacturer's liability cannot depend solely on the relatively accidental consideration of how the component parts are put together [references omitted]. But it is clear that the Eighth Civil Senate was dealing only with the case before it and had no intention of laying down definitive tests, as is shown by its subsequent decision of 5 July 1978. Then it allowed the purchaser of a used car to sue the seller in tort for the harm suffered in an accident due to the fact that the rear tyres were not in conformity with regulations. In both decisions the court expressly stated that it was not laying down definitive criteria.

(b) The adoption of a common-sense or economic standpoint will often enable one to say whether the harm in suit is substantially identical with the undervalue due to the original defect [reference omitted]. Thus substantial identity will be found where the defective component is so integrated into the composite or so unified with the part now damaged but originally undefective that separation is impossible without great economic loss (BGH 24 June 1981, NJW 1981, 2248, 2249). So, too, where it would make no economic sense to make the defect good (this may have been the case in the decision of the Seventh Civil Senate on 25 May 1972 (BauR 1972, 379) where the foundations underneath the whole of the extension were inadequate). Other cases where the distinction is hard to draw must be determined in accordance with the principles stated in 1(b) above, taking into account the nature and extent of the damage in suit, the nature of the defect to which it was due, the effect of the defect on the condition of the thing, and, as reflected in these factors, the extent of the manufacturer's duty in tort which here, as in other cases, is affected by the purpose of the product, the consumer's expectations of it and even, under certain circumstances, its price [reference omitted].

(c) In this case we need not ask whether the throttle was a functionally distinct component of the motor car in the sense of BGHZ 67, 359, or whether the Court of Appeal was right to suppose that it was not. For the purposes of this appeal we must take the accident to have been caused by a defect which inhibited the flow of petrol, and in such a case the common-sense observer could disregard the nature and origin of that defect and say that the harm to the car was substantially different from the undervalue which the defect caused to the owner's interest in its being worth what he paid for it. The critical feature in this case is that the vehicle remained roadworthy despite the defect in the throttle, which by no means rendered the vehicle valueless from the outset, and that the inherent risk of damage could have been allayed by prompt discovery of the defect and its repair at little cost and without damage to other parts of the car. The accident to the car was far from being a necessary manifestation of the undervalue of the car owing to the defect in the petrol supply; the harm was rather due to the concurrence of regrettable circumstances which could and would have been avoided had the plaintiff become conscious of the danger in good time.

We need not decide whether the manufacturer's liability for property damage resulting from a defect exists only if the damage or disturbance occurs in a *violent* manner (for example, through fire, explosion, or similar events) [reference omitted]. But certainly when the defect in a component is apt to lead to the destruction of a valuable chattel such as a motor car or damage to it in a 'violent' manner such as occurred here, then this clearly speaks for the liability of the manufacturer: the duty breached by the manufacturer in putting into circulation a vehicle with such a noxious defect was imposed on him not just because people are interested in the usability and value of their chattels but also because the owner or possessor has an interest in their well-being.

Case 52

BUNDESGERICHTSHOF (SIXTH CIVIL DIVISION) 14 MAY 1985*
NJW 1985, 2420

In April 1980 the plaintiff bought a compressor from the defendant manufacturer. In March 1982 its diesel motor suffered considerable damage, because it had run for a time without lubricant. This was because oil had leaked out owing to the fracture of the oil-conduit at the point where it joined the sump. The plaintiff maintains that it was a fault in design that the oil-conduit was fixed at only one point, namely where it entered the motor—or compressor—housing, and that it would not have broken under the vibrations set up by the prolonged running of the motor if it had been affixed to the chassis as well.

The plaintiff claimed damages of DM 5730.28 for damage to property (cost of substitute motor, expenses of experts, and rental of replacement).

Reasons

1. The Court of Appeal was of the opinion that, accepting the plaintiff's allegations as true, the damage to the compressor's motor was not damage to the plaintiff's interest in the integrity of his property such that the defendant was under a tort duty to take care to avoid it. If, as he alleged, the compressor was unfit for prolonged use as envisaged, he must bring a claim in respect of his interest in the usability and value of a merchantable compressor.

* Translated by Tony Weir.

II. The judgment of the Court of Appeal is unsound in law.

1. The first points made by the Court of Appeal are correct enough.

(*a*) The Court of Appeal followed decisions of this Division to the effect that the manufacturer of a product can be liable under § 823 I BGB for harm to a consumer's property if the damage to or destruction of the property represents damage which it is the duty of the manufacturer to take care to avoid in the interest of the acquirer in the integrity of his property [references].

(*b*) The Court of Appeal correctly distinguished those cases where the damage consisted simply of the fact that the defect in the thing made it less valuable and constituted an infringement of the acquirer's interest in usability and value for money, since it is not the function of duties imposed by the law of tort to protect a purchaser's interest in having a thing to use which is free from defects.

(*c*) As to whether or not the damage represented an invasion of the plaintiff's interest in the integrity of his property the Court of Appeal was right to adopt the test whether the damage was identical with the loss of value of the compressor due to its initial defect, i.e. whether it was 'substantially similar' to the loss in value *quoad* usability and value for money represented by the defect.

2. The Court of Appeal was nevertheless wrong to infer from the fact that the initial defect in the compressor only manifested itself in the loss of its value the conclusion that in this case there was no invasion of the plaintiff's interest in the integrity of his property.

(*a*) The Court of Appeal was wrong to suppose that the primary test as to whether the harm which later manifests itself is identical with the loss of value due to an initial defect, that is, whether they are 'substantially similar', is whether the thing was fit for prolonged use. What really counts is the comparison between the damage which is in issue and the disvalue of the product at the time of transfer, namely the amount by which the defect renders it less valuable. The diminution in value due to the defect and consequently the harm to the interest in value for money can be tested by the principles applied when abatement of the price is sought for breach of warranty (§ 472 I BGB) [references]. While it is true that in making this assessment the fact that the defect will reduce the useful life of the product can materially increase the initial shortfall in value, it is only if the entire thing or component for which compensation is sought is affected from the economic point of view by the non-durability that the short life expectancy will be *fully* expressed in the diminution of value and thus establish *complete* 'substantial similarity' between loss of value and damage to the thing. Where the initial defect which carries the risk of premature breakdown affects only part of the product and is quite curable, and only later destroys the product or damages other parts of it, the undefective part of the product has a value sufficiently distinct from the shortened life due to the defect that there is no complete identity between the damage and the shortfall in value.

That was the case here. Taking the material facts as found below, the component parts of the compressor which the plaintiff bought from the defendant manufacturer were individually faultless and it was initially quite functional. The only trouble was the inadequate anchorage of the oil-pipe which rendered it likely to break under the stress of operation and let the oil escape. This could have been avoided by the simple welding job of making an additional fixing to the chassis. Only the oil-pipe was non-durable, not the compressor as a whole or even the motor. As the defect, viz. the inadequate and easily curable fixing of the oil-pipe, could only damage the motor if its fracture and the consequent loss of oil remained unnoticed, the loss of value due to the defect at the critical moment, namely the transfer of ownership, was limited to the cost of occasional replacement of the pipe during the normal life of the compressor, or alternatively the cost of installing an additional fixing.

(b) Contrary to the view of the Court of Appeal, the plaintiff's claim is not simply for an invasion of his interest in the usability and value for money of a functioning compressor. This case differs from the '*hydraulic jack*' case, cited below, in which this Division dismissed a damages claim for damage to property where the jack was not usable (NJW 1983, 812 = VersR 1983, 346). A point sometimes overlooked by critics is that the defendant in that case had restored the jack to its original condition after the collapse of one of the supports, so that the plaintiff was in possession of a jack with just the original defect and no more, namely the design or construction fault in its undercarriage. It is true that as this defect was not remedied by the manufacturer the plaintiff did not use the jack for a long time for fear that a support might again give way under the weight of the vehicle. In such a case the purchaser suffers no harm over and above the original defect in the product, whereas in our case, as explained above, the damage is significantly greater. This demonstrates that the plaintiff here is not complaining simply of an invasion of his interest in having a functional compressor to use.

(c) This case differs in two respects (neither of which affects the outcome) from previous decisions of this Court where it was held that there had been an invasion of the plaintiff's interest in the integrity of his property (BGHZ 67, 359 = NJW 1977, 379 (thermostat); BGHZ 86, 256 = NJW 1983, 810 (accelerator pedal); NJW 1978, 2241 = BB 1978, 1491 (rear tyres)).

(*aa*) In the accelerator pedal case 'a risk of accident arose through a combination of unfortunate circumstances'. As the court below correctly held, that was not the case here.

It cannot be a precondition of a damages claim that *further* special circumstances be required before any damage occurs [reference]. Even in the absence of further special circumstances defect and harm lack 'substantial identity' if, as explained above, a curable defect initially affects only a particular part of this product.

Furthermore, it must be irrelevant to the question of the congruence of initial defect and subsequent harm whether or not the harm occurs by means of an accident or results from a 'violent' occurrence. This senate in BGHZ 86, 256 (273) = NJW 1983, 810 left it open whether it was only in such circumstances that the manufacturer's liability arose. But just as tort liability cannot depend on whether the defect in part of a product endangers *other* interests of the consumer or third party, that is, poses a risk to the environment and not just to the product itself (BGHZ 86, 256 (258) = NJW 1983, 810, criticized by Hager, *AcP* 184, 417), so it cannot be relevant to liability that the harm occurs by means of an 'accident' or by 'violent' damage to or destruction of other parts of the product. That would introduce into the law of tort a criterion foreign to its general principles.

The principle is that the acquirer's interest in the thing not being damaged or destroyed by reason of a fault of design or manufacture deserves as much protection as his interest that such fault not damage other property acquired elsewhere, and the manufacturer's liability cannot sensibly depend on whether the defect in manufacture damages other property of the consumer or only the product itself [references]. Likewise, the victim's interest in the integrity of his property and its protection by the law of tort cannot depend on whether the thing is damaged or destroyed 'violently' or gradually over a period of time. After all, the manufacturer's liability for damage to other property of the consumer does not depend on whether the damage is sudden or gradual; nor does it where the damage is to the product itself. For damage to the product the manufacturer is liable in tort as well as in warranty unless the plaintiff never had an undamaged product and so cannot complain of any impairment in his interest in the product remaining undamaged, that is, unless the subsequent damage was so inherent in the original undervalue of the product that any damages awarded must be for his failure to acquire an undamaged thing rather than for invasion of his interest in the thing not being damaged.

(*bb*) Finally it is immaterial that in this case the damage to the compressor's motor occurred through the *absence* of an *additional* fixing for the oil-pipe, rather than through the presence of a defective or unsuitable component which threatened the whole. Here the damage was as much an invasion of the plaintiff's interest in the integrity of his property, which the manufacturer was under a duty to respect, as in cases where an original defect in a component affects the whole or other parts of the thing. The case is like those in which a thing is badly constructed because one of its parts is too weak to work or otherwise unsuitable (BGHZ 67, 359 (362) = NJW 1977, 379). This distinction can have no effect on tort liability.

Reversed and remanded for further findings of fact.

Case 53

BUNDESGERICHTSHOF (SIXTH CIVIL DIVISION) 24 MARCH 1992*
NJW 1992, 1678

Facts

The plaintiff brought an action for damages against the defendants arguing that he had suffered an interference with his property interest in a car engine which had been damaged as a consequence of a faulty mounting by the defendant. On April 8, 1989 the plaintiff purchased a car engine from Firm P which an acquaintance then installed in his motor vehicle. This engine had previously been given a general overhaul by the defendants and delivered by them as a so-called replacement engine to Firm P. After 9,500 km had been registered on the clock, serious damage to the engine occurred on January 18, 1990. The plaintiff attributes the occurrence of loss to the fact that the defendants had not put in place the fastening screw of the camshaft driving wheel, so that this slipped off the camshaft. He claimed compensation from the defendant in the amount of DM 6,870.39, covering the costs of repair and the provision of an expert report, damage resulting from loss of use, and telephone expenses.

The LG rejected the claim. The plaintiff's appeal to the OLG was unsuccessful. His further appeal to the BGH resulted in the quashing of the judgment and its remission to the lower court for reconsideration.

For the following

Reasons

The OLG found a failure of the pleadings to state a cause of action as a matter of law. In its view the defendants are to be seen as the manufacturers of the engine. However, they are not liable on the basis of § 823 I BGB because only the plaintiff's financial interest ('*Äquivalenzinteresse*') and not his interest in the integrity ('*Integritätsinteresse*') of his property were

---

* English version by Ms J. Shaw.

affected. There was an 'identity of substance' between the damage and the alleged defect in the product. In other words, the initial loss in value corresponded to the loss which occurred.

The initial lack of value of the engine was not restricted to the costs of putting in place the missing fastening screw. Such an approach would only be appropriate where the absence of the screw was known or should have been apparent in the context of the normal usage of the motor, for example, during a service. According to the pleadings of the plaintiff, this was precisely what did not happen. The subsequent sequence of events—the slippage of the camshaft drive wheel—was inevitably going to occur. A defect which is not discoverable cannot be removed. In that case, therefore, the plaintiff's financial interest coincided in full with the subsequent (large scale) loss. In addition, it was relevant that from the beginning the plaintiff had not acquired a properly functioning engine, since the risk of the destruction of the engine existed at all times. The drive wheel, which was only secured by the cable attached to the camshaft, could have fallen off immediately after the engine was put into service, so that this was not a case of 'creeping loss'.

II. The judgment of the OLG is incorrect in law and must be quashed. The plaintiff has implicitly satisfied the basic conditions of an adequate plea for damages based on § 823 I BGB.

1. Any person who manufactures a product may be liable in damages in respect of loss which occurs to the product itself after it has been delivered on the grounds that the property of the purchaser has been damaged in accordance with § 823 I BGB. This is the case where the damage to or destruction of the product results in a form of damage (creeping loss) which, because of the purchaser's interest in the integrity of his property, should have been avoided by the producer who is under a duty to take care. In contrast, there is no right to compensation in tort in respect of losses which merely represent a 'lack of value' of the product and which merely affect the purchaser's interest in usability and financial interest as a consequence of the defect in its condition [references omitted].

The OLG likewise based its decision on these principles. In that context it was right to hold that the defendant is subject to a tortious duty of care in respect of the engine to which it had given a 'general overhaul', which it sold and delivered as a 'replacement engine' and which it guaranteed as being free from defects. This is the case irrespective of whether the defendant had renewed only a limited number or all of the components of the engine in the context of the overhaul and in so doing had made use of materials supplied by third parties; for the defendant in any case took responsibility for the assembly of the components which it had prepared [references omitted].

2. However, the arguments on the basis of which the OLG reached the conclusion that there was no interference with the plaintiff's interest in the integrity of his property—namely that the ultimate damage (damage to the engine) and the defect in the product (the missing fastening screw) are 'identical in substance', and that therefore the 'lack of value' corresponded to the loss which occurred are not free of errors in law.

(*a*) In its case law, this court has described the financial destruction of the interest of the purchaser which was already disappointed when the property was acquired [reference omitted] as 'identical in substance' to the initial 'lack of value' [references omitted]. Consequently, there will be 'identity of substance' where, viewed from an economic perspective, the initial defect affects the whole object in respect of loss for which compensation is now claimed [reference omitted] because for instance the object as a whole from the beginning is not at all or only in part usable for the purpose for which it was intended because of the defect [references omitted]. In this category are included also the cases in which the elimination of the defect (even if it only affects a part of the object) is not technically possible; the same view is gaining ground in respect of those cases where the defect cannot reasonably be eliminated without excessive expenditure [references omitted]. If, however, the defect is confined to a part of the product and is therefore capable of rectification according to the principles set out here and if it only subsequently leads to the destruction of the product or to damage to other parts of it, then that part of the object which was not initially tainted by the defect has its own value; the 'lack of value' does not therefore correspond to the damage [reference omitted].

(*b*) The OLG correctly uses these principles as the basis for its judgment, but makes the mistake of treating the absence of the fastening screw on the camshaft driving wheel as a defect which cannot be rectified, which leads to the view that the damage is identical to the 'lack of value' attributable to the defect. The conclusion of the OLG cannot be followed where it essentially focuses on whether the defect could have been discovered in the context of the normal use of the engine, for example, during a service.

It is not, in legal terms, of relevance for the question whether it is the purchaser's interest in the integrity of his property or only his financial interest in the usability of the product which has been impaired, whether he could or could not have discovered the defect before the loss occurred in normal circumstances; the subjective ability to discover is not relevant. What is essential is that the defect—from an objective technical standpoint—could have been identified even if only when it was specifically being sought, so long as that would not have involved a disproportionately high cost in terms of time and expenditure. Only from the latter perspective can it be relevant to the economic value of a defect in what circumstances a presumed defect can be discovered. For in the case of a defect which can only be identified with difficulty, as defined here, the possibility of rectifying the defect can be challenged on technical or economic grounds [reference omitted]. The initial 'lack of value' and the damage will coincide where the search for the defect and its elimination cause costs which are, for example, equal to or even greater than the cost of the whole product [reference omitted].

(*c*) The factual circumstances based on the plaintiff's pleadings which the OLG uses as the basis for its decision do not justify the conclusion that the defective securing of the camshaft driving wheel could not have been eliminated on technical or economic grounds. The OLG bases the adoption of this position solely on the allegation made by the plaintiff that the absence of a screw on the camshaft would not have become apparent if the servicing of the engine had been carried out in accordance with the instructions given in the service booklet.

It is incorrect to conclude that there is a defect the elimination of which is excluded on technical or economic grounds and which consequently taints the whole product with an initial 'lack of value', simply because it is not known whether the product actually has a defect or because the defect did not become apparent in the context of normal servicing work which the manufacturer would expect to be undertaken, in other words, in the context of normal usage. As the BGH decisions on 'creeping loss' have so far shown this will normally be the case [reference omitted].

There is in this case no support to be derived from the findings of the OLG or from the pleadings of the parties, which are focused purely on the foreseeable servicing work, that the absence of the fastening screw could not have been discovered without economically disproportionate expense.

3. This court is also unable to follow the arguments of the OLG to the effect that the engine delivered by the defendants was entirely unusable from the outset, because from the beginning there was an inherent danger of its destruction thus making this not a case of 'creeping loss' and that it was coincidental that the initial propensity of the product to be damaged was only subsequently realised. It is true that the engine was defective in the sense that it lacked a screw which should have secured the driving wheel to the camshaft. The rest of the engine, however, was fit and had, as a whole, considerable value. The defect affected only a small portion of the product at first—namely the driving wheel which was not properly secured and which therefore ran the risk of breaking away from the camshaft—but not the product as a whole, even if—as is, in fact, always the case with 'creeping loss'—there is from the outset the risk of significant damage to the whole

product (which is otherwise free from defects). The question of when this risk might be realised, and in particular the question of whether the defect might be timely discovered and eliminated (for instance in the context of repair work otherwise necessitated) was uncertain. The facts of the case, on which the OLG based its decision having regard to the pleadings of the plaintiff, show that the damage to the whole product did not in fact occur immediately after it was put into operation, but the engine proved capable—for whatever technical reasons—of providing 9,500 km of usage over 19 months. In these circumstances, it cannot be said that the 'lack of value' of the engine from the outset was so high that the damage which later occurred could be regarded as 'identical in substance' with this 'lack of value' and as merely the expression of the plaintiff's financial interest.

III. The OLG also concluded—logically from its standpoint—that it should leave open the question disputed by the parties as to whether in fact the fastening screw for the camshaft driving wheel was in fact missing when the defendant delivered the engine. The appeal judgment must therefore be quashed and the decision sent back to the OLG so that the necessary findings of fact can be made.

Case 54

BUNDESGERICHTSHOF (THIRD CIVIL DIVISION) 27 MAY 1963
BGHZ 39, 358 = NJW 1963, 1821 = JZ 63, 707 (with a critical note by H. H. Rupp = VersR 1963, 973)

The plaintiff site-owner claimed damages from a local authority which had issued a building permit without adequately checking the architect's calculations regarding the load-bearing capacity of the foundations, as marked on the plan. Because of this error, the building collapsed while in process of construction, and both the builder and the architect were insolvent.

The plaintiff's claim was dismissed by the trial court and his appeal was also dismissed for the following

Reasons

1. The trial court was correct to hold that in checking and authorizing the plans for the building, the supervisory authorities are exercising a governmental function. In consequence, as the Appeal Court agrees, the plaintiff's claim against the defendant can only be based on the rules relating to the liability of officials (§ 839 BGB in connection with Art. 34 GG); it must be shown that one of the defendant local authority's officials in the exercise of the public function attributed to him was in breach of an official duty which he owed to the plaintiff . . .

2. In approaching the question whether, in giving building permission when it should not have done so, the local authority was in breach of official duties owed to the plaintiff, the trial court correctly started by considering the purpose served by the official duty [reference]. In the first instance, official duties are imposed in the interest of the State and the public. If the sole function of an official duty is to promote public order, the general interest of the commonwealth in orderly and proper government, the satisfaction of exigencies within the service, or the maintenance of a properly organized and functioning administration, then there is no question of any liability to third parties for its breach, even if its exercise has adversely affected them or their interest. Liability exists only where the official duty which was broken was owed by the official to the third parties themselves. Whether this is so and how wide the range of protected persons may be are questions which must be determined in accordance with the purpose served by the official duty. This purpose is to be inferred from the provisions on which the official duty is based and by which it is delimited, as well as from the particular nature of the official function in question. If, in addition to satisfying the general interest and public purposes, the official duty has the further purpose of safeguarding the interests of individuals, this is sufficient, even if the affected party had no legal claim that the official act in question be undertaken (BGHZ 35, 44, 46–47; BGH VersR 1961, 944).

Before a building permit is issued, the plans must be checked for conformity with all building regulations of public law (§ 2 II Provincial Building Ordinance). Such an investigation must encompass the structural safety of the building (§ 15 I *e*, § 61 Provincial Building Ordinance); as the Court of Appeal was right to emphasize, with reference to Pfundtner/Neubert [reference omitted], concern for safety is one of its most important aims, since unsafe buildings pose a direct threat to life and health, the value of physical property and safe conduct of business. The supervision of buildings thus permits the avoidance of dangers (BGHZ 8, 97, 104; see Baltz/Fischer, *Preussisches Baupolizeirecht* I ff.). The provisions requiring the verification of the calculations concerning the load-bearing capacity of buildings are directed to the dangers which threaten the public from the collapse of unsafe constructions. While these provisions and the official duties which they impose serve the protection of the public—the 'public interest' (Baltz/Fischer, ibid.)—they also protect every individual member of the public who might be threatened by its unsafe condition, that is, every person who comes into contact with the building as inhabitant, user, visitor (RG Recht 1929 no. 757, SeuffArch 83 no. 134; JW 1936, 803, BGHZ 8, 97, 104), neighbour (BGH VersR 1956, 447), passer-by (LM to BGB § 839 Fe no. 1), or workman, and who relies on its being safe. The owner or developer may also be a beneficiary of this protective function if he suffers damage to his body, health, or property as a result of a collapse while he is visiting the building or inhabiting it, but only if the harm is a consequence of the danger from which it is the function of the official verification of the technical specifications to protect the public and hence the individual endangered. That is not the case here. It is true that the plaintiff has suffered damage as a result of the collapse of the building, but he is not a victim of the danger from which, as a member of the public, he was entitled to be protected by the official duties and the provisions which created them, since it was only the building itself and no other property of his which was damaged.

Case 55

BUNDESGERICHTSHOF (SEVENTH CIVIL DIVISION) 30 MAY 1963
BGHZ 39, 366 = NJW 1963, 1827 = VersR 1963, 933, 1024

In 1951 the plaintiff contracted with the defendant builder to have a house built on his land and with the defendant architect to have the construction supervised. Cracks appeared in the ceilings because the concrete used was well below the requisite strength. The plaintiff claimed damages for the reconstruction of the ceilings which were in danger of collapse. Because he was out of time for a contract claim the plaintiff based his claim on the delictual provisions § 823 I BGB and § 823 II BGB in connection with § 330 of the Criminal Code (StGB) or § 367 no. 15 StGB.

Reasons

The Court of Appeal was right to find that the facts disclosed no tort on which the plaintiff's claim for damages could be based.

1. There is no question of a claim for damages under § 823 I BGB on the basis that the plaintiff's property (*Eigentum*) has been damaged by fault. The land owned by the plaintiff, as compared with what it was, has suffered no harm through the defective method of construction. In so far as the land has been built on, as the Court of Appeal rightly stated, the plaintiff never owned it in an undefective condition. As the building proceeded, the plaintiff's ownership attached to each part of the building as it was constructed in the condition in which it was constructed, with all the qualities and defects resulting from the incorporation of the building materials. To make someone the owner of a defective building is not to invade an already existing ownership (compare RG JW 1905, 367; OLG Karlsruhe NJW 1956, 913).

The decision of the Senate in LM no. 4 to § 830 BGB was a different case; there defective concrete balconies which had been built onto the top storey caused the collapse of the whole building.

2. The Court of Appeal was also right to reject the claim for damages based on § 823 II BGB in connection with § 330 StGB. Under this last-named provision a person 'who in supervising or erecting a building in breach of generally recognized rules of building practice acts in such a way as to cause danger to others' is guilty of an offence. The trial court found that a danger existed within the meaning of this provision and this finding is not subject to review. But as the Court of Appeal stated, § 330 StGB is solely designed to protect the lives and health of individuals [references]. It is only to this extent that the provision is a protective statute whose breach can give rise to a claim for damages under § 823 II BGB. Damages can only be claimed under this text if the harm takes the form of the invasion of a legal interest for whose protection the rule of law was enacted (BGHZ 19, 114, 126; 28, 359, 365 f.). The claim before us is for compensation for harm to an interest other than the legal interest protected by § 330 StGB.

Nor is the claim for those damages justifies by the consideration that the replacement of ceilings which are in danger of collapse is necessary to save the users of the rooms from imminent danger. It still remains the case that the cost of rendering the ceilings represents a harm which affects only the pecuniary interests of the plaintiff. This is evident if one imagines that a ceiling collapses and injures an individual; then certainly the harm attributable to the personal injuries must be compensated under § 823 II BGB and § 330 StGB; but there would still remain the material harm requiring the replacement of the ceilings, and this would still affect only the economic interests of the plaintiff.

3. The plaintiff finally relies on § 823 II BGB in connection with § 367 I no. 15 StGB. This provision provides, *inter alia*, that it is an offence for a builder or building worker to construct a building in deliberate deviation from the building plan approved by the authority. According to the plaintiff, an offence was here committed because the approval of the plan was based on specific calculations, incorporated in the submission, relating to the load-bearing capacity of the construction, and these calculations were in turn based on the quality of the concrete to be used.

It is not necessary to decide whether the use of concrete inferior to that on which the stress calculations were based constitutes a deliberate deviation from the authorized plan. We agree with the Court of Appeal that § 367 I no. 15 StGB is not designed to offer protection against harm of the sort for which the plaintiff claims damages.

It is true that in its decision reported in LM no. 1 § 823 (Bb) BGB the Bundesgerichtshof recognized that § 367 I no. 15 StGB was a protective statute; that case, however, involved personal injuries suffered by a worker employed on the building site.

In the view of the Court of Appeal, § 367 I no. 15 StGB is like § 330 StGB in offering protection only to the human person.

This view is open to criticism. The final Courts of Appeal have accepted that the cognate provision of § 367 I no. 14 StGB exists for the protection of property as well and that a breach of the provision may also give rise to claims for damages in respect of property damage under § 823 II BGB (RGZ 51, 177–8, BGH, LM no. 2 to § 823 Bd BGB). Both these decisions were concerned with harm caused to neighbouring buildings adjoining the building site and vested in third parties.

Thus it may be taken that the protective purpose of § 367 I no. 15 StGB is also to be construed to guard against damage to property as well as damage to persons. In the present case, however, as has already been stated, there is no damage to property but a pecuniary loss attributable to the defective execution of the building work in breach of contract . . .

Notes to Cases 48–55

1. Cases 48–53 deal with damage *to* the product and not damage caused *by* the product and must be compared with the decision of the US Supreme Court in *East River* reproduced in Addendum 2 to this section. Cases 54 and 55 face an analogous problem in the context of immovables. The questions here are basically two: (i) is this economic loss or physical damage and (ii) should the answer be left to the law of contract or be found in an extended law of tort? If the answer favours tort, should the tort duty be determined, both in its scope and extent, by the underlying contract?

2. First, as to defective premises since German law seems quite settled on this point: *Dutton* v. *Bognor Regis UDC* ([1972] 1 QB 373) held that the ultimate purchaser of a house that had been built on a rubbish tip and subsequently developed cracks had suffered material damage that could be claimed in tort. (A key extract from Lord Denning's judgment is reproduced below in Addendum 3.) The House of Lords, in those days in frequent disagreement with the Court of Appeal, approved: *Anns* v. *Merton London Borough Council* ([1978] AC 728. These cases stand in stark contrast with the German decisions whose reasoning was: (*a*) superior and (*b*) transplantable. In fact English law has, thirteen years later, moved much closer to the German approach, though it has done so gradually (some would say confusingly slowly) and in much more expansive judgments. (See: *Peabody Donation Fund* v. *Sir Lindsay Parkinson and Co. Ltd.* ([1985] AC 210); *Curran* v. *Northern Ireland Co-Ownership Housing Association Ltd.* ([1987] AC 718); *D and F Estates Ltd.* v. *Church Commissioners* ([1988] 3 WLR 368; and, most significantly, in *Murphy* v. *Brentwood DC* [1991] 1 AC 398). The basic tenets nowadays are clearly two: (*a*) the harm suffered by the plaintiffs in these cases is pure financial harm and not, as originally believed, property

damage, and (*b*) the purpose behind the supervisory powers over building operations conferred by the legislature on local authorities is to protect occupiers of buildings and the public against dangers to their health and personal safety and nothing more.

3. On the *Dutton, Anns, Murphy* problem, American courts have not been able to come up with a uniform answer, so all one can do here is to warn of the diversity of answers. Thus, at one end of the spectrum, many state courts have allowed recovery of economic losses resulting from defects in buildings. See: *Sewell* v. *Gregory* (1988) 371 SE 2d 82, 84–5 (West Virginia); *Cincinnati Riverfront Coliseum* v. *McNulty and Co.* (1986) 28 Ohio St. 3d 333, 504 NE 2d 415, 419; *Keel* v. *Titan Construction Corp.* (1981) 639 P. 2d 1228 (Oklahoma). Probably more courts have opted for the exact opposite view, denying all recovery. See: *Atherton Condo. Bd.* v. *Blume Development Co.* (1990) 115 Wash. 2d 506, 799 P. 2d 250, 262; *Ellis* v. *Robert C. Morris Inc.* (1986) 513 A. 2d 951 (New Hampshire). Cf., however, *Lempke* v. *Dagenais* (1987) 547 A. 2d 290 (allowing recovery for breach of warranty even in the absence of privity). In between these two extremes, one also finds compromise permutations—for instance recovery for remedial work for life-threatening defects. See: *Council of Co-Owners* v. *Whiting-Turner Constructing Co.* (1986) 308 Md. 18, 517 A. 2d 336, 344–5. These problems are discussed by Jones, 'Economic Loss Caused by Construction Deficiencies: the Competing Regimes of Contract and Tort', 59 *Univ. of Cincinnati L. Rev.* 1051 (1991); Libertucci, 'Builders' Liability to New and Subsequent Purchasers', 20 *Southwestern University Law Rev.* 219 (1991); Yuen, 'Absent Privity of Contract Contractors may not Recover Economic Damages caused by an Architect's Negligence', 60 *Cincinnati L. Rev.* 565 (1991).

4. These cases, however, also show that accidents cannot always be neatly categorized. A television set explodes and injures my child: this is product liability and the damage is clearly personal injury (if it damages my table, it is property damage). The same television does not function when switched on. This (according to the better view) is economic loss and the remedy should best be sought in the law of sales, the UCC etc. In this sense: *Spring Motors Distributors Inc.* v. *Ford Motor Co.* 489 A. 2d 660 (1985); *Henry Heide, Inc.* v. *WRH Products Co. Inc.*, 766 F. 2d 105 (1985). For a systematic analysis see *Two Rivers Co.* v. *Curtiss Breeding Serv.*, US Ct. of App., 5th Cir. (Tex., 1980), 624 F. 2d 1242. For Germany see Hager, 'Zum Schutzbereich der Produzentenhaftung', *AcP* (1984), 413.

5. In between are cases like 48, 49, 50, 51, 52, where a defective component causes further damage to the product but no other damage to persons or other property. This borderline case has caused its problems; and it is here that tort is increasingly used to invade the province of contract law. This

unease is reflected in the German cases reproduced in this book. (Note, for example, case 46 and, incidentally, note how superficially (by English standards) earlier case law is brushed aside. This 'summary' way that earlier 'precedents' are handled by German courts is a subject worthy of further study.) Thus it is said that if the defect and the damage caused by it are not 'substantially the same' then recovery for the latter is possible in tort. And conversely, if there is 'substantial identity' (*Stoffgleichheit*) between defect and subsequent harm, then no tort action will be allowed. So where asbestos tiles attached to the plaintiff's house released in rainy weather a substance which silted up his windows, a tortious claim was successful (BGH NJW 1981, 2250). But in another case (BGH NJW 1981, 2248) insulation material built into a roof caused it to crack as temperature variations produced expansion and contraction. The defect and the damage it caused were here considered to be 'substantially the same' so the tort action failed.

6. Decisions such as the above provide illustrations (see also BGH NJW 1983, 812); but the criterion of 'substantial identity' has much troubled the German courts as cases 48–52 clearly show. Their study makes hard reading but, basically, one detects an unease with the whole subject evidenced by changing tests and underscored by academic doubts (see, for example, Deutsch, *JZ* 1984, 308, 311; Stoll, *JZ* 1983, 501). Thus, originally, the defective part had to be a 'functionally limited unit' of the whole product in order to be classed as damage to property when it spread and 'infected' the rest of the product. In the *Gaszugfall* case (51) the court decided that one should not focus exclusively on the idea of a 'functionally limited unit' but one should, instead, adopt an economic approach. The question to be asked was thus whether the defective part could be separated from the rest of the product without considerable economic loss (see section II.2(*b*) of case 51). The *Kompressorfall* case (52) now introduces a new test which requires the court to compare the defect of the product when acquired with the damage done when the defect has spread.

7. This German case law has proved highly controversial with academics, but their criticisms have left the judges unmoved. In the light of this, an outside observer must be cautious in expressing his views and should, perhaps, limit his observations to three points. Thus, *first* comes the advice to the reader to familiarise himself with as much of this literature as possible. The references given in the next paragraph (8.) are meant to assist this process; and the study of foreign laws can only enrich this understanding. *Secondly*, the reader will be assisted in his task by the comments that Professor Kötz volunteered (in a private letter to the author; *Addendum 1*) and which refer to the *Schwimmerschalter* case (no. 45, above). The main thrust of his objections (and further references) can also be found in his invaluable *Deliktsrecht*, 5th edn. pp. 28 *et seq. Finally*, despite the force of these

arguments, the reader will also benefit from looking at these developments from a broader perspective. Thus, another distinguished comparatist, (Professor Fleming in (1989) 105 *LQR*, 508–511; *Addendum 2*) seems to regard this case law as a reaction (perhaps inept but, arguably, inevitable) to the restrictive regime that the Code has adopted towards the problem of pure economic loss. Seen in this light, these developments may thus also contain important lessons for Common lawyers.

8. See, more recently: BGH VersR 1989, 91 (*Fischfutter*); BGH NJW 1990, 908 = VersR 1980, 204 (*Weinkorken*); BGH VersR 1990, 1283 (with disapproving note by E. Lorenz); BGH VersR 1992, 758 (*Nockenwellensteuerrad*); BGH VersR 1992, 837 (*Kondensator*); Steffen, 'Die Bedeutung der "Stoffgleichheit" mit dem "Mangelunwert" für die Herstellerhaftung aus Weiterfresserschäden', *VersR* 1988, 977; Kullmann, 'Die Rechtsprechung des BGH zum Produkthaftpflichtrecht in den Jahren 1991/92', *NJW* 1992, 2669; v. Bar, 'Probleme der Haftpflicht für deliktsrechtliche Eigentumsverletzungen,' *Mannheimer Vorträge zur Versicherungswissenschaft* (1992).

Addendum 1 (From Professor Dr Hein Kotz)

'It might shed some . . . light on the *Schwimmerschalter* decision if one bears in mind that the parties in that case were the buyer and the seller of the product in question and that the buyer had lost his contractual remedy only because he had failed to bring his action within the six-month period laid down in § 477 BGB. Nobody would have raised an eyebrow if the Court had said: "We are sorry that we cannot help the plaintiff since he failed to bring his action within the limitation period of § 477 BGB." Nobody would have raised an eyebrow if the Court had added: "This is a harsh result since in this case a reasonable man would have been unable to detect the defect before the end of the six-month period, let alone bring an action before that date. We cannot do anything about it, but we ask Parliament to look at the problem and devise a solution, perhaps along the lines of Art. 39 of the Vienna Sales Convention." It would have been somewhat bolder but perfectly acceptable if the Court had said: "We interpret § 477 BGB restrictively so as to let the six-month period start running not at the time of the delivery of the product but, in the event of a reasonably undetectable defect, at the date at which the buyer did detect it or, as a reasonable man, should have been able to detect it." The Federal Court, however, did not choose any of these solutions, but came up, quite unexpectedly, with a disastrous fourth solution.

In later cases, the Federal Court applied the *Schwimmerschalter* rule to cases in which the parties were not linked by a contract but the plaintiff was a buyer further down stream. It follows that a seller may do what he pleases in order to exempt himself from both contractual and tort liability by way of a contractual agreement with his direct customer. All this, however, will not help him at all if a downstream buyer suffers damage to the defective product itself. Let me add that the limitation period for a tort claim is of course three years after detection of the damage and the [identity of the] person responsible for it (§ 852 BGB). In my view, this makes no sense.'

Addendum 2 (Professor John Fleming)

'This line of attack [contained in the *Kompressor* case] is reminiscent of the equation of "property damage" with structural change in the pre- *D and F Estates* cases, also of Justice Traynor's view in the leading American case of *Seeley* v. *White Motor Company* 63 Cal. 2d 9 (1965) distinguishing between a claim by a purchaser of a defective truck for the cost of repairs in a causally related accident and a claim for loss of profit due to inability to haul the expected quantity of loads.

What is at issue here is not so much the precise formula suggested by the German court as its willingness, indeed eagerness, to extend tort protection for damage to the defective thing itself. It is the more remarkable because of the Civil Code's categorical exclusion of tort damages for purely economic loss and the great weight reputedly given by German law to theoretical orthodoxy over pragmatism. Clearly English law would not have to go to the same pains to justify similar results: only traditionalists have to seek refuge in abstractions. The answer is found in a search not for what the law had been thought to be, but what we want it to be. There clearly are options.'

Addendum 3

1. Extract from Lord Denning MR's judgment from *Dutton* v. *Bognor Regis UDC* (CA) [1972] 1 QB 373, 396.*

Mr Tapp [attorney for the defendant local authority] submitted that the liability of the council would, in any case, be limited to those who suffered bodily harm: and did not extend to those who only suffered economic loss. He suggested, therefore, that although the council might be liable if the ceiling fell down and injured a visitor, they would not be liable simply because the house was diminished in value. He referred to the recent case of *SCM (United Kingdom) Ltd.* v. *W. J. Whittal & Son Ltd.* [1971] 1 QB 337.

I cannot accept this submission. The damage done here was not solely economic loss. It was physical damage to the house. If Mr Tapp's submission were right, it would mean that if the inspector negligently passes the house as properly built and it collapses and injures a person, the council are liable: but if the owner discovers the defect in time to repair it—and he does repair it—the council are not liable. That is an impossible distinction. They are liable in either case.

I would say the same about the manufacturer of an article. If he makes it

---

* In this case Mrs Dutton bought a house, which had been negligently built on a rubbish tip, not from its builder but from an intervening purchaser. The building inspector, acting for the local council, failed to notice the inadequate foundations. The walls later started to crack. The action against the *builder* was compromised, and the above extracts come from the Court of Appeal judgment dealing with the action against the local authority. Lord Denning's characterization of Mrs Dutton's loss as 'physical damage' was subsequently approved by the House of Lords in *Anns* v. *Merton London Borough Council* [1978] AC 728. But was it 'physical damage'? See Lord Denning's extra-judicial views in his book *The Discipline of the Law* (1979), 264.

negligently, with a latent defect (so that it breaks to pieces and injures someone), he is undoubtedly liable. Suppose that the defect is discovered in time to prevent the injury. Surely he is liable for the cost of repair.

2. Uniform Commercial Code, § 2–318
Third-Party Beneficiaries of Warranties Express or Implied

Alternative A

A seller's warranty whether express or implied extends to any natural person who is in the family or household of his buyer or who is a guest in his home if it is reasonable to expect that such person may use, consume, or be affected by the goods and who is injured in person by breach of the warranty. A seller may not exclude or limit the operation of this section.

Alternative B

A seller's warranty whether express or implied extends to any natural person who may reasonably be expected to use, consume, or be affected by the goods and who is injured in person by breach of the warranty. A seller may not exclude or limit the operation of this section.

Alternative C

A seller's warranty whether express or implied extends to any person who may reasonably be expected to use, consume, or be affected, by the goods and who is injured by breach of the warranty. A seller may not exclude or limit the operation of this section with respect to injury to the person of an individual to whom the warranty extends. As amended 1966.

3. *Restatement Second, Tort*, § 402A
Special Liability of Seller of Product for Physical Harm to User or Consumer

(1) One who sells any product in a defective condition unreasonably dangerous to the user or consumer or to his property is subject to liability for physical harm thereby caused to the ultimate user or consumer, or to his property, if

(*a*) the seller is engaged in the business of selling such a product, and

(*b*) it is expected to and does reach the user or consumer without substantial change in the condition in which it is sold.

(2) The rule stated in subsection (1) applies although

(*a*) the seller has exercised all possible care in the preparation and sale of his product, and (*b*) the user or consumer has not bought the product from or entered into any contractual relation with the seller.

Addendum 4

East River SS Corp. v. *Transamerica Delaval* 476 US 858, 106 S. Ct. Rep. 2295

Justice BLACKMUN delivered the opinion of the Court.

In this admiralty case, we must decide whether a cause of action in tort is stated when a defective product purchased in a commercial transaction malfunctions, injuring only the product itself and causing purely economic loss. The case requires us to consider preliminarily whether admiralty law, which already recognizes a general theory of liability for negligence, also incorporates principles of products liability, including strict liability. Then, charting a course between products liability and contract law, we must determine whether injury to a product itself is the kind of harm that should be protected by products liability or left entirely to the law of contracts.

I. In 1969, Seatrain Shipbuilding Corp. (Shipbuilding), a wholly owned subsidiary of Seatrain Lines, Inc. (Seatrain), announced it would build the four oil-transporting supertankers in issue—the TT Stuyvesant, TT Williamsburgh, TT Brooklyn, and TT Bay Ridge. Each tanker was constructed pursuant to a contract in which a separate wholly owned subsidiary of Seatrain engaged Shipbuilding. Shipbuilding in turn contracted with respondent, now known as Transamerica Delaval, Inc. (Delaval), to design, manufacture, and supervise the installation of turbines (costing $1.4 million each, see App. 163) that would be the main propulsion units for the 225,000-ton, $125 million (ibid.) supertankers. When each ship was completed, its title was transferred from the contracting subsidiary to a trust company (as trustee for an owner), which in turn chartered the ship to one of the petitioners, also subsidiaries of Seatrain. Queensway Tankers, Inc., chartered the Stuyvesant; Kingsway Tankers, Inc., chartered the Williamsburgh; East River Steamship Corp. chartered the Brooklyn; and Richmond Tankers, Inc., chartered the Bay Ridge. Each petitioner operated under a bareboat charter, by which it took full control of the ship for 20 or 22 years as though it owned it, with the obligation afterwards to return the ship to the real owner. See G. Gilmore and C. Black, Admiralty §§ 4-1, 4-22 (2nd edn. 1975). Each charterer assumed responsibility for the cost of any repairs to the ships. Tr. of Oral Arg. 11, 16–17, 35.

The Stuyvesant sailed on its maiden voyage in late July 1977. On December 11 of that year, as the ship was about to enter the Port of Valdez, Alaska, steam began to escape from the casing of the high-pressure turbine. That problem was temporarily resolved by repairs, but before long, while the ship was encountering a severe storm in the Gulf of Alaska, the high-pressure turbine malfunctioned. The ship, though lacking its normal power, was able to continue on its journey to Panama and then San Francisco. In January 1978, an examination of the high-pressure turbine revealed that the first-stage steam reversing ring virtually had disintegrated and had caused additional damage to other parts of the turbine. The damaged part was replaced with a part from the Bay Ridge, which was then under construction. In April 1978, the ship again was repaired, this time with a part from the Brooklyn. Finally, in August, the ship was permanently and satisfactorily repaired with a ring newly designed and manufactured by Delaval.

The Brooklyn and the Williamsburgh were put into service in late 1973 and late 1974, respectively. In 1978, as a result of the Stuyvesant's problems, they were inspected while in port. Those inspections revealed similar turbine damage. Temporary repairs were made, and newly designed parts were installed as permanent repairs that summer.

When the Bay Ridge was completed in early 1979, it contained the newly designed parts and thus never experienced the high-pressure turbine problems that plagued the other three ships. Nonetheless, the complaint appears to claim damages as a result of deterioration of the Bay Ridge's ring that was installed in the Stuyvesant while the Bay Ridge was under construction. In addition, the Bay Ridge experienced a unique problem. In 1980, when the ship was on its maiden voyage, the engine began to vibrate with a frequency that increased even after speed was reduced. It turned out that the astern guardian valve, located between the high-pressure and low-pressure turbines, had been installed backwards. Because of that error, steam entered the low-pressure turbine and damaged it. After repairs, the Bay Ridge resumed its travels.

II. The charterers' second amended complaint, filed in the United States District Court for the District of New Jersey, invokes admiralty jurisdiction. It contains five counts alleging tortious conduct on the part of respondent Delaval and seeks $3.03 million in damages, App. 73, for the cost of repairing the ships and for income lost while the ships were out of service. The first four counts, read liberally, allege that Delaval is strictly liable for the design defects in the high-pressure turbines of the Stuyvesant, the Williamsburgh, the Brooklyn, and the Bay Ridge, respectively. The fifth count alleges that Delaval, as part of the manufacturing process, negligently supervised the installation of the astern guardian valve on the Bay Ridge. The initial complaint also had listed Seatrain and Shipbuilding as plaintiffs and had alleged breach of contract and warranty as well as tort claims. But after Delaval interposed a statute of limitations defense, the complaint was amended and the charterers alone brought the suit in tort. The non-renewed claims were dismissed with prejudice by the District Court. Delaval then moved for summary judgment, contending that the charterers' actions were not cognizable in tort.

The District Court granted summary judgment for Delaval, and the Court of Appeals for the Third Circuit, sitting *en banc*, affirmed. *East River SS Corp.* v. *Delaval Turbine, Inc.*, 752 F. 2d 903 (1985). The Court of Appeals held that damage solely to a defective product is actionable in tort if the defect creates an unreasonable risk of harm to persons or property other than the product itself, and harm materializes. Disappointments over the product's quality, on the other hand, are protected by warranty law. Id., at 908, 909–10. The charterers were dissatisfied with product quality: the defects involved gradual and unnoticed deterioration of the turbines' component parts, and the only risk created was that the turbines would operate at a lower capacity. Id., at 909. See *Pennsylvania Glass Sand Corp.* v. *Caterpillar Tractor Co.*, 652 F. 2d 1165, 1169–70 (CA3 1981). Therefore, neither the negligence nor the strict liability claims were cognizable.

III. . . .

B. [2] The torts alleged in the first, second, third, and fifth counts clearly fall within the admiralty jurisdiction. . . .

C. [3] With admiralty jurisdiction comes the application of substantive admiralty law. . . . Absent a relevant statute, the general maritime law, as developed by the judiciary, applies. . . . Drawn from state and federal sources, the general maritime law is an amalgam of traditional Common-law rules, modifications of those rules, and newly created rules. . . .

[4] The Courts of Appeals sitting in admiralty overwhelmingly have adopted concepts of products liability, based both on negligence . . . and on strict liability. . . .

We join the Courts of Appeals in recognizing products liability, including strict liability, as part of the general maritime law. . . . Our incorporation of products liability into maritime law, however, is only the threshold determination to the main issue in this case.

IV. Products liability grew out of a public policy judgment that people need more protection from dangerous products than is afforded by the law of warranty. See *Seely* v. *White Motor Co.*, 63 Cal. 2d 9, 15, 45 Cal. Rptr. 17, 21, 403 P. 2d 145, 149 (1965). It is clear, however, that if this development were allowed to progress too far, contract law would drown in a sea of tort. See G. Gilmore, *The Death of Contract*, 87–94 (1974). We must determine whether a commercial product injuring itself is the kind of harm against which public policy requires manufacturers to protect, independent of any contractual obligation.

A. [5] The paradigmatic products-liability action is one where a product 'reasonably certain to place life and limb in peril', distributed without reinspection, causes bodily injury. See e.g. *MacPherson* v. *Buick Motor Co.*, 217 NY 382, 389, 111 NE 1050, 1051, 1053 (1916). The manufacturer is liable whether or not it is negligent because 'public policy demands that responsibility be fixed wherever it will most effectively reduce the hazards to life and health inherent in defective products that reach the market'. *Escola* v. *Coca Cola Bottling Co. of Fresno*, 24 Cal. 2d, at 462, 150 P. 2d, at 441 (concurring opinion).

For similar reasons of safety, the manufacturer's duty of care was broadened to include protection against property damage. See *Marsh Wood Products Co.* v. *Babcock & Wilcox Co.*, 207 Wis. 209, 226, 240 NW 392, 399 (1932); *Genesee County Patrons Fire Relief Assn.* v. *L. Sonneborn Sons, Inc.*, 263 NY 463, 469–73, 189 NE 551, 553–5 (1934). Such damage is considered so akin to personal injury that the two are treated alike. See *Seely* v. *White Motor Co.*, 63 Cal. 2d, at 19, 45 Cal. Rptr., at 24, 403, P. 2d, at 152.

In the traditional 'property damage' cases, the defective product damages other property. In this case, there was no damage to 'other' property. Rather, the first, second, and third counts allege that each supertanker's defectively designed turbine components damaged only the turbine itself. Since each turbine was supplied by Delaval as an integrated package, see App. 162–3, each is properly regarded as a single unit. 'Since all but the very simplest of machines have component parts, [a contrary] holding would require a finding of "property damage" in virtually every case where a product damages itself. Such a holding would eliminate the distinction between warranty and strict products liability.' *Northern Power and Engineering Corp.* v. *Caterpillar Tractor Co.*, 623 P. 2d 324, 330 (Alaska 1981). The fifth count also alleges injury to the product itself. Before the high-pressure and low-pressure turbines could become an operational propulsion system, they were connected to piping and valves under the supervision of Delaval personnel. See App. 78, 162–3, 181. Delaval's supervisory obligations were part of its manufacturing agreement. The fifth count thus can best be read to allege that Delaval's negligent manufacture of the propulsion system—by allowing the installation in reverse of the astern guardian valve—damaged the propulsion system. Cf. *Lewis* v. *Timco, Inc.*, 736 F. 2d 163, 165–6 (CA5 1984). Obviously, damage to a product itself has certain attributes of a products-liability claim. But the injury suffered—the failure of the product to function properly—is the essence of a warranty action, through which a contracting party can seek to recoup the benefit of its bargain.

B. The intriguing question whether injury to a product itself may be brought in tort has spawned a variety of answers.[3] [Footnote omitted.] At one end of the spectrum, the case that created the majority land-based approach, *Seely* v. *White Motor Co.*, 63 Cal. 2d 9, 45 Cal. Rptr. 17, 403 P. 2d 145 (1965) (defective truck), held that preserving a proper role for the law of warranty precludes imposing tort liability if a defective product causes purely monetary harm. See also *Jones and Laughlin Steel Corp.* v. *Johns-Manville Sales Corp.*, 626 F. 2d 280, 287 and n. 13 (CA3 1980) (citing cases).

At the other end of the spectrum is the minority land-based approach, whose progenitor, *Santor* v. *A and M Karagheusian, Inc.*, 44 NJ 52, 66–7, 207 A. 2d 305, 312–13 (1965) (marred carpeting), held that a manufacturer's duty to make nondefective products encompassed injury to the product itself, whether or not the defect created an unreasonable risk of harm.[1] See also *LaCrosse* v. *Schubert*, 72 Wis. 2d 38, 44–5, 240 NW 2d 124, 127–8 (1976). The courts adopting this approach, including the majority of the Courts of Appeals sitting in admiralty that have considered the issue,[2] e.g., *Emerson GM Diesel, Inc.* v. *Alaskan Enterprise*, 732 F. 2d 1468 (CA9

---

[1] Interestingly, the New Jersey and California Supreme Courts have each taken what appears to be a step in the direction of the other since *Santor* and *Seely*. In *Spring Motors Distributors, Inc.* v. *Ford Motor Co.*, 98 NJ, at 579, 489 A. 2d, at 672, the New Jersey court rejected *Santor* in the commercial context. And in *J'Aire Corp.* v. *Gregory*, 24 Cal. 3d 799, 157 Cal. Rptr. 407, 598 P. 2d 60 (1979), the California court recognized a cause of action for negligent interference with prospective economic advantage.

[2] Most of the admiralty cases concerned fishing vessels. See *Emerson GM Diesel, Inc.* v. *Alaskan Enterprise*, 732 F. 2d 1468, 1472 (CA9 1984) (relying on solicitude for fishermen as a reason for a more protective approach). Delaval concedes that the courts, see *Carbone* v. *Ursich*, 209 F. 2d 178, 182 (CA9 1953), and Congress, see 46 U.S.C. § 533, at times have provided special protection for fishermen. This case involves no fishermen.

1984), find that the safety and insurance rationales behind strict liability apply equally where the losses are purely economic. These courts reject the *Seely* approach because they find it arbitrary that economic losses are recoverable if a plaintiff suffers bodily injury or property damage, but not if a product injures itself. They also find no inherent difference between economic loss and personal injury or property damage, because all are proximately caused by the defendant's conduct. Further, they believe recovery for economic loss would not lead to unlimited liability because they think a manufacturer can predict and insure against product failure. See *Emerson GM Diesel, Inc.* v. *Alaskan Enterprise*, 732 F. 2d, at 1474.

Between the two poles fall a number of cases that would permit a products-liability action under certain circumstances when a product injures only itself. These cases attempt to differentiate between 'the disappointed users . . . and the endangered ones', *Russell* v. *Ford Motor Co.*, 281 Or. 587, 595, 575 P. 2d 1383, 1387 (1978), and permit only the latter to sue in tort. The determination has been said to turn on the nature of the defect, the type of risk, and the manner in which the injury arose. See *Pennsylvania Glass Sand Corp.* v. *Caterpillar Tractor Co.*, 652 F. 2d 1165, 1173 (CA3 1981) (relied on by the Court of Appeals in this case). The Alaska Supreme Court allows a tort action if the defective product creates a situation potentially dangerous to persons or other property, and loss occurs as a proximate result of that danger and under dangerous circumstances. *Northern Power and Engineering Corp.* v. *Caterpillar Tractor Co.*, 623 P. 2d 324, 329 (1981).

We find the intermediate and minority land-based positions unsatisfactory. The intermediate positions, which essentially turn on the degree of risk, are too indeterminate to enable manufacturers easily to structure their business behavior. Nor do we find persuasive a distinction that rests on the manner in which the product is injured. We realize that the damage may be qualitative, occurring through gradual deterioration or internal breakage. Or it may be calamitous. Compare *Morrow* v. *New Moon Homes, Inc.*, 548 P. 2d 279 (Alaska 1976), with *Cloud* v. *Kit Mfg. Co.*, 563 P. 2d 248, 251 (Alaska 1977). But either way, since by definition no person or other property is damaged, the resulting loss is purely economic. Even when the harm to the product itself occurs through an abrupt, accident-like event, the resulting loss due to repair costs, decreased value, and lost profits is essentially the failure of the purchaser to receive the benefit of its bargain—traditionally the core concern of contract law. See E. Farnsworth, *Contracts* § 12.8, pp. 839–40 (1982).

We also decline to adopt the minority land-based view espoused by *Santor* and *Emerson*. Such cases raise legitimate questions about the theories behind restricting products liability, but we believe that the countervailing arguments are more powerful. The minority view fails to account for the need to keep products liability and contract law in separate spheres and to maintain a realistic limitation on damages.

C. Exercising traditional discretion in admiralty, see *Pope and Talbot, Inc.* v. *Hawn*, 346 US 406, 409, 74 S. Ct. 202, 204, 98 L. Ed. 143 (1953), we adopt an approach similar to *Seely* and hold that a manufacturer in a commercial relationship has no duty under either a negligence or strict products-liability theory to prevent a product from injuring itself.[1]

'The distinction that the law has drawn between tort recovery for physical injuries and warranty recovery for economic loss is not arbitrary and does not rest on the "luck" of one plaintiff in having an accident causing physical injury. The distinction rests, rather, on an understanding of the nature of the responsibility a manufacturer must undertake in distributing his products.' *Seely* v. *White Motor Co.*, 63 Cal. 2d, at 18, 45 Cal. Rptr., at 23, 403 P. 2d, at 151. When a product injures only itself the reasons for imposing a tort duty are weak and those for leaving the party to its contractual remedies are strong.

The tort concern with safety is reduced when an injury is only to the product itself. When a person is injured, the 'cost of an injury and the loss of time or health may be an overwhelming misfortune', and one the person is not prepared to meet. *Escola* v. *Coca Cola Bottling Co. of Fresno*, 24 Cal. 2d, at 462, 150 P. 2d, at 441 (concurring opinion). In contrast, when a product injures itself, the commercial user stands to lose the value of the product, risks the displeasure of its customers who find that the product does not meet their needs, or, as in this case, experiences increased costs in performing a service. Losses like these can be insured. See 10A Couch on Insurance §§ 42: 385–42: 401, 42: 414–17 (2nd edn. 1982); 7 Benedict on Admiralty, Form no. 1.16–7 (7th edn. 1985); 5A Appleman, Insurance Law and Practice § 3252 (1970). Society need not presume that a customer needs special protection. The increased cost to the public that would result from holding a manufacturer liable in tort for injury to the product itself is not justified. Cf. *United States* v. *Carroll Towing Co.*, 159 F. 2d 169, 173 (CA2 1947).

Damage to a product itself is most naturally understood as a warranty claim. Such damage means simply that the product has not met the customer's expectations, or, in other words, that the customer has received 'insufficient product value'. See J. White and R. Summers, Uniform Commercial Code 406 (2nd edn. 1980). The maintenance of product value and quality is precisely the purpose of express and implied warranties.[2] See UCC § 2–313 (express warranty), § 2–314 (implied warranty of merchantability), and § 2–315 (warranty of fitness for a particular purpose). Therefore, a claim of a non-working product can be brought as a breach-of-warranty action. Or, if the customer prefers, it can reject the product or revoke its acceptance and sue for breach of contract. See UCC §§ 2–601, 2–608, 2–612.

---

[1] We do not reach the issue whether a tort cause of action can ever be stated in admiralty when the only damages sought are economic. Cf. *Ultramares Corp.* v. *Touche*, 255 NY 170, 174 NE 441 (1931). But see *Robins Dry Dock and Repair Co.* v. *Flint*, 275 US 303, 48 S. Ct. 134, 72 L. Ed. 290 (1927).

[2] If the charterers' claims were brought as breach-of-warranty actions, they would not be within the admiralty jurisdiction. Since contracts relating to the construction of or supply of materials to a ship are not within the admiralty jurisdiction, see *Thames Towboat Co.* v. *The Schooner 'Francis McDonald'*, 254 US 242, 243, 41 S. Ct. 65, 66, 65 L. Ed. 245 (1920); *Kossick* v. *United Fruit Co.*, 365 US 731, 735, 81 S. Ct. 886, 889, 6 L. Ed. 2d 56 (1961), neither are warranty claims grounded in such contracts. See 1 Benedict, Admiralty § 188, p. 11–36 (7th edn. 1985). State law would govern the actions. See *North Pacific SS Co.* v. *Hall Brothers Marine Railway and Shipbuilding Co.*, 249 US 119, 127, 39 S. Ct. 221, 223, 63 L. Ed. 510 (1919). In particular the Uniform Commercial Code, which has been adopted by 49 States, would apply.

Contract law, and the law of warranty in particular, is well suited to commercial controversies of the sort involved in this case because the parties may set the terms of their own agreements.[1] The manufacturer can restrict its liability, within limits, by disclaiming warranties or limiting remedies. See UCC §§ 2–316, 2–719. In exchange, the purchaser pays less for the product. Since a commercial situation generally does not involve large disparities in bargaining power, cf. *Henningsen* v. *Bloomfield Motors, Inc.*, 32 NJ 358, 161 A. 2d 69 (1960), we see no reason to intrude into the parties' allocation of the risk.

While giving recognition to the manufacturer's bargain, warranty law sufficiently protects the purchaser by allowing it to obtain the benefit of its bargain. See J. White and R. Summers, *supra*, ch. 10. The expectation damages available in warranty for purely economic loss give a plaintiff the full benefit of its bargain by compensating for forgone business opportunities. See Fuller and Perdue, 'The Reliance Interest in Contract Damages' *1*, 46 *Yale LJ* 52, 60–3 (1936); R. Posner, *Economic Analysis of Law* § 4.8 (3rd edn. 1986). Recovery on a warranty theory would give the charterers their repair costs and lost profits, and would place them in the position they would have been in had the turbines functioned properly.[2] See *Hawkins* v. *McGee*, 84 NH 114, 146 A. 641 (1929). Thus, both the nature of the injury and the resulting damages indicate it is more natural to think of injury to a product itself in terms of warranty.

A warranty action also has a built-in limitation on liability, whereas a tort action could subject the manufacturer to damages of an indefinite amount. The limitation in a contract action comes from the agreement of the parties and the requirement that consequential damages, such as lost profits, be a foreseeable result of the breach. See *Hadley* v. *Baxendale*, 9 Ex. 341, 156 Eng. Rep. 145 (1854). In a warranty action where the loss is purely economic, the limitation derives from the requirements of foreseeability and of privity, which is still generally enforced for such claims in a commercial setting. See UCC § 2–715; J. White and R. Summers, Uniform Commercial Code 389, 396, 406–10 (2nd edn. 1980).

In products-liability law, where there is a duty to the public generally, foreseeability is an inadequate brake. Cf. *Petitions of Kinsman Transit Co.*, 388 F. 2d 821 (CA2 1968). See also Perlman, 'Interference with Contract and Other Economic Expectancies: A Clash of Tort and Contract Doctrine' 49 *U. Ch. L. Rev.* 61, 71–2

---

[1] We recognize, of course, that warranty and products liability are not static bodies of law and may overlap. In certain situations, for example, the privity requirement of warranty has been discarded, e.g. *Henningsen* v. *Bloomfield Motors, Inc.*, 32 NJ 358, 380–4, 161 A. 2d 69, 81–4 (1960). In other circumstances, a manufacturer may be able to disclaim strict tort liability. See e.g. *Keystone Aeronautics Corp.* v. *R. J. Enstrom Corp.*, 499 F. 2d 146, 149 (CA3 1974). Nonetheless, the main currents of tort law run in different directions from those of contract and warranty, and the latter seem to us far more appropriate for commercial disputes of the kind involved here.

[2] In contrast, tort damages generally compensate the plaintiff for loss and return him to the position he occupied before the injury. Cf. *Sullivan* v. *O'Connor*, 363 Mass. 579, 584–6, 588, n. 6, 296 NE 2d 183, 187–8, 189, n. 6 (1973); Prosser, 'The Borderland of Tort and Contract', in *Selected Topics on the Law of Torts* 380, 424–7 (Thomas M. Cooley Lectures, Fourth Series 1953). Tort damages are analogous to reliance damages, which are awarded in contract when there is particular difficulty in measuring the expectation interest. See e.g. *Security Store and Mfg. Co.* v. *American Railways Express Co.*, 227 Mo. App. 175, 51 SW 2d 572 (1932).

(1982). Permitting recovery for all foreseeable claims for purely economic loss could make a manufacturer liable for vast sums. It would be difficult for a manufacturer to take into account the expectations of persons downstream who may encounter its product. In this case, for example, if the charterers—already one step removed from the transaction—were permitted to recover their economic losses, then the companies that subchartered the ships might claim their economic losses from the delays, and the charterers' customers also might claim their economic losses, and so on. 'The law does not spread its protection so far.' *Robins Dry Dock and Repair Co.* v. *Flint*, 275 US 303, 309, 48 S. Ct. 134, 135, 72 L. Ed. 290 (1927).

And to the extent that courts try to limit purely economic damages in tort, they do so by relying on a far murkier line, one that negates the charterers' contention that permitting such recovery under a products-liability theory enables admiralty courts to avoid difficult linedrawing. Cf. *Ultramares Corp.* v. *Touche*, 255 NY 170, 174 NE 441 (1931); *State of Louisiana ex rel. Guste* v. *M/V Testbank*, 752 F. 2d 1019, 1046–52 (CA5 1985) (*en banc*) (dissenting opinion), cert. pending, no. 84–1808.

D. For the first three counts, the defective turbine components allegedly injured only the turbines themselves. Therefore, a strict products-liability theory of recovery is unavailable to the charterers. Any warranty claims would be subject to Delaval's limitation, both in time and scope, of its warranty liability. App. 78–9. The record indicates that Seatrain and Delaval reached a settlement agreement. Deposition of Stephen Russell, p. 32. We were informed that these charterers could not have asserted the warranty claims. See Tr. of Oral Arg. 36. Even so, the charterers should be left to the terms of their bargains, which explicitly allocated the cost of repairs.

In the charterers' agreements with the owners, the charterers took the ships in 'as is' condition, after inspection, and assumed full responsibility for them, including responsibility for maintenance and repairs and for obtaining certain forms of insurance. Tr. of Oral Arg. 11, 16–17, 35; App. 86, 88, 99, 101, 112, 114, 125–6, 127. In a separate agreement between each charterer and Seatrain, Seatrain agreed to guarantee certain payments and covenants by each charterer to the owner. App. 142–6. The contractual responsibilities thus were clearly laid out. There is no reason to extricate the parties from their bargain.

Similarly, in the fifth count, alleging the reverse installation of the astern guardian valve, the only harm was to the propulsion system itself rather than to persons or other property. Even assuming that Delaval's supervision was negligent, as we must on this summary judgment motion, Delaval owed no duty under a products-liability theory based on negligence to avoid causing purely economic loss. Cf. *Flintkote Co.* v. *Dravo Corp.*, 678 F. 2d 942 (CA11 1982); *S. M. Wilson and Co.* v. *Smith International, Inc.* 587 F. 2d 1363 (CA9 1978). Thus, whether stated in negligence or strict liability, no products-liability claim lies in admiralty when the only injury claimed is economic loss.

While we hold that the fourth count should have been dismissed, we affirm the entry of judgment for Delaval.

17. CAUSATION

Case 56

REICHSGERICHT (THIRD CIVIL DIVISION) 13 OCTOBER 1922*
RGZ 105, 264

On 2 January 1920, as the plaintiff's husband was about to alight from a tram, he was shot in the arm above the elbow by a policeman aiming at an escaping criminal. He was taken to hospital, contracted influenza (then prevalent in the hospital), and died on 18 March of a suppuration which developed in the chest in connection with the influenza. The plaintiff claims from the Prussian State under the Act of 1 August 1909 compensation for the loss arising from the death of her husband, caused by the fault of the policeman. The Landgericht granted her claim in part; the Court of Appeal rejected it completely. The plaintiff's application for review succeeded for these

Reasons

The Court of Appeal agreed with the Landgericht in finding it proved that the policeman who shot the plaintiff's husband was guilty of a negligent breach of his official duty. Unlike the Landgericht, however, it denied the causal connection between that shooting and the husband's death. It regarded the influenza, from which the victim died, as a mere 'subsequent accidental illness' and continued: At a time when the influenza epidemic was so widespread throughout Germany, no particular causal significance can be attached to the fact that at that time the influenza was fiercely raging in the hospital and especially in the ward into which the plaintiff's husband was taken. The risk of infection was the same inside the hospital as it was outside. Moreover, it is generally accepted that in hospitals the better hygienic arrangements and the continuous medical assistance if anything reduce such risks. Further, the applicant's case was not strengthened by the argument that the weakening of the victim's system by the shooting affected his resistance to infection or the illness that followed it.

The applicant rightly complains that in this way the Court of Appeal makes too rigorous demands for the acceptance of a causal connection. There is no doubt that between the shooting and the death of the plaintiff's husband a causal connection in the natural, mechanical sense does exist: the plaintiff's husband was taken into the hospital because he was shot. In the hospital he was attacked by the outbreak of influenza and succumbed to that illness. That causal connection was not excluded by the mere possibility

---

* English version by F. H. Lawson and B. S. Markesinis.

that he could have contracted influenza elsewhere, and also without the shooting.

Moreover, according to case-law the causal connection—the so-called adequate connection—exists here. The taking of the injured person to the hospital was an unobjectionable (even though not absolutely necessary), appropriate, and normal consequence of the injury. However, once in hospital he was, contrary to the opinion of the Court of Appeal, exposed to the risk of infection by a complaint prevalent to a particularly high degree because he could not escape from the company of the sick, as he might otherwise have done. He had to stay night and day in the ward where the influenza raged. That fact involved an enhancement of the risk of infection, according to human experience, and cannot be outweighed by any hygienic arrangements in the hospital or the care of the doctors and nurses. It must also be accepted that an injury, such as here existed, even if its cure progressed favourably, is in general not without effect on the resistance of the injured person against otherwise injurious influenza and that, therefore, the risk of an infection and its consequences is much greater than if there had been no injury. Accordingly, in agreement with the Landgericht, the shooting must be in law found to have been a contributory cause of the death of the plaintiff's husband.

Case 57

REICHSGERICHT (SIXTH CIVIL DIVISION) 22 JUNE 1931*
RGZ 133, 126

The facts appear in the

Reasons

The only point in dispute in the appeal is whether the fault of the plaintiff contributed as a cause to the automobile accident of 9 November 1928 (§ 9 Automobile Act, § 254 BGB). The Court of Appeal, which decided in the plaintiff's favour, denied this for the following reasons. Admittedly he acted carelessly, for that as a pedestrian he failed, before crossing the road, to ascertain whether an automobile was approaching. The co-defendant driver, however, was not prevented from avoiding the accident, which he could easily have done, and which was his duty. No adequate causal connection, therefore, existed between the plaintiff's conduct and the accident.

The complaint that in these explanations the concept of adequate causal connection was misunderstood is well founded. There can be no doubt that a natural causal connection existed between the plaintiff's conduct and the accident, for if he had not crossed the street at the very moment that the

* English version by F. H. Lawson and B. S. Markesinis.

defendant's automobile overtook J's cart, he could not have been struck by it. That was apparently the view of the judge of First Instance. But the facts must also be regarded as showing an adequate causal connection. Such a connection exists where an act or omission, generally, not only under especial and quite improbable circumstances which are not to be anticipated in the regular course of things, is capable of producing the result that occurred [references]. But in view of present traffic conditions, it cannot be accepted as inconceivable, that at the moment a pedestrian crosses the road, an automobile will pass over the same spot. The appellate judges seem to have been of the same mind; for they found a lack of foresight in the plaintiff's not looking round for any approaching automobiles, and therefore held him to have been at fault (§ 276 BGB).

Accordingly, the causation and fault of both parties must be balanced against each other according to § 9 of the Automobile Act and § 254 BGB. This balancing is essentially a matter for the trial judge and is reserved to the court below.

Case 58

REICHSGERICHT (SIXTH CIVIL DIVISION) 26 APRIL 1937*
RGZ 155, 37

[The facts of the case are not entirely clear but what appears to have happened is that the plaintiff suffered from morbid disturbances which impaired her earning capacity. The part of the judgment that is reproduced here discusses a causal point, namely whether her state is due to the defendant's negligence or should be attributed to her nervous disposition induced by her pregnancy.]

1. . . .

2. . . .

3. . . .

4. The plaintiff submits the opinion and report of the director of a university women's clinic and has nominated him as a witness. Although a judge of fact is entrusted with the choice of experts the Court of Appeal in the present case has rejected the request with a reasoning extracted from the factual content of the opinion, but which is legally objectionable. That reasoning is, according to the final sentence of the opinion, that the plaintiff's present state is conditioned by the pregnancy that produced twins. The expert's explanation must however be understood in its context. He says: the possibility remains open that the lady, affected mentally and bodily by the

* English version by F. H. Lawson and B. S. Markesinis.

accident, was burdened by the beginning of the pregnancy, in which she was carrying twins, to quite an exceptional degree; but one can best account for the plaintiff's condition by assuming that she had received severe damage by the accident, especially to her nerves. Moreover, there were also some slight bodily changes. So the opinion says: 'If the lady with her delicate constitution had not become pregnant, all consequences of the accident would probably have been made good. However, her present state is conditioned by the pregnancy, especially as she was carrying twins.' It would follow from this that the accident was still *one* condition of the plaintiff's present state. The pregnancy would indeed have affected the course of her state of health; but her present state would not have come into existence without the accident. That the causal connection was broken by the pregnancy cannot be said: the cause of her present state can still be adequately linked to the accident.

5. The Court of Appeal further admits that the origin of nervous disturbance which really existed, is to be traced to the accident, that the plaintiff, however, had a nervous predisposition and that it combined with her fantasies to affect the extent of the disturbances. The Court of Appeal is only willing to take all these disturbances into account down to the end of July 1933, in assessing medical expenses relying for that on the opinion of the expert K. Indeed, he too admits that the accident precipitated in the susceptible patient a lively 'mental reaction' with various morbid excitable states, but is of the opinion that the accident was not responsible for the plaintiff's especial mental disposition which was at the root of her nervous disturbance. This view is based on a legal error. If any accident strikes a person in a weakened state of health and the consequences have been so serious because of that state of health that his earning capacity is diminished, the law treats that diminution entirely as a consequence of the accident; in other words: anyone who commits an unlawful act against a person in weakened health has no right to be placed in the same position as if he had injured a person in perfect health.

Case 59

REICHSGERICHT (EIGHTH CIVIL DIVISION) 29 APRIL 1942*
RGZ 169, 117

On 20 January 1937 the plaintiff (a chimney-sweep) was struck down by a lorry owned by the second defendant and driven by the first; he suffered various injuries. The accident was caused by unlawful driving on the part of the first defendant, who was convicted of an offence under § 335 StGB. The plaintiff claims damages for this accident; he demands RM 6000 for pain

* English version by F. H. Lawson and B. S. Markesinis.

and suffering and RM 1725 for loss of earnings until 30 June 1938 and monthly payments of RM 100 from 1 July. The Landgericht allowed the claim in general but fixed the damages for pain and suffering at RM 3000. On appeal by the defendants, the Oberlandesgericht reduced the damages for pain and suffering and the compensation for the period until 30 June 1938 to one-half, the monthly payments for the period from 1 July to 31 December 1938 to RM 50, from 1 January 1939 to 30 June 1940 to RM 17.50, from 1 July to 30 November to RM 10.50, and from 1 December 1940 onwards to RM 7.50.

On the plaintiff's application for review, the Landgericht's decision was restored as regards the capital payments claimed; as regards the monthly payments the case was sent back to the Oberlandesgericht for these

Reasons

The defendants no longer object to the order obliging them to pay compensation for the damage done by the accident; nor is any doubt cast on the first defendant's conviction. The dispute between the parties is limited to whether the pain and suffering and loss of earning capacity are to be traced to the accident. While the Landgericht recognized this to the full extent, the Oberlandesgericht, on the basis of a fresh expert opinion of University Professor Dr von G, adopted a division of percentages. According to that opinion, the plaintiff suffered from a disease called *arthrosis deformans* (deforming arthrosis with degeneration of the joints), which is to be traced to a predisposition. But, in addition, down to the end of 1938 there were signs of so-called arthritis which arose from the accident. Moreover, sciatica on the left side, which also occurred down to the end of 1938, was produced by a predisposition but was brought into the open as an illness by the accident. According to the expert's opinion, the sick state of the plaintiff was traceable in equal shares to his predisposition and the accident. With this predisposition the plaintiff's illness was suddenly brought into the open by the accident which he suffered; besides, experience shows that those signs appeared in much greater degree, developed more quickly, and resulted as a rule in a more protracted illness than if it had developed only from the predisposition. Accordingly, the expert holds that down to the end of 1938 the illness was due about 50 per cent to the predisposition, the rest to the accident. Afterwards, when the arthritic complaints faded away, he traces the plaintiff's condition as 75 per cent to his predisposition and only 25 per cent to the accident. According to his opinion even without the accident, which brought it into the open, his illness would conceivably have broken out in the course of 1937 or 1938 from some other cause (by catching a cold or the like). In accordance with this opinion, the Oberlandesgericht awarded to the plaintiff, who had had to employ an assistant because of his illness, only half the damages for pain and suffering, assessed at RM 3000, and half of the expense of employing assistants in 1937 and 1938, and as regards the monthly payments demanded for the following period only 25 per cent of his shortfall, which it assesses at 70 per cent of the payments demanded.

The applicant for review rightly takes objection to this partition of the damage suffered by the plaintiff. The Court of Appeal misunderstands the concept of causal connection, as it has been shaped by the writers and the courts. The court has to answer the question of causal connection not only according to the view of the medical expert but independently by having regard to the relevant legal prerequisites, which may lead to deviations from the medical view (*JW* 1938 (no. 4), 105; SeuffArch. 95, no. 9). It is recognized that even illnesses that are brought to light by an accident, only because there was a predisposition thereto in the injured person, are treated by the law as consequences of the accident to their full extent; anyone who commits an unlawful act against a person in weak health has no right to be treated as though he had injured a completely healthy person (RGZ 151, 283; 155, 41; SeuffArch. 95, no. 9). The causal connection between the act of the person inflicting the damage and the damage is also not excluded because the particular consequence that followed from the injurious act could have occurred through another event that definitely happened later on (RGZ 141, 365; 144, 80 and 348; similarly *Kommentar zum ABGE* 4, n 1d to § 1294). For that other event, the occurrence of which without the injurious act of the first defendant the Court of Appeal regards as certain in agreement with the expert opinion (catching cold and the like), would not have deprived the first defendant's act of its causal responsibility for the damage; instead that act has prevented the second event from being itself the cause of the damage. The accident to the plaintiff, which induced the illness, must, therefore, be looked upon as itself causing the damage that occurred in full even if the consequences could have been produced without the accident by a cold or the like because of the plaintiff's predisposition— an occurrence which the Court of Appeal took into account without more ado. The plaintiff's predisposition is important only in so far as, like advancing old age, in course of time and without the intervention of anything particularly inducing illness, reduces earning capacity and so influences the amount of damage. Only with this limitation is it right for the appellate judge to form the opinion that, where symptoms of illness are brought to light by an accident which triggered them off, the person to blame can be made liable only for the portion of its consequences that can be traced to it but not for those that are brought about by the predisposition. A partition of the consequences of an accident by percentages, as where the injured party shares the blame, is quite impossible in such cases.

In the present case the damage to the plaintiff consists in his no longer being able to undertake the heavier work of chimney-sweeping, in particular climbing up the chimney and therefore being greatly hindered in the exercise of his craft since bent chimneys (*Schiefkamine*) are common. To carry on with his business he has had to employ an assistant. It is a question of how long the plaintiff would have been able to expect to carry on his business without help but for the accident, and when therefore his predisposition would, even without the accident, have made it impossible for him to attend the cleaning of *Schiefkamine*. According to the expert's opinion the arthritic symptoms which made him unable to work are traceable to the accident. These symptoms, which must be judged to be a development of the pre-existing arthrosis—which did not affect his ability to work—lasted until the end of 1938. Since then only the arthrosis remains to which, though its effects were exacerbated by the accident, he is substantially predisposed. Hence it can now be said that the damage sustained by the plaintiff down to 30 June 1938 is traceable to its full extent to the accident and must, there-fore, be made good by the defendants. The same applies to the damages the plaintiff claims for pain and suffering. The judgment appealed against, which remains unaltered in so far as it orders payment by the defendants, must therefore be modified as regards the damages for pain and suffering and the amounts claimed for the period down to 30 June 1938. As concerns the monthly payments for the period from 1 July 1938 onwards, further elu-cidation is needed up to what time the plaintiff might have been expected, without the accident, to be in a position to devote himself without assistance to his occupation, and from what date the natural development of his pre-disposition to arthrosis would have made it impossible for him to carry on his business without assistance. Up to that moment he must be awarded the monthly payments that he claims, the Court of Appeal having fixed the cost of an assistant at over RM 100 a month; for the subsequent period (irre-spective of the amounts already awarded him with final effect) he has no longer a claim.

Case 60

BUNDESGERICHTSHOF (FIRST CIVIL DIVISION) 23 OCTOBER 1951[*]
BGHZ 3, 261 = VersR 1952, 128

On 27 July 1948 six ships entered down stream the Datteln lock of the Lippe Side Canal. The first, the tug *Dollart*, was moored to barges *Gesine* and *Heinrich Hirdseg* (*HH9*), which were moored behind each other to the south wall. In the fourth place followed the MS *Edelweiss*, laden with 360 tonnes of wheat, on the way from Bremen to Rüdesheim. The *Edelweiss* lay on the

[*] English version by F. H. Lawson and B. S. Markesinis.

starboard side of the *HH9* and was moored to the north wall. Finally came the motor ships *Weser I* and *Nixe* moored behind each other to the north wall. The walls of the Datteln locks are strengthened towards the bottom so that their chambers have a conical instead of a rectangular cross-section. As the water-level then stood, with a difference of 7.46 m between high and low water, the clear distance between the wall diminished from 12.77 m above to 12.31 m below. For that reason the lock personnel were instructed to pass through ships side by side of the overall breadth of 11.75 m only.

In the absence of the lock-keeper, the lock was operated by the subordinate T. He asked the skippers of *HH9* and *Edelweiss* beforehand about the breadth of their craft. *Edelweiss* gave her breadth correctly as 6.67 m, whereas the skipper S gave the breadth of *HH9* incorrectly as 5 m. It was actually 5.87 m. The pump operator M received the same answers to his questions. The subordinate T accepted the declared overall breadth as satisfactory, shut the upper gate, and emptied the lock chamber. As the water dropped, *Edelweiss* and *HH9*, which originally floated freely, were pressed together and also left rubbing marks on both walls. They were disregarded and the process was continued until the lower water level was reached. It was only when the skipper of the tug *Dollart* tried to drag the barges *Gesine* and *HH9* that it was noticed that the latter was stuck fast to the *Edelweiss* and could not be moved. So *Dollart* dragged only *Gesine* out. Thereupon T and M, in the lock-keeper's absence, decided to free the ships by raising the level of water in the lock chamber. The lower gate was shut and the sluice-boards of the upper gate raised 19 cm. The water level rose at a rate of 25 cm in a minute and a half. But the boats that were stuck together did not float up evenly. They were lifted like a roof along their common surface of contact but with their other surfaces listed, hanging on the lock walls. The *Edelweiss*, which had only a 15 cm freeboard, was threatened with flooding. Despite persistent danger signals the lock personnel failed to stop the rush of water in time. The *Edelweiss* filled with water and sank. Only the crew could be saved.

The plaintiff, who had insured the owner of the *Edelweiss*, indemnified him and claimed DM 103,605 as compensation from the defendant as owner of the *HH9*, on the ground that the damage had been caused by its skipper's incorrect statement of its breadth. The defendant rejected the claim, disputing the causality of the incorrect statement and attributed the damage exclusively to the unskilful steps taken by the lock personnel.

The Navigation Court declared the claim (originally only for a part claim amounting to DM 10,000) against the defendant and the skipper S justified in full against the latter, but limited as to the defendant to the ship and cargo or their value. Only the plaintiff and the defendant appealed. The Court of Appeal allowed in full the claim, extended in the second instance to the total damage, and now directed only against the defendant, and rejected the defendant's appeal.

The application for review resulted in the decision being quashed and the case being referred back for the following

Reasons

The Court of Appeal holds that the master's incorrect statement of the *HH9*'s breadth was the immediate and adequate cause, not only of the jamming together of the ships, but also of the additional damage that arose from the loosening of the ships from the jam. It went on to say that jamming on leaving a lock, though infrequent, was not extraordinary, and that the instructions to the lock personnel took account of such an occurrence. In any case, the removal of the jam by letting the water in was not an extraordinary but the only solution. Risks in operating locks are always a matter of practical experience. These risks are multiplied if one of the foreseen dangers, here the jamming, intervenes and must be removed in a usual way, in accordance with practical experience. In so doing increased account must be taken of a failure, at the same time both human and technical in character. That is not at all improbable and should, according to general human experience, have been recognized by the bargemaster. Accordingly, the failure of the lock personnel was not enough to break the causal connection between the incorrect information about the breadth and the sinking of the *Edelweiss*.

It must be conceded to the applicant that the statements concerning the causal connection as a presupposition of the defendant's liability are not free from legal error. To begin with, the assumption that the blameworthy conduct of the master S was the immediate cause of the damage is not correct. S did nothing to lay *Edelweiss* alongside *HH9* and thereby provide the first condition for the subsequent jamming. The choice of the berth depended on the free decision of the master of *Edelweiss*. Likewise, the placing of the boat at that spot depended on the decision of the lock personnel, who alone had to determine the occupation of the lock and approved the laying side by side, so as to make better use of the space. However, S's incorrect statement of the breadth led to that decision and in that way indirectly caused the jamming. It is certain that the lock personnel would not have allowed the boats to be placed side by side, if they had known the correct breadth of the *HH9*. The incorrect information was therefore, in spite of its merely indirect operation, a *conditio sine qua non* of the further course of events.

However, this alone does not prove that S caused the damage in such a way as to incur liability. It has long been undisputed in legal literature and case-law that the scope of such natural logical causes is commonly far too wide for all their consequences to be imputed to the person causing them. Hence the jurists have elaborated the concept of adequate causation, which, according to the Reichsgericht's decision of 18 November 1932 [reference],

should make it possible to exclude some conditions, which from the point of view of natural science were conditions of a certain consequence, and without whose existence the consequence would not have occurred, for the purpose of causal connection in a legal sense; and the conditions which are logically most remote from the consequence should be excluded, because a consideration of those conditions would also lead to legal results that are at variance with equity.

Adequate cause has been formulated mainly by von Kries, Rümelin, and Traeger (cf. summary in Lindenmaier, 'Adequate cause and proximate cause' in *Festschrift für Wüstendörfer, Zeitschrift für das gesamte Handelsrecht und Konkursrecht* 113, Heft 3/4 (Stuttgart 1950)). Common to these formulations is the valuation of a concrete *conditio sine qua non* on the basis of its tendency to favour the consequence according to general standards. They differ according to the point of view from which the valuation is undertaken. While von Kries, the creator of the concept of adequate cause, prefers to undertake a valuation on the basis of all circumstances known or knowable individually to the originator of the condition at the time of its entry (*ex ante*), and also taking into account general practical knowledge (*ex post*) based on experience, Rümelin puts forward the theory of 'objective hindsight'. For the formation of a judgment of possibility he prefers to have regard to the whole empirical knowledge of mankind and all the circumstances anywhere to hand at the time the condition occurred, whether they were recognizable by the most superior discernment or had first become recognizable *ex post* from events following the condition in question.

Von Kries's individual foresight proved to be too narrow for private law cases of objective strict liability and contractual liability, Rümelin's objective hindsight too wide, to exclude with certainty the inequitable results of the condition theory. Rümelin himself accordingly found it necessary to curtail his doctrine, in so far as by the condition in question the injured party was brought into contact in time or in space with the damage-producing event. Traeger avoided the defects in both formulations with the following formulation (*Kausalbegriff im Zivil- und Strafrecht* (1904), 159): An event is an adequate condition of a consequence if it has in a general and appreciable way enhanced the objective possibility of a consequence of the kind that occurred. In making the necessary assessment account is to be taken only of:

(*a*) all the circumstances recognizable by an 'optimal' observer at the time the event occurred, (*b*) the additional circumstances known to the originator of the condition.

The factual situation so established is, according to Traeger, to be examined by applying the whole human experience available at the time a decision is made to see whether it appreciably favoured the occurrence of the damage-producing event (cf. Lindenmaier, op. cit., 223–6).

Traeger's formulation has been followed in essentials by the Reichsgericht since the decision in RGZ 133, 126, 127, more recently in the form that there is an adequate connection 'if a fact in general and not under special peculiar quite improbable circumstances, to be disregarded according to the regular course of things, was apt to produce a consequence'.

This formulation expressed until now unaltered in essentials in many decisions (RGZ 133, 126; 135, 154; 148, 165; 152, 49; 148, 38; 168, 88; 169, 91) has also been followed by this Senate, maintaining the grounds for decision laid down by Traeger. Admittedly—as Lindenmaier points out (op. cit., 239, 241)—one must not forget the starting-point of the inquiry: namely the search for a corrective that restricts the scope of the purely logical consequences, in order to produce an equitable result to the imputable consequences. Only if the courts are conscious of the fact that it is a question here not really of causation but of the fixing of the limits within which the originator of a condition can equitably be presumed liable for its consequences, and therefore of establishing in reality a positive condition of liability (Larenz, *Vertrag und Unrecht* 12, 14; Lindenmaier, op. cit., 239, 241–2), will the danger of a schematization of the formula be avoided and correct results be guaranteed.

That in the case before us the jamming of the boats was an adequate consequence of the incorrect information (concerning the breadth of the vessel) was accepted by the Court of Appeal without error of law. But the jamming produced no provable damage, since matters were at a standstill and the boats lay quietly on an even keel in the lock chamber. However, the first real damage-producing consequence came later, and in assessing them the Court of Appeal did not pay sufficient attention to the possibly necessary restriction of liability, when, while recognizing it the court declined to consider the failure of the lock personnel. It is true that the Reichsgericht has repeatedly recognized that anyone who has caused an accident must also answer for such consequences as are first produced in the course of conduct made unavoidable by the accident, through an intervening lack of skill, because according to human experience it must be taken into account that not all conduct will necessarily be perfect and accompanied by the desired result (RGZ 102, 230; 105, 264; 119, 204; RG HRR 28, 831; RG JW 1911, 755). This principle, however, does not apply without exception and cannot lead to saddling the person responsible for an accident indiscriminately with all consequences that, without his doing, are brought about in a completely unusual and inappropriate way by persons who are completely unauthorized to intervene (cf. the aforementioned decisions RGZ 102, 230 and JW 1911, 755).

The defendant had pointed out that such an unusual and grossly incorrect intervention of the lock personnel did occur and the Court of Appeal should therefore have made a detailed examination of their behaviour, instead of contenting itself with the remark that 'no matter how significant the signs of the failure of the lock personnel they did not suffice for a break in the causal connection, above all because there could be no question of the accident being intentionally brought about by the lock personnel'.

The question raised by the concept of intentional conduct has no place in this connection, which is concerned only with the concept of causation. It requires only an examination of whether an 'optimal' observer would normally have been able to take into account the behaviour of the lock personnel as it is presented—and, for the most part, undisputed—at the moment the condition on which liability was based—i.e. the incorrect declaration of breadth—occurred. The omission of that examination not only justifies the procedural objection raised by the application for review that the factual situation was not exhaustively dealt with, but leads to a recognition that the Court of Appeal did not apply the correct standard for distinguishing between imputable and inadequate consequences.

Among the circumstances which could form independent causes of damage according to the factual situation, the following were to be examined:

1. the fact that the lock-keeper neglected, contrary to § 2 no. 2 of the service instructions, to supervise the operation of the lock in person, that he left the operation to the subordinate who had not been appointed as his representative and who had continued it although the marks of rubbing on the lock walls ought to have made him notice that the boats were jammed;

2. the fact that after the jamming the lock personnel and the pump engineer had, of their own volition and contrary to an express prohibition in the service instructions, tried to break the jam by letting in the water, without warning the lock-keeper, who was alone empowered to do so by the instructions, and leaving to him the removal of the obstacle, and all of it although there was no occasion for precipitate action, since the course of events had come to a standstill once the lower water-level had been reached;

3. the fact, asserted by the defendant and established by evidence, that the lock-keeper would have been able to break the jam without danger to the boats, as he had done on several previous occasions, perhaps by removing obstacles created by good fenders and coverings and by carefully raising the water-level, if need be by manually working the sluice-boards;

4. the fact that the raising of the water-level was so quick that within one and a half minutes the freeboard of the *Edelweiss*, which was only 15 cm high, was bound to be flooded if the jam were not broken and the boats did not float up as intended;

5. the fact of the failure in the electricity supply, which remains unexplained, when and why it happened . . .

It may be that one or even several of these facts fall within the scope of the dangers which experience would lead one to expect, so that their fore-seeability, taken one by one, could be affirmed. Nevertheless it should have been examined whether the coincidence of these manifold conditions, in part possibly accidental, were not unusual and outside the scope of normal risks. In that connection it should be noted that conditions were under con-sideration which reinforced each other and only in combination led to the perilous aggravation of the situation that had little to do with the original creation of the jam.

The Court of Appeal's findings of fact do not go far enough to enable the court of review to decide finally the question of causal connection. The part played by the lock personnel in the course of the accident must be eluci-dated, if need be with the help of independent experts, and then a fresh con-clusion reached on the responsibility of the defendant.

Case 61

BUNDESGERICHTSHOF (SIXTH CIVIL DIVISION) 24 APRIL 1952*
NJW 1952, 1010 = VersR 1952, 352

The husband/father of the plaintiffs was in 1937 struck by an automobile belonging to the defendant. In consequence of the accident, his right leg was amputated; he bore therefore an artificial leg and had to walk with the aid of two sticks. In a lawsuit it was established that the defendant was obliged as a joint debtor to make good all the damage arising from the accident of 1 February 1937.

In 1945 the husband/father of the plaintiffs was injured by artillery fire and died of that injury. He used at the time in question to set out in the evening to go to a bunker with the plaintiffs. In the afternoon of 31 March 1945 the place lay under artillery fire. The plaintiffs' family first stayed at home, and only when the firing stopped, set out for the bunker. While the three of them were on their way, the firing suddenly started up again. The first plaintiff ran to a house where he took shelter. The second plaintiff hur-ried to the bunker. The husband/father of the plaintiffs set out on the road

---

* English version by F. H. Lawson and B. S. Markesinis.

but could cover the ground only slowly because of his lameness. Before he reached either a house or the bunker he was injured by a shell fragment.

The plaintiffs, considering the death of their husband/father as a further consequence of the 1937 automobile accident, demanded of the defendant compensation for the support they were deprived of in consequence of the death.

Reasons

Even if the laming of the first plaintiff's husband is looked upon as a *conditio sine qua non* (BGHZ 2, 138, 140 ff. = NJW 51, 711) for the injury from the shell fragment, it cannot be the basis for the defendant's liability, for there is no adequate causal connection between the laming due to the accident and the death resulting from the artillery fire. An adequate connection exists only 'if according to general experience and not under especially peculiar, quite improbable circumstances, not to be contemplated according to the regular course of things, were apt to produce a consequence' (RGZ 113, 126, 127 and the later constant case-law of the RG). Whether there is 'adequacy' is not really a question of causation but of setting the limits within which liability can equitably be attributed to the originator of the condition. Since in so doing we are concerned with an assessment which of its nature affords some room for judicial discretion, an element of uncertainty cannot be excluded, especially at the lower limit, in deciding whether the condition favoured the result to an appreciable degree. Such an uncertainty cannot be avoided either by applying other important legal concepts such as offending against good morals, important reason and, above all, against the principle of good faith. Only the idea of adequate causation can provide a sufficient guide. The question whether and in what measure a causal connection induces liability can never be exhaustively answered by abstract rules but can be decided in doubtful cases only by the judge according to his unfettered discretion having regard to all the circumstances; and only when it is borne in mind that the doctrine of adequate causation as a way of limiting liability is based on § 242 BGB, will the danger of schematizing the formula be avoided and correct results obtained (BGHZ 3, 261, 267; Lindenmaier in *Zeitschrift für das gesamte Handelsrecht und Konkursrecht* 113, 239–43).

In agreement with both courts below, an adequate causation must be rejected, without any need to go into the formulations set out in the books, which are concerned with whether foreseeability of the consequence must be required and by what rules it must be determined. 'Adequacy' is here excluded because the laming, by its general nature, did not enhance in what experience would show to be an appreciable degree, the probability of being struck by artillery fire. For a causal connection exists in a legal sense, as has already been mentioned, only when the condition originated by the person doing the damage is in a general way apt to produce the damage in question—especially peculiar and quite unusual circumstances which would not be taken into account in the regular course of things, being excluded. In examining, therefore, the facts, it must be determined whether a 'general' favourable tendency exists, but a tendency will be disregarded which is so considerable that no account would be taken of it in ordinary experience (Lindenmaier, op. cit., 227; Enneccerus-Lehmann, *Schuldrecht* (13th edn., 1950) 63, fn. 6). Such a consequence, outside ordinary probability, must be treated as accidental and not imputable. That is so in the present case because a laming as such cannot in any case according to general experience be regarded as enhancing to an appreciable extent the danger of being wounded. Shell fire may make anyone, even healthy persons, liable to be hit. It is in no way foreseeable how hostile fire may be directed. For the civil population being struck by a shell was a 'new and independent event' of a purely accidental character. The danger might be avoided to a certain extent by seeking shelter at once. Whether it was generally 'right' to run to a neighbouring house or a bunker could be at least doubtful. The probability that the plaintiffs could be hit, when they ran to seek shelter, was, according to general experience, not less than the danger for the injured party in case he remained standing or lying down. In view of this 'accidental effect' of a few shots happening at short intervals, running away might have proved 'wrong' and standing or lying down 'right'. In view of the combinations of purely accidental conditions the injury to the first plaintiff's husband from shell fragments can no longer be regarded as an imputable consequence of the 1937 traffic accident.

Case 62

BUNDESGERICHTSHOF (THIRD CIVIL DIVISION) 25 SEPTEMBER 1952*
BGHZ 7, 198 = NJW 1953, 700 = VersR 1952, 430

The orphan plaintiffs claim compensation from the defendant for the damage they suffered from their mother's death as the consequence of an abortion carried out by the defendant. She felt herself pregnant in May 1949 as a result of intercourse with Sp. The defendant, who practises as a doctor, was at her request ready to perform an abortion in consideration for a fee. For that purpose he visited Frau S at Sp.'s home and with his help operated on her. He felt, but misunderstood, a peculiar structure in her womb and thought he noticed the remains of an afterbirth. After douching the womb with Sp.'s help he placed the patient on a sofa, and ordered her to rest in bed for three days and to see him in his surgery in 14 days. He left the house a few minutes before 4 p.m. Some 20 to 25 minutes later the patient

---

* English version by F. H. Lawson and B. S. Markesinis.

complained of severe pains in her abdomen. At her request, Sp. hurried to the defendant's surgery, reported that Frau S was in pain, and obtained from him a pain-killer. When, after about an hour's absence, he came home, he found that her condition had deteriorated further. When a gynaecologist was eventually called in, arriving about 6 p.m., he found a severe internal haemorrhage, so he arranged for an immediate transfer to a hospital; and after about three-quarters of an hour he operated and found a rent in the womb and ascertained that the womb artery had been torn. Although he bandaged the source of blood and made a blood transfusion, the plaintiffs' mother died before the operation was complete.

The plaintiffs claimed compensation from the defendant in contract and delict for medical and hospital expenses together with payment of an annuity and also a declaration that they were entitled to be compensated for all further damage.

Both instances rejected the claim; the appellants demanded the case be sent for reconsideration.

Reasons

1. The Court of Appeal agreed with the Landgericht that the defendant caused the death of Frau S from loss of blood by piercing the wall of her womb and thus damaging the womb artery. It came, however, to the conclusion that he was not at fault in causing the injury.

The experts were unanimously of the opinion that an injury such as happened here could have been inflicted by even the most conscientious and experienced medical man in the course of an abortion; in following it the Court of Appeal made no mistake of law. Thus, such an injury *could*, but *need not*, have resulted from a careless and improper use of the instruments. The Court of Appeal acted consistently in examining whether such a careless act of the defendant in the present case was to be inferred either according to the prima-facie evidence or by way of circumstantial evidence. It said no to both questions.

(*a*) Whether this was a typical course of events affording sufficient prima-facie evidence required, in the first place, a formulation of the results of experience and then its application to the present situation. Such a formulation is a conclusion of fact inferred from general circumstances and can, in these proceedings, be checked for correctness only in so far as it is drawn from established facts. The facts themselves cannot be checked; they must be proved by the person who seeks to found on them a prima-facie case. The burden of proof is thus on the plaintiffs just as the other party must prove the possibility of a deviation from the typical course of events. When, therefore, the Court of Appeal reached the result, on the basis of expert opinions, that 'no formulation from the results of experience can be established that the piercing of a womb in an abortion can as a rule be traced to a careless use of instruments by a doctor', the unassailable finding of fact followed, that according to medical experience the injury in question was 'possible even with a careful use of instruments' and could 'find its explanation in the peculiar characteristics, not visible to the doctor, of the womb'. That under these circumstances experience afforded no prima-facie evidence was based on no error of law.

(b) The Court of Appeal considered that the defendant was at fault in not affording the required medical care after finishing the operation. But it declined to attribute fault to the general conduct of the defendant, which would also provide, as the plaintiffs contend, prima-facie evidence of a faulty use of the instruments and therefore of his being to blame for the injury.

The court took into account various surprising and irregular circumstances such as the use of a camphor injection before the operation; the suspicion that a miscarriage was beginning; the failure to recognize the rupture of the artery; the leaving of an alleged afterbirth in the womb; and finally the omission still to be discussed, of an immediate reference to a hospital. While it adhered to the opinion that they did not constitute errors in medical practice, it saw in both of the last circumstances two blameworthy omissions; yet it considered that they did not disclose a general prolonged lack of medical conscientiousness or care, and that there was, as a whole, no typical conduct justifying a prima-facie presumption that the defendant did the injury to the wall of the womb and the opening of the artery through a careless use of instruments.

Here also no objection can be taken on legal grounds to the Court of Appeal's decision . . .

(c) It is on the other hand possible to treat fault in such a situation as an indication that the doctor was not careful in the operation itself. That point also was not missed by the Court of Appeal. But it considered the evidence insufficient to afford it the necessary certainty. It considered that the proved omissions predominantly disclosed a lack of conscientiousness in the *aftercare* of the patient, whereas a fault in the abortion itself would consist in lack of care in the use of the instruments. The basis of the fault in the two cases would be too different to enable secure enough conclusions to be drawn from the one to the other. The court was entitled to value the indication as a means of information, and that valuation could not be checked in these proceedings, so that no legal error can be found to exist in its judgment.

II. The Court of Appeal, however, rightly found that the defendant was at fault in his neglectful conduct after finishing the actual operation. He ought not to have left a doubtful situation without getting rid of the afterbirth, and he ought, by that time, to have had the patient sent at once to a hospital. That he did not do so was described by the expert, Professor Ph., as 'unintelligible', and the Court of Appeal rightly agreed with him. Complications had ensued which required further treatment in hospital, in relation to which it was irrelevant whether the defendant was to blame for them or not.

The Court of Appeal likewise declined to infer liability for the consequences because it denied causality. It inferred indeed from the opinions of the experts that an immediate transfer to the hospital would have improved the patient's chances of survival. But it held that death might have occurred even if there had been immediate transfer after the abortion and an operation without delay. It could 'not decide beyond reasonable doubt that if the defendant had done his duty immediately after the operation or even when informed by Sp. that the patient was in pain, her life would have been saved'.

These considerations do not make it quite clear whether the Court of Appeal had sufficiently in mind what was needed to prove causation. According to longstanding case-law it is not the strict rule of evidence in § 236 ZPO but that in § 287 that applies here . . . Under § 287 ZPO the court is not prevented from being convinced by the evidence and the circumstances that there is an adequate causal connection, even if the possibility cannot without reasonable doubt be excluded that the damage could have occurred without the defendant's fault. If, as here, the blameworthy conduct consisted in an omission, the question of adequate causation ought to be formulated as 'whether that omission was in the ordinary way capable of producing a result, and not only under peculiar, quite improbable circumstances, not to be contemplated in the normal course of events'. It is not, therefore, a question of whether other, not remote circumstances could have produced the result, but whether the injurious consequence could not have occurred in the normal course, or rather would have been produced only by special circumstances of that kind. Here the Court of Appeal had merely found that a dutiful conduct would not certainly have prevented the result, and that finding cannot be regarded as sufficient to exclude the omission as the cause of the result. The Court of Appeal ought to have considered in accordance with § 287 ZPO—if need be after further questioning the experts—whether it could have produced such a result.

III. The Court of Appeal started from the position that the operation was an unlawful attack on the mother's bodily integrity, and therefore an infringement of the protective enactments §§ 223, 218 StGB. Yet, it was unwilling to infer any liability from them because it did not see any causal connection between the operation and its fatal outcome. It explained that the defendant undertook the abortion as a doctor and carried it out according to the rules of medical art and science. Permitted abortions with the object of saving the life and health of the patient would be conducted in the same way. According to the expert, Professor Ph., injuries could occur outside the actual purpose of treatment. The doctor need not, however, as a rule take account of them when he started. In particular, complications dangerous to life were conditional on the intervention of peculiar or unfortunate circumstances, such as an opening of the womb artery through an injury to or spontaneous cleavage of the wall of the womb, which must in the normal course be disregarded. Even when such dangerous circumstances occur, the doctor would have means at his disposal to prevent a fatal outcome with some, though not absolutely sure, prospect of success. Thus, the possibility that an abortion undertaken by a doctor would lead to a patient's death was too remote for the assumption of a causal connection, giving rise to liability, between the operation and its fatal outcome.

1. These explanations exaggerate the requirements for adequate causation . . . It need not be decided whether there are medical operations in which complications dangerous to life can be produced only through the intervention of quite unique, quite improbable circumstances which can be disregarded according to the regular course of things. For an operation such as an abortion this was evidently assumed neither by the expert nor the Court of Appeal, for both reckoned with the possibility of such dangers and omitted to consider them only because in this case the doctor had appropriate means at his disposal, to which however the Court of Appeal accords only 'some, though not a certain prospect of success'.

If one starts from the position—as one must—that the entry of the aforementioned dangerous circumstances falls within the adequate consequences of an abortion, the further adequate causal connection cannot be denied on the ground that there was some possibility of preventing the fatal outcome. This denial of a causal connection is based on a fallacy similar to that which appeared in relation to the causality of the delayed transfer to the hospital. Once a danger to the patient's life appeared in any way, no peculiar and quite improbable circumstances were needed to lead to death, but, on the contrary, medical skill was needed to prevent it. Whether the prospects of success in those attempts to avert it were more or less great cannot alter the fact that a failure is the adequate consequence of a danger to life.

2. Moreover, the liability of the defendant cannot be denied on the ground that there was no causal connection between the illegal operation and its fatal outcome. That connection would be unimportant only if the operation was not illegal on the ground that the deceased not only agreed to but

expressly wished it. The Court of Appeal was able to refuse to go more deeply into the question of what significance that wish had. It confined itself to the statement that consent to an abortion is forbidden and therefore legally inoperative . . . A consent is inoperative not only when influenced by a defect of the will, but also when it is repugnant to a legal prohibition or good morals and is therefore invalid (§§ 134, 138 BGB). That presupposition is here affirmed by the Court of Appeal on the ground that an infringement of § 218 StGB makes both the doctor and the patient punishable.

It is also not a defence to a claim that a plaintiff is acting deceitfully and in bad faith if he claims damages from a person whom he asked to afford a particular kind of medical assistance, so long as he keeps within what he was asked for. This invocation of good faith must also be denied to one who so severely infringes a prohibition of the Criminal Code. The legal position is not altered by the fact that a portion of the public, for various reasons, demands an abolition of the prohibition.

3. By undertaking the operation, the defendant not only deliberately injured the body of Frau S, but also infringed the protective enactments contained in §§ 233, 218 StGB. Although the second paragraph aims in the first place at protecting the living embryo, it serves also to protect the pregnant woman; and that is enough to satisfy the conditions of § 823 II BGB. If, however, they are satisfied, it follows, as the Reichsgericht has pertinently said . . . that the defendant is liable for all the injuries caused by his operation, even if they are not his fault. That, contrary to the Court of Appeal's opinion, there was a causal connection between the death of Frau S and the operation is shown above at (1).

For these reasons also the legal dispute is not yet ripe for decision, since the defendant can rely on the consent and wish of the deceased in so far as that, too, implied fault in the undertaking of the operation. As matters stood, if she had not energetically desired the operation, the defendant would not have performed it . . . That fault will have to be balanced against the defendant in respect of causality (§ 254 BGB), and the defence arising from it must affect the plaintiffs also in accordance with § 846 BGB.

Case 63

BUNDESGERICHTSHOF (THIRD CIVIL DIVISION) 17 OCTOBER 1955[*]
BGHZ 18, 286 = JZ 1956, 177 (with approving note by K. Sieg)

In 1946 the husband and the father of the plaintiffs had to undergo the general inoculation against typhus, which was carried out in virtue of an ordinance of the Oberpräsident of the then province of Hanover of 22 January

[*] English version by F. H. Lawson and B. S. Markesinis.

1946 with the approval of the British military government. He had three inoculations in all, after which he suffered an illness, in the course of which a malignant swelling appeared. On 27 February 1948 he died.

The plaintiffs claimed compensation from the defendant State on the ground of its breach of official duty and—in a subsidiary way—for public sacrifice in being deprived of their right to support by the death of their breadwinner. They alleged that the death of their husband and father was caused by the typhus inoculation and the doctor was to blame for the death.

The lower courts applying the rules on sacrifice for the public good declared the claim justified in principle but otherwise dismissed the action.

The defendant's application for review failed for these

Reasons

I. . . .

II. In agreement with the Landgericht the Court of Appeal finds it proved, on the basis of the evidence adduced, that the typhus inoculations applied to the deceased produced a staphylococcus suppuration which within $1\frac{1}{2}$ to 2 years developed into a malignant swelling of sarcoma appearance, from which death resulted. Against this interpretation of the evidence no doubt is raised by the applicant. An attack is made on the view taken by the Court of Appeal that the inoculation constitutes not only an incontrovertible condition in the physical sense (*conditio sine qua non*) for the death, but also the cause in the legal sense, i.e. an adequate condition for the occurrence of the death. That attack is, however, unfounded. In this connection it is of importance—as the Court of Appeal conclusively observed—that the inoculation led to the death not through the intervention of independent acts of third persons or the deceased himself, but that death ensued without the co-operation of any further intervening causes. Admittedly the findings of the Court of Appeal must lead to the conclusion that a staphylococcus suppuration only seldom results from a typhus inoculation and also, in particular, that the development of such a suppuration into a fatal sarcoma belongs to the class of rare medical phenomena. All the same, neither such a suppuration nor its further development into a fatal sarcoma can be regarded as circumstances outside all medical experience which, according to the case-law of the Reichsgericht, further developed by the Bundesgerichtshof (cf., e.g., BGHZ 3, 261, 265–7) could not be described as an adequate casual connection. It must be noted that the question of adequacy between condition and consequence cannot be answered in a purely logical, abstract way by numerically computing the frequency of the occurrences of such a consequence, but that in a value-judgment those out of the many conditions in a physical sense must be excluded which on a reasonable view of things cannot be regarded as circumstances giving rise to liability; in other words, the limit must be found by a value-judgment 'up to which a liability for the consequences of a condition can be equitably imputed to its originator' (BGHZ 3, 267). In making such a value-judgment it must be of importance (for the purposes of setting the limits of liability) whether the originator of the condition consciously took into account the more or less remote possibility of damage resulting from it or would not have acted otherwise if he had thought of the possibility of such damage. In that case the limit of liability may be set relatively wide. There would have been no decision not to order a general typhus inoculation if a possibility—though extremely rare—of death had been envisaged. Accordingly, the typhus inoculation (carried out in virtue of an official ordinance) must be imputed to the State as the cause creating the death, even though the manner in which the inoculation led to the death belonged to the class of exceptional medical phenomena.

Moreover, for the following reasons a liability-creating causal connection between the inoculation and the death cannot be called in question: That an inoculation—whatever be the kind—leads to the death of the person inoculated does not lie beyond the bounds of experience. That is the ground for example for § 6 of the North Rhine–Westphalian Act on Inoculation Injuries of 10 February 1953 (GVBl 166). If, therefore, an inoculation has directly caused a death, i.e. without the co-operation of further intervening causes, an adequate causal connection between inoculation and death must be said to exist irrespective of the precise manner in which it came about (e.g. through infection, as in this case, or because of a particular predisposition of the inoculated person).

III. The applicant goes on to object that the Court of Appeal granted to the plaintiffs a claim for compensation, as only indirectly injured, by an analogous application of § 844 BGB. The Senate, however, shares the Court of Appeal's opinion.

The right to compensation is, indeed, governed by the principle that only the person directly injured is entitled to compensation. None the less we have here to do with the exceptions contained in §§ 844, 845 BGB. These exceptional provisions, which in the case of a person's death afford compensation to persons who suffer indirect damage, correspond to the quite general opinion prevalent before the BGB came into force, which developed at a very early date in modification of Roman law and had already found a place in the positive law of different countries (cf. for the historical development RGZ 7, 139, 141–4). Parties of the kind of interest here, who have suffered only indirect damage are allowed damages not only in the case of culpable unlawful acts but also where the duty to compensate rests exclusively on strict liability (§ 3 II Haftpflichtgesetz: § 10 II StrVerkG; § 21 II

LuftVerkG of 21 August 1936). Further, the principles laid down in §§ 844, 845 BGB apply, if not generally, certainly partly to the law of contract by virtue of express provisions (§ 618 III, § 62 III, § 76 I BGB) and are to that extent regarded as capable of an analogous application (RGZ 167, 85, 89; BGHZ 5, 62 ff., with further references). Likewise, it is generally recognized that these principles are also to be applied in the sphere of public law (RGZ 11, 22, 23 and 112, 290, 297); Enneccerus-Lehmann, *Recht der Schuldverhältnisse* (1954) 971). Our law is accordingly widely governed by the principle that, where compensation is payable to the injured party for bodily injury, compensation must also be afforded in a case of death to those deprived of their legal right to maintenance. This principle, according to what has been said, cannot without further ado be applied to all cases in which compensation would have to be paid for a mere bodily injury (e.g. not simply in the field of pure contract law). If, however, in general a claim for compensation is afforded for violent attacks on bodily integrity, then within the scope of compensation claims a corresponding application of § 844 BGB to killing cannot be refused. The state of facts that gives, outside all contractual relations, a claim for compensation on the ground of sacrifice for the public good for attacks on bodily integrity are from the points of view of interest here so close, both in law and in fact, to the states of fact in which compensation is to be paid for similar damage under §§ 823 ff. BGB or on the basis of strict liability that those who are legally entitled to support in case their breadwinner is killed cannot in any circumstances be denied redress for the loss of their right to support. The legal result is unacceptable that, on the one hand, interference by a public authority with corporal integrity leading to an injury must be compensated while, on the other hand, if the interference leads not only to corporal injury but to death, and the person concerned has made a far bigger 'sacrifice' the relatives entitled to maintenance, who are only affected indirectly but particularly hard by this sacrifice should be left wanting. Such a result would also, as the Court of Appeal has already conclusively remarked, be incompatible with the principle of a social law-abiding State (Art. 20 GG) and would clash with the constitutionally guaranteed protection of the family (Art. 6 GG). The Court of Appeal, therefore, rightly awarded to the plaintiffs (i.e. the widow and the sons of the deceased) compensation on the ground of sacrifice for the public good in compliance with § 844 BGB.

The amount of compensation to be awarded to those entitled to support in accordance with the general rules on sacrifice for the public good by the analogous application of § 844 BGB, already limited by § 844 to the actual loss of support cannot—as the applicant would wish—be further limited quite generally by the courts, to conform to the corresponding rules of social insurance law. That can only be done by express legislative provision, such as is, for example, contained in § 6 of the North-Rhine–Westphalian Act on Inoculation Injuries.

Case 64

BUNDESGERICHTSHOF (SIXTH CIVIL DIVISION) 22 APRIL 1958*
BGHZ 27, 137 = NJW 1958, 1041 = JZ 1958, 742 (with lively approving article by G. Boehmer)

The plaintiff's motor cycle collided on a main road passing through a village with a motor-car coming in the opposite direction which belonged to the defendant's husband, since deceased, as the latter turned left to enter a side street. The plaintiff was injured. Both vehicles were damaged.

Criminal proceedings were instituted against both drivers. The defendant's husband was convicted of causing bodily harm in a negligent manner but then died.† The death was not connected with the accident and occurred before the order of the court could be served upon him. The plaintiff was also sentenced by the Amtsgericht to pay DM 30 for speeding. On appeal the Bavarian Oberstes Landesgericht quashed this judgment and remitted the case to the Court of First Instance for rehearing. The plaintiff was then acquitted for lack of evidence.

He claimed from the defendant, as heir of her husband, compensation for the costs he had incurred in defending himself in the criminal proceedings.

The Landgericht declared his claim justified as to four-fifths and rejected any further claim. On appeal by the defendant, the Oberlandesgericht rejected the claim for the costs. The plaintiff lost his appeal against the decision for the following

Reasons

The parties are still in dispute only over the question whether the defendant must also pay the plaintiff four-fifths of the costs which he had to pay to defend himself in the criminal proceedings. The Court of Appeal gave a negative reply on the ground that no causal connection existed between the bad driving of the defendant's husband and the incurring of the defence costs. Whether the attacks against this decision of the Court of Appeal are justified may be left undecided since in any case the view of the Court of Appeal that this claim for compensation of the plaintiff is to be rejected must in the result be approved.

A finding of adequate causation is not decisive for the decision of the dispute. The current mode of thought which looks at the question of limiting

---

* English version by F. H. Lawson and B. S. Markesinis.

† In the case of certain minor offences, it is possible for the court to impose a penalty—usually a fine—without a proper hearing though the person 'penalized' can object to this once the court's order is served on him. A proper hearing will then follow.

liability only from the point of view of adequate causation is not always capable of providing a proper solution . . . In previous judgments the Bundesgerichtshof has already made clear its view that the formula of adequate causation does not suffice to solve the problem of limiting liability (cf. BGHZ 8, 325, 329; 10, 107, 108; 20, 137, 142, 143). In a search for other means, von Caemmerer has justly focused on the question whether the facts for which compensation is demanded lie within the area of the protection of the rule that has been broken. This formulation of the question is commonly applied and recognized in determining liability for breach of a protective statute (§ 823 II BGB). Here, as this Senate also declared in its judgments (BGHZ 12, 213, 217 and 19, 114, 126), following the case-law of the Reichsgericht, it is a condition of liability that the damage lies within the scope of the interests protected by the protective enactment, that is to say that the damage arises from the injury to a legal interest for the protection of which the rule was made. This limitation applies no less, if, as here, claims are raised under § 823 I BGB. Here, too, it must first be asked whether the damage in question lies within the protective purpose, in other words whether it concerns dangers which fall within the scope of the risks for which the rule was made. For this reason the sense and scope of the rule violated by the defendant must first be inquired into . . .

The plaintiff, in demanding compensation for his defence costs, in claiming that damage be made good that he suffered in his estate, that is to say economic damage. It is generally accepted that by § 823 I BGB, under which he primarily makes his claims, the estate as such is not protected. The only question therefore is whether the damage falls within another aspect of the field of dangers dealt with in § 823 I BGB, namely the integrity of the body, health, and property. Its intention is to protect against all risks that arise from an infringement of those rights. Only the consequences of that infringement are imputed to the wrongdoer and only within that scope are the interests of the injured party protected by it.

If anyone, like the plaintiff, is injured in an accident and his motor vehicle is damaged, the costs of restoring his health and repairing the vehicle are undoubtedly within the protective purpose of § 823 I BGB. That applies also to his loss of earnings, because his injury makes him unable to continue his calling, and also to the loss of the use he makes of the vehicle in his business. All of these are consequences of the accident which are connected with the personal injury and the damage to the vehicle. Although to some extent economic damage is involved, they fall within the protection of § 823 I BGB. It is quite different with the expenditure the criminal proceedings brought upon the plaintiff. So far no dangers that were protected against by the law have materialized through the accident. This had nothing to do with the personal injury and property damage suffered by him through the accident, for it arose from his being suspected of committing a criminal offence and from the decision of the prosecuting authority to institute proceedings against him. The risk of becoming involved in criminal proceedings is a general risk that affects every citizen. It is independent of the personal injury and property damage suffered in an accident, for it occurs even where an accident produces neither of them, and even when the driving complained of leads to no accident at all. The risk of having to spend money in defending oneself against a criminal charge is not one that the law intends to avert when casting the protection of § 823 I BGB over the integrity of health and property. Thus that provision disappears as a foundation for a claim to have that damage made good, irrespective of whether there is an adequate causal connection between the conduct of the wrongdoer and the damage done by him.

Moreover, the plaintiff cannot claim compensation for his defence costs under § 823 II BGB, in combination with § 13 StVO. For § 13 StVO . . . apart from protecting the orderly movement of traffic, also protects only the health and property of those engaged in it, but not their economic interests. The only damage that is still in dispute, the defence costs, touches neither the health nor the property of the plaintiff, but interests that are not protected by it . . .

None of the legal considerations that have been adduced support the plaintiff's claim to have his defence costs made good.

Case 65

BUNDESGERICHTSHOF (SIXTH CIVIL DIVISION) 16 FEBRUARY 1972*
BGHZ 58, 162 = NJW 1972, 904 = JZ 1972, 559 (and important article by E. Deutsch in JZ 1972, 551 = VersR 1972, 560)

On 21 June 1968 there was a traffic accident on L Street in B. A lorry of the Dutch armed forces, in an attempt to overtake an automobile which was in course of parking, collided with an oncoming car. Both drivers left their vehicles in the narrow passage made by the parking vehicle, waiting for the arrival of the police. In consequence the highway was, for the time, blocked for the following car drivers. Thereupon several drivers, who could not make headway because of the lorry in front of them, drove round on to the sidewalk to the right of the scene of the accident. About fifteen minutes later, when the police arrived, substantial damage had been done to the sidewalk. The city of B, as owner of the highway, had to spend DM 1736.58 to clear it up.

The drivers who drove on the sidewalk have not been identified.

The Bundesrepublik, under the provisions of NATO Armed Forces

* English version by F. H. Lawson and B. S. Markesinis.

Statute, compensated the owner of the car struck by the army lorry. The plaintiff city contended that the Bundesrepublik must also make good the damage done by those drivers in driving on the sidewalk.

Whereas the Landgericht rejected the claim, the Oberlandesgericht allowed it.

On appeal, by leave of the Oberlandesgericht, the Bundesgerichtshof restored the judgment of the Landgericht for the following

Reasons

The Federal Republic, as is agreed between the parties, has, under the provisions of the NATO Armed Forces Statute, assumed liability for damage done by the lorry of the Dutch armed forces as if it had been done by a lorry of the German forces. The claim is based on § 839 BGB, in combination with Art. 34 of the Constitution, so that liability under §§ 831, 823 BGB combined with the provisions of the Road Traffic Ordinance is excluded. According to the second sentence of § 839 I BGB, the plaintiff city would have had to show that it could not have obtained compensation in any other way for the damage—in particular, not from the drivers who had actually caused the damage and who, if they had been ascertained, would doubtless have had to make it good.

There is no dispute between the parties that the conditions for this liability are satisfied. For, as the judgment under attack establishes, the driver of the lorry was even at fault, since the strict liability is not excluded by unavoidable circumstances (§ 7 II StVG). The only question is whether the damage that the drivers who were forced to halt behind the lorry did in driving round on the sidewalk would be traced back to a conduct giving rise to liability, in this case the occupational hazard of this lorry, for which the operator is responsible. The Court of Appeal said yes.

II. This standpoint cannot be accepted.

1. Admittedly, approval must be given to the Court of Appeal's holding that the causal connection between the conduct of the lorry-driver and the damage to the sidewalk was even in this case adequate (the decision of the District Court of Düsseldorf in the 'Greenbelt' case, is, to this extent, sound). It is well known that in cases like this drivers constantly—no doubt in breach of traffic regulations and subject to punishment for malicious damage (§ 303 StGB)—do not wait long enough for passage to be possible or for a diversion to be allowed by the traffic police. In view of the experience that the conduct of such drivers will always recur, it may also be assumed that a driver must foresee that an accident caused by him in the flow of traffic may lead to such reactions on the part of following drivers, with ensuing damage to the public streets, private front gardens, fences, and

so on. Nevertheless, in the present case, there is no absolute need to discuss fault as a ground for liability, because the plaintiff city can base its claim on § 7 StVG.

The appeal wrongly casts doubt on the view of the Court of Appeal that the lorry was 'in operation' when such drivers passed over the sidewalk. The lorry had not been taken out of circulation when it came to a stop but prevented other vehicles from going forward. For the purposes of § 7 StVG the operation of an automobile lasts as long as the driver leaves it in circulation and the danger involved by it persists (BGHZ 29, 163, 166). Moreover, the diversion made by the impatient drivers is still in close connection, in both time and place, with the collision caused by the lorry (cf. BGHZ 37, 311, 318). If a following automobile, in an attempt to avoid striking the lorry in front of it, braked and skidded and so invaded the sidewalk, the damage caused would certainly fall within the operational hazard of the lorry. Nor would it be different if a following driver, in order not to collide or not to be overrun by subsequent participants in the traffic, had deliberately turned on to the sidewalk.

2. If, therefore, the adequate causal connection and the connection with the operational hazard of the lorry are admitted to exist, the decision of the dispute depends on whether such consequences also can be imputed to a causer of damage as rest upon the 'free' decision of a third party (so-called 'breach of the causal connection' or 'no recourse'). That question does not depend, in cases of this kind, on whether the injured party bases his claim on § 823 II (in combination with the provisions of the StVG) or on § 823 I BGB or on § 839 BGB or, as here on the ground that the highway was blocked by an automobile, on §§ 7, 18 StVG.

(*a*) Despite the contention of the appellant this imputation is not to be rejected on the ground that such impatient drivers acted deliberately and unlawfully in driving on the sidewalk.

The imputation of damage is not automatically excluded by the intervention of a third party (BGHZ 12, 206, 211; 17, 153, 159; 24, 263, 266). Only when the causal nature of the first state of facts is completely irrelevant to the second event can it be said that the causal connection is 'broken' (BGHZ 3, 261, 268; 17, 159). That is not the case here. That such drivers caused the damage unlawfully does not stand in the way of the imputation. Whether the intervention of the third party was unlawful is of no decisive importance for the question of imputation.

Just as irrelevant is it that a person is acquitted of liability for damage done by a third party on the ground that the latter acted wilfully. Accordingly, the driver and operator, whose automobile collided with a lorry so that its load fell on to the highway, must compensate not only for the goods that were damaged by the fall, or could not be put in safe-keeping, but also the goods stolen from among those strewn on the high-way. There the person liable for the fall cannot refer the injured party to his claim against the thieves; that damage also may be imputed to him, on the ground that he created the danger of their being stolen. That those conse-quences of his conduct causing liability (that is to say the operation of the damage-causing automobile, or the traffic blunder of his driver) no longer fell into the class of risks for the avoidance of which rules of liability are pre-scribed (§§ 7, 18 StVG; §§ 823 ff. BGB, in combination with the provisions of the StVG), cannot be accepted (cf. BGHZ 27, 137, 140). Such duties to assume risks may also be established by statute. Thus, under certain circum-stances, the duty of care of a person participating in traffic may extend so far that he must take care that he does not, by defective behaviour, induce third parties to contravene wilfully the road traffic rules. Above all, the operator of an automobile is answerable for all damage that is connected with the operation of his vehicle, irrespective of the way its dangerous char-acter has caused damage in a particular case; he is liable also for damage a joy-rider knowingly and deliberately causes by his vehicle, even for the reck-less killing of a human being (BGHZ 37, 311, 316/317).

(*b*) On mature consideration, however, the case to be decided appears to be different. The drivers, once they came to a halt on the road, drove onto the sidewalk of their own free will. That was connected with the accident, and so with the manner of driving the lorry and the operational hazard involved in it, only so far as the accident and its blocking of the road pro-vided an occasion for the behaviour of the drivers. This was, however, no more than an external circumstance which gave the motivation for wilful conduct, without regard for the public safety, of the drivers. It cannot, therefore, be regarded as a sufficient foundation for an imputable connec-tion (cf. also BGHZ 25, 86, 90; Senate decision of 12 February 1963—VI ZR 181/62). Above all, it cannot be said here that the conduct of the lorry-driver and the blocking of the highway 'provoked' the conduct of the dri-vers (cf. BGHZ 57, 25, 28). The blocking of the highway did not constitute such a situation compelling the intervention of the third parties. As regards the damage to the border strip, the impatient drivers alone, and not the lorry-driver, were 'masters' of their injurious conduct. Accordingly, the pre-sent case affords no opportunity for examining whether, in discussing 'provocation' of the reckless conduct of a third party, effect should be attributed to the degree and importance of the danger caused to the prop-erty of others. The decision of the dispute follows from the principle that the activities which are important in deciding the imputation of a damage must always be made the subject of a valuation (BGHZ 18, 286, 288; 30, 154, 157;

Senate decisions of 8 January 1963—VI ZR 80/62 and 12 February 1963—VI ZR 181/62—823 BGB).

In making the valuation there is no connection sufficient to ground liability between the conduct of the lorry-driver and the damage, even if, in the plaintiff's interest, attention is focused not only on § 7 StVG, but also on the fault of the lorry-driver which led to the collision. Here the law, and above all the traffic ordinance, clearly distinguished the spheres of liability: the driver and operator of the lorry were liable for the collision and its consequences to others involved in the accident as well as for all objects thereby damaged. For the damage to the sidewalk on the other hand, only the drivers who drove on it are answerable. The current instructions and prohibitions applicable to the lorry-driver protected the interests of those who, with their property, were near the highway only to the extent that the driver was not allowed to invade the pedestrian path with his lorry or to afford an occasion for other vehicles to swerve onto the ground next to the road in order to avoid a collision. But what happened after the accident, as a result of other vehicles driving over the sidewalk in order to get on more quickly, does not fall within his sphere of duty. The lorry-driver was not in a position either in fact or in law to hinder them. That the imputation made by the Court of Appeal goes too far is also plain because the plaintiff city, if it were correct, could claim also against the operator of the car with which the lorry collided, if he did not succeed in exonerating himself under § 7 II StVG; and in certain circumstances the concurrent liability of the automobile which was being parked on the right might have to be considered. It would also be going too far to hold an operator liable for the damage done by the following drivers driving onto the sidewalk if, as a result of failure in its equipment, the lorry had slid across the road.

3. After all, it was not here the operational hazard of the lorry or the driver's way of driving that in any imputable way led to the damage of the sidewalk. That might, to be sure, have happened because the driver of the lorry left it standing until the police arrived in answer to their call. If the resulting hindrance to traffic (cf. § 1 StVG) had no longer had a reasonable justification, this conduct could have created a liability for the damage done by the impatient drivers (§§ 823 I and II, 839 BGB), so that the operator also (according to § 831 BGB, here the defendant according to Art. 34 of the Constitution) might be liable. But a liability on this ground must be legally distinguished from the liability due to the preceding conduct for the actual consequences of the accident. The liability could also affect anyone who blocked the highway not by a vehicle or had not been to blame for the accident.

Under what conditions such a liability should be allowed to exist needs no examination here. The plaintiff city has made no complaint against the driver on these lines.

III. The plaintiff city therefore can have recourse to those drivers only for the damage done by them. It runs the risk, if their identity can no longer be ascertained, of having ultimately to bear the damage. That is, however, a general loss that falls on anyone who has property adjoining a road used for traffic and one that it cannot shift off onto the defendant. In consequence the decision appealed from cannot stand.

Case 66

COURT OF APPEAL OF STUTTGART, 24 NOVEMBER 1964*
OLG Stuttgart = NJW 1965, 112 = VersR 1965, 296

The defendant drove his car, in which were two workmates, down a street in Heilbronn. Unfit to drive because he had a blood–alcohol proportion of 1.80, he drove into a stationary lorry. In the collision his car caught fire. The plaintiff, who saw the accident from his parents' petrol station, hurried with an extinguisher and, together with a passer-by, rescued the defendant and his two passengers from the burning car . . . He suffered severe burns and was unable to work for two weeks.

The defendant's insurer paid compensation for the pecuniary damage, but denied liability to pay for pain and suffering. The Landgericht rejected the claim, but the plaintiff succeeded on appeal for the following

Reasons

In so far as compensation was awarded to the plaintiff for his material damage, the judgment was not attacked by the defendant. The plaintiff has appealed against the rejection of his claim to be compensated for his pain and suffering.

Contrary to the view of the Landgericht, the plaintiff is also entitled to be paid for his pain and suffering in delict under §§ 823 I, II, and 847 BGB. The finding that the defendant's driving while unfit to drive did not afford an adequate cause for the plaintiff's injury cannot be accepted. Admittedly, it is not every *conditio sine qua non* that constitutes an adequate cause, but only such a one as, generally and in accordance with an objective judgment or experience, is apt to produce such a consequence, or one that in general appreciably enhances the possibility of its occurrence, and therefore adequate causes do not include conditions which according to general human experience are completely irrelevant to its occurrence that according to common opinion they cannot reasonably be taken into account. All the

---

* English version by F. H. Lawson and B. S. Markesinis.

same, the finding cannot be accepted that in the present case the bodily injuries to the plaintiff lay outside what was to be normally and objectively expected as a consequence of the accident. It is of course true that it occurred here only because of a further act, due to the free decision of the plaintiff, namely his intervention in order to rescue the defendant and his passengers. That does not, however, exclude an adequate causal connection between the unlawful act and the consequences. It is not correct that where there is an independent and voluntary intervention by a third party an adequate causal connection can only be recognized to exist if the intervention served to ward off an especial danger to the public and therefore was in performance of a legal or moral obligation. Admittedly in RGZ 29, 121 and 50, 223, where an adequate connection was held to exist between the insufficient securing of a team of horses drawing a vehicle and the injuries to a person who tried to hold them up, attention was directed to the fact that the rescuer had acted in performance of a legal or moral duty. In RGZ 50, 223 attention was also expressly directed to the fact that the injured party had intervened to avoid a threatened accident to persons in the village street, and especially children coming out of school precisely at that moment. Nevertheless the Bundesgerichtshof in NJW 1964, 1363, when holding that an adequate causal connection existed between the conduct of a hit-and-run driver and an accident to a pursuing driver caused by an increase of speed, expressly said that the recurrent allusion in those decisions of the Reichsgericht to the fact that the rescuer's intervention had been in accord with a legal or moral duty should not be understood to limit liability to such cases, but only to show that in such cases the intervention of the self-sacrificing third person is nearly always automatic, so that the injuries suffered in doing so were undoubtedly adequate consequences of the wrongful act. In the above-mentioned decision, the court drew the conclusion that in less threatening situations it turns on the circumstances whether the situation produced by the wrongdoer is generally to be considered apt to produce rescues by third persons and, if so, in the present form. In the case then decided the court went on to say that after a sufficiently serious traffic accident it is not at all unusual for other drivers to take up the pursuit of a hit-and-run driver independently, and that such traffic camaraderie, even if it may not reach the level of moral duty, is a fact which prevents us from regarding such a pursuit of the escaping driver as the quite improbable and gratuitous intervention of a third party in the causal continuity. Thus, one may start from the position that even where such an intervention is the immediate cause, an adequate connection may be held to exist between the damage and the event that was the initial occurrence, if the conduct of the third person was justifiable. It is therefore irrelevant that in the present case the plaintiff was not expected to assist and, therefore, under no legal duty to help. It can also be left undecided whether there was a moral duty to rescue. In any case there was a justification. Indeed morally his conduct was of a high standard. Although in the circumstances his intervention required considerable courage and intrepidity, one cannot agree with the Landgericht that the possibility of it must have appeared to an observer so remote that it could not reasonably have been taken into account . . .

Moreover, one cannot agree with the judgment under appeal in regarding the injury to the plaintiff as not an imputable consequence of the defendant's unlawful act . . . It shows a misunderstanding of Larenz's position in invoking his opinion that even where there is an adequate causal connection between the rescue by the plaintiff and the defendant's unlawful act, that act must be regarded as a meaningless condition of the rescue and the ensuing injury to the plaintiff, which must no longer be imputable as a consequence of the unlawful act, since although the defendant could in any case be blamed for negligence in relation to the plaintiff's injuries, the latter bears the full responsibility for his deliberate conduct and therefore a quite predominant share of responsibility falls on him. As the plaintiff in his grounds for appeal aptly says, Larenz was merely upholding the view that even where several persons caused, because they one after another provided conditions for the eventual consequence, one of them can be regarded as its author because he intended the act as his own and thereby reduced the condition that the others provided to the status of an indifferent and legally meaningless condition; side by side therefore with the responsibility of the one who deliberately produced the consequence by his unlawful act, that of another person who merely provided an adequate condition, even though he acted negligently, appears meaningless, so that the consequence cannot be imputed to him as his act. Thus, the Landgericht failed to see that the plaintiff, who, as has already been explained, had a justification for his deliberate intervention, and whose conduct was of a high moral order, acted neither contrary to law nor in blameworthy fashion. Moreover, it failed to see that Larenz, when referring to the above-mentioned decisions of the Reichsgericht in RGZ 164, 125, expressly said that the free but faultless act of a third party did not exclude the imputation to the one who had provided an adequate condition . . . Further, the defendant was also to blame for the damage to the plaintiff through his negligence, because it was foreseeable not only objectively, as has already been said, but subjectively, and here also, just as objective foreseeability is required for an adequate causal connection, infrequent and exceptional consequences are to be taken into account and only quite remote possibilities are to be left out of account. Such a remote possibility, however, as has already been discussed in connection with the intervention of the plaintiff, was, neither objectively nor, from the defendant's point of view, subjectively, in question.

The defendant, therefore, is liable for the damage suffered by the plaintiff under § 823 I and II BGB. The plaintiff, therefore, is entitled to damages for pain and suffering under § 847 BGB. Admittedly, in the cases decided by the Bundesgerichtshof (NJW 1964, 1363) only compensation for material damage was dealt with and not pain and suffering. There was no question at all of personal injury to the driver pursuing the hit-and-run driver, but only damage to his car. This, however, seems immaterial. What is essential is that the court affirmed liability for a delict.

It follows that where a person suffers personal injuries he can claim damages for pain and suffering. Moreover, the Reichsgericht, in the case already mentioned of the rescue of passengers from a burning vehicle (RGZ 164, 125), expressly awarded damages for pain and suffering to the injured rescuer against the objection of the defendant.

Since the plaintiff's claim for damages for pain and suffering is based on an unlawful act, there is no need to go more deeply into whether a claim for damages for pain and suffering also lies under the head of *negotiorum gestio*. [Discussion followed about the amount of damages for pain and suffering.]

Case 67

BUNDESGERICHTSHOF (SIXTH CIVIL DIVISION) 30 JUNE 1987*
JZ 1988, 150

A medical practitioner who culpably removes the sole kidney of a child is liable for the damage which the mother suffered by donating a kidney of her own.

When 13 years of age, on 6 February 1976, the plaintiff was injured while engaged in sport. Since it was suspected that her spleen had been damaged the doctor attending the accident sent her to the hospital in E which is run by the rural district. The surgeon Dr H, in his capacity as the Second Senior Registrar acting in the absence of the Chief Surgeon, examined the plaintiff and decided to open the abdominal cavity. Finding that the left kidney had been damaged, he removed it. On the following day the plaintiff was transferred to the University clinic in H as a result of acute renal failure. It was discovered there that she lacked a right kidney from birth and that consequently her only existing kidney had been removed in the District Hospital in E. In the hospital in H she was first treated temporarily by means of an artificial kidney. Upon the advice of the resident medical staff the plaintiff's mother expressed her readiness to donate one of her own kidneys. On 31 March 1976 one of her kidneys was removed and implanted in the plaintiff. At the end of April the plaintiff was sufficiently well to be discharged from the hospital for further treatment at home.

* English version by Kurt Lipstein.

The plaintiff sued Dr H and the District Council for damages in respect of her own economic loss and for pain and suffering. To that extent the action has been concluded. As a result it is also undisputed that the removal of the plaintiff's kidney constituted a negligent course of treatment. If the correct medical procedure had been followed, the kidney could have been saved. The plaintiff now asks for a declaration that the defendant Rural District must compensate her mother for any economic damage which the latter suffered as a result of the removal of her own kidney on 31 March 1976, subject to any assignment of the claim—by operation of law—to the authority administering social security. For this purpose the plaintiff has accepted an assignment of her mother's claims.

The District Court allowed the action for a declaration. The appeal by the defendant was rejected by the Court of Schleswig. At the same time, on an appeal against a supplementary judgment of the Court below it, the Court of Appeal increased the assessment of costs. A second appeal by the defendant against these decisions remained unsuccessful.

Reasons

I. The Court of Appeal, whose decision dated 3 October 1986 was published in FamRZ 1987, 384 and NJW 1987, 710, has held that the mother's claim for damages is well founded. Its conclusions amount in essence to the following:

The action for a declaration was admissible, irrespective of who was entitled to assert the claim. Even if she had not been assigned the claim, the plaintiff had a legal interest of her own in the declaration demanded by her if for no other reason than because she was then potentially exposed to future claims by her mother on the ground of *negotiorum gestio*. The need to avoid that any claims for damages might be caught by the rules on limitation of actions was, in itself, a reason for an immediate declaration. A real possibility existed that the plaintiff's mother would suffer physical damage.

The plaintiff's mother was entitled to damages in her own right against the defendant by virtue of §§ 31, 89, 823 I BGB in respect of that damage which could not be treated as expenses in restoring the plaintiff's health.

The surgeon Dr H, acting on his own responsibility in his capacity of deputy of the chief medical officer of the hospital's surgical department, was to be regarded as a representative of the defendant Rural District which was responsible for his wrongful treatment. As in the cases of action to save a person or to assist in an emergency, considered by the practice of the courts and in the literature, the donation (by the mother) of one of her kidneys was called for by the tort committed against the plaintiff. Despite the voluntary character of the decision of the plaintiff's mother, a causal link (operating mentally) existed between the tort attributable to the defendant, the physical damage resulting from the donation of a kidney, and the requisite connection between them. Nor did the mother's consent to the operation to remove the kidney exclude the illegality of the bodily injury as far as the defendant was concerned.

II. The objections against these conclusions put forward in the second appeal are unfounded. The Court of Appeal has held correctly that the action for a declaration, which has as its object any future physical damage to the plaintiff's mother, is well founded. This Senate also holds that the plaintiff's mother has to this extent a claim of her own for damages according to §§ 31, 89, 823 I BGB which the plaintiff, as an assignee, may pursue by way of an action for a declaration.

1. Contrary to the view expressed by the appellant, no objections exist against the admissibility of the action for a declaration. The fact that the Court of First Instance by its decision, which has since obtained the force of *res judicata*, has held the defendant liable in respect of future physical damage is not an obstacle. It only dealt with damage suffered by the plaintiff, but did not include damage suffered by the plaintiff's mother, which is in issue here. As the Court of Appeal has stated correctly, the plaintiff may, in certain circumstances, be exposed to subsequent claims by her mother based on *negotiorum gestio*, if the latter incurs expenses in consequence of the loss of the kidney which she donated.

2. The question, denied by the Court of Appeal, as to whether the plaintiff's mother also has claims against the defendant based on *negotiorum gestio* in view of §§ 683, 670 BGB in respect of future expenses resulting from the loss of the kidney need not be examined here. As the Court of Appeal has held correctly, she is entitled in any event to claim compensation in tort, according to § 823 I BGB from the defendant in respect of future damage as a result of the physical injury caused culpably by Dr H.

(*a*) Contrary to the view put forward by the appellant, such a claim is not excluded on the ground that the surgeon Dr H was not to be regarded as an organ representing the authority responsible for the hospital where he removed the kidney. In the absence of the chief medical officer of the surgical department, Dr H, in his capacity as the latter's deputy, was charged with the function of a chief medical officer. In law his position does not differ from that of the chief medical officer himself, had he been present. In so far as the appellant doubts whether also the chief medical officer in charge of a department of a hospital (and not only the chief medical officer in charge of the entire hospital) acts as an organ of the authority responsible for the hospital, his references are to a judicial practice which is outdated and has been abandoned [references]. The question, which had been left open by the Federal Supreme Court [reference], has been decided in the meantime by the present Senate to the effect that the heads of individual sections of a hospital must be regarded as the properly appointed representatives of the local authority responsible for the hospital [references]. This certainly holds good as long as the authority responsible for the hospital does not show that in the particular instance the organization of the hospital must lead to a different conclusion. The defendant has not made any allegations to this effect in the court below dealing with the facts. On the contrary, the liability of the defendant according to §§ 31, 89 BGB for its organs was never disputed in respect of the culpable acts of Dr H.

(*b*) When the Chief Medical Registrar, Dr H, removed the plaintiff's only kidney in violation of a medical practitioner's duty of care, he did not only damage the plaintiff's body and health. In addition he thereby created a dangerous situation which could, above all, cause near relatives of the plaintiff to accept an injury to their own body in order to save the life and health of the plaintiff, by offering a kidney for implanting into the plaintiff. This enforced sacrifice of personal bodily integrity is an injurious act. Leaving aside some special aspects remaining to be discussed, which cannot however lead to a different legal assessment, it can, as in other cases of rescue and emergency, also result in a duty of reparation on the part of the person responsible for the situation calling for rescue or emergency—assistance towards those engaged in the rescue or assistance towards those who suffer injury in the course of it.

(*aa*) There can be no question that a causal nexus, which is relevant for the purpose of legal liability, exists between the removal of the plaintiff's sole kidney, for which the defendant must assume responsibility, and the mother's donation of her kidney. The possibility of a kidney transplant, including a donation by a living person, was known at the time, and the donation of a kidney by a close relative was not so remote as to leave it out of legal consideration. Contrary to the appellant's view, it is to be expected that, upon the advice of medical practitioners, a mother will be prepared to make this sacrifice for her child. Nor is the causal nexus broken by the fact that the donation of the kidney was due to a voluntary decision of the plaintiff's mother; this decision was solely induced by the dangerous situation, for which the defendant is responsible, faced by the mother as a result of the wrong medical treatment, which alone led to the rescuing action. As the practice of this Senate shows [reference], a mentally induced cause can also suffice to establish liability. Writers agree almost unanimously on this. Nor does the appellant challenge this conclusion.

(*bb*) The practice of the Federal Supreme Court, too, has recognized for a long time that the resolution to expose oneself to the risk of injury in order to rescue another who is in danger does not in principle create a new chain of causation which attributes liability for injuries of this kind to the 'rescuer' himself and relieves from liability the person who is responsible for endangering the 'object of the rescue'. On the contrary it was the *Reichsgericht* which extended the liability of the latter to injuries of this kind suffered by the 'rescuer', at least in those cases where the act of rescue was not disproportionate to the impending danger and its prevention (RGZ 28, 120 ff.: restraining bolting carriage horses; RGZ 50, 219, 223: restraining bolting riding horses; RGZ 164, 125 ff.: saving passengers in a bus; OLG Stuttgart NJW 1965, 112: saving passengers in a burning motor-car). This Senate followed that practice in the so-called pursuit cases [references]; and at least in principle it is approved unanimously by writers [references]. It is true, as this Senate has made clear on another occasion, that no duty exists to protect others against harming themselves and, conversely, no general prohibition against inducing another to imperial himself [references]. Social co-existence involving manifold contacts between human beings means that one person may influence another in many ways, without having to incur liability. Only if the person causing the injury is to be *blamed* for having created a dangerous situation which is so serious and calls so urgently for action by the rescuer and emergency-helper the risk assumed by the latter, together with the danger created for the person to be rescued, must be attributed to the person causing the injury, having regard to the circumstances. He must be held liable for any self-inflicted injury of the rescuer and emergency-helper. The reason is that he has created a situation which, although the rescuer and emergency-helper are not required to intervene, at least makes such intervention reasonable and praiseworthy. In such circumstances, it is no longer permissible to consider the intervention on the part of the rescuer and emergency-helper in isolation, distinct from the creation of the 'aggravated dangerous situation' [reference] by the person inflicting the injury. Thus the present Senate has repeatedly spoken of a culpable 'challenge' by the person inflicting the injury to the injured party to imperil himself.

(*cc*) In order to give concrete expression to this assessment of liability this Senate has already formulated a number of principles. The intervention of the rescuer and emergency-helper must not be completely of his own accord; it must have been suggested by the initial act and been 'challenged' by it, as this Senate has expressed it in the decisions referred to above. In addition the acceptance of the peril and the injury to oneself must be commensurate with the possible success of the intervention, and its motivation must at least be acceptable according to the recognized rules of social conduct [references]. In the absence of these criteria limiting liability, which in their formulation are only defined very generally and require to be developed in greater detail in each individual case, the liability of a person who has injured another for the resulting intervention by a third party would no longer be covered by the protective range of the duty of care not to bring about situations which constitute a call for rescue or emergency aid. Outside this range, the fact that a rescuer or emergency-helper imperils or injures himself will fall within his own sphere of action for which he is only responsible to himself. He acts 'at his own risk'. (For the necessary restriction of liability in the case of a mentally transmitted causality see *inter alia* [references].)

(*dd*) These legal principles permit it, in the case for decision involving the donation of a kidney and the injury to the body and the health of the plaintiff's mother, to attribute legal liability to the defendant in respect of the conduct of the Senior Medical Registrar, Dr H. The donation of the kidney was caused precisely by the fact that Dr H, by injuring the child, placed the plaintiff's mother in a situation in which she may have felt called upon to make such a sacrifice. Undoubtedly her conduct must deserve high praise morally and must therefore be approved and recognized by the law. The attempt, which was medically indicated, to improve the plaintiff's physical and health situation by the donation of a kidney and at least to shorten the period of treatment by dialysis, is reasonably and proportionately commensurate with the injury to herself which the mother accepted. Her decision was based specifically upon the detailed advice by the medical officers attending the plaintiff.

(*ee*) Contrary to the appellant, the causal nexus is not to be denied on the ground that the mother did not make up her mind to donate a kidney under the direct impression of an acute emergency but that she had time to consult the medical officers and could ponder the grounds for and against. If an intervention by the rescuer and emergency-helper is suggested, it is irrelevant whether the latter has acted, so to say, on the spur of the moment or whether he was able to assess in advance the chances and risks of his intervention. This does not alter the 'challenging situation' in any respect; and the causal nexus between the damaging act of the injuring person and that by which the rescuer and emergency-helper imperils or injures himself remains in any event. It is not unusual for a rescuer to have sufficient time for reflection. It must be admitted that the notion of 'rescue', understood as an induced intervention for the purpose of averting or containing of damage resulting from a perilous situation brought about culpably by the person committing the injurious act, normally does not extend to help in overcoming the damage, especially if it represents mere assistance in restoring it. From the point of view of legal liability, such assistance can no longer be attributed to the damaging act by the person inflicting the injury. The answer to the question as to when the sacrifice by a person who wishes to reduce the actual damage or at least to contain it still amounts to a rescue and to emergency aid requires an assessment which must take into account the intimate relationship with the challenge of the situation and undoubtedly also the connection in time and space. Regarded from this angle, the donation of a kidney by a near relative—in this case by the mother—for the benefit of the injured child can still be held, without straining the argument, to have been a measure, responding to a challenge, of rescuing the child whose life and health was imperilled. The mother's sacrifice is directly connected with the dangerous situation caused by the defendant medical practitioner by removing the child's only kidney. The delay in making the sacrifice is due not so much to the fact that only after the child's health had been damaged remedial measures were initiated, but that in the circumstances the rescuing donation of the organ could not be carried out immediately, but only after some time. For this reason, the donation of the kidney by the plaintiff's mother is to be regarded in the case for decision as a consequence of the injurious act for which the defendant must assume liability. (To the same effect Deutsch, *Arztrecht und Arzneimittelrecht*, 1983, p. 205 marginal note 305; in Anglo-Saxon law on the basis of the 'rescue doctrine' *Urbanski* v. *Patel*, Manitoba Queen's Bench, 25 January 1978, 84 DLR 3d 650 on the one hand; *Sirianni* v. *Anna* 21 December 1967, 55 Misc. 2d 553, 285 NYS 2d 709 (1967); *Moore* v. *Shah* 30 December 1982, 458 NYS 2d 33; 90 AD 2d 389 and *Ornelas* v. *Fry*, Court of Appeals of Arizona 6 May 1986 (151 Ariz. 324), 727 P. 2d 819 on the other hand.) It need not be considered whether the Senior Medical Registrar Dr H or the defendant authority responsible for the hospital were under a legal *duty* to arrange for a kidney transplant. This consideration cannot serve as the criterion whether the plaintiff's mother made an 'induced sacrifice'.

(*ff*) Contrary to the arguments of the appellant, the claim of the plaintiff's mother does not fail for the reason that she accepted not only the possibility of injuries to herself, as it seems to happen in most cases of rescue and emergency aid, but that she submitted to this injury by donating her kidney, thus sacrificing her health with her eyes open. This fact, too, does not modify in any respect the challenge of the situation nor does it give cause for assessing liability restrictively. Any restriction of liability could only be justified if the self-inflicted injury was disproportionate to the chance of saving the injured person or if the self-inflicted injury exceeded the boundaries of moral approval. Neither is the case here. On the contrary, this Senate has no doubt that the necessary nexus with the tort for which the defendant is responsible is not disproportionate and not reprehensible.

(*gg*) Finally, this Senate cannot accept the appellant's contention that, from the legal point of view the plaintiff's mother has not suffered a bodily injury giving rise to damages because she consented to the operation for the removal of the donated kidney. It is true that therefore the surgical removal of the kidney by the medical practitioner entrusted with this task was lawful. The author of the injurious act who has caused, and is liable for, what from this point of view is a voluntary sacrifice of health and a consensual bodily injury, is precluded on his part from arguing that the bodily injury of the intervener was voluntary and therefore lawful. He cannot do so either if, as in the case, another person must first commit an act of bodily injury in order to enable the rescuer and emergency helper to carry out his rescue operation. In agreeing to the removal of a kidney the plaintiff's mother did not also give her consent to Dr H to being placed in a situation where she had to sacrifice her health in order to save her child. Therefore the tort committed against her retains its illegal character.

Case 68

BUNDESGERICHTSHOF (SIXTH CIVIL DIVISION) 29 FEBRUARY 1956*
BGHZ 20, 137 = VersR 1956, 305

The plaintiff, born in 1911, suffered a fractured skull when he was twelve years old. On 2 April 1940, while riding a motor cycle, he collided with a railway belonging to the defendant mining company and suffered an injury to the right side of his forehead coupled with a concussion. By a judgment which has the force of *res judicata* it was held that the defendant is liable to pay three-quarters of the damage suffered by the plaintiff. Up to 31 December 1944, the defendant made to the plaintiff periodic payments.

The plaintiff contends that as a result of the accident he became permanently unfit for work and demands a monthly payment of DM 300 from 1 January 1951 until he reaches the age of sixty-five. The defendant alleges that all the effects of the accident had long disappeared and, in particular, that the plaintiff's ability to work is no longer restricted.

The claim was rejected by the District Court of Essen and by the Court of Appeal of Hamm. A second appeal was also unsuccessful for the following

Reasons

I. . . .

* English version by Kurt Lipstein.

2. . . .

3. . . . the question is whether the Court of Appeal, relying on its own findings and of the observations of the expert, Professor Dr K, rightly rejected the plaintiff's claim. The appellant denies this and refers to the well-known practice of the Reichsgericht in the matter of accident neurosis. He contends that according to this practice the existence of a causal nexus must be admitted between the accident of 2 April 1940 and the condition of the plaintiff which, while constituting a neurosis inspired by the device to obtain periodical payments, was nevertheless one which paralysed the plaintiff's working capacity and power of mental resistance.

It is true that contrary to the previous practice of the Reich Insurance Office [reference] the Reichsgericht held in principle that a causal connection exists even if the accident was suffered by a person who, owing to his neurotic and labile condition, could not resist sufficiently purpose-and-desire-inspired fantasies. In particular, the Reichsgericht pointed out repeatedly that it is not possible to limit liability to pay damages to physically ascertainable injuries and to exclude nervous or emotional disturbances caused by the accident on the ground that they are due to a special predisposition of the victim. According to the Reichsgericht, a tortfeasor who has injured a person weakened by bad health cannot expect to be treated as if the victim had been healthy. It made no difference whether the fact of bad health was caused by a physical ailment or by an emotional weakness based on his personal make-up [reference].

This point of view was consistently opposed by the medical profession; the dispute was further seriously complicated by the fact that the two sides relied on different notions of causality. In the face of these attacks and the change in the practice in matters of social insurance the Reichsgericht adhered to its view and pointed out, in particular, that a court must always determine in accordance with legal considerations whether a causal nexus exists. Nevertheless, in special cases the Reichsgericht approved a refusal to grant damages [references] and showed in its decision [reference] a clear tendency to restrict liability in the light of a 'purely external nexus' between the accident and the neurotic condition. Further, the Reichsgericht sought to counter an excessively broad liability by relying on § 254 BGB. This Division, in its decision of 8 July 1953 [reference], agreed in principle with the practice of the Reichsgericht and affirmed the possibility that an adequate causal connection can exist between an accident and a 'psycho-reaction' initiated by it.

It would be unnecessary to reopen this question if it were evident that the plaintiff consciously practised deception in simulating the existence of complaints . . . However, the observations of the Court of Appeal in connection with the expert evidence appear to permit only the conclusion that the conduct of the plaintiff borders on simulation and conscious aggravation, but yet that it is primarily to be characterized by the fact that the plaintiff, who is emotionally labile, influenced by purpose-and-desire-inspired fantasies had acquired and retained the fixed idea that he suffered from the consequences of an accident and . . . the fluid transition from intentional to automatic effects is characteristic [of this illness]. The exaggerated symptom results finally in a childish psychotic state akin to pseudo-dementia, in which the patient remains caught. It is therefore impossible to reject a claim for damages in reliance on § 254 BGB without further considerations; contributory negligence could only be held to exist if it could be said that a neurotic person is able to control his will in response to the requirements of the situation and to resist effectively his wishful fantasies. Especially those whose neurotic tension makes them take refuge in the fantasy that they are sick and are entitled to claim against the community or against the tortfeasor to have their livelihood guaranteed are unable to exercise this control and to offer this resistance [reference].

This Division reaffirms the principle that a tortfeasor must also pay compensation for any damage resulting from emotional reactions of the victim if the accident constituted the adequate cause. The fact alone that a certain behaviour is interpreted as a psychogene reaction does not necessarily rule out a connection between the occurrence which caused the accident and the condition which inhibits the ability to work and to resist. Much as the courts must familiarize themselves with the new ideas of medical and psychological sciences about the nature and the causes of neurotic conditions of behaviour, it must not be forgotten that the question of causality is a legal question, and from the legal point of view causality is not restricted to the functioning of the body and its organs. The attempt to restrict liability for neurosis on the ground that these are 'outwardly connected only' does not supply a test for achieving a correct delimitation. If this should mean that the existing complaint and inhibitions would in all probability have manifested themselves even if the accident had not occurred, the court in the exercise of the power conferred by § 287 of the Code of Civil Procedure to assess the evidence quite independently, in particular the conclusions of the medical experts, can deny the existence of a causal nexus altogether. If, on the other hand, it would appear in favour of the plaintiff that his emotional condition which impedes his integration into working life would not have arisen without the occurrence of the accident, the causal nexus cannot be denied, even if the emotional disposition of the plaintiff was an important contributory factor.

If, therefore, it is useless to attempt to limit liability for neurosis by reference to considerations of causality, it is necessary nevertheless to restrict liability for other reasons. In according a claim for compensation to a victim of a corporeal injury, the law wishes to assist him and to facilitate his speedy recovery. It would be contrary to the purpose of the claim for damages if the fact that another must pay the damages would render integration into social life and obligations more difficult or even impossible. For this reason medical opinion points out regularly that the legal regulation of damages must not result in supporting the flight into illness of neurotics set on obtaining damages by way of pensions and in assisting their 'infantile regression . . .' [reference]. If the expert evidence shows that the psychological state of the plaintiff, especially his apathy, is to be explained primarily by his—admittedly unconscious—aim to obtain an advantageous settlement of his livelihood or as a fixation on an imaginary legal position—the accident forming an excuse for avoiding the struggle of daily life—it is equitable not to attribute these consequences to the tortfeasor. For the latter cannot be required to contribute to the perpetuation of a condition which, in the end, is harmful to the physical and mental health of the plaintiff. For this reason claims of neurotics with a fixation on asserting legal rights and damages by way of pensions must be set a limit inspired not by the absence of a causal nexus but by the purpose of compensation owed by equitable considerations. As the First Division of the Federal Supreme Court has pointed out appositely [reference], similar considerations moved legal theory and practice to restrict liability for damages to the adequate consequences of the occurrence which caused the damage, although the Code does not lay down such a restriction. If the principle of liability is not to be extended excessively, as it would if the court were to follow the test of strict causality, liability to pay damages must also be limited correspondingly in the present case. Thus the justified interests of social medicine are also satisfied.

Naturally, only a very detailed and careful assessment of the plaintiff's personality will make it possible to determine correctly the manner and the causes of his neurotic condition. For this purpose, it will be particularly important to establish the boundary between the emotional disturbance caused by the gravity of the accident, the resulting shock, or the physical medical treatment and that which is inspired, following the ensuing legal position, by fantasies of demands [reference].

4. Even if the Court of Appeal has not considered the decisive legal problems correctly in every respect, its findings suffice to enable it to reject the claim for damages in respect of loss of earning capacity . . . The Court of Appeal was therefore correct in the result in rejecting the claim of the plaintiff for damages in respect of loss of earning capacity.

Case 69

BUNDESGERICHTSHOF (FIRST CIVIL DIVISION) 29 JANUARY 1969*
NJW 1969, 789 = VersR 1969, 406

[A collection of jewellery owned by the plaintiff was being carried in the trunk of a car by their traveller K, then a general agent and now a partner in the firm. In the middle of June 1965 K hired a room in the defendant's hotel, as he had often done before. On returning to the hotel one evening at about 10 p.m., he gave the night porter the keys of the car (including the key of the trunk) and told him to have the car garaged. The garage in question was nearby but it was not part of the hotel: it belonged to B, a firm which serviced and rented cars. If a guest wished his car garaged, this was the garage which the defendant hotel used. The porter called B and had the car fetched by one of his employees. There were notices in hotel rooms about this service in June 1965. They said 'Contract Garaging. Day and Night. Cars Fetched and Returned'.

One of B's employees collected the car and the porter handed him the keys of the car and its trunk. The car was returned next morning by a different employee at about 9 a.m. and left in front of the hotel. In the middle of the afternoon K and his colleague T drove to H to see a customer, and when T went to the trunk to collect the jewellery he found it locked. K and T then looked through the collection and saw that a number of wristwatches had been stolen from it. The lock of the trunk was undamaged, and police enquiries proved fruitless.]

The plaintiff claims compensation both in his own right and as assignee of the rights of K. The Landgericht dismissed the claim and the Oberlandesgericht dismissed the appeal. On the plaintiff's appeal, the judgment below is reversed and the case remanded.

Reasons

I. . . .

II. 1. . . . 2. . . .

3. (*a*) The Court of Appeal clearly assumed that if the defendant were liable in contract for the loss of the wrist-watches the plaintiff could claim for its loss on the basis of an assignment to it by K. This is correct. The principle of *Schadensliquidation des Drittinteresses* is applicable. It is implicit in the agreement between the defendant and K, already a contractual guest in the defendant's hotel, for the deposit of the car for reward, that the defendant's contractual liability for the protection of the car applies even if the car

* English version by Tony Weir.

belongs to a third party, it being irrelevant whether the defendant knew or should have known or had any ground for supposing that it did so belong (BGHZ 15, 224, 228).

(*b*) On the other hand, there are objections in law to the view of the Court of Appeal that the contract of deposit in this case did not cover the contents of the trunk. By its very nature the contract of deposit applies to the moveable which is handed over to the depositee for protection as an entirety, whether it consists of a single object, a collection of objects which are legally or physically discrete, or of one single thing which contains a number of objects which are legally or physically separate. So far as can be seen, this has never been doubted before (see BGH NJW 1968, 1718). Thus the defendant's contractual duty extended to safeguarding the contents of the trunk.

Given the findings made by the Court of Appeal, that the watches were stolen while the car was in B's garage, the defendant had the burden of proving that its inability to return the property was not due to matters for which it was responsible (§ 282 BGB). It is not enough for the defendant to prove that it took all necessary care, which in any case it has not yet done. The circumstances here (the trunk being opened without harming the lock, the removal of the more valuable objects from the collection, the employment in the garage of a person who, according to the district attorney was 'well known to be a burglar and confidence trickster') strongly suggest that it was the fault of the defendant or one of its agents for performance (§ 278 BGB) that the goods have gone, so the defendant can exculpate himself only by proving what in fact caused their loss (RGZ 149, 284 ff.; BGH NJW 1952, 1170). This has not been done.

(*c*) The outcome of the case now depends on whether the defendant has a total or partial defence on the ground that the plaintiff or its partner K was at fault under § 254 BGB. This defence was raised by the defendant, but the Court of Appeal naturally did not consider it.

As will be seen, this court cannot conclusively apportion responsibility for the harm under § 254 BGB, since the requisite facts have not been found by the Court of Appeal. The judgment of that court must therefore be vacated and the matter remanded to it for further proceedings and decision on the merits and on costs, taking the following considerations into account.

4. The Court of Appeal will have to verify whether fault on the part of K or the plaintiff contributed to the loss in issue, so as to reduce, perhaps to nothing, the damages payable by the defendant (§ 254 BGB). Given such a fault, then the amount of responsibility to be attributed to K and therefore to the plaintiff depends in the first instance on how far the harm was preponder-

antly caused by one or other party; the critical factor here is whether the conduct of one party not only enabled the harm to occur but made its occurrence substantially more probable than did the behaviour of the other party. The temporal order of the events which caused the harm is not critical (BGH NJW 1952, 537, 539; NJW 1963, 1447, 1449). Only if one cannot conclude from the respective causal efficacy of the conduct of both parties that the harm was preponderantly caused by either of them should the degree of fault of the two parties be considered. Then the first thing to do, before proceeding to apportionment, is to determine the amount of the fault of each party.

The first factor to consider is that K left the jewellery in the trunk of the car without telling the porter or anyone else on the defendant's staff that it was valuable and that the risk of loss was consequently very high (§ 254 II 1 BGB). If the trunk had a separate key—this is not clear—the fact that K gave it as well as the car key to the porter would increase the plaintiff's contribution.

K's behaviour seems intrinsically to be grossly negligent of his own interests, but various considerations, some undisputed, others inferable from the plaintiff's evidence, make it seem less grave. There is the standing of the hotel to be considered and the quality of service which guests would expect. Guests want to be spared the bother of parking their car, but they also expect it to be safeguarded as they themselves would do. According to the defendant, the garage ticket states that no liability is accepted for the contents of the trunk, but since the plaintiff's evidence is that the ticket was not handed to K before, or even at the time when, the car was handed over, the defendant would not be showing the careful service to be expected of such a hotel unless he told K that the garage-owner's exclusion of liability make it risky to leave things in the trunk. There is the further fact in this case, according to the plaintiff, that K had been a frequent guest in the defendant's hotel in recent years. It was known to the hotel staff who looked after him that he carried a valuable collection of jewellery with him in the car and they never sought to dissuade him from leaving it in the trunk, as he sometimes did. Furthermore, on the present occasion the staff knew that K had the jewellery with him. It is true that K did not always leave the jewellery in the car, but he may have been induced to believe that when the car was securely garaged the jewellery in its trunk would also be safe. It is not clear on the evidence whether K knew where the car was garaged or how it was secured, so he could perhaps infer from the information provided in the hotel that his car would be looked after in a manner appropriate to its standing. The Court of Appeal will have to investigate these circumstances, determine the causal potency of the conduct of both parties, and apportion the responsibility between them.

Case 70

REICHSGERICHT (THIRD CIVIL DIVISION) 27 JUNE 1913*
RGZ 83, 15

In December 1908 the plaintiff, a travelling decorator, suffered an injury to the little finger of his right hand, and went to the defendant for medical treatment. The defendant washed the wound with raw carbolic acid, and put a carbolic acid bandage on it for over twelve hours. As a result there developed a so-called carbolic gangrene which required prolonged medical attention. The finger-nail came off and the finger itself became pink and shiny, thick in parts and stiff overall. To the plaintiff's claim for damages the defendant objected that the plaintiff would be able to work just as well as before the accident if only he had the finger amputated. It was clear, according to the defendant, that the plaintiff would have had the finger amputated if the injury had been due to an accident or something of the sort and there were no third party to pay for his loss of earnings. Experts would testify that the operation was simple and free from risk. Of course there was no question of forcing the plaintiff to undergo the operation, but if there was some method by which his loss of earning capacity could be reduced and he chose not to employ it, this must be at his own expense and not at the expense of the defendant. The plaintiff could therefore claim compensation for only such loss of earning capacity as would subsist after such an operation.

The plaintiff contested this defence. Experts would testify that the operation was attended with pain and risk, and that so far from necessarily improving his earning capacity as travelling decorator, it might lead to the whole hand becoming stiff; under these circumstances he could not be expected to expose himself to the danger and trouble of an operation.

The defendant was held liable at first instance and in the Court of Appeal, but his further appeal to this court is now allowed. The decision of the courts below is vacated, and the case is remanded for further proceedings and judgment.

Reasons

The appellant first complains that the Court of Appeal paid no attention to his defence that all or most of the harm in respect of which the plaintiff is suing would have been avoided by the amputation, partial or total, of the useless little finger on his right hand, since such an operation would restore or greatly improve his ability to work . . . This defence the Court of Appeal

---

* English version by Tony Weir.

wholly ignored, to the extent of not even referring to it in its judgment. It will be clear from what follows that the point raised by the defendant cannot be so easily passed over.

In RGZ 60, 147, the Sixth Civil Senate considered the rights of the parties when a person who has been injured in an accident at work refuses to enter a hospital for medical treatment although the prognosis of a cure of great improvement is good. They held that a person who is responsible for the consequences of an accident has a defence under § 254 BGB if a treatment exists which experts agree would lead to a cure or significant diminution of the injury, and if the victim should have been aware of the existence of, and in a position to benefit from, such treatment. If this is established, then a victim who has declined to undergo this treatment must explain why. The court must then weigh his reasons in order to determine whether a reasonable man who was paying due attention to the interests of the party responsible for the harm would likewise refrain from having the treatment in question. A reasonable person would certainly have such treatment if it involves no risk to life, no great bodily pain, and no expense—the expense being borne by another (RGZ 60, 151, 153). The same Senate of the Reichsgericht, in JW 1907, 740 no. 6, applied this principle to operations of the kind in question before us, and approved the formula enunciated by the Court of Appeal: a victim can be expected to undergo an operation if its success is guaranteed—so far as guarantees can exist in medical matters— and if the victim is convinced that the operation is free from risk. The Senate added that all the circumstances of the individual case must be taken into account, including the gravity and danger of the operation and the greater or lesser prospect of success.

These principles must now be amplified and defined with greater particularity. We must remember, when a defendant invokes § 254 II BGB against a victim of personal injuries whose capacity to earn could be restored or improved by undergoing an operation, that the victim has a basic right to decide freely and at his own discretion whether he wishes to undergo such an invasion of his bodily integrity. Before the BGB came into force, lawyers therefore used to hold that it was wrong to treat a victim as being at fault if in the exercise of his free right over his body he refused to undergo a surgical operation simply to reduce the liability of the person responsible for the harm. There was the additional consideration that even in the case of operations which are normally safe, some unforeseen circumstance may cause further harm, even death, and that it may not be as successful as expected. It was thus unjustifiable, they believed, to use the threat of refusing full compensation for all the victim's harm in order to cause him to undergo an operation, even one which is normally safe and effective, just to protect the tortfeasor.

This is a one-sided view which takes account only of the victim's rights, and since the BGB came into force, writers and courts alike have rightly abandoned it. There must be some limit to the victim's right of free self-determination over his body, and that limit is reached when the exercise of this right is purely capricious, a selfish and inconsiderate exploitation of the fact that the defendant is liable. The right is not to be used to equip the victim with the means of living a life of idleness when his capacity to work could be restored by a safe and relatively painless operation. This is required by *Treu und Glauben*, a principle to which the exercise of the right to claim compensation for harm is subject. We can leave aside the question whether a passion for a pension is, as we have recently been taught, an actual disease, so-called compensation hysteria, and to be treated as such. For our purposes the only thing that counts is the objective situation in the individual case.

It follows that certain requirements must be fulfilled before the victim's failure to undergo an operation can constitute a defence. First, the operation must, in the view of experts, be free from danger in so far as in the current state of medical knowledge any operation can be said to be free from danger, that is, it must be safe in the absence of unforeseen circumstances. This removes from consideration immediately any operation which calls for a general anaesthetic, as opposed to a purely local anaesthetic, for with chloroform there is always a risk of death even if the preliminary physical examination of the patient is carried out with scrupulous care. This is in line with the decisions of the *Reichsversicherungsamt* [reference omitted]. Next, the operation must be one which does not involve any significant pain; after all, it is only as a result of some act for which the defendant is responsible that the victim is in the situation where he must take steps to restore his earning capacity, so the principle of *Treu und Glauben* can hardly require him to undergo significant pain for the defendant's benefit. Thirdly, the operation must, on the evidence of experts, be sure to bring about a major improvement in the victim's earning capacity, that is either restore it completely or improve it very greatly. Finally, the defendant must have let the victim know that he is ready to arrange for the operation to be carried out at his expense in an appropriate place and by professional doctors, or to pay the cost of the operation in advance and let the victim arrange it himself; for a victim whose recovery is otherwise complete is not obliged to use money of his own to have an operation carried out simply to reduce the liability of the defendant who, whether he be the person actually to blame or only the party responsible for him, is bound to make good the harm.

Often, it is true, a victim proceeds spontaneously to an operation just to relieve an intolerable physical condition, and then he is personally responsible to the surgeon for the fee; but cases of that sort are not before us now.

It follows that if, contrary to expectation, the operation fails, the defendant is automatically responsible for any further harm it may cause, for such harm is also in a causal relationship with the original injury for which he was responsible. His liability follows naturally from his requiring the victim to undergo the specified operation in order to restore or improve his earning capacity.

If the defendant makes a demand which satisfies these requirements and the victim refuses to undergo the operation in question, the defendant has a good defence to the victim's claim for damages to the extent that the victim's earning capacity would have been restored or improved by the operation. It is then for the victim by way of reply to explain the special reasons for his refusal, as laid down by the Reichsgericht in RGZ 60, 151 ff. . . .

Case 71

BUNDESGERICHTSHOF (SIXTH CIVIL DIVISION) 14 MARCH 1961 *
BGHZ 34, 355 = NJW 1961, 655 = JZ 1961, 602 (with approving note by W. Flume)

The plaintiff in this claim for damages was involved in a motor accident when he was sixteen-and-a-half years old. Like the first defendant, then nearly twenty years old, he was an apprentice motor mechanic in a workshop in H. Every week they had to visit D in order to attend the local training college there. On 21 February 1957 they drove to school in a colleague's Volkswagen. The first defendant, who was at the wheel, was the only one with a driving licence. In the lunch break he suggested to the plaintiff and to two other fellow apprentices, the second defendant and J, then nearly seventeen and seventeen-and-a-half years old respectively, that they should drive to V to have lunch with his parents. On the way there, the second defendant entreated the first defendant to allow him to drive the car but the first defendant refused because, like the plaintiff, he knew that the second defendant had no driving licence. On the way back, however, the second defendant renewed his entreaties and the first defendant relented and allowed him to take the wheel for a spell. They changed places with the motor still running. Though the road was quite steep, the second defendant drove down it at about 60 km per hour, and failed to reduce this speed a few hundred metres on where the road curved slightly to the left. He lost control of the car, and it crossed the highway and struck a tree. The second defendant suffered a cranial fracture, the first defendant a knock on the head, and J a bruise to the left eye. The plaintiff suffered brain damage and a severing of the left ocular nerve: vision in his left eye is reduced to about 10 per cent and is unlikely to improve.

---

* English version by Tony Weir.

The plaintiff alleged that he had warned the second defendant against driving, though only from fear of a police check.

Accepting that he was 20 per cent to blame, the plaintiff claims appropriate damages for pain and suffering from the defendants as common debtors, and seeks a decree that they are liable as common debtors for four-fifths of any harm he may suffer in the future.

The defendants urge that the claim be dismissed on the ground that the plaintiff was acting at his own risk: not only did he consent to the wheel being taken by the second defendant despite his having neither experience nor a licence, but he himself had even sought to drive and so put his companions at risk.

The Landgericht awarded DM 4000 as damages for pain and suffering and decreed that the defendants were liable as common debtors for two-thirds of any future harm suffered by the plaintiff.

On appeal by the defendants the Court of Appeal dismissed the plaintiff's claim in its entirety. The plaintiff now appeals to this court. The judgment below is vacated and the case is remanded.

Reasons

I. The Court of Appeal held that there was no implied agreement which excluded the defendants' liability in tort, any such agreement by a minor like the plaintiff being in any case invalid without the consent of his legal representative. But the court held that the defendants were nevertheless entitled to be relieved from liability on the ground that the plaintiff had been acting at his own risk. The plaintiff had sufficient insight, so the court found, to appreciate the clear risk involved in the second defendant's taking over the wheel. Just as he himself had been ready to imperil his companions by driving the car, so it was in full knowledge of the risk that he had agreed to the second defendant's attempting to drive despite his lack of skill and experience. Though he objected at first, this was only through fear of a police check, and even this objection he did not maintain. The accident was due exclusively to the second defendant's being an inexperienced and incompetent driver. This being so, it would be contrary to *Treu und Glauben* to hold the defendants liable for the results once the risk materialized. Since it was reasonable that the defendants be released from liability, their release should not be prejudiced by the application of § 107 BGB, which need not be applied where there was a 'community of danger among the young', as here. So to hold was consistent with the view recently adopted by the courts, that the effect of a young person's consent to surgery depends not on the law relating to contractual declarations but on his factual ability to appreciate the situation (BGHZ 29, 33).

II. We quite agree with the Court of Appeal that the defendants' liability was not effectively excluded by contract. However, its observations on the doctrine of acting at one's own risk require us to make a decision of principle.

At present lawyers speak of a person as acting at his own risk when, without any sufficient reason, he puts himself in a position of imminent danger although he is aware of the particular circumstances which make for the danger in question. If this risk results in injury, the question arises whether the injured party can claim damages from another person who would otherwise be liable, whether under the law of strict liability or under the rules of contract or tort law. At first the courts applied § 254 BGB in such cases unless they found an implicit contractual exclusion of liability, which they were very reluctant to do. The doctrine of acting at one's own risk only became an independent force in litigation when the Reichsgericht used it to avoid imposing *strict* liability towards a victim who had consciously exposed himself, without any legal, professional, or moral obligation, to a hazard he might well have avoided (RGZ 130, 162). This was a way of avoiding the imposition of strict liability in cases to which the legislative reason for imposing strict liability did not seem to apply. The Reichsgericht adopted the idea that a conscious exposure of oneself to danger might amount to acting at one's *own* risk in order to mitigate strict liability in accordance with the supposed purpose of the legislature. In so doing the Reichsgericht emphasized that when the defendant's liability arose under § 823 BGB, the fact that the plaintiff had acted at his own risk need not necessarily lead to a dismissal of his claim for damages: in such a case there might be an apportionment under § 254 BGB which could take account of the particular facts (RGZ 130, 162, 169; see also RG JW 1911, 28).

Not until its judgment of 19 June 1933 (RGZ 141, 262) did the Reichsgericht . . . adopt the view that a person who rides in a vehicle with knowledge of special attendant dangers thereby consents to any personal injury which may arise therefrom during the journey. If the agreement was valid and relevant, it neutralized the illegal quality of the defendant's conduct with the result that though he caused the harm, he was not liable for it. Such consent to an invasion of a legal interest was a declaration of will, needing to be received by its addressee and, if uttered by a person with limited legal capacity, valid, in view of its adverse effect, only if his statutory representative agreed to it. The Reichsgericht adhered to this view (RGZ 145, 390), and the Third Civil Senate of the Bundesgerichtshof adopted it in BGHZ 2, 159 (see also BGH VersR 1952, 420). This Senate has assumed the soundness of the doctrine that acting at one's own risk is a complete defence, although in none of the cases it has decided were its requirements found to be satisfied. We permitted the plaintiff to appeal in this case because we wish to depart from the decisions of the Reichsgericht and the Bundesgerichtshof.

III. As long ago as 25 March 1958 (NJW 1958, 905), this Senate expressed doubts about the way of treating conscious self-imperilment introduced by the Reichsgericht in RGZ 141, 262, and scholars have increasingly objected to treating a person who 'acts at his own risk' as giving a consent to a possible invasion of a legal interest which operates as a justification. They stress that it is artificial and unrealistic to view the situation in this way, that it is inappropriate to employ the concept of the 'legal act', and that this construction tends to lead to unsatisfactory results [references omitted]. We agree with these criticisms and now depart from the doctrine of the Reichsgericht.

1. The commonest case involves carriage by an incompetent driver. Here it is clearly unrealistic to suppose that the passenger who is aware of the driver's incapacity is consenting to the personal injuries which may arise during the journey. It is normally a case of conscious negligence rather than of conditional intention, to use a distinction which is drawn when one person injures someone else rather than himself: the passenger is aware of the danger, but hopes that it will not materialize. We blame him because in imperilling himself he is acting recklessly: it is normally a gross fiction to hold that such conduct by the passenger constitutes a consent to personal injury.

2. Furthermore, it is only within the rather narrow limits of §§ 134, 138 BGB and § 226a StGB that any such agreement could serve as a justification for the defendant's conduct. Should the injury prove fatal, the defendant's conduct clearly cannot be justified by any such agreement (BGHSt 4, 88, 93). And if the resulting personal injuries are serious, especially if they involve loss of vital organs, the victim's agreement still cannot justify their infliction, since this is morally offensive and legally discountenanced, regardless of the victim's consent (see BGHSt 6, 232, 234 [other references omitted]). Thus to treat putting oneself at risk as raising an issue of consent inevitably makes the legal outcome depend on the gravity of the harm, which for tort lawyers should be irrelevant. Furthermore, there is no need for any justification at all in cases of strict liability, since strict liability does not depend on the illegal nature of the conduct (GSZ in BGHZ 24, 21, 26).

3. Another unsatisfactory consequence of treating a person's consent to the invasion of a legal interest as constituting a declaration of will is the requirement that it needs to be received and must therefore 'reach' the addressee. There can be no good reason for making the defendant's liability depend on whether *he* knew or could have known that the victim was consciously

putting himself at risk (compare the facts of the case before the Senate on 8 December 1954 (VersR 1955, 120)) . . .

4. Nor is the doctrine any better when the victim is under age. Why should liability towards minors, who are themselves capable of being liable in tort, depend on whether their statutory representative consents which is in practice extremely uncommon since normally the decisions involved are sudden and spontaneous?

5. In cases involving drunk-driving the view we now reject meant that whether there was a complete defence or a more elastic apportionment under § 254 BGB depended on whether the passenger, himself often drunk, was conscious of the risk or whether he had simply rendered himself incapable through gross negligence of appreciating it. This is a very subjective matter, and in cases like these where things happen very quickly it is hard to come to any firm conclusion on it. Thus even in the typical case the test which stems from RGZ 141, 262 proved impracticable: applying it led to unpredictable results.

6. We note finally that the view of the Reichsgericht leads to a difference in the way the illegality of an actor's conduct is judged in private and in criminal law. In criminal law the victim's conscious self-exposure to harm is not accorded the same justificatory force where personal injuries are negligently inflicted as it has been in private law since RGZ 141, 262 (see BGHSt 4, 88, 90 [other reference omitted]). Furthermore, in dealing with consent to an invasion of one's corporeal integrity, the criminal law does not invoke the private law principles of *Willenserklärung* at all [reference omitted]. Thus so long as a person's exposure of himself to danger is to be treated as a justificatory declaration of will, our legal system can never achieve a unitary method of judging the illegality of conduct.

IV. In the view of this Senate, the problem under discussion gives rise to issues of illegality and justification only when the victim's conduct really and without any artificial construction amounts to a consent to an envisaged invasion of his legal interest. This may happen in certain dangerous sports (compare BGHSt 4, 88, 92), but in the common case before the courts today the sole question is almost always whether, and if so to what extent, a person's liability in damages is affected by the fact that the victim had consciously exposed himself to the danger when it was imminent. If in such cases it seems more or less offensive that the damage should be shifted from the victim to the other party, that is because in claiming compensation the victim is acting in a manner inconsistent with prior conduct of his own and for which he is answerable. To go against one's own act conflicts with the principle of *Treu und Glauben*, and it is this which makes it wrong for the victim to invoke the liability of the defendant without taking account of the fact that he himself consciously created or helped to create the dangerous situation which enabled the defendant's contribution to it to cause the harm. Once this is realized, we see that the correct way to deal with the problem is by means of the value-judgment expressed in § 254 BGB. This rule, which provides that a defendant's liability may be affected, or even extinguished, if conduct for which the victim is responsible, especially his capricious exposure of himself to danger, contributes to the harm, is essentially based on the concept of inconsistent behaviour which is rooted in § 242 BGB. Specific application of this principle to damages law is found in § 254 BGB [references omitted]. Thus if a judge, in apportioning responsibility under § 254 BGB, gave great weight to the views here put forward, he would not be invoking any consideration extraneous to that rule; on the contrary, if he failed to take sufficient account of the victim's conscious exposure of himself to the danger and his inconsistency of conduct, the judge would not be doing justice to the particular circumstances in which the harm, and responsibility for it, arose.

It is true that if the commonest cases of self-exposure to danger are to be dealt with under § 254 BGB, we will be abandoning the familiar rigid principle that to act in the knowledge of specific existing danger is to act at one's *own* risk and thus to forfeit one's claim to damages. But in our view it will do nothing but good if this principle is abandoned. Even the practice of the courts hitherto has failed to give effect to this principle in a full and logical manner; they have been forced to adopt unrealistic exceptions in order to limit its effect. Furthermore the courts have tended to set almost impossibly stringent requirements for the proof of the plaintiff's knowledge of the special source of danger, simply because they wished to be free to apply § 254 BGB, which they believed to be more appropriate.

As to the question when liability should be *excluded* in a case where the victim has exposed himself to danger, and when there should simply be a *reduction* of the damages, we are of opinion that no precise rule can be laid down. The types of case involving conscious self-endangerment are so various that clarity and certainty of law could not be achieved by any inflexible and uniform rule. Certainly, when a victim has clear knowledge of a specific danger and exposes himself to it without any good reason and is hurt, or indeed when he helps to create the dangerous situation, there will be good reason to relieve the defendant of all liability. But it would be one-sided to concentrate, to the exclusion of all the other features of the individual case, on the fact that the plaintiff voluntarily endangered himself. Other factors may be of great weight, for instance how the danger arose, how much the defendant was to blame for the existence and actualization of the risk, what the relationship between the parties was, and how obvious the danger was (see also the decision of this Senate on 2 December 1958 (VersR 1959, 368)). A person's psychological state is very hard to ascertain, and a decision which focused exclusively on the plaintiff's attitude at a particular moment of time would often be unrealistic and unfair. § 254 BGB permits the trial judge to do justice in the particular circumstances of the individual case in a judicially responsible manner, and he will be assisted in making a just and proper exercise of his discretion in applying this provision if he pays attention to the principles evolved by the courts in relation thereto and to the principle of inconsistency in conduct.

The Third Civil Senate has stated that it no longer wishes to adhere to the doctrine of 'acting at one's own risk' as laid down in BGHZ 2, 159, so it is unnecessary to convoke the Great Senate for Civil Matters under § 136 GVG.

V. It is well-established law that if the victim is a minor, his contributory fault under § 254 BGB is to be judged in accordance with the relevant principles of delictual law. If a sixteen-and-a-half-year-old like the plaintiff is personally at fault in consciously putting himself at risk, one must therefore look to his actual ability to recognize the dangerous nature of his conduct and to behave accordingly. To this extent we agree with the Court of Appeal. But as has been explained in **IV**, above, we cannot follow the Court of Appeal in holding that the defendants must be released from liability just because the plaintiff consciously endangered himself. This very case shows how unjust a result may follow from undue concentration on this point.

The following factors in particular should be noted. It is true that the plaintiff's failure to maintain his objection to the second defendant's taking over the wheel counts against him, as does the fact that he himself was ready to take the wheel in lieu of the second defendant and so imperil his fellow-travellers. On the other hand, the plaintiff was not the first to suggest that someone other than the first defendant should drive. In view of the way young people behave, the conduct of the plaintiff as a whole, while certainly culpable, is not incomprehensible. Young people like the plaintiff are especially ductile if an older comrade sets a bad example. In the circumstances, the plaintiff's fault in remaining in the vehicle when the second defendant was driving it certainly cannot be described as gross. The second defendant, by contrast, was the origin of the suggestion that an unqualified person should drive, and it was his unreasonable and incompetent driving which caused this serious accident. The first defendant was especially to blame, for it was he who had control of the car; furthermore, as the only person with a driving licence, he must have known the probable consequences of letting the second defendant drive; finally, he was the oldest of the group and should have asserted himself more strenuously.

These observations are not intended to prejudge the final decision which in view of the change in the law and the possibility of further evidence must necessarily be left to the trial judge. We make them only in order to show that on the evidence so far adduced it would be wrong that the defendants, who have apparently suffered only slight injuries, should be entirely released from liability to the plaintiff, who is maimed for life. This case is entirely different from the hypothetical case put by the Court of Appeal, where three youths of the same age who do not know how to drive and have no licence take turns at driving a car they have stolen and are badly injured in an accident while one of them is at the wheel. There is really no comparison between the situations. Nor does the very vague idea of 'community of danger among the young', which weighed with the Court of Appeal, provide any legal basis for refusing to hold the defendants liable to the plaintiff.

Case 72

BUNDESGERICHTSHOF (SIXTH CIVIL DIVISION) 17 SEPTEMBER 1991[*]
NJW 1991, 3275

Facts

The plaintiff *Land* brought a claim for damages by way of the right of subrogation in respect of injuries suffered by K who was injured in a road accident on 11 February 1962. At the time of the accident, K was employed by the *Land* as a police officer. As a result of the consequences of the accident, K had to take early retirement on 1 February 1964. The defendants in the action were the insurers of R (the other driver), whose responsibility for the accident is not in dispute. As a result of a declaratory binding judgment dated 9 January 1969, the defendants are obliged to compensate the plaintiff *inter alia* for the costs which the latter will incur up to 30 November 2000 in respect of maintenance payments which it must make to K. The amount of the compensation payable is the difference between what K would have earned as a police sergeant and his earnings as a computer programmer. This is because since July 1964 K has been working as a programmer at the firm of T. Soon afterwards K was earning more in his new job than as a police officer. On 1 March 1982, however, he left the employment of T and joined the firm of S, owned by his brother. The intention was that after about one year's experience working for this firm he would take over the management of a newly established subsidiary company of S. Soon after opening, this subsidiary had to cease trading as its economic prospects were poor. K left the employment of S on 30 September 1983. Subsequently, he was employed as a sales representative for a publishing company, and then

* English version by Ms J. Shaw.

as an insurance agent. Since 1984 his income has been less than that of a police sergeant. The plaintiff therefore sought to recover in respect of the maintenance payments made between 1984 and 1987, based on the difference between what K actually earned and the earnings of a police sergeant, namely DM 101,219.69.

The LG gave judgment for the plaintiff; the OLG rejected the defendants' appeal. The defendants' appeal to the BGH was successful.

For the following

Reasons

I. The judgment of the OLG is based on the assumption that were it not for the accident, K would have remained in the police force and during the period of time in question would have had the earnings of a police sergeant. The claims for loss of earnings brought by the plaintiff by way of the right of subrogation (§ 99 NRWBG) were losses resulting from the accident. An adequate causal link exists between the loss and the accident. Developments such as those which have occurred in a case like the present one, whereby the professional activity initially taken up is subsequently abandoned with the result that the victim has a lower level of earnings, are not wholly improbable. There were therefore no grounds for the defendants to be exonerated from the duty to make good the damage resulting from K's loss of earnings according to the principles which have been developed by the case law on the protective scope of the norm and on the breaking of the chain of causation.

II. The judgment of the OLG is incorrect in law. The defendants' appeal must succeed and the claim must be rejected.

1. The OLG is correct to affirm that the pre-requisites are satisfied which would normally suffice for the defendants to be liable, such that they would be responsible for the loss of earnings in accordance with the provisions of § 823 I and § 842 BGB read in conjunction with § 3 of the Act on Compulsory Insurance (PflVG). Thus it is not in dispute that the defendants are bound to make good in full the loss of earnings suffered by K as a result of the accident. In contrast to the view put forward at the oral hearing on behalf of the applicants, it must also be assumed that K's accident is a scientific and factual cause of the loss of earnings for which the claim has been brought. For the OLG has established—and its underlying procedure has not been called into question by this appeal—that this loss would not have occurred but for the road accident. The judgment of the OLG is also correct in holding that there is an adequate causal link between this loss and the accident. It is not wholly improbable (to use the general definition [references omitted]) that a person injured in an accident who can no longer exercise his earlier profes-

sion because of the injuries he has suffered and must therefore earn his living in a different way, may also give up this professional activity, even if it is better paid, in order to seek greater job satisfaction elsewhere or in order to earn more, but that the result of the further change in job may be that his earnings fall behind what he was earning previously. Such a chain of events lies within the sphere of what experience has indicated can be expected to occur.

2. These general preconditions for liability will not, as this court has repeatedly stated, suffice in every case as the basis for the tortfeasor's duty to make good a particular consequence of the accident. Even though the loss may have been 'adequately' caused by the accident, there may not, in exceptional cases, be the necessary internal connection between the infringement of the legally protected interest and the 'resulting loss' as defined by § 823 I BGB for which the injured victim claims compensation required to generate a duty to compensate on the part of the defendants. If, as appears from the evaluation so far made of the facts, there is no more than a purely external, so to speak coincidental connection between the conduct which caused the injury and the consequential loss for which recovery is sought, then there is no relevant justification for attributing responsibility for this consequence of the original accident to the tortfeasor [references omitted]. Such is the case here.

(*a*) The necessary connection, such as is required for there to be a duty to compensate on the part of the defendants, with the range of risks to which the defendants, through their tortious conduct, subjected the victim, may be missing, in particular where the victim himself decides to take a certain course of action and thus himself has been the true cause of the consequential loss for which he now seeks recovery. In such a set of circumstances, an evaluatory assessment can lead to the conclusion that the loss thereby caused belongs exclusively to the normal risks of life of the victim himself. Thus it is recognised that the causal connection with the original tortious act is broken where conduct of the victim which causes the loss is wholly unusual or inappropriate [references omitted]. The same may apply where a decision of the victim which brings about the loss is so far removed from the risk created by the tortfeasor and is embedded within the victim's own sphere of risk such that the tortfeasor cannot legitimately be made liable for this consequence. It was with this reasoning and in the same circumstances as those at issue here, in which the victim of the accident changed job and thus suffered loss, that this court decided that further consequential loss fell outside the sphere of risk for which the defendant was responsible, provided that the change of professional activities was such that the accident was no more than the external trigger for this development (NJW-RR 1991, 854).

Such an exception will only apply subject to strict conditions. The principle of full compensation which applies to the law of damages requires that such an evaluation can only be undertaken in exceptional cases. It is necessary that there is a clear break which is externally visible, which shows that the injured person has accepted as his own the risks resulting from his decision to pursue a different professional goal [reference omitted].

If in a particular case there are unequivocal factors which indicate that with his decision to change careers the victim separated his future professional activities from the accident, then the principle of full compensation does not require the victim to be exonerated from the negative consequences of his career choice or the tortfeasor to take the burden of those consequences which, on an evaluatory assessment, have nothing more to do with the injury which was suffered or with the career change which this brought about, simply because the victim's career took a different path as a consequence of the accident and there is thus a causal connection with the loss. Where there is such a change of career, the victim—who may benefit from increased promotion and earning opportunities without being asked to account for these [references omitted]—acts at his own risk. He is not protected by the liability of the tortfeasor against the effects of all the incorrect vocational decisions he may make or against all the misfortunes which may occur from the moment of the accident to the time when he ceases work.

(b) In the case in question, K took up a post as a programmer in Firm T after the accident; he worked there for nearly 18 years. Soon afterwards, he earned more than in his previous job as a police sergeant. It is not claimed, nor is it the case, that K did not feel 'wholly valued' in his new job or that he did not have the same social standing as in his previous job [references omitted]. K's decision to leave Firm T in 1982 and to switch to his brother's Firm S was not for instance based on any continuing effects upon his health of the road accident which occurred long before, but was simply based on K's wish to take up a new job which promised success and higher remuneration. These circumstances, taken as a whole and evaluated as this court is entitled to do on the basis of the findings of fact of the first instance court, make it apparent that there is a break in the chain of causation between the road accident on 11 February 1962 and the professional failures of the plaintiff after 1982. By taking a decision, which was no longer influenced by the accident, to leave his established job of 18 years with Firm T and to switch to his brother's firm, K decided to take his subsequent professional fate into his own hands, as would have been the case if any employee of Firm T, regardless of whether he or she had suffered a road accident, had decided to change jobs. So long as he was earning the level of salary paid by Firm T, K was suffering no loss of earnings as a consequence of the accident. There is evidence that this would not have changed up to the end of working life. If, in these circumstances, K were to feel the need to change jobs, then he was free to do so; however, there is no question of him making the person who caused an accident which happened 20 years earlier responsible for his professional failures which were caused by a decision by K which was brought about neither by the injuries caused in the accident, nor by any alleged 'lesser value' of his work for Firm T. The road accident and K's subsequent employment at Firm T which was brought about by the accident were only relevant to his renewed decision to change jobs and work for Firm S to the extent that were it not for the accident he would have shied away from the possibility of working in his brother's business, given his permanent position in the public service as a police sergeant. This circumstance alone does not change the position as regards the factors set out above which indicate clearly that K was acting on his own responsibility, and does not undermine the argument that the chain of causation is broken between the road accident and the loss of earnings which is claimed. It follows that the disadvantageous consequences can no longer, with regard to the accident, be construed as 'damage arising therefrom'.

(*c*) Contrary to the view put forward by the respondent in its argument, it is not necessary to reach a different conclusion on the grounds that his professional situation with Firm T might have been a contributing factor in K's decision to move to his brother's business and that consequently it was necessary to establish the facts further in this respect. It is not necessary to decide whether the tortfeasor will always be liable in respect of the loss of earnings suffered by the victim which might occur considerably later after his forced change of job as a result of a reorganisation by his new employer. For the decision of the OLG does not leave it open as to whether the reason for K's move to his brother's business was attributable to his professional situation with Firm T, but rather it stated in the grounds for decision—and these were not challenged in the appeal—that K gave up his job as a programmer *in order* to take up a senior post in another business. In addition, as was apparent from the facts presented in the OLG judgment, the plaintiff, himself, did not even argue that K would no longer have been able to work for Firm T when it moved its data processing department, in which he worked, to the town of W; on the contrary, the plaintiff argued that the reason for K's move to his brother's business was that K did not want to move to W. Whether this would suffice as a ground for imposing the burden of the consequential loss of earnings which would have resulted from K's refusal and the subsequent change of job upon the person who caused the accident can be left open in this context since, as was said, the OLG found that the reason for K's change was his decision to take up a senior post in his brother's business. The professional misfortunes which resulted from this decision are, as stated here, no longer attributable to the acts of the tortfeasor.

Notes to Cases 56–72

1. The eighteen cases reproduced above deal with various aspects of causation: cases 68 and 60 contain oft-quoted definitions of the adequate cause theory; cases 64 and 65 provide the leading examples of the operations of the 'scope of the rule theory' of causation; 58 deals with the problems of predispositions, while no. 68 discusses the thorny question of accident neurosis; case 66 looks at the issues associated with rescues; case 70 deals with the plaintiff's duty to mitigate his loss and so on. All these points have been developed in section A of Chapter 2, 5, above; and excellent collections of American materials can be found in: Franklin and Rabin, 282; Epstein, 363; Henderson and Pearson, 127; Posner, 543; Prosser, Wade, and Schwartz, 265 etc. Prosser and Keeton, *On Torts*, still provide one of the clearest textbook accounts. All of these also give abundant references to the rich periodical literature, so these notes can be kept to a minimum.

2. The literature may be extensive and some of the problems intellectually fascinating, but causation must be approached with the following warning in mind:

The problem [of causation] is a difficult one, but the length of the treatment in this casebook and the amount of time allocated it in most courses may perhaps give an exaggerated impression of its importance. In the great majority of negligence cases, the problem does not arise at all; it comes up only in the fraction of negligence actions that involve unusual fact situations. (Prosser, Wade, and Schwartz, 337.)

This down-to-earth remark applies equally to German and American law.

Prosser also states in his case-book that 'The principle task of the court is to do justice as between these parties in their present situation. For this purpose, a weighing evaluative process is required, rather than a clear-cut rule of law'. This is not so different from the point the German Federal Court made in its famous judgment of 23 October 1951 (case 60) where, after reviewing the many variants of the adequate cause theory, it concluded that the answer must, in the end, be found in common sense and a reasonable choice between competing policy factors. Once again Americans and Germans are thus not so far apart. For in both these countries academics have not managed to conceal their fascination with the subject which, in the end, they are forced to admit is of relatively small practical value and should be approached in a common-sense way (Hart and Honoré, ch. 2).

3. The differences between adequate causation and foreseeability have been discussed above (Ch. 2, section 2.A 5(*b*)). 'But foreseeability', to quote Prosser again (ibid. 338), 'is an accordion concept, depending upon the

detail and precision with which foresight is required.' In modern times it has thus been stretched (over-stretched in some cases, see, for example, *Meah* v. *McCreamer* [1985] 1 All ER 367), so that it is legitimate to enquire whether it has lost much of its usefulness as a device controlling liability. Was not that one of the reasons why the *Re Polemis* rule [1921] 3 KB 560 was abandoned in England (but not the USA; see Friendly J.'s remarks in *Petition of Kinsman Transit Company* 338 F. 2d 708 (1964)) by the *Wagon Mound (No. 1)* [1961] AC 388? In Germany, von Caemmerer has reached the same conclusion about the effectiveness of the adequate cause theory ('Das Problem des Kausalzusammenhangs' *Gesammelte Schriften* I, 395, 402, 408); and the German Federal Court is not tuning down its doubts about the concept of adequacy in general (for example see BGHZ 79, 259). Not unnaturally, the search for more normative theories of causation can thus be found in both systems, though once again the similarity between the views of Rabel and Green is, to say the least, coincidental but uncanny. Such theories, as we have seen, can help keep liability under control; but they can also lead to irreconcilable decisions: cf., for example, *de Haen* v. *Rockwood Sprinkler Co.* 258 NY 350, 179, NE (1932); *Di Caprio* v. *New York Central Rly.* 231 NY 94, 131 NE 746 (1921); *Kernan* v. *American Dredging Co.*, 355 US 426, 78 S. Ct. 394 (1958) and, of course, the classic English case of *Gorris* v. *Scott* LR 9 Exch. 125 (1874). Little wonder that in view of such ambiguities and uncertainties some authors have expressed open scepticism about the utility of the notion of causation (see, for example, Coase, 'The Problem of Social Cost' 3 *J. Law and Econ.* 1, 2 (1960); Calabresi, *The Cost of Accidents* 6, n. 8 (1970). But can terms like 'cheaper cost avoider' avoid causal language?

4. In view of this, the selection of cases translated above more than usually reflects personal tastes and predilection. But even here a note of warning must be sounded. The judgments reproduced usually deal with one facet only of the problem selected for inclusion and discussion. For example, take the rescue case reproduced above (no. 66). This obviously invites comparison with *Wagner* v. *International Rly.* 232 NY 176, 133 NE 437 (1921). The result is the same, since the policy behind the judgments is the same. But the terminology is different (causative language instead of duty of care). The use of the one rather than the other does not really matter, as most American books which discuss the problem say quite categorically. (In any event, terms such as 'duty', 'foreseeability', 'adequate causation' in these cases barely conceal policy dictates.) But the difference in literary style cannot be passed unnoticed. Cardozo's romantic imagery has justly been immortalized; dry causative language, on the other hand, can only make the law appear even more remote from real people and their problems than most of us perceive it to be.

Giving a rescuer an action is right only under certain circumstances. The German judgment, along with other different systems, hints that the solution will be different if his intervention is rash or the result of pure intermeddling with the affairs of others. Other problems arise. What, for example, if the person rescued negligently puts himself in a position of danger? What if the rescuer injures the rescued person or a third person? What about the rescuer's rescuer? In the casuistic Common law, most of these problems have been litigated (see Prosser, Wade and Schwartz, 331–3); in German law the answers are usually canvassed in the literature; but in practice the solutions, again, should not be different, since the same policy issues are at work in both systems. The references given in the principal German case confirm this.

5. Foreseeability and rescue have also been considered in a novel context that has arisen, in part, because the law has not kept up with the rapid forward leaps of medical technology. The point can be easily put: should a medical practitioner who culpably removes the *sole* kidney of an injured child be liable for the damage which a close relative (typically mother or father) suffers by donating one of his kidneys? Case 67 and Canadian law (*Urbanski* v. *Patel* 84 DLR 3rd 650, 671 (1978)) have said 'yes' to such claims—the courts in the USA have decided otherwise. (See *Sirianni* v. *Anna* 285 NYS 2d 709; *Moore* v. *Shah* 458 NYS 33 (1982); *Ornelas* v. *Fry* 151 Ariz. 324, 727 P. 2d 819 (1986).) What are the arguments for and against recovery?

First, there is a hint, but no more than that, to suggest that the donor's intervention may be unforeseeable and unexpected. This must have been particularly true when cases like *Sirianni* v. *Anna* (1967) were decided when organ transplants were still rare. This argument, however, is unlikely to carry much weight today when, as the Canadian Court put it in *Urbanski* v. *Patel*, 'a kidney transplant is an accepted remedy in [cases of] renal failure'.

A second argument, considered in *Moore* v. *Shah*, was that foreseeability alone is not enough to lead to the discovery of a 'duty of care' and thereby to the imposition of liability. This is certainly true as far as English law is concerned though it is somewhat surprising to see it coming from the pen of American judges. For, as Professor John Fleming has put it, 'In California [at least] foreseeability has for most purposes become a sufficient test for "duty"' (*The American Tort Process* (1988), 118). Equally surprising is the fact that American judges, who are in practice quick to usurp the (inactive) legislature's role, are in this context suggesting that if a remedy is needed it should come from the legislator (*Sirianni* v. *Anna* at p. 713).

A third objection considered by the *Moore* court is that the imposition of liability would extend the physician's liability 'beyond manageable limits' since they could not 'foresee each and every person other than his patient who might conceivably be affected by his negligence'. But quite apart from the fact that the floodgates argument has never held out much appeal in instances involving physical injury, the fact is that in these cases one is only concerned with a limited and usually identifiable group of close relatives who, for medical reasons (tissue matching), or from an understandable moral compulsion, are, in practice, the only ones likely to come forward in order to save the injured primary victim. In any event, the floodgates argument seems to be effectively countered by the criteria which the German courts say must be evaluated *ad hoc* before the rescuer's intervention is deemed worthy of support.

The fourth objection is that in the view of the American courts this situation is incompatible with Cardozo's phraseology in the *Wagner* case. There Cardozo had talked of 'the act of rescue, *if only it be not wanton*, is born of the occasion'; and 'wanton' was in the kidney cases interpreted to mean 'wilful', later elaborated into 'wilful, intentional, voluntary'. Do you think that is what 'wanton' means? Since every rescue, even one attempted on the spur of the moment, is intentional and voluntary, should not 'wanton' here be taken to imply 'reckless'?

Fifthly, in the USA the rescue doctrine was not applied to the present situation on the grounds that the rescuer/donor had time to reflect on his action. How does the German court counter this point? Which view do you find more convincing?

Finally, the sixth objection against recovery is the presence of consent on the part of the donor/plaintiff. With respect, however, the argument is misleading. For no one is saying that the kidney was removed without consent; if it had been, there would be an action for battery! What one is saying is that the defendant's negligence placed the donor in a position in which, morally and socially, he felt compelled to act the way he did. Indeed, wider policy considerations should encourage such donations, not penalize them by not rewarding them. The German court, influenced by such motives, had no doubt that 'consent' could not in this case be used as a defence. Do you agree with its view or do you prefer the American reasoning? How much has policy influenced the outcome of those cases? Which view do you think the English courts should/will adopt?

6. The problem of accident neurosis is represented in this selection by one case only. Given the limitations of space this is inevitable; but it is also regrettable since the interaction of law and medicine is here, as elsewhere, fascinating. The medical aspects of this problem are discussed by a consultant neurologist in a book which is intelligible even to non-specialists (Trimble, *Post Traumatic Neurosis* (1981)); and one of the points made there is that attitudes towards this problem are changing. Thus, while during the

nineteenth century stress was put on 'organic' material changes, during the greater part of our century the emphasis has shifted to psychological interpretation of the symptoms. More recently, however, there is a certain return towards more 'organic' interpretations as the functioning of the human brain becomes better understood. The notion that in most of these cases plaintiffs are not guilty of malingering may, in part, explain the greater willingness to provide compensation. Certainly medical science has shown that illness following injury seems susceptible to manipulation by compensation factors. Clearly there is here more room for interdisciplinary work.

Illustrations

Bismarck and Emperor William I

BISMARCK, Otto Eduard, Leopold Prince von Bismarck-Schönhausen (1815–1898). Bismarck's life and personality are fascinating not only to the politician and the historian but also to the lawyer, first because the political unification of Germany which he helped forge in the 60's and 70's gave the decisive push towards the drafting of the Civil Code, and secondly because of his politically motivated but pioneering social legislation (which is discussed briefly in chapter 3 of this book.) The Nobel laureate Thomas Mann, in a little-known essay entitled *Goethe, das deutsche Wunder* (reprinted in Thomas Mann *Dichter und Herrscher. Europäischer Geist in Fünf Jahrhunderten.* Ausgewählt von Rudolf Hochhutch *Buchgemeinschafts-Ausgabe* p. 9) reflecting on the three creators of modern Germany (Luther, Goethe and Bismarck) has given us the best ten-line description which deserves to be quoted in full.

'. . . a phenomenal political genius of German stock who, in three bloody wars, forged the Prusso-German domination and secured its hegemony in Europe for decades . . . A historical colossus with a high-pitched voice; brutal, sentimental, and prone to nervous fits of weeping, all at the same time; a giant of unfathomable cunning and of such cynical candour of speech that it was not advisable to report on it officially (according to Lord Russell); a misanthrope and subduer of men through charm and force; a go-getter, realist, utter anti-idealogue; a personality of inordinate, almost superhuman dimensions, the absolute ego, who infected everyone around him with enthusiasm but also set them quaking.'

WILLIAM I, seventh King of Prussia and First German Emperor (1797–1888). An old fashioned king who led his troops to such decisive victories as Gravelotte and Sédan. He was physically and morally an upright King which gave Bismarck precisely the kind of cover he needed to implement his machiavellian plans. The crowning of Wilhelm as Emperor of the reborn Reich offers a telling illustration of the two main personalities. For Wilhelm was more interested in remaining King of Prussia; and he also objected to the idea of receiving the Imperial Crown from Parliament and People. It would be otherwise, however, if it were offered to him by King Ludwig of Bavaria, the senior German King. Bismarck sensed this and enticed Ludwig to make the offer in exchange for paying off Ludwig's private debts. The money came from the famous 'reptile fund' which consisted of the sequestered assets of the deposed king of Hanover administered by Bismarck's Jewish personal banker and financial adviser Gerson Bleichroder. Thus, as Edward Crankshaw tellingly remarks in his readable biography *Bismarck* (at p. 294), 'Hohenzollern robbed Guelph to pay Wittelsbach.' Bismarck's intriguing relationship with Bleichroder is superbly described in Fritz Stern's *Gold and Iron. Bismarck, Bleichroder and the building of the German Empire* (1977).

The watercolour portrait was painted by Konrad Siemenroth and shows the two men in the historical Corner Room of the Royal Palace. The original is in the Bismarck museum in Friedrichsruh, near Hamburg.

A NOTE ON THE JURISTS THAT FOLLOW

Selection is an invidious task; and it becomes almost impossible to perform when the list of distinguished German jurists is so extensive. From the outset, it was clear to me that focusing on the better known names of the 19th century would have been wrong on two counts. First and foremost this is a work on contemporary German law. Secondly, to concentrate on the past would imply that the present offers unworthy successors. This is patently wrong; and a variety of factors, including the cultural 'fall out' of the Second World War, can account for the fact that modern German law (and its lawyers) is less known in the university class rooms of today. Incidentally, from the moment the decision was taken to include pictures of distinguished German jurists, I was clear in my mind that I would not include jurists, however distinguished they might have been, who had played an active part in the National Socialist regime in the thirties and early forties.

A second question that had to be resolved was whether this 'pantheon' should be limited to academics. Given the strong academic content of German law, such a decision would have been perfectly possible and defensible. Yet one of the theses of this work is that modern German law is highly dependent on its case law. So judges had to be included, though that did not answer the question how to select those who merited inclusion.

The difficulty is caused by the fact that no individual judgments are delivered in the German Courts (except the Constitutional Court); and it is difficult to trace an individual's contribution in a collective judgment. The possibility of finding in German law an individual stylist such as Cardozo's or Holmes', Blackburn, Atkin or Denning simply does not exist. After consulting my German friends, I decided that selecting from those who had served as Vice President's or Presidents of the Federal Supreme Court in the fifties and sixties was an objective a criterion as I could get. Their short biographies that I have prepared to accompany each photography shows that all were not only senior judges but also had impressive academic credentials. If my list is still not to everyone's liking, the possibility of a fourth edition of this book is the only hope of redemption that I can offer.

Friedrich Carl von SAVIGNY (1779–1861). He was a descendant of a family from Lorraine which moved to Germany in 1630 because of its protestant beliefs. He studied law in Marburg between 1795 and 1799 and then held Chairs in Marburg (1803), Landshut (1808), and Berlin (from 1810 where he co-founded the Prussian University and was its first rector from 1812–1813. He was the founder of the Historical School and the *Zeitschrift der Savigny-Stiftung für Rechtsgeschichte.* He taught the Crown Prince – subsequently King Frederick William IV of Prussia. When in 1814 Thibaut, a Professor at Heidelberg wrote his famous tract *Über die Nothwendigkeit eines allgemeinen bürgerlichen Rechts für Deutschland*, proposing a general Civil Code for Germany along the lines of the recently enacted French Code, Savigny replied with his polemical tract *Vom Beruf unserer Zeit für Gestezgebung und Rechtswissenschaft* arguing that the time was not ripe for such a project which should be preceded by a thorough study of the existing, indiginous legal material. Savigny's *magnum opus* was his *System des heutigen römischen Rechts* published in 8 volumes between 1840 and 1849 (the last chapter of which on conflict of laws was translated into English.)

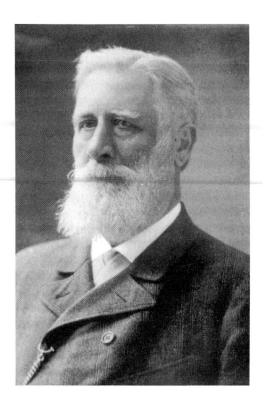

Otto von GIERKE (1841–1921). Son of a Prussian judge who served first as Associate Professor in Berlin (1866) and then as full Professor in Breslau (1872), Heidelberg (1884) and Berlin (from 1887). His principle work was his *Genossenschaftsrecht* in 4 volumes which appeared between 1869 and 1913. He provided a useful contribution to the preparation of the Code through his polemical piece *Der Entwurf eines Bürgerlichen Gesetzbuchs und das deutsche Recht* published in 1889. He was a severe critic of the 19th century bourgeois liberal ideas that came to be enshrined in the Code; and as the leading 'Germanist' of his age, he often criticised the predominant influence that Roman law had on the drafting of the new Code.

Hans Carl NIPPERDEY (left) (1895–1968). Started his legal career as an Associate Professor in Jena. His first major work which brought him to national attention was published in 1920 and was entitled *Kontrahierungszwang und diktierter Vertrag*. From 1925 onwards he was Professor at Cologne mainly writing on the General Part of the Civil Code (Ennecerus/Nipperdey *Allgemeiner Teil des Bürgerlichen Rechts*) and (with Alfred Hueck) on labour law (*Lehrbuch des Arbeitsrechts*). From 1954 to 1963 he held the post of President of the (supreme) Federal Labour Court and concentrated his efforts on developing the uncodified labour law on a case-by-case basis, paying particular attention to the constitutionally guaranteed basic rights.

Werner FLUME (right) (1908–). He was a pupil of the famous Romanist Fritz Schulz. In the beginning, his career under Schulz flourished with a scholarly work on the accessory nature of guarantee stipulations in Roman law. After 1933, however, the persecution of Schulz by the Nazis affected his career as well and he had to earn his living as a practising lawyer specialising in business and tax law. Academic recognition finally came in 1945 when he was elected to a Chair in the University of Bonn. Important works followed: in 1948 his *Eigenschaftsirrtum und Kauf* and later (between 1965 and 1977) his three-volume *Allgemeiner Teil des Bürgerlichen Rechts* along with numerous articles on company and tax law. Flume spoke on a number of occasions to the German Association of Lawyers giving his views on many matters of tort law, his severe criticism of the 'Gentleman Rider' case being one of them.

Ernst von CAEMMERER (1908–1985). Born and raised in Berlin. Studied law in Munich and Berlin and then became judge at the Berlin Landgericht. Later he became legal adviser to the Dresdner Bank. While in Berlin he met Ernst Rabel and was persuaded to join as an Assistant the famous Kaiser Wilhelm Institut für ausländisches und internationales Privatrecht. In the long run, Rabel's influence on von Caemmerer and his work proved decisive. But in the thirties his association with this great jurist (who had by then sought refuge in the United States) hindered his career which seemed to be grinding to a halt. During the war he served as a naval officer on a mine sweeper. The breakthrough came in 1946 when he completed his *Habilitation* in Frankfurt under Walter Halstein (who was later to become Germany's first Foreign Affairs Minister) and a year later was called to a full Chair in Freiburg where, despite many attempts to entice him away, he stayed for the rest of his life. Von Caemmerer defies the usual pattern of a German academic career depending for advancement on the writing of learned monographs or large treatises. But his influence on the German law of torts, unjust enrichment, and the law of international commerce was enormous and it came through numerous scholarly articles and notes which still attract much attention in Germany.

Robert FISCHER (left) (born in 1911) in Hessen studied law in Tübingen and Breslau. His doctoral thesis in 1935 was on a subject of company law which qualified him well for his subsequent work in the Legal Department of the *Deutsche Bank*. From 1945 to 1950 he served as the Director of the Landgericht of Göttingen and then was offered a seat in the Bundesgerichtshof becoming the youngest person ever to reach such a post at the age of thirty-nine. He subsequently turned down an offer of a Chair at Cologne University choosing, instead, to concentrate his efforts on his work as President of the Second Civil Senate. Between 1968 and 1977 he served as President of the entire Federal Court. His influence on the court's case law, especially in the areas of commercial and company law, was very great.

Bruno HEUSINGER (right) (1900–1975). Originated from Lower Saxony. Studied history at the University of Göttingen where he wrote a doctoral dissertation on the *Servitium Regis* (dealing with the economic relations of the German Monarchy between 900 and 1250 A.D.) He later switched to law and from 1929 he served as judge in the *Landgericht* and later in the Oberlandesgericht of Braunschweig of which he had become president by 1934. In that year, however, the Nazis demoted him to his first rank. It was not until 1948 that he was allowed to return to his earlier judicial post as president of the Court of Appeal, a post which was followed by that of President of the Oberlandesgericht of Celle. Two years later the supreme recognition of a distinguished judicial career finally came with his appointment as President of the Bundesgerichtshof a post which he held until his retirement in 1968.

Map 3. The German Confederation in 1815

Map 4. Development of the Prussian–German Customs Union

Map 5.   The Unification of Germany, 1867–71

Map 6.   Divided Germany after 1945

Map 7.   Re-united Germany

Pre-codification map of Germany reproduced by kind permission of the Niedersächsische Staats-und Universitätsbibliothek in Göttingen.

3

Stricter Forms of Liability

SECTION A. COMMENTARY

1. §§ 831 AND 278 BGB

Select Bibliography

Von Caemmerer, 'Wandlungen des Deliktsrechts, Hundert Jahre deutsches Rechtsleben', *Festschrift zum 100 jährigen Bestehen des Deutschen Juristentages* II (1960) 49, 115 ff., reproduced in his *Gesammelte Schriften* (1968) 452; idem, 'Reformprobleme der Haftung für Hilfspersonen' *ZfRV* (1973) 241; Deutsch, 'Die neuere Entwicklung der Rechtsprechung zum Haftungsrecht' *JZ* 1984, 308, 314 ff.; Diederichsen, 'Zum Entlastungsbeweis für Verrichtungsgehilfen' *ZRP* (1968) 60; Hassold, 'Die Lehre vom Organisationsverschulden' *JuS* 1982, 583; Helm, 'Rechtsfortbildung und Reform bei der Haftung für Verrichtungsgehilfen' *AcP* 166 (1966) 389; Hübner, 'Zur Reform von Deliktsrecht und Gefährdungshaftung' *NJW* 1982, 2041; Jakobs, 'Über die Notwendigkeit einer Reform der Geschäftsherrenhaftung' *VersR* 1969, 1061; Kiser, 'Die Haftung des Fuhrparkhalters nach § 831 BGB hinsichtlich Auswahl und Beauftragung des Fahrers' *VersR* 1984, 213; Kupisch, 'Die Haftung für Verrichtungsgehilfen (§ 831 BGB) *JuS* 1984, 250; E. Schmidt, 'Zur Dogmatik des § 278' *AcP* 170 (1970) 502, 520 ff.; Steindorff, 'Repräsentanten- und Gehilfenversagen und Qualitätsregelungen in der Industrie' *AcP* 170 (1970) 93; Weitnauer, 'Aktuelle Fragen des Haftungsrechts' *VersR* 1970, 585, 593 ff. For comparative discussions see Eörsi, in *International Encyclopedia of Comparative Law* XI, ch. 4; Kötz, 'Strict Liability in German Law', *In Memoriam Jean Limpeus* (1984) 75 ff.; Lawson and Markesinis, *Tortious Liability for Unintentional Harm in the Common Law and the Civil Law* (1982), I, 163 ff.; Zweigert and Kötz, *An Introduction to Comparative Law* (1977) II, 293 ff. (with further references to English and French literature).

(a) General observations

Up to now we have been envisaging liability for one's own acts or omissions. Its importance remains crucial in today's world; and in fairly primitive or simple societies, with agrarian economies and a fairly elementary system of labour, it was the *most* crucial form of tort liability. But economic growth, industrialization, the increase of commerce and of economic activity in general, necessitated the introduction of a more elaborate system of work which enabled one person or business entity to use the services of other persons in the furthering of their economic interests. Since these persons or entities—the masters—derived the benefit from the services of those working for them—the 'servants' or employees—it was only natural to think of making the former liable for the harmful conduct of the latter. Besides, the masters were often in a position to take steps to prevent the harm or—at a later stage—to carry insurance against the risk. Such a way of looking at things also offered considerable advantages to the victim, for he was thus offered a person worth suing in the place of the often impecunious servant who had actually caused him the harm. Arguments such as these led to the strengthening and extension of what Common lawyers call vicarious liability; subject to the points made below, they are to be found as much in German law as they are in the other systems.

But the urge to make the 'master' liable instead of or in addition to the servant could be approached in two ways. The one most consistent with the reasons we gave above was to make the master liable *strictly* for the faults of the servants. His own liability, therefore, was strict in the sense that it did not depend on any fault on his part; but fault there had to be on the part of the servant. This is, indeed, the position taken by most of the legal systems of the world. But the German Civil Code opted for a weaker rule of 'vicarious' liability: the master's liability would be based on his *own* fault of bad selection or supervision of the servant but it would be rebuttable in accordance with what will be said very shortly.

There are a number of reasons that account for this different approach. An historical explanation lies in the fact that the nineteenth-century Pandectists had convinced themselves that the doctrine of *culpa in eligendo*, which they were introducing into § 831 BGB, was the only one known to Roman law. That this was so in a number of individual factual situations is beyond doubt; but to develop from the casuistic Roman approach a generalized doctrine that the master could *only* be liable if he himself was at fault was incorrect. (For more details see Seiler, 'Die deliktische Gehilfenhaftung in historischer Sicht' *JZ* 1967, 530; Kaser, *Das römische Privatrecht* (1955) I, 527 ff., and, in English, Lawson and Markesinis, op. cit., I, 160–3.)

A more pragmatic objection to the introduction of the 'true' notion of vicarious liability was the fear that it would bring in its wake unwanted economic consequences, and in particular, increased economic burdens for small industry. And it was the aspirations and interests of this small industry, the rising middle class, that the Civil Code had at heart. Not for the first time, therefore, the Code was to give effect to these ideas, almost oblivious to the fact that in the wider industrial field the enactment of such statutes as the Imperial Liability Act of 1871 had imposed strict liability on railway companies and, in this context, completely overtaken the notion of fault. In the end, therefore, the Code chose, as we shall see in section A.3, below, to leave the regulation of special matters to specialized legislation and to sanction as a general principle the idea that the master would be liable for the unlawful conduct of his servants only if fault could be imputed to him, personally, (or, if the master was a legal entity, to his 'duly' appointed representatives: § 31 BGB) in the choice and supervision of the servants.

We shall discuss this subject under four headings (b)–(f): (b) master–servant relationship; (c) damage in the course of employment; (d) unlawfulness; and (e) the master's exculpatory proof. A concluding section (f) will deal with the many ways devised to overcome the unfortunate effects of § 831 BGB.

(b) Master–servant relationship

For the master to be liable, the damage must have been caused by a person to whom the master had 'entrusted the performance of a function' (*zu einer Verrichtung bestellt*). Who qualifies as a servant (*Verrichtungsgehilfe*) is a mixed question of law and fact for the court to determine. The most widely applied test, used to determine this relationship, is that of 'direction and control' which means that salaried and wage-earning employees will, invariably, be classed as servants. (A classic formulation can be found in RGZ 92, 345, 346.) The limitations of this test, in a society with sophisticated labour and economic relations, have become apparent in Germany as they have elsewhere. The need was thus felt to widen the test so as to render, for example, hospitals liable for the wrongs of their surgeons, anaesthesiologists, and technical staff over whom, obviously, the master (hospital) had no direct and detailed control. Thus, it has on several occasions been stressed that the right to direct and control need not cover details. In one case (No. 59) the court expressly said that the right to give instructions need not cover details. It is sufficient that the master has the right to limit the worker's activity or withdraw it or circumscribe it as to time or circumstances (BGHZ 45, 311).

Clearly, even this redefined test will not solve all difficulties, and borderline cases will always exist. So, for example, a problem area well known to Common lawyers can be found in cases dealing with 'borrowed servants' (usually 'let out' by their masters with complicated modern machinery). If they cause damage while operating this machinery, who will be held responsible—the permanent or temporary master? Much will depend on the facts of each case but as in England (see *Mersey Docks and Harbour Board* v. *Coggins and Griffith (Liverpool) Ltd.* [1947] AC 1), so in Germany (BGH VersR 1956, 322) there is a certain tendency to retain the responsibility of the permanent master since he usually retains the greater degree of overall control. However, the solution adopted sometimes in the USA, to hold *both* employers liable to the employee and then let them sort the situation out among themselves (as in *Strait* v. *Hale Constr. Co.* 26 Cal. App. 3rd 941, 103 Cal. Rptr. 487 (1972)), does not appear to have been followed. It will be noticed, however, that there is an increasing tendency to think in terms of the possibility of command and not, necessarily, actual command—a development which tends to extend the area of vicarious liability.

This trend is further reinforced by the fact that *actual* and not *legal* subordination will suffice to render the master liable (see Enneccerus, Kipp, and Wolff (Lehmann) 980; cf. *Restatement of Agency, Second* (1959) § 220, which talks in terms of 'control or *right* to control'). Moreover, the subordination need not be constant: a student working on a part-time basis may render his employer liable and this even if the services he is rendering to him are gratuitous.

Determining whether a person is a servant or, alternatively, what Common lawyers would call an independent contractor, is essential, since in *principle* there will be no liability for the wrongs committed by the latter category. To achieve this, German lawyers are increasingly following the Common law example and looking at the entire economic relationship, not merely enlarging or adapting the control and direction test. Thus, von Caemmerer has candidly suggested ('Reformprobleme der Haftung für Hilfspersonen' in *Zeitschrift für Rechtsvergleichung* 1973, 241, 254) that this enquiry should be directed towards such matters as which person is in a better position to carry the risk or is economically more suitable to take out insurance. Once again, though individual solutions may occasionally receive a different answer, the German approach is, on the whole, quite similar to that taken by Common law lawyers, so no further details need be given.

This similarity is also to be found in the exceptions to the rule that one is not, in principle, liable for the torts of independent contractors (cf. §§ 410–29 *Restatement of Tort, Second*). However, here, too, German lawyers have felt the need experienced by their Common law colleagues to develop rules of responsibility analogous to our non-delegable duties. Thus, the master will be liable if he himself has negligently selected the independent contractor and, on occasion, also if he failed to control him in the exercise of his task. The extent and nature of this duty will vary from case to case, but in cases of large building works—especially when neighbouring buildings or their foundations are endangered—such additional obligations will readily be imposed on the employer of the independent contractor. The decision of the Bundesgerichtshof of 7 October 1975 (*JZ* 1975, 733) provides another illustration, akin to the English notion of extra-hazardous activities. In that case, a chemical factory engaged a firm of specialist contractors to dispose of some very toxic waste for their benefit. The waste was improperly removed and the chemical factory was held responsible for this bad execution of the work. It will be noticed that, as in English law, these duties are *stricter* than the normal duties of care in so far as they impose a duty to see that care be taken; but that they do not actually impose truly *strict* liability. Some German writers, however, have advocated that a strict duty be imposed in such cases upon the employer (see Vollmer, *JZ* 1977, 371).

(c) *The damage must have been inflicted by the servant 'in the exercise of the function assigned to him'*

Behind this not very informative expression lies one of the most litigated aspects of the whole law of vicarious liability as Common lawyers who have grappled with the equivalent notion of 'course of employment' will readily understand. To solve it the courts have used—as we shall note below—a variety of terms or notions, but perhaps we could attempt to simplify the problem by saying that in practice there is one rule: either the servant is within the 'course of employment' (and so if the other conditions are satisfied will render his master liable), or he is not (in which case there is no liability for the master). Whether he is in the course of his employment or not is really a question of fact and, in a sense, the situation is not dissimilar from that found when discussing the elements of negligence or carelessness where, also, there is a simple rule: if a person has behaved carelessly, he is liable (subject to certain other conditions being fulfilled); if he was not careless, he is not liable. The question whether his behaviour was careless or not is one of fact. Just as there are guide-lines (not rules) to help in determining carelessness, so there are guide-lines, and no more, which help in determining 'course of employment' (or the equivalent German expression). The decision is, therefore, often impressionistic and the only permissible generalization is that the area of activity falling within the 'scope of employment' seems to be widening, partly as a result of the increase in motor traffic (and the compulsory insurance schemes that go with it) and partly because the scope of acceptable risk has widened as legal entities have taken over from human beings the position of 'master'.

However, one must immediately qualify the last sentence by pointing out that German law has consistently taken a stricter view on this matter than other systems have done (e.g. the French) and has excluded acts done by the servants merely because their employment provided them with the occasion or opportunity for performing these acts (Enneccerus, Kipp, and Wolff (Lehmann) 979; Larenz I, 20, viii, p. 401; II, 649 n. 2; see, also, case 74, below). Thus, if the wrong is something incidental to the work assigned (*bei Gelegenheit der Verrichtung*) to the worker, his master will not be 'vicariously' liable (under § 831 BGB) for it, unless it can be shown that he himself was at fault (§ 823 I BGB) in introducing this risk. A practical joke played by one employee on another will therefore not justify the employer's vicarious liability though it may attract his own personal liability if it can be shown that he was aware of the employee's mischievous or irresponsible propensities. (For English law see *Hudson* v. *Ridge Manufacturing Co. Ltd.* [1957] 2 QB 348 (personal liability); *Chapman* v. *Oakleigh Animal Products* (1970) I KIR 1063 (vicarious liability).)

On the other hand, the employer's liability may be engaged even if the act accomplished by his employee is not *exactly* the one he was entrusted to perform, so long as it falls within the range of measures which can be properly linked to the exercise of the entrusted functions (see BGHZ 49, 19, 23). Sometimes this idea is also expressed in causal language. This is so whenever the court speaks of an internal, direct connection between the function assigned to the servant and the activity that has caused the harm—(BGH NJW 1971, 31). In practice this means that if the servant's act amounts to a *bad* way of performing the entrusted function (rather than doing something completely different), the master will—all other conditions being satisfied—be liable for the wrongful result. So, using a vehicle of the employer's in a forbidden manner will not necessarily absolve the employer from all liability (see BGH VersR 1966, 1074; BGH NJW 1971, 31). On the other hand, if the servant gives a free ride to the injured plaintiff in the employer's car, despite the latter's express prohibition, then the employer *may* not be liable (BGH NJW 1965, 391). (Compare and contrast the following English cases: *Limpus* v. *London General Omnibus Co.* (1862) I H. & C. 526; 158 ER 993 and *Conway* v. *George Wimpey & Co. Ltd.* [1951] 2 KB 266. More recent pronouncements can be found in *Rose* v. *Plenty* [1976] I WLR 141.) The same is true of the so-called 'deviation' cases where the servant while on duty deviates from the prescribed route or even goes off on a trip of his own and then causes damage. The answer here will largely depend on the extent of the deviation (see RG LZ 1930, 589).

The case-law on this topic is, as one would expect, rich (see also RG DR 1942, 1280 and cf. OLG Munich MDR 1959, 391) and, it is submitted, not all decisions can be reconciled with one another. On the other hand, as already noted, this is something which should not cause too much consternation; and the Common lawyer will again realize that this is almost inevitable in this area of the law. (For a brief comparison with English law see Markesinis and Deakin, *Tort Law* 3rd edn. (1994), 485 *et seq.*; for a summary of American law see Prosser and Keeton *On Torts* (5th edn. 1984), 501–8.)

(d) 'Unlawful' damage

§ 831 BGB further requires that the damage caused by the servant be inflicted 'unlawfully'. The element of unlawfulness and the element of *culpa* (fault, which is *not* mentioned in § 831 BGB) were discussed in Chapter 2 under the heading of § 823 I BGB, but since they raise difficult problems in this context as well, they must be re-examined briefly.

It will be remembered that there exist two theories on the definition of 'unlawfulness': the traditional one, which looks at the *result*, and if this is an interference with one of the interests enumerated in § 823 I BGB, then the element of unlawfulness is satisfied; and the more modern theory which looks at the *conduct* and treats as unlawful only those interferences with the enumerated interests which also amount to a breach of one of the duties of care. It will be remembered also that we stressed that, according to the traditional theory, the element of *culpa*—fault—is only considered *after* the element of unlawfulness is satisfied in accordance with the above, whereas according to the new theory, unlawfulness and *culpa* tend to be merged into the same phase of the enquiry. Finally, it will be remembered that we said that save in some exceptional circumstances the two theories will almost certainly produce the same practical results.

§ 831 BGB is one of those exceptional circumstances where the two theories *could* produce different results. This is because, § 831 BGB, unlike § 823 I BGB, makes no mention of *culpa*—and, apparently, only requires an unlawful infliction of damage on the part of the servant. If unlawful is taken to mean a simple interference (even if committed without fault) with one of the enumerated interests, then the master will be presumed liable unless *he* can then adduce his exculpatory proof in accordance with what we shall say below under (*e*). To put it differently, a logical application of the traditional theory on unlawfulness would require the plaintiff/victim *merely* to prove that he had been injured, even by a non-faulty act of the servant, and then the presumption of fault (of the master) under § 831 BGB would come into play and it would be for *him* to adduce the exculpatory proof envisaged by this provision.

The new theory on unlawfulness would look at things in a different way. An interference with one of the protected interests of the plaintiff is not, *per se*, unlawful; it will be so if, in addition, the servant does not attain the standard of care required in the circumstances. To put it differently, if the servant's activity was in breach of one of the duties of care and also interfered with an enumerated interest, then and only then would it be unlawful. Both these things are matters for the plaintiff/victim to prove and only if they are established will § 831 BGB be invoked and the defendant/master will have to produce the required exculpatory proof.

The different distribution of the burden of proof, resulting from the application of one or other of the theories of unlawfulness, can have important practical consequences. A servant/driver, for example, who *through no fault of his own*, injures the plaintiff because black ice forces his car into a skid, will have acted unlawfully if the traditional theory is applicable, but lawfully if the new theory is used to determine the nature of his conduct. Let us take another example from a case decided by the Bundesgerichtshof in 1954. The plaintiff was injured by a telephone post which collapsed due to a heavy storm. The interference with the plaintiff's life and limb was clear, and according to the traditional view, the element of unlawfulness was satisfied; § 831 BGB should have been applicable, and the defendant/Post Office (owner of the post that had collapsed) should have been called upon to adduce the exculpatory proof envisaged by § 831 BGB. The Bundes-gerichtshof, however, felt that this stage had not been reached since the plaintiff had not shown that the accident was also due to a fault on the part of the team of employees responsible for the maintenance of the posts (BGH NJW 1954, 913). Unfortunately, the problem of who has to prove exactly what is not only linked with the view one takes on the notion of unlawfulness. In fact our last illustration reveals the kind of uncertainties and difficulties that persist in this field.

In a decision handed down in 1957, the Great Senate of the Federal Supreme Court (see Fig. 1 at p. 2) had to deal with the following problem (see the judgment reproduced below, case 87). The plaintiff was injured while getting into a tram due to the fact that the tram departed before the plaintiff had completed his entry. It could not be established whether the plaintiff's injury was caused because he tried to jump onto the tram after it had started moving, or whether the accident was the result of the conductor giving the departure signal prematurely. If the old theory of unlawfulness was applied, then the servants of the defendant (tram) company had acted unlawfully and the burden of producing the exculpatory proof of § 831 BGB would have shifted to the defendant company. If, on the other hand, the new theory applied, then the defendant would not have to be called to pro-duce such evidence, since the plaintiff had not proved (nor, given the uncer-tainty we mentioned, could he prove) that the conductor had culpably and prematurely given the departure signal.

The Great Senate clearly opted for the new theory on unlawfulness and, as we have already noted, this has commended itself to most modern lawyers (but not all lower courts). But when it came to applying it to the burden of proof it did not take the attitude that has been described above but chose, instead, a different manner of distributing the burden of proof. The injured party was thus merely obliged to prove an interference with one of his protected rights. It was then for the *master to prove* that the conduct of his servant was correct in the circumstances and thus *not* unlawful. If he did not do this (and, in the present case, given the uncertainty as to what had happened, he could not), then he would have to rebut the presumption of his own fault in accordance with § 831 BGB.

The convoluted reasoning as well as the result has not been welcomed (except for the part of the judgment that sanctioned the new theory of unlawfulness). The reason is clear. As Professor Kötz has remarked

(*Deliktsrecht*, no. 281), 'this decision has the absurd consequence that where the facts of the accident are not clear, the injured party will be in a more favourable position if his injuries have been caused by the servant, and not the master himself'. For if a pedestrian is run down by a van belonging to a pharmacist and it is not clear whether the accident could be attributed to the driver, the condition of the van, or the pedestrian himself, then the pedestrian's claim will be rejected if the pharmacist (master) was at the wheel himself (since the action would be based on § 823 I BGB) and the plaintiff would have to prove the defendant's fault. (Incidentally, for the reasons we shall give below, section A.5 (iii), the Road Traffic Act 1952 might also not be applicable in this case.) If, on the other hand, the van was driven by the pharmacist's servant, then the victim would (by invoking § 831 BGB) be able to see his claim succeed *unless* the pharmacist could produce the exculpatory proof.

(e) The master's exculpatory proof

If all the above-mentioned conditions are satisfied, the defendant/master will be presumed at fault and will be made liable unless *he* shows that (i) he was careful in the selection, instruction, and training of his servants and that he properly supplied them with the right kind of equipment or, failing that, (ii) the damage or injury would have occurred even if he (the master) had fulfilled the above-mentioned duties.

Producing evidence that the servant was properly selected, instructed, and supervised has become an increasingly heavy burden for employers—especially in those cases where the accident is caused in the context of carriage of passengers by buses, trains, trams, and the like. Here, as the cases reproduced below (83 and 84) show, the degree of supervision required is very high, and includes such things as random checks and regular warning notices (e.g. BGH VersR 1966, 364; BGH VersR 1969, 518; KG NJW 1966, 2365; more recently BGH VersR 1984, 67 contains a good description of the master's duties to select and supervise his employees carefully). When such accidents occur, and the action proceeds on § 831 BGB, the attention of the court is thus switched away from the details surrounding the accident, which the victim could conceivably discover or reconstruct, and is, instead, focused on the kind of internal supervision system that the defendant/master had devised in order to avoid or minimize the chance of the accident. In these cases, however, the plaintiff/victim has little knowledge and often, rather than be faced with such uncertainties and the cost of prolonged litigation, he will settle for the lesser sums provided by the strict liability Acts such as the Road Traffic Act or the Strict Liability Act (discussed below, section A.4 (iii)).

Where large organizations are concerned, proof that *every* employee has been carefully selected or supervised is, of course, impossible and the practice developed in Germany of allowing the master to show that the selection of the 'leading employees', who stand in a hierarchically intermediate position (for example a foreman who had chosen and was supervising the 'guilty' servant) had been properly chosen and supervised. This system of 'decentralized exoneration' (*dezentralisierter Entlastungsbeweis*), which substitutes the intermediary employee for the 'real' master and makes the former liable instead of the latter, is undesirable both economically and in terms of labour–management relations and, not surprisingly, has not been followed by other systems, such as the Swiss who in this area of tort law have otherwise closely followed the German model (Oftinger, *Schweizerisches Haftpflichtrecht* II, I (2nd edn. 1960) 139, 159). But German lawyers as well have come to realize the unfortunate nature of this rule, and the Supreme Court itself discovered a way to neutralize it by finding fault in the real master for the way he has organized his business and thus made the accident possible. Falling back on § 823 I BGB has in this way provided a way around the provision of § 831 BGB. (See BGHZ 4, 1, 2 below, case 85. See also BGH VersR 1964, 297 and BGH NJW 1980, 2810, 2811.)

(f) Methods developed in order to avoid the effect of § 831 BGB

It will have been noticed that despite the fact that the German courts impose strict requirements for the exoneration of masters, the possibility of such proof being adduced is always there with the result that the victim can then only sue the usually penniless employee. This result is not only incompatible with the rationale of true vicarious liability; it is also economically unsound given the employer's greater ability to insure and to spread the cost with a minimum of social dislocation. The courts were therefore eager to discover ways to bypass § 831 BGB and three of them will be discussed here.

The *first* was particularly applicable to legal entities of a private (§ 31 BGB) or a public law (§ 89 BGB) character. (BGH NJW 1985, 1838.) The legal entity's liability for the torts committed by its organs, i.e. members of its board, or other 'duly appointed representatives', is absolute without any possibility of exoneration so long as the tort was committed by the representative in the 'carrying out of his duties'. The potential sphere of application of this provision was, initially, rather limited, but in more recent times it has been expanded considerably, especially by giving a very wide meaning to the phrase 'duly appointed representative'. Consequently, the original requirement that this liability be applied only for the acts of organs who had a legal power to represent the legal entity in legal transactions was abandoned in favour of a wider definition (see RG, 25 Oct. 1943, DR 1944, 287; BGHZ 49, 19, 21 reprinted as case 74, below). Representatives who have the right to make independent decisions in their own sphere of work, subject only to general instructions, will thus be included in the definition even though they may not have the wider power of legal representation and their powers are not specifically defined in the articles of association. And the legal entity may also be liable for the torts of persons who have been authorized to act for it *ad hoc* in lieu of the person who should have acted in accordance with its articles (RGZ 157, 228, 235 ff.). Liability of the entity for its *own* defective organization, in accordance with what is said in the next paragraph, may also be invoked.

The *second* way round § 831 BGB is by discovering a 'defect in the structure of the enterprise' for which the master/entity is made liable. We are here talking of liability under § 823 I BGB and no longer of liability under § 831 BGB. Two cases reproduced below (77 and 78) show how effective is this method of bypassing § 831 BGB.

In the first case (BGH NJW 1956, 1106; case 77) the plaintiff was hurt while in the defendant's hospital as a result of risks inherent in the treatment he was receiving but of which he had not been adequately warned. The defendant/hospital was successful in adducing the exculpatory proof required by § 831 BGB but was found liable under § 823 I BGB for its own culpable failure to guide its doctors as to how they should discharge their duties to warn and explain matters to patients. Similarly, in the second case (BGH NJW 1971, 1313; case 78) the defendant's employees carelessly damaged an underground gas-pipe which caused an explosion which led to the destruction of the plaintiff's house. The track record of the employees was perfect and the defendant was able to adduce the exculpatory proof imposed upon him by § 831 BGB. The Supreme Court, however, was not interested in this line of reasoning and chose to hold the defendant liable for his own fault.

It should be noted that though the grounds of liability are distinct, there is no reason why in practice the result could not be based on both. A decision of the Supreme Court in 1955 (BGHZ 17, 214) illustrates this. In that case, the Federal Railways used wagons to transport animal foodstuffs. The wagons had not been properly cleaned and the foodstuffs were contaminated, thereby causing serious damage to the plaintiff's cows. Both the Court of Appeal and the Supreme Court had no difficulty in holding the defendant railway company liable on both grounds, i.e. liable for not properly inspecting their employees (§ 831 BGB) *and* for their own failure to adopt a safe system of work (i.e. liability under § 823 I BGB).

2. FROM TORT TO CONTRACT: § 278 BGB

The third way of evading § 831 BGB is for comparative law purposes the most intriguing. In one sentence, it meant invoking the adaptable law of contract in order to remedy the deficiencies of the law of tort. This, of course, is not the first time a civil law system has had to turn to its law of contract in order to remedy the shortcomings of its law of tort. For example, we have already noted how the non-recognition of purely economic loss as a compensatable type of harm under § 823 I BGB forced German (and French) lawyers to 'discover' contracts in the negligent misstatement cases which, in the Common law system, are resolved through the law of tort. The converse was true of the Common law systems: the doctrine of consideration—especially where it was taken rather seriously (e.g. in *English* Common law)—meant that contracts could not be discovered where the plaintiff had not 'paid' for the information he received. The law of product liability is another example, for in this area as well, civil law has shown a tendency to extend the law of contract to do the work of the law of tort. We have noted (above, ch. 2, section A.4 (*c*)) how German law has moved away from this position; but in French law the ultimate purchaser's rights in product liability cases are still in most instances viewed as an extension of the rights conferred by the law of sale to the immediate purchaser (Arts. 1641 ff. French CC) though in recent years tort law has reasserted its position in the field. The problems posed by § 831 BGB provided the third, though by no means least, important impetus to side-step tort law and have recourse to contract; § 278 provided the much-needed escape provision.

§ 278 BGB states that a 'debtor'—which in the instances that concern us means the employer—'is responsible for the fault of his statutory agent and of persons whom he employs in fulfilling his obligation, to the same extent as for his own fault'. It thus imposes upon the debtor 'strict' liability for *faults of the persons he uses in the course of fulfilling his contractual obligations*. The possibility of exoneration, which can be found in § 831 BGB, is absent in this case. Moreover, the terms used in § 278 BGB suggest that the debtor's liability may cover the faults of persons whom he uses in the performance of these obligations, but who may not, strictly speaking, be 'servants' (in the sense of § 831 BGB). Both these points, and especially the first, make the plaintiff's position more advantageous than it might otherwise be if his action were based on § 831 BGB. There are other advantages for the plaintiff who can shift in this way the basis of his claim from tort to contract. It will suffice to mention three. First, pure economic loss is more easily recoverable in a contract action. Secondly, the *contractual* period of limitation will usually—though not always (see BGHZ 61, 227 and § 558 BGB)—be longer (cf. § 195 BGB and § 852 BGB; thirty years instead of three). Finally, the burden of proof may be more favourable for the plaintiff if the action is based on § 278 BGB (see § 282 BGB and BGHZ 66, 51; BGH NJW 1976, 712, case 90). But these advantages for the plaintiff are also bought at a price: § 278 BGB will *only* apply in the fulfilment of a *contractual* obligation; and the range of remedies it may offer the victim/plaintiff may be more restricted than it would be if the action were based on tort. These two points require further elaboration.

Since § 278 BGB requires a contract (or, more precisely, a *Schuld-verhältnis* = a relationship creating obligations), in order to come into force, the courts set about discovering such contracts where none would be immediately obvious to a Common lawyer. This meant extending the contract to the precontractual phase and also extending its scope to include persons other than the immediate contracting parties. Eleven cases dealing with these types of situations are reproduced below (section B.2) so here we shall limit our remarks to a few general points.

The famous linoleum case (RGZ 78, 239, case 89) marks historically the first attempt to extend contractual remedies to the precontractual phase of negotiations through the concept of *culpa in contrahendo*. This doctrine, initiated by the famous German jurist Rudolf Jhering (*Culpa in contrahendo, oder Schadenersatz bei nichtigen oder nicht zur Perfektion gelangten Vertraegen*, in *Jahrbuecher für die Dogmatik des heutigen römischen und deutschen Privatrechts* (1861)), was extended from certain contractual situations to cases, such as the one before the Reichsgericht in 1911, which were essentially delictual in nature. In that case, the prospective purchaser entered the store, asked to inspect some carpets and, while doing so, was injured by two rolls which fell from the shelf. The court took the view that the demand to see the carpets and the fulfilment of this demand resulted in a relationship preliminary to the sale and similar to a contract and imposed duties of care with respect to the person and property of the parties. The wording of this judgment makes frequent references to the 'prospective purchaser' and, therefore, makes it clear that this extension of the 'contract' to the precontractual phase will not be attempted in all instances. The demarcation line is left for future courts to draw. (See also BGH NJW 1976, 712.) Probably, the same *contractual* protection will be extended to cover not only the prospective purchaser who, for example, is queuing to pay for the goods he has already selected, but also the 'potential purchaser' who enters the shop 'to look around' but with as yet no fixed intention to purchase anything in particular. The shop-lifter, on the other hand, who slips on spilt yoghurt, will not be protected in this way (BGH NJW 1976, 712 *obiter*). In between these 'extremes', one can envisage other possibilities, for example the citizen who seeks refuge in the store during a heavy storm. The solution and the casuistic approach of the German courts should neither surprise nor disturb the Common lawyer. Given the greater willingness to discover 'duties of care' these days, the answer to our hypothetical problem should be sought in the law of delict and not the law of contract. And the disadvantage that this might create for the plaintiff—the return to § 831 BGB—

und Adäquanz in der neueren Rechtsprechung des BGH' *VersR* 1984, 1133; Ullmann, 'Gefährdungshaftung in der Schiffahrt?' *VersR* 1982, 1020. Will, *Quellen erhöhter Gefahr* (1980, with complete comparative references). *In English:* Zweigert/Kötz, *An Introduction to Comparative Law* (Eng. trans. by T. Weir), II, 1977, para. 19; Lawson and Markesinis, *Tortious Liability for Unintentional Harm in the Common Law and the Civil Law* (1982) I, 142 ff. Finally, for the historical background see Bienenfeld, *Die Haftung ohne Verschulden* (1933); Ogorek, *Untersuchungen zur Entwicklung der Gefährdungshaftung im 19. Jahrhundert* (1975); Rümelin, 'Culpahaftung und Causalhaftung' *AcP* 188 (1988) 285.

(a) General observations: the statutory method

Tort liability was in German law traditionally based on fault. This was certainly true of the *lex Aquilia*, in a sense the *fons et origo* of Roman law which, in its turn, became the basis of the *Gemeines Recht* that prevailed in a large part of Germany during the pre-codification era. The Prussian Code, in force in other areas, had also based tort liability on fault; and so, of course, had the French Code which, as we have noted, had also been adopted by yet another group of German States. Apart from history, logic also dictated—and dictates—that 'bad' people must pay for the harm they cause and, usually, the greater the degree of their blameworthiness the greater the amount that they have to pay. But during the nineteenth century—especially in the latter half—the reverse of this proposition was also advocated by many lawyers: if there was a fault there should be no liability and the loss should be left to lie where it fell. The mixture of moralistic, economic, and other arguments that led to the adoption of this attitude are reviewed by Professor Tunc in his excellent introductory chapter to the tort volume of the *Encyclopedia of International and Comparative Law*. But, as Tunc has shown—and his observations though couched in broad comparative terms, also apply to German law—these arguments are hardly convincing.

It could, of course, be argued that it would be asking too much of the nineteenth-century draftsmen of the German Civil Code to see the weaknesses of the proposition that there can be no liability where there is no fault. The nineteenth century was the century when the fault rule reigned supreme. Yet, interestingly enough, some courts did make limited attempts to introduce strict liability *automatically* by discovering fault in particular activities. (Much later, and in the context of liability towards guest passengers in cars, the French courts adopted the theory of *faute virtuelle* to achieve more or less the same result.) More importantly, during the latter part of the nineteenth century the German Parliament had enacted a number of specific but important statutes which introduced risk liability (*Gefährdungshaftung*). So, if there was one national legislator in Europe at that time that had realized the limitations of the fault principle, it was the German. The problem of the foundation of tortious liability could thus have received a more unified and innovating treatment than was, in the end, actually accomplished. But legal tradition prevailed. Apart from one minor exception in the Code (§ 833 BGB dealing with certain kinds of animals, namely 'luxury animals'; other animals used for the keeper's professional business (e.g. milk cow, guard dog, etc.) will only render their keeper liable if he is at fault, though according to § 833 sentence 2, BGB such fault is presumed), which was justified by reference to Roman and ancient German law, the Code refused to be moved from the principle that liability for fault was the only acceptable basis for any obligation to compensate the victim. The specific legislation alluded to above was treated as exceptional and denied the moral superiority attributed to provisions found in the Code itself. This approach had many consequences; notable among them are two: first it set the pattern of the future development of strict liability in German law and in this respect set it apart from other civil law systems, notably the French; second, it created a dual regime of liability, partly to be found in the Code and partly in specific statutes, with resulting difficult problems of demarcation. The difficulties of demarcation, and the gaps that have resulted from this dual system of treating accidents, will be noted later on as particular aspects of these enactments are considered more closely. Here suffice it to note that the Janus-like nature of the German legislator, displaying a 'social' outlook in his special legislation, while remaining strongly 'individualistic' in his general Code, did not pass uncriticized even at the time. An extract from Gierke's scathing comments brings out clearly the inconsistencies and dangerous consequences of this approach. He wrote:

[I]t is a fatal error—an error committed by the draft of the German Civil Code—to think the social work can be left to special legislation so that the general private law can be shaped, without regard to the task that has thus been shifted, in a purely individualistic manner. There thus exist two systems ruled by completely different spirits: a system of the general civil law that contains the 'pure' private law, and a mass of special laws in which a private law, tarnished by and blended with public law, governs. On the one side a living, popular, socially coloured law full of inner stimulus, on the other an abstract mould, romanistic, individualistic, ossified in dead dogmatics. The real and true private law can now develop in all its logical splendour oblivious of the heretical special laws . . . But the general law is the native soil out of which the special laws also grow. By contact with the general law our youth learn legal thinking. The judges take their nourishment from it. What a fatal abyss opens before us! What a schism between the spirit of the normal administration of justice and the administrative jurisdiction that is being extended further and further! What a . . . danger of stagnation and degeneration of jurisprudence . . . (*Die soziale Aufgabe des Privatrechts* (1889) 16–18; trans. by von Mehren and Gordley, *The Civil Law System* (2nd edn. 1977), 693.)

In the remainder of this subsection we shall concentrate on the peculiarly German method of introducing strict liability in the legal system. Then, in the next subsection (ii) we shall note some features shared by these enactments and, finally, in subsection (iii) we shall take a closer look at two of the most important statutes: the Strict Liability Act and the Road Traffic Act.

The passing of strict liability statutes is not a phenomenon unique to Germany. One can find specific statutory interventions in the Common law system (for example the English Animals Act 1971), and in other civil law systems (for a list of French statutes see Viney, *Les obligations: la responsabilité* (1982) 25 ff.). What is, however, typically German is the development of a legal tradition, going back to the first Prussian Railway Act of 1838, that the introduction of strict liability into the legal order is a prerogative of the legislature. This mentality, along with the carefully, and on the whole restrictively, drafted articles of the Civil Code, made it impossible for the German judges to develop the kind of general, all-embracing rules which their French counterparts were able to create thanks to the wide if not amorphous delict provisions of their Code. As a result, though there are a number of situations where *fault* can be presumed, there is no general presumption of *liability* for damage caused by things (whether dangerous or not) under one's control analogous to that established by the famous first line of Art. 1384 French CC, or any general rule dealing with 'extra-hazardous' activities. Nor has German law adopted the bold attitude taken by the French Supreme Court in the *Desmares* decision (and subsequently incorporated in the 1985 French Road Traffic Act) to ignore the contributory negligence of the victim in certain instances of strict liability. Once again, clear statutory provisions to the contrary make this impossible.

The next thing to note is that the introduction of strict liability was the result of different though not necessarily mutually exclusive factors which influenced the mind of the legislator. (Indeed, looking at the strict liability acts one can trace the evolution of industrial and technological developments in modern Germany.) So, for example, it has for some time now been recognized that the social security legislation of the early 1880s, namely the Sickness Insurance Act of 1883 (*Krankenversicherungsgesetz*) and the Accident Insurance Act of 1884 (*Unfallversicherungsgesetz*), was largely prompted by Bismarck's political calculation that the satisfaction of certain legitimate needs of the working classes concerning conditions of work and accident insurance would go a long way in 'taking the wind out of the sails' of the socialist movement which was at that time, in Germany and elsewhere, slowly gaining wider political support. (For further details see Lawson and Markesinis, op. cit. I, 158.)

In other instances it was the novelty of the danger coupled perhaps with the risk of serious injury resulting from the operation in question. This was

so, for example, in the case of the Prussian Railway Act of 1838 (later incorporated in the Imperial Act on Liability of 1871) and the Road Traffic Act
(*Strassenverkehrsgesetz*), both of which dealt with potentially dangerous
(and, at the time of their enactment, also novel) activities. In all instances,
however, the utility of rail and, later, motor vehicle transportation was perceived. Clearly, increased benefit was accompanied by increased dangers.
The solution was obviously to permit these activities and, indeed, to encourage them in various ways, but only on condition that they were saddled with
the cost of the risks they entailed.

In yet another group of cases the enormity of the possible damage resulting from the activity in question was such that the activity could only be
allowed to continue 'at a very high price'. The 'Act Relating to the Peaceful
Use of Nuclear Energy and the Protection Against its Dangers' (*Gesetz über
die friedliche Verwendung der Kernenergie und den Schutz gegen ihre
Gefahren*) 1959—more briefly referred to as the Nuclear Energy Act—therefore imposes absolute liability on the operator of installations which are
concerned with nuclear fusion or fission. This is also the case according to
§ 33 ff. of the Air Traffic Act (*Luftverkehrsgesetz*) of 1936. In both these
instances, liability is truly 'absolute' in the sense that even the defence of
force majeure is denied to the 'operator' (of the nuclear installation) and
custodian (of the aircraft). Finally, the enormity of the potential harm that
can be caused by water pollution must explain the (financially) unlimited
liability imposed by the Water Supply Act of 1957 (*Wasserhaushaltsgesetz*)
on anyone who 'introduces' substances into water (which includes lakes,
rivers, streams, ponds etc.), thereby altering the quality of the water so as to
render it harmful.

The Imperial Act on Liability of 1871 (*Reichshaftpflichtgesetz*), which
originally imposed strict liability for death or personal injury suffered by
persons 'in the course of operation of a railway' (§ 1), and its subsequent
extensions in 1940 to cover property damage and in 1943 to cover death or
personal injury caused, under certain specific circumstances, by gas, electricity, or steam, were enacted with a variety of policy aims in mind. (The present version—the *Haftpflichtgesetz* of 1978—includes harm caused by gases,
fumes, and piped fluids.) Notable among them was the desire to facilitate
the evidentiary burden of proof cast on the unfortunate victims of what the
French, at that time, called the 'anonymous accidents' caused by modern
industrial machinery. (See Josserand, *Cours de droit civil positif français*
(2nd edn., 1933) ii, no. 415.) To some extent the same is also true of the
most recent of these strict liability statutes—the Act on Pharmaceutical
Products of 1976 (*Arzneimittelgesetz*). But arguably from the beginning,
and certainly, with the passage of time, it became obvious that the imposition of strict liability in the above instances also aimed at placing the risks of

these activities on the shoulders that could best carry them. For all these industrial concerns were in a far better position to spread the cost of accidents either by reflecting it in the form of minute increases in the cost of their products or, later, by their greater ability to insure. The same motive can also be found in modern product liability law though the 1989 Product Liability Act has as its immediate cause the EEC's desire to try to achieve greater harmonization of the law of the Member States. Be that as it may, the fact is that in our modern mechanized society a variety of policy aims accounted for the steady increase of legislative enactments, each dealing with a fairly narrowly defined activity or risks emanating from ownership of potentially dangerous things or substances. Some of the problems raised by this patchy growth of the law will be noted in the next subsections.

(b) Some general characteristics shared by all or most of these enactments

(i) Similar or analogous clauses

Though one of the ideas behind specific legislation is to allow the legislator to word his provisions in a way most appropriate to the particular risk or industry being regulated, this has not prevented the appearance in most of these enactments of almost identical provisions. One such provision— imposing maxima for monetary compensation—can be found in all but one of the statutes, and because of its importance it will be discussed separately, below. Another common provision (for example § 12 of the Strict Liability Act 1978; § 16 of the Road Traffic Act 1952) preserves the validity of the 'Common law'—which, in effect, means the Civil Code—so that a victim can recover further sums by relying on the fault-based articles of the Code. This, as we shall note, is often necessary not only because of the monetary maxima imposed by these statutes which will be discussed below; but also because of the fact that compensation under them does not include sums for pain and suffering which are thus claimable only if the fault-based provisions of the Code can be successfully invoked. (The only exception to this last rule can be found in § 53 III of the Air Traffic Act.) It is, perhaps, worth observing at this stage that other Germanically orientated systems which have, on the whole, adopted the German way of introducing strict liability by means of specific statutes, have not followed the German example of imposing monetary maxima or excluding from the statutory provisions compensation for pain and suffering. As a result of this arguably more logical approach to the problem, these systems have been able to provide for the exclusion of the ordinary rules of civil responsibility. The Swiss Road Traffic Act—in force in its latest form since 1 August 1975—provides such an example. (For a good summary of Swiss law see Deschenaux and Tercier, *La responsabilité civile* (1975) 138 ff.)

A third type of common clause reduces the liability of the tortfeasor by taking into account the contributory negligence of the victim. (See, for example, § 2*a* of the 1871 Imperial Act on Liability—now § 4 of the 1978 Strict Liability Act; § 27 of the 1959 Nuclear Energy Act.) The reduction of the damages awarded to the victim will be decided in accordance with § 254 BGB after weighing the victim's own fault against the typical risks connected with the activity in question (the so-called 'business risk') and the causative connection with the victim's hurt (BGHZ 2, 355). In extreme cases this could mean either that the victim could lose his entire claim for compensation (see, for example, BGH VersR 1963, 874) or the reverse, i.e. receive full compensation despite some negligence on his part (see, for example, BGH VersR 1969, 736). In the context of traffic accidents, the recognition of this defence has meant a net increase in contested cases since there is hardly such an incident in which the keeper of the vehicle will not invoke this defence and start a usually lengthy dispute into the exact facts of the accident. Many of the advantages of a strict liability statute can thus soon be lost in a controversy over facts which have little or reduced significance given today's insurance background. *In this context*, it is therefore important to note with approval the solution advocated by the Court of Cassation in the *Desmares* decision which refuses to take into account the victim's own fault in the realization of his harm (see Cass. 2ème civ. 21 juillet 1982, *D.* 1982, 449; see, also, the Law of 6 July 1985, reprinted as Addendum 2 to B. 3).

(*ii*) *Monetary maxima imposed on compensation paid under these statutes*

Save in the case of the Water Act (and also in the case of § 833 BGB), all other strict liability statutes impose maximum amounts which can be paid in the form of compensation under these provisions. However, recourse to the fault-based provisions of the Civil Code for additional compensation for pecuniary losses, as well as for pain and suffering, is in all cases expressly permitted. (See §§ 12 of the 1978 Strict Liability Act; 16 of the 1952 Road Traffic Act; 37 of the Air Traffic Act; 31, 38 of the Nuclear Energy Act.) Here the only limitation on the tortfeasor's liability is, practically speaking, his capacity to pay or, if he is insured, the ceiling of his insurance coverage. Thus, if a person is killed or injured through the operation of electricity, gas, steam, or current escaping from a cable or a pipeline or a plant for the provision of such energy or material (§ 2 of the Strict Liability Act, 1978), then the concern in question will be liable to indemnify to the full his medical expenses (§ 6) and to compensate him for his lost earnings by paying him an annuity of not more than DM 30,000 per annum. (At the time of writing—October 1993—1 US$ = DM 1.6.) And the liability under the Act (§ 10) for property damage will not exceed DM 100,000. In the case of motor vehicle accidents, to which the 1952 Traffic Act applies, the sums are DM 30,000 in the form of an annuity or a maximum lump sum of DM 500,000. Where several persons are killed or injured in the same accident, the annual periodic payment cannot exceed DM 45,000 and the total lump sum the figure of DM 740,000. The total liability under the Act for damage to property is, again, DM 100,000 and this even where several objects are damaged in the same accident (§ 12 I; see also § 37 of the Air Traffic Act and § 30 of the Nuclear Energy Act). These figures represent true maxima so that if, for example, more than one person or car is injured or damaged in the same accident the total amount available will have to be shared between them all. Who, in the case of a traffic accident, is responsible to pay these sums will be discussed in greater detail in subsection 3, below. Here suffice it to state that since the enactment of the Obligatory Insurance Act in 1939, the 'holder' of any car is obliged to take out third-party insurance which, as a *minimum*, covers the above sums. Needless to say, the growing cost of road accidents, coupled with the very real possibility of the 'holder' of the car being made *additionally* liable under § 823 I BGB, has meant that insurance policies covering risks in excess of one million marks are becoming increasingly common. (In practice the extra coverage, typically of the order of 2 million DM, can be obtained at a very small extra premium.) Incidentally, these maxima can be (and have over the years been) readjusted by governmental decree in order to take into account inflation and other rising costs.

As stated, the regulation of compensation through statutory maxima makes it increasingly likely that in cases of serious accidents the Common law—the BGB—will be invoked. This, of course, means that the victim is thrown back into the fault system with all the theoretical and practical disadvantages that this entails (delays, costs, uncertainty of result, increasing the load of court work). Even so, the victim's position has, once again, been improved in recent years by the development of three devices: (i) the 'discovery of new duties of care' (discussed above, in Ch. 2, section A); (ii) the treating of many of the provisions of the Road Traffic Act as 'protective laws' allowing the victim to bring an action under § 823 II BGB (discussed in the next chapter); and, finally, (iii) by an increasing use of the doctrine of prima-facie proof—analogous to our doctrine of *res ipsa loquitur*—which can often result in the surreptitious introduction of strict liability in a system which, judging by its Civil Code, remains faithful to the idea of fault.

(iii) The courts' role in defining the precise ambit of the statutes

As one would expect, all these enactments contain terms or notions which, though simple and obvious at face value, have given rise to many difficulties of proper demarcation. In the face of these observations, the courts have not been inactive and the rich case-law that has emerged clearly presents great interest both to the academic and practising lawyer. Here, for reasons of space, we shall limit our observations to three points: (1) the use of normative theories of causation as a means of defining the proper ambit of the statute in question; (2) the occasional tendency to construe narrowly certain provisions; and, finally, (3) the tendency in other, more numerous instances, to define more widely a particular statutory term and thus, to enlarge the scope of the statute in question. In all these instances we find illustrations of how the courts have exercised the rather limited role ascribed to them by legal tradition in the area of strict liability.

1. Compensation under the strict liability rules will clearly be limited to the extent that the harm complained of represents the realization of precisely that danger which prompted the legislator to enact the strict liability rule. The search for the protective aim of the violated norm thus becomes as important in this area of the law as it is when discussing causation problems arising from the violation of fault-based rules (§ 823 I and II BGB; see above, Ch. 2, section A.5). The limits of the liability will, therefore, be determined by discovering whether the type of harm in suit and the manner of its infliction was of the kind which the statute wished to prevent. The search for an answer to such questions will, obviously, start by looking at the wording of the relevant statute—for example was the plaintiff injured 'in the course of the operation of a motor vehicle' (§ 7 I of the Road Traffic Act); or was he killed 'in the course of the operation of a railway' (§ 1 of the Strict Liability Act)—but the end-result will largely be determined by the judge's value-judgment of the situation which will often lead him to an interpretation of the enactment against the background of *contemporary* socio-economic demands. A decision of the German Supreme Court in 1959 brings this point out very clearly (BGHZ 29, 163). The court in that case had to decide whether a *stationary* vehicle could be brought under § 7 I of the Road Traffic Act. This, as will be explained below, imposes strict liability upon the keeper of a motor vehicle which 'in the course of *operation*' injures or kills another person. In the court's view since

the legislator has not provided any . . . explanation, it is for the judge to interpret this ambiguous rule [accident in the course of operation]. The judge is, therefore, not prohibited from interpreting § 7 StVG broadly if in so doing he conforms to the sense and purpose of the enactment to protect participants in traffic against the dangers of motor traffic. It is therefore entirely within the scope of permissible interpretation if this protection . . . is extended also to the dangers produced by stationary vehicles in present-day traffic conditions.

Clearly, continued the court, 'even if the legislator of 1909 saw the chief danger of motor vehicles, in their rapid movement due to engine power . . . that would not exclude the adaptation of the concept "in the operation of a motor vehicle" to the experiences and requirements of present-day traffic'.

In the end, therefore, the use of normative theories of causation can lead—as Anglo-American lawyers have also discovered—to a considerable flexibility which, in turn, can produce an extension (and not only a restriction) of liability, rendering the defendant liable for all the 'typical' consequences inherent in his business activity. (Cf. in this respect the views of Ehrenzweig in his *Negligence Without Fault* (1951) reprinted in 54 *Cal. L. Rev.* 1422 (1966); see also 'Vicarious Liability in the Conflict of Laws—Towards a Theory of Enterprise Liability under "Foreseeable and Insurable" Laws III', 69 *Yale L. J.* 978, 989 (1960).)

2. An example of narrowing liability can be found in the area of application of § 833 BGB in so far as it imposes strict liability. Here, it must be shown that the harm caused was the result of the specific dangers arising from the animal's nature. Damage caused by a bolting horse—even where the cause of its fright is an external noise—or from a biting dog, would clearly be the kind of typical harm that animals of this kind can cause. But the injury suffered by a rider who borrowed from a friend a horse, which he knew to be unruly when ridden by strangers, in order to demonstrate his greater riding skills, would not lead to strict liability of the owner of the horse (BGH NJW 1974, 234; NJW 1977, 2158). Nor, as Professor Kötz has suggested (*Deliktsrecht*, no. 360), would a cyclist, who collided in darkness with the corpse of a dead dog, be able to sue its owner under § 833 BGB (though he might, of course, be able to make him liable under § 823 I BGB) since the hurt of the plaintiff cannot in this case be traced back to a special risk inherent in the animal. (But see OLG Celle VersR 1980, 431.) The same reasoning produced the same (negative) conclusion in a case where the plaintiff's cellar was flooded as a result of his drains being blocked by cow-dung from the defendant's cows (LG Köln, 13 July 1960, MDR 1960, 924).

At this point a brief excursus can show how the same kind of legal reasoning can be found in precisely the same area of the law in the Common law system. Thus, s. 4 I of the Animals Act, enacted in England in 1971, imposes strict liability for 'damage' done by straying livestock 'to the land or to any property on it'. The definition of damage in this section is narrower than the general definition given in s. 11 which includes personal injury and disease. The narrower definition of s. 4 I is generally taken to prevail in this case since it is regarded as *lex specialis*. (For example, Winfield and Jolowicz, *On Tort* (12th edn. by W. V. H. Rogers) 469 and n. 52.) For our purposes, however, it could be seen as a statutory embodiment of the scope of the rule theory. In other words, it can be said that the legislator wished to impose strict liability *only* when the typical consequences resulting from cattle trespassing actually occurred (damage to land, crops etc.). When other harmful consequences flowed from such straying livestock (e.g. human beings were trampled down) then liability should be based on the possible fault of their owner and not on the statute.

A similar narrow interpretation of the rules of strict liability has been adopted in other instances outside the area of the Civil Code. The Water Supply Act imposes, as we have seen, strict liability on anyone who 'introduces' (*leitet ein, bringt ein*) substances into water, thereby prejudicially altering its physical, chemical, or biological characteristics. The deliberate discharge by factories of pollutants into nearby rivers, lakes, ponds, or estuaries is, of course, caught by this provision. But so is the discharge of substances which do not affect the quality of water and marine life therein, even if its effects are not known to the person (legal or physical) who is carrying on these activities. On the other hand, the courts insist that for harmful conduct to be brought under this statute it must be shown that there was 'a positive act objectively aimed at the water'. As stated, this would include the above activities of 'discharge' of substances, but would exclude, for example, a collision between two petrol tankers which led to one of them falling into a nearby river and thereby accidentally emptying its contents into the water. (See Larenz, *Schuldrecht*, § 77.VIII; idem in *VersR* 1963, 593, 602. (In the 12th edn., § 17. ix, p. 731, another illustration is given: bridge collapsing under the weight of a petrol tanker.) See also BGHZ 46, 17; 57, 170, 173; 62, 351, 355. For other examples see the discussion in 3(iii), below.)

3. More often than not, however, the courts use the avowed purpose of the rule imposing strict liability in order to give an extended meaning to a term or phrase to be found in one of the enactments. A number of illustrations will be given in 3(ii), below, when we talk about traffic accidents, so here we shall concentrate on one of the best-known examples which can be found in the definition of a 'railway' in § 1 of the old Imperial Act on Liability—now included in the 1978 Strict Liability Act.

Today, there is no doubt that 'railway' includes all types of transport moving on rails—whether wide or narrow gauge, or moving above or beneath the metal rails in question; indeed, the Strict Liability Act has made this clear by expressly including cable-cars and suspension railways. But the statute also requires that the accident happened 'in the course of the operation of a railway . . .' and the question thus arises whether this statute can be extended to cover other activities carrying with them risks not unrelated to the kind of dangers peculiar in some sense to the operation of a railway. This question as to whether the accident can be regarded as a 'business accident' (*Betriebsunfall*) and thus covered by the statute was, in a sense, linked with the question of proper definition of a railway and both were raised in one of the early cases that came before the Reichsgericht in 1879 (RGZ 1, 247). In that case the defendant, a building contractor, was engaged in the business of constructing a railway and was moving earth around in tippingwagons operated on a narrow-gauge rail when the accident occurred. The Court of Appeal refused to apply § 1 of the Imperial Act on Liability of 1871. Its decision was reversed by the Reichsgericht in a judgment most notable for its polemical style against all attempts (favoured by some judges and academics) to give a narrow interpretation to the recent Imperial enactment. The Supreme Court openly alluded to the policy factor briefly mentioned at the beginning of this paragraph, and concluded that any narrow interpretation of the wording of the statute, of the kind adopted by the Court of Appeal, would lead to the emasculation of the new statute and should, therefore, be rejected. As a result of this bold judgment and after many others that took a similarly broad view of the notion of 'business accident', German law has now come to include under the protective ambit of this paragraph not only typical accidents connected with railways, such as deaths or injuries resulting from sudden application of brakes (even where this is caused by the totally unexpected appearance of a child or animal on the tracks: RGZ 54, 404; BGH VersR 1955, 346), swaying or swinging of carriages, derailments, or accidents caused by faulty signalling; but also cases where passengers are injured on platforms when jostled by other passengers during rush-hour, so long as there exists a 'direct external local and temporal connection between the accident and a particular business procedure or business installation belonging to the railway' (BGHZ 1, 17, 19). This rather verbose statement can lead to some fine distinctions so that, for example, if the plaintiff's injury is caused by the kind of jostling that takes place in crowded stations or results from an uneven or slippery surface of the platform, the railway concern will be liable. But if the injury resulting from the fall was caused by, say, the presence of black ice, formed by freezing rain, then the liability of the railway would have to be based on fault (i.e. pleaded under § 823 I BGB). However, it is always possible in this case to try and argue that the water that froze, and caused the fall of the plaintiff, came from a railway engine or found its way onto the platform because of a defect in the station roof. If such an allegation is substantiated, then one could again be back under the heading of 'business accident' and thus be able to invoke strict liability. Given the desirability of avoiding such niceties and, one might add, given the prevalence of modern insurance, it is not surprising to note a very clear tendency to interpret the statute 'generously' and thereby afford maximum protection to victims. A result, one might add, that the French courts have also very largely managed to achieve through the medium of Art. 1384 French CC, or the discovery of implied contractual terms (*obligations de sécurité*) in the contract of carriage. (For a summary of the different French approach see Weill and Terré, *Les Obligations* (1980) 369, 400.)

(*iv*) *Is analogical extension of the statutory rules possible?*

We have already noted how the German courts carved out for themselves an important area of activity in this otherwise statute-dominated part of the law. Yet they stopped short of taking the most vital step, which would have placed them on an approximate par with the legislature, when they refused to arrogate to themselves the right to extend analogically specific statutes to new situations raising similar issues of public policy. The important judgment of 1912 (RGZ 78, 171) that marked the beginning of this judicial attitude towards this matter, is reproduced below as case 106. (For other instances see RGZ 147, 353; BGHZ 54, 332.) The litigation was provoked by an accident caused when one of Count von Zeppelin's experimental airships was forced by bad weather to land and then broke its moorings, injuring one of the many spectators who had spontaneously gathered to witness this novel sight. An attempt to extend analogically the recently enacted (3 May 1909) Road Traffic Act was rejected by the Supreme Court on the ground of the exceptional nature of this piece of legislation. Yet, the policy reasons behind the legislator's decision to enact the Traffic Act (novel form of transport, increased dangers etc.) were, arguably, equally to be found in airships; and, indeed, other German-inspired systems, such as the Austrian, have allowed their courts to extend analogically statutes imposing strict liability (see cases cited by Zweigert and Kötz, *An Introduction to Comparative Law*, 2nd edn., 351–3). In 1912, however, the German Supreme Court refused to accept this and has since repeatedly adhered to this position (see, for example, BGHZ 55, 229 and cases cited previously). The 'tame' language employed in that famous judgment thus stands in stark contrast to the 'bold' approach adopted some thirty years earlier when, for a moment, the court seemed to indicate its willingness to play a part in expanding the grounds of strict liability.

(*v*) *A critical epilogue**

Though necessarily brief, our sketch of the German way of introducing strict liability has already revealed some of the system's cardinal weaknesses. The notion that only the legislator can introduce strict liability has resulted in a delayed, patchy, and complicated system for handling accidents resulting from new technology and more generally, the risks of modern life. It has been *delayed* because, inevitably, there always was, and always will be, a time-lag between new technological developments and the

---

* Professor Kötz's stimulating proposals for reform of the existing law (see Select bibliography) and Dr Hübner's critical review of these and other suggestions to reform German tort law (see Select bibliography) will repay careful reading and will complete this summary account of the weaknesses of the present law.

time when the legislator intervenes in order to regulate them. The result is that until such intervention occurs, the courts have to step in and handle as best they can the problems posed by new technology. (Some illustrations can be found in RGZ 17, 103 (protection of property before the enlargement of § 1 of the Imperial Act on Liability, discussed in section (iii) and below); RG JW 1938, 1234; RGZ 147, 353 (liability of electricity companies before the 1943 extension of the Imperial Act on Liability); RG DJZ 11, 1316 (car accident before the enactment of the 1909 Road Traffic Act).)

It was *patchy*, since each statute only handled specific problems, on the basis of scientific and technological information available at the time of their enactment, while leaving often related activities or risks outside their purview. The inability to extend these enactments analogically only aggravated the difficulties. Thus Professors von Caemmerer, Kötz, and others have for some time now been pointing out the capriciousness of the existing law and advocating the adoption of a more generalized provision to deal with this subject. So, for example, why cannot the dangers inherent in operating an explosives factory be assimilated to those of the gas industry dealt with by § 2 of the Strict Liability Act? Could it not be said that the operation of a large river dam poses risks broadly analogous to those found in nuclear stations regulated by § 25 of the Nuclear Act? Should the spraying of a poisonous insecticide lead to strict liability only if it contaminates water, in accordance with § 22 of the Water Supply Act, but not when it destroys or dangerously contaminates useful crops? Or why should a contractor using a tipping-wagon for the construction of a *railway* be strictly liable for any damage he causes, but only be liable upon proof of fault if he is simply helping build a *factory* or a large block of *flats*? Other systems—including the Civil Code of the (former) German Democratic Republic (East Germany)— have provided for strict liability not only in the case of specifically mentioned activities, but also in all those instances where an activity carries with it an increased danger for others (see §§ 334–7 of the Code of the former East Germany).

Finally, the system is *complicated* because the imposition of maxima for monetary compensation and the exclusion under these statutes of all compensation for pain and suffering often means recourse to the ordinary, fault-based liability rules to be found in the Civil Code. If these 'limitations' imposed by the statutes were dictated by fears of unlimited liability and unbearable economic consequences, especially at a time when insurance was not as widely spread as it is today, then the time has surely come to reconsider the validity of this kind of argument. Certainly, the absence of any maxima in compensation paid under the Water Act has caused no problems; in motor vehicle insurance, coverage in excess of the maximum amount provided by the statute (i.e. DM 500,000) is widely obtained without a considerable increase in premium cost; and, finally, the Swiss experience, quite different in this respect from the German, has not justified the fears expressed in Germany concerning an extension of the rules of strict liability. A more unified treatment of its problems would, it is submitted, be a considerable improvement on the status quo. But, despite many rumblings, and even more proposals for reform, the present system seems unlikely to be greatly changed in the near future. Thus, in this as in so many other areas of civil liability (e.g. § 831 BGB; express recognition of the right of personality etc.) the codal framework has proved too resistant to much-needed change.

(c) Two specific statutes on strict liability

(i) The Strict Liability Act 1978

It was stated earlier in this section that the history of the German strict liability statutes follows closely the development and expansion of modern industry. The Strict Liability Act of 1978 brings this point out very clearly.

The origin of this Act can, in a sense, be traced back to the 1838 Prussian Railways Act—by any reckoning, a most pioneering enactment. For when it was enacted, the Kingdom of Prussia had less than 100 kilometres of rail tracks so there was really no pressing practical need for such a measure. But capitalism in those days also had its paternalistic aspects; and, in any event, the economic consequences resulting from the imposition of strict liability for harm to persons or property 'resulting from carriage on the railway' (§ 35) hardly affected the mainly landowning dominant class.

The importance of the railway system for the economy and, later, the defence of the realm, was quickly perceived by the German leaders. The investment in an efficient national railway system was considerable and with the unification of the Reich, the 1838 enactment was to serve as the model of the Imperial Insurance Act of 1871. This statute introduced strict liability for railway carriage throughout the entire Reich; but it was also narrower than its model—which remained in force in Prussia and certain other parts of Germany (and also served as the model of an Austrian enactment of 1869)—in so far as § 1 of the 1871 Act limited strict liability for death or personal injury only (and not property damage) resulting from the 'operating of the railway'. This discrepancy between the old, geographically limited but in this respect wider statute and the Imperial enactment posed difficult problems which a number of courts tried to resolve by extending strict liability to property damage caused by the operation of railways (cf. RGZ 17, 103). These attempts, however, achieved only limited success and, on the contrary, attracted some hostile academic criticism. It was not, therefore, until the enactment of the 1897 Commercial Code that some measure of uniformity was achieved in the area of liability for carriage of goods and this trend was firmly consolidated in 1940 when a special statute, amending the 1871 Imperial law, introduced strict liability for property damage, as well (*Gesetz über die Haftpflicht der Eisenbahnen und Strassenbahnen für Sachschäden*). This position is, of course, now also clearly reflected in § 1 of the 1978 consolidating enactment.

Apart from this 'retrograde' step, connected with the exclusion of property damage from the scope of the statute, the Imperial Insurance Act was a far-reaching enactment. § 2, for example, imposed what we would call true vicarious liability on the operators of mines, quarries, pits, and factories for the damage caused by the *faults* of their authorized agents or representatives. For the persons working in these industries and most exposed to their dangers, this was a great step forward, especially when coupled with another set of provisions of the Act—§§ 6 and 7—which greatly increased the discretion of the courts in evaluating the evidence and the amount of damages to be awarded. This 'free evaluation' principle, as it became known—a great innovatory step when compared with the rigid rules of procedure applicable at the time—was subsequently widely adopted by the Code of Civil Procedure of 1871 and thus §§ 6 and 7 of the Imperial Insurance Act became redundant and were abolished. But the more equitable treatment of industrial accidents did not stop there. The passing of the social security legislation of the early 1880s gave even greater protection to the working classes for accidents at work, and the consolidation of the entire law of social insurance by the 1911 *Reichsversicherungsordnung* removed accidents at work from the province of the law of tort. A bird's-eye view of this system will be given in the next subsection.

The expansion of the Imperial Insurance Act continued well into the twentieth century. Apart from the enlargement that took place in 1940 in order to include property damage, a further amendment in 1943 extended the ambit of the statute to cover injury to persons or damage to property resulting from the operation of electricity, gas, steam, or current escaping from cables, pipelines, or plants for the provision of such energy or materials (see § 2 of the 1978 statute). The 1978 *Haftpflichtgesetz* extended strict liability further so as to include gases, fumes, and piped fluids but in other respects it can be regarded as a consolidating act.

Finally, one should note that the Strict Liability Act contains the usual defences—contributory fault of the victim (§ 4) and *force majeure* (§ 3), which is interpreted in a very stringent manner. Thus, in one case (BGHZ 7, 338) the young plaintiff was electrocuted when his kite—secured by a metal wire and not, as is usual, by a string—came into contact with an overhead electricity cable. Though the facts of the case were, clearly, very atypical, the Supreme Court refused to treat this as a case of an unavoidable accident and held the electricity operators liable to the victim. (For the full text of the 1978 statute see section B.4.)

(ii) An excursus: accidents at work and social security legislation in modern German law

As already stated, since 1884 Germany has had a no-fault compulsory insurance scheme covering accidents at work. This has been amended and expanded in various ways by subsequent enactments and now forms part of a wider and more comprehensive system of social security that covers such things as permanent incapacity for work as well as sickness. Here we shall limit our comments to the treatment given to accidents at work, a phrase which should be taken to include not only injuries sustained while actually at work but also accidents occurring while travelling to and from work. (Hence, in practice, a considerable overlap here with the compensation system established by the Traffic Act discussed below.)

Compensation in the above cases is made through various schemes which are administered by trade co-operatives or institutes (*Berufsgenossenschaften*) which are separate legal entities, usually in close contact with one another, and under the general supervision and responsibility of the Minister of Labour and Social Security. The institutes function on a territorial basis and are organized to cover different commercial or other activities. There are in all some thirty-four industrial accident insurance institutes; nineteen agricultural institutes; thirteen municipal accident insurance organizations; eleven State funds; four Federal insurance institutes; and a number of other smaller autonomous funds—some ninety institutes in all (the first two of these, however, are the most important, covering between them some 90 per cent of work accident insurance). These institutes are self-governed by boards or councils, usually composed of equal numbers of employers and employees. Every employer is automatically a member of the institute appropriate to his firm's activities in the locality in which it carries on its business. Institutes may provide voluntary insurance for the self-employed in their areas and some actually make this compulsory.

The financing of the various institutes is a complicated affair. Generally speaking, revenue from taxes funds those institutes which insure public employees; and the funds of agricultural institutes are subsidized by the central (Federal) government. The thirty-four industrial accident insurance institutes, on the other hand, derive their funds entirely from contributions made by employers, though there is the possibility (realized once only) of mutual financial help. The contributions vary depending on the risk factor attendant on the branch of industry to which the member belongs as well as on the risk-rating of the firm in question. These figures are reviewed periodically and contributions tend to vary from 1 to 12 per cent of earnings.

The awards are made by the officials of the appropriate institutes and there is an intricate system of appeals to local State and Federal courts. A basic assumption of the system is that, save in cases of intentionally inflicted injury, the injured victim cannot claim any further compensation by relying on the ordinary tort rules of the BGB. To make up for this, the system of awards tends to be closely connected with the victim's pre-accident earnings and the sums recoverable can thus often be quite generous. Moreover, pensions and other periodic payments are index-linked. Awards are made to all those in paid employment (whether German nationals or not) and, since 1971, children and students have been covered by the schemes. What is awarded depends largely upon whether the case is one of personal injury or death.

Awards for personal injuries will cover medical costs, including the costs of nursing, convalescence, and rehabilitation. The vast majority of cases will be dealt with under the general sickness insurance schemes (which are financed by contributions from both employers and employees). But the accident insurance institutes will meet all costs after the eighteenth day and, in about 15–20 per cent of the cases, depending on the type and seriousness of the injury, they take over responsibility from the outset and handle the case through their own specialists and hospitals. The institutes will also pay varying sums for loss of wages depending on the degree of invalidity incurred and the period it lasts, but during the first six weeks of incapacity the employer remains responsible for paying the victim's wages. Total incapacity will usually produce approximately 65 per cent of the pre-accident wages for the first thirteen weeks of the incapacity and from then onwards a pension equal to two-thirds of the pre-accident wages within certain maximum limits. In the case of partial incapacity, the sums payable represent the proportion of the sum payable in the case of total incapacity that corresponds to the actual degree of incapacity and these sums are increased by small amounts if the injured person has dependants. In the case of fatal accidents, a sum equal to one month's earnings plus the funeral expenses becomes payable immediately. In addition to this sum, a widow would receive a pension which is usually 30 per cent of the deceased husband's pre-accident income; but this sum can be increased to 40 per cent where the widow is over the age of forty-five or her own earning capacity is reduced by at least 50 per cent, or if she has children to look after. Children can also receive a pension which is higher where both parents are dead and lower if one of the parents has died. The sums are, once again, calculated on the pre-accident earnings of the parent, are index-linked, and cease to be paid when the child becomes eighteen. A widower, too, can claim a pension, but only where he can show that his wife was mainly responsible for the maintenance of the family and that he is, through incapacity, unable to support himself.

Naturally, this applies if the wife died in an industrial accident as defined above.

(iii) The Road Traffic Act 1952

(a) *General observations.* The twentieth century presented tort law with challenges never before encountered during its long history. A set of legal rules, originally devised for human beings, were increasingly applied to legal entities; rules which are meant to regulate the consequences of blameworthy conduct were used to determine the allocation of risks; modern insurance and social security meant that more and more of those who met the cost of accidents were innocent absentees. One could go on and on with this list with the intention either to criticize the 'antiquated' tort system and recommend its reform or abolition or, alternatively, to marvel at its ability to survive such changes. This is not the place to do either; but it is, perhaps, appropriate to remind the reader that the topic that has revealed the greater weaknesses of tort law, has prompted some of its most imaginative writing, and has proved a veritable hot-bed for ideas for reform, is the law of traffic accidents.

The practical significance of the topic is undisputed. In West Germany, with whose systems we are here primarily concerned, the cost of car accidents, in both human and financial terms, is enormous. In the early 1980s, in a country with some 60 million inhabitants and 30 million licensed cars of all types, nearly 12,000 people were killed every year on the roads and just under 480,000 were injured. Given the complexity of the compensation system—which draws its funds both from social security and private insurance—it is difficult to give an accurate idea of the financial cost. What is clear, however, is that insurance payments for personal injury, death, and property damage were around 5.6 billion DM per annum during the late 1970s.

Clearly, the topic is one of those that could justify on its own an 'advanced course in tort law'. Here we shall only outline the German approach under three headings. In the first we shall sketch briefly the gradual expansion of the statute law in order to assure a more comprehensive protection of victims of car accidents. In the second, we shall describe the main liability provisions of the Road Traffic Act of 1952. In the third, we shall consider some of the shortcomings of the present law in the light of some brief comparative observations. Before tackling these points, however, some reference must be made to the very rich legal literature on this subject.

Further reading

On German law (written in *German*) see Bauer, *Die Kraftfahrtversicherung* (1976); Becker, *Kraftverkehrs-Haftpflichtgesetz* (18th edn., 1992); Drees/Kuckuk/Werny,

Strassenverkehrsrecht Kommentar (7th edn., 1992); Gelhaar/Thuleweit, *Das Haftpflichtrecht des Strassenverkehrs* (1969); Gessner/Kötz, 'Verkehrsunfälle vor Gericht. Eine rechtstatsächliche Untersuchung' *JZ* 1973, 82; Grossfeld, 'Haftpflichtversicherung im Wandel' *VW* 1974, 693; Hanau, 'Rückwirkungen der Haftpflichtversicherung auf die Haftung' *VersR* 1969, 291; Jagusch/Hentschel, *Strassenverkehrsrecht* (31st edn. 1991); Weyers, *Unfallschäden, Praxis und Ziele von Haftpflicht und Vorsorgesystemen* (1971); Wussow, *Das Unfallhaftpflichtrecht* (13th edn. 1985).

For a brief account in *English* see Pfennigstorf, 'Analysis of the German Auto Accident Compensation System' in *Comparative Studies in Automobile Accident Compensation*, 33 ff., published by the US Department of Transportation in 1970; idem, *German Insurance Laws* (trans. and annotated in English) and published by the American Bar Foundation in 1975 and 1977 (Supplement).

For proposals for reform of the German law see von Caemmerer, *Reform der Gefährdungshaftung* (1971); Güllemann, *Ausgleich von Verkehrsunfallschäden im Licht internationaler Reformprojekte* (1969); von Hippel, *Schadensausgleich bei Verkehrsunfällen, Haftungsersetzung durch Versicherungsschutz* (1968); idem, 'Schadensausgleich bei Verkehrsunfällen, Mögliche Wege einer Reform' *ZRP* 1973, 27; Kötz, 'Empfiehlt sich eine Vereinheitlichung und Zusammenfassung der gesetzlichen Vorschriften über die Gefährdungshaftung im BGB' *Gutachten und Vorschläge zur Überarbeitung des Schuldrechts* (1981) 1779; Krause, *Das Risiko des Strassenverkehrsunfalls, Zuordnung und Absicherung* (1974); Schmeer, 'Haftungsersetzung durch Versicherungsschutz?' *VersR* 1973, 390; 'Soziale Sicherung gegen Unfälle im Strassenverkehr?' *Verhandlungen der Tagung des Deutschen Sozialgerichtsverbandes in Berlin am 17./18. 10. 1974* (1975).

Finally, excellent comparative law insights can be obtained by reading Professor Tunc's 'Traffic Accident Compensation: Law and Proposals' in vol. XI, ch. 14 of the *International Encyclopedia of Comparative Law* (1971) and the most recent collection of essays on his latest proposals on the subject entitled *Pour une loi sur les accidents de la circulation* (1981).

(*b*) *Increasing protection through statutory interventions.* We have already noted that the introduction of strict liability in German law has been a closely guarded legislative prerogative. In this area of the law, legislative intervention on two fronts (the purely delictual and the insurance front) has been coupled with a close regulatory function on the part of the State. In different ways both have tried to improve the protection given to victims, the public in general, and in some cases, the insured keepers of the cars.

The process has been a gradual one. The first attempts to introduce strict liability were made nearly two years after the BGB came into force, when a conference of lawyers passed a resolution demanding the extension of the Imperial Insurance Act of 1871 to motor vehicles (even though at that time there were less than 2000 cars on the road) and, what is particularly interesting, proposing the creation of a mandatory co-operative risk-spreading association. (*Verhandlungen des Sechsundzwanzigsten Deutschen*

Juristentages I, 27–55; III, 163–207 (Berlin 1902, 1903).) The idea met with some success with the government which even went so far as to present Parliament in 1905 with a Bill. But by that time the motor car lobby was also gaining strength and the Motor Vehicle Act (*Gesetz über Verkehr mit Kraftfahrzeugen*) that was finally enacted on 3 May 1909, was a compromise in so far as (i) it introduced maxima for monetary compensation, which the 1871 Imperial Liability Act *in its original form* did not contain; (ii) it included no proposals for some kind of insurance scheme (as proposed by the 1902 conference), and (iii) it excluded from its application death or injuries suffered by the driver or non-paying passengers. The idea behind this last restriction was that the *rationale* of strict liability for car accidents was the danger posed to road-users by fast-moving objects. Strict or stricter forms of liability by means of specific statutes were first introduced by Denmark in 1903 (and were considerably extended by a 1918 amendment). Sweden followed suit in 1906 (and its statute was further amended in 1916), then came Greece in 1911, Norway in 1912, Finland in 1925, Switzerland in 1932, and the Netherlands in 1935. A readable account of the very different evolution of the English Common law during this same period can be found in an article written by J. R. Spencer in 42 *Cambridge Law Journal* 65 ff. (1983).

After various amendments and re-enactments, the 1909 Motor Vehicles Act became in 1952 the Road Traffic Act (*Strassenverkehrsgesetz*) and has since then survived basically unchanged. But the introduction of strict liability helps the victims of traffic accidents only so long as the tortfeasors can and will pay. In the absence of obligatory insurance this could not originally be guaranteed, even though many German drivers voluntarily obtained insurance coverage after the enactment of the 1909 Act. In the 1930s, however, a new trend started to manifest itself. In 1931 warehouse operators were, under certain circumstances, obliged to carry insurance; in 1936 the same was true for airplanes. Obligatory third-party liability insurance for cars was clearly not far away and, in fact, it became a reality on 7 November 1939, when the first Obligatory Insurance Act came into force imposing on the 'keeper' of a motor vehicle an obligation to carry insurance for himself and for the *authorized* driver of his vehicle. But there were still important gaps and, following the 1959 European Convention on Compulsory Insurance against Civil Liability in Respect of Motor Vehicles (*European Treaty Series* no. 29), the 1939 Act was revised and re-enacted under the short title *Pflichtversicherungsgesetz* of 5 April 1965. The main two loopholes that were closed by this enactment concerned (i) uninsured cars and (ii) hit-and-run accidents. In effect, the Act 'legalized' an unofficial agreement that the insurance industry had operated since 1955. A private non-profit corporation, controlled and managed by the insurers, was created and compensation was provided out of its funds to the victims of the above-mentioned type of accidents. But compensation from the fund was limited in two important ways. First, it was entirely secondary in nature and could be claimed only if no compensation could be obtained from any other source. Second, it was limited to the statutory maxima (now, as we have seen, DM 500,000) and was and is further limited to claims for actual pecuniary damages arising from death or injury. Property damage, therefore, and pain and suffering are not compensated under this scheme save in very exceptional circumstances of real hardship. The other insurance gap that remained to be filled was connected with the possibility of an insurance company going bankrupt and being unable to meet its obligations. Though not something that has happened frequently—indeed so far as one can discover there exists only a handful of such incidents—German insurers decided to intervene in this area as well. Thus, in 1968 they created a private law corporation known as the Aid for Traffic Victims Fund (*Verkehrs-opferhilfe e.V.*) which meets to the full all claims made against insolvent members, subject to a small deduction.

The increased legislative intervention described in the preceding paragraphs has created a regulatory background against which the modern insurance market operates under the supervision of a Federal Office situated in Berlin. The intricate nature of the rules so established stems partly from the need to regulate the interrelationship with the social security system of compensation, notably through the establishment of a complicated system of subrogations and, partly, through the desire to protect at one and the same time the interests of (i) the public at large, (ii) the injured person, and (iii) the insured himself.

The protection of the public at large is assured first of all by the creation of the obligatory system of liability insurance. (Only the Federal State, the States of the Federal Republic and certain public institutions are exempt from this requirement.) Second, this protection is ensured by imposing an obligation on insurers to provide the minimum mandatory coverage (application for insurance coverage cannot be refused except in certain narrowly defined cases given in § 6 of the 1965 Obligatory Insurance Act). Third, the protection is ensured by the establishment of an elaborate administrative system by which no car is put on the road without a valid licence and, for this to be obtained, a valid certificate of insurance must be produced. Operating a car in contravention of the above is made a criminal offence, and penalties are also imposed if the termination of an insurance policy is not notified without delay to the licensing authority.

The protection of the injured person is, clearly, also furthered by all the above rules. In addition, however, since 1965 the victim has been given a direct right of action against the insurer (§ 3 I of the Obligatory Insurance

Act). Moreover, the victim's rights against the insurer are protected against the risk of the contract being void or voidable or the insurer having some other defence against the insured. Since 1965 the insurer is also liable for the damage caused by unauthorized drivers of vehicles for which their keeper is not liable under § 7 III of the Road Traffic Act. Finally, the victim can rely on the insurance policy even after its cancellation, but only if the claim is made within one month from the cancellation being notified to the licensing authority. It should be noted, however, that the insurer's liability to the victim is limited to the amounts, if any, that the victim cannot recover from other sources—notably the social security system. This means that in most cases the victim's medical expenses and even lost earnings are met by the appropriate social sickness insurance or social accident insurance. Given the dominant role in the compensation system played by the various social security schemes, the insurance companies tend to be brought into the picture at a later phase when the social insurance carrier wishes to be subrogated to the compensation claims of the insured. (A brief description in English of these complicated subrogation agreements can be found in Pfennigstorf's account of German law quoted in the Further Reading above.) Needless to say, an insurer who has paid the victim or his social security carrier may, in his turn, seek reimbursement from the insured person in accordance with the relative insurance laws. In practice this will happen in cases where the insured is in some way in breach of the contract of insurance: car used by unauthorized or unlicensed driver, or used for unauthorized racing; contract concluded under fraud or misrepresentation; failure to pay agreed premium etc. (For further details see Kötz, *Deliktsrecht*, nos. 418 *et seq.*)

Finally, the interests of the insured (and, arguably, once again the public at large) are safeguarded by a stringent supervisory control exercised over the one hundred or so insurance companies that are involved in the car insurance field. Though this regulatory function has since the early 1960s decreased somewhat, it remains by any standard quite stringent and includes such things as the control of the standard terms of insurance contracts as well as an effective control on premiums to be charged and the criteria for differentiating between premiums. Needless to say, this last point has been very controversial, critics of the existing regime arguing that it prevents effective competition between insurance companies and thus helps keep insurance premiums unrealistically high. (For further details on this see Gärtner, *Privatversicherungsrecht* (1976) 235.)

(*c*) *The salient features of the Road Traffic Act 1952.* The leading provision of this enactment is, undeniably, § 7. (The full text of the liability section of the Act is reproduced below, B.4.) § 7 imposes upon the 'keeper' or 'holder' (*Halter des Fahrzeugs*) of a 'motor vehicle' strict liability for personal injury, death, and property damage resulting from the 'operation of a motor car'. These three terms must be examined more closely.

Motor vehicle. This includes, according to § 1 II of the Act, all land vehicles which are driven by mechanical force and are not attached to railway tracks. § 8, however, excludes from the purview of the Act all slow-moving vehicles, i.e. those whose maximum speed at ground level does not exceed 20 kilometres per hour (12.5 m.p.h.).

Keeper. The liability is primarily imposed on the keeper of the car. The keeper is the person who uses the car at his own expense and who has the power of disposal that goes with such use (see RGZ 127, 174, 175; BGHZ 13, 351 etc.). The owner is usually deemed, but need not always be, the keeper. Cars driven by the employees of the keeper and causing damage will render him liable under the Act, the defence of bad selection or supervision, provided by § 831 BGB (discussed in Ch. 3, section 3 A.1), not being available in this case. A person using a car on a short-term hire agreement will, usually, not be treated as its keeper (see BGHZ 32, 331; 37, 306); but in the case of a long-term hiring agreement, the user of the car may become its keeper if he is saddled with all the running costs. If the car is used with the consent of the keeper, or it has been stolen because the keeper's negligence facilitates such a theft, the keeper will remain liable under the Act (§ 7 III). But if the car is used without the keeper's knowledge and consent—by a so-called 'joy-rider' (usually a thief)—then that person and not the keeper will be liable under the Act. The danger that could result from this rule to a victim of a car accident (impecuniosity of the 'joy-rider' and, hence, inability to meet the victim's claims) has, as we have seen, been removed by the insurance legislation of 1965 which renders the insurer liable. The German statute—unlike those of Austria and Switzerland—also regulates in § 18 the liability of the driver. This, however, is only a prima-facie liability which the driver can rebut by proving that he was not negligent when driving the car. In practice this exculpatory proof is very difficult to adduce, the courts imposing on drivers a very high standard of care indeed, and thus rendering the driver jointly liable with the keeper of the vehicle. When this is so, § 17 is brought into operation and the extent of the compensation to be paid as between keeper and driver will be determined in accordance with the usual rules of contributory fault (§ 254 BGB).

Damage caused in the course of the operation (running) of the car. This is the last positive requirement for strict liability to be imposed on the keeper. As already indicated, this term has given rise to a very rich case-law which is marked by the courts' desire to extend the protection of the victims of traffic accidents. (Though, once again, their value-judgments are often couched in causative language. See, for example, BGH NJW 1972, 1808.) Naturally, the term 'in operation' includes the typical way harm is caused, namely through collisions with moving or even immovable objects (other cars, cycles, pedestrians, sign-posts etc.). But no contact with the car that causes the injury is required; for example a sudden turn of a car which causes a cyclist, who is coming behind it, to swerve, lose his balance, and fall can render its driver liable under the Act. A leakage of oil on the road or dropped cargo, which then causes an accident, can also be brought under this heading. An accident is caused by the 'operation' of a car even where the car is stationary and not, strictly speaking, 'running' on the road. Abandoned stationary vehicles (because the driver is having a rest or because they have broken down) which have caused an accident have thus also been brought under this heading (see, for example BGHZ 29, 163, case 100); though a police car or a motor cycle which was parked in the middle of the road with its lights on to serve as a 'signal' that there was an accident ahead, was not included under the term 'in operation' (BGH VersR 1961, 369; likewise OLG Celle DAR 1973, 183, 187 quoted by Kötz, *Deliktsrecht*, 5th edn. no. 388). The case-law, in its desire to invoke the strict liability of the Act and afford greater protection to victims has, in fact, gone even further than the above examples may suggest (though these results have not escaped criticism). In one case when a tank smashed a paddock fence thereby enabling a horse to escape into the highway causing an accident, it was held that the accident had occurred in the course of 'operating a motor vehicle' (OLG Celle NJW 1965, 1719). In another, more extreme case, the same was held to be so when the car that caused the plaintiff's death was deliberately driven into him in order to facilitate the driver's escape from arrest. But it remains very doubtful that this was the type of 'mischief' that prompted the legislator to impose strict liability. A proper application of the scope of the rule theory should have then produced the opposite result. Thus, in other cases a more correct result has been reached by observing the proper purpose of § 7 of the Road Traffic Act. One such case is BGH NJW 1975, 1886, which is reproduced below (case 102), not only because it illustrates the point just made, but also because it shows how casuistic the approach of German courts is in this respect. In that case the engine of a stationary specialized motor vehicle was kept 'running' in order to help to discharge its cargo in a silo. One of the questions the court had to decide was whether damage caused during this operation could render the keeper of the vehicle liable under § 7 of the Road Traffic Act. The Supreme Court, overruling the Court of Appeal, held that it could not since, in principle, the statute only applied to 'such perils . . . which emanate from the motor vehicle in its capacity of an engine serving transport'. The court continued, 'Since our legal system does not know of a general principle of strict liability for operating engines supplying power at work, § 7 of the Road Traffic Act cannot be applied to accidents which occur in consequence of technical processes which cannot any longer be reasonably connected with the character of the engine employed as part of a motor vehicle.'

If the above requirements are satisfied, then the keeper of the vehicle will, usually, be liable to the extent provided by the Act (see §§ 10, 11, and 12) and perhaps, additionally (see § 16 of the Act) in accordance with the general rules of the law of delict (namely § 823 I or II BGB). But the liability under the 1952 Act will be excluded if he, the defendant, succeeds in proving that the accident was caused by an unavoidable event. An 'unavoidable event' is defined by § 7 II 2 as 'an event that (*inter alia*) . . . is due to the conduct of the injured party or of a third party (who is not an employee) or of an animal and if both the keeper and the driver of the vehicle have applied that care which is required in the light of the circumstances'. This last sentence has been interpreted in a very strict way, the courts demanding proof of 'extreme concentration and circumspection' on the part of the driver (BGH VersR 1962, 164). And, it is made even harder by expressly stating (§ 7 II 1) that an event is *not* unavoidable if it is due to a defect in the construction of the vehicle or a failure of one of its component parts (e.g. defective axle, brake failure, etc.). Moreover, the courts have assimilated to this 'mechanical' failure of the car any 'human' failure of its driver so that, for example, the loss of consciousness on the part of the driver, perhaps because of a sudden and unexpected brain haemorrhage, will *not* count as an 'unavoidable event' (BGHZ 23, 90). In practice, therefore, adducing this exculpatory proof is difficult though not necessarily impossible, e.g. unexpected appearance of black ice. (See Kötz, op. cit., no. 394, p. 145 and references given therein.)

Apart from the above—and the exclusion of the liability of the keeper for damage caused by a 'joy-rider'—the Act also contains one more important exceptional case where its application is excluded. This can be found in § 8*a* which states that the Act does not apply (i) to injury or death caused to any non-paying passenger travelling in the car (and this is taken to include the driver—see BGHZ 37, 311, 318) and (ii) to damage to property carried in the car unless it is carried by a paying passenger on himself. Naturally, in these cases the victim's claims can be based on the ordinary provisions of the Code (§ 823 I and II BGB).

Finally, according to § 9 of the Act, the injured party's contributory fault will also be taken into account. This can mean that, either this fault will be deemed to be the sole or main cause of the accident and thus bring into operation the defence of 'unavoidable event' (which will totally exonerate the keeper); or, more likely, the victim's fault will be considered as a contributing factor to his hurt and the damages awarded to him will be reduced in accordance with § 254 BGB.

(*d*) *A comparative epilogue*. Despite the fact that over the years a number of loopholes affecting traffic accident victims have been closed, German law on this subject still retains much of its vitality and controversial nature. Many of the criticisms have been voiced in a comparative way and it is appropriate in a book such as this to adopt a similar attitude.

The German approach to traffic accidents via a strict statutory liability is not unique. As already noted, Austria, Greece, the Netherlands, Switzerland, and the Scandinavian countries have all followed the same path and one can find quite similar (though not German-inspired) enactments even in the Common law world (the Saskatchewan Motor Vehicle Insurance Act 1947 being, probably, the best-known example). This way of regulating traffic accidents is markedly different from the French approach through the Code (but see now the 1985 Act at p. 854 below) and the Common law's persistent tendency to treat traffic accidents as a branch of the law of negligence. But in addition to being different, the German approach was, despite gaps, also pioneering in so far as it introduced strict liability at a very early stage in the life of the motor car. (The Scandinavian countries took a similar approach at about the same time.) Yet, even allowing for the progressive closing of the gaps of the original enactment and recognizing as undeniable the extension of the protection given to car accident victims, German law still remains, in some respects at least, less wide and less generous to victims than some of the more contemporary European systems. Two of its main weaknesses will be discussed below while a third—the extreme complexity of the compensation system—will be ignored since this accusation can also be levied against the English and French systems.

The first weakness of German law is the exclusion from the Traffic Act of injuries suffered by non-paying passengers. True, the position of the gratuitous passenger may not be as bad as it can be in some US jurisdictions where his recovery will depend on proof of gross negligence on the part of the driver; but it does remain unjustifiable given modern insurance practice. By contrast, in this area the most conceptually antiquated French system managed to break new ground when in the late sixties it decided to extend the strict liability of Art. 1384 CC to such cases (subsequently, most Canadian provinces moved more or less towards the same direction; see Linden, *Canadian Tort Law* (2nd edn., 1981), ch. 16). The older arguments invoked against such an extension (consent of the victim; impropriety of suing one's 'benefactor' without at least proving some fault on his part), advanced in all systems, have been increasingly recognized for what they are—fictions, appropriate to an era when third-party liability insurance was not compulsory, but objectionable relics now that modern insurance practices have transformed this part of the law. Old practices, however, die hard, especially when the insurance lobby wishes to retain them.

Insurance arguments also point to another weakness of the German system; the decision to reduce (and in extreme cases even eliminate) the victim's damages because of his own contributory fault. The abolition by the courts of this defence is impossible in German law given the express statutory provisions of the main Act; but even the desire to do this has often been lacking. For proposals for reform have always been met with moralistic arguments that any such move would not only increase the number of accidents but it would also sap tort law of much of its moral content. Empirical evidence, however, has shown that the first objection at least is not convincing and many would nowadays be prepared to treat the legalistic arguments in favour of retaining the defence of contributory fault as a smoke-screen concealing the vested interests of certain members of the legal profession who vehemently oppose the abolition of this lucrative source of revenue. Tort law is thus increasingly seen in the area of law accidents as little more than a 'forensic lottery' (the title of a pioneering monograph by Professor Isson); tort litigation (especially in France and in Common law jurisdictions) has cluttered the overburdened courts even further; and tort law has itself been forced to encourage the growth of fictions (e.g. the tendency to discover negligence in cases of unfortunate but statistically inevitable inattentions) in order to avoid the harshness of its rules. Here, again, French law has proved its flexibility and given a lead by recently advocating the abandonment of the defence of contributory fault. True, the pioneering decision of the Second Chamber of the Court of Cassation was rendered in a car accident case based on Art. 1384 CC; and the problem now exercising the French courts is whether it should be limited (as Professor Viney has argued in *Dalloz Chronique* 1982, 201) to cases where insurance is obligatory or, at least, widely prevalent. That it should is not seriously disputed though *how* this can be achieved, given the wide wording of Art. 1384 CC ('One is responsible for the damage caused by the things in one's care'), is another difficult matter (see Durry, 1983 *Rev. trim. dr. civ.*, 752). But whatever the difficulties of delimitation, the fact remains that the French experiment (which has still to receive the blessing of the plenum of the Court of Cassation) has given an interesting lead and has generated legal literature which can be consulted with profit even by the non-comparatively minded Common lawyer. (See now the 1985 Act reproduced below at p. 854.)

This brings us to the next point that at least American students of the modern civil law should bear in mind. The study of the European systems (including the English), fruitful as it may be, must always be undertaken bearing in mind some essential differences in the legal background. Thus it must be remembered that in Europe (including England) civil action claims arising from car accidents are not tried by juries; that the contingent fee system for legal remuneration is banned, and most importantly that a highly developed social welfare system plays an important part in the overall compensation of car accident victims. All these factors can help to explain the lower levels of awards and other differences in the substantive law. Finally, though Germany (like the USA) is a Federal State, tort law (and hence, traffic accident law) is the same in all the States of the Federation. Thus, one does not find in Germany the regional variations that the American (or Canadian) lawyer has come to accept in his own system.

This comparative epilogue should, perhaps, end by reminding the reader that, once again, the study of the subject can be greatly enhanced by an interdisciplinary approach. The contact with insurance, in particular, must never be forgotten; and it could provide the 'unifying link' in any comparative study that sought to argue that legal borrowing is possible even in an area where historical and conceptual differences might at first sight seem to discourage it.

SECTION B. CASES

1. § 831 BGB

Case 73

BUNDESGERICHTSHOF (SIXTH CIVIL DIVISION) 7 OCTOBER 1975*
JZ 1975, 733

The plaintiff, the Gas–Electricity and Waterworks of the City of K, as holders of the right to draw water for their undertaking, claimed damages in respect of expenses incurred or likely to be incurred in the future as a result of the pollution of the water-table by petroleum waste. The plaintiff alleged that the fourth defendant, a petrochemical enterprise, had engaged the first defendant on the recommendation of the second defendant—an independent expert on damage by mineral oil and *de facto* manager of the first defendant—to carry and safely to dispose of their oil waste consisting mainly of a mixture of oil and water. In carrying out this assignment, the first defendant had installed ovens and barrels in a gravel-pit filled with refuse situated in an area which had been designated by the government as a protected water-zone for the use of the waterworks. No licence had been obtained, although the first defendant had been given to understand by the competent authorities that it would be forthcoming, if certain conditions were complied with.

On being alerted by an outsider that the oil waste had not been disposed of expertly, the plaintiff caused boreholes to be sunk and excavations to be

---

* English version by Kurt Lipstein.

made which disclosed that the water-table was covered by an extensive body of oil. In the action against the fourth defendant the plaintiff sought to be reimbursed for the expense of drilling observation wells and of collecting and examining samples of water and soil.

The District Court, by a separate judgment, rejected the claim against the fourth defendant while allowing the other actions to proceed. On appeal by the plaintiff, the Court of Appeal of Cologne quashed the judgment of the District Court and referred the case back. A second appeal was unsuccessful for the following

Reasons

I. The Court of Appeal has held that the fourth defendant is liable in tort (§ 823 I BGB), as well as on the ground that the plaintiff had acted on his behalf in his interests and in accordance with his actual or presumed intention (§§ 683, 677, 670 BGB), to pay the expenses claimed by the plaintiff if further evidence to be obtained by the District Court reveals that the first defendant has contaminated the water-table to the plaintiff's detriment by disposing inexpertly of the waste entrusted to him.

1. The plaintiff's pleadings do not support any liability of the fourth defendant according to the provision of § 22 of the Water Preservation Act (WHG) which establishes extensive strict liability for such expenses in the instances enumerated there.

(a) § 22 I WHG cannot serve as a basis of the claim, if for no other reason, because no act of the fourth defendant was objectively capable of allowing the waste produce to seep into the water-table [references]. The fourth defendant has not even envisaged and accepted the possibility that the oil waste might be disposed of in this manner nor were the measures taken by him for the destruction of the waste in fact capable of allowing the waste to seep into the water. The circumstance that by handing the waste over to the first defendant he enabled the latter to dispose of it improperly, contrary to a contractual arrangement, does not suffice to attract liability under § 22 I WHG. This provision was not intended to create such an extensive liability for the unauthorized conduct of third parties . . .

(b) The fourth defendant cannot be held liable under § 22 II WHG because the noxious substances infiltrated into the water-table from the *first defendant's* installation but not from that of the fourth defendant from which they had already been carried away.

2. Liability for damage caused by the fact that waste materials seeped into the water-table is not, however, confined to the situations enumerated in § 22 WHG. This provision was intended to reinforce the protection against

interference with the quality of water by introducing strict liability; in the absence of an express statement to this effect this provision, like any other establishing strict liability, does not preclude claims based on tort or on quasi-contract [acting for another without authorization; references].

The Court of Appeal was also correct when considering this ground of liability that the right of the plaintiff enjoyed by virtue of §§ 46 ff., 200, 203 of the Prussian Water Act was not affected by subsequent legislation [references]. The right to extract water is an absolute right in the meaning of § 823 I to be respected by everybody [reference], capable of being violated by the pollution by noxious substances to the water-table in the area of the intake operated by the plaintiff's waterworks [reference]. The Court of Appeal was right in holding consequently that the fourth defendant must prevent as far as possible any such interferences with the right to extract water by waste products and that if he fails to act in accordance with the care required in daily life he must, *inter alia*, pay for the necessary measure to avert the danger to the supply of drinking-water by the waterworks as a result of a pollution of the water-table [references].

II. 1. As stated, the producer of such industrial waste which is a source of danger to the environment in the absence of special measures is liable, irrespective of other special rules of conduct and of the legal consequences resulting from their infringement under § 823 I BGB, to take the necessary steps in the execution of the general duty of care to safeguard the public in general [*Verkehrssicherungspflicht*] derived from § 823 I BGB to avoid that the (potential) danger results in damage to third parties. Just as the producer of goods is subject to this duty in respect of goods introduced into commerce [references] the producer of industrial waste must also seek to avert within the limits of what is practicable any usual dangers emanating from by-products 'of negative value'. It is irrelevant in this connection that they are not for sale, as is also that their manufacture is allowed. The fact alone determines that the manufacturer has created the source of danger and must render it safe for third parties within the limits of what is possible and can be expected of him. This general principle of the law of tort [reference] has its counterpart, as regards objective imputation, in the maxim which also dominates in public law relating to the environment to the effect that he who causes damage to the environment must also pay for it [references] . . .

2. The Court of Appeal has found, without contravening the law, that the waste containing petroleum constitutes a special danger for the maintenance of the water-table if it is stored or destroyed inexpertly. Given the danger to the environment, especially having regard to the quantity of petroleum waste products produced by the fourth defendant (about 570 tonnes in approximately two months), strict care was required in storing and dispos-

ing of it. The Court of Appeal stressed correctly in this connection that a harmless disposal of the waste was technically difficult and therefore demanded a special method and a special installation for destroying it if the danger of inexpert or incomplete destruction was to be avoided; and that at least greater storage capacity and longer storage was necessary with its attendant perils.

3. The Court was right, moreover, in holding that the fourth defendant was not obliged to store, and dispose of, the waste himself, but could delegate this task to an independent enterprise which could not be regarded as its aide in the meaning of § 831 [*editor's note*: the judgment refers wrongly to § 832] BGB in the absence of a relationship of dependency. In such circumstances, the fourth defendant was, however, bound to see to it that the necessary safety measures were taken properly in order to prevent damage to third parties by the disposal of the oil waste.

(*a*) Naturally the supervision of a specialized enterprise is limited by the need for a trusting collaboration, and by the independence and the immunity from orders of the agent; it would mean straining excessively the requirements of care in the face of economic and technical reality if the principal were asked to control at every step the manner in which the agent operates. On the other hand, those subject to duties of care to safeguard the public in general are not always released of their responsibility for the sources of danger which they have created if another is equally bound to take safeguarding action by virtue of a contract. Instead they may be obliged, if the circumstances so require—as for instance in an acutely dangerous situation [reference: fireworks] or if serious reasons exist for doubting whether the agent will take sufficient account of the dangers and the need to safeguard against them [reference: Mosel Lock construction]—to control the work by the enterprise entrusted with it or to intervene in case of necessity [reference]. In particular, the duty is not discharged if an enterprise is employed which does not offer a sufficient guarantee that the necessary safety measures will be taken; for in those circumstances the delegation to such an enterprise of the duty to safeguard the public only increases the danger of damages to third parties. In such a case those subject to a duty of care to safeguard the public in general cannot plead that by the interposition of an independent enterprise their power controlling the source of danger has been curtailed. They had the opportunity to select the agent carefully; the more their influence is limited by the independence of the enterprise to which the task is delegated, the more the duty to select the enterprise carefully must be taken seriously. They are liable if the danger materializes, since they themselves brought it about by employing an unreliable enterprise.

(*b*) The appellant argues that petroleum waste is no more dangerous than the petroleum produced by the fourth defendant. Since the fourth defendant cannot be held liable for damage caused by an inappropriate use of the petroleum after it has been delivered to his customers he cannot be liable either if an enterprise engaging in the destruction of waste employed by him disposes of the waste in an improper manner contrary to a contractual arrangement.

This argument cannot be accepted—at least in this generalization. It need not be decided whether and to what extent the manufacturer of goods can also be held liable for damage to third parties when the product is used contrary to its intended use, if the manufacturer ought in this respect to have had doubts about the reliability of the customer [references]. In determining and delimiting the respective spheres of liability it is decisive that the waste incidental to the manufacture of petroleum and its disposal are, so to say, the 'negative aspect' of the manufacture and that, according to the general view, its destruction is and remains a matter for the manufacturer, while the 'destruction' of the petroleum is in the hands of the customer according to its purpose. If a manufacturer decides to engage in the production of petroleum, he must provide for safe destruction of waste, the more so since this normally requires special measures; certainly resort may also be had to his liability in private law if somebody is damaged by the waste. If the manufacturer employs a third party for the disposal of the waste, he complies with his *own* duty to safeguard the public in general through the interposition of the third party . . .

4. No legal objections exist against the finding of the Court of Appeal that in the course of the enquiries, which were necessary and could be expected to be carried out before delegating the task, the fourth defendant should have realized that the enterprise employed by him did not at the time offer a sufficient guarantee that the waste would be disposed of safely and that, if the enterprise should have disposed of it in the way the plaintiff alleges, dangers did materialize for which the fourth defendant is liable, not having used sufficient care in selecting the enterprise.

(*a*) The Court of Appeal is correct in law when it bases its critical appreciation of the first defendant's action on the primitive conditions in which the installation, established provisionally only, was operated . . . This method did not comply with the provisions of § 34 II 1 WHG according to which even outside a water protection zone materials may only be stored or deposited so as not to create the fear that the water-table may become polluted or that its quality may be affected in any other way. The fact that the installation was set up on a foundation of clay which had been spread over the refuse did not exclude with the necessary degree of certainty a pollution of the water-table—by seeping oil—if only as a result of mixing it with oil [reference], the more so since it was uncertain whether the layer was resistant to water and fluids throughout [reference]. For this reason special measures had to be taken for the protection of the water-table so as to prevent effectively that oil should escape because the containers begin to leak as a result of corrosion, of defective materials or construction, or in consequence of spilling in the course of filling or emptying [references] . . .

At all events the fourth defendant should have realized, when he gave the order, that the installation lacked the simplest safety mechanism for protecting the water-table and that in its actual state the harmless destruction of the waste was not guaranteed, keeping in mind the amount of waste to be destroyed. If so, he should have entertained doubts about the reliability of the management of the enterprise which has so flagrantly disregarded the simplest requirements of safety. In view of such manifest flagrant omissions the fourth defendant could also have foreseen that the first defendant in destroying the oil waste would not seriously consider the protection of the water-table . . .

(b) Having regard to its duty to safeguard the public in general [*Verkehrssicherungspflicht*], the fourth defendant was obliged to inform himself of the operational conditions of the first defendant before entrusting him with the waste oil. The fact that at the time malpractices in disposing of industrial waste had not seriously concerned the public and the industries involved, as the appellant contends, does not relieve the fourth defendant; given his experience he must have been aware of the possibility and the resulting danger of an improper destruction of such waste . . .

In agreement with the Court of Appeal it must be held that the fourth defendant could not rely on the recommendations of the second defendant, even if he got to know him as a reliable expert on the prevention of damage by oil and that he had been recommended as such by the water authorities and by the department head of the fourth defendant's insurers. Whether the same considerations would apply also if the second defendant had not been personally connected with the first defendant need not be decided here. At any rate . . . the fourth defendant knew that the second defendant had founded the enterprise together with his wife, who was only nominally the manager, and that in fact he managed the affairs of the first defendant himself.

III. 1. In view of those considerations, the Court of Appeal had held correctly that if the fourth defendant had applied the standard of care required of him, he should not have left it to the first defendant to dispose of the waste, at least not without taking special measures for controlling the destruction. Consequently, the fourth defendant is liable, certainly from the angle of damages due according to § 823 BGB, to compensate the plaintiff for the expenses necessarily incurred in restricting the dangers to the supply of drinking-water, in so far as they are caused by the alleged inexpert operations of the first defendant and would not have occurred if the fourth defendant had properly complied with his duty of care to safeguard the public in general.

Case 74

BUNDESGERICHTSHOF (SEVENTH CIVIL DIVISION) 30 OCTOBER 1967*
BGHZ 49, 19 = NJW 1968, 391 = VersR 1968, 92

The plaintiff finances hire-purchase agreements of motor-cars by providing loans for the purchasers. The money representing the loans is paid direct to the vendors in discharge of the purchase price. The plaintiff only grants a loan if title to the motor vehicle is transferred to him by way of security, if the seller becomes a surety, and if a report concerning the purchaser's creditworthiness is favourable.

The defendant carries on the business of an information agency with branches in sixteen cities of the Federal Republic. The branch in Bonn was managed from 1955 onwards by Z, its 'commercial representative' (until he died in March 1962). For many years Z provided the motor car dealer F— who has since lost his fortune and was adjudicated bankrupt at his request—with 'information concerning the financial standing' of about 1500 clients of F. This information was supplied on paper with the name of the defendant at the letter-head. In twenty-six cases the information was invented; the persons did not exist; in five other cases the persons existed, but the information was too favourable. In these twenty-six cases Z wrote the letters at short notice without having engaged in any enquiries or examination, relying exclusively on the information supplied by F, and concealed their existence from the defendant. Using these letters, F deceived the plaintiff into making him pay over the 'loan'. The District Court found, and it is now undisputed, that Z was aware of the danger to the plaintiff's assets as a result of his conduct, but that he took the risk.

The plaintiff claims from the defendant damages in respect of the loss, alleged to be DM 201,145.08, caused by F and Z. The defendant disputes the claim both as to its basis and its extent. He also pleads contributory negligence . . .

The District Court and the Court of Appeal of Frankfurt rejected the claim. Upon a second appeal the claim was admitted in principle and the case referred back to ascertain the amount for the following

* English version by Kurt Lipstein.

Reasons

The plaintiff argues that the defendant is liable under § 31 BGB for the torts committed by Z to the detriment of the plaintiff. The Court of Appeal denies this.

1. It holds that Z is not the defendant's representative appointed in accordance with the statutes in the meaning of § 31 BGB. He lacked the necessary independence in his dealings with third parties and a sphere of administration of his own within functions of management of the defendant.

These arguments are not free from error in law. The facts as found by the Court of Appeal compel the conclusion that Z was the representative of the defendant in the meaning of § 31 BGB.

(*a*) According to this provision, a legal entity is responsible for the damage to a third party by its representative, appointed in accordance with the statutes, as a result of an act 'in the execution of the duties allotted to him' which engages liability to pay damages. The legal concept of 'representative appointed in accordance with the statutes' has been extended increasingly in practice and in the literature. The Court of Appeal has overlooked this.

Representatives appointed in accordance with the statutes are not only those persons whose activities are envisaged by the statutes of a legal entity, nor need they possess the right to represent the entity in legal transactions. It is not necessary either that the range of tasks falls within the managerial administration of the legal entity. It suffices if the representative is entrusted with handling important and essential functions of the legal entity by the general system and functioning of the enterprise [references]. In such circumstances it would be inequitable to permit the legal entity to exonerate itself in reliance on § 831 BGB.

(*b*) These conditions were fulfilled in the present case as regards Z.

(*aa*) It is undisputed that he managed the office of the defendant in Bonn as a 'one-man business' in complete independence. With the permission of the defendant he described the office as a 'branch' of the latter. In agreement with the defendant he used the latter's business stationery and reference forms and a stamp to the same effect. Thus, in his dealings with third parties he clearly did not act as an 'independent commercial agent' on behalf of the defendant; the Court of Appeal was wrong in holding that in fact he managed the defendant's office in Bonn as an independent agency of information.

(*bb*) In view of the agreed conduct in dealings with third parties, it is irrelevant that, as between Z and the defendant, their legal relationship was governed by the 'contract of agency' of 11 August 1955 in accordance with the law relating to commercial agents. This does not rule out the conclusion that in his relations with third parties Z was the representative of the defendant in accordance with § 31 BGB.

(*cc*) By providing references on paper bearing the letter-head of the defendant, Z made the statements contained therein *in the name of the defendant*. Nothing in these letters indicates that these are not statements of the defendant, but only of Z. Obviously, the value of these references for the recipient consisted in the fact that they emanated from the reputable defendant, a big information agency known throughout the world. It is not disputed that the defendant knew of this general practice of Z, although the particular thirty-one 'references' which form the basis of the present claim were concealed from him.

(*dd*) The Court of Appeal has found that the defendant himself engages in the business of an information agency, that he has set up and maintains a network of information offices, that it provides these offices with the sources from which to draw their information and permits these offices to use its business name. In so doing it has, to a wide extent, delegated to the managers of its 'offices' the independent discharge of its characteristic functions (to provide information). Thus, the defendant has also delegated to Z the task of supplying references independently in the area of Bonn. It need not be stressed that the provision of references on creditworthiness by an information agency is a very responsible activity; if carried out carelessly much damage can be caused, as the present case shows clearly.

2. By way of a subsidiary argument the Court of Appeal denies that the defendant is responsible for Z under § 31 BGB on the ground that his torts had not been committed 'in the execution of the functions allotted to him', but only on their 'occasion'. This conclusion, too, is wrong having regard to the facts as found by the Court of Appeal.

(*a*) An act is done in the execution of the duties entrusted to a person if it remains within the range of measures which constitute the execution of the functions entrusted to him. The act must be in close objective connection with those measures. The liability is not excluded if the order is exceeded or the power is abused. An international tortious act may well be committed in close objective connection with the allotted functions; this is the case, in particular, if the tortious act violates the allotted specific duties [references].

(*b*) The defendant refers to the decision [references]. However, that case must be distinguished. A credit agent who had been entrusted with a single sale of a motor vehicle had falsely represented to a third party that the order had been carried out, in order to get hold of the moneys involved. In so doing, the agent had severed himself from his allotted range of functions objectively as well. As is pointed out in that decision, the conclusion would have been different if he had sold the vehicle intentionally on his own account and had embezzled the purchase price; this act would still have been sufficiently connected with the functions allotted to him. This is not the case here. It is true that Z gave false references, but they were references and thus he operated exactly within his real sphere of functions. The close objective connection is not destroyed by the fact that he exceeded his powers arbitrarily and intentionally illegally.

3. The Court of Appeal relies on an additional subsidiary argument to the effect that the plaintiff's contributory negligence excludes altogether a possible obligation of the defendant to pay damages . . .

The judgment of the Court of Appeal does not show clearly whether this statement refers only to liability under § 831 BGB or whether the Court of Appeal also wishes thereby to rule out any claim under § 31 BGB which, as was shown here, is alone in issue.

If the latter should be the case, the decision of the Court of Appeal cannot be approved. Faced with intentional acts of representatives appointed in accordance with the statutes in accordance with § 31 BGB, contributory negligence on the part of the injured party can never be regarded as so serious as to preclude a claim for damages altogether.

Case 75

BUNDESGERICHTSHOF (SIXTH CIVIL DIVISION) 6 OCTOBER 1970*

NJW 1971, 31

For the purposes of his business the defendant owns a lorry and a lorry-train consisting of a lorry with a trailer. In addition to a number of drivers employed by him, he is assisted by his brother. He instructed the latter on 16 June 1965 to fetch 10 tonnes of coal. The brother used the lorry-train and not the single lorry, which would have required two journeys. Since the trailer was parked on the market in K, he fetched it from there and drove the empty vehicle to the place where the coal was located. On the way he had to pass through a village where the road made a sharp bend to the left. Since the road was wet he braked. As a result the trailer skidded on to the left side of the road and collided with the plaintiff's car. The plaintiff suffered severe injuries, and his car was badly damaged.

The defendant's brother was fined for negligently causing bodily harm. In these proceedings an expert stated that the brakes of the trailer were too weak with the result that it tended to skid on a wet surface and to leave its

---

* English version by Kurt Lipstein.

side of the road. In these circumstances the defendant insurer refused to pay for the entire damage and has only accepted liability in favour of the plaintiff up to DM 150,000 in accordance with §§ 158 ff. of the Act concerning Contracts of Insurance.

The plaintiff sued the defendant's brother and the defendant claiming damages amounting to DM 24,216 and asking for a declaration that both brothers are also liable to compensate him for any other damage arising or likely to arise in connection with the accident. The plaintiff also sued the defendant's brother for damages for pain and suffering.

The District Court, dealing with part of the claim, allowed damages for pain and suffering as well as DM 14,363 in respect of general damages and reserved its decision as regards the remaining DM 9853. In addition it granted the declaration asked for by the plaintiff.

After the brother of the defendant had paid the sum of DM 14,363, the defendant lodged an appeal limited to the grant of the declaration that he was also liable to the plaintiff in respect of future damage. The Court of Appeal of Düsseldorf rejected the appeal. A second appeal was unsuccessful for the following

Reasons

B. . . .

II. Contrary to the contentions of the appellant, the Court of Appeal applied § 831 BGB correctly.

1. It is undisputed that the defendant, in asking his brother to fetch the coal with the motor vehicle, appointed him to execute a function. The appellant questions, however, whether the brother of the defendant acted illegally in the meaning of § 831 BGB [reference] and argues that the brother had been engaged in a 'frolic of his own' [*Schwarzfahrt*] for which the defendant was not liable. In both respects the Court of Appeal was right.

(*a*) The brother of the defendant has injured the plaintiff illegally. Even if the test employed here is not that of an 'effect tort', i.e. whether the plaintiff was injured, the defendant must prove at least that his brother observed 'proper traffic practices' when he passed the sharp bend with his lorry-train. This is not, however, the case, even if he had not hit the plaintiff's motor car. If a motor vehicle skids and bars the road, it cannot be said that the driver—whose personal culpability is not immediately relevant in applying § 831 BGB—drove in accordance with 'proper driving practices'. Even if the defendant's brother had examined the brakes of the trailer before starting and had found them in good order, it has not been shown and proved that his manner of driving at the time of the accident complied with the legal regulation of traffic to such a degree that it could not be condemned as illegal. This would only be the case if the brother of the defendant had acted in a manner which complied entirely with the demands and prohibitions of the traffic regulations [reference]. In the present case the question remains open, to the detriment of the defendant, whether his brother entered the sharp bend at an excessive speed in contravention of § 9 of the Road Traffic Act with the result that despite the dangerous wet road he had to apply the brakes of the lorry-train—with the behaviour of which he was not familiar in any case, as the defendant alleges. The Court of Appeal is therefore justified in stating that the insufficient operation of the trailer's brakes had been a 'contributory cause' of the accident.

(*b*) It is true that the reversal of the burden of proof laid down by § 831 BGB only affects the principal if the person entrusted with the execution of a function has caused the damage in the course of executing the function, and not merely on its occasion. A direct intrinsic connection must exist as to manner and purpose between the function entrusted to him, on the one hand, and the injurious act on the other hand [references]. Contrary to the objections raised by the appellant, the Court of Appeal has correctly found that such a connection exists.

It must be admitted that the keeper of a motor vehicle is not liable for a 'frolic of his own' by the driver against his will; the principle is that he is not liable either under § 7 of the Road Traffic Act or under § 831 BGB [references]. However, in the present case the brother of the defendant was not on a 'frolic of his own'; he had undertaken the journey not against his brother's will, but with his consent; both the time of the journey as well as the route chosen by him corresponded to the latter's intention. It is true that the principal may not be liable in certain circumstances for the faults of his assistant if the damage would not have occurred had the driver followed a certain prohibition imposed by his principal. This Division has so held in a case in which the driver, in disregard of a prohibition, had given a ride to an acquaintance who was injured in an accident [references]. The appellant is mistaken in contending that the present case is similar. In the former case, the injured party had accepted a lift by a driver on a journey on which only goods were to be transported; in the present case the third party was injured not in the course of making use of the vehicle, but as a road-user. It must be assumed in favour of the defendant that his brother fetched the trailer which caused the accident in disregard of the express prohibition by the defendant and connected it. According to a constant practice, however, acts of a person entrusted with the execution of certain functions do not fall outside the range of these functions even if he contravened the principal's orders intentionally and on his own [references]. In the present case, when the brother of the defendant hitched on the trailer contrary to his orders, he did so in order to avoid having to make two journeys, and thus in order to carry out the task more quickly. Therefore this, and in particular the journey, in the course of which the accident occurred, stood in a relation not only of adequate causality but also, which is decisive, of intrinsic connection with his order to fetch 10 tonnes of coal. The fact is irrelevant that the defendant, as he alleges, forbade his brother to take the trailer because he did not wish to entrust him with driving the lorry with a trailer on the grounds of his advanced age.

Case 76

BUNDESGERICHTSHOF (THIRD CIVIL DIVISION) 14 JANUARY 1954*
BGHZ 12, 94 = NJW 1954, 913

The plaintiff, who was insured by M, while riding his motor cycle at night collided with one of four telegraph poles which were lying across the road and suffered a severe fracture of his skull. The District Court allowed his claim for damages, but the Court of Appeal of Frankfurt rejected it. Upon a second appeal the judgment below was quashed and the case referred back for the following

Reasons

I. The defendant, the Federal Post, is only liable for the consequences of the accident if the case falls within the ambit of a particular statutory provision. The law in force at present does not provide for liability 'according to general principles'; in particular it does not contain a principle that everybody is liable to make good any damage caused by his property unless he can prove that he is not to be blamed for the fact that the location of the property imperilled others. Absolute strict liability of the defendant in respect of the telephone lines maintained by it deserves even less consideration.

II. The plaintiff complains that the defendant did not maintain its installations in a safe condition for traffic and that its employees did not take measures for removing the recent obstacle to traffic. None of these considerations is sufficient to hold the defendant liable under § 839 BGB and Art. 131 of the Constitution of Weimar; even in the case of public operations both the duty to maintain an installation adequately for traffic purposes as well as the duty to remove sudden obstacles to traffic are obligations which do not arise out of a special relationship of protection between the public authority and a third party who happens to have been affected accidentally; the real reason is that objectively a dangerous situa-

---

* English version by Kurt Lipstein.

tion has been created. Where such obligations to take safeguarding measures are concerned public corporations are not to be treated differently from private persons, even if the activity in question may bear the character of an act *jure imperii*. The liability of the public corporation is therefore governed by §§ 823, 831 BGB. Following the practice of the Reichsgericht, this Division in its decision [reference] has given detailed reasons for so holding; the observations made there as to the duty to safeguard the public in respect of a public path apply here as well. The appellant is wrong in relying in this connection on the argument that according to the practice of the courts the activity of the Federal Post has been regarded increasingly as being exercised *jure imperii*. The appellant is also wrong in referring to the decision of the Reichsgericht [reference]; it is there stated expressly that the principle set out here applies also to damage caused by the laying of telephone cables; as regards 'third-party outsiders' no liability arises under § 839 BGB; liability in the exercise of official functions to protect a third party against damage exists only in favour of those who are obliged, by virtue of the Law concerning Telegraph Lines to suffer interference with their property. However, this is not the case.

III. The Court of Appeal has held correctly that the defendant is not liable for having failed to remove the fallen telegraph poles from the highway in time.

1. The objection of the appellant to the conclusion of the Court of Appeal that the defendant is not liable under § 831 is unfounded.

(*a*) According to a constant practice no liability arises under § 831 BGB, even in the absence of separate evidence in exoneration, if the employee has acted in such a manner as any carefully selected person would have done [reference].

(*b*) The technical supervisor acted, however, as any other employee, including he who acts with the necessary care, would have acted. It may be that the night in question was stormy and that this could also be observed at the Post Office in L. It cannot be said, however, that in these circumstances an employee of the Post Office, acting with the necessary care, on noticing a partial disruption of the telephone lines would have dispatched immediately a repair column during the night. Since only seven out of thirty lines failed to function, it could not be assumed that poles had fallen and that the lines had collapsed. The defendant has stated, and the plaintiff has not disputed it, that such interruption had also occurred previously due to the fact that damp had penetrated the cables and because 'lead fatigue' had affected the strength of the cables. The parties agree that during the night when the accident happened the weather was wet. It is understandable, therefore, that the technical supervisor also attributed this disruption of the lines to the causes which had been observed previously. It must be conceded to the defendants that little purpose would have been served in attempting to remedy this disruption if a repair column had been sent on a search errand during the night. The Act on Telegraph Lines, too, assumes, as § 12 III shows, that disruptions are normally dealt with during daytime only.

2. In these circumstances, the appellant is wrong in contending that the telephone business had been supervised inadequately by the defendant and that it was therefore liable for the damage—directly in accordance with § 823 BGB—thus ruling out the need to prove that one of its organs had been at fault. Such liability has been held by the practice to exist, e.g. if a public corporation has failed to take any measures at all which serve to control its installations in order to ensure the safety of traffic [references]. During the night from 15 to 16 February 1948, too, an employee of the Post Office had been charged with supervising the functioning of the telephone lines. It need not be decided whether the technical supervisor could be regarded as an 'organ' of the defendant in the meaning of §§ 89, 30, 31 BGB; the Court of Appeal has rightly denied that he acted negligently. The observations made above in respect of the question whether a carefully chosen employee would have acted in the same way have shown that he did not act culpably. It has not been demonstrated either that during the night when the accident occurred another employee of the defendant or one of his organs negligently omitted to attend to the telephone lines. No claims arise therefore on the ground that the obstacle to traffic had not been discovered and removed in time.

IV. The plaintiff also bases his claim on the ground that the defendant had not maintained its telephone poles properly; the accident had occurred because the storm had felled a rotten pole which by means of the telephone cable had in turn pulled down the other poles which had been secured inadequately. This allegation has not been considered entirely satisfactorily by the court below.

1. The Court of Appeal does not consider this allegation as forming a basis of the claim because in its opinion the fact has not been proved and is incapable of being proved that the accident actually occurred in the way alleged by the plaintiff; the possibility should not be ruled out that an American lorry had collided with a pole and had thus caused the collapse of the telephone lines.

In so far as the appellant argues that the Court of Appeal had misunderstood the burden of proof, seeing that faced with an actual situation in violation of the traffic rules the defendant bore the burden of proof 'that it is not responsible for the dangerous condition of its installation', his contention cannot be accepted. It is for the plaintiff to prove that the damage was caused by faulty maintenance of the installation not only where the claim is based on § 823 BGB but also in the case of § 836 BGB [reference]. This follows from the principle that a claimant must prove that the factual conditions exist for the creation of a right.

2. The Court of Appeal overlooks, however, that the defendant may be liable even if an American lorry had collided with the pole, thus leading to the collapse of the telephone lines. The Court of Appeal is of the opinion that the possibility of the lorry by colliding with it made a strong impact on one of the poles is to be ruled out. In the absence of any traces on one of the collapsed poles, experience shows that, if at all, the collision would only have had a weak impact on the pole. If, however, even a slight impact with the pole could have resulted in a complete collapse of a part of the installation, the possibility would exist that inadequate maintenance of the installation was in fact a contributory cause of the accident. It must be considered whether the rotten condition of one of the poles, conceded by the defendant itself, was so considerable and, apart from this the other poles had been secured insufficiently so as to render them no longer safe for traffic. It need not be decided whether the storm or the lorry broke the pole. Neither does a natural event create liability nor does the act of a third party exclude liability in all cases. This principle applies also in respect of § 836 BGB. In dealing with the question of causality, the determining factor is whether the structure was so inadequately maintained or secured that even a minor impact, to be taken into consideration as normal, could lead to its collapse. The 'last' cause may perhaps never be ascertained, and yet liability may not be excluded for this reason.

If upon further examination it should appear that the telephone poles were deficient in the sense indicated here, the defendant would be liable under § 823 BGB in conjunction with §§ 89, 31, 30, unless it proves that none of the organs is to blame; the fact alone that another dangerous situation was allowed to persist is a sufficient indication that the care was lacking which is required for safeguarding traffic . . .

In view of the special features of this case, liability under § 823 BGB would exist if it should be established that the telephone lines were inadequately maintained, unless the defendant can exonerate himself. In these circumstances it is unnecessary to discuss the question raised by the appellant as to whether liability under § 836 BGB can arise even if the damage has not been caused by the 'mobile force' of the collapsing structure but by the fact that the collapsed structure is allowed to lie on a road which carried public traffic. § 836 does not involve a different type of case but only a reversal of the burden of proof [reference]. Thus § 836 can be disregarded if within the framework of § 823 BGB the debtor is called upon exceptionally to prove that he is not to blame.

Case 77

BUNDESGERICHTSHOF (SIXTH CIVIL DIVISION) 10 JULY 1954*
NJW 1956, 1106

The plaintiff was a patient in the neurological clinic of the Municipal Hospital in B between 25 May 1951 and 9 February 1952. He suffered from introspective-endogenous depressions. On 24 May 1951 he received electro-shock treatment and on 28 May 1951 he underwent a lumbar puncture. On 6 and 7 June the electro-shock treatment was repeated. In the course of it he suffered a fracture of the twelfth vertebra from which he recovered after having lain in plaster for six and a half months. Since then his right leg is paralysed and he suffers from intestinal and heart trouble. The medical expert of the Social Insurance Office of the Land regards him as incapable of work. The Court of Appeal of Bremen allowed the plaintiff's claim for damages against the hospital of the defendant. A second appeal was unsuccessful for the following

Reasons

The Court of Appeal has found that the plaintiff entered the clinic of the defendant as a patient supported by social security. It has held correctly that in these cases the legal relationship between the municipal hospital or clinic and the patient is of a private law nature. According to a constant practice of the Reichsgericht, followed by the Federal Supreme Court [references], the reception of a patient supported by social security creates a contract with the hospital in favour of the patient with the result that the patient acquires a right of his own to be treated expertly. If a doctor, who has been charged with the treatment of such a patient supported by social security commits a mistake culpably, the defendant as owner of the clinic is liable according to § 278 BGB for the mistake of the doctor appointed by him to perform the duties of the latter.

On the other hand, as the Court of Appeal has pointed out, a claim for pain and suffering against a doctor in charge on the ground of assault causing bodily harm cannot be based on § 278 BGB, but only on § 831 BGB, unless direct liability under § 823 BGB is in issue.

II. 1. The appellant is wrong in alleging that the plaintiff had validly consented to the electro-shock treatment and that this consent could only have

* English version by Kurt Lipstein.

been annulled in accordance with §§ 161 ff. BGB. This view would only be correct if

(*a*) the plaintiff had been aware of the typical dangers of electro-shock treatment and, in particular, of a fracture of the spine and if with knowledge of these dangers his consent had included these factors, or

(*b*) the doctor in charge could so understand and interpret the general conduct of the plaintiff in the particular circumstances of the case and having regard to the views current in human relations between reasonable people that the plaintiff was aware in outline of the dangers connected with shock treatment and that he had accepted the risk.

As to (*a*): It is a constant practice in cases where a passenger in a motor vehicle is injured that an exemption from liability based on the assumption of a risk can only be presumed if the victim went on the journey conscious of the possibility of danger and thus consented expressly or tacitly to a possible danger arising out of the driver's conduct, whether culpable or not. Such a consent does not include dangers which the victim merely ought to have noticed [references]. Similarly, the Reichsgericht has pointed out [reference] that physical treatment by a doctor involving the corporeal inviolability of a patient is only covered by the contract and not illegal in so far as the consent of the patient extends to it. According to the Reichsgericht, [reference] before applying any physical treatment the doctor must make certain of the patient's consent, which must be done based upon correct ideas concerning the nature and consequences of the treatment, even if naturally it does not cover all details. In [reference] the Reichsgericht upheld this view. The Federal Supreme Court has affirmed this view [reference], even if in the case before it the existence and the extent of the consent was not in issue, but whether it was void on the ground of illegality or contrary to *bonos mores*. These principles must be applied here. The Court of Appeal agrees [reference] . . . by requiring that a valid consent presupposes that the person who gives it knew the significance and the extent of the physical treatment by the doctor, at least in outline. No objections can therefore be raised against its legal conclusions.

As to (*b*): As the Reichsgericht [reference] and the Federal Supreme Court [references] have stated, the declared and not the subjective intention of the plaintiff counts. The Court of Appeal has found that the doctors administering the treatment assumed that the plaintiff had consented. However, according to the Court of Appeal they should have realized that real consent was lacking. They had therefore assumed negligently that consent had been given. This conclusion cannot be faulted in law. The court has thereby correctly made it clear that all the plaintiff's declarations, oral, tacit, or to be presumed, could not and should not have been regarded by the doctors

2. These statements do not suffice, however, to show that the first defendant has discharged the burden of proof incumbent upon him for exonerating himself. Instead, the undisputed pleadings themselves disclose that the first defendant's organization is to blame.

(*a*) According to the practice of the highest courts and to the dominant view in the literature, civil engineers undertaking construction work on public roads of cities must take into account the existence of subterranean service ducts and must exercise the utmost caution in the knowledge of the exceedingly great danger which can be caused if electricity, gas, water, or telephone lines are damaged. The life and health of human beings is imperilled if such works are carried out inexpertly, especially through contact with power cables or the escape of gas. Moreover, the failure of the supply lines often causes considerable damage to industrial and commercial enterprises, to hospitals and others. Consequently, civil engineers whose work brings them into contact with supply lines, especially by the use of excavators and similar heavy gear, are under a particularly heavy duty to make enquiries and to take safety measures concerning any existing supply lines; a civil engineer is obliged to obtain the information within the limits of general technical experience which is necessary for the safe execution of the operations to be carried out [reference].

In this connection a civil engineer is bound, in particular, to acquaint himself adequately with the lay-out of the gas pipes as well as the other supply lines by inquiring at the place where the relevant reliable details are available.

Since supply lines are normally laid down and maintained without the collaboration of the communal building authority, it is not sufficient to make enquiries with the latter; instead, information must normally be obtained from the competent supplier of the services. In a number of cases evidence of this can be found, as is shown by the cable information leaflet of the electricity works of Koblenz . . . These instructions do not have the character of legal rules. They show, however, the extent of the duty to safeguard the public in general (§ 823 I BGB) incumbent upon civil engineers using excavators. If the necessary information cannot be obtained by inspecting the documents in the possession of the supplier of the service, the position of the supply lines must be ascertained by other means before the excavators begin their work . . .

In general, an inspection of these maps will provide the civil engineering enterprise with a sufficient amount of information concerning the position of the subterranean lines and individual connections with houses . . .

It must not be decided either whether their duty to obtain information, which the first defendant had assumed, additionally by contract [reference] is always incumbent upon the management *itself* of the civil engineering enterprise [references]. In the case of enterprises which are as big as the first defendant, this may be difficult, even if the manager of the branch in K should be regarded as its statutory representative. In any event, if the gathering of information is delegated to employees, the civil engineering enterprise must give clear, emphatic instructions to the local construction manager and to the supervising foreman when and how they must ascertain the position and extension of the supply lines, including the individual connections of houses on the basis of reliable documentation by the supply undertakings in question. In view of the particularly grave danger if gas, water, and power installations are damaged, the instructions must point out imperatively not to be satisfied with oral information of a general kind not containing specific figures—especially as to the depth at which the ducts are located—which is clearly not based on maps.

Such a duty to ascertain the location of the existing supply lines must be said to exist where the excavations involve the creation of a ditch to a depth of 0.60 metres, especially if it is to run under the pavement and thus in the neighbourhood of connections with houses; experience shows that the latter run at a lesser depth than the main ducts.

The duty to make enquiries existed even if information was supplied by . . . on the occasion of a previous examination. When as a result of the extension of the order for excavations—as it was in the present case—the danger is increased, the additional operation requires further information if on the previous occasion only oral information of a general kind was provided without precise details and also clearly without the assistance of maps or other papers. Moreover, the first defendant should have given general instructions to the two other defendants concerning the need for a renewed investigation if an additional order of this kind is received.

The defendant failed to give instructions dealing with the various aspects as was required here.

The first defendant would not be exonerated if, as he contends, the connection of the gas pipe with the house was located at a depth of 45 centimetres. It is not true that if a ditch is dug by an excavator to a depth of 60 centimetres, the possibility of hitting a gas pipe could be disregarded altogether . . . [references]. The first defendant should therefore have considered the possibility that gas pipes, particularly connections with houses, may be located at a depth much less than one metre.

(*b*) The failure to give the necessary instructions to the second and third defendants also constituted the cause of the damage which occurred . . .

Case 79

BUNDESGERICHTSHOF (SIXTH CIVIL DIVISION) 3 NOVEMBER 1964*
NJW 1965, 391

Reasons

. . .

II. The second appeal by the first defendant must succeed.

1. The legal position would be favourable to the plaintiffs (the dependants of O, who was killed), if they could rely on the liability under § 831 BGB. The District Court gave judgment against the first defendant on the basis of this provision. The Court of Appeal did not consider this aspect. In the light of the facts as found it is indeed not possible to hold the first defendant liable on the strength of § 831 BGB (in conjunction with § 844 BGB). It is true that the Reichsgericht has held occasionally that an employed driver continues to act 'in the execution of the function entrusted to him', if contrary to his instructions he gives a lift to outsiders in the course of a journey ordered by his employer [references]. In the opinion of this Division it cannot be stated generally, at least, that in such cases the employer is liable for the damage, unless he has been able to exonerate himself. In the present case, the first defendant had ordered the second defendant to *transport goods* and has expressly forbidden him to carry persons other than those connected with the business in his lorry. Having regard to the circumstances of the journey it was not reasonable either for O to assume, without making further enquiries, that the first defendant would agree to it that O would be carried in his lorry over a considerable distance at night. O entrusted himself exclusively to the second defendant, who was an acquaintance of his. In these circumstances the employer of the driver, and owner of the lorry, cannot be held liable for the personal safety of O. If the functions of the driver have been restricted by his employer, these restrictions are also effective in relation to such a user. Consequently a direct connection between the activity entrusted to the driver and the damage cannot be said to exist, even if the journey itself was not undertaken outside the scope of the employment [reference]. Even if in the absence of exoneration (§ 831 I first sentence BGB) the first defendant would be liable to a person in the street who had been injured owing to the negligence of the second defendant, irrespective of the fact that the latter had deviated from the timetable fixed by the office [reference], it does not follow that the first defendant is similarly liable to an unwanted passenger. His position is different; in so far as he is concerned, the employee entrusted with the execution of tasks allotted to him

* English version by Kurt Lipstein.

[*Verrichtungsgehilfe*] has exceeded his function, a fact which is relevant in excluding liability, seeing that the passenger's damage falls outside the operational risk attracting liability under § 831 BGB [reference]. Therefore claims by the dependants under §§ 831, 844 BGB are also excluded.

Case 80

BUNDESGERICHTSHOF (SIXTH CIVIL DIVISION) 11 DECEMBER 1956
NJW 1957, 499 = VersR 1957, 165

Reasons

According to § 17 I of the Rules for the Prevention of Accidents issued by the Bavarian Builders' Confederation in the wording of 1 July 1941, then in force, unauthorized persons were to be prohibited by notices from entering a building site. The District Court has found that this was done in the present case. Thereby the builders involved in the conversion of the house have complied with their duty to safeguard the public in general [*Verkehrssicherungspflicht*] in so far as third persons are concerned who were not employed on the building site. By means of the warning notices they indicated in a usual and generally comprehensible way that the parts of the building which were being converted were barred to 'unauthorized persons' in view of the danger connected with the building operations. The plaintiff, too, was to be regarded as an unauthorized person, although she came to speak to her husband who was employed on the site. This follows clearly from § 17 II of the Rules for the Prevention of Accidents according to which even insured persons are only permitted to visit building sites if this is necessary in the performance of tasks allotted to them.

No need existed according to § 17 I of the Rules for the Prevention of Accidents cited above to protect the building site against the entry of third parties otherwise than by the erection of warning notices. In particular it was unnecessary to specify particular rooms in the course of conversion or to indicate the particular dangers which threatened unauthorized visitors, for they came within the danger zone if they obeyed the general prohibition of entry. The plaintiff cannot therefore base her claim on § 70 of the Rules for the Prevention of Accidents which requires special safety measures for rooms with ceilings or floors which are not load-bearing; these provisions exist to protect persons who are endangered while entering the room with permission, i.e. primarily workers operating there. It is neither the purpose of the Rules for the Prevention of Accidents to protect unauthorized visitors against the many dangers lurking on a building site, nor can the owner or the builders employed there normally do so or be expected to do so. It is unnecessary to determine here whether stricter requirements exist in special circumstances, as for instance if children play frequently near a building site, for the plaintiff is an adult who could understand the meaning of the warning notices on the building site and who did so, as the Court of Appeal found, despite her simple-mindedness.

Case 81

BUNDESGERICHTSHOF (SECOND CIVIL DIVISION) 27 FEBRUARY 1952*
BGHZ 5, 321 = NJW 1952, 658 = VersR 1952, 166

In late November 1946 the plaintiff hurt his right hand and went as a private patient to Dr D, a senior doctor in the defendant hospital. A few days later the plaintiff became an in-patient in the defendant hospital in one of Dr D's private beds. On 9 December he there received a blood transfusion administered on Dr D's instructions by an assistant, Dr J. The donor of the blood was A, who had given blood at the defendant hospital on many previous occasions. In 1948 it was discovered that both A and the plaintiff were suffering from syphilis. A had first given blood at the defendant hospital in early August 1946. On that occasion, the only test administered to him was a Wassermann reaction test, which proved negative: there was no visual inspection or any other kind of examination. Between August 1946 and November 1947, A gave blood on twenty-five occasions for twenty-four different recipients, twenty of these occasions being at the defendant hospital. During this period he had no further tests. Only in the middle of January 1948 did a different doctor cause blood tests to be made on A. In both cases the Wassermann test proved to be extremely positive, a fact which A communicated to Dr J on 14 February. Dr D then examined the plaintiff and ascertained that he too had syphilis.

The plaintiff asserts that his infection resulted from the blood transfusion effected in the defendant hospital on 9 December 1946. He asserts that the defendant was at fault in failing to follow the requirements of the Blood Donor Ordinance of 5 March 1940 [reference omitted] and in particular in failing to give A the prescribed tests. The serious result of this was that the disease was diagnosed in the plaintiff only at a very late stage, when the prospect of cure was much poorer. The plaintiff sought a decree that the defendant hospital, Dr D, and Dr J were liable to him as common debtors in respect of all the resulting harm, as well as for damages for pain and suffering.

The Landgericht held that the claim was well-founded. The Oberlandesgericht dismissed the defendant hospital's appeal by separate decree. The hospital's further appeal is now dismissed for the following

* English version by Tony Weir.

Reasons

1. The appellant's first objection is to the Court of Appeal's finding that it was under any contractual obligation to the plaintiff regarding the provision of medical treatment. When the plaintiff became one of Dr D's private out-patients in late November 1946, a contract for medical treatment was formed between him and Dr D, a contract which was not terminated on 7 December 1946 when the plaintiff was admitted to the defendant hospital. It followed, according to the appellant, that the contract whereby he was admitted to the hospital did not extend to any medical treatment, the plaintiff's medical treatment being a matter for Dr D alone, but simply called for the provision of bed and board.

We cannot agree with the appellant.

(*a*) We need not decide whether the contract which the plaintiff made with the hospital on 7 December 1946 was what is called a 'total hospital contract' which involves the provision of medical treatment, for even if one accepts the appellant's assertions that in a case like the present the contract formed between doctor and patient before the patient is admitted to hospital is not affected by his admission to the hospital, it does not at all follow that the contract by which the patient later enters the hospital covers only bed and board. On the contrary, the in-patient who has made an independent contract with his doctor for medical treatment and then makes a further contract with a hospital for nursing care expects the hospital to provide him with all necessary medical treatment which is not provided by the doctor himself but is usually provided by hospital staff using hospital equipment. This would include administering drugs, giving injections, taking X-rays, and much else. The hospital itself evidently has the same expectation, since it makes the equipment available and not only performs these tasks but charges for them as well. Into this category fall blood transfusions such as the present plaintiff had, for the apparatus required for blood transfusion is normally found only in hospitals and the transfusion itself is normally performed by someone other than the principal doctor. There is therefore no doubt that Dr J, the doctor who carried out the blood transfusion in this case, was acting as the defendant hospital's contractual assistant. The defendant is therefore responsible under §§ 276, 278 BGB for any mistakes which Dr J made in carrying out the transfusion.

The Court of Appeal held that in performing the transfusion, the assistant, Dr J, failed to follow the safety procedures laid down in the Decree of 5 March 1940. Like any other doctor in charge of a blood transfusion, Dr J should have been aware not only of how the transfusion should be effected from the technical point of view but also what steps were required for it to be effected with the greatest safety. The Court of Appeal also held that in failing to follow the prescribed tests and other safety measures, Dr J was at fault and that this fault was a cause of the plaintiff's being infected with syphilis. The Court of Appeal was therefore correct to hold that the defendant's liability for faulty breach of its contractual duty to afford the plaintiff proper medical treatment was established.

(b) But the defendant's contractual liability can be based also on the fact that it failed to take care to bring to the notice of the doctors in the hospital the provisions regarding the safety rules to be followed in giving blood transfusion. The failure was due to Dr L, who from 1940 to 1946 was the doctor in charge of the hospital and one of its statutory representatives under § 31 BGB. In this capacity he became aware of the Decree of 5 March 1940 regarding the precautions to be taken in blood transfusions, but he culpably failed to pass this information, which was important to all doctors, to the other departments in the hospital. It was his duty to do this even though his position vis-à-vis the other senior doctors was not that of a director. Since the hospital's contractual duty remained unfulfilled by reason of a faulty omission on the part of one of its statutory representatives, the hospital is liable (RG DR 1941, 1937).

The Court of Appeal was thus correct to hold that the failure to inform the doctors in the surgical and gynaecological departments of the hospital of the provisions of the Circular of 5 March 1940 was a cause of A's being used as a blood donor for the plaintiff and also of the plaintiff's being infected by A's blood. This was not, however, as suggested by the Court of Appeal and the appellant, a so-called organizational fault but rather a breach of the defendant hospital's own duty through a member of its executive committee, the said Dr L. This failure is equally a basis for the defendant's liability.

2. But Dr L's negligence renders the defendant hospital liable to the plaintiff not only in contract but also, and more extensively, in tort. The Court of Appeal established that it was because the doctors in the surgical department of the defendant hospital were not informed of the security precautions required by the Minister in cases of blood donors that Dr D and Dr J were insufficiently apprised of these security measures and therefore failed to check that the prescribed tests had been administered to A. It was therefore a cause of syphilis being transferred from A to the plaintiff. It follows that the defendant is liable for the harm suffered by the plaintiff under §§ 31, 843 I, 847 I BGB as well.

Case 82

BUNDESGERICHTSHOF (SEVENTH CIVIL DIVISION) 30 JUNE 1966*
BGHZ 45, 311 = NJW 1966, 1807 = JZ 1966, 645 = VersR 1966, 959

Defendants G and T are partners in civil law (*Gesellschafter einer Gesellschaft des bürgerlichen Rechts*) in a motor vehicle garage. The plaintiff had an accident as a result of defects in repairs to his automobile that had been made at the garage. He brought a claim for damages against the defendants. The Oberlandesgericht adjudged G and T liable to pay for only half the damages in view of the contributory fault of the plaintiff. On the revision brought by the defendants, the liability of defendant G for damages was denied.

The court holds that defendant T, who actually repaired the vehicle, is liable under § 823 BGB for defects in the repairs which caused the brake fluid to leak out and the brakes to fail at the time of the accident. The court also holds that defendant G is not liable under § 823 BGB since he did not repair the vehicle, and that he cannot be held liable under § 31 BGB since that section does not apply to his partnership.

Accordingly, [with respect to G] only liability under § 831 BGB comes into consideration. The appellate court held that such liability existed. Nevertheless, the factual basis for imposing it is absent.

One assigned a task within the meaning of § 831 BGB is simply one who is dependent upon the instructions of the person assigning it. The right to give instructions need not extend to details. It is sufficient that the worker's activity may be limited at any time or withdrawn or circumscribed as to time and circumstances. These requirements are not met with regard to the work which defendant T did on the plaintiff's automobile. Dependence in the sense just described cannot be deduced from the fact that both defendants bound themselves to a partnership contract in which each had the obligation to conduct repairs pursuant to the purpose of the partnership. In such cases, as a rule, two prerequisites for imposing liability under § 831 BGB are absent, namely the possibilities of limiting the task by use of an authority to give instructions and of ordering that the task not be performed. [Citations omitted.]

* This, and the following four translated *extracts*, are taken from von Mehren and Gordley's *The Civil Law System* (2nd edn.) and are reproduced here with the authors' kind permission.

Case 83

BUNDESGERICHTSHOF (SIXTH CIVIL DIVISION) 18 FEBRUARY 1969
VersR 1969, 518

A bus owned by the defendant pulled up to a bus-stop without coming close enough to the kerb to enable passengers to step directly from the kerb into the bus. Plaintiff, a sixty-year-old woman, stepped into the street to board the bus and slipped on a patch of ice. As the plaintiff was regaining her feet, the conductor of the bus gave the signal to start the vehicle, the driver set the bus in motion, and the bus struck the plaintiff. She sued the bus company under § 831 BGB for her injuries. The court held that 'in view of the great danger of accidents [during departures at icy bus-stops], and especially of accidents caused by inopportunely placing the bus in motion, it is not enough that, as witness J testified, the driver received instructions during his training as to the need for appropriate conduct'. The defendant had to supervise the driver and conductor on a continuing basis.

The appellate court correctly reasoned that, from a practical and legal standpoint, the measures for training and supervision demonstrated by the first defendant are insufficient to guarantee sufficiently the proper conduct of bus personnel and, in particular, their conduct in stopping and supervising departures from the bus at icy bus-stops. In view of the great danger of accidents during these departures, and especially of accidents caused by inopportunely placing the bus in motion, it is not enough that, as witness J testified, the driver received instructions during his training as to the need for appropriate conduct. Unless the driver and the conductor were given continual oral reminders, it was at least required that a written notice be kept before them in an accessible place advising them of precisely these dangers and the means for avoiding them. The first defendant, who has the burden of exoneration, has presented no evidence on such measures, and has also failed to prove that the personnel were instructed concerning the special dangers of icy bus-stops.

The appellate court also justifiably criticized the proof offered on the grounds that the inspections, which were only described in the testimony of witness J, should have been directed to the proper starting of the vehicle and to the attention required at icy bus-stops. Finally, the appellate court correctly reproached the defendant for not having been able to present any evidence of both occasional unanticipated inspections and occasional covert inspections (the latter being normally impossible when personnel known to the driver are used). In view of the special responsibility of public commercial enterprises, such inspections by reliable employees cannot be neglected.

Case 84

BUNDESGERICHTSHOF (SIXTH CIVIL DIVISION) 25 JANUARY 1966
VersR 1966, 364

[The first defendant was employed by the second defendant as a butcher boy and driver. While delivering a load of meat and sausage, the first defendant negligently collided with a vehicle parked by the kerb. The owner of the vehicle brought suit, and the second defendant, arguing that his employee had been adequately selected and supervised pursuant to § 831 BGB, prevailed in the lower courts. The plaintiff's *Revision* was unsuccessful.]

Notwithstanding the opinion of the *Revision*, the conclusion of the appellate court that the second defendant adequately supervised his driver can be supported without proof being made of unexpected or covert inspections. The judge of the facts was aware that particular observation of a driver's conduct is frequently necessary in order to satisfy the strict requirements governing supervision of one employed as a driver. He nevertheless held that the question whether such additional measures were taken no longer arises when the employer and his representative—here the second defendant's brother—participate in the trips so frequently that their presence is no longer perceived as an inspection and the vehicle driver accordingly drives so as to show his customary behaviour. If no objection arises to his behaviour after this sort of observation, then no further information should be expected from following the driver occasionally in another vehicle, a procedure in which the possibilities for observation are limited. This point of view is in agreement with the decisions of this Senate which have repeatedly emphasized that, although supervision must be strict, it must still be conducted in accordance with what the individual case requires and that no simple catalogue of required measures can be given. Thus, in a very similar case, it was held to be sufficient that the driver had proved his ability by making trips for about two years without any accidents and that the owner or his representative had provided continual supervision by frequently accompanying the driver on these trips. Under such circumstances, it would be exaggerated to require particular inspections in addition, such as those conducted for the most part in large businesses and in any event in public enterprises. It has also been decided that a well-founded belief in the ability of the driver, based on careful selection and supervision, could possibly make exceptional and unexpected inspections unnecessary. The same must apply to the training, instructions, and supervision of speed which the *Revision* asserts is lacking here. If a need for such measures does not arise when the owner and his representative accompany the driver on trips that are no longer perceived as supervision, then the question whether such additional measures were taken cannot be decisive. The plaintiff has not cast doubt on the fact that the first defendant was actually supervised in the manner alleged without any objections arising to his conduct. Accordingly, there are no legal grounds for objecting to the conclusion of the appellate court that the second defendant has fulfilled his duty of oversight.

Case 85

BUNDESGERICHTSHOF (THIRD CIVIL DIVISION) 25 OCTOBER 1951
BGHZ 4, 1 = NJW 1952, 418 = VersR 1952, 166

The defendant is the owner of an estate. His manager, K, assigned B, a six-teen-year-old agricultural labourer employed on the estate, to transport gasoline. B used a cross-bred horse. The horse bolted and seriously injured the plaintiff.

The defendant contests the plaintiff's claim on the grounds that the horse had been gentle, B had been a careful driver who was accustomed to driving horses, and the horse had pulled a milk wagon every day and was accus-tomed to jolting vehicles.

The Landgericht denied recovery, the Oberlandesgericht reversed, and the *Revision* results in reversal and remand.

Reasons

The appellate court held that the proof of exoneration required of the defen-dant had not been made because the defendant had paid no attention to the transport of the gasoline. It held that the defendant has violated the duty of supervision incumbent on him because he himself did not take care that his manager gave adequate instructions to the boy for the particular trip with the cross-bred horse, which was not without its dangers. The appellate court thought it had been demonstrated that manager K told B that he should drive carefully on this trip; however, it is thought that this instruction was not sufficient and that, in view of B's youth, the disused street, and the use of a cross-bred horse (which, as a matter of common experience, is difficult to ride), K ought to have given more particularized instructions.

In so far as the appellate court derived the liability of the defendant from the fact that he did not personally concern himself with the trip, its opinion cannot be accepted.

In the present case, the manager hired B and supervised his work. He intervened as an intermediate party between B, the worker, and the defen-dant, the proprietor. According to the decisions of the Reichsgericht, the proprietor of a large enterprise is not to be expected to select and supervise the entire personnel. If a number of persons are employed in a manner such that one is subordinate to another, then the employer's proof of care extends only to the selection and supervision of the higher employee chosen by him, the manager.

This easier proof for purposes of § 831 BGB is to be permitted, in the Reichsgericht's view, on the basis of what is equitable and consonant with the section's purpose. It is certainly true that the employer must institute a system of controls sufficient to guarantee reasonable supervision and conduct of business. Even if only the manager were required to exercise immediate personal oversight of the agricultural labourer, it remains the task of the estate owner to attend to the general regulation of the supervision which provides the guarantee for orderly conduct of the enterprise. If there is a defect in the organizational structure, then the employer is liable for negligence in providing general oversight as required by § 823 I BGB.

Some writers have opposed the Reichsgericht's basic principles for the liability of large enterprises. They feel that this easier burden of proof is inequitable and inconsistent with the Code. If an intermediary between the employer and the worker is employed, then it should not be sufficient for the employer to prove that he carefully selected and supervised this intermediary, but he should also prove that the intermediary acted carefully in the selection of subordinate employees. If the employer had appointed a legal representative (*Vertreter*) to make this selection, he would answer for the fault of this representative as though it were his own (§ 278 BGB); otherwise, moreover, one would reach the inequitable result that an entrepreneur with large capital resources could escape liability even though the higher employees were not in a position to pay large damages.

Nevertheless, these objections do not provide a basis upon which the Reichsgericht can discharge its task of deciding cases. Prevailing law distinguishes as to whether the basis for liability for the conduct of employees rests on contractual or on non-contractual principles. If the provisions of § 278 BGB, which pertain to contractual liability, are applicable in a variety of cases involving relationships similar to contracts, such as the public law responsibility for the safekeeping of objects (*Verwahrungsverhältnis*), it is still not possible to expand these provisions to cover the case of tortious liability for which the code has expressly provided the particular dispositions of § 831 BGB. This provision makes it possible for the employer to make a proof of exoneration, and also provides that his liability does not rest on whether his employee has committed a fault. This general principle of § 831 BGB is not dependent on the size of the enterprise. There were large enterprises in existence at the time the Civil Code was enacted, and it was impossible then, in these enterprises, for the selection and oversight of every single employee to be left to the owner or a legal representative (*gesetzlicher Vertreter*) chosen pursuant to § 831 BGB. If establishment of a particular rule governing such enterprises had been desired and, in particular, if the expansion of the legal concept contained in § 278 BGB to include delictual liability had been desired, it would have been expressed in the Code.

Accordingly, in the present case, the principal matter to be demonstrated was whether the defendant used the requisite care in the selection and supervision of his manager K. . . .

Case 86

BUNDESGERICHTSHOF (SIXTH CIVIL DIVISION) 11 NOVEMBER 1956
MDR 1957, 214 (with approving note by Josef Esser)

In February 1952, as the plaintiff was leaving a house on S Street in Hamburg where he had been visiting his sister, he slipped on a walk which bordered the house and was separated from the sidewalk of S Street by strips of greenery, and suffered a compound fracture of the upper thigh.

He contends that his fall was caused by a slippery patch of snow. He claims the defendant is liable for his accident as owner of the house and sidewalk because of a violation of a duty to sand the walk.

The Landgericht rejected the claim. The appellate court held the claim for damages to be legally grounded. It granted the demand for a fixed sum of money and periodic payments, provided the claim was not paid by a publicly owned insurer. It also entered a judgment subject to the same reservation, declaring the defendant to be liable.

The *Revision* is without success.

Reasons

The appellate court found that it had been demonstrated that the walk had a slippery patch of snow and had not been sanded and that the defendant was under a duty to pay compensation under § 823 BGB because, as owner of the walk which was used by the general public and, in particular, by the residents of neighbouring houses and the customers of three stores located in them, the defendant had a duty to clean and sand the sidewalk according to the provisions of the Hamburg Road Cleaning Ordinance of 10 January, 1940 [reference] and regulations made under this Act on the same day [reference]; and that the responsibility falls on the defendant for not having taken care to fulfil the duty to sand the walk in the required way.

[The court rejects the defendant's contention that sanding the sidewalk was not required on the day of the accident under the Act and regulations just cited, because weather conditions that day would have made the sanding of the walk useless.]

Moreover, the conclusion that the defendant committed a fault stands up against legal scrutiny.

In this regard, the appellate court maintained that the assignment of the duty to clean and sand the walk to a married couple, W, living on the ground floor by a contract of lease had legal effect only in relations between the defendant and these lessees. The prerequisites for finding that the married couple W had a duty with public law effects to clean and sand the sidewalk under the provisions of the Road Cleaning Ordinance are absent. Therefore, as what is involved is a violation of a duty required of the defendant itself, and as the plaintiff's claim for compensation is based on § 831 BGB, the case does not turn on proof of exoneration under § 831 BGB. The defendant, indeed, is a large enterprise, which must employ the help of others to fulfil its duty to sand. The appellate court did not reject that the defendant had entrusted the lessees of the buildings with this task. But it correctly took as its premise that the defendant must organize the carrying out of the duty to sand so as to guarantee that it will be reliably performed.

The appellate court found that the defendant apparently placed the duty to clean and sand walks on the inhabitants of the ground floors of its buildings by simply inserting such provisions in form contracts of lease, and that the married couple W became obligated in this way without regard to whether the wife W, after the death of her husband and after attaining the age of seventy-six, still possessed the physical ability to do the cleaning. The appellate court took the view that the method used by the defendant for the employment of persons for sanding the walk does not satisfy the requirements imposed on him.

The *Revision* contests this view as too extensive, arguing that the customary practice in Germany is for the lessee living on the ground floor to be responsible for the performance of the duty to clean and sand the sidewalks, and that an objection to this practice should not be made if the owner of the building demonstrates that the lessee adequately performs this duty by himself or with the help of a third person.

The question can be left open whether placing the duty to clean and sand the sidewalks on the person living on the ground floor by a form contract of lease is consistent with the content of the duty of care in selecting persons to sand the sidewalks, a duty which concerns the building owner in the area of its responsibility under § 823 BGB to no less extent than the duty of care which falls on the employer under § 831 BGB concerning the selection of an employee. The owner of the building has at the least a duty of supervision which is sufficiently broad for it to be required to ensure that the lessee actually performs—or has another perform—the obligations assigned the lessee in a regular manner. The duty of general supervision rests on one who makes a careful selection of persons to whom he, as the one responsible for fulfilling a general duty, assigns the actual performance of this duty. This applies particularly and in very large measure when regard to the competence and reliability of these persons was not a decisive factor at the time they were employed.

According to the findings of the appellate court as to the factual situation, the defendant failed to provide the supervision required of it. The measures taken by the defendant consisted of the employment of a building manager for three different blocks of housing, located six to ten minutes apart and containing a total of thirty separate buildings. It need hardly be argued here that, as a general rule, it must be held insufficient for an enterprise leasing houses to employ only one man for a housing area of this size to supervise the performance of the duty to clean and sand walks by lessees. The manner in which Mrs W performed the duty assigned her of cleaning and sanding the walks had given cause for complaints before the day of the accident— that the place where the accident occurred was often not adequately sanded. The defendant could not have remained in ignorance of this if it had organized supervision in the manner required by the duty just described to provide oversight. As a result, the conclusion of the appellate court that the plaintiff's accident was caused by the neglect of the defendant must be accepted. The defendant is accordingly liable on the basis of §§ 831 and 823 BGB.

Case 87

BUNDESGERICHTSHOF (DECISION OF THE GREAT SENATE) 4 MARCH 1957*

BGHZ 24, 21 = NJW 1957, 785 = JZ 1957, 543 (see article by F. Wieacker in JZ 1957, 535 = VersR 1957, 288, 517, 783)

Reasons

1. The case submitted to the Great Senate for Civil Cases is based on the following facts:

The plaintiff took part in a family celebration and intended about 1.30 a.m. to return on the tramway run by the defendant enterprise from the 'Apotheke' stopping-place. When he tried to mount the forward platform of the tramcar he fell: he was run over by a car and his right foot so severely injured that his leg had to be amputated below the knee. The plaintiff made the defendant, the driver, and the conductor of the vehicle responsible for the damage and put forward the following grounds for his claim:

The fall occurred because the tramcar started too soon. The conductor gave the departure signal and the driver started although both could have seen that the plaintiff was still just about to mount the forward platform. He had stood in front of the door when it started and had already grasped both

---

* English version by F. H. Lawson and B. S. Markesinis.

the entrance handles. The driver did not stop immediately on getting the emergency signal from the conductor.

In his action the plaintiff demanded damages from the defendant, the driver, and the conductor of the tramcar.

The defendant, the driver, and the conductor admitted his claims in part . . . Otherwise they claimed that the action should be dismissed and urged that:

The conductor gave the signal to start and the driver set the tramcar in motion only after the invitation to enter had been given and no one else was prepared to enter. The plaintiff had been standing by a group of persons who had not intended to ride, but had then hurried after the moving tramcar and tried to jump on. When the emergency signal was given the driver stopped at once. The plaintiff had been drunk and had only himself to blame for the fall.

The Landgericht allowed the claim, reduced to one-half.

On appeal by the plaintiff and counter-appeal by the various defendants, the Oberlandesgericht dismissed the action against the driver and conductor and declared the defendant tramway company liable to pay compensation up to two-thirds.

On appeal the defendant company moved for a complete dismissal of the action.

2. It was disputed in the first place whether the defendant company also was liable under § 831 BGB for the damage caused by its employees. This question required examination because the plaintiff's claims were not completely supported by the *Reichshaftpflichtgesetz*, in particular in so far as he demanded damages for pain and suffering.

The Court of Appeal found that the defendant company was responsible under § 831 BGB for the damage to the plaintiff, because the driver, and perhaps also the conductor, had caused the physical injury unlawfully and because the defendant company had not produced the proof necessary for exonerating itself under § 831 I sentence 2, case 1 BGB from liability for its 'employees'. The Court of Appeal came to the conclusion that the way the fall occurred was not clear. It was possible that the plaintiff's allegations of fact were correct, but it was also possible that the accident happened in the way described by the defendant. In view of this negative result of the evidence, the Court of Appeal felt that the possibility could not be excluded that a causal connection did exist between a presumable failure of choice and supervision on the defendant company's part, and the occurrence of the damage (§ 831 sentence 2, case 2 BGB).

3. The Sixth Civil Senate had doubts whether to follow the Court of Appeal's findings of law. The doubts were directed above all against the

view that an 'employee' (for the purposes of § 831 BGB) engaged in tramway or railway traffic did damage unlawfully merely by causing physical injury. It is a matter for discussion whether the basis of the unlawfulness must be further gone into in order to show whether the conduct of the employees is objectively contrary to good traffic practice. For that purpose, reference is made to the traffic rules which regulate the conduct of participants in traffic in ever-greater detail. Recourse must also be had to the legal concept of social adequacy and to developments in modern criminal theory, more especially because according to this the concept of negligence includes essential requirements which relate to unlawfulness and not to fault. If a finding of unlawfulness in traffic accidents does not automatically follow from the resulting consequence but (is satisfied) only if a breach of the traffic regulations has occurred, then it seems probable, in view of the report laid before us, that the conception of the burden of proof hitherto followed in applying § 831 BGB can no longer be upheld. That must be true in particular of cases which resemble the one in question and are distinguished by the fact that, in view of the failure to clarify what happened on the occasion of the accident, no objectively irregular conduct on the part of the 'employees' can be established.

The Sixth Civil Senate attaches fundamental importance to the clarification of these questions of law. In accordance with § 137 GVG it submits them for decision to the Great Senate for Civil Cases and formulates them as follows:

Does a person employed in tramway or railway traffic do damage unlawfully to another within the meaning of § 831 I BGB merely by injuring his life, body, health, or property? Or is it a further condition of unlawfulness that the participant employed in the traffic conducted himself in an objectively irregular way? Is the employer who fails to exonerate himself from the charge of defective selection or supervision liable under § 831 BGB even if according to the evidence the possibility remains open that the 'employee' observed the objective duties of care and, in particular, the rules governing highway or rail traffic?

1. When § 831 BGB makes the employer's liability depend on whether his 'employee' did unlawful damage to another person in executing his task, this requirement connects it with the factual situations of the law of delict in which the unlawful acts involving a duty of compensation are described and delimited. Not every doing of damage produces liability, but only such as falls within a liability situation of the law of delict, and, therefore, is an 'unlawful act' in the sense of §§ 823 ff. BGB. Accordingly, for the purpose of traffic accidents as here in question, in the first place a reference is needed to § 823 BGB, especially § 823 I. Claims for damages are constantly recurring from injuries to life, body, health, or property in tramway and railway traffic. Now the wording of § 823 I BGB requires that the injury to the enu-

merated legal interest be unlawful, that is to say repugnant to the legal order. The legislator, however, when describing in legal terms the factual basis of illegality, indicates that he regards the breach of the legal interests listed in § 823 I BGB as normally unlawful. By adding 'unlawful', however, he indicates that the mere breach does not necessarily involve unlawfulness, but that unlawfulness can for special reasons not exist. It may be questionable whether that indication was needed. It is certainly useful in applying the law, by making judges attentive to the fact that any factual description of unlawful conduct is bound to be incomplete and that therefore they are under a duty to examine whether a finding of unlawfulness based on a fulfilment of the factual conditions must be withdrawn on special grounds. Further, the BGB does not provide an exhaustive formulation for defining when there is a legal justification. The initial provision about consent as a justification was struck out in the discussion of the draft because it was desired to leave to practice the task of marking out the limits of justification. Moreover, the jurists and judges have also developed slowly those principles to which they may have resort for the purposes of excluding unlawfulness, such as on the basis of *negotiorum gestio*, the protection of vested rights, or the balancing of interests. There is, therefore, no exhaustive legal catalogue of justifications, no *numerus clausus* which would set limits to legal development. Accordingly, the matter must be gone into now that the report of the Sixth Civil Senate has submitted for discussion the question whether, in the special field of tramway or railway traffic, conduct fulfilling on its face the factual condition of § 823 I BGB must no longer be adjudged unlawful if it was in harmony with the legal regulations laid down for the traffic.

The line of thought in that direction found in the report must in principle be approved. The draftsmen of the BGB may indeed not have recognized that these are matters for discussion which concern objective unlawfulness and not merely fault in the sense of personal blameworthiness. Only with the technical development of traffic and the increase in its dangers did modern mass traffic produce problems calling for regulatory legislation. The legislator was faced with the need to regulate by increasingly detailed provisions the duties of participants in traffic, so that the possibilities of danger should be reduced to a minimum. At the same time, the legal provisions dealing with liability for risks were developed in order to apportion with social fairness in their economic effects the dangers and risks rendered inevitable by modern traffic. In the process, it was more and more recognized that what was in question was not a liability for wrong but a duty on those in control of dangerous operations to assume responsibility for certain typical risks. With that legal development there is no longer any place in the law of delict for a doctrine that looks upon unavoidable injuries in tramway and railway traffic as unlawful injuries to persons or property and denies liability only for lack of fault. The legal order, in permitting dangerous traffic and prescribing in detail to its participants how to conduct themselves, declares that conduct conforming to those prescriptions is within the law. It is not right that conduct which takes full account of the orders and prohibitions of the traffic regulations should nevertheless be adjudged unlawful. The actual consequences do not afford sufficient ground for it, for, in deciding whether conduct is unlawful within the meaning of the BGB provisions about delicts, one cannot leave unconsidered the act that produced the consequences. The rule must therefore be laid down that orderly conduct of a participant in tramway or railway traffic conforming to traffic regulations does not produce unlawful damage.

Whether the result implies a special application of the legal idea of so-called social adequacy may be left unanswered. Since the question here is restricted to the field of traffic law, there is also no need to go into whether the same result could equally be obtained through reliance on modern criminal theory, which splits up the concept of negligence by treating the enquiry into the observance of objectively required care as appertaining to unlawfulness, and only the question whether the disapproved conduct should be imputed to *an individual doer* as an inquiry into fault. Doubt must in any case be expressed as to whether, if this complex concept of negligence in modern criminal theory were to be taken over into civil law, in the law of civil responsibility, also, under cover of a special enquiry into fault, a special standard of judgment should be imposed on the conduct of the doer of damage that took account of his personal characteristics. That might, indeed, appear to harmonize the legal concepts, but it would not allow for typical differences which arise from the specific characteristics and purposes of two different branches of the law. In particular, this view would not be in accord with the provisions of § 276 I 2 BGB as it has always been understood in applying the law.

2. The question submitted to the court now makes it necessary to enquire what are the consequences produced by the standpoint adopted for apportioning the burden of proof. Here it must be recalled that the legislator, by establishing a separate factual basis for delicts, intended to lighten the judges' task of examining whether a wrongful act exists or not. Unlike the cases where delict is governed by a general clause, leaving a wide scope for judicial interpretation (§§ 823–25 BGB), in describing casuistically the wrongs giving rise to liability, the legislator affords a solid basis for applying the law, by suggesting, at least provisionally, the criterion of unlawfulness. Thus, an injury to one of the legal interests especially named in § 823 I BGB to which the law affords a preferred protection, needs a special justification if it is not to be adjudged unlawful. That applies irrespective of whether the

act was done intentionally. This relation of rule and exception established as part of the system of our law of delict and upheld in its application has, in accord with the recognized principles of the law of evidence, the consequences that the proof of a justification is for the person who infringes a protected legal interest. In this respect, the justification afforded by conduct according to rules in tramway and railway traffic can claim no separate status.

This apportionment of the burden of proof in applying § 823 I BGB to traffic accidents means that the doer of damage can provide a basis for justification by proving that his conduct conformed to traffic rules. If the proof is supplied, proof of fault ceases to have any substance, because there is to start with no unlawful infliction of injury. If on the other hand the question whether his conduct in traffic was regular is not cleared up, one starts with an unlawful injurious act. The question of liability however is not yet decided; for § 823 I also requires the injurious act to have been intentional or careless. The injured party must therefore prove that the doer acted intentionally or negligently, in the meaning of § 276 I 2 BGB, that is to say omitted to take the care required in daily intercourse. For that enquiry also it will, of course, be essential to know whether the provisions of the traffic regulations have been observed. That the question of conduct according to the traffic rules can be significant for unlawfulness and fault is due to the shape and legal classification of the concept of negligence. For the practical application of the law it remains that the injured party must prove in full the conditions of a claim for compensation under § 823 I BGB and that accordingly—unless there is a prima-facie case—an insufficient elucidation of the facts is to his disadvantage.

The apportionment of the burden of proof in applying § 831 BGB is different. There the legislator consciously made the employer's liability depend only on the 'employee's' acting unlawfully and not also on his doing the damage intentionally or negligently. In so far therefore as concerns the 'employee's' conduct, only those principles governing the burden of proof apply that affect the sphere of unlawfulness. Thus, the injured party must prove that the 'employee' by an adequately causal act injured one of the legal interests protected in § 823 I. On the other hand, it is for the employer to prove that the 'employee's' conduct was regular, because it conformed to the legal rules of tramway or railway traffic. So far, doubt is to the disadvantage of the employer. On the other hand, if regular conduct of the 'employee' is proved, the conditions for a claim under § 831 BGB are unfulfilled, so that there is no longer any need to go into whether proof can be provided that there was no causal connection between the prima-facie presumption of faulty selection or supervision, and the damage. From that last-mentioned point of view the Reichsgericht had denied the employer's liability when the judge was convinced that even a carefully chosen and supervised 'employee' could not have acted differently in the given case. That the production of the exoneratory proof under § 831 I and II BGB makes it unnecessary to go into the question of unlawful injury is self-evident.

It is clear that as regards a traffic accident the cause of which remains obscure, the regulation of the burden of proof set out above makes it better for the injured party if the 'employee' and not the employer himself has caused the accident. In the latter case the employer's liability is as a rule excluded, because no fault can be established, whereas where it is caused by the employee, the employer is liable if he cannot exonerate himself from the charge of imperfect choice and supervision. This preferential treatment was clearly intended by the legislator, for there is here a certain allowance for the fact that otherwise the injured party's legal position is quite unfavourable because exoneration is possible and usually successful. It is precisely for that reason that it would be wrong in applying the law to do away with the part favourable to an injured party in the regulation of the BGB of delictual liability for 'employees'. If one observes that emphasis is there placed—even though incompletely—on responsibility for enterprise risks, it is not unfair to impose on the one in whose sphere of influence the risk originated the burden of proof about the way the damage occurred, which he is usually, though not always, in a better position to satisfy than the one to whom it occurred. Also so far as the provision of 'appliances and implements', which include the means of transport, is concerned, the law has for the same reason imposed on the employer within the framework of § 831 BGB an enhanced duty of elucidation and proof. If the evaluation of the employee's conduct is under discussion, attention must also be paid to the point of view that the employee—that is the meaning of the reversal of the burden of proof—must be considered to have been unfit for his task, until the employer proves that he showed the care described more fully in § 831 I 2 BGB.

Case 88

BUNDESARBEITSGERICHT 24 NOVEMBER 1987*
NJW 1988, 2816

Facts

The defendant was employed whilst a student as an occasional driver by the plaintiff's mini-cab firm. On September 20, 1980, around 10 p.m., he was driving a radio-controlled mini cab. At a road junction he failed to give way to other traffic as required and collided with another car. The plaintiff

---

* English version by Ms J. Shaw.

claimed damages in the amount of DM 8500 from the defendant in respect of the damage caused to the mini cab. He alleged that the defendant acted with gross negligence since, as a cab driver of relatively long standing, he was familiar with the junction; moreover, the visibility and weather conditions at the time of the accident were good.

The Arbeitsgericht (ABG) accepted the plaintiff's claim in part, awarding damages to the amount of DM 4250. It accepted that the defendant was negligent. However, since the accident occurred in the context of work which tends to be dangerous ('*gefahrgeneigte Arbeit*'), and since he was not guilty of gross negligence, the damages were reduced by 50 per cent. The Landesarbeitsgericht (LAG) allowed the appeal of the defendant, and held that the defendant should pay compensation for the loss up to the amount of DM 2000; the plaintiff was to be treated as if he had taken out comprehensive motor vehicle insurance with the insured's contribution towards the loss set at the first DM 2000. In his further appeal to the Bundesarbeitsgericht (BAG) the defendant argued that the damages should be further reduced to DM 1000. In an application made out of time, he applied for the claim to be rejected or, in the alternative, for it to be rejected in so far as it exceeded DM 1000. The defendant's appeal was rejected.

For the following

Reasons

B. The appeal fails on the substance. The defendant must pay damages in the amount of DM 2000 to the plaintiff.

I. As the LAG correctly asserted, the defendant is liable to the plaintiff in respect of the damage caused to his vehicle. There are two bases for this conclusion: positive breach of contract (§§ 280 and 286 BGB applied by analogy) and tort (breach of § 823 I BGB).

II. The reasoning of the LAG should also be followed in as much as it concluded that the defendant should be liable only in respect of part of the loss, as this occurred in the context of work that tends to be dangerous work and that consequently the defendant should be regarded as guilty of an ordinary negligence.

1. The LAG was correct to accept that when he was driving the radio controlled mini cab, the defendant was undertaking work that tends to be dangerous work. In reaching this conclusion, the LAG followed the established case law of the BAG in which the work of a driver of a motor vehicle is in normal circumstances regarded as tending to be dangerous, unless there are facts which justify making an exception [refs. omitted]. No such circumstances are apparent in this case.

2. Furthermore, there are no grounds in law for reversing the conclusion of the LAG that the defendant caused the accident negligently (§ 276 I BGB), although he was not guilty of gross negligence (§ 277 BGB). (Further discussion omitted in case report).

3. The LAG also states that in the context of conduct displaying such a degree of fault, the defendant has some proportionate responsibility for the damage caused to the plaintiff's vehicle. In reaching this conclusion it followed a consistent line of case law developed by the BAG which was itself based upon the decision of the *Großer Senat* of the BAG of 25 September 1957 (BAGE 5, 1; other refs. omitted). According to this line of case law, loss caused by the gross negligence of an employee in the context of work that tends to be dangerous will normally be borne by the employee alone. Loss caused by an employee in the context of work which tends to be dangerous and where the conduct of the employee reveals a 'normal' degree of fault (which could also be termed normal, slight or average negligence or average fault) rather than gross negligence, will normally be apportioned between the employer and the employee. In this context, all the circumstances of the case are to be taken into account, in particular the cause and extent of the loss, bearing in mind what might fairly and reasonably be expected of each of the parties. Where the fault of the employee is only slight (also termed '*leichteste Fahrlässigkeit*', very slight negligence) it is for the employer alone to bear such losses [references omitted]. This is the approach taken by this Chamber.

III. The liability of the employee is not ruled out simply because he did not act with gross negligence.

1. As the defendant points out, it is true that the 7th Chamber of the BAG in a judgment of 23 March 1983 (BAGE 42, 130 = NJW 1983, 1693) altered the existing case law principles governing the liability of employees in the context of work which tends to be dangerous. That Chamber resolved that the loss caused by an employee undertaking work that tends to be dangerous, who is not acting intentionally or with gross negligence, falls within the sphere of risk attributable to the employer's business and is therefore to be borne by the employer alone. In a further judgment of 21 October 1983 (BAGE 44, 170 = NJW 1984, 2458L) the 7th Chamber confirmed this view. This Chamber cannot follow this line of case law.

(*a*) The reasoning of the 7th Chamber was as follows [an English version of the decision can be found in the 2nd edition of this book, page 571]. The easing of the liability has, since the decision of the BAG of 28 April 1970 (AP § 611 BGB—*Haftung des Arbeitnehmers*—Nr. 55) been derived from the business risk which operates as an independent factor justifying the attribution of responsibility to the employer irrespective of fault where § 254 BGB can be applied by analogy. This excludes the possibility that the employee may be subject to fault-based liability in cases of less than grave fault. 'Less than grave fault', as defined by the *Großer Senat* in its decision of 25 September 1957 (BAGE 5, 1 = NJW 1958, 235), includes in conceptual terms not only the very slightest degrees of fault, but also average negligence. An assessment of the attribution of the business risk on a case-by-case basis, which was previously the approach taken in cases of normal negligence in accordance with the established case law of the BAG, no longer represents an appropriate resolution of the problems of employee liability because of the increased risks of liability associated with technological development. On the contrary, a comprehensive attribution of the business risk in cases which fall below the level of gross negligence can be justified by the argument that within the business it is division of labour by the employer which subjects the employee to certain work-specific risks, which the employer himself would be required to incur in the absence of such a division, and the employer can use his rights of ownership and power of management in order to determine how the work of the business is to be organised. The employer can reduce the specific business risks through appropriate technical and organisational measures and, where necessary, he can insure against loss. It is further relevant that the level of the loss incurred is decisively determined by the technical and organisational form of the business. In almost all sectors of the economy, technological developments have led to a reduction in the numbers of persons employed, which means that individual employees who use valuable machinery are subject to ever greater risks of liability. Since, on the other hand, such technical rationalisation is reducing the employer's expenditure on wages, it is right that the increased risk of loss should fall on him where the employee who has caused loss has acted neither intentionally nor with gross negligence. Finally, such a comprehensive attribution of risk accords better with the requirements of legal certainty and clarity than will a case-by-case evaluation of the risks.

(*b*) The exclusion of the liability of the employee in cases involving an average degree of negligence cannot be supported on the basis of these arguments under the current law.

(*aa*) The general attribution of risk, which according to the view of the 7th Chamber should in the future be made in place of the previous practice of assessing risk in each individual case, cannot be deduced from an application by analogy of § 254 BGB. This provision only justifies the judicial apportionment of the loss between the tortfeasor and the injured party in individual cases. This Chamber is adopting in this respect the unanimous criticism which the reasoning given by the 7th Chamber has encountered in the literature [references to literature omitted]. Furthermore, § 254 BGB represents an exception to the principle of full compensation (§ 249 BGB). Moreover, there is nothing in the legal principle set out in § 254 BGB which indicates that one should apply a degree of fault on the part of the defendant which differs from that prescribed in § 276 BGB.

(*bb*) The 7th Chamber was likewise in error when it held that 'less than grave fault' within the meaning of the decision of the *Großer Senat* of the BAG of 25 September 1957 [references omitted] should in conceptual terms be regarded as including also normal negligence. The *Großer Senat* in fact decided that an employee is not liable where his fault is 'not grave in the circumstances of the case.' It expressly avoided making use of the concepts of slight and gross negligence in order to set the division between liability and the exclusion of liability. In order 'to leave the maximum degree of discretion' for later decisions, it chose instead to use the 'indeterminate' term of 'less than grave fault' in order to describe the range of circumstances in which the employee is not liable [reference omitted]. The conclusion drawn by the 7th Chamber is therefore not justified. It is, moreover, one which the specialised Chambers of the BAG have declined to draw during the 25 years which followed the decision of the *Großer Senat* [references omitted].

(*cc*) The argument that a general attribution of risk leads to greater legal certainty and clarity does not justify the result reached by the 7th Chamber. Apart from the fact that the uncertainties of differentiation, which have so far been caused by the threefold division of negligence, could be reduced by one to the important distinction between gross and average negligence [references to literature omitted], the principle of legal certainty can make no greater claim in the present context than it can in the context of the direct application of § 254 BGB. In that context, also, the legislature has seen fit to subordinate this principle to that of an appropriate apportionment of loss.

(*dd*) No position needs to be taken in this case on the other arguments which the 7th Chamber puts forward to support its solution [references to literature omitted], namely that its approach could in an individual case lead to effective loss distribution within the business. However, these arguments do not justify making the employee liable only for harm caused intentionally or with gross negligence.

2. There is likewise no justification to be found in the law as it applies at present for making the employee liable only for intent or gross negligence.

(*a*) It is said in the literature that with regard to employees the legal system offers support only for the position which restricts liability to intention and gross negligence. This is said to be apparent from Art. 34, 2nd sentence of the Constitution and § 640 I RVO [references to literature omitted]. The parties to collective agreements likewise have chosen to draw this distinction wherever they have sought to restrict the liability of the employee [references to literature omitted]. The earlier case law has thus, it is said, proceeded on the basis of two concepts which do not exist within the legal order, namely the concepts of work which tends to be dangerous and average negligence [references to the literature omitted]. Finally, it is argued that in discussions around proposals for reform, support is likewise given to the restriction of the liability of employees to cases of intention and gross negligence.

(*b*) This view could only be supported if the [appropriate] pre-requisites existed for the judges to undertake a further development of the law which would go beyond the actual statutory text [references omitted]. Such a development would go beyond the point reached by the judgment of the *Großer Senat* of 25 September 1957 discussed above (BAGE 5, 1 = NJW 1958, 235) and the decisions of the individual specialised chambers of the BAG taken on a case by case basis the law concerning the liability of the employee towards his employer by altering the principles contained in §§ 276 and 249 BGB. These are changes which have been loyally followed elsewhere in legal practice for more than 20 years. It is possible that in this way customary law has evolved [reference omitted] although, arguably, it only allows complete exclusion of liability in cases of very slight negligence [reference omitted].

3. Such pre-requisites are not, however, present for a more extensive judicial development of the content of the law whereby an employee is only liable to his employer in respect of loss inflicted in the context of work that tends to be dangerous where he has acted intentionally or with gross negligence.

(*a*) The Federal Constitutional Court has always accepted the authority of the courts to develop the law [references omitted]. The case law which underlies the binding force of Art. 20 III of the Constitution is legitimate and justifies the bringing to light, and the implementation in individual decisions, of value judgments which are inherent within the constitutional order but which are not expressed or only incompletely expressed in the text of written laws, by means of an act of evaluatory recognition which also involves elements of intention. Of course, in that context the judge must avoid making arbitrary decisions; his decision must rest upon rational arguments. It must be possible to show without doubt that the written law is not fulfilling its function, which is that of resolving a legal problem appropriately. The judicial decision then closes the gap in the law according to the standards of practical reasons and the acknowledged general values of justice adhered to within society [references omitted]. A limitation placed by the judges upon the liability of the employee and restricting it to cases of intent and gross negligence, is not possible according to these principles. The situation lacks the necessary general legal conviction [references omitted]. Furthermore, such a judicial evaluation of the law would distance itself from the written law to an extent which exceeds what is permissible in the interests of doing justice in individual cases [reference omitted]. For the purposes of satisfying the established general principles of justice, it is necessary only that the liability of the employee should be qualified, by way of a departure from the principles contained in §§ 276 and 249 BGB. It is at present a very controversial question whether under the present law the employee is wholly exonerated from liability if he is guilty only of average negligence. Amongst those who deny this, it is furthermore a matter of controversy whether such a rule should be introduced by the legislature. The previous practice of reducing the employee's liability by reference to the circumstances of the individual case, which rests on the legal principles contained in § 254 BGB, represents the less serious departure from the written law.

(*b*) There is no general conviction within the law that the liability of the employee should be limited only to cases involving intent or gross negligence. This is demonstrated by how the discussions regarding legal policy and legal doctrine have developed since the decision of the *Großer Senat* of 25 January 1957 [reference omitted].

(*aa*) At the 45th *Deutscher Juristentag* in 1964 which discussed *inter alia* the issue of whether it is desirable that the liability of the employee towards the employer should be regulated in a manner which departs from the general rules of the BGB [particularly § 254 BGB], there was no consensus on whether the rules governing the liability of the employee to be adopted by the legislature should be based on the threefold division made in the case law or upon the general focus of liability upon average negligence, as the Rapporteur had proposed [reference omitted].

(*bb*) The preliminary draft of a second amending labour law drawn up by the Federal Ministry of Labour and Social Affairs in 1970 [reference omitted] provided that in cases where there was no gross negligence, the employee should not be liable to pay compensation [normally a contribution to his employer] where and to the extent that it would be inequitable to impose such an obligation upon him, having regard to the circumstances.

(*cc*) The draft published by the *Deutscher Gewerkschaftsbund* [the German T.U.C.; reference omitted] in 1977 proposed in contrast the restriction of the employee's liability to cases of intent and gross negligence.

(*dd*) Similar rules were proposed in the draft of a labour code—general law of the contract of employment—drawn up by the Labour Code Commission which was published by the Federal Minister for Labour and Social Affairs in September 1977.

The Federal Association of German Employers' Organisations spoke out against such a reformulation of the rules [reference omitted]. This body complained that the preventative functions of liability, namely to encourage careful conduct, to avoid damage to the employer and third parties, and to restrict the risks of accidents and injuries resulting from such damage would no longer be guaranteed; the creation of a sphere within which the employee would be wholly exonerated in respect of a negligence would encourage careless driving and the careless use of machines and other equipment; the economic consequences of such a rule would affect the quality of work and of products and would consequently affect the general interests of the consumer; the loss of the preventative functions of liability would also be contrary to the employee's own best interests, since it would lead to an increase in the risk of accidents where several workers were working together; finally the granting of such a privilege to the employee with regard to the question of negligence would have consequences also outside the world of work, and for example lead to a general impairment of traffic safety where the employee was using a vehicle on the highway.

(*ee*) It is not possible to derive from the collective agreements which have so far been introduced that the parties to these agreements, whose general views would be decisive *inter alia* for the purpose of determining whether a development of the law in the field of labour law was permissible [reference omitted], have over the years, come closer to adopting a position under which liability is limited to intent and gross negligence.

In the private sector, it appears that there are only a few liability-limiting clauses which provide that the employee is responsible only for intent and gross negligence [reference omitted].

Collective agreements applicable to the public sector likewise do not reveal a common intent on the part of the parties to these agreements to restrict the liability of employees in general to intent and gross negligence. With regard to the liability of employees for damage which they cause, they refer to the rules which currently apply to the public officials employed by the relevant employer (cf. e.g. § 14 BAT, § 11a MTB II, § 11a MTL II, § 9a BMT-GII). It follows from this that for these employees, when they act in the exercise of the sovereign power of the state, the restriction of liability and the right of indemnity to cases of intention and gross negligence (which is provided for in Art. 34 second sentence of the Constitution and in the law governing public officials: cf. § 46 I 2 and II BRRG and e.g. § 78 I 2 and II BBG) will apply. In other cases, i.e. those not involving the exercise of sovereign powers, employees are liable under the same conditions as private sector employees. For even public officials must make good loss which they wrongfully (i.e. including slight negligence) inflict upon their employers in breach of duty (cf. e.g. § 46 I 1 BRRG and § 78 I 1 BBG), and in this context it is common practice to apply by analogy to public officials the labour law principles which govern the liability of employees in the context of dangerous work [references omitted]. It would appear that there are exceptions to this general rule only in the *Länder* of Berlin, North Rhine-Westfalia and Schleswig-Holstein. In those parts of the country, the liability of public officials to their employers is subject to a general restriction, applicable in respect of actions undertaken in the exercise of both sovereign powers and also fiscal powers, limiting the liability of public officials to intentional and grossly negligent breaches of duty [references omitted]. If it is assumed that these provisions are valid, although they deviate from the norm laid down in § 46 I BRRG [references omitted], then in these *Länder* the amended adoption of these provisions into the relevant collective agreements means that the liability of the employee employed in the public service is subject to a general restriction limiting liability to responsibility for intention and gross negligence. This does not, in itself, however, provide evidence of a common conviction held by the parties to the collective agreements that the liability of employees should in general be restricted in this way. Rather, the provisions governing the public service referred to create a legal situation which would have corresponded since 1 January 1982 to the provisions of the State Liability Act of 26 June 1981 (BGBl. I, 553) if the latter had not been declared invalid by the Federal Constitutional Court [reference omitted]. § 27 of this Act sought to restrict the liability of public officials even beyond the realm of sovereign powers to cases of intention and gross negligence. However, this was only intended to further the conventional purpose of the limitation upon the liability of public officials, namely the strengthening of the power of decision-making willingness of public officials to take responsibility and to eliminate the distinction between private law and sovereign activities which had previously been considered to be inappropriate [reference omitted]. This provision contained no indication of how the liability of employees should, in general, be formulated. This applies likewise to the regulations framed on the basis of the *Staatshaftungsgesetz* in Berlin and North Rhine-Westfalia as well as the older rules of Schleswig-Holstein. It is also not possible to attribute to the collective provisions, which are in force in these *Länder* by virtue of the reference to country-wide collective agreements governing the public service, any more extensive meaning.

(*ff*) The question of whether an employee should be wholly exonerated from responsibility for damage which he has caused neither intentionally nor through gross negligence remained controversial even after the two 1977 draft laws cited above and in particular following the decision of the 7th Chamber of the BAG of 23 March 1983 (BAGE 42, 130 = NJW 1983, 1693). This dispute concerned not only whether it was the case under the current law that the employee is wholly exonerated from responsibility in the case of average negligence, but also whether it would be desirable to have a statutory rule to this effect from the point of view of legal policy.

One section of the literature regards the exclusion of liability in a case involving average negligence as [already being] either the present rule or, at least, the desirable rule [references omitted], and in that context Kothe goes so far as to state that the liability of the employee for gross negligence is excluded and in this context refers to the assessments contained in §§ 553 and 723 RVO which in his view should be applied also to the liability of the employee towards the employer (cf. Kothe, *AuR* 1983, 229 *et seq.*).

The contrary position not only sees the restriction of the liability of the employee to gross negligence and intention as an infringement of the present law, but also, in part, regards such a rule as undesirable from the point of view of legal policy [references omitted] or, at least, doubts whether the legal development undertaken by the 7th Chamber was permissible [references omitted].

At the 56th *Deutscher Juristentag* in 1986 in Berlin, the question remained unresolved. It is true that there was a majority in favour of an immediate statutory rule being introduced [reference omitted] and in that context there was support for an exclusion of the liability of the employee for slightly negligent breaches of duty [reference omitted]. However, the *Deutscher Juristentag* did not see this rule as representing the present law, for it rejected by a majority the further evolution of the rules on liability by the judiciary [reference omitted].

(*c*) This court cannot, therefore, establish any general conviction that the employee should in every case involving less than gross negligence be wholly [and automatically] exonerated from economic loss incurred by the employer. There is unanimity only in cases of average negligence that contrary to the rules in §§ 276 I and 249 BGB the liability of the employee should not encompass the whole loss.

4. If, therefore, the constitutional prerequisites are not present for the development of the law on the liability of employees to make them liable only for intentional and grossly negligent conduct, it follows that the view put

forward by the 7th Chamber in its decisions of 23 March and 21 October 1983 (BAGE 42, 130 = NJW 1983, 1693; BAGE 44, 170 = NZA 1984, 82 = NJW 1984, 2488L) lacks any legal foundation. Were this court to carry forward this line of case law, this would amount to a substantive determination of the content of the principle of the 'social state' which may be demanded in policy discussions but which does not correspond to general convictions as to the positive law. For this reason therefore, if none other, it is a determination which is not appropriate for judicial formulation but which represents a task for the formal legislature [reference omitted].

Since there is, however, a unanimous view that the liability of the employee should be limited in accordance with the principles pertaining prior to the decision of the 7th Chamber of the BAG as expressed in a consistent line of case law since the decision of the *Großer Senat* of the BAG of 25 September 1957 [reference omitted] and even prior to that date [reference omitted], this court will follow these case law principles. At least the court sees no justification emerging from the case to be decided here involving the liability of an employee in the context of work tending to be dangerous and an average degree of negligence, for departing from these principles. As formulated in the recent case law of the BAG, these principles focus on a distribution of the loss in a case such as the present one which is based on all the circumstances and, by means of an application by analogy of § 254 BGB, takes into account, on the part of the employee, the degree of his fault and, on the part of the employer, the business risk [reference omitted]. This later concept should be understood in this context as a criterion for assessing responsibility and not in its otherwise understood meaning as the risk of the employer that he may have to pay the employees' salary in the event that the performance of their obligations becomes impossible [references omitted]. In so doing, this concept takes account of the value judgments contained in Arts. 1 I, 2 I and 28 I of the Constitution which do not find expression in the rigid principles set out in §§ 276 and 249 BGB. By making reference to the legal principles encapsulated in § 254 BGB which, with the exception of the special rules governing strict liability, represents the only departure within the law of damages from the governing principle that the loss should be compensated in full or not at all, the principles contained in the case law fall closely in line with the case expressly dealt with in the BGB and thus observe the constitutional law principle that judicial legal development should only depart from the written text of the law to the extent necessary to do justice in a particular case [reference omitted].

IV.–V. [Sections IV and V deal, *inter alia*, with the ability of the Chamber to reach a decision which differs from that of the 7th Chamber without referring the issue to the *Großer Senat*.]

VI. As in the decisions of the 7th Chamber of 23 March 1983 and 21 October 1983 there is no question here of considering whether the restriction upon the liability of the employee should be extended beyond the category of work tending to be dangerous, as set out in the decision of the *Großer Senat* of 25 September 1957 [reference omitted] and as so far respected by the case law, to cover also other business activities [reference omitted].

VII. There are no grounds in law to query the decision of the LAG regarding the quantum of the claim in this appeal.

1. The LAG accepted that the loss resulting from the accident should be borne equally by the two parties. Factors favouring the defendant were that he was a student and relatively young, that he had a small income, that he only drove at weekends, and that a sudden error on the part of such an employee can often lead to devastating consequences. Factors favouring the plaintiff were that the damaged motor vehicle was the basis for his economic existence. There was no question of imposing too great an economic burden upon the plaintiff in the respect of his small business. It should also be taken into account that the plaintiff had renounced his claim to a considerable portion of his claim for damages, including the loss of earnings and the costs of the expert report. However the LAG reduced the damages awarded by the ArbG to DM 2000 because, having regard to the fact that the vehicle involved in the accident was worth DM 10,500 at the time of the accident, the plaintiff must be treated as if he had concluded comprehensive motor vehicle insurance with the insured paying the first DM 2000 of the claim. In that context, it was to be assumed that the defendant had the average earnings of a driver. The fact that the defendant was only an occasional driver could not be taken into account, because the plaintiff could not be expected to adjust the comprehensive motor vehicle insurance in each case to the specific nature of the particular employment relationship of the driver.

2. The court has examined and affirmed these conclusions.

(*a*) The arguments which led the LAG to the conclusion that the parties were in principle equally responsible for the loss are not flawed in law. The attribution of responsibility for loss within the framework of § 254 BGB is first and foremost the task of the judge of fact. The Court of Appeal may only examine whether the judges of fact have properly assembled all the documentation, have evaluated this documentation in the context of the evaluation of the case, and have not infringed the principles of logic or precedent [references omitted]. This applies also where, within the framework of the equalization of the loss within a business, it is the fault of the employee which must be set against the business risk of the employer by analogy with § 254 BGB. If this restricted measure of review is used, there is no cause for objecting to the conclusion reached by the LAG which weighed up the fault of the defendant, the business risk of the plaintiff, and the economic and personal circumstances of the parties, and concluded that the parties were each responsible for half of the loss. It is apparent from these arguments that the LAG has taken into account the circumstances of the infliction of the loss and the consequences of the loss which are decisive for such an evaluation [reference omitted].

(b) The LAG has also not made an error in concluding that the defendant should make good the plaintiff's loss to the amount of DM 2000, which represents the equivalent of the insured's contribution under a comprehensive motor vehicle insurance policy. The defendant cannot claim a further reduction in his liability. The court has shown (cf. above VII 2a) that in the case of loss which was caused by an employee in the context of work tending to be dangerous, but where he acted neither intentionally nor with gross negligence, the result of the assessment of all the circumstances may be that the employer can claim compensation in the amount of the loss which would not be covered by the insurer if he were comprehensively insured. This court adopts this assessment likewise as the basis for this dispute. The LAG put forward the view that with regard to what was then the value of the vehicle involved in the accident that the plaintiff could and should have bought comprehensive motor vehicle insurance with the highest possible level of contribution, namely DM 2000, and that the remaining risk in the amount of DM 2000 is reasonably borne by the defendant having regard to the earnings of a driver. This approach is not flawed in law. Consequently, the application by the defendant to have his liability reduced to DM 1000 should not, as appears from the above considerations, succeed.

2. § 278 BGB (OR § 831 BGB)

Case 89

REICHSGERICHT (SIXTH CIVIL DIVISION) 7 DECEMBER 1911*
RGZ 78, 239 = JW 1912, 191

Reasons

According to the findings of the Court of Appeal the plaintiff, after making several purchases in the defendant company's department store, went to the linoleum department to buy linoleum floor-cover. She mentioned this to W, the sales assistant who served there, and looked through the patterns which he displayed for her to make a choice. W, in order to pull out the roll she

---

* English version by F. H. Lawson and B. S. Markesinis.

pointed to, put two others aside. They fell, hit the plaintiff and her child, and struck both of them to the floor. The purchase of the linoleum was not completed because, in the plaintiff's words, she became seriously disturbed by the fall.

The Court of Appeal rightly attributed the plaintiff's accident to W's fault, on the ground that he had put the rolls, which were not stable enough because of their relatively small bulk, insecurely on one side, instead of furnishing them with lateral protection on leaning them against the wall, and this even though he could have foreseen that the plaintiff, as usually happens with the buying public, would approach the place where the goods she had asked to be displayed were stored. The Court of Appeal's view is comprised in the simple conclusion that the rolls would not have fallen if W had placed them carefully and regularly on one side.

The Court of Appeal's opinion that the defendant company is liable for W's fault under § 278 BGB cannot, in spite of the appellant's contention, be rightly objected to; and it conforms to the case-law of this Senate. W was acting for the defendant company (§ 164 BGB, § 54 HGB) when he entered into negotiation with the plaintiff. The plaintiff had asked for a piece of linoleum to be laid out for inspection and purchase. W had acceded to her request in order to make a sale. The proposal and its acceptance had for their purpose the conclusion of a sale, and therefore the production of a legal transaction. That was no mere factual proceeding, a mere act of courtesy, but a legal relationship came into existence between the parties in preparation for a purchase; it bore a character similar to a contract and produced legal obligations in so far as both seller and prospective buyer came under a duty to observe the necessary care for the health and property of the other party in displaying and inspecting the goods.

The judgments of this Senate have already proceeded on similar grounds, and it has been recognized in several decisions of the Reichsgericht that duties of care for the life and property of the other party can arise from bilateral or unilateral obligations, which have nothing to do with the legal nature of the relation in a narrower sense, but nevertheless follow from its factual character.

The defendant company made use of W's services for the fulfilment of the aforesaid obligation to the prospective purchaser, and is therefore answerable for his fault. This is in line with the thought expressed in § 278 BGB, that whoever himself owes a performance that he must carry out with the required amount of care must, when he makes use of an employee, answer for his careful performance, and that accordingly the other person to whom the performance is due must not be put in a worse position because he does not do it himself but commits it to an employee. It would be contrary to the general feeling of justice if in cases where the person in charge of the business of displaying or laying out goods for exhibition, sampling, trial, or the like carelessly injures a prospective purchaser, the proprietor of the business—with whom the prospector wished to make a purchase—should be answerable only under § 831 BGB and not unconditionally, so that the injured person should, if the proprietor succeeds in exonerating himself, be referred to the usually impecunious employee.

There is no need to go here into the legally questionable view of the Court of Appeal that the mere entry into a department store of a prospective purchaser or even a visitor without any intention of buying creates a contractual relation between him and the proprietor, including the widely discussed duties of care . . .

Case 90

BUNDESGERICHTSHOF (EIGHTH CIVIL DIVISION) 28 JANUARY 1976*
BGHZ 66, 51 = NJW 1976, 712 = JZ 1976, 776 with approving note by K. F. Kreuzer =
VersR 1976, 589

The plaintiff, who at the time of the accident was fourteen years of age, went with her mother to a branch of the defendant's, a small self-service store. Whilst her mother, after selecting her goods, stood at the till, the plaintiff went round to the packing counter to help her mother pack the goods. In doing so she fell to the floor and suffered an injury which necessitated lengthy treatment. Alleging that she had slipped on a vegetable leaf, she sued the defendant for breach of his duty to provide safe access. The Court of Appeal, having dismissed as time-barred the claim for damages for pain and suffering, the parties are now in dispute only on the question whether the defendant is obliged to compensate the plaintiff for her economic loss as well as prospective damage.

The Landgericht rejected the claim as time-barred. The Court of Appeal granted it—after deducting one-fourth for contributory fault. The defendant's further appeal was unsuccessful for these

Reasons

I. The Court of Appeal found as proved that the plaintiff slipped on a vegetable leaf lying on the floor near the packing counter and suffered injuries which necessitated the expenditure in question and may possibly lead to future loss. These findings disclose no legal error; they are in fact undisputed on appeal.

II. According to the Court of Appeal's opinion the defendant had not furnished the proof incumbent on him that he had taken all necessary care for

---

* English version by F. H. Lawson and B. S. Markesinis.

the safety of movement in his store and that the accident could only be attributed to the fact that another customer had shortly before let a vegetable leaf fall to the floor. These findings also cannot be faulted legally. They conform to the settled case-law of the BGH (NJW 1962, 31; cf. also RGZ 78, 239) both on the duty of a shopkeeper to ensure safety of movement and on the reversal of the burden of proof required by § 282 BGB in cases of claims for damages based on *culpa in contrahendo*. This point also is not contested on appeal.

III. The defendant therefore is liable—so continued the Court of Appeal—after taking the contributory fault of the plaintiff into account, for three-quarters of the existing and prospective loss, and that not only in delict, but also for fault in concluding contract, since in opening the self-service store he infringed the contractual duty of protection and care which he had undertaken to the plaintiff. Moreover, the plaintiff also has a claim for damages under a contract with protective effects towards a third party because her mother was during the accident preparing to contract with the defendant and the plaintiff was being included as an assistant within the scope of that contract-like obligation. For claims, however, arising from fault in concluding a contract the limitation period is thirty years, so that the claim was brought in good time.

IV. These explanations stand up to examination—at least in result. Admittedly, the main line of the Court of Appeal's reasoning, that the defendant is directly liable to the plaintiff for fault in concluding the contract, irrespective of whether a contract with protective effects towards a third party needs to be brought into the picture, gives rise to doubts. Liability for *culpa in contrahendo*, which in cases like the present one is more favourable to a plaintiff than the general liability in delict for breach of the duty to provide safe access—because of the increased liability for employees (§ 278 BGB in contrast to § 831 BGB), the longer limitation period (§ 195 BGB in contrast to § 852 BGB), and the reversal of the burden of proof (§ 282 BGB)—rests on a legal obligation created by way of supplement to the written law. It arises from the process of bargaining for a contract and is largely independent of the actual conclusion or efficacy of a contract (BGHZ 6, 330, 333). The liability for a breach of the duties of protection and care arising from this obligation finds, in cases of the present kind, its justification in the fact that the injured party entered the other party's sphere of influence for the purpose of negotiating for a contract and can therefore rely on an enhanced carefulness in the other party to the negotiation (cf. also BGH NJW 1960, 720). This is borne out exactly by the present case in which the mother entered the sales department of the defendant for the purpose of making a purchase and in doing so had to subject herself to a risk involved in the increased congestion, especially near the till, in a self-service store. It is, however, always a presupposition of liability for *culpa in contrahendo* in this type of contract of sale that the injured party enters the sales department with the purpose of contracting or of entering into 'business contacts'—and therefore at least as a possible customer, though perhaps without a fixed intention to purchase (cf. BGH NJW 1962, 31). It need not be decided whether it is enough, in view of the peculiarities of sale in a self-service store, for a customer (when entering the sales department) to have intended at first only to have a look at the objects offered and be possibly stimulated to buy or only to make a preliminary comparison of prices with those in competing enterprises. In any case there is insufficient justification for a contractual liability for *culpa in contrahendo* stretching beyond liability for delict when the person entering the store never intended to buy, perhaps because—leaving aside the shop-lifter mentioned by the Court of Appeal—he is sheltering from a shower or using the store as a way through to another street or even only to meet other persons. The line may be difficult to draw in particular cases, above all because it depends on the difficult proof of unexpressed intention. In the present case, however, it is beyond dispute that the plaintiff from the start did not intend to make a contract herself but only to accompany her mother and help her in buying. A direct application of liability for fault in concluding a contract with the defendant is therefore excluded.

V. Nevertheless, the appellate judgment is proved right in result, because it is supported by supplementary considerations.

1. If the plaintiff's mother had been injured in the same way as her daughter, there would have been no objection to making the defendant liable for *culpa in contrahendo*—as is also clearly stated in the appeal. In that case nothing need be said about the question, disputed in academic circles, whether in a self-service store the display of the goods constitutes an offer and the contract of sale is concluded by the buyer's accepting it in presenting the selected goods at the till—thus reserving a final decision until that moment—or whether the display of the goods constitutes only an invitation to make offers, which the customer for his part makes by showing them to the cashier and the latter accepts by registering it on behalf of the self-service store. In any case, the general run of the reasons for the judgment, even though it contained no express statement by the Court of Appeal, makes it obvious that at the moment of the accident the goods intended for the purchase had already been finally chosen and a legal obligation already existed between the defendant and the plaintiff's mother justifying liability for *culpa in contrahendo*.

2. It is on the legal obligation that the plaintiff can rely to justify her contractual claim for damages. It accords with the long-standing case-law of this Senate in particular that in special circumstances even bystanders who do not themselves participate in a contract are included in the protection afforded by it, with the consequence that although they have no claim to have the primary contractual duty performed, they are entitled to the protection and care offered by the contract and can make good in their own name claims for damages arising from the breach of those subsidiary duties ... It is not necessary to consider here the theoretical question whether such a contract with protective effects toward third parties, on which the courts have proceeded hitherto, is derived from the supplementary interpretation of a contract incomplete to that extent (§§ 133, 157 BGB), or whether, as is increasingly accepted in the literature, direct quasi-contractual claims arise on grounds independent of the hypothetical intention of the parties, perhaps from customary law, or on the basis of legal developments by the courts. In any case, according to both views it is essential that the contract, according to its sense of purpose and the requirements of good faith, demands an inclusion of third parties in its sphere of protection; and that one party to the contract can in honesty—and in a manner discernible by the other party—expect that the care and protection owed to it will be equally extended to a third person. There is no good reason to exclude sales in general from this legally possible configuration as this is shown in particular by sales in shops to which buyers, in certain circumstances, must enter the sphere of influence of the seller. And that is also the view of the Sixth Senate in BGHZ 51, 91, 96.

3. Admittedly the inclusion of third persons in the sphere of protection of a contract—if the contract between contractual and delictual liability established by the legislator is not to be destroyed or blurred—needs to be confined to narrowly defined cases. Whether the mere fact that the customer makes use of a third person in initiating and concluding a purchase in a self-service store is enough for the protected effect to be accepted as possible may be left undecided; for in the present case it must be added that the plaintiff's mother was responsible for her daughter 'for better or worse' (BGHZ 51, 91, 96) and therefore—and this should be known to the defendant also—for that reason alone it could reasonably be inferred that the daughter accompanying her should enjoy the same protection as herself. In such a close family relationship the courts have always seen themselves justified in extending contractual protection.

4. That in the present case the sale was not concluded at the moment of the accident is, in the result, unimportant. If one looks upon the duty of protection and care as the determining element of the legal obligation based on

negotiating for a contract, and if one considers that the other party owes this duty of care both before and after the conclusion of the contract, the inclusion of third persons (who are equally worthy of protection) in the obligation follows. Moreover, there would be no rational ground for making the contractual liability depend on the chance of whether the negotiations had already led to a contract when the damage occurred; that is impressively shown by the present case, where the 'sale negotiations' had, in essence, been completed and the conclusion of the contract—possibly subject to a delay on the mother's part in completing it at the till, and for which the plaintiff's mother was not responsible—was in any case imminent. The appellant's contention that a cumulation of liability for *culpa in contrahendo* and inclusion of a third party in the protective effect of a contract would lead to an unforeseeable widening of the risk on a seller, is directed in principle against justification of both institutions in general. The danger of a flood of litigation, which cannot be dismissed out of hand, has, as has already been explained, long been taken into account by the courts, which have imposed strict requirements on the inclusion of third parties in the protective sphere of a contract. As regards to merely precontractual relations some reservation may be indicated. But in any case with so narrow a limitation there is no objection to an extension of protection if—as here—the person causing the damage could not reasonably have opposed any desire expressed by the mother, when negotiating for a contract, to have from the start the same protection expressly given to the child who was subsequently injured herself. Finally, in so far as the appellant contends that the long limitation period—combined with the reversal of the burden of proof—would intolerably worsen the evidentiary position of anyone sued for damages in such situations, the remedy must be found in laches (*Verwirkung*) of the existence of which there is no indication in this case.

Case 91

BUNDESGERICHTSHOF (THIRD CIVIL DIVISION) 10 MAY 1951*
BGHZ 2, 94 = NJW 1951, 596

The plaintiff was leaving the hospital where his wife was a private patient when he fell and suffered concussion, a fractured skull, and a cerebral haemorrhage. He alleged that the accident was due to the dangerous condition of the main entrance of the hospital, and claimed damages from the defendant. So far as his action was based on breach of contract it was dismissed at all levels of jurisdiction.

* English version by Tony Weir.

Reasons

The Court of Appeal held that the defendant was not liable on its contract with the plaintiff for the hospitalization of the plaintiff's wife. It accepted that under a contract of *lease* the tenant's family have a contractual claim against the landlord if there is a defect in the leased dwelling or its approaches which is attributable to him and they suffer harm thereby; and it agreed that the hospitalization contract is like a lease in certain respects; it found, however, that the lease features of a hospital contract are really very subsidiary: the patient has no claim to any particular form, and the primacy of the medical treatment reduces the significance of the premises as compared with a contract of lease. Therefore no contractual liability of the defendant arose under § 278 BGB.

In contesting these views, the appellant emphasizes the fact that he himself made the contract whereby his wife was taken in by the defendant as a private patient. The contract bound him to pay the hospital bill and bound the defendant not only to care for his wife (§ 328 BGB), but also, as a subsidiary duty, to enable him to visit his wife in safety. Given that he was a principal contracting party, it is irrelevant, says the plaintiff, whether, had he not been, the defendant would be liable to him under § 328 BGB in the way the landlord is liable to the tenant's family.

Contrary to the appellant's view, the contractual liability of the defendant for the accident which the plaintiff suffered as he was leaving the hospital by the front steps cannot depend on whether it was the plaintiff himself or his wife who entered into the hospitalization contract. It is true that a contract is formed when a private patient is taken into a hospital, even a hospital run by a public body (RGZ 64, 231; 83, 72; 111, 263; see also RGZ 108, 87), and that the plaintiff as husband acquired contractual rights against the defendant (RGZ 64, 233); yet it is not from the formation of the contract but from its content that a duty to take care of the plaintiff's safety must arise. If in addition to the primary obligation towards the patient to give him medical treatment, the terms of the contract include an obligation towards certain third parties, the hospital would be contractually liable to those third parties regardless of whether they had participated in the formation of the contract or not.

The hospitalization contract is doubtless a contract of services (*Dienstvertrag*) (RG JW 1938, 1246 [other references omitted]), whereby the patient is to be provided with bed and board as well as with medical treatment and care. The medical treatment is, however, the essential and critical element, the bed and board being by contrast rather subsidiary (see RGZ 112, 60 [other references omitted]). There is thus no occasion to infer any subsidiary *contractual duty* to ensure that the patient's husband be safe in visiting the hospital. But the result would be just the same even if one held, in view of the purposes of the hospitalization contract, that there was an independent contract for lodging and meals collateral to the main contract for medical services; the result would be the same, too, if a separate contract with different terms were made with a doctor (RG JW 1936, 3182 no. 6), for example, if the patient were taken into the hospital on the referral of the doctor treating her so that the treatment could be continued there. For even if there were a separate contract with the hospital for lodging and meals, the plaintiff as husband would have no contractual claim to safe access to his sick wife, despite the lease features of the contract. It is true that under the law of lease the tenant's family have the same rights against the landlord regarding the safety of the premises as the tenant himself (RGZ 91, 21, 24; 102, 232; 152, 177; 169, 87 [other reference omitted]). In accordance with the purpose of the contract, rights are granted under § 328 BGB to those who belong to the tenant's household, members of the family and domestic help; but no such rights are granted to guests: the precondition is living together in the rented premises. The tenant intends (and his intention, though inexplicit, is perceptible by the landlord) to have the lease include the members of his family and respect their needs; to persons outside the home, who stand in no particular relationship to the leased premises, this does not apply. The recognition of the tenant's implicit contractual purpose to put his family in the optimum legal position may have led to giving a child a direct claim for proper medical treatment when the treatment is arranged by its statutory representative (RGZ 152, 175), but even so it is only the child being treated who has a direct claim for the contractual performance arising out of the contract. When the husband takes his wife to hospital, he admittedly has a contractual claim that she be properly treated, but apart from that he is in no special relationship with the hospital and has no contractual claim for care towards his own person; and therefore cannot demand safe access to his wife in the hospital on the basis of the hospitalization contract. We need not decide whether it would make any difference if the husband, with the consent of the hospital management, had stayed in the hospital, even overnight, in order to be near his wife. On the facts, the plaintiff had no claim against the defendant for breach of a contractual duty of care.

Case 92

OBERLANDESGERICHT DÜSSELDORF, 3 OCTOBER 1974*
NJW 1975, 596 = VersR 1975, 863

The plaintiff's son was stabbed in a brawl and was taken to the defendant's hospital where the chief surgeon saw to the stab wound in the skin and

* English version by Tony Weir.

stomach-lining. The youth died. At the post-mortem it transpired that there were other wounds which had not been cared for, in the rear stomach-lining, in the upper and lower intestine, and in the left kidney. The plaintiff asserted that the chief surgeon had caused his son's death by failure to attend to these wounds, and claimed damages for loss of support.

The Landgericht rejected the claim. Before the Oberlandesgericht the plaintiff sought to answer the defendant's proof of exculpation under § 831 BGB, first by asserting that the defendant was also to blame in failing to provide an assistant surgeon for the operation, and then by arguing that the defendant was personally liable in contract and must answer for the fault of the chief surgeon as its agent for performance. The plaintiff's appeal was dismissed.

Reasons

The plaintiff has no claim for damages against the defendant. There can be no claims under §§ 242, 276 BGB for breach of contractual duty since there was no contract between the parties. The hospitalization contract with the defendant under which the plaintiff's son received medical treatment and care in the hospital was made not with the plaintiff but with the local General Health Insurance Scheme (AOK). It is true that the AOK did not actually refer the plaintiff's son to the hospital—this was an emergency case—but the contract was formed later when AOK agreed to pay the bill. It is not argued that any contractual negotiations took place between the parties, and it is clear that there were none.

Nor did this contract have any protective effect for the plaintiff. Such protective effect only applies to the insured and not to his dependants (RG JW 1937, 926; BGHZ 2, 94). Normally, the protective effect of a contract is limited to those persons who, by their connection with the creditor, come into contact with the debtor's performance, and whose safety is, to the debtor's knowledge, as important to the creditor as his own. This requirement is normally met only when the creditor has a joint responsibility for the protection and care of the third party (BGHZ 51, 91, 96; BGHZ 56, 269; BGH NJW 1959, 1976; 1970, 38). This is not the case with the plaintiff here. The decision of the Bundesgerichtshof to which the plaintiff refers (NJW 1959, 1676) is of no assistance to her, for in that case the third party was one of the plaintiff's employees, that is, a person who came into contact with the debtor's performance through the creditor and to whom the creditor owed a duty of care and protection. These preconditions are not satisfied here: the defendant's performance did not affect the plaintiff and AOK is not bound to afford her care and protection. Nor can it be said that the plaintiff was 'close to the performance' (*Leistungsnähe*). The performance which was owed by the defendant, namely medical care and attention in its hospital, did not affect the plaintiff. She was not the patient. Furthermore, the plaintiff in this case was in no relationship to the creditor AOK. She cannot acquire a claim against the defendant by founding it on her relationship with the third party, her son (under § 328 BGB), or on *his* duties towards her . . .

Case 93

BUNDESGERICHTSHOF (SEVENTH CIVIL DIVISION) 7 NOVEMBER 1960*
BGHZ 33, 247 = NJW 1961, 211 = JZ 1961, 169
(with approving article by W. Lorenz)

On 11 April 1953 two adjoining ferro-concrete plates became loose from the 16–18 m high roof of the steelworks at W belonging to the Siemens-Martin-Stahlwerk and fell on two persons at work in the works, namely the works engineer S and the steel-worker L. S died at once, leaving a widow and two children. L was severely injured.

The roof had been erected by the defendant company between October 1952 and March 1953. In making use of the old roof construction, ferro-concrete plates developed by the defendant company were substituted for the former concrete layers (which formed the ceiling).

The plaintiff association claims to be recouped for the payments made as an accident insurer to the surviving relatives of the works engineer S and to L.

It bases its claim on delict and on a 'positive breach of contract' (*positive Vertragsverletzung*) (§§ 328, 618 BGB), in each case in combination with § 1542 RVO (right of subrogation).

The defendant company denies that it did an unsatisfactory job in performing the steelworks contract. It pleads in addition that the steelworks were jointly at fault in defectively altering the roof. This share of the fault must be imputed to the plaintiff. The defendant company also pleads that the claim is time-barred.

The Landgericht dismissed the claim. On appeal, the Oberlandesgericht found the claim for payment justified in principle and granted the declarations applied for.

The defendant company's appeal led to the decision being quashed and the case being sent back for reconsideration for the following

Reasons

1. (*a*) The Court of Appeal left open the question whether the claim in delict of the injured parties (and therefore of the plaintiff) was time-barred. It granted them a direct claim against the defendant company on a 'positive breach of contract' under §§ 328, 618 I and III, 844 BGB. The contract between the defendant company and the steelworks included a subsidiary

* English version by F. H. Lawson and B. S. Markesinis.

duty on the defendant company to see that no damage should occur to the other party in doing the job. That obligation bound the defendant company under § 618 I BGB to the customer's work-force also; they had acquired direct claims for damages through the breach of the obligation.

(b) That is in conformity with the opinion developed in the case-law of the Reichsgericht and the Bundesgerichtshof. According to it the basis of this liability is a contract for the benefit of third parties in the sense that in its protection are included the persons to whom the promisee on his part owes essential duties of care and protection.

(c) The Court of Appeal was not in error in including those injured in the accident within the circle of those so benefited. That circle must of course be limited and easily ascertainable. But it was so here. Both the victims belonged to the work-force and were employees who were regularly active in the shop roofed by the defendant company. It was a numerically limited and spatially confined group to which the employer owed a special duty of care in fitting out the workshop. It was only that circle that the Court of Appeal included in the protection afforded by the construction contract, not, as is said in the appeal, the several thousand employees of the steelworks' work-force.

2. Nor was the Court of Appeal in error in affirming the transmission of the claims of the injured persons to the plaintiff under § 1542 RVO. That paragraph is, as the Senate has already decided (BGHZ 26, 365), applicable also to claims for contractual damages.

3. The Court of Appeal properly held that the defendant company contributed by its fault to the accident and was therefore bound to make good the damage on the ground of a 'positive breach of contract' [point discussed but not reported].

4. It left open the question whether the steelworks contributed at all by their fault to the accident, because in its opinion this was irrelevant.

That was rightly attacked in the appeal.

The question whether in such a case the injured third party must have imputed to him under § 254 BGB a contributory fault of the other party to the contract with the person causing the damage has been answered in the affirmative by the Reichsgericht and the Bundesgerichtshof only where that party is the statutory representative or the employee of the injured party (BGHZ 9, 316; 24, 325; LM No. 2 to § 254 BGB) that 'inclusion of the plaintiff in the contractual protection' implies that 'he must along with the widening of his legal protection, take into account the legal disadvantages bound up with it' points in this direction and shows also that the solution found here conforms to equity.

It follows that the judgment under attack, in so far as it disregards any contributory fault of the steelworks, cannot be upheld.

5. It could of course stand if the plaintiff's claim could also be supported in delict, for to that extent the contributory fault of the steelworks must not affect the liability of the defendant company.

The Court of Appeal—consistently with its standpoint—did not examine that question. In particular, it had left open the question whether this claim was time-barred. For want of the necessary findings, the Senate is itself not in a position to arrive at a decision.

The judgment under attack must therefore be set aside and the matter referred back to the Court of Appeal.

The view is taken further in the legal literature that the person who owes compensation may quite generally, even when the other party to the contract—as here—is not the statutory representative or the employee of the injured third party, plead against the latter under § 254 BGB the contributory fault of that party to the contract.

That view must—contrary to the Court of Appeal's opinion—be accepted. As in every contract for the benefit of third parties, so also in a contract of the kind in question, the protected third party derives his rights against the doer of the damage only from the contractual relations between the immediate parties. That follows already from the legal principle underlying § 334 BGB, according to which defences under the contract available to the promisor can also be pleaded against the third party. The words in the decision of the Bundesgerichtshof in LM 2 of § 254 BGB(E) that 'the inclusion of the plaintiff in the contractual protection' implies that 'he must along with the widening of his legal protection take into account the legal disadvantages bound up with it' points in this direction and shows also that the solution found here conforms to equity.

It follows that the judgment under attack, in so far as it disregards any contributory fault of the steelworks, cannot be upheld.

6. It could of course stand if the plaintiff's claim could also be supported in delict, for to that extent the contributory fault of the steelworks might not affect the liability of the defendant company.

The Court of Appeal—consistently with its standpoint—did not examine that question. In particular it had left open the question whether this claim was time-barred. For want of the necessary findings, the Senate is itself not in a position to arrive at a decision.

The judgment under attack must therefore be set aside and the matter referred back to the Court of Appeal.

Case 94

REICHSGERICHT (SIXTH CIVIL DIVISION) 10 FEBRUARY 1930*
RGZ 127, 218 = JW 1930, 1720 (with approving note by A. Elster)

The plaintiff acted from the middle of April until the end of June 1926 as daily help to the widow M. On 10 and 11 August 1926 she was helping Frau M to move to a new dwelling; as from 15 August she had accepted a new post as a maidservant. Frau M had employed the defendant firm to move the gas meter in the bathroom of her new dwelling. At the end of July the firm instructed their leading fitter B to do the job. On 11 August the plaintiff noticed a smell of gas in the dwelling, as she had done the day before. To discover the place of the leak she climbed a ladder in the bathroom and lit the gas burner with a match. The leaking gas was set alight and the plaintiff suffered appreciable damage to the upper part of her body. The gas escape was due to the looseness of an overflow screw on the meter. The screw had been installed by B. The Court of Appeal found that he had been grossly negligent in the unworkmanlike execution of the job.

The plaintiff first sued the widow M for damages in preliminary proceedings. At that stage the present defendant firm appeared as 'co-defendant' with Frau M. The action was dismissed on the ground that in any case the plaintiff was predominantly to blame (§ 254 BGB).

The plaintiff now sued the firm B & R and also B as co-defendants for damages and an annuity, and for a declaration of liability for further damage.

The Landgericht found the claim against both defendants justified as to two-thirds. The Oberlandesgericht reduced the award to one-half.

The appeal of the firm B & R (hereinafter called the defendant) was unsuccessful, apart from a determination of the duration of the annuity.

Reasons

The essential grounds on which the Court of Appeal based its judgment were the following. The defendants were strictly liable without exoneration for damage caused by B under the contract made with Frau M. That contract bound the defendants to take the care normally required in carrying out the job; moreover, in performing that duty they made use of their employee B and must therefore take responsibility for him under § 278 BGB. Not only was Frau M entitled as a contracting party to have that care taken, and to be compensated for the damage caused by the neglect of it, but the plaintiff was also entitled in so far as the contract must be taken to have been a contract for the benefit of third parties.

* English version by F. H. Lawson and B. S. Markesinis.

STRICTER FORMS OF LIABILITY

Whether a contract was intended to bring § 328 I BGB into operation, so that the third party should acquire directly a right to claim the promised performance must, under § 328 II BGB and in the absence of any special provision, be decided on the facts of each case, with particular reference to what can be recognized by both parties to have been the purpose of the contract.

The contractual purpose here signifies the objective means of determining the terms of the contract so that an agreement must be taken as covered by the contractual intention which the contracting parties could have arrived at if they had faced up to the elaboration of the details according to the purpose of the contract. Whether the extent of their agreement had actually been realized was beside the point. The application of these principles led to the conclusion that there was here a contract for the benefit of third parties. When a contract is made for the execution of a job in a customer's dwelling the danger is involved for anyone using it, the customer must be assumed to have intended—and this intention is capable of being observed by the contractor—that the interest of relatives living with him would be respected and that they should, for this purpose, have the same rights as he himself has to be compensated for damage done to them through the performance of the job. For without such an extension of the contractual duties, injured dependants would be limited to non-contractual claims. Such a different treatment of the customer and his dependants would offend against a sound instinct for justice and be out of accord with the contractual intent of the customer who, as the contractor must have been aware, would not wish to place his dependants in a worse position than himself as regards claims for compensation.

The position of the customer's domestic servants is the same. Here, too, the intention—capable of being recognized by the contractor—must be implied that he will respect the interest of the domestic staff, who must work on the premises where the contractor does the job and would have a claim to a safe system of work against the customer (§ 618 BGB). Where the customer contracts for a performance of a dangerous character, the contractor must know that he intends the performance to be carried out so as not to cause damage either to himself or to the members of his family or domestic staff, and that he is to stand in no better position than those belonging to his immediate household.

Now the plaintiff was indeed not a domestic servant but only a daily help, and therefore, was not a member of the domestic community. But, when making the contract, the head of the household must have intended—and this intention must have been understood by the contractor—to ensure that, over and above the circle of family dependants and domestic staff, all those persons to whom a master owes a duty of protection shall enjoy the special protection of a personal claim to have care taken of them under § 618 BGB. The daily help belongs to that class. This interpretation, however, must be subject to the limitation that only such persons must be regarded as benefiting from § 618 BGB as stand towards their employer in a relationship of some duration from which arises at least a moral duty on the employer to increase his protection. For a master must not be taken to intend to contract for the benefit of persons who serve only occasionally and temporarily on his premises and with whom he does not form any close attachment, such as arises from a longer use of their services and a more frequent contact, and even the creation of personal relations. The plaintiff stood in no passing relation to Frau M for she was in regular service with her for about a quarter of a year and was also, as is stated more fully, in a long-standing relationship with her.

But even if that no longer applied to 11 August 1926—so says the appellate decision—a contract for the benefit of third parties would exist as regards the plaintiff. For during the removal and the putting in order of the new dwelling, the dangers involved in the furnishing were so much greater than in ordinary housekeeping that the occupier must be taken to have intended to provide special protection to all taking part in the removal. The contract for the benefit of third parties must be taken to have imposed a duty of care upon all taking part in it.

Against this the appeal contends that a contract for a job of work cannot be taken to include the protection of all those permanently or temporarily in a dwelling; for principles worked out for leases cannot be applied to contracts for a job of work.

This attack cannot succeed, in particular because the appellate judge's interpretation of the contract of work between the defendant and the widow M, to the effect that it was a contract of work for the benefit of the plaintiff is free from legal error, above all in his application of §§ 133, 157, 328 BGB. Whether his definition of the circle of those benefited was entirely correct need not be discussed. In any case it includes persons who are entitled to damages from the customer under § 618 BGB.

The fundamental considerations on which the Court of Appeal proceeded are to the point, and are established by case-law of the Reichsgericht. It is in particular correct that the contract for the benefit of a third party can be an implied one and that the decision whether a contract is to be regarded as having been made for the benefit of a third party also and whether the third party shall acquire rights immediately against the promisor depends essentially, in the absence of a special term, on a finding of the facts in each case. For that purpose, regard must be had to the intention of the parties, the purpose of the transaction, and business usages; especial attention must be paid to the supplementary interpretation of contracts. The business intention of the parties provides an objective indication; whether the parties were aware when contracting of the scope of their declarations is irrelevant. Finally, there is no requirement that the identity of the third party should be ascertained when the contract is made; it is enough for it to be ascertainable.

On this basis, more recent judgments of the Reichsgericht have followed its earlier case-law in recognizing more and more contracts for the benefit of third parties in cases where a third party has suffered damage [there follows an exposition of the slowly developing practice of the Court].

If, now, one comes to decide the present case, one arrives at the following conclusions. The plaintiff was a daily help in a long-term relationship with the widow M. Accordingly she was entitled and obliged, in the interest of her own health but also in the furtherance of her employer's business, to enter the bathroom from which the smell of gas seemed to come. The gas escape rendered the premises in which she was bound to serve unfit to afford her protection against danger to life and limb. The unfitness was due to the grossly negligent way B, the defendant's 'employee', performed the job of fixing the gas meter (§ 278 BGB). Under § 618 BGB Frau M was subjected to obligations which the legislator considered so essential that their exclusion or limitation by contract was made illegal (§ 619 BGB). Under them Frau M was liable to compensate the plaintiff, although she was not herself to blame. For liability under § 618 BGB is contractual and hence § 278 is applicable, so that Frau M had to answer the plaintiff for the defendant's fault.

Now, Frau M's purpose, as the defendant could well realize, in making the contract was to have the gas meter properly fixed, and in particular that the execution of the job should produce no danger to life and limb either to herself or to any persons to whom she might become liable under § 618 BGB. No obligation to point of law can be taken to the further finding that the appellate made in interpreting the contract by way of supplementation, according to § 157 BGB, that Frau M and the defendant would have agreed to the direct liability of the latter for all damage for which Frau M might become liable to compensate persons through an improper fitting of the gas meter, if the parties, when making the contract, had contemplated such a possibility. For Frau M would have made the assumption of such direct liability a term of the contract and the defendant would, in order to get the order, have accepted such a term, all the more so because he had in any case to do a perfect job and it made no essential differences to him whether he exposed himself to a direct claim for damages by the employee of Frau M or for an indemnity by the latter.

Case 95

REICHSGERICHT (THIRD CIVIL DIVISION) 3 JUNE 1921*
RGZ 102, 232

The plaintiff and her husband lived on the third floor of a house belonging to the defendant and rented from him by the husband. On the morning of 23 October 1918 her husband was found dead and she was found unconscious in their bedroom. This was due to gas poisoning, the gas having come, according to the plaintiff, from the floor below. On the floor below the defendant was having gas replaced with electricity, and had retained G, a master plumber, to remove the gas pipes. At the end of his work on 21 October, one of G's workmen failed to plug the gas pipe leading from the gas meter to the apartment of one Gr., a publican. The gas meter was turned off at the time, but it was turned on by Gr. on 22 October, and gas then flowed out of the unstopped pipe and filtered through the ceiling into the living quarters above, those of the plaintiff and her husband as well as those of Gr. himself.

The plaintiff claimed compensation for her own illness and for the loss she suffered through her husband's death, the claim being based on the contract of lease which her husband had entered as well as on tortious negligence. The defendant denied the plaintiff's assertions about the gas poisoning and contended that the accident had occurred because a gas tap in their apartment had carelessly been left on either by the plaintiff or by her husband.

Both lower courts dismissed the claim, but the plaintiff's appeal was allowed.

Reasons

The Court of Appeal accepted the plaintiff's version of the cause of the gas poisoning. It held, in accordance with decisions of this court (see, for example, RGZ 91, 24), that the contract of lease concluded by the plaintiff's husband was one for the benefit of the plaintiff under § 328 BGB and that therefore the plaintiff had a personal contractual claim against the landlord for breach of his contractual duty of care under §§ 536, 538 BGB. It is held, correctly, that the landlord was contractually bound to each of his tenants not to damage them by works being effected on the premises and to indemnify them for any harm due to culpable breach of his duty. The court nevertheless rejected the plaintiff's claim because the defendant was neither personally at fault nor liable for the negligence of an agent for performance (§ 278 BGB). There was no personal fault in the defendant because the person to whom he had entrusted the work, the master plumber G, was a

---

* English version by Tony Weir.

specialist. He had thereby fulfilled his duty of care to see that the works were carried out properly and in a manner not involving risk to the occupants of the house, all the more so since what was involved was a simple and easy task which the chosen specialist could be expected to carry out properly. It was not common practice for the landlord himself to supervise specialist tasks which he was in no position to evaluate, nor to appoint a representative to do so for him. It therefore could not be expected that the defendant should supervise G's work. Nor was the defendant liable under § 278 BGB, because the work being done on the gas pipes was not in execution of any duty owed by the defendant to the plaintiff, but of a duty owed by the defendant to the occupant of the lower apartment; G and his workmen could therefore not be regarded as the defendant's agents for performance *vis-à-vis* the plaintiff.

The appellant criticizes the Court of Appeal's opinion of both points. Criticism of the finding that the defendant was not personally at fault is without merit. In the case of work such as was here entrusted to the master plumber G, the defendant was under no duty, either personally or through a clerk of works, to see that the work was being carried out properly or to check it as soon as it had been completed. A subsequent inspection, perhaps in the defendant's own interest, would not have prevented the accident.

On the other hand, the appellant is right to say that there has been misapplication of §§ 278, 536, 538 BGB. The Court of Appeal itself recognized that the landlord has a contractual duty to all his tenants not to injure them by work being done on the premises. This duty stems directly from the basic duty imposed on the landlord by § 536 BGB, which is not simply to make the rented property available at the outset of the lease in a condition suitable for use in accordance with the contract, but also to maintain it in this condition for the duration of the lease. But this is not a duty merely to avoid doing harmful work on the premises, it is a positive duty to see that the rented property is maintained in a condition suitable for contractual use. It therefore includes the duty to take care that the tenant's use of the premises is not unacceptably affected by any work being done on the premises, including the work done in parts of the building other than those demised to the tenant for his exclusive use. If the landlord allows work to be done in the house which runs the risk of affecting the tenanted premises, he is bound under the contract of lease so to effect these works that this danger is averted, regardless of where in the house or why the work is being done. The landlord of a house whose ground floor needed strengthening or whose gas or water supply was defective at any point would clearly be contractually bound as against tenants anywhere on the premises who were endangered thereby to do any repairs properly. If he entrusts the work to someone else he is using that other person for the performance of his duty towards all such tenants: he must therefore answer for his assistant's fault under § 278 BGB as if it were his own. The same is true if the danger arises from works undertaken in rooms rented to others. For example, suppose a supporting wall on the ground floor is to be removed in order to enlarge the window. The landlord's contractual duty to do these works is owed only to the tenant of the ground floor and not to other tenants, but if he actually engages on the work, he owes to all the tenants in the house a contractual duty so to manage it that the rooms they rent are not adversely affected. To this extent, therefore the workmen whom the landlord employs for modification of the building are his agents for performance under § 278 BGB not only as against the tenants of the ground floor but also as against all tenants whose rooms could be affected by the work of reconstruction. So here, taking the plaintiff's assertions as true, although the defendant was indeed under no contractual duty towards the plaintiff to replace the gas pipes by electric wiring, he was responsible to the plaintiff and to the other tenants in the house for seeing that the gas pipes were removed without risk of gas flowing into their rooms. Those persons to whom the defendant entrusted the removal of the gas pipes were consequently his agents for performance *vis-à-vis* the plaintiff too.

Such an application of § 278 BGB in respect of the landlord's obligation to maintain the leased property so that it remains fit for contractual use is correlative to the tenant's liability for his employees arising from his duty to treat the leased property properly: those whom the tenant engages in the business he runs on the tenanted premises are his agents for performance of his duty to treat the premises properly, even if he owes the landlord no duty whatever to run the business in which those persons are employed (see RGZ 84, 222) . . .

Case 96

REICHSGERICHT (SIXTH CIVIL DIVISION) 7 JUNE 1915*
RGZ 87, 64 = JW 1915, 1018

On 20 July 1913, there was a collision between a tram belonging to the plaintiff and a taxi belonging to the first defendant and driven by the second defendant. The passengers in the taxi, Sch., an accountant, and his wife and daughter, were injured. They claimed damages from the plaintiff tram company under the Imperial Act on Liability. The plaintiff now alleges that the accident was entirely due to the fault of the second defendant, for which the first defendant is responsible, and seeks a declaration that the defendants are bound to indemnify it for all loss arising from the accident.

* English version by Tony Weir.

The lower courts granted the claim, and the defendant's appeal is dismissed.

Reasons

1. The court below did not misapply § 278 BGB, as the appellant contends. Doubts may certainly be entertained about the reasoning of the Court of Appeal that in a case like the present the taxi-driver may regard all of his passengers as contractors, and may look to each of them for the fare. We need not decide this, however, since in any case there is no doubt that a contract was made with the accountant Sch., who boarded the taxi at the same time as his wife and daughter. But that does not mean that he is the only person with a contractual claim arising out of the contract of carriage. On the contrary, the contract of carriage is a contract in favour of the wife and daughter who were travelling with him; they were 'third parties' under § 328 BGB, and acquired a direct right to demand performance, namely proper and safe carriage. There is therefore no reason to doubt the Court of Appeal's conclusion that the first defendant was liable under the contract of carriage to all three passengers, and that he must answer for the fault of the second defendant, who in this respect was his agent for performance under § 278 BGB . . .

Case 97

REICHSGERICHT (THIRD CIVIL DIVISION) 5 OCTOBER 1917
RGZ 91, 21 = JW 1918, 95 (with approving note by K. Friedrichs)

The male plaintiff is a senior assistant on the railways. When he was moved to J, he was provided with accommodation which had previously been used by Dr., the station supervisor. A few months after moving in, his daughter, the female plaintiff, contracted tuberculosis, and had to go on a voyage for her health. The plaintiffs attribute this illness to the fact that the dwelling was infected with tuberculosis bacilli, Dr.'s wife having had pulmonary trouble, and that the defendant State failed to disinfect the dwelling until five or six days after they moved in. They therefore claim damages for the loss attributable to the disease, not all of which may have manifested itself.

The Landgericht allowed the claims. The Oberlandesgericht rejected the defendant's appeal in respect of the male plaintiff's claim, but allowed it in respect of that of the female plaintiff, whose claim was therefore dismissed. The female plaintiff's appeal was allowed, and the defendant's appeal was dismissed.

Reasons

On the basis of the evidence, the Court of Appeal concluded that the female plaintiff became ill because the service dwelling in which she lived had been infected with tuberculosis bacilli during the illness of Mrs Dr., but it held that the only person to whom the defendant was liable was the male plaintiff: he had a claim, based on an analogous application of §§ 618, 278 BGB, for the damage he had suffered through his daughter's illness. The court said that the delay in disinfecting the house was due to the fault of Dr D, the railway doctor appointed by the defendant who attended to Mrs Dr. It was the duty of Dr D to inform the railway authorities of all cases of tuberculosis which came to his notice in his capacity as railway doctor, and if he had performed this duty, the house would have been disinfected at the right time. But the Court of Appeal disallowed the female plaintiff's claim for damages on the ground that she had no contractual or similar relationship with the defendant, and that her claim in tort failed because the defendant, having adduced exculpatory proof under § 831 BGB, was not liable for Dr D.

So far as the male plaintiff's rights are concerned, the Court of Appeal was correct in the result but wrong in the reasons, and so far as the female plaintiff's rights are concerned, it was wrong in both regards.

Since the male plaintiff is an official, the solution must be looked for in public law; and since there are no relevant tests, it must depend on the principles which emerge from the nature of the case in the light of the legal ideas which control decisions in analogous relationships subject to private law. It is established by the Reichsgericht that the State and other bodies of public law owe their officials a duty of care such as is implied into the contract of employment by § 618 BGB. Thus it has been held that under the Prussian Act on Conditions of Service of Teachers in Public Schools of 3 March 1897, local authorities are bound to ensure that the accommodation they provide for teachers are safe and properly maintained, and that they are liable for any injury or illness caused to the teacher by culpable breach of this duty (RGZ 71, 243). This duty of care is closely related to the fact that the accommodation is provided so as to enable the occupant to perform his service obligations or to perform them more easily. Being required to use the service dwelling for the performance of his duties, the official can expect the local authority to protect him adequately against defects in the dwelling which imperil his health. This leads to the conclusion that in respect of official accommodation, the State owes the same duty of protection to the dependants whom the official is entitled to lodge in the dwelling as to the official himself. For if the official is bound to use the accommodation provided, so, too, are they, in the interests of maintaining the family community.

So far as the official himself is concerned, the protective duty owed to him means that he can hold the State responsible for its breach, not only when his own health suffers but also when he suffers loss through injury to the health of a dependant. Just as the official's entitlement to compensation when his own health is affected is based on the application of § 618 BGB by analogy so, when a dependant's health is affected, private law powerfully suggests that the dependant has a claim for damages as well as the official himself. If a landlord is responsible for unhealthy conditions on the leased premises and a member of the tenant's family suffers thereby, the tenant can sue the landlord under § 538 BGB for the consequent harm he may suffer (RGZ 77, 99, 101). But in addition the dependant himself can normally sue the landlord for his own harm (though not for his pain and suffering). Unless very peculiar circumstances indicate a different conclusion, the tenant of a family dwelling who concludes a lease must be taken, as the landlord must know, to intend to obtain the maximum protection for the members of his household and to acquire for them the same rights in relation to the safety of the premises as he himself enjoys against the landlord (§ 328 BGB). If the landlord's contractual duties are not extended in this manner, injured dependants would be restricted to claim in tort, and would not have the benefit afforded to the tenant by §§ 278, 538 BGB, that the landlord is strictly liable for any defects in the premises existing at the time of the contract. To give such different rights to the tenant and to his dependants is offensive to proper legal sentiment and false to the tenant's purpose in contracting, for, as the landlord is bound to know, he wants his dependants to be as well placed as himself to sue for damages. So, too, in the contract of employment of private law where the employer provides the employee with a family house so as to facilitate the rendering of the contractual services, the employee must be taken to intend the employer to assume the duty, as regards the condition and maintenance of the living quarters, to protect his dependants from danger to life and limb to the same extent as himself (§ 618 BGB) and to have them acquire rights of their own to this effect. Now, if an official who is directed to live in service quarters could not claim from the State protection against dangerous defects in the living premises for those dependants who are entitled to stay in the dwelling, and if his dependants did not have a claim of their own to the effect, there would be an intolerable difference in the treatment of cognate legal relationships in public and private law. Such differential treatment would be all the more unjustifiable as the official and his dependants do not have the freedom of choice which is open to the tenant or employee and their dependants, but are bound to use the accommodation provided. This extension to the dependants of the State's duty of care is also in line with the development in public law of the state's duty to look after the family of its officials.

It is one of the benefits to which officials are entitled, not by way of contractual counter-performance for their services, but as a means of assuring their position in life.

In the case for decision, the State has failed to satisfy its duty of care, since it failed to take steps to ensure that its service accommodations were disinfected sufficiently soon after the departure of an occupant in whose family tuberculosis had broken out. The rules certainly provide that in such a case the station-master is to undertake the disinfection. A duty is also imposed on railway doctors and supervisors to inform the railway authorities of any cases of tuberculosis in the families of railway employees which come to their knowledge. If this duty is performed, the railway authorities would be in a position to give the station-master due notice of any required disinfection. But if no such notification is given, as may easily happen, the regulations make no provision for securing the object in question. The dangers to which officials are exposed in the absence of such notification is such that the defendant should have provided for steps to be taken which would permit the premises to be disinfected at the right time, possibly by making inquiry of the station doctor before assigning accommodation to a new occupant.

Case 98

BUNDESGERICHTSHOF (SECOND CIVIL DIVISION) 11 APRIL 1951*

BGHZ 1, 383 = NJW 1951, 798

The plaintiff, who had ingrowing toe-nails, was referred for out-patient treatment to the defendant city's hospital by the local Medical Union of which he was a member. He was made to sit down on a three-piece settee, about 30 inches high, designed for gynaecological examinations but used as an auxiliary operating table, the back part having been fixed in a horizontal position. The second defendant, who had been the hospital's chief doctor for many years, gave the plaintiff a local anaesthetic, an injection of 2 per cent novocaine solution, in either one big toe or both. While waiting for this to work, the plaintiff suddenly lost consciousness and fell off the settee. He injured his cervical column in the fall, and has since experienced severe stiffness and loss of function in both arms. At the time of the accident, the second defendant was standing at the door of the small operating theatre, speaking to his chauffeur, and the operating sister was quite close to the plaintiff, treating a patient for burns.

The plaintiff claims that the defendants are liable on the following grounds. No one told him to lie down after the injection, so he was still sitting when he suddenly became unconscious. Had he known he should lie

* English version by Tony Weir.

down, he would have done so, and not fallen. The second defendant should have realized and guarded against the risk of a sudden faint, in particular by making him lie down, but instead of taking any such steps he left the plaintiff to his own devices after giving him the injection. This was the sole reason for the accident, which had rendered him wholly and, as it seemed, permanently unfit for work. The plaintiff claims an annuity for lost earnings and damages for pain and suffering from both defendants.

The Landgericht rejected the claim, but the Oberlandesgericht held the plaintiff entitled to a monthly sum for loss of earnings and damages for pain and suffering. The defendants' appeal was successful only in part.

Reasons

The plaintiff has a good contractual claim against the first defendant. The Reichsgericht always held that when a General Health Insurance Scheme (AOK) refers a member to a hospital, the contract it makes with the hospital is one in favour of the patient whereby, under § 328 BGB, the patient acquires a direct claim to proper treatment against the operator of the hospital (RGZ 165, 106). The first defendant entrusted to the second defendant the treatment of the National Health patient referred to it, so he became the first defendant's agent for performance and the first defendant is accordingly responsible to the plaintiff under § 278 BGB for any fault committed by the second defendant in the execution of his professional medical activity.

Between the plaintiff and the second defendant there were no direct contractual relations. A hospital doctor's contractual duty to undertake the proper treatment of National Health patients is normally owed only to the hospital which appoints him. But if a hospital doctor actually does embark on the treatment of a union patient and injures him in his health by infringing a widely recognized rule of medical science, he is liable to the patient under §§ 823 ff. BGB, whether or not he has any contract with the patient. It is immaterial whether the fault of the doctor is one of commission or of omission. The doctor may be under no obligation to the patient to treat him at all, but if he does so, he must avoid injuring him in body or health by breach of the rules of medical science [reference omitted].

In the instant case the Court of Appeal was right to find that it was the second defendant's fault that the plaintiff did not lie down after the injection; he should have told him himself or got the operating sister to do so.

The appellant contends that the failure to tell the plaintiff to lie down was not an adequate cause of the consequent harm. This is not so. The decisions of the Reichsgericht cited by the appellant on consequences for which the actor is not responsible because the causal connection is not adequate refer to consequences which occur only under extremely peculiar circumstances and through quite improbable concatenations of events and which can be ignored in the normal course of things. The consequences here, according to the expert, are not of this kind. On the contrary, the expert expressly emphasized that the reason for the good old rule that a patient should always be prone or supine during all manipulations and injections is precisely the possibility of a faint and a fall; it may be true that this rule cannot always be observed in practice and often is not, but such practical considerations cannot relieve the doctor of the charge that he ignored a duty of care. In such a case there can be no question of any interruption of the adequate causal connection. The appellant is also wrong to say that the Court of Appeal pitched the doctor's duty of care too high. The court was right to follow the expert, whose evidence was based on his knowledge of the rules of the medical art, and who stated in clear terms that there was undeniable negligence in this case unless perhaps it could be proved that the sister had been enjoined to attend to the patient and that the patient had disobeyed her instruction to lie down.

It follows that the plaintiff's claim for monthly payments is established against the first defendant under §§ 276, 278 BGB and against the second defendant under § 823 BGB. However, the second defendant alone is liable for the damages for pain and suffering under § 847 BGB. Only under § 831 BGB could the first defendant be held liable for such damages. The defendant city asserts that it has satisfied the requisite exculpatory proof. We agree. It was common ground that the second defendant had been chief doctor in the first defendant's hospital for many years and that the nurse had served as operating sister for nine years without any criticism. The plaintiff did not even assert, much less prove, anything that tended to show that the second defendant had been guilty of any fault during his twenty years' service in the defendant city's hospital. Under such circumstances, the hospital management cannot be expected to adduce any further exculpatory proof.

Case 99

REICHSGERICHT (THIRD CIVIL DIVISION) 8 JANUARY 1926*
RGZ 112, 290

On 8 January 1919 and the following days several people went to the All Saints Hospital in B to be treated for scabies. They were rubbed with an ointment which, though thought to be the normal sulphur ointment, was in fact extremely poisonous with chromium. The treatment resulted in the death of Joh. Sch. and of Ha., a coachman, whose mother and heirs are respectively plaintiffs, and in severe injury to Miss Ch. H. The fatal ointment had been supplied to the city B by an independent apothecary.

* English version by F. H. Lawson and B. S. Markesinis.

These are suits for damages against the city B. Miss Ch. H seeks an indemnity for her medical expenses, loss of earnings, and damaged clothing, as well as damages for pain and suffering and a decree that the defendant is liable for any future damage due to the chromium poisoning. Mrs Sch. claims burial expenses and an indemnity for the support her son would have provided had he lived. Ha.'s widow and children likewise claim for loss of support.

The Landgericht gave judgment for all the plaintiffs. The Oberlandesgericht dismissed the claims of Ch. H and of Ha.'s heirs, and dismissed also the city's appeal in the case of Frau Sch. Appeal has been brought to this court by Ch. H, the heirs of Ha., and the city. The judgment below is vacated, and the matter remanded to the Court of Appeal for further proceedings.

Reasons

All Saints Hospital is primarily a charitable institution through which its owner, the city B, performs its public welfare functions by providing poor patients with free medical treatment and, in suitable cases, free board and nursing as well. Its relationship with these patients is purely one of public law with no private law elements. But other patients pay a fee, fixed according to a sliding scale, for treatment and nursing in the hospital, and these people are admitted under a contract of private law, whether of services or of some other kind (see RGZ 64, 231; 83, 71; 91, 134 and 263). Thus the duties of the city and the consequences of their breach are determined for the first class of patients by public law, and for the second class by the contract law of the BGB, unless, of course, tort law applies.

Ch. H, Joh. Sch., and Ha. were treated in the All Saints Hospital with a poisonous chromium mixture instead of the normal sulphur ointment. Sch. and Ha. died, but Ch. H regained her health after a long period in hospital. The fatal ointment was first used on 8 January 1919. According to the Court of Appeal, the mere fact of this occurrence betokens no fault on the part of the city. The court accepted the testimony of Professor J that the nurses who were applying the ointment would not be alerted by the fact that it was greenish in colour rather than yellow: the usual ointment used to vary in colour because the Vaseline used during the war and immediately thereafter was not uniform. The poisonous ointment was purchased from an independent apothecary. Of course, the hospital doctors were not bound to test the ointment before using it: it would take far too much of a doctor's time and energy if he had to check the composition of every medicament he prescribed. For this occurrence, then, only the apothecary is responsible.

But the Court of Appeal found that on the first application of the ointment on 8 January, many of the patients screamed and one of them had a fit of vomiting. Such reactions are normally rare and sporadic, so the number of them on this occasion should have led the nurses to inform Dr U or some other doctor in the hospital immediately, and the doctor should then have had the ointment checked forthwith. Then its odd colour would have confirmed the suspicion that it had been incorrectly made up. Had this happened, the Court of Appeal found, the poisonous quality of the ointment would have been discovered that very day, and the fateful events of the following two days would have been avoided. As it was, either the nurses failed in their duty to inform the doctors, or the doctors failed in their duty to investigate.

Up to this point the views of the Court of Appeal are logical and correct, but hereafter their analysis of the case, both factually and legally, is inadequate.

1. When the clinic accepted Ch. H for treatment as a charity patient, there arose between her and the city a relationship in public law which imposed on the city a public law duty to treat her in an appropriate way without endangering her life and limb, and gave Ch. H a right in public law to have such treatment. Thus there was superimposed on the city's general welfare duties a specific obligation to Ch. H with a defined content such as to render the city liable if this obligation were broken by the fault of the person whose services the city used in the performance of its obligation. As this Senate held on 11 March 1921 (RGZ 102, 6; see also RGZ 98, 343), the legal idea which applies in private contract law by reason of its expression in § 278 BGB applies in public law relationships as well, unless there is some special feature in a case which excluded its application. No such feature is present here; indeed, to hold that the principle of law contained in § 278 BGB was inapplicable to the public law relationship between a commune and a charity patient in a communal hospital would be to pervert the very notion of welfare.

Ch. H was given the ointment treatment on 8 January, and very early on that day, since she presented herself at the clinic at 7 a.m. and was back home two and a half hours later. As has been established, neither the nurses nor the doctors were negligent in the original treatment, but if the requisite care had been taken and the ointment investigated, then, as the Oberlandesgericht found, the dreadful mistake made by the apothecary would have been discovered that very day. The city should then have informed Ch. H immediately—for her name and address were in their books—of any possible countermeasures. This would have been not just an act of humanity, but part of its public law duty towards her. The judges of fact must therefore investigate, with the aid of experts if need be, whether Ch. H's injuries could have been avoided or reduced if such a communication had been made, that is, whether and how far the failure to make it was a cause of the plaintiff's suffering. Even if this question is resolved in favour of Ch. H, however, she will still have no claim for damages for pain and suffering, for according to § 253 BGB, money damages can be awarded for non-economic harm only in the cases prescribed by law. The idea here expressed by the legislator is that in the normal case one does not have to pay for the so-called immaterial harm one may cause. An exception is made in § 847 BGB which imposes an obligation to repair such harm in cases of injury to body and health, but it only applies when such harm results from an unlawful act as laid down in the BGB. Thus § 847 BGB cannot give rise to a claim when the defendant's liability is based only on faulty breach of a contractual obligation (see RGZ 65, 17; JW 1910, 112 no. 13). Just as this exceptional rule cannot be applied by analogy to breach of contractual duties, so it cannot be applied to faulty breaches of public law obligations.

Only if the city were liable in tort as well as for breach of its public law duties would Ch. H's claim for damages for pain and suffering be good. On this point also the views of the Court of Appeal seem inadequate. There is nothing wrong with its finding that the city was free from fault with regard to the provision of the ointment, and in its choice and appointment of its doctors and nurses. There was no need to direct or supervise the application of the ointment, as such a mechanical task was well within the competence of trained nurses. Thus the city cannot be made liable under § 831 BGB. But that does not conclude the matter. One must distinguish between the duty of a business or institution to supervise the performance of individual tasks and its general duty to supervise, monitor, and instruct, for breach of which it may be liable under § 823 BGB, a liability which attaches to a commune if the breach is due to one of its constitutional representatives under §§ 31, 89 BGB. What the precise implications are of this general duty of supervision must depend on the individual case, and especially on whether the execution and supervision of tasks has been entrusted to knowledgeable persons who are familiar with them and who have proved themselves reliable. It will only be very rarely that a business or institution will be able to exempt itself entirely from its duty to exercise this control (see RGZ 53, 53 and 276; 82, 206; 95, 181; 96, 81; JW 1906, 547 no. 13; JW 1906, 75 no. 16; JW 1909, 659 no. 10).

In the present case, the city is performing a welfare function, and poor patients trust it with their greatest assets, namely their health and life. It follows that the city must issue instructions through its top management that it is the duty of nurses to inform the doctors whenever any medicament has an unexpected effect and whenever anything unusual occurs on its being administered and that it is the duty of the doctors, if so informed, to make an immediate investigation. But this does not exhaust the city's duties in the matter. It is not enough simply to issue these instructions: the city must also see to it by suitable occasional checks that they are being followed. From the opinion below we cannot tell whether the city has satisfied its general duties of instruction and supervision, any breach and its causal effect being for the plaintiff to establish, with any possible assistance from the rules regarding prima-facie proof. The tort aspects of Ch. H's suit therefore require further investigation.

2. With regard to the death of young Sch., the Oberlandesgericht held that although he paid no fee to the hospital when he was accepted for treatment, he thereupon entered into a private law contract with the city. Were this so, then his mother's suit must fail, for in a contractual claim she could only claim for the harm which her son had suffered as a result of breach by his contractor, and her claim was for a loss which had befallen the mother rather than the son, namely the loss of the support which Joh. Sch. would have been bound to provide had he lived. Such a claim, which is at odds with the general principle that compensation may be claimed only by the person directly affected, could only be based on § 844 II BGB, and that provision requires that her son's death be attributable to a tort for which the city is responsible through its constitutional organs. § 844 II has no application in the law of contract, any more than § 844 I (see JW 1907, 710 no. 18; JW 1908, 9 no. 9). Now the Oberlandesgericht gave no reason for holding that there was a private law contract in this case. One almost has the impression that the only reason was that unlike Miss Ch. H, Sch. did not return home after the treatment but was kept in hospital while the scabies were to be cured. But gratuitous admission to the hospital is just like gratuitous treatment to an out-patient: it is an act of public law welfare which gives rise to public law relations between the in-patient and the city. But even though the Court of Appeal was wrong to invoke private law, the decision it reached is correct in public law.

The poisonous ointment was applied to Sch. on 9 January, so his death was indubitably due to negligence on the part of either the doctors or the nurses. Now just as the principle that a debtor must answer for the fault of his assistants as he does for his own applies in public as well as private law, so do the legal ideas expressed in § 844 BGB. If it were otherwise, public law would be intolerably and unjustifiably defective. Nevertheless, we cannot yet affirm the decision of the Oberlandesgericht in favour of Frau Sch. since it is possible that even though Sch. did not actually pay the hospital as required by the tariff for money patients, he might nevertheless be under a duty to pay and so have entered into a private law contract with the city. Thus in this case also we need further facts, including whether the city was guilty of any breach of its general duty of supervision (see §§ 823, 31, 89 BGB) . . .

Notes to Cases 89–99

1. Most of these cases illustrate (i) the difficulties experienced by German law as a result of § 831 BGB and (ii) the ways used by the courts to produce a more sensible result. Thus, cases 78, 83, 84, and 85 show how the employer must supervise his employee properly and constantly or otherwise run the risk of being held liable under § 823 I BGB for breach of his own primary duty; case 74 discusses issues relevant to § 31 BGB; cases 76 and 87 discuss the thorny question of 'unlawfulness' in the context of § 831 BGB (though much of the reasoning in the latter case appears to have become obsolete); cases 89–99 illustrate what is, perhaps, the most ingenious way of bypassing § 831 BGB, namely by invoking the aid of the law of contract. As Zweigert and Kötz have put it (*An Introduction to Comparative Law*, 2nd edn. II, 147):

The sole purpose of these decisions is to put the accident victim in a better position than if his only claim for damages were based on delict. Under German law, with regard to prescription, burden of proof and especially vicarious liability, a victim is in a much better position to claim damages if he can claim in contract for the harm he has suffered. Not the slightest blame attaches to the German courts for using the contract for the benefit of third parties in order to get round the misconceived legal policy contained in § 831 BGB; nor is there anything wrong with what they have done as a matter of positive law. Nevertheless, it must be seen that these are cases where the harmful consequences of accidents are attributed to the person responsible, not because he is guilty of any breach of specifically contractual duties but because he has committed a breach of general duties of care imposed by the law of delict. The position of German law may be excused by the necessity caused by the unfortunate policy of § 831 BGB, but the comparative lawyer has to classify problems according to the true significance of their actual facts. These cases must therefore be put in the law of tort, as is done everywhere else in the world. In doing so, the comparatist must realize that it may be necessary to study a person's contractual relations with third parties in order to discover *to whom* he owes his delictual duties of care not to cause harm.

But this solution is, at best, only a partial one. Claims formed in contract cannot, because of another troublesome provision (§ 253 BGB), compensate the plaintiff for his pain and suffering (contrast § 847 BGB). The return to the law of delict thus not only produces an intellectually neater classification; it can also benefit the victims (see case 98). The growing tendency to invoke § 823 I BGB, by discovering what the Common lawyers would call non-delegable duties, may then be described as a move in the right direction (for illustrations see cases 73, 79, 92, 93 etc.). From the little said in this paragraph, it should be clear that these cases must be read in close conjunction with the text of Ch. 3, section A.

2. The cases and the preceding commentary make it clear that there exist some important structural differences between German law on the one hand and the Common law on the other. One further difference of classification must also be noted with American Common law: in the latter, vicarious liability is a subject which is shared between agency and tort and the two relative Restatements. Thus, the master–servant relationship and the notion of 'scope of employment' are defined in §§ 220 and 229 of the *Restatement of Agency, Second* (and are reproduced below in Addendum 1). On the other hand, liability for independent contractors is treated in §§ 409–29 of the *Restatement of Torts, Second*. Tort books that discuss (briefly) the matters raised in this chapter include Prosser and Keeton, *On Torts* (5th edn. 1984) 499 ff.; and Henderson and Pearson, ch. 3.

3. Once the above points are well digested, the comparatist should experience no difficulty in understanding what is happening in 'the other system', the differences being differences in emphasis or detail rather than substance. Thus, the rationale for imposing vicarious liability is the same everywhere: the belief that it is more efficient to place the risk on the employer's shoulders than on the employee's. The same rationale also seems to favour the more modern tendency not to allow masters (or, more likely, their insurers) the right to claim contribution or an indemnity from the servant unless the latter's conduct was intentional and grossly negligent. (For English law see Markesinis and Deakin, *Tort Law* 3rd edn. (1994), 517; for American law see Comment 34 *La. L. Rev.* 79 (1973); Note 53 *Ore. L. Rev.* 366 (1974).) The tendency to make employers rather than employees liable also accounts for the increased willingness to give a wide meaning to such inherently ambiguous notions as 'course of employment'. As already noted, German law is, perhaps, the strictest in this respect, with French and American law showing a clear willingness to include even acts of violence which the servant's employment merely gave him the opportunity to commit. The French decision which held the employer of a cinema attendant vicariously liable for the latter's rape of a cinema patron (Crim. 5 nov. 1953, *D.* 1953, J. 698) has happily not been followed in the US: see *Mays* v. *Pico Finance Company, Inc.* 339 So. 2d 382 (La. App. 1977). But there are other just as grotesque examples; thus in *Miller* v. *Keating* 349 So. 2d 265 (La. 1977) the attempted murder of a company employee by some of his co-employees was held to be within the scope of their employment since the corporation (the Common employer) was the beneficiary of the victim's insurance policy—a conclusion which led one commentator to remark that 'cynicism reaches new heights when attempted murder becomes regarded as "fair and reasonably incident" to corporate offences'! (Comment 52 *Tul. L. Rev.* 443, 450 (1978).) But, as stated in Section A of Chapter 3, this point need not be laboured too much: aberrant cases can

always be found and the vagueness of such notions as 'course of employ-ment' may also be their main virtue since it provides the desirable degree of flexibility in decisions. (For French law and the possibility that the insur-ance factor may in some cases account for such wide interpretations see Hassler, 'La responsabilité des commettants' *D. Chron.* (1980) 125–8; Markesinis, 'La perversion des notions de la responsabilité civile délictuelle par la pratique des assurances' *Rev. int. dr. comp.*, 301 (1983).)

4. Lack of space prevents a more detailed annotation of the cases but three more points can be made briefly. First, in the case of borrowed ser-vants, American law until recently took a different view from English and German law and tended to make the 'special or temporary employer' liable for the torts of the borrowed servant on the grounds, *inter alia*, that he had (at the moment of the accident) the benefit of the services of the borrowed servant. See *Lewis* v. *Potter* 149 Mont. 430, 427 P. 2d 306 (1967). Recent decisions, however, suggest an opposite movement (for example, *Salsgiver* v. *E. S. Ritter Co.* 42 Ore. App. 547, 600 P. 2d 951 (1979); *LeSuer* v. *LeSuer* 350 So. 2d 796 (Fla. App. 1977)); and, as stated, Californian courts have favoured plaintiffs further by allowing the victim to sue *both* employers and then let them solve their internal relationship: *Strait* v. *Hale Constr. Co.* 26 Cal. App. 3d 941, 103 Cal. Rptr. 487 (1972).

Secondly, American courts have developed the family purpose doctrine which, in some circumstances, makes car owners vicariously liable for harm caused by persons to whom the vehicles were loaned or made available. Although attempts to introduce the doctrine in England were made by Lord Denning MR in *Launchbury* v. *Morgan*, they met with the disapproval of the House of Lords which felt that the matter should best be left to the leg-islator to settle. Needless to say, the legislator these days does not have the time to intervene in such matters of relative detail with the result that in cases such as these the English victim may be in a less favourable position than his American counterpart.

Finally, § 831 BGB and the growth of the non-delegable duty device in Germany and England must be compared carefully with §§ 409–29 of the American *Restatement of Torts, Second.* The text of the basic rule (§ 409 on liability of torts of independent contractors) and the exceptions are repro-duced below in Addendum 2. A glance at these rules makes it clear that the exceptions are gradually swallowing up the rule, a result which led one American court to say that '. . . it would be proper to say that the rule is now primarily important as a preamble to the catalog of its exceptions' (*Pacific Fire Ins. Co.* v. *Kenny Boiler & Mfg. Co.* 201 Minn. 500, 277 NW 226 (1937)).

Addendum 1

Restatement of Agency, Second

§ 220. *Definition of servant*

(2) In determining whether one acting for another is a servant or an independent contractor, the following matters of fact, among others, are considered:

(*a*) the extent of control which, by the agreement, the master may exercise over the details of the work;

(*b*) whether or not the one employed is engaged in a distinct occupation or business;

(*c*) the kind of occupation, with reference to whether, in the locality, the work is usually done under the direction of the employer or by a specialist without supervision;

(*d*) the skill required in the particular occupation;

(*e*) whether the employer or the workman supplies the instrumentalities, tools, and the place of work for the person doing the work;

(*f*) the length of time for which the person is employed;

(*g*) the method of payment, whether by the time or by the job;

(*h*) whether or not the work is a part of the regular business of the employer;

(*i*) whether or not the parties believe they are creating the relation of master and servant; and

(*j*) whether the principal is or is not in business.

§ 229. *Kind of conduct within the scope of employment*

(1) To be within the scope of employment, conduct must be of the same general nature as that authorized, or incidental to the conduct authorized.

(2) In determining whether or not the conduct, although not authorized, is nevertheless so similar to or incidental to the conduct authorized as to be within the scope of employment, the following matters of fact are to be considered:

(*a*) whether or not the act is one commonly done by such servants;

(*b*) the time, place, and purpose of the act;

(*c*) the previous relations between the master and the servant;

(*d*) the extent to which the business of the master is apportioned between different servants;

(*e*) whether or not the act is outside the enterprise of the master or, if within the enterprise, has not been entrusted to any servant;

(*f*) whether or not the master has reason to expect that such an act will be done;

(g) the similarity in quality of the act done to the act authorized;

(h) whether or not the instrumentality by which the harm is done has been furnished by the master to the servant;

(i) the extent of departure from the normal method of accomplishing an authorized result; and

(j) whether or not the act is seriously criminal.

Addendum 2

Restatement of Tort, Second

§ 409. *General principle*

Except as stated in §§ 410–29, the employer of an independent contractor is not liable for physical harm caused to another by an act or omission of the contractor or his servants.

§ 410. *Contractor's conduct in obedience to employer's directions*

The employer of an independent contractor is subject to the same liability for physical harm caused by an act or omission committed by the contractor pursuant to orders or directions negligently given by the employer, as though the act or omission were that of the employer himself.

§ 411. *Negligence in selection of contractor*

An employer is subject to liability for physical harm to third persons caused by his failure to exercise reasonable care to employ a competent and careful contractor

(a) to do work which will involve a risk of physical harm unless it is skilfully and carefully done, or

(b) to perform any duty which the employer owes to third persons.

§ 412. *Failure to inspect work of contractor after completion*

One who is under a duty to exercise reasonable care to maintain land or chattels in such condition as not to involve unreasonable risk of bodily harm to others and who entrusts the work of repair and maintenance to an independent contractor, is subject to liability for bodily harm caused to them by his failure to exercise such care as the circumstances may reasonably require him to exercise to ascertain whether the land or chattel is in reasonably safe condition after the contractor's work is complete.

§ 413. *Duty to provide for taking of precautions against dangers involved in work entrusted to contractor*

One who employs an independent contractor to do work which the employer should recognize as likely to create, during its progress, a peculiar unreasonable risk of physical harm to others unless special precautions are taken, is subject to liability for physical harm caused to them by the absence of such precautions if the employer

(*a*) fails to provide in the contract that the contractor shall take such precautions, or

(*b*) fails to exercise reasonable care to provide in some other manner for the taking of such precautions.

§ 414. *Negligence in exercising control retained by employer*

One who entrusts work to an independent contractor, but who retains the control of any part of the work, is subject to liability for physical harm to others for whose safety the employer owes a duty to exercise reasonable care, which is caused by his failure to exercise his control with reasonable care.

§ 414A. *Duty of possessor of land to prevent activities and conditions dangerous to those outside of land*

A possessor of land who has employed or permitted an independent contractor to do work on the land, and knows that the activities of the contractor or conditions created by him involve an unreasonable risk of physical harm to those outside of the land, is subject to liability to them for such harm if he fails to exercise reasonable care to protect them against it.

§ 415. *Duty to supervise equipment and methods of contractors or concessionaires on land held open to public*

A possessor of land who holds it open to the public for any purpose is subject to liability to members of the public entering for that purpose for physical harm caused to them by his failure to exercise reasonable care to protect them against unreasonably dangerous activities of, or unreasonably dangerous conditions created by, an independent contractor or concessionaire employed or permitted to do work or carry on an activity on the land.

§ 416. *Work dangerous in absence of special precautions*

One who employs an independent contractor to do work which the employer should recognize as likely to create during its progress a peculiar risk of physical harm to others unless special precautions are taken, is subject to liability for physical harm caused to them by the failure of the contractor to exercise reasonable care to take such precautions, even though the employer has provided for such precautions.

§ 417. *Work done in public place*

One who employs an independent contractor to do work in a public place which unless carefully done involves a risk of making the physical condition of the place dangerous for the use of members of the public, is subject to liability for physical harm caused to members of the public by a negligent act or omission of the contractor which makes the physical condition of the place dangerous for their use.

§ 418. *Maintenance of public highways and other public places*

(1) One who is under a duty to construct or maintain a highway in reasonably safe condition for the use of the public, and who entrusts its construction, maintenance, or repair to an independent contractor, is subject to the same liability for physical harm to persons using the highway while it is held open for travel during such work, caused by the negligent failure of the contractor to make it reasonably safe for travel, as though the employer had retained the work in his own hands.

(2) The statement in subsection (1) applies to any place which is maintained by a government for the use of the public, if the government is under the same duty to maintain it in reasonably safe condition as it owes to the public in respect to the condition of its highways.

§ 419. *Repairs which lessor is under a duty to his lessee to make*

A lessor of land who employs an independent contractor to perform a duty which the lessor owes to his lessee to maintain the leased land in reasonably safe condition, is subject to liability to the lessee, and to third persons upon the land with the consent of the lessee, for physical harm caused by the contractor's failure to exercise reasonable care to make the land reasonably safe.

§ 420. *Repairs gratuitously undertaken by lessor*

A lessor of land who employs an independent contractor to make repairs which the lessor is under no duty to make, is subject to the same liability to the lessee, and to others upon the land with the consent of the lessee, for physical harm caused by the contractor's negligence in making or purporting to make the repairs as though the contractor's conduct were that of the lessor.

§ 421. *Maintenance of structures on land retained in lessor's possession necessary to tenant's enjoyment of leased land*

A possessor of land who, having a part of the land, is under a duty to maintain in reasonably safe condition the part retained by him, and who entrusts the repair of such part to an independent contractor, is subject to the same liability to the lessee, and to others upon the retained part of the land with the consent of the lessee, for physical harm caused by the negligence of the contractor in failing to maintain such part of the land in reasonably safe condition, as though the lessor had himself retained the making of the repairs in his own hands.

§ 422. *Work on buildings and other structures on land*

A possessor of land who entrusts to an independent contractor construction, repairs, or other work on the land, or on a building or other structure upon it, is subject to the same liability as though he had retained the work in his own hands to others on or outside the land for physical harm caused to them by the unsafe condition of the structure

(*a*) while the possessor has retained possession of the land during the progress of the work, or

(*b*) after he had resumed possession of the land upon its completion.

§ 422A. *Work withdrawing lateral support*

One who employs an independent contractor to do work which the employer knows or should know to be likely to withdraw lateral support from the land of another is subject to the same liability for the contractor's withdrawal of such support as if the employer had retained the work in his own hands.

§ 423. *Making or repair of instrumentalities used in highly dangerous activities*

One who carries on an activity which threatens a grave risk of serious bodily harm or death unless the instrumentalities used are carefully constructed and maintained, and who employs an independent contractor to construct or maintain such instrumentalities, is subject to the same liability for physical harm caused by the negligence of the contractor in constructing or maintaining such instrumentalities as though the employer had himself done the work of construction or maintenance.

§ 424. *Precautions required by statutes or regulation*

One who by statute or by administrative regulation is under a duty to provide specified safeguards or precautions for the safety of others is subject to liability to the others for whose protection the duty is imposed for harm caused by the failure of a contractor employed by him to provide such safeguards or precautions.

§ 425. *Repair of chattel supplied or land held open to public as place of business*

One who employs an independent contractor to maintain in safe condition land which he holds open to the entry of the public as his place of business, or a chattel which he supplies for others to use for his business purposes or which he leases for immediate use, is subject to the same liability for physical harm caused by the contractor's negligent failure to maintain the land or chattel in reasonably safe condition, as though he had retained its maintenance in his own hands.

§ 426. *Negligence collateral to risk of doing the work*

Except as stated in §§ 428 and 429, an employer of an independent contractor, unless he is himself negligent, is not liable for physical harm caused by any negligence of the contractor if

(*a*) the contractor's negligence consists solely in the improper manner in which he does the work, and

(*b*) it creates a risk of such harm which is not inherent in or normal to the work, and

(*c*) the employer had no reason to contemplate the contractor's negligence when the contract was made.

§ 427. *Negligence as to danger inherent in the work*

One who employs an independent contractor to do work involving a special danger to others which the employer knows or has reason to know to be inherent in or normal to the work, or which he contemplates or has reason to contemplate when making the contract, is subject to liability for physical harm caused to such others by the contractor's failure to take reasonable precautions against such danger.

§ 427A. *Work involving abnormally dangerous activity*

One who employs an independent contractor to do work which the employer knows or has reason to know to involve an abnormally dangerous activity, is subject to liability to the same extent as the contractor for physical harm to others caused by the activity.

§ 427B. *Work likely to involve trespass or nuisance*

One who employs an independent contractor to do work which the employer knows or has reason to know to be likely to involve a trespass upon the land of another or the creation of a public or a private nuisance, is subject to liability for harm resulting to others from such trespass or nuisance.

§ 428. *Contractor's negligence in doing work which cannot lawfully be done except under a franchise granted to his employer*

An individual or a corporation carrying on an activity which can be lawfully carried on only under a franchise granted by public authority and which involves an unreasonable risk of harm to others, is subject to liability for physical harm caused to such others by the negligence of a contractor employed to do work in carrying on the activity.

§ 429. *Negligence in doing work which is accepted in reliance on the employer's doing the work himself*

One who employs an independent contractor to perform services for another which are accepted in the reasonable belief that the services are being rendered by the employer or by his servants, is subject to liability for physical harm caused by the negligence of the contractor in supplying such services, to the same extent as though the employer were supplying them himself or by his servants.

3. ROAD TRAFFIC ACT OF 19 DECEMBER 1952 (BGBL. I 837)
(AS AMENDED)*

CONTENTS

I Traffic rules

* A revised version of the Act concerning the Circulation of Motor Cars of 3 May 1909 (RGBl. 5, 437). English version by Kurt Lipstein and B. S. Markesinis.

II Liability

§ 7 *Liability of the Keeper of a Vehicle*

(1) If in the course of the operation of a motor vehicle a person is killed, the body or the health of a person is injured or an object is damaged, the keeper of the motor vehicle is obliged to compensate the injured party for the damage resulting therefrom.

(2) The duty to compensate is excluded, if the accident was caused by an unavoidable event which is not due to a defect in the construction of the vehicle or to the failure of its mechanism.

An event is deemed to be unavoidable in particular if it is due to the conduct of the injured party or of a third party who is not an employee or an animal and if both the keeper and the driver of the vehicle have applied that care which is required in the light of the circumstances.

(3) If somebody uses the vehicle without the knowledge and consent of the keeper of the vehicle that person is liable to pay compensation for the damage in the place of the keeper; in addition the keeper himself remains liable to pay compensation if the use of the motor vehicle was facilitated by his negligence. The first sentence of this paragraph does not apply if the person using the vehicle was employed by the keeper for the purpose of operating the vehicle or if he was entrusted with the vehicle by the keeper.

§ 8 *Exceptions*

The provisions of § 7 do not apply, if the accident was caused by a vehicle which cannot proceed at a speed exceeding 20 kilometres on level ground or if the injured person was employed in operating the motor vehicle.

§ 8a *Liability to Passengers in the Course of Commercial Transport of Persons*

(1) If a passenger in a motor vehicle has been killed or injured, the keeper of the vehicle is only liable in accordance with § 7 if a commercial transport of passengers for remuneration is involved.

If an object has been damaged which was carried by a motor vehicle, the keeper of the vehicle is only liable under § 7 if a person who is carried in the vehicle in the circumstances envisaged in § 7 carries the object on himself or with himself.

The commercial character of a transport of passengers in the meaning of the first and second sentences is not excluded by the fact that the transport is performed by a corporation or institution governed by public law.

(2) The duty of the keeper to pay compensation in respect of the death or injury suffered by a passenger in accordance with para. 1, final sentence, in

conjunction with § 7 cannot be excluded or restricted. Any provisions or arguments to the contrary are invalid.

§ 9 *Contributory Negligence of the Injured Party*

If the injured party contributed to the damage by his negligence, § 254 BGB applies with the proviso that if an object was damaged, negligence on the part of the person exercising factual control over the object is treated as equivalent to negligence on the part of the injured party.

§ 10 *Extent of Liability in the Case of Death*

(1) In the case of death, damages to be paid comprise compensation for the expenses of an attempted cure and for the economic loss which the deceased has suffered because his earning capacity was destroyed or reduced during his illness or because his needs were increased. The person liable to pay damages must also reimburse the cost of the burial to the person responsible for it.

(2) If at the time of the injury the deceased stood in a relationship to a third party by virtue of which he was legally bound to maintain the latter, or might become so liable, and if as a result of the death the third party has lost the right to maintenance, the person liable to pay compensation must pay damages to the third party to the extent that the deceased would have been liable to pay maintenance during the probable duration of his life. The duty to compensate arises even if the third party was conceived at the time of the injury, but had not yet been born.

§ 11 *Extent of Liability in the Case of Injury to the Person*

In the case of injury to the person or to health, the damages comprise compensation for the expenses of the cure and for the economic loss which the injured party suffered because his earning capacity was temporarily or permanently destroyed or reduced as a result of the injury or because his needs have increased.

§ 12 *Maximum Amount of Liability*

(1) The person who is bound to pay compensation is liable to pay:

1. Where one person was killed or injured a lump sum of up to DM 500,000 and no more or periodic payments up to DM 30,000 per annum;

2. Where several persons were killed or injured in the same event, notwithstanding the limits laid down in (1), a total lump sum of DM 750,000 and no more or periodical payments of DM 45,000; this restriction does not apply, however, in the cases of § 8a, para. 1, first sentence in so far as the liability of the keeper of the vehicle is concerned;

3. Where an object was damaged, up to an amount of DM 100,000 even if several objects were damaged in the same accident.

(2) If the damages to be paid to several claimants involved in the same event exceed in total the maximum amount enumerated in 2., first part of the sentence, or in 3., the damages payable to each individual are reduced in proportion of the total in relation to the maximum amount.

§ 13 *Periodical Payments as Damages*

(1) In the future, damages in respect of the loss or the reduction of earning capacity or because the needs of the injured party have increased as well as the damages due to a third party under § 10, para. 2, must be paid by way of periodical amounts.

(2) The provisions of § 843, II to IV of the BGB apply by way of analogy.

(3) If at the time when judgment was given for periodical payments the judgment debtor was not asked to give security, the person entitled to the payment may demand security nevertheless, if the circumstances of the judgment debtor have deteriorated considerably; in the same circumstances he can demand that the security fixed by the judgment should be increased.

§ 14 *Period of Limitation*

The period of limitation is determined by the analogous application of the rule of the Civil Code governing the limitation of actions in tort.

§ 15 *Duty to Give Notice—Laches*

The claimant for damages forfeits the rights granted by the provisions of this law, unless he had given notice of the accident to the person liable to pay compensation within six months after having ascertained the damage and the identity of the person liable to pay compensation. Forfeiture does not take place if the failure to give notice was due to circumstances for which the claimant for damages is not responsible or if the person liable to pay compensation has come to know of the accident by other means during the period set out above.

§ 16 *Liability due to Other Legal Provisions*

Any Federal provisions are unaffected according to which the keeper of a motor vehicle is more extensively liable for damage caused by the vehicle than according to the provisions of the present law or according to which another person is liable.

§ 17 *Contribution among Several Persons Liable to Pay Compensation*

(1) If damage is caused by several motor vehicles and if the keepers of the vehicles involved are bound by law to pay compensation to a third party, the liability to pay compensation of the keepers of the vehicles and the extent of the compensation to be paid as between themselves depends upon the circumstances, especially according to whether the damage has been caused predominantly by one or the other of the parties. The same applies to the liability of one of the keepers of the vehicles if the damage was caused to another keeper of a vehicle involved in the accident.

(2) The provisions of para. (1) apply by way of analogy if the damage is caused by a motor vehicle and an animal or by a motor vehicle and a railway.

§ 18 *Liability of the Driver to Pay Compensation*

(1) In the circumstances covered by § 7 I, the driver of the motor vehicle is also liable to pay compensation in accordance with the provisions of §§ 8–15. No liability exists if the damage was not caused by the blameworthy conduct of the driver.

(2) The provisions of § 16 apply by way of analogy.

(3) If in the circumstances covered by § 17 the driver of a vehicle is also liable to pay compensation, his liability in relation to the keepers and duties of the other vehicles involved, to a keeper of animals or a railway undertaking is determined by the analysis application of the provisions of § 17.

§ 19 (Abrogated.)

§ 20 *Local Jurisdictions*

Claims based on this Act fall also within the jurisdiction of the court of the district in which the event occurred which caused the damage.

III Provisions concerning penalties and administrative fines

§ 21   *Driving without a Licence*

§ 22   *Prohibited Manufacture, Sale or Issuing of Number Plates*

§ 23   *Commercial Sale of Components of Motor Vehicles not bearing Official Marking of Type Approved*

§ 24   *Contravention of Traffic Regulations*

§ 24a   *Limit of 0.8 Pro-mille of Alcohol in Blood*

Case 100

BUNDESGERICHTSHOF (SIXTH CIVIL DIVISION) 9 DECEMBER 1959*
BGHZ 29, 163 = NJW 1959, 627

The plaintiff's lorry (motor vehicle and two trailers) remained stationary on the right side of the Karlsruhe–Frankfurt autobahn in the night of 7–8 March 1951 because of damage to the engine. About 1.15 a.m. the carrier K—husband of the defendant Sophie K and father of the defendant Herbert Bernhard K—driving a motor lorry with a trailer ran into the plaintiff's stationary lorry. Both lorries sustained considerable damage. K, who had been driving his lorry, suffered such serious injuries that he died on the way to hospital.

The plaintiff contends that the collision is exclusively attributable to the fault of K; for he would have been bound, if he had been attentive enough, to notice the red light of the stationary lorry and the hurricane lantern which had been set up, and could have deviated in time on to the lane for overtaking. He demanded damages from K's heirs.

The District Court upheld the claim in principle. The Court of Appeal, on the other hand, in principle affirmed the defendant's liability in damages, limited only as to one-half. The plaintiff's application for review, in which he sought to have the judgment of the District Court restored, failed for these

Reasons

I. According to the findings of the Court of Appeal the carrier K, with his long-distance lights turned on, ran with the whole width of his vehicle into the stationary lorry, without braking in time or turning off to the left.

---

* English version by F. H. Lawson and B. S. Markesinis.

During the previous one and a half hours several other vehicles had driven past the plaintiff's lorry, whilst it stood on the autobahn. According to the Court of Appeal's view K also would have been bound to notice the stationary lorry if he had been attentive enough, even if it had been completely unlit, and could then still have moved on to the lane for overtaking. It went on to say: the fact that K did not react at all to the obstacle before him proves that he was guilty of gross inattention or, alternatively, that despite his being blinded by the light of oncoming vehicles he drove on with undiminished speed into a space where he could not see. On the basis of the established facts, this view of the Court of Appeal is unexceptional in law. It therefore also held rightly that the defendants, as heirs of K, must under §§ 823, 1967 BGB make good the damage to the plaintiff.

II. The applicant for review objected that the Court of Appeal applied § 17 StVG and awarded to the plaintiff in principle compensation for only half his damage.

He alleges that §§ 7, 17 StVG are not applicable, because the plaintiff's lorry was no longer in operation and urges that a vehicle is no longer in operation, even when it has not reached the end of its journey, if it has come to a full stop from lack of fuel or a mechanical fault. Even if a failure of its engine causes it to stop on a traffic highway and it stays there for a not wholly inappreciable time, it is generally regarded as no longer in operation, since it has lost the capacity to move.

This view of the appellant corresponds in result to the practice of the Reichsgericht and of several Courts of Appeal. According to that practice, a vehicle is no longer in operation in the sense of § 7 StVG if it is reduced to a complete standstill and owing to failure its engine can be set again in operation only after considerable time (e.g. RGZ 122, 270; 333, 132, 262). In so holding, the Reichsgericht also did not start from the engineering notion of operation, according to which a vehicle is in operation only as long as the engine is working directly or indirectly. It preferred the traffic-orientated point of view and even then attributed an accident to the operation of a motor vehicle if it stood in a close local and temporal connection with a particular operation or a particular operating mechanism, irrespective of whether the engine propelled the vehicle or not. According to the Reichsgericht's point of view, approved by the Bundesgerichtshof, the operation of a vehicle is therefore not interrupted as a rule when it stops on the highway with the engine switched off. But even in adopting this traffic-orientated point of view, the Reichsgericht has interpreted the concept of the operation of a motor vehicle strictly, and assumed that the operation comes to an end when, for more than a short time, the vehicle can no longer move under its own power because of engine failure or lack of fuel.

The Bundesgerichtshof is unable to follow this practice of the Reichsgericht because, in view of the enormous increase of motor traffic and its dangers, it no longer conforms to the sense and purpose of § 7 StVG. The purpose of the Act, to protect participants in traffic against the increasing dangers of present-day motor traffic, makes it necessary to give a broad interpretation to the concept 'in the operation of a motor vehicle' [references]. In that decision this Senate denied that the vehicle was inoperative and so exempt from strict liability where a driver has left his lorry on the carriageway of a federal highway to have a good night's rest. The Senate also attributed the accident that ensued because a car ran into the stationary lorry to the operation of the stationary vehicle in the sense of § 7 StVG. No other conclusion can be reached if similarly an accident occurs because a lorry remains standing for a considerable time on the carriageway of a high-speed highway owing to engine failure. The case that now calls for decision differs from the earlier one only because the lorry here had lost the capacity to proceed under its own power, whereas there, although its engine was turned off, it was ready to move on the highway. That distinction is irrelevant in applying § 7 StVG if one looks at the concept of operation in that provision from the traffic-orientated point of view, as the prevailing opinion now does. The risks which the motor vehicle produces in traffic emanate not only from the engine and its effect on the vehicle but, with the increase of traffic, more and more from its general flow and in particular from motor vehicles which stop or park on the carriageway portion of a high-speed highway. It is precisely on the autobahn on which the present accident occurred that stationary vehicles raise a typical risk for other participants in the traffic. In this case, as the Bundesgerichtshof observed in its judgment of 8 April 1957 [references] the risk of a stationary motor vehicle may even be greater than of a moving one. It is therefore permissible and justified by the sense and purpose of the provisions on liability of the Road Traffic Act to attribute an accident produced by a collision with a stationary vehicle not only to the operation of the moving but also of the stationary vehicle and hence to make both drivers strictly liable in damages. It is irrelevant whether the driver voluntarily pulled up for a break or was forced to stop on the carriageway owing to a defect in the vehicle. The decisive factor is that in both cases other participants in the traffic are put at risk by his vehicle standing on the highway. That an accident due to a defect in the vehicle or a failure of its mechanism should lead to liability of the driver is clear from § 7 StVG which expressly denies that this case constitutes an avoidable event which excludes liability. This liability for accidents which are attributable to a technical defect in the vehicle would, as the Court of Appeal of Karlsruhe (VersR 1956, 260) accurately emphasizes, be rendered nugatory to a considerable extent if it were held that an accident during a halt due to a technical failure was not within the operation of the vehicle and therefore did not lead to liability under § 7 I StVG. The wording of section II of that provision shows that the strict liability established by it extends also to accidents of this kind.

This result follows a line which originated with the decision of the Reichsgericht, RGZ 170, 1. There the Reichsgericht held that an accident was within the course of operation of a lorry in a case where a railway train collided with a lorry stuck in a hole in the road, the left rear part of its loading flap extending over the rails and unable to move under its own power because the lifting arrangement had been torn off. In that case, the Reichsgericht held that the operation of the motor vehicle continued. It explained that the lorry had moved to the place of accident and had thereby in the course of its operation set the cause which produced the collision. It is not essentially different when a lorry, as in the present case, blocks a portion of the highway because of engine failure. Here also the lorry drove up to the place of accident and therefore produced in the course of its operation a situation endangering traffic.

In examining the question whether in such a case § 7 StVG is to be applied, one cannot neglect the criterion of how long a motor vehicle stands on the carriageway. If the defect in the vehicle can be remedied in a short time and it can soon go on its way, it is now generally accepted in accordance with the practice of the Reichsgericht that the operation of the vehicle, for the purpose of § 7 StVG, is not interrupted by that halt (cf. *inter alia* RG JW 1929, 2055 no. 7 in a case where the petrol lead was blocked). If now one considers that the dangers from a stationary vehicle increase the longer it forms an obstacle for other participants in the traffic, it would be illogical from the traffic-orientated standpoint to treat favourably as regards liability the driver of a vehicle which is stationary for a longer period and which therefore creates a greater risk. It is wrong to exempt him from liability while a slighter operative risk of the vehicle attracts strict liability. If, as in the present case, a vehicle must stay for a longer time on the carriageway because it cannot be repaired at once, then if another vehicle collides with the obstacle, that accident must also be attributed to the operation of the stationary vehicle [references]. The operation of this vehicle continues as long as the driver leaves the vehicle in the midst of the traffic and the dangerous situation thus created continues. For the purpose of § 7 StVG the operation is only interrupted when the vehicle is withdrawn from the carriageway and is placed somewhere away from the regular traffic. Only thus the interruption of the operation is made known to others, but also that typical risk is eliminated which arises if motor vehicles are stopped or parked on the fast traffic lane of the carriageway. Whether as Walther [reference] contends, the answer should be different when an unauthorized user leaves a vehicle standing in the middle of the traffic, never to use it again, need not be examined since such a case is not in issue here. In the case for decision the lorry was on the way to a particular place and it was planned to continue the journey.

This view is criticized by Roth Stielow [reference] on the ground that it goes beyond the limits which the judge must observe in interpreting legislation. He starts by assuming that there is a 'clear statutory direction to the contrary' which it infringes. But this starting-point is wrong. The enactment does not provide a detailed definition of the concept 'in the operation of a motor vehicle' and, as Boehmer (*VersR* 1957, 587) correctly explains, says nowhere that it only constitutes an accident within the operation if the vehicle is in motion or its engine is running. But if the legislator has not provided any further explanation, it is for the judge to interpret this ambiguous concept. The judge is therefore not prohibited from interpreting § 7 StVG broadly if in so doing he conforms to the sense and purpose of the enactment to protect participants in traffic against the dangers of motor traffic. It is therefore entirely within the scope of permissible interpretation if this protection of the participants is extended also to the dangers produced by stationary vehicles in present-day traffic conditions.

Even if the legislature in 1908 saw the chief danger of motor vehicles in their rapid movement due to engine power and hence regarded the mechanical aspect of the concept of operation as paramount, that would not exclude the adaptation of the concept 'in the operation of a motor vehicle' to the experiences and requirements of present-day traffic. As was already emphasized in another connection, according to experience modern traffic risks arise, not only from the engine as such and its effect on the motor vehicle, but from the movement of traffic as a whole. The motor vehicle itself creates a substantial danger as part of the traffic. Accordingly, Wussow [reference] rightly remarks that it is precisely from the point of view of risk, which the legislator takes as his starting-point, that the traffic-orientated aspect becomes much more prominent than the danger produced by the engine. The judge would not be true to his task if under these circumstances he clung to the concept, which is far too narrow, of a mechanical operation. His duty towards legislation and to law (Art. 20 II GG) allows him not only to develop the law by interpretation in the direction of its further evolution, but obliges him to do so if the finding of a just decision requires it. The wording of the enactment gives way to its sense and purpose. To give effect to them in applying the law in the individual case and to provide an equitable and reasonable solution to the dispute is the judge's task [references]. As Radbruch [references] expresses it, not only must he follow the thoughts of the legislature, but he must also think them through to their final conclusion. But the judge does nothing else when he adapts the concept of operation in § 7 StVG to the experiences and requirements of the modern age in order to give effect to the legislative intent which is to afford extensive protection against the dangers of motor traffic.

In any case, it cannot be assumed that the characterization of the concept of operation from the traffic-orientated point of view, which has long prevailed in the courts, conflicts with the intent of present-day legislature, for while it has repeatedly altered other provisions of the Road Traffic Act, it has retained the wording of § 7 I StVG, although it was aware of the long-standing practice concerning the term 'in the operation of a motor vehicle'.

III. In view of these considerations, the Court of Appeal was right in dividing the damage of the plaintiff according to § 17 StVG, and, when examining how far it was caused predominantly by the one or the other side, considered in the first place the risk arising from the operation of both lorries. [A discussion of the apportionment follows.]

Case 101

BUNDESGERICHTSHOF (SIXTH CIVIL DIVISION) 23 NOVEMBER 1955*
BGHZ 19, 114 = NJW 1956, 217 = VersR 1956, 36, 126

On 23 December 1948 the A. H. Limited Partnership held a Christmas party for its personnel in a restaurant. E, the partner personally responsible, instructed the defendant, a bookkeeper in the firm, to take home two drunken employees, Sch. and H, in the firm's car. The car was struck by a train on a level-crossing and H was killed.

The appropriate professional association claimed from the plaintiff reimbursement of its payment under § 1542 of the Imperial Public Insurance Act (henceforth referred to as RVO) and the provisions of the Reichshaftpflichtgesetz. The plaintiff, the German Federal Railway, met the claim of the professional association. It demands of the defendant compensation for its disbursements on the ground that he had alone caused the accident by his gross negligence.

Its claim for compensation failed in all instances for these

Reasons

I. The Court of Appeal rightly proceeded from the principle that the plaintiff can under § 17 of the Road Traffic Act (StVG) claim from the defendant compensation for the payments made to the professional association only if the defendant as driver of the car involved in the accident was bound by statute to make good the damage suffered by the dependants of the deceased. For that purpose it is material whether H lost his life in an

---

* English version by Kurt Lipstein.

industrial accident and whether the defendant's liability is excluded by § 899 RVO in combination with § 898 RVO.

1. The appropriate professional association acknowledged that the fatal accident of H was an industrial accident requiring compensation. The court is bound by this decision under § 901 RVO.

If the defendant were to be regarded as an agent or representative of the entrepreneur, or as a superintendent of his business and work, he would be liable to H's dependants under § 899 in combination with § 898 RVO only if it was established in criminal proceedings that he caused the accident intentionally. Since no such finding was made, and the defendant was only convicted of a criminal act committed negligently, it is necessary to examine first of all whether the defendants belong to one of the classes of persons who are assimilated to the entrepreneur in § 899 RVO.

The Landgericht and Oberlandesgericht regarded the defendant as a superintendent of the business and work. The Court of Appeal came to that conclusion on the basis of the following findings:

The defendant supervised the whole business in the absence of the managing partner. He had prepared and carried through the staff Christmas party on the entrepreneur's instruction. That the managing partner, on leaving the party about four o'clock in the morning with his co-partners, entrusted to the defendant, and not to one of the professional drivers who were present, the task of taking the drunken employees home was not only because he seemed to be quite sober but because the whole conduct of the party had been placed in his hands. The managing partners, on leaving the party, had wished to hand over the responsibility for its smooth ending to the man who possessed the highest authority in their absence. By virtue of the order given him, the defendant had to perform independently and responsibly the task of getting the inebriates properly and safely home and, in accordance with the entrepreneur's duty of care, to assure the safety of the employees who were his passengers.

Contrary to the view of the applicant for review, these findings justify the conclusion that the defendant enjoys the protection of § 899 RVO.

The applicant maintains that the Court of Appeal drew the character of superintendent too widely and therefore misunderstood it. That is not correct. In its judgment the Court of Appeal accurately started from the principles regarding the notion of character of a superintendent of business and work developed by the Reichsgericht in its decision RGZ 167, 685 and 170, 159. It did not fail to realize that the only person who can be regarded as a superintendent is a member of the work-force who has the duty to supervise others so engaged or at least one of the departments of the enterprise. As the Reichsgericht (RGZ 170, 159) correctly states, he must stand out from among the other employees by the fact that he must care for the co-operation of several employees or for the smooth interlocking of the establishment and the plant, and therefore for the harmonious interplay of personal and technical forces and must be responsible for these. It must be conceded to the appellant that this is of course not generally the case of a car driver who has no other duties. The performance of the necessary journeys and the care and upkeep of the car are not a supervisory activity contemplated by § 899 RVO. It is established, however, that the defendant was not appointed as chauffeur. As the Court of Appeal found, even when he undertook the fatal journey he did not act only as a chauffeur but was engaged in a task that exceeded the general duties of a driver. As the Court of Appeal found, he was given the responsibility for the smooth ending of the party after the managers had left, and therefore a position was entrusted to him that raised him above the other employees. The applicant is in error in maintaining that the order did not fulfil the conditions for rendering him responsible for the regular co-operation of several employees or the smooth interlocking of the establishment and the plant, for such a range of duties demanded a delegation of at least some duration. There is no need here to decide whether the position of a superintendent of business and work requires that the responsibility is to be delegated for a longer period, for in the present case there is a finding, overlooked by the applicant, that the defendant had the task not only for the time being, but generally of supervising the business in the managing partner's absence. In this situation the Court of Appeal's characterization of the defendant as a superintendent of business and work is free from objection. It can therefore be left undecided whether he was also an agent in the sense of § 899 RVO, because in driving several employees home on the order of the entrepreneur he discharged the latter's duty of care. In any case, the finding of fact makes it free from doubt that, even on the journey which led to the accident, the defendant acted as a person assimilated to the entrepreneur as mentioned in § 899 RVO.

2. Moreover, the application of §§ 898, 899 RVO is not excluded by § 1 second sentence of the Act of 7 December 1943 (RGBl. I 674) on the extended admission of claims for damages arising out of service and industrial accidents. According to that provision, insured persons and their surviving dependants can make good their claims for compensation without limit against the persons mentioned in §§ 898, 899 RVO, if the accident occurred when they were participating in general traffic. On this point the Court of Appeal followed the case-law of the Supreme Court for the British Zone, according to which there is no participation in the general traffic if the injured person was a passenger in a private vehicle driven by the person who caused the injury and the injured party stood in causal and organic

connection with the employment (BGHZ 1, 245 = NJW 1949, 263). It assumed that such was the case here.

The present Senate decided (BGHZ 8, 330, 336 ff.) that so-called works traffic (constant transport of workers in a works vehicle to the place of business) constitutes transport within the business and that the transported workers do not participate in general traffic. It left unanswered the question whether also in the case dealt with in the Supreme Court of the British Zone, in which the entrepreneur took an employee from the place of work in his own car, there was no participation in the general traffic. In the dispute between the present parties there is also no need to decide whether the principle established by the Supreme Court is invariably to be followed. In any event in the present case, in agreement with the Court of Appeal, no participation in the general traffic can be said to have taken place.

The Act of 7 December 1943 deals principally with accidents suffered by a worker on the way from or to the place of work and which count as industrial accidents according to § 543 RVO. If an entrepreneur or a person assimilated to him (§ 899 RVO) should run down an employee on the way to the place of work, §§ 898, 899 RVO would exclude claims of a private law nature against the entrepreneur and the persons mentioned in § 899 RVO, although in such cases only a slight connection exists between the accident and the worker's activity in the business. The Act, according to its preamble, wishes to do away with the unfairness that was produced because in cases of this kind a person injured in the course of service or work is placed in a worse position than other participants in traffic. This unfair disadvantage was to be removed in all cases where the accident occurs in the course of participation in general traffic. As this Senate has already said (BGHZ 8, 330 [337]), in deciding whether there is such participation it must first be asked whether the insured person suffered the accident as an ordinary participant in traffic or as an employee. Whether the former or the latter is the case or predominates must be decided on the facts of the particular case. If an employee, like H in the present case, is driven home after a staff party in a works car on the entrepreneur's order, that journey is occasioned by the operation of the enterprise and is so closely connected with the enterprise and with the injured party's membership of the enterprise that the character of the passenger as a participant in the traffic recedes into the background. That applies especially if the journey, as here, served only to take the employees home and, as the Court of Appeal also found, was ordered out of a feeling of care for the drunken employees. That an insured person in a case of this kind does not participate in the general traffic, in the meaning of § 1 II of the Act on the extended admission of claims for damages arising from service and industrial accidents, conforms to the principles on which both the courts and writers proceed in similar cases. The prevailing opinion recognizes that taking an employee home as a passenger from the place of work in the works car is not a participation in the general traffic [references].

The Court of Appeal thus held correctly that the Act of 7 December 1943 on the extended application of claims for damages arising out of service and industrial accidents does not stand in the way of applying §§ 898, 899 RVO in the present case.

II. The applicant for review also asks for an examination as to whether the statutory exclusion of liability in § 898 RVO affects the claim for compensation at all. He refers to the judgment of 3 February 1954 (BGHZ 12, 213) in which this Senate decided that a contractual exclusion or reduction of liability, e.g. between driver and passenger, cannot adversely affect the claim for contribution by a second tortfeasor under § 17 StVG or § 426 BGB. The applicant wishes to apply to the present case the notion that the effectiveness of such an exclusion of liability would stultify the equitable contribution intended by the legislator, and maintains that since the entrepreneurs and those assimilated to them under § 899 RVO are liable to the professional association for his expenditure according to § 903 RVO, the limitation of liability under §§ 898, 899 RVO is only justified in relation to the person directly injured in order to avoid litigation within the enterprise. But the legislator, the applicant continues, cannot have intended by this provision to interfere with the rights of third persons and thus to curtail provisions whose purpose is to produce an equitable compromise. Since the professional association sought the reimbursement of its expenditure from the plaintiff only but did not make any claims against the defendant under § 903 RVO, the plaintiff, who was responsible only on the ground of strict liability, was saddled with the damage, whereas the defendant, who was to blame, was not called upon to pay. The applicant regards this as unfair and as an infringement of §§ 898, 899 RVO and 17 StVG.

These arguments of the applicant for review cannot be of help to it. It may, of course, at first sight appear unfair that the plaintiff, who has to answer for the damage only on the basis of strict liability, must perform in full, whereas the defendant, who was to blame, is relieved of responsibility. But this objection of the applicant does not take sufficiently into account the special conditions of accident insurance law, which consciously aims at protecting the entrepreneur, agent, and business superintendent against claims exceeding the liability under § 903 RVO [reference]. The provisions, indeed, of §§ 898, 899 RVO serve also, as must be conceded to the applicant, the purpose of avoiding, in the interest of industrial peace, disputes between workers and employers over the responsibility for business accidents (BGHZ 8, 330 [339]) . . . It is, however, essential here that the Act has in relation to industrial accidents excluded claims for compensation by injured parties against an entrepreneur because the latter has to bear the burden of accident insurance and because the insured are allowed claims for compensation when the entrepreneur and his agents are not to blame and even if the employer himself has caused the accident through his own negligence. Likewise § 899 RVO in principle relieves agents as well as business and work superintendents of liability towards the workers because under § 903 RVO they must reimburse the professional association the expenses incurred by the latter, if they caused the accident intentionally or by carelessly neglecting their official, professional, or industrial duties. Hence the exemption of the entrepreneur as well as his agents and superintendents from liability towards the injured constitutes a compensation for the latter in return for their statutory liability to the professional association (RGZ 170, 159 [160]; cf. also RGZ 153, 38, 41, 42 and BGHZ 8, 330 [338]). This compensation would only be incomplete if the entrepreneur, agents, and superintendent were exposed, along with the liability under § 903 RVO, to a further claim and had to pay damages to a second wrongdoer in whole or in part by way of compensation. That would contradict the purpose of the law of social insurance, for the protection afforded by it to the business entrepreneur and those assimilated to him according to § 899 RVO would in that way be nullified again. That cannot be the intention of the statute. It shows that as a rule the insured has no claim against the individual entrepreneur, agent, or superintendent and that such a claim lies only in the exceptional case, not in issue here, where the entrepreneur, agent, or superintendent causes the accident intentionally (cf. RGZ 153, 38 [43]). If, however, the injured party has no claim whatever against them, an essential condition is lacking for a claim to contribution by the second wrongdoer. Contribution is a consequence of the common duty of several wrongdoers to pay damages and hence presupposes as a matter of principle that several wrongdoers are liable as joint debtors for the damage (BGHZ 11, 170 [174] and 12, 213). Since in the case to be decided the liability of the defendant to the injured party's surviving dependants is excluded, a joint debt is lacking and with it the foundation for a claim to contribution.

It is another question whether the plaintiff could have resisted the professional association's claim to payment, on the ground that it would be contrary to good faith, in spite of the possibility of recourse against the defendant (§ 903 RVO) to claim the full payment from the plaintiff. That question, however, need not be decided here.

III. The applicant for review now maintains that the claim has none the less a basis in § 426 II BGB. Both parties are alleged to be liable to the professional association as joint debtors, the defendant under § 903 IV RVO and the plaintiff because the claim of the surviving dependants under § 1542

RVO had been assigned to the professional association. Since the plaintiff has satisfied the association, their claim has passed to the plaintiff under § 426 II BGB.

It must be conceded to the applicant that both parties were debtors of the association for the reasons adduced by it. But that could lead to a duty of contribution between them under § 426 BGB only if to that extent they had stood in a true joint debtor relationship towards the association (BGB RGRK 10 edn. § 426 n. 1 and § 421 n. 1*c*). That, however, is not the case. A true joint debtor relationship presupposes an internal connection of the two obligations in the sense of a legal community of purpose (BGHZ 13, 360 [365], Great Civil Senate with references to practice of the Reichsgericht). That is missing from the obligations on which the claims were based which the association had against parties to the present dispute. It has lodged against the plaintiff a claim of the dependants of the injured party which is based on the Reichshaftpflichtgesetz and falls within the sphere of private law; it had been assigned to the association by operation of law (§ 1542 RVO). On the other hand, the association had against the defendant in its own right a claim to compensation of a special kind based on a statutory provision forming part of public law (§ 903 RVO) against which a contributory fault of the injured party could not be pleaded (RGZ 96, 135; 144, 31 [35]). It is adapted to the structure of accident insurance in the Reich Insurance Ordinance and to the relationship of the association to enterprises belonging to it which must pay contributions and has the purpose of indemnifying the association for its expenditure arising from the accident. Admittedly the existence of a true joint debt is not absolutely excluded by the differing bases of the obligations and of their origins. Instead it is decisive that in the present case an internal connection is lacking between the two obligations in the sense of a legal community of purpose. Both claims stand only in loose economic connection with each other, for they both had for their object the reimbursement of payments which the association was bound to make on the occasion of the accident arising out of the enterprise. The plaintiff and the defendant thus owed identical performance to the same creditor (the professional association) to the extent that the economic purpose of the obligation is attained by a single performance to the creditor who can therefore claim only one payment. This happened, however, without the internal connection required for a true joint debt. Since there was no legal community between the debtors, which is required by § 426 BGB as a presupposition for a duty to contribute (cf. BGHZ 13, 360, 365), only a joint debt in an untechnical sense can be envisaged. §§ 421 ff. BGB, and in particular the regulation of contribution in § 426 BGB, do not cover a relationship of this kind. Hence there is also no room for an analogous application of that provision.

This emerges also from another point of view. The Reichs Insurance Act does not wish to force the professional association to make claims on its members to cover its expenditure if they only acted negligently. Accordingly § 905 RVO provides that the meeting of members of the professional association or, if the by-laws so permit, the directors can renounce their right to recourse. If the directors wish to claim reimbursement, § 906 RVO allows the person liable to appeal to the meeting. Accordingly, the question whether a claim should be made on a member of the association under § 903 RVO is referred to the exclusive decision of the association. If the plaintiff were to be granted a claim for contribution by an analogous application of § 426 BGB, that would indirectly involve an outsider bringing a claim against the tortfeasor indirectly, which the professional association did not wish to make. This would be an admissible attack on the insurer's authority to decide.

This view of the Senate that the plaintiff cannot bring a claim for contribution under § 426 BGB conforms to the practice of the Reichsgericht. It took the same standpoint in its decision in Seuffarch, 65 no. 32; and in its judgment published in DR 1940, 1779 no. 10 dealing with a similar case without, however, going more deeply into the matter it came to the same result that no joint debt and therefore no duty to contribute existed [reference].

IV. Before the Court of Appeal the plaintiff, by referring to the fact that the defendant had endangered transport, also based its claim on § 823 II BGB. The Court of Appeal regarded this as a modification of the claim which was inadmissible owing to irrelevance (§ 264 ZPO). It can be left undecided whether the arguments of the Court of Appeal on this question merit approval, for even from that legal standpoint contrary to the view of the applicant, a claim by the plaintiff for the reimbursement of its expenditure is not well founded.

The plaintiff does not allege that as a result of the defendant's conduct it suffered damage to its locomotive or any other direct damage to itself. It relies only on the damage which is suffered because it was called upon to pay under the Reichshaftpflichtgesetz. A claim for compensation of that damage cannot be derived from § 823 II BGB in combination with §§ 315, 316 StGB. It is true that those criminal law provisions are protective statutes, which also serve to protect the plaintiff. Moreover, the mere circumstances that the sum which the plaintiff claims involves indirect damage does not, contrary to the view of the respondent, lead to a rejection of the claim, since, according to a general principle of civil law, a person who has suffered direct damage can claim compensation not only in respect of any direct but also of any indirect damage which he suffered. It is however always a presupposition that the damage falls within the scope of the interests protected by the protective statute, i.e. that it arose from the invasion of a legal interest for the protection of which the legal rule was enacted [references]. In the case for decision the danger which the protective statute is intended to avert did not in fact arise. The provisions on endangering the operation of a railway (§§ 315, 316 StGB) protect the health and property of railway entrepreneurs and the other persons directly affected by railway traffic, but not their general economic interests [references]. The damage that the plaintiff suffered through the claim for compensation on the basis of the Reichshaftpflichtgesetz affects only its general economic interests and therefore a sphere of interests which is not protected here. Hence § 823 II BGB, in combination with §§ 315, 316 StGB, also fails to provide a legal basis for the claim made in the plaintiff's action.

Case 102

BUNDESGERICHTSHOF (SIXTH CIVIL DIVISION) 27 MAY 1975[*]
NJW 1975, 1886 = VersR 1975, 945

The plaintiff owned a chicken-farm. The hens were housed in a building where they were arranged in so-called batteries. The first defendant supplied the plaintiff with concentrated chicken feed. On 8 September 1969 the second defendant, employed by the first defendant, delivered ten tons of chicken feed loaded on a lorry which was equipped with two tanks in which the feed was contained. The chicken feed was to be deposited in a silo attached to the building. The walls of the silo consisted of chipboard sheets of a thickness of 20 millimetres. On the outside of the silo, a feed-pipe leading to within 70 centimetres below the roof turned vertically into the silo and terminated at a distance of 1.25 millimetres from the opposite chipboard wall. The second defendant connected the tanks of the lorry with the feed-pipe by means of a hose-pipe. Using a compressor attached to the lorry, he blew the feed into the feed-pipe in order to deposit the feed in the silo. The force of the pressure broke the chipboard sheets of the opposite wall and the escaping feed was deposited on the adjacent roof of the building which collapsed under the weight. Many laying hens were killed or had to be destroyed. The plaintiff claimed damages in respect of the damage to the roof and to his livestock.

The Court of First Instance allowed the claim and the Court of Appeal of Aldenburg rejected an appeal by the defendant. Upon a second appeal the judgment below was quashed and the case referred back for the following

[*] English version by Kurt Lipstein.

Reasons

I. The Court of Appeal left it open as to whether the first defendant is liable in contract, as the Court of First Instance has held. Instead it found that the first defendant was liable under § 7 I of the Road Traffic Act because an object belonging to the plaintiff had been damaged 'in the course of operating the defendant's motor vehicle'. According to the Court of Appeal, the necessary connection existed in space and time between a certain operational use or installation and the accident, at any rate if, as in the present case, a load was discharged from a vehicle with the aid of a motor, thereby causing an accident.

II. These conclusions cannot be maintained in face of the objections raised by the appellant. It is impossible to accept the view of the Court of Appeal that the accident occurred 'in the course of operating a motor vehicle' in the meaning of § 7 I of the Road Traffic Act.

1. According to the so-called engine-orientated view, which was enlarged by the traffic-orientated view first put forward by the Reichsgericht [reference] and subsequently adopted and developed by the Bundesgerichtshof [reference] in respect of certain cases, a motor vehicle is 'in operation' if its motor has been started and moves the vehicle or one of its operational parts. To that extent, as the Court of Appeal states correctly, it makes no difference whether during the operational activity the motor vehicle is located on a public highway or (as here) on private land (building site [reference]; works compound [reference]).

As a result of technical developments, the motor power of motor vehicles is being used not only to transport persons and goods, but also for other works processes which can hardly be regarded as merely loading or unloading goods for transport. Thus many specialized vehicles exist today which are constructed for special tasks but serve ordinary purposes at the same time. The heavy goods lorry of the defendant was also such a specialized vehicle, since it was fitted with special containers for transporting feed and was provided, *inter alia*, with a mechanical installation for discharging it. If an accident occurs in the course of employing operational installations of such special vehicles which do not serve directly the purpose of transport, it is not obvious that such an accident has occurred 'in the course of operating a motor vehicle' in the meaning of § 7 of the Road Traffic Act. In the present case, this cannot be said to have happened, contrary to the view of the Court of Appeal.

(*a*) The Court of Appeal, too, states that the question is whether the accident is still to be regarded as arising from the operation of the motor vehicle. According to the Court of Appeal the test is whether the accident was 'closely connected in space and time with an operational process' of the heavy goods vehicle (for this notion see the decisions of this Division [reference]). This formula indicates, in the first place, that a link of adequate causality must exist between the operation of the motor vehicle and the actual damage. However, the meaning of this formula is not completely expressed thereby. To that extent it only defines a minimum requirement for a causal link to exist. In addition, the effect caused by the operation of the motor vehicle for which damages are to be paid must be covered by the meaning and the purpose of the rule creating liability, i.e. by the protective range of § 7 I of the Road Traffic Act [references]. It is insufficient for the Court of Appeal to argue that the process of discharge falls within the sphere of operation of the lorry because the compressor employed for the purpose of discharging the load was impelled by the motor of the lorry. This establishes only the causal link between the operation of the motor and the damage which, however, cannot be in doubt. On the other hand, contrary to the opinion of the Court of Appeal, the occurrence is not to be attributed to the operation of the lorry, against the danger of which § 7 I of the Road Traffic Act is to provide protection, as the appellant correctly points out.

(*aa*) It is true that in accordance with the recent practice of the Courts of Appeal the discharge of a vehicle with the assistance of its motor constitutes a use of an operative installation corresponding to the purpose of the vehicle and therefore takes place 'in the course of its operation' [references—all concerning either the loading or discharging of oil by a tanker lorry]. These decisions are frequently cited in the literature, albeit without a more detailed discussion of possible objections against them [references]. This Division has expressly left the question open in the cases which have come before it hitherto on appeal from the Courts of Appeal of Nürnberg and Hamm as to whether an accident caused on the occasion of oil being loaded or discharged by a road-tanker can be also attributed to the operation of the latter in the meaning of the Road Traffic Act [references]. The decision of this Division dated 25 April 1956 [reference] also does not show any other attitude in principle. It is true that this Division held that a 'close connection in space and time with the operational process' existed in the case where a motor lorry dropped its load on a rubbish dump with the help of its engine power and thereby caused an accident. However, in that case, too, this Division observed that no need arose to decide whether such a connection 'always' exists when damage is caused on discharging a motor lorry.

(*bb*) Whether, as in the present case, an accident caused in the course of the unloading of a specialized motor vehicle with the assistance of its engine is still to be attributed to the operation of a vehicle in the meaning of the Road Traffic Act depends upon the answer to the question against what perils § 7 of the Road Traffic Act is to provide protection and whether the user of this 'operative installation' which led to the accident still falls within this range of protection. Naturally only such perils are involved which emanate from the motor vehicle in its capacity of an engine serving transport (see §§ 1, 2 of the Road Traffic Act). As soon as a connection no longer exists with the purpose of the motor vehicle as a means of transport in traffic, and the motor vehicle is only used as a means of performing work, the danger emanating specifically from a motor vehicle used for its natural purpose has ceased to exist. (See also the Reichsgericht [reference omitted], concentrating on the nature of a motor vehicle as a means of transport.) Since our legal system does not know a general principle of strict liability for operating engines supplying power at work, § 7 of the Road Traffic Act cannot be applied to accidents which occur in consequence of technical processes which cannot any longer be reasonably connected with the character of the engine employed as part of a motor vehicle. As this Division has already stated in its decision of 10 January 1961 [references] it is not decisive that the engine of the motor vehicle has been started up if this is done independently of an operational process characteristic of a motor vehicle for purposes other than moving it [reference]. In the case referred to, the engine of a moped served only to operate its lights which were required as a source of illumination for purposes other than to drive the moped (but see critically Boehmer [reference]).

In what circumstances the power of the engine and the operational installations of the vehicle driven by it have lost their connection with the latter's function as a means of transport and with road traffic, with the result that from the point of view of legal liability only the function of the engines as a source of power is in issue, can only be determined in the individual case, having regard to all the circumstances. If, as in the present case, the engine is used for purposes of unloading, it will be decisive whether the damage was caused by the special construction of the vehicle and the operational installations connected therewith (as for instance in the case of discharging a load with the help of a tipping-device; see the decision of this Division of 25 April 1956 [reference] or in the case of a towing vehicle equipped with a crane or of a vehicle for transporting long loads which is provided with a grip [reference]) or whether its function as a source of working power was predominant, as for instance in the case of a mobile building-crane.

If the present case is examined in accordance with these principles it follows that it is not to be regarded as part of the operation of a motor vehicle if feed is blown into a silo with the engine of the motor vehicle running the compressor. The occurrence of damage is entirely independent, both technically and legally, of the specific peril emanating from a motor vehicle, be it even a specialized vehicle. Instead, the only peril is that flowing from the engine providing power for work, which is supplied by the engine of the motor vehicle. The damage thus caused does not come within the range of protection provided by § 7 of the Road Traffic Act.

(b) The traffic-orientated approach to the term 'operation' in § 7 of the Road Traffic Act does not lead to any different conclusion. It was developed for the protection of those involved in traffic in order to cover the after-effects of the perils created by a motor vehicle present in the area of public traffic, even if the motor vehicle which had been put 'in operation' had come to a standstill [reference]. A dangerous situation of this kind has not occurred in the present case. The motor vehicle was standing on private land belonging to the plaintiff and did not represent an obstacle for other users of the road in the place where it stood.

Case 103

BUNDESGERICHTSHOF (SIXTH CIVIL DIVISION) 6 JUNE 1989*
NJW 1989, 2616

Facts

The plaintiff, who suffered from high blood pressure, was involved in a road accident around midnight on 28 April 1984 while driving his wife's car. His car collided with another vehicle driven by M. The liability insurer for this car was the defendant. Soon after the accident had occurred and the police had taken the details of the accident, the plaintiff suffered a stroke. Since then, he has been unable to work and draws disablement benefit. Between the parties it is not disputed that the defendant must compensate the plaintiff for all the damages of the accident. On the basis of these facts, the plaintiff claimed from the defendant compensation for his loss of earnings, a declaration of the defendant's continuing responsibility for the loss since the claim was brought, and damages for pain and suffering; in particular the plaintiff made the following allegations: the stroke, which occurred as a result of the rupture of a blood vessel and a resulting brain haemorrhage, was caused by the excitement brought on by the conduct of M and his three passengers after the accident and the measures taken by the police officer who was at the place of the accident in order to test whether the plaintiff was driving under the influence of alcohol. After the accident, M and his passengers approached the plaintiff in a threatening manner. One of the passengers ran at him and shouted, incorrectly, that he was driving too fast.

* English version by Ms J. Shaw.

Another of the persons accompanying M drove his vehicle to the side of the road, so that he feared that it would no longer be possible for the facts of the accident to be clarified. All four occupants of M's vehicle falsely alleged to the police that he was under the influence of alcohol; that caused the police officer to breathalyse him, although the results of the test were negative. As a consequence of this test and the subsequent conduct of M and his fellow passengers, the shock which he had suffered as a result of the accident grew more intense. When he later drove on, he experienced symptoms of paralysis which were the symptoms of his stroke.

The plaintiff's claim was unsuccessful in both lower courts, and his application to the BGH was rejected.

For the following

Reasons

I. [According to the OLG] . . . the claim as a whole had no legal basis. A direct claim against the defendant on the basis of § 3 Nr. 1 PflVG [*Pflichtversicherungsgesetz* = Act Concerning Compulsory Insurance] failed because the loss claimed by the plaintiff was not suffered as a consequence of the operation of the vehicle insured by the defendant (§ 10 I AKB [*Allgemeine Bedingungen für die Kraftverkehrsversicherung* = General Conditions for Motor Vehicle Insurance]). Furthermore, M himself was not liable to the plaintiff. There was no liability under §§ 7 and 18 StVG [*Strassenverkehrsgesetz* = Road Traffic Act] because the invasion of his health alleged by the plaintiff did not occur in the context of the use of the vehicle by M. There was no liability under § 823 I BGB because there was no basis for holding that M was at fault. A claim for compensation based on § 823 II BGB failed because even if there were a breach of a protective law (§§ 164 and 185 *et seq.* StGB = Criminal Code), a reasonable bystander would not have expected the occurrence of a stroke as a consequence of the damage inflicted upon the plaintiff.

II. The plaintiff's appeal fails. The judgment of the OLG is correct in its result, even if not in its reasoning (§ 563 ZPO).

The claim has no basis in law. The prerequisite for a claim against the defendant on the basis of § 3 Nr. 1 PflVG is that the plaintiff has claims for compensation in respect of the alleged loss against M or the keeper of the vehicle driven by M (§§ 823 *et seq.* BGB and §§ 7 and 18 StVG) and that the loss is caused in the context of the operation of the motor vehicle insured by the defendant (§ 1 of the PflVG; § 10 I AKB). That is not, however, the case here.

1. A claim for compensation against M based on tort (§§ 823 *et seq.* BGB), which is the only way a claim for damages for pain and suffering could be justified (§ 847 BGB), has no basis in law.

(*a*) Loss of earnings and non-pecuniary loss on the part of the plaintiff should not be recoverable from M under § 823 I BGB simply because M caused damage to the plaintiff's property as a consequence of the crash caused by his fault and was consequently guilty of an interference in the *ownership* rights of the plaintiff and because the impairments claimed by the plaintiff could be seen as *consequential* loss. First, the property damage caused by M to the car driven by the plaintiff was suffered not by the plaintiff, but by his wife as the owner of the vehicle. Furthermore, there is no evidence from the pleadings that the state of excitement which the plaintiff believes led to his stroke was in any way caused by his being upset by the *damage to the vehicle* [emphasis added].

(*b*) The plaintiff's request for damages is furthermore not justified in so far as it is based on an argument that there was an invasion of the plaintiff's *health* actionable under § 823 I BGB.

(*aa*) Following the plaintiff's arguments, and rejecting the view of the OLG, it must be concluded that M did make a contribution to the injury to the plaintiff's health in so far as he acted unlawfully and negligently by contravening the priority rules (§ 8 StVO = *Strassenverkehrsordnung*) and consequently causing the crash. For by causing the accident he led the plaintiff to become upset and thus created one precondition which, in conjunction with the consequent conduct of M and his passengers, and the attendance at the accident by the police, caused the plaintiff to suffer a critical increase in blood pressure in his brain and led to the rupture of the blood vessel and the consequential brain haemorrhage when the plaintiff later drove away from the accident [references omitted]. It is not relevant to his responsibility in tort that M did not cause the impairment of the plaintiff's health through a physical invasion of his bodily integrity; an invasion of the plaintiff's health can occur, as here, through a psychological impact upon the victim [references omitted].

Contrary to the view of the OLG, it is equally irrelevant to the tortious responsibility of M that the impairment to the plaintiff's health may only have occurred because, unbeknown to M, the plaintiff was suffering from high blood pressure. For it is established case law that a person who causes loss must also take responsibility for those consequences of his actions which are the result of the fact that the victim is already suffering from some form of bodily injury or some other weakness in his constitution [references omitted]. A tortfeasor must always reckon with the possibility that a person affected by his breach of the priority rules may be a person suffering from high blood pressure. It is also not wholly unforeseeable that as a consequence of the upset caused by the accident that such a person may suffer impairment to his health. It is not necessary to foresee the precise circumstances in which this might occur or how the risk might result in the occurrence of damage [references omitted].

(*bb*) The linkage of the invasion of health suffered by the plaintiff and the infringement of the priority rules by M for the purposes of liability is, however, precluded by the fact that this damage in fact only occurred as a result of the conduct of M and his passengers after the accident and the events which occurred when the police attended the scene of the accident. For the traffic rule contained in § 8 StVO breached by M is not intended to provide protection against the possibility that an accident caused by a failure to observe this provision leads to the plaintiff suffering a stroke in the manner alleged by the plaintiff as a consequence of pressures experienced by the victim solely as a result of the upset occurring in the context of the aftermath of the accident.

It is also established case law that in the context of damages claims which are based on § 823 BGB it should be examined whether the event in respect of which compensation is claimed falls within the protective scope of the norm, and thus whether the risks materialised through the event which breached the rule of conduct was intended to protect against [references omitted]. This condition is not satisfied here. For the provision contained in § 8 StVO breached by M is intended, according to the basic principle set out in § 1 II StVO, to protect above all the bodily integrity of other persons; its protective scope extends, however, as is apparent from § 1 I StVO, to cover only the prevention of the risks of accidents and the prevention of injuries to health associated with primary threat to life and health. These can include those injuries which occur in the aftermath of the accident, for example in the context of salvage work or while making the accident report, which themselves constitute the realisation of one of the risks of road traffic at the scene of the accident. It is the view of this court that this argument cannot extend to cover psychological pressures associated with disagreements regarding the clarification of how the accident occurred or regarding the question of fault, such as those which were primarily responsible for the plaintiff's stroke, leaving aside the impairment of his condition caused by the accident itself. In this case the plaintiff, himself, admitted that the breach of the priority rules by M engendered in him merely a state of general excitement which, in itself, did not represent an invasion of his health [references omitted]. The fact that this state of excitement became more intense as a consequence of the subsequent conduct of M and his passengers before and during the presence of the police, and the fact that this led to the plaintiff suffering a brain haemorrhage leading to a stroke, fall beyond the protective scope of § 8 StVO. It is not the task of this provision of road traffic law to protect the person who had priority on the highway against the psychological and physiological impairment which he might suffer as a consequence of a criminal investigation or criminal proceedings being mounted against him, or against his own need to take action in civil or criminal proceedings to recover his loss. Nor is this provision aimed at providing protection against an invasion of the plaintiff's health suffered as a consequence of a state of excitement regarding the police attendance at the accident, whether this is caused by measures taken by the police, or by statements made by the tort-feasor or third parties which make it more difficult to clarify the issue of responsibility. Protection against detriment stemming from errors or attempts to manipulate the facts when the circumstances of the accident are being clarified is subject to separate rules; it is not included within the scope of the rule of conduct contained in § 8 StVO which is intended to ensure the safety of traffic on the roads.

Having regard to the assessment which has been made, it must be concluded that as a matter of the ascription of responsibility, the stroke suffered by the plaintiff was linked to the conduct of M and his passengers *after* the accident. However, even from this perspective the conduct of M cannot give the plaintiff an action for damages under § 823 I BGB. For the fact that, as the plaintiff alleges, M and his fellow passengers might have given an incorrect description of the accident to the police officer charged with making a report after the crash or might have 'invented' allegations about the plaintiff having driven too fast or being under the influence of alcohol does not, of itself, render their conduct unlawful. Such an attempt by those using the highway to shift the blame for an accident onto the other side does not in itself violate, in the absence of other circumstances, the standard of conduct which is to be expected of every person who uses the roads but who has no claim for compensation, after an accident. The same applies to the unsubstantiated allegation made by the plaintiff (though only before the OLG) that the passengers in the other vehicle came towards him 'in a threatening manner' [references omitted].

Finally, it is not possible to conclude that the conduct of M after the accident was unlawful simply because the OLG, when it was examining the plaintiff's claims which it ultimately rejected, reached the conclusion under § 823 II BGB that M and his passengers had breached the protective laws contained in §§ 164 and 185 *et seq.* StGB as a result of their conduct following the accident. Quite apart from the fact that the defendant, as the insurer, could only be liable for the conduct of M and not for that of his fellow passengers (cf. § 10 I d AKB), the findings of the OLG should be viewed as findings of law, not as findings of fact, that is as a presumption of the truth of the plaintiff's allegations. For the facts as pleaded by the plaintiff reveal no evidence of a breach of the provisions of the criminal law by M.

2. As a result, the OLG was correct to deny, on the basis of § 3 Nr. 1 PflVG, a claim for compensation by the plaintiff leading to the liability of the defendant under §§ 7 I and 18 I StVG. Such a claim, which in accordance with § 11 StVG can in any case only extend to compensation for *pecuniary* loss, presupposes that the invasion of the plaintiff's health occurred in the context of the operation of the vehicle driven by M and that the loss claimed by the plaintiff is attributable to the risks associated with the operation of this vehicle. The OLG was wrong to conclude that the first condition was not present; the second requirement is not, however, fulfilled.

(*a*) Damage occurs 'in the context of the operation' of a motor vehicle where the risk which emanates from the vehicle as such has had an impact upon how the damage actually happened, and thus where the occurrence of damage has in this way been (partially) shaped by the motor vehicle. Evaluated from this perspective, the case law of this court leads to the conclusion that the condition of liability that the damage must occur 'in the context of the operation' of a motor vehicle must in principle be construed extensively in accordance with the broad protective scope of § 7 I StVG [references omitted].

(*b*) In this case, however, as was stated above in the context of liability under § 823 BGB, the accident caused by M's operating the vehicle in breach of the road traffic rules did contribute to the stroke suffered by the plaintiff as a result of the impairment of the general condition of a victim such as the plaintiff who suffered from high blood pressure. However, as with liability in tort, the responsibility of M under §§ 7 and 18 StVG requires that the loss suffered should fall within the protective scope of the norms in question [references omitted]. Any attribution of this loss to the risk of the operation of the vehicle driven by M must, however, be denied on the same grounds as those which justified the refusal to link, as a matter of the law of tort, the loss with the wrongful breach by M of the provisions of § 8 StVO. For since liability under § 7 StVG represents, so to speak, the price for the fact that the use of a vehicle on the roads offers a permissible source of risk, then the responsibility of the keeper and the driver which is based on this provision must be limited to those losses which represent the realisation of precisely those risks which result as such from motor vehicles. It is not possible to establish the necessary internal link between the risks of operation of a motor vehicle and the loss in the form of the plaintiff's stroke and the damaging consequences of that stroke. In this context, rather, it is a separate sphere of risk which is involved also as regards the risk-based liability contained in the Road Traffic Act, and this sphere of risk must, according to the standards imposed for this form of liability, be attributed to the general risks of life.

Case 104

BUNDESGERICHTSHOF (SIXTH CIVIL DIVISION) 13 APRIL 1956*
BGHZ 20, 259

In order to enter a private driveway, the defendant made a sharp left-hand turn from the right-hand side of the highway. The plaintiff came round a bend behind him on a 490 cc. motorcycle, and struck the defendant's vehicle near the left-hand kerb. The plaintiff was thrown on to the sidewalk and suffered serious injuries.

The Landgericht granted the plaintiff's claim for damages for pain and suffering, and held the defendant liable for all other damage as well. On the defendant's appeal, the Oberlandesgericht held that the claim for damages for pain and suffering should be allowed only as to two-thirds, and that the defendant was liable only for a like proportion of the other harm suffered by the plaintiff. The plaintiff sought to have the decision of the Landgericht reinstated and the defendant sought to have the claims dismissed. Both appeals were unsuccessful.

Reasons

It was alleged that the plaintiff could and should have foreseen the defendant's improper left turn in time to brake or swerve and so avoid the collision. The trial judge, however, held—unobjectionably in law—that this was not established. But an accident does not constitute an 'unavoidable event' in the sense of § 7 II KrfzG (Motor Vehicle Act) (now StVG (Road Traffic Act)) just because the plaintiff is not proved to have been at fault in contributing to it. Supposing that the defendant, as is possible, had put out his direction indicator and was proceeding slowly, and that the plaintiff had been driving with abnormally scrupulous care, alertly and attentively focusing all his faculties on the situation (NJW 1954, 185 no. 1), then the plaintiff might, despite the unexpectedness of the defendant's manoeuvre, have avoided the damaging collision by braking or swerving, given that his own speed was perhaps only 20 m.p.h. If in this sense the accident could possibly have been avoided by the plaintiff, the danger attributable to his motorcycle is a factor which must be taken into account in any claim he may make (BGHZ 6, 319).

It is true that some writers have criticized the decisions of the Bundesgerichtshof (BGHZ 6, 319; VersR 1953, 337) to the effect that, except in the case of an unavoidable event, the claim of the injured custodian is subject to reduction by reason of any contribution made to the accident by the danger due to his vehicle (references omitted), but despite these criticisms this

_____
* English version by Tony Weir.

senate proposes to adhere to the established case-law. If someone else as well as the custodian of a car is liable to an injured third party and the question is how the loss should be borne as between the two of them, it is quite obvious that the custodian will have to bear part of his loss. The same must apply when the custodian of a vehicle which the legislature has stigmatised as dangerous, suffers damage while in the vehicle whose dangerous nature contributed to the accident, even if he himself was not at fault, or not provably so. Theoretically one might avoid splitting the loss in this way by drawing a distinction between the capacities of custodian and occupant, and attaching strict liability only to the capacity of custodian, but this would be unduly theoretical and quite unrealistic. The danger attributable to the custody of a motor vehicle exists equally if the custodian happens to be in his own car, as passenger or driver, and so in such a case also he must bear the consequences which flow from having it in his custody. It is irrelevant that § 8 StVG exempts him from liability to any other occupant. Berchthold is wrong to draw the conclusion that even a scrupulously careful custodian will always have to bear part of the loss he suffers (see also BGH VersR 5, 251, 253), since if the event is unavoidable, the dangerous nature of the vehicle has no part to play. If the danger does fall to be taken into account, the trial judge must in each case determine whether and to what extent the loss should be divided. Even then, as Gelhaar and Wussow have pointed out with reference to decisions of this senate, the custodian is not inevitably saddled with part of his loss. As against a tortfeasor whose conduct was gross or reckless, it might be right to ignore an insubstantial contributory danger. On the other hand (and this supports the view here put forward), it would not be right to require a person who has been only slightly negligent to bear the whole of the custodian's loss when the custodian's vehicle made a significant contribution to the harm.

The same must apply when a custodian-occupant brings a claim for damages for pain and suffering. It is true that in JW 1931, 3315, the Reichsgericht stated that the loss should not be divided unless the custodian would have been liable to any third party injured in the accident, and it refused to use § 17 KrfzG to curtail the claim for damages for pain and suffering brought by an injured custodian who was responsible for nothing other than the custody of a dangerous motor vehicle. On the other hand, in RGZ 149, 213, the Reichsgericht held that the part of the loss which an injured custodian must bear if he himself was in part responsible was not subject to the monetary limit laid down by § 12 KrfzG. To this extent, therefore, according to the Reichsgericht, different rules may apply on the same facts depending on whether the issue is one of liability to a third person or of the duty to bear part of one's own loss. It is certainly clear that the main reason the legislature set the monetary limit on the strict liability introduced by the KrfzG was to enable custodians of vehicles to insure themselves against liability without undue cost (see RGZ 149, 213, 215 and the reasons there given).

But the idea of so limiting the amount of a claim based on strict liability has no application when the question is whether the plaintiff should bear an appropriate part of his own harm. It would be irrational to say that the custodian need not bear any part of his loss when his claim is based on the BGB (loss of income, § 842; loss of services, § 845; damages for pain and suffering, § 847) but that his claim is reduced if it is based on the StVG when it is in any case limited in quantum (§§ 10–12 StVG). The result would be that a reduction would take place only in those very claims whose satisfaction the legislature thought particularly urgent, as the enactment of the KrfzG/StVG shows. The legislature cannot have intended this result to flow from the limitation on the amount of the defendant's liability. It is rather for the judge whenever the situation is appropriate for a division of the loss between the victim and the person who caused the injury, to apply § 17 I, 1 StVG, which is analogous to § 254 BGB, and decide whether the victim is to bear an equitable part of his own loss.

This conclusion is logically consistent with the decisions of the Bundesgerichtshof on the question of contribution between common debtors liable for the same harm under § 17 StVG (BGHZ 6, 319, 322). The relationship between common debtors and their respective contribution claims depends exclusively on the actual facts, especially the extent to which they respectively contributed to the harm, and not on the basis of their legal liability to the victim; the adjudication of contribution claims is entirely divorced from the legal basis of the individual debtor's liability, to the point where it is irrelevant whether the actual causes of the harm were a ground of liability to the victim (reference omitted). Now, since the same considerations apply, and the results should be the same, when one is weighing up the respective responsibility for harm as between several common debtors on the one hand (§ 17 StVG) and as between those causing and suffering harm on the other (§ 254 BGB), so in the latter case also one should take no account of the basis of liability, but only of the totality of the facts, especially the extent to which each contributed to the harm as a matter of causation (reference omitted). Just as one is to ignore the legal basis of liability in the individual case when it comes to dividing the loss (BGH VersR 5, 163), so one should ignore the question whether the harm is of such a kind that a third party could claim in respect of it. The only safe way to an equitable division of the loss is to have the judge make the custodian bear part of it by applying the standards of § 17 I, 1 StVG, as would be the result of applying § 17 StVG and § 254 BGB [reference omitted].

Accordingly, the Court of Appeal was right to hold that the plaintiff's claim for damages for pain and suffering was also affected by the danger contributed by his motor cycle.

About 9 p.m. on 5 September 1952 the plaintiff was riding his moped out of town on V. St. He crossed the intersection with I. St., and was about to pass the E. gas station on his right when the defendant E. drove out of the gas station in his Opel Olympia 1937 and turned right into V. St. in front of him. In overtaking E.'s car, the plaintiff got between the tramlines in the middle of the highway. He overtook E.'s car but had not yet regained the right hand side of the road when he collided head-on with B.'s Mercedes 170S, 22 metres before the intersection with E. St. The plaintiff suffered serious injuries in the collision, and his left leg had to be amputated.

The plaintiff asserts that E. came out of the gas station right in front of him, so that he was forced to overtake. In doing so the plaintiff had to get between the sets of tramlines in the middle of the road, because E.'s left hand wheels were over the right hand tram lines by reason of cars parked on the right hand side of the road. The plaintiff took some time to overtake because E. accelerated as he was doing so, and he was therefore unable to regain the right hand side of the road in due time. The defendant B. had also crossed the tramlines while overtaking a car in front of him, and would have seen the plaintiff if he had been paying proper attention.

The plaintiff claims compensation from the defendants for one-half of the damage he suffered, and the defendants answer that the accident was entirely due to the plaintiff's fault.

The Landgericht dismissed the claim against E., and granted the claim against B. as to one-fifth of the total damage.

On appeal by the plaintiff and B., the Oberlandesgericht held that both defendants were liable under the Strassenverkehrsgesetz (StVG) for two-fifths of the total harm, and that the defendant B. was also liable under the Civil Code (BGB) for two-fifths of the amount claimed by the plaintiff.

The defendants' appeals were allowed in part, the Bundesgerichtshof holding that while each defendant was liable for one-fifth of the total damage, they were not together liable for more than one-third.

Reasons

The Court of Appeal was right to hold that the defendant E. was liable for one-fifth of the plaintiff's total damage, so E.'s appeal on this point must be

_____

* English version by Tony Weir.

dismissed. B.'s appeal equally fails in so far as it argues that he is not liable at all.

The Court of Appeal then added together the two liabilities for one-fifth each, and consequently held the defendants jointly liable for two-fifths of the total harm (four-fifths of the amount actually claimed by the plaintiff, for he claimed for only one-half of his harm). The defendants are right to object to this.

1. The Court of Appeal was right to start out by weighing the plaintiff's contributory fault against each of the defendants separately, and correctly applied § 254 BGB first as between the plaintiff and E., and then as between the plaintiff and B. This separate apportionment is necessary because the plaintiff has an independent claim for compensation against each defendant. Each defendant is responsible for providing an adequate cause of the harm, and has thereby met the conditions of statutory liability (§ 823 BGB, §§ 7, 18 StVG). Had the plaintiff sued only one of the defendants, he could claim only one-fifth of his total damage (= two-fifths of the sum actually claimed). The fact that he sued both defendants in one suit does not justify an apportionment under § 254 BGB on the basis that the responsibility of the two defendants should be treated as a unit and compared as such with that of the plaintiff.

Where several persons have caused harm, there is only one case where it is right to combine their spheres of responsibility and thus make each responsible for the contribution to the harm made by the others, and that is when the requirements of § 830 I, 1 BGB are met, namely that the various persons causing the harm caused it by means of 'a wrongful act committed jointly'. There is no question of that here. Indeed, it may be that this provision is inapplicable on the mere ground that whereas E. was guilty of an unlawful act in the sense of § 823 BGB, B. was liable only on the basis of the strict liability in §§ 11, 18 StVG. Be that as it may, there was here no 'act jointly committed' by the defendants. True though it is that together they produced the harmful result, this was through different independent individual acts, not through a common act. To several acts of negligence of this kind (*fahrlässige Nebentäterschaft*), § 830 I, 1 BGB is not to be applied [reference omitted]. If in RGZ 58, 357 the Reichsgericht indicated otherwise, this court cannot agree. When the harm has been caused by the concurrence of several individual acts, the fact that these acts may coincide closely in time and place does not justify an apportionment which burdens each debtor with the contributions of the others. Nor did the Reichsgericht itself hold that when several drivers had caused an accident by various independent acts of bad driving they were 'joint actors' (*Mittäter*) in the sense of § 830 I, 1 BGB.

2. The Court of Appeal believed that § 840 BGB empowered them to add together the portions of the harm, namely one-fifth each, for which the defendants were responsible. In this they failed to see that since under § 840 I BGB the debtors' obligations must coincide before there can be a relationship of common debt, the defendants could be common debtors only in respect of one-fifth of the plaintiff's harm. In contrast with § 830 I BGB, there is here no legal basis for treating the contributions of the two defendants as a unit imputable to both and opposing it to the plaintiff's quota of responsibility. Such a solution is irreconcilable with the recognised principles concerning the factors relevant to an apportionment under § 254 BGB. It would improperly extend the limits within which the law of tort allows the imputation to one person of another person's fault. And it is inequitable because each of several *defendants* would bear the risk of the insolvency of the others, whereas the *plaintiff* would not be exposed to this risk at all, even though he was equally to blame, if not more so.

3. According to the decisions of the Reichsgericht and those of the Bundesgerichtshof hitherto (BGHZ 12, 213, 220; VersR 1957, 167), several tortfeasors whose liability as a result of the individual weighing process is equal in amount (as with the defendants here, one-fifth each) are liable for that amount as common debtors under § 840 BGB, and the plaintiff must bear the remainder of the loss himself. This is an unsatisfactory solution, because it gives the victim less than he should, if one views the accident as a whole, recover. The example given by Dunz in *JZ* 1955, 727 makes this quite clear. If ten people, all equally at fault, cause damage to an eleventh, the victim can claim the full amount of his loss from any of the ten. But if one of the ten who are equally careless is himself the victim, the result of the individual weighing is that each of those causing the harm is liable to the plaintiff for half of his harm. If we apply the rule of common debtors as the courts have done until now, the victim recovers only half of his harm altogether whereas, if all the debtors are solvent, he should get nine-tenths. On the other side, the effect of contribution proceedings would be that each person causing the harm would pay only one-eighteenth of it.

The main reason for the unsatisfactory nature of the law hitherto applied in such cases is that the rules of common debt have been applied too soon and too formalistically. Of course § 840 I BGB applies in the case of several as well as joint tortfeasors (see BGHZ 17, 214). This makes for no difficulty if the several tortfeasors are each liable for the whole harm, for then we have the situation which is characteristic of a common debt, namely that performance by any one debtor satisfies the whole of the creditor's interest. But this identity of the content of performance is lacking to some extent if the victim is himself guilty of contributory fault so that his damages claims against the several tortfeasors fall to be reduced under § 254 BGB. It is also lacking in the case before us today, for the one-fifth for which E. is liable as a result of the individual apportionment is neither economically nor legally identical with the one-fifth of the harm which B. has to pay. Payment of one of these two parts of the harm does not give the victim of the accident all he ought to get from E. and B. together. This is the second reason for the unsatisfactory nature of the law applied until now: the traditional comparison of the contribution of the victim with that of each individual causing the harm fails to give a global view of the accident and leads to a division of the loss which, on a global view, is unsatisfactory.

4. It might seem that one could equitably deal with the consequences of an accident by dividing the harm between the parties involved in the occurrence of the harm in relation to their respective contributions to it, and burdening each only with the appropriate portion of the harm he has caused. In support of such a view one might adduce the idea that all those involved in an accident, including the responsible victim (§ 254 BGB, §§ 7, 17, 18 StVG), form a kind of community, entailing a duty to resolve it so that no member has to bear more of the loss than is appropriate under § 17 StVG or § 254 BGB. Such a method brings the apportionment of the loss between the various persons who caused it (the inner or contribution relationship) into the suit brought by the victim against any or all of the persons causing the harm (external liability). There are several reasons which render this unacceptable.

There is no statutory basis for such apportionment proceedings. In admiralty law, indeed, there is such a rule (§ 736 HGB): if a collision between two or more vessels results from the fault of the crews involved, the owners of these ships are only liable in proportion to the gravity of their respective faults, at any rate so far as concerns damage to the ships themselves or to property on board, personal injury being dealt with otherwise. Here, several liability is introduced in lieu of joint liability, and the division between external liability and internal contribution which the law has maintained for good reason in other areas is abolished. But § 736 I HGB only applies in this particular area of admiralty law: it cannot be applied to the law of road traffic or to the general law of tort. Certainly nothing in § 17 StVG would justify abandoning the distinction between external liability and internal contribution in the case of a collision between motor-cars and making the drivers and custodians involved in the accident liable to the victim only for their several parts (see also BGHZ 15, 123, 135). Several liability such as is exceptionally provided for by § 736 I HGB would often be detrimental to the victim, for it would deprive him of the security and advantages offered to him by the principle of joint liability and by the separation of external liability and internal contribution. To take Dunz's example once again, if several liability existed, the plaintiff could recover only one-tenth of his harm from each person causing it; yet each of them had provided an adequate cause for the harm and was, in relation to the plaintiff, as much to blame for it as the plaintiff himself, so it would seem right to give him a claim for half his harm against each individual causing it. Finally, several liability would greatly complicate the trial of many tort cases. Very frequently, the victim does not sue all those liable for the harm resulting from an accident; to minimise the risk, he often sues only the person whose liability can most easily be established. Now if the principle of several liability applied, one could only decide how much the defendant must pay by ascertaining the extent to which all the other persons responsible for the accident were to blame and contributed to it as a matter of causation. Thus in every traffic accident case, one would have to ask whether anyone not in court might be liable for the harm, though any such determination would lack the force of *res judicata* against such a person. Wide-ranging enquiries would often be necessary although the actual issue was quite simple. To complicate matters like this would conflict with the policy of the Code, especially § 421 BGB, to assist the victim, even when he, too, is at fault, for it is in the victim's interests to limit the issues in trial and to make a quick decision possible.

For all these reasons the principle of several liability does not provide a solution.

5. Solutions are suggested by Dunz (*JZ* 1955, 727 and 1957, 371) and Engelhardt (*JZ* 1957, 369) but as Dunz himself admits in his second article, they are not ideal.

6. In order to achieve a satisfactory result one must somehow harmonise the principle of common debt (joint liability) with the principle of apportionment of § 254 BGB (§ 17 StVG) and combine the individual apportionment with a global apportionment achieved by looking at the accident as a whole. An example may make this clear. Suppose that A is injured in an accident due to his own carelessness and the careless driving of B and C. If the contribution of all three parties is equal, and the damage suffered by A amounts to DM 3,000, the individual apportionment will be that A's contribution to the accident is equal to that of B (1:1). A may therefore claim DM 1,500 from B. The same applies as between A and C. Now if A claims damages from B and C together, one must follow this individual apportionment by taking a global view of the accident, and asking how much each of them contributed to it. Since from this point of view A, B and C are each responsible for one-third, A should have to bear only one-third of his harm (DM 1,000) and should be able to claim a total of two-thirds (DM 2,000) from

the others. The results of these two processes of apportionment (the individual and the global) leads to the conclusion that: 'B and C together must pay A a total of DM 2,000, but neither of them need pay more than DM 1,500', or, to put it another way: 'A may claim DM 1,500 from B, and he may claim DM 1,500 from C, but he may not claim more than DM 2,000 in all.' The question of contribution between B and C remains a matter of their relationship *inter se*. If B has paid A the DM 1,500 he owes him, then C owes B DM 500 as contribution under § 17 StVG. C remains liable to A, but only for DM 500, since A has already received DM 1,500 from B.

While maintaining the legal structure of joint liability, this solution accommodates it to the particularities of the law of tort liability arising from the principle of apportionment of § 254 BGB and related provisions, and the solution is a just one in that all those involved in an accident bear the loss in a measure which reflects their responsibility for it. By linking individual and global apportionment, it avoids the disadvantages to which the victim has hitherto been exposed when claiming damages from several defendants (hitherto A has obtained judgment for DM 1,500 against B and C as common debtors, and had to bear half his loss himself). On the other hand, the individual apportionment ensures that no person causing the harm pays more to the victim than is fair in view of their relationship *inter se* (B pays A here DM 1,500, and so does C). So far as these debts overlap, the victim has the security and other advantages which the principle of joint liability is designed to give him (§§ 840, 421 BGB).

The step of making the global apportionment and ascertaining the respective quotas of harm is naturally only to be taken when the victim sues several persons at the same time, or if there are successive suits.

7. We can now apply these principles to the case in hand, taking the individual apportionments made by the Court of Appeal as correct in law. Here as between plaintiff and E. the total harm must be divided in the proportion 4:1, and likewise, under the StVG, in the same proportion of 4:1 as between the plaintiff and B. Taking the global view next, as we must, the harm must be divided between the three parties involved so that the proportion of the harm borne by the two defendants remains the same and that on the other hand the proportion of four to one is maintained both in the relationship between the plaintiff and E., and in the relationship between the plaintiff and B. It follows that the global apportionment must be in the ratio 4:1:1. This means that the plaintiff is responsible for four-sixths (= two-thirds) and the defendants are each responsible for one-sixth. In the end result, the plaintiff will have to bear two-thirds of the total loss, and the defendants must make good one-third, though each defendant is liable only for one-fifth of the harm and B. is liable only under the StVG. The plaintiff's claim

being limited to half of his total harm, the end result is that his claim succeeds against E. for two-fifths and against B. for two-fifths under the StVG, subject to this, that the total sum he may recover from both is not to exceed two-thirds of the sum he has claimed.

Notes to the Road Traffic Act

1. Traffic accidents represent a major area of accident compensation; arguably, they have also presented traditional tort law with its major challenge. The result was inevitable: revealing empirical studies, a vast literature, and numerous proposals for reform. Comparing the German law with other systems of compensation (whether in existence or merely proposed) makes it look both pioneering and in need of further reform. But change is hard to achieve and the role of a reformer is rarely a happy one. In some countries such as the USA no-fault statutory schemes have been challenged on constitutional grounds. See, for example, *Kluger* v. *White* 281 So. 2d 1 (Fla. 1973); *Lasky* v. *State Farm Insurance Co.* 296 So. 2d 9 (Fla. 1974). In other countries, like France for example, proposals for reform have met with strenuous if not at times undignified reactions on the part of various specialized pressure groups (insurers, practising lawyers).

2. Any comparative summary of such a topic is bound to be incomplete if not misleading. The decision was thus taken to depart from the pattern adopted throughout this book. Instead of comparing German law with Common law, the reader is invited to look at an imaginative French proposal and then compare it with German law and his own law.

3. The French proposal can be best understood by looking at the French legal background and discovering its own deficiencies. Good brief accounts of this can be found in von Mehren and Gordley's *The Civil Law System* (2nd edn. 1979), ch. 9, and Lawson and Markesinis, *Tortious Liability for Unintentional Harm in the Common Law and the Civil Law*, ch. 3. Professor Tunc—the author of the proposed French Bill—has also provided more detailed accounts in 31 *American Journal of Comparative Law* 489 (1983) and in 16 *Rev. Jur. Uni. Interam. Puerto Rico* 125 (1981). André Tunc is also responsible for a masterly comparative account of the subject in vol. XI, ch. 14 of the *International Encyclopedia of Comparative Law*. The literature in French on the Tunc proposals is enormous. One of the most recent and interesting collections of essays on the proposed Bill have been published under the editorship of Tunc under the title *Pour une loi sur les accidents de la circulation* (1981). The reader is invited to compare Tunc's proposals (Addendum 1) with (*a*) the *Desmares* decision and (*b*) the 1985 Act (Addendum 2). The difficulties caused by some of the Act's terms (particularly the words *faute inexcusable*) have given rise to much case-law reviewed by Margeat, Landel, Thiry, and Besson, *Accidents de la circulation: Loi du 5*

juillet 1985—Bilan et perspectives, published in 1988 by the Gazette du Palais.

Addendum 1

A BILL CONCERNING THE COMPENSATION OF VICTIMS OF ROAD TRAFFIC ACCIDENTS, PROPOSED BY ANDRÉ TUNC[*]

Part I. Obligation to insure

Article 1

Every owner or possessor of a motorized vehicle must, before putting it into 'circulation', take out an insurance policy covering, according to the provisions of the present law and despite all contrary clauses, the damages that may result from a road traffic accident in which the said vehicle is involved.

For the purposes of the present law, the word 'vehicle' denotes a motorized land vehicle, its trailer, or semi-trailer and their load; any vehicle not immobilized in a private garage is considered to be in circulation.

For the purposes of the present law, public bodies exempted from the obligation to insure their vehicles, will assume with regard to their vehicles the rights and obligations of an insurance company.

Part II. Corporeal damage

Article 2

Every victim of personal injury, resulting from a road traffic accident in which a vehicle has participated, has the right to be compensated in accordance with the provisions of articles 3–12, below.

Article 3

The victim has a right to be reimbursed for all expenses reasonably incurred as a result of the injury, whether for care, rehabilitation, aid, special equipment for or adaptation of the home, travelling expenses for members of the family, repair or replacement of clothes, or items worn at the time of the accident and damaged as a result of the latter.

Article 4

The victim has the right to be compensated for loss of salary or professional earnings resulting from a temporary disablement.

Article 5

If the victim is permanently disabled, he has the right:
(*a*) to be compensated for the loss of salary or professional earnings

---

[*] English version by B. S. Markesinis.

which would arise from the normal course of events concerning a person in the same position as himself;

(*b*) to compensation for purely physiological harm in accordance with a table taking into account the degree of his disablement and his age—this table, and also the medical scale used to calculate the degree of his disablement, to be established by Decree.

Article 6

Loss of salary or professional earnings in the sense of articles 4 and 5, above, should be taken to mean only the actual loss not compensated by employers' contributions, social security, or any other organization for social welfare.

Article 7

Compensation will only be paid for loss of salary and professional earnings not exceeding x times the index-linked minimum wage.

Article 8

When the permanent disability of the victim entails the loss of salary or professional earnings of at least 30 per cent, compensation of this loss will take the form of an index-linked annuity in accordance with the provisions of the law of 27 December 1974, and will be reviewed as the victim's physical condition develops.

This annuity will be liable to be reduced should the beneficiary refuse without valid reason a measure of examination, observation, treatment, or adjustment reasonably suggested by the insurance company.

It will not be subject to attachment any more than would have been the salary or professional earnings it is meant to replace.

Article 9

When the victim dies as a result of the accident, his heirs and next of kin are entitled to be reimbursed for expenses which they must reasonably have incurred as a result of the accident. The persons who paid the funeral expenses are entitled to be reimbursed.

Article 10

The persons who as the result of the victim's death are deprived of (financial) assistance which they were receiving or could reasonably have expected to receive from him are entitled to compensation within the limits provided by article 7 of the present law. This compensation will take the form of an index-linked annuity in accordance with the provisions of the law of 27 December 1974.

Article 11

The obligation to pay the compensation envisaged in articles 3–10 of the present law falls upon:

(*a*) the insurer of the vehicle in which the killed or injured victim was being transported or,

(*b*) if the victim was not being transported [in a vehicle], the insurer of the vehicle which participated in the accident.

When more than one vehicle has participated in the accident, each insurer will be obliged to compensate the victim (to the full extent), the cost of the damages to be divided either in equal parts or in proportions to be agreed amongst them.

Article 12

When a stolen vehicle has participated in an accident, the thief and the handler of the stolen car forfeit all rights to compensation under the present law.

Part III. Material damage

Article 13

Damage suffered by colliding vehicles is compensated in accordance with percentages determined by types of circumstance fixed by Decree. The same Decree will specify the elements of compensatable loss.

Damage occasioned to goods carried in or on vehicles will only be compensated in cases of collision with or transport by professional carriers and then only within the limits laid down by Decree, subject to any more extensive compensation envisaged by the contract of insurance.

All other material damage caused by a vehicle (to a furnished building) must be compensated.

Part IV. Miscellaneous provisions

Article 14

The rights provided for by the law exclude all other rights of compensation resulting from a road traffic accident with the exception of the following:

(1) the victim has a right to seek further compensation in accordance with the ordinary rules of civil liability against the manufacturer, seller, or repairer of the vehicle;

(2) the insurer, obliged to pay compensation under the provisions of this law, is entitled to be subrogated against:

(*a*) any person who intentionally caused a type of damage covered by this law;

(*b*) the manufacturer, seller or repairer of the vehicle, responsible under the ordinary rules of civil liability;

(*c*) the highway authorities under the ordinary rules of civil liability. These subrogation rights will be for lump sums even where the compensation is to be paid in the form of an annuity.

Article 15

Whenever a person is, because of his involvement in an accident, condemned to imprisonment of . . . [a certain period] the criminal court can order as an additional penalty the payment of a sum not exceeding 50,000 fr. to be made to the *Fonds de Garantie*.

Article 16

The courts cannot be seized of a dispute arising from the application of this law until it has been submitted to a Commission for Reconciliation, the membership and functions of which will be decided by Decree.

Article 17

The actions of personal injury and property damage are statute-barred in three months and one year respectively from the moment the victim becomes aware of the damage.

Article 18

The premium to be paid by the insured will be adjusted every twelve months depending on the number of accidents in which the vehicle has participated. A Decree will regulate such details as no-claims bonuses and upward adjustments of premiums.

Addendum 2

Law no. 85-677 of 5 July 1985*

Aiming at the improvement of the position of victims of traffic accidents and the acceleration of the compensation process. (JO of 6 July 1985, 7584.)

Chapter 1. Compensation of traffic accident victims

Article 1

The provisions of the present chapter apply to victims of traffic accidents, whether transported by virtue of contract or not, involving (*impliqué*) a land

---

* English version by B. S. Markesinis.

motorized vehicle as well as trailers and half-trailers with the exception of trains and trams running on fixed rails.

Section 1. Provisions relating to compensation.

Article 2

The driver or guardian of a vehicle mentioned in article 1 above cannot plead against victims, including drivers, [the defence] of *force majeure* or act of a third party.

Article 3

Victims, excluding the drivers of motorized land vehicles, are compensated for damage resulting from injuries to their person without it being possible to invoke against them their own fault with the exception of their inexcusable fault [negligence] in so far as it was the exclusive cause of the accident.

The victims designated in the preceding sub-paragraph, whenever they are below the age of sixteen or over that of seventy, or whenever, irrespective of their age, they have at the time of the accident been recognized as suffering from a permanent incapacity or invalidity of at least 80 per cent, will in all cases be compensated for damages suffered as a result of personal injuries.

However, in the cases envisaged in the preceding sub-paragraphs, the victim will not be compensated by the tortfeasor for harm resulting to his person when he voluntarily sought the damage that he suffered.

Article 4

The fault committed by the driver of a motorized land vehicle has the effect of limiting or excluding the compensation of the damages that he has suffered.

Article 5

The victim's [contributory] fault results in the exclusion or limitation of his compensation for damage suffered by his property. However, compensation for supplies and equipment provided on medical prescription is made in accordance with the rules applicable to compensation for personal injury.

Wherever the driver of the motorized land vehicle is not its owner, the fault of such driver can be opposed against the owner for compensation of damages caused to his vehicle. In such cases the owner has a right to sue the driver.

Article 6

The loss suffered by a third party as a result of the damage caused to the direct victim of the traffic accident is made good by taking into account the limitations or exclusions applicable to the compensation of such damage.

Section 2. Provisions relating to insurance and fonds de garantie.

Articles 7–11 contain amendments and conditions to the Code of Insurance.

Section 3. Concerning the offer to pay compensation. ·

Article 12

The insurer who guarantees the civil liability resulting from a motorized land vehicle is bound, within a maximum period of eight months from the date of the accident, to make an offer of compensation to the injured victim. In the event of death of the victim, the offer is made to his heirs and, where appropriate, the spouse.

The offer must also be made to the other victim within a period of eight months reckoning from the date of the request for compensation.

The offer includes all compensatable headings of damage including the elements relating to property damage whenever they have not been the object of preliminary settlement.

They may be of a provisional nature whenever the insurer has not, within three months of the accident, been informed of the stabilization of the state of the victim's [health]. The definitive offer for compensation must in this case be made within five months of the insurer being informed of such stabilization.

In the case of plurality of vehicles, and if there are many insurers, the offer is made by the insurer authorized by the others.

The preceding provisions are not applicable to victims to whom the accident caused only property damage.

Article 13

On the occasion of his first correspondence with the victim, the insurer is bound [subject to] relative nullity of any agreement that might be reached [result] to inform the victim that he can obtain through a simple request a copy of the report of the police enquiry and to remind him that he may obtain the assistance of a lawyer and, in the case of a medical examination, [the assistance] of a doctor.

Under the threat of the same penalty, the above-mentioned correspondence must inform the victim of the provision of sub-paragraph 4 of article 12 and of article 15 [of this law].

Article 14

When the insurer could not, without fault on his part, have known that the accident had occasioned disbursements to the paying third parties envisaged in articles 29 and 33 of the present law, these [third parties] lose all rights of reimbursement against the insurer and the author of the damage. However, the insurer cannot invoke such ignorance *vis-à-vis* organizations that make social security payments.

In all cases, failure to produce the claims of paying third parties, within a period of four months from the moment of the request made by the insurer, will entail the forfeiture of their rights against the insurer and the author of the damages.

In the case where the demand that emanates from the insurer does not mention the stabilization of the victim's health, the claims made by the paying third parties may have a provisional character.

Article 15

Whenever, through the conduct of the victim, the paying third parties have not been able to assert their claims against the insurer, they will have a right of recourse against the victim to the extent of the indemnity he has received from the insurer under the same heading of damages and within the limits provided for by article 31. They must act within a period of two years from the demand of payment.

Article 16

When the offer has not been made within the period allowed by article 12, the amount of compensation offered to the victim by the insurer or granted to him by the judge, automatically attracts interest at double the rate of the legal interest from the moment of expiry of the permissible period up until the moment when the offer or the judgment becomes definitive. This penalty can be reduced by the judge because of circumstances not attributable to the insurer.

Article 17

If the judge who determines the compensation is of the view that the offer made by the insurer is manifestly insufficient, he will, of his own initiative, condemn the insurer to transfer to the *fonds de garantie* envisaged by article 420-1 of the Code of Insurance a sum of at [most] 15 per cent of the compensation awarded [by the court] without prejudice to any damages and interest due to the victim for this conduct.

Article 18

The insurer must submit to the *juge des tutelles* or the *conseil de famille*—depending on which of the two is appropriate—all proposals of settlement concerning minors or adults subject to guardianship [*tutelle*]. Similarly, he must give informal notice to the *juge des tutelles*, at least fifteen days in advance of the payment of the first instalment of an annuity or of any sum due to be paid as compensation to the legal representative of the protected person.

Any payment which has not been preceded by the requisite notice or any unauthorized transaction can be annulled at the request of any interested party or one of the *ministère public* but not of the insurer.

Any clause by which the legal representative of a minor or of an adult subject to guardianship, guarantees the ratification [by the said persons] of the acts mentioned in the first sub-paragraph of this article is void.

Article 19

The victim may, by means of a registered letter accompanied by a request for its receipt, denounce the settlement within fifteen days of its conclusion.

Any provision in the settlement that deprives the victim of this right is void.

The above-mentioned provisions reproduced very clearly in the offer proposing a settlement and in the settlement itself [at the risk of] relative nullity of the latter.

Article 20

Payment of the agreed sums must take place within one month from the expiry of the period within which denunciation is permitted according to article 19. Sums not paid will automatically [produce] interest at 50 per cent above the legal rate for the first two months [of the delay] and twice the legal amount for any period thereafter.

Article 21

In the event of payment being ordered by the court (even by a provisional decision)* the rate of legal interest is increased by 50 per cent after the expiry of two months and it is doubled after the expiry of four months counting from the day when the decision was made whenever the case was contested. In all other cases [time runs] from the day on which the decision was notified [to the defaulting party].

Article 22

The victim can, within the period provided for by article 2270-1 of the Civil Code, demand from the insurer compensation for the increase of the damage he has suffered.

Article 23

Whenever the insurer invokes an exception of legal or contractual guarantee, he is bound to comply with the provisions of articles 12 to 20 on account of the party concerned; the resulting settlement can be contested before the

---

* This may, for example, happen because the victim's position has not 'stabilized' [e.g. art. 12 IV] or a doctor has not yet been able to report on the future consequences of the injury.

judge by the person on whose account it was made without challenging the amount of money allocated to the victim or those deriving rights from him.

Article 24

For the purposes of articles 12 to 20, the State and all public entities, enterprises or organizations not obliged to carry insurance or having by virtue of article 211-3 of the same Code obtained [a waiver from the duty to take out insurance] are assimilated to an insurer.

Article 25

The provisions of articles 12 and 13 to 22 are applicable to the *fonds de garantie* in its relations with the victim and those deriving rights from him. However, the times provided for in article 12 run against *le fonds* from the day when it has received information justifying its intervention. The application of articles 16 and 17 are not obstacles to the [specific] provisions that cover actions against the *fond*. Whenever the *fonds de garantie* is bound to pay the interest provided for by article 17, this is payable to the Treasury.

Article 26

Under the control of public authority a periodic publication will provide an account of the amounts of compensation awarded by the courts or agreed upon as a result of private settlements.

Article 27

A degree of the Council of the State will fix the necessary measures for the application of this section. In particular it will list the causes of suspension and prorogation of the delays mentioned in article 12 as well as the reciprocal information that must be supplied by insurer, victim and paying third parties.

4. STRICT LIABILITY ACT 1978

(HAFTPFLICHTGESETZ) OF 4 JANUARY 1978

(BGBl. I, 145—as amended)*

§ 1. *Liability of the entrepreneur*

(1) If in the conduct of a railway or cable-way a human being is killed or suffers injury to body or health or a thing is damaged, the entrepreneur [the undertaking] is bound to make good to the injured party the damage arising therefrom.

* English version by F. H. Lawson and Kurt Lipstein.

(2) The duty to make good is excluded if the accident was caused by *force majeure*. Nevertheless in so far as the railway was operated within the travelled portion of a public highway, the duty to make good is excluded if the accident was caused by an unavoidable event which is due neither to a defect in the condition of the vehicle or lay-out of the railway nor to a failure of its management. An event is deemed to be unavoidable in particular when it is traceable to the conduct of the injured party or of a third person not concerned in the undertaking or of an animal and both the entrepreneur and the persons engaged in the undertaking observed the care required of them by the circumstances of the case.

(3) The duty to make good is also excluded if:
    1. an object accepted for safekeeping is damaged;
    2. an object being transported is damaged, unless a passenger is wearing or carrying it with him.

§ 2. *Liability of the proprietor of an energy establishment*

(1) If a human being is killed or suffers injury to body or health or an object is damaged through the operation of electricity, gas, steam, or current escaping from a cable or pipeline or a plant for the provision of such energy or material, the proprietor of the plant is bound to make good the damage arising therefrom. The same applies if the damage, without being due to the operation of the electricity, gas, steam or current, is traceable to the existence of such plants, unless they were in a proper state when the damage was caused. A plant is in a proper state as long as it conforms to the recognized technical rules and is intact.

(2) Subsection 1 does not apply to plants which serve only for the transmission of signs or sounds.

(3) The duty to make good under subsection 1 is excluded:
    1. if the damage occurred inside a building and is traceable to a plant discoverable therein (subsection 1) or if it occurred inside a plot in the possession of the proprietor of the plant;
    2. if the damage was caused by *force majeure*, unless it is traceable to fall of cable wires.

§ 3. *Liability of other entrepreneurs*

Anyone who operates a mine, quarry, pit, or factory is liable to compensation if an authorized agent or representative or anyone employed in the direction or supervision of the undertaking or of the workmen causes by a fault in the carrying out of the service arrangement, death or bodily injury to a human being.

§ 4. *Contributory fault*

If a fault of the injured party contributed to the occurrence of the damage § 254 BGB applies; where an object is damaged, the fault of the person who exercises the factual control over it is equivalent to the fault of the injured party.

§ 5. *Extent of the compensation for death*

(1) In the case of death, compensation must be made by making good the cost of the attempted cure as well as of the pecuniary damage which the deceased has suffered therefrom by having his earning capacity destroyed or diminished during the illness, or by having his personal needs increased. The person bound to make compensation must also make good the funeral expenses to the person who is under a duty to bear those expenses.

(2) If the deceased at the time of the injury stood to a third party in a relation by virtue of which he was, or could have become under a statutory duty of maintenance, and if the third party is deprived of the right to maintenance as a result of the death, the person bound to make compensation must compensate the third party for the period of the deceased's presumed life expectancy. The duty of compensation arises also if the third party at the time of the injury was conceived but not yet born.

§ 6. *Extent of the compensation for bodily injury*

In case of bodily injury, the compensation (§§ 1, 2, and 3) must be made by making good the cost of cure as well as the pecuniary damage which the injured party suffers by having his earning capacity temporarily or permanently destroyed or diminished or by having his personal needs increased by reason of the injury.

§ 7. *Compulsory law*

The duty of compensation under §§ 1–3 of this Act may not, in so far as personal injury is concerned, be either excluded or restricted for the future. The same applies to the duty of compensation under § 2 of this statute to damage to objects, unless the exclusion or restriction of liability has been agreed to between the proprietor of the plant and a public corporation or fund or a businessman by the terms of a contract relating to the conduct of his business. Provisions and agreements to the contrary are void.

§ 8. *Money annuity or lump sum settlement*

(1) Compensation for destruction or diminution of any earning capacity and for increase in the personal needs of the injured person as well as

compensation to be paid to a third party under § 3 II is due only for future losses and payments must take the form of an annuity.

(2) The provisions of §§ 843 II–IV BGB apply *mutatis mutandis*.

(3) If in the sentencing of the person bound to pay a money annuity no decision is made as to the provision of security, the person entitled to compensation can nevertheless demand that such security be provided if the financial status of the person bound to pay it has appreciably worsened; in similar circumstances, he can demand an increase in the security fixed by the judgment.

§ 9. *Limit of liability*

The entrepreneur or the proprietor of the plant indicated in § 2 is liable in cases under § 8 I only up to an annuity of DM 30,000 for each person killed or injured.

§ 10. *Limit of liability for damage to objects by energy plants*

(1) The entrepreneur or the proprietor of a plant listed in § 2 is liable for property damage only up to the sum of DM 100,000, even if several objects are damaged by the same event.

(2) If, by reason of the same event, compensation is payable to several persons, which together exceeds the highest permissible sum of DM 100,000, the individual awards are reduced in the proportion to which their total sum stands to the highest permissible sum.

§ 11. *Prescription*

With regard to prescription the provisions of the BGB applicable to unlawful acts apply *mutatis mutandis*.

§ 12. *Further liabilities*

Statutory provisions remain unaffected according to which a person bound to make compensation is liable to a greater extent than under the provisions of this Act or another person is responsible for the damage.

§ 13. *Several persons liable*

(1) If several persons are bound to make good property damage to a third person, as regards the mutual relations of those bound to make compensation, the duty to compensate and its extent depend on the circumstances, and in particular on how far the damage was caused by one or the other. The same applies if the damage occurred to one of those bound to compensate, to the liability that attaches to another of them.

(2) Subsection (1) applies *mutatis mutandis* where, along with those bound to compensate under §§ 1 and 2, another person is legally responsible for the damage.

§ 14. *Optional jurisdiction*

Actions based on these provisions may also be brought in the court, in whose district the event causing damage took place.

Case 106

REICHSGERICHT (SIXTH CIVIL DIVISION) 11 JANUARY 1912*

RGZ 78, 171

On 5 August 1908, while flying from Mainz to Friedrichshafen, the defendant's airship was forced by engine failure to land on a field near Echterdingen. Since thousands flocked to see the sight, the landing area was sealed off by the military, while the fire brigade, and various army units were placed at the defendant's disposal. Around 3 p.m. a sudden storm caused the airship to break loose from its moorings and to be dragged for some 1200 metres before exploding and burning up. The plaintiff, who was among the spectators standing near the place of anchorage, was struck by the anchor-chain. He sued the defendant for damage alleging that the accident was caused by the defendant's negligence.

Both lower courts rejected the plaintiff's claim and his application for review was denied for the following

Reasons

1. The claim was considered by the Court of Appeal in the light of §§ 823 and 831 BGB and it refused to consider the applicability of other statutory provisions imposing liability for dangerous objects (*Gefährdungshaftung*). This conclusion is entirely justified by existing law. In cases such as this, where the plaintiff's injuries have been sustained outside any contractual relations, the provisions of the Civil Code dealing with torts are the only ones that can apply. According to these provisions, however, the defendant can only be liable to the plaintiff if the latter's damage is due to the former's culpable conduct. Special provisions of the Civil Code imposing liability without fault, e.g. § 833 BGB concerning the liability of keepers of animals, the principles of the Imperial Act on Liability (*Reichshaftpflichtgesetz*), or of the statute of 3 May 1909 (*Strassenverkehrsgesetz*) concerning automobile accidents, which (statutes) impose liability based on risk, cannot be applied to aerial navigation given their exceptional character.

---

* English version by F. H. Lawson and B. S. Markesinis.

2. With regard to liability for damages resulting from illegal acts, the older view can no longer be accepted which postulated with respect to the dangerous nature that constitutes a fault (*Verschulden*). Consequently, it cannot be said that because aerial navigation is fraught with great dangers the defendant, as initiator of this dangerous undertaking, can be regarded as being at fault in the sense required by § 823 I BGB. This approach has not been misapplied by the Court of Appeal taking the view, which pays due attention to the requirements of general safety and which is legally correct, that in the circumstances the defendant was under a duty to take particular care. The Court thus held the defendant was under a duty to take exceptional care, not least because at the time of the accident there was little experience in landing such an airship . . .

3. Given that in view of the above points the position taken by the Court of Appeal is free from legal error, the question arises whether the findings of fact justified it in holding that the defendant had discharged this duty. The plaintiff denies this on two grounds.

(*a*) First, he insists that the defendant was at fault, if for no other reason than the fact that he decided to go ahead with the flight even though he had insufficient experience in landings. In his appeal he therefore alleges that the defendant should not have gone ahead on the assumption that everything would necessarily proceed smoothly. At the very least he should have, from the outset, warned the public of all incidental dangers; and, if common sense and experience suggested that such warning of possible dangers would not be sufficient to avert them, then he should have cancelled the flight altogether.

This argument is misconceived. The facts of this case show that the defendant embarked upon this journey, which would have lasted for several days, in excellent weather conditions and was aided by an experienced crew. As the Court of Appeal suggested, he had every reason to believe that a carefully executed landing would pose no dangers to any crowd assembled for the spectacle. His principles of anchorage were correct and his means for anchoring were ample. And the defendant knew that wherever this happened competent assistance would be on hand. In his opinion his experience in such matters was more than adequate and he entertained no doubt that, even in the event of a storm he would be able to anchor his airship safely. Given all this he could undertake this flight without hesitation. And past experience had also shown that public warnings against possible future risks were ineffective. Instead he is entitled to believe that if need be injuries could be prevented by a cordon and by warning the crowds.

In view of the above no legal error can be found in the conclusion that the defendant's conduct during the preparation of the flight was careful in the sense of § 276 BGB. The applicant's view that the defendant should have had absolute certainty that the flight posed no dangers whatsoever is too far-fetched. Any enterprise of this type is bound to entail some dangers, also for third parties, and this could never be entirely eliminated, even if great care was taken. In the circumstances, therefore, it would be unjust to demand that such flights were banned altogether because their inherent dangers cannot be entirely eliminated. All that one can demand is that all care required in the circumstances should be taken. This, indeed, occurred since the defendant undertook the flight after proper preparations were carried out in accordance with prevailing experience. The flights went ahead when the weather conditions were good and everything could normally be expected to go well and safely. Consequently, he is not guilty of any recklessness constituting a danger to the community nor, indeed, can he be regarded as having carelessly breached his duty to take care.

(b) The applicant's second complaint is against the finding of the Court of Appeal that the defendant took sufficient measures at the landing-field both in respect of his anchoring his airship and in cordoning off the landing-space.

This argument, too, is unacceptable. With regard to the anchoring the Court of Appeal found the following facts. Prevailing experience, on which the defendant was entitled to rely, clearly suggested that since the emergency landing was only expected to last a few hours, the airship was quite properly anchored. Thus at the front, where it pointed downwards, the ship was secured to the ground by means of an anchor and posts and sacks while at the rear end the airship was held down by men, and deliberately kept in suspension so that it could swing in the direction of the wind. Forty men held the anchor rope and the front cabin of the ship while thirty men, properly instructed as to how to handle the side-movements of the airship, controlled the ship's rear cabin. And reinforcements were also at hand should the need arise. When the defendant left the airfield, the weather did not indicate that there might be any change in the direction of the wind, but even if such a change occurred, the airship was sufficiently secured to remain on the ground so long as its back remained free to swing in the new direction of the wind. The Court of Appeal also examined how, despite the above, the airship could cut loose from its anchor. In its view what happened was that the first gust of wind was quite suddenly followed by a second and extraordinarily violent gust which hit the airship on its side before it had time to swing to its direction and raised it with great force. Whatever method of anchorage was adopted there was no absolute proof that it would have managed to secure the ship to the ground.

The applicant is also wrong in arguing that since no one was to be responsible to the defendants for such extraordinary occurrence, he should have taken precautions against such an exceptional situation. This allegation is unsupported by the findings of facts. For given the initially prevailing favourable weather conditions, no sudden changes of wind were foreseeable at the time of the landing; thus, the defendant was not in breach of the duty of care required in the circumstances given that he had anchored his ship in accordance with the dictates of human experience and knowledge believing that his anchor could hold well even in a storm. That the airship was nevertheless torn away, as a result of the unexpected and violent gust of wind, and would probably have been torn away whatever system had been adopted for the anchoring, must be seen as the consequence of an act of God (*höhere Gewalt*).

As for the cordoning off of the landing-place, the Court of Appeal admitted that the plaintiff would probably not have been hurt if the cordon had been considerably wider. But again it is established that in taking these measures the defendant had done all that could have been expected of him. Thus, towards Echterdingen—from where the wind was blowing—ropes were used and soldiers were employed, while in the direction of Berhausen soldiers alone were posted at a close distance since no more ropes were available to drive the surging crowds back over and over again.

Nevertheless, the applicant feels that the defendant took insufficient precautions in this respect and insists that ropes should have been used in the direction of Berhausen; and soldiers could also have been used at much shorter intervals. But on the findings of facts this argument, too, fails. For as stated, the defendant cordoned off the place with all disposable means and achieved this as best he could despite the fact that curious crowds kept surging in the direction of the airship. If this forced landing, which was only meant to last for a few hours and carried out in favourable weather conditions, had not been disturbed by an unforeseeable change of weather, taking place against all reasonable expectation, the cordon would have been perfectly sufficient and no accident would have occurred. The defendant had no reason to anticipate that a storm, the result of an act of God, would suddenly blow up and tear his airship away from its moorings and then carry it over the heads of the public at such low height as to cause injury to some bystander. The requisite standard of crew did not, therefore, require the taking of such precautions that might protect the public against dangers which could in no way be foreseen as the likely consequence of a more or less normal forced landing . . .

Notes to the Strict Liability Act

I. Reading the text of the Strict Liability Act in conjunction with the commentary in Chapter 3, above, one immediately becomes aware of the considerable historical and methodological differences that exist between the German law on the one hand and the French and Common law on the other in the area of strict liability. For the French, unlike the Germans, have, by skilfully developing—one might even say perverting—an unpromising provision of their Code, brought strict liability within the codal context. This technique, however, has not blinded them to the advantages of special legislation dealing with specific areas where strict liability is desirable.

By contrast, the English Common law has experienced some difficulty in abandoning the idea that where there is no fault there can be no liability. On the whole, the attack on the notion of fault has not been a frontal one, but has taken the form of guerrilla warfare (waged through the concept of *res ipsa loquitur* and the objectivization of the notion of negligence) thus affecting the fringes only of the notion. The position is considered by many to be unsatisfactory; and the Pearson Committee recommended that strict liability should be introduced in a number of areas of tort law. At the time of writing, however, the prospects of that happening appear slim with the result that in English law strict liability can only be found in a limited number of statutes (e.g., the Nuclear Installations Acts 1959–65); in the rule of *Rylands* v. *Fletcher* (1868) LR 3 HL 330 (considerably restricted over the years by successive timorous judicial pronouncements); and in certain instances of damage caused by animals. Incidentally, this latter subject is now embodied in the Animals Act 1971—a prime example of the long-winded and unnecessarily complicated English drafting techniques.

2. As is often the case, the position in the United States is much more interesting and, indeed, advanced than it is in England. The traditional strict liability areas—animals, *Rylands* v. *Fletcher*—can be found there, as well. But the reception that the latter rule has had in the different parts of the United States has varied depending on the prevailing socio-economic and geographical conditions of the area in question. A well-known extract from *Turner* v. *Big Lake Oil Co.* 128 Tex. 155, 96, SW 2d 221 (1936) makes this clear:

In *Rylands* v. *Fletcher* the court predicated the absolute liability of the defendants on the proposition that the use of land for the artificial storage of water was not a natural use, and that, therefore, the landowner was bound at his peril to keep the waters on his own land [Citations omitted]. This basis of the English rule is to be found in the meteorological conditions which obtain there. England is a pluvial country, where constant streams and abundant rains make the storage of water unnecessary for ordinary or general purposes. When the court said in *Rylands* v. *Fletcher* that the use of land for storage of water was an unnatural use, it meant such use was not a general or an ordinary one, not one within the contemplation of the parties to the original grant of the land involved, nor of the grantor and grantees of adjacent lands, but was a special or extraordinary use, and for that reason applied the rule of absolute liability. This conclusion is supported by the fact that those jurisdictions which adhere to the rule in *Rylands* v. *Fletcher* do not apply that rule to dams or reservoirs constructed in rivers and streams, which they say is a natural use, but apply the principle of negligence. [Citations omitted.] In other words, the impounding of water in streamways, being an obvious and natural use, was necessarily within the contemplation of the parties to the original and adjacent grants, and damages must be predicted upon negligent use of a granted right and power; while things not within the contemplation of the parties to the original grants, such as unnatural uses of the land, the landowner may do only at his peril. As to what use of land is or may be a natural use, one within the contemplation of the parties to the original grant of land, necessarily depends upon the attendant circumstances and condition which obtain in territory of the original grants, or the initial terms of those grants.

In Texas we have conditions very different from those which obtain in England. A large portion of Texas is an arid or semi-arid region. West of the 98th meridian of longitude, where the rainfall is approximately 30 inches, the rainfall decreases until finally, in the extreme western part of the State, it is only about 10 inches. This land of decreasing rainfall is the great ranch or livestock region of the State, water for which is stored in thousands of ponds, tanks, and lakes on the surface of the ground. The country is almost without streams; and without the storage of water from rainfall in basins constructed for the purpose, or to hold waters pumped from the earth, the great livestock industry of West Texas must perish. No such condition obtains in England. With us the storage of water is a natural or necessary and common use of the land, necessarily within the contemplation of the State and its grantees when grants were made, and obviously the rule announced in *Rylands* v. *Fletcher*, predicated upon different conditions, can have no application here.

Again, in England there are no oil wells, no necessity for using surface storage facilities for impounding and evaporating salt waters therefrom. In Texas the situation is different. Texas has many great oilfields, tens of thousands of wells in almost every part of the State. Producing oil is one of our major industries. One of the by-products of oil production is salt water, which must be disposed of without injury to property or the pollution of streams. The construction of basins or ponds to hold this salt water is a necessary part of the oil business. . . .

Other references are given by Leon Green, 'Tort Law Public Law in Disguise', 38 *Texas Law Rev.* 1, 5 (1959), who puts great stress on the 'environmental factor'. But not all courts have taken such a hostile view and the trend is to adopt in substance, if not always in name, the *Rylands* v. *Fletcher* rule. See, for example, *Cities Service Co.* v. *State* 312 So. 2d 799 (Fla. App. 1975). But if the accumulation and escape of liquid substances have at times left the courts divided, blasting operations have been dealt with with greater severity and uniformity. See, for example, *Sullivan* v. *Durham* 161 NY 290, 55 NE 923 (1900) (and many others since). The underlying idea here is that extra-hazardous activities must pay their own way (cf. *Smith* v. *Lockheed Propulsion Co.* 247 Cal. App. 2d 774, 56 Cal. Rptr. 128 (1967)).

The *Restatement of Torts, Second* has phrased the rule, which stems from

Rylands v. *Fletcher* but is also stripped of many of its limitations, in the following way:

§ 519 (1) One who carries on an abnormally dangerous activity is subject to liability for harm to the person, land, or chattels of another resulting from the activity, although he has exercised the utmost care to prevent such harm.

(2) Such strict liability is limited to the kind of harm, the risk of which makes the activity abnormally dangerous.

§ 520. In determining whether an activity is abnormally dangerous, the following factors are to be considered:
  (*a*) whether the activity involves a high degree of risk of some harm to the person, land, or chattels of others;
  (*b*) whether the gravity of the harm which may result from it is likely to be great;
  (*c*) whether the risk cannot be eliminated by the exercise of reasonable care;
  (*d*) whether the activity is not a matter of common usage;
  (*e*) whether the activity is inappropriate to the place where it is carried on; and
  (*f*) the value of the activity to the community.

3. For further discussion of the rich case-law see Franklin and Rabin, 442 ff.; Henderson and Pearson, 677 ff.; *Rylands* v. *Fletcher*, and its reception in the USA, has given rise to an interesting socio-legal literature. Thus see, *inter alia*, Bohlen, 'The Rule in *Rylands* v. *Fletcher*' 59 *U. Pa. L. Rev.* 298, 373, 423 (1911); Molloy, '*Fletcher* v. *Rylands*—A Re-examination of Juristic Origins' 9 *U. Ch. L. Rev.* 266 (1941).

4. In addition to the above-mentioned developments of 'traditional' strict liability doctrines, one can also find in the US new areas of strict liability. The modern law of product liability offers such an example in the key provisions of the *Restatement of Tort, Second*. Good accounts and further references to this dynamic part of modern tort law can be found in all the textbooks and case-books referred to throughout this work.

One must further note the existence of new compensation systems which have emerged as alternatives to the system of tort liability based on fault. Some of these, e.g. workers' compensation schemes (replacing in all but some isolated instances the Common law tort action) have already acquired a respectable history. The Massachusetts statute enacted in 1911 (Mass. Gen. Laws, ch. 152) is a fairly representative example and is discussed by Henderson and Pearson, 845–54. No-fault automobile insurance is, on the other hand, a relative newcomer and despite many statutory variations and even more proposals for reform, has never quite aspired to replacing tort law completely. (Interesting discussions can be found in Franklin and Rabin, ch. 11, and Henderson and Pearson, 861 ff.) Finally, what was in the 1970s described as the 'medical malpractice crisis' prompted many to contemplate the possible advantages of a no-fault system of compensation for this type of injury. An example of such thinking can be found in a feasibility study prepared in 1979 by the American Bar Association on Medical Professional Liability and is discussed briefly by Henderson and Pearson, 887 ff. The American Bar Association has published useful annotated bibliographies of the growing literature on this topic under the title *Tort Reform and Related Proposals: Annotated Bibliographies on Product Liability and Medical Malpractice*, ed. B. A. Levin and R. Coyne (1979).

5. The legal aspects of case 106 are discussed at p. 704; but its non-legal background is also interesting for the accident described in the case happened in the process of perfecting the lighter than air dirigible aircraft first manufactured by the Frenchman Giffard in 1852—his airship was steam-powered and could travel at 5 m.p.h.—but perfected by the German Count Ferdinand von Zeppelin. (The British did not, initially, enter this Franco-German race; and it was only in 1917 that their first airship—the R33—was successfully launched, though its design was based on a German Zeppelin—the L33—which was brought down in England in September 1916 in an almost intact condition.)

The accident described in the leading case happened as the airship was returning to its base in Friedrichshafen, the old capital of Württemberg, on the north-eastern side of lake Constance where Zeppelin had set up his famous factory. During the First World War the Zeppelin was put to military use; and some fifteen years later, again in Friedrichshafen, another lethal air machine—the Dornier—was manufactured.

The French competed with the Germans not only in the manufacture of these dirigibles but also in making legal history through their misfortunes. See: *Coquerelc. Clément-Bayard*, Cass. Req. 3 août 1915, D.P. 1917, 1. 79.

5. ENVIRONMENTAL LIABILITY ACT OF 10 DECEMBER 1990*

(Translated from the German by The Cologne Re.)

With the consent of the *Bundesrat*, the *Bundestag* has enacted the following into law:

Article 1

Environmental Liability Act (ELA)

§ 1. *Facility liability for environmental impacts*

If a person suffers death or injury to his body or health, or if property is damaged, due to an environmental impact that issues from one of the facilities named in Appendix 1,† then the operator of the facility shall be liable to the injured person for the damage caused thereby.

§ 2. *Liability for non-operating facilities*

(1) If the environmental impact issues from a facility that is not yet completed and arises from circumstances forming the basis of the hazard posed by the facility after completion, then the operator of the not yet completed facility shall be liable pursuant to § 1.

(2) If the environmental impact issues from a facility that is no longer in operation and arises from circumstances forming the basis of the hazard posed by the facility prior to its ceasing operations, then the operator of the facility at the time of the ceasing of operations shall be liable pursuant to § 1.

§ 3. *Definitions*

(1) Damage arises from an environmental impact if the damage is caused by materials, vibrations, noises, pressure, rays, gasses, steam, heat, or other phenomena that have been dispersed in soil, air, or water.

(2) Facilities are permanent structures such as plants or storage facilities.

(3) Facilities include:
   (a) machines, instruments, vehicles and other mobile technical structures, and
   (b) ancillary structures

that stand in a spatial or operational relation to the facility or part thereof and could be significant for the occurrence of an environmental impact.

---

* As printed in Bundesgesetzblatt, Jahrgang 1990, Part I, p. 2634.

† These are defined in a very detailed manner in Appendix 1 which, for reasons of space, is omitted from this book.

§ 4. *Exclusion of liability*

No liability shall exist insofar as the damage has been caused by *force majeure*.

§ 5. *Limitation of liability for property damage*

If the facility has been operated properly (§ 6 II second sentence), then liability for property damage shall be excluded if the property has only been impaired insignificantly or to a degree that is reasonable according to the local conditions.

§ 6. *Presumption of causation*

(1) If a facility is inherently suited, on the facts of the particular case, to cause the damage that occurred, then it shall be presumed that this facility caused the damage. Inherent suitedness in a particular case is determined on the basis of the course of business, the structures used, the nature and concentration of the materials used and released, the weather conditions, the time and place at which the damage occurred, the nature of the damage, as well as all other conditions which speak for or against causation of the damage in the particular case.

(2) Paragraph (1) shall not apply if the facility has been properly operated. A proper operation is present if the special operational duties have been complied with and no disruption of operations has occurred.

(3) Special operational duties are those duties imposed by administrative permits, requirements, and enforceable administrative orders and regulatory laws, insofar as their purpose is to prevent such environmental impacts that could be considered to be the cause of the damage.

(4) If, for the purpose of supervision of a special operational duty, controls are prescribed in the permit, in requirements, in enforceable administrative orders or in regulatory laws, then compliance with this operational duty shall be presumed, if:

1. the controls were carried out during the period in which the environmental impact in question may have issued from the facility, and these controls give rise to no inference of a violation of the operational duty, or

2. at the time the claim for compensation is made, more than ten years have passed since the environmental impact in question occurred.

§ 7. *Rebuttal of the presumption*

(1) If multiple facilities are inherently suited to cause the damage, then the presumption shall not apply if another circumstance is, on the facts of the particular case, inherently suited to cause the damage. Inherent suitedness

in a particular case is determined on the basis of the time and place at which the damage occurred, the nature of the damage, as well as all other conditions which speak for or against causation of the damage.

(2) If only one facility is inherently suited to cause the damage, then the presumption shall not apply if another circumstance is, on the facts of the particular case, inherently suited to cause the damage.

§ 8. *Injured party's right to disclosure from facility operator*

(1) If there are facts justifying the assumption that a facility has caused the damage, then the injured party may demand information from the operator of the facility insofar as this is needed to determine the existence of a claim for damages pursuant to this Act. The demand shall be limited to data about the structures used, the nature and concentration of the substances used or emitted, and other effects issuing from the facility as well as the special operational duties as provided in § 6 (3).

(2) The right to disclosure pursuant to paragraph (1) shall not exist to the extent that the events must be kept secret pursuant to legal norms or the countervailing interests of the facility operator or of a third party requiring secrecy.

(3) The injured person may demand from the facility operator an opportunity to review existing documents insofar as the assumption is justified that the information provided is incomplete, incorrect, or insufficient, or if the information is not provided within a reasonable time. Paragraphs (1) and (2) shall apply accordingly.

(4) §§ 259–261 of the Civil Code shall apply accordingly.

§ 9. *Injured party's right to disclosure from administrative agency*

If the facts justify the assumption that a facility has caused the damage, then the injured party may demand information from administrative agencies that have issued a permit in respect of the facility, that supervise the facility, or that are responsible for recording impacts on the environment, insofar as this is needed to determine the existence of a claim for damages pursuant to this Act. The agency shall not be required to provide information if to do so would impair the performance of the tasks of the agency, if the disclosure would disserve the wellbeing of the Federal Republic or of a state thereof, or to the extent that the events must be kept secret pursuant to law or due to their nature, in particular due to lawful interests of the parties or of third parties. § 8 I, second sentence, shall apply accordingly for those agencies which have issued a permit in respect of the facility or which supervise the facility; information regarding the name and address of the facility operator, his legal representative, or agent for service of process may be demanded from these agencies.

§ 10. *Facility operator's right to disclosure*

(1) If a claim pursuant to this Act is brought against the operator of a facility, he may demand from the injured person or from the operator of another facility information or an opportunity to review documents or demand information from the agencies named in § 9, insofar as this is needed to determine the scope of his liability to the injured person or of his claim for indemnity against the other operator.

(2) The provisions of § 8 (2), (3) sentence 1, and § 8 (4) shall apply to the right to disclosure from the injured person; § 8 (1) sentence 2 and (2)–(4) shall apply to the right to disclosure from an administrative agency pursuant to § 9.

§ 11. *Contributory negligence*

If the fault of the injured person contributed to the cause of the damage, § 254 of the Civil Code shall apply; in case of property damage, the fault of the person having actual control of the property shall be considered to be the fault of the injured person.

§ 12. *Scope of liability for death*

(1) In case of death, compensation shall be paid for the costs of healing efforts as well as for the financial loss which the deceased suffered because his earning capability was eliminated or diminished or his needs were increased during the illness. In addition, the liable person shall pay funeral costs to the person who has to bear these costs.

(2) If, at the time of injury, the deceased stood to a third party in a relationship whereby he was obligated to that person, as a matter of law, to provide support or could become so obligated, and if the third party is deprived of the right of support as a consequence of the death, then the liable person shall pay to the third party damages to the extent that the deceased would have been obligated to provide support during his presumed lifetime. Liability shall also attach if, at the time of the injury, the third party was conceived but not yet born.

§ 13. *Scope of liability for bodily injury*

In case of bodily injury or injury to health, compensation shall be paid for the costs of treatment as well as for the financial loss which the injured person suffers thereby because his earning capability is eliminated or diminished temporarily or permanently or his needs are increased.

§ 14. *Compensation by annuity*

(1) Future compensation for elimination or diminution of earning capability and for increased needs of the injured person, as well as future compensation to a third party pursuant to § 12 (2), shall be provided by means of an annuity.

(2) § 843 (2) of the Civil Code shall be applied accordingly.

§ 15. *Maximum limits of liability*

The person liable shall be liable for death, bodily injury or injury to health only up to a maximum amount of 160 million Deutsche Mark and also for property damage only up to a maximum amount of 160 million Deutsche Mark, insofar as the damage is caused by a unitary environmental impairment. If the multiple losses to be indemnified on the basis of a unitary environmental impairment exceed the applicable maximum amounts provided in the first sentence, then the amount of each indemnification shall be reduced in the proportion that the total bears to the maximum amount.

§ 16. *Expenses incurred for restoration measures*

(1) If damage to property also impairs nature or scenery, then, insofar as the injured person restores the condition that would exist but for the occurrence of the impairment, § 251 (2) of the Civil Code shall apply, but the expenses incurred for restoring the prior condition shall not be considered unreasonable for the sole reason that they exceed the value of the property.

(2) Upon demand by the person entitled to compensation, the person liable shall make advance payment for the necessary expenses.

§ 17. *Limitation of actions*

The limitation provisions of the Civil Code pertaining to torts shall apply accordingly.

§ 18. *Effect on liability under other laws*

(1) This Act shall have no effect on liability arising under other legal provisions.

(2) This Act shall not apply in case of a nuclear event insofar as the Atomic Act applies in connection with the Paris Convention on Atomic Liability of 29 July 1960 (as published on 15 July 1985, BGBl. 1985 II p. 963), the Brussels Convention on Reactor-Powered Ships of 25 May 1962 (BGBl. 1975 II p. 957, 977) and the Brussels Convention on the Transportation of Nuclear Materials by Sea of 17 December 1971 (BGBl. 1975 II p. 957, 1026), as amended.

§ 19. *Provision of coverage*

(1) The operators of facilities named in Appendix 2 shall ensure that they are able to fulfil their legal obligation to provide compensation for damages that arise from a person suffering death or injury to his body or health, or from property being damaged, as a result of an environmental impact that issues from the facility (provision of coverage). If a facility that is no longer in operation presents a special hazard, the competent administrative agency may order the person who operated the facility at the time of the ceasing of operations to provide for coverage for a period of up to ten years.

(2) Coverage may be provided

1. in the form of liability insurance issued by an insurance company licensed to do business in the territory in which this Act applies;

2. in the form of an indemnity agreement or guarantee made by the Federal Government or by a state; or

3. in the form of an indemnity agreement or guarantee made by a credit institution licensed to do business in the territory in which this Act applies if such agreement or guarantee provides security comparable to that provided by liability insurance.

(3) The persons named in § 2 (1), Nos. 1 to 5 of the Compulsory Insurance Act as published 5 April 1965 (BGBl. I p. 213), last amended by the Act of 22 March 1988 (BGBl. I page 358), are exempt from the duty to provide for coverage.

(4) The competent administrative agency may prohibit, in whole or in part, the operation of a facility named in Appendix 2 if the operator does not comply with his duty to provide for coverage and fails to prove, within a reasonable time to be set by the competent agency, that coverage has been provided for.

§ 20. *Authorization to issue executive orders*

(1) The Cabinet shall, with the consent of the Upper House of the German Parliament, issue executive orders regulating:

1. the point in time after which the operator of a facility shall be required to provide for coverage pursuant to § 19;

2. scope and amount of the provision of coverage;

3. the requirements to be set for indemnity agreements and guarantees by credit institutions;

4. the procedures and powers of the administrative agency having jurisdiction to monitor the provision of coverage;

5. the proper office pursuant to § 158 c (2) of the Insurance Contract Act and the giving of notice pursuant to § 158 c (2) of the Insurance Contract Act;

6. the duties of the operator of a facility, of the insurance company, and of a person making an indemnity agreement or guarantee to the administrative agency having jurisdiction to monitor the provision of coverage.

(2) Any executive order shall be presented to the Lower House before presentment to the Upper House. The order may be amended or rejected by resolution of the Lower House. The resolution of the Lower House shall be presented to the Cabinet. If, after three session weeks following receipt of an executive order, the German Lower House has not deliberated on it, the order shall be returned to the Cabinet unamended. The Lower House shall deliberate on an executive order upon petition by the number of members required for forming a parliamentary group.

§ 21. *Criminal penalties*

(1) Any person who

1. fails, wholly or partly, adequately to provide for coverage in violation of § 19 (1), sentence 1, in connection with an executive order pursuant to § 20 (1), No. 1 or 2; or

2. violates an enforceable order issued pursuant to § 19 (1), sentence 2, shall be imprisoned for a term not to exceed one year or fined.

(2) If the violation is committed negligently, the imprisonment shall not exceed six months or the fine shall not exceed 180 day-sentences (*Tagessätze*).

§ 22. *Administrative penalties*

(1) Any person who violates an executive order pursuant to § 20 (1), Nos. 3 to 6, commits an administrative offence insofar as the particular order refers to this provision on administrative penalties for a specific violation.

(2) The administrative offence may be penalized with a fine of up to ten thousand Deutsche Mark.

§ 23. *Transitional provisions*

Where the damage was caused before the entry into force of this Act, this Act shall not apply.

Article 2

Amendment to the Code of Civil Procedure

The Code of Civil Procedure, as revised and published in the *Bundesgesetzblatt*, Part III, 310–14, most recently amended by Schedule 1, Chapter III, Area A, Section II No. 1 of the Unification Treaty of 31 August 1990 in connection with Article 1 of the Act of 23 September 1990 (BGBl. 1990 II pp. 885, 921), shall be amended as follows:

The following shall be inserted after § 32:

'§ 32a Jurisdiction in actions against the operator of a facility named in Appendix 1 of the Environmental Liability Act seeking compensation for damage caused by an environmental impact shall be vested exclusively in the court sitting in the district in which the impact issued from the facility. The aforesaid shall not apply if the facility is located abroad.'

Article 3

Transitional Provision

Insofar as the damage was caused before the entry into force of this Act, the Code of Civil Procedure, unamended by this Act, shall apply.

Article 4

Amendment to the Federal Emissions Protection Act

The Federal Emissions Protection Act, as published on 14 May 1990 (BGBl. I p. 880), as amended by Schedule 1, Chapter XII, Area A, Section II of the Unification Treaty of 31 August 1990 in connection with Article 1 of the Act of 23 September 1990 (BGBl. 1990 II pp. 885, 1114), shall be amended as follows:

The following § 51b shall be inserted after § 51a:

'§ 51b Provision for service of documents

The operator of a facility for which an operating permit is required shall ensure that certain documents may be served on him within the territory to which this Act applies. If service may be ensured only by the appointment of an agent for service, then the operator shall provide the name of the agent to the competent administrative agency.'

Article 5

Entry into force

This Act shall enter into force on 1 January 1991.

Notes on the German Environmental Liability Regime

William C. Hoffman, International Legal Counsel, Cologne Reinsurance Co., Cologne, Germany

1. *Introduction*

This note describes briefly the provisions of civil liability under current German law for injury arising from harm to the environment. The basic features of civil environmental liability under laws in force prior to 1991 will be described first. Particular attention will then be given to the Environmental Liability Act of 1990 (ELA), which became effective on 1 January 1991. Finally, several comparative observations and conclusions are made. The titles of the sources referenced herein are listed along with other useful references in a short bibliography.

2. *Environmental Liability under German Law Prior to 1991*

Environmental liability in the Federal Republic of Germany has been the subject of many provisions widely dispersed throughout public and private law. Numerous public law provisions prohibit specific polluting activities, and various civil liability laws require polluters to compensate for losses caused by pollution. See Kloepfer, *Umweltschutz* (collecting texts from over 100 separate pieces of German legislation regulating and providing liability for activities harmful to the environment).

Thus, German environmental law in force prior to 1991 consists of a patchwork of various laws, each having a relatively narrow scope of application. Many individual federal laws regulate single activities, such as construction, mining, railroads, streets, hunting, hotels, x-rays, and the removal of animal bodies, to name only a few. Each law contains restrictions deemed appropriate to curb pollution with respect to the particular activity. As a result, approximately 30 separate federal laws regulate water pollution arising from different sources and activities.

As will be discussed below, the ELA is an attempt to provide a broader and more comprehensive liability scheme supplementing the numerous pre-existing laws. An understanding of the ELA therefore requires a review of the most significant pre-existing laws, including: (1) state police power, (2) §§ 906 and 823 BGB, and (3) special laws providing strict liability for damage caused by water pollution or (4) by certain inherently dangerous facilities.

2.1. *Police Power to Prevent Pollution*

The several states (*Länder*) of the Federal Republic have police power to regulate directly conduct causing pollution, including conduct that threatens to pollute. Liability is strict, and *force majeure* generally is not a defence;

in many cases, no proof of causation is required at all. The police power is, however, generally preventative only, and permits State and local authorities only to issue orders enjoining future pollution but not to order the clean-up of past pollution or to order payment of police-response costs. See Schmitt, *Haftungs- und Versicherungsfragen* at 50–3, 58.

In short, while public liability for police-response costs does not exist *per se*, in some cases authorities can, in effect, order 'clean-up' operations by reference to a future threat to public health. However, the police power is not a source of tort law, and does not provide for civil damages as compensation for injury to persons or property. For a damages remedy, the claimant must sue under the various liability laws.

2.2. *§§ 906 and 823 BGB*

A claim for nuisance arises under § 906 of the German Civil Code (*Bürgerliches Gesetzbuch—BGB*). Liability for nuisance is strict. The action will lie where one landowner infringes the right of another to make use of the land. Generally, however, the offending neighbour is liable only for emissions that *substantially* deprive the claimant of use of the land. Liability arises under § 906 I only if 'unweighable materials' (*unwägbare Stoffe*), such as airborne substances, vibration, noise, or similar emissions from another plot cause an impact which 'not insubstantially impairs' (*nicht unwesentlich beeinträchtigt*) the use of the land. § 906 II further restricts liability to those cases in which the emissions exceed levels customary for the area and in which it is also economically reasonable to require the offending landowner to reduce the emissions. Otherwise, an injunction is possible if it is reasonable to require a reduction of emissions.

Thus, § 906 BGB affords protection to private use interests in land and does not extend to other kinds of injuries that pollution can cause. Personal injury or damage to personal property cannot give rise to a claim under § 906 BGB. For example, in the 'Smelting Oven' (*Kupolofen*) case, see BGHZ 92, 143 (1985), the German High Court held that an industrial landowner could not be held liable under § 906 for damage which airborne ashes, emitted by its facility, caused to the paint of cars parked on neighbouring industrial property.

§ 823 BGB provides a broader basis of liability in tort. Wrongful death, personal injury, damage to personal and real property and injury to other private interests may give rise to a claim for damages under § 823. Liability is based on a negligent or intentionally 'wrongful act' (*unerlaubte Handlung*) causing such injury. In the environmental area, most claims under § 823 will be based on negligence, and therefore require proof of fault as well as of causation.

Proving the elements of fault and causation can be exceedingly difficult in environmental cases, but plaintiffs in environmental cases may now benefit from a reversed burden of proof in respect of fault. Traditionally, under § 823, the burden of proof is on the claimant with respect to each element of a tort claim. However, in the 1985 *Kupolofen* case, *supra*, the court held that if, under § 823, the defendant raises the defence that the emissions were within the legal limits, then the burden of proof on the issue of the legality of the conduct is on the defendant. Nevertheless, as for the element of causation, the claimant still bears the full burden of proof.

Increasingly in recent years, the German legislature has responded to the inherent limitations of §§ 906 and 823 BGB as provisions of environmental liability law by enacting a number of pollution laws of special scope.

2.3. *Water Resources Act*

By far the most significant civil environmental liability act in force prior to 1991 is the Water Resources Act of 1957 (WRA) (*Wasserhaushaltsgesetz*), effective as from 1 March 1960. § 22 WRA imposes strict liability for bodily injury, property damage and—unlike §§ 906 or 823 BGB—pure economic loss resulting from any change in the physical, chemical, or biological composition of a water source. Liability for pure economic loss may arise under the WRA where, for example, water contamination causes a loss of income to a fisherman or to another business dependent on the water source.

§ 22 I WRA provides for non-facility liability and § 22 II for facility liability. Multiple tortfeasors are jointly and severally liable. Further, in 1971 the German High Court construed the WRA to give rise to a presumption of causation. If the polluting substance is 'inherently suited' (*geeignet*) to cause the harm suffered, then causation may be presumed. See 57 BGHZ 257, 264 (1971). This presumption applies, however, only if the claimant names multiple possible polluters; if only a single defendant is named, then the claimant bears the full burden of proving causation. This presumption, if applicable, reverses the burden of proof, shifting to the defendant the task of disproving causation.

2.4. *Facility Liability*

Other strict liability laws enacted since the WRA have also used the 'facility liability' approach. These laws apply only to certain types of facilities deemed inherently dangerous. Usually, the types or categories of facilities are listed in an appendix to the law. Under the most significant of these laws, strict liability exists for injury or damage arising from mining facilities (*Bundesberggesetz*), from nuclear reactors (*Atomgesetz*), from electricity plants and other energy production facilities (*Haftpflichtgesetz*), and from certain other facilities that release emissions harmful to the environment (*Bundes-Immissionsschutzgesetz*).

3. *The Environmental Liability Act*

As shown, the state of German environmental law in force prior to 1991 was a patchwork of numerous individual provisions enacted piecemeal and each having a relatively narrow objective. This state of the law gave rise to a need for a single, broader and more comprehensive liability law.

On 1 November 1986, the Rhine was severely polluted following a fire at a large chemical plant in Schweizerhalle, Switzerland. Water that had been used for extinguishing the fire drained into the river, washing highly toxic substances released during the fire into the environment. As a result, from Basel, Switzerland to Rotterdam in the Netherlands, the Rhine became extremely contaminated and virtually all fish and much other wildlife were destroyed. This event prompted the German government to announce, in 1987, that a strict liability law was desired, not only for water damage but also for damage caused by air and soil pollution.

The act that emerged after a hotly debated legislative process is the Environmental Liability Act of 1990 (*Gesetz über die Umwelthaftung*), enacted 10 December 1990 and effective as from 1 January 1991. The ELA is not, it must be kept in mind, a public, criminal or administrative law. The ELA is a liability law providing a civil damages remedy for harm caused by pollution of air, soil or water. As such, the ELA has a broader scope than prior liability laws but it does not preempt or supersede any of the prior laws. Rather, the ELA coexists with and complements them, although some overlap is apparent.

3.1. *Nature, Scope and Elements of Liability Under the ELA*

The ELA imposes strict liability of up to DM 160 million for bodily injury and DM 160 million for property damage caused by any one environmental impact on air, soil or water. Liable persons are the 'operators' (*Inhaber*) of certain facilities listed in Appendix 1 of the Act. Thus, facility operators may be liable for a total of up to DM 320 million per impact, per facility.

Unlike the WRA, however, the ELA does not provide for recovery of damages for pure financial loss. A claimant seeking compensation for pure financial loss must therefore establish liability under other provisions permitting recovery for such losses, such as the WRA (permitting recovery of pure financial loss caused by water pollution) or § 847 BGB (permitting recovery of non-economic loss for pain and suffering in personal injury cases).

The nature and scope of liability under the ELA in general are set out in § 1 of the Act, which provides:

If anyone suffers death, personal injury, or property damage due to an environmental impact emitted from one of the facilities named in Appendix 1, then the operator of the facility shall be liable to the injured person for the damages caused thereby.

Liability is 'strict' under § 1 ELA because no fault is required. Polluters are liable for damage caused by their pollution regardless of whether the environmental impact was intended or negligent, known or unknown, occurred within a short span of a few minutes or over a prolonged period of many years. Causation alone, if proved under the ELA's provisions discussed below, provides the basis of liability. Further, the ELA as enacted contains no development risk exclusion, so that it is no defence against liability to assert that the state of scientific or technical knowledge at the time did not permit the defendant to know of the potential harm to the environment. Moreover, strict liability can attach under the ELA for amounts of pollution that are authorized or tolerated by existing regulatory laws, if the claimant can establish the element of causation.

Liability is joint and several among multiple defendants under the ELA. A draft bill containing a pro rata apportionment among multiple defendants was blocked by the Upper House in October 1990, and one of the provisions that were unacceptable to the Upper House was the pro rata provision. That provision was deleted from the ELA as enacted, with the result that multiple ELA defendants are subject to general tort principles, including joint and several liability under § 840 BGB. This means that any one of several defendants held to be jointly liable may be liable for the entire amount given by the judgment (regardless of what percentage of the damage that particular defendant might have caused in fact).

Several exclusions from liability delimit the scope of the ELA. § 4 ELA excludes liability for damage caused by *force majeure* (*höhere Gewalt*). Further, § 5 ELA excludes liability for property damage that is 'only insubstantial' or that the impairment is 'reasonable according to the local conditions' if the facility was 'operated properly', i.e., according to all applicable regulations and no interruption of operations has occurred. Finally, § 15 ELA limits, as mentioned above, liability to a combined total of DM 320 million for all bodily injury and property damage per impact, per facility.

In order to establish liability under the ELA, a claimant must prove three elements: (1) that the defendant operates a *facility* named in Appendix 1; (2) that *an environmental impact was emitted* from the defendant's facility; and (3) that this environmental impact *caused* the damage complained of. The following paragraphs examine each of these elements briefly.

3.2. *Facility*

The ELA applies only to a 'facility' as defined in its provisions. Because the ELA imposes liability on a 'per impact, per facility' basis, the definition of 'facility' would play an important role, for example, in determining whether the ELA defendant might be subject to multiple limits of liability, e.g., where more than one 'facility' may be said to have given rise to an 'environmental impact'.

§ 3 II ELA defines 'facility' (*Anlage*) to mean a 'permanent structure such as a place of business or warehouse'. The same provision states that 'facility' also includes any 'machines, instruments, vehicles and other mobile technical structures', and 'outbuildings' which 'stand in a spatial or technical relation to a facility or part thereof and could be significant for the occurrence of an environmental impact'. Thus, the existence of a 'facility' seems to be tied to a structure, vehicle, or instrument of some kind. Under § 2 ELA, uncompleted or unfinished facilities and finished facilities no longer in use are included in the definition.

Appendix 1 of the ELA contains a list of 96 specific types of facilities. These are grouped into ten general categories of facilities engaged in the processing, manufacture, or handling of certain materials and include industries engaged in:

(1) mining, energy and heat production;
(2) the manufacture of products from stone, earth, glass, ceramic, and other construction materials;
(3) the processing and manufacture of steel, iron, and other metals;
(4) the manufacture of chemical, pharmaceutical, or petroleum products or their further processing;
(5) treatment with organic materials and the manufacture of artificial materials;
(6) the processing of wood and wood pulp;
(7) the production of food, feed, and agricultural products;
(8) the treatment of waste;
(9) the storage and disposal of certain materials; and
(10) other facilities, including paint, printing ink, asphalt, etc. production.

This list of facilities is more extensive than prior facilities appendices, and includes certain toxic waste disposal and burning facilities not previously subject to major environmental legislation.

3.3. *Environmental Impact*

§ 3 I ELA defines 'environmental impact' (*Umwelteinwirkung*) to mean an impact from 'material, vibration, noise, pressure, rays, gasses, steam, heat, or other phenomena which are emitted into soil, air, or water'. Thus, the ELA applies to all emissions already specifically prohibited by § 906 BGB, and also overlaps with the remedy for bodily injury and property damage caused by water pollution under the WRA. Strict liability for bodily injury and property damage resulting from impacts on soil and air is, however, new under the ELA.

3.4. *Causation*

The element of causation presents the core problem of proof under the ELA. Causation can present nearly insurmountable difficulties in cases of gradual pollution arising from sources located far away, such as chemical emissions from a distant smokestack, toxic waste seeping into a water source, etc. The drafters of the ELA drew on the experiences from the WRA and attempted to compensate for this difficulty with a presumption of causation.

At the time of its passage through the legislature, the ELA's most controversial provisions were those located in § 6 ELA. § 6 I ELA provides that the element of causation will be presumed upon a prima facie showing that the particular facility is 'inherently suited' (*geeignet*) to cause the damage. Thus, the drafters of the ELA codified the judge-made presumption of causation that had its origins under the WRA in the 1971 decision, cited *supra*. This presumption reverses the burden of proof: it eases the claimant's evidentiary burden by shifting to the defendant the task of showing an absence of causation. However, unlike its predecessor under the WRA, the presumption of causation under § 6 I ELA applies equally in cases against single facilities. Once the presumption applies, the defendant may be held liable unless the presumption can be precluded or rebutted.

§§ 6 II, III and IV ELA provide that the presumption of causation set out in § 6 I is precluded from arising, and has therefore no application, if the defendant can show that his facility was 'properly operated'. 'Proper operation' means that the facility fulfilled all 'special operational duties' and that no disruption of operations occurred. 'Special operational duties' refers to all applicable administrative regulatory duties aimed at preventing pollution. In a subpresumption aiding the defence, the ELA provides that compliance with a 'special operational duty' may be presumed for purposes of excluding the presumption of § 6 I. If (1) documented checks are required by law and (2) such checks do not allow for an inference of a violation, then compliance with the applicable laws will be presumed.

A defendant may rebut the presumption of causation under § 6 I by using the provisions of § 7 ELA. In cases of single or multiple facilities inherently suited to cause the claimant's damage, the presumption of causation is rebutted if another 'circumstance' (*Umstand*) also appears 'inherently suited' to be the cause.

Substantively, perhaps the most far-reaching effect of the ELA's presumption of causation occurs in connection with joint and several liability. In cases against multiple defendants, the presumption may form the basis of liability as against all defendants who fail to exclude or rebut it.

It must be noted, however, that neither §§ 6 II–IV ELA nor § 7 ELA operates as a defence. In other words, even if a defendant successfully precludes § 6 I's presumption of causation from arising under §§ 6 II–IV, or rebuts it under § 7, this alone will not necessarily relieve a defendant of liability. Rather, the effect of these provisions is merely procedural; the claimant thereby loses the benefit of the reversed burden of proof. In such a case, the claimant bears the full evidentiary burden on the element of causation which, if met, nevertheless establishes liability.

Perhaps the drafters of the ELA did not foresee that § 7 ELA may turn out to be the exception that swallows the rule. The broader the courts construe the language 'inherently suited' in § 6 ELA, the easier it will be for a defendant to point to facts giving rise to a 'circumstance' to rebut the presumption under § 7. With a little imagination, a clever defendant might easily point to facts raising an issue as to whether another 'circumstance' satisfies a broadly construed 'inherent suitedness' test. Thus, § 6 I's presumption, together with § 7's rebuttal thereof, could operate to blunt the teeth of the ELA. However, as the language 'multiple facilities' in § 7 makes clear, in no case can another defendant facility be the other 'circumstance' justifying the exclusion. Thus, § 7 prevents multiple defendants from using each other to deflect use of the presumption.

3.5. *Right to Disclosure*

In a highly unusual provision for German law, the ELA confers on claimants and defendants rights to obtain information pertinent to ELA claims. Generally, German civil procedure does not provide for party-initiated fact gathering. See J. Langbein, 'The German Advantage in Civil Procedure', 52 *Univ. of Chicago L. Rev.* 823, 824 (1985). However, §§ 8 and 9 ELA grant claimants a right to seek disclosures from facility operators and from administrative agencies. § 10 ELA grants defendant facility operators a similar right. In further provisions, these rights are made subject to other laws, more firmly imbedded in German legal tradition, providing for secrecy. See §§ 8 II, 9, and 10 II ELA.

3.6. *Mandatory Insurance of ELA Appendix 2 Facilities*

§ 19 ELA imposes a provision-of-coverage requirement for the facilities named in Appendix 2 of the Act. The operators of those facilities must ensure that compensation will be provided for losses caused by an environmental impact issuing from such a facility. This § 19 ELA coverage may take the form of (1) a liability insurance provided by an insurance company licensed to do business in Germany; (2) an indemnity agreement with the federal government or a state; or (3) an indemnity agreement with certain credit institutions if the security provided is comparable to an insurance coverage.

The mandatory insurance requirement of § 19 ELA will not come into effect until the Ministry of Justice issues a decree setting the terms of the insurance. The decree has not been issued as of 1 October 1993. When issued, it will establish, for example, what coverage limits will be required. If the recently issued genetic damage insurance regulation is any indication—and some believe that it is—the mandatory minimum amount of coverage might be between 10 million and 30 million DM. On the other hand, one cannot dismiss summarily the view that the special hazards posed by ELA Appendix 2 facilities may prompt the Ministry of Justice to require some higher amount of coverage, particularly since the ELA itself imposes a potentially far greater amount of liability.

The drafters of the decree will also resolve issues arising from the nature of mandatory insurance of ELA Appendix 2 facilities. For example, § 19 I ELA provides in part: 'If a facility that is no longer in operation presents a special hazard, the competent public agency may order the person who operated the facility at the time of the ceasing of operations to provide for coverage for a period not to exceed ten years.' Based on this provision, the Ministry of Justice could require facility operators to purchase an 'extended reporting period' of up to ten years for claims based on damage caused by a facility's operations but discovered after operations cease.

3.7. *Competence of the Court and Extraterritoriality*

Generally, the proper German court for a claim in tort is the *forum delicti commissi*. See Code of Civil Procedure (*Zivilprozeßordnung*) § 32 (1981) (the proper court is the court of the district 'in which the tort was committed').

This rule does not always designate a single forum in environmental cases because damage occurring in one forum may be due to pollution emitted in another. As with other multijurisdictional torts, the *locus delicti* (or 'place where the tort occurs') can be either the place of the emission or the place where the claimant's damage is located. A claimant in a border-straddling case therefore may choose the more favourable of two proper courts. This forum-shopping is permitted by the German courts in domestic and international cases under § 32 of the Code of Civil Procedure, see 1 Baumbach, *ZPO* § 32 at 81 (1981), as well as in those international cases in which the 1968 European Community Convention on Jurisdiction and Enforcement of Judgments in Civil and Commercial Matters, Title II, Ch. 2, Art. 5 (3), applies.

However, the ELA abolished the claimant's choice of forum in domestic cases. § 2 of the ELA amended the Code of Civil Procedure to provide that an ELA action must be brought in the district court where the facility emitting the pollution is located. If, however, the facility emitting the pollution is located beyond German borders, then this rule does not apply. Thus, in cases of emissions from abroad causing damage in Germany, the general procedural rule of claimant's choice of forum applies.

On this procedural basis the ELA's substantive provisions have, in international cases, extraterritorial reach. German choice of law rules provide for application of German substantive law in cases involving damage resulting in Germany. See: Introductory Act to the Civil Code (*Einführungsgesetz zum Bürgerlichen Gesetzbuch*), § 2. Thus, operators of facilities located outside Germany not only may be sued in the German courts for compensation for damage occurring in Germany, but they will have to answer according to the provisions of the ELA. The ELA is more stringent than existing laws in many of the countries surrounding Germany, and so the ELA's standards of strict and joint and several liability, as well as its presumption of causation, may be a trap for the unwary owners of facilities beyond Germany's borders, as well.

4. *Conclusion*

Comparatively speaking, Germany is a leader in matters of environmental liability legislation in Europe. Indeed, German law has provided for strict liability for a wide variety of environmentally-related damage since the WRA entered into force in 1960. Thus, German strict environmental liability pre-dates by many years the experience of the United Kingdom under the Environmental Protection Act 1990 and of the United States under the Comprehensive Environmental Restoration, Compensation and Liability Act of 1980 (CERCLA). On the European Continent, Germany is far in advance of most other countries in this regard.

However, it must be noted that the patchwork of German environmental laws seems to result in a less comprehensive body of law than, say, in the United States, where civil liability, police power to order clean up, and enforcement provisions are combined in CERCLA. In Germany, civil liability for harm caused by pollution arises under entirely separate laws than does the power to order clean up. Whether or not this patchwork approach makes a substantial difference in the effectiveness of German law to regulate and deter pollution, as well as to compensate for pollution-related harm, is a far more difficult question, the answer to which will have to be based in part on future experience under the ELA.

Further reading. A. Texts of German Environmental Laws: M. Kloepfer, Umweltschutz, Textsammlung des Umweltrechts der Bundesrepublik Deutschland (1993) (looseleaf collection of virtually all German environmental laws); *B.* Books: G. Landsberg and W. Lülling, *Umwelthaftungsrecht—*

Kommentar, Umwelthaftungsgesetz, Haftung nach dem Gentechnikgesetz, sonstige Umwelthaftungsvorschriften, Materialien (1991) (the first and best commentary on the ELA co-written by one of the drafters of the ELA); P. Salje, *Umwelthaftungsgesetz—Kommentar* (1993) (recommended); J. Schmidt-Salzer, *Kommentar zum Umwelthaftungsrecht* (1992); A. Schmitt, *Haftungs- und Versicherungsfragen bei Umweltrisiken* (1990); C. Articles: U. Diederichsen, 'Die Haftung für Umweltschäden in Deutschland' *Produkthaftpflicht international* (PHI 5/92) (Sept. 1992); W. Hoffman, 'Germany's New Environmental Liability Act: Strict Liability for Facilities Causing Pollution', 28 *Neth. Int'l Law Review* 27–41 (1991) (a fully annotated text providing the basis for this note); W. Hoffman, 'Environmental Liability and its Insurance in Germany', 43 *Fed'n of Ins. & Corp. Couns. Q.* 147–65 (1993); R. Renger, 'Überlegungen zur Verordnung über die Deckungsvorsorge nach dem Umwelthaftungsgesetz', *Produkthaftpflicht international* (PHI 3/92) 86 (May 1992).

4

The Remaining Provisions of the German Civil Code

SECTION A. COMMENTARY

I. TWO MORE GENERAL CLAUSES

(a) § 823 II BGB

This important provision of the BGB imposes an obligation to make amends on anyone who violates a statutory provision intended for the protection of others. The element of unlawfulness which, as we saw in the context of § 823 I BGB, is defined by reference to the violation of the specifically enumerated interests, is here made to depend upon the notion of a violated protective norm (*Schutzgesetz*). This is taken to refer to statutes (of private and public law), government decrees, local by-laws, food and drugs regulations, and police orders. On this important paragraph there is an extensive literature. See, *inter alia*: Bistritzki, *Voraussetzungen für die Qualifikation einer Norm als Schutzgesetz im Sinne des § 823 Abs. 2 BGB* (Diss. München 1981); Knöpfle, 'Zur Problematik der Beurteilung einer Norm als Schutzgesetz im Sinne des § 823 Abs. 2 BGB' *NJW* 1967, 697; Peters, 'Zur Gesetzestechnik des § 823 II BGB' *JZ* 1983, 913. A list of laws recognized as containing protective norms in the sense of this paragraph can be found in: Palandt, § 823 no. 145 ff. and in the *Münchener Kommentar* (Mertens) § 823 no. 166 ff. (See Ch. 1.7, Bibliographical Survey.)

Civil liability for violation of a protective norm under § 823 II BGB may overlap with liability arising from the violation of some other provision of the Code. For example, in the chicken-farm case (case 43) we saw that the manufacturer of the defective vaccine that killed the plaintiff's poultry was in breach of a special statute which was held by the court to be a protective statute in the sense of § 823 II BGB. However, readers will also remember that his liability overlapped with liability based on § 823 I BGB and in fact it was this part of the judgment that made history. Sometimes the overlap may exist with the provisions of some other enactment. As already stated, a breach of the Road Traffic Act (or police regulations made pursuant to it) will often be treated as a breach of a protective norm. In such cases liability for a breach of the Road Traffic Act will co-exist with liability based on § 823 II BGB. Indeed, liability may further be based on § 823 I BGB. § 823 II BGB is thus an additional cause of liability, not a reason for excluding liability that may arise from another legal source.

This overlap, however, does not mean that the requirements of liability are the same in all these cases. As we have already noted, liability under the Road Traffic Act does not depend on fault. On the other hand, liability under § 823 I and II BGB is fault-based liability. The second sentence of § 823 II BGB makes this abundantly clear by stating that where breach of a particular statute can engage liability irrespective of fault—something which often happens these days—additional civil liability under § 823 II BGB will be imposed only if some fault can be found in the wrongdoer. In this instance, however, the case-law has reversed the onus of proof and placed it squarely on the defendant. So fault will be presumed unless the defendant can positively disprove any fault on his part (BGHZ 51, 91; BGH NJW 1968, 1279). In this sense, therefore, § 823 II BGB is more favourable to the plaintiff. But it is also more favourable in another respect as well, notably in its recognition of the compensability of purely economic loss. This explains why the plaintiffs in the cable cases, reviewed earlier on (cases 9 and 10), tried to base their claims on § 823 II BGB. These observations, however, should not be taken to imply that plaintiffs can, as a matter of course, base their claims on this paragraph of the BGB every time there has been a violation of some statute. The requirement that the violated statute is a protective norm provides the greatest obstacle and the most interesting condition of this provision of the Code. It is to this, therefore, that we must now turn our attention.

Now the first thing to note in this respect is that the German legislator expressly states that, subject to what is said below, the breach of a particular statute will always give rise to a civil remedy. By so doing he has successfully avoided one of the problems that has literally plagued the English courts and forced them to search for the real or imaginary intention of the legislator on this matter. (See in this respect Lord Denning's remarks in *Ex. p. Island Records* [1978] ch. 122, 135A.) But the civil remedy will be granted only if the violated norm was a protective statute. This means that the plaintiff must show that the mischief that occurred was in fact the one that the legislator wished to avoid. Moreover, he must show that he himself belongs to the class of persons to which the legislator intended to grant a civil remedy. Both of these propositions are quite simple to state; and they contain nothing that will surprise a Common lawyer. But the answer to these questions is by no means easy to find; it invariably involves difficult questions of statutory construction which varies from case to case and in practice it has given rise to a very rich case-law. The detailed study of this case-law presents little interest to any course of lectures or book that aims at introducing students to the study of foreign or comparative law so we shall limit ourselves to a few illustrations. (For further details see Peters, 'Zur Gesetzestechnik des § 823 II BGB' *JZ* 1983, 913.)

When looking at these cases, the first thing one can note is the fact that a statute meant to protect the public at large does not necessarily mean that it was not also intended to include within its protective ambit a particular (legal or physical) person. For example, during the First World War the German Government imposed stringent regulations concerning meat imports. Powers to control such imports, regulate their qualities and internal distribution (in order to avoid food shortages), and if necessary to confiscate illegally imported consignments of meat, were vested in a state-owned Central Purchasing Corporation. On one occasion one of the Corporation's employees, working near the Netherlands border, wrongfully authorized the import of an excessive quantity of meat which reached an accomplice of his and was subsequently sold to their mutual gain. The Corporation's action for damages against both these persons was successfully based on § 823 II BGB in conjunction with the relevant government order that had created the Corporation and vested in it the powers described above (RGZ 100, 142, 146). As the court said, the fact that the order creating the Corporation was issued for the protection of the common well did not prevent it from conferring a special right of action on the Corporation in accordance with § 823 II BGB. It would be wrong, however, to argue the reverse and say that all statutes passed in the interest of the public at large also automatically conferred rights on its individual members. This point was made very clear in one of the cable cases which has been reproduced above (case 9) and need not be repeated here.

The question whether the particular plaintiff is included in the protective ambit of the violated statute naturally turns on the wording and the often elusive intention of the legislator. The search for this can be aided by consulting the *travaux préparatoires* but if these, too, are ambiguous then 'the question must be attacked directly, whether the creation of an individual claim for compensation appears meaningful, sensible, and tolerable in the light of the whole system of liability' (BGHZ 66, 388; see, also, BGH NJW 1980, 1792). Three cases, reproduced below (cases 107–109) provide interesting illustration of how the above guiding principles are applied in practice.

In the first case (BGHZ 26, 42), the defendant was granted under statutory powers a licence to operate a bus service, but was prohibited from operating on a regular line between points A and B. Despite this express prohibition, he did operate that line and was sued by the Federal Railways.

One of the questions before the court was whether the Federal Railways could base their claim under § 823 II BGB and the violation of the Act on Carriage of Persons on Land under which the original licence had been granted. The main question was connected with the proper construction of the law subjecting land transport to State licensing and regulation. In the court's view this was meant to protect the interests of the general public in the establishment of an orderly transport system which has always occupied a special position in the country's transport policy. The action by the Railways was thus accepted.

In another case (BGHZ 15, 315), an association was formed in order to protect the interests of tenants of leased premises. Among the services that the association provided for its members was the availability of legal advice on legal points and this was done in consideration of a fee which was fixed in accordance with the professional fee-scales applicable to the members of the Bar. The plaintiffs, another association formed to protect the economic and professional interests of the members of the Hamburg Bar, applied for an injunction requesting that the defendant tenants' association cease to provide legal counselling services. Once again, the outcome depended on discovering the purpose of the relevant statute concerning the provision of legal services by qualified members of the Bar. The court took the view that this had a double purpose; first, to ensure that the public received proper counselling from a well-qualified and disciplined body of professionals, but secondly, also, to protect the interests of the Bar against competition coming from persons or bodies who were not subject to the same disciplinary and other restrictions as were professionally qualified lawyers. The claim that the association of tenants could not charge full fees was accepted, though the court also took the view that a more modest charge could be made simply in order to cover the association's expenses.

BGHZ 29, 100 (case 109) is our last example. In that case the plaintiff, an unsecured creditor of a company in liquidation, sued one of its directors alleging that in breach of statutory duty (§ 64 of the Companies Act) he had failed to commence liquidation proceedings at a given date and, as a result, the plaintiff had suffered financial loss by advancing credit to the company. The defendant's argument, that the obligation to commence liquidation proceedings on time was solely meant to safeguard the public interest, was not accepted. The court took the view that the purpose of this enactment was also to safeguard the position of creditors of the company against precisely this type of risk. Moreover, this was true even for those creditors who had advanced credit *after* the date when the liquidation proceedings ought to have been commenced. (See, further, Medicus no. 622 giving further references at p. 306. See, also, the recent decision BGHZ 100, 19.)

It is not enough for the plaintiff to prove that he belongs to the class of persons that the violated statute wished to protect; he must also show that the mischief that has occurred was the one that the statute wanted to avoid. Only if both these points are proved will the plaintiff be able to base his claim on § 823 II BGB.

The liquidation case, mentioned in the previous paragraph, provides an illustration for this point as well. Another and arguably better example can be found in one of the cases discussed earlier under the heading of manufacturers' liability (BGHZ 39, 358, case 54). It will be remembered that in that case a local authority was being sued because cracks appeared in a building, the foundations of which had not been properly inspected. No personal injury or damage to other property was pleaded and the claim was rejected. For the court took the view that the purpose of the statute imposing upon local authorities an obligation to inspect foundations was to prevent injury to human beings and damage to *other* property but not to safeguard potential buyers against the risk of paying an excessive price for a worthless building. (For another illustration see BGHZ 66, 388, BGHZ 19, 114, 125 and cases 9 and 101 respectively. Deutsch, *JZ* 1984, 308, 311–12 and *JZ* 1990, 733, discusses briefly some of the most important recent cases.)

(b) § 826 BGB

Select bibliography

Braun, *Rechtskraft und Restitution. Erster Teil. Der Rechtsbehelf gem. § 826 BGB gegen rechtskräftige Urteile* (1979); Kohte, 'Rechtschutz gegen die Vollstreckung des wucherähnlichen Rechtsgeschäfts nach § 826' *NJW* 1985, 2217; Larenz, 'Grundsätzliches zu § 138 BGB' *Juristenjahrbuch* 7 (1966/7) 98; Sack, 'Das Anstandsgefühl aller billig und gerecht Denkenden und die Moral als Bestimmungsfaktoren der guten Sitten' *NJW* 1985, 761; Simitis, *Gute Sitten und ordre public. Ein kritischer Beitrag zur Anwendung des § 138 I BGB* (1960); Teubner, *Standards und Direktiven in Generalklauseln, Möglichkeiten und Grenzen der empirischen Sozialforschung bei der Präzisierung der Gute-Sitten-Klauseln im Privatrecht* (1971); Wolf, 'Der Ersatzberechtigte bei Tatbeständen sittenwidriger Schädigung' *NJW* 1967, 709.

This is the third and last general provision of the Code and was, in fact, intended from the outset as an all-purpose residual provision, able to accommodate future expansion in the growth of the law of torts. In the event, however, the limitations built into this provision did not facilitate such growth, with the result that some of the most significant extensions of tort liability have been achieved either through § 823 I BGB, or the expansion of the law of contract into what otherwise would properly be described as the province of the law of torts.

§ 826 BGB is subjectively the narrowest of the three general provisions, since it will be satisfied only if intention can be shown to exist. For present purposes, mere negligence is thus not an acceptable *mens rea*. Intention is taken to include *dolus directus* and *dolus eventualis*. An example of the first can be found whenever the defendant knows the consequences of his conduct and wishes to bring them about; an illustration of the latter can be seen in those cases where the defendant is aware of the consequences of his conduct which he accepts as inevitable even though he may not specifically desire them. What must be intended is the damage in suit, though its full extent and the precise way it is brought about need not have been specifically anticipated.

Though subjectively narrow § 826 BGB is objectively wide—in fact the most general, indeed amorphous provision of the Code. In this instance the pervading notion of unlawfulness is not determined by reference to the violation of a carefully enumerated list of protected interests; nor is it linked with breaches of statutory provisions to be found outside the Code. Here, the determination of the element of unlawfulness is left to the judge to decide by reference to the flexible notion of *boni mores*. Though as we shall see this does not mean that the outcome depends on the personal views and predilections of the judge, in practice this formula does confer wide praetorian powers.

It will have become obvious from the above that intentionally inflicted loss will not, of itself, bring § 826 BGB into operation. Economic competition—the basis of all modern free economies—often means that the economic ruin of one person is the price of success for the competitor. Though nowadays there is an increasing tendency to limit some of the excesses of capitalism, the fact remains that in all systems intentionally causing economic loss to another person will not alone suffice to create tortious liability. Thus, just as English law imposes the additional requirement that the loss be inflicted 'unlawfully', so does German law require that the activity be intentional and *contra bonos mores*. This, then, becomes the crucial notion of this paragraph: crucial and, one should also add, elusive.

The difficulty of definition lies largely in the fact that because of historical reasons, German law chose to cover a multitude of wrongs under one broad and abstract formula instead of treating each factual situation as giving rise to different torts and requiring its own concepts and definitions. To put it differently, this separate pigeon-hole approach which can be found in England did not commend itself to the Germans. Thus deceit, passing off, intimidation, procuring a breach of contract, unfair competition, malicious prosecution, etc., which are all actionable as separate torts in the Common law, in German law are brought under one heading. Clearly, these wrongs are so disparate that if one formula is to cover them all it has to be a very wide one. This, as stated, accounts for the different approach and, indeed, has encouraged the abstract if not philosophical writings on the subject. But whatever the merits or demerits of this different approach—and one is inclined to think that in this instance the English casuistry has its advantages—the problems (and often the solutions) are quite similar in both systems. But to return to the basic notion: when is an activity *contra bonos mores*?

Apart from a brief interlude during the Nazi period, when this provision of the Code (as so many others) was subverted to the cause of national socialism (cf. RGZ 150, 1, 4), good morals have received a fairly constant definition. Thus 'the sense of propriety of all good and right-thinking members of society' (BGHZ 17, 327, 332) has often been quoted as the yardstick to be used in these cases. This is a flexible test, capable of accommodating change, and particularly useful in the context of problem situations which arise within the context of family life (e.g. RGZ 58, 248; BGH NJW 1962, 958). But in a modern pluralistic and less homogeneous society, is it always possible to discover a prevailing morality? Or is it practicable to introduce 'moral' considerations in the most typically litigated disputes involving some kind of excessive or improper competition? Should the actual practice of businessmen be used as the model instead? Or should the standard be derived not from extra-legal rules of morality but from the various rules of the positive legal system, including the Constitution itself? The idea that good morals is a notion much more akin to the English concept of public policy or the French *ordre public* has gained support, and in turn, become the target for criticism. It is difficult—especially for a Common lawyer looking at the German law—to say which of the many theories best explains the case-law. It is safer to assert with some measure of confidence that (i) the notion of *boni mores* has undergone some change since the War and, perhaps, (ii) that no one theory can be said to be able to cover the whole spectrum of disparate cases. To use Dean Prosser's description of the tort of nuisance, this is not a tort but a field of tortious liability. Perhaps, therefore, the best one can do is to give a series of examples from actually litigated cases and thus demonstrate to the Common law student the amplitude of this provision. For convenience's sake these illustrations are grouped under four headings.

(i) Misstatements

1. If a person gives in good faith false information and then subsequently becomes aware of its falsity he may, under certain circumstances, be under a duty to correct it and if he does not do so he will be liable under § 826 BGB (RGZ 76, 318; BGH JZ 1979, 725).

2. If an art expert deliberately values highly a fake painting so that his report can be shown to a third person and entice him to buy the picture, he will be liable to that third party under § 826 BGB.

3. If the directors of a company produce what to their knowledge is a false balance sheet in order to attract a potential investor they will be liable under the same paragraph (RG JZ 1908, 448).

4. If an employer intentionally gives to a third party an untrue reference about one of his employees he may be liable to the third party for the loss resulting therefrom (RG DJZ 1905, 697; see also BGH NJW 1970, 2291).

5. If a person gives recklessly false information about the credit of a third person he may be liable to the recipient of this information under § 826 BGB (BGH WM 1956, 1229).

6. Failure to disclose relevant information in the course of a business transaction may be actionable under § 826 BGB, especially where the defendant's conduct constitutes an abuse of his dominant economic position. (BGH NJW 1982, 2815.)

7. For other decisions under this broad heading see: BGH NJW 1983, 1850; BGH WM 1984, 221.

(*ii*) *Obtaining a judicial decision by fraud etc.*

1. If a person perjures himself and thereby causes another to be condemned to pay a debt which that other has in fact already discharged, he will be liable to that person for the loss suffered thereby (RGZ 46, 75).

2. A person who obtains a divorce by fraud can be liable under this paragraph (RGZ 75, 213).

3. A person who executes a judgment which he knows to be wrong can be liable under § 826 BGB, though this heading and the conditions that have to be satisfied, are controversial (BGHZ 50, 115; BGHZ 101, 380; BGHZ 26, 391, 396. See also OLG Celle MDR 1982, 408; BGHZ 112, 56, 56).

4. An execution of a judgment given in the case of a contract *contra bonos mores* is itself *contra bonos mores* (OLG Düsseldorf NJW 1985, 153; OLG Karlsruhe NJW 1985, 744; OLG Frankfurt NJW 1985, 745; OLG Stuttgart NJW 1985, 2273; but cf. OLG Düsseldorf NJW 1985, 747, 748; OLG Hamm NJW 1985, 749).

(*iii*) *Inducing breach of contract and other trade disputes*

Liability under § 826 BGB may be incurred in the following situations:

1. Intimidation of employers by trade unions not to employ non-union members (RGZ 104, 327).

2. Boycott (under certain circumstances) (RGZ 60, 94, 104; 64, 57, 61; 66, 379, 384; 76, 35; 86, 152; 105, 70; BGHZ 19, 72; BGH NJW 1985, 60, 62).

3. Inducing breach of contract (RG JW 1913, 866; RGZ 78, 14, 17; RG JW 1913, 326; BGH NJW 1981, 2184). Mere 'co-operation' in the breach of a contract with a third party will not suffice (BGH NJW 1969, 1293 ff.). In reaching a decision all the surrounding circumstances must be considered. (BGH NJW 1981, 2184.)

4. Under certain circumstances, strikes can also be caught by this provision (RGZ 130, 98).

5. A person who induces a vendor of sold but undelivered goods to hand them over to him (rather than to their purchaser) (RG JW 1931, 2238).

6. Disclosing confidential information acquired during previous employment may be actionable in contract (§ 74 HGB and § 242 BGB) as well as being actionable under § 826 BGB (BAG NJW 1983, 135). BGH NJW 1981, 1089 ('Wallraff-Fall') is particularly noteworthy not only because of the public interest it attracted, but also because it discussed the position of § 826 BGB within the context of the wider constitutional order. In that case Wallraff—the second defendant—wrote a book, which was to be published by the first defendant, and in which he described how a well-known Hanover newspaper was run. This information he had acquired while working under a false name for the editor of this newspaper. The latter's action— based *inter alia* on § 826 BGB—to prevent the publication of the said account was dismissed on the grounds that § 826 BGB in this instance had to give way to the constitutionally protected freedom of expression (*Meinungsfreiheit*) (Art. 5 I of the Constitution of Bonn). See BVerfG NJW 1984, 1741.

(iv) Miscellaneous matters

1. Malicious falsehood (RGZ 76, 110).

2. Abuse of rights (BGHZ 26, 391, 396).

3. Passing off (RGZ 144, 41, 45).

4. Malicious prosecution (BGHZ 17, 327; BGH NJW 1951, 597).

5. Wrongful use of monopoly power (RGZ 132, 273; cf. BGH MDR 1980, 121).

6. Other underhand activities (OLG Celle NJW 1983, 1065; BGH WM 1984, 850 (touting)).

7. Rejected applications to join business or social 'societies' or 'clubs' can also under certain circumstances found actions on § 826 BGB (BGHZ 29, 344 ff.; BGH NJW 1969, 316 ff.; BGH NJW 1980, 186).

2. OTHER HEADINGS OF TORTIOUS LIABILITY

(a) Instances where the onus of proof is reversed or strict liability is imposed

The Code provides for the reversal of the onus of proof in three more situations; § 832; §§ 833–4, and §§ 836–8 BGB.

§ 832 BGB makes those who are under a duty to supervise other persons (minors, mentally or physically incapacitated human beings etc.) liable for the damage caused by these persons to third parties or to their property. The obligation to supervise may stem from the law (e.g. the parents of a legitimate child: § 1626 II; § 1631 I BGB; the mother in the case of an illegitimate child: § 1705 BGB; legal guardian: §§ 1793, 1800 BGB etc.; courts have taken a stern view in cases of damage caused by children playing with matches: BGH NJW 1983, 2821; OLG Karlsruhe VersR 1985, 599); or it may derive from contract (e.g. kindergartens, boarding schools but not State schools (BGHZ 13, 27), private nursing-homes, and the like; for doctors and nurses in psychiatric hospitals see: BGH NJW 1984, 2574; NJW 1985, 677). In yet other instances, difficult demarcation problems may arise (e.g. a grandparent or a neighbour looking after a child: is this always a purely factual situation or can it amount to a legal relationship bringing into operation § 832 BGB?) (On this see Larenz II, 647 and the cases cited in n. 1. For further details on § 832 see: Albilt, *Haften Eltern für ihre Kinder?* (1987); Dahlgrün, *Die Aufsichtspflicht der Eltern nach § 832 BGB* (Diss. München 1979); M. J. Schmid, 'Die Aufsichtspflicht nach § 832 BGB' *VersR* 1982, 822.)

The liability of the supervisor arises the moment the 'tortfeasor' has realized the *objective* conditions of a particular rule of liability. If such an unlawful infliction of loss has occurred, the supervisor will be presumed to have culpably failed to discharge his own duty to supervise and will be liable to the victim, either solely or jointly with the 'tortfeasor' depending on whether the latter is capable of some fault (§§ 827–8 BGB). The requisite standard of care in supervision obviously varies from case to case, the Reichsgericht having stated that it will depend on 'the age, disposition, characteristics, development, education, and all other individual features of the minor' (RGZ 52, 73). The vagueness and flexibility of such phrases is deliberate but it should not conceal a discernible trend in recent cases to raise the standard of care expected of modern parents. (See Larenz II, 648 and cases cited in nn. 4–7.) In BGH VersR 1983, 734 the court held liable the parents of a seven-year-old child which started a fire having got hold of an easily accessible box of matches. But see OLG Stuttgart NJW 1982, 2608 (no duty of parents to supervise a fifteen-year-old boy playing football).

If the supervisor succeeds in exculpating himself, and the 'tortfeasor' is incapable of all fault (and, therefore, not personally liable), the innocent victim might run the risk of being left without any compensation. This, in fact, was the solution adopted by French law until the Court of Cassation changed its case-law in 1964 (Cass civ. 2ème 18 déc. 1964, *D.* 1965, J. 191). The German legislator, however, foresaw this eventuality and included a provision in the Code—§ 829 BGB—which enables the judge to take into account the financial position of the parties (including the insurance situation) and to oblige the innocent tortfeasor to pay the equally innocent victim/plaintiff such compensation as equity demands.

§§ 836–8 BGB impose a similar presumption of fault in the context of damage or personal injury caused by collapsing buildings, or man-made structures (e.g. walls, fences, flag-poles etc.) (See, BGH WM 1990, 1878.) Responsibility here is placed on a number of persons meticulously defined in §§ 836–7 BGB. Thus, while the person usually liable will be the owner, liability may also be imposed on a mere possessor (§ 836 I and III BGB), a former possessor (§ 836 II BGB), or even a builder or constructor (§ 837 BGB) who at Common law would, for certain purposes, probably be treated as the occupier of the premises.

These provisions, which derive in part from Roman law and can also be found in a less elaborate form in civil codes such as the French, do not impose risk-based liability, but in reality, widen the area of liability for unlawful omissions which is further intensified by a presumption of fault. Thus, the possessor will be held responsible for personal injury and/or property damage suffered by a third party as a result of the collapse of a building on his land. Such liability, however, will be avoided if the possessor proves that he took all necessary steps to avert the danger. Where a former possessor is being sued, he must prove that he took all necessary steps while he was the occupier of the premises or that a later possessor could have avoided the danger by observing the appropriate standard of care. In any event, the liability of the former possessor is potentially limited to damage caused within one year after the termination of his possession (§ 836 II BGB).

The wording of § 836 BGB makes clear its potential limitations. The damage must be the result of the collapse of a building (or part thereof) or some other structure attached to land, and to the consequence of defective construction or inadequate maintenance, not otherwise. Thus, for example, the Federal Supreme Court has ruled that building material falling as a result of *demolition* work will not be included in the protective ambit of this provision (BGH VersR 1978, 1160). In this case liability, if any, will be imposed on the demolition contractor and will be based either on the breach of some statutory duty or the violation of the general duties of care (§ 823 I and II BGB). One must, therefore, be always alert to the in-built limitations of this provision and be prepared to consider the alternative or parallel application of the general rules of liability. All in all, however, the resulting intricate web of overlapping legal rules is not a feature unique to German law. English Common lawyers in particular have been faced with similar problems and have had to combine different torts (like negligence or private or public nuisance) with statutory interventions (like the Occupiers' Liability Act 1956 or the Defective Premises Act 1972) in order to solve the potential liability of owners, occupiers, possessors, or landlords of dangerous or defective premises towards (i) their visitors; (ii) their next-door neighbours; and (iii) users of adjoining public roads.

§§ 833–4 BGB are the last provisions to be discussed under this subheading. Here a distinction has to be made between § 833 sentence 1 and 2 BGB. For the first imposes genuine risk-based liability (the only one to be found in the Code) for damage caused by certain kinds of animal whereas the second merely establishes a rebuttable presumption of fault against the keeper of 'domestic animals'. The term 'domestic animals' refers not just to tame animals (or animals domesticated in Germany in the sense that the English Animals Act uses this notion) but tame animals that are used 'to aid the business, the earnings, or the prosperity of the keeper'. Thus a gamekeeper's dog, a farmer's pigs or herd of cows, a shepherd's dog will come under this category; but dogs (generally), cats, or birds, which simply provide for their owner's pleasure, come under § 833 sentence 1 BGB. In between one finds some doubtful cases. For example, there is some ambiguity as to which part of § 833 should apply to a blind man's guide-dog. On the other hand a policeman's dog or horse, assisting him in the execution of his professional duties, have been brought under the second sentence of § 833 BGB (RGZ 82, 226). (Comparison with the Common law and the English Animals Act 1971 is fruitful and can reveal some interesting differences but cannot be attempted here. For further detailed discussions see: Baumgärtel, 'Neue Tendenzen der Beweislastverteilung bei der Tierhalterhaftung' 25 *Jahre Karlsruher Forum, Sonderbeilage zu VersR* (1983) 85; Deutsch, 'Die Haftung des Tierhalters' *JuS* 1987, 673; idem, 'Gefährdungshaftung für laborgezüchtete Mikroorganismen' *NJW* 1976, 1137; Dunz, 'Reiter wider Pferd oder Versuch einer Ehrenrettung des Handelns auf eigene Gefahr' *JZ* 1987, 63; Herrmann, 'Die Entwicklung der Tierhalterhaftung nach § 833 s. 1 in der modernen Judikatur und Literatur' *JR* 1980, 489; Honsell, 'Beweislastprobleme in der Tierhalterhaftung' *MDR* 1982, 798.)

(b) Other specific torts of the BGB

§ 824 BGB imposes civil liability for oral or written statements which are likely to endanger the credit of another person or otherwise damage his earnings or prosperity. Liability under this heading may overlap with the crime of insult or defamation (§§ 185, 186 StGB) and the civil consequences envisaged by the treatment of these provisions as protective statutes within the context of § 823 II BGB. But § 824 BGB is also wider in so far as it covers (i) intentional and negligent activities and (ii) statements which may endanger a person's credit or economic interests, even if they do not actually affect his reputation.

The statement must refer to an identified or identifiable plaintiff and not merely a wider class to which he belongs. Moreover, § 824 BGB refers to statements of facts and not expressions of opinion or other value-judgments. (See BGH NJW 1987, 2225.) The truth of the asserted fact will, normally, provide a full defence. If the facts are untrue—and the burden of proving their inaccuracy lies on the plaintiff—the maker of the statement may still avoid liability if he or the receiver of the communication had a lawful interest in it. But this privilege only applies if the maker of the statement did not know that his statement was incorrect. The defence of 'justified interest', as this defence is called, will be upheld only where an 'objective assessment of the contents of the communication, its form and all the surrounding circumstances suggest that it is the appropriate and necessary means for achieving a legally acceptable objective' (BGHZ 3, 281). If the elements of liability are satisfied, the plaintiff will, normally, be entitled to demand the retraction of the statement and compensation for costs reasonably incurred in order to mitigate his loss (§ 249 II BGB). In some (but not all) of these cases the courts have also allowed the plaintiff the costs of inserting a 'correcting statement' in the national press (see on this BGHZ 66, 182, 191 ff.).

§ 825 BGB contains the elements of another specific tort: the unlawful inducement of a woman to extra-marital cohabitation. The gist of the tort lies in the unlawful means used to coerce the woman's will: cunning, threats etc. Compensation for this tort will include economic loss (e.g. medical expenses incurred for curing a sexually transmitted disease; miscarriage or costs of giving birth to a child) as well as appropriate damages for pain and suffering and impairment of the victim's reputation (§ 847 BGB). The antiquated nature of the tort and the emergence of the new and wider right to one's personality have rendered this provision almost entirely obsolete in practice.

§ 839 BGB—dealing with liability for breach of official duty—is, by contrast, of considerable significance and has given rise to a rich case-law. Before analysing the elements of liability, three preliminary observations should be made. (For more detailed discussions see the references in Larenz II, 652, n. 3.)

First, one must note that this paragraph provides for the *personal* liability of the official. In most cases, however, the victim/plaintiff will be anxious to engage the liability of the State (or other local authority or agency). When and how this can be done depends on the *nature of the act* of the official.

This brings us to the second preliminary observation. The official may be exercising a 'sovereign act' or he may be pursuing ordinary, private law activities on the part of the State. The distinction between acts *iure imperii* and *gestionis*, never entirely satisfactory, has become more difficult in recent time as the modern State has entered the market-place. Nevertheless, as we shall note further on, the distinction is of great significance in the context of § 839 BGB.

Finally, one must always remember that § 839 BGB is a specific enactment and as such overrides the provisions of the other more general clauses of the Code (BGHZ 3, 94, 102; BGH NJW 1971, 43, 44). This is important to bear in mind since often the same act (by the official) can be brought under §§ 839, 823 I or II, or 824 BGB. Where this is the case, § 839 BGB will prevail and this may have serious repercussions on the position of the plaintiff given the various restrictions of liability provided in § 839 BGB. In this sense, therefore, § 839 BGB represents a narrowing of liability. On the other hand, the paragraph is also wider than some of the other general clauses (e.g. § 823 I BGB) in so far as it imposes liability for *any damage* arising from the unlawful conduct of the official, which means that under this heading even claims for negligently inflicted purely economic loss may succeed.

Turning now to the wording of § 839 BGB, we note once again that it refers to the liability of the 'official' for breach of official duty. In practice, however, it is the State that is made liable for his conduct. This is because of Art. 34 of the Constitution of Bonn of 1949 which provides that

If any person, in the exercise of a public office entrusted to him, violates his official obligations to a third party, liability shall rest in principle on the State or the public body which employs him. In the event of wilful or grossly negligent conduct, the right of recourse shall be reserved. In respect of the claims for compensation of the right of recourse, the jurisdiction of the ordinary courts must not be excluded.

Thus, the Constitution in effect shifts the responsibility of the official under § 839 BGB onto the State (or other official body). In fact it goes further since it also makes clear (i) that the State is liable instead of the public official; (ii) that the official himself is not in principle to be held liable to the third party (BGHZ 4, 45); (iii) that the claim against the State can, despite its public law nature, be pursued before the ordinary civil courts; and (iv) that the right of recourse against the official himself is severely limited. On the other hand, the courts have consistently taken the view that the State's liability is limited in exactly the same way as is the liability of the official under § 839 BGB (BGHZ 4, 46; 10, 138).

It is important to note that the liability of the Federal Government (State or other public body) is not limited to the acts of State officials (as the term is defined in administrative law) but can include the conduct of any other person, including a private enterprise or private individual, so long as they are performing acts which fall within the realm of 'sovereign' activities of the State. The position is different when officials (in the public sense) breach official duties while pursuing the private law interests or obligations of the State. For such acts the State can only be liable, either under § 31 BGB (acts of a constitutionally appointed representative) or under the rules of vicarious liability of § 831 BGB, both of which have been discussed in Chapter 3. Whether and how the liability of the State can be engaged will thus depend on how the activity will be characterized. Since the distinction between sovereign and private law acts is not clear, a rich case-law has, inevitably, developed in this area. Thus, some activities (e.g. running the police, the post office, etc.) are described as sovereign acts attracting the direct liability of the State under Art. 34 of the Constitution, while others (e.g. running the Federal Railways system (but excluding the activities of the railway police), the maintenance of public buildings, operation of State hospitals, etc.) are treated as private law acts leading first and foremost to the liability of the official under § 839 and, possibly, the State under §§ 31 or 831 of the BGB. (For further illustrations and references see Larenz II, 657–8.)

The State's activity cannot be engaged if the requirements of § 839 BGB are not satisfied. Looking at them, however, one sees clear signs of a protective philosophy which may have made sense at the turn of the century but which nowadays appears less convincing, leaving the Treasury as the only beneficiary. For example, the official will only be liable if he has *culpably* breached his duty. This makes sense in a system of individual responsibility based on fault (which is the one adopted by the BGB) but does it also make sense when the rule is applied to the modern State? It would appear that in many cases it does not, hence the courts' tendency to raise significantly the standard of care, at times to near-strict liability. On the other hand, where the official is given a discretion and acts within the proper limits of such discretion, or when he is called upon to apply a rule which is unclear (or is only subsequently clarified in litigation) he and the State will not be liable for any damage or loss caused thereby.

A second important limitation contained in § 839 BGB can be found in sub-section 1. Its effect is to render the official liable only when the victim cannot obtain redress from another source (which includes private insurance, social security etc.). This rule, introduced before Art. 131 of the Constitution of Weimar of 1919 first established State liability, was meant to shield public officials from excessive liability which might lead them into complete inactivity out of fear of being held civilly responsible for their conduct. But now that the State's liability has been substituted for that of the individual official, the continuation of this rule appears to be unnecessary.

Finally, in section 3 of this provision one finds yet another limitation: the right to claim compensation is lost if the victim has either intentionally or negligently omitted to mitigate his loss by making use of any other legal remedy available against the official in question (e.g. to demand his reprimand or the annulment of the decision in accordance with the rules of administrative law).

The last point that must be stressed is that it is not enough for the plaintiff to prove a culpable breach of an official duty: he must also prove two further requirements: first, that the duty was owed to him (or the class to which he belongs) and, secondly, that the damage in suit falls within the protective ambit of the violated norm. For example, the duty of the Public Prosecutor's Office to prosecute certain crimes is one that is owed to the community at large and not to an individual citizen who thus cannot complain if it is not exercised (RGZ 108, 249; 154, 268). On the other hand, State supervision over certain banking activities is instituted not only in the interests of the public at large but also in the interests of creditors of these institutions who may suffer loss as a result of an unlawful activity on their part (BGHZ 68, 142). The inefficient inspection of building foundations by local authorities provides an excellent illustration of the second requirement: namely that the damage that has occurred must fall within the protective object of the violated norm. Reading cases 54–55 shows that purely economic loss resulting from such bad inspections is not recoverable under these paragraphs. (From the large literature see: Engelhardt, 'Die neueste Entwicklung der Rechtsprechung zum Staatshaftungsrecht' *NJW* 1985, 621; Jacobs, *Staatshaftungsrecht* (1982); idem, *Neuere Entwicklungen im Staatshaftungsrecht* (1984); Krohn, 'Zum Stand des Rechts der staatlichen Ersatzleistungen nach dem Scheitern des Staatshaftungsgesetzes', *VersR* 1991, 1085; Ossenbühl, *Staatshaftungsrecht* (4th edn., 1991). In English: Council of Europe (ed.) *The Liability of the State* (1981).)

(c) Remaining provisions of the Code

In an introductory book such as this, the remaining provisions of the Code need not concern us for long. Thus, §§ 827, 828 BGB deal with cases of infliction of damage by persons of diminished responsibility—in the case of the former paragraph because of mental disturbance preventing the free exercise of the will, in the case of the latter paragraph because of youth. Under certain circumstances, no liability will be imposed for harm thus caused, though another person may be made liable for such loss, for example, under § 832 BGB. Alternatively, § 829 BGB may be relied upon in order to make the innocent tortfeasor pay the equally innocent victim equitable compensation.

§§ 830 and 840 BGB deal with the important practical problems raised by torts committed by several persons, their liability to the victim and their rights and duties against each other.

The first of these paragraphs deals expressly with the problem of joint tortfeasors. This is the case where the parties commit a breach of a joint duty or act in pursuance of a common design. If this element of common design is satisfied it is irrelevant how significant is the contribution of each party in causal terms. Even mental participation in the form of helping out with the planning of the act or merely providing friendly support will suffice. § 830 II BGB treats instigators and accomplices in the same way.

§ 830 I, second sentence, applies the same rule to a different situation where several persons participate in a course of conduct which, though not unlawful in itself, is potentially dangerous to others. The difference between this and the previous situation lies in the fact that whereas in the former case of joint tortfeasors the loss is caused by several persons acting in consort, in the latter case only one person has caused the loss but it is difficult if not impossible to say which one has done so. (The classic illustration is that of the huntsmen who discharge their guns simultaneously and the pellets from one unidentifiable gun hit an innocent passer-by.) In this case, as well, § 830 BGB adopts the same rule and makes all the participants liable to the victim for the full extent of damage.

The problem of several concurrent tortfeasors (*Nebentäterschaft*) does not receive express treatment by the Code but in principle there is little doubt as to how it should be dealt with. In the absence of specific proof showing what damage each tortfeasor caused, the courts will apply the rules stated above and hold them all responsible for the full amount.

§ 840 BGB deals with the status of joint debtors and their internal claims for adjustment. Joint debts will arise in many ways: the tortfeasors may be joint tortfeasors, they may be several concurrent tortfeasors, or they may have participated in a dangerous activity as described in the previous paragraph. Alternatively, the joint debt may arise because of a master–servant relationship (§ 831 BGB) or because one debtor is the owner of an animal (§ 833 BGB) that has caused damage and the other is its custodian (§ 834 BGB). The possessor of a building may also be liable along with a former possessor or a constructor (§ 836 BGB) and the owner of a vehicle may be liable under the Road Traffic Act along with the driver who may be liable under § 823 I BGB (though in this case the first debtor's liability will be subject to the statutory maxima provided by the Road Traffic Act). All of these persons will be liable to the victim for the full amount of his loss. As between themselves, § 426 I BGB envisages equal contributions unless otherwise provided. §§ 840 I and II and 841 BGB do, in fact, specify certain exceptions. The text of these provisions is set out in Ch. 1, section 3, above; and for a fuller discussion of these issues the reader must consult more specialized works. Larenz I, § 37, II; II, § 74 gives further references. For interesting causative explanations of these solutions see Honoré in *International Encyclopedia of Comparative Law* XI, ch. 7 *passim*. For discussions in German see: Bodewig, 'Probleme alternativer Kausalität bei Massenschäden' *AcP* 185 (1985) 505; Brambring, *Mittäter, Nebentäter, Beteiligte und die Verteilung des Schadens bei Mitverschulden des Geschädigten* (1973); Brehm, 'Zur Haftung bei alternativer Kausalität' *JZ* 1980, 585; Weckerle, *Die deliktische Verantwortung Mehrerer* (1974).

3. COMPENSATION AND SATISFACTION*

Select bibliography

Berger, 'Abkehr von der konkreten Schadensberechnung?' *VersR* 1985, 403; Ebel, 'Schadensersatz bei Personenschäden (§§ 844–6 BGB)' *Jura* 1985, 561; Flessner, 'Geldersatz für Gebrauchsentgang' *JZ* 1987, 271; Grunsky, 'Neue höchstrichterliche Rechtsprechung zum Schadensersatzrecht' *JZ* 1986, 170; idem, *Aktuelle Probleme zum Begriff des Vermögensschadens* (1968); idem, 'Neue höchstrichterliche Rechtsprechung zum Schadenersatzrecht' *JZ* 1983, 372; Lange, *Schadensersatz* (2nd edn. 1990); Egon Lorenz, *Immaterieller Schaden und 'billige Entschädigung in Geld', Eine Untersuchung auf der Grundlage des § 847 BGB* (1981); Medicus, 'Naturalrestitution und Geldersatz' *JuS* 1969, 449; idem, 'Schadensersatz und Billigkeit' *VersR* 1981, 593; Mertens, *Der Begriff des Vermögensschadens im bürgerlichen Recht* (1967); Schiemann, *Argumente und Prinzipien bei der Fortbildung des Schadenrechts* (1981); Sturner, 'Der Erwerbsschaden und seine Ersatzfähigkeit' *JZ* 1984, 412–16, 461–8; Wussow/Küppersbusch, *Ersatzansprüche bei Personenschäden* (5th edn., 1990). For comparative analysis see Fleming, 'Damages or Rent' 19 *Univ. of Toron. L. Jour.* 295 (1969) and McGregor and Stoll in vol. IX, chs. 9 and 8 respectively of the *International Encyclopedia of Comparative Law*.

(a) Preliminary observations

The concluding section of this book deals with the scope and extent of remedial relief that a victim of a proved tort may claim from his tortfeasor. Clearly, the two main issues that have to be discussed here are compensation for personal injury and for damage to property. Before this is done, however, it is advisable to make a few preliminary observations.

The first thing to notice is that for the traditional Common law everything that pertained to the notions of damage and damages was within the province of the jury and not the judge. As a result, the elaboration of legal principles has been weak or, at times, non-existent. This statement must now be qualified as far as the English Common law is concerned. The abolition of juries in personal injuries cases may be a recent phenomenon (it was

---

* This section substantially reproduces the text of an article of mine published in *Studi Senesi* (1985) pp. 7–46.

decided by the full Court of Appeal in *Ward* v. *James* [1966] 1 QB 273; see especially Lord Denning's reasons at 299–300); but, remarkably perhaps, in the 28 years that have elapsed since this important decision was handed down, a clear body of legal principle has emerged, making the comparison with German law easier than it would have been in days gone by. Indeed, in the pages that follow, the presentation of German law has been accompanied by frequent excursus into English Common law in order to show how a different history and a different methodological approach have, yet again, failed to produce significant differences in outcome. Indeed, in many respects the similarities between the two systems is quite remarkable.

However, we must immediately stress how very different is the methodological approach adopted by the two systems. German law, a creation of the universities and the product of a constant move towards abstraction and systematization, immediately reveals these features in its law of damages. For it is these characteristics that account for the reduction of the vast English casuistry into a mere handful of articles: §§ 842–7 BGB dealing with personal injury; §§ 848–51 BGB dealing with damage to property. However, provisions dealing directly or indirectly with compensation can also be found in the various strict liability statutes, e.g. the Strict Liability Act §§ 5–10; Road Traffic Act §§ 9–13; Air Traffic Act §§ 35–8, 46–51, etc. (Incidentally, one should note that though §§ 842, 843 BGB are in the tort section of the Code, many authors believe that they contain rules of general application and that they are, therefore, also relevant to the law of contract.) And it is the tendency to be ruthlessly systematic and logical that accounts for the fact that the provisions that crucially supplement the above-mentioned articles of the Code are to be found in the general part of the law of obligations and not in the tort section of the BGB. Thus § 249 BGB states that a person who is obliged to make compensation must restore the situation which would have existed if the circumstances which render him liable to make amends had not occurred; this is to be found in the general part of the law of obligations quite simply because an obligation to pay compensation can arise from breach of contract and/or the commission of a tort. The second point that must be stressed, therefore, is that once again the Common lawyer must be prepared to find the guiding principles in different parts of the Code.

A rule that must satisfy both contract and tort inevitably must be widely phrased and very abstract. Abstract generalizations, however, may be good for codes but are of little use to practitioners. Often they must be transformed into concrete rules of thumb, especially if out-of-court settlements are to be encouraged. Theory must yield to the demands of practice and the codal bones must acquire flesh and muscle before they can function properly. Indeed, the regulation of compensation by the Code hardly does justice to the subject (though, on the other hand, it is infinitely more detailed than the French civil code which is entirely silent on this matter!). This is where the courts come into the picture and it is through their work that the comparative lawyer can start to perceive the real similarities that the abstract apparatus of the Code tends to obscure. Once again the understanding of foreign law is enhanced if it is studied through its case-law.

Another area in which the two systems come closer together is where 'satisfaction' takes over from 'compensation' and the court is instructed by the legislator to weigh all the surrounding circumstances when deciding the level of the award. In those cases, as we shall note later on, insurance considerations at last come to the surface of the German judgments, giving a greater sense of reality to what the judges are really trying to achieve. Even the legal literature—traditionally sombre and concept-orientated—can reveal a refreshing interest in the problems of real people and real life.

The third point that must be made absolutely clear is that the advent of social security and private insurance has dramatically affected the function and purpose of the rules concerning compensation. This is, of course, true in all systems; but it is particularly noticeable in Germany where these days social security and insurance cover most of victims' needs and then take over the tort actions against their tortfeasors. (Sozialgesetzbuch of 1980 as amended in 1982, para. 116 of Book 10.) The typical feminine designation *die Klägerin* (which usually refers to either *die Kasse*, the social security carrier, or *die Gesellschaft*, the private insurance company) underscores the fact that the bulk of the personal injury litigation is these days undertaken by these two types of subrogees. In such circumstances, compensation of the victim can no longer be the prime purpose of the compensation rules. Rather, they have come to form a part of the intricate complex of rules which help allocate risks or, in some cases, seek to promote deterrence. To put it differently, the tort action, when it is taken over by the social security carrier or the insurer, helps to put the cost of accident back on the shoulders of the wrongdoer (or his insurer). Of course, if allocation of risks and costs is nowadays a prime purpose of tort law one should perhaps discuss at the liability phase of the enquiry which of the two parties is in a better position to carry the risk or channel the loss. But with few exceptions, such an open economic approach to tort law does not figure in German tort books; nor is it greatly favoured by the courts. American ideas tend to reach Europe with a jet-lag of about twenty years or more. In practice, therefore, actions by injured victims against their wrongdoers only take place whenever the social insurance scheme has not fully covered the actual loss.

Be that as it may, the fact remains that modern tort law has been forced to take into account the fact that its rules are no longer the only ones that determine compensation for loss. The need to regulate the interrelationship between all these disparate rules of compensation has thus arisen in Germany as it has elsewhere and it has been approached with one guiding principle in mind: the tort victim must be indemnified for his loss but he must not make a profit out of it (e.g. Kötz, *Deliktsrecht*, no. 508 *et seq.*). In this respect German law is different from American law since, on the whole, the latter appears to take a very generous view about cumulation of different benefits partially, no doubt, because a substantial part of the award goes towards financing the costs of tort litigation. Though this 'background' difference (between English and American law) may thus seriously affect the operation of tort law in practice, it seems rarely to be openly acknowledged. There does, however, exist the occasional, frank judicial admission which make such an idea plausible and thereby underscores the need to study legal rules within their wider political and socio-legal context in which they operate. Thus, in *Helfend* v. *Southern California Rapid Transit District* (2 Cal. 3d 1, 465 P. 2d 61 (1970) the Supreme Court of California argued that 'Generally the jury is not informed that plaintiff's attorney will receive a large portion of the plaintiff's recovery in contingent fees or that personal injury damages are not taxable to the plaintiff and are normally deductible by the defendant. Hence [the plaintiff] rarely actually receives full compensation for his injuries as computed by the jury. The collateral source rule partially serves to compensate for the attorney's share and does not actually render "double recovery" for the plaintiff.'

The general approach of German law is, in this respect, much closer to English law than it is to American law. Historically, however, there were also differences as to how one should avoid double compensation. Thus, originally, English law provided that in the case of certain benefits there should be a partial deduction from damages for personal injury, amounting to half the social security payments made to the plaintiff up to a maximum period of five years from the cause of action. Benefits both paid and likely to be paid after the judgment were deductible, but in calculating future benefit entitlement, no account was taken of likely increases in the levels of payment. The courts read the Act as implying that beyond the five year period, no deduction was to be made in respect of the specified benefits. (S. 2(1) of the Law Reform (Personal Security) Act 1948). This rule was widely criticised, partially on the ground that it 'subsidised' tortfeasors and, eventually, it was replaced by the Social Security Act 1989 which, in s. 22, changed the law by introducing a scheme of state 'recoupment' of social security benefits from damages awards above a statutory threshold set initially at £2,500. All the significant benefits which are concerned with income replacement and with the expenses of accident victims are included in the scheme. The court must now disregard these specified benefits when making its assessment of damages. However, the tortfeasor must then pay to the Department of

Social Security the full amount of any of the benefits which the plaintiff has received in respect of his injury or accident. The Department of Social Security is not formally subrogated to the plaintiff's claim (as in German law) but the effect is very similar. Thus, the tortfeasor must now pay in full but, as a result of these reforms, the plaintiff is worse off than he was under the old regime as a complete reduction of benefits is made. This scheme applies to accidents and injuries occurring after 1 January 1989.

As already suggested, this is not the German approach. Here, the entity (social security, insurance) that has compensated the victim will be subrogated to his tort action and will be able to claim from the tortfeasor the full amount that it has paid to the victim. According to the German Insurance Act of 1908 the same, broadly speaking, is true of payments made by a private insurer. The position more precisely is as follows: in respect of certain types of insurance contracts (e.g. loss insurance but *not* personal injury insurance), the insurer has a legal right (*cessio legis*) to be subrogated to the rights of the insured to the extent that he has indemnified the latter. In other types of insurance contracts, however, e.g. medical costs insurance, only 'conventional' subrogation is envisaged, i.e. the right of subrogation depends upon the insured having contractually conferred on the insurer a legal right to take over his claim. In this latter case the victim will thus have to cede to the insurer his right of action against the tortfeasor and will not be entitled to cumulate the insurance benefit and the tort damages. The point is widely accepted as just, though one could argue against it that the insurance money is the product of the victim's own thrift and foresight and that it is bad policy to take it away from him. (For further details Kötz, *Deliktsrecht*, nos. 506–12.)

The last preliminary point that has to be made is that the plaintiff's damages will be reduced (and in some circumstances even completely wiped out) in order to take into account his contributory fault. The term 'contributory fault' is here used instead of the more familiar Common law term 'contributory negligence' not only because it is the one employed by German (and, incidentally, French) law; but also because it is wider than the Common law term in at least two respects. For in the first place contributory fault includes intentional as well as negligent conduct. Secondly and, perhaps, more importantly it includes the conduct of the injured party/plaintiff *after* the occurrence of the initial harm as well as *before* it. However, though the German Code distinguishes the fault of the injured party that positively contributes to his harm and his failure to minimize it once it has happened, it subjects both these types of contributory fault to the same rules.

In the matter of contributory fault, German law departed from the old Roman law rule (also found in pre-1945 English Common law and still accepted by those American jurisdictions that have not introduced the notion of comparative negligence) according to which the injured party could not recover if his injury was due to his own fault unless the tortfeasor's conduct was intentional. Instead, § 254 I BGB states that 'if any fault of the injured party has contributed to the occurrence of the damage, the duty to compensate and the extent of the compensation to be made depend upon the circumstances, especially upon how far the injury has been caused predominantly by the one or the other party'. In this respect the German approach could be termed to be more 'modern' than that of traditional Common law; but German law has not taken the next step to ignore altogether the fault of the victim. This, it has been noted, has already happened in French law; and according to the view of some German authors it should also be introduced in German law, especially in the context of traffic accidents. For there appears to be hardly a traffic accident case which in theory should be dealt with expeditiously under the strict liability of the Road Traffic Act but which in practice does not become a prolonged and convoluted affair because the defendant raises the plaintiff's contributory fault.

When is there such contributory fault? In Common law there has been some discussion as to whether negligence in the defendant is the same thing as negligence in the plaintiff. The answer is negative since in the former but not the latter case a breach of a duty has to be proved. Likewise, in Germany it has been debated whether fault in the context of § 254 BGB has the same meaning as it has in § 823 I BGB—the better view being that a negative answer is appropriate since the notion of unlawfulness is relevant only in the latter instance. (See Kötz, *Deliktsrecht*, nos. 552–3.)

The answer to the question when is there fault on the part of the victim depends on the facts of each case. Certain factual situations, however, have come almost automatically to indicate that there is fault on the part of the plaintiff/victim. So, for example, a *motor cyclist* who does not wear a crash helmet will be deemed to be at fault (BGH NJW 1965, 1075) and the same rule applies to mopeds (BGH NJW 1979, 980). The occupants of a vehicle will also be contributorily negligent if their injury can be partly attributed to not wearing safety belts. (BGH VersR 1979, 536; BGHZ 74, 25.) But an injured *cyclist* is not guilty of contributory fault if he is not wearing a helmet (BGH NJW 1979, 980); nor will a passenger who had not fastened his seatbelt have his damages reduced if he can show that his injuries would have occurred even if he had secured his seat-belt (BGH NJW 1980, 2125 and cf. *Froome* v. *Butcher* [1976] QB 286). Incidentally, the wearing of seat-belts became compulsory in German law in 1976 (new § 21a of the Road Traffic Ordinance (Strassenverkehrs-Ordnung = StVO).

The vast majority of illustrations of contributory fault comes from traffic accident cases but one group of cases which is not always connected with accidents arising from cars deals with incidents involving infants. The case-law is clear that an infant's contributory fault will be taken into account only if he was capable of committing fault in accordance with § 828 II BGB and had acted culpably in the sense of § 276 BGB. § 828 II BGB adopts a rather arbitrary test by providing that 'A person who has completed his seventh year but not his eighteenth year of age is not responsible for any damage which he does to another if, at the time of committing the damaging act, he did not have the understanding necessary for realizing his responsibility . . .'. Academics, on the other hand (e.g. Esser/Schmidt, *Schuldrecht* I, 36), are not so categorical, some arguing that the infant's contributory negligence should be counted against him even where he was incapable of recognizing the danger to himself, while others maintain that policy reasons require that it should be ignored.

Contributory fault may, as has already been stated, arise after the damaging occurrence and will consist in the victim's own failure to mitigate his loss (§ 254 II BGB). Thus, if the plaintiff's vehicle is damaged in an accident and can be repaired he will, normally, have the right to have it repaired at the defendant's expense. But if the cost of repair significantly exceeds the cost of replacement of the car with another one of approximately the same value, he will be obliged to mitigate his loss and opt for the lower cost of replacement (cf. *Darbishire* v. *Warran* [1963] 1 WLR 1067, which reached the same result and with the same reasoning). Difficulties, however, can arise when the destroyed item is unique and the question how the replacement value will be calculated can also raise nice problems (on which see Kötz, 'Die Abwicklung des Kraftfahrzeug-Totalschadens' in *Festschrift Hauss* (1978) 181).

The same duty to mitigate the loss arises in personal injury cases so that, for example, an injured person must where reasonable obtain medical treatment as soon as possible (RGZ 139, 131, 136) and submit himself to any reasonable operation that could help restore his health (RGZ 129, 398; OLG Oldenburg NJW 1978, 1200). (For further references Stürner, 'Der Erwerbsschaden und seine Ersatzfähigkeit' *JZ* 1984, 412 ff. and 461 ff.) What of course is reasonable depends on a variety of factors, such as the age of the person injured, the degree of danger involved in the operation, the chances of acquiring alternative employment after the operation (which may depend on the condition of the labour market), and so on (RGZ 129, 398; cf. also OLG Oldenburg NJW 1978, 1200). Equally, the injured person must mitigate his loss by seeking alternative employment, which if necessary may even mean changing his profession (BGHZ 10, 18 though this again may raise nice problems); or take part in a retraining scheme, naturally at the defendant's expense (RGZ 160, 119; BGHZ 10, 18); and, in another case (BGH VersR 1971, 82) it was said that a self-employed individual may have to employ an assistant rather than give up his business altogether. The similarities here with Common law are such that they need not be laboured any further.

(b) Personal injury (pecuniary losses)

Personal injury can cause primary and consequential loss. The first term is taken to refer to such items as medical expenses incurred as a result of the injury and compensation for the injury itself (loss of an arm, eye, etc.). On the other hand, the second heading would include future loss of earnings and expenditure incurred as a result of further deterioration in the health of the victim flowing from the accident itself, e.g. subsequent development of epilepsy as a result of severe cranial injuries. This distinction between primary and consequential loss, with its strong causal undertones, is made both in cases of personal injury and damage to property and is usually adopted by textbook writers. Here, however, we shall adopt the English distinction between pecuniary and non-pecuniary losses, partly because it appears to be neater but mainly because it will help in the comparative presentation of the German law.

When the injured party's loss is pecuniary, i.e. it can be estimated in money terms, then the guiding principle is that of *restitutio in integrum*. This is true of English law (*Livingston* v. *Rawyards Coal Co.* (1880) 5 App. Cas. 25, 39 per Lord Blackburn) as it is of German law. § 249 I BGB expressly authorizes the restoration of the *status quo ante* which in personal injury cases means ordering the defendant to meet the plaintiff's costs (see § 249 II BGB). It follows that all reasonably incurred medical expenses, including such items as hospitalization, nursing, physiotherapy, radiotherapy, postoperative convalescence, the acquisition of special, e.g. orthopaedic aids, cosmetic surgery etc., will be met by the tortfeasor or, more likely, his insurer etc. (Once again, the position is identical in England: see Markesinis and Deakin, *Tort Law* (1994), 710 *et seq.*) The cost of private medical care may also be claimable if reasonably incurred and is usually claimed and awarded in the more serious types of injury where long and costly treatment or convalescence is necessary (see BGH VersR 1964, 257). In England failure to use the facilities of the National Health Service will not affect the reasonableness of the plaintiff's expenses which will thus be claimable (see *Harris* v. *Brights Asphalt Contractors Ltd.* [1953] 1 QB 617, 635 per Slade J.). In German law medical expenses can, on occasion, be also claimed even if they have not been actually incurred. So if, for example, cosmetic surgery is recommended because of the severity of the plaintiff's injuries, their cost may be claimable even if there is no likelihood of his actually agreeing to the operation (OLG Celle VersR 1972, 468; OLG Stuttgart VersR 1978, 188). The wisdom of this solution is, however, doubtful. (Cf. Kötz, *Deliktsrecht*, no. 515 with references.)

Lost future earnings often form the largest item and in their calculation, increases in pay, promotions, and the like will be taken into account. Income from an illegal or immoral source, however, tends not to be taken into account (see, however, the controversial decision of BGHZ 67, 119 dealing with the income of an injured prostitute). Damages are not awarded (or are reduced) if the defendant can show that the injured party/plaintiff would have lost his income in any event, e.g. through an imminent dismissal (BGHZ 10, 6; BGH VersR 1963, 674—predisposition). Where lump sums are awarded the annual income tends to be computed with a figure (capitalization factor) arrived at in a manner not very dissimilar to the English method. Useful guidelines were laid down by the BGH in its decision of 8 January 1981 (BGHZ 79, 187).

Not infrequently, relatives of the victim come to his assistance thereby incurring travelling expenses and often more serious loss of income (e.g. mother giving up her job to look after her injured child). German and English law are, in principle, at one on this by accepting that the victim may recover from the tortfeasor these expenses (see BGH VersR 1961, 272; VersR 1964, 532 and cf. *Donnelly* v. *Joyce* [1974] QB 454, also BGH NJW 1989, 766; BGH VersR 1991, 559, and Seidel, 'Der Ersatz von Besuchskosten im Schadensrecht', *VersR* 1991, 1319); though a fair number of decisions also seem to take a harsher view on such claims whenever the visits cannot be genuinely linked to the condition of the victim (BGH NJW 1990, 1037; NJW 1991, 2340). Both systems also agree that if compensation is then decreed for the victim it is then for him to decide whether he will reimburse these relatives with the sums he has recovered from the tortfeasor. But in both systems attempts have been made to impose a *legal* obligation on the victim to reimburse the relatives who have come to his aid and thereby suffered loss. In Germany this could arguably be satisfied by having recourse to § 683 BGB (management without mandate) and in England by utilizing the trust mechanism (see *Cunningham* v. *Harrison* [1973] QB 942, 952 per Lord Denning MR). In both these systems, however, these attempts have met with little success in the courts. (Cf. Esser/Weyers § 46 II 2.)

As already stated, the victim's loss (including his lost earnings) are often met by some social security carrier or insurer who is then subrogated to the victim's tort action to the extent that he has indemnified him. If the social security carrier has only partially compensated the victim the latter naturally retains his tort action for the difference. German law, however, also *imposes a legal obligation* on employers to continue paying the wages or salaries of their injured employees for a minimum period of time (usually not less than six weeks). (See for example § 616 II BGB; § 63 of the *Handelsgesetzbuch* (Commercial Code); § 1 of the Lohnfortzahlungsgesetz of 1969 (BGBl. I 946).) In such cases the loss is therefore incurred by the employer and not the injured employee and it should be the former who should have a right to take over the tort action to the extent that he has paid the victim/employee. The net result is accepted by the courts (cf. BGHZ 43, 378) though it has been questioned by some writers, not least because the loss suffered by the employer (paying wages without receiving any services in exchange) is purely economic loss and, as we have seen, not covered by § 823 I BGB. Perhaps the way to explain the above undoubtedly sensible result is to say that the employee retains his independent action against the tortfeasor but implicitly assigns it to his employer. This 'legal construction' means that in the event the tortfeasor is made to pay; the victim is not doubly compensated; and the employer is not left to carry the loss (cf. BGHZ 7, 30; 42, 76; 43, 378). It should be noted that in English law *whenever* the employer is under a legal duty to continue paying the wages of the injured employee the latter cannot claim them from the tortfeasor. (Since it would appear that the employer is equally unable to recover sums thus paid, the only one who stands to gain from such an arrangement is the tortfeasor.) But where the employer has made *ex gratia* payments, these will probably not be set off against the lost earnings (*Dennis* v. *London Passenger Transport Board* [1948] 1 All ER 779; *Cunningham* v. *Harrison* [1973] QB 942. Likewise in German law: RGZ 92, 57; BGHZ 10, 107).

Up to this point the presentation of German law will have caused no difficulties to the Common (especially English) lawyer. When we move, however, to the form of the award and the method of its calculation, some important differences of approach become obvious. Surprisingly, however, once again they seem to be attenuated in practice. The source of the difference lies in the attitude any given system is prepared to take towards lump-sum awards and periodical payments. Of course, whenever a debate about this issue takes place one must remember that it refers to the form the compensation will take for *future economic* loss. For no system objects to capitalizing earnings lost up to the time of the judgment. And the same is true for sums awarded to 'compensate' for pain and suffering—the relevant paragraph of the BGB (§ 847) being silent on this point. The dispute as to the form the payments should take is thus limited to such items as loss of future earnings, future medical expenses, and in the case of wrongful death loss of future support.

The question 'what form should these payments take?' can receive four possible answers. At the one extreme one finds Common law systems with their unequivocal preference for lump-sum awards. (For American law the last illustration can be found in *Slater* v. *Mexican National RR Co.* 194 US 120, 24 S. Ct. 581 (1904).) At the other end of the spectrum one finds certain socialist systems which only allow periodical payments or annuities, as they are most commonly called. (Rudden, *Soviet Insurance Law* (1966), ch. 7;

idem, 'Soviet Tort Law' 42 *NYUL Rev.* 583, 609 ff. (1967).) In between lie the vast majority of legal systems, though their approach can be further divided into two categories: the first includes those systems which are, technically speaking, neutral as to what form the award will take, accepting that either lump sums or periodical payments are perfectly acceptable. (France and Switzerland belong to this category.) The systems that belong to the second group, in which we find German law, accept that awards can take either form but expressly state their preference for periodical payments. §§ 843 I BGB and 844 II BGB state this preference in unequivocal terms. (According to §§ 843 II and 760 BGB annuities are paid three months in advance (but monthly annuities are commonly *agreed*).) The only exception is provided in § 843 III BGB where it is stated that a capital sum can be allowed instead of a periodical payment only if 'a serious reason' exists (*ein wichtiger Grund*). (Accident neurosis has for a long time been recognized as a sufficient ground for granting a capital sum: RGZ 73, 418, 420; 136, 373. The danger of the defendant going bankrupt would also constitute a serious reason: OLG Stuttgart OLGE 2, 440, 441. The victim's wish to use his compensation award to start a new professional life has also been accepted (RG JW 1933, 840) as has the fact that the person paying the compensation normally resides abroad or changes his residence permanently: OLG Nürnberg FamRZ 1968, 476, 478. See also RGZ 93, 209, 210 and Palandt, *Bürgerliches Gesetzbuch* (52nd edn., 1992, § 843 no. 6). According to Larenz II, 676, the cost of retraining for a new job in order to pursue gainful employment after the injury would also justify the demand of a lump sum.) This different approach calls for a number of observations.

The first is to invite the reader to examine the merits and demerits of the lump sum versus the periodical payments method of compensation and consider whether in the light of comparative observations the controversy can be seen in a different light. (For an excellent study see J. Fleming, 'Damages or Rent' 19 *UTLJ* 295–325 (1969).) Such a comparative approach can reveal that some of the disadvantages of the periodical payments system of compensation (which are correspondingly treated as advantages of the lump-sum method) can effectively be countered in practice. For example, the alleged disadvantage of the annuity system that it can expose the plaintiff to the danger of the defendant going bankrupt can be countered partly by the fact that defendants nowadays tend to be insurance companies (which, in theory, are less likely to go bankrupt than ordinary individuals) and partly by the courts' power to order defendants to provide adequate security to ensure the continued payment of the award. § 843 II BGB expressly gives this discretionary power to the court, though it is generally taken not to confer upon the plaintiff a right to demand that he be provided with such a security. (By contrast, the Swiss Code of Obligations makes the provision of security mandatory in such cases: Art. 43 II CO). Another supposed disadvantage of the annuity system, namely that it requires defendants to set up complicated and time-consuming mechanisms for the continued payments of awards, also appears to be less convincing when, once again, one realizes that the typical defendants are insurers who are equipped to deal with the problems of periodical payments. The finality of the award is also widely regarded as the real virtue of the lump-sum method of compensation. In a sense, it is also its great drawback, since it does not allow the court (or any other body) to correct errors in the forecasts that the judge has to make when fixing the lump sum. Thus, the medical condition of the plaintiff may get better or worse and thus prove the award too generous or inadequate. The same can happen with the plaintiff's employment prospects.

These imponderables affect the English Common law method of calculation of future pecuniary losses. The multiplier and multiplicand method of compensation (described in detail in Markesinis and Deakin, *Tort Law* 3rd edn. (1994) 713 *et seq.*) allows the judges to reflect all these imponderables in their rough-and-ready calculations. Moreover, the Administration of Justice Act 1982 has provided a new mechanism which is limited to certain instances of personal injuries and which allows the court to abstain from this guessing game and make an award on the basis that the feared eventuality (deterioration of health of the victim) may not be realized. But if it is (for example the plaintiff's cranial injuries caused by the defendant lead many years later to the development of epilepsy), the plaintiff will be given the chance to return to the court and seek an upward adjustment of the award.

This does not mean that the German method of calculating the annuity is less complicated. German judges, too, have to indulge in all sorts of calculations before they can reach a final figure for the annuity. In this they are greatly assisted by the traditional requirement that the plaintiff itemize his losses as precisely as possible, something which has led to an almost complete neglect of § 287 ZPO and the discretion it offers judges to estimate freely the amount of damages. But at least they do have the possibility of adjusting the amounts upwards or downwards so as to take into account changes in circumstances. (Incidentally, in French law an award can only be adjusted upwards.) And in one area at least, this different method of payment has altogether avoided a problem which has caused considerable difficulties to many Common law judges. The problem we are referring to is linked with the judge's duty to evaluate the chances of remarriage of a widow when assessing the size of the lost dependency. This unsavoury exercise led to the partial abolition of this duty in English Common law by the Law Reform (Miscellaneous Provisions) Act 1971 (now § 3 II of the Fatal Accidents Act 1976)—judges nowadays not being obliged to take into account the remarriage of the widow or her prospect of remarriage. But the duty to indulge in this exercise remains when the courts have to evaluate the chances of remarriage of a widower (claiming loss of economic support from his deceased wife) and, more importantly, when calculating the loss of support of orphaned children (since if their mother remarries and the new father takes them into his home he assumes a legal obligation to maintain them). The old law was, as already stated, greatly resented by judges and feminist organizations; but the new solution, partly because of the inconsistencies mentioned above, and partly because it can lead to over-compensation, is also treated as an anomaly. German law, on the other hand, with its attachment to the periodical payment system, seems to have avoided this problem altogether as it has avoided another problem that occupied English courts in the 1970s, namely that of inflation.

The final observation that one may make is, perhaps, the most intriguing of all. For despite the differences of approach that have been described, and the apparent superiority of the rent system over the lump-sum award, the Germans (and the French) whenever possible seem to opt for the lump-sum method of payment. Thus Professor Fleming has estimated that in Germany 99 per cent of all compensated claims take the form of a lump-sum award. Practice has in his words 'dwarfed [the codal orthodoxy] into statistical insignificance'. (Dr McGregor in his excellent chapter 9 of vol. XI of the *International Encyclopedia of Comparative Law*, 26 states that the same figure applies to French law, as well; see also Nehl's 'Kapitalisierung von Schadensersatzrenten' *VersR* 1981, 407, 412.) It thus becomes essential to enquire first why practice has bypassed the codal solution and secondly the way this evasion has been accomplished given the clear contrary wording of the Code.

The deviation from the wording of the Code is clearly due to the fact that whatever the theoretical merits of the rent system, both plaintiffs and defendants prefer the lump-sum award. Thus defendants (though in practice insurance companies perfectly able to cope with the mechanics of periodical payments) are, understandably, anxious to 'close their books'—something which only lump-sum awards allows them to do for two reasons. The first is because they are encouraged in this by their lawyers who know that their fees, which will come out of the award, will be met more promptly and with less resentment if they are taken out of a large lump-sum award rather than from periodical payments. The second is due to the attractions offered by larger awards. This is particularly true in Germany where as we have seen the bulk of medical and other pecuniary losses will be paid by a social secu-rity carrier in the form of periodical payments. With his basic needs thus being met, it becomes particularly attractive to a plaintiff to receive the top slice of the future economic loss award (along with the compensation for pain and suffering) in the form of a large lump sum which may enable him to indulge in purchases etc. which before the accident may have been entirely outside his financial means.

As for the method of circumventing the wording of the Code this can be found in the practice of extra-judicial settlements which are encouraged or even 'suggested' by the courts. In other words, once the liability issue has been determined, the lawyers and the court may encourage the parties to agree on a lump-sum award and even 'suggest' its level. As a result, in Professor Fleming's words (op. cit., 299) 'the lump-sum settlements have like termites reduced the rent system to but a hollow shell'.

This then is an area of the law of torts where the use of the comparative method can be profitably employed by both legal families (Common law and civil law) since both could benefit from the study of each other's weaknesses and strengths. For example, would it not be preferable if each system (English, German) adopted a more flexible mixed system which would allow the parties (or, in the last resort, the court) to decide which method of payment was more appropriate in their case, than opt for rigid schemes or preferences. From a didactic angle the study of this topic is also useful in so far as it reveals to the Common lawyer (and, perhaps, to the civil lawyer) how unrealistic the treatment of the law can be in civil law textbooks. For their emphasis on what the law is according to the code rather than how it works in practice can be misleading to say the least. The subject we have just briefly discussed offers an excellent illustration.

(c) Personal injury (pain and suffering)

Personal injury does not only lead to pecuniary losses of the kind described above; typically it also entails pain and various forms of mental suffering. The indemnification of the victim for such losses has caused difficulties of a similar kind both in England and in Germany. For though both systems, unlike those of the socialist and Islamic worlds, are prepared to take cognizance of such losses, both realize that they are dealing with unquantifiable items of loss where *restitutio in integrum* is not possible. Instead, the idea of 'fair compensation' or satisfaction is introduced into the legal vocabulary, suggesting not only an inability for precise calculation, but also a desire for a certain degree of uniformity of awards. (Once again, where, as in America, juries have the last word, such uniformity is often impossible to attain and, in turn, its absence must hinder the out-of-court settlement process.) The above, however, should not be taken to suggest that money paid for pain and suffering is an insignificant part of the total award; on the contrary, there is a clear tendency to increase the size of the awards under this heading, and academic opinion is, on the whole, firmly behind this trend (see Teplitzky, 'Umwelt und Recht', *NJW* 1966, 388; Kötz in *Festschrift von Caemmerer* (1978) 389 etc.).

Fair compensation for injury to body or health or for deprivation of liberty is expressly provided for by § 847 BGB. Section II of this article, displaying its rather antiquated origins, provides the same for a woman who has been the victim of an immoral crime or has been induced by cunning or threats or abuse of a relationship into an extra-marital cohabitation. These provisions were necessary because of the general principle enunciated by § 253 BGB which prohibits the award of monetary compensation for non-pecuniary losses except where the law expressly provides for an exception. It must be also remembered that a claim under § 847 BGB will be allowed only if the tort action is based on the breach of one of the tort provisions of the Civil Code. If, on the other hand, the tort is based on the violation of one of the provisions of a strict liability statute, then no claim for pain and suffering will be allowed. (The only exception can be found in § 53 III of the Air Traffic Act. For further details see Ch. 3, section A.5.)

Unlike § 844 II BGB which, as we have seen, expresses a clear preference for the annuity system, § 847 BGB is silent as to the form the award has to take. In the event, it provides one of the clearly exceptional cases where the lump sum is the solution both favoured by theory and adopted by practice. This, however, does not mean that annuities cannot be paid in addition to or in lieu of lump-sum awards if the circumstances of a particular case make this the more appropriate form of payment (see BGH NJW 1957, 383). But annuities for pain and suffering cannot be index-linked (BGH NJW 1973, 1653).

The leading case on this topic (BGHZ 18, 149) is reproduced in full (case 110) and it deserves careful reading. In the words of the Great Senate, '. . . damages for pain and suffering have a dual function. They are meant to provide the injured party with adequate compensation for that kind of damage. At the same time, however, they are meant to indicate that the tortfeasor owes the victim "satisfaction" for what he has done to him.' This latter element, however, brings the tort award into the realm of criminal law and since punitive damages in civil actions are, on the whole, frowned upon in the civil law systems, this heading has caused considerable discussion. (See, however, BGHZ 35, 363; von Bar, 'Schmerzensgeld und gesellschaftliche Stellung des Opfers bei Verletzungen des allgemeinen Persönlichkeitsrechts', NJW 1980, 1742; Egon Lorenz, *Immaterieller Schaden und 'billige Entschädigung in Geld'. Eine Untersuchung auf der Grundlage des § 847 BGB* (1981).) Apart from this doubtful situation therefore, the notion of punitive damages in a civil action, so well known to American law, is (in theory) ignored by the German system. (The role of insurance in the context of § 829 BGB was recently reconsidered by the Federal Court in the important decision published in BGHZ 76, 279; NJW 1980, 1623.)

Fair compensation and satisfaction are notions so inherently vague that they inevitably allow much room for judicial discretion. One of the most important elements that can be taken into account is the relative economic strength of the parties so that on occasion it may be equitable to increase the tortfeasor's liability in a way that will reflect his economically robust position. Whether the tortfeasor is insured or not is also a factor that can be taken into account and this irrespective of whether the insurance is obligatory or simply widespread (BGHZ 18, 149, 165). Apart from § 829 BGB, this is the only other paragraph in the Code that allows such economic factors to be *openly* considered by the courts when determining the level of awards.

In fixing these awards the German courts tend to attach much importance to the pain suffered by the victim. Great intensity and duration will thus help grant larger awards (BGH VersR 1960, 401; BGHZ 18, 149). Generally speaking, this is regarded as a subjective heading of damage so that if pain is not experienced, either because the victim was rendered unconscious by his injuries or because pain-killers have helped reduce his pain, the sum awarded can be diminished or even be obliterated (see BGH NJW 1982, 2123, case 111). Not all cases, however, can be easily reconciled with this rule. In some rather isolated instances (BGH NJW 1976, 1147; contrast BGH NJW 1982, 2123) the BGH has felt that some money should be awarded as a 'symbolic atonement' 'for the interference with rights and interests unconditionally protected by the legal order' even if the victim is unconscious. Such phrases, however, help to confuse rather than clarify the issue. In particular the use of words such as 'atonement' can again appear to be trespassing into the area of criminal law. Moreover, it could be argued that German law, which on the whole does not always adhere rigidly to the kind of headings adopted by English law, could in cases such as the above really have been trying to compensate the victim for his loss of amenity and not for pain and suffering which he clearly is not experiencing. Where such an interpretation is possible, the result will, once again, approximate that achieved in England (*West* v. *Shephard* [1964] AC 326). For here, too, loss of amenity is compensated objectively, i.e. irrespective of whether the victim is aware of the loss, though *de lega ferenda* it could be argued that it does not make much sense to award enormous amounts in such cases. (On the above see E. Lorenz, op. cit.)

Apart from pain, mental suffering is also compensated. English law usually tends to use a global term such as 'loss of amenity' or 'enjoyment of life' for all sums given to the victim to alleviate his anguish for loss of a particular enjoyment or pastime or pleasure. Clearly, a footballer who has lost his legs or a pianist who has lost his fingers will have to receive additional compensation for these very personal losses. This is certainly true in German law as it is in English law, though in the former mental suffering appears classified under different subheadings. Thus mental suffering occasioned by disfigurement (especially in the case of a woman) will be compensated; and this sum will be additional to any economic loss claimable as a result of the disfigurement (BGH NJW 1959, 1031; OLG Celle NJW 1968, 1677, but see Larenz's doubts, op. cit. II, 675). Mental suffering caused by loss of marriage occasioned by disfigurement will also be compensatable (BGH NJW 1959, 1031). On the other hand, German law has not known (as English law did until the Administration of Justice Act 1982 abolished it) an independent heading for 'loss of expectation of life'. But anguish caused by the realization of a shorter life expectancy can be and has been taken into account when calculating the sum for satisfaction (BGH VersR 1961, 374).

Perhaps one should conclude by saying that the above are mere illustrations of some of the headings of recoverable harm. For a fuller list one must consult the case-law and the 'Tables of Damages for Pain and Suffering' which are customarily used by judges as the starting-point for their calculations.

So far we have been considering the case of an accident victim who survives his injuries. If the victim dies, problems of a different nature arise. Some of them are related to the new cause of action which is given to his dependants and will be discussed in the next section (in English law known as the Fatal Accident action). The problem that will be dealt with here, however, is different and concerns the issue of active transmissibility of the victim's action to his heirs. (Since the Law Reform (Miscellaneous Provisions) Act of 1934 English law has recognized this possibility without any restrictions, save that in the case of defamation the cause of action dies with the injured person; also penal damages cannot be claimed by the estate.)

Until recently the position of German law was opaque and unsatisfactory. This was because according to § 847 I, 2 BGB the right devolved upon the victim's heirs only if the injurer recognized this by contract before the victim's death or if a legal action had been commenced before that time. Whatever the original justification for this limitation, in practice it caused much dispute and an unsavoury scramble to institute actions as soon as possible after the accident lest the victim die too soon (see BGHZ 69, 323; BGH NJW 1984, 2348). The position was thus deemed unsatisfactory (see Deutsch, *Haftungsrecht* I (1976), 477; Kötz, *Festschrift von Caemmerer* (1978) 389, 404) and, in the end, transmissibility facilitated by the legislative abolition of § 847 I 2 on 14 March 1990. (BGBl. I, 478.) For more details on the old position see page 684 of the 2nd edition of this work.

(d) Ricochet damage in the context of fatal accidents

When the victim dies from his injuries, third parties can suffer further loss. A young girl may lose her father's much needed financial support; an ageing relative the services of a younger member of the family; an employee may see his job disappear as a result of the death of his employer; a football club may be deprived of a sizeable transfer fee when one of its star players is killed (the facts of a classic French case: Colmar, 20 avril 1955, D. 1956, 723). The list of ricochet victims can be endless; the harm they suffer can range from emotional distress to severe pecuniary loss. Three main questions arise under this heading: the first is whether a *new* cause of action should be created for this type of situation, the second is to whom should it be given, and the third is what should it be for. An important supplementary issue is connected with the victim's own fault and the effect it should have on the dependant's claims. We shall look at all these points in turn.

The first question is whether a new cause of action should arise whenever there is a fatal accident. The answer given by all systems is a positive one, but the ways this result is achieved differ. In one group of systems (French, Belgian) the amorphous delict provisions of the Code (e.g. Art. 1382 French CC) are used to justify this extension. Another way, favoured by the English Fatal Accident Acts and their American derivatives, is to opt for specific statutory enactments expressly creating such rights. Yet a third group of systems include special provisions in the delict sections of their Codes. Germany belongs to this group and, incidentally, so do Austria (Art. 1327 Austrian CC), Switzerland (CO Arts. 45, 47), and Greece (Art. 922 Greek CC).

German law, always striving for logic and terminological precision, makes a distinction between loss of support, which is regulated in § 844 BGB, and loss of services, which is the subject of separate treatment (§ 845 BGB). The former, as we shall note below, typically consists of an action brought by a wife and/or child for the loss of the breadwinner/father; the latter, more rare in practice, is brought by an elderly person for the loss of the services of a younger member of the family. Natural and adopted children are, in certain circumstances, under a duty to provide such services: see §§ 1619 and 1754 BGB. When the wife is injured she can claim under § 842 BGB for amongst other things her inability to continue to provide services to her family; but where she is killed a claim for loss of support under § 844 II BGB can be brought by her husband (BGHZ 51, 109). Since similar rules apply to both §§ 844 and 845 BGB and cases tend to overlap it is not entirely clear that anything is really gained by this distinction between loss of support and loss of services.

To the second question mentioned above—who will be given the new right of action—three answers are, once again, possible. The most generous, adopted both by a number of German-inspired systems (e.g. Swiss CO Art. 45 III; former East German Code, § 332 II) as well as by the Romanistic legal family (France etc.), grants this action to anyone who can actually prove to have suffered a loss. This approach may, in theory, cause some uncertainty to the extent that the courts have to deal with each case on its merits, but it can also produce more equitable results. Besides, its apparent disadvantages can be exaggerated by ignoring the fact that in practice the courts have, through a cluster of causative notions, managed to keep liability very much under control. (On this see B. S. Markesinis, 'A Comparative Look at Certain Problems of Pure Economic Loss', published in *The Cambridge Lectures* 1981 (ed. N. Eastham and B. Krivy) 45–61.)

The exact opposite way is to leave it to the legislator to determine which persons will be classified as dependants in law and be given the right to sue. This is the Common law method as seen in the Fatal Accident legislation. Interestingly enough, however, the list of dependants in these Acts has been greatly widened over the years and in practice the results reached by English and French law are more similar than the different starting-points would suggest.

German law has opted for a third method. According to § 844 II BGB only those persons to whom the deceased owed a statutory duty to provide support will be allowed to sue. (Typically this includes spouses (§ 1360 BGB) and children (including adopted children and adopted parents: § 1766 BGB).) This right of maintenance must exist at the time of the *injury*, so if a couple gets married after one of them has been injured and then dies, the surviving spouse will not have a right of action since there existed no right to support at the time of the injury. But if the legal relationship, from which the duty to support flows, exists at the time of the injury, then the right to sue will not be affected by the fact that at that time no support was yet being provided. English law would in this respect appear to be stricter than German law in so far as it requires that the claimant is a dependant in law *and* in fact at the time of the death of the victim (though cases like *Taff Vale Rly.* v. *Jenkins* [1913] AC 1 suggest that a reasonable expectation of a future pecuniary benefit may (in some circumstances at least) suffice. But see BGHZ 4, 133 and Staudinger-Schäfer, 12th edn. § 844 no. 60). An important group of potential claimants who are thus left without an action in German (and, very likely, English) law are fiancés (of both sexes) since before their marriage there is no obligation to provide support (KG NJW 1967, 1089). Mistresses are also treated with similar harshness and, for the same reasons, denied any right of action. Finally, to give one last example, stepsons are also denied compensation even where it can be shown that the deceased had maintained and would have continued to maintain his stepson to whom he was very attached. In the last two instances (mistresses, stepsons), English, French, and Swiss law would provide an action. In practice the right to sue under § 844 BGB will thus be given to surviving spouses, direct relatives, and adopted children since in all these cases there is a statutory duty to support (see §§ 1360, 1601, 1766 BGB). To foreign eyes, German law thus appears excessively preoccupied with legal certainty even if this can lead to injustice in a number of deserving cases.

What will the 'dependants' be allowed to claim? Once again there is no unanimity in the systems. For some (e.g. Common law) the action should be limited to 'pounds, shillings and pence' though most recently the English Administration of Justice Act 1982 (new s. 1(A) of the Fatal Accidents Act 1976) recognized a right to claim a fixed sum (at the moment £3500) for bereavement. Rather anomalously, however, this new right is limited to a spouse claiming for the loss of the other spouse or parents claiming for the loss of a child, but not vice versa. (For details see Markesinis and Deakin, *Tort Law* 3rd edn. (1994).) French law, on the other hand, is again the most generous, allowing a claim for both pecuniary losses and moral damage. The German solution is very much like Common law, though where the victim has suffered nervous shock as a result of the death of a relative, he may be able to claim for it under § 823 I BGB. Perhaps, at this stage, we should make it clear that we are always talking about the dependants claiming for their moral damage in a fatal accident action. The victim's own damages (for the period during which he was alive) will, of course, now be claimable by his estate.

The last point to which we must turn our attention is that of contributory negligence on the part of the deceased/victim of the tort. Once again, there is an express provision in the Code that deals with this matter in conjunction with § 254 BGB. This is § 844 II BGB which, quite simply, declares that the dependants' claim will be reduced to take into account the victim's own fault in the realization of the harm. The solution is similar to that adopted by the English Fatal Accident Act 1976 and is irreproachable. More dubious, however, is the recent extension of this principle to another factual situation (see BGH NJW 1971, 1883). Thus, it will be remembered that the widow of a victim cannot claim for her mental anguish under the German fatal accident action but can claim under § 823 I BGB for the nervous shock that she may have suffered as a result of seeing or being told of her husband's death. § 846 BGB, discussed above, will not be applicable here since the widow is not suing under § 844 BGB but issuing under § 823 I BGB. Nevertheless, the Supreme Court held that reasons of equity dictated that once again the deceased person's own contributory fault should be taken into account and reduce accordingly the widow's own claim under § 823 I BGB. This result, which is not compatible with earlier decisions (e.g. RGZ 157, 11), has been severely criticized by Professor John Fleming in 20 *American Journal of Comparative Law* 485 (1972).

(e) Interference with honour and reputation

This subsection deals briefly with indemnification for interference with the general right to one's personality. This has already been discussed in Ch. 2, section A.2, 3(iv) so the comments made here must be read in conjunction with the earlier observations and the notes accompanying the translated cases reproduced in Ch. 2, section B.10.

The starting-point must again be § 249 BGB which, as already stated, ordains restitution in kind. In most of these cases this will mean the publication of a correction of the statement or representation that gave rise to the dispute. The correcting statement must, normally, receive the same prominence as the offending statement and it is usually the defendant who is asked to publish the correction in his paper or journal. If he refuses to do so, the complainant may claim from him the cost of a correction inserted by him. But this cost must be reasonable, so in one case where the plaintiff tried to correct his tarnished image by inserting full-page statements in some fifteen national papers, he was not allowed to claim his enormous cost of about DM 300,000 (BGHZ 66, 182).

Monetary compensation is, therefore, treated as the ultimate remedy and is most commonly claimable where pecuniary loss results from the offending statement. This will clearly arise where, for example, the victim/plaintiff has lost a lucrative contract as a result of the statement made about him. But substantial amounts have, as we have seen, been awarded in cases where no proof of such loss was forthcoming. (See, for example, the case of the Canon Law Professor, no. 31.) Here damages are awarded to provide 'satisfaction' to the plaintiff rather than compensation so they are, as the Common lawyers would put it, at large (note the Supreme Court's views in the 'Gentleman rider' case (no. 30, above), to provide guide-lines for the calculation of the awards). This development, of course, meant bypassing the obstacles posed by § 253 BGB; but common sense dictated this result and we have seen that the Constitutional Court gave it its blessing.

A more important limitation in the granting of monetary compensation is the court's insistence that the tortfeasor's fault be *serious* and the intrusion into the victim's private sphere *objectively* serious. The laudable purpose of these limitations is to prevent individuals making capital out of the slightest intrusion into their private lives. The ultimate decision is thus made to turn on the facts of each case. BGH NJW 1971, 698 (case 111) offers an excellent illustration. In that case, a professional actress took part in a sex education film which involved some rather explicit sexual scenes. Provocative pictures from this film were subsequently used by the defendants without her permission in order to advertise a certain product. For this she brought an action complaining of unauthorized invasion of her privacy and she succeeded. In reaching the conclusion that the interference was both grave and unwarrantable the Supreme Court took into consideration the following factors: (i) the wide circulation of the magazine that carried the advertisements; (ii) the impression given that the actress had given her permission for the use of the photos in consideration for a fee; (iii) the desire to make a large profit from the advertisement (which contrasted sharply with the educational aims of the film-makers); and, finally, (iv) the effect that this affair could have on the plaintiff's future career as a serious actress. The case is thus typical of the careful balancing of interests that is attempted by the courts in this part of the law when deciding (*a*) the issue of liability and (*b*) the quantum of damages appropriate under this heading. Overall, one could conclude this section by saying that there are, apparently, no empirical studies available providing details of such awards, the average amount is rather low (estimated DM 6–7,000). Few awards seem to exceed DM 10,000 and there seems to be less than a handful of cases that have surpassed DM 50,000. On the other hand, the reader must be reminded that there are the sums awarded for 'pain and suffering' resulting from the actionable invasion of one's privacy and that further financial losses are recoverable if properly proved. (See, for example, OLG München NJW 1988, 915.)

(*f*) *Damage to property*

Once again the rather inadequate delict provisions of the Code (§§ 848, 849 BGB) must be supplemented by the general provisions found in §§ 249–52 BGB. The starting-point is, in fact, the restoration of the status quo (§ 249 I BGB). Taken literally, it suggests that the defendant must through his own efforts restore or repair the damaged property; in practice, however, it is the plaintiff who has his property repaired or replaced and then seeks to recoup his expenditure from the defendant. Once again, therefore, what is presented by § 249 II BGB as the possible exception to § 249 I BGB is, in practice, the rule. Monetary compensation is, however, openly recognized to be the rule where restoration in kind is impossible (§ 251 I BGB); or requires a disproportionate economic expenditure (§ 251 II BGB).

The defendant's obligation is to make good all primary and consequential losses occasioned by the damage to the plaintiff's property, subject of course to the rules of legal cause. Normative theories of causation (such as the scope of the rule theory) can, once again, be used to impose effective legal limits on the extent of the obligation to compensate. The evaluation takes the form of a mathematical calculation which estimates the difference between the state of the damaged property if the damaging act had not occurred and the actual state of the property after the damaging act or event, though a more recent trend favours a more liberal assessment of the damage. Older codes—e.g. the Prussian Code of 1794—made the compensation of lost profits depend on other factors (e.g. a higher degree of fault: §§ 287 1, 5, 288, and §§ 7 1, 6, 10–15; see also §§ 1325, 1331 of the Austrian Civil Code of 1811); but § 252 BGB specifically authorizes the compensation of actual damage and of lost profits. According to the second sentence of § 252, 'Profit is deemed to have been lost which could probably have been expected in the ordinary course of events, or according to the special circumstances, especially in the light of the preparations and arrangements made.' However, even though this rule favours the injured plaintiff, it does not allow him to claim for a possible chance. Thus the BGH has ruled that a tenderer to a public contract which was unjustifiably cancelled could not claim his costs for preparing his offer so long as he could not establish that he would have been awarded the contract (BGH NJW 1981, 1673). The loss of a 10 per cent chance of receiving an X DM amount will not entitle the victim to 10 per cent of that amount. For losses that are certain to arise in the future but have not yet arisen at the trial, plaintiffs are often advised to seek declaratory judgments stating their relevant rights.

The bulk of claims for damage to property arise in the context of car accidents. (There were, for example, 1.98 million traffic accidents in the FRG in 1987, 83 per cent involving only material damage. The annual payout by the insurance companies for this period was 10 billion DM.) This then is an important topic on which we can concentrate for our illustrations. But it is also interesting from a didactic point of view to focus our attention on this topic since it reveals very clearly how the needs of practical life (quick settlements of disputes) have helped fashion a series of detailed rules that concretize the rather abstract provisions of the Code.

Clearly, one of the primary losses likely to be suffered by the owner of a damaged vehicle is the cost of repair. This will be borne by the defendant even if the plaintiff carried out the necessary repairs (KG NJW 1970, 431). The amount claimable in such cases will be equal to the sum that the garage would have charged had it carried out the repairs (the figure, rather oddly, will also include the VAT sum that the garage would have added to its bill: BGH NJW 1973, 1647; BGH NJW 1982, 1864). Where the cost of repair and replacement are approximately the same, the owner of the damaged vehicle will be free to decide what he will do. It must be remembered, however, that § 254 II BGB always obliges the plaintiff to mitigate his loss so that if, for example, the cost of replacement is considerably lower than the cost of repair, the owner of the vehicle will have to take the former option, however much he may wish to repair and retain his original car. (A similar solution was reached in the Court of Appeal in *Darbishire* v. *Warran* [1963] 1 WLR 1067.) Unique items (e.g. vintage car), however, are not covered by this rule (cf. *O'Grady* v. *Westminster Scaffolding* [1962] 2 Lloyd's Rep. 238).

The cost of repair is also claimable even where the owner of the damaged vehicle decides not to have it repaired; or when he legally deprives himself of the chance of carrying out the repairs, for example, by selling the damaged vehicle (BGHZ 66, 239). The cost of repair can also include what is sometimes referred to as the 'commercial inferiority' of the repaired vehicle. This occurs whenever the damaged vehicle, though fully repaired, becomes 'marked' as a repaired vehicle and thereby loses some of its resale value (BGHZ 35, 396).

More problematical, though equally well compensated in practice, are the so-called 'consequential' losses. § 252 I BGB makes it clear that lost profits—for example resulting from the immobilization of a van during its repairs—can be claimed from the tortfeasor. According to this paragraph, 'profit is presumed to have been lost which could probably have been expected in the ordinary course of events, or according to special circumstances, especially in the light of the preparations and arrangements made'. This presumption, however, can be rebutted by showing, for example, that the owner of the damaged van had other spare vans that could be used for the same purpose.

The same is true where the owner of the damaged vehicle is a private individual rather than a commercial firm. In this case what can be claimed is the cost of hiring an appropriate substitute which, quite simply, means that the owner of a damaged Volkswagen cannot go out and hire a Rolls-Royce at the defendant's expense. All this, however, must be constantly viewed against the duty to mitigate so that, for example, a plaintiff who happens to have an extra car available, will have to use it and will not normally be allowed to claim the cost of substitute hire. But what if the plaintiff deliberately keeps and maintains an extra vehicle precisely for this eventuality? Can he in such a case claim from the tortfeasor the monthly cost of maintenance of this spare vehicle? The point is disputed (and from a theoretical point of view it is difficult to see how an expense incurred *before* the accident can be treated as its consequence). But the Supreme Court has on occasion sanctioned such claims (BGHZ 32, 280; cf. also BGHZ 79, 199).

From the above it should be clear that additional expenditure incurred as a consequence of damage to vehicles can, in principle, be claimed. But what if the owner of the car has incurred no such expenditure because, for example, he has not hired a substitute vehicle or could not have used it anyway since he himself was injured in the same accident? The case-law is rich on the subject, and generalizations can be misleading. In principle, however, one can say that the Supreme Court has characterized the 'loss of the possibility of using a car' as property loss and thus treated it as an indemnifiable item of damage (BGHZ 40, 345; BGHZ 45, 212). But if the owner of the vehicle would not or could not have used it anyway, a claim will not usually be allowed (BGH NJW 1968, 1778). It will have been noticed that by calling this type of loss 'property loss' the courts have bypassed once again the obstacles of § 253 BGB. But this 'evasive' action is not always possible. (This highly controversial problem is thoroughly reviewed in BGH NJW 1986, 2037 = VersR 1986, 189 and, in a less clear manner, in BGH NJW 1987, 50 = JZ 1987, 306, reproduced below as cases 114 and 115.) Thus, a damaged car may frustrate a family's carefully planned holiday arrangements. Can the 'lost holiday' be claimed as consequential loss? The answer really depends upon whether we are faced here with a claim for disappointment and frustration or something which is capable of being equated with a pecuniary loss. Where there is no wasted expenditure incurred prior to the accident, the better view is to deny such claims (BGHZ 60, 214). But in another famous case (BGH NJW 1956, 1234) the German customs authorities were held liable under § 839 BGB to a young married couple whose luggage was delayed as a result of their negligence thereby ruining their honeymoon in the Canaries. (In BGHZ 86, 212 the Supreme Court tried to reconcile BGHZ 60, 214 with BGH NJW 1956, 1234.) Perhaps one should add that in recent times a number of decisions *pleaded on breach of contract* have allowed sums for 'disappointed holidays'; and an enactment—the *Reisevertragsgesetz* of 4 May 1979, § 651 f II BGB—has adopted the same view in the narrow context of travel contracts. But what is particularly interesting in these judgments is a growing tendency to look at holidays as representing a pecuniary interests which can give rise to material loss if they are wholly or partially ruined (BGHZ 63, 98; in similar vein BGHZ 77, 116; 80, 366; 82, 219; 85, 50). This must suggest that the recognition of such claims in tort actions may be imminent though a recent decision (BGHZ 86, 212, case 112), *pleaded in tort*, refused to sanction such a development. Until this happens, German law will thus differ from English law. (See *Jackson* v. *Horizon Holidays Ltd.* [1975], 1 WLR 1468 (in contract); *Ichard* v. *Frangoulis* [1977], 1 WLR 556 (in tort).) From the extensive literature on these problems see: Brinker, *Die Dogmatik zum Vermögensschadensersatz* (1982); Dunz, 'Schadensersatz für entgangene Sachnutzung' *JZ* 1984, 1010; Flessner, 'Geldersatz für Gebrauchsentgang' *JZ* 1987, 271; Jahr, 'Schadensersatz wegen deliktischer Nutzungsentziehung—zu den Grundlagen des Rechtsgüterschutzes und des Schadensersatzrechts' *AcP* 183 (1983), 725; Hagen, 'Entgangene Gebrauchsvorteile als Vermögensschaden?' *JZ* 1983, 833; Kötz, *Deliktsrecht*, nos. 481 *et seq.*; Lange, *Schadensersatz*, § 6 VII 4b; Larenz, *Schuldrecht* I, 14th edn. (1987) § 29 II (p. 499); Medicus, 'Nutzungsentgang als Vermögensschaden' *Jura* 1987, 240; Ott/Schäfer, 'Begründung und Bemessung des Schadensersatzes wegen entgangener Sachnutzung' *ZIP* 1986, 613; Schwerdtner, 'Grundzüge des Schadensersatzrechts' *Jura* 1987,

143, 304, 475; Weber, 'Entschädigung für den entgangenen Gebrauch eines Kraftfahrzeuges' *VersR* 1985, 111.

SECTION B. CASES

1. § 823 II BGB

Case 107

BUNDESGERICHTSHOF (SIXTH CIVIL DIVISION) 12 NOVEMBER 1957*
BGHZ 26, 42

The defendant was the owner of a business running omnibuses. On 6 February 1950 he was granted a licence by the competent authority permitting him to operate two omnibuses to be employed for hire or on excursions. The licence stated expressly that the employment of the buses on regular service between specified places was prohibited.

The plaintiffs, the German Federal Railways, alleged that the defendant had regularly conveyed persons between G and L with his buses. They argued that, since most of these persons would otherwise have used the Federal Railways, they had suffered damage as a result of this unlicensed regular traffic. The plaintiffs asked for an account of the number of journeys and passengers and claimed a sum representing part of their damage. The defendant denied that he carried on regular services and contended that the Act on the Carriage of Persons is not a law serving to protect the German Federal Railways. Moreover it violated the Constitution by restricting the commercial activities of transport undertakings.

The District Court rejected the claim, the Court of Appeal of Hamm allowed it. A second appeal was unsuccessful for the following

Reasons

1. The Court of Appeal was correct in regarding as a protective law in the meaning of § 823 II BGB in favour of the plaintiffs the provisions of the Act concerning the Transport of Persons on Land which require a licence by the administrative authorities for the operation of regular traffic with land-based vehicles and provide penalties for such operations without a licence. The crucial question is whether the legislature, in providing regulations for public traffic, also wished to protect the special interest of the Federal Railways [reference]. This question must be answered in the affirmative without hesitation. The special position of the German Federal Railways within the legal framework of public passenger transport is shown

* English version by Kurt Lipstein.

by the fact that § 14 of the Act on Passenger Transport exempts them from licensing and that § 27 II only requires them to give notice of the intended establishment of a regular route. According to § 5 of the Decree for the Execution of the Act on Passenger Transport, the Federal Railways must be consulted if a dispute arises as to whether a traffic undertaking is subject to the provisions of the Act on Passenger Transport or to which type of traffic the traffic undertaking belongs. § 9 I 2 of the Decree requires the competent regional directorate of the Federal Railways to be heard if an application is submitted for a licence to operate a regular cross-country route. According to § 11 II of the Decree a licence for a regular service is not to be granted if a new enterprise constitutes inequitable competition for an existing traffic undertaking. Together these provisions show clearly that in the proceedings of consultation the Federal Railways are granted a right to intervene as the guardian of the public interests concerning traffic but that they may *also* plead any adverse effects upon their own interests. This is the reason why the Federal Railways are accorded the right to start proceedings in the administrative courts if their objections have been overruled [references]. The fact that according to §§ 17 and 24 of the Act on Passenger Transport the administrative authorities also control the price and the conditions of travel is a safeguard against a ruinous competition by undercutting at the expense of the Federal Railways. The importance of the Act on Passenger Transport consists precisely in the fact that it restricts competition between the various transport undertakings because the legislature allots to each branch of transport those tasks which it can fulfil best within the framework of traffic as a whole and of the economy. In so doing, the legislature has attached special significance to the interest of the Federal Railways on the assumption that the maintenance of their efficiency must be assured in the public interest.

2. The appellant is wrong in asscrting that the provisions of the Act on Passenger Transport which pursue this goal contravene Art. 12 of the Constitution (GG). Article 12 I of the Constitution guarantees the right to choose an occupation freely but reserves the exercise of an occupation or trade for regulation or statute. It is generally recognized that the legislature is not prohibited in principle from regulating, in particular, the conditions for carrying on a profession or exercising a trade and from requiring a licence by the administrative authorities for commercial activities. It is equally recognized that in establishing the conditions for exercising a profession the legislature is not completely unfettered and that the essence of the fundamental right to carry on a trade must not be touched [reference]. Opinions are divided as to how the limits set for the legislature are to be drawn in detail and as to when, in particular, the essence of the right to

carry on an occupation is being fettered. In this controversy the view of the Federal Administrative Court which grants the legislature a considerable measure of discretion is to be contrasted with the very restrictive view of the First Civil Division of the Federal Supreme Court expressed in its references to the Federal Constitutional Court, but these do not bind this Division [references].

The first opinion stresses that all fundamental rights contain their own intrinsic limits and is less concerned with the compelling reasons for these restrictions than with the problem of what remains of the fundamental right, once these restrictions have been recognized.

The restrictive opinion allows fundamental rights to be limited for reasons of urgent necessity only and requires the encroachment to be as small as possible in the light of the circumstances, guided by the desire to leave the fundamental right an extensive scope. Nevertheless, the First Division [references] acknowledges that the legislature may also enact laws in the interest of individual groups if this should be necessary in the public interest and does not arbitrarily detract from the interest deserving protection of other parties. In its decision the First Division also recognizes that the legislature enjoys a measure of discretion in the sphere of Art. 12 I of the Constitution and points out that the judicial control of the legislature is limited correspondingly.

It is unnecessary here to discuss in detail the many attempts to determine and to circumscribe the extent of the prohibition expressed by Art. 19 II of the Constitution. Even if a statutory restriction of occupational activities is only regarded as constitutional within narrow limits, it cannot be said that the Law on Passenger Transport has infringed illegally the essence of the fundamental right enshrined in Art. 12 I of the Constitution by having made the commercial operation of a regular traffic route of land-based vehicles subject to a licence for the reason, *inter alia*, in order to save the Federal Railways from inequitable competition by motorized traffic undertakings. In this connection it is important that despite an increase in motorized traffic the Federal Railways deal with the major portion of public transport. The pre-eminent interest of the community in the efficiency of the Federal Railways is expressed in the organization of the Federal Railways by the Act of 13 December 1951 concerning the Federal Railways. The act treats the discharge of the functions of the Federal Railways as a public service and requires that in the administration of the Federal Railways the interests of the German economy are safeguarded [references]. For this reason, the operation of the Federal Railways is subject to a number of restrictions which could not be justified from a purely commercial point of view. They cannot in their discretion discontinue routes which are unprofitable and, in particular, they are not free to determine the fares. (Fares must be established, must be equal, serve social needs, and must offer free passes.) Moreover the Federal Railways are burdened with extensive maintenance obligations towards their present and past employees which private traffic operators do not have to carry. The Federal Railways would no longer be able to fulfil their function in the service of the community if private commercial motor transport operators were allowed to exploit the economically profitable routes, which alone are of interest to them, with the result that the Federal Railways would be relegated increasingly to carrying out less profitable transport services. For this reason alone, the legislature must be interested in the maintenance of the efficient operation of traffic by rail, since the service of mass traffic by the railways is indispensable in present conditions and since any interruption in the ability of the railways to function would lead to a crisis. In this connection it is relevant that any shift of public passenger traffic from the railways to motor vehicle traffic is restricted if for no other reason than because the capacity of the German road system is strictly limited. The special character of public transport makes it appear unlikely that the regulating effect alone of offer and demand can achieve a satisfactory solution to the far-reaching problems of public transport which satisfies the needs of the community. This explains why § 99 of the Act against Restrictions of Competition of 27 July 1957 [reference] does not apply to the Federal Railways and other public traffic institutions.

The Federal Administrative Court has pointed out rightly that the safeguarding of orderly operations of public traffic is one of the protected legal interests essential for the existence of the community [reference]. It is a primary task of the legislature which is concerned with maintaining and extending an efficient transport system to regulate and to plan public transport by a process of adjustment and balancing [references]. This Division cannot discern in the discharge of this task by the legislature, which must necessarily include the regulation of the competition between rail and road traffic, an act of unconstitutional interference in the freedom of commerce, all the more since public transport had already been regulated by statute at the time when the Constitution was being enacted. Moreover, it does not appear that in enacting the Constitution the intention was to question the validity of this regulation on the ground that freedom of occupation was being restricted or to restrict the legislature and the administration to measures for controlling safety and the proper conduct of trade [references]. If the public interest in an efficient system of passenger transport must be the principal object of the legislation measure for regulating traffic, the legislature was justified for this reason in regarding the protection of the Federal Railways as especially important where route transport is concerned and in fashioning its traffic regulations accordingly [reference].

The enactment of the Act on Passenger Transport does not constitute a closure of the occupation for private transport enterprises but the control of their commercial activity dictated by the overriding interests of the community. This control does not interfere with the essence of the fundamental right enshrined in Art. 12 I; on the contrary, in the opinion of this Division the statutory provisions fall within the framework of the task set for the legislature by Art. 12 II inasmuch as, by requiring the consent of the administration, the legislature wishes to ensure that the Federal Railways are protected against inappropriate competition and that every traffic institution is allotted that task which it can best perform in the interest of the common good.

. . . even if the refusal of a transport licence on the sole ground of insufficient need is regarded as illegal, the need for a licence remains justified in the opinion of this Division inasmuch as, apart from other reasons, the just interest of the Federal Railways in averting inequitable competition must be taken into consideration. Consequently there are no objections from the point of view of Art. 12 of the Constitution against regarding the penal provision of § 40 I of the Act on Passenger Transport as a valid protective law in the meaning of § 823 II BGB in favour of the Federal Railways by penalizing unlicensed route transport (as the dominant practice holds [references]). The view taken by this Division is in keeping with its decision of 27 March 1956 [reference] where the comparable provision of the Act concerning Milk and Fats regulating that market were found to protect by an action in tort dairies, the economic activities of which had been interfered with in the absence of a licence [reference]. Finally, the First Civil Division in its judgment [reference] allowed a claim under § 823 II BGB by chemists against drug stores which had contravened the Act on Medicaments.

3. . . .

Case 108

BUNDESGERICHTSHOF (FIRST CIVIL DIVISION) 30 NOVEMBER 1954*
BGHZ 15, 315

The plaintiff is a registered association founded in 1946. According to § 1 of its statutes its purpose is to protect and to further the professional and economic interests of the Hamburg Bar.

The third defendant is an association founded in 1890 as a legal entity. According to § 2 of its statutes its purpose is to better the 'tenancy and housing conditions' of the population and, especially, to protect the legitimate

* English version by Kurt Lipstein.

interests of its members. According to § 2(*d*) and (*e*) of its statutes this goal is to be achieved by providing free oral advice as well as written advice for a fee for all members of the association; in addition it offers to represent them for a fee in dealings with public authorities, civil and administrative courts. The fees payable to the association are the same as those charged by legal counsellors.

The first and the second defendants are the legal advisors of the third defendant who are entitled, according to § 8(6) of the statutes, to represent the members before public authorities and courts. Until 1 October 1952 they were paid their own expenses and 80 per cent of the fees after deducting the expenses incurred by the association. The parties disagree as to what fees are paid to them after 1 October 1952.

The plaintiff contends that the first and the second defendants have contravened the Act against Abuses in the Field of Legal Advice and the Unfair Competition Act (UWG) and that the third defendant had enabled them to carry on their illegal activity, and had assisted them.

The plaintiff has asked that the first and second defendants be ordered to desist from advising the members of the third defendants gratuitously or against a fee and from representing them in court and to order the third defendant to desist from according to the first and second defendants the right to give free advice or advice for a fee and to represent it in court.

The defendants have denied that the plaintiff has a legal interest calling for protection. They argue that the first and second defendants do not give legal advice on a commercial or professional basis. Nor did their conduct constitute unfair competition.

The District Court rejected the claim. On appeal, the plaintiff has asked as an alternative to prohibit the third defendant from handling legal matters professionally, especially by charging fees similar to those of procedural representatives or the like, and to prohibit the first and second defendants from collaborating with the third defendant in handling legal matters. The Court of Appeal of Hamburg rejected the entire claim. The plaintiff's appeal was successful in most respects for the following

Reasons

The plaintiff has based his claim for orders to desist primarily on § 823 II BGB in conjunction with § 1 I of the Act concerning Legal Counsellors. Since this act aims at protecting the citizen against the dangers arising from the employment of unqualified and unreliable persons, but also seeks to protect the Bar against competition by such persons who engage in legal advice who are not subject to the constraints relating to professional etiquette, fees, and the like created in the interest of the administration of justice, it cannot be doubted that it bears the character of a protective act . . .

The appellant is wrong in contending that the third defendant must not demand any 'consideration', for his legal services, not even to reimburse him for his expenses.

The claims of the members of the association to receive assistance in legal matters follows from their membership. The expenses incurred by the association in satisfying this claim must naturally be covered somehow, be it by contributions by *all* members, or by special payments to those members who ask the association for assistance in legal matters. It is an internal matter to be decided as such by the association as it sees fit. The question as to whether in so doing it exceeds the limits set by § 7 I of the Act concerning Legal Counsellors is not necessarily identical with that as to whether the association may only provide 'gratuitous' assistance in legal matters or whether it can do so also for 'remuneration'. For, as will be shown later on, even to claim actual expenses only, i.e. to provide assistance in legal proceedings gratuitously in the strict meaning of the word, may be illegal in certain circumstances; e.g. if the association grants the persons who act for it in assisting in legal proceedings a remuneration in accordance with the scale of fees for lawyers or for legal counsellors and then seeks to recover it from the members as actual expenses. The plaintiff contends, in agreement with the literature and practice, that 'remuneration' in the meaning of § 7 I of the above-mentioned law consists of any money payment by a member of the association, even if it only represents a reimbursement of expenses and not a genuine remuneration. However, this Division cannot accept his view that the assistance in legal proceedings by the association must be 'gratuitous' in this sense.

Contrary to the view of the appellant the wording of § 7 I of the Act concerning Legal Counsellors . . . does not indicate that this exceptional provision is to apply only if the assistance in legal matters is 'gratuitous'. In so far as § 1 VII of the Act concerning Legal Counsellors permits the association concerned acting within the limits of their established task to 'provide' advice and assistance in legal matters for their members, the word 'provide' does compel the conclusion that the legislature only wished to allow a gratuitous activity . . . The Court of Appeal was therefore correct in holding that a comparison of § 7 I and § 1 I does not lead to the conclusion that the advice and assistance must only be gratuitous. . . .

Nevertheless, the objections of the appellant must succeed in so far as they are directed against the assessment of the remuneration in accordance with the official scale of fees. The appellant is right in stating that to allow remuneration to be charged on the scale of charges fixed for legal counsellors (§ 2(*e*) of the statutes) is incompatible with the provision of § 7 I of the Act concerning Legal Counsellors and therefore illegal.

§ 7 I of the above-mentioned Act is based on the consideration that voluntary legal assistance is to be judged by different standards than those activities which, in looking after the legal affairs of others, serve a gainful purpose [reference]. An association is only exempt from the need to have a licence if advice and assistance is provided within the framework of its professional duties. Its activity must be strictly limited to these tasks; it becomes illegal if the association, in exceeding the limits set to it, e.g. by the way in which it regulates the remuneration payable by its members, participates in the pursuit of economic gain, which in the case of legal advice is only permitted by the law in strictly fixed circumstances.

According to § 1 I of the above-mentioned Act, not only physical persons but also legal entities and other associations which intend to act for others in legal matters require a licence. In this connection the legislature has established special protective measures for entities which appear in the form of corporations, especially private companies and similar associations of persons. The grant of the licence depends not only on the consideration that the circumstances of the individual case justify the desired legal form for the operation [reference] but it presupposes also that the exercise of the profession is limited to the persons who are designated by name in the licence [reference]. Moreover, like individuals these associations are subject to the supervision by the President of the District Court and are controlled as to the proper conduct of their operations [reference]. The intention of the legislature expressed in these provisions to protect the community against damage and to protect the Bar which is subject to extensive restrictions against competition by an immeasurable number of persons must not be evaded or frustrated. § 7 I of the Act concerning Legal Counsellors must be interpreted in accordance with this purpose of the law. The meaning and the purpose of this Act would be reversed if the associations which have a professional basis were allowed to exercise an activity which, in the main, distinguishes them no longer from the circle of persons who require a licence. If an association with a professional or similar basis looks after the legal affairs of others in a manner which comes near to the activity of an individual or association requiring a licence to such an extent that a member of the association occupies a position in relation to the association which does not differ essentially from that towards a person covered by § 1 I of the above-mentioned Act, that association can no longer claim that its activity is permitted by § 7 I. Such is the case, in particular, if the professional association which looks after the affairs of a member demands a fee which is assessed on the scale of fees for advocates and legal counsellors. Only advocates and, to a certain extent [reference], legal counsellors [reference] may claim fees on this scale. The reason is that this profession, which is required for the administration of justice, must be guaranteed an adequate remuneration for its service and thus a dignified position in life [reference]. This consideration does not apply, however, to an association formed in accordance with § 7 I of the above-mentioned Act. It is true that such an association cannot be prohibited from seeking reimbursement for those expenses and costs incurred in the course of safeguarding the legal interests of their members. The association must therefore remain entitled to bill its members—either all of them or only those requiring legal assistance—for the salaries actually paid to its employees and for the compensation paid to an agent as well as for other general office expenses by apportioning them in its discretion without undue need for restrictions. However, the association exceeds the legal limits set for its operations if it provides assistance and support for its members on the basis of a scale of fees which is only permitted in entirely different circumstances to a circle of persons to which admission is by registration or by a licence according to § 1 of the above-mentioned Act. It is irrelevant in this connection whether in the end by using this scale of fees the association *in fact* made a profit by rendering assistance in legal proceedings. It is common experience that a scale of fees of this kind at least encourages the tendency to make a business out of looking after the legal affairs of others. If so, all the dangers facing those seeking advice would be allowed to materialize which persuaded the legislature to require a licence for gainfully engaging in looking after the legal affairs of others. If the professional associations were given dispensation by § 7 I of the above-mentioned Act from the need to apply for a licence the reason was because, and to the extent that, a genuine activity of assistance appeared to exclude these dangers from the outset. This privilege is, however, no longer justified if as a result of the method of determining the remuneration for its activities the association creates the same dangerous situation which the requirement of a licence sought to meet in the case of non-privileged individuals and associations.

By providing in its statutes that its fees are to be those applicable to legal counsellors, the third defendant has therefore contravened § 1 I of the above-mentioned law in conjunction with § 823 II BGB. He is therefore obliged to refrain from doing so in so far as he allows his members to be advised or to be represented in court by the first and second defendant in consideration of fees as they are established for legal counsellors . . . Since it may be assumed without hesitation that the first and second defendants were familiar with the statutes of the third defendant, they are equally liable for having contravened § 823 II as accomplices or accessories and are therefore equally under the obligation to desist.

Case 109

BUNDESGERICHTSHOF (SIXTH CIVIL DIVISION) 16 DECEMBER 1958*
BGHZ 29, 100

The defendant and B, a merchant, were the sole shareholders and directors of a . . . private company [GmbH]. On 17 July 1954, on the application of the company, bankruptcy proceedings were started against it.

The plaintiff, who had supplied raw materials to the company over many years, claimed DM 26,604 as a non-privileged creditor. According to the report of the trustees in bankruptcy, the assets only sufficed to satisfy in part the claims of the privileged creditors.

Claiming only part of the sum registered in the bankruptcy proceedings, the plaintiff sued the defendant personally on the ground that he had neglected in several respects his duties as a director of the company and that the plaintiff had suffered considerable damage as a result. In particular he had failed, in contravention of § 64 of the Act relating to Private Companies [henceforth cited as GmbHG] to initiate bankruptcy proceedings in time, although the company had been insolvent and overburdened with debts for some time.

The District Court rejected the claim; the Court of Appeal of Hamburg allowed it. Upon a further appeal the judgment of the Court of Appeal was quashed and the case referred back for the following

Reasons

I. The managers of a private company are obliged under § 64 I GmbHG to apply for the start of bankruptcy proceedings as soon as the company becomes insolvent or if the annual or an interim balance sheet shows that the debts exceed the assets . . . The Court of Appeal regarded this provision as a law for the protection (§ 823 II BGB) of the creditors of a private company and held that the defendant had culpably violated his duty to initiate bankruptcy proceedings . . .

II. The appellant denies that § 64 I GmbHG is a protective law in the meaning of § 823 II BGB in favour of the creditors of a private company. He contends that this conclusion was ruled out by § 64 II GmbHG which hardly made any sense if § 64 I bore a protective character. This view cannot be accepted. § 64 II GmbHG only establishes the consequence as between the directors and the company if bankruptcy proceedings are begun too late. It provides that the directors must compensate the company in respect of payments made after the company became insolvent or overburdened with

---

* English version by Kurt Lipstein.

debts if these payments cannot be reconciled with the case of a merchant. It does not follow therefore that this provision determines exhaustively the responsibility of the directors for their dereliction of duty and that the creditors of the company are denied protection in their own right. The Act relating to Private Companies does not state whether the directors are liable to the creditors, and this question must therefore be determined in accordance with the general principles of private law [references].

The plaintiff may claim damages based on a violation of § 64 I GmbHG in conjunction with § 823 II BGB if this provision of the Act relating to Private Companies is also intended to protect the creditors of a private company and to afford them the type of protection which the plaintiff claims for himself [references]. Whether this is so must be determined in the light of the substance and the purpose of § 64 GmbHG.

1. § 64 I GmbHG provides that the directors must initiate bankruptcy proceedings as soon as the private company becomes insolvent or if the balance sheet discloses that the debts exceed the assets. If the directors fail to initiate these proceedings in time they are liable to imprisonment or a fine in accordance with § 84 I GmbHG. Clearly these provisions are intended to protect the creditors of the company as well. They, in particular, always suffer damage if bankruptcy proceedings are not begun or are not begun in time. It is obvious that the duty to apply to the court laid down by § 64 I GmbHG is also to protect them. This protection of the creditors is all the more called for as the partner shareholders of a private company are not liable personally for the debts of the company. The Reichsgericht, too, has held in a constant practice that § 64 GmbHG is a law for the protection of the creditors of the company. It has held that, while this provision does not protect everyone, particularly not those persons who are extraneous to the company, it is intended to protect not only the interests of the company but also the creditors [references].

2. The appellant argues further that even if § 64 GmbHG bore the character of the protective law, it could only protect the creditors existing at the time when bankruptcy proceedings should have been begun. If, as the Court of Appeal has held, the defendant should have started bankruptcy proceedings in January 1954 at the latest, the plaintiff could not, as regards claims arising after this date, be placed in a better position than other subsequent creditors for the reason that other claims of his were of an earlier date. At best he could claim damages in respect of the loss resulting from the fact that the dividend in respect of his claims outstanding in 1954 was smaller owing to the delay in starting bankruptcy proceedings than it would have been otherwise. However, the plaintiff had not incurred such a loss for he had admit-

ted himself that his claims arising during the period up to January 1954 had been satisfied. As regards goods supplied between 31 January and 15 July 1954, which were alone in issue, the plaintiff could not claim any damages against the defendant on the basis of § 823 II BGB, § 64 GmbHG.

The appellant is wrong in believing that § 64 GmbHG only protects those persons who were already creditors of the company when the conditions for the operation of § 64 I GmbHG materialized [reference]. The duty of the directors to start bankruptcy proceedings continues even after this date, as long as the company's debts exceed the assets or the company is insolvent. No reason exists for restricting this continuous duty to apply to the court to the claims of old creditors, that is to say, creditors whose claims already existed at the time in which the delay occurred in making the application. The duty of a director to initiate bankruptcy proceedings exists also towards a creditor who after this date supplies goods to the company on credit or who becomes its creditor otherwise. As a present creditor of the private company he is protected against subsequent infringements of § 64 I GmbHG in the same way as are old creditors. Therefore, contrary to the appellant, the protection accorded to the plaintiff extends also to claims against the private company which arose after 31 January 1954.

3. The question remains as to how far the protection extends which the plaintiff enjoys for this period by virtue of § 64 I GmbHG. The plaintiff seeks as damages the full price of the goods which he supplied after 31 January 1954, i.e. after the date when, in the plaintiff's opinion, the defendant should have started bankruptcy proceedings at the latest. The plaintiff can claim compensation for this damage on the strength of § 823 II BGB only if the entire damage falls within the range of dangers to protect against which § 64 GmbHG was enacted [reference]. If a statute serves to protect certain persons they can only claim compensation for such damage which occurred within the range of the interests protected by the statute. Therefore, before it is possible to apply § 249 BGB on which the plaintiff relies, it is necessary first to examine the range of protection afforded by § 64 I GmbHG and to determine, first of all, whether this provision is intended to provide that protection which the plaintiff claims in his favour.

In examining the question of the meaning and the purpose of this provision it appears, first of all, that the purpose of the legislature is to secure a prompt initiation of bankruptcy proceedings in the case where the debts are no longer covered by the assets. Therefore, the legislature in requiring the directors to start bankruptcy proceedings as soon as the annual balance sheet or an interim balance sheet discloses an excess of debts over the assets, clearly aims primarily at preventing that the company assets necessary for satisfying the creditors are not available for this purpose. The intention is to preserve the company assets for the benefit of the creditors so as to allow them to receive payment and to protect them against excessive losses as a result of the bankruptcy. This protection alone, which is clearly the primary purpose of the Act, cannot assist the plaintiff, however, for the plaintiff's claim for damages is not based primarily on the ground that owing to the delay in initiating bankruptcy proceedings the assets available to the creditors have been diminished and that therefore his claim lost totally or partially. Instead the plaintiff holds the defendant liable in the first place for the fact that the plaintiff still gave a credit to the private company, the debts of which exceeded the assets. According to § 823 II BGB the defendant is only liable to pay damages for loss occasioned thereby if § 64 I GmbHG protects the interests of the creditors also in this respect, i.e. if it seeks to protect them quite generally against the dangers resulting from the continuing operation of a company the debts of which exceed its assets. It is true that the community is in fact protected in this respect as well as by the existence of § 64 GmbHG. This fact alone cannot suffice, however, to attribute to § 64 GmbHG the character of a protective act having such an extensive range. For this purpose not the effect of the law but its substance and aim must be considered, more particularly whether the legislature intended to provide such a far-reaching protection or at least accepted it [references]. This cannot be assumed, however. Confidence in the solvency and the creditworthiness of another does not enjoy special protection in trade and commerce. He who makes a mistake and suffers a loss must normally prove that § 826 BGB or § 823 II BGB in conjunction with § 263 of the Criminal Code applies, unless he can rely on contractual claims. The Act does not indicate that a different rule is to apply in relations with private companies and that those dealing with private companies are to be given more extensive protection. Gadow and Weipert [reference] and Bergenroth justify the need for special protection of the public on the ground that public and private companies are legal entities whose shareholders are not liable for the debts of the company with their entire assets. It must be admitted that a need exists for this reason to protect the creditors. The legislative history of the Act concerning Private Companies [GmbHG] shows that the fact that only the assets of a private company are liable for its debts led to the provision that bankruptcy proceedings are to be begun against the company not only if the company is insolvent, but also if its debts exceed its assets [references]. No indications exist that in enacting § 64 I GmbHG the legislature also intended, in addition to the protection mentioned above, to protect the creditors against giving credit to a private company which is overburdened with debts or from entering into business relations with it at all. If they suffer damage in this way such creditors, like creditors of an individual or of a partnership, are therefore restricted to the protection offered by § 826 BGB and by other provisions such as § 823 II BGB in conjunction with § 263 of the Criminal Code, leaving aside any contractual claims.

It follows that the plaintiff can only claim damages against the defendant on the basis of § 823 II BGB in conjunction with § 64 I GmbHG if, and to the extent that, at the time when his claim for the payment of goods sold arose he would have participated in the distribution of the assets. It is not clear whether and to what extent this was the case. Certainly the plaintiff cannot, on this interpretation of the law, contrary to the view of the Court of Appeal, receive the full price of the goods sold, which he claims as damages. Therefore, the judgment appealed against cannot be maintained, having regard to the reasons given by the Court of Appeal . . .

Notes to Cases 107–109

1. In all the systems under comparison a rich case-law can be found under the heading of tort liability for breach of statute, but there is no need to give more than a few illustrations. For, as Professor Medicus has said about German law (op. cit., no. 621), each case turns on its facts and the construction of the wording of the statute in question. Yet, some basic principles do exist and they have been discussed briefly in Ch. 4, section A1(*a*), above. For English law see the very useful account by John Spencer in Clerk and Lindsell, *On Torts* (16th edn. ch. 13), and the older but seminal article of Glanville Williams, 'The Effect of Penal Legislation in the Law of Tort,' 23 *MLR* 233. For American law see Prosser, Wade, and Schwartz, 220, with further references at 231 and 247.

2. As we have already noted, German judges are spared the need of discussing whether the legislator intended to allow a civil remedy when a particular statute has been breached—§ 823 II BGB providing, subject to what we said above, a clear positive answer. But the court still has to discover the purpose of the statute: Was the mischief that occurred the one the statute wished to avoid? Was the plaintiff the person the statute wished to protect? (For an illustration see BGHZ 108, 134.) Cases 107–109 give some idea of how the German courts tackle these problems; but other decisions, reproduced elsewhere, have also discussed this problem. (See, for example, cases 9 and 54.)

3. The search for the purpose of the statute only thinly disguises the value-judgments that have to be made in each case by the court. Policy thus strongly determines the result, though it is done under the guise of statutory construction. Thus, where more valuable interests are at stake (e.g. life and not just the protection of property) the courts tend to construe the statute in a way that is favourable to the plaintiff (cf. *Kernan* v. *American Dredger Co.* 355 US 426, 78 S. Ct. 394 (1958) with *Gorris* v. *Scott* LR 9 Exch. 125

(1874)). And where certain types of plaintiffs are involved (e.g. children, workmen etc.) the courts will, again, have their interests very much at heart when 'construing' the relevant enactments. (See Prosser, Wade and Schwartz, 246.)

4. Courts often talk of the 'purpose' of a statute, but is there any reason why a statute should not have more than one? (See, for example, *Hines* v. *Foreman* (Tex. Comm. App. 1922) 243, SW 479.) Could it be that looking for 'one' aim or purpose makes it easier to limit liability, if that is what the judge wishes to achieve?

2. COMPENSATION AND SATISFACTION

Case 110

BUNDESGERICHTSHOF (GREAT CIVIL DIVISION) 6 JULY 1955*
BGHZ 18, 149

The Great Civil Senate has answered as follows the question referred to it by the Sixth Civil Senate as to whether in assessing the amount of reasonable compensation in money in accordance with § 847 BGB all the circumstances must be taken into account, including the financial circumstances and the degree of blameworthiness of the person liable to pay damages:

In assessing equitable compensation in money in accordance with § 847 BGB all circumstances of the case can be taken into account, among them the degree of blameworthiness of the person who is liable and the financial circumstances of both parties. In this connection account must also be taken of the extent to which the person who is liable is indemnified by a liability insurance or a claim for redress.

Reasons

According to § 847 BGB 'equitable compensation' in money may be claimed in case of injury to the body or to health even in respect of damage which is not pecuniary. The older view, held in particular by the Reichsgericht, was that compensation under § 847 BGB must be 'equitable' in respect of *all* the circumstances which characterize the damaging event in issue; it therefore took into account not only the extent and the duration of the pain, disfigurement, suffering, and intrusion, which were always matters of primary concern, but also particularly the economic situation of the injured party and of the tortfeasor, the degree of blameworthiness, and the circumstances which led to the damage (e.g. gratuitous transportation). According

* English version by Kurt Lipstein.

to a more recent view the compensation must only be 'equitable' with reference to the purpose, which is to compensate non-pecuniary damage; it therefore only takes into account the extent and the duration of the pain, disfigurement, suffering, and intrusion as well as the means necessary to compensate for non-pecuniary damage; thus it takes into account only the general circumstances of the injured party. This more recent view was adopted by the Third Civil Senate in its decision of 29 September 1952 [reference] to the extent that in assessing the amount of damages for pain and suffering it did not take into account the economic circumstances of the tortfeasor, while leaving open the question as to whether the degree of this blameworthiness should also not be considered.

I. 1. The modern practice bases its view on the ground that claims for damages for pain and suffering, too, are true claims for damages; it therefore regards as decisive the non-pecuniary damage which the injured party suffered as a result of the tort; as in all cases of claims for damages it seeks to take into account only those consequences which the act giving rise to damages has had for the injured party.

This view assumes correctly that as a result of the treatment of the Civil Code of claims in respect of torts—including those based on non-pecuniary damage—it is impossible to attribute to them a direct penal function. This applies equally to claims for non-pecuniary damage. However, by denying the penal character of claims for non-pecuniary damage no final answer has been given to the question for decision in the present case which is in respect of what circumstances damages to be awarded under § 847 BGB must be 'equitable'.

2. First of all the provision of § 847 BGB must be considered as part of the system of the Civil Code as a whole, which in the most diverse places determines the extent of a performance in accordance with 'equitable discretion' or allows 'equitable compensation'. In these cases the Code intends normally that account should be taken of all the circumstances of a case which are relevant according to equitable considerations, and more particularly the situation of all the parties involved.

(a) If a performance is to be fixed in accordance with 'equitable discretion', as §§ 315, 317 BGB require, or an act must be carried out in accordance with 'equitable discretion', as §§ 1246, 2048, 2156 BGB demand, it means undoubtedly in these cases that not only the economic circumstances of the creditor, but also those of the debtor must be taken into account.

(b) In connection with claims for damages, too, the Civil Code refers not only in § 847 but also in §§ 829, 1300 to equitable compensation or to damages in accordance with the requirements of equity.

When § 829 BGB speaks of equitable considerations, the Code refers expressly to 'the circumstances of the parties involved', and thus the economic circumstances of the parties must also be taken into account. It is true that normally § 847 BGB presupposes that the tortfeasor is to be blamed, while § 829 establishes strict liability. Moreover, according to § 829 both the ground for holding a person liable as well as the extent of his liability are determined according to the principles of equity, while according to § 847 only the extent of liability is so to be fixed. Nevertheless, it is the express intention of § 829, also in so far as it determines the extent of the claim for damages in accordance with equity, that the circumstances of those involved should be taken into account, albeit on the basis of detailed particulars. It is not possible either to refer to § 829 in order to further the argument in support of a restrictive interpretation of § 847, as adopted by the more recent practice, if only for the reason that the Civil Code by requiring that something is to be performed in accordance with the principles of equity intends not only in that case, but regularly, that all circumstances are to be taken into account which may be relevant.

(*c*) A closer connection than that between § 847 and § 829 BGB exists between the claims arising under § 847 and the claim for defloration under § 1300 BGB, in respect of which the law provides also that 'equitable compensation' in money is to be granted. It must be admitted that the liability under § 1300 arises from the breach of an agreement which forms part of Family Law while that under § 847 is based on a tort. However, in both cases the extent of liability is to be determined in accordance with equity.

This history of § 1300 BGB shows that the legislature intended the considerations which had led it to allow 'equitable compensation under § 1300' to apply equally to 'equitable compensation in § 847'. Thus the proposal to replace the expression 'equitable compensation' in what is now § 1300 by the term 'adequate compensation' was rejected together with the further proposal to grant, instead of 'equitable compensation', 'compensation which takes into account the financial circumstances of either party to the engagement to marry as well as the reduced expectation of another marriage'. One of the reasons was that § 831 of the Bill, now § 847, which was followed by § 1283 of the Bill, now § 1300, also referred to equitable compensation and that in the case of a claim for damages under what is now § 1300, which follows closely the claim for damages under what is now § 847, no danger existed that the previous practice (opposed by the second proposal) in the case of claims for defloration would be continued.

The substantive considerations expressed in respect of § 1300 and applicable also to § 847, as appeared above, emerge from the reasons which accompany the rejection of the proposals referred to above. The first of these proposals was rejected on the ground that 'the term "equitable" had a clear established technical meaning'. The second proposal was met by the argument that 'it was not just in assessing the damages to take no notice at all of the financial circumstances and the situation in life of the girl, as might be feared, if the proposal were accepted; the best means of ensuring the development of a realistic practice of the Court was not in any way to restrict the judges in assessing damages'. Another proposal to fix the damages under § 1300 at a minimum of fifty times the normal local daily wage was 'countered by the argument that individual provisions concerning the assessment of damages were not advisable . . .'.

Therefore the preparatory materials for the Civil Code permit the conclusion in respect of § 847 as well that it was the intention of the legislature not to constrain the courts to disregard certain circumstances in assessing damages for non-pecuniary losses. This means that in fixing equitable compensation the courts may, as a matter of principle, take into consideration all the circumstances which may arise.

3. Contrary to the modern view the same conclusion follows from the legal purpose of damages for pain and suffering. In law damages for pain and suffering have a dual function. They are meant to provide the injured party with adequate compensation for that kind of damage, for those handicaps which are not of a pecuniary nature. At the same time they are meant to indicate that the tortfeasor owes the victim satisfaction for what he has done to him.

Of these two functions that of compensation or redress is prominent. The purpose of the claim is redress for the loss suffered. The latter cannot, however, be assessed arithmetically. The underlying idea may perhaps be formulated as follows: the tortfeasor, who has not only inflicted pecuniary damage upon the injured party but also gravely affected his life, is to help the latter by his payments to alleviate his burden as far as possible. Having regard to this purpose of damages for pain and suffering it must be admitted that considerations of the seriousness, acuteness, and duration of the pain, suffering, and the disfigurement constitute the main basis for assessing equitable damages. The sum required to provide this redress, therefore, depends primarily upon the extent of this damage. It is the merit of the decision of the Third Division of this court [reference] to have shown this, with the result that damages for pain and suffering were treated more seriously than hitherto not only as to their legal significance, but also as to their factual evaluation. Since, however, the Code requires equitable compensation in the meaning set out above (**I.**2), the purpose of making good cannot determine alone the amount of damages, particularly since this purpose is insufficient alone to fix the amount with something approximating certainty.

Furthermore, even if claims in tort for damages, including damages for non-pecuniary losses, no longer bear any penal character directly, nevertheless something inherent in the purpose of making good is a reminder of its former function as a fine or, to use the apposite term of the corresponding Swiss institution, as satisfaction. Legal history shows that damages for pain and suffering have their origin in criminal law and that in the laws of the German States in modern times different types were fashioned according to the respective stages of development, which still reflect in some respects their antecedents in criminal law. The following is significant: wherever damages for pain and suffering were not excluded altogether, as for instance in § 112 I 6 of the Prussian Allgemeines Landrecht of 1792 in respect of the persons other than 'peasants or common citizens' or in Art. 14 of the Württemberg Act concerning the effects in private law of crimes and penalties of 5 September 1839 [reference], the laws provided expressly that in assessing the amount of damages also certain circumstances were to be taken into account which cannot be reconciled with a limited notion of damages restricted to making good. Such are the degrees of blameworthiness mentioned in §§ 168, 125 I 6 of the Prussian Allgemeines Landrecht, or the degree of blameworthiness and 'the financial circumstances of the tortfeasor' as stated in § 15 of the Baden Act concerning the effects in private law of crimes of 6 March 1845 [reference] or if, according to the Saxon decree of 1 August 1856 [reference] damages were to be fixed 'in the discretion of the judge, having regard to the pain inflicted on the victim', which latter provision was interpreted to mean that the status and the financial circumstances of the claimant were to be taken into account [reference]. Similar considerations influenced the unanimous view of the practice of the courts and writers up to the thirties of this century in dealing with § 847 BGB to the effect that in assessing damages for pain and suffering all circumstances must be taken into account which colour the individual case.

It is true that the legislature has given the claim for pain and suffering the form of a claim for damages according to private law. However, in substance it does not bear the character of a usual claim of this kind, which is for compensation in respect of pecuniary damage. Its purpose to effect restitution cannot be achieved through restitution in kind, as is the case where the damage is pecuniary. To that extent restitution is impossible. Certainly an attempt is to be made to make good, but it cannot be done arithmetically. It is impossible to concentrate on the notion of making good, because non-pecuniary damage can never be expressed in terms of money and since the possibility itself of making good by means of money payments is very limited. Contrary to a view to be encountered occasionally, non-pecuniary losses concern 'assets not to be valued in money terms'. The amount of money necessary to make good cannot be determined by 'so to say balancing pain with those pleasures which are intended to wipe out the victim's memory of his sufferings'. Even where it is to a certain extent possible to compensate physical and mental suffering by amenities and comforts, widely differing possibilities almost always exist as to how redress is to be effected and the purpose alone of the damages to make good does not provide a sufficient measuring-rod. The purpose of making good alone only provides a very rough standard for assessing damages the greater the non-pecuniary loss. This appears particularly if the non-pecuniary loss is so extensive that it is difficult to conceive of making it good, as for instance when restitution can hardly be achieved because the body of the victim has been extensively destroyed. This becomes particularly clear where the type of non-pecuniary damage cannot be made good at all, as for instance frequently in the case of psychological effects. It is generally recognized that damages for non-pecuniary losses must also be awarded if an assault, false imprisonment, or interference with physical integrity resulted in psychological and not in physical injuries. Especially in the case of psychological disturbances it will frequently be impossible to compensate the feelings of unhappiness since the injured party himself is not conscious of his damage. Nevertheless, damages for pain and suffering have been rightly awarded even in this case. The award of damages under § 847 BGB, it must be admitted, serves to make good non-pecuniary loss; it is not, however, a condition for awarding damages for non-pecuniary loss that this purpose can be achieved. The same would be the case if the injured party is so situated financially that no amount of money could raise a sense of happiness which would make good his non-pecuniary damage.

Precisely in these situations of non-pecuniary damage, the function of making good, which is intimately connected with the legal regulation of damages for non-pecuniary loss, acquires its special significance. The function of making good underlines that the injurious act has created a certain personal relationship between the tortfeasor and the victim—which, by its nature demands that in assessing how much the tortfeasor must pay the victim *all* the circumstances of the case must be taken into account. This appears also from the special provision that this claim dies with the claimant and cannot be assigned.

II. In accordance with the foregoing observations, the severity and the extent of the reduction in the enjoyment of life must be considered in the first place for the purpose of assessing damages for pain and suffering. This is the preponderant aspect. In addition, other circumstances may, however, be taken into account as well which are salient features of the injurious act.

1. One of these is the degree of blameworthiness on the part of the tortfeasor. The degree of blameworthiness is not only relevant, as the more recent

interpreters of § 847 BGB would have it, with regard to its effect upon the injured party: the fact that the injury was caused by the reckless or even intentional behaviour of the defendant, may naturally have left the injured party embittered, while he may be more inclined to accept as his fate an injured caused by slight negligence. Leaving aside the reaction of the injured party, it may accord with equity and the notion of satisfaction in assessing compensation under § 847 BGB if, in the individual case, intention and recklessness count against the tortfeasor, while especially slight negligence counts in his favour. It would be incomprehensible if the trial judge could not award higher damages for pain and suffering in the case of a crime than where the external consequences are the same, but occurred as result of an error in normal human intercourse which might be committed by anybody. For this reason many foreign legal systems, too, have taken, and still take, into account the degree of blameworthiness of the tortfeasor in assessing the amount of damages payable by him. The fact that German law does not offer this opportunity where the damage is pecuniary does not preclude its use where the Code offers it in arriving at the equitable compensation for non-pecuniary loss. On the contrary, this possibility is a great merit of the regulation of damages for non-pecuniary losses.

Apart from the degree of blameworthiness, the cause of injury or of the injurious act may be relevant in certain circumstances. Even if the degree of blameworthiness is the same, different acts may bear very different characteristics (injury in the course of the enjoyment of some pleasure on the one hand, or in connection with the exercise of a profession, the administration of help, or any other necessary activity on the other hand). This is particularly valid in those cases in which the tort was committed on the occasion of an activity which the tortfeasor carried out in order to oblige the injured party and which the latter welcomed—perhaps even gratefully—as, for instance, where the victim suffers an injury on the occasion of a journey as a gratuitous passenger in the car of the tortfeasor as a result of the latter's negligence who sought to do him a favour. In such a case it may even be inequitable if the victim claims damages for pain and suffering to an amount equal to that which a pedestrian could have claimed who had been run down by the tortfeasor.

2. Possibly the economic circumstances of the injured party may also influence the assessment of damages on grounds of equity.

The economic circumstances of the victim may, for instance, affect the notion of making good inasmuch as the function of making good is less significant if, for example, the injured party is so favourably circumstanced economically that sums of money paid by the tortfeasor can hardly make good the non-pecuniary damage suffered to him. In such cases the function of damages as satisfaction assumes primary importance. On the other hand, it is not impossible that in individual cases the higher standard of living to which the victim is accustomed may also lead to increased damages for pain and suffering.

3. Finally, the economic circumstances of the tortfeasor may also be taken into account in assessing the damages under § 847 BGB.

(a) Viewed from the angle of equity, i.e. by taking into account the circumstances of both parties, the idea of making good should not normally result in the tortfeasor's serious and lasting penury. It is true that here, too, the need to offer satisfaction and to make good the damage is preponderant. The fact that the tortfeasor is not well off must be of greater or lesser importance having regard to the cause of the damaging event, and especially to the degree of blameworthiness. Any behaviour of the tortfeasor which is especially reprehensible, such as inconsiderate recklessness or, even more so, acting intentionally, may consign into the background any concern to preserve him from economic distress. On the other hand, if the tortfeasor's economic situation is particularly favourable it may appear equitable in the exercise of the court's discretion to award higher damages. Moreover, the smaller the amount of damages required to make good non-pecuniary losses, the more it will be possible to disregard the economic circumstances, in particular those of the tortfeasor. Equally the economic circumstances of the victim may be relevant in this connection. If the victim is comfortably off, it may appear equitable in assessing the damages to exercise in favour of the tortfeasor the power of discretion inherent in the consideration of the economic circumstances. On the other hand, if the victim is in straitened circumstances it may seem equitable to exercise this discretion in favour of the tortfeasor to a lesser extent than if the victim is well situated financially. However, even if the tortfeasor is penniless considerations of his financial position can never release him from the duty to pay damages for pain and suffering, for the financial position of the tortfeasor constitutes only one aspect among many, and not even the most important, which must be taken into account.

(b) Any such consideration of the economic circumstances of the parties involved is not contrary to the intention of positive law—express or implied. It is, however, true that in the case of a debt consisting of fungibles the debtor is always liable, even if he cannot supply them and that therefore in the case of a debt of fungibles, he cannot plead his adverse economic circumstances. The significance of any considerations of the economic circumstances of the tortfeasor, is, however, completely misunderstood by those who argue that, as a result of his adverse economic circumstances damages for non-pecuniary loss which are appropriate 'as such' are reduced and that therefore the victim is receiving less than is due to him 'as such'. This view assumes that in fixing equitable damages *only* the extent of the losses is to be taken into account. In reality the amount of damages for pain and suffering is ascertained only when *all* the circumstances of the individual case have been considered. Taking into account all the financial circumstances of the tortfeasor does not reduce in any way the damages which are appropriate 'as such'; instead 'equitable damages' are being assessed for the first time in accordance with § 847 BGB by taking into account all circumstances which can be evaluated, including the economic circumstances of the parties involved; without considering all the circumstances, and thus also where appropriate the economic circumstances, no assessment would be possible. For this reason it cannot be contended that such an interpretation amounts to 'breaching the principle which governs the entire area of law in the matter, which is that the extent of an obligation is always independent of the ability of the debtor to perform'. This principle applies to pecuniary damages. On the other hand, the Code intends the extent of the damages for non-pecuniary losses envisaged by § 847 BGB to be assessed having regard to all the circumstances of the case. For the same reason it follows that an injured party whose economic circumstances are taken into account in his favour cannot be awarded more than his damage. The decision DR 1941, 280 does not permit the conclusion that the Reichsgericht abandoned its current practice and assumed that there is something like damages for pain and suffering 'which are appropriate as such'. If such a complete change of practice had taken place, it would certainly have been accompanied by more detailed arguments; where the Reichsgericht employed the term 'damages for pain and suffering which are appropriate as such', it clearly used an imprecise formulation.

If it is acknowledged that the economic circumstances of the parties involved may be taken into account as one of the possible bases for assessing the amount of pecuniary damages for non-pecuniary losses, this constitutes a facet of the facts before the court, as are also the extent of the non-pecuniary damages and the possibility of providing an opportunity for making good. It is therefore wrong to say that it is contrary to the principle of equality to take the economic circumstances of the parties into account; for if the same victim suffers non-pecuniary damage inflicted by two tortfeasors whose economic circumstances differ from each other, the two situations are not identical. It is not clear why, as is said occasionally, the consideration of the economic conditions of the parties involved should be regarded as unsocial. Surely the fundamental principles of a social state based on law are not violated if in assessing damages the economic circumstances of the parties involved are balanced against each other.

(*c*) Considerations of the economic circumstances of the parties do not lead to insoluble difficulties either.

The view that considerations of the economic conditions of a penniless tortfeasor must—in strict logic—lead to a complete denial of damages under § 847 BGB has already been refuted above.

The view is also incorrect that the principle of taking into account the economic conditions is breached in those cases where the Fiscus is the tortfeasor. It must be conceded that in these cases, and also where the tortfeasor is a 'charitable institution' of public law, the practice of the courts, especially that of the Reichsgericht, does not take notice of the financial situation of the tortfeasor. The reason is that the assets of the Fiscus serve public purposes and are tied to this extent. The conclusion is drawn therefrom that these assets do not reflect a financial situation in the nature of private enterprise; they cannot therefore be related to the assets of the victim, representing private enterprise, so as to balance them against each other. In the light of this view of the assets of the Fiscus, the financial situation of the Fiscus and that of the injured party are so different as to preclude a comparison. In these cases the tortfeasor (i.e. the Fiscus) lacks a characteristic (i.e. the economic circumstances) which, if existing, would have to be taken into account where engaging in considerations of equity. In the case of the Fiscus 'economic' circumstances defy evaluation. They mitigate neither in favour of nor against the Fiscus as a debtor. The Fiscus can never plead straitened economic circumstances, just as the victim cannot point to the particularly favourable circumstances of the Fiscus which is liable to pay damages for pain and suffering.

No objections can be raised against the admissibility of considerations concerning the economic circumstances of the parties on the possible ground that the assessment of damages for non-pecuniary losses, which is difficult in any event, will be 'rendered unpredictable and complicated' if the economic circumstances of the parties are taken into account. Apart from the fact—stressed more than once before—that the amount of damages depends primarily on the extent of the damage, the possibility of making good, and the amount of the means necessary to achieve this, none of these conceivable difficulties rules out the admissibility of considering economic circumstances, now that the legislature has abolished the more or less fixed rates for assessing damages to be awarded for non-pecuniary losses. The view that 'non-pecuniary damage can be assessed and also that certain maximum and minimum amounts can be laid down as to how objectively ascertainable non-pecuniary losses can be compensated' results of necessity in the readoption of the fixed tariffs which were established by the law of some German States (e.g. §§ 113, 118 I. 6 of the Prussian Allgemeines Landrecht;

§ 1497 of the Saxon Civil Code) which were abolished by the Civil Code. Not only does the variety of possible non-pecuniary losses preclude the adoption of such 'maximum and minimum tariffs' altogether or the latter would not do justice to the individual character of non-pecuniary damage, but it restricts the opportunity created by the code of reaching a decision based on the discretion of the court.

Moreover, the fact that the adverse economic circumstances of the tortfeasor are taken into account does not make it difficult or inequitable if later on, in the course of execution (by way of a judicial adjustment, a composition with creditors, or of bankruptcy), the tortfeasor seeks to obtain a reduction of his debts and thus also of his liability to pay damages under § 847 BGB which had already been fixed as appropriate in view of his unfavourable economic situation. The conclusion derived therefrom that in these cases the adverse financial position of the tortfeasor leads twice to a reduction of the claims under § 847 BGB is influenced by the incorrect assumption that damages which are appropriate 'as such' are being reduced if the economic circumstances of the tortfeasor are taken into account. Here, too, the damages awarded under § 847 BGB are 'reduced' only once, i.e. in the course of execution. Moreover, regarded from the economic point of view, the same result is reached not only in § 847 BGB but wherever the amount of the performance owed depends upon the economic circumstances of the debtor, as for instance where the extent of a performance or act is to be determined 'in accordance with equitable discretion under §§ 315, 317, 1246, 2048, 2156 BGB, where a contractual penalty is to be reduced in accordance with § 343 BGB, or where damages for breach of promise under § 1300 are in issue'.

(*d*) Once it is realized that where the claim is for non-pecuniary losses, damages which are appropriate 'as such' do not exist and cannot therefore be increased or reduced in view of the economic circumstances of the parties, the case where several tortfeasors acting together have committed a tort resulting in non-pecuniary damage—which is that before this court—can be solved without difficulty. Here, too—if necessary—damages under § 847 BGB must be assessed independently in respect of each tortfeasor. The same task is incumbent upon the courts if, as regards pecuniary damage, one tortfeasor is only liable under § 7a of the Haftpflichtgesetz (Strict Liability Act), § 12 of the Strassenverkehrsgesetz (Road Traffic Act), or § 23 of the Luftverkehrsgesetz (Air Traffic Act) while the other has incurred more extensive liability under § 843. The two tortfeasors are only liable as debtors in common to the extent that the amount of their liability is the same; as regards the excess, that tortfeasor is only liable who must pay higher damages.

In taking into account the economic circumstances, the question may arise as to whether in so doing the possibility of compensation between the tortfeasors should be considered. Since the fact that the economic circumstances are taken into account means that economic potential counts and since, on the other hand, economic potential is increased if enforceable claims for redress exist against the co-tortfeasor, it follows naturally that such enforceable claims for redress must be taken into account in determining economic potential. It must be admitted that if several tortfeasors who are liable in common have claims for redress against one another, each is liable in the end to pay only a portion of the total damages. The reason is that even in the presence of several tortfeasors the victim can only demand to be compensated once. This principle is not violated if the damages for non-pecuniary loss are fixed at a higher level because the value of the claims for redress against other tortfeasors is taken into account in determining the economic potential of one of the tortfeasors. In this case, too, the injured party can only recover once the sum of money which was awarded to him in respect of non-pecuniary losses. Therefore, no principle of positive law is being violated in this respect either.

(*e*) It was much disputed—especially in recent times—whether in considering the economic circumstances of the tortfeasor it is relevant that he is insured against liability.

The view was expressed in particular by the Reichsgericht at an early stage, that the claims of the tortfeasor arising out of liability insurance could not be taken into account since the purpose of liability insurance was to indemnify the insured in respect of payments which the latter was obliged to make because he was liable, and that this must be established first. However, this view concentrates exclusively on the relationship between the tortfeasor and the insurer of his liability; in reality the question must be as to whether and how the fact that the tortfeasor is insured against liability can affect the extent of his liability towards the injured party. For this purpose the following consideration applies quite generally to damages according to § 847 BGB: a tortfeasor who is entitled to be reimbursed by the insurer against liability to the extent of the amount insured is in a more favourable financial position than a tortfeasor who carries himself alone the burden of paying damages. The claim acquired by the payment of premiums to protection by the insurer is a financial asset in so far as any payment of compensation for damage caused is concerned.

Since in taking this financial approach it is only relevant whether the tortfeasor must bear the cost of the damages himself or will be reimbursed—at least in part—on the strength of his liability insurance, it can make no difference whether the insurance against liability is voluntary or compulsory.

Finally, it cannot be concluded that liability insurance must be disregarded because the assets of the insurer against liability constitute a special fund which is dedicated to a special purpose, similar to the assets of the Fiscus, which must be disregarded. This view overlooks that the assets of the Fiscus are not assets in the meaning of private law for the reason that they are not only dedicated to a special purpose, but because the special purpose is a public one. Therefore they cannot be related to the assets of the injured party, which are within the private sector, so as to balance them. The assets of a liability insurer, however, contrary to those of the Fiscus fall within the private sector. For this reason alone the reference to the treatment of Fiscal property is inappropriate. Moreover, in taking into account the existence of liability insurance no 'purpose linked special fund' of the insurer is being considered, but the claims of the tortfeasor to be indemnified by the liability insurer.

Consequently it is admissible in assessing damages under § 847 BGB to take into account also that the tortfeasor can demand an indemnity from the insurer—up to the amount of the sum insured.

(f) In taking into account the economic circumstances of the tortfeasor it may be relevant that the damages for pain and suffering are not being awarded in the form of a lump sum but of periodic payments. Thereby the result can be achieved in some cases that the victim receives damages for pain and suffering which are largely in keeping with their purpose, namely to make good, even if the tortfeasor's financial circumstances are unfavourable, seeing that such periodic payments do not burden him that heavily for the time being. If damages for pain and suffering are assessed in the form of a right to periodic payments the question arises, however, as to whether a subsequent change in the financial circumstances of the tortfeasor must be taken into account under § 323 of the Code of Civil Procedure [ZPO]. The answer must be in the affirmative. It is true that when the amount of damages for pain and suffering is fixed by a judgment or a compromise, the claim for damages in respect of non-pecuniary loss loses its character as a claim for damages in money; thus the amount of the claim under § 847 BGB is henceforth fixed for the future, at least in principle. However, just as any consequences of the injurious act which occurred or manifested themselves subsequently, and therefore had not been taken into account in assessing damages under § 847 BGB, may give rise to a supplementary claim under § 847 BGB, so no objections exist in principle against reviewing the periodic payments if the conditions laid down by § 323 ZPO are fulfilled, especially if a fundamental change in economic circumstances has occurred, in particular on the part of the tortfeasor.

4. As stated above on several occasions, among the circumstances to be taken into account on grounds of equity, the extent, the severity, and the

duration of pain and suffering must always contribute the determining criteria; the non-pecuniary damage inflicted, the adverse effect on life always occupies the first place among the circumstances to be taken into account. For the rest, it is impossible to establish a general order of priorities among the circumstances to be considered, for their extent and importance in assessing equitable compensation emerges only when they coincide in the individual case, as was shown above, especially in **II.** 3 (*a*). It is therefore necessary to consider the individual case. The extent to which the circumstances enumerated previously, or any other which may be relevant, affect the assessment of damages for pain and suffering must be determined in accordance with equity. Such an examination may also lead to the conclusion that certain circumstances, as for instance the financial situation, should be disregarded in fixing damages for pain and suffering.

In the light of the foregoing, the question had to be answered in the general terms in which it had been formulated by the Sixth Senate of the court, for only thus the substance of the question could be treated exhaustively. Nevertheless, it seemed appropriate to stress already by the manner in which the answer is formulated that not all the circumstances which have been mentioned must be taken into account in each individual case, but only that they may be considered, having regard to the facts. In order to eliminate doubts it also appeared appropriate to include at this stage the treatment of possible claims of the tortfeasor for an indemnity under a policy of liability insurance or for redress against other tortfeasors.

Case 111

BUNDESGERICHTSHOF (SIXTH CIVIL DIVISION) 22 JUNE 1982*
NJW 1982, 2123

In January 1977 the defendant ran down with his motor car the plaintiff, then three and a half years of age, who had suddenly darted into the road, and injured him severely. By a decision of the Court of Appeal of Düsseldorf, limited to the merits and to part damages, which has since obtained the force of *res judicata*, the defendant was condemned to pay DM 1000 as part payment in respect of damages for pain and suffering. The dispute between the parties is now confined to the amount of additional damages for pain and suffering. The plaintiff contends that, having regard to his serious irremediable injuries, damages by the way of a lump sum of DM 100,000 and monthly payments of at least DM 500 are indicated. Apart from several fractures and other injuries which have since healed, the stem of the brain was damaged. This resulted in an expression aphasia, incontinence of urine and stool, a spastic tetraparesis with a right-sided predominance, and in occasional epileptic absent spells. The plaintiff can move

* English version by Kurt Lipstein.

about with difficulty in an invalid chair, is incapable of speaking, and must rely for the rest of his life upon assistance and care by others. The details of his handicaps are in dispute.

Reasons

I. In assessing the amount of damages for pain and suffering the Court of Appeal relies on the expert evidence of Professor P . . . As a result it concludes that the plaintiff has suffered extremely severe physical injuries which are irremediable. However, the Court of Appeal is of the opinion that the plaintiff is not incapable of experiencing sensations and therefore not only nominal damages for pain and suffering must be considered . . . An award for considerable damages for pain and suffering—also by way of periodical payments—could contribute to give pleasure and to make up for the loss of amenities of life. It could provide the plaintiff with those facilities according to his age which the centre for rehabilitation where he was housed could not afford to supply on its own, but which the plaintiff would clearly appreciate as such . . .

II. These conclusions cannot be supported upon a further appeal.

1. The Court of Appeal holds correctly that damages for pain and suffering according to § 847 **BGB** are meant to compensate the plaintiff for non-economic losses and to provide additional satisfaction for the suffering which has been inflicted. These considerations are in accordance with an established practice of this Senate. Nor does the Court of Appeal fail to appreciate that compensation and satisfaction can no longer serve their purpose if as a result of extremely severe brain damage the injured party can no longer be aware of them. In these circumstances the award of damages for pain and suffering constitutes merely a symbolic act of reparation which must be reflected in the amount of the award [references].
2. The Court of Appeal is mistaken in holding that in the present case a symbolic act of reparation is not involved. The appellant objects with justification that in effect the plaintiff is being awarded damages for pain and suffering to an extent which would normally be awarded for the most severe injuries of a permanent kind, but that no reason has been given how such high damages can compensate the plaintiff for his physical and mental suffering or to what extent satisfaction can be provided for the plaintiff which can be appreciated by him.

(*a*) It is possible that the Court of Appeal is of the opinion that in assessing damages for pain and suffering no differentiation is any longer admissible if the injured party is not completely 'incapable of any sensations' (or perhaps more precisely: if apart from maintaining purely vegetative functions he cannot notice anything and cannot assimilate it intellectually in any form); and that the same amount must be awarded as would be allowed in the case of an injured person who has the mental capacity to appreciate intellectually his injuries and their causes, and who suffers on that account. Such an approach would not be justifiable in law. Instead it must always be examined in borderline cases involving an injured person who merely vegetates as a 'living corpse' and who is owed symbolic reparation to what extent damages for pain and suffering can fulfil their purpose beyond this amount. If this can only be achieved to a very limited measure, this factor must affect the extent of the sum to be awarded.

(*aa*) Having regard to the so-called *compensatory* function this means: compensation is to be granted for any detriments experienced by the injured person consisting in physical suffering, such as pain and other disagreeable sensations, in mental suffering, such as a feeling of disadvantage compared with other healthy persons, and in a sense of dependence upon existence by others. The award of a high lump sum cannot compensate for this if the injured person cannot feel these detriments and is not aware of them.

Moreover, if he cannot employ the high damages usefully and others can also not employ them in alleviating his sufferings, the compensatory function of damages for pain and suffering is ineffective. All the more no substantive reason exists for awarding damages for pain and suffering by way of *periodical payments* if the injured party does not suffer from the consequences of his injuries by being aware of them permanently and constantly. In the present case the Court of Appeal should not have restricted itself to the finding that the plaintiff was generally susceptible to physical and mental sensations in order to allow him on this basis the amount claimed by him. Since the very fact of his injuries excludes any compensation of his non-economic damage or permits it to a very limited extent only, the equitable compensation in money due to the plaintiff must be assessed in figures which are considerably lower than those regarded by the Court of Appeal as appropriate.

(*bb*) Having regard to the so-called purpose of *satisfaction*, the judgment of the Court of Appeal fails to show to what extent it could serve a useful function in assessing damages for pain and suffering beyond constituting a symbolic reparation. For the purposes of the court it is accepted that the plaintiff has suffered very severe brain damage which precludes him from perceiving the full force of his handicaps and from connecting them with the damaging event and with the participation of the defendant. As this Senate has stated before in its decision [reference] referred to above, this circumstance must be taken into account in assessing the amount of damages for pain and suffering. In cases where the injured person cannot really experience satisfaction, the amount of damages which is necessary and appropriate to compensate non-economic loss must be less than that which is usual in other cases.

3. . . .

Case 112

BUNDESGERICHTSHOF (SIXTH CIVIL DIVISION) 11 JANUARY 1983*
BGHZ 86, 212

The plaintiff, a general medical practitioner, was run down by a lorry on 20 September 1976 while walking in Bad Schönborn. The lorry was insured against accidents by the defendant who admitted liability in principle without reservation. The injuries of the plaintiff consisted in several abrasions, bruises, and haemorrhage; in addition he alleges that he suffered a renewed and more severe attack of tachycardia and palpitations, while the defendant denies that these are the results of the accident.

In the proceedings before the Court of First Instance the plaintiff claimed damages on the ground that between 20 September and 19 October 1976 he was not able to attend to his practice and had thus suffered a loss of income.

The District Court of Karlsruhe rejected the claim on the ground that the allegation of the plaintiff in specifying his damages had not been proved. On appeal the plaintiff pursued his claim to a reduced extent only. He pleaded now—correctly, as the defendant admits—that he had closed down his practice as early as 15 September 1976, when he started his vacation for reasons of health in Bad Schönborn. As a result of the accident he had lost twenty-one days of vacation.

The plaintiff contends that the sum of DM 10,873 represents the expenses of a resumed holiday on the basis of the hypothetical cost of a *locum tenens* and in running expenses for employers and maintenance. He argues that the lost vacation must be compensated according to these principles.

The Court of Appeal of Karlsruhe rejected the appeal to this effect. A further appeal by the plaintiff was unsuccessful for the following

Reasons

I. The Court of Appeal has held that the plaintiff's claim for 'spoilt holidays', which admittedly he did not resume, is not justified, even having

* English version by Kurt Lipstein.

regard to the practice initiated by the decision of the Federal Supreme Court [reference]. It referred to the criticism of this decision in the literature and is of the opinion that in any case these principles cannot be extended to the sphere of unjustifiable enrichment. In this context, non-economic damages are here in issue which according to § 253 BGB could only be recovered where an express provision so required.

II. The decision under review cannot be faulted, at least in the result.

1. The Court of Appeal rightly starts from the premiss that the plaintiff cannot claim damages equal to the 'value of the vacation' for having suffered the loss of a holiday which was not taken up later on.

(*a*) In so far as the law of tort is concerned, the damages for the economic consequences to be recovered in the case of injury to the person are mainly restricted to losses of gains and future earnings (§ 843 BGB). The practice of the courts has with good reason interpreted these notions broadly. However, this has not modified the principle that according to the intention of the legislators all loss of enjoyment can only result in damages for pain and suffering (§§ 253, 847 BGB). Thus a direct 'commercialization' assessment of the vacation is excluded.

Accordingly, the Federal Supreme Court has, for instance, denied damages if, as a result of his injuries, a person could not exercise his licence to hunt which he had acquired for payment [reference]. The Court also denied damages for the loss of use of a damaged motor car if during the period in question he was unable to use it—even if the inability of the plaintiff to use the motor car was the result of a personal injury suffered on the occasion of the same accident [references]. The temporary inability to work, too, does not constitute a recoverable head of damages, unless it results in a loss of income [reference].

Similarly, the Federal Supreme Court has disallowed damages for the 'value of a vacation' resulting from damage to an object (a motor car) [reference]. This judgment shows that the Third Civil Senate also shares the opinion that generally a lost period of vacation cannot be treated as an economic loss resulting from the violation of the legal interests mentioned in § 823 I BGB. Normally the same applies in the case of violations of protective laws (§ 823 II BGB). The fact that in an earlier decision [reference] . . . the Third Civil Senate held differently in a case of liability for the violation of official duties (§ 839 BGB) may perhaps be explained by the special connection between the error committed by the customs authorities and the vacation; however, it is unnecessary in this context to discuss this question any further.

(b) This practice is to be maintained in the sphere of torts having regard also to the more recent pronouncements of the Seventh Civil Senate. According to the chain of authorities initiated by the decision [references], it is indeed admissible to claim damages for 'lost holidays' as economic loss if breaches of contract are involved concerning the arrangement for or the performance in kind or by means of services connected with the form of the holidays. These efforts of the Seventh Civil Senate to start a new practice have been superseded by the statutory regulation of the travel contract (§ 651a–k), but its substance has been maintained in essence.

The Seventh Civil Senate clearly intended to create a solution for *this* (contractual) sphere in particular, which satisfies the interest concerned in the absence of a statutory regulation to this effect. The legislature, too, has restricted to this area the new rule, which may be said to limit to a certain extent the principle expressed in § 253 BGB, which also applies in principle to the law of contract. The Seventh Civil Senate did not regard its practice established before the legislative change as conflicting with the practice regarding the law of tort referred to in (a) above, of which it was aware [references]; the reason was that it did not regard itself as precluded from adhering to this practice because it was only concerned with contractual claims. Moreover, it regards its aim as mainly satisfied by the new regulation in the Civil Code which is limited to the law of contract [reference].

Consequently, the present Senate is not precluded from adhering to its practice pertaining to the law of tort. It is unnecessary to determine whether the above-mentioned decisions of the Seventh Civil Senate and the majority of writers [references] have only sought to find a solution by relying on a notion of economic damage which is devised to be of general validity. Objections might be raised against such an attempt. Less emphasis must be placed on the notion of economic damage, the details of which have given rise to theoretical disputes, and stress should be laid on the question whether, having regard to the purpose of the respective grounds of liability, any deleterious effect is still to be treated as economic damage. (For the attribution of consequential damage in the light of the purpose of liability in general, see the recent decision of this Senate—reference.) Accordingly, it seems entirely appropriate to treat the enjoyment of holidays in commercial terms *when*—and only when—the enjoyment of holidays has been made directly or indirectly the object of a contractual performance and if this obligation has been breached. To this extent such a close and clear relationship exists between the contractual duty to act and the interest in enjoying the holiday which had, so to say, been entrusted to the other contracting party that it appears justifiable to attribute to the enjoyment of vacations a commercial character based on the contractual agreement. This court finds support for its view in the observations of Stoll [reference] which are shared to a great extent by Lange [reference]; see also Steffen [reference]; Hagen [reference]. The need to relate the commercial qualifications of damages for loss of enjoyment to the purpose of the basis of liability is also underlined by the decision of the Third Civil Senate of 3 November 1980 [reference] which—contrary to the above-mentioned judgment of this Senate [reference]—envisaged the possibility of damages in respect of the loss of the pleasure of earning a licence to hunt in a case where this licence to hunt had been frustrated illegally.

If it is correct that the loss of enjoyment (in the present case as regards the period of vacation) can only be taken into consideration if another legally protected interest has been violated (e.g. in the present case by injuring health, but also where an object is damaged, such as a motor car needed for holiday travel), it remains necessary to observe the purpose of the provision of § 253 BGB in the absence of a special statutory rule. This is not only in accordance with the statute, but takes into account the undisputable consideration that otherwise an unpredictable expansion of liability in tort would have to be expected. The practice of the Seventh Civil Senate does not fail to perceive this either [references]. The reason is that the loss of the enjoyment of holidays is only one of many conceivable cases in which the loss of enjoyment, while not directly capable of being assessed in economic terms, can nevertheless be attributed a 'commercial' value in certain circumstances. The fact that the area of damage may be incalculable is absent precisely in those cases where the enjoyment of a vacation is directly and clearly connected with the failure to perform contractual duties.

Consequently, this Senate does not believe that its view conflicts with the results of the decisions of the Seventh Civil Senate. The fact that in their reasoning these decisions differ in part from its own considerations is not determining in the view of this Senate, which approves the results reached by those decisions. Therefore they are not opposed to the present decision.

2. The foregoing considerations would not, however, exclude the possibility that in assessing the amount of damages for pain and suffering due to the plaintiff account may be taken of the fact that his injuries (which have proved to have been relatively light) have resulted in the loss of three weeks' vacation . . .

Case 113

BUNDESGERICHTSHOF (SIXTH CIVIL DIVISION) 26 JANUARY 1971*
NJW 1971, 698

The plaintiff is an actress who participated in 1968 in the production of a film for sex education. In a printed sheet advertising the film her picture appeared on the back page in a close embrace with her partner. The defendant sells aphrodisiacs. In nos. 10, 11, and 23 of the 1969 issue of the periodical *Stern* the defendant published advertisements which contained a picture measuring 12 by 50 millimetres, the price (DM 24), and the defendant's address together with the following text:

'Paris love potion. The intimate means for men and women. A modern inducement to love. Overwhelming—seductive—irresistible. A few drops suffice for an immediate reaction'.

The picture included in the advertisement consisted of a partial reproduction measuring 12 by 35 millimetres of the above-mentioned picture of the plaintiff and her partner which figured in the printed sheet advertising the film. The plaintiff did not give her consent to the reproduction of her picture for the purposes of the defendant.

The plaintiff claimed DM 8000 as damages of non-economic loss. The court awarded the plaintiff DM 4000 in respect of non-economic loss and rejected any further claim. The Court of Appeal of Munich rejected the claim in its entirety. The Federal Supreme Court admitted a second appeal, quashed the judgment, and referred the case back to another Senate of the Court of Appeal.

Reasons

The plaintiff does not claim compensation for economic loss which she may have suffered because as a result of the unauthorized publication of her picture she failed to receive a fee. Instead, her claim is expressly for pecuniary compensation in respect of non-economic loss. This is undisputed by the parties. The Court of Appeal, too, proceeds from this assumption.

I. 1. Contrary to the Court of First Instance, the Court of Appeal has rejected the claim simply because it refuses as a matter of fundamental legal principle to award pecuniary damages in cases of violations of the right to personality as compensation for non-economic loss. The Court of Appeal acknowledges that in so holding it acts contrary to a constant and well established practice of the Federal Supreme Court.

2. As the Federal Supreme Court, and in particular this Senate, has consistently held, a person whose right to his personality has been severely vio-

* English version by Kurt Lipstein.

lated in a culpable manner may demand pecuniary compensation for non-economic loss if it is otherwise impossible to compensate satisfactorily for the inflicted harm. The court has felt entitled and also bound in accordance with Art. 1 III of the Constitution to grant this extended remedy in order to take into account in the sphere of the protection of personality of the principles expressed in Arts. 1 and 2 I of the Constitution. The Federal Supreme Court has responded repeatedly to the attacks directed against this development of the law [references]. The observations in the decision appealed against which reproduce a summary of these opinions and adopt them in the result do not constitute a reason for this Senate to discuss this problem again in detail. Its practice, which has since become well established, will be maintained [references].

Other Senates of the Federal Supreme Court have also followed the same practice in principle [references], as has a considerable number of writers [references].

3. In so holding the consideration that an imperative need must exist for granting compensation of this kind is taken into account by two restrictions.

In the first place, the victim of an attack on his right of personality is not to be awarded pecuniary damages unconditionally and in all cases. Instead certain aggravating circumstances must exist if an imperative need is to be recognized for allowing the injured party at least a limited amount of compensation for his non-economic loss by awarding him pecuniary damages. This is only the case if the injury is to be regarded as severe [references].

Further, according to the practice of this Senate the victim of a severe culpable attack upon his right of personality can only demand payment of pecuniary damages by the tortfeasor if the harm which has been inflicted cannot be compensated sufficiently by other means [references]. The grant of a right to pecuniary compensation is based in essence on the idea that otherwise the right of personality would lack sufficient legal protection. In the light of this consideration, the right to pecuniary damages is to be postponed if the injury can be compensated sufficiently by other means; according to the facts of the case the right to demand an order to desist and in particular to retract—rights which have equally been developed by the courts by way of an extension of the law some time ago—may supply an adequate and suitable measure.

In this connection the Court of Appeal is of the opinion that it is sufficient if the victim can redress his injury by means of the other 'remedies' (*Rechtspositionen*) provided by private law, and it refers to the (prevention) injunction. This overlooks that the possibility of applying for an order to desist is directed, according to its purpose and function, against the future infliction of harm but does not affect harm which has already been caused. Moreover—and for this very reason—this possibility fails if there is no danger of repetition. The additional possibility of asking for a retraction is also not suitable in many cases of violation of the right of personality to provide sufficient compensation [reference]. This applies also when—as in the present case—a retraction cannot be considered having regard to the nature and the manner of the injury (by violation of the right to one's own likeness).

4. In the limited circumstances mentioned above, an award of pecuniary compensation for non-pecuniary damage must also be considered in principle when the violation of the right of personality consists in an infringement of the right to one's likeness, as is the case here [references].

5. For these reasons alone the decision of the Court of Appeal, which relied on the arguments set out above, cannot be upheld. Since additional facts must be considered and ascertained, this Senate cannot pronounce itself a final judgment in this matter.

II. The Court of Appeal, correctly having regard to its point of view, did not examine whether by this conduct the defendant has culpably violated the plaintiff's right of personality (§ 823 I BGB) by violating the plaintiff's right to her own likeness (§ 22 of the Act on the Copyright in Works of Art); nor did the Court of Appeal investigate whether according to the principles established by the Federal Supreme Court the existence of non-pecuniary damage suggests a claim to pecuniary damages.

1. The Court of First Instance held that the right to one's own likeness had been violated. The defendant denied this in the proceedings before the District Court but did not argue this point before the Court of Appeal. There are indications that the defendant himself now admits that the plaintiff's right of personality has been violated at least *objectively*. At any rate, the facts before this Senate are sufficient to permit the court below so to hold, at least initially.

(*a*) The court below will have to ascertain as a fact whether the plaintiff could be identified in the advertisement complained of. The circumstance that the partial reproduction was small in size does not exclude that the plaintiff's features are visible and therefore recognizable [reference]. Even if in the present case the picture was published without appending a name, the features taken from the film and reproduced on the back of the sheet advertising it, which has a wide circulation (*Film Kurier*), can lead to the identification of the plaintiff. It suffices for a violation of the right of personality if the person represented by the picture has reasonable grounds for believing that, having regard to the manner of the picture, he can be identified [reference]. Thus this Senate has also stated [reference] that the person affected cannot be required to prove who of the many spectators—the reproduction of a picture in a cinema was in issue—had recognized him in the weekly review of events and had gained the impression that he was a murderer.

(b) It is undisputed that the plaintiff did not consent to the reproduction of her picture for the purposes of the defendant (§ 22 of the Act on the Copyright in Works of Art). It cannot either be disputed seriously in law that the reproduction in issue here was not included by the consent given to the producer of the film. This consent did not extend to a publication which merely served to advertise a product which is not connected with the film, moreover in a manner which violated the right of personality in a particularly harmful manner, as will be shown below. For this reason alone the plaintiff has not lost her entitlement to the rights arising out of such a violation, as the defendant has argued before the Court of First Instance, quite apart from the fact that in the present case her claim for compensation in respect of non-economic loss resulting from an invasion of the right to her personality is in issue.

The publication was also not lawful without her consent (see § 23 of the Act on the Copyright in Works of Art). Even if, as the defendant argued in addition before the Court of First Instance, the plaintiff was to be counted among the personalities of contemporary history—in the meaning of § 23 I, no. 1, of the Act on the Copyright in Works of Art, which need not be decided here, the publication by the defendant is not covered by this exceptional position. The anonymous picture of the plaintiff was not reproduced in her capacity as a personality of contemporary history, as the manner of the publication shows. The publication served exclusively the business interest of the defendant and not a justifiable need of the public to receive objective pictorial information [references].

Furthermore, § 23 II of the Act on the Copyright in Works of Art would create an obstacle. Even if he is a personality of contemporary history, the person whose picture is published can decide whether he is willing to allow his picture to be used as an advertisement for goods or for commercial services.

2. By reproducing the picture of the plaintiff her right of personality was infringed. The infringement is characterized, in particular, by the fact that the defendant used the plaintiff's picture for the purpose of advertising, particularly in a denigrating manner. The publication in the form of a pictorial supplement to the advertisement for the 'Paris love potion' offered by the defendant could lead to the misleading inference that for a consideration the plaintiff had given her consent to an advertisement of this kind.

3. The Court of Appeal, correctly having regard to its point of view, has also not considered and determined whether an objective infringement of the plaintiff's right of personality can be imputed to the defendant as a culpable act in the meaning of § 823 I BGB. When considering this aspect the court below will have to take into account the following:

Having regard to the previous decisions alone, the defendant, acting in accordance with the care required in mutual dealings, could not assume that he was entitled to reproduce the picture of the plaintiff without the latter's consent [reference]. The main question is, however, whether the defendant has failed in his duty of care by omitting to ascertain that the plaintiff had given her consent before he reproduced the preview of the film. Generally speaking, a person who wishes to publish a picture of another must examine of his own motion the extent of his right to reproduce. Consequently, it can be stated with some certainty that, observing the necessary care in mutual dealings, the defendant should have enquired of the printers that supplied the matrix whether the plaintiff had given her consent [reference]. This would seem to apply even more so in the present case, where a photograph of a woman is employed to advertise an aphrodisiac potion.

However, even if the court below should come to the conclusion that the plaintiff's right of personality has been infringed culpably and that therefore liability exists according to § 823 I BGB, the plaintiff is not entitled to a pecuniary compensation in respect of non-pecuniary damage as a matter of course and in all circumstances.

4. According to the practice of the Federal Supreme Court, and in particular of this Senate, as was pointed out before, the imperative need to grant the injured party at least a certain amount of compensation for non-pecuniary loss by awarding pecuniary damages is to be admitted in special aggravating circumstances. As this Senate has stated on several occasions, it must be examined in each individual case, having regard to the manifold possibilities of infringement of the right to personality, whether the injured party whose non-pecuniary loss cannot be compensated by other means is to be awarded pecuniary damages on equitable grounds. An affirmative answer can only be given if the violation is to be regarded as severe. The question as to whether it is to be treated as a severe invasion of personality as a separate protected interest can only be answered on the basis of *all* the facts of the individual case. For this purpose the manner and the severity of the harm inflicted and the degree of blameworthiness must be considered in particular, as well as the cause and the nature of the act. (Constant practice [references].) On this basis the results of the proceedings hitherto

disclose that the following aspects may be significant for the court below in reaching a decision:

In order to assess the *severity of the infringement* it may be relevant that the plaintiff was associated with an advertisement for an aphrodisiac. The impression was created that against payment she allowed her person to be used for such an advertisement by means of her picture. This unfavourable impression was possibly increased by the fact that five additional advertisements by the defendant on p. 156 of *Stern* no. 11, where the advertisement complained of was published, make it clear to the reader that the defendant, as a mail order business also sells other sex appliances and explicit sex literature.

In this connection the contention of the plaintiff may also be relevant that she was known as a film actress and that she appears in the theatre in classical plays. The plaintiff has stated further that she had gone through an apprenticeship in classical works and that in the theatre where she had her first engagement she had played almost exclusively classical roles. In this capacity in particular she had also appeared as a guest in various theatres. The discriminatory (*sic*) publications had, above all, placed her guest engagements in jeopardy. Finally, the *objective* severity of the infringement may be gauged by the fact that the advertisement appeared in three successive issues of the magazine *Stern* which has a big circulation, and that therefore it became widely known.

As regards the *degree of blameworthiness* of the defendant—an affirmative finding in principle to this effect still remains to be made by the Court of Appeal, as was pointed out before—the Court of Appeal will have to consider whether the failure to make enquiries may not have to be regarded as negligent in the light of the special circumstances. The First Civil Senate has given an affirmative answer to this effect in [reference] and has characterized the blameworthiness of the defendant in that case as gross negligence. In this connection the statement of the plaintiff may assume additional relevance that by a letter dated 14 March 1969 written by her lawyer she had warned the defendant after the first advertisement had appeared on 9 March 1969, no. 10 of *Stern*.

The *cause and the motive* of the defendant in acting as he did were clearly egotistic commercial interest and not the satisfaction of a need deserving legal protection to provide information. It certainly does not exclude a finding that the infringement was severe in the meaning of the practice of this court.

Case 114

BUNDESGERICHTSHOF (FIFTH CIVIL SENATE) 22 NOVEMBER 1985*
NJW 1986, 2037

The following questions are submitted to the Great Senate by the Fifth Civil Senate:

1. If the owner of a thing which he uses himself, such as an owner-occupied house, is temporarily unable to use it by reason of a tortious interference with his ownership, does this represent a compensatable economic loss in the absence of any extra expenditure or lost revenue?

2. If such a loss of use is compensatable, how is it to be quantified?

Facts

The plaintiff owns a plot of land on which there is a substantial and well-appointed dwelling, with a living area of about 260 square metres. On the land sloping steeply away from the plaintiff's property the defendant was building some terraced houses. The excavations were improperly executed and the plaintiff's house was rendered temporarily unstable. The city issued an evacuation order, prohibiting occupation of the house between 12 August and 16 September 1981. Repairs to the façade and interior of the house cost DM 5851.75 and DM 340 respectively. In addition to these sums and interest, the plaintiff claimed DM 3000 as compensation for the fact that during the validity of the evacuation order she and her husband had had to live in their dormobile nearby.

The Landgericht upheld the claim for repairs of DM 5998.29, but dismissed the rest of the claim. The Oberlandesgericht dismissed the plaintiff's appeal, but allowed the defendant's appeal on the ground that the plaintiff had received 'new for old' and reduced the damages to DM 3334.90. With the leave of the Oberlandesgericht the plaintiff appealed only as to the claim for DM 3000 for loss of use of the house. The Fifth Civil Senate laid the matter before the Great Senate for Civil Matters.

Reasons

II. As regards the claim in issue the court below found that between 12 August and 16 September 1981 the plaintiff and her husband were unable to occupy their house by reason of the local authority's evacuation order, and had instead lived in their dormobile which was equipped with all proper conveniences. The court held that the temporary loss of use of their

---

* Translated by Tony Weir.

dwelling, though complete, did not constitute an economic loss but only a non-economic loss incapable of compensation.

III. The Fifth Civil Senate was of the same opinion but regarded the question as one of principle and sought a decision from the Great Senate for Civil Matters as being necessary to resolve divergent views in the courts (§ 137 GVG).

IV. There is indeed a divergence of views between five of the senates of the Bundesgerichtshof on the question of damages for loss of use of chattels and realty.

1. At the outset we have decisions of the Third and Sixth Civil Senates on the temporary loss of use of a motor vehicle involved in an accident [references].

(*a*) Decisions of 1964 and 1966 [references] recognize that the owner of a motor vehicle, including one for private and personal use, which he is unable to use while accident damage is being repaired can claim lump-sum damages for economic loss even when he has not hired a substitute or incurred extra expenditure or lost any income (most recently BGHZ 89, 60 (63) = NJW 1984, 722).

(*b*) In order to stem the tide of liability numerous limitations have been introduced, as to the basis and *quantum* of the claim. Money damages (§ 251 BGB) are awarded only if the loss of use is 'actually felt' by the victim (ibid.). No compensatable harm thus arises when a purely abstract possibility of use is frustrated (BGHZ 45, 212 (219) = NJW 1966, 1260) or when a power of disposition is affected (BGHZ 55, 146 (150) = NJW 1971, 796— the hunting rights case); the courts require an ability and an intention to use (BGH NJW 1985, 2471—military ambulance). Compensation has even been refused when the reason the owner could not have used his vehicle while under repair was that he himself had been injured (BGH NJW 1968, 1778).

Exceptions to these exceptions are made where the vehicle would have been used by members of the owner's family or even his fiancée (BGH NJW 1975, 922).

Damages for loss of use were denied in a case in which the victim could reasonably be expected to use a second car which was not needed for other purposes [references]. In other cases damages for the maintenance cost of a vehicle held in reserve have been allowed (BGHZ 32, 280 (284) = NJW 1960, 1339—tram in Bremen; BGHZ 70, 199 (201) = NJW 1978, 812—bus in Bremen; see also BGH NJW 1985, 2471).

A victim who rents a smaller car cannot add to the actual hire costs a sum representing the difference in use-value of the two vehicles (BGH NJW

1967, 552) but instead of claiming the hire for the rented car he may claim a lump sum for the loss of use of his own car (BGH NJW 1970, 1120).

If purely personal reasons prevent the owner from using his vehicle, for example where his driving licence has not been properly safeguarded, the Third Civil Senate finds no compensatable harm (BGHZ 65, 170, 173 ff. = NJW 1975, 2341), but if there is an invasion affecting the thing itself, the loss of use is in principle compensatable, and the courts find such an invasion even where there is no physical damage but use is prevented by some factual or legal obstacle (see BGHZ 85, 11 (15, 16) = NJW 1982, 2304; but note that the Fleet case there mentioned (BGHZ 55, 153 (159) = NJW 1971, 886) was a case of lost profits under § 252 BGB). The Third Civil Senate has occasionally allowed cases where the car's documents were withheld (BGHZ 40, 345 (351) = NJW 1964, 542) or a garage entry blocked (BGHZ 63, 203 (206) = NJW 1975, 347).

(c) The Bundesgerichtshof has also sought to limit the amount of the lump sum payable for loss of use. In order to avoid any element of profit, the Sixth Civil Senate deducts from the gross hire charges for a comparable substitute all the elements of cost which the commercial hirer adds to the 'true use value' (BGHZ 45, 212, 220 = NJW 1966, 1260; BGHZ 56, 214, 218 ff., 222 = NJW 1971, 1692), and makes a further deduction for the plaintiff's savings, taking the notional rental cost of a similar car as merely an 'indicator' (see BGH NJW 1970, 1120). Finally it regarded as sufficient a sum 'well in excess of the cost of a car not in use' (BGHZ 56, 214 (215 ff.) = NJW 1971, 1692). In the end result the daily tariff amounts to 25–30 per cent of the hire cost of a comparable vehicle. The details are given in tables prepared for the use of liability-insurers and the courts, and endorsed by the Bundesgerichtshof as legally accurate [references].

2. The Eighth Civil Senate has carried these decisions over into the area of contractual liability and extended them to cases where a debtor is in delay in delivering a car or its documents (BGHZ 88, 11 = NJW 1983, 2139, where the Court of Appeal awarded DM 21.50 per day, a total of DM 1075 for 50 days' loss of use).

3. In cases involving chattels other than motor cars the Bundesgerichtshof has not yet treated loss of use as a form of economic harm.

In BGHZ 63, 393 (= NJW 1975, 733) the purchaser of a fur coat in a claim for damages for non-performance sought DM 1700 because the coat had been unusable for four years while futile alterations were constantly being made, but the Eighth Civil Senate held that this was not economic harm. The same Senate held likewise in the caravan case (BGHZ 86, 128 (130) = NJW 1983, 444) where a camping site operator who had leased space for the caravan refused access to it for 311 days under the pretext that the rent had not been paid. Here the plaintiff claimed DM 311 × 15 = DM 4665.

In the motor-boat case (BGHZ 89, 60 = NJW 1984, 722) the boat was damaged in a road accident and rendered unavailable for the owner's holiday and subsequent weekends. He claimed DM 6160 as forty days' loss of use at DM 154 per day (the daily hire cost for a similar boat being DM 280), but the Sixth Civil Senate saw in the temporary loss of use only a 'diminution of the individual's pleasure' and a 'non-economic harm'.

4. Divergent decisions have also been rendered in cases involving temporary loss of use or deprivation of enjoyment of real property.

(*a*) In the case decided by the Third Civil Senate on 11 July 1963 (NJW 1963, 2020) the plaintiff property owner had been badly affected by excessive noise and small emanating from an official military clubhouse, but had remained in occupation and had not had to accept a lower price for the house. The Third Civil Senate did not award damages for economic harm, but awarded compensation for the reduction of the 'monthly enjoyment-value of the property'. In BGHZ 91, 20 (28) = NJW 1984, 1876 the Third Civil Senate awarded 'compensation for expropriatory invasion' to the owner-occupier of a dwelling affected by smells emanating from a communal distillery, and approved the quantum awarded by the trial court with reference to the probable reduction in the monthly rent hypothetically obtainable.

(*b*) When an owner was temporarily unable to use his house owing to malfunction of the heating due to the fault of the outgoing tenant, the Eighth Civil Senate awarded him damages for the abstract loss of use, and said that it was immaterial if the house had been used for purposes other than occupation (NJW 1967, 1803). Whether the same result would have been reached in tort was left open.

(*c*) The Fifth Civil Senate has twice denied the existence of economic harm in assessing damages for delay. In BGHZ 66, 277 = NJW 1976, 1630 a person for whom a dwelling was being constructed could not move into it until seven months after the due date, owing to the contractor's fault, and had to stay in his previous smaller house during that period. The Senate denied that the loss of enjoyment, valued at a monthly rental of DM 2000, constituted economic harm. The decision was the same in BGHZ 71, 234 = NJW 1978, 1805, concerning a claim by the purchaser of an apartment yet to be constructed, where the Senate said that neither the servicing of the capital deployed during the eight month delay (for the price had been paid on time) nor the community taxes assessable during that period constituted economic loss.

(*d*) In the swimming-pool case (BGHZ 76, 179 = NJW 1980, 1386) the Seventh Civil Senate hesitated to adopt the view of the Fifth Civil Senate that temporary loss of the chance of using a dwelling or apartment does not constitute economic harm, but found no economic harm when a private swimming pool for a housing complex had been badly designed and was unusable for the eight months it took to put it right. By contrast in a decision on 10 October 1985 (NJW 1986, 427) the Seventh Civil Senate, applying the law relating to the contract for work and materials, held that economic harm did exist when an underground garage with six parking places to service an apartment block was unusable for twenty-two months because of inadequate corrective measures.

(*e*) In a tort case of blast-damage (BGHZ 75, 366 (370 ff.) = NJW 1980, 775) the Fifth Civil Senate held that there was no economic harm where the use of property had been partially obstructed rather than totally prevented. In that case the authorities had temporarily forbidden the use of a house in danger of collapse, but the owner had nevertheless established a bedroom in the cellar and had continued to occupy half of the ground floor despite the prohibition.

V. This divergence of decisions in the Bundesgerichtshof on the question of damages for loss of use is not calculated to advance legal certainty. The decisions contain no clear criterion to distinguish between economic harm and non-economic harm (§ 253 BGB) or to distinguish the different types of case; nor is it clear whether the question should be treated differently in contract and in tort. The variety and incompatibility of the reasoning offered in support of the decisions reflects itself in different tests for the *quantum* of recovery.

. . .

VI. 1. According to the decisions of the Bundesgerichtshof the question whether compensatable economic harm has occurred is to be answered with reference to the *theory of difference*: one compares the economic situation produced by the occurrence said to involve liability with the situation which would exist had it not occurred [references] . . .

2. According to the theory of difference no economic harm exists in the present case . . .

3. There do not seem to be any plausible, let alone compelling, reasons for holding that the mere loss of the benefit of use constitutes economic harm calling for compensation . . .

[The Senate discusses invasion of 'exclusive rights' and industrial property rights.]

(*bb*) To recognize as compensatable the harm consisting of loss of use in these cases would conflict with the principle of the law of liability expressed in § 252 BGB. It is true that § 252 sentence 2 BGB modifies the burden of proof in cases of lost profit (BGH NJW 1983, 758) but it permits rebuttal. If the victim intended to profit from the use of the thing (such as a commercial vehicle) during the period it was out of commission he is entitled to the profit presumed by the law unless the defendant proves that that profit would not have been made even if the damage had not occurred. The money damages legally due are payable not for the abstract loss of a possibility of use but because in the particular circumstances the occurrence probably made an economic difference [references]. The loss of the possibility of use is a source of potential harm, not an economic harm in itself [references]. The law allows the defendant to show that the planned used would have been wasteful rather than profitable [references]. Otherwise the law of liability would be preferring consumption to production, and nothing in the positive law justifies such a paradoxical result. Only in certain exceptional cases does the law provide for computation of harm *in abstracto* in order to facilitate the disposition of certain obligational relationships, usually arising by way of contract (see § 376 II, III HGB).

(*ee*) In sum, the values implicit in the law afford no basis for saying that in cases of invasion of an absolute right of disposition, damage to use in the abstract should be recognized, let alone at the rate of a hypothetical rental. All the more recent cases avoid adopting such a wide principle which would indeed undermine the effort of all the Senates concerned to restrict the extension of liability for loss of use.

(*b*) In its decision of 11 July 1963, already cited, the Eighth Civil Senate invoked decisions of the Bundesgerichtshof relating to loss of use of motor vehicles. Even in the special area of motor accidents the reasoning is open to question, and the desirable tendency of several Senates of the Bundesgerichtshof has been not to generalize this principle but to confine it to that particular area (most hesitant, BGHZ 66, 277 (279 ff.) = NJW 1976, 1630; 'The doctrinal basis for decisions concerning the use-potential of motor cars is insufficiently insecure to justify its extension to other areas').

(*aa*) The main argument which already figures in BGHZ 45, 212 (216) = NJW 1966, 1260 was one of fairness, that it is an 'unsatisfying result' to allow the tortfeasor (and his liability insurer) to escape all liability for lost use simply by an unjustified refusal to meet the (temporary) claim for natural restitution in the form of provision of, or payment for the hire of, a substitute vehicle under § 249 sentences 1 and 2 respectively BGB. But this is to ignore the basic distinction drawn by the legislator: whereas the primary remedy of restitution *in natura* is not limited to the replacement of economic losses and provides certain other advantages, the secondary and subsidiary remedy of money damages (§§ 251, 252 BGB) expressly excludes compensation for non-economic harm. Such differences as exist between restitution *in natura* and compensation in money result from the structure deliberately adopted by the legislator.

A further argument of fairness has appeared since BGHZ 56, 214 (216) = NJW 1971, 1692, namely that it is unfair that the tortfeasor should benefit from the victim's decision to forgo the convenience of a substitute vehicle. But this is inconsistent with the legislator's decision that compensation for mere inconvenience and discomfort can be granted only in the exceptional cases of §§ 847, 1300 BGB (see now § 651 BGB). This argument loses its force where liability is strict, as in the case of the guardian of a motor vehicle under § 7 StVG, and is in any case incompatible with the attempt of the courts to grant only the cost of keeping, not using, the car rather than the full cost of a hypothetical rental: for this too confers a deplorable 'benefit' on the tortfeasor and his insurer.

(*bb*) The so-called 'commercialization' idea is not convincing either (leading case: BGH NJW 1956, 1234; followed in BGHZ 40, 345 (349 ff.) = NJW 1964, 542). This holds that a pleasure or convenience, far from being uneconomic, constitutes an independent economic value if it is commonly capable of being obtained for money, that is 'bought' or 'commercialized'; to diminish such a pleasure is to depreciate its monetary equivalent. Writers have rightly criticized the baselessness of the premise that economic harm arises every time anything 'commercialized' is affected [references]. So many pleasures today are to be had for money that this test hardly serves to distinguish economic from non-economic harm, and recent cases, rather sceptical of the 'commercialization' idea, use it as subsidiary, if at all [references]. This Senate shares such reserve [references].

(*cc*) The prevalent view of the Bundesgerichtshof is that the only valid and decisive touchstone for discerning economic harm as regards compensation for loss of use of vehicles and other things, moveable or not, is 'public perception'. (The Fifth Civil Senate has stood aloof (BGHZ 66, 277 (279) = NJW 1976, 1630).) The Third Civil Senate [references] and even more the Sixth Civil Senate [references] find it decisive that in the public perception today, the temporary loss of use of a vehicle is seen as economic loss because the availability of a car is apt to save time and effort even outside working hours so that the advantages thereby afforded are regarded as 'money' [references].

. . .

As a matter of principle it must be said that 'public perception' is not a source of law . . .

One factual objection is that this 'public perception' is not usually ascertained empirically but is simply assumed by the judges in the case. Reference to 'public perception' not empirically ascertained may often be a shorthand justification for a solution prompted by the value-judgments of the court [references]. This can lead to an unacceptable degree of legal uncertainty, and has actually done so on this very question. Courts that actually wanted to ascertain the relevant 'public perception' would be led into an unduly and impractically wide range of related sociological questions.

(*ee*) In order to limit liability for loss of use several Senates of the Bundesgerichtshof have adopted the test of whether it was 'actually felt'. This is inconsistent with positive law.

Thus in BGHZ 40, 345 (353) = NJW 1964, 542 the Third Civil Senate said that there were cases 'in which the temporary loss of possession or potential use of a vehicle was not felt by the victim and so involved, from the economic point of view, no loss'. The Sixth Civil Senate has adopted this test (BGHZ 45, 212 (219) = NJW 1966, 1260), and both Senates have drawn consequences from it, some of which limit its scope.

These limitations may have been necessary as a matter of policy in order to contain the spread of liability in cases of motor accidents, but this is only a further indication that the original decisions on loss of use of a vehicle went too far. The requirement that an economic loss be 'felt' in order to be compensatable is foreign to the law of liability. A millionaire who loses a small profit can claim compensation for that loss by the clear terms and obvious intent of § 252 BGB even if the effect of his failure to increase his wealth is imperceptible to him; at the other end, a person hopelessly burdened with debt can claim compensation for a further liability even if it does not perceptibly worsen his economic plight [references]. To limit compensation for harm to such harm as is 'actually felt' runs counter to the legal principle of reparation in full [references].

(*c*) Finally, it is not really a question whether any standards otherwise recognized by law can be found for the evaluation in money terms of a temporary loss of use [references]. The absence of such standards indeed suggests that loss of use is not a separate economic loss [references], but not *vice versa*. The value of the use of a thing is not a value separate from and independent of the value of the thing itself, but is indiscernibly involved in its market value. A diminution of the value of the use of a thing usually leads to a drop in its market value, and making up the market value automatically compensates for loss of use-value [references].

As a matter of accounting there is an additional loss related to the duration of the loss of use which is not compensated if the loss is subsequently made good, namely periodic costs not related to actual use, which must be incurred if the thing is to be available for use [references]; in the case of a motor vehicle these would include the vehicle licence fee and the liability insurance premium. These are independent of the individual circumstances of the owner and, unlike purchase price where there is no price control, can be compensated without practical difficulties because they are the same for all and are easily ascertained. Nevertheless, there are serious objections to giving damages even in respect of these items.

These costs are not caused by the occurrence which leads to the loss of use [references], and in principle damages are payable only for harm caused by the occurrence which entails liability [references]. To the extent that the basic cost of keeping a vehicle in reserve in order to forestall harm is treated as compensatable [references] this is because of the close connection between preventing harm and mitigating harm (as required by § 254 BGB; see BGHZ 32, 280 (295) = NJW 1960, 1339); these decisions can also be justified on causal grounds if one regards the deployment of the reserve vehicle as an effect of the tortious occurrence [references].

. . .

One can get round these causal problems by concentrating not on the expenditures themselves but on their 'equivalent', namely the use of the thing so facilitated, and treating the expenditures as a measure of the monetary value of the loss of use [references]. This does not, however, get us any further forward. It is true that a rule limited to these basic costs (tax, insurance) is not open to the usual objection that a thing does not have value simply because money has been spent on procuring it, much less the value of the expenditure [references]. But it *is* open to the objection that contrary to the principles of the law of liability it leads to a preference for consumption over production (see above **VI.** 3(*a*), (*bb*)). In the case of a thing put to commercial use, such as an apartment block used for rent, these basic costs reduce the profit and so diminish the damages payable for lost profits, the only compensatable item (§ 252 BGB); thus these costs are at the risk of the owner. It would be inconsistent with this legislative apportionment of risks to make the tortfeasor pay for the 'frustrated' basic costs in cases of the loss of consumer use of goods.

. . .

VII. Should the Great Senate decide, on whatever grounds, to hold that damages may be claimed in tort for loss of use of things used by their owner personally, such as an owner-occupied house, there will be the further problem of the quantification of such loss.

. . .

2. In the light of the decided cases the position of the Fifth Civil Senate is as follows:

(*a*) The Sixth Civil Senate is right to hold that the notional rental value of a substitute (or the reduction in rental value in cases where enjoyment is merely impaired) cannot be used directly as a standard of measurement. The enjoyment of a thing by its owner is not profit-orientated but constitutes consumption of investment in future enjoyment, so no loss of profit is involved in the temporary loss or impairment of enjoyment. Since tort law must not result in enrichment, the notional rental must be purged of all elements of profit. Accordingly the notional rental cannot, contrary to the view of the Seventh Civil Senate, be treated as the 'decisive' factor in the computation [references].

(*b*) The best approach is that of the Sixth Civil Senate, namely to do the sums 'from the bottom up', though indeed the basic costs (tax, insurance) are non-compensatable in the light of § 252 BGB, as was shown by the comparison with loss of use of commercial property (above **VI.** 3(*a*), (*bb*)). But the idea of 'modest addition' must be rejected as unsupported by any sound doctrine, despite the attempts by Dunz to support it [references]. For Dunz the 'addition' is simply 'a rebuttable lump-sum for typical consequential harm' [references]. In relating this 'addition' to the extra time and effort spent by the victim on the widespread assumption that 'time means money' even outside working hours, Dunz is being inconsistent with positive law (above **VI.** 3(*b*), (*dd*)). To the extent that he has in mind extra expenses such as tram tickets and gratuities to courtesy drivers, one would have to set against them the petrol costs, maintenance costs, wear and tear and other, probably higher, expenses, involved in using one's own vehicle. The 'modest addition' is unjustified and unnecessary.

Case 115

BUNDESGERICHTSHOF (GREAT SENATE) 9 JULY 1986*
NJW 1987, 50

The Fifth Civil Division submitted the following questions to the Great Senate:

(1) If the owner of a thing which he uses himself, such as an owner-occupied house, is temporarily unable to use it by reason of a tortious interference

* Translated by Tony Weir.

with his ownership, does this represent a compensatable economic loss in the absence of any extra expenditure or lost revenue?

(2) If such a loss of use is compensatable, how is it to be quantified?

The Great Senate gave the following answer:

The owner of property which he himself uses, such as an owner-occupied house, who is temporarily deprived of its use as a result of a tort may be able to claim damages therefore as constituting an economic loss, despite the absence of extra expense or lost revenue.

Reasons

. . .

III. The Great Senate is of the view that, leaving aside cases involving cars for personal use, a compensatable economic loss arises when the owner of a thing is temporarily deprived of its use by a tort if (1) his domestic economy depends on the constant availability of the thing, such as the house he occupies, and (2) he would actually have used it during the period of deprivation. With this limitation the award of damages is permitted by law and does not imperil legal certainty; indeed, it is necessary to give compensation for such deprivations in order to ensure the full and just compensation of economic losses.

1. The BGB does not define the concepts of 'patrimony' or 'economic harm', but leaves it to writers and courts to flesh them out. In order to ascertain whether the plaintiff has suffered patrimonial harm, the Bundesgerichtshof generally follows the Reichsgericht in applying the 'difference method', and compares his present economic situation with what it would have been had the harmful occurrence not taken place. The Fifth Civil Division is right to say that the temporary loss of personal use is not reflected in such a computation, which apart from replacement costs discloses only the income lost if the thing would have been used to produce income or the savings made if it would have involved costs and liabilities.

(*a*) But the Bundesgerichtshof has come to realize that while this accounting operation is value-neutral, the courts must still determine what items are to be included in the account in the light of the protective function of tort liability and the compensatory function of damages.

In this sense the difference method, which is not actually enjoined by the law [references], takes on a normative aspect [references]. While it is true that economic loss will always reflect itself in an increase on the debit side or a decrease on the credit side, it is for the law to decide what items are to be included on the balance-sheet for the purposes of compensation.

(b) Such a balance-sheet must take account of the fact that wealth is significant not just in its actuality but also in its potentiality, as enabling its owner to realize his goals in life [references], a function protected by law.

If, looking only to money, the system gave compensation only for loss of the commercial use of property, it would be ignoring the gain that comes from domestic use also, deprivation of which, though not expressed in loss of income, can comparably affect the owner's economic sphere. Thus a motor vehicle not only often represents the major item in a private person's property but is commonly the very basis of his domestic economy and lifestyle, especially if he uses it for his profession. Even more clearly, the decision to answer one's living needs by buying a home is largely based on economic considerations.

The price reflects the market's valuation of such goods precisely as domestic goods, and recognizes their temporary loss as a devaluation of them. If it puts an evident constraint on the owner's housekeeping, as when he would otherwise have used the thing, only an approach which dealt exclusively in monetary loss and gain, an approach not required by the notion of 'patrimony', would regard this as economically insignificant.

2. Nor is § 252 BGB compelling here. Where a thing is put to productive commercial use, loss of use is essentially shown by loss of profit, compensation for which is expressly provided for by § 252 sentence 1 BGB. This provision emphasises the importance attached by the legislator to loss of productive use in goods in commerce, and there is no comparable provision for the domestic use of goods.

But we cannot agree with the Fifth Civil Division that the law has set its face against damages for deprivation of domestic use of goods not resulting in any loss of income. Unlike provisions in earlier codes, § 252 BGB is principally designed to make it clear that damages extend to the whole economic loss regardless of the degree or type of fault which causes it [references]; to this extent the provision follows through the mandate of full compensation implied in § 249 BGB; § 252 sentence 2 BGB fits into this scheme, though hitherto the courts have seen it only as alleviating the burden of proof so as to let the plaintiff obtain proper compensation for harm which is often difficult to prove, an aim also furthered by § 287 ZPO [references]. Though the law is geared to productive use, it can be extended so as to embrace analogous domestic use without putting such a claimant in a better position as regards proof as feared by the Fifth Civil Division provided that damages are not given *in abstracto*, which the BGB permits only exceptionally (see §§ 288, 290, 849 BGB). For this purpose the courts have added the requirement, in the case of motor vehicles, that the loss of use be 'actually felt', that the victim was willing and able to use the vehicle during the period of deprivation and would actually have used it. If this limitation is carried over to other property, the victim's position as regards proof will be comparable in cases of commercial and domestic use respectively, and it will be easy enough to relate damages for loss of domestic use to the actual harm affecting the victim's estate without setting up any tariff for different types of case.

. . .

4. Any such extension of the law must certainly be limited to property on whose continuing availability domestic arrangements typically depend. Further extension would go beyond the need to give similar treatment to commercial and domestic property and might lead to granting compensation for non-economic harm, contrary to § 253 BGB; the law might become unpredictable and damages difficult to assess.

(*a*) In permitting compensation only for economic loss, § 253 seeks to limit damages to cases where objectively measurable harm occurs: when awarding damages the judge should find not on the uncontrollably subjective valuation tendered by the victim but on the valuation generally attributed to that interest by the market. The legislator also wanted to avoid any monetization of 'ideal' interests [references]. If things one uses in private life are rendered unusable, one's mode of life is inevitably affected, but compensation cannot be given for all such inconvenience without giving damages for purely personal harm, which § 253 definitively renders non-compensatable, in cases of tort at any rate. It may be different on contract cases since the parties may contract out of § 253 just as they may agree that economic interests should have less protection. But so far as goods of vital importance to general daily living are concerned, there is no risk of an undue extension of damages in the non-economic area, for not only does their use in the domestic economy clearly relate to the economic sphere [references] but their prevalence and function make it possible to measure at least their economic core by means of objective standards, eschewing subjective factors peculiar to the victim personally. To this extent, at any rate, the fact that such anfractuosities would not show up in a commercial balance-sheet is not a conclusive argument against their compensatability.

. . .

(*c*) Decisions of the Bundesgerichtshof have staked out the bounds of liability for loss of use of motor vehicles, a situation where the plethora of cases makes it necessary to ignore some of the differences between individuals as regards the importance of the thing.

We need not now determine the range of property, apart from motor cars, whose temporary loss of use calls for compensation on the principles already stated. But the temporary loss of use of a home tortiously affected, as in the case in hand, can clearly constitute an economic loss.

It hardly needs saying that one's domestic economy and mode of life centre on the home and that its continuing availability for occupation is a central item in daily life and intrinsic to one's whole wealth. This very instance shows how unfair it would be to limit damages to loss of commercial use, to regard loss of domestic use not as a loss in itself but only as a source of possible loss, and to leave uncompensated the person who forbears to rent alternative accommodation: it would be an unjustifiable preference for investment in production over investment in consumption. It may be justifiable to refuse damages in cases of temporary impairment of use which the victim can reasonably temper by alternative measures he can be expected to adopt, but where the house in which the owner would have lived is rendered wholly uninhabitable even for a time, the principle that economic harm must be paid for in full requires compensation to be made.

IV. It must be for the courts to work out on a case-by-case basis methods for quantifying loss of use which are suited to the kind of property involved and the way it is treated. The only legal constraints are that quantification must satisfy the requirements of compensation, that is, apply objective standards as indicated by § 253 BGB and treat like cases alike.

It would be wrong in principle to grant damages on the basis of what it would have cost the owner to rent a substitute article for the period of deprivation. We are concerned with compensation, not reparation, and compensation is based not on the savings effected by having a thing of one's own but on the monetary value of having one's own thing to use. Nor can the owner claim what he might have charged the tortfeasor for the use of the thing. Such a method of computation may be justified in special instances of conflicting interests, but it is inconsistent with the general principles of damages law. Compensation is for the loss of domestic use, not for the loss of profit from a rental contract with a third party which the owner never dreamed of entering.

Nevertheless the rental market may provide a basis for measuring the loss once the rental charge has been carefully purged of all elements related to profit-making. So, too, may the basic post-acquisition costs related to the period of loss of use (interest in capital tied up, recurrent costs of keeping the property available, depreciation). And, contrary to the view of the Fifth Civil Division there is nothing wrong in this context with adding a modest supplement to the minimum sum at which the market would put the basic costs of having a thing to use, in order to take account of the fact that the fall-out effects on a person's economy of the unavailability of such property may be very difficult to track down in detail. The mention of these possible ways of measuring the loss is not, however, intended to exclude other appropriate methods.

5

Annex: Recent Decisions

Case III

BUNDESGERICHTSHOF (SIXTH CIVIL DIVISION)
16 NOVEMBER 1993*
NJW 1994, 788

Facts

THE first and second plaintiffs are the parents of a girl born in 1982 with a mental and physical handicap. Suspecting that they might have an abnormal genetic disposition, they were, in August 1983, referred by their GP to the Department of Clinical Genetics (run by the first defendant) of the Institute of Anthropology and Human Genetics of the University (third defendant), because they wished to be advised, prior to deciding on a second pregnancy, of the possibility of an adverse hereditary disposition. The second defendant, a doctor at the Institute's clinic, made tests and on 27 October 1983 and wrote a report, which was signed by himself and the first defendant. Copies of this report, informing the two plainitffs that an inherited adverse disposition was very unlikely and that the couple should not be dissuaded from further pregnancies, were also sent to their GP. On 6 March 1985, the third plaintiff was born with the same mental and physical handicaps as the first child. The plaintiffs, believing that the genetic consultation and advice had been faulty, claimed damages from the defendants. The first and second defendants requested the court to clarify whether they were liable to make compensation for any current and future material losses stemming from the third plaintiff's brain damage, as far as these claims have not been transferred to the social security bodies. The second and third plaintiffs also demanded damages for pain and suffering.

---

* Translated by Irene Snook.

The Landgericht rejected the claim. On appeal by the first and second plaintiff, the Oberlandesgericht declared that the first defendant must compensate the (first and second) plaintiffs for all current and future losses originating from the birth of the third plaintiff, including the entire costs of living. The Court also decided that the first and second defendant are liable as joint and several debtors to pay the second plaintiff damages for pain and suffering for the birth of the third plaintiff. The Court rejected all other claims. By this further appeal, the first and second defendants requested that the Landgericht decision be restored; the first and second plaintiff (hereinafter: 'the plaintiffs') claimed that the third defendant should be included in the decision on liability. The third plaintiff's further appeal was withdrawn. This Division only accepted the first defendant's further appeal in so far as it concerned the claim for financial losses. The further appeal was unsuccessful.

Reasons

I. The Appeal Court held that the first defendant was liable for his breach of the consultation contract, including his liability for the breach committed by the second defendant as employee perfoming his obligation (§ 278 BGB).
. . .

II. The further appeal fails to challenge the Appeal Court's reasoning.

1. In respect of the contract of genetic consultation, the further appeal unsuccessfully challenges the first defendant's status as the mainly liable contractual partner. . . .

According to the findings of the Court of Appeal, the plaintiffs were referred for genetic counselling by their GP to the department run by the first defendant of the institute run by the third defendant. The Appeal Court also correctly ascertained that the first defendant was authorised by the National Health Service to provide this kind of service. . . .

In view of this situation, the Appeal Court followed the principle repeatedly expressed by this Division (BGHZ 100, 363 [367 *et seq.*]; BGHZ 105 , 189 [194]; BGHZ 120, 376 [382 *et seq.*]) that the first and second plaintiffs only entered into a contract with the first defendant, since the out-patient treatment of National Health patients is not first and foremost the duty of the body running the hospital, but is rather that of the approved National Health doctor or the chief consultant appointed for National Health patients. As a result, a National Health patient only enters into a contract with the chief consultant running the out-patient National Health department, and not with the hospital even where the GP's referral names the hospital (BGHZ 105, 189 [194]). . . .

A genetic consultation is not an alternative to out-patient and in-house treatment but is rather a form of out-patient treatment . . . The first defendant, not the Institute itself, was the person authorised by the National Health organisation to provide such counselling, . . . Internal arrangements as to payment between the doctor and the Institute cannot alter the fact that as regards the consultancy contract, the duly appointed chief consultant was the plaintiffs' contractual partner.

2. The further appeal unsuccessfully challenges the opinion of the Court of Appeal that the counselling by the second defendant (for which the first defendant is reponsible) was wrong . . .

(a) . . . According to the undisputed findings of the Court of Appeal, the question whether the first-born child suffered from genetic or prenatal damage was at the time of consultation left unanswered. The Appeal Court, therefore, held that the letter written on 27 October 1983 by the first and second defendants, stating that (a) an adverse inherited disposition was extremely unlikely and an as yet unknown prenatal damage was the most likely cause of the disabilities; (b) a repetition was not to be expected; and (c) a further pregnancy should not be dissuaded, misrepresented this uncertainty. In view of the open-ended medical results, the advice which the parents derived from this letter was not sound enough. The genetic counselling should have made this point clear.

The further appeal submits that the letter had been sent to the GP, and the plaintiffs had only been sent a copy of it . . . In view of the clear statements contained in the defendants' letter, the further appeal fails to show how the GP could have advised his patients as to possible risks along any other lines . . . For its opinion that the risks had been assessed too optimistically and that the recommendations had been insufficiently safe, the Appeal Court could unreservedly rely on expert advice. . . .

The Court of Further Appeal does not doubt that the lower court's findings show a connection between the tortious act (the wrongful consultation) and the resulting damage; had the consultation been complete and correct, the plaintiffs would not have had another child. The Appeal Court correctly held that the damage claimed resulted from a breach of duty which the first defendant had under the consultancy contract, since the genetic consultation was intended to prevent the birth of a genetically damaged child by allowing the parents to make a reasoned decision. The Appeal Court held that there existed a sufficient with the protective purpose of the consultancy contract if any kind of genetic damage to the third plaintiff was at least a factor contributing to any mental or physical handicap. In view of the facts of the case this could be easily ascertained: both children had the same symptoms of damage, suggesting a combination of genetic and exogenic damage. As regards the third plaintiff, mere prenatal damage could, for all intents and purposes, be ruled out . . .The fact that the exact nature of the third claimant's established genetic damage could not be exactly ascertained, prevents neither the finding of a causal connection between the wrongful advice and the birth of a genetically damaged child, nor the inclusion of the damage to health under the scope of protection of theconsultancy contract since by this contract all possible genetical damage was to be excluded . . .

3. The further appeal fails in so far as it opposes the finding that the plaintiffs' claim for damages comprises the total costs of living necessary for the third plaintiff. . . .

(b) In view of the findings of the Court of Appeal that the plaintiffs would have refrained from having another child if they had fully and correctly been advised on the genetic implications, the opinion of the Court of Appeal is in line with the case law of this Division, according to which the costs of maintenance resulting from the birth of the further child can be claimed from the wrongly advising doctor as damages for breach of the consultancy contract. This Division has decided this point on a number of occasions for comparable groups of cases, i.e. for cases of (a) wrong advice on the prevention of the birth of a severely prenatally damaged child (BGHZ 86, 240 et seq.; BGHZ, 89, 95 et seq; NJW 1987, 2923), (b) failed sterilisation (BGHZ 76, 249 et seq.; BGHZ 76, 259 et seq; VersR 1980, 719; NJW 1981, 630; NJW 1981, 2002 ; NJW 1984, 2625; NJW 1992, 2961), and (c) failed (permissible) abortions (BGHZ 95, 199; NJW 1985, 2752; NJW 1985, 671; NJW 1985, 2749; VersR 1986, 869; NJW 1992, 1556). The facts of this case provide no reasons why the principles developed for those cases cannot be applied to a case where the parents of a handicapped child, before procreation of another child, undergo genetic counselling in order to prevent the risk of giving birth to a second handicapped child.

(c) The Second Division of the Bundesverfassungsgericht (Federal Constitutional Court) in its decision of 28 May 1993 (NJW 1993, 1751 et seq.*), headnote no. 14, and in its reasons under D V 6, expressed its doubts as regards the decisions of this Division. Although the remarks of the Bundesverfassungsgericht are not binding on this Court, and this Division has already repeatedly and critically reviewed its own previous findings (see BGHZ 76, 249 [252] and NJW 1984, 2625), a further detailed analysis of the legal position is called for.

The Bundesverfassungsgericht decided that the legal possibility that a child's existence may be a source for damages is constitutionally barred under Article 1 I GG. The duty of all organs of the state to honour every

---

* See case 112 below.

human being in its existence, (and here reference is made to Part I 1 a) of the decision) prohibits, in itself, the view that maintenance of a child can be seen as financial loss. The case law of the civil courts on liability for medical errors in counselling on failed abortions should therefore be reviewed.

This Division fails to find this remark of the BVerfG a reason why in the case here under investigation expenses for maintenance cannot be seen as financial loss.

(*aa*) The legal classification of expenses for maintenance proceeds from the contractual liability of the doctor to fulfil all medical requirements in order that the treatment or consultancy undertaken by him be successful. Such legal liability can, however, only be used as a starting point for contracts whose legality is not in question. As regards abortions without legal justification which, as a result of the Constitutional decision of 1993 must now be regarded as illegal (for instance because the previously applied justifications are no longer accepted as valid . . .), this Division can here leave undecided, whether in such cases the need to prevent economic loss arising from a child's existence is at all relevant for the contractual relationship and, even where such need existed, if it could be the starting point for a claim for damages.

On the other hand, (a) consultancy contracts intended to prevent, as here, the procreation or, in other cases, the birth of a genetically damaged child; or (b) sterilisation contracts aimed at preventing the birth of any, or any further, children or (c) contracts for the legally permitted abortion of a pregnancy, (for instance in cases where such termination is undertaken for criminalogical or embryopathic reasons), are all contracts intended to reach a legally permissible objective. If there are no qualms about the legal validity of a contract for sterilisation (see this Division BGHZ 67, 48 [51 *et seq.*] and *NJW* 1984, 2625), there should, *a fortiori,* be none in cases like the present. The plaintiffs' intended to have a second, but not as handicapped child as their first, and in order to prevent the damage feared as a result of the first child's handicap, they wished to make procreation dependant on the outcome of a consultation. Such intentions cannot meet with moral qualms. Such behaviour is due to a high degree of parental responsibility.

Where a contract is geared to reaching a legally permitted aim, i.e. the birth of a child (in this case potentially genetically impaired), the doctor is responsible for obtaining the contractually agreed aim by fulfilling his accepted duties. The Division cannot see any constitutional doubts. In the cited decision, the BVerfG in its reasons expressly points out that faulty performance of medical duties in respect of treatment or advice can in principle lead to civil liability. The constitutional and general legality of contracts such as the ones described above is reflected in the contents of these contracts in so far as they are geared to prevent economic burdens incurred from the birth of children. Where this was properly contractually agreed, such economic protection is part of the duties which the doctor accepted and the legal order condones. Thus, this Division adheres to its previously reasoned opinion that the doctor's liability includes liability for the prevention of this economic consequence where, as part of the specific aims of the contract for treatment and consultation, he had also accepted that of the pevention of such losses. This Division has affirmed this result for cases of sterilisation for reasons of family planning (BGHZ 76, 249 [256]; 76, 259 [263 *et seq.*]; *NJW* 1981, 630; *NJW* 1981, 2002 and *NJW* 1984, 2625). In a case similar to this one, where during pregnancy a consultation took place aimed at preventing the birth of a severely disabled child, this Division (BGHZ 89, 95 [104 *et seq.*] held that even in such cases the prevention of economic burdens is part of the protection envisaged by the consultancy contract, even where this is not its paramount reason, as in cases of sterilisation for economic reasons.

Where in the course of such contracts the doctor commits a medical error leading to the birth of a child, his liability includes his duty to reimburse the contractual partner for all economic losses which the contract was intended to prevent. Accepting a medical duty aimed at attaining a permitted contractual purpose makes the doctor legally responsible and has consequences for his liability. In the last instance the protection afforded to the contractual partner, which stems from the doctor's liability, is a consequence of medical progress which, within the boundaries of the law, opened up the possibility of preventing the birth of a child.

(*bb*) Given these facts, it would be a grave incursion into the parties' contractual interests if the doctor were free from consequential liability in cases of culpable breach of contractual duties. Even when considering the BVerfG's opinion, this Division cannot detect any constitutionally-based reason why such a grave incursion into contractual liability is needed. Here, protection of a nasciturus from abortion is not at issue. This point of view is also obviously not the starting point of the BVerfG's criticisms, which are directed, without differentiation, at this Division's jurisdictional principles. Nor can an opposing constitutional reason be derived from the view that the economic burden which must be borne by the doctor as a result of his breach of contract actually consists of the costs of living of a child.

(i) This Division shares the views underlying the reasoning of the BVerfG in its decision of 28 May 1993 (*NJW* 1993, 1751 *et seq.*) that it is constitutionally prohibited (Art. 1 GG) to classify the very existence of a child as damage, even within the laws of contract and tort. This Division has repeatedly expressed this view (BGHZ 76, 249 [253 *et seq.*]; *NJW* 1984, 2625).

But in its leading decision (BGHZ 76, 249) this Division has already pointed out that to use the slogan 'child as damage' is an inappropriate and legally useless way of looking at the problem. Instead, the Court in this and later decisions, especially in its decision of 19 June 1984 (*NJW* 1984, 2625) declared that the damage consists of the costs of maintenance incurred by the unplanned birth of the child. The Court held that in this respect the distinction between the child's existence and its undoubted value as a person on the one hand, and the parents' maintenance burden on the other, does not represent an artificial disintegration or a 'dissection of the child's personal integrity' (see for instance Lankers in *FamRZ* 1969, 384), but is rather a logical consequence of looking at the problem from the point of view of the law of damages. In order to reach the consequences of the law of damages here under discussion, neither the legal provisions of the law of damages nor those of family law, nor an unrestrained contemplation of the entire facts, require that the very existence of the child is seen as the damaging event. It is only the ensuing financial burden to the parents, i.e. the cost of maintaining the child, which represents the damaging economic loss. The provisions on liability do not exonerate the parents from their own duty to provide maintenance for their child. Their own duty to the child and their costs in maintaining the child are only partially met by the doctor's liability.

    (ii) According to the opinion of this Division, considerations of liability and damage are not precluded by the fact that the economic burden takes the form of maintenance for a child. The legally necessary comparison of the economic situation with and without the damaging event does not mean that the child's existence and its non-existence are compared in the sense that the child's non-existence is regarded as a positive and its actual existence as a negative economic factor. This point of view would certainly meet with constitutional objections under Article 1 GG. But such a comparison would also be wrong under the law of damages. When the considerations of liability and damage are solely restricted to the economic side of the complex facts which the birth of a child involves, the conclusion is reached that for the person liable to provide maintenance, the comparison of the two economic situations needed to determine the actual loss merely comprises the economic situation with and without the duty to provide such maintenance.

In this respect, the Division is aware that the economic burden is only brought about by the child's existence. But this is merely a causal link provided by natural science, which in itself is free from value judgments. Even in the case of a 'longed-for child', the parents' duty to provide maintenance is expressed as a burden on their finances without any negative consequence for the relationship between the parents and the child. Moreover, even in cases where the BVerfG has expressly acknowledged the duty to compensate for losses incurred in connection with the birth of a child, the birth must be seen as the 'source of loss' intended by the BVerfG, if this expression has any relevance at all to the law of damages (for the different view held by Deutsch, see *NJW*, 1993, 2361 [2362]). This Division has also contemplated whether in consultancy cases such as this one or in cases of failed family planning, it could, for constitutional reasons, be necessary to acknowledge a claim to fair monetary compensation for immaterial damages on the basis of breach of the parents' personal rights, as has been considered in academic literature (see Diederichsen, *VersR*, 1981, 693 [696]; Stürner *VersR* 1984, 305 and *FamRZ* 1985, 753 [760 *et seq.*]; H. Lange, *Schadensersatz*, 2. edn., Sec!!! 6 IX 7h). However, this point of view does not dispense with a comparison with the situation had the child not been born. A classification as immaterial damage to its parents would have a more direct and graver effect on the child as a person than the ascertainment of the parents' economic burden for which the doctor must (partially) relieve them. Moreover, as regards questions of liability, such a stance seems rather dubious, since the economic burden arising from the birth of the child would indirectly affect the calculation of compensation, since under this legal concept (damages for pain and suffering) compensation for economic losses is not possible. The differences between economic and immaterial losses would be blurred.

(*c*) In cases where the burden of the costs of living was meant to be prevented through a contract with a doctor, an economic approach in assessing the burden does not negatively affect the views of the value of the child's person and existence. According to the compensatory nature of the law of liability and damages, the doctor's share of the economic burden is reduced to a mere financial obligation which neither taints the child nor questions its right to live. Neither the law nor the practice on damage and compensation links the term 'damage' to such negative value judgements; if this were the case it would necessarily be prohibited to classify the birth of a child as damage. The classification of maintenance costs as losses in the relationship between parents and doctor means, however, neither that a value judgment is made in respect of the child nor that its personality is degraded by connection with the term 'damage'. According to the opinion of this Division, the term ' damage' does not include such connotations which, in the light of the Constitution, would in any case be objectionable. When the BGB was enacted, the legislator deliberately refrained from clearly defining the terms 'financial and economic losses' and instead left their interpretation to jurisprudence and the courts. From the very beginning the courts interpreted economic losses as the diminution of assets and the increase of debts, calculated by way of a mathematical comparison between the economic situation brought about by the damaging event and the situation which would have existed had the event never occurred (*Großer Senat für Zivilsachen*

BGHZ 98, 212 [217 *et seq.*]). This method of calculating the difference through a neutral mathematical operation cannot, however, dispense with an assessment of the various mathematical positions to be employed when calculating the difference; these need to be evaluated according to the protective purpose of all liability and the compensatory function of damages (BGHZ 98, 212 [217 *et seq.*]) But where a contract with a doctor was intended to prevent the parents being burdened with maintenance costs, and this burden is incurred as a direct result of a breach of contract, the protective purpose of the contract and the purpose of damages as equalisation of burdens demand that it be seen as economic loss. The fact that this balancing of losses cannot result in a 'negative value judgement' of the child as a person follows from the above-outlined restriction of the assessment of losses to the economic aspect of the facts of the case. Nor does this comparison under the law of damages between the two economic situations reduce the human existence in a degrading manner to a mere item of accounting and balancing. The comparison is merely the basically value-free method of calculating economic consequences on which the law of damages always relies and whose classification as a mere tool for establishing facts affects the meaning of term 'loss'. This is the ultimate purpose of the law of damages; to compare economic situations and to provide economically expressed differences for the purposes of the law of liability which then establishes who is responsible for the creation of the burden and to whom it must accordingly be attributed. This function of the law of damages does not involve a negative value judgement of the economic difference as 'loss'. If compensation is nowadays understood as a just allocation of burdens according to the various criteria of liability, and not as a sanction for damaging behaviour, this Division sees no reason why the classification of maintenance costs as 'loss' should be detrimental to the honour of the child.

This Division is rather of the opinion that, especially in cases such as this, granting compensation not only has no detrimental effect on the child, but can rather be beneficial to it, since it improves its financial situation and possibly even its standing within the family. The shifting of the maintenance burden to the attending doctor appears especially satisfactory where, due to his faulty consultation, he is co-responsible for the economic burden which, if a severely handicapped child is in constant need of care, can even threaten the family's existence. As this Division has previously stated (BGHZ 76, 259 [266 *et seq.*]), even in cases where the doctor is fully liable for all extra expenditure calculated by means of an economic comparison, the parents are still burdened with the total personal care of the child and also with a certain amount of financial losses and sacrifices which they cannot transfer to the person who created the damage. The Court fails to detect any constitutionally objectionable attack on the honour of the child from this partial

economic alleviation of the parents' burden. Should the parents in fact treat the child badly because they blame it for the additional maintenance costs, such behaviour would not be improved by the legal order refusing to shift some of the burden to the person who, by his breach of contract, created it.
. . .

4. As regards consultancy contracts of the kind here under investigation, the compensatory purpose of damages prohibits a restriction of the claim for damages to the amount of extra expenditure incurred by reason the child's congenital handicap . . .

(b) As this Division has previously stated, a doctor who culpably breaches his duty to provide a proper consultation, and who is therefore liable for maintenance costs, must, within the limits set out by this Division, pay compensation for the entire maintenance costs of the child and not only for the additional expenditure caused by the handicap. After a further review, the Court has decided to uphold its previous opinion even for cases such as the present. As far as liability is concerned, there are no grave differences between the two cases of consultancy. In both instances the parents required medical advice in order not to give birth to a congenitally damaged child. If, in view of the risk of having a second handicapped child, they intended to forego a second pregnancy if the doctor advised them in that direction, it is clear that they would not have given birth to the child had they been correctly advised. According to the parties' intentions, the scope of protection afforded by a consultancy contract always includes those losses arising from financial expenditure on severely handicapped children which the parents intended to prevent, for themselves and the child, by consulting a doctor. As this Division stated in its decision (BGHZ 89, 95 [105]), these maintenance costs cannot be split into those which are legally expected to be incurred by parents of a (hypothetically healthy) child and the additional costs which stem from the child's handicap. The necessary expenditure for safeguarding the existence of a severely handicapped child is indivisible. Moreover, this Division is of the opinion that it is irreconcilable with the respect for the child's person in the sense of Article 1 I GG to measure its existence and the various corresponding needs by using the yardstick of a 'normal' child. Compensating the parents for the entire costs of maintenance is thus no disregard of the child's honour but rather an appropriate means of protecting it from losses, and of guaranteeing such protection.

BUNDESVERFASSUNGSGERICHT (SECOND DIVISION)
28 MAY 1993*

BVerfGE 88, 203

Reasons

D V 6. The duty of the State to protect the nasciturus does not require that contracts are classed as non-binding which were concluded with doctors and hospitals for abortions which are not punishable under the (new) counselling program. The program rather requires that the mutual tie of obligations between doctor and patient take the form of a legal relationship so that all obligations are fulfilled for valid legal reasons. Irrespective of any specific contractual consequences, §§ 134, 138 BGB are inapplicable. Doctors and hospitals only take part in abortions on the basis of a valid contract which safeguards their claim for payment and outlines their duties. It is in particular the doctor's duty towards the unborn child and the patient's health which needs contractual safeguards. As a consequence, faulty performance of the duties to provide counselling and treatment must in principle be able to trigger contractual and tortious sanctions.

However, in the light of the Constitution this result needs to be differentiated. A civil law sanction for faulty performance of the contract or for tortious infringement of the patient's physical integrity is basically necessary; this entails not only the duty to pay back any wasted fees, but also the duty to compensate for damage under the provisions of §§ 823, 847 BGB, including compensation for pain and suffering resulting from a failed abortion or from the birth of a handicapped child. But as a result of Article 1 I GG, the child's existence cannot legally be classified as damage. The duty of all public bodies to respect every human being for its own sake, prohibits maintenance for a child to be classified as damage. In the light of this fact, the case law of the civil courts on liability for medical mistakes in counselling or in peforming failed abortions needs to be reconsidered (see for abortion BGHZ 86, 240 *et seq.*; 89, 95 *et seq.*; BGH NJW 1985, 671 *et seq.*; VersR 1985, 1068 *et seq.*; VersR 1986, 869 *et seq.*; VersR 1988, 155 *et seq.*; NJW 1992, 1556 *et seq.*; for sterilisations see BGHZ 76, 249 *et seq.*; 76, 259 *et seq.*; BGH NJW 1984, 2625 *et seq.*). However, the doctor's duty to pay damages

* Translation by Irene Snook

to the child for damage caused in the course of an unskillfully attempted and thus failed abortion remains unaffected (see BGHZ 58, 48 [49 *et seq.*]; BGH NJW 1989, 1538 [1539]).

Case 113

BUNDESGERICHTSHOF (SIXTH CIVIL DIVISION)
19 DECEMBER 1995*
NJW 1996, 1128

Facts

In these proceedings the plaintiff, *Caroline of Monaco*, is objecting to the publication of certain photographs distributed in Germany and France by the defendant, the publishers of the magazines *F* and *B*. In issue no. 30 of the *F* magazine, dated 22 July 1993, the defendant published a total of five so-called 'paparazzi' photographs which show the plaintiff with the actor *Vincent Lindon* in a garden restaurant in *S*. (France). On the front page, next to a large photograph of the plaintiff (the use of which is not impugned in these proceedings) is a photograph of her, accompanied by reference to an article entitled 'The most tender photographs of her romance with Vincent'. The series of four photographs on pages 4 and 5 is entitled 'These photos are proof of the most tender romance of our time'. In issue no. 32, dated 5 August 1993 of the illustrated magazine *B*, the defendant published on page 88 a photograph of the plaintiff on horseback and on page 89 a photograph of the plaintiff with her children *P*. and *A*.; these photographs belong to an article entitled 'Caroline: I don't think I am the ideal wife'. In issue no 34 of the *B* magazine, dated 19 August 1993, the defendant published an article with several photographs entitled 'Simple happiness', showing the plaintiff with her daughter in a paddling boat, going for a walk alone, carrying a wicker basket, riding a bicycle, together with *Vincent Lindon* in a pub, with *Lindon* and her son *P.*, and, finally, with another woman in the market. After a lengthy dispute over the admissibility of these publications, the defendant brought an action against the claimant before the Landgericht of Munich requesting that the Court make a declaratory judgment to the effect that the defendant need not in future abstain from publishing these photographs. By these proceedings the plaintiff, who

* Translation by Irene Snook

claims that the publication of these photographs infringes her right to personal privacy, requests under German and French law that the defendant in future abstain from any further publication of the photographs. The plaintiff claims that even as an 'absolute person of contemporary history' she does not have to put up with the publication of photographs of herself. All of these photographs had been taken from a great distance, without her knowledge, and are said to belong to her private life. The plaintiff is constantly followed by photographers leaving her in no peace outside of her home. Even for her, there must be a protected private area outside of her own home.

The Landgericht found in favour of the plaintiff as far as the distribution within France is concerned but otherwise rejected the claim. The plaintiff appealed against this decision, and the defendant cross-appealed. The Oberlandesgericht has rejected the claim. The further appeal, in so far as it was accepted, is partially successful.

Reasons

III. The reasoning of the Appeal Court is, in legal terms, partly flawed. The further appeal rightly claims that the photographs which show the plaintiff in an outdoor restaurant with *Vincent Lindon* fall into the sphere of her private life. Their publication infringes her right to personal privacy and is thus prohibited. The other photographs are legally unobjectionable.

A. 1. As far as the distribution of the magazines in Germany is concerned, the Appeal Court has rightly based its decision on German law. According to the principles of international private law, for claims based on tort and therefore, as here, claims to desist from certain actions (*Unterlassungsanspruch*) said to violate the right to one's own personality (references omitted), the law of the place where the tort was committed applies. For products of the newspaper industry, the place of commission is the place where the product was published and every other place where it was distributed (Senat, NJW 1977, 1590 with further references). As regards the magazines distributed in Germany, the place of commission and the place where the effects of the tort were felt are both in Germany, so that German law applies at least for the German area of distribution. . . .

2. According to German law, the distribution of the photographs referred to above is illegal. In particular, it is not covered by the guarantee of press freedom set out in §§ 22, 23 of the Artistic Creations of the Act (KUG) or Article 5 I, Constitution.

(*a*) In principle, pictures of a person may only be distributed with the permission of the person depicted (§ 22 KUG). The right to one's own image forms a particular aspect of the general right to one's own personality. It follows that basically only the person depicted is entitled to decide whether and in what way his picture will be shown to the public (references). There is no doubt that the plaintiff has not given such permission.

(b) Pictures belonging to the sphere of contemporary history may, however, be distributed or shown without permission of the person involved, unless legally protected interests of the person depicted are thereby infringed (§ 23 I, No.1, II KUG). Pictures of persons regarded as 'absolute contemporary persons' form part of contemporary history. The plaintiff belongs to this group of persons. The further appeal wrongly disputes this fact. Decisive for the classification of a person as an absolute person of contemporary history is the fact that the public regards his pictures as important and worthy of note just because of the particular person shown. The public has a justified interest, based on a real need for information, in seeing pictures of these persons (BGHZ 20, 345, 349 *et seq.*; Senat, NJW 1996, 985). In particular Monarchs, Heads of State, and eminent politicians belong to this group (see KG *JW* 1928, 363—*Kaiser Wilhelm II*; AG Ahrensboeck DJZ 1920, 596—*Reichspräsident Ebert* and *Reichswehrminister Noske*; Senat NJW 1996, 593—*Bundeskanzler*; OLG München UFITA 41 [1964] 322—*Kanzlerkandidat*). As the eldest daughter of the reigning Prince of Monaco, the plaintiff belongs to this circle of persons as she, herself, has acknowledged. The Senat's decision of 12 December 1995 (NJW 1996, 985) is based on this view.

(c) There are, however, limits to the publication without permission of pictures of persons who form part of contemporary history. According to § 23 II KUG publication is prohibited where the justified interests of the person shown outweigh the other interests at stake. Whether or not this is the case here, must be decided through a process of weighing up the various rights and interests involved so that in each individual case it is established whether the public interest in information protected by the freedom of the press (art. 5 of the Constitution), which the defendant can cite as justification, has precedence over the plaintiff's right to her personality (Art. 2 GG) to which she refers. (BVerfGE 34, 269, 282; BVerfGE 35, 202, 221; Senat, NJW 1994, 124; BGHZ 128, 1, 10.)

(aa) The protection of a person's private sphere of life is of special importance when the two legal interests are weighed against each other. The right to respect one's own private sphere of life is an emanation of the general right to one's own personality, which grants every person an autonomous area of personal life within which he can develop and experience his own individuality, free from the interferences of others. The right to be left alone and 'to belong to oneself' forms part of this area (BVerfGE 34, 238, 245 *et*

seq.; BVerfGE 35, 202, 220; for the right to be left alone as part of the right
to privacy under American law see *Katz* v. *United States* 389 Supreme Court
(1967), 347, 350 *et seq.*; Warren/Brandeis, 4 *Harvard Law Review* [1980] 193
et seq.; Götting *Persönlichkeitsrechte als Vermögensrechte*, 1995, 168 *et seq.*,
174). As a result, since 1954, the German courts have, especially in the area
of civil law consistently given particular weight to the right to respect one's
own private sphere of life, i.e. treated it as a basic right, guaranteed by the
constitution, which includes the right to one's own image (BVerfGE 27, 1, 6;
BVerfGE 34, 269, 282 *et seq.*; BVerfGE 35, 202; BVerfGE 44, 353, 372;
BGHZ 24, 200, 208 *et seq.*; BGHZ 27, 284, 285 *et seq.*; BGHZ 73, 120, 122
et seq.; Senat JZ 1965, 411, 413—*Gretna Green* ; OLG Hamburg UFITA 78
[1977] 252, 257; OLG Hamburg UFITA 81 [1978] 278, 285; OLG Hamburg,
NJW 1970, 1325—*Haus Hohenzollern*).

(*bb*) The right to respect one's own sphere of private life can be claimed
by anyone, and can therefore be claimed by the plaintiff, even if she is a person of contemporary history. For even such persons need not tolerate pictures which depict central aspects of their private life, for instance their
domestic surroundings, being taken for later publication without their permission (BGHZ 24, 200, 208; BGH GRUR 1962, 211, 212—*Hochzeitsbild*;
BGH NJW 1965, 2148—*Spielgefährtin*). Only in exceptional circumstances,
can the distribution of pictures from this area be permissible, i.e. where an
overriding public interest justifies such an intrusion (see Senat JZ 1965, 411,
413—*Gretna Green*; OLG Hamburg UFITA 78 [1977] 252, 257—*Grace
Kelly*; OLG Hamburg UFITA 81 [1978], 278, 285; OLG Hamburg NJW
1970, 1325; OLG München UFITA 41 [1964] 322, 324).

(*d*) The Appeal Court applied these principles. But it was of the opinion
that the public's justified interest in information ends 'at the doorstep' of the
person depicted and, therefore, extends to places open to anyone, e.g. as
here, 'in front of' a garden restaurant which is open to public view. The
Appeal Court, therefore, resticted the private sphere of life to places inside
people's homes from which the public is excluded. This view has been
widely adopted by the courts and is shared by the legal literature. (KG in,
Schulze *UrhRspr. KGZ* 14; Schricker/Gerstenberg, *UrheberR*, 1987, § 23
KUG, n. 35; Wenzel *Das Recht der Wort- und Bildberichterstattung*, 4. edn.
[1994], n. 5.46 and 5.60; Evers, *Privatsphäre und Ämter für Verfassungsschutz*, p. 44.)

This Division cannot share this view. A spatial restriction of the private
sphere of life to the domestic area cannot have been intended under the
KUG, since the explanatory notes to that Act state that the safeguards of
the justified interests of the person depicted, set out in § 23 II KUG, were
intended 'especially to prevent events being shown to the public which
pertain to the personal and domestic life' of that person (reference). This

formulation in no way limits the protection of the private sphere of life to the domestic area but, rather, leaves room for a wider interpretation. The necessity of protecting the private sphere of life outside the domestic area is also partially recognised by legal writers, though for different reasons and with varying intentions (Allfeld DJZ 1920, 702; Evers *Privatsphäre und Ämter für Verfassungsschutz*, 44; Hubmann *Das Persönlichkeitsrecht*, 2d edn., (1967), p. 322; Helle *Besondere* Persönlichkeitsrechte im Privatrecht, 1991, 180; Paeffgen *JZ* 1978, 738, 740; Prinz NJW 1995, 817, 820; Siegert *DB* 1958, 419, 421; Siegert NJW 1963, 1953, 1955. Likewise LG Köln AfP 1994, 166, 168; see also BGHSt 18, 182, 186—*Callgirlaffäre*). This Division shares the view that there is a private area worthy of protection outside that of the purely domestic area. This is the case, where a person has retreated to a place of seclusion where he wishes to be left alone, as can be ascertained by objective criteria, and in a specific situation, where he, relying on the fact of seclusion, acts in a way in which he would not have done so in public. An unjustified intrusion into this protected area takes place where pictures of that person are published if taken secretly or by stealth.

(*aa*) Like anyone else, persons who are part of contemporary history have the right which must be respected by all third persons to retreat to places outside their own home where they wish to be alone or, at least, left secluded from the general public. This can even occur in places which are open to the public, i.e. in public places. But this presupposes that in the place and at the point in question the person 'shut himself off' somewhat from the public at large; and this seclusion from the public must have been objectively obvious to third persons. This can, for instance, be the case in separate rooms of a restaurant or in hotels, sports grounds, telephone booths, under certain circumstances even in the open, as long as the person does not appear more than just another member of the public.

(*bb*) Moreover, the right to demand that other persons respect one's privacy presupposes that the situation in which the person [observed] finds himself is one of a typically private nature. This is the case where a person, relying on the seclusion of the specific place where he finds himself in, behaves in a manner which he would not normally adopt in full view of the public. This may be the case whenever [the observed person] expresses personal emotions which are clearly not intended for the eyes of third persons or is acting in an 'unrestrained' manner. Only in such situations can it be assumed and objectively verified that the person did not intend to allow other persons sharing the moment. In such circumstance he is entitled to have the chosen seclusion respected.

(*cc*) It is an unjustified infringement of the sphere of privacy which is worthy of protection if, for reasons of personal gain, pictures are taken/published which exploit the innocence of the person depicted who believes himself unobserved. This is always the case where the person is observed almost as if through a keyhole, or is surprised by the surreptitious taking of the pictures. The same applies where the picture is taken openly but so suddenly that the person photographed has no time to prepare himself. A restriction of the prohibition to these particular circumstances is justified because protection of the private sphere of life is here extended to places which are in theory open to everyone. In these cases the person's privacy is only unjustly infringed where the intrusion happened surreptitiously or by surprise. The courts have always held that the surreptitious taking of photographs by secret means is illegal (BGHZ 24, 200, 208; Senat NJW 1966, 2353, 2355—*Vor unserer eigenen Tür*; OLG Frankfurt NJW 1987, 1087; see also BGHZ 27. 284—*Tonbandaufnahme*; BGHZ 73, 120—*Telefonabhören*; BAG JZ 1988, 108). Up to now, this only applied to the private domaine within one's home, where the depicted person's consent was always required for the taking of photographs. But the same protection can legitimately be demanded in circumstances where persons, so to speak, transfer their private sphere of life to a place outside of their home. For the same reasons, photographs may then and there be taken, and later published, only if prior consent was given.

3. In the light of these principles, the weighing up of the rights and interests involved in this case leads to the conclusion that the plaintiff's protected sphere of privacy was violated by photographs taken in a garden restaurant and published in issue no. 30 of the magazine *F.* under the headline 'These photos are the proof of the most tender romance of our time'. The plaintiff can prohibit any future publication of these pictures. . . .

(*b*) When weighing up the various interests involved, the information value of the events depicted plays a significant role. The greater the interest of the public in being informed, the more the protected interests of the person of contemporary history must recede in favour of the public's need for information. Conversely, the need to protect the depicted person's privacy gains in weight as the value of the information which the public obtains from the photographs decreases. In this case, the photographs which show the plaintiff with *Vincent Lindon* in a garden restaurant contain little, if anything of value. Here, according to the Appeal Court, mere prying and sensationalism, and the public's wish to be entertained, outweighed all other considerations. Such motives, especially the mere wish of the public to be entertained, which is to be satisfied by pictures of totally private events of the plaintiff's life, cannot be recognised as worthy of protection. Our courts have repeatedly acknowledged this. (BVerGE 34, 269, 283; BGHZ 24, 200, 208; BGHZ 128, 1, 12; BGH NJW 1965, 2148, 2149; BGH JZ 1965, 411; OLG Hamburg AfP 1992, 376, 377).

4. However, the further appeal is unsuccessful in respect of the photographs in the other magazines since these are not concerned with the plaintiff's protected private sphere of life.

(*a*) . . . The plaintiff cannot prohibit the publication of such pictures. As a person of contemporary history, she must accept that the general public has a justifiable interest in knowing where she goes and how she behaves herself in public, be it during shopping trips in the market square, in a cafe or during sporting or other activities of daily life. This includes the picture reproduced in the issue no. 34 of the magazine *B*, taken in a restaurant and showing the plaintiff sitting at a table with other persons. This picture differs from the ones taken in the garden restaurant because here the characteristics which made the other ones an unjustifiable intrusion are missing. For here, the plaintiff had not retreated to a place secluded from the general public, and secondly the situation in which she was photographed was not of a somewhat private nature in the sense outlined above. The fact that the plaintiff was not aware of being photographed does not, in itself, provide a reason for demanding that the photo remain unpublished, since persons of contemporary history must normally tolerate unnoticed or even clandestine photographs of themselves if they appear in public (Frank *Persönlichkeitsschutz heute*, 1985, p. 118, n.280).

(*b*) However, what all these pictures have in common is the fact that they do not show the plaintiff performing a public function. They are, instead, concerned with her private life in the wider sense of the term. The plaintiff wishes to prohibit generally the publication of these photographs in Germany and France. But this is not possible under German law. In France under Article 9 of the Code Civil, which is intended to protect private life (*vie privée*), the publication of a picture requires in principle the consent of the person shown. This can even apply to monarchs and other public figures, unless they are shown performing a public duty (see Cour de Cassation, *Bulletin des arrêts* Chambres civiles, No 98, p. 67—*Farah Diba;* Tribunal de grande instance de Paris *Recueil Dalloz Sirey* 1977, Jur. p. 364 *et seq.—Caroline de Monaco*; see also Hauser, *GRUR Int.* 1988, 839, 840; Ehlers/Baumann *ZvglRWiss* 1978, 421 et seq; Codes Dalloz, Code civil, 92. ed., [1992–1993], Art. 9, n. 9).

Under German law (§ 23 KUG*)*, this result is not possible. As this Division stated in its judgment of 14 November 1996 (NJW 1996, 539), under German law the public can have an undisputed interest in seeing photographs of an 'absolute person of contemporary history'. There is no further requirement that that person be performing a public function. As a consequence, within the scope of § 23 I No. 1 KUG, the public's interest in information which is worthy of protection can be assumed even where the photograph merely shows how a well-known person acts in normal public surroundings, i.e. when not performing public functions. This interest in being informed only needs to give way where, in quite specific situations, the justified interests of the person shown take precedence (s. 23 II KUG). This does not, however, apply to the photographs shown in issues nos. 32 and 34 of the magazine which are in fact quite flattering.

B. As far as distribution of the magazines in France is concerned, contrary to the plaintiff's contentions in this further appeal, the Court need not decide whether or not the plaintiff's claim would succeed if French law were applied.

I. As the Appeal Court rightly held, to apply French law in deciding in favour of a claim for an order to abstain from an action is barred by Article 38 EGBGB. According to this provision, claims based on tortious acts committed abroad against a German citizen are limited to the remedies available under German law. This principle also applies in favour of the defendant, a legal person domiciled within Germany (RGZ 129, 385, 388; OLG Hamburg IPRspr. 1930, No. 155; see also BGHZ 86, 234, 237). A comparison of the results under German and French law is thus superfluous when it is clear, as here, that German law provides no basis for a claim (BGHZ 71, 175, 177; BGHZ 86, 234, 237; BAG NJW 1964, 990, 991; Prof. v. Bar *JZ* 1985, 961, 963.

INDEX